THY WILL BE DONE

Also by Gerard Colby
DuPont: Behind the Nylon Curtain

THY WILL BE DONE

The Conquest of
the Amazon:
Nelson Rockefeller
and Evangelism
in the Age of Oil

GERARD COLBY

WITH

CHARLOTTE DENNETT

HarperCollins*Publishers*

Grateful acknowledgment is made for permission to reprint portions of the following:

The Rockefellers by Peter Collier and David Horowitz. Copyright © 1976 by Peter Collier and David Horowitz. Reprinted by permission of Henry Holt and Company, Inc.

Navigating the Rapids, edited by Beatrice Bishop Berle. Copyright © 1976 by Beatrice Bishop Berle. Reprinted by permission of Harcourt Brace and Company.

FIRST EDITION

Designed by Michael A. Lebrón

The authors and publishers wish to thank the following for permission to use their artwork:

Garfield Davis: p. 755.

Carol Keller: pp. 45, 109, 213, 277, 286, 297, 303, 338, 365, 373, 462, 463, 502, 506–7, 518, 526, 527, 550–51, 554, 572, 604, 605, 649, 682, 683, and 808.

Ted Keller: pp. 127, 488, 612, 621, 661, and 713.

Library of Congress Cataloging-in-Publication Data
Colby, Gerard, 1945–
    Thy will be done : the conquest of the Amazon : Nelson Rockefeller and
  evangelism in the age of oil / by Gerard Colby with Charlotte Dennett. —
  1st ed.
      p. cm.
  Includes bibliographical references and index.
  ISBN 0-06-016764-5
    1. Rockefeller, Nelson A. (Nelson Aldrich), 1908–1979. 2. Townsend,
William Cameron, 1896–1982. 3. Wycliffe Bible Translators. 4. Petroleum
industry and trade—Amazon River Region—History—20th century. 5. Indians
of South America—Missions—Amazon River Region. 6. South America—
Politics and government—20th century. 7. Amazon River Region—History.
I. Dennett, Charlotte. II. Title.
E748.R673C55   1995
973.925'092—dc20   93-48360

95 96 97 98 99 ❖/RRD 10 9 8 7 6 5 4 3 2 1

To the forty-seven journalists killed while reporting in Guatemala during military dictatorships between 1978 and 1985, and to their colleagues of the press who have died similarly in Brazil and other countries, trying to bring to the world the news of what is happening in the frontiers of "developing" nations.

> The loss of liberty in general would soon follow the supression of the liberty of the press; for it is an essential branch of liberty, so perhaps it is preservative of the whole.
>
> —JOHN PETER ZENGER
> (1697–1746)

By the descriptions of all who had seen them, there were no more inoffensive and charming human beings on the planet than the forest Indians of Brazil, and brusquely we were told they had been rushed to the verge of extinction. The tragedy of the Indian in the USA in the last century was being repeated, but it was being compressed into a shorter time. . . . The official report said pioneers leagued with corrupt politicians had continually usurped Indian lands, destroyed whole tribes . . . in which bacteriological warfare had been employed, by issuing clothing impregnated with the virus of small pox, and by poisoned food supplies. Children had been abducted and mass murder gone unpunished. The Government itself was blamed to some extent for the Indian Protection Service's increasing starvation of resources over a period of thirty years. The Service had also had to face "the disastrous impact of missionary activity."

Norman Lewis
The Sunday Times (London)
February 23, 1969

CONTENTS

IV

PROPHETS OF ARMAGEDDON

V

THE DAY OF THE WATCHMAN

VI

THE SLAUGHTER OF THE INNOCENTS

VII

A NEW WORLD ORDER

VIII

DAYS OF JUDGMENT

Photographs follow pages 272 and 528.

ACKNOWLEDGMENTS

This is a great "How" age. But "Why" remains unanswered,
and will doubtless again claim attention.

—Malcolm Muggeridge, 1958

There is a subtlety about time that can break the heart, and it is hard to believe that eighteen years have passed since this journey of discovery began, and even harder to believe it is over. In 1976 the authors traveled to the Amazon to seek out the truth behind allegations in the Latin American press that members of the Wycliffe Bible Translators (known abroad as the Summer Institute of Linguistics), American corporations, and the Central Intelligence Agency had been involved in the destruction of Indian life and culture in the Amazon basin countries. The charges were widespread and, given the nature of revelations at the time about CIA abuses of authority, including assassination plots, mind-control experiments on unwitting citizens, and use of missionaries as sources of intelligence, they could not be ignored. Was there any truth to American involvement in a crime so serious as genocide or its cover-up, and if so, why?

The research trip to the Amazon was supposed to take six weeks; it ended up consuming six months, involving some 170 interviews in eight countries, including visits to Wycliffe's jungle bases in the five Amazon basin countries of Ecuador, Peru, Bolivia, Brazil, and Colombia. In the years that followed, research also took us throughout the United States, particularly the South and Southwest, and parts of Europe and southern Africa, as well as several more trips to Latin America. After realizing the story was much more complex and richer in themes than we originally thought, we returned our advance on royalties to one publisher in order to avoid rushing to print. Our search for the right publisher required us to change literary agents twice. Finally, through word of mouth at a National Writers Union conference on censorship, we received the referral that helped make this book possible.

We wish, therefore, to thank first of all our able literary agent, Chris Tomasino of RLR Associates, whose wisdom and responsiveness to our concerns set a standard for mutual respect between authors and agents. She found us an editor who was familiar with many of the names in our initial prospectus and understood the research requirements of this book.

Our next thanks go, therefore, to Hugh Van Dusen, our editor at HarperCollins, for his untiring belief in this book and for the long-suffering patience he showed while waiting for its delivery.

We are grateful to the Fund for Investigative Journalism, particularly its former directors, Howard Bray and John Hanrahan, for supporting the "Amazon Project," as we called it, since our first visit to Latin America in 1976, and to the staff of the International Indian Treaty Council for their encouragement and advice.

Our deep appreciation also goes to the Reverend William Wipfler, formerly of the Latin America and Human Rights offices of the National Council of Churches and vice chair of Amnesty International, whose dedication to the cause of human rights has been an inspiration.

For profound insights into American anthropology, as well as the Wycliffe Bible Translators and their work with American oil companies, we are indebted to anthropologist and filmmaker Scott S. Robinson. His movie, *Sky Chief,* depicting the disastrous impact of Gulf Oil's and Texaco's operations on the environment of the Ecuadorian Amazon and the Kofan Indians, is a classic in documentary filmmaking.

Kenneth Kensinger's explanation about why he left Wycliffe provided us with a look into the utilitarianism that can prevail even among sincere missionaries when confronted with questions that get in the way of their mission.

The missionaries we met were uniformly hospitable and gracious. We could not help but be impressed by their willingness to endure many lonely years with remote tribes in the jungle. These were not people who fit the stereotype of the fanatical missionary; they were thoughtful, kind, considerate people who had studied hard to learn the linguistic skills that had earned them Ph.D.s and their reputation as the crème de la crème of the Fundamentalist missionary world. Yet their sincere dedication to bring about what they believe is good for the Indian cuts both ways. When we first met them, they were clearly struggling to cope with a modern world that questioned their vision of "enlightened" Christianized tribes being the key to fulfilling a biblical prophecy of the Second Coming of Christ. There was also, beyond the determined naïveté apparent to many observers, the reality of power, both political and technological, that Wycliffe enjoyed. Never, in our collective ten years of investigative journalism, had either of us encountered so much fear surrounding a religious organization; in country after country respected critics were vanquished.

The truth behind this remarkable organization lies beyond the claims of miraculous interventions and hometown support for its field missionaries. Some of this truth could only be found in the papers of Wycliffe's founder, William Cameron Townsend, at the headquarters of its Jungle Aviation and Radio Service (JAARS) outside Waxhaw, North Carolina. Unfortunately, some of Townsend's documents could not be quoted directly but had to be paraphrased in this book, because Wycliffe elders, describing the documents as "sensitive," refused to grant permission to quote. Nevertheless, we are grateful for Wycliffe's cooperation throughout most of our research.

We are also grateful to those who supported our work on this project during many difficult financial times. For sheer perseverance and unquestioning support over many, many years, we are greatly indebted to Carol and William Ferry, Robin Lloyd, Ted and Georgia Keller, Robert and Barbara O'Connor, and Beverly Jacobson. They have been outstanding friends. We also wish to thank Sallie Bingham, John Bloch and Rebecca Sheppard, Rev. Philip and Susan Wheaton, John Douglas, Joan and Stuart Eagle, Ed Everts and Deb Davis, Ben Ptashnik, Jean Hardisty, Jonathan and Roxanne Leopold, Maya Miller, Peter Shepherd, Michael Howard, Olivia Robinson, John Puleio, Jerry Shields, Dwight and Barbara Steward, William Hoffman, Jim Gosdin, Ann Dunlop, Steve Freeman, John and Patti Gallagher, Jeff Weaver, Lesli Myers, Terry Allen, Warren King, Jackie Harman, Kim Chase and Don Odell, Jack and Tina Mulvey, Anthony Pollina and Deborah Wolfe, Philip Caleb and Anna Taylor Caleb, Judith and Richard Dewey, Eddie Becker, Michael Parenti, Gloria Perez, David and Donna McWilliams, Bob and Kathleen Engstrom, Al Salzman, Ed Krales, Mary Anne Holowaty, Paul Abbott, Christine Wood, Terry Dugan and Larry Klein, Barry Kade, Jim Higgins, and Louise and Anala Ferland, *Toward Freedom* magazine, Dan Higgins, Jane Kramer, Roz Payne, Cameron O'Connor, Richard Geidel, the Rainforest Action Network, the PEN Writers Fund, and—for its support to *Toward Freedom* for a slide show based on the contents of this book—the Haymarket Foundation.

Special thanks are due also to the O'Connors and Beverly Jacobson for their helpful suggestions after reading portions of the manuscript, to Cynthia Merman for a superb job in paring it down to a manageable size, to Trent Duffy for his careful final review of the entire manuscript and its graphics, to Stephanie Gunning for her coordination of the book's production, and to attorneys Jenie Gavenchak and Sara Pearl for their meticulous legal review.

For the actual creation of many of the book's maps and charts, we would like to express our appreciation to Carol Keller for her artistry and patience, and to Ted Keller for his always resourceful advice and assistance.

For the powerful art and design of the book's jacket, and for the book's interior design, we are indebted to Michael Lebrón.

Our appreciation also goes to the following people for their kind efforts to assist our research: Scott S. Robinson of Mexico City, Professor Robert Wasserstrom and Jan Rus in Mexico, anthropologist Richard Chase Smith in Peru, James and Marge Goff of Latin America Press in Lima, Nemesio Rodrigues of the Centro Antropologico de Documentacion (CEDAL) in Mexico City, Robert Fink of Washington, D.C., and the staffs of the Washington Office on Latin America and the Bolivian Action Coalition of Vancouver, Canada.

For keeping us updated on the conditions of indigenous peoples and violations (including massacres) of their human rights during the writing of this book, we thank Erik Van Lanep of Arctic to Amazonia (Stafford, Vermont), Stephen Corry of Survival International (London), John Friede of Amanakáa (New York), and Betty Mindlin of the Instituto de Antropologia e Meio Ambiente (São Paulo).

We wish to acknowledge our debt to the works of scholars who wrote what can only be described as great books: David Stoll, author of *Fishers of Men or Builders of Empire?: The Wycliffe Bible Translators in Latin America* (1982); Shelton Davis, author of *Victims of the Miracle* (1977); Jan Knippers Black, author of *United States Penetration of Brazil* (1977); and David Horowitz and Peter Collier, authors of *The Rockefellers: An American Dynasty* (1976).

Our thanks also to the veteran journalist Norman Lewis, for permission to quote from his 1969 article in *The Sunday Times* of London, "Genocide," and for insights gained from his subsequent investigative reporting on violations of Indian human rights in Paraguay and Bolivia; to the courageous anthropologists and human rights defenders who contributed to the World Council of Churches' *The Situation of the Indian in South America* (1972) and *Genocide in Paraguay* (Richard Arens, ed.); and to Lucien Bodard for the rare poetic power of his *Green Hell* (1971).

None of the above people, however, are responsible for the opinions and conclusions expressed in this book by the authors.

The Rockefeller aspect of this story developed five years after the research for this book began. Nelson Rockefeller was not originally a character in this book. How we came to Rockefeller's extraordinary role in shaping much of what happens in this book must be the subject of another story. Suffice it to say that our discovery of Rockefeller's involvement during World War II in an "Amazon development plan" that the Brazilian government had already rejected occurred only after following a long trail of leads. Most important were the papers of Adolf Berle at the Franklin D. Roosevelt Library and the National Archives' declassified holdings of Rockefeller's papers when he was the Coordinator of Inter-American

Affairs.* After examining these extensive collections, we took up our next research task at the Rockefeller Archive Center. When we began our research there in 1984, Nelson Rockefeller's personal papers were still not open, but those of his private aid agency in Latin America, the American International Association for Economic and Social Development, were.

We visited the Rockefeller Archive Center many times over the years. Each time we found the center's archivists professionally dedicated, courteous, and helpful. Their ability to aid researchers was limited, however, by the Rockefeller family. After Nelson Rockefeller's death in 1979, all his papers, including those he had made available to researchers, who quoted from them in books, were withdrawn by the family and sent to the Center for processing. For much of the next decade, they remained closed to the public; as of this writing, despite the processing and release of a substantial amount of Rockefeller's documents, many of his private and government papers still remain closed, as are records of his brother Winthrop's involvement in Nelson's and David Rockefeller's million-acre ranch in Brazil's western frontier, Fazenda Bodoquena, a subject of undoubted future interest.

We spent many days trying the patience of staffs at presidential libraries, archives, museums, newspaper morgues, and university and other libraries in the United States, Latin America, Europe, and southern Africa. We owe much to the professionalism of the archivists and librarians of the following institutions: the Rockefeller Archive Center (particularly Harold Oakhill and Tom Rosenbaum), the Townsend Archives (particularly Cal Hibbard), the National Archives (particularly John Taylor), the Washington Federal Records Center, the Franklin D. Roosevelt Library, the Harry S. Truman Library, the Dwight D. Eisenhower Library, the John F. Kennedy Library, the Lyndon B. Johnson Library, the Nixon Presidential Materials Project at the National Archives, the Gerald R. Ford Library (particularly Helmi Raaska), the Inter-American Indian Institute in Mexico City, the New York Public Library (particularly David Beasley of the Economics Division), the Boston Public Library, the Library of Congress, the National Library of Peru, the National Library of Ecuador, the National Library of Colombia, the Securities and Exchange Commission's research office in New York, the Zurich municipal library, the British Museum, the Chicago Historical Library, the corporate records divisions of

---

*A note of style seems appropriate here. We have elected to use CIAA, the acronym that was employed by Nelson Rockefeller's wartime colleagues and his biographer Joe Alex Morris, for the office of the Coordinator of Inter-American Affairs, which he headed from 1940 to 1945. Subsequent to Rockefeller's elevation to assistant secretary of state in 1945, the title of the agency was changed to the Office of Inter-American Affairs (OIAA), the name subsequently adopted by the National Archives as the title for the agency's entire collection of records. Given that the CIAA years covered four out of five years in the collection, we elected to retain the original acronym.

ACKNOWLEDGMENTS

the Departments of State of the states of New York, Massachusetts, Florida, and Missouri, the North American Congress on Latin America, NACLA-West, the University of Vermont's Bailey Howe Library, Yale University, Yale Divinity School, Harvard University, Dartmouth College, the University of Texas at Austin, Trinity College (Connecticut), the University of California at Irvine, the University of Oklahoma at Norman, the University of North Carolina at Charlotte, the University of Massachusetts at Amherst, the University of Florida at Tampa, the Scripps Institution of Oceanography, the Summer Institute of Linguistics at Yarinacocha (Peru), *La Prensa* (Lima, Peru), *Alternativa* (Bogotá, Colombia), the *St. Louis Post Dispatch,* the *Charlotte News Observer,* the *Dallas Morning News,* the *Houston Chronicle,* and the *Johannesburg Star.*

During our research we met some extraordinary individuals who took risks to get additional information. Most have requested confidentiality. Some are included in the list of interviews, most of which took place between 1976 and 1980. For insight into the Bolivia of the Banzer dictatorship, however, we would like to acknowledge particularly Father Roy Bourgeois, who paid dearly for his criticism of the CIA's compromising and undermining of missionary work in Bolivia and for his efforts among Indians in the hills above La Paz: he was imprisoned, tortured, and, fortunately, through the intervention of church leaders, deported. Father Bourgeois's arrest came after he challenged the presence of a CIA officer, the embassy's labor attaché, at a meeting between Maryknoll missionaries and the U.S. ambassador that took place before our interviews with him. Since returning to the United States, Father Bourgeois has been imprisoned for showing his opposition to military aid to the government of El Salvador by protesting before visiting Latin American military officers at the Special Warfare Training Center at Fort Bragg, North Carolina.

Trying to persuade others of crimes against humanity is not an easy task, especially when these crimes occur in distant lands and powerful names at home are raised.

In Brazil, documents that might have been useful in naming those who were responsible for high crimes against Indian peoples perished in a mysterious fire at the archives of the government's Service for the Protection of the Indian. Fortunately, reports by anthropologists and unusual political circumstances prompted Brazil's attorney general to conduct his own investigation.

But the conquest of the Amazon is not only about the Brazilian Amazon. The Amazon River basin, including the mighty river's tributaries, also spans much of Peru, Colombia, Ecuador, Bolivia, and part of Venezuela, an area the size of the United States. Nor is conquest just about atrocities. Reports by anthropologists and government officials often described genocide and ethnocide as an unnecessarily cruel *process* of frontier development. By the end of our investigation, we had discovered that this process bore striking similarities to the conquest of the American West and involved some of the same powerful North American economic and political forces.

In the Amazon basin countries, the conquest followed the general trend of exploring for oil, rubber, and minerals, building roads and airstrips, backing surveys for colonization, expanding cash agriculture (to the detriment of indigenous subsistence agriculture), razing the rain forests, and U.S. competition with other big powers over geopolitical spheres of influence. All this was assisted by a foreign aid system which was gradually crafted over thirty years by Nelson Rockefeller, beginning as Roosevelt's Coordinator of Inter-American Affairs during World War II and as Truman's foreign aid architect.

The missionaries came in on the cultural, social, and political side of the conquest, their leader influenced by Rockefeller philanthropies and a counterinsurgency network shaped by Nelson Rockefeller's development goals. Summer Institute of Linguistics (SIL) was hired by military dictatorships and civilian governments, often headed by Nelson's allies, to pacify the tribes and integrate them into national economies increasingly being brought into the North American market. SIL used the Bible to teach indigenous people to "obey the government, for all authority comes from God."

In our research we found that those who challenged this assumption and the legacy left behind by Rockefeller and Townsend often paid the price of rejection through criticism, denial, or, worse, deafening silence. We remember particularly the late Michael Lambert, a former ethnobotany graduate student at Harvard University who did field research in the Amazon; he will be remembered for his quiet determination to bring the genocide of Amazonian Indians to the attention of his Harvard colleagues. He described his experience as painful.

No one, however, has suffered more pain than indigenous people. Unlocking the secrets took too many years, for us, but ultimately for them. If this book makes future inquiries easier and wiser, then it will have served its purpose.

January 1995

INTRODUCTION

The dark, comforting silence of the confessional shattered as the tiny sliding door rapped open, spraying light through a small screen.

"Yes, my son?" encouraged the priest when the male voice, whispering, faltered.

Then, out of the shadows it came, a torrent of crimes so overpowering that Father Edgar Smith's vow of silence shook to its Jesuit foundations.

Murder, the man explained, mass murder had been committed, and he, Ataide Pereira, had taken part. He could no longer live with his conscience. Besides, he had not been paid the $15 he was promised.

The victims were Cintas Largas, a small Indian tribe in the Brazilian Amazon. Named for the broad belts of bark that were their only clothing, this group of some 400 souls had lived for centuries along the Aripuanã River, hunting and fishing with arrows dipped in curare, successfully resisting all intruders. But now Brazilian and foreign companies coveted their lands. The Indians were marked for removal. Since Brazilian law technically protected the Indians as wards of the state, only surreptitious violence could be used.

It was a common enough solution. The general overseer of a local rubber company, Francisco de Brito, had already earned the local title of Champion Indian Killer by taking any Indians he captured on "a visit to the dentist": the victim was forced to "open wide" and shot through the mouth with a pistol. But one band of Cintas Largas had eluded the final solution by living deep in the jungle. Fortunately for de Brito, a man was found who knew enough of the culture of the Cintas Largas to tell him the precise day when most of the people of this village were likely to gather. The occasion would be deceptively joyful: their annual family reunion. The Indians would gather in the center of the village to pray, feast, and consult ancestral spirits represented by masquerading dancers.

De Brito concluded that the ceremony would be the perfect target for an aerial bombing. He hired a pilot and a commercial Cessna that flew over the village on the holy day, dropping sugar on the first pass and dynamite on the second. To hunt down the survivors seen fleeing into the jungle, de Brito turned to his underling, Chico, a man with a fondness for the machete. Pereira was one of Chico's recruits.

"We went by launch up the Juruena River," Pereira said.

> There were six of us, men of experience, commanded by Chico, who used to shove his tommy gun in your direction whenever he gave you an order.
>
> It took a good many days upstream to the Serra do Norte. After that we lost ourselves in the woods, although Chico had brought a Japanese compass with us. In the end the plane found us.
>
> It was the same plane they used to massacre the Indians, and they threw us down some provisions and ammunition. After that we went on for five days. Then we ran out of food again.
>
> We came across an Indian village that had been wiped out . . . and we dug up some of the Indians' manioc for food and caught a few small fish. By this time we were fed up and some of us wanted to go back, but Chico said he'd kill anybody who tried to desert. It was another five days after that before we saw any smoke. Even then the Cintas Largas were days away.
>
> We were all pretty scared of one another. In this kind of place people shoot each other and get shot, you might say, without knowing why. When they drill a hole in you, they have this habit of sticking an Indian arrow in the wound, to put the blame on the Indians.

The men hacked their way through the jungle, fighting off hordes of insects, enduring heat and downpours. "We were handpicked for the job, as quiet as any Indian party when it came to slipping in and out of trees.

"When we got to Cintas Largas country, there were no more fires and no more talking. As soon as we spotted their village, we made a stop for the night. We got up before dawn, then we dragged ourselves yard by yard through the underbrush until we were in range, and after that we waited for the sun to come up."

The clamor of the jungle night hushed as dawn broke over the village. A young Indian boy of about five had just stepped out to watch his elders work on the new huts they were building, when a murderous barrage of bullets poured on the village, cutting the men down where they stood. Armed whites appeared among the huts, firing their weapons indiscriminately, until only the boy and a young Indian girl (to whom he had fled for safety) were left. The terrified child was "yelling his head off." Pereira tried to stop Chico when he moved on the children, but Chico shrugged him off.

Chico shot the boy through the head. Pereira pleaded for the girl's life, reminding Chico of de Brito's penchant for prostituting Indian girls and of their own sexual appetites. Chico was unmoved. He gained sexual satisfaction through violence.

"We all thought he'd gone off his head," Pereira said,

and we were pretty scared of him. He tied the Indian girl up and hung her head downward from a tree, legs apart, and chopped her in half right down the middle with his machete. Almost with a single stroke I'd say. The village was like a slaughterhouse.

He calmed down after he'd cut the woman up, and told us to burn down all the huts and throw the bodies into the river. After that we grabbed our things and started back. We kept going after nightfall, and we took care to cover our tracks. . . . It took us six weeks to find the Cintas Largas, and about a week to get back.

When they arrived at Aripuanã, a tropical Dodge City, Chico brought samples of ore he found in the area to de Brito "to keep the company pleased."

Father Smith kept his head. Using all the powers of absolution at his command, he prevailed on Pereira to repeat his story on tape. "I want to say now that personally I've nothing against the Indians," Pereira claimed. But the Indians' lands were rich in gold, diamonds, and rare minerals. "The fact is the Indians are sitting on valuable land and doing nothing with it. They've got a way of finding the best plantation land, and there's all these valuable minerals about, too. They have to be persuaded to go, and if all else fails, well, then, it has to be force."[1]

Father Smith turned over the tape to local authorities, demanding an investigation, but for years the 1963 massacre of the Cintas Largas was covered up. Three prosecutors had withdrawn from the case, claiming conflicts of interest. Only when a congressional outcry over the growing sales of Amazonian lands to foreign companies prompted revelations in 1968 by the interior minister of widespread Indian genocide did the attorney general press for a trial. The Cintas Largas massacre turned out not to be an exceptional case.

More than $62 million worth of Indian property had been stolen in the previous decade, and at least 1,000 crimes—ranging from embezzlement to murder—were laid at the doorstep of the government's world-acclaimed Indian agency, the Service for the Protection of the Indian (SPI). A special commission had spent fifty-eight days traveling 10,000 miles to survey the Indian tribes, visiting more than 130 posts.

The evidence of genocide was overwhelming. Twenty volumes of evidence had been collected, documenting the destruction of whole tribes. Attacks by outsiders using everything from poisoned food to clothing infected with smallpox had resulted in Indian deaths by the tens of thousands. Anthropologists' estimates of the Indian population in Brazil ranged from just below 100,000 to a high of 200,000 Indians in 1957.[2] By 1968, these estimates had been cut by 50 percent[3]: anywhere from 40,000 to as many as 100,000 men, women, and children had died. The Indians north of the Amazon River had suffered particularly after 1964, when a military coup overthrew the elected government. Now nationalist army officers, led by General Albuquerque Lima, the interior minister, wanted the holocaust stopped—along with the foreign corporate penetration of the Amazon that, they claimed, had fanned the flames.

By then, however, most of the witnesses of the Cintas Largas massacre, as well as Father Smith, either had disappeared or were dead. The archives of the SPI had been destroyed in a mysterious fire. Finally, guns and tanks intervened. A military coup in December 1968, the second in four years, deposed the nationalist attorney general and the interior minister. None of the 134 SPI officials charged with crimes would ever stand trial. The attorney general's charge that SPI had been corrupted by starvation of government resources and "the disastrous impact of missionary activity" remained officially ignored. So did the claim of *Jornal do Brasil* in 1968 that "in reality, those in command of these Indian Protection posts are North American missionaries—they are in all the posts—and they disfigure the original Indian culture and enforce the acceptance of Protestantism."[4] But officials of the American Fundamentalist missionary organization that worked with the SPI among the tribes—the Summer Institute of Linguistics (SIL), known in the United States by its less scientific alias, the Wycliffe Bible Translators—denied that any genocide took place. The head of SIL's branch in Brazil disclaimed all reports of genocide,[5] and the founder of SIL, William Cameron Townsend, denied any knowledge of the massacres at all.[6]

The Cintas Largas case—and the Indians themselves—seemed slated for oblivion until *The Sunday Times* of London resurrected the genocide charge in 1969. Norman Lewis again raised the specter of foreign companies moving into the Brazilian Amazon. He reported that "deposits of rare metals were being found in the area [of the Cintas Largas]. What these metals were was not clear. Some sort of security blackout has been imposed, only fitfully penetrated by vague reports of the activities of American and European companies, and of the smuggling of planeloads of the said rare metals back to the U.S.A."[7]

A little over a year later, the International Police Academy, a school in Washington sponsored by the Agency for International Development (AID) but actually run by the CIA,[8] would report that a new Indian Guard was being trained in Brazil.[9] The Indian Guard, modeled after the Tribal Police of the U.S. Bureau of Indian Affairs (BIA), was placed under the authority of the regime's hurried replacement for the disgraced SPI, the National Foundation for the Indian (known in Brazil by its Portuguese acronym, FUNAI). FUNAI, in turn, was placed under the command of the former chief of military intelligence. It would take another two years before a top FUNAI agent would reveal that the Indian Guard was rounding up resisting Indians for "reeducation" at a concentration camp at Crenaque in the mining state of Minas Gerais.[10] "I am tired of being a gravedigger of the Indians," the agent stated on resigning from FUNAI. "I do not intend to contribute to enrichment of economic groups at the cost of the extinction of primitive cultures."[11] By then, FUNAI had adopted the BIA's policy of leasing Indian lands to mining companies, while its military superiors in the interior ministry in Brasília were cooperating with the U.S. Geological Survey in an AID-sponsored aerial survey of the Amazon.[12]

Among the American companies that would be allowed to enter the Cintas Largas reservation to explore for cassiterite, a vital component in tin production, was a firm partly controlled by a friend of Nelson Rockefeller.

In June 1969, a huge silver jet bearing the words "The United States of America" descended toward the airport of Brasília, the nation's futuristic capital in the Amazon basin. As the airliner's shadow passed over the shining steel and glass buildings that symbolized Brazil's pledge to conquer its wild interior, thousands of soldiers surrounded the ultramodern airport and lined the streets. *Air Force Two* landed with a screech and rolled toward the crowd of dignitaries waiting near the terminal. A door swung out and a man, his familiar square jaw cradling a wide smile, stepped briskly down the ramp. Nelson Rockefeller had arrived.

To most of the American Embassy staff, Rockefeller was just another powerful politician who happened to be a very wealthy man. He was the Republican governor of New York who had twice failed to win his party's presidential nomination. By all accounts, he was not through yet. His presence here on a presidential fact-finding tour left little room for doubt about his political ambitions.

But to many of the Brazilian dignitaries on hand, Nelson Rockefeller was much more than a rich politician. He was, to a degree, a personification of their fondest hopes in a troubled world. Perhaps more important, he was also a living symbol of the past, beginning thirty years before when they knew him simply as the Coordinator.

These Brazilians were aware of another, much less public Rockefeller: the Latin American Rockefeller. During World War II, as U.S. Coordinator of Inter-American Affairs, he had waged relentless economic and psychological warfare across the hemisphere against striking Indian workers and Nazi sympathizers with seemingly equal zeal. Then, as Franklin Roosevelt's assistant secretary of state for Latin America, he had launched the Cold War before it had even been declared, fusing hemispheric unity against the Soviets at the Pan American Conference in 1945 and that year's founding conference of the United Nations. His success in laying the legal foundation for a regional military pact paved the way for the Organization of American States (OAS), for the North Atlantic Treaty Organization (NATO), and for the Southeast Asia Treaty Organization (SEATO), which became the raison d'être for the war in Vietnam. Here was a proven ally against communists, whether homegrown or foreign.

He was also a valued economic ally. His personal sense of mission, inherited from his family's religious traditions and their unswerving Calvinistic belief in the uplifting capacities of capitalism, had been tempered by a respect for Latin culture rare among North Americans. His almost evangelical enthusiasm for developing capitalism in the Third World had been vital in launching America's foreign aid programs, especially Harry Truman's Point Four program. Under Dwight Eisenhower, he took this commitment to unparalleled if hidden heights as the president's personal liaison with the CIA as special assistant for Cold War strategy and psychological warfare. Long a confidant to presidents and business leaders throughout Latin America, Rockefeller was a trusted partner and quiet owner of vast ranches, giant banks, mines, and even—through IBEC, one of the hemisphere's largest diversified corporations—supermarkets. An heir to oil holdings in Central and South America, he was also brother of David Rockefeller, chairman of one of the region's prime sources of capital, Chase Manhattan Bank.

Nelson Rockefeller was, in short, Richard Nixon's perfect emissary to the southern American hemisphere's most powerful circles. He was a vigorous enthusiast schooled in the mutual subtleties of high finance and foreign aid, steeped in the rich cultural and political life of Latin America, and privy to the most secret U.S. intelligence operations in the region—an insider among insiders on the president's Foreign Intelligence Advisory Board. All this power, in turn, stemmed from the wealth created by Standard Oil, the firm his legendary grandfather had founded and steered toward its eventual dominance over Latin America's oil trade.

It was to his grandfather that Nelson owed his presence in Brazil this day. John D. Rockefeller, Sr., was the source of his power and the inspiration of his life. Strategically poised like a medieval robber baron at the crossroads of an industrializing world, the elder Rockefeller had extracted a personal treasure larger than anything the world had ever seen and—in relative terms—would probably ever see or allow again. From his steel will an empire had been forged, stretching along rail lines across America and then beyond, to the oil seeps of Latin America and the markets of the world.

Oil had brought Nelson Rockefeller to Brazil decades before, and the country had always been one of his favorites. Its vast Amazonian heartland held the shining dream of a new frontier for the Western world, much as the American West had captured the imagination of his grandfather's generation. The challenge of the West, symbolized by the Indians and the virgin lands they defended, had been met not just by troops and railroads; the religious missionaries funded by Grandfather and the secular missionaries sent out by Grandfather's great foundation had played vital roles. Now the missionary zeal powered Nelson's drive into the Amazon. And for this zeal, Nelson owed a great debt to his childhood memories of the world of his fathers.

I

THE LEGACY

We are only in the very dawn of commerce, and we owe that dawn, with all its promise to the channels opened up by Christian missionaries. . . . The effect of the missionary enterprise of the English speaking peoples will be to bring them the peaceful conquest of the world.

—REV. FREDERICK GATES
Letter to John D. Rockefeller, Sr.,
April 17, 1905

1
THE BAPTIST BURDEN

On the first day of July 1924, as the sun neared the end of its long span over the New Mexico desert, the Indians of Taos Pueblo awaited an important visitor. Most, like their war chief, Antonio Romero, hoped the man would become their ally.

The Pueblos were in desperate need of allies. Some of their best irrigated lands, occupied by Anglos and Mexican Americans, were on the verge of being lost forever without compensation. Their traditional religion was under attack by Christian Fundamentalist missionaries and the Bureau of Indian Affairs. Federal marshals could appear at any moment to end their defiance of the BIA's ban on their "pagan" ceremonies. Their children were undernourished and sick, some dying of tuberculosis, others blinded by trachoma. Now, the Pueblo way of life was threatened with extinction. The Pueblos needed friends in the powerful white world. And this man was very powerful.

As dusk neared, Indians on the roofs of their adobe homes noticed three twisting billows approaching from the distance. When they could see that these billows were unusually large automobiles, the pueblo exploded with excitement. By the time the expensive touring cars pulled up in a whirl of dust, a crowd had gathered.

Out stepped a small middle-aged man. He smiled shyly at the Indians. If they had not been apprised earlier of who he was, they would never have guessed that here was the richest man in the world.

John D. Rockefeller, Jr., gestured, and three adolescent boys joined him from the other cars. The eldest, tall and lean, seemed as shy as his father. Eighteen-year-old John carried his grandfather's name into the third generation and already seemed bent under the burden. The smallest boy, fourteen-year-old

Laurance, held a promising glint of mischief in his eyes, but had a habit of looking toward an older boy standing next to him for what to do next. This middle brother, a husky sixteen-year-old, beaming with animal confidence, was clearly the leader. His eyes quickly took in the crowd, one eye strangely bluer than the other. But what really set him apart was the square-jawed grin that flashed a fearless geniality. His father introduced him as Nelson. Nelson Aldrich Rockefeller, named after the maternal grandfather who had been the most powerful man in the United States Senate, already commanded attention.

Nelson's need for attention was precisely what made his father uncomfortable. It had been a source of strain for the father ever since the boy's early childhood, when Nelson's rebelliousness surfaced. This trip, far from their Manhattan home and the special relationship Nelson enjoyed with his mother, had been the father's attempt to gain a closer relationship with his elder boys, particularly this most troublesome second son. Yet the very fact that the Rockefeller males had arrived in different cars—the father riding with officials of a mining company, the boys following in tow—underscored how hard it was for the father to break with the corporate responsibility of being John D. Rockefeller's only son, even during a vacation. Try as he might, Rockefeller, Junior, seemed incapable of moving out of the shadow of his father, the founder of the family fortune. Even in the family office, he was referred to as "Mr. Junior"; as Junior himself once explained, there could be only *one* John D. Rockefeller. If Junior was hurt that Nelson looked up to his grandfather, not to him, as the family's role model, he had only himself to blame.

This western trip did not bring the father and son closer. On the contrary, it only strengthened the boy's identification with Rockefeller, Senior. All that Nelson had seen so far—and would see—that was symbolic of Rockefeller power, including the mining company that had furnished the cars and drivers for this visit to the Indians, was really a testament to his grandfather. Even the Indians who had gathered to meet them were attracted not to the little man who was his father, but to the magic of Grandfather's name.

The day had been long, and Nelson, as usual, was hungry. Beneath large cottonwoods deep rooted in the Indian soil, the Rockefellers dined, watching the sky over the pueblo fade from crimson to deep violet.

Then, as stars sprayed over the Pueblo canyon, the fun began for the boys. Around a crackling campfire in the woods, Indians performed ceremonial dances in their traditional garb. Nelson was entranced. The bright colors of their costumes dazzled in the firelight as the Indians moved with the ancient rhythms, the music echoing off the canyon walls like spirit voices. When the dancing ceased, Romero stepped forward and presented his own warbonnet to Nelson's father, a rare honor. The man received the headdress with proper grace. He was impressed.

"No government official has ever been presented with a present that is valued as highly by the Indians," Junior was later told by a proud executive of

Colorado Fuel and Iron Company.[1] The Rockefeller-owned CF&I, which ran mining operations in the Colorado mountains to the north, was a power in the region. Unknown to Nelson or his brothers, the company had secretly contracted through the BIA for the dances, paying the Indians thirty dollars.

It was a pittance for what a BIA official called the most elaborate entertainment that Taos Pueblo had ever put on for visitors. Warned by a CF&I official against jeopardizing "future courtesies" the Indians might extend to the Rockefellers, Junior showed his appreciation. The next day he returned with the boys. In true GI fashion he distributed seventy pounds of candy to squealing crowds of children.

If the Indian children's parents had hoped for something more substantial, they would be disappointed. Junior would not assist them in their struggle against the Baptist missionaries and the BIA. In fact, he was secretly funding the missionaries.

The Religious Rockefellers

Nelson's father had been raised within the moral confines of the northern Baptist church. Everything in life was severely measured, everything reduced to its place within the safe clockwork universe of a Newtonian God. Pocantico, Grandfather's 3,600-acre estate overlooking the Hudson River, symbolized this passion for order. Surrounded by tall fences and guarded gates, Pocantico was a world apart, isolated from the chaos of nature. Formal gardens, acres of flower beds and carefully manicured lawns, and shrubs and transplanted trees positioned at strategic points along paved roads all spoke of the steely will of the Calvinist ex-bookkeeper who had founded Standard Oil. On top of the tallest hill stood the huge stone chateau Junior had built for his father in atonement for the wooden mansion that had accidentally burned down during one of his summer stays there. Beneath Grandfather's mansion, cradled in the valley below, Junior built his own home, its modest size appropriate to his station in the family's patriarchy.

Here, under the long shadow of their grandparents' frill-less religion, Nelson and his brothers and sister were raised. Each morning, precisely at 7:45 A.M., Junior would lead them in prayer and Bible readings around the breakfast table; each evening before dinner, they would pray again. Between Junior's exhortations on the importance of keeping accurate accounts of their allowances and the occasional reward for killing flies at a penny apiece, the children were drilled in Bible verses written on cardboard file cards. Sunday evenings, after the obligatory state dinner with Grandfather on the hill, were often given over to singing hymns. Nelson, the most effusive of the children, suffered terribly. "We sang hymns tonight," he once wrote his mother, Abby Rockefeller, after one such night when she could not attend, "but luckily Pa had to go to church so we stopped at a quarter of eight."[2]

Junior was not simply a churchgoer; he was a church leader. For years, he ran a Bible class for aspiring young men at the Fifth Avenue Baptist Church in New York City. He was a heavy contributor to the Northern Baptist Convention and its missions. He also gave millions to the Young Men's Christian Association. It was at a YMCA meeting at Brown University, in fact, that Junior delivered a famous address comparing the elimination of small-business competitors to the pruning that made the American Beauty rose possible.

Yet, because of his liberal education at Brown University, Junior also developed a keen appreciation of the modern sciences. He had, with his father, become more sympathetic to the "higher criticism" of the Bible that rejected the literal, ahistorical interpretation of the Scriptures favored by Fundamentalist preachers. By the time Nelson had reached his teens, the Baptist ministers and ministers' sons who had guided most of the Rockefeller family's business investments and philanthropic affairs had been replaced by younger men, such as lawyer Raymond Fosdick and his brother Rev. Harry Emerson Fosdick, the liberal theologian.

This did not sit well with the Baptist elders, especially when Ray Fosdick advised Junior to give $1,000 to the liberal and often controversial American Indian Defense Association. Rockefeller support for any Indian civil rights movement could do great damage to the missionaries' hold over the reservations. Missionaries, through their schools, already controlled the education of Indian children; now they sought to break the back of Indian culture by prohibiting traditional Indian religions.

Six months before Nelson and his brothers arrived with Junior at Taos Pueblo, a pitched battle had broken out between liberals and conservatives over the mind of the only son of the founder of Standard Oil. The stakes were high: control over a fortune approaching $1 billion. Junior needed a bevy of advisers to guide him through the mounting tangle of financial and social responsibilities that accompanied the family's transition from provincialism to world power. The summer of 1924 found Junior torn between safety in the traditions of his Baptist past and the exigencies of stewarding his family's wealth through a tumultuous, technology-driven decade.

Feeling the looming presence of Senior over his shoulder, Junior was terrified of controversy. Decisions did not come easily to the Rockefeller heir. In the previous decade he had committed a series of blunders. On the advice of the Baptist minister who ran the family office, he had fought a union drive and triggered a massacre of miners and their families at CF&I. On the advice of John Mott, evangelical leader of YMCA, he had tried to launch a Christian missionary crusade to save the world from communism, only to see it collapse in debt and scandal. Now he was worried that he had gone too far in the opposite direction and gotten his name involved with an extreme liberal—John Collier, the founder of the American Indian Defense Association. Junior's Baptist friends were warning him that Collier's unbridled defense of the Pueblo Indians was threatening to explode in scandal.

Conservative Baptist missionaries had recently joined the U.S. Department of the Interior in publicly accusing Collier's beloved Pueblo of performing acts of "pornography" and "obscenity" in their ceremonial dances. Worse, the Indians' white allies were being accused of "communism." The country was still reeling from the government's massive nationwide raids during the post–World War I red scares, and those who participated in the smears carried a wide brush. Rumors had begun circulating about Collier, and Junior's anxiety about his own respectability was mounting. Junior could prevent his sons from knowing, but how long could he hide the truth from someone like his father? He decided to deny future funding to Collier and his Indian Defense Association. At this stage in his life, when Senior was finally turning over his private fortune to Junior, fear of controversy was a guiding light.

So were old family habits. John D.'s family had traveled a long way within Baptist traditions. They relied on the advice of church elders when it came to Indian missions and the promotion of the "uplifting" Protestant work ethic. Ever watchful of the evils that paganism and drink did to the work ethic, Junior's temperance-obsessed mother, Laura Spelman Rockefeller, had been the catalyst for many of the Rockefeller contributions to Baptist missions in the West.

The location of the Indian missions, however, indicated that she was not the sole inspiration. The missions were in areas where her husband had been quietly planning investments.

The Secular Rockefellers

In the nineteenth century, when white America galloped mercilessly through what Helen Hunt Jackson called its "Century of Dishonor" with Native Americans, the Rockefeller family's investments were at the forefront of the commercial conquest of the West. While his brothers William and Frank speculated in the commercial beef ranches that were replacing the Indians' buffalo-hunting lands, John D. Rockefeller focused on iron, coal, and lead mines and the railroads that serviced them, along with the new oil fields being found in Kansas and Oklahoma.[3]

During those years, the elder Rockefellers had used missionaries to gather intelligence about insurgences in the West or to discourage them. As far back as 1883, after word reached Cleveland, Ohio, of a rebellion on the Creek reservation in Oklahoma Territory coinciding with Geronimo's headline-making war against encroaching silver miners in Arizona, Rockefeller took a sudden interest in one of his wife's missionary friends. He wrote Rev. Almon A. Bacone, who ran

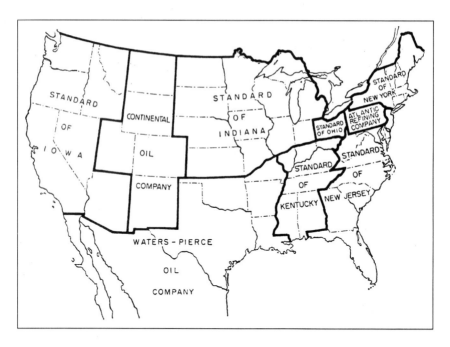

The conquest of the American West and Standard Oil's expansion into the West, carving up territories among its subsidiaries, was accompanied by Rockefeller support for northern Baptist Christian missions.

Source: (*top*) Standard Oil Company, 1899, in Continental Oil Company, *Conoco: The First One Hundred Years* (New York: Dell, 1975); (*above*) Interchurch World Movement, *World Survey, American Volume* (New York: Interchurch Press, 1920).

an Indian school not far from the rebellion in Oklahoma, asking for information. Bacone replied with details on the rebellion's exact location and the impact it had on the region. Bacone's years of fruitless entreaties to the oil tycoon were over; the next thing he knew, Rockefeller's check for $5,000 had arrived on his desk.[4] Rockefeller's contributions mostly were channeled through the American Baptist Home Mission Society, inspiring Bacone to name his school's first major building after Rockefeller. Rockefeller philanthropies would continue donations to Bacone College, but by 1890, as the site of insurgency moved north to Chicago's factories, Rockefeller shifted his attention to Dwight L. Moody, a forerunner of Billy Graham. The fiery Chicago evangelist exhorted workers "to higher thoughts than labor agitation."[5] Delighted with this otherworldliness, Rockefeller funded Moody until the orator died in 1899. In the same period, Rockefeller money went to Baptist missionaries working among the restless miners, loggers, and Chippewa Indians in the Lake Superior region, where Rockefeller's newly acquired Mesabi iron mines were located.[6] Bacone's school, meanwhile, prospered under the BIA's aegis beside the Kansas-Texas Railroad, in which Rockefeller had a sizable investment. Bacone had tried to ingratiate himself with Senior by giving him hot tips on Indian land speculation. Cherokee land, he advised Rockefeller, was selling for $6,000, and "government warrants will rise" once the "Cherokees sell their strip."[7] Rockefeller declined. Trading in real estate did not interest him. Oil did.

By 1924, when Nelson and his brothers arrived in the Southwest, a forest of Grandfather's derricks covered Indian reservation lands in Oklahoma. Standard Oil's drills were also boring into the Navajo reservation in New Mexico that Junior and the boys visited before coming to Taos. Just the previous October, BIA Commissioner Charles Burke had auctioned off twenty-two Navajo oil tracts. One oil structure, called Rattlesnake Dome, near Shiprock, New Mexico, was sold for $1,000 to friends of the BIA's new commissioner for the Navajo, only to be resold for $4 million to Continental Oil, a spinoff of the old Standard Oil Trust, in which the Rockefellers had a substantial holding. In 1926, when Continental Oil completed a pipeline from Shiprock south to the railroad junction at Gallup for shipments of oil to Standard Oil's refineries in New Jersey, Junior would drive along its route with Abby and the younger children, having incorporated Shiprock into his tour of the Navajo Reservation. To keep his vacation as productive as possible, he would also include Bartlett Ranch north of Taos Pueblo, a coal-rich miniempire that had been proposed as an investment.[8]

As the Rockefeller caravan sped away from Taos, Nelson only vaguely comprehended his elders' capacity to turn a profit on the Indians' desperation. He did witness his father purchasing old Navajo blankets, a rug, and silver objets d'art as well as Yaqui blanket-rugs and 100-year-old Chimayó blankets at BIA-sponsored shops in Santa Fe and Grand Canyon National Park, but he had no notion of the BIA-sponsored oppression that was behind these shops. Instead, "primitive art" caught his fancy. And just as Nelson at an impressionable age had watched his father finger the Indian artifacts with more than casual intent, so his own future son, Michael, would also embrace the trade. In Michael's case, however, his hunger for primitive art would consume not just his interest, but his life.

THE RECKONING

From Taos and more Indian dances in the cliff dwellings of Mesa Verde canyon, Junior took the boys north into the rugged foothills of southern Colorado for their first tour of an underground mine. Donning coveralls and miners' caps with headlamps, they plunged wide eyed into the bowels of CF&I's Walsenburg mine. As their coal cars raced beneath timbers holding up tons of rock, the boys were fascinated by the eerie lights and the tough miners with mineral-blackened faces.

But the dark caverns held poignant memories for their father. It was just twenty-five miles south of here, at the CF&I mines in Ludlow only ten years earlier, that forty striking miners were killed and countless wounded by company gunmen and state militiamen shooting machine guns. When the miners' families picked through the smoldering ruins of their camp the next morning, they found more horror: Eleven children and two women, trying to hide from the bullets, had taken refuge in their tent's dugout; the bullets had set fire to the tent above, suffocating them.

Ludlow had threatened to bring as much disgrace to the second generation of Rockefellers as Standard Oil's competitive ruthlessness had brought to the first. Junior saw the killings and the public hearings that followed as "one of the most important things that ever happened to the Rockefeller family,"[9] forcing their first fledgling steps toward corporate liberalism.

Junior was trying to build a new image of the Rockefellers in the public eye. He was seen visiting the CF&I hospital with the boys and meeting members of the company union that he had set up for the miners. Later he and the boys would climb aboard a private Pullman and speed to Montana for the boys' final treat: camping and horseback riding in Glacier National Park and meeting more Indians. Junior's struggle between corporate liberalism and Baptist conservatism had already been tested by the Pueblos. In that case, he resolved the conflict by withdrawing support from a cause tainted by the reputed radicalism of the Indian Defense Association. For the rest of the century, the Rockefellers would shun extremes of either side. With the Blackfeet in Montana, Junior would avoid controversy by simply exposing his sons to Indian ways without committing himself one way or the other. Even this was an act ahead of its time, however.

Except for Indian agents and missionaries, few white men would be seen mingling their families with "redskins."

Junior arranged day-long visits to the Blackfoot reservation. The Indians, led by a former tribal judge, Wolf Plume, "received us in their war paint and beaded clothes with great ceremony," Junior noted in his diary, "and were most friendly."[10] The Indians gave each of the Rockefellers a Blackfoot name. Junior was named "Little Dog"; John, "Buffalo Teeth"; and Laurance, "Rider-of-a-Sorrel Horse." Nelson's name had a prophetic charm: Sikiopio-Kitope, "Rider-of-a-White Horse."

This was Nelson's last childhood experience with Indians, and one that would influence his political life in more ways than he ever guessed.

The Priming Sting

Back in New York, Nelson returned to school and the joys of owning his first car, a hiccuping old Ford roadster. His relations with his father did not improve any more than did his grades. Increasing his studies to two hours a day and cutting off the radio and phonograph during the week did not help fend off Junior's steady barrage of criticisms. Authoritarianism, not liberalism, ruled the Rockefeller household.

Nelson's problems with school stemmed mostly from dyslexia, a developmental anomaly in the cerebral cortex of the brain that transposes the order of numbers, letters, and words when reading. Junior only aggravated this condition by trying to force the boy's left-handedness into the right-handed standards of society. Junior's remedy was pain. Each night, Nelson was forced to sit at the family dinner table with an elastic band around his wrist. Attached to the band was a string that led to the head of the table. When the boy instinctively raised his left hand to eat, Junior jerked the string, snapping the elastic band against Nelson's wrist with a sharp sting.

"My father didn't believe in people being left-handed, " Nelson confided years later to interviewer David Frost.[11]

From the time Nelson could count, he learned that Junior dispensed emotional rewards as meagerly as Junior's own father had allowed waste. When Junior did show fatherly affections, they were as strictly rationed as the twenty-five-cent allowances he distributed to the children each week, minus five-cent fines levied on Nelson for his perennially poor bookkeeping.

Lincoln School, an experiment of Columbia University's Teachers College, was Abby's one opportunity to provide an escape for her son. It proved to be a godsend. It allowed each student to progress at an individual pace. True to founder John Dewey's theories about the importance of education in preparing a citizenry for democracy, Lincoln rejected Latin and the classics favored by educators of the previous century and emphasized instead the sciences, history, and modern topics. It also prepared the mostly upper-class heirs for their future social responsibilities by exposing them to ethnic and class diversity through a democratic sprinkling of immigrant children from New York City's vast working class.

Abby's troubled teenager flourished in his newfound freedom. The family's life soon revolved around shuttling the youngest boys, Laurance, David, and Winthrop, between Lincoln and Junior's Fifty-fourth Street town house, Abby's top-hat-shaped electric-powered "box car" eventually replaced by the watchful limousine that dutifully followed the roller-skating children to and from school. Junior once again had to concede that in the raising of his sons—as in his religious, philanthropic, and labor policies—his Baptist authoritarianism had to give way to a science-based liberalism if order and respect were to be maintained. But his bond with Nelson was never to be intimate.

Conversely, Nelson's admiration for Grandfather was unbounded. Junior and Senior were studies in contrast. Whereas Junior was cautious to the extreme, Senior in his younger days had been legendary in Cleveland for his readiness to crack a whip over his horses for a buggy race with any neighbor who dared challenge him.

Nelson grew up sheltered from his grandfather's antics in the early oil wars. Never once, in all the Sundays that he and his brothers and sister were bundled up and driven to their grandfather's mansion for dinner, had Nelson ever heard the old man speak of Standard Oil. And Senior certainly did not cut a figure that suggested great power. The world's titan of oil was by then cadaverously thin and bony, and he had lost all his hair to alopecia. Where eyebrows once fixed a penetrating gaze over a handsome face sporting a thick brown mustache, now only scars remained like etching on dried parchment.

Nelson, in the requisite Eton collar, coat, and pin-striped pants, was awed. He noted the great respect his father showed the old man and considered himself special for having been born on Grandfather's birthday. Every sabbath, when Senior was in residence at Pocantico, the patriarch would preside at the head of the long table in his ornate dining hall, spinning tales. Senior would often spring up from his chair to act out scenes, joking in his dry midwestern humor. Despite his advanced years, his disdain for reading, and his penchant for idle gossip, there was an unsettling sharpness in his mockery of the idiosyncrasies of his associates. Beneath his white wig, which was often askew, startlingly clear blue eyes peered out from sunken sockets, betraying the intelligence that still worked feverishly behind them, formulating plans and mapping strategies as seriously as it did forty years before.

And now, as Junior tried to protect his father's traditional influence in the northern Baptist church and its missionary programs, the whole Fundamentalist movement among missionaries fell under the old man's steady gaze.

2

THE FUNDAMENTALIST CONTROVERSY

THE FUNDAMENTALIST CHALLENGE

At eighty-five, Senior was still playing eighteen holes of golf and capable of dancing a jig after sinking a twenty-foot putt. He had retired long ago from any official role in the Standard Oil Trust, but not from keeping a watchful eye on the thirty-nine companies it spawned or on his other holdings. He retained his seat on the New York Stock Exchange, dabbling with a $20 to $30 million kitty he had taken out of his $1 billion fortune.

He still made headlines as easily as he made money. Ivy Lee, the father of corporate public relations, had been generously paid to convert Rockefeller's image from the black-caped mustached villain with a top hat who tied young women tenants to rails in front of approaching trains. The tycoon was now photographed as a smiling gentle old soul who handed out dimes to curious bystanders and tens of millions to educators, healers, and scientists.

But even the wizardry of Ivy Lee could not control the deeper forces that pulsed beneath the glittering skin of the prosperous 1920s, powers of an earlier rural age that resented the Industrial Revolution that finally had conquered America. Since the first decade after the Civil War, John D. Rockefeller had symbolized this revolution. His ruthlessness in the new oil business that fueled this revolution had earned him the fear of small businessmen across the nation. The rebates he forced on railroads, accounting for at least some of the higher freight charges the railroads imposed as compensation on everything from grain to furniture, had stirred the ire of populist farmers for over half a century. From these farmers had come the greatest political challenge to the new eastern wealth

Rockefeller represented, a giant rural movement led by Nebraska's Senator William Jennings Bryan, the hero of the breadbasket states and their marrying priesthood, the Fundamentalist preachers of the literal Bible.

Hardly a season passed during his adolescence when Nelson did not read newspaper accounts of Fundamentalists attacking his family. In the midst of Nelson's junior year at Lincoln, in December 1924, Dr. John Roach Stratton, a leader of the Baptist Bible Union, and pastor of Manhattan's Calvary Baptist Church, delivered a scathing assault on Nelson's father.

"Conditions today are appalling," he said of the hedonistic roaring twenties, "and are enough to awaken even a self-complacent and somnolent Modernist like John D. Rockefeller, Jr. The Rockefeller money is the greatest curse that rests upon the Baptist denomination. Through the infidel University of Chicago and the unbelieving Union Theological Seminary of this city, it is doing more to blight us and blast us than all other forces combined."[1]

Behind these ravings was an economic and political conflict unknown to Nelson, but not to Senior or Junior.

Across the nation, rural Fundamentalist ministers reacted angrily to what they perceived to be the vice and venality of the cities and the cities' impact on their farming congregations. Steeped in a literal Bible unencumbered by science or historical insight and unaware of its scriptural contradictions, the inhabitants of America's closed frontiers found their most cherished institutions being destroyed by what the Rockefellers called progress. In the ensuing struggle between traditionalism and modernism for control of America's soul—and future—one man, perhaps more than any other, stood in the middle before he, too, succumbed to the Rockefellers' quest for new frontiers. His name was Frederick Gates.

The son of a Baptist missionary sent to the "destitute of the West," Gates had risen to the secretaryship of the American Baptist Education Society. In 1887, Gates and other Baptist leaders had convinced the elder Rockefeller to finance the founding of the West's first great Baptist university, the University of Chicago. The university was given the mission of influencing the religious development of the new states being carved out of lands of the defeated Indians.

But Gates was not exclusively Baptist. Taking over Rockefeller's secondhand "retail charity" and transforming it into a prime-mover "wholesale philanthropy," he urged the Rockefellers to break through the walls of Baptist sectarianism and donate to the missions of other denominations in the "one great preconceived plan." These contributions included $100,000 in International Harvester bonds to the Congregationalist Foreign Missions Board in 1905. That it was rejected as "tainted money," coming as it did on the heels of Ida Tarbell's exposé, *The History of the Standard Oil Company,* did not deter the minister. Gates, sensing Junior's crushing sense of guilt and lack of worth under the shadow of his father, convinced him to pay his moral debt by responding to the "white man's burden" of expanding Christian civilization. By secularizing the Christian mission through corporate philanthropy and empowering it with the wonders of modern medical science, God's work could be done for the benefit of humanity, the Rockefeller name, and Junior's immortal soul.

Like the Brown-educated heir, Gates had studied the "higher criticism" of modernist Protestant theologians who found a literal interpretation of the Bible incompatible with history or science. He saw science as God's light shining in a world of dark passions. "In these sacred rooms," Gates wrote after inspecting the Rockefeller philanthropy, the Rockefeller Institute for Medical Research, "He is whispering His secrets. To these men He is opening up the mysterious depths of His Being,"[2] and, apparently, to Fundamentalist schools, His wrath. Scores of medical schools run by Protestant denominations succumbed under the competition for students posed by such science-based, Rockefeller-favored institutions as the University of Chicago, Johns Hopkins, Yale, and St. Louis's Washington University.

Next on Gates's streamlining list was the General Education Board itself, formed "to promote a comprehensive system of higher education in the United States." Gates believed that only a fourth of the country's colleges and universities were qualified to be incorporated into the GEB's system, which would emphasize the social and physical sciences, rather than religious interpretations of phenomena. Once again, the Fundamentalists howled.

Finally, Gates antagonized Fundamentalist southern businessmen by invading the area with Rockefeller investments. The South was being rediscovered as a new frontier of cheap labor and raw materials for northern capital investments along J. P. Morgan's reorganized Southern Railway. The GEB was, in fact, inspired by Junior's trip on the "Millionaire's Special," a train tour through the cotton mill towns of the southern Piedmont. The founding of the GEB coincided with Gates's steering Rockefeller money into the South. At least $4 million worth of stock in the Virginia-Carolina Chemical Company gave the Rockefellers a stake in one of the nation's largest fertilizer firms, with phosphate holdings and fertilizer plants throughout the South. Other agribusiness investments included the Southern Cotton Oil Company, makers of Wesson oil, the American Agricultural Chemical Company, and the American Linseed Company, which used linseed oil as a primer in paints and varnishes, and refined Hawaiian coconut meat and peanut oil to create "Nucoa Butter" margarine. And $30 million was invested in the International Harvester Corporation, the new holding company that J. P. Morgan had organized for the Rockefellers' McCormick in-laws.[3]

By 1911, the new Rockefeller interest in cash agriculture had blossomed into another secular mission for the GEB: a program of model farms across the South, designed to demonstrate the value of farm machinery, fertilizer, and scientific methods of crop rotation to fight the boll weevil's ravages of cotton crops.

This crusade for productivity was complemented by the Rockefeller Sanitary

Commission's extraordinarily successful drive to eradicate the mysterious cause of the South's notorious "germ of laziness," hookworm. Armed with science and the Standard Oil fortune, the Rockefeller campaigns swept away all opposition.

The Arms of the Octopus

But the ground they broke in southern agriculture also held the hot coals of rural resentments. After World War I, the cultural battle rolled over into the field of economics and politics, where farmers had forty years of bitter experience with Standard Oil's manipulation of rail freight charges. Fertilizer companies and farm machine giants, such as International Harvester, had increased the productivity of acreage so much that the agricultural markets were flooded, and prices were lowered. Although much more than the Rockefellers were responsible, they were easily identifiable targets for populist organizers of small farmers who could not afford to purchase the expensive machinery, fertilizer, or more land.

At the same time, the government's postwar red scare resulted in bizarre allegations against the family. It was during these years that the Rockefellers were transformed in the minds of many rural Fundamentalists from the ogres of monopoly capitalism into secret financiers of an international communist conspiracy. The germ of this remarkable metamorphosis lay in the Fundamentalists' confusing the centrally planned *publicly* owned economy, promoted by socialists (and later by communists), with the centrally planned *privately* owned economy, promoted by many corporate leaders. Given the limited access to information about the critical differences in the programs (both of which, after all, came from the hated big cities of moneyed elites) and the farmers' own bitter experiences with the all-powerful corporate trusts, it is understandable that the frustrations and fears of rural people were so easily channeled by demagogues posing as populists and that this confusion was actively encouraged by even sincere populists.

Rev. William Riley, speaking at Moody Memorial Church in Chicago, charged the Rockefeller family with "standardizing" religion, just as it had the oil industry. Within the space of only a few years, Fundamentalist distrust of the Rockefellers evolved into a near-pathological conviction that the Rockefellers were not religious at all, but promoters of a vast communist conspiracy to seize control of their churches and impose atheism on their schools. Riley claimed that the culprit was William R. Harper, president of the University of Chicago, and his theories of "progressive education."

"If it were American education only, the situation would not be so bad, but our foreign denominational schools are feeling the pull of these same coils and are rapidly being converted into the flesh and blood of Modernism through the

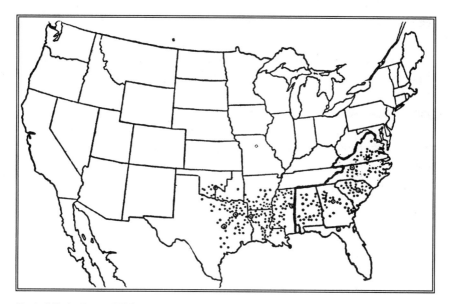

Rockefeller's General Education Board established farm demonstrations throughout the South between 1904 and 1914, extolling virtues of machinery, fertilizers, crop rotation, and other techniques. Rockefeller investments in International Harvester and fertilizer companies also occurred during this period.

Source: Abraham Flexner, *The General Education Board, 1902–14.*

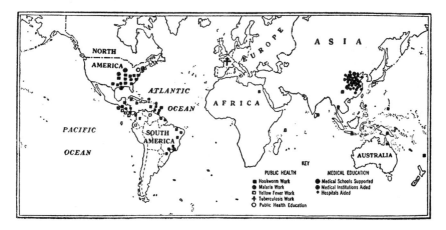

Rockefeller secular missions soon expanded beyond their social laboratory in the American South to overseas lands where Standard Oil was active.

Source: Alan Nevins, *Study in Power: John D. Rockefeller, Industrialist and Philanthropist*, vol. 2 (New York: Charles Scribner's Sons, 1953), p. 393.

Harper-Rockefeller movement." America, claimed Riley, was being threatened by an "Octopus of unbelief."[4]

Despite all Junior's philanthropic efforts to clear the family name, the tainted legends surrounding his father's rise to power would continue to haunt his own children. Worse, Senior would soon find out. Junior had heard that Fundamentalists had scored an unprecedented victory at the recent Northern Baptist Convention in Des Moines. An anonymous gift of $1,750,000 was accepted by the Baptists in return for a pledged adherence to the Fundamentalist creed by recipient lay missionaries and ordained ministers. Few were fooled by the donor's insistence on anonymity. Milton Stewart, brother of Lyman Stewart, the founder of Union Oil of California, had recently financed a tour of Protestant missions in China by Fundamentalist leaders and had imposed identical conditions for receiving Stewart's donations.

If anything could waken the ire of Senior, it was the Stewarts. Not only did they fund the Rockefellers' most vehement Fundamentalist critics, but they were the biggest thorn in the side of his favorite offspring from the oil trust, Standard Oil of California. Since 1904, when Lyman Stewart's son, W. L. Stewart, beat out Standard Oil for the crude oil of independent producers in the San Joaquin Valley, Union Oil had proved to be a powerful competitor.[5] The Stewarts held a personal grudge against the Rockefellers as well, having been among the independent producers of Titusville, Pennsylvania, that succumbed to the Standard Oil Trust.

Junior had hesitated to tell Senior about the Fundamentalists' successes at the Northern Baptist Convention. He had never felt adequate to the task of running his father's empire—and for good reason. Senior had not taken the time to prepare Junior for empire. "Father never said a word to me about what I was to do in the office before I began work there," he once confessed.[6] A traditional father, Senior had left the task of child rearing to Junior's mother, Laura Spelman Rockefeller. But there was a price for being the only son of the hated John D. Rockefeller: isolation. Tutored on the Rockefeller estate outside Cleveland, where Standard Oil's first refinery was located, Junior was fawned upon like a "Crown Prince," as his older sister, Edith, put it.

He was chagrined by reversals so soon on the heels of large donations to the Baptists by his father and the Laura Spelman Rockefeller Memorial Fund. Only six months before, Senior had given $500,000 each to the American Baptist Foreign Mission Society, the American Baptist Home Mission Society, and the Ministers and Missionaries Benefit Board of the Northern Baptist Convention. He had also made an unconditional gift of $100,000 to the Relief and Annuity board of the Southern Baptist Convention in Dallas.[7] Junior had been one of those who encouraged his father to make the gifts unconditional. Now he felt humiliated by Stewart's "Fundamentalist-only" gift to the Northern Baptists.

There was no way out. Junior summoned his courage and wrote his father, acknowledging that Senior had "doubtless" been told of the Fundamentalist victories and the conditional gift. He suggested that Senior invoke a clause in his letter of bequest allowing the money to be withdrawn if it should "cease to be needed." He ended with a shameless apology. "If I had ever dreamed that the Home Mission Society would have accepted a gift on such conditions, permanently binding its trustees to the holding of such narrow views, I would have strongly urged you not to make the gifts to it which you have recently made."[8]

Rockefeller's reply from Pocantico makes Junior's consternation understandable. It was a remarkable demonstration of just how much the octogenarian patriarch was still in command.

The senior Rockefeller had no intention of retreating and suggested that Junior get his lawyers ready for action. He had decided to "get the consent of the Mission Societies for modified conditions of our gifts, possibly without delay, so as to forestall, if possible, the ill effect that their still treacherous action may have on the final carrying out of our ideas."

His tactic was vintage Rockefeller: the subtle approach, requesting only a change in the terms of his gifts. But the implication was clear: A refusal of his terms by the missions would jeopardize further gifts. The real substance of the tactic, however, was its breadth. Rockefeller's request would go to *all* Protestant missionary organizations that had accepted his gifts, not just to the Baptists, so "that if we go about it wisely we may secure still further protection against possible inroads by the group to which you refer."[9]

The Fundamentalists had awakened an enemy far more formidable than they realized. For here was a veteran of wars more bloody and ruthless than most ministers had ever encountered. Rockefeller had built an empire by crushing stronger men than Rev. Riley. The old warrior's blood had been stirred, and he would, as usual, battle with all the legendary powers at his command.

His wrath was unconcealed, but measured. Money could keep the mainstream denominations in line. And behind money was oil, still the bulk of the Rockefeller fortune. As the family began unloading its holdings in domestic agricultural firms to escape the postwar collapse of agricultural prices, oil, particularly foreign oil, would remain the source of its power. Oil's role in the postwar realignment of power around the world would be crucial, and the Rockefellers intended to play a big part in that realignment.

Standard Oil counsel and Rockefeller Foundation trustee Charles Evans Hughes recently had become President Warren G. Harding's secretary of state. Hughes had initiated an era of policy and style that prompted a member of the British Foreign Office to complain that "Washington officials begin to think, talk, and write like Standard Oil officials."[10]

The Prince of Modernism

On the religious front, it was left to Rev. Harry Emerson Fosdick, brother of Junior's closest adviser, to fire the first shot in the Rockefeller counterattack that soon was called "the Fundamentalist Controversy."

Although an ordained Baptist minister, Fosdick had accepted the pulpit of a liberal Presbyterian church in Manhattan. Fosdick had already earned criticism as the "Prince of Modernism" for the liberal views on evolution he espoused in a speech before the Northern Baptist Convention in 1919 and for making no secret of his disdain for the ethnocentrism and intolerance he witnessed during a trip to China secretly funded by Rockefeller Junior. These experiences influenced one of his first sermons at the First Presbyterian Church in Manhattan, entitled "Shall the Fundamentalists Win?" Fosdick actually appealed to Christian unity, but under a modernist banner; he argued persuasively for an educated science-based faith and liberal tolerance of other cultures in the world.

Fosdick's sermon might have gone unnoticed except for the intervention of Junior and Ivy Lee, the master propagandist. Lee prepared, and Junior paid for, a mass mailing of the sermon.

The Fundamentalists took the bait and quickly overplayed their hand, launching a campaign that revealed the full vehemence of their intolerance. Led by former Secretary of State and Klan-sympathizer William Jennings Bryan, they even tried to seize control of the 1924 Northern Presbyterian General Assembly, but were cleverly foiled by a young Wall Street lawyer named John Foster Dulles. Dulles, a future secretary of state, used his formidable legal skills to shift the issue of debate from modernism to Fosdick's connection with the Baptist church. Fosdick accepted his role as sacrificial lamb for a modern science-based Protestantism and resigned from the New York presbytery. The Fundamentalists won the battle, but lost the war of public opinion. The Rockefellers had again emerged triumphant. That was in 1925, the year that William Jennings Bryan suddenly died right after convicting John Scopes in the "Monkey trial." With Bryan's death, the Fundamentalist movement was decapitated and was not to reemerge as a serious political force until half a century later, when Nelson Rockefeller would be denied the vice presidential nomination after Fundamentalist intervention.

The family's problems with the Baptist church were not over yet. The indecisive Junior got into trouble again, this time over the conditions of Indian reservations.

Cutting the Last Cord

In the spring of 1926, Junior was preparing for his third trip west in six years, when he received a letter from Wolf Plume, the Blackfoot leader, and Black

Bull, another elder. "We are extremely under hard circumstances as we go without eating for three or four days at times. . . . We hope you will be able to see your way clear to aid us this spring."

Junior was on the fence. The Indians' circumstances again forced him to contend with old Rockefeller traditions. He did not want to answer the letter. But his silence could be taken as insensitive by a number of people, foremost among them his sons.

The Indians struck this tender chord themselves in their letter. How would you feel, they asked, if "you were in our state of circumstances"? Then they moved in on Junior's soft spot: "Wolf Plume wants to know how your little son [Laurance] is getting along whom Wolf Plume christened."[11]

Typed on the stationery of the Indian Protective Association of Montana, the letter indicated that influential whites, as well as Indians, were waiting to see how Rockefeller responded, if at all.

Since his children were involved, Junior also had to consider the feelings of their mother. Abby was a conspirator of sorts with the children against Junior's Baptist authoritarianism and bristled at anything hinting of racial discrimination. "Put yourself in the place of an honest, poor man who happens to belong to one of the so-called 'despised' races," she wrote Nelson, Laurance, and John during these years.

> Think of having no friendly hand held out to you, no kindly look, no pleasant, encouraging word spoken to you. What I would like you always to do is what I try humbly to do myself; that is, never to say or to do anything which would wound the feelings or the self-respect of any human being, and to give special consideration to all who are in any way repressed. That is what your father does naturally from the fineness of his nature and the kindness of his heart. I long to have our family stand firmly for what is best and highest in life. It isn't always easy, but it is worth while.[12]

Junior thought it might be wise to make inquiries. He passed Wolf Plume's letter on to the BIA. Fearing more requests for aid, Junior suggested that something should be done to "strike more at the root of the matter."[13] The response was defensive, rooted as always in the Calvinist notion of self-sufficiency: "Where the Indians have invested in sheep on the reimbursable plan, they are getting along very nicely. . . . If these Indians will get down to business and help themselves just a little, they can get along alright."[14]

Another response to his inquiries was less quieting. One of his guides in 1924 confirmed that Wolf Plume's band "is in a worse way now than for some time past [and] may be going hungry part of the time." But the problem was in the Indians themselves and their culture. "The band you saw are all fullbloods, all related or mostly so and that's the reason Wolf Plume and Big Spring may be hard up now, because they have shared with the others. Your old time fullblood will always share with his people." The selfish individualism that accompanied property ownership had not taken root with the older Indians.

He advised the Rockefellers not to send money to these "simple minded children." He pledged "to admonish" them "not to write you in this way again." It was "the Government's place and duty to look after these people and not you."[15] Junior agreed.

There is no record that Junior ever answered Wolf Plume's letter.

While Nelson was in France that summer, his alter ego, Laurance, was to return West with his parents and younger brothers. Junior came up with a solution. He simply decided not to include the Blackfoot reservation in their itinerary.

But the Indians could not be so easily controlled. Their revolt was in full swing and making headlines. Taos Pueblo leaders, backed by John Collier's Indian Defense Association, had been jailed for resisting the missionaries and the BIA, and the Indian rebellion was spreading to the Great Plains tribes and beyond, to tribes in California. The threat that the Rockefeller name would again be linked to violent repression emerged. Once more, Junior's options seemed split between following Baptist leaders or heeding the advice of liberal aides like Ray Fosdick, the man who had encouraged Junior's $1,000 donation to John Collier two years before.

It had been a short honeymoon for the Rockefellers and the thin, stoop-shouldered Collier. In 1924, shortly after the BIA started leasing Navajo reservation lands to oil companies, Collier's request to Rockefeller for an additional $10,000 to investigate Indian conditions was rejected. Instead, Junior launched his own probe—of Collier. He dispatched an aide to Washington to confer with Interior Secretary Herbert Work and BIA Commissioner Charles H. Burke. Their attack on Collier bordered on slander, Burke calling Collier "an agitator" and denouncing the Indian Defense Association's efforts as "destructive."[16]

Probably the loudest criticism came from Charles L. White, executive secretary of the American Baptist Home Mission Society. Although White personally did not have much influence with the Rockefellers at the time, because of his flirtation with Fundamentalist donors, Junior wanted to keep his own power over the direction of the Baptist missions from being further eroded by Fundamentalist attacks. He listened as White severely impugned Collier's character and even suggested that Collier had misappropriated funds.

Those voices from the political and religious establishment were enough for Junior. He turned down Collier's request and cut off further funding to his organization. Instead, he shifted his support to the Baptist missionary-oriented Indian Rights Association, which White had just recommended to Fosdick.[17]

It was one of Junior's greatest blunders. The Indian Rights Association had taken up the earlier unsubstantiated claim of a Fundamentalist missionary, Rev. William "Pussyfoot" Johnson, that Christian Indian converts were being forced to participate in "obscene" dances that allegedly caused the pregnancy of young girls.

The missionaries demanded that all "pagan" dances end. They were also pressing for federal marshals to be sent in to seize children from Pueblo parents who had always temporarily removed their boys from BIA schools to initiate them through religious rites of passage. This custom was vital to the survival of Pueblo culture, and the missionaries knew it. The campaign by the Indian Rights Association, its president stated proudly, was designed to "make the pagan reactionary element in Santo Domingo [a center of Pueblo resistance] feel that the United States laws are to be obeyed, and that Christian progressive Indians will be protected in their rights."[18]

Meanwhile, John Collier was not silently sitting by. As far as he was concerned, both the Indian Rights Association and the BIA were bandits. The Indian Rights Association was attempting to "split the Pueblos asunder" to "paralyze" the Indians from benefiting from his organization's legal services. And it was doing so at the very moment that the "final settlement of the land controversies" was occurring.[19] Over the past forty years, Indians had lost some 40 million acres of parceled tribal lands in sales to whites and, through BIA-coerced leases, had lost the use of most of the land they still owned.[20]

In 1926, these leases—and particularly the new oil leases—were the focus of escalating attacks by John Collier and his chief ally in Congress, Rep. James A. Frear. Frear called for a joint congressional investigation of the BIA's support for the Indian Oil Bill that attracted speculators like "a cloud of buzzards obscuring the sun." Then the two men conducted their own survey of twenty western reservations, traveling over 4,400 miles by car. They found that the conditions were worse than they had feared: For example, the Sioux were starving, and 25 percent of the Crow Indians were in danger of being blinded by trachoma. The BIA, Collier insisted, was destroying the Indians because it still had a "hangover" from the "original military policy which regarded the Indian as an outlaw and danger to society."[21]

By this time, Junior had returned from the West and concurred with Fosdick that support for the conservative Indian Rights Association had been an error. The missionaries' attacks on Indian traditions were counterproductive; worse, one of the Indian Rights Association's most strident officials, Clara D. True, who previously had been sued by the federal government for misappropriating BIA funds, had been indiscreet about the Rockefellers' funding.[22]

If Baptist missionaries could no longer be relied upon to prevent violence or scandal from looming over the Rockefeller horizon, then Junior had little choice but to turn to other, more scientifically objective sources.

Fortunately, Rockefeller money had already ensured that those sources were on hand. Interior Secretary Work, sensing that he was losing the initiative to John Collier and hoping to forestall a congressional investigation of the BIA and its Navajo oil leases, invited the Brookings Institution for Government Research to conduct a survey of Indian conditions, a survey independent of the BIA, but beholden to the Rockefellers to the tune of $125,000.

This time Junior had made a safe bet. The Brookings Institution's board of trustees included Raymond Fosdick and Jerome Greene, two members of Rockefeller's inner legal circle, along with such familiar names as Carnegie Institute president John C. Merriam (who had advised Junior on his Western itinerary).

Under Lewis Meriam's direction, the report of the survey, *The Problem of Indian Administration*, was widely hailed when it was published in 1928. But as Collier had feared, the Meriam Report spared the top BIA officials from criticism for the conditions it described. Instead, it chose to follow the BIA's and missionaries' line that Congress was to blame for the Indians' misery. Congress, for its part, conducted its own investigation, holding hearings that led to the resignation of BIA Commissioner Charles H. Burke. For a brief while, it appeared to Collier that the reign of big money and missionaries over Indian affairs might be over.

He was wrong. In 1928 the American people, beguiled by the prosperity of the twenties and the promise of a "chicken in every pot and a car in every garage," had elected conservative Herbert Hoover president. To lead the BIA, Hoover appointed Charles J. Rhoads, a wealthy banker and treasurer of the Indian Rights Association, who did address grievances, but not with protective legislation or Indian empowerment. But the Indian Rights Association had received its last funds from Junior. From then on, the Rockefellers would increasingly turn away from the Baptists. They preferred more secular missions at home and abroad as they took command of the age of oil.

3

RETHINKING MISSIONS

IN SEARCH OF A MISSION

In these early years, Nelson Rockefeller did not understand the global implications of the "Indian Problem" confronting his father's generation. As a sixteen-
year-old on his first trip west in 1924, he had been little more than a rapt observer
of Indian life. By the summer of 1929, when he and his brother Laurance joined
missionary doctor Sir Wilfred Grenfell on one of his famous expeditions to the
Eskimos, his childlike wonder had faded into cynicism. "The natives . . . just sit
around and go fishing when the spirit moves them. . . . Why, if any of them were
half way ambitious he could make some money. But I suppose there is no use getting excited about it. Perhaps they get more out of life that way than we do rushing around." [1]

Nelson's letter to his parents revealed the same conflict between conservatism and liberalism that tormented his father. His disdain for the rural native's
lack of ambition reflected America's Calvinist thinking since the landing of the
Pilgrims: One's success in life is measured by the amount of money one has made
and the property one has acquired. But no sooner had Nelson's own words of
contempt spilled onto paper than he checked himself, as if nudged by some silent
moral mentor to keep an open mind. Two motivations—profit and humanitarian—would war within Nelson as he followed his father into the rough-and-tum-
ble of world power.

For a time, an uneasy truce had reigned between Nelson and his father. At
Dartmouth, Nelson even managed to charm Junior when he wrote his economics
thesis on Standard Oil. Junior was delighted by the shameless apology, drawn

heavily from an unpublished biography of Senior that Junior had commissioned.

But it soon became obvious that the world of business did not hold the same lure for Nelson that it did for other Rockefellers. "I only hope that I shall grow up and live a life that will be worthy of the family name," he wrote from France one summer after inspecting the restoration work at Versailles and Rheims that his father had financed. "I'm sure [brother] Johnny will because he already thinks and acts exactly like you, Pa. . . . But as for myself—well, I'm a lot different and I don't think the same way."[2]

When senior year and graduation approached, he was even more explicit. "Frankly, I don't relish the idea of going into some business. . . . Just to work my way up in a business that another man has built, stepping from the shoes of one to those of another, making a few minor changes here and there and then, finally, perhaps at the age of sixty, getting to the top where I would have real control for a few years. No, that isn't my idea of living a real life."[3]

Such zest for life had been the attribute most often associated with his mother. Abby Rockefeller was the opposite of her husband, imbued with a fearless sense of adventure. She refused to allow her compassion for the less fortunate to be hardened by the Rockefeller obsession with the "correct" Puritan stewarding of wealth. Her greatest gift to Nelson was a quiet but enduring resistance to the sterner Rockefeller tradition.

Nevertheless, for Nelson power beckoned. It was ordained not only by the august Rockefeller name, but by the heady political legend of his namesake, his maternal grandfather, Nelson Aldrich. For thirty years Nelson Aldrich had been one of the most powerful figures in the U.S. Senate, renowned for his friendships with bankers and heads of sugar companies and a political career that had started with humble resources and ended with a $50 million fortune.

By his senior year, Nelson had caught the bug. He made two feverish runs for the presidency of his class. Both were failures. As in the broader political arena to come, young Nelson Rockefeller had to settle for the vice presidency.

THE PEACEFUL CONQUEST OF THE WORLD

In December 1929, Junior received an urgent letter from one of his most trusted envoys. John Mott had just returned from a tour of Protestant missions in Asia, and he was quite agitated. Mott was a millenarian who hoped to hasten the Second Coming by evangelizing the world "in this generation." But he was not a Fundamentalist; he believed that science was the probing of God's mind, and the strident proselytizing he had witnessed among Fundamentalist missionaries in China deeply worried him. Unless more tolerance and social concern were shown by American missionaries throughout the Third World, the missionaries would find themselves facing the same kind of angry nationalistic reaction he had just witnessed.

After popular revolutions had broken out in both Mexico and China in 1910, Junior sent Mott to set up a China Medical Board to blend medical science and religion into a powerful new institution, the Peking Union Medical College. "If we wait until China becomes stable," Mott told the members of Junior's China Medical Board at the board's first meeting, "we lose the greatest opportunity that we shall ever have." Mott understood that the Rockefeller fortune could shape the political future of the world's most populous nation. "That nation will have only one first generation in its modern era," he wrote after the proclamation of the Chinese Republic in 1911. "The first wave of students to receive the modern training . . . will set the standards and the pace."[4]

To realize his vision, Mott became a shrewd fund-raiser among rich men like the Rockefellers. He incorporated the sales pitch of a Wall Street broker. "To ask money of a man for the purposes of the world-wide Kingdom of God is not to ask him a favor," he once wrote. "It is to give him a superb opportunity of investing his personality in eternal shares." Money was "so much stored-up personality," he argued, accumulated days of human labor that survived its owners and therefore could be used after death to extend the owner's life on earth.

This concept of the transubstantiation of money into an immortal soul bore a striking resemblance to the family's rationale for a perpetual Rockefeller Foundation; indeed, Standard Oil was Mott's organizational model. He incorporated the culture and methods of corporations into the missionary movement. Over the years, millions of Rockefeller dollars poured into Mott's pursuit of a streamlined, efficient evangelism.

Two significant factors lured Mott into locking himself firmly within the Rockefeller orbit. One was the global vision of Senior's closest investment adviser, Baptist minister Frederick Gates. The other was China and its huge potential harvest of souls, which had obsessed the mind of American Protestantism since its first missionaries boarded the clipper ships of the China trade sailing out of New England's harbors.

Gates had been captivated by the thought of the family fortune moving into foreign markets. With Standard Oil taking the lead, he argued that the advance of the American corporation represented the Will of God. Standard Oil's kerosene had literally lit the lamps of China since the 1890s, inspiring the company to commit its own form of blasphemy by lifting its product's slogan from the New Testament: "the Light of the World."

To Gates, the growing cultural interdependence of the global market and the accompanying spread of "English-speaking" Protestant missions bore evidence of "one great, preconceived plan." A "study of the map of the world" disclosed to the cleric that the different missions were really a single "invading army," whose "masterfulness of strategy and tactics . . . [was] controlled and directed by one master mind," God.[5]

If Senior was put off by this unreconstructed Calvinist doctrine of predestination, Gates's emphasis on the relationship between missionary efforts and commercial conquest had a more practical saving grace:

> Quite apart from the question of persons converted, the mere commercial results of missionary efforts to our own land is worth, I had almost said, a thousand-fold every year of what is spent on missions. . . .
>
> Missionaries and missionary schools are introducing the application of modern science, steam and electric power, modern agricultural machinery and modern manufacture into foreign lands. The result will be eventually to multiply the productive power of foreign countries many times. This will enrich them as buyers of American products and enrich us as importers of their products. We are only in the very dawn of commerce, and we owe that dawn, with all its promise to the channels opened up by Christian missionaries. . . . The effect of the missionary enterprise of the English speaking peoples will be to bring them the peaceful conquest of the world.[6]

Mott shared Gates's vision, but not its complacency. Since Christian traditionalists, backed by Lyman Stewart of Union Oil, had published *The Fundamentals* of their faith before World War I, Mott had noticed a stiffened intransigence among Christian missionaries abroad. These missionaries drew strength from the movement of rural ministers at home, who now officially called themselves Fundamentalists and attacked Darwin's science of evolution and the modernist Protestant currents that had converged with Rockefeller funding into the Federal Council of Churches.

Fundamentalists were building dams of intransigence before the ever-swelling tide of anticolonialism. John Mott witnessed the upsurge of nationalism in China and predicted the impending explosion. American missionaries were sure to suffer the most, simply because of their number: Sixty-five American mission societies were functioning in China, almost twice the number of British societies.

The West had badly underestimated the strength and intensity of Chinese patriotism, and now the Chinese were insisting on a national educational system stripped of Western control. American missionaries, who between 1925 and 1928 numbered 4,000 to 5,000 out of the 9,800 Americans in China and owned property worth at least $43 million,[7] were being forced to reevaluate their position. The nationalist revolution of 1910 ushered in Chinese boards that merely set the stage for the immediate nationalization and eventual secularization of the missions. Some Christian Fundamentalists, seeing evangelization as the sine qua non of a Christian education, refused to bend, increasing the Chinese resentment.[8] And not without cause. Two-thirds of the 4,375 Christian missionaries in 1928 were concentrated in 176 prosperous commercial centers, where only 25 million people, just 6 percent of the Chinese population, lived.[9]

Modernist missionaries had recognized the crisis. They called for a cooperative approach in the rural areas, advocating health surveys, agricultural work, and bilingual education.

But the modernists' efforts were crippled by the lack of funds and support from their colleagues. Most missionaries in the Far East were traditionalists and recent converts to the Fundamentalist cause; they preferred to concentrate on saving souls by evangelism alone, assuming the imminence of the Second Coming. Meanwhile, Chinese communists who had survived Chiang Kai-shek's massacres at Shanghai and Canton and had followed Mao Tse-tung into the countryside were winning thousands of recruits by assisting peasants who were struggling against wealthy landlords.

Mott was shocked and concluded that time was running out for American missionaries all over Asia. He wanted Junior to convene a meeting at the Rockefeller town house to discuss the urgent need for another great mission: modernizing the world's Christian missions to the Third World.

Secularizing Foreign Missions

When John Mott made this proposition to Junior, Riverside Church was nearing completion. The concept of this church, honoring not only Christian leaders but founders of the great Eastern religions and scientists (including the despised Darwin), symbolized the Rockefeller family's broadening, global perspective. The international power of the Rockefeller fortune was just asserting itself in the 1920s, joining the general thrust of American corporate wealth in expanding overseas.

World War I had reversed American business's dependence on Europe for capital. From 1920 to 1929, the United States' direct investments abroad rose $40 million, to over $600 million; trade and investment overseas grew over 700 percent.

The Standard Oil companies, of course, led the way for the Rockefellers. Besides the New Jersey company, by 1926 Standard Oil of California held 575,000 acres in Venezuela and 200,000 acres in Mexico. Standard Oil of New York had penetrated markets from the Balkans, through the Middle East, down to South Africa, and east through India and Indochina to the Philippines and the Dutch East Indies.

Standard Oil of New Jersey was growing into the oil colossus of the Western Hemisphere. Its area of new exploration was Latin America.

In Bolivia's arid Altiplano around Lake Titicaca, the highest lake in the world, Standard Oil of New Jersey was busy refining and marketing.

Peru had been entered back in 1913. And in Colombia, where tempers still flared over the ripping away of the Panamanian isthmus in 1903 by an American-financed "revolution," backed by nine U.S. gunboats, Standard concentrated on getting the Harding administration to pay a $25 million indemnity in 1921 to soothe Colombia's pain. Then the company obtained a government concession to the 2,000-square-mile De Mares oil field along the Magdalena and Carare rivers, where oil seepages had been observed by local Indians since the days before the Spanish Conquest. Within a year after Nelson's trip out to the West, the De Mares field had become Standard Oil's largest foreign source of oil.

Through all these successes, the Rockefellers and their tax-free philanthropies profited enormously. The oil companies were now giant machines of human labor, pumping millions of dollars in dividends and capital gains into interlocked coffers. The Rockefeller Foundation owned stock in thirteen oil companies and nine pipelines in the United States, as well as thirty-five railroads and thirty-five other corporations that were involved in everything from steel and gas to banks and real estate. Many of these companies were doing substantial business in Latin America or the Far East by the mid-1920s.

As the oil companies expanded abroad, the family's concern for foreign missions, both secular and religious, intensified. In Latin America, missionaries in the Rockefeller philanthropic orbit were well aware of the heightened interest by corporations in the southern hemisphere. John Mott's Committee on Cooperation in Latin America was perhaps the most forthright, reporting in its 1919 Annual Report:

> Capitalists, manufacturers, steamship directors, food economists, political leaders of nations that need an outlet for surplus goods and populations, all are planning intensive activities in these fallow, underdeveloped southern lands of promise. . . .
>
> With modern agricultural inventions and the development of sanitation, the tropics are no longer uninhabitable for the white man and may be looked upon as an open field for his future activities.

The Rockefeller Foundation, headed by the astute Raymond Fosdick since 1921, was at the vanguard of turning Latin America into this "open field."

Guatemala was at the center of Rockefeller attention. Standard Oil had begun exploratory drilling in this mostly Indian country, whose border with Mexico was the focus of concern over the spread of diseases both political (revolution) and viral (yellow fever). Enlisting the assistance of the commander of Guatemalan troops along the border, Rockefeller's International Health Board (IHB) succeeded in getting revolutionary Mexico quarantined on health grounds. A *cordón sanitario* allowed martial law to be imposed on the restless towns and sugar and coffee plantations along the route of United Fruit Company's International Railways.

From its reported success in the coffee *fincas* and plantations in now-"eradicated" Guatemala, IHB launched campaigns against the other great mosquito-carried disease, malaria, throughout Central America. The foundation's antimalaria campaign would eventually spread to some forty-five warm-climate countries and territories around the world.

The eradication of hookworm had also become a worldwide campaign, again, first in Guatemala, where $165,000 was all it took to examine more than 227,000 people and treat 132,000. It remained one of Senior's great medical bargains for spreading goodwill. And it gave him a foothold in the region.

The political content of the foundation's work in Latin America was never stated publicly, but in private correspondence it was blatantly expressed. The IHB's Dr. E. I. Vaughn considered the people of Guatemala "the cream of Central America," where "the unfortunate mixture of negro blood so common in Spanish countries is almost nil." The white population were "direct descendants of the original Spanish colony . . . A large percentage of the better classes are blonde and of decidedly Basque facial characteristics." The racist myth of Nordic superiority, championed by the early eugenics movement and Frederick Gates, lingered among Anglo-Saxons in the Rockefeller employ and shaped their political hopes for Latin America. Guatemala's military dictatorship had recently been overthrown, and the white propertied minority was enthusiastic about the future: "The general feeling among the whites is that a nightmare has passed and now is the psychological time to make Guatemala the leading country in Central America."

And what of the vast Indian majority? "The Indian is beginning to realize that he is something better, and intended for something better, than a beast of burden," continued Vaughn, "and he has only been able to express his primitive soul by clamoring for education for his children and becoming a mild Bolshevik. I am confident that the seed cast by the International Health Board has fallen on fertile ground, and I can make only one recommendation, and that is *Patience.*"[10]

Patience, however, was a luxury few Indians could afford. The aggressive expansion of plantations growing cash crops for export disrupted the Indians' traditional land tenure and the subsistence agriculture of village life, increasing malnutrition and susceptibility to disease. Company-owned shantytowns seldom had adequate sewer and sanitation systems, intensifying the hookworm infestation. The spread of communicable diseases and mosquito-bearing fruit trains and ships along the new commercial trade routes and railroad towns of coastal Latin America only aggravated the chronic health problems in densely populated areas.

The Rockefeller Foundation's projects in sanitation, health, and medicine attacked these symptoms, but not their social causes. They were designed to ease the human suffering that accompanied the dramatic socioeconomic changes brought about by American corporate investment and the expansion of the commercial market system into the interior. The goal of healthy workers combined moral imperatives with the businessman's concern for productivity.

To modernist liberals, Rockefeller's measures in Latin America seemed infinitely preferable to the "Big Stick" of Theodore Roosevelt. A post–World War I movement to change the methods and style of U.S. intervention from gunboat diplomacy to dollar diplomacy was led by Raymond Fosdick and other Wilsonian liberals who had supported the League of Nations and were now associated with

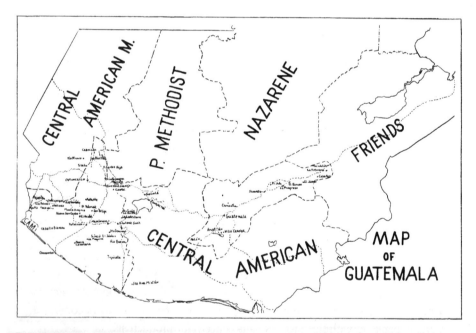

Rockefeller-sponsored cooperation between formerly competing Protestant missions in Mexico (*top*) established a successful standard for penetrating "heathen" lands, and was soon applied to Guatemala (*above*).

Source: (*top*) Interchurch World Movement, *World Survey, Foreign Volume* (New York: Interchurch Press, 1920); (*above*) Gennet Maxon Emery, *Protestantism in Guatemala*.

the Rockefellers' Council on Foreign Relations. Through their efforts, Latin America became a sort of laboratory to test strategies for future foreign policy toward the Third World in general.

Junior was open to Mott's concerns about sectarian missions and American inflexibility to nationalist sentiments in underdeveloped countries. Nine years had passed since their last crusade, when Mott had warned hundreds of businessmen, politicians, and ministers that they must move beyond old sectarian principles and denominational rivalries if they were to defeat the specter of revolution.

"Some of us were in Russia shortly after the outbreak of the Revolution," Mott told the group, "where we saw the beginning of that fell influence that has swept over the world and that we now speak of as Bolshevism. We recognized its menace, but little did we realize that so soon it would spread like some great disease from nation to nation." In the Russian Revolution, Mott saw an internationalist force that went beyond being just another case of nationalist uprising in an underdeveloped, oppressed land.

"The object of Lenin, as I see it, has been not to divide the peoples vertically into compartments [national states], but to cut a great horizontal cleavage across the entire human race, arraying class against class with growing bitterness."[11]

To match the international alliance of lower-class revolutionists, Mott had urged corporate leaders to close ranks in their own international Christian entente. "Against that evil," agreed former Secretary of State Robert Lansing, "the churches should battle as they battle against every evil that flows from the devil."[12]

Now, nine years later, America's Protestant lay leaders who had not listened to Mott's original warning seemed more receptive. The stock market had crashed just two months before, in October. Antagonism between the classes would grow again in the United States, just as nationalist resentments were already reappearing abroad. Christ's message of love was needed for all. Mott was right. It was time to act.

The Manifesto

But not in public. Junior did not wish to rekindle Fundamentalist fires. He convened a gathering of well-heeled northern Baptists at his Manhattan town house on January 17, 1930, to allow Mott to make his pitch. They decided to include other mainstream northern Protestant denominations in a formal interchurch commission to oversee the Laymen's Foreign Missions Inquiry. And Junior, of course, agreed to pick up the entire tab, which by the end of the year came to $320,000.[13]

The Laymen's Foreign Missions Inquiry sent out its survey team to Asia in September 1930. It returned nine months later and issued its report, *Rethinking Missions*, in 1932.

"Rumors were abroad that things were not well on the foreign field," a spokesman explained at the report's formal presentation. "There were ominous stories of trouble in China, and in India and in Japan. Students were uprising, communism was rampant; missionaries themselves were disturbed, and the Boards did not seem to know how to direct their own efforts and activities."[14]

Rethinking Missions recommended reforms that few Fundamentalists could accept: an end to segregation from Asian cultures and appreciation of elements in Asian faiths that were kindred to Christ's message; more quiet lessons of examples and programs in education, medicine, and agriculture and less evangelical prose-lytizing; more cooperation and efficiency to reduce the wasteful overlap of pro-grams; and, most important, a gradual transfer of power to indigenous churches.

The report was a bombshell, running through ten printings in six months. Junior read sections of the manuscript before it was released. "I have done so with a lump in my throat," he wrote the commission's members, "and with a fervent song of praise in my heart."[15]

Those who were deep in the ranks of Fundamentalism openly criticized the report. Dr. Nelson Bell, a medical missionary in north Jiangsu province in China, rejected the report's argument that "the use of medical or other professional ser-vice as a direct means of making converts . . . in wards and dispensaries from which patients cannot escape is subtly coercive and improper." To Bell, it was "the *preaching* of the Cross, the Gospel of redemption from sin through faith in the shed blood of the Savior, which is the power of God."[16]

Bell's heavy emphasis on "the Word," the literal Bible, to convey the message of Christ was symptomatic of the entire Fundamentalist movement. With Bell, it would have a powerful voice through his editorship of *Christianity Today* and through his son-in-law, Billy Graham.

In the coffee hills of western Guatemala, however, another young Fundamentalist missionary could understand Mott's call for indigenous control over institutions founded by foreign missionaries. And he had learned the value of the Rockefellers' philanthropies for his own mission. In the years ahead, he would ally himself with Bell, his funder J. Howard Pew of Sun Oil Company (Sunoco), and Billy Graham to build America's largest and most politically controversial mis-sionary organization, the Summer Institute of Linguistics. One day he would be called by evangelicals "the greatest Apostle since Saint Paul." He would also be Fundamentalism's greatest paradox, inadvertently serving the interests of Nelson Rockefeller as "the Apostle of the Lost Tribes."

His name was William Cameron Townsend.

4

THE APOSTOLIC VISION

THE ROCKEFELLER PILLARS

In May 1930, when Fundamentalist missionaries from around the world gathered at Moody Memorial Church in Chicago to attend its Annual Missionary Rally, many of them were angry about the growing power of Rockefeller-funded modernism. The unholy trinity of Rockefeller, money, and modernism was symbolized by Riverside Church's gothic spires climbing ever higher over upper Manhattan as the church neared completion. But few were prepared for the dissent that erupted from within their own ranks. One of them, in fact, their most successful young colleague, was about to stun them with an act of rebellion unheard of in Moody's fifty-three-year history.

Anguished over his future in Guatemala under the thumbs of Fundamentalist elders, William Cameron Townsend announced to a hushed audience that he intended to leave one of their most important missions in Latin America. At age thirty-six, he had spent thirteen years promoting God's Work in Guatemala, and now it was time to move on. He wanted to evangelize the lost tribes of the Amazon, he explained, and he wanted to do it with airplanes.

His listeners were aghast. Oil geologists had been killed by Amazonian Indians, protested a twenty-five-year veteran of South America. "It is impossible to reach them."[1] The missionary urged Townsend to stay with the Cakchiquel Indians. "Now that you've finished the New Testament, your work is just beginning. You know their language and their ways. They believe in you. Go back and train more preachers."[2]

Townsend already had, but not to preach as vassals under an American supervisor. He had been won over to the modernist concept of the indigenous church. He had heard all the Fundamentalist warnings about potential heresies. But he had also learned that the condescension with which mixed-blood *ladino* preachers regarded the Indian was undeserving of respect. His first Indian companion, Francisco Diaz, had convinced him of the value of the Indian preacher soon after he arrived in Guatemala. "He's eager, industrious, and skillful in missionary work. What the Lord could do with a hundred like him! They could evangelize their own people in their own language."[3] It was at Diaz's urging that Townsend had decided to leave his job as a Bible salesman for the Los Angeles Bible House and set up his first "School of the Prophets" in Diaz's hometown, San Antonio de Aguas Calientes, just west of Antigua, Guatemala's old colonial capital. Since then, a decade of hard work had built up a strong church with an active indigenous clergy, who did not need an American overlord.

Townsend, however, was momentarily subdued by the force of his elders' convictions. In Moody Church's auditorium, while a prayer meeting was under way, "I felt a chill come over my soul. The old fervor and burden for the unreached tribes was gone." Like Dwight Moody, who once went into a crisis during a failing fund drive, Townsend shuddered and cried for the return of "the warmth of soul that has accompanied the vision of pioneering." If purpose would return, he would go where the Lord sent him "even though the task seems impossible." At last he felt the zeal return. "I knew that God had called," he recalled later.[4]

Throughout his life, William Cameron Townsend had accepted God's Word in the Bible without question. He owed his beliefs to his father. The elder Townsend had wrestled with poor harvests, debts, and nagging dreams of the Promised Land for years as an itinerant farmer. All had driven him farther and farther west, from Kansas to Colorado and finally to southern California. There, under the shadow of the great citrus plantations that dominated the Santa Ana River Valley, he scratched out a living growing vegetables until, deaf and aging, he met hard times again. Only this time there was no new frontier; the Pacific had put a stop to that. So he fell back on the three things he knew best: his Bible; his family; and a stubborn belief that honesty, temperance, and a prairie-born populist justice would somehow, someday, prevail. These were the values that Will Townsend drilled into his oldest namesake son, called Cam to distinguish him from his father. And Cam buried them deep in his heart and carried them to Guatemala and unparalleled Fundamentalist success among the Indians of the Mayan highlands.

But in spite of Cam's lifelong reverence for the Word, his work had come under growing scrutiny by his mission elders over the past five years. Locked in battle with modernists abroad as well as at home, Cam's Fundamentalist superiors were doubtful of his doctrinal purity.

And they had reason to be. Since sailing to Guatemala in 1917, Cam had shown hints of dangerous modernist traits, such as donning Indian clothes and showing an appreciation of Indian culture. Even his inspiration for becoming a missionary had been John Mott. Mott had delivered a passionate speech before Cam and other students at Occidental College on "evangelizing the world in this generation." Cam, "impressed by how little I had done to witness my faith," took up the call, asked for a draft deferment, and moved to Guatemala to sell Bibles. When he arrived, he found his superiors at the Central American Mission (ironically referred to as C.A.M.) to be unwavering in their adherence to Fundamentalist tradition.

The Central American Mission was a conservative body. Although it reluctantly agreed to collaborate with John Mott's Committee on Cooperation in Latin America during World War I and joined other missions in dividing up Central America like pieces of cake, the mission had never forgotten its roots in the Moody Church, the cathedral of Fundamentalism.

Cam did not question the tenets of C.A.M.'s founder, Cyrus Scofield, a former Indian hunter turned preacher among Texas land boomers and merchants. Scofield and his *Reference Bible* prophesied that the Millennial Kingdom of peace and justice would come only after Christ's Second Coming, not before, as millennialists had traditionally taught. This meant that scriptural commands to give up the pursuit of wealth also applied only to that distant Kingdom, when the Lord would rule, and not before. Thus Scofield preserved for his donors as well as his missionaries the central thesis of the Puritan ethic: By living one's life according to the Book, one could avoid social reform and still win both riches and the keys to heaven. Social reform was deemed impossible in a world ruled by Satan and "Man's Fallen Nature," so why try? Wealth became not only God's reward for a holy life in a sinful world, but a sign of His grace for answering in one's chosen work some particular "calling" in His Great Plan.

Cam wondered why such a powerful message in the Bible should be useful only to those already assimilated into Euro-American culture, not full-blooded Indians living in the more remote, traditional villages.

Spanish-language Bibles were useless to most of the Indians, who spoke their own native tongues. To reach them with God's Word, a missionary had to learn their languages and reduce them to some written form so that the Bible could be translated into words and cultural terms the Indians could understand.

Thousands of highland Indians who worked seasonally in the plantations along Guatemala's Pacific coast had been overlooked by missionaries in favor of their mixed-blood ladino overseers. Cam was raising a new church, an Indian church, on the four pillars of linguistics, education, health reform, and economics.

In health care, Cam discovered a direct means of supplanting the authority of traditional Indian healers. When he first arrived in Guatemala, he traveled along the route of the sanitary cordon established by the Rockefeller Foundation's doctors and witnessed the foundation's programs against hookworm and malaria. Soon he was campaigning for the government to drain the mosquito-infested swamps and dispensing quinine for malaria and modern chemistry for hookworm.

"The Rockefeller Foundation has found that 80 percent of the Indians have the hookworm,"[5] he reported in C.A.M.'s *Central American Bulletin*. Armed with chenopodium and quinine, his Christian campaign against traditional Indian healers advanced steadily. Elvira Malmstrom, a Moody Church missionary whom he married, assumed the part of nurse.

"This has been a week of great blessing," he wrote home. "Through sickness on all sides many homes continue to be opened to us." A native healer soon succumbed to the competition. Although "still doctoring many by her magic arts," he explained, "when she herself . . . gets sick she comes for Elvira. We are now being called upon to doctor many cases other than malaria."[6]

Since the days of the conquistadores, disease had played an important role in the European conquest of the Americas. By inadvertently introducing European diseases, such as smallpox, a tiny minority of Spaniards overwhelmed millions of Indians and the sophisticated Aztec, Inca, and Maya civilizations that had no immunity to alien diseases. Indian tribes in Mexico watched the new white God kill Aztecs, but leave Spaniards unharmed; suddenly the Aztec gods, like the Aztec king, no longer looked invincible. The Indians allied with Spaniards by the thousands, to their later regret.[7] This scenario for cultural conquest was replayed in the American West—and in the Cakchiquel hills of Guatemala through missionaries like Townsend administering the white man's modern medicine, compliments of the Rockefeller Foundation.

Cam's linguistics, too, had a Rockefeller connection. For his breakthrough in analyzing the Cakchiquel language, Cam was indebted to a visiting American archaeologist who warned him that he was trying to force the Indians' oriental-sounding language into the Latin mold. The archaeologist recommended the less ethnocentric approach of Edward Sapir, the leading linguist of the University of Chicago.

Sapir had established a new standard in linguistics by phonetically describing languages in terms of their "own genius," rather than in ways that European culture considered important. Words spoken in any culture, Sapir maintained, evolved as having importance in a language because they allowed communication within a given perspective on the world, a perspective that might look at the universe quite differently from the way European culture did. To understand the structure of a language, therefore, you had to step out of a European perspective and accept that another perspective had given certain words status as means of communication. Important words that were keys to a language structure had status not simply because they existed, but because they could be shared by the people who used them. In language, as in most tools of a culture, it was sharing, cooperation, that was the hallmark of human culture's success as an adapting mediation with the nat-

The Rockefeller Philanthropies' Influence on W. C. Townsend

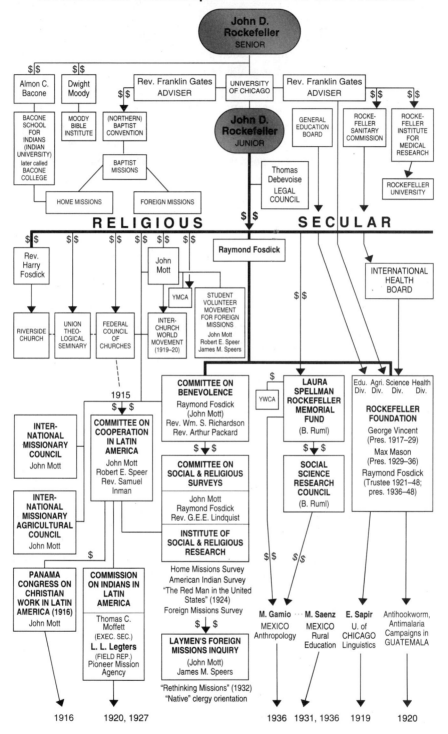

ural environment, not the crude competition of "the survival of the strongest" championed by the social Darwinists of the imperial Victorian age. The strongest, as the dinosaurs' extinction proved, were not always nature's fittest.

Using Sapir's approach, Cam soon grasped that the tone, inflection, and words of the Cakchiquels' language was as purposefully specialized as the colors and pattern in the clothes worn in each of their villages. The language was incredibly rich and sophisticated. Unlike English, the possibilities of combinations to express different meanings and subtle nuances were much more complex. Ideas, such as time, location, the number of subjects, and types of actions, could be collapsed into a single verb. The possible combinations of ideas were staggering. Cam estimated that one verb could be conjugated into 100,000 forms, not even counting compounds.

Cam combined his new understanding of linguistics with his limited knowledge of Jerome's translation of the Gospel of St. Luke gained from his college course on New Testament Greek. He worked hard to render as accurate a translation of Mark as possible into Cakchiquel. When he finished four chapters, Elvira typed them, following each page of Cakchiquel with its Spanish equivalent. The Townsends had adopted bilingual education.

This was a decidedly political act, an announcement of Cam's commitment to the assimilation of the Indian into the culture and political life of the Spanish-speaking minority who ruled Guatemala. It won him the immediate support of many ladinos, including the mayor of Antigua.

But it was through economics that he probably won the most adult male converts. Cam founded a coffee cooperative. This project was also the result of his ability to call upon American resources, in this case a St. Louis coffee company owned by a mission-minded Baptist, Alexander E. Forbes. Moved by Cam's call in the *Christian Herald* for help in economically uplifting his Indian converts, Forbes had a ready solution. His family fortune had been built on processing coffee into liquid concentrates and soluble powder for "instant" coffee. Forbes had been buying coffee from Guatemala since at least 1890. He therefore suggested that if Townsend could persuade his converts to grow and pick their own coffee and combine their harvests into a cooperative, he would donate a sheller and a turbine; all he asked in return was the Indians' coffee. He got it.

THE MISSION'S BURDEN

It was precisely Cam's success by such unorthodox ways that had whipped both Catholic clergy and his fellow Fundamentalists into a jealous froth. His quoting the good deeds of the Rockefeller Foundation to mission magazines; welcoming Indians into his home (originally a cornstalk house, like the Indians'); wearing their costumes; departure from mission policy by fund-raising among local merchants; commitment to training a native clergy by setting up the Robinson Bible Institute (named after a close missionary companion); and, above all, intention to perpetuate the culture of the backward Indian by having his Cakchiquel translation of the New Testament put in print had inspired angry protests to the mission's home office.

But the fact was that Townsend was the Central American Mission's success story. Despite his youth, Cam had, in a remarkably short period, acquired, by risk and hard work, an unparalleled breadth of knowledge of Indian conditions throughout the interior of Central America. He had traveled through jungles, swamps, and mountains and had visited the Indians where they worked in mines and plantations and where they lived in the high *altos*. He had won their respect and even their assistance and counted 2,000 of them as converts. He was friendly with the U.S. ambassador and with Guatemala's president, who had helped the Protestant missions thrive by deporting Catholic priests. The mission board not only voted in Cam's favor by a majority of six, but the following year named him administrative secretary of C.A.M.'s central district.

Now, five years after his first confrontation with his Fundamentalist elders, the maverick missionary was back, promoting his new idea of flying missionaries into the Amazon jungle. Here, he urged, were a thousand Bibleless tribes roaming a green hell. Cam owed this dark vision to L. L. Legters, a former Presbyterian missionary to the Comanche and Sioux Indians who had surveyed Mexico and the Amazon as a director of Philadelphia's Pioneer Mission Agency. Hoping to set up a neutral missionary agency for Indians that might transcend the Fundamentalist-modernist schism, Legters had won backing from John Mott's Committee of Cooperation in Latin America. Impressed by Cam's work in Guatemala, Legters sent Cam pictures he had taken of "fine, stalwart, naked Indians" bereft of God's Word in the isolated Xingu River Valley of the Brazilian Amazon. These, he told Cam, were only a few of the thousand tribes who waited for brave young men like Townsend.[8]

Cam was more than ready and willing. In fact, he was desperate. Pioneering a new exotic field for Bible translation with modern airplanes was far more exciting than administering C.A.M.'s missionary routines in Guatemala.

Cam's inspiration for planes was less spiritually inspired: the U.S. invasion of Nicaragua. For the first time in its relations with Latin America, the United States used warplanes in attempting to crush the resistance forces of General Augusto Sandino. In January 1927, while two American destroyers arrived off the shores of Nicaragua, American warplanes also landed in Guatemala City. Cam was on hand to greet them. The planes were on a "goodwill" flight of navy pilots to demonstrate American aerial might in Latin America and, according to the secretary of war, to test amphibian airplanes for the War Department.[9]

Cam introduced himself to the commander, Major Herbert Dargue, and told him about his mission work among the Indians. He asked the major for cost estimates for an aviation program in a jungle area. Cam was already dreaming beyond Guatemala.

Dargue promised to put together some facts and figures. Months later, Dargue's reply came, outlining a program that required much more than the missionary had anticipated: a jungle airstrip with a hangar, an outpost, three amphibian airplanes, pilots, mechanics, radio operators, repair facilities, posts, fuel, insurance, and medical personnel. And that was before operations could safely begin; three years of operating expenses would cost another $134,000.

With that kind of expense, Cam's proposal for the Amazon's tribes was doomed before it echoed off Moody Church's stately walls.

But the Townsends refused to give up. At the church's Missionary Union, they spoke of their dream and of the power of airplanes to reach it. Cam asked them for permission to use the mission's name to raise money for a plane in northern Guatemala. His vision could not be dimmed, and he showed it. "The jungles and rivers there are like Amazonia,"[10] he explained.

MUTINY IN THE MISSION CHURCH

Carrying the mission's reluctant endorsement, Cam returned to the Guatemalan highlands the Cakchiquels called home. The village elders welcomed Cam "as a beloved brother. The old men poured out their grievances to him as they couldn't to the Spanish-speaking missionaries."[11] The Indians wanted to assume responsibility for their church "because the mission had everything." They "wanted their own organization."[12] Cam sympathized with the Indians' aspirations, but he knew that the attitude of his colleagues at the Central American Mission would not be so kind. He advised the Indians to surrender authority over the church to the C.A.M. mission. "You can do better working with them than against them."[13] Because the Indians trusted him, they acquiesced.

Cam eagerly awaited the arrival of his Cakchiquel New Testament. He found the Bibles buried in the archives of Guatemala City's post office, all eighteen copies of the American Bible Society's advanced shipment long overdue. He caressed the leather-bound books, marveling over their beauty, then hurried to make sure that one man in particular heard the message first. This man was not an Indian, but one of their oppressors: the new dictator, General Jorge Ubico.

Ubico had come a long way since getting his first political break in 1918, when lightning struck in the form of the Rockefeller Foundation anti-yellow fever campaign. As military overseer of the campaign, he often subjected the Indians to extreme measures of disease eradication, including burning their homes "as the only way out."[14] Ubico was now the third largest landowner in Guatemala and president to boot, having recently seized power by overthrowing the latest dictatorship.

Late in the afternoon of May 19, 1931, General Ubico received Cam

Townsend, the Caribbean secretary of the American Bible Society, and Trinidad Bac, a Cakchiquel who helped Cam with his tribe's language and was now an evangelical preacher. Cam had the Indian formally present the book, then made a short speech himself and had Ubico pose with them for a picture for a front-page story in the next day's newspaper. It was a scene Townsend would repeat many times with dictators in years to come.

Now that the translation was done, Cam's vision expanded. "The tribes of South America will have the Bible. And North America, Africa and Asia also."[15]

Cam was thinking of airplanes and of specially constructed steamboats that would haul missionaries up and down the great Amazon of South America. "There is surely some Christian oil man who would give us a plane," Cam's brother Paul pleaded in a Presbyterian newsletter,[16] but there was only silence and Cam's swelling frustrations.

Then one day Cam noticed a stranger taking pictures in Panajachel, a resort town west of Guatemala City on Lake Atitlán, where he ran a small school for the Cakchiquel. The man introduced himself as Moisés Sáenz from Mexico.

A Beacon from Mexico

Cam recognized the name immediately. Moisés Sáenz had gained quite a reputation for himself heading Mexico's rural education program, the first concerted effort to bring education to Mexico's Indians. Like many educators after the Mexican Revolution, Sáenz was a Protestant, in fact, a Presbyterian like Townsend. Sáenz had graduated from a private Protestant secondary school in Monterrey and from Presbyterian Theological Seminary in Coyoacán, a fashionable suburb of Mexico City. He was also American trained, having done postgraduate work at Washington and Jefferson College in Pennsylvania before returning to his homeland, then in the throes of revolution. This liberal educator also believed in Protestant evangelism.

Cam took Sáenz on a tour of the Cakchiquel, visiting the school and the mission at San Antonio. Sáenz was delighted when the children sang in both Cakchiquel and Spanish. He was also impressed by Cam's books and curriculum and the medical clinics Cam had established in other villages. The Maya people here were linguistically similar to some of the Indians in his own country. Sáenz invited his fellow Presbyterian to come to Mexico. After he returned north, he sent a letter from his office repeating the invitation, as Cam had requested. That simple letter, written on official Mexican stationery, was to prove fateful for Cam and tribal peoples the world over.

The road Cam had been searching for suddenly flashed before him. If he was not immediately drawn to Mexico, he was at least aware that there were horizons beyond the elusive Amazon.

And beyond the Central American Mission. The mission's executive committee sent him a disappointing Christmas present in 1931. He was to remain in the Cakchiquel work until "adequate leadership" could replace him.

"What they mean is missionary bosses," he told his wife, Elvira. "They should let the Cakchiquels themselves take over. They have enough well-trained leaders, and more being turned out every year. They have the New Testament. Why do they need American overseers?

"And they want me to do 'occasional exploration into unoccupied fields.' How can I do that, when 500 tribes in Latin America await God's word?"[17]

A few weeks later, Cam suffered another blow. Word arrived from California that his mother was dead. She had been fighting cancer for months, but he had been sure that Jesus would heal her. His mother had always had faith in him. Now he had to make the greatest decision of his life—whether to leave Guatemala—without her advice.

Cam reflected on his future. His Cakchiquel translation had given him enough confidence in his skills to move on to other New Testaments and other tribes, far from the dictates of his Fundamentalist elders.

Elvira was delighted. The pace of Cam's work had driven the small, round-faced woman almost mad. She had begun to have explosions of anger, most of them directed at Cam. Her protests escalated to violence; one day she even kicked her husband. She had never adjusted to the Indians' culture, preferring the work among ladinos that she had expected to do when she first came to Guatemala.

Whatever hesitation Cam felt about leaving ended when disaster struck. On January 21, 1932, the Volcano of Fire above his mission in San Antonio erupted in flames, along with the entire volcanic chain that stretched south toward Guatemala's border with El Salvador.

Soon after, word came from across the border of an even greater disaster. Thousands of Pipil Indians, whom Cam had surveyed for the mission in 1925, were being butchered by the military dictatorship after the Indians attempted a revolt led by local communists. The conspiracy had even spread to Guatemala, claimed President Ubico, who had the foresight to arrest and execute labor organizers in the plantations. Cam and Elvira quickly decided to move to the lowlands for their health, explaining that Cam had contracted tuberculosis.

They spent five months there, pondering their future with the Central American Mission. Despite ongoing support from several of his supporters there, Cam knew that it would be difficult to fulfill his solemn vow "to work in perfect harmony with the Central American Mission."[18]

When Cam and Elvira left Guatemala for home in mid-1932, they discovered that Elvira's emotional strain had a physical basis: She was suffering from heart pains. His sister Lula and her husband, Eugene Griset, offered their small Santa Ana farm to the couple. Elvira was bedridden for seven months, forcing

Cam to deal with the drudgery of housework that had been Elvira's burden. A brief career as a radio evangelist, appealing vainly for funds and translators to reach the Amazon, added to his frustrations.

It was not surprising, then, that when L. L. Legters showed up in February 1933 Cam greeted him with a shout of joy.

Eight years had passed since Legters had visited Townsend after completing a survey of the Indians of the Brazilian Amazon for the Inland South American Missionary Union. "Look at the map," he had said as he spread it out before Cam's hungry eyes. "The Amazon basin covers two and a half million square miles. There must be Indian tribes all over the area."[19]

But it was not to the Amazon that Legters now wanted Townsend to go. Legters and his Commission for Indian Work in Latin America had a new target: Mexico.

"There are at least fifty Mexican Indian tribes. I'm told there are 300,000 Mayans in Yucatán alone. Tell you what; you go, and I'll help raise support."[20]

Cam agreed. But he saw a larger task. Linguistics was the ark of his covenant with the Bibleless tribes. There were too many tribes in Mexico and beyond for him and Elvira to take on alone. What was needed was a summer school to train young missionaries how to translate the Scriptures into native tongues. Would Legters have his fund-raising organization, the Pioneer Mission Agency, sponsor a summer school for recruits?[21]

Legters immediately caught Townsend's vision, one which would soon give birth to the Summer Institute of Linguistics. They agreed to leave for Mexico the following fall to get permission for operations from the government of the new Mexican president, General Lázaro Cárdenas.

They prayed for guidance. A great adventure was about to begin.

Nelson Rockefeller was also embarked on a great adventure at this time, one that would shape the lives of both these men once their paths converged in Latin America.

5

THE RITES OF POLITICAL PASSAGE

Passage to India

Mohandas K. Gandhi watched the unusual couple work their way through the crowd of green-uniformed guards and his white-robed colleagues in the court-yard and approach him.

Their friendly confidence was rare for foreigners these days, especially Westerners dressed as well as these. Only last month bomb threats and demonstrations had greeted visitors at the opening of the new British seat of government a few miles south, at New Delhi. Many Indians took to the streets to show their displeasure with an Indian legislature granted only limited powers through Britain's "Indirect Rule." More than 100,000 people had followed Gandhi to jail in the last year to protest British rule of any kind. And now that the tense negotiations for independence had taken a bad turn, no one could be sure that Gandhi and his compatriots would not be in prison—or worse—before the week was out.

Against this mood of dread, the buoyant steps of these young Westerners were a relief. The woman, tall and thin, seemed caught in two eras: While dressed conservatively, she wore her brown hair in the short fashion of the Roaring Twenties. She held her back straight and head high, much like the British aristocrats Gandhi had recently had to face in negotiations. She had, in fact, been raised on an estate that was given to her family by King George III.

Her escort seemed more convivial, perhaps even brash. He returned stares with an easy smile. Introduced to the wizened man, he spoke English with the flat nasal tone of an American from New York. Gandhi recognized the name immediately: It symbolized immense wealth and power. But he only nodded his bald head while his fingers continued to work the cotton on the spinning wheel before him. Monday was Gandhi's day of silence, reserved for meditation and restoring internal peace. His spinning spoke for him, an eloquent protest against cheap British cloth that used India's cotton to ruin its own village textiles. To set an example for reviving local weaving to restore the economy and self-respect of the rural villages, Gandhi had assigned a daily quota to himself. This commitment, like his vow of silence, was not to be broken for anyone, even this couple. Instead, he scribbled a note and handed it to the young man: "Come back tomorrow. I'll talk to you."[1]

Nelson Rockefeller was not used to having his presence treated so casually, let alone dismissed. Kings, presidents, prime ministers, industrialists, bankers, scholars, poets, religious leaders—all had welcomed him warmly during this global honeymoon. All seemed to respond to his father's name as if it could work magic. Even Lord Irwin, viceroy of India and Gandhi's powerful opponent, had shown the Rockefellers the courtesies due their august station, seating Mary "Tod" Rockefeller beside him at the royal banquet at the new Viceregal Palace.

The seriousness of resolve he sensed around Gandhi was in marked contrast with the expensive week-long festivities he and Tod had participated in, celebrating the opening of New Delhi's vast government forum. Gandhi had denounced "the waste of money on architectural piles" that had no relation to India's villages, the source of Indian identity. His colleague, Jawaharlal Nehru, had been more blunt; he condemned the "elaborate show" and derided the Viceregal Palace where Nelson and Tod dined with Lord Irwin and eighty others as "the chief temple where the High Priest officiated."[2] Now, in this simple courtyard, Nelson stood before a half-naked old man who held the loyalty of millions of Indians.

Nelson agreed to return. For the first time in his twenty-two years, he was personally witnessing a fateful confrontation in world affairs, one that controlled the prospects for peace—or mass violence—for a whole subcontinent. He was fascinated.

Nelson had been a boy during World War I, and his family's enormous wealth had insulated him from the harsher realities of the world. Dartmouth had not altered this innocence. Nestled in the green hills of New Hampshire far from the challenge of urban life, Dartmouth was one of the more sheltered Ivy League schools. But now that he had graduated and married, Nelson Rockefeller was determined to see more of the tumultuous side of life.

Through the Twilight of Colonialism

From the beginning, it was not as Nelson and Tod had expected. From the day that one of Junior's chief aides saw the newlyweds off at the railroad station with a bouquet of flowers, the couple found themselves shadowed by people associated with Rockefeller interests or entranced by the power of his grandfather's name.

Nelson quickly learned that Rockefeller was more than a famous name; it was a symbol of something deeper, almost mysterious. In his eagerness to join the adult world, he had plunged into marriage without understanding the enormity of his inheritance. It was only on this trip that he was introduced to the first and most obvious reality of his name: that his life, his destiny, was to be bound to an empire from which there was no escape. At almost every stop or port of call from Hawaii to Manchuria, the newlyweds were greeted by officials of Standard Oil or by doting representatives of the railroads and steamship lines they used. And through most of their honeymoon, they were shepherded by a distinguished-looking white-haired man and his wife.

The older couple were charming and informative, but it was obvious that the man was more than a traveling companion. George Vincent, until the previous year president of the Rockefeller Foundation, had a mission. The Rockefeller fortune and its philanthropies had changed course, toward the Third World. This decision would profoundly influence the future not only of Nelson Rockefeller, but of the world.

Their trip was more an inspection tour by visiting royalty than a honeymoon. Like suffering royalty, the newlyweds endured the heavy schedule of up to seven events a day, racing through an endless series of visits to heads of state, educators, and scientists. After a brief escape through a typhoon to the Philippines, they steamed south into the Dutch East Indies, where Nelson bought his first piece of primitive art, a portentous knife handle shaped like a shrunken head. Standard Oil of New Jersey was here, too. The company had recently used State Department pressure on Holland to obtain the rights to 625,000 acres, a refinery for its oriental markets (then, one-third of all its foreign sales), and a joint marketing subsidiary with Standard Oil of New York.

Junior may have hoped that this trip would deepen Nelson's appreciation of his heritage by giving him a sobering taste of the non-European world, but it accomplished the opposite. In Bangkok, the new U.S. ambassador, a veteran of Latin America, was trying to warn his fellow diplomats that time was running out for colonialism. Shortly after the Rockefellers arrived, he threw a Christmas party on the embassy grounds, which drew a large crowd of Siamese children. The ambassador personally served American ice cream and showed Hollywood movies.

Nelson was impressed at "this unheard of contact with the masses." He had begun to have a different view of European diplomats since his wide-eyed tours during college vacations. American diplomats aping British ways looked less impressive in the Third World, where Victorian arrogance won few friends and much enmity. Nelson bristled at this narrow-mindedness of American businessmen, and the disinclination he already felt toward a business career stiffened.

"I'm sorry to say," he wrote his father from Sumatra, "that seeing and hearing so much about . . . business doesn't make me very keen to go into it. It seems to squeeze all other interests out of the men's lives that are in it."[3]

It was in the realm of politics that the honeymoon probably had its greatest impact on Nelson's life. The trip awakened his interest in foreign affairs and developed his sensitivity toward nationalist feelings. Nelson saw the inglorious side of European colonialism and was particularly disturbed by the racial discrimination of expatriates toward the people of their host countries. On a boat ride up Burma's Irrawaddy River, for instance, young European aristocrats on board loudly mocked the Burmese. Nelson winced when even the captain of the boat, trying to fend off the arrogance they directed at him, joined in, calling his Burmese crew "worthless" and claiming that they constantly needed his discipline. Members of the crew, he assured Nelson and Tod, were not allowed in the captain's office unless they removed their shoes.

Nelson was mortified, and he showed it. His sympathy for the crew may have saved his and Tod's lives. At Bhamo, a small town at the northern tip of their trip, "we were walking on shore when one of the crew ran to tell us to turn back because there was plague in the village. . . . It was a very decent thing for him to do."[4]

Nelson could not help contrasting the thoughtful behavior of nationals with the arrogance of British colonialists, especially when he and Tod discovered "that the British considered us as colonials."[5]

He also witnessed the sad indignity of U.S. foreign officers mimicking the attitudes and practices of their British mentors. "All of these things left a very strong impression," he confessed, "and one which we felt boded little good for future relations with those countries. It was evident we were not handling ourselves as a people abroad in a way that developed confidence or respect."[6]

Nelson found nationalism sweeping Asia, where local communists were willing, with alarming frequency, to take personal risks to lead anticolonial movements into broader social revolutions. Yet it was Gandhi, a pacifist, who gave young Rockefeller his most stirring experience with the growing power of anticolonial movements.

THE GANDHI ENCOUNTER

At the time of their visit, Gandhi had just been released from a British jail. In contrast to American businessmen and their Tory mentors, Britain's new Labor government was offering valuable lessons in a more modern method of colonialism in the Third World. The MacDonald government was attempting to implement Indirect Rule. Since the murderous debacle of World War I had stripped Europe of its aura of moral superiority—along with much of its treasure—the British Empire's subject populations had proved less willing to be made over in the image of white Europeans.

Diehard colonialists, like characters in E. M. Forster's recent *A Passage to India*, could still seize the arguments of social Darwinists for the need for firm guardianship over, rather than "sentimental" compassion for, the "children of the dark world." But the higher echelons in the Labor government had come to realize that such an attitude, although sufficient to motivate British colonial officers in the field, could no longer work as an effective colonial policy. They desperately wanted to end the huge civil-disobedience campaigns being led by Gandhi.[7] Britain was "anxious to retain the cooperation of moderate politicians at least in creating the new constitutional structures which it hoped would be the buttress of a new imperial order. Consequently the British did a deal with Gandhi. They resurrected their old technique of alliance with a notable who could bring his followers with him, and in so doing reinforced his continental standing."[8] Within two years, they would discard Gandhi, choosing to repress the 1932 civil-disobedience campaign and refusing to deal with him.

Nelson was prepared to sympathize with Gandhi. He gained an invitation through a visit to Ambalal Sarabhai, one of the many Indian textile manufacturers who hoped to gain control over India's economic policies by funding the nationalist movement, believing that Gandhism was the only alternative to communism. Accompanying Sarabhai's family on the train to Delhi, Nelson and Tod were again confronted with British racism. "We created quite a stir on the way as it seems the English don't exactly travel in company with Indians," he recalled. "Something like our colored situation— and, of course, we ate with them in the diner."[9]

Nelson's meeting with Gandhi, which had to be delayed for two days because of the tense negotiations and conferences with other Congress leaders, left a strong emotional impression.

"Gandhi came out looking pretty tired, but very cheerful," Nelson wrote home. The Mahatma had just completed his most critical meeting with the British viceroy, Lord Irwin, at two o'clock that morning and gotten to bed at 4 A.M. only three hours before the Rockefellers arrived. They drove to an old Mogul fort at the edge of Old Delhi, where Gandhi liked to walk. A dark bank of clouds had rolled over the city; Indra, the ancient Hindu god of war, began thundering her drums in the heavens.

"We have finally come to our agreement with the Viceroy," Gandhi said, his eyes shining behind gold-rimmed spectacles. "There will be one more conference later today to arrange all the details."[10] It had been a critical meeting, one that would cement Britain's most important colony to an indefinite future, but under Indirect Rule.

Gandhi walked with the Rockefellers, answering their questions. "He told us his whole background, his relation with the British," Nelson later recalled. "It gave me the Indian point of view."[11] Gandhi spoke about the negotiations, praising Lord Irwin; he had been elated by the outcome.

As Gandhi and the Rockefellers returned to the house where he was staying, Gandhi concluded by explaining that the Indian people could never fulfill their destiny within the British Empire. Then he said good-bye and walked back to his colleagues in the courtyard.

Sunlight broke through the clouds, and Nelson was swept with the feeling that he had been privileged to witness a rare moment in history. The initiative seemed to belong to Gandhi and Lord Irwin. Through anguish and turmoil, the British had learned, in India at least, how to strike a modus vivendi with nationalist uprisings through Indirect Rule. It was a lesson not to be forgotten.

Humiliations by the British had cemented Nelson's antipathy toward colonialism. They nurtured in him a growing conviction that Americans, with their anticolonial origins as a nation and their uncommon wealth and military power, had something unique to offer the Third World.

It was only natural, then, that having discerned in Asia the twilight of Victorian colonialism, Nelson would, on returning home, also wonder what would replace the British Empire. Was there an inheritance even larger, historically greater, and more urgent than that of his family?

Facing the Indian Revolution

After his return from his honeymoon, Nelson threw himself into the operations of Rockefeller Center. Derided by one architect as a "graceless bulk," it was rising into the skies above midtown Manhattan. To many, the erection of the Center's five buildings—particularly its seventy-two-story skyscraper—in the midst of the Great Depression was itself a travesty, the giant proportions of its architecture symbolic of the previous decade of sin. Nelson worked feverishly to attract tenants in a city that simply did not need new office space. Rumors soon began to fly of Nelson's aggressive ways.

Junior's misgivings grew. There had been other disagreements in the family office, including Nelson's decision to accept a seat on the board of the Metropolitan Museum of Art. In fact, Special Work, his real estate firm for the Center, had become Nelson's excuse for escaping the staid office and its constraints. If his older brother, John 3rd, wished to accept a life sentence, so be it. But Nelson had bigger dreams.

His mother, Abby, had always encouraged those dreams in her favorite boy. A lover of the arts and one of the founders of the Museum of Modern Art, she backed Nelson's election to the museum's board in 1932. It was through this shared appreciation of modern art, which his father loathed, that Nelson first came in contact with Mexico's most celebrated artist, Diego Rivera. He did not foresee that the part-Indian artist would be the catalyst for his first confrontation with Latin America's spreading revolution.

Nelson did not come up with the idea of a Rivera mural for the Center. That suggestion came from a representative of the Rockefeller Foundation in Mexico,

Mrs. Francis Flynn Paine. Through Paine's influence, Rivera had been commissioned to paint the murals in the San Francisco Stock Exchange and Henry Ford's Detroit Technical Institute. Impressed by the power of his work, Paine recommended Rivera to Abby, sure that his murals would conform to the orthodox version of American history and "progress as accelerated by the discovery and large use of petroleum."[12]

Junior, as usual, objected futilely. Backed by his mother, Nelson prevailed. Abby was intrigued by Rivera. High spirited and possessed of a streak of bohemianism, Abby had little trouble asserting her independence from her husband when it came to art.

Nelson had reasons beyond art for selecting Rivera, business reasons. Diego Rivera represented exactly the kind of mix of controversy and quality that the new Rockefeller Center needed to draw crowds of tourists.

As soon as Rivera arrived in March 1933, a furor of speculation erupted over what he was going to paint. Day after day, Nelson would pass by the painter's tall scaffolds in the Center's lobby and crane his neck to watch Rivera's assistants sketch the outline of a great scene across 63 feet of wall 17 feet high. At first it was difficult to make out the shapes. But contrary to his later claims, Nelson knew most of what would appear. In November, Abby had approved Rivera's sketch for the mural and its accompanying synopsis. The mural was to be a salute to science, with Jupiter capturing lightning as a source of electricity and the "Man of Science" presenting "the scale of Natural Evolution, the understanding of which replaces the Superstition of the past." It was also to present a vivid political portrayal of tyranny, war, and rebellion by the laboring classes.

"My panel will show the Workers arriving at a true understanding of their rights regarding the means of production," Rivera wrote Abby. "It will also show the Workers of the cities and the country inheriting the Earth. . . .

". . . on the left, a group of unemployed workers in a breadline. Above this group . . . an image of War, as in the case of Unemployment, the result of the evolution of Technical Power unaccompanied by a corresponding ethical development."[13]

The Rockefellers, of course, had another, less concrete vision: "Our theme is NEW FRONTIERS," they wrote Rivera during the negotiations, ". . . Man cannot pass up his pressing and vital problems by 'moving on.' He has to solve them on his own lot. The development of civilization is no longer lateral, it is inward and upward. It is the culmination of man's soul and mind, and coming into a fuller comprehension of the meaning and mystery of life."[14]

It was, in many ways, a statement reflecting its time. The Great Depression was viewed as the punishment of an angry God against a decade of hedonism. Reform, personal and national, was now the order of the day, the New Frontier having become internal and spiritual, rather than external and materialistic.

Junior and the Center's executives had chosen black and gray stone for the lobby to convey conservative dignity. To Rivera, the lobby looked like a tomb. Upon his return from Italy, he had rediscovered the "great force and genius" of pre-Columbian Indian art and was influenced by the "barbaric" colors found on the walls of Mayan and Aztec pyramids.[15]

After a few days of self-restraint, he could bear it no longer. Suddenly, the giant wall sprang alive with colors and sweeping shapes, causing a sensation in New York's art world. Hundreds of artists and students came to watch the Mexican paint his great allegory of the world war and the Roaring Twenties. Nelson, never one to let an opportunity for promotion pass, issued about a hundred tickets a day. One day in April, Abby came by and climbed up the metal scaffold to watch the artist work. She was enthralled.

Whatever Nelson's initial feelings, his opinion changed after an article appeared on May 3 in the *New York World Telegram* under the headline, RIVERA PAINTS SCENES OF COMMUNIST ACTIVITY AND JOHN D. JR. FOOTS BILL. The *Telegram* attacked the mural for vividly depicting "poison gases used in war" and "prostitutes infected with venereal diseases so placed as to indicate them as the results of a civilization revolving around nightclubs." The reporter saw red everywhere, "red headdress, red flags, waves of red," and "iron-jawed policemen, one swinging his club" at what the reporter described as "a Communist demonstration."[16] The article created the impression that the Rockefellers had been duped.

Nelson responded immediately—to Rivera. He wrote Rivera that while visiting "Rockefeller Center yesterday viewing the progress of your thrilling mural, I noticed that in the most recent portion of the painting you had included a portrait of Lenin. The piece is beautifully painted but it seems to me that his portrait appearing in the mural might very seriously offend a great many people." Nelson asked him "to substitute the face of some unknown man where Lenin's face now appears."[17]

A figure of Lenin had been included in Rivera's earliest sketches. Nelson's sudden turnabout convinced the artist that something terrible was afoot. His response was to work at a frenzied pace. He wanted to finish his painting before it could be aborted. He offered to add a portrait of Lincoln surrounded by abolitionists and the slave-revolutionary Nat Turner. But he would not destroy any part of his painting, including the portrait of Lenin. It had been there for a month without any previous objection by Nelson or his mother and represented to the artist a prophecy of an anti-Nazi alliance between Russians and Americans.

Nelson was not amused. He pressured Rivera with personal pleas, but Rivera kept painting.

A week later, matters were taken out of Nelson's hands. Rivera received a letter from Hugh Robertson, executive manager of the Center, insisting that there had been "not the slightest inclination either in the description or in the sketch that you would include in the mural any portrait or any subject matter of a controversial matter."

At 9 P.M. the next night, a messenger scurried up the scaffold with a smug smile and summoned Rivera, still working, to Robertson's office. There Rivera was handed a check for the $21,500 contract and ordered to leave. Demonstrations immediately broke out in front of the RCA building, demanding that Rivera's art be saved. The Rockefellers promised that "the uncompleted fresco of Diego Rivera will not be destroyed or in any way mutilated."[18] But the public was not allowed to view it, nor were photographs permitted. A drab canvas was draped over the entire wall, like a shroud. Most understood its meaning.

Almost a year later, at the lonely hour of midnight, February 9, 1934, workmen appeared under orders to chip the painting off the wall. In its place, a politically safer mural in sepia was done by José Maria Sert. This time, it was Robertson who did the hiring.

BIRTH OF AN ALIAS

For a time, the specter of the Rockefellers destroying Rivera's mural haunted the embassy in Mexico City, casting a shadow over Mexican-American relations. But one day, U.S. Ambassador Josephus Daniels greeted two Americans "who were quite interesting and unlike any other visitors I had had since I have been here."

William Cameron Townsend and L. L. Legters arrived at the embassy. As Cam had done with the dictator of Guatemala, he presented the ambassador with a copy of his Cakchiquel translation of the Bible. Here, Legters found it unnecessary to hide their intention to proselytize Mexico despite its anticlerical laws. He freely identified himself as the field secretary of the Pioneer Mission Agency, whose "settled point of mission is to translate the Bible into the Indian tongues."[19]*

Daniels was a North Carolinian with strong Fundamentalist leanings. He was moved by the miracle of faith. When he asked Townsend and Legters where the money came from to pay their expenses and the "expenses of other translators," Legters did not mention Pioneer's primary role as a financial conduit for missionaries. Legters replied only that "We do not trouble about money; the Lord will provide."

"I have not seen so great faith," Daniels wrote, "no, not in Mexico," and added wistfully, "I wish I could have as undimmed faith as they seemed to have."[20]

Townsend's and Legters's faith in the divine origin of their mission was real.

---

* Cam was less candid. He described himself as having been "in South America " as well as Guatemala "for some time." According to Daniels, "Mr. Townsend told me he was present when Geronimo died and buried him." If Townsend's South American residence was fanciful, his presence at Geronimo's death must have been miraculous; Geronimo died at Fort Sill, Oklahoma, in 1909, when thirteen-year-old Cam had yet to venture beyond Long Beach, California.

The previous November, Cam and Elvira had traveled to Dallas for a rendezvous with Legters and his wife at the headquarters of the Central American Mission. From Dallas, Cam went on a speaking tour in Wichita Falls. There he met an Episcopalian rector who was fascinated with the Aztec religion and wrote on a card an introduction to the Episcopalian dean of Mexico City "to put you in touch with some influential people."[21]

It was the break Cam needed.

He would not be delayed. Even Elvira's ailing heart could not dissuade him. He sent Elvira home to her family at the Moody Church in Chicago. By the middle of the month, he and Legters were trying to cross the border at Laredo, but were stopped by suspicious customs officials. Only by producing his dog-eared letter from Moisés Sáenz, the Mexican director of rural education he had met in Guatemala, did Cam persuade them to wire Mexico City for instructions. The response from Mexico's director of immigration was cautious. The government had learned of the Americans' missionary goal from an article Cam had recently published, and proselytizing by foreign missionaries was against the law. The two men were permitted entry on the condition that they would neither preach nor study Indian languages. They agreed.

That evening Townsend and Legters pulled into Monterrey, the Protestant stronghold of northern Mexico. The men spent an anguished night battling doubts with comforting passages from the Bible; the next morning they continued south over the uncompleted Pan-American Highway. Along the way, Cam noticed that the Indians working beside the road were similar to those in Guatemala: poor.

But there the similarity ended. The political conditions in Mexico and Guatemala were very different for American missionaries.

Mexico was then at the height of its antipathy toward foreign missions, and every missionary Cam had spoken to in the capital confirmed that residence visas were impossible to get.

There was more bad news. Moisés Sáenz was no longer on hand to help. Since 1932, Sáenz had come under increasing pressure to match his ideals as Mexico's rural educator with a commitment to use his schools as a means of changing the economic system that exploited the Indians. Even the appointment of Moisés's brother, Aarón, as *superintendente,* or mayor, of the Federal District of Mexico City could not save Moisés's position. In January 1933, citing philosophical differences, Moisés resigned as director of rural education.

By the time Cam arrived in Mexico City the following November, Aarón Sáenz's political future was also being rapidly eclipsed by the rise of General Lázaro Cárdenas. Aarón Sáenz was committed to the growth of a native Mexican capitalism; Cárdenas was committed to the laboring classes, the increasingly ignored backbone of the Mexican Revolution.[22]

With the Sáenz family out of favor, Cam fell back on his only hope for an entrée into Mexican high society: his card of introduction to the Episcopalian dean. The next Sunday, Cam slipped into the dean's service at the Episcopalian cathedral and presented his card. When the cleric heard of Cam's interest in Mexico's Indians, he invited him to dinner the following Tuesday to meet Bernard Bevans, an English ethnologist who was studying the Indians. At the dinner, Cam sat next to Bevans and pleaded his case. Bevans agreed to hold a small luncheon for Cam; one of the people he invited was Dr. Frank Tannenbaum of Columbia University. That luncheon proved to be one of the decisive moments of Cameron Townsend's life.

Tannenbaum was among the many American anthropologists who had fanned out across Latin America in search of clues to unravel the mysteries of human origins. He rebelled against the persistent assumption that tribal peoples represented a "primitive" stage in the evolution of human culture that ascended, quite conveniently, to the Euro-American zenith.

Tannenbaum was impressed by the Indian campesino's central role in the Mexican Revolution. While Mexican intellectuals had turned toward Europe and remained out of touch with the rural peasants of their country, small groups of Indians under anonymous leaders had been mounting the revolution of 1910. Without intellectuals, however, the Indian revolution was voiceless.

The one exception was Emiliano Zapata. An Indian of humble peasant origins, Zapata had formulated the only clear plan for agrarian reform based on the *ejidos*, or common lands, of the villages. Between 1911 and 1919, his forces constituted the only government in the state of Morelos, the vast valley south of the capital where expanding sugar plantations sent their product to the Colossus of the North via an American-owned railroad.

To counteract this Indian-led revolution, Mexico City's successive regimes engaged in a war of extermination against the villages of Morelos. As late as 1923, four years after federal troops killed Zapata, Tannenbaum saw an inscription on a wall in Cuernavaca: "Rebels of the South. It is better to die on your feet than to live on your knees."[23]

From the 1920s on, the prospect of more Indian revolutions spreading through Central and South America haunted U.S.-Latin American relations. Tannenbaum was one of the first U.S. anthropologists to realize that Zapata's challenge would continue from the grave if the misery of Mexico's landless Indian peasants was allowed to fester.

Sponsored by the Social Science Research Council and the Brookings Institution (both Rockefeller-funded institutions), Tannenbaum conducted an intensive study of Mexico's Indians that brought him into close contact with Moisés Sáenz.

Tannenbaum's study decried Mexico's 12,479 rural schools as "a fraction of Mexico's needs" and called for land grants for community-built school buildings and vegetable gardens. The success of Mexico's rural education program would depend on the possession of land by the villages, he argued, and the rural communities could not have a successful school unless they had *ejidos* to feed the population. "The rural community must support the school in the future," he wrote with double economic and cultural meaning, "the way it supported the church in the past."[24]

At the luncheon, Tannenbaum wrote an endorsement of Cam's work for Rafael Ramírez, Moisés Sáenz's replacement as director of rural education. From Tannenbaum, Cam learned that Ramírez would be in Monterrey on November 23.

Cam and Legters were at Monterrey when Ramírez arrived. The Mexican educator was reluctant to expose Indians to American missionaries, especially Fundamentalist Bible translators. But then he noticed that Cam was carrying Tannenbaum's book.

"He's a good man," Ramírez commented. "Understands our Revolution. Most people in the States don't."

Cam showed him Tannenbaum's endorsement. Ramírez's attitude shifted.

"Tannenbaum's word is good enough for me," Ramírez said. "I think I'll invite you to study our rural education, but not the Indian languages. You can visit areas where Indians live and see what we are doing. Maybe you can write some articles."[25]

The missionary was happy to oblige. Following a six-week tour of rural schools in the states of Campeche, Yucatán, and Chiapas, Cam returned to Elvira in Chicago and brought her down to the warmer climate of Sulphur Springs, Arkansas, where his brother Paul was now director of the Fundamentalist John Brown Academy. From there, he wrote articles on Mexico's expanded school system for the *Dallas Morning News* and *School and Society* magazine. He passed them on to Ramírez, who responded warmly, noting the missionary's "deep sympathy."

Encouraged, Cam now pressed forward with his plans to hold his first "summer training camp for prospective Bible translators." One of the John Brown Academy's revivalist song leaders pitched in, offering the use of a nearby farm. Cam now saw the hand of Providence at work everywhere and rushed a catalog through a printer.

The catalog was the first of its kind in the evangelical world, offering courses on Indians' history, their customs, their psychology, and evangelization by Legters; "practical problems" by Cam's brother Paul; and Spanish by Cam's Cakchiquel language informant, Joe Chicol, who had followed Paul to John Brown Academy. Cam's own ambitious courses were the core: the economic and cultural status of the Indian, government programs, translation techniques, and how to conduct a literacy campaign. Little here smacked of the old missionary approach.

Yet, to attract students, Cam had to seek support from the pillars of Fundamentalism. The new Dallas Theological Seminary approved of Cam's decision to enter Mexico "as linguists rather than as missionaries,"[26] as did Charles Fuller, director and leader of the California Orange Growers Association, a hotbed of planter reaction against collective bargaining by Mexican field workers. Another important backer was Will Nyman, a former lumber executive who had retired to California to become secretary of the Missions Committee of Lyman Stewart's wealthy Church of the Open Door. Moody Church's pastor, Rev. Harry Ironside, also OK'd the project.

The "open door to Mexico" Cam had prayed for with Legters had at last been cracked, thanks not to Fundamentalists, but to a book by a "radical" anthropologist backed by Rockefeller-funded organizations.

Providence Calls

In 1981, while the CIA's contra war raged in Nicaragua, Wycliffe Bible Translators republished Cameron Townsend's only novel. Half a century had passed since the events that inspired it, but its message was still fresh to Fundamentalist missionaries aiding the CIA's war: A world communist plot was behind the revolutions in Central America, and the only antidote besides U.S. armed intervention was Christ's Word in the Bible. It was a strange theme for a professed admirer of the Mexican Revolution to pen when knocking on its door.

The first summer school had so charged Cam and Elvira with expectation that in the fall of 1934 they decided to drive to Mexico to follow up the contacts he had made the previous year. Mud slides along the unfinished Pan-American Highway, however, forced them to hold up in Monterrey for two months. Cam became acquainted with the large Protestant community of that town, the home of the Sáenz family. It was here that he wrote his "autobiographical novel," *Tolo: The Volcano's Son.*

The novel purported to present an account of the Indian revolt in El Salvador that had helped persuade Cam to leave Guatemala in 1932 and argued for Cam's own Bible translation mission as a response to similar insurgencies.

Tolo mentioned how an American Bible translator in Guatemala had long seen the danger of creeping radicalism among the Indians. In describing this missionary's activities, Townsend offered to posterity an account of his own counterinsurgency doctrine: "Guatemala would find that in the human mass she had relegated to brute exploitations, she had prepared a pile of tinder in readiness of a spark of radicalism from across her northern frontier. The translator had labored feverishly to avoid this danger; his greatest hope was the Bible. . . . Through its influence, he hoped to see nuclei of newborn men and women formed in all the towns to labor in behalf of progress. These would counteract extremists, should they come."[27]

Though filled with innuendos and inaccuracies,* *Tolo* was a useful entrée to

---

*A few examples: a Russian spy who never actually existed; an international communist conspiracy in Guatemala and El Salvador when Stalin and the Comintern had written off Central America as lacking the proper revolutionary conditions; and Cam's own ignoring reports by a fellow Central American missionary in C.A.M.'s bulletin of atrocities by the Salvadorian army, including the machine-gunning of 300 men and

self-proclaimed "Christian businessmen" who were caught in the throes of their own political crises during the Great Depression. The millenarian *Revelation* magazine published the novel in serial form for seven consecutive months, starting in April 1936. The timing was propitious. During those months, one of Cam's key backers, Charles Fuller, was locked in a battle with Mexican field workers who harvested his citrus plantations. Orange County's prosperity of neat white-fenced farms and quaint Christian steeples rested on a foundation of low wages. In June 1936, 2,500 citrus workers went on strike in Orange County for a wage increase. They wanted to increase their wages from twenty-five cents to forty cents an hour. The California Orange Growers Association, which Fuller headed, refused to bargain. Supported by local Protestant clergy and the Associated Farmers of California (a growers' organization financially backed by Standard Oil of California),[28] the growers instead pointed to the Mexican composition of the workforce and the presence of Communist party members among the organizers of the farmworkers' union. That was all they needed to justify calling in the Orange County sheriff. Four hundred armed deputies descended on the farmworkers' shantytowns with tear gas and clubs. Men were beaten, and women and children were gassed. Santa Ana, the quiet town where Cam had biked to high school and reposed with his Griset in-laws after leaving Guatemala in 1932, was transformed into the site of a concentration camp, where 115 workers were herded into a stockade built just *before* the strike commenced. The strikers were then marched into court and summarily found guilty by the same Anglo judges and juries who had imposed segregation on them.

Cam kept silent on what was happening in his home state. *Tolo's* anticommunism spoke for him in American Fundamentalist circles where growers like Charles Fuller could savor its political message.

In Mexico, where anger arose over the repression in southern California and the deportation of some 200,000 countrymen from the United States, Cam kept his beliefs to himself. This was not out of character with what he had already proposed—and Fuller endorsed—when he first set up his summer camp: the use of linguistics as a disguise for his proselytizing goals. The Word *would* be brought to the Bibleless peoples before this century was out, Cam insisted. And it was he who had been called to be the Lord's messenger.

This divine calling had never seemed more certain than during the second camp for prospective Bible translators, now called Camp Wycliffe, in honor of John Wycliffe, the sixteenth-century translator of the Bible into English. At the suggestion of a visiting lecturer from the Bible Institute of Los Angeles, Cam was leading his students in prayer for an "open door" to Mexico for Protestant missionaries. For

---

slaughter of 400 boys in the town of Nahuizalco. Some 2,500 died in this town; the total slaughtered has been estimated from a low of 8,000 to as many as 40,000 people, most of them Indians.

a full, aching morning, the faculty and students knelt. And no sooner had they risen at noon for lunch than "someone arrived from town to report" that the local radio station had announced that President Cárdenas had fired his entire cabinet. Elated, the students were eager to follow "Uncle Cam" into Mexico that autumn. God, it seemed, had answered their prayers with a miracle. What better sign could there be that Cameron Townsend's vision had the Lord's blessing?

Cam did not tell the youths that the news was only late in arriving at Sulphur Springs. Cárdenas, in fact, had fired his cabinet weeks before, in early June, and one of his officials had already written Townsend of the turn of events. The news had already been printed in the national press. Why it was not reported in Sulphur Springs until that miraculous day of prayer was never discovered.

When his students followed Cam to Mexico City that September, they thought that the "fanatical atheists" were out. They were wrong. Rafael Ramírez, the atheist who had succeeded to Moisés Sáenz's old post as director of rural education, was still in.

This situation was actually to Cam's benefit. Cam had cultivated Ramírez as his means of boring into Mexican officialdom. It was Ramírez, in fact, who wrote Townsend on June 4 of the cabinet shake-up.[29]

CAM'S "LINGUISTIC INVESTIGATORS"

A few months later, Cam and his recruits were in Mexico City to attend the seventh Inter-American Scientific Congress at the Palace of Fine Arts. The missionary, spotting Ramírez, worked his way through the crowd and, in front of everyone, embraced him like an old friend. Ramírez, apparently taken aback, responded cordially. But he did introduce Cam to three powerful officials in the Cárdenas government: the secretary of labor, the secretary of the Congress's Division on Indians, and the director of the Mexican Institute of Linguistic Investigation.

Although these men came from three separate fields—labor, anthropology, and linguistics—they were all dedicated to pursuing Cárdenas's interest in setting up a Department of Indian Affairs along lines originally proposed by Moisés Sáenz: educating and integrating the Indian into modern Mexican society. A key component of this process was linguistics. When Cam heard from the officials that the Mexican government was interested in pursuing linguistic studies among the Indians, he leaped at the opportunity. He presented his followers as "linguistic investigators," rather than missionaries.[30]

If this linguistic cover was not deep (since the Mexicans already knew of Cam's interest in Bible translation), it at least carried the option of plausible denial for Mexican officialdom. So did Cam being invited to join the Linguistic Society of America, a small organization founded the year before by the father of modern anthropology, Franz Boas. Cam immediately saw the advantage of membership in the society and put it to use: The society became the official sponsor of Townsend's group and the financial conduit for donations from Legter's Pioneer Mission Agency.[31]

Years later, the Inter-American Scientific Congress would be described by Townsend's followers as the birthplace of the Summer Institute of Linguistics (SIL). It was also the birthplace of SIL's active collaboration with Rockefeller allies. Here Cam gained entrée to the Rockefeller-funded world of *indigenismo*, an international movement of liberal anthropologists and other social scientists in the Americas.

Foremost among the movement's Mexican adherents was Moisés Sáenz. Sáenz was aware of the recommendations of the 1926 survey of American Indian conditions that had been funded by John D. Rockefeller, Jr. Released in 1928, Lewis Meriam's *The Problem of Indian Administration* grasped a central truth: The fundamental grievance among America's restless Indians was the loss of their lands. Meriam called for the curtailment of leasing Indian land to white settlers, repeal of the Dawes Allotment Act that had seized and parceled communal land, and revolving loans to help Indians buy back lands and administer their resources with government aid.[32]

At the same time the Meriam report was circulating among *indigenistas* in North and South America, Sáenz was exploring the return of Indian village communal lands, or *ejidos*, to their original owners in Mexico. He had discussed these policies with Frank Tannenbaum when the latter was doing his survey of Mexican conditions in the late 1920s, and he had exchanged ideas with John Collier during the latter's visits to Mexico in 1930 and 1931. In 1934, Collier, by then Roosevelt's commissioner of Indian Affairs, invited Sáenz to Washington to participate in a conference devoted to overhauling a corrupt BIA with major social and economic reforms.[33] After consultations with leading social scientists in the Rockefeller funding orbit, Collier devised the Indian Reorganization Act of 1934, which included, among its most far-reaching reforms, the restoration of tribal lands, Indian self-government, and the creation of economic cooperatives.

What Cam found in Mexico was strikingly similar. President Cárdenas intended to go beyond Sáenz's proposals; he advocated not only the greater return of *ejidos*, but also granting Indians control over their agricultural and industrial production and a larger share of their revenues. By breaking up haciendas and redistributing land, the government could also give the Indians some measure of economic power, perhaps enough to facilitate their entry into local and national decision-making circles on a more equal basis.

At the Inter-American Scientific Congress, Cam got his first look at Lázaro Cárdenas, a husky, big-boned man with dark brown hair and a short bushy mustache. Cam whispered to his students that Cárdenas was called "the 'Peasant's President.' He shocked the Mexican aristocracy by moving from the presidential palace into a middle class home."[34] Sáenz, however, was not at the Congress. (He was serving as Cárdenas's Mexican ambassador to Ecuador.) The mantle of indigenismo leadership in Mexico had fallen on the shoulders of Dr. Manuel Gamio, a man long associated with Rockefeller-funded institutions.

Gamio's record was impressive. During the 1920s, he completed a monumental study of the Mayan civilization and its descendants in Yucatán, inaugurating an interdisciplinary approach by integrating archaeology, history, anthropology, and sociology. He subsequently renewed his association with the University of Chicago, for which he undertook to study the conditions of Mexican immigrant workers in the United States, funded by the Laura Spelman Rockefeller Memorial Fund. Gamio's next foreign study was a trip to Japan in 1929 to examine soybean production on the invitation of the Rockefeller-funded Institute for Pacific Affairs.[35]

Now, under Cárdenas, Gamio's star was again in ascendance. Within a few years, as wartime head of the Inter-American Indian Institute, he would play an important role in the growth of Cameron Townsend's influence in the hemisphere.

The Inter-American Scientific Congress was a turning point in Cam's life. It provided him with contacts and scientific insights about assimilating Indians that few of his missionary peers possessed. This exposure to social science would give his SIL followers a scope and depth of knowledge unique within the Fundamentalist mainstream, helping ensure their status as the crème de la crème of American Fundamentalist missionaries.

Another great unseen but felt authority over the congress was Dr. Robert Redfield of the University of Chicago. Redfield had pioneered the Mexican field for American anthropology, first, as a compiler of oral histories of Mexican immigrants and then as an investigator of Tepoztlán, a village south of Mexico City. Since his arrival there in 1926, Redfield had witnessed the painful effort of its people to return to normalcy after the civil war that followed the revolution of 1910. Redfield realized that as the pace of change quickened with Euro-American expansion into Third World countries, so would the need for individuals who could accommodate themselves to—rather than resist—the change.

The implications of all these factors for the indigenous nonwhite majority of the world were enormous. The penchant for social engineering, whether exercised by "enlightened" missionaries like Cameron Townsend or future foreign policy architects like Nelson Rockefeller, would never be fully overcome.

Peaceful integration, respect for Indian culture, reforms in education—these made up the heady brew Cam gulped down at the congress. Kenneth Pike, his most promising young translator, was deeply impressed. The would-be missionary had already decided to say good-bye to his fellow Camp Wycliffe students when they left for home and to proceed south to the mountains of Oaxaca to study the language of the Mixtec Indians.

For Townsend, there would be less isolation from the seat of power and more collegial comfort. He had been advised at the congress to start his work in the Aztec village of Tetelcingo, sixty miles south of Mexico City. Tetelcingo was described as one of the most "backward" Indian villages in Mexico, a euphemism for those traditional communities that were less assimilated into the national culture and its political consensus. In fact, it was a hotbed of Zapatism in the most revolutionary valley in rural Mexico, Morelos.

BEHIND THE MIRACLE OF TETELCINGO

As Cam and Elvira's Buick and trailer descended 3,000 feet into Morelos, the valley offered an imposing panorama. Blessed with a pleasant climate, thermal waters, and fertile soil with luxurious vegetation, Morelos had been called the "Site of Eternal Spring" by the Aztecs. It had been a center of Indian settlement for centuries before Hernán Cortés marched his conquistadores through the valley, attacking the Indians' adobe villages and erecting his palace in the resort town of Aztec royalty, Cuernavaca.

Tetelcingo was one of the 5,000 other Indian villages in Mexico that still collectively owned some 45,000 square miles in 1854. Then the descendants of Spanish settlers declared themselves independent of Madrid, and in the name of liberty, equality, and a free market, civil communities were barred from holding lands. In a precedent for what would happen thirty years later in the United States under the Dawes Act, communal land was seized, subdivided, and parceled out to individual Indians. Most of the Indians of Morelos saw their lands fall into the hands of speculators and giant plantations, or haciendas. By 1910, more than 90 percent of the population was landless and desperately poor, a direct result of the spread of haciendas that made Morelos, after the new U.S. colonies of Hawaii and Puerto Rico, the third largest producer of sugar in the world.[36]

This was the reason the valley gave such widespread support to Emiliano Zapata. With his wide-brimmed sombrero perched above fiery dark eyes and a long, bushy mustache, Zapata was the giant of the Mexican Revolution. His program of land reform based on *ejidos* repossessed from the haciendas struck terror in privileged circles. Zapata became the living symbol of peasant revolution in the Third World and of the specter of Indian revolt that had always hung over the Americas. But to most of the Indians of Morelos, the illiterate Zapata was simply a son of the valley, a courageous and brilliant man who had dared to lead their resistance against exploitation and dictatorship.

For almost a decade, while the United States looked on with increasing anxiety, twice sending in forces to intervene in the civil war in the north and east, the campesinos of Morelos in the south fought back the armies of four central governments that repeatedly attacked and sacked the villages for daring to follow Zapata's land reform.

Zapata was assassinated in 1919, betrayed into an ambush by forces loyal to

President Venustiano Carranza's "Constitutionalist" government. Carranza, in turn, was overthrown the following year by two of his top generals. One, Alvaro Obregón, became president. The other, Obregón's chief of staff, was Aarón Sáenz. Aarón would become one of Mexico's wealthiest sugar barons. He would also become an ally of William Cameron Townsend.

Defeated and subdued, the people of Morelos began to stream down from the hills where they had taken refuge during the war. They found razed homes, slaughtered cattle, and an annulled agrarian reform.

The memory of Zapata still haunted the valley when the Townsends arrived in 1935. The Great Depression had devastated world sugar prices for the smaller cane growers in Morelos. It also meant rising unemployment and fewer, larger refineries, with ownership concentrated in fewer hands. The real power in Morelos, Cam learned, was an American, William Jenkins, owner of the region's largest sugar mill at Atencingo in the fertile valley of Matamoros. A rich American getting richer off Indian labor and 304,000 acres of once-Indian lands, Jenkins was a predictable target for protests. Zapatista villagers challenged his Atencingo landholdings, and soon Zapatistas in Morelos were also challenging his control over the sugar haciendas. The distribution of fertile lands had been slow, and the villagers had become increasingly militant in their demands. President Cárdenas was suddenly confronted with the prospect of severe unrest.

Once again, the seeds of Indian revolution surged through the valley. Violence was also intensifying between Zapatistas and right-wing religious fanatics. Former members of the Catholic Cristero movement of the 1920s had murdered seventy-five rural teachers in the past year.[37]

These were not the kind of conditions that inspired foreigners, much less a gringo with an ailing wife, to go to Morelos. But years later, Cam would claim that he accepted the Morelos challenge so Elvira's heart condition could benefit from Tetelcingo's climate. He seemed untroubled by those who questioned this or his other rationale, the need to bring the Bible to Bibleless tribes. But if there was any urgent need for Bible translators in Morelos, the facts did not suggest it. Illiteracy did afflict 60 percent of the population, but Morelos was more literate than twelve other states, seven of which were areas with higher Indian populations. In Morelos, in fact, just 1 percent of the state spoke only an indigenous language, whereas in other states, the need for translators was much greater. Yet Morelos became the launching pad for Cam's success.

Decades later, Cam offered a clue to the riddle of his appearance in Tetelcingo. After moving into the valley, he paid a visit to the U.S. Embassy at Ambassador Daniels's request and prepared a report for Washington on the effect of Cárdenas's programs on the Indians of Morelos.

Townsend's four-page report reflected the ambassador's concerns that

Cárdenas, like Roosevelt, was under unfair criticism from conservative business-men for alleged "communistic" policies.

"Certain radical elements in the Cabinet were endeavoring to use the school system for communistic and atheistic propaganda," the missionary wrote. But now "the radical leaders had been dismissed from office and the bitter broadsides of atheism and communism with which official and semi-official periodicals have been filled before were little in evidence. There seemed to be in progress a swing back to the original principles of the Mexican Revolution and away from the extreme ideals which are Russian rather than Mexican."

Cam was not shy about revealing his vast ambitions. "Indo-America presents a vast field for linguistic research which is almost untouched and our Institute hopes to locate five hundred trained linguists during the next two decades among primitive tribes not only of the three Americas but also the Philippine Islands, the East Indies."[38] This was Cam's first serious attempt to impress upon U.S. govern-ment officials his usefulness as an informant on local conditions.

Washington had always relied to some extent on the political intelligence provided by travelers and missionaries, such as Townsend. On the interna-tional level, Mexico was potentially the most powerful Caribbean nation, and certainly the most avowedly revolutionary. Cárdenas, like Roosevelt, repre-sented a chance for peaceful reform without scrapping the general framework of private enterprise.

This was true for U.S. domestic politics as well. Back in the United States, Roosevelt was trying to resist growing pressure from business and Catholic circles to intervene militarily in Mexico. He knew that winning allies in Latin America was contingent on a policy of nonintervention. Now he was facing a tough reelec-tion. It helped having a firsthand report by a Fundamentalist missionary that chal-lenged tales in the U.S. press of Mexican girls being forced to parade naked in public schools for the "sex education" of boys[39] or charges that religious persecu-tion continued under Cárdenas.

Cam, aided by gifts from the Ministry of Labor (including a truck, no mean symbol of prestige, which Cam taught villagers to drive) and by money from the director of rural education to buy plants and fruit trees, worked hard at planting a garden in the town square. With the mayor as his language informant, Cam tried to master Tetelcingo's melodious Aztec dialect. The garden served as proof that Cam was the exception to the revolutionaries' rule that "religious workers were parasites."[40] Even Elvira was encouraged to start a sewing class for the Indian women.

But for all their efforts, they remained gringos, living out of their trailer in the center of a town of cornstalk huts with thatched roofs. Elvira spent much of her time in bed, seldom mixing with the villagers. Cam's vegetable garden, for all his work, was not a permanent change; it disappeared after his departure. But his vegetables had served another purpose by then: impressing Cárdenas with his earnestness, for Cam's embassy report had reached the president, and the Protestant chief of state decided to honor the American missionary with a visit.

The Ultimate Miracle

Behind this monumental moment in Cam's life was the threat of a coup. After Cam called on him in early December, Ambassador Daniels toured northern Mexico with Cárdenas to show U.S. support as the president took his case for reform into the stronghold of business critics. They capped their tour with a stop at the industrial center of Monterrey, the home of the Sáenz family. Right-wing demonstrations had recently ended there in violence. The political nature of these protests was clearly stated in a leaflet given to Daniels charging that "the entire people endure with profound loathing the application of the theories and principles which have converted Russia into an inferno, and which threaten to convert Mexico into the Russian branch of America. . . . When twelve million Indians and half-breeds scarcely removed from savagery hurl themselves on cities and towns in a wave of destruction, then it will be too late to save ourselves; now there is still time."[41]

Daniels was alarmed and promptly dispatched the leaflet to Secretary of State Cordell Hull. Then the climate got uglier. Ex-president General Plutarco Elias Calles returned from an expedition to southern California, charging that Mexico was going communist. Cárdenas appeared confident before Calles's charges, but by the end of December it was clear that he was facing a crisis.

A month later, on January 21, 1936, Cam was plucking a chicken for dinner when two black limousines pulled up to Tetelcingo's square. People immediately gathered around a tall man with dark hair and a mustache leading four companions toward the schoolhouse. Cam recognized the man and hurriedly worked his way through the crowd and extended his hand.

"Buenos días, Señor Presidente," Cam said. Cárdenas turned and looked him right in the eye.

"Buenos días, Señor Townsend."

Cam was stunned.

They talked for more than an hour. Cárdenas appreciated Cam's report to Ambassador Daniels, as well as his articles praising the rural school system in the *Dallas Morning News*. He was glad that Cam's bilingual Aztec-Spanish primer had just been printed. (Cam's new friends from the Scientific Congress had arranged for its publication by the Ministry of Education and the University of Mexico as "an early demonstration of their linguistic programs for Indian education.")[42]

"Will the young people you want to bring do this type of thing for other Indian towns?" Cárdenas asked while inspecting Townsend's garden.

"I can assure you that they will. We read in the Bible that 'the Son of man came not to be ministered unto, but to minister.' The linguists we bring will follow His example by carrying out practical projects for the benefit of the people in the communities where they live."

"Then bring in all you can get!"[43]

A strange friendship, with unforeseen dire consequences for tribal peoples around the world, had begun.

Expanding with American Horizons

When Cam returned to Mexico from the third Camp Wycliffe in September with ten young translators, he found President Cárdenas in good spirits. Cárdenas's drive to build a loyal Indian constituency by improving their lives had won international acclaim.

His popularity soaring, Cárdenas was also able to prevail against Calles, who on April 10, 1936, found himself driven under armed guard to the airport and sent into exile to the United States.

Cárdenas invited Townsend and his group to lunch at Chapultepec Castle, the palace that Emperor Maximilian had built on the site where young Mexican cadets were slaughtered by U.S. forces during the Mexican-American War. Arriving in their Sunday finery, the translators were treated to a nine-course banquet. Cárdenas then offered modest salaries for eight of the translators. Cam was delighted, but two of the translators were not. They had gone to Camp Wycliffe to become Bible translators, not employees of a self-declared "revolutionary" government. They were uncomfortable with the emphasis Cam gave to their linguistic, rather than their missionary, goals.

The youths had already been recruited into the Mexico mission when Cam formalized this seeming duplicity with a new name that sounded more scientific than religious. Legters had told Cam that the board of the Pioneer Mission Agency wanted him to set up his own committee to accept their funds, rather than continue behind the facade of the American Linguistic Society. Cam was happy to oblige. He called his group the Summer Institute of Linguistics, a name less pretentious and less alarming, he explained. And to make sure he was not under Pioneer's control, he informed the agency that SIL was a "field committee," controlled by its members in the mission field. By placing the director (who would, of course, be himself by reason of experience) under an executive committee and having both the director and the committee periodically elected at an annual business conference of the membership, Cam won over the students. What Pioneer had always feared was finally taking shape: Cameron Townsend was setting up his own mission, and under what appeared to be false pretenses.

If that was not bad enough, his recruits were being told that they were working for the Mexican government, and under an alleged Communist party sympathizer, at that. For two of them, it was too much to take. "Uncle Cam, we cannot do it," they told him, and resigned.[44] The rest accepted Cam's dual-identity strategy and fanned out to tribes across Mexico.

In only two years, Cam had established a beachhead in Latin America. To protect it, he would have to be of service to his current benefactors, Ambassador Daniels and President Cárdenas. When he paid a courtesy call to Cárdenas before leaving for the fourth summer session of Camp Wycliffe, the president was again in a crisis with the United States. The issue was a familiar one in Mexican-American relations: oil. The combatants were Mexico's striking oil workers and foreign-owned companies that, explained Cárdenas, "refuse to submit to our courts."[45] The most powerful of these companies was Standard Oil. Perhaps there was some way Cam could help.

6

GOOD NEIGHBORS MAKE GOOD ALLIES

The Learning Center

Nelson watched, amazed, as Texas Congressman Dick Kleberg flipped a silver dollar up, quickly pulled out his gun, and shot it out of the air. Nelson had come to Texas only because his uncle, Winthrop Aldrich, wanted him there. The dapper chairman of Chase National was on a bankers' tour of the country. The United States was a vast buyers' market in December 1934, and the Rockefellers were one of the few families who could still afford to be big buyers. Chase, now under Rockefeller leadership, was about to back oil in a big way, in both the United States and Latin America, and Aldrich was shopping for bargains in the depressed economy. He had just inspected Standard Oil's huge oil strike on the Klebergs' 2,000-square-mile King Ranch. Dallas reporters sensed a story in Nelson Rockefeller's accompanying the banker.

Aldrich tried to downplay Nelson's presence. "We just brought him along to see the country."[1]

Nelson had reason to be wary of reporters. Since the Diego Rivera debacle, his name had become a focus of controversy. The midnight destruction of Rivera's mural sparked an international furor, and charges of "cultural vandalism" would dog Nelson for the rest of his public life. It was a bitter lesson. "Mother's museum," he later put it, was where "I learned my politics."[2]

Rockefeller Center was the workshop of Nelson's stormy apprenticeship. After the draping of Rivera's mural, Nelson took a month-long "vacation" in Mexico trying to make amends with Rivera's fellow artists by dispensing checks for their paintings for Mother's museum.[3] He returned not to his Special Work office, but to the family office, which Junior had recently moved from the Standard Oil building on lower Broadway to Rockefeller Center in midtown.

Nelson had become interested in assuming greater responsibilities. The Special Work office was now running smoothly and required little attention from him. He wrote Junior: "I hope that I will be able to be of distinctly more assistance to you. . . . For the immediate future, my plan is to become more familiar with all phases of your real estate interests and to avail myself of every opportunity to get acquainted with your oil, coal and banking interests."[4]

Nelson quickly learned that the Rockefeller holdings in real estate, oil, coal, and banking were more than extensive. They constituted an empire.

Nelson's deepening involvement in Rockefeller real estate interests also led him into a closer relationship with the family bank, Chase National, and its president, his uncle Winthrop Aldrich.

Aldrich had been selected to run Chase when Junior decided it was necessary to save the Rockefeller-controlled Equitable Trust bank from the depression's tidal waves of loan defaults. In 1930, the Rockefellers' Equitable took shelter within the much larger Chase National.

Over two decades, Chase's chairman, Albert H. Wiggin, had piloted Chase into the Caribbean, a balmy sea with a capacity for overnight turbulence. The riches of its lands seemed worth the risk. American oil companies (led by Standard) and sugar and fruit plantations were quickly displacing Spanish and German coffee haciendas. American corporations were also entering into joint ventures with British companies in mining and tobacco. The Caribbean basin, in fact, was the host for most of the initial American capital that penetrated Latin American markets after the Spanish-American War. By 1928, direct investments by American corporations had grown to $5.4 billion, larger than American corporate holdings in either Europe or Canada.[5] All these investments required banking, and hungry Chase got the lion's share.

Wiggin's strategy was to build a powerful alliance of mining, steel, sugar, and chemical companies that could act independently of the titan of Wall Street, J. P. Morgan & Company. This strategy appealed to the Rockefellers' antipathy for the Morgan monopoly over Wall Street. Senior had been anxious to break Morgan's hold over corporate financing since at least 1921, when he expressed concern over Standard Oil of New York's growing reliance on Morgan. Moreover, the Morgans were in the way of Rockefeller expansion into Latin America's riches, particularly its oil. The House of Morgan had long-established ties with British interests, which aggressive American companies like Jersey Standard and banks like Chase and National City Bank (the old Standard Oil Trust's bank in New York, controlled by the Stillman family and the family of John D. Rockefeller's brother, William) wanted to replace.

By 1930, Chase had more than $2 billion in assets and the deposits of giant clients like Bethlehem Steel, the leading rival of Morgan's U.S. Steel. Its board of directors included representatives of some of the most powerful corporate forces in America.

Equitable Trust, meanwhile, was by 1929 the nation's eighth largest bank with some $250 million in deposits. That December, its president died. Junior, discerning the opportunity for personal control, tapped Aldrich to take the helm. Less than a year later, Equitable and Chase merged, and Aldrich was in command of what was then the world's largest bank in assets. In 1932, the last obstacle to the Rockefellers was removed with the retirement of Albert Wiggin, who got a $100,000 lifetime annuity and a pat on the back. Within a year, however, as congressional investigators focused on bankers' use of their depositors' money to speculate in the stock market, Wiggin found himself abandoned by the Rockefellers. Aldrich in his testimony publicly distanced himself from Wiggin—and soon became Chase's new board chairman.

In 1935, Nelson went abroad to work full time for Chase at the advice of family *consigliere* Thomas Debevoise. This was no sudden appreciation of his elders' advice. He had met Joseph Rovensky, the head of Chase's foreign department. A shrewd, tight-lipped man wise in the myriad ways of financing American corporations abroad, Rovensky became one of Nelson's closest advisers. He encouraged Nelson's interest in the Rockefeller operations overseas by giving him contacts among the leading personalities in the raw materials and oil cartels. Officially, Nelson's job for Chase, as at Rockefeller Center, was public relations, and no financial genius was required for a banker named Rockefeller to throw successful parties in London and Paris.

What really caught Nelson's attention, however, was oil, and in both Paris and London all the talk was about the incredible pool found beneath Lake Maracaibo in Venezuela. Since the first big strikes in 1922, Dictator Juan Vicente Gómez—called El Brujo (the Sorcerer) by his countrymen—had shown himself amenable to the demands of the 100 oil companies that flocked to the lake. By 1935, predatory competition and corruption in Gómez's court had whittled that number down to just three giant rivals: the Mellon family's Gulf Oil, which controlled 12.4 percent of Venezuela's crude; British-owned Shell, which owned 36 percent; and the big winner at 49 percent, Creole Petroleum. Standard Oil of New Jersey had purchased Creole from Standard Oil of Indiana following Junior's much heralded purge of Indiana's maverick president, who had made the mistake of building Indiana and buying huge oil reserves in Mexico and Venezuela without giving a cut of his business to his supposed competitors at the old Standard Oil Trust. Caught in the Teapot Dome oil scandal of bribes and kickbacks from raids on naval oil reserves, Indiana Standard ultimately lost both its president and its Venezuelan oil, just when the boom around Lake Maracaibo was taking off.[6]

Nelson got caught up in the excitement surrounding Venezuela's oil and opted to take the plunge. He wrote his father, asking if some of the Standard shares Junior had recently used to set up a trust fund for Nelson and his brothers could be exchanged for a large interest in Creole. Junior happily agreed, and Nelson, now only twenty-seven years old, was placed on Creole's board.

It was a fateful move. In December 1935, the quarter-century-long spell of the Sorcerer was broken by his death. A torrent of pent-up aspirations poured onto Venezuela's political stage. Much of this new popular unrest drew inspiration from the Mexican Revolution.

Creole officials remained complacent. Their Jersey Standard superiors in New York continued to invest capital as they shifted the focus of their international operations from turbulent Mexico to the more hospitable shores of Venezuela. In doing so, they cut back on operating expenses in Mexico, including wages. Like any capital-intensive industry, Standard Oil was driven by a heavy debt load and dividend-demanding stockholders into the search for an ever-rising bottom line.

It was not the first time such a quest had led to political shortsightedness, or power to arrogance. But it would be the last time for Standard in Mexico. Standard had made a tactical blunder of incalculable proportions, one that would embroil both Nelson Rockefeller and Cameron Townsend in the destiny of the entire hemisphere.

The Spell of the Incas

The Indians had seldom seen so huge a boat on this part of the river. Venezuela's Orinoco, though one of South America's longest and widest rivers, was relatively unused in 1937. A ninety-foot yacht in the middle of the jungle was a rare spectacle. For a few moments the Indians sat still in their dugout canoes, their paddles out of water, their eyes fixed warily on the steamer as it glided by like some giant fish of prey. On board, white faces shone in the fierce sun, serene and seemingly oblivious to the Indians' naked presence. The boat slipped past, slicing the gentle brown current as it pushed upriver. The colossal jungle screamed with monkey cries as the boat went by, followed by a clatter of colorful wings exploding into the sky. Then, as suddenly as it had appeared, the yacht was gone. A profound silence closed over the daylit forest, entrancing the Indians with the illusion of restored tranquility, even as they were forced to dip their paddles to steady their canoes, rocking in the ship's wake.

"We have been coming down the most beautiful tropical river all day in the Standard Oil Company's yacht," Nelson wrote his parents that night. The steamer had laid anchor between two giant walls of black vegetation that howled and splashed with a riot of jungle noises that fascinated young Rockefeller. "We spent the last two days visiting the oil fields in the interior of eastern Venezuela in the company's planes and then went on the boat last night. . . . This is low swampy country, a dense overhanging growth which changes character from time to time. The trees are full of monkeys and birds of all descriptions and colors, big and small. There are alligators on the banks. . . . But most interesting of all are the Indians. They live in little palm leaf huts along the river, wear practically no clothes and paddle around in hollowed out logs. They spend their time getting bark, from which is made tannic acid, and fishing. . . . The pelicans do a much better job of the latter."[7] Nelson Rockefeller's love affair with Latin America had begun.

The Indians had captured Nelson's interest throughout this grand tour of South America with Tod. Most of Nelson's three-month tour—considered by many biographers a turning point in his life—had traced the route of European settlement of the continent. Along the coasts, whites or mixed-blood *mestizos* ruled cities that looked out upon oceans that provided commercial and cultural ties to European homelands. But in the interior, radiating from the refuge of its giant Amazonian heartland out to the surrounding river valleys and the cathedral Andes to the west, lived another America, an Indian America, whose historic presence neither European plagues nor genocidal wars had been able to extinguish.

This Indian presence was hardly ever acknowledged along the coast. Wherever Nelson went, he noticed that most government officials of Spanish descent tended to look down on the Indians. Yet it was these people who were the continent's original inhabitants and still made up most of the population along its Andean spine and in its vast interior of jungles and prairies. And it was their pre-Columbian civilization that gave the continent its oldest and most distinctly American heritage.

In the city of Lima, for instance, once the proud Pacific capital of the Spanish empire in South America, government officials were reluctant to spend money to save mummified remains found at Paracas. Here were the desert tombs of more than 100 leaders of the ancient Nasca Indian civilization, famous for its ceramics and the Nasca Lines carved out of the stony desert, which are so huge that they can be appreciated only from the air. These sun-worshiping people had flourished along the southern coast a thousand years before the arrival of Francisco Pizarro. Later they had spread into the interior's high plateau to inspire the temples, pyramids, and Gate of the Sun of the Tiahuanaco culture around Lake Titicaca, the highest lake in the world. The Tiahuanaco culture, in turn, may have given rise to the famed Inca civilization of the Cuzco basin to the north at the end of the eleventh century.

Nelson had been greatly impressed by the Incas. The Inca empire was one of the largest planned societies on earth, with a form of social security and roads that stretched 3,000 miles along the Andes, from what is now coastal Chile to Ecuador.

Nowhere was the romance of the Indian past stronger than in Cuzco, the ancient Inca capital, perched 11,000 feet on the eastern slope of the Andes.

Nelson wanted to see Cuzco. He hired a Ford trimotor airplane, stripping it of most of its seats so it could clear the Andes' soaring peaks. The Rockefeller party had no sooner landed in Cuzco than Nelson was beside himself with excitement. The city's architecture was colonial Spanish now, but it literally rested on the Indians' ancient glory: along almost every street the smooth, perfectly fitted giant stones of the Incas still served as foundations for the Spaniards' cruder adobe buildings. The aura of an enduring, permanent Indian presence permeated Cuzco, quietly understated in its Inca walls, arches, and amphitheater and even in the flocks of llamas brought in from the countryside by Indians who still spoke the language of the Inca empire, Quechua.

Nelson plunged into the Indian textile market, happily emerging with arm-loads of colorful Indian blankets and serapes. Nelson was now treasurer of the Museum of Modern Art and was eager to bring his new finds home to New York, even to the point of risking his party's lives by insisting upon a return flight over the Andes in a dangerously overloaded plane.

Back in Lima, Nelson's fascination with Inca art led him into a confrontation with dictatorial power in Latin America. Nelson met the archaeologist who had found the threatened Paracas mummies. Dr. Julio César Tello poured out his grievances, explaining that the mummies and their pre-eighth-century wrappings were an international treasure. But Tello was now out of favor—and out of money. He had recently lost his seat in the Peruvian Senate and his job as director of the Archaeological Museum. Tello's fall was only one of many examples of repression in Peru since General Oscar Benavides had seized power through an armed coup four years earlier.

Nelson was sympathetic. He decided to use the power of the Rockefeller name to intervene. Unlike his older brother and father, Nelson did not feel any real burden in being a Rockefeller; in fact, he reveled in it. "I never in my life felt any conscious embarrassment or concern about the family name or the family's money," he later remarked. "I never felt any different from other people—not even when I was with the Indians in the Andes Mountains."[8]

When he met the bull-necked Benavides on a courtesy call, Nelson simply donned one of his many Rockefeller hats. He was developing plans, he quietly explained, for closer cultural ties between South America and New York's muse-ums, for two of which he was a trustee. One, the Metropolitan Museum of Art, would be interested in helping preserve the mummies.

"It is my intention to provide the money,"[9] he announced to the startled dic-tator, assuming, he added, that the Peruvian government could house and main-tain the collection. That meant the Archaeological Museum and Dr. Tello, Benavides realized. But it was an offer he could not refuse. He could bask in the prestige of saving a national treasure. It might even help placate his critics.

It was Nelson's first diplomatic victory in Latin America, the first of his interventions into the destiny of its Indians. The cruel irony, that it was Indians long dead who made it possible, was not yet apparent.

For Nelson Rockefeller had not come to South America to see Indians.

The Power of Indirect Rule

Nelson's real purpose was to inspect Standard Oil's operations in South America, particularly Creole's in Venezuela. This purpose was reflected in the presence in the party of two top lieutenants in the Rockefeller empire: Jay Crane, treasurer of Standard Oil of New Jersey, and Joseph Rovensky, vice president and head of the foreign department of Chase National Bank.

Of all nations in Latin America, Bolivia probably caused Nelson the greatest concern that spring of 1937. On March 13, Bolivia stunned the world with the news that it was nationalizing Standard Oil's properties.

Only a month later, Nelson was flying in a Standard Oil plane over eastern Venezuela's Oficina field north of the Orinoco River. Oficina was Creole's newest jewel, with its superior light oils and low sulphur content. Nelson, however, saw a bigger political picture, and it troubled him. "We met the President and all the members of his cabinet and called on the Governors of four states," he proudly reported to his father, "plus talking at great length to many men in the Standard Oil Company. . . . Unless something unforeseen happens, it looks as if this would turn out to be one of the soundest . . . countries in the world—and there's certainly plenty of oil here."[10]

The unforeseen was another Bolivia or worse, a revolution, perhaps led by Venezuelan communists or radical socialists.

Throughout his tour of Latin America, Nelson had seen again and again that executives of American companies tended to model their behavior after their British counterparts. They held themselves aloof from all but the top echelons of local society. They seldom learned Spanish and relied instead on local autocratic managers to communicate with the workers. He cringed at the sight of barbed-wire fences erected around Standard's American compounds. The barbed wire imposed a racial segregation that was not only crudely blatant, but carried the suggestion that violence might be vested upon trespassers from the shantytowns that inevitably sprung up outside the company's gates.

Nelson had seen such foreign compounds in the British colonies during his honeymoon in the Far East, and he knew the anger that was stirred by such haughty behavior.

One day, while still taking notes on Creole's operations, he received an urgent telegram from his father. Senior had passed away in a coma in the early morning of May 23. Junior had been with him at the end.

Nelson flew back for a private funeral service at Pocantico conducted by

Riverside Church's Rev. Harry Emerson Fosdick and attended by relatives from William Rockefeller's line and families of Standard Oil Trust's partners.

Some weeks later, Nelson saw the descendants of his grandfather's old partners again, and this time he was challenging them. Since his return from Latin America, he had been conveying a message to friends, business associates, and family members with evangelical fervor: Reform was needed. The old British blueprint for colonial operations had been a disaster. If it had not been for the dedication of American missionaries, teachers, and doctors, such as those of the Rockefeller Foundation, a hurricane of anti-Yankee rage would have long ago swept over Latin America—and Standard Oil.

Nelson presented his sense of urgency to the executives of Standard Oil of New Jersey and offered to address its foreign-branch officers at Standard's annual meeting. Since Rockefeller family members held 8.69 percent of New Jersey Standard's stock and controlled another 4.82 percent through shares owned by the Rockefeller Medical Institute, the General Education Board, and the Rockefeller Foundation,[11] the oilmen were in no position to refuse. But after Nelson had delivered his address, entitled "The Social Responsibility of Corporations," they may have wished they had.

Before 300 executives of what was then the largest industrial corporation in America, Nelson challenged the men to develop a sense of responsibility that went beyond the well-being of the machine and the size of the shareholders' dividends. His concern was for "ownership of property anywhere in the world. Such ownership," he explained, "can only be justified if the property serves the broad interests of the people in the host country. This means recognition of obligations to the public welfare."[12]

Nelson Rockefeller was far from naive, and he made this clear in practical terms, addressing political power. Laws could protect a corporation only if the people were convinced that its success was being used in their best interest. Laws, one way or another, he warned ominously, can and would be changed. "We must recognize the social responsibilities of corporations and the corporation must use its ownership of assets to reflect the best interests of the people. If we don't, they will take away our ownership."[13]

The older Standard officials refused to listen. They believed they were already paying their social obligation to the people of host countries by bringing in the capital and expertise to develop the oil and by paying taxes and wages that would otherwise not exist.

Nelson knew from Bolivia and Venezuela that this arrogance was suicidal. The unparalleled wealth and abundance that accompanied modern industry allowed for more flexible strategies than the traditions of strictness and thrift forged by an earlier age of scarcity. The continued existence of inherited fortunes despite the Great Depression enabled younger heirs like Nelson Rockefeller and

William Averell Harriman to rise to the challenge of public leadership with a confidence and optimism their elders did not enjoy.

Nelson's warning before the Standard Oil hierarchy revealed a self-conscious sense of noblesse oblige. It reflected the political maturity of not just the third generation of Rockefellers, but of an American industrial gentry coming of age. This, clearly, was not a manager speaking, but a member of Old Wealth with a traditional concern for retaining power. What seemed simplistic to the uninitiated actually was profoundly fundamental, and fundamental strategic truths were often what field generals lost in the heat of battle.

Grandfather bequeathed a board made up of company men set in their ways, and Nelson walked away from the Jersey Company's 1937 annual meeting in defeat. Before another year would pass, Standard's general staff would flout the laws of both Venezuela and Mexico. In Venezuela, they would get away with it. But in Mexico, where the Supreme Court ruled in favor of the striking oil workers, they faced a stronger president, Lázaro Cárdenas.

CRUSADERS FOR CÁRDENAS

In February 1938, Cam and Elvira were about to sit down to lunch in their trailer at Tetelcingo when they heard a knock. Cam's eyes widened as he opened the door. There, with his wife, stood the president of Mexico.

Cárdenas had found in Cam Townsend a stalwart supporter. The missionary even allowed the Mexican government to review the contents of his personal appeal to evangelical missionaries in Mexico before he sent it out, calling on them to join him in "doing my bit to help in the crusade of reform headed by President Cárdenas."[14] The president now was seeking Townsend's help.

After lunch, the men moved to shade behind the trailer. In grave tones, Cárdenas explained to Cam that the oil crisis was nearing its climax. Standard Oil and a dozen other American and British companies had refused to sign a general labor contract with the new oil workers' union, despite repeated concessions by the workers in their contract proposals.

Cárdenas was caught between the companies' belligerence and the threat of political instability. Unless there was obedience to the law and some compromise, the president would have to act and risk armed U.S. intervention. Cárdenas clearly empathized with the oil workers. As a young army officer stationed at Tampico, he had witnessed firsthand the low wages, disease, and dangerous conditions the workers experienced.

His words fell on sympathetic ears. Cam, too, had flinched at the misery he saw during his visits to the oil regions. He was aware that bribes had been behind many of the concessions won by the American companies during the pre-Revolution regime of Porfirio Díaz.

"If I could just reach the stockholders of these companies," Cárdenas said, "instead of their high-salaried agents who refuse to concede the justice of our demands."[15]

Cam had only prayers to offer, to which Cárdenas responded with a pledge to remove duties on Bibles. Then the old warrior presented Townsend with the fountain pen he had used to sign the land decrees of the past three years. Cam resolved to do more than pray.

A scandal was brewing involving the American oil companies.

Lombardo Toledano, head of the Mexican Workers Confederation, charged that Standard Oil was withdrawing funds from Mexico (later confirmed by the companies) and had even tried to remove equipment. Because of Venezuelan oil, new explorations for oil in Mexico were down. The oil workers then announced their intention to strike at midnight, March 18. The impending strike confronted Cárdenas with the imminent paralysis of a major industry on which much of the transport for Mexico's agriculture and mines depended.

By March 1938, the very sovereignty of the nation had been flouted by the companies' refusal to abide by a Supreme Court decision awarding oil laborers 2.6 million pesos. Moreover, Cárdenas was convinced that the companies' transfer of funds out of Mexico was causing a serious flight of capital.[16] In an interview with the president, the executives of the oil companies made their final mistake. Cárdenas had just offered guarantees against further wage demands and tax increases, but he warned the oil executives that the Supreme Court's decision would also be guaranteed. The oil officials asked who would enforce these guarantees.

"Me," answered Cárdenas, "the President of the Republic."

"You!" a British oilman scoffed.

Cárdenas rose from his chair. "Gentlemen," he said icily, "we have finished."[17]

His expropriation decree shortly followed.

The reaction in Washington was swift. Secretary of State Cordell Hull persuaded Treasury Secretary Henry Morgenthau to suspend U.S. purchases of Mexican silver.

Reaction to that suspension was swifter. "I cannot convey to you the feeling here," Ambassador Daniels gravely wrote President Roosevelt, "that a friend has struck a blow more devastating than he can conceive. It hurts economically and reduces [the] ability to give employment and meet obligations, but it hurts worse in a conviction that it is the end of the Good Neighbor Policy and a replacement by the old policy of the Big Stick and the patronizing Big Brother policies." He asked Roosevelt to resume silver purchases.[18]

Roosevelt agreed. He accepted Cárdenas's expressed willingness eventually to provide compensation and had a chagrined Hull send a note to that effect on March 30. Cárdenas, having feared a U.S. invasion, was elated. "Today my

Country is happy to celebrate without reservation the proof of friendship which it has received from yours," he wrote Daniels the following day, "and which will be carved in the heart of its people."[19]

Such presidential exchanges only made Standard's executives more furious at both Cárdenas, the "communist," and Roosevelt, "the traitor to his class." They decided to retaliate with their own foreign policy, refusing to supply oil products to Mexico's new national oil company, PEMEX. Twenty-one other companies joined the boycott.

By May, the oil companies would escalate their retaliation beyond boycotts. They would be plotting coups.

Roosevelt adviser Adolf Berle, summoned to Washington in February 1938 to help in the mounting crisis, had noted in his diary that "we prefer not to have a revolution and to ride out the confiscation of the oil companies. Again the oil companies prefer a revolution, not understanding that they may uncork a civil war of some magnitude."[20]

It was in this tense political climate that Cam met with President Cárdenas before returning to Arkansas for the 1938 Camp Wycliffe. The missionary offered to form an "Inter-American Brigade" of young Americans paid by Mexico to assist Cárdenas's social projects. He also proposed a trip to Washington and New York to lobby on Cárdenas's behalf.

The president was so taken with these ideas that he handed Cam a $1,000 check to pay for a new automobile. "I don't want your sick wife riding in a bus," he explained.[21]

Before leaving, Cam conferred with Ambassador Daniels. The black-tie southerner was populist enough to back Cárdenas's agrarian reforms. And his bonds to modernist Protestants, who were likely to share his sympathies, were still strong. The ambassador offered Cam advice on whom to see and scribbled a note of introduction to President Roosevelt's appointments secretary, Steve Early.

Cam dropped off Elvira in Sulphur Springs and headed east alone. His goal: to lobby John D. Rockefeller, Jr., and President Roosevelt personally on Cárdenas's behalf.

On June 1, Junior received an urgent cable from Townsend, requesting a meeting the next day.

Cam knew that it would take a miracle for an unknown missionary to get an appointment with John D. Rockefeller, Junior, especially in one day. And this time the Lord did not oblige. When Cam called Junior's office the next day, an aide put him off and referred him to Standard Oil's headquarters in the same building. Townsend walked past the sepia mural where Rivera's bright colors had once been and took the elevator to Standard's offices. There he was told that

Standard's demand for the return of its oil holdings in Mexico was not negotiable. It wanted them back.

Standard's intransigence had a ruthless quality about it. In fact, it had been just that attitude which prompted Cárdenas to nationalize Standard's properties in the first place.

Cam next tried to gain entrée to the White House. But even with Ambassador Daniels's backing, he got nowhere. He left Washington in defeat and drove home to Arkansas for the Summer Institute of Linguistics. He felt some joy when he discovered that SIL's membership had expanded to thirty-two that summer.

He could not shake off his worries about Cárdenas's crisis with Washington. Should Mexico's relations with the United States deteriorate, SIL's future would be in doubt. He wrote the Mexican president on July 25 of his concern that the agrarian reform was adversely affecting large American holdings. Cárdenas replied patiently that the Mexican government would pay indemnities but only "as the economic condition of the country will permit." It was not possible "to delay the giving of land to the villages, nor to wait until the necessary funds for an immediate indemnization are in hand."[22] The one bright point for Cam was Cárdenas's belief that Cam's trips to Washington and New York were "very important."

Cam took the hint. In September he read that Secretary of State Hull was demanding that Cárdenas repay an old $10 million debt. This was at the very time that Mexico was suffering from a severe depression and the collapse of the purchasing power of its peso, caused in no small measure by Hull's cessation of silver purchases. Cam fired off an indignant wire to Hull, followed by a four-page, single-spaced letter containing the kind of strategic wisdom for American corporations that someone like Nelson Rockefeller would have appreciated. "They [the oil companies] had better decide right now to give the Nationals of all Latin America a share in the industry," he warned, "or they will be kicked out bag and baggage sooner or later."[23] A year and a half later, in January 1940, Roosevelt himself would echo these sentiments, proposing "a new approach . . . to these South American things. Give them a share."[24]

Ambassador Daniels did his best to enhance Townsend's prestige with the State Department. He sent a glowing report on "Plans of the Townsend Group for Educational Work among the Primitive Tribes in Mexico" that was read at the Bureau of Indian Affairs. He also arranged a commendatory review of SIL in the *American Foreign Service Journal*. Undaunted by the State Department's hostility toward Cárdenas, Cam recruited seven youngsters to an Inter-American Service Brigade and repeatedly pushed the brigade concept during the next two years.

The idea would languish in Washington's limbo for two decades, until its spirit was resurrected in the Peace Corps.

Roosevelt Moves Toward Fortress Inter-America
—and Rockefeller

If Cameron Townsend's political creativity was frustrated by the Roosevelt administration during these prewar years, he was not alone. Samuel Inman of the Committee on Cooperation in Latin America also had failed to get Roosevelt's ear for his idea of a division in the State Department devoted exclusively to improving U.S. cultural relations with Latin America.

This emphasis on the cultural over the commercial was no new goal of Inman's committee. As early as 1929 the committee's annual report had expressed dismay that "the sad part about the foreign missionary enterprise is that too often not the spiritual forces but the driving economic agent is the best known of American representatives abroad."[25] Originally, the committee had hoped to take advantage of American corporate expansion into Latin America. Only the previous year, the committee had noted the "opportunity" presented to American missionaries to stimulate interest in "our southern neighbor"* by a Commerce Department report. "Citizens of the United States," the committee noted from the report, "now own a considerable proportion of the wealth and receive a proportionally large part of the income of most Latin American countries."[26]

But by 1934, the blush was off the corporate rose. The revelations of Senate munitions hearings in 1934 had deeply shaken the missionaries. Not only had such a respectable company as Du Pont profited $250 million off the world war—overcharging the U.S. government to the point that Secretary of War Newton Baker called the family a "species of outlaws"—but Du Pont had become deeply involved in the postwar international munitions traffic and spread the arms bazaar to Latin America, setting up explosives plants in Chile and Mexico.[27] The Committee on Cooperation asked missionaries like Townsend to consider the grave implications. "What are the legitimate hopes that missionaries in Paraguay and Bolivia may advance the Kingdom of God in those lands, while their fellow North Americans as munitions salesmen are providing the means for wholesale slaughter?"[28]

In an age that seemed to be rolling uncontrollably toward the unbelievable—another world war—the Committee on Cooperation in Latin America turned desperately to cultural exchanges as a major means of promoting public support for peace treaties. Yet it was in the commercial realm that men in

---

*The field surveyor for the committee's Commission for Indian Work in Latin America, Rev. L. L. Legters, had taken this vision to William Cameron Townsend in 1929 and focused it on the Amazon. Legters, in fact, had been visiting Townsend when Legters's colleague in the commission's survey of Indian tribes in the Brazilian Amazon had been killed by Nambikuára Indians. From that tragedy, Townsend's own vision widened to airplanes. Cam was convinced that bush airplanes, like the U.S. military planes he saw passing over Central America, somehow could have made a difference in the missionary's fate.

Washington were most interested. Roosevelt handed the job of engaging in commercial warfare in Latin America to the new assistant secretary of state for Latin American affairs: Adolf Berle.

Roosevelt had been pushed to this point by domestic as well as foreign considerations. In 1937, accepting Treasury Secretary Morgenthau's prognosis that the United States was moving out of the depression and that mounting inflation had to be reined in, Roosevelt had returned to fiscal conservatism. He slashed federal spending, cutting the budget of Harry Hopkins's Works Progress Administration and almost ending Harold Ickes's Public Works Administration. But he moved too late as far as corporate leaders were concerned, and they were still unsatisfied with Roosevelt's progressive tax reforms. With the Federal Reserve tightening the money supply and consumer spending slowing again, the "strike of capital" continued, drying up investments. In July 1937, Japan invaded China. The following month, nervous American investors began unloading stocks to grab whatever profits they could.

The result was the most brutal drop in industrial stocks in the nation's history. By December the crash had wiped out all the gains the stock market had made since 1935, and 2 million people had lost their jobs. As the crisis became publicly known as "Roosevelt's Depression," the President decided that his predecessor's emphasis on foreign markets might have been right all along.

In any case, he saw there was no alternative. Everything in his cultural training, from his Calvinist Reformed Dutch religion to his education in the most aristocratic U.S. schools, made it impossible for Roosevelt to step any further in the socialistic direction of some of his advisers. Nor could the American economy return to a nineteenth-century republic of competing small producers. Domestic policy alone would not suffice. Foreign markets had to be expanded, and the aggressive behavior of the Axis powers no doubt gave urgency to Roosevelt's increased concern with defending corporate America's economic frontiers.

Standard Oil's operations in China brought this point dramatically home on December 12. Japanese warplanes bombed and sank the U.S.S. *Panay* while it was escorting Standard Oil tankers up the Yangtze River. Standard's tankers, the real targets, were also attacked. Hull demanded, and got, an immediate Japanese apology and complete repayment of the losses. But from then on Roosevelt was oriented increasingly toward the strategy of a Fortress America, which soon became a Fortress Inter-America. For help, he turned to Adolf Berle. Berle's arrival at the helm of Latin American affairs symbolized this move, as well as the return to business-government "cooperation" that had marked the first phase of the New Deal that Berle had helped usher in as a member of the original Brain Trust.

The son of a minister and a lay missionary to the Sioux Indians, Berle could never shake the hope that the regeneration of the businessman would bring about the reforms the United States needed. He had been a member of Thomas

Debevoise's law firm; it was he who had steered John Collier in 1924 to Ray Fosdick for a Rockefeller grant. Berle and Fosdick had both served in the U.S. delegation to the Versailles Peace Conference and shared a disgust for the uncompromising and avaricious terms imposed by the Allied victors and their betrayals of wartime promises of self-determination for colonies like Vietnam and India that had fought for the Allies. Modern corporate society could afford to be more generous, they believed; otherwise, not only renewed war, but revolutions, such as those that erupted in Russia, China, and Mexico, could spread.

Berle at first took a conservative stance toward Cárdenas's nationalization of American-owned sugar plantations. But he ascended to the higher wisdom of accommodation in the face of the rising menace in Europe. If the fleets and merchant marines were to move about the ports of Latin America unharassed to support the fighting in the North Atlantic and the South Pacific, the cooperation of Latin America was essential. Making Fortress Inter-America a reality required the strengthening of the goodwill brought about by the Good Neighbor Policy.

For this delicate task of public relations, Berle was unsuited: He simply brought too much baggage with him from the business community and his participation in the U.S. financial pressure and the gunboat diplomacy that replaced the civilian government of Ramón Grau San Martín with the military dictatorship of Fulgencio Batista. A new face was needed, and one that belonged to a mind that appreciated Latin American culture, nationalist sensitivities, and the importance of American business in tying the knot between development south of the Rio Grande and restored prosperity north of it.

7

THE MEXICAN TIGHTROPE

THE VENEZUELAN CONNECTION

Nelson realized by 1939 that time was running out in Venezuela. Here he was, arguing with communist labor organizers right in Creole's own oil fields, and still he couldn't get Standard Oil's hierarchy in New York to listen. If reforms were not initiated, and soon, the very thing these communists were pressing for—elimination of Yankee ownership over oil, just as Cárdenas had done in Mexico—would happen in Venezuela.

For weeks, Nelson had walked around with a copy of Marx's *Capital* under his arm. He was so disturbed by the book's analysis of capitalism that he insisted that his chief associates read it. He realized, however, that what would have the greatest influence on the restless oil workers' minds was not ideology or analysis but improving the actual conditions of their lives. He toured Creole's operations, warning the American managers behind their barbed-wire compounds about the lessons of Mexico. He had been greatly impressed by a book exposing Standard's abuses in that country. He made his people read that, too.

Labor unrest, not Axis espionage, was Nelson's biggest concern in Venezuela. As in Mexico, oil workers were experimenting with an explosive blend of nationalism and communism. Nationalism had even spread to the military and was now threatening to be not only anti-Yankee, as in Bolivia, but anticapitalist as well.

Nelson's presence was not yet appreciated by either local Creole managers or anticommunist nationalists like Rómulo Betancourt, editor of *Ahora* and leader of the left-of-center opposition party, Acción Democrática. But it could not be ignored. "After looking over his vast oil properties," Betancourt wrote of

Rockefeller, ". . . he will return to his office atop Rockefeller Center, to the warm shelter of his home, to resume his responsibilities as a philanthropist and Art Maecenas. Behind him will remain Venezuela producing 180 million barrels of oil for the Rockefellers. . . . Behind him will remain Venezuela with its half million children without schools, the workers without adequate diets . . . , its 20,000 oil workers mostly living in houses . . . better called 'over-grown match-boxes.'"[1]

Nelson's Creole also left behind a thick sludge of oil over the surface of Lake Maracaibo. In December, for the second time that decade, the oil scum caught on fire; the shacks that oil workers had built on stilts over the lake exploded in flames, roasting hundreds of families alive.

Townsend, then in Mexico, was appalled. "The thing was outrageous enough in itself, but since it happened to be the second occurrence of the awful catastrophe within a decade it was nothing short of criminal. If the men, women, and children who were burned to death had been English, Dutch or American, a furor of protest would have been raised against the carelessness of the companies, but they were 'just Venezuelans,'" he wrote.[2]

A furor did break out over Venezuela, however. Whatever resistance to Nelson's reforms remained among Creole's managers collapsed after the fire. Down came the barbed wire. Up went public health clinics modeled after the Rockefeller Sanitary Commission. A dozen Berlitz teachers arrived from New York to begin teaching Spanish, which was now mandatory, to Creole executives. Job discrimination against Venezuelans in heavy drilling operations was phased out. To answer criticisms that Venezuela had become a monoindustrial society dominated by oil, Creole brought down an engineering firm to survey the economy and recommend developments for agriculture and the diversification of industry.

To fill the financial vacuum in that area, Nelson stepped in with his own firm, the Compañía de Fomento Venezolano (Venezuelan Development Company). "Such a company," an aide suggested to Nelson, "would give us the perfect excuse to get around the country to get to know the local political and business people in the rest of Venezuela, and, as always, to keep our eyes open for other possibilities for ourselves."[3] Some of these "other possibilities" included food distribution, asbestos, and pharmaceuticals.[4]

As the Nazi blitzkrieg swept over France, Compañía officials began looking toward a possible postwar era in which Rockefeller interests would be competing peacefully in Venezuela with the companies owned by triumphant Nazis. Nelson sent Carl Spaeth to Caracas to evaluate the feasibility of further investments in light of the war. Spaeth was enthusiastic. "To postpone such programs as ours until after the war is to lose an excellent opportunity to get in a substantial position in advance of German commercial interests . . . in the event Germany wins the war."[5]

Later, even after taking public office in Washington, Nelson would commission Spaeth to investigate the potential for private investments. To avoid a legal conflict of interest, Nelson would not actually pursue these Venezuelan options until after the war.

As the elections of 1940 approached, two powerful groups with overlapping concerns were emerging to formulate a new U.S. strategy toward Latin America.

One group, led by Undersecretary of State Sumner Welles, Assistant Secretary Adolf Berle, and Pan American Union head Leo Rowe, was visible to the public and the press. The other group met in private corporate offices and centered on Nelson Rockefeller. Outsiders called it "the Group," but it called itself the Junta. And its convener was not Rockefeller, but a social scientist turned businessman who represented the point of contact between the two groups: Beardsley Ruml.

The Junta Meets Roosevelt

Ruml was Nelson Rockefeller's advance man in Washington. Considered brilliant, Ruml had won a reputation in higher circles as an idea man, and his newest idea was a Rockefeller-led commercial and cultural assault on Axis influence in Latin America. By the end of 1938, Ruml was trying to get young Rockefeller the proper entrée into the Democratic White House through Harry Hopkins.

Hopkins was the perfect choice. Since Roosevelt had elevated him from chief of the Works Progress Administration to secretary of commerce in 1938, Hopkins had allied himself with Adolf Berle in fostering a new policy of closer cooperation with big business. The policy recommendations he received were increasingly focused on Latin America.

Hopkins shared Berle's distress over German competition in Latin America. He agreed with the assistant secretary's view that German commercial rivalry was a threat to U.S. national security, remarking to the press that "today foreign trade is being used by some countries as a vehicle to support political and cultural penetration."[6] This was the perfect climate for Ruml to introduce Nelson Rockefeller to the White House's inner circle.

"Congratulations!" Ruml wrote Hopkins in December 1938. "If you are to be in New York soon, I think it would be well worth it for you to spend about two hours at leisure with Nelson Rockefeller to hear his views on U.S. commercial relations with South America, a subject on which he is well informed and very much interested. Nelson Rockefeller would esteem it a privilege and I should be delighted to arrange."[7]

"I would like very much to see Nelson Rockefeller," Hopkins replied in January.[8] By March, Nelson was standing before the president of the United States.

Roosevelt's curiosity about Rockefeller had actually been piqued the previous summer, when he was told that Nelson Rockefeller was "sympathetic—he feels quite differently from some of the members of his family."[9] Now, following

Nelson's meeting with Hopkins, an appointment was set up with the president, apparently at Rockefeller's request.

Roosevelt had personal reasons for wanting to meet Nelson. The president was seeking an unprecedented third term in 1940. Winning over an heir of the family that was doing its most to make Wall Street stockbroker Wendell Willkie his Republican successor would be a coup. It might even encourage support from some business circles.

By the time Nelson left the White House, the president had agreed to participate in an international radio broadcast celebrating the new home of the Museum of Modern Art (MOMA). His participation in the broadcast would greatly enhance Nelson's reputation across the United States. Nelson also planned to use the museum to ingratiate himself with Latin America.

Roosevelt's fifteen-minute congratulatory speech on May 10 was politically innocuous enough, but Nelson's own address caused quite a stir among devotees of art. Nelson neglected to mention that the museum was ten years old or that others had helped to found it. "'It sounded as though the Museum had just opened that night,' a member of the audience later reported. 'It came as quite a surprise to the staff.'"[10] To Latin Americans who listened, MOMA *had* just opened that night, and Nelson Rockefeller was the assumed benefactor. This event set the stage for Nelson's surprising move into international diplomacy: He offered the Cárdenas government, in the middle of the oil crisis, a MOMA exhibition on twenty centuries of Mexican art. President Roosevelt, he promised, would again be the star draw.

At the beginning of 1940, Nelson flew to Mexico with Tod to discuss the matter with the Mexican government. But their companions on this trip, Mr. and Mrs. Walter C. Douglas, indicated that a larger political goal was being pursued.

Douglas was a director of the Southern Pacific Railroad, which had properties in Mexico and a big stake in Mexican trade with the United States. Douglas was convinced that a Rockefeller intervention in the Mexican oil crisis would benefit everyone concerned. The failure of the negotiations was evident. New blood was needed.

Nelson was happy to give diplomacy a crack. If it worked, he would be pulling off the diplomatic coup of the decade. He spent a month working out terms acceptable to Standard Oil, and then he and Tod flew to Mexico with the Douglases.

Cárdenas greeted them with typical Mexican warmth at his new home in the village of Juquilpan de Juárez beside Lake Pátzcuaro. Here, at last, was the kind of stockholder Cárdenas had sent Cam Townsend to New York to seek out. Nelson, however, played it coy. He identified himself only as the president of MOMA and confined his comments to the show on Mexico's cultural history. He asked Cárdenas to match the museum's $20,000 contribution to the cost. When Cárdenas readily agreed, Rockefeller next turned to another concession he wanted. The Rockefeller Foundation was having difficulty with the seniority hiring requirements of Mexican labor law that prevented young Mexican physicians who were trained in the United States by the foundation from stepping into top positions in rural health care.

Again, Cárdenas agreed to make the necessary exceptions.

When there was still no mention of oil, Cárdenas invited the couples to spend the night. But even after dinner Nelson did not bring up the oil crisis. Since Nelson was in the stronger position, he could afford to wait. It was a tactic that had given Senior the edge in so many deals.

The following morning, Cárdenas decided to flush Nelson out. He directly raised the issue of the expropriation of oil.

"I'm here as a private citizen, and have no official connection with the oil companies," Nelson said disingenuously. That pro forma disclaimer aside, he launched into a four-hour discussion.

"Your businessmen don't associate with our government officials or with our business community," Cárdenas told Nelson. The arrogance of foreigners aside, Mexico's claims had a historical basis that stemmed from its struggle for independence. "You have to remember that in the background is the seizure of Texas in 1836, the United States action in taking New Mexico and California in 1846, in sending your army against [Pancho] Villa in 1916. Then you have to remember that our revolution ended the domination of the Spanish ruling class in Mexico and restored the self-confidence of our people. That was our liberation from domination in our own country." But that liberation meant that the economic domination by American companies and banks also had to end, from the railroads to the sugar estates and henequen plantations to even the oil companies, the most arrogant of all. "We must retain ownership even if the oil has to stay in the ground. Better that than for the people to lose their dignity."[11]

Nelson was stunned. Cárdenas's convictions were so earnest and basic that they were overpowering. Nelson tried to negotiate terms that left Standard and the other oil companies with majority control, but the Mexican president would not hear of it. Forty-nine percent was his maximum concession. Mexican oil must remain Mexican.

Nelson went away defeated, but wiser. He returned to New York and reported the results. His faith in his mission was not shaken; if anything, it was confirmed. He was now convinced that the United States needed his leadership, at least with respect to Latin America.

Beardsley Ruml had already begun holding meetings of the Junta at his Greenwich Village home. Here were Nelson's closest advisers, men who had participated in the first 1937 trip through Latin America and shared Nelson's concerns about expanding American business in the region. They wanted to stop the growth of German and Italian investments and find some way of accommodating Latin America's rising nationalism before socialist currents became too strong to reverse.

The meetings of the Junta soon moved from Ruml's home to Rockefeller's luxurious Fifth Avenue apartment. There, surrounded by paintings by French and American masters and beneath the Matisse mural that adorned the living room, they shaped a series of proposals that were to influence the course of history. Then Ruml and Rockefeller took the proposals to Washington to discuss them with two of Roosevelt's advisers. Nothing came of them.

Finally, in May, Ruml and Rockefeller decided to turn again to Hopkins. The busy Hopkins asked them to distill the Junta's proposals into a policy paper. Ruml set to work on what turned out to be a broad and far-reaching plan for a "Hemisphere Economic Policy."

Nelson arrived at the White House on June 14 and was escorted immediately to the Lincoln Room. Hopkins was there to greet him.

As Nelson drew out the three-page memorandum from his briefcase, Hopkins leaned back in his chair and gravely asked him to read it aloud.

"Regardless of whether the outcome of the war is a German or Allied victory," Nelson said, "the United States must protect its international position through the use of economic means that are competitively effective against totalitarian techniques." Like Cameron Townsend's cabled pleas to Secretary of State Hull a year and a half earlier on the need to preserve Latin American friendship as a counterweight to Axis influence, Rockefeller made the pitch for hemispheric cooperation. But instead of moral arguments, Nelson's case had a cold, hard economic thrust.

"If the United States is to maintain its security and its political and economic hemispheric position," Nelson continued, "it must take economic measures at once to secure economic prosperity in Central and South America, and to establish this prosperity in the frame of hemisphere economic cooperation and dependence." This statement was from one of America's emerging political powers with a wealth of resources literally at his fingertips. Hopkins was now listening closely.

Since the British blockade had cut off Latin America's traditional European markets, he continued, emergency action had to be taken to stimulate the flow of trade between the United States and the rest of the hemisphere. Tariff walls had to come down. An "open door" policy had to be initiated to permit American corporate investments in the southern lands. Latin American surplus products had to be absorbed. The consular service had to be augmented by a bold new program of increased cultural, educational, and scientific programs. Moreover, these programs should stimulate production to meet the needs of American industry and its people, while drawing on the expertise of existing private agencies. Finally, to coordinate all these efforts, a small advisory committee, directed by a presidential assistant with direct access to the president, would be required.[12]

It was obvious to Hopkins whom Nelson had in mind for that job and what the composition of the advisory committee would be if left to the Junta. There was no doubt also that the Rockefeller Foundation could be expected to play a leading role and that American corporations, including those controlled by the Rockefeller financial interests, would rush into Latin America to fill the void left by the loss of European markets and investors.

Hopkins agreed to bring the subject up with "the Boss." Within twenty-four hours, the Rockefeller group's plan was on the president's desk.

Roosevelt read the document and passed it along to Hull at State, Morgenthau at Treasury, and Wallace at Agriculture. There were objections to the proposal, but as far as the president was concerned, they simply could not outweigh the formidable opportunity that the power of the Rockefellers offered. The president ordered the new economic program to begin on June 28.

What made the Rockefeller-Ruml proposal unique was its proponents' independence from bureaucratic infighting and their enormous financial power. Nelson, however, was passed over for the top job. "Nelson doesn't have the kind of ability needed for the job," said presidential aide James V. Forrestal.[13]

Nelson had little cause for celebration when his thirty-second birthday arrived on July 8. His memorandum had gotten him nowhere. His broad free-trade proposal ran contrary to Undersecretary of State Welles's previous policy of sticking to tariff agreements that were strictly reciprocal in nature. It was just the beginning of a Welles-Rockefeller antagonism that would flare up throughout the war.

Nelson's own attempt to build cultural bridges with the Cárdenas government through the MOMA Mexican art exhibit had also been rebuffed. The State Department prevented President Roosevelt from being a sponsor of the show. To make matters worse, Nelson's negotiations with Cárdenas on behalf of the oil companies had failed, too.

In fact, the only recent case of collaboration between the Rockefeller Foundation and Washington was a Rockefeller grant to anthropologist Mary Doherty, at the Institute of Current World Affairs, for her investigation for the Bureau of Indian Affairs (BIA) of Latin American government programs for Indians. This survey was a key component of a broader intelligence operation by Washington. The Indians of the Americas had been decreed honorary Aryans by the Nazis as part of Hitler's propaganda drive among the major labor force of the Andes and Central America.

This did not seem a promising start for his generation's efforts to safeguard the Rockefeller family's interests in Latin America, much less move into the new inter-American endeavors Nelson wished to pursue.

Nelson could never have anticipated how crucial that survey would be for Washington's leadership of the upcoming First Inter-American Conference on Indian Life in Mexico or for the fate of tribal peoples in the Americas. He had not guessed its importance for his own "Hemisphere Economic Policy" when his birthday party was suddenly interrupted by a phone call. It was from White House aide James Forrestal. Could he come down to Washington? He was there the next day. Nelson Rockefeller's political career had begun.

Setting the Indian Stage

Three months earlier, when Cárdenas had appealed to the 400 delegates of the Inter-American Conference on Indian Life at Pátzcuaro, Cam could not help feeling anxious for the survival of the Good Neighbor Policy.

Here was his friend, the president of Mexico, pleading for justice for the hemisphere's Indian peoples before the greatest assemblage of government experts on Indian affairs ever gathered in one place. It should have been a sympathetic audience. All the delegates were aware that what was at stake was the survival not only of the Indians of America, but, in the age of Hitler, of the democratic aspirations of the entire Western world.

And yet, as the delegates listened to the part-Indian president, the taut expressions on some of their faces gave a hint of the underlying conflict between the Mexican and American perspectives. Cam had hoped that by now Washington would understand the depth of Mexico's resolve about controlling its own natural wealth—and paying its creditors at the same time. Two years ago, in a stirring oration before hundreds of thousands of cheering Mexican workers and peasants following Mexico's expropriation of Standard Oil, Cárdenas vowed "to make it known to all the countries of the world, that Mexicans will honor their foreign debts."[14] And the Mexicans did.

"Checks were written in four figures from people who were not exactly wealthy," Cam reported to his Fundamentalist brethren back home. "The poor came forward with their pesos. School children brought pennies. Women gave their earrings, bracelets, stickpins and odds and ends of value. Peasants brought chickens, pigs or vegetables. . . . I could not help but think that the executives of the petroleum companies might have seen the sight of barefoot Indians dropping a mite or two into the fund for economic redemption."[15]

But Standard Oil had refused to accept compensation for a majority ownership of its Mexican holdings. It wanted to retain control. Cárdenas had broken Standard's international embargo on Mexican oil by selling oil directly to Japanese companies. This action prompted Rep. Hamilton Fish to call on the floor of Congress for an invasion of Mexico. At Townsend's personal request shortly after Nelson Rockefeller's departure for New York, Cárdenas had delayed the sale until Standard's response to a final appeal could be heard. The answer had again been negative.

Because of the U.S. embargo, Cárdenas had already begun selling oil to Germany. In principle, this was no different from the thriving business Standard Oil itself was doing with Germany. As late as 1939, Jersey Standard had favorably reviewed the cartel agreement it had signed in the 1920s and 1930 with I. G. Farben, a major backer of Hitler, and, in fact, renewed it in a secret meeting in Holland just as the war broke out. Worse, Junior's long-time publicity adviser, Ivy Lee, had, at Standard's behest, accepted Nazi money for advice on improving

Hitler's international image. Lee had recommended interpreting the Nazi rearmament program as a plea for "equality of rights" among nations and an effort at "preventing for all time the return of the Communist peril."[16]

Standard's apparent lack of aversion to Nazism, however, did not prevent the company from assailing Cárdenas for his barter agreement with Germany. The anger fomented by the conservative press in the United States had further chilled relations between the State Department and Cárdenas.

Cam and Ambassador Daniels were deeply worried about this cold war against Mexico. Rumors were circulating in Mexico City of covert manipulations by the oil companies in Mexico's presidential campaign, then in full swing. Both men tried to reassure their respective religious and political networks back home of Cárdenas's good intentions toward Roosevelt's policy of Inter-American solidarity. Daniels wrote repeatedly to Roosevelt, praising his restraint, while reminding the self-righteous Hull that "we cannot properly object to such [Mexican] sale because the Standard Oil Company sold to Japan and Germany before the expropriation."[17]

Shortly after the Inter-American Indian Conference, Cam published a daring pamphlet entitled *The Truth About Mexico's Oil*. The pamphlet showed that much of his father's prairie populism was still alive in Cam. "Cárdenas gave in [and sold oil to German companies] when he found that there were almost no buyers in the democratic nations that were sufficiently free from the control of the oil trusts to be able to bid for Mexican oil," he argued. "We have no one but the oil companies to blame for this."[18]

Ironically, the oil embargo, Cam noted, forced Cárdenas to initiate his own Good Neighbor policy to develop a Latin American bloc of support for Mexico's territorial integrity and to procure markets for oil. Of the three nations involved, Bolivia was the most worrisome to the State Department. The military regime there had not only nationalized Standard Oil's properties, but had close ties to European fascism. Its powerful Falange party was modeled after Mussolini's Fascists. Mussolini's army officers had settled in as official advisers to the Bolivian air force. And Bolivia's only airline was German owned, which could give Hitler control over refueling stations and airdromes at the strategic point of intersection of South America's air routes. It could also give him potential aerial control over the export of strategic minerals out of Bolivia's highest plateau, the Altiplano, which had some of the world's richest tin and copper mines and a network of attendant railroads vital to the Allied war effort. Nazi propaganda among overworked and underpaid Indian miners in the Patiño tin mines was making inroads; spreading strikes hampered production in 1940, threatening to cut off Britain's tin supply.

Cárdenas's concern for Latin America's Indians was worrisome here, too. In March 1939, Cárdenas had sent a mission of linguists to consult Bolivia on its rural school system for Indians, who constituted more than 70 percent of the population. Bolivia responded by sending teachers to Mexico to study the system that Moisés Sáenz had initiated. It was not surprising, then, that when Bolivia, facing its own powerful pro-Axis lobby, decided not to honor its agreement to host the first Inter-American Indian Conference and General Jorge Ubico refused the Indianists access to Guatemala, Mexico's invitation was readily accepted by Latin America. To Washington's growing concern, most of the Western Hemisphere now looked toward Mexico for leadership in the *indigenismo* movement.

America's Indianist

BIA Commissioner John Collier drafted the proposal for this conference that was presented to the 1938 Pan American conference in Lima by the U.S. delegation headed by Hull and Berle. Collier characteristically underplayed his role. Like Cameron Townsend, his appearance was deceptive. A thin, stoop-shouldered man with often unruly brown hair and a corncob pipe in his mouth, Collier liked to wear comfortable baggy clothes. But these disarming features hid strong organizing skills motivated by a passion for reform and a vision of European social democracy transplanted to America through the American Indian. He had devoted his life to public service, eventually focusing his attention on the plight of the Indian. After Roosevelt's election, his friendship with the new interior secretary, Harold Ickes, a charter member of Collier's American Indian Defense Association, convinced the president to accept Collier as Ickes's commissioner of Indian affairs.[19]

Collier's tenure was a whirlwind of controversy. Collier forced through many changes in the BIA's heavy-handed administration of the reservation system, including the Indian Reorganization Act of 1934. But some of his programs were arbitrary, and a few even bordered on the scandalous.

Thousands of Navajos had lost a primary source of income, clothing, and milk when Collier, at the behest of the Soil Conservation Agency, advised them to kill 400,000 sheep and goats to prevent further soil erosion on their lands.[20] Behind the slaughter was a grimmer reality: the familiar greed of the white man. Commercial ranchers had refused to sell Indians land that had passed into their control since the breakup of tribal lands under the Dawes Allotment Act of 1887. Since the Navajo reservation could not expand enough, overgrazing by the herds was inevitable. The herds, in turn, impinged on the plans of agribusiness. Overgrazing had created such extensive soil erosion along the Colorado River that silt was undermining the usefulness of the new Hoover Dam for the irrigation and development of southern California's Imperial Valley.

The slaughter of the Navajo herds would haunt Collier for the rest of his life and might have shattered his ability to continue had it not been for his success in implementing a wide range of health and economic reforms on the reservations. His "Indian New Deal" of 1934 won acclaim throughout Latin America and enhanced the prestige of the Roosevelt administration. Most of the delegates to the Inter-American Indian Conference knew and admired Collier's work.

Eighteen other governments had sent delegates, and forty-seven Indians were there representing tribes in the hemisphere. Seventy-one social scientists also were on hand, ready and willing to promote *indigenismo* with an ideological enthusiasm. From such Rockefeller-endowed centers of learning as the University of Chicago, Harvard, Yale, Columbia, and Johns Hopkins came a new school of anthropology and linguistics that proclaimed its dedication to incorporating the Indian peoples into the mainstream of Western society through their tribal cultures, not despite them. Gone were the overt expressions of white supremacy.

All these people would do most of the work of spreading Collier's "ethnic laboratory" beyond the United States and Mexico to the rest of the hemisphere. Ethnic diversity was central to his Darwinist understanding of the successful evolution of humanity as an adaptable, culturally mutating social animal. He was convinced that through the Indians, diversity would blossom in Western societies, not despite conscious cooperative planning, but because of it.

But only a few of the delegates could play coordinating roles as inter-American leaders of Indian assimilation. Men of such international stature as himself, Moisés Sáenz, and Manuel Gamio were obvious candidates. A balding American Fundamentalist missionary named Cam Townsend was not.

The Summer Institute of Linguistics (SIL), significantly, was the only large missionary delegation present. Yet, even though it lacked the prestige that comes with advanced degrees or official recognition of one's government, Cam's group had direct access to some of the highest officials in Mexico, an influence of which few non-Mexican delegates were aware.

The Dawn Within the Dusk

Ambassador Daniels, who hosted Collier at the embassy, was an exception. He had watched the number of Townsend's linguists grow to thirty-seven by 1940 and he had never seen the missionary commit a diplomatic blunder. Cam took the success of his mission too seriously to allow the Fundamentalist proclivities of his followers to jeopardize it by proselytizing or criticizing the Cárdenas government. Instead, at every opportunity, Cam heaped praise on the Mexican president.

Although he was an unabashed promoter of Cárdenas, Cam demanded "strict neutrality" on government policies from his followers in an effort to silence dissenters. "After all," he wrote his translators, "who called us to pass judgment upon rulers? Are we not commanded to obey and pray for them?" Cam finally arrived at the bone of contentious debate within SIL: "There is too much at stake for this [criticism] to continue. Twenty million Indians in Latin America wait to see the spirit of the Gospel demonstrated in a way they can comprehend and to read the Word in a language they can understand." He characterized the criticism of Cárdenas as "half-cocked" and "unbecoming of us who have received so many courtesies from the government of Mexico." He asked them to trust God and "recognize your mistake."[21]

A few could not, convinced they were being asked to trust Cameron Townsend, not God. They left.

Yet in the conference's rosy dawn of Pan-American Indianism, even these losses seemed endurable. Seventy-two resolutions were drafted, laying the foundation for a hemispherewide Indian policy covering bilingual education, cultural survival, rural medicine, schools, and the setting up of national Indian institutes. And, of central importance to SIL's future, an Inter-American Indian Institute was to be based in Mexico City to carry on the hemispheric work, to serve as a clearinghouse for information, and to convene future Inter-American Indian conferences. The Institute would also publish a bimonthly *Boletín Indigenista* and a quarterly *America Indígena* to spread the secular good cheer of Indian administration as an experiment in social action research—and benevolent control—that would turn all Latin America into a vast laboratory of ethnic relations.

Cárdenas provided the top personnel, proposing an eight-person executive committee composed of two Mexicans and six men from countries with large Indian populations. There remained only the crucial ingredient of U.S. financial and technical support for the many programs Collier envisioned. Standing in the way of that support was the unresolved issue of the properties of Standard Oil and the other American companies.

Cam attempted to surmount this barrier by writing a straightforward defense of Cárdenas to President Roosevelt. He used the occasion to castigate the oil companies and their "insidious anti-Mexican propaganda" for creating "a very dangerous situation." He incorporated the letter in *The Truth About Mexico's Oil*, which his newly created Inter-American Fellowship sent to every member of Congress. This gave the letter—and him—a prominence beyond the actual limited role he was playing in the international debate. It was a brilliant tactic.

But there was also a desperate tone in Cam's pamphlet that may have been prompted by angry reactions in the American colony to the recent decisive breakthrough in the oil crisis. On May 1, Sinclair Oil accepted $8.5 million in a separate agreement with Cárdenas.

Standard Oil was furious. So was Secretary of State Hull, who had publicly intervened on April 3 to prevent just such a settlement. Standard's reasons were obvious. Ambassador Daniels had conveyed them to Roosevelt as early as 1939. The oil companies were "waiting for two elections . . . in the United States and in Mexico. They hope you will be succeeded by an apostle of the imperialistic Old Stick, and that the successor of Cárdenas will be a rightist who would undo the policies of President Cárdenas."[22] To Cam's and Daniels's great relief, the Mexican and American elections of 1940 ended any hope that Standard Oil held for the return of the Mexican oil fields. General Manuel Ávila Camacho won. Cárdenas stood firm for constitutional succession and was confident that Camacho could return the oil wells only at the risk of his head. The Mexican people would simply not allow it.

Then Franklin Roosevelt was elected to an unprecedented third term in November. As evidence of his support to the Mexican government, he sent Vice President-elect Henry Wallace to join Daniels in toasting Camacho's inauguration. It was one of the few times that the teetotaler Daniels lifted a glass of champagne.

Cam sensed that as a new era was opening, another had closed. There was no sudden light on a road to Damascus turning him toward the Amazon, or even particularly Peru, his next destination. Rather, there was a growing uncertainty in Mexico, as the guiding lights that had led him so far so quickly faded on the stage of power.

Cárdenas's influence was diminishing rapidly as Camacho consolidated power. Mexico's "Great Commoner" betrayed a deep sense of bitterness and foreboding in a final message of congratulations to the reelected President Roosevelt:

"As a citizen of a country which has lived a constant tragedy under the pressure of an international capitalism which aspires to control of national, public, and private economies, I also hope that the policy of your government will be affirmed in the sense of a just attitude toward the American countries which have felt themselves crushed under the same pressure."[23]

A year later, Cárdenas was physically removed from the political scene when he accepted President Camacho's appointment to head Mexico's coastal defenses from a headquarters in Baja California.

The U.S. Embassy was also undergoing a change. Daniels wanted to return home because of his wife's health. Before he left, the ambassador tried to ease the transition for friends, including the Townsends. He had the missionaries over for dinner, attended a luncheon Cam threw on the roof garden of Hotel Ontario for Mexican officials, and even agreed to take up with Washington Cam's request for draft exemption for his male translators. Then Daniels was gone.

Cam was approaching a new stage in his life. And Moisés Sáenz was leading the way, pointing him toward the next field of battle for the Lord. Sáenz had been appointed Mexico's ambassador to Peru, a land of fabled riches and naked Amazonian warriors who knew none of the borders white men drew on maps.

As his yearnings turned toward Peru's Bibleless tribes and the wider opportunities offered by the Inter-American Indian Institute, Cam also turned away from the political sympathies that Cárdenas represented. In 1937, he and Cárdenas had visited the site of Zapata's assassination. The group photograph Townsend took that day shows the grimly determined president surrounded by proud peasants. In his letter to Roosevelt on behalf of SIL's Mexican benefactor, Cam had spoken freely of the monopolistic nature of the trusts, of "privileged interests that had established strangleholds upon those lands when they were minors . . . dissidents [who] possess such great financial power that they have been able not only to challenge the very sovereignty of these lands but also to wield a disproportionate influence over our press, our people and our legislators."[24]

He would never utter such words again.

Instead, he would set his course along that of the institute Collier and Sáenz had started. He could not foresee the tragedy that was enveloping Collier and his BIA or understand the implication of Collier's incorporating Beardsley Ruml's Social Science Research Council into the governing board of the institute's U.S. section, the National Indian Institute. Alone, now without friends in high places, Cam Townsend did not know that the National Indian Institute was secretly being funded by the president's new defense-oriented Coordinator of Inter-American Affairs, Nelson Rockefeller.

II

WORLD WAR II: THE CRUCIBLE

The average man can hardly realize how widespread is the idea, even in the U.S., that the settling of South America's interior would give another breathing spell to our civilized world. . . . I find myself confronted at every turn by the romantic argument that the conquest of South America's wilderness would do for the Western Hemisphere what the conquest of the West did for the United States at a critical time.

—EARL P. HANSON, *JOURNEY TO MANAOS* (1938)

8

THE COORDINATOR

A Debt Unpaid

Nelson Rockefeller owed his life to an Indian—twice. In 1939, he rented an amphibious plane and flew to a remote lake in the mountains of Alaska to hunt big game with three friends and an Indian guide. On the third day Nelson and the guide came upon two bears, a brown grizzly and a giant Kodiak. Nelson chose the larger trophy. He lifted his rifle, sighted on the Kodiak's huge bulk, and heard the crack of his gun and the whump of a bullet striking home. The bear fell. With the grizzly fleeing into the woods, Nelson thought he was safe.

It all happened so fast that the Indian could not stop him. Nelson leaped forward to check out his prize when the beast, now all hatred and rage, sprung alive.

"Shoot again!" the Indian shouted.

Nelson did, but he was nervous and missed. The wounded bear charged. Nelson just stood there in shock watching almost a ton of claws and teeth roaring down on him. The Indian dropped on a knee to steady his aim and fired. The Kodiak collapsed.

A few days later, Nelson was pursuing easier prey, mountain goats, when he froze on a narrow cliff ledge above a 400-foot drop. Only after five minutes of reassurances was the Indian able to coax him slowly down to safety.

Less than a year later, when asked to help Indians, Nelson was reluctant. Bureau of Indian Affairs Commissioner John Collier wanted Nelson to arrange federal funding for the new National Indian Institute mandated by the Pátzcuaro Conference. Nelson, as head of Roosevelt's new Office of the Coordinator of Inter-American Affairs (CIAA), refused until Roosevelt ordered him to stop stalling.[1]

When Collier wanted Nelson to support a nutrition study and a soybean project among the impoverished Otomi Indians of Mexico, he again declined. Only public pressure and presidential intervention turned Rockefeller around.

Nelson's interest in Indians was expedient. He was primarily concerned with extracting the minerals and natural resources from Latin America needed by the U.S. war machine.

Nelson was "the Eager Beaver to end all EB's," recalled future Atomic Energy Commission Chairman David Lilienthal. But he was not alone; the Junta came with him. They frequently traveled to Washington, staying at Nelson's large home on Foxhall Road. Almost all the top CIAA aides stayed there, too, Nelson turning the place into a kind of boardinghouse until late 1941, when Tod and the children came down to stay with him. Nelson had been dutifully productive for the family tree: There were now four offspring.

But Nelson had little time for Tod and the family now. His day began at 6:00 A.M., when he rose to listen to news broadcasts while tanning himself under a sunlamp. Sometimes he raced off to a brisk match of tennis doubles with Vice President Henry Wallace against any two CIAA aides who were naive enough to mention their interest in the game. By 7:45 he had returned, showered, and inspected a lineup of the children at the breakfast table. Here the Rockefeller tradition of reading morning verses from the Bible was continued, supplemented with the innovation of Nelson reading the children articles from the newspapers. While eating, Nelson answered their questions and wrote memos. Then he was off to the office by 8:00 A.M., stuffing packed briefcases into his car and picking up as many as four assistants for a harrowing ride at excessive speed into the capital. "The rest of us were always cringing and mentally putting on the brakes," one aide remembered. "He didn't seem to give a damn. But he never had an accident."[2]

In his large office in Harry Hopkins's Commerce Department building, Nelson had adapted the Rockefeller Foundation's surveys to a military style proper for a wartime commander. The briefing room had the shape of a war room. Mechanical layouts, maps, charts, and graphs recorded the progress of all projects with military precision. A large conference table was hurriedly set up, and lights and a movie projector were installed.

Staff briefings were rehearsed like Radio City musicals. By 10:30 A.M., when top CIAA personnel and representatives from other government offices and departments filed in for their daily briefing, Nelson's show ran as slick as oil. It was like a never-ending Broadway hit, subject to instant rewriting by the director.

Even lunch offered no relief, limited to a sandwich at the desk over a bull session on ideas, with Nelson making the final decisions and giving the marching orders. The rest of the day was crowded with meetings and lobbying the Hill, offering Nelson his first look at the back rooms of the White House, Washington's labyrinth of departments and agencies, and the congressional cloakrooms where he

Office of Coordinator of Inter-American Affairs (CIAA)

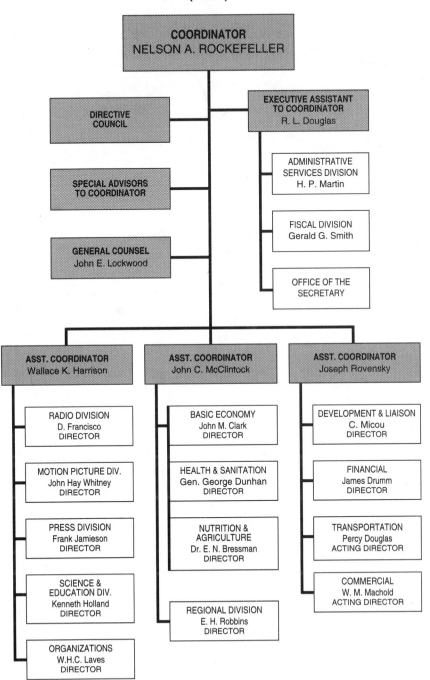

COORDINATOR
NELSON A. ROCKEFELLER

DIRECTIVE COUNCIL

SPECIAL ADVISORS TO COORDINATOR

GENERAL COUNSEL
John E. Lockwood

EXECUTIVE ASSISTANT TO COORDINATOR
R. L. Douglas

ADMINISTRATIVE SERVICES DIVISION
H. P. Martin

FISCAL DIVISION
Gerald G. Smith

OFFICE OF THE SECRETARY

ASST. COORDINATOR
Wallace K. Harrison

RADIO DIVISION
D. Francisco
DIRECTOR

MOTION PICTURE DIV.
John Hay Whitney
DIRECTOR

PRESS DIVISION
Frank Jamieson
DIRECTOR

SCIENCE & EDUCATION DIV.
Kenneth Holland
DIRECTOR

ORGANIZATIONS
W.H.C. Laves
DIRECTOR

ASST. COORDINATOR
John C. McClintock

BASIC ECONOMY
John M. Clark
DIRECTOR

HEALTH & SANITATION
Gen. George Dunhan
DIRECTOR

NUTRITION & AGRICULTURE
Dr. E. N. Bressman
DIRECTOR

REGIONAL DIVISION
E. H. Robbins
DIRECTOR

ASST. COORDINATOR
Joseph Rovensky

DEVELOPMENT & LIAISON
C. Micou
DIRECTOR

FINANCIAL
James Drumm
DIRECTOR

TRANSPORTATION
Percy Douglas
ACTING DIRECTOR

COMMERCIAL
W. M. Machold
ACTING DIRECTOR

OIAA RADIO

LOCAL RADIO STATION COVERAGE

PROGRAMS SPONSORED BY
CIAA LOCALLY:

REBROADCASTS OF SHORTWAVE PROGRAMS

TRANSCRIPTIONS

*SPECIAL LOCALLY PRODUCED SHOWS: news,
commentaries, drama, music.*

*Size of circle represents coverage in miles,
and is determined by kilowatt power.*

Rockefeller's CIAA produced radio programs that were broadcast throughout Latin
America during World War II.

Source: CIAA Files, U.S. National Archives.

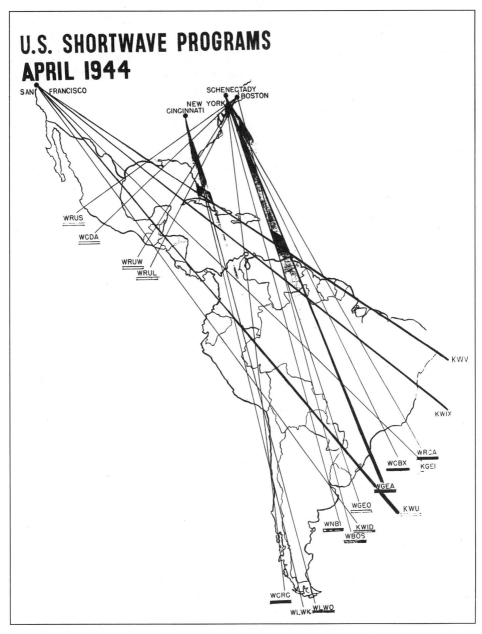

U.S. SHORTWAVE PROGRAMS
APRIL 1944

SAN FRANCISCO

SCHENECTADY
BOSTON

NEW YORK
CINCINNATI

WRUS

WCDA

WRUW
WRUL

KWV

KWIX

WRCA
WCBX   KGEI

WGEA

WGEO   KWU

WNBI   KWID
WBOS

WCRC
WLWK WLWO

Rockefeller's CIAA shortwave radio programs blanketed Latin America with propaganda during World War II.

Source: CIAA Files, U.S. National Archives.

enlisted men like Texas's Sam Rayburn and Rayburn's protégé, Lyndon Johnson, on his behalf. Nelson was always pushing his ever-lengthening agenda for Latin America. Starting with the meat and potatoes of trade and culture, it soon included the exotic spices of intelligence gathering on political and economic developments, large heaps of propaganda and control over Latin America's press, and even a liberal dash of postwar economic development. In other words, "a reorientation of the whole Latin American problem from the viewpoint of National Defense."[3]

NELSON'S GRAND ALLIANCE

Within three months of his becoming Coordinator of Inter-American Affairs, Nelson was suddenly threatened with eclipse by another rising star in wartime Washington, General William J. Donovan. Nelson's senior by twenty-five years and a man of wide experience, Donovan was the president's newly appointed Coordinator of Information.

"I think there will be a transfer of the Latin American information program from your office to ours," he bluntly told Rockefeller.[4] In desperation, Nelson suggested that they see the president together to resolve the dispute. Donovan rejected the idea. The subject, Donovan announced, was closed.

Nelson was shocked. He had worked hard to build CIAA's information division. He had expanded shortwave broadcasting facilities to Latin America. He distributed carefully selected recordings and transcripts to radio stations in Latin America for rebroadcasting. He persuaded Hollywood to deny films to theaters showing German or Italian movies and newsreels. The CIAA filled the news vacuum with its own propaganda, producing newsreels, political cartoons, and films featuring the rosier side of American culture and Latin American governments.

Rockefeller's press division was another big hit. Every month, it saturated Latin America with news and feature stories, locking in about 1,200 newspaper publishers who were dependent on CIAA-subsidized shipments of scarce newsprint on U.S. flagships. Nelson even published his own monthly magazine, aptly entitled *En Guardia* ("On Guard"), with a circulation of 80,000 by the summer of 1941.

This was an opinion-molding empire Nelson Rockefeller was not about to surrender without a fight.

William Donovan, aged fifty-eight, was a formidable opponent. He had earned the nickname "Wild Bill" in Mexico while serving in General John Pershing's 1916 expedition against Pancho Villa and had commanded the "Fighting 69th" in World War I. He was respected on Wall Street as one of its cleverest lawyers and had been the Republican party's conservative candidate to replace Roosevelt as New York's governor in 1932. Moreover, Donovan had won wide acclaim in intelligence circles by carrying out sensitive missions to Britain, the Mediterranean, and the Middle East in 1940–1941.

But Nelson had one thing Donovan did not: friends in the Democratic party who were in the president's inner circle. These friends persuaded Roosevelt to get some more opinions.

Adolf Berle was only too happy to give his. Berle believed, with some cause, that Donovan was a usurper of power, including his own as founder of the State Department's Bureau of Intelligence.

Berle enlisted the FBI's J. Edgar Hoover, who threw his formidable weight behind Nelson. At Berle's suggestion, Roosevelt had given Hoover power to establish a "Special Intelligence Service" that would extend FBI activities throughout Latin America.

Donovan never really had a chance. Roosevelt acceded to the demands of vested interests, including Nelson's domain over psychological warfare. "I continue to believe that the requirements of our program in the [Western] Hemisphere are quite different from those of our programs to Europe and the Far East," the president wrote Donovan. "In order that information, news and inspirational matter going to the other American republics . . . may be carefully adapted to the demands of the Hemisphere, it should be handled exclusively by the Coordinator of Inter-American Affairs in cooperation with the Department of State."[5]

Donovan did not talk to Rockefeller for two years.

This was the last serious challenge to Nelson Rockefeller's power over Latin American affairs during the war. Donovan would have to content himself with control over the intelligence and paramilitary operations in the war theaters through the newly created Office of Strategic Services (OSS).

The OSS's Latin American Division was restricted to passing on information on Axis sympathizers to the FBI and the CIAA for them to follow up in their counterintelligence and economic warfare programs or financially supporting CIAA's propaganda efforts.

The Business Imperative

Of all U.S. agencies, the CIAA may have been the most prepared when war actually came. Throughout Latin America, the CIAA team was headed by efficient business executives. With their hands already on the levers of local power, such businessmen facilitated the CIAA's transition to wartime operations. But Nelson paid a price for this readiness: He had already gained a reputation for being politically too timid in his economic programs, too oriented toward American businesses and not enough toward the economic needs of the countries in which they functioned.

"Most problems," one CIAA staff member remembered, "were approached from a business point of view at first. They reflected a viewpoint . . . that you mustn't do anything to disturb business. Whenever anybody had a new idea, Rockefeller's first reaction was to ask whether it would hurt business—not his

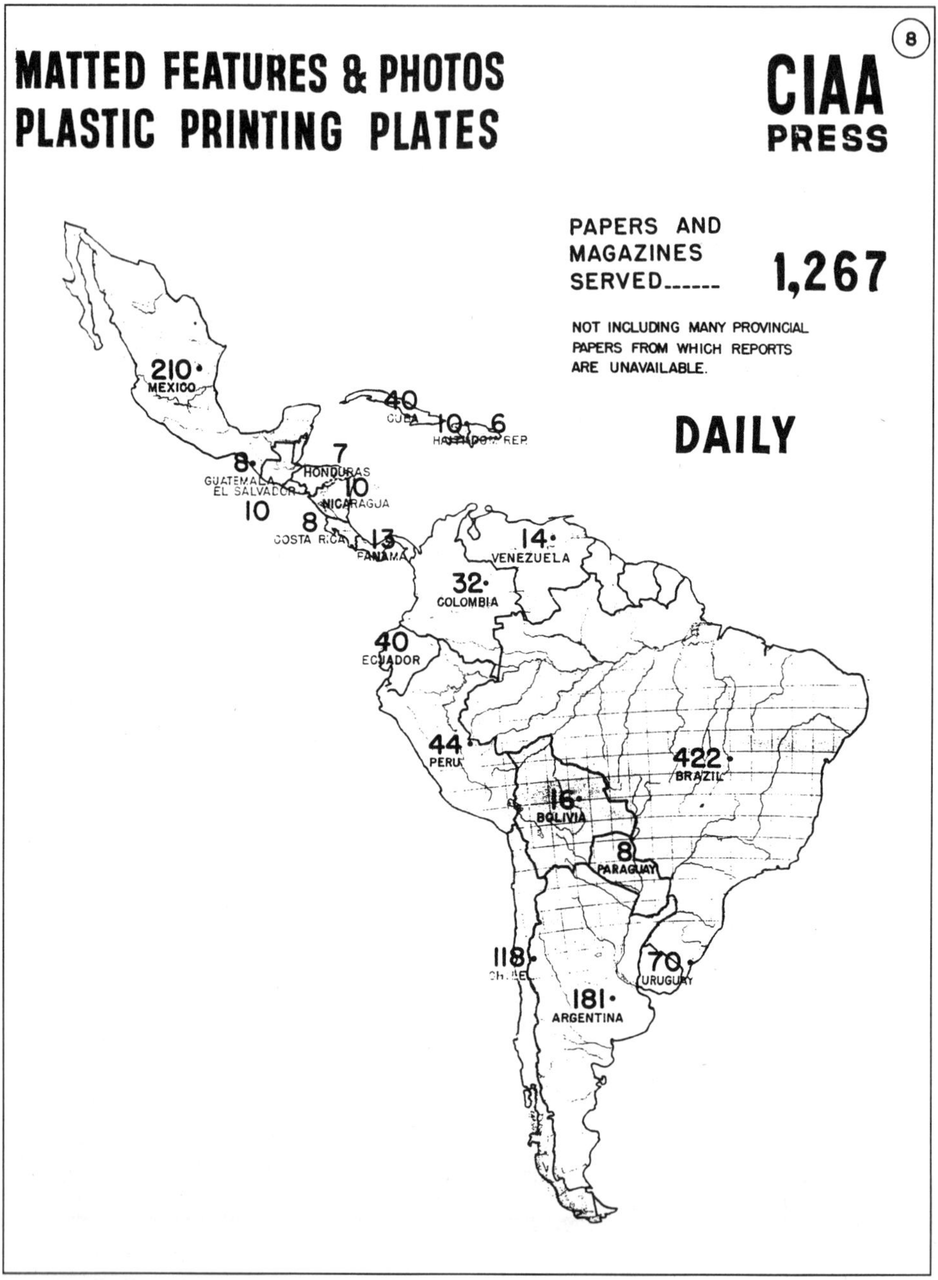

MATTED FEATURES & PHOTOS PLASTIC PRINTING PLATES

CIAA PRESS

PAPERS AND MAGAZINES SERVED------ **1,267**

NOT INCLUDING MANY PROVINCIAL PAPERS FROM WHICH REPORTS ARE UNAVAILABLE.

DAILY

210· MEXICO

40 CUBA

10· 6
HAITI DOM. REP.

8· GUATEMALA
EL SALVADOR

7 HONDURAS

10 NICARAGUA

10

8 COSTA RICA

13 PANAMA

14· VENEZUELA

32· COLOMBIA

40 ECUADOR

44· PERU

422· BRAZIL

16· BOLIVIA

8 PARAGUAY

118· CHILE

70 URUGUAY

181· ARGENTINA

Rockefeller's CIAA influence over Latin America's press during World War II was extensive.

Source: CIAA Files, U.S. National Archives.

own personal business, mind you, but the business community generally. Only Pearl Harbor changed all that."[6]

The accusation was untrue. Nelson was just as pro-business after Pearl Harbor as before. In fact, the CIAA became one of the largest and most glamorous bureaucracies in Washington, with art exhibits, university professors, dancers, singers, and authors touring in almost every country in the hemisphere, coordinated by branch offices in every U.S. embassy in Latin America.

At first glance, the programs appeared merely to emphasize the need for cultural ties. Behind this concern for cultural ties, of course, was business. Nelson, who initially was told that his annual budget would be about $3.5 million, had spent $140 million by 1944. He could have never gotten approval for such expenditures if his activities were only the cultural events most people saw. Underpinning these activities was a hidden economic agenda: drawing Latin America into the economic matrix of the war-supplies programs being run by corporate leaders.

The "coordinating committees" that the CIAA set up in Brazil and elsewhere were "composed of the biggest businessmen," a State Department official complained. "They have very definite ideas as to what our general policy should be and in general their ideas have been the most reactionary."[7]

Josephus Daniels was equally worried.

"I believe," he wrote Roosevelt, "that entrance into this war by the United States would witness the return of the forces of privilege in control of our government, as occurred after the war of 1914–1918, and all the reform measures which have been obtained at a great price will be dethroned, . . . with monopoly strongly entrenched in business, manufacturing, finance and government."[8]

Perhaps more than anyone, Nelson Rockefeller represented those forces. Besides assistants from the immediate Rockefeller financial group, CIAA's top positions were filled with captains of industry like financier and movie producer John Hay Whitney; Texas cotton king Will Clayton (who worked with CIAA's Raw Materials and Commodities Division); and Otis Elevator's exports manager, Percy Douglas. Business expertise came not only into the CIAA, but out of it as well. Assistant Coordinator John C. McClintock, for example, helped United Fruit run its vast plantations in Latin America after the war, often serving as a liaison with the CIA. Investment banker Paul Nitze was director of the CIAA's financial division; representing Nelson on the Board of Economic Warfare gained him expertise in metals and minerals purchases that he later took to the War and State departments as an armaments expert.

Nelson's four brothers were fully supportive, particularly Laurance, who was always Nelson's closest ally in both personal and business affairs.

As in so many other things since childhood, Laurance was, in a sense, Nelson's junior partner. By devoting himself almost exclusively to investments, he became Nelson's arm in the business world. Laurance shared Nelson's interest in venturing beyond the family's traditional preoccupation with oil. In 1938, he made the first modest move by his generation to diversify the Rockefeller fortune, joining a syndicate being organized by World War I ace Eddie Rickenbacker to purchase Eastern Airlines from the Du Pont interests. Laurance put only $10,000 into the venture pool, but it was the first step toward eventually becoming Eastern's largest stockholder.

Laurance learned from Nelson and other sources the importance that aviation would hold for penetrating the interior of South America. So with another $10,000, he backed an engineer named James S. McDonnell. McDonnell was gearing up for production of a newly designed warplane in anticipation of orders from the War Department.

Laurance by then could see both Nazis and profits approaching over the horizon. Wanting to take advantage of opportunities created by the void of British capital and the British sale of corporate holdings in Latin America, he took an air tour of South and Central America in March 1941, after which he bought a controlling interest in 1.5 million acres of prime agricultural land on the Magdalena River in Colombia. Laurance's interests ranged from harvesting rich mahogany timberlands to building a hotel on the projected Pan-American Highway to raising cattle,[9] complementing Nelson's own newly acquired ranch in Venezuela, Monte Sacro, once owned by Simón Bolívar.

But it was in aviation that Laurance's entrepreneurial passions melded most directly with Nelson's political designs for Latin America—and into direct confrontation with German corporate expansion in Latin America.

The Secret War for the Skies

In April 1939, when Adolf Berle was gathering his forces to "clear out" the German airlines from Latin America, Laurance Rockefeller was invited to lunch by Robert W. Johnson, founder of Johnson & Johnson drug company. In itself, there was nothing unusual about a corporate official meeting with one of the Rockefeller boys. But what Johnson had to say to Laurance was.

Johnson & Johnson did a large business in South America. Its greatest competitors were German companies, particularly Bayer. Like most drug companies, it depended on the Amazon to supply most of the plants used in the drugs it manufactured. It also had two manufacturing subsidiaries in Brazil and Argentina, run with army-like precision by a West Point graduate with a penchant for intelligence gathering named John Caldwell "J. C." King.

Johnson was worried about reports of a growing German corporate presence in Latin America. German airlines had greatly increased their trunk and local services in Latin America. Recognizing that Latin America could become a source of raw materials second only to southeastern Europe, Berlin had spurred an enormous

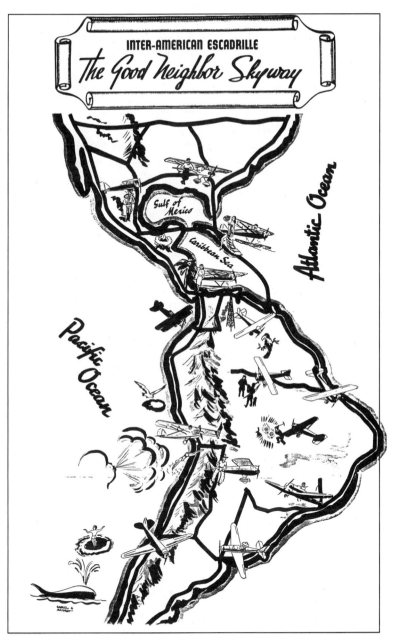

INTER-AMERICAN ESCADRILLE
The Good Neighbor Skyway

The Good Neighbor Skyway, promoted by the Rockefeller-backed Inter-American Escadrille's 1940 flight around Latin America, had objectives beyond those pushed in this map—airplane sales and tourism. Among the hidden goals were the creation of local aviation clubs with ties to American aviation companies and sympathies for the United States, the replacement of German corporate influence over Latin American aviation, and the integration of Latin America into the United States' hemispheric air defense system and the Allies' global air supply system.

Source: Rockefeller Archive Center.

growth of trade. Latin Americans had found this trade a welcome relief from the fall in Anglo-American purchases during the depression. By 1940, many Latin American countries were selling twice as much to Germany as Germany sold to them.

German airplanes were among the more expensive finished goods sold to Latin America. These sales helped redress Germany's trade deficit with the hemisphere while increasing Latin American dependence on German technology and parts. It also allowed the Nazis to score propaganda victories.

For this reason Johnson had revived a little-known organization called the Inter-American Escadrille, a trade association of American airline executives promoting the expansion of civil aviation in Latin America. Founded in 1934, the Escadrille had floundered until 1939, when the outbreak of the European war opened a window of opportunity for American companies seeking some way to stop growing German competition in the hemisphere's skies.

Johnson outlined a plan to send an airplane on tour of Latin America to boost the growth of civil aviation with ties to American aviation. As a director of Eastern Airlines, would Laurance help with an endorsement?

Laurance did more. He joined the Escadrille's board of directors, which soon emerged as a powerful lobby. Adolf Berle had already taken the initiative against the German airlines. By 1942, Colombia, Bolivia, and Brazil would remove Germany from South American skies. In its place would be American, or American-financed, airlines, including Pan American Airways, Lloyd Bolivian Air, and Avianca.

What made smooth transitions of ownership practical was the intensive training of Latin American pilots, technicians, and managers inspired by the Inter-American Escadrille. And behind this training was the Rockefellers.

On March 5, 1941, Nelson smiled for photographers as he shook hands with General Frank McCoy of the Foreign Policy Association and other members of the crew before the Escadrille plane left Washington for Latin America.

The trip was a publicist's dream. Everywhere they stopped, the Escadrille team was toasted by local government officials and executives of American companies doing business there. Air clubs were formed into "wings," with each country's chief of state named honorary chairman. At a reception in the home of a vice president of an American gold mining company in Nicaragua, glasses were raised to the health and happiness of "Frank [Roosevelt] and Tacho [Somoza], the two champions of inter-American solidarity." The toasts were always the same, whether it was Ubico of Guatemala or Camacho of Mexico, and they all created an atmosphere conducive to the expulsion of German companies.

Nelson appropriated $50,000 to help bring hundreds of Latin American students to the United States to be trained as pilots, mechanics, and engineers. The air forces of Latin America were integrated into a coordinated coastal defense plan worked out by the War Department at its new Pentagon headquarters in Washington.

In 1945, amid State Department charges that the Escadrille was being used as a "high pressure group to sell airplanes"[10] to Latin America, Nelson ceased all CIAA funding. But then the job was complete.

Laurance, resigning from Escadrille's board to accept a commission to help run the navy's aviation buildup and later oversee aircraft production in California, was candid. "The work of the Escadrille has been assisted by the Office of the Coordinator of Inter-American Affairs and other government agencies and now seeks the cooperation of manufacturers who have an interest in the post-war market for United States aircraft products in Latin America."[11]

Beyond testimonials, the Escadrille's officers accrued nothing. The program, abandoned to its boosters, quickly died. Meanwhile, some leaders of Escadrille's local country "wings" returned from training in the United States to work for the local subsidiary of Pan American. For it would be Pan Am—and Laurance Rockefeller's Eastern Airlines in Puerto Rico and Mexico—that would reap most of the harvest of Latin America's skies.

WINGS OVER THE AMAZON

The vast Amazonian heartland of South America would also be harvested. One of the glaring problems the Escadrille's flight revealed in early 1941 was the absence of airfields. In addition, crews dreaded the jungle, with its boa constrictors, piranhas, jaguars, and "fleas that crawl right into the flesh under the skin and raise young ones there."[12]

But their greatest fear was the silent, unseen presence of tens of thousands of armed Indians roaming beneath the endless green canopy.

The greatest of the jungle's known natural resources was rubber. What had once built fortunes (and an opera house) in the middle of the jungle had, over the past thirty years, suffered a steep decline after Amazonian seeds had been smuggled out of Brazil to British plantations in the Far East. Now, with the war, these British plantations had been overrun by Japanese troops, and the Amazon's abandoned wild rubber trees were once again in demand. Washington hurriedly set up the Rubber Reserve Corporation and assigned Nelson Rockefeller the task of ensuring safe, healthy, and thereby productive working conditions for armies of harvesters.

Of all the rubber-bearing countries whose borders melted into the Amazon's Green Hell, Peru had rulers with seemingly the least antipathy toward American ambitions. The restlessness of Peru's Quechua Indians in the American-owned silver, zinc, and copper mines and the impoverished villages of the Andes required President Manuel Prado to find some solution to his country's pressing economic problems. He believed that he found it in the Amazon frontier. Not only did the Amazon hold rich reserves of rubber. Here also were some of the world's largest stands of timber that, if cleared, could end Peru's dependence on foreign suppliers for 95 percent of her lumber.[13]

But, above all, here was oil. In 1939, oil was struck at the Ganso Azul (Blue Goose) Dome near Pucallpa, a small town on the Ucayali River, a tributary of the mighty Amazon. Prado, who hailed from a powerful Lima banking family, dreamed of a new frontier of farms and subterranean riches sending back oil, cereals, beef, and even leather from a tanning industry built out of the jungle's deer, peccary, and alligators. All he needed was a road across an Andean mountain range averaging 13,000 feet high.

Conquering the Amazon was not a new dream for Peru's rulers. It had already inspired a war with Colombia in a futile effort to seize that country's strategic (and only) port on the Amazon, Leticia. Another more successful war had been fought in 1941 with Ecuador over jungle believed to cover oil. But oil at the Ganso Azul field was not mere conjecture. It was real. And Prado knew that it was the only proved source of petroleum in the entire Amazon basin. It would be needed for any rubber program that the United States launched in the Amazon, including one in Brazil.

The only thing standing in Peru's way was roads—there weren't any. Prado's predecessor, dictator Oscar Benavides, understood that "without roads, commerce is asphyxiated, industries lead an anemic existence, the farmer lives under constant worry about the fluctuations of foreign markets, because for him the internal market is inaccessible."[14] Prado agreed, but he added a new twist in their direction, pointing them east instead of west, to the Amazon, the new frontier. He had only to get the Americans, who already had $81.5 million in direct investments in Peru and owned another $54 million worth of Peruvian bonds,[15] to build his road to the Amazon.

On January 21, 1942, Nelson Rockefeller received a note from President Roosevelt about Peru. The president wanted the United States to assist the development of Peru's economy and set up cultural exchanges.[16] Rockefeller replied that the CIAA was contemplating a bilingual language project through the Peruvian-American Association.[17] Before the year was out, Nelson would also arrange funding for a new trans-Andean highway to Pucallpa, passing within fifteen miles of the Ganso Azul oil field, to which a service road was built.

Peru had already agreed in principle to stimulate rubber production. Now Prado agreed to sell all Peru's surplus rubber and allow the U.S. Rubber Reserve Corporation to launch a $1.2 million program to increase the production of wild rubber. In May, Prado authorized U.S. construction of an airport at Iquitos, the Amazon's last deepwater port capable of handling oceangoing ships. To organize the collection of rubber, the Peruvian Amazon Corporation was founded.

Now all that remained was to find some way of dealing with the Indians who stood in the way. One organization was already becoming known in Lima, having been promoted by Mexico's ambassador to Peru, Moisés Sáenz.

Its name was the Summer Institute of Linguistics.

9

THE SWORD OF THE SPIRIT

FORGING THE LINGUISTIC WEAPON

Washington was a blur of bustling uniforms in 1943 when Ken Pike arrived at CIAA offices carrying his mentor's dream of an Amazon conquered for Christ. Cameron Townsend wanted the young linguist to go to Peru to convey his vision of Amazonian tribes pacified by the Word of the Bible. The American Bible Society had offered Pike the perfect opportunity by asking him to do a field survey of Indian languages in Peru, Bolivia, and Ecuador. But Pike, doubting his own abilities, had hesitated—until Uncle Cam insisted.

There was only one remaining obstacle, and for most young Americans it might have been insurmountable. Pike was of draftable age, and Mexico's antimissionary sentiments had made ordination—and clerical exemption—impossible. Although Cam's personal appeal to Ambassador Daniels had helped spare the young man of army duty, Pike could not travel to South America during wartime without getting Washington's approval. And that meant getting the OK of the man who ran Washington's cultural relations with Latin America, Nelson Rockefeller.

Cam was confident of Pike's chances. Pike had helped write textbooks for the CIAA to teach English to Latin Americans, part of Rockefeller's response to a burgeoning political crisis.

By 1943, some 200,000 Mexican agricultural workers had crossed the border into the American Southwest to fill jobs left vacant by workers drafted into the war. Their sudden arrival, however, triggered racial backlashes and rioting.

If Nelson Rockefeller had learned anything from Lincoln School, it was that education has the power to break down cultural barriers and isolation and bring people into the active mainstream of American life, a prerequisite to building loyalty. Education in English further ensured the isolation of Mexican Americans. To encourage an alternative, Rockefeller turned to one of America's most distinguished linguists, Charles Fries. With $20,000 in CIAA funds approved in August 1942, Fries's English Language Institute hurried the preparation of new textbooks.[1] Fries's right-hand man was Kenneth Pike.

Fries's word carried weight in Washington. Armed with an introduction from Fries, Pike went to see the head of cultural relations for inter-American affairs to get approval to travel to South America.

"Your passport has to come across my desk," the official said. "When it does, I will okay it."[2]

BUILDING THE ARMY OF THE LORD

Pike's collaboration with Fries had already been valuable to Cam. It was through their association that Cam had escaped the Ozarks for the limelight at the University of Oklahoma at Norman. Oil money had built Norman's land-grant college into a university, and by 1940 it was poised to become the leading educational institution in the Southwest east of the Rockies.

This oil-fired growth was accompanied by the militarization of the campus as war approached. By 1942, the U.S. Navy had taken over the airfield for training navy pilots. Within two years, even Norman coeds were being recruited into the Sooner Squadron of the Army Transport Command, while Latin American coeds were paying hospitality visits to officers from South American armies being trained at nearby Fort Sill.

Into the middle of this wartime fervor marched Cam's missionaries. The recruiting officer for the Summer Institute of Linguistics (SIL) was Roy Temple House, Norman's most promising professor of modern languages. House's ambition was to make Norman *the* linguistic center for the study of American Indian languages. In 1940, he finally got permission to offer a course in Cherokee—if he could find a teacher. He sent a colleague on an odyssey into the rarefied world of linguistics. She quickly found SIL and Ken Pike. House offered to find room at Norman for SIL sight unseen, along with college credit for students. To Cam, it all sounded like the horns of Jericho, tumbling the walls of anonymity. He immediately grasped the significance of what Norman offered SIL: academic respectability.

The following summer, Cam and Pike traveled to Oklahoma and into success. They taught more than 130 students. With its Bible Belt location in the middle of a population sympathetic to Fundamentalism, Norman doubled SIL's enrollment in a single year.

Cam now moved rapidly to stake his claim for independence. Having already been pressed by the Pioneer Mission Agency to handle his own funds, he took the occasion formally to proclaim the dual identity of his organization. He worked out a delicate formula whereby those who supported his evangelical goals but were less keen on a scientific emphasis could be reconciled with those who supported SIL's work but were leery of a scientific organization focusing on the Bible. Cam's solution was simple: two organizations, both incorporated in California, one retaining SIL's name and 1937 constitution, the other adopting intact the old doctrinal statement of the China Inland Mission and the name Wycliffe Bible Translators. The organizations would have the same members and interlocking boards, but they would also offer the membership and its supporters two faces, one turned toward science, the other toward God.

There was another obvious boon to the Janus-like identity: The religious face, Wycliffe, could be turned toward Fundamentalist donors in the United States; the scientific face, SIL, now officially sanctioned by a major American university, could simultaneously turn toward Latin American governments that had to coexist with powerful Catholic bishops.

For the first time, Cam was not worried about money. He had recently won over Al Johnson, a retired Chicago millionaire, who, approaching Heaven's Gate, offered Cam financial support. Better still, one of Cam's oldest backers, citrus king Charles Fuller, had just helped establish a powerful new organization, the National Association of Evangelicals.

Cam's ambitions were afire. "Who will open Tibet, or claim the last acre of the Amazon, the hills of central India, the jungles of Borneo, the steppes of Siberia—the merchant or the missionary?" he challenged his followers. "When the war is over, let us take up the Sword of the Spirit and march."[3]

The military atmosphere of those days permeated the young organization. Terms like *occupation,* to describe the entry of missionaries into a land, were revived with vigor. Cam's new *Translation* magazine would soon encourage supporters in 1944 to pray "to weaken the enemy, enabling us to take his long-prepared and well-fortified positions. . . . Your praying for us should be so fervent and so concentrated and continuous that the enemy may be blasted out of the positions that we are preparing to take: in all the tribes of Mexico, in the continent of South America, and beyond."[4]

Adding flesh to the vernacular were the Navigators, an organization of Fundamentalist servicemen founded by Dawson Trotman, a Long Beach, California, evangelist. One of Trotman's converts had joined SIL in 1940, and the Navigators underwrote his translation work among the Yaqui Indians of Mexico. Through Trotman, Cam could have access to a huge number of women and men with skills in everything from nursing and mechanics to flying, providing SIL with a practical balance to the academic talents of less worldly men like Pike.

Cam dashed off a letter to Trotman, inviting him to come down to Mexico that fall to see SILers in operation and minister to them. Trotman arrived in time to attend the annual meeting and left a member of Wycliffe's board. The harvest of Navigators would be rich for Cam, including five future SIL pioneers who would go on to Cam's first beachhead in the Amazon: Peru.

The twin pillars of SIL's growth, the university and the military, were now in place. Cam next set up his own permanent organization with a home board where his largest donors were, in southern California. The $2,400 per month minimum that Cam projected SIL as needing was easily met by heaven. "As a matter of fact," he cheerily announced to his followers, "God is sending in through the Glendale office and direct to our workers well over $4,000 a month."[5] All that remained was for Peru to extend an invitation.

An invitation from Peru was no longer as simple as it once had seemed. Moisés Sáenz had returned to Peru as Mexico's ambassador after hosting the Pátzcuaro Conference. But Sáenz had died unexpectedly in the fall of 1941, leaving the missionary without an avenue to Lima's higher circles.

The American Bible Society's request to Pike in 1943 to go to the Andes, therefore, seemed a bolt from the hand of God. It left Cam breathless with praise for the Lord—and soon for Nelson Rockefeller as well.

By late 1943 Pike was in Lima standing nervously before Education Minister Enrique de la Rosa. But his association with the CIAA, where the Peruvian president's son worked, again cast its spell. He spoke of the bilingual education program in which he and Fries were involved and then told de la Rosa of the University of Oklahoma's SIL. De la Rosa was impressed. He invited Pike to give a series of lectures to all teachers of high school English in Peru and then did one better: He suggested that SIL enter Peru to work with the jungle tribes.

Cam was overjoyed. After two frustrating decades, the Amazon was at last beckoning.

He now allowed himself to return to an idea he had proposed to L. L. Legters many years before: a jungle training camp. The Amazon was no quiet Indian village in Mexico. The tribes there were armed and resisted intruders to the point of hunting heads. The jungle they lived in was a seething mass of poisonous snakes, insects, and wild animals, including jaguars that still ran off with children. If his young recruits were to have any chance of surviving, they would need training in more than linguistics—and in more than an academic environment.

Cam needed a jungle.

Intrigue in the Jungle

Far to the south, in Mexico along the border of Guatemala, was just such a place, a tropical rain forest botanically almost an extension of the Amazon. Here, in the state of Chiapas, where more than 80 percent of the population was Indian, lived the mysterious Lacondóns, a small tribe of robed, long-haired descendants of the Maya who burned incense and prayed to homemade clay figures of Mayan gods. This isolated tribe lived within a rich mahogany and chicle forest whose harvesting the Camacho government wanted to control.

Chiapas had always been a scene of Indian suffering. Bishop Bartolomé de Las Casas had waged his famous campaign for Indian survival in this state, only to see his efforts steadily undermined. Over the succeeding four centuries, landowning *criollos,* who considered themselves direct descendants of the conquistadores, thought they had a right to outdo their forebears when it came to exploitation. Other Mayan tribes also came under the Spanish yoke. But the Lacondóns never surrendered. Instead, they retreated deeper into the rain forest of their Mayan ancestors, inspiring still one more legend about a lost tribe of Israel.

It was in 1944, the same year that Kenneth Pike suddenly chose to study Mayan languages, that Cam decided to search the Lacondón forest for a suitable site for SIL's jungle training camp. And in this effort, as in so many other things, his way was paved by the Rockefellers.

Nelson Rockefeller had encouraged U.S.-sponsored archaeological expeditions into Latin America during the war. These expeditions generated useful data on local customs and resources, as well as headlines complimentary to the United States.

In 1942 Nelson took an interest in Chiapas that extended beyond the intellectual. The area was reported to be a hotbed of Nazi spies. German-owned *fincas* had dominated coffee production in the area, just as they had in neighboring Guatemala, one of the first non-Axis countries to recognize Franco's fascist Spain.

"German interests in Chiapas almost broke up an Indian Congress called by the Mexican Department of Indian Affairs," an official of the Bureau of Indian Affairs (BIA) had reported to Rockefeller in December 1941, "and continue to impede the Government's program in that native region. . . . Friction among the natives along the borders of Guatemala and Mexico is reported as foreign inspired. Falangist periodicals such as 'Reconstruction,' 'Hispanidad,' 'El Sinarquista' and others have given considerable attention to the Indians."[6]

Rockefeller believed in fighting propaganda with propaganda. He arranged a screening of *The Road to Mayapan* for President Roosevelt at the White House. The film depicted the Lacondóns as a lost tribe that had built a Mayan "Lost City." Mayapan, however, was in the Yucatán peninsula, far to the north and east of Chiapas, and the filmed city actually turned out to be the well-known ruins of Tonalá, on the Pacific Coast east of the Sierra Madre mountains and far from the Lacondóns.

The film was nevertheless purchased by the CIAA to stir public interest in the Lacondón Indians. It provided a scientific rationale for American presence in their jungle, just as the first of three American expeditions within a period of two years penetrated the Lacondón forest.

Funded by the Rockefeller Foundation, the first expedition was led by Sol Tax, one of five members of the Anthropology Advisory Committee to the new National Indian Institute funded by the CIAA. Before the expedition even set off, however, its leader was mired in controversy.

Tax had recently astounded colleagues by claiming that there was no racial problem in Guatemala's treatment of Indians. "The 'race problem' had solved itself," he asserted, through intermarriage.[7]

In denying the Indians' racial identity, Tax was providing a scholarly rationale for undermining their untitled land claims and hastening their assimilation as a cheap labor force. His position offended many Indianists, chief among them BIA Commissioner John Collier. Collier accused Tax of speeding up the disappearance of Indian culture, whitewashing the Indians' annihilation by accepting the destruction of their cultures as inevitable. He, on the other hand, advocated the preservation of Indian culture through nation-building, a role Collier hoped the Inter-American Indian Institute would embrace. Denying the Indians their unique identity, in Collier's view, was racism pure and simple.

The debate was irrelevant; Rockefeller money had already tipped the balance in favor of Tax. Tax's claim that language was the only remaining barrier to assimilation for the Indian had gotten him named head of the Rockefeller Foundation's Yucatán Linguistics Surveys,[8] and money was sent down to Mexico to create five anthropological fellowships.

The following year, Tax led his first column into the Lacondón jungle, successfully made contact with the Indians, and returned to Mexico City's accolades. He spent 1943 studying his notes and lecturing as a guest professor at the National School of Anthropology under a Rockefeller grant. Another guest professor that year was SIL's own Kenneth Pike.

The Drafting of SIL

By 1943, the CIAA, working with the Rockefeller-financed American Council of Learned Societies (ACLS) and the Office of Education, incorporated linguists, such as Pike and Fries, into an entrenched Intensive Language Program. The program was now militarized into courses for both United States and Latin American military officers. With the dramatic turn in the war and the eventual Allied victory in sight, the threat of invasion was removed from the Americas. Yet the training of Latin America's military intensified, but as the beginning of what would become a postwar regional military pact.

In November, as the CIAA reviewed the progress of an intensive English course for Ecuadorian pilots,[9] SIL was asked to join in the militarization. Cam snapped up the offer. America's traditional separation of church and state had already been compromised by the stipends and university facilities received from

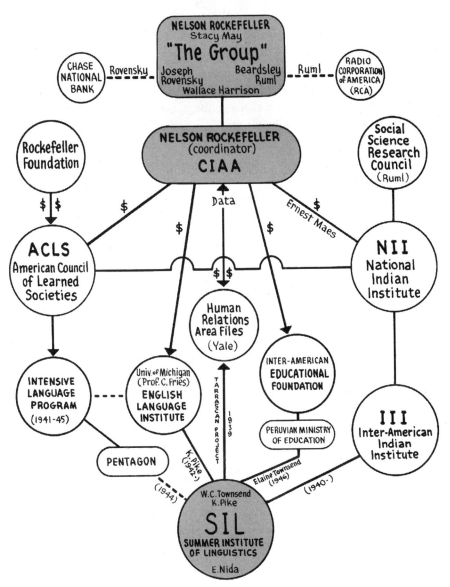

Rockefeller Wartime Network of Influence and SIL
(1940–1946)

the state of Oklahoma. To avoid crossing over the line would have required an understanding of the republic's foundations and of the founders' warning against state-sponsored religion. What SIL saw, instead, was an opportunity for money and recruits, rather than a peril to the neutrality of its religious identity in foreign lands.

This was not the first time that SIL had served U.S. government intelligence purposes during the war. In 1942, after discussions in Washington with "some men who are interested in furthering good will between our countries," Cam specifically requested SIL's Mexico City office to solicit reports from "any of our workers who may have observed efforts on the part of anyone to make the Indians think that Americans are not their friends." Cam's directive ended with a message, "Please give my regards to Mr. Lockett in case you should see him in this connection."[10] Thomas Lockett, commercial attaché, was Cam's confidential contact at the embassy after Ambassador Daniels departed in 1941. Lockett carried out intelligence missions for Washington, identifying suspected Nazi sympathizers and their companies for Berle and Rockefeller.[11] SIL was one of his intelligence sources.

SIL had helped gather anthropological information on the Tarascan Indians that ended up in Nelson Rockefeller's intelligence files. The files contained cross-references to reveal behavioral patterns among Indian peoples in everything from socialization (including aggressive tendencies) and personality traits, drives, emotions, and language structure, to political intrigue, kinship ties, traditional authority, mineral resources, exploitation, and labor relations. Rockefeller called these data the Strategic Index of Latin America.[12]

Indians in general, precisely because of their oppression and poverty, were suspected of being susceptible to both fascists on the right and communists on the left.[13] The CIAA noted that "the strategic importance of the Indians has not been overlooked by friends of the Axis powers. The German courts have decreed Indians to be Aryans. Anti-American and anti-democratic propaganda addressed to or against Indian groups is widespread. . . . Already German propaganda among Indians has resulted in sabotage of tin production in Bolivia, and similar difficulties can be expected in other areas."[14]

The Inter-American Institute, which coordinated research with the CIAA on Indian conditions in Latin America, was to become a "clearinghouse of information" for leading anthropologists, providing "analysis on failure and success of Indian work."[15] This pragmatic approach to Indians—regarding them as objects of study to meet strategic wartime needs—coincided with the growing popularity of "applied anthropology" on both sides of the Atlantic during the war. Developed first by the British to meet the needs of colonial administrators, applied anthropology was embraced by a wide array of U.S. government agencies during World War II. Harvard anthropologist Clyde Kluckhohn explained why: "If we know a culture, we know what various classes of individuals within it expect from each other—and from outsiders." As an example, he offered the dilemma of American

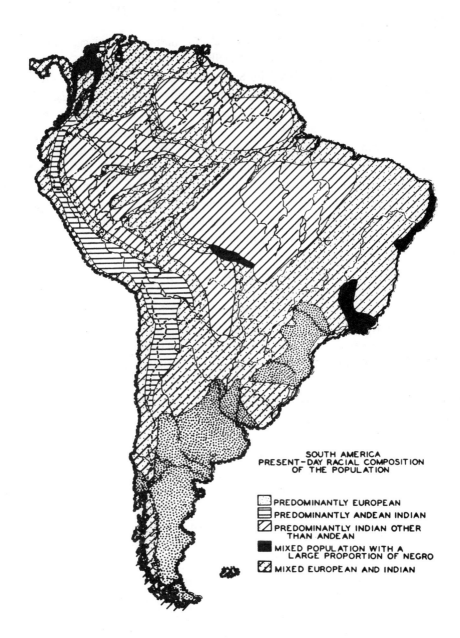

SOUTH AMERICA
PRESENT-DAY RACIAL COMPOSITION
OF THE POPULATION

☐ PREDOMINANTLY EUROPEAN
⊟ PREDOMINANTLY ANDEAN INDIAN
▨ PREDOMINANTLY INDIAN OTHER
      THAN ANDEAN
■ MIXED POPULATION WITH A
      LARGE PROPORTION OF NEGRO
▨ MIXED EUROPEAN AND INDIAN

As U.S. war industries geared up for increased extraction of South America's natural resources during World War II, Rockefeller's CIAA was sensitive to racial compositions of targeted South American labor force

Source: CIAA Files, U.S. National Archives.

army paratroopers dropped in a remote jungle in Thailand. What kind of reception would they receive?

The U.S. government left nothing to chance, hiring anthropologists, according to Kluckhohn, to serve in "Military Intelligence, the Department of State, OSS, Board of Economic Warfare, the Strategic Bombing Survey, the Military Government, Selective Service Organization, Office of Naval Intelligence, the Office of War Information, the FBI, . . . the medical branch of the Army Air Forces and Chemical Warfare Division."[16]

SIL, with its growing expertise in linguistics, proved equally useful. "The U.S. Government," Cam announced to SILers in November 1943, "has asked the Summer Institute of Linguistics to give its courses to one hundred army and navy officers, beginning May 1st. . . . The Government will pay $1,000 a month for the instruction." Cam hoped for a quid pro quo. "May we not expect that some of the officers will become Bible translators after the war?"[17]

The Lacondón Challenge

While Cam's SIL was being drawn into Rockefeller's orbit, Cam's old friend, Frank Tannenbaum, remained true to John Collier's progressive wing of the Indianist movement. As if in response to Tax's 1942 expedition, Tannenbaum joined archaeologist Franz Blom and Mexico's J. E. Palacios in their own expedition to the Lacondóns in 1943.

Blom was an old hand. He had first entered the jungles of southern Mexico in 1919 when oil, not Indians, was his primary concern. Intrigued by the Mayan ruins he found, Blom gave up oil and took up archaeology. He was the first man to map the Lacondón area as part of a 1925 ethnographic survey of the Maya.

The results of Blom's current expedition belied SIL's raison d'être among the Lacondóns. The Lacondóns, the expedition found, were living under better conditions than when they were last studied by the government in 1936. Now crops were in evidence, and the whiskey that reflected the exploitation of lumber and gum in the mountains was gone. And, most important, Spanish was now widely spoken.[18]

Cam nevertheless thought that Bible translators were needed for the Lacondóns. His belief was confirmed when Ken Pike returned with the good news from Peru. Cam showed his followers that, for SIL at least, more was at stake with the Lacondóns than their souls. As Tax began his second Rockefeller expedition to the Lacondóns in 1944, Cam traveled to the end of the Lacondón jungle, to the Bulnes family's Finca El Real, and sought out its owner, Jaime Bulnes.

Jaime's mother was an American named Mannie Flanagan, a claimed relative of the McCormicks, Nelson Rockefeller's cousins and owners of large henequen plantations in the Yucatán. Bulnes & Company had some unused land[19] that Cam wanted. It was a choice parcel. Called "Yashaquintala," or "where the green water flows," by local Tzeltal Indians, it was a beautiful site beside a large river that led into the Lacondón forest, perfect for canoeing and camping. It also had enough cleared land for a landing strip for the airplanes Cam still envisioned crossing the jungles.

Jaime Bulnes was at first reluctant to sell. But Cam soon convinced Bulnes to travel with him back to Mexico City. Whomever Cam took Bulnes to see was persuasive: Bulnes not only gave Cam a long-term lease, but built huts for SIL's first training session. These huts constituted the Main Base. Deeper in the jungle, and barred to outsiders, was the crux of the operation: the Advance Base.

The new recruits would call it Jungle Camp when they arrived the following year. But it was really SIL's boot camp, a grueling initiation rite into a closed society where mostly young recruits from suburbs and small towns were thrown on the mercies of SIL leaders for survival. Trainees were put through endurance swimming, steering down rapids in dugout canoes, and an intensive physical workout each day. At night they were required to take turns giving testimony to their surrender to the Lord. As the physical training exhausted their bodies, lectures and confessions around nightly campfires exhausted their emotions. The only respites were evenings spent alone in the black jungle, suspended in hammocks under trees alive with howls and gnats, or with one of the Tzeltal families whom Cam had recruited into a network of language informants for the trainees to use for linguistic drills. Hikes were arranged to visit Lacondón homes, among whom Cam had already placed two translators; to help Tax and Blom excavate a Mayan pyramid; or to help mahogany lumbermen survey a river valley so that more of the Lacondóns' forest could be cut away.[20]

Like U.S. Marine recruits at Parris Island, trainees forged personal bonds that would last a lifetime; unlike U.S. Marine recruits, however, SILers seldom experienced anything in the future as punishing as Jungle Camp.

But SILers came out of it well prepared for the worst, perhaps too well prepared—their cultural insularity was actually reinforced. And with few exceptions, they also came out loyal to their new Wycliffe "family," even to the point of accepting SIL's censorship of their letters used as circulars to friends and family back home who financially supported the missionaries.

Christmas 1944 saw the Townsends at Al Johnson's spacious Hollywood home, where Cam set to work on a biography of Cárdenas. On December 23, just as Cam and Elvira were climbing into bed, Elvira collapsed in Cam's arms gasping for air. Within twenty-four hours, she was dead. Cam's hectic pace had finally exacted its toll.

At the Johnson-paid funeral in Glendale, California, Cam was too shattered to speak. He had written an eloquent speech, but it was more about himself than his wife and ended in a passionate call not for Elvira, but for his own crusade. Dawson Trotman read it for him:

> If I have permitted hardships, dangers, pleasures, and the powerful chords of human love to swerve me at times from full obedience, henceforth, "none of these things shall move me." . . .
>
> This pledge is not taken lightly. It has been burned into my soul, and though the branding processes have not been easy, the pain now seems like nothing as I visualize the fruit and joy of a truly all-out effort for my Savior and the unevangelized tribes that need Him so.
>
> The task of giving God's Word to all the peoples of the earth can be finished in this generation.[21]

Elvira was then lowered into her grave.

Cam would remarry within a year and a half, this time to one of his young recruits, a strong woman half his age who, his biographer would affirm, "never questioned his leadership."[22]

Like all his recruits, she followed him into the Green Hell.

10

THE SHINING DREAM

The Rubber Ploy

At the end of 1941, Berent Friele, the CIAA man in Brazil, received a letter from Brazil's agricultural director for the Amazon. It was a rapturous description of the immense riches of the Amazon:

> petroleum at the sources of the Juruá; rubber at the head of the Madeira river, north of Mato Grosso; gold in the bowels of the formation of our Amazon archaean . . . as well as in the virgin lands of Rondonia; fibers for coarse textiles, from the archaean to the quartenary lands of the Amazon valley; meat of every sort to be obtained from the transformation of the forests of the low Amazon into ever green pastures; coal in the Pennsylvanian canals of the Amazon Basin; aluminum, in the form of an island, facing Maranhao; vegetable oils, fish, entomotoxic plants throughout the whole region—everything that can represent the wealth of an immense empire is kept intact waiting for the elements of man and capital in order to be transformed in utilities for civilization which today clamors desperately for American action.[1]

Not that Nelson needed to be seduced. The vast Amazonian region had caught Nelson's attention in 1940. With Japanese armies overrunning the rubber plantations of French Indochina and British Malaya, Brazil's president Getúlio Vargas saw an opportunity to earn badly needed foreign exchange by reviving rubber production in the wild rubber forest of the Amazon. By the time he paid a personal visit to the Amazon in October, however, his vision for Amazonian development extended far beyond rubber.

"I did not come to the Amazon region as a tourist who finds here so many reasons to be dazzled and overcome," he told an audience in Pôrto Velho, rubber capital of the Madeira River Valley. "I came with the purpose of learning the practical possibilities of putting into execution a plan for the systematic exploitation of the riches of the great valley and its development." Vargas's plan consisted of two parts—sanitation and colonization—and he promised free land and farm tools to the homesteaders he had transported from Brazil's impoverished Northeast.

But his most surprising announcement was that he planned to "intensify industrial exploitation" of the Amazon by American corporations. "To that end there are already arriving at the government's invitation North American industrialists interested in collaborating with us in developing the Amazon region, where their capital and technical resources find a continuing profitable application."[2]

This was a new turn for a leader who had been considered a fascist sympathizer. Vargas had come to power in 1930 with an aura of intense nationalism, leading an army of gauchos from the south and enjoying the support of Brazilian Germans and disgruntled homesteaders who had been squeezed out of the São Paulo–led export-oriented economy by the world depression.

Once in office, President Vargas initiated a series of drastic measures that not only restored Brazil's economy, but enhanced Germany's participation in its growth. After 1934, Hitler made Brazil Germany's leading trade partner in South America.[3]

Germany, which replaced the United States as Brazil's top source of foreign trade, was not alone. In 1934, Mussolini sent the longest and largest flight of military planes in history to Rio de Janeiro to flutter the hearts of the Brazilian military. This performance was outdone in 1938 by a greater display of *machismo* affection: he launched his son, Bruno, fresh from aerial heroics over defenseless Ethiopian villages, on a trans-Atlantic flight. When Bruno at last descended on an anxious Rio, he donated his plane to Vargas's "New State," triggering a delirium of enthusiasm.

Vargas's romance with the Axis powers suddenly turned sour when the fascist Integralista party tried an insurrection in 1938. If this attempted coup was a splash of cold reality, American dollars soon provided the fount of warmer relations, with the development of the Amazon high on Vargas's list of priorities.

Up to that point, the only significant American investment in the Amazon was Ford Motor Company's failed Fordlândia rubber plantation, covering 7,943 square miles along the east bank of the Tapajós River, a tributary to the Amazon River in the northern state of Pará. The terrain was too steep to allow easy operations, and the local soil was deemed unreceptive to the *Hevea brasiliensis* rubber tree. In fact, the clearing of the rain forest had removed the plant and animal diversity that had allowed most rubber trees to survive attacks by insects and disease, particularly *dothidella vlei*, commonly known as South American leaf blight. Overconcentrations of rubber trees made them too vulnerable to survive in the Amazon. After his first plantation was almost destroyed, a second 800,000-acre tract was carved out of the jungle ninety miles downriver at Belterra, but Ford could not find enough men who were willing to work for low wages. The only labor sources were Indians and descendants of runaway African slaves who had intermarried with the Indians. Although they were good workers, a U.S. Embassy report in 1938 reviewed by the CIAA noted that "life is sustained at their jungle homes with so little effort that employment for wages is not attractive."[4] The blight struck again, and Ford had all but abandoned the plantations when World War II created rubber shortages, convincing him to hold on, claiming patriotic reasons, not the hope of recovering the $9 million he had already invested in the Amazon venture.

At first, Rockefeller showed little interest in either the Amazon or the rubber crisis, even after Japanese invasions and U-boat sinkings of Allied shipping disrupted rubber supplies to the United States. He left the matter to Agriculture Secretary Henry Wallace, who got a $500,000 appropriation to send rubber technicians to Latin America. But when CIAA aide Earl Parker Hanson brought news that Vargas was seriously proceeding with his Amazon development plan, Nelson suddenly made rubber—and development of the whole Amazon valley—a priority. He adopted Hanson's suggestion that Berent Friele should "ask his Brazilian friends if they want a major survey. . . . Get together a hell of a big party or even organize a corporation, jointly with Brazil immediately."[5]

Friele was the perfect man to present the Amazon development program to the Brazilians. He had been president of the Brazilian-American Association of New York and, not coincidentally, of the American Coffee Corporation as well. He represented the largest American company engaged in the largest American trade with South America's largest country.

Nelson wrote a four-page memorandum in September 1941 for Friele to circulate in Brazil, offering to cooperate "in the development of the Amazon along the lines suggested by the Brazilian Government"[6] and proposing a survey of the Amazon basin's resources and problems. Friele passed it on to the U.S. Embassy for review and held his breath.

The response from Ambassador Jefferson Caffery, one of the State Department's top troubleshooters in Latin America, was wary:

> Survey findings would, indirectly at least, be critical of many existing conditions in the Amazon, and recommendations as to solutions of existing problems would, in many cases, inevitably arouse the antagonism of established interests and officialdom. The survey, if undertaken, should therefore be handled as a joint project, and should have as a prerequisite the full backing of the Brazilian Government.[7]

Nelson had no such intentions. Joint sponsorships, yes; joint control, never.

Besides, Nelson had submitted his proposal to Brazilian Finance Minister Arthur de Souza Costa and President Vargas and had gotten their approval. The Rio newspapers were already full of approving editorials and headlines.

Nelson sincerely favored joint ventures. He and Ambassador-to-Mexico Josephus Daniels had convinced President Roosevelt that more was to be gained against the Axis powers by actually *helping* Latin American governments to develop their resources than by insisting only on reciprocal trade agreements.

Therefore, a series of agreements were struck. The first rubber agreement with Brazil in October 1940 pledged to assist the long-term development of Brazil's rubber industry. In return, Brazil cut off rubber sales to the Axis powers and reserved rubber for the United States, with the U.S. Rubber Reserve Corporation acting as the purchasing agent for Firestone and Goodyear. The rubber pact was then expanded into a broader agreement on strategic materials in May 1941. According to that agreement, Brazil provided iron ore and other strategic minerals in return for more than $20 million in financing for its Volta Redonda steel project, funds that private American steel companies had refused to provide.

Nelson pursued this dual policy of protecting American corporate markets and encouraging the diversification of Latin American economies through 1941. But after Japan's attack on Pearl Harbor, Washington began to view economic development as either a luxury it could no longer afford or one that had to be subsumed under American war priorities.

Brazilians now began to worry that rubber and inter-American solidarity might be used as a wedge to open their Amazon territories to American control.

Brazil also was concerned that the involvement of other Amazon basin countries whose governments were less strong and more susceptible to U.S. pressures might result in either U.S. control or territorial claims by these governments on the Brazilian Amazon. Peru and Ecuador were at the time engaged in just such a border dispute over Amazonian lands that were believed (correctly, it turned out) to contain oil deposits.

Amazon rubber production would indeed require cross-border operations. A young American botanist at Harvard's Peabody Museum, Dr. Richard Evans Schultes, had recently toured Mexico (including Chiapas) for the Rockefeller Foundation's Agricultural Survey[8] and was already at work gathering seven tons of rubber seeds in the tropical Putumayo and Vaupés regions of southern Colombia— and passing on intelligence on the political sympathies of his Colombian colleagues.[9] This was not out of character for the American war effort. Shortly after Pearl Harbor, Nelson authorized the Department of Agriculture's request for a special $100,000 allocation to employ spies for the strategic-materials stockpile program to obtain military and naval intelligence.[10]

The authorization of spying was precisely what the Vargas government feared. Since the CIAA had assisted in removing German influence from Brazil's airlines, its intelligence-gathering and propaganda capacities were no secret. The Brazilian people were also bitter about the British smuggling rubber seeds out of Brazil at the turn of the century to cultivate plantations in British colonies in the Far East. These actions spelled Waterloo for the wild Brazilian species, triggering an economic decline in the Amazon.

Brazil therefore tried to confine Rockefeller's activities to supplying technicians who would be under Brazilian control. Nelson, however, was not easily deterred. He saw rubber as merely the opening wedge into the Amazon.

The Amazon Plan

On Christmas Day, 1942, the jungle seemed a long way off as Nelson watched his children frolicking around the Christmas tree. But the Amazon suddenly burst into his thoughts when he tore open the wrappings of a small gift from Berent Friele, the CIAA's man in Brazil. It was a copy of *Journey to Manaos*, CIAA aide Earl Parker Hanson's account of his 1931–1932 trip to the Amazon.

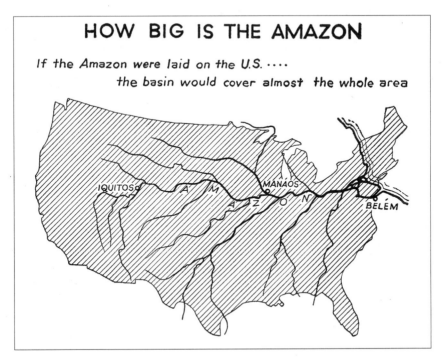

HOW BIG IS THE AMAZON

*If the Amazon were laid on the U.S. ····
the basin would cover almost the whole area*

IQUITOS   A M A Z O N   MANAOS   BELÉM

CIAA adviser Earl Parker Hanson used this map to help promote Amazon development.
Source: Earl Parker Hanson, *The Amazon: A New Frontier* (New York: Foreign Policy Association, 1944).

Hanson believed that "the settling of South America's interior would give another breathing spell to our civilized world. . . . I find myself confronted at every turn by the romantic argument that the conquest of South America's wilderness would do for the Western hemisphere what the conquest of the West did for the United States at a critical time."[11]

Friele knew Nelson would want to have this book. He had been alerted to it by Morris L. Cooke, who was now in Rio heading the U.S. Industrial Mission to Brazil. Cooke had proposed that a giant series of locks and canals could link the oil fields of Venezuela's Orinoco with the Amazon basin without having to brave the German submarine wolf packs off the Atlantic Coast. The project was discussed during Nelson's recent visit to Rio to sign a health-and-sanitation agreement with the Brazilian government. Nelson had immediately grasped the enormous economic implications and embraced the idea as a CIAA project.

"You may well have inspired Nelson with the shining dream of regional development,"[12] Friele wrote Cooke.

Nelson's "shining dream" had, in fact, been percolating for well over a year, since Hanson had warned him that Vargas was making his own plans for the Amazon. Vargas, for his part, had been thrown into a quandary as soon as Nelson's proposals for an Amazon survey had begun to circulate in the fall of 1941.

On the one hand, Foreign Minister Oswaldo Aranha had urged Vargas to allow the Americans to develop the Amazon. On the other hand, Finance Minister Souza Costa had urged caution and the principle of Brazilian control. Vargas decided to send Souza Costa to Washington into the bear's den.

Nelson summoned all the forces at his command before this meeting with Souza Costa. He then had a formal resolution hurriedly drawn up for members of his Policy Committee, allocating $200,000 for a "comprehensive survey study of the Amazon basin, the survey to be used as a basis for carrying out specific cooperative projects." Rockefeller wanted to send down survey teams of experts in agriculture, tropical settlement, tropical disease, transportation, nutrition, and labor, as well as economists to study the "present status of land ownership in various states of the Amazon basin," all "under the guidance of an outstanding qualified administrator."[13] Nelson had already decided who that special someone would be: J. C. King. King was vice president of Johnson & Johnson, in charge of operations in Brazil and Argentina. He had a reputation among businessmen in both countries as a man who could get difficult projects under way. Most important for Rockefeller's purposes, he also knew the Amazon, the source of most plants used in the preparation of medicines. His work had also placed him at the cutting edge of American penetration of the South American drug market and of Western medicine's advance into the jungle interior.

He appreciated that Brazilian sensitivities would require a Brazilian president of his Amazon Valley Corporation. But that was all right; the real power would be in the hands of the managing director, King. True to his West Point training, King would also be loyal to his superior, namely, Nelson Rockefeller. "Nelson doesn't expect you to be a yes-man," one CIAA aide explained, "but he does expect you to be a Rockefeller man—first, last, and always."[14]

Everything was in place as Nelson set up the first of his lunch meetings with the visiting Brazilians. All the CIAA's rubber technicians were ready to go. King was waiting only for his appointment to be formalized, and he would begin his survey. Texas Congressmen Dick Kleberg and Sam Rayburn were also on board, thanks to Nelson's backslapping and Friele's "confidential" report to the Texans on the potentially explosive "Brazilian Political Situation" of an alleged 250,000 German and Japanese in the Amazon area.[15] Rockefeller had also recruited high-level talent from the Department of Agriculture and other agencies.

Backed by some of the most powerful men in the U.S. government, Nelson tried to impress upon Souza Costa that "comprehensive development had to be under the direction of American experts."[16] He walked out of the conference convinced that his charm and power had won the day. He was wrong. Nelson had failed to line up the most important people of all: the Brazilians.

Souza Costa bought time by suggesting that the Americans put their proposal in writing. The CIAA drew up the proposal, got the approval of the other agencies, and set up another meeting. This time Souza Costa was ready. Nelson submitted a proposal for a joint $1 million Amazon Development Corporation to administer $5 million in loans from the Federal Loan Agency. There were three hitches: (1) the United States would name the managing director, (2) Brazil would have to establish and maintain a quota for the internal consumption of rubber, and (3) all the surplus would go to the United States.

The Brazilian representatives, although willing to try to get Vargas's assent to the last two conditions, had no authority to agree to them. But they immediately took exception to losing control over the development of most of their own country.

Nelson dug in. He insisted that "we should be entitled to name the managing Director in a true charge of operation," since "by far the greater part of the funds of the corporation would be advanced by us." Besides, the Brazilians had allowed a "past history of decline in Amazon rubber production," and the war created an "urgency compelling us to take no chances of its repetition." He agreed only to "give the aspect of control further consideration."[17]

Nelson believed that he held the trump card: $100 million in U.S. credits already offered to Brazil. Cotton magnate Will Clayton, now deputy administrator of the Federal Loan Agency, proposed that Nelson simply set up the Amazon Valley Corporation himself and use $5 million that could be advanced from the Rubber Reserve Corporation. It was a classic case of American big-businessmen thinking money could buy anything.

But to patriotic Brazilians in the Vargas government, Brazil's Amazon—seen then as Brazil's future—was not for sale. Nelson had lost their trust. As long as Vargas was in power, it would never be completely regained.

State Department Undersecretary Sumner Welles took matters into his own hands. Although Nelson looked upon Welles as a mentor, the undersecretary was not prepared to sacrifice Brazilian cooperation to Nelson's personal agenda for the Amazon. He ignored Rockefeller's and Clayton's proposals, conducted his own negotiations, and concluded an agreement with Souza Costa on March 3 that scrapped the idea of the Amazon Valley Corporation and gave the funding and carrying out of the rubber project to the Rubber Reserve Corporation. This left the approval of all Amazon projects in the hands of the Brazilians.

In his heart, Nelson never accepted the State Department's edict about the Amazon. But when it came to policy, Roosevelt had already made it clear that the State Department had the last word.

"Look, Nelson," the smiling president said from behind his big desk, "I know that you're in a difficult situation in regard to State. . . . But understand this—it is up to you to get along with them because if it ever comes to a show-down between your office and State, I will have no choice but to back the Department and Mr. Welles."[18]

Nelson consulted with Welles. He wanted to use his $200,000 allocation for the Amazon survey. But his ambition had already poisoned the well. Welles did not see any need for the survey. If tropical products needed to be developed, the new Rubber Development Corporation should easily be able to carry out the task with its $100 million. Asked by Welles to specify what tropical products were so important to require King's survey, Nelson agreed to send him a list. He never did.

Time was running out. Friele and King decided to go ahead with the survey Rockefeller wanted. King left immediately for Brazil.

The Valley of Death

J. C. King was excited at the prospect of boarding a riverboat in Belém, Brazil's major port on the Amazon. From here he would plunge into the interior, traveling more than 4,000 miles, surveying the people and resources as part of his month-long secret mission. Both he and Nelson knew that the Amazonian rain forest held many more secrets beneath its dense undergrowth than the locations of the ubiquitous rubber plant.

But he had barely stepped on board when he became uneasy. "I examined [the] crew of [the] ship," he wrote Friele. "Out of 35, 24 admitted to syphilis, 22 have, or had, gonorrhea. Only 4 disclaimed either. . . . Every boy waiting on passengers' table was syphilitic. Crew had 522 children; 20 dead."[19]

It was a ship of death, taking souls into a Green Hell.

As he cruised deeper into the jungle, he passed whole towns that seemed to be dying. At ports where the boat stopped to pick up fuel and passengers, he confirmed his worst suspicions: The rampant disease he had found aboard was only a token of the horror on shore.

None of the villagers had received any medical aid. Nurses and doctors were unheard of, and medicine was nonexistent, "although several people offered to pay for anything I could supply. Besides malaria (and possible typhoid), people complained of liver, kidneys, intestines, young women of irregular periods or complete stoppage with accompanying symptoms.

". . . There is some rubber in the district, prices are high," he reported, "but there is a feeling of hopelessness and abandonment, for what good is money if they keep on dying. . . . No new people have come in years for who would care to live in a village of despair and death."[20]

What made the suffering of the Amazon Valley all the more tragic was its chronic nature. Like so many travelers before him, King was familiar with the Amazon's tormented past. In his report to Nelson, he summarized it in the terse economic terms a Rockefeller could understand:

> Before the conquest, two million Indians in 500 thriving villages lived between the moribund town of Guripa, on the Zingu (Xingu) and São Louis de Maranhão. A century later, the sword and the white man's disease had reduced their numbers to 800 fighting men. After 400 years of civilized rule, the population is less than when Orellana crossed the Andes from Peru, in 1540, to descend the entire length of the Amazon. A well balanced economy was destroyed. Today a large part of the food consumed is imported. . . . The economic history of Brazil is a mirror of its racial origin. . . . Her record of internal migration is a record of pursuit of immediate wealth, from the sugar of Pernambuco to the gold of Minas (Gerais), to the cotton of the northeast, to the rubber of the Amazon.[21]

The situation did not improve when King boarded the J. P. Morgan-financed railroad at Pôrto Velho. Thousands of people had died building this railroad for rubber barons. At first, they were veterans from the Panama Canal, confident as they again pounded rails into ties between tropical hills. However, the night became a singing nightmare of millions of hungry mosquitoes. When these men were dead, their place in the Amazon sun was taken by sons of southern Germany and Italy, peasants dispossessed of their lands and hopeful of a new start in the New World. They found only an old one of exploitation and a final reward among rows of lonely crosses.

"Morgan's Folly," as it came to be called, slowly, mercilessly, bored its way through rivers and valleys, turning each hill it passed into a cemetery. Civilization had at last arrived, a Prometheus bound by iron pounded into wood at the cost, so legend said, of a human life for every tie.

King headed west into Acre, where the rubber forests were richer. Over and over, his notes were the same:

> Of *seringueiros* [rubber collectors] moved in last year to Abuna region, 10% had died, 20% were non productive because of illness. This was normal.
>
> . . . Seven families: Child mortality: 15 living, 5 dead; one girl under 21, 5 children, 2 dead. Now pregnant.
>
> . . . Four families: Child mortality: 11 living, 9 dead. Was asked by father to help lovely one year old girl, dying.
>
> . . . Nova Vida, 67 children alive, 53 dead. . . . Leprosy is said to be spreading on the Purus.

And what of the working conditions themselves?

> The *seringueiro* is expected to work twelve hours daily from May until December, six days a week. He is exposed to the dangers of poisonous snakes, poisonous insects, poisonous worms, poisonous water, wild animals—sometimes wild Indians—and worst of all, to the deadly fevers. His only protection is his knowledge of the jungle, the quickness of his eye and hand, and the use of his knife and gun. There is no doctor—he is simply in the hands of God. For food and supplies he may pay double—triple—eight times the prevailing market of the big cities. For his rubber he gets a half to a fifth of the same market. And when his day's work is ended he returns to his barraca, set on stilts—with its porch, the bedroom and kitchen. He goes to the nearby stream or river to bathe—careful of the alligators, water snakes, man-eating fish and electric eels. If he has been so fortunate as to kill a wild animal on the trail that day he will have meat for supper. . . . Many a time he has left at dawn, his breakfast a cup of black coffee and farina, his knapsack empty of food. Usually he has a bottle of one of the vilest and most powerful of all drinks—cacheca—his week-end companion and solace. His main fruit is the banana, sometimes an orange, seldom a lemon. Lemons are common, but he is convinced that they weaken his sexual powers, and it is for sex that he lives. . . .
>
> The life of the *seringueiro* is the life of the far frontier; removed from all legal and moral restraint, a life of struggle and violence—a twentieth century replica of our old Wild West.

If that were ever to change, "the love of land, so necessary to build an agricultural economy, the backbone of any nation,"[22] had to be developed. In his report to Rockefeller, King outlined his scheme: "At the same time every effort is made to increase the extraction of wild rubber, the ground work should be laid for small experimental stations in three or four key spots, there to serve as a foundation of a vast post-war program for expansion and colonization. These stations would serve equally for experiments with all tropical products supplemental to the economy of the United States of America."[23]

Despite all the horror he had witnessed, King emerged from the Amazon with dreams of a sweeping development that rivaled, indeed surpassed, the settling of the American West.

> The Amazon basin, with its 2,772,000 sq. miles of almost unpopulated and undeveloped land, offers our greatest challenge and hope. Capable of supporting a hundred million people, a vast new outlet for industrial America, a giant reservoir of raw materials to the tropics, the Amazon stands today, the white man's greatest failure. . . .
>
> No plan for the development of the Amazon Valley, however sound in theory, can be successful unless provision is made for an infusion of new blood by selected immigration on a major scale, from impoverished Europe, under the direction of honest, intelligent, public-spirited men, free from selfishness, corruption, indifference and cruelty to man.
>
> We, the United States, are facing one of the great opportunities of history—an opportunity of changing the balance of good and evil—by building a vital force—created from the energy, industry and genius of oppressed millions, whose love of freedom and strength of spirit will urge them to seek new horizons.

All the lofty ideals in this vision could not hide King's Euro-American ethnocentrism, and it was not surprising that the State Department, duly warned by Ambassador Jefferson Caffery, would worry that such plans hatched out of the Rockefeller office might trigger an adverse Brazilian reaction that could jeopardize its cooperation in the war effort, including the rubber-procurement programs. Caffery's experience in Latin America was appreciated. As ambassador to Colombia, he helped Gulf Oil secure the giant Banco concession; in El Salvador, he had prevented the dictator from drawing in U.S. troops during the Pipil Indian insurrection of 1932. His voice was listened to in Washington, and now he was drawing the line in the Brazilian sand against Nelson Rockefeller's plans for the Amazon.

By the time King returned to the United States, Washington was buzzing with anticipation of a coming battle. Ambassador Caffery had alerted Secretary of State Cordell Hull that Rockefeller might try to resurrect his Amazon Development Corporation despite the Brazilian government's objections.[24]

The Indian Question

During his month in the Amazonian interior, King's thinking had ventured beyond the health conditions of prospective rubber workers. He also made contacts with Brazilian businessmen and government officials. Years later, when King, by then the CIA's Chief of Clandestine Services for the Western Hemisphere, commanded CIA covert operations in Latin America, he created precisely such networks, so casually obtained in pursuit of seemingly liberal goals.

King appreciated that "Problem No. 1 is manpower." And the number-one manpower question was whether the Amazonian Indians would be used.

To get some idea, King visited the director of Indian affairs for the state of Pará. The director worked for the renowned Service for the Protection of the Indian (SPI), whose founder, General Cândido Rondon, operated on the pacifist principle "Die if it be necessary, but kill never."*

Having just set up new posts in the Xingu and Tapajós river valleys, the director of Indian affairs in Pará was anxious that Americans not undo all he had begun. The Indians of these valleys were nomadic and elusive and would attack, he told King. "The hostile attitude is justified," King reported to Rockefeller, "because of ill-treatment from whites. On the river Araguaya [Araguaia], twelve Indians were killed brutally eight years ago. They recently killed twelve whites. Reprisals are certain."

"Before the Indian can be civilized the white settler must be. The present white habits of drink and transmission of venereal disease is serious."

The SPI director saw "no possibility of permanent white colonization until further [health and sanitation] protection is afforded [the] *seringueiro*," King wrote. "Predict new colonists . . . will not become permanent settlers until government action is taken."[25]

King's report came at a time when the Amazonian Indian had become a sensitive issue for Nelson Rockefeller. In March, the CIAA had received a telephone call from Charles Collier, John Collier's son and the secretary of the National Indian Institute, inquiring about the status of the Indian in the Amazon region.

Because of past CIAA-BIA collaboration, Charles Collier's inquiry was totally proper. Rockefeller's CIAA had funded the BIA's 1941–1942 survey of Indian programs in Latin America done by Ernest Maes.[26] Maes reported extensively on relations between Venezuela's Carib Indians and the Orinoco oil operations of Nelson's Creole Petroleum, on Indian agricultural production in Colombia, and on the mobilization of Indians in Ecuador for the border war with Peru. Maes's reports also inspired Nelson to fund a visit by nine Latin American Indian admin-

* Rondon's strategy—developed within the rubber zone between 1890 and 1910—was based on the principle of keeping Indians at bay while protecting their lives. Rondon ordered his men to leave gifts on trails for Indians hidden in the jungle, and if attacked, to offer no resistance. Rondon's success in pacifying the tribes won official acclaim in June 1910, when the Brazilian government established the SPI. The government appointed him head of the SPI and decreed that Indians could live peacefully in assigned territories and would work only of their own free will. The government further maintained that the Indians had full right to profit from their work and controlled access to SPI assistance in agriculture, hunting, and education. SPI's new director in Pará intended to revive this tradition

istrators to the United States, where they were given a tour of BIA reservations with special emphasis on John Collier's reforms.[27]

But when it came to Maes's proposals for improving Indian diets, Nelson flatly refused. All John Collier's arguments about improved wages and better nutritional standards increasing markets for U.S. and Latin American products* may have had some interest for Nelson before Pearl Harbor. After war was declared, however, Nelson tried to stay in line with Washington's preoccupation with immediate military goals. If he made an exception, it was to pursue his own goals or the White House's, not the postwar political goals of New Deal Democrats like Secretary of the Interior Harold Ickes or John Collier.

The elder Collier had tried unsuccessfully to appeal directly to Nelson's worries over Nazi propaganda among the Indians.

Then Ickes tried, fitting his beliefs within the War Department's myopia: "In many Latin American countries, the long range hopes for democracy lie in the Indian population . . . [which is] more than 28% of the entire population of Latin America. It is 80% in Peru, Ecuador and Bolivia; 75% in Guatemala; more than 50% in Honduras, Mexico, Nicaragua and El Salvador; 44% in Paraguay."[28]

The appeal failed,[29] and would continue to be rejected until President Roosevelt intervened.

Charles Collier was aware of Rockefeller's lack of interest when he called to ask what was being done to protect the Amazonian Indians from the revival of the rubber business. Collier received a typical bureaucratic runaround, but, wise to the ways of Washington, would not be put off.

He had learned from the Department of Agriculture that there had been no discussion of the status and conditions of the Indians. He asked whether that was true.

It was.

Confirmation that Rockefeller was planning to use Indians merely as rubber gatherers deeply disturbed Collier. The last time Amazonian Indians had been used as labor for rubber gathering, they had been enslaved and killed.

The Wood that Wept

An estimated 2 million Indians lived in Brazil at the time Columbus landed in the Americas. By 1900, 90 percent had "disappeared," lured by Portuguese mis-

---

* "It is not only an important factor in our political and cultural relations with Latin America," Collier wrote Robert G. Caldwell, chairman of CIAA's Cultural Relations Program, in November 1940, "but it is also of supreme importance to the economic stability of the entire Western hemisphere. In addition to the untapped productive energy and material resources of these thirty million Indians, we have a great potential undeveloped market which, by educating the Indians to desire an improvement in their standard of living and by increasing their purchasing power, would relieve greatly the economic strain caused by the loss of European markets." See John Collier to Robert G. Caldwell, November 13, 1940, Brazil—Rubber 1942–1945 folder, RG 66, Box 92, National Archives.

sionaries or dragged at gunpoint from the interior to clear the forests or work the coastal sugar and cotton plantations. As the Indians died of disease, floggings, enslavement, and despair, they were replaced by black slaves brought over from Portugal's African colonies. It was not until 1888 that Brazil abolished slavery, the last country to do so in the Western Hemisphere. Slavery nevertheless continued.

What Eli Whitney's cotton gin had done to revitalize slavery in the U.S. South, Charles Goodyear's vulcanizing of rubber in the United States now did for de facto slavery in Brazil. As the evil-smelling liquid was bled from the jungle and passed down the Amazon through Belém to foreign markets, the former slave town awoke from its slumber. The blood of the Indians' *cahuchu*, "the wood that wept," attracted ravenous companies from across the seas. Armies of *pistoleiros* (hired guns) and workers again swept up the Amazon, probing its furthermost tributaries in the heart of the continent.

The Indians soon became targets of slavers who were armed with the same Winchester "repeater" rifles used to kill Indians in the U.S. West. Flesh and trees alike were gashed, blood and latex so intimately mingled that the rubber workers became known as *seringueiros*, the "blood-letters" of the jungle. Battalions of these impoverished men were commanded by respectable businessmen serving the tire and rubber-hose industrialists of the United States and Europe, where the real fortunes were made for men with names like Firestone and Goodyear and, unknown to most, Rockefeller.[30]

For over a quarter of a century, Indians were exploited without any censure by the government. Manaos, the central port on the Amazon, named after the "vanished" Manao Indians, became a boomtown. Rubber barons sent their shirts to London to be ironed, installed the first trams in South America, imported Sarah Bernhardt for their listening pleasure, and offered Enrico Caruso a small fortune to travel from Italy for a single night's performance in their gilded opera house, Teatro Amazonas (he refused).[31]

It was behavior like this, past and present, that infuriated Indianists like the Colliers. Nelson, for his part, was careful to avoid controversy, perhaps learning a few lessons from his father. He did not personally respond to any of the Colliers' concerns; he merely sent their remarks on to his aides. But he knew he had to be careful.

Nelson's silence did not ease the Colliers' concerns, but the long socioeconomic report from Maes in June 1942 did.

Maes pointed out that the Indians at the newer Ford plantation at Belterra were fast workers, tapping 400 trees in six hours, compared to the usual 250 trees elsewhere. "Their long experience with Amazon labor has convinced the management of this enterprise that there is no better labor anywhere if provision is made for its health and an adequate food supply." If Rockefeller's CIAA provided health and sanitation programs, Maes asked, could not SPI's many posts in the rubber areas protect the new workforce against exploitation by expanding the definition of the Indian? SPI had already recommended setting up twenty new SPI posts "to control the purchase of rubber from the Indian collectors."[32]

John Collier urged Nelson to accept Maes's proposal. "The use of this important population is essential to the success of the rubber program. The rubber program in turn is potentially dangerous to the welfare of this population." Collier then made his pitch for the SPI, calling it "the only official Brazilian agency responsible for the protection of the Indian population."[33]

For a week there was stony silence. Rockefeller had one of his aides draft a reply the next day, but it was held for a week while Nelson went over King's report. In it, King had ignored the dangers the rubber program held for the Indians.

Nelson flatly rejected Maes's proposal to use the SPI. Worse, he planned to use the Ministry of Labor as the Indians' sponsoring authority, even though Maes had reported that this was the very agency that almost let SPI die in the 1930s.

"While not under-estimating the fine accomplishments of the Indian Service, we are inclined to look to the Ministry of Labor first in this matter," Nelson wrote. The rubber program planned to use workers "drafted from Ceara, where the proportion of Indian blood is not generally high." Ignoring information to the contrary, Nelson also insisted that "the Indian Service has few, if any representatives in the high-yield rubber areas of the Amazon where it is proposed to concentrate the effort to expand production; this, of course, arises out of the fact that there are relatively few Indians in those areas."[34]

The CIAA had a map of the Brazilian Amazon giving population counts and the possible number of Indians who could be recruited from each area to tap rubber. The total was close to 10,000, or 10 percent of a grossly conservative estimate of 100,000 Indians in prewar Brazil.* Nelson recruited some well-known anthropologists into the rubber effort, including Charles Wagley, who was on close terms with SPI's leaders, and former BIA tribal arts official René d'Harnoncourt, both of Columbia University. Harnoncourt eagerly advised Rockefeller on BIA proposals, sometimes to the detriment of Collier's efforts at the Inter-American Indian Institute. Harnoncourt undermined Collier's role in the institute by denying the BIA the sole authority to control the training program. It was the beginning of Collier's eventual demise as BIA commissioner.

Rockefeller was not without his own disappointments. He had been forced to accept a drastic scaling down of his Amazon Development Project, focused now on getting rubber out of the jungle, and his direct role was limited to health and sanitation.

---

*The map drew on reports by American and Brazilian anthropologists and ethnographers found in the Strategic Index of the Americas. Nor was the CIAA's study limited to Brazil. Other countries touching the Amazon basin were also seen as sources of Indian rubber gatherers: 2,000 in Venezuela, 6,000 in Colombia, 2,500 in Ecuador, 7,000 in Peru, and 6,000 in Bolivia—over 33,000 Indians in all.

Nelson did enjoy a moment of personal triumph over Ambassador Caffery, however. The ambassador had so resented Nelson's muscling into the Amazon rubber project that for a year he had sat on Vargas's invitation for Nelson to visit Brazil. Now Nelson had a chance to meet prominent Brazilians, and he worked hard on a speech.

The lunch, with forty-eight of the most powerful men in Brazil, could have

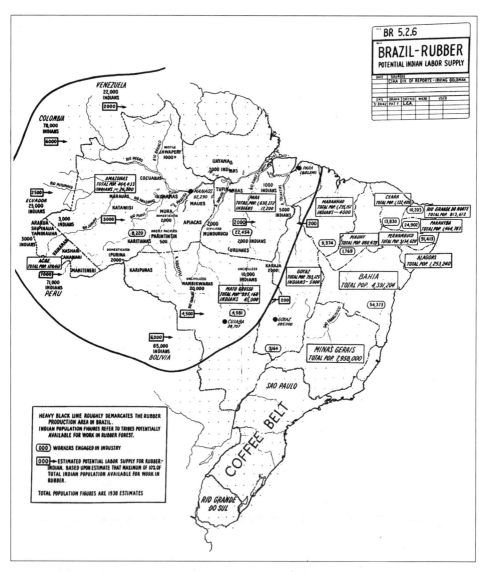

CIAA map identifying locations of potential Indian labor supply for rubber collection.
Source: CIAA Files, U.S. National Archives.

been Nelson's triumph or an American disaster. Caffery was deeply worried about what Nelson might say and how the nationalists around Vargas might react. At the last minute he decided to intervene. He told the Brazilian foreign ministry that he could see no reason for any political speeches and even advised the officials that it was not necessary for anyone to meet Rockefeller at the airport.

At the luncheon, Nelson found Caffery poised but defiant. As Nelson rose to speak, the ambassador created a diversion, calling loudly for cigarettes and engaging a Brazilian official in a conversation across the table. For a moment, Nelson just stood there at the lectern, his eyes fixed on Caffery. The Brazilians fell silent. Then Nelson began to talk—not about Brazil, but about Caffery. Nelson poured praise over Caffery and kept pouring it until it seemed that the ambassador would drown in embarrassment. Five minutes passed before he turned to his prepared speech. When it was over and the audience was clapping, Caffery was beaten. From then on, he stayed out of Nelson's way—and soon, out of Nelson's hemisphere. He was transferred with a demotion in rank to liberated France in 1944.

J. C. King had less to celebrate. He had wrapped up his work at Johnson & Johnson and had completed his brief survey of the Amazon. But Sumner Welles had never relented on Nelson's ambitious Amazon Valley Corporation. So King opted for active military service. He asked if Rockefeller could put in a good word for him with Secretary of War Henry Stimson.[35]

King's march to the pinnacles of power in the CIA had begun.

11

THE DANCER[1]

THE RED MAN'S BURDEN

For most men of humble origins who rise to the thin air of world shakers, war is often the rocket they ride to glory; for Nelson Rockefeller, born richer than most princes on earth, World War II was merely a confirmation of destiny. Backed by loyal expertise from Rockefeller businesses and family institutions, Nelson possessed—indeed, his very name symbolized—resources that none of his rivals or allies in Washington had. This, more than any other factor, accounted for his longevity in the Democratic administration despite his inexperience and tendency toward rashness and the Republican activism of his family elders.

Latin America's Indians were one of Nelson's major instruments in proving his worth to President Roosevelt in a time of cabinet shake-ups and resignations in Washington between 1943 and 1944. In his drive to extract the most strategic resources from Latin America with the least expense, he spared no means. The nutritional plight of the Otomi Indians in the Mezquital Valley south of Mexico City held little interest for him, but when the argument was framed within the context of labor productivity, light shone upon the Coordinator's deliberations. A CIAA aide wrote:

> By reason of undernourishment, these laborers are far less effective than they would be if improvement could be made in the food supply of the Indians of the Valley. This project, therefore, has an important bearing upon the mining of strategic materials in which the United States is interested. . . . It is important that they not become victims of Nazi or Falangist propaganda which is apt to be most successful when applied to hopeless and hungry people.[1]

Increased productivity was also the motive for the CIAA's food and health programs in the jungles of eastern Peru, where the humble *Nelson Rockefeller* plowed Amazonian waters along with five other launches dispensing medicine to sick rubber workers. At an experimental agricultural station set up to look into rubber products, cash crops, and food production, the CIAA built the area's only hospital. Smaller facilities were set up in two other towns close to the Ganso Azul oil field

At this point, in 1943, the legacy of the cheery Inter-American Escadrille,

Under the Inter-American Cooperative Health Program, CIAA health stations were set up to protect the health of U.S. armed forces and "workers on strategic products."
Source: CIAA Files, U.S. National Archives.

sponsored by Nelson and Laurance Rockefeller two years earlier, descended upon the Amazon's Indians like an avenging angel of progress. The Escadrille's William Barkley Harding—the Smith, Barney investment banker who had been instrumental in the reorganization of Eastern Airlines that gave Laurance Rockefeller a controlling interest (and in the reorganization that purged Lloyd Aereo Boliviano of German influence)—now arrived to advise the U.S. Rubber Reserve Corporation's new offshoot, the U.S. Rubber Development Corporation, on aviation in the Amazon. Harding's recommendations, submitted to the corporation as well as to Nelson Rockefeller, required the installation of runways and wireless radio stations at key points throughout the Amazon basin to tie together the rubber producing areas of Brazil, Peru, Bolivia, and eastern Colombia. Manaus was chosen as the center of this integrated transportation and communications system, maintaining regular communication with Washington via New Orleans.

This was the beginning of the end of the Indians of central Brazil. With the U.S. rubber programs as the impetus, Brazil's President Vargas established the Central Brazil Foundation to sponsor the approaching conquest of the Amazonian interior. In 1943, the "Great Expedition of Central Brazil and Xingu-Roncador" was ready to go.

After a patriotic send-off by Vargas, the bewildered small army spent a year chopping their way through jungle and building airstrips and new roads. In 1944, they crossed the dread Rio das Mortes (the River of Deaths) and plunged into the land—and arrows—of the mighty Xavante tribe. Five times, Indians desperately charged the Brazilians' hastily dug trenches, only to flee when a volley of gunfire was loosed over their heads. Perhaps because of the size of the Brazilian force, the Xavante relied on frontal assaults to overwhelm the invaders, rather than previously successful hit-and-run ambushes. Eight months later, facing superior weaponry and the invaders' steady advance, the Xavante surrendered to the proclaimed love of the SPI advance team. The Indians agreed to let the expedition pass, naively believing the promise that they would then be left in peace. It was history in deadly repetition: the American West, Africa, the South Pacific, only now the means were more subtle, the emphasis on psychology rather than bullets. The goal, however, remained the same: penetration and, ultimately, conquest.

Instead of telegraph lines, strategically placed airdromes, concrete runways, and wireless stations and radio beacons were strung across the Amazon. Anthropological reports on the Amazon's Indians, like its "useful" flora, were entered into the CIAA's Strategic Index of the Americas.[2] The mysteries of the Amazon were at last being unveiled.

Colombia also surrendered her rubber trees and other natural resources to the American industrial war machine. The plight of the Indians facing this invasion, though undoubtedly felt by the CIAA men working with the rubber program, went unmentioned in their official reports to Washington. But by January

1943 Brazil's General Rondon was so disturbed by reports on the exploitation of Indian labor that he pleaded in the Inter-American Indian Institute's *America Indigena* for an extension of SPI's techniques to the rubber frontiers of Peru and Colombia.[3] To no avail. Nelson's CIAA was concerned only with production.

As the Amazon jungle's Indians were left to their fate with the white man's microbes, the Andes mountains' Indians were left to their silicosis and other lung diseases. Rockefeller's *Servicios* set up clinics for the copper and tin mines of mostly American corporations and dispensed medicines and improved food supplies, but funds to improve ventilation and working conditions in the antiquated mines of Peru and Bolivia were never put in the budget of the CIAA or any other government agency.[4]

In Bolivia, however, Indians in the mines and plantations had increasingly asserted their rights—despite repression by the military regime of General Enrique Peñaranda and his claim of imminent Nazi revolution.

The Ghosts of Rebellion

In 1942, two major events took place that would soon have a major impact on Nelson's operations. First, under the auspices of the Federal Labor Union of Chuquisaca Workers, Andean Indians convened the First Congress of the Keschua [Quechua] Language. Representing Indian communities from the Bolivian Andean mining states, the delegates confronted the entire industrial white world with basic democratic demands: an end to child labor, evictions from the land, forced labor, price gouging, and private tolls on public roads; they asked for tenants' rights, maternity leave, irrigation for their farms, and a government investigation of the "ridiculous" twenty cents a day wages paid on plantations.

Nothing like this had been seen from Indians since Emiliano Zapata led the villages of Morelos to revolution in Mexico. The Inter-American Indian Institute noted the seriousness of the Indians' resolve: "The Congress passed posthumous homage to . . . the leaders of the great revolution of the Indians against Spanish domination who gave their lives for this great cause."[5]

Any passing of the torch of Zapata to the Indians of the Andes was cause enough for alarm in Washington in normal times. But these were not normal times. Since the fall of Malaya to the Japanese in early 1942, Bolivia's Indians produced 67 percent of the world's tin concentrates. They were, literally, the greatest source of tin imported into the United States.

All this came crashing home to Nelson in December, when the second event involving Bolivian Indians that year shook the foundations of the Good Neighbor Policy. Overworked Indian miners, who faced an average life expectancy of fewer than forty years, refused to work at the Patiño Company mine at Catavi. The U.S. ambassador intervened on the side of Patiño. The Peñaranda regime, now confident of U.S. support, unleashed its troops on the miners' camp on December 21. When the smoke lifted, hundreds of miners and their families lay dead.

The Catavi Massacre made headlines around the world. And in the furor that followed, a startling discovery was made: One of Nelson Rockefeller's top aides, Joseph Rovensky, was a director of the Patiño Mines. An assistant coordinator of the CIAA, Rovensky had been involved in negotiations with the Export-Import Bank for financing for the Patiño Mines, one of Nelson's earliest concerns.[6] Rovensky had to go, but not too far; he returned to his duties in Manhattan at Chase National Bank.

The loss of Rovensky came at a difficult time for Nelson. The Coordinator's far-flung enterprise felt its first shudder of imminent collapse with the winding down of the war in 1943. For the first time since Nelson took office, the CIAA's budget began to contract, not expand.

Berent Friele was the first to grasp what this would mean for Nelson's relations with his Latin American constituency and alerted him of the need for a tactful withdrawal. Promises had been made and hopes raised, especially for U.S. cooperation in Brazil's development of its Amazonian interior. Now, as Washington's concerns switched from winning the war to how its interests would best be promoted in the postwar period, the year-long honeymoon with Vargas since Brazil's August 1942 declaration of war would soon be over.

"As the postwar transition develops," Friele confidentially wrote Nelson, "there can be expected to be a considerable amount of criticism, blame and complaint. Since the Americans are almost the only foreigners who have been active here for many months now, most of the blame for the difficulties and problems of any character can be expected to be placed on the United States."

Friele recommended closing down CIAA's fieldwork as soon as possible to avoid "discredit," transferring the expensive food and sanitation programs to the Brazilians and the information, science, and education programs—those most useful to intelligence gathering and psychological warfare—to the U.S. Embassy. He considered an "organized aggressive public relations program on behalf of the U.S. Government a matter of prime necessity," conceding that it would be "an extremely difficult job."[7]

It was an impossible job. The expansion of aviation in the interior was curtailed on the grounds that the waterways of the Amazon basin were sufficient for handling the rubber shipments. Then Rockefeller's Inland Waterways Project linking the Oficina oil fields of Venezuela's Orinoco River with the Amazon was canceled on the grounds that the Brazilian navy had successfully cleared the coast of German submarine wolf packs. Finally, the rubber program itself was slowed.

It took only two months for the Vargas government to pick up the signals from Washington. It was a bitter reminder of the last time the Amazon had been used and abandoned.

Nelson had always been convinced that abandonment of the Good Neighbor Policy would spell disaster for American business interests, including Standard Oil, in Latin America. But now he also had a large personal stake. His meteoric rise in Washington had been tied to Latin America. Should the hemisphere's place in Washington's galaxy of stars fall, so would Nelson's career.

It was impossible for Nelson to challenge the prominence of Europe in the minds that ruled the White House. The war in Europe had always been the main object of the CIAA's programs in Latin America, and the keystone of the Grand Alliance that arched across the Atlantic was Anglo-American cooperation with the Soviet Union, the ally that bore the brunt of the fighting.

In 1943, Nelson saw just how much importance the president placed on this alliance with the Soviets. Two of Nelson's closest mentors at the State Department, Assistant Secretary for Latin America Adolf Berle and Undersecretary of State Sumner Welles, lost their jobs over it.

ALLIES LOST FOR ALLIES GAINED

Adolf Berle owed his fall from grace in the Roosevelt administration largely to a scandal involving Standard Oil.

In 1942, the Justice Department had revealed that Standard Oil had refused to surrender its control over patents for making Buna artificial rubber, patents it had obtained years ago in a deal with Germany's giant chemical combine, I. G. Farben, with no apparent regard for American national security.

Farben, at Hitler's behest, had refused to turn over information on the actual manufacturing processes. Standard Oil not only acquiesced, but continued to provide Farben with technical data on its own research, including the development of synthetic rubber.[8]

All this, and the fact that the Nazi company was the second largest stockholder in Jersey Standard (the Rockefellers being first), was revealed in March 1942 by the Attorney General's office. Members of the Senate Special Committee to Investigate the National Defense Program were so stunned that Chairman Harry S. Truman left the hearing angrily talking about "treason." Criminal charges were filed against Standard Oil for knowingly joining with the Germans in a conspiracy to restrain trade and competition between American companies, delaying the manufacture of Buna in the United States.

Two years later, the U.S. government would receive confirmation that Farben used slave labor from the Auschwitz concentration camp to manufacture Buna and synthetic gasoline at adjacent new factories.[9] Those not working were gassed with Zyklon B, which Farben also supplied.

While Standard Oil's patent deal with the Germans was exploding in the nation's headlines, a respected gadfly newsman, I. F. Stone, wrote an open letter of protest to Nelson's father. An agitated Junior insisted that Standard Oil's board should improve the company's public image.[10] For a family disclaiming any control over Jersey Standard, their intervention worked marvels. Jersey Standard's old guard suddenly crumbled.

Adolf Berle stumbled into the controversy. As German tanks overran eastern Russia to meet the Soviets' last stand at Stalingrad, Berle, as head of State Department intelligence, opposed the administration's decision to provide the Soviets with what the Germans already had: Buna artificial rubber. Berle's ideological war against communism could brook few compromises between the Allied powers. He had already caused a sensation for defying Roosevelt's July 25, 1941, order to turn I. G. Farben's synthetic oil process over to the Soviets.[11]

Berle's fate, no doubt, was sealed by the resignation in September 1943 of his mentor, Undersecretary Sumner Welles. The austere, courtly Welles had earned Secretary of State Cordell Hull's enmity for taking a soft stand against the pro-Axis government of Argentina at the Foreign Ministers Conference in Rio de Janeiro in January 1942. Welles hoped to coax Argentina gently into the Anglo-American camp. But Hull would have no part of it. Argentina's return to the fold could spell disaster for the Grand Alliance. The Soviets would view it as a betrayal of the Anglo-American pledge to fight fascism to the end. Worse, a U.S.-led inter-American alliance containing a pro-Axis power as a major military component would signal that Washington already was preparing postwar regional military pacts with reactionaries who were hostile to the Soviets. Hull believed that such an alliance would endanger the war effort and destroy the postwar cooperation between the Allies that was essential if the proposed international successor to the defunct League of Nations, the United Nations, was to have any chance of success. Hull insisted that Argentina first break relations with the Nazis before U.S. relations with Buenos Aires could be improved.

As Nelson and Berle watched anxiously from the sidelines, matters came to a head when the seventy-two-year-old Hull, claiming illness, told Roosevelt that he would be unable to attend the Allies' Foreign Ministers Conference in Moscow. But when Hull heard that Welles had been asked in his stead, he informed President Roosevelt of his readiness to attend the conference "anywhere between here and Chungking." This vote of no confidence from his boss was more than Welles could take. His resignation was announced by the president on September 25.[12]

Nelson Rockefeller quickly took stock of his declining fortunes. His CIAA was winding down its operations. His major supporters in the State Department, Welles and Berle, had either been purged or stripped of influence, leaving him alone to face Hull in the department. Since his base of support in the department was eroding, there was only one direction he could go: up. He had to try to succeed Berle as the assistant secretary of state for Latin American affairs. His ambition, however, was too desperate not to be obvious.

"I particularly remember a weekend with Nelson Rockefeller," William O. Douglas recalled years later. Roosevelt had invited Nelson to his mountain retreat, Shangri-la, now Camp David. "Nelson asked me what I thought his chances were. I replied, 'Nelson, if FDR was going to make you Assistant Secretary of State he would not bring you down here for a weekend, keeping you full of suspense.'

" 'Then why was I invited?'

" 'I'm not sure, but I think it's a consolation prize.' "[13]

Nelson Rockefeller had never been satisfied with consolation prizes.

The Betrayal of Hull

Bolivia's Indians provided Nelson with the perfect opportunity to get his foot in the door of the State Department. In December 1943, just one year after the Catavi Massacre, Indian miners supported young military officers in overthrowing the pro-American regime of General Peñaranda. The loss of his regime was looked upon with deep suspicion by Secretary Hull. Rumors of Axis subversion flew wild in Washington. The officers, in fact, saw themselves as continuing the "military socialism" of the previous Bolivian president who had nationalized Standard Oil's properties. They encouraged the miners to organize more of their own democratic trade unions and to present their grievances to Patiño Mines and the other corporations.

Nelson, sensing his opportunity to curry favor, leaped onto Secretary of State Hull's bandwagon, fanning popular paranoia of Nazi intrigue in Argentina as a prelude to turning that paranoia against "fascist influences" in Bolivia. In a reversal of previously held positions, Nelson proclaimed Argentina a nest for Axis subversion of its neighbors. He proposed a full economic boycott.

As could be expected, Hull was delighted with Nelson's conversion and scurried off to the White House to show Nelson's memorandum to the president. Roosevelt, just as expectedly, was wary. He sent the proposal off to London and got a predictable reply. No, cabled Winston Churchill, a boycott of Argentine beef and grains was exactly what Britain did *not* need. Its need for food was more important than its need to chastise Argentina.[14]

Both governments quickly bent, anyway, to the pressure of Hull's broad brush painting them pro-Nazi. Bolivia got renewed credit by proclaiming loyalty to the Allied war effort. Argentina broke off diplomatic relations with the Axis powers and then, logically enough, sought closer ties with the United States, including military aid.

Hull now made the first of a series of mistakes that would end his career. He delivered a blustering note to Argentina, attacking her neutrality in tones just short of a tirade. Latin America was aghast. A significant move had been made by Argentina toward inter-American solidarity. Instead of encouraging it, Hull had condemned it, and with the imperiousness of the American bully of old. Was the Good Neighbor Policy dead?

The following month, Argentina's President Pedro Ramírez, in the midst of a dispute with Minister of War Juan Perón, was overthrown. But Hull did not see this as an opportunity for a fresh start. He not only continued to withhold recognition, but he got Roosevelt to agree to impose limited economic sanctions partly along the lines Nelson had proposed.

Rockefeller's partial triumph quickly became Hull's diplomatic disaster. Churchill again refused to go along with the sanctions. So did Bolivia, Chile, Paraguay, and Uruguay.

As inter-American unity began to crumble in Hull's hands, the architect of the secretary's policies basked in the anti-fascist limelight. On the night of May 8, Nelson stood before a crowd gathered to do him honors. The Pan American Society, which the CIAA had funded, presented him with its gold medal "in recognition of his efforts toward inter-American unity and cooperation."[15]

Junior and Abby were in the audience. Abby beamed with pride. But Junior sat with his back to Nelson, his arms crossed, his chin resting pensively on one raised hand. The distance between father and son was greater than ever.

The next day Junior attempted one last time to reach out in his old age with a letter that was rare for its expression of emotion. He had chafed over the scandal surrounding Standard Oil's relations with I. G. Farben and the Nazis. Recognition of Nelson's service helped restore the family's honor:

> I was very proud of you last night, proud of the recognition . . . proud of the appreciative words spoken about you; proud of the wholly charming, modest manner in which you accepted . . . proud of the many expressions of affection and devotion to you. . . . I never was surer of the importance of friendly relations among the various countries of the Western Hemisphere than I am today. You have proved to the world that such relations are possible. . . . And so, with a full heart of pride, joy and gratitude, I say: "Well done, my son, you have wrought a good work . . . you have brought added credit to the family name." Affectionately, Father.[16]

It was too late. Nelson had, on his own, arrived at a sense of his worth, but through an appreciation of power, of how he could use the enormous wealth and influence of his family to accomplish his own ends.

Nelson's ambition was a fire burning so brightly that it inspired some, frightened others, and blinded most. It was not that his devotion to the war effort was so much different from that of other dollar-a-year men of wealth in Washington. What was troubling was the rapidity and ease with which he discarded principles he had earlier proclaimed. Each new course of action, no matter how contradictory to what preceded it, was described with such dedication that there could be no doubt of its momentary sincerity. Others with less moral resilience watched in awe, terror, or sometimes disgust.

WORLD WAR II: THE CRUCIBLE

J. D. Le Cron, for one, discovered that all food projects of his Food and Supply Division had to be oriented toward extracting the maximum amount of natural resources out of Latin America for U.S. industries. He concluded that Latin America's economic development was not Nelson's true concern, and resigned.[17] Nicolo Tucci, director of the State Department's Bureau of Latin American Research, also resigned. "I became aware rather slowly that these [CIAA] people were only after their own interests," he recalled years later, "and that they were sort of sorry that they had to fight the Nazis."[18]

Nelson had caught the drift of a new attitude toward Argentina—an inclination toward cooperation—as postwar planners became more concerned about regional spheres of influence and maintaining security within them than with past ideological differences. Washington had changed a great deal during the

Sources of Essential Raw Materials in Latin America
An American view of natural resources in Latin America during World War II
Source: National Industrial Conference Board, *Foreign Trade and Hemisphere Unity*, May 1941.

war, much as Josephus Daniels had feared. The change was readily apparent in the increase in the number of military officers and corporate lawyers. War had turned the close cooperation between business and government, advocated by Roosevelt during the prewar New Deal, into an almost incestuous relationship. Not only were businessmen wearing braids and brass, but the Pentagon seemed a vast daytime hotel for corporate lawyers negotiating fine, profitable points into contracts.

Corporate net profits from the 1940–1945 boom amounted to $117 billion, a staggering 450 percent increase over the $26 billion made between 1934 and 1939.[19] But a dark side to all this prosperity loomed beyond the day when the last of 400,000 crosses replacing lost American lives would finally be planted. Paradoxically, prosperity carried the seed of its own destruction, for its corporate form demanded the same level of profit performance in peacetime as in war, lest private investors sell their declining stocks to minimize their losses.

As postwar planners began to realize the full social, and hence political, implications of the new, highly productive technology brought into American factories by war contracts and government subsidies, subliminal warfare broke out in Washington's bureaucracies between big-business lobbyists, who sought to delay the reconversion to peacetime production, and small-business advocates, who wanted to speed it up. Big firms like General Electric prevailed, taking longer to convert precisely because of their deep profitable involvement in war production. It was a sign of just how far Washington had come since the New Deal ended that it was Roosevelt's former corporate foes, not his New Deal friends, who won.[20] Reconversion was delayed, heralding the coming of age of a new behemoth in American life: the military-industrial complex.

It was in this political climate that Nelson attended meetings of the National Defense Council and the Inter-American Defense Board, where he listened, fascinated, to geopolitical predictions of a postwar rivalry between the superpowers.

Rockefeller was a powerful name, but in these circles only one among many. Even the president, in his need for wartime cooperation in 1941–1942, had been obliged to defer to business leaders, such as U.S. Steel's Edward Stettinius, in their preference for a slow conversion to military production. Big business was like a giant ocean liner whose course could be turned only with time, but once done, plowed a mighty wake and carried most of America's businesses with it. Gradually, the larger meaning of Welles's replacement by Stettinius as Hull's undersecretary of state became apparent. Hull was a politician, not a direct representative of business. Stettinius, with a permanent power base, would have considerable influence on the president.

This was borne out a few weeks after Nelson's Pan American Society dinner. On May 29, without inviting or even consulting the United States' Good Neighbors, Hull announced the opening of the Dumbarton Oaks talks with

RAILROAD PROJECTS
STATUS JAN. 31, 1945

IN PLANNING   IN PROGRESS   COMPLETED

Rockefeller's CIAA railroads tapped resources of Latin America using Indian and *mestizo* labor.
Source: CIAA Files, U.S. National Archives.

Britain, the Soviet Union, and China on organizing the United Nations. Was the United States abandoning the inter-American system? Hull had already rejected the proposal by Mexican Foreign Minister Ezéquiel Padilla for an inter-American conference to mend the growing breach because Hull had not wanted to give Argentina a forum. The Latin Americans felt taken for granted. As the rent in hemispheric unity widened, Hull's prestige in Washington quickly took on water. Nelson's, conversely, continued to rise.

Nelson now did not just jump the sinking ship; he helped sink it. He met with Hull on August 19 and again proposed a full boycott of Argentine goods.

Hull said no.

Nelson then cheerfully proposed an exactly opposite alternative.

"We must call a conference of foreign ministers of all the American republics, put the Argentine situation up to them and be guided by their joint decision."

When Hull again refused, Nelson argued for consistency in policy and returned again to the impossible alternative of the boycott.

"I believe it would help rather than harm the Administration in the coming election."[21] Hull wasn't buying it.

With Hull ensnared in the contradiction between the impossible and the unsavory, Nelson struck home. He went directly to Roosevelt, demonstrating both his antifascist credentials over Argentina and his own freedom, unlike Hull, to act on Padilla's proposal for a conference to affirm hemispheric solidarity.

Nelson charged that Hull had failed to come up with a way of giving concrete support to those nations that might suffer reprisals if they broke relations with Argentina. Nor had he developed any alternative machinery for establishing an overall Latin American policy. Moreover, the organization of the department around tasks meant that programs took on an ad hoc nature, leaving the regional "big picture" ignored and authority fragmented.

Roosevelt was impressed. It was Nelson's breakthrough in showing the president that he had administrative capacities that might be useful beyond the CIAA. When Nelson suggested that he put his critique in the form of a formal memorandum, Roosevelt nodded his consent.

Nelson's six-page analysis must have been a shocking blow to Cordell Hull, especially when the president approved the criticism by this man almost half his age and with only four years of political experience. It was tantamount to a vote of no confidence. Hull submitted his resignation three weeks later. Roosevelt accepted.

By mutual agreement, Hull's departure was not announced until after the November elections. His replacement, Stettinius, was Harry Hopkins's candidate.[22] So was the president's choice for assistant secretary of state for Latin America: Nelson Rockefeller.

12

PREEMPTING THE COLD WAR

In Search of New Enemies

Nelson's rise to power was not greeted warmly in Washington. Returning from Haiti, where he launched a rubber project that would displace some 100,000 people and end in disaster,[1] he found that a political chill had gripped the capital. Liberal Democrats had been disappointed that summer when Roosevelt bent to pressure from southern delegates to the national Democratic convention and dumped Vice President Henry Wallace for the more conservative Harry S. Truman. Now, after solidly trouncing Thomas Dewey in the general elections, Roosevelt gave his liberal followers another jolt by appointing conservative businessmen to the four top positions in the State Department. Nelson shrugged off liberal complaints and eagerly readied himself for his new position.

At just thirty-six years of age, Nelson was now a prime mover in the destiny of an entire hemisphere. Even before his confirmation, he had begun to act with astonishing decisiveness. After consulting Mexico's Ezéquiel Padilla, he got Edward Stettinius and the president to agree to revive Padilla's proposal for an inter-American conference of foreign ministers in Mexico City. By excluding Juan Perón, he explained, terms for Argentina's reentry into the inter-American system could be worked out with the other countries. The only problem was convincing them to come. Some South American governments might be afraid of offending Argentina; others, without the spirit of Latin American solidarity, simply might not want to come at all.

Nelson raised the problem with Costa Rica's ambassador, Rafael Oreamuno, a friend from his Inter-American Development Commission. Oreamuno's solution was simple: flattery. Personal contact with the new assistant secretary, so rare during the Hull era, would delight the ambassadors of three key countries. The right-wing government of Chile had become more cooperative as Germany's fortunes declined; Colombia and Peru were already reliable allies.

On December 21, one day after his confirmation, Nelson Rockefeller, without the knowledge of President Roosevelt, committed the United States to a fateful course. Hosting the four ambassadors at luncheon, he made his pitch for a conference that would exclude Argentina. When the men raised their fears of Argentine reaction, Nelson promised military aid. When the men raised their fears of a Bolivia-type revolution, Nelson promised more military aid. The transformation of South America into an armed camp dependent on the United States was now one step closer to realization.

By the time they got to dessert, Nelson had their approval for the conference's agenda. He then trotted off to all the other ambassadors from Latin America. One by one, Nelson "gave each the feeling of having been consulted and of having contributed to the plan."[2] They all came on board.

Nelson had big plans for the inter-American conference, exactly the kind of plans the State Department was worried about: turning a sphere of influence into a military alliance. Roosevelt endorsed regional agreements within the framework of the U.N. Charter. But he hadn't decided what to do about military commitments beyond mere promises of "support." Rockefeller arranged for Roosevelt to talk to former President Eduardo Santos of Colombia, a so-called moderate liberal.

But not a true liberal. Santos was actually the leader of the right wing of Colombia's Liberal party; as president, he had resisted social reforms

Roosevelt was pale and tired when he greeted Santos on January 9. With Rockefeller by his side, Santos brought up the subject of military commitments by appealing to Roosevelt's Wilsonian liberalism. Recent U.S. military aid to Latin America, he argued, encouraged military dictatorships that were prone to adventures and border wars. "The best hope for the future lies in the idea of President Wilson for a mutual guarantee of borders. Do you think that you or Secretary Stettinius might mention such an idea at the Mexican conference?"[3]

Roosevelt, knowing that Latin American memories of U.S. Marine interventions could be stoked alive, was reluctant. But he liked the idea of order, world order, hemispheric order. He turned the tables on Santos. Why shouldn't Santos's own government introduce a resolution along those lines? If it did, the United States would go along.

"I believe Colombia might introduce the resolution," Santos said, "but we probably would want to have Venezuela join with us."

"This is a wonderful example of the spirit of cooperation in the Western Hemisphere," Roosevelt said. "I think I will discuss the principle with Stalin and Churchill at Yalta."

He turned to Nelson. "Will you follow up on this talk for us?"[4]

Nelson was only too glad to do so, but the State Department's International Division got wind of what was afoot and objected. Was Rockefeller building a voting bloc for the founding conference of the United Nations, scheduled for May in San Francisco, and one tied into a military pact? That would be 19 votes added to western Europe's 9, against the Soviets' expected 3 votes, blatant overkill. The Soviets would quickly size up this maneuver as "ganging up" on them. Rockefeller's maneuver could sabotage years of work in building a delicate but effective wartime trust between the great powers. It could destroy exactly what the president was hoping to achieve—a United Nations, made effective by continued postwar cooperation among the Allies.

But Rockefeller had never conceived that such cooperation was even possible. He had read J. Edgar Hoover's feverish reports on suspected communist subversion in Latin America. The war had created an atmosphere of secrecy and intrigue within Washington. As the Nazis faded as a plausible rationale for every Indian miners' revolt or resistance to rubber roads cutting into their forests, Nelson began to perceive that Russian hands would replace those of the Germans. As early as 1943, his fear had grown so acute that even Adolf Berle, who was not immune to fits of paranoia, had to steady Nelson's keel by warning him not to take seriously charges that communists were sabotaging the Mexican railroads.

Cooperation with communists in Latin America, who could be seen only as puppets of the Soviet Union, was difficult enough to accept during wartime. After the war, it would be impossible, and Nelson once said so to Roosevelt. He simply did not agree with Roosevelt's opinion that the evolution of the Soviet and American economies could create enough common ground to make a working arrangement feasible in the world. "My feeling," he told Roosevelt, "is that the liberal leadership of this hemisphere should be provided by the United States and that it is not in the interest of any American country to have the people look to or be led by a nation outside the hemisphere."[5] National sovereignty could be ignored if countries strayed toward accepting peaceful coexistence, much less socialism.

To the horror of the State Department's International Division, Nelson took this vision with him to the inter-American conference in Mexico City as the official leader of the U.S. delegation. There was no one to stop him. His immediate superiors were with the president at Yalta.

At the outset, Nelson broke the rules of diplomacy with typical flair. He turned the flight to Mexico into a junket for his Latin American friends, personally chartering a plane to take them all down as a group to promote "togetherness." It was the kind of spendthrift flamboyance both his grandfather and father frowned upon. The State Department saw it as a paternalistic breach of protocol. But to Nelson it was simply fun.

On February 18, their plane landed at Mexico City. No sooner had the diplomats settled into their rooms than Nelson sent word that they should be careful what they said because their rooms might be bugged, like his.[6] Even certain tables at popular restaurants, he warned, were wired. Meanwhile, Mexican students began demonstrating in the streets against Argentina's exclusion from the conference. An aura of intrigue settled over the conference, making Nelson's Latin American friends from Washington even more psychologically dependent on his leadership.

TRIUMPH AT CHAPULTEPEC

That something new was happening in Washington—especially to the Good Neighbor Policy—was indicated by the unusual composition of Nelson's delegation. The official leadership was virtually all Republican. Nelson had also diluted the State Department's influence by insisting on including a fifteen-member advisory group of his powerful personal allies in Congress, business, and labor.

If there were any doubts as to the Americans' line of march, they were dispelled during the first days of the conference at Chapultepec, the same palace where Townsend's missionaries had once dined with then-president Cárdenas. The conference's direction had been decided in advance. Most of the 180 resolutions that had been prepared by the twenty countries to promote industrialization and improve their terms of trade with the United States died in committee for lack of U.S. support. Cuba's popular resolution to emphasize state supervision of foreign investments was throttled. Brazil's similar resolution also languished on the table. Chile's visionary "American Industrialization Plan" was consigned to oblivion.

Dominating the American delegation's concerns was the worry that the Great Depression would return with the end of the war boom. The United States had plenty of ideas, workers, and products. What it needed was markets. Nelson was looking, he said, for "frontiers."

Edward O'Neal, president of the American Farm Bureau Federation, was even more candid about the political implications of all this expansion of the Monroe Doctrine. "Let us spread it all over, let us run it into China, if necessary, and turn it around into Russia." The farm surpluses "will wreck our economy, unless we can find sufficient outlets in foreign markets to help sustain the volume of production."[7]

With rare unanimity of opinion, Rockefeller felt free to insist on an Open Door to the markets of the world, including Latin America, with commensurate influence on foreign governments, while demanding that the Western Hemisphere be closed to that world for the almost exclusive benefit of American interests.

At Chapultepec, therefore, Latin America's resolutions on tariff protection met an early death. Instead, the U.S. delegation championed the improvement of

HIGHWAY PROJECTS
STATUS JAN. 31, 1945

Rockefeller's CIAA highways, built to serve the U.S. war effort, became springboards for industrial and commercial penetration of Latin America.
Source: CIAA Files, U.S. National Archives.

roads as commercial arteries and health, sanitation, nutrition, and food-supply programs that supported the construction of the roads and the mostly extractive industries they served—all programs on which Rockefeller's CIAA had focused during the war. Chapultepec, Aztec for Grasshopper Hill, was living up to its name; the day of the locusts had arrived.

The impact that these roads might have on the health and land tenure of Indians of the Andes and the Amazon was ignored. Dismayed officials from the Inter-American Indian Institute were not given the opportunity even to present their concerns.

Accordingly, the Indianists were unimpressed with Nelson's overgeneralized approach toward sanitation and health problems. "Similar general health measures have been recommended on numerous occasions at previous congresses, especially intended to benefit white or *Ladino* peoples," they protested. "Rarely have suggestions been made to benefit Indians specifically. The result: thousands of Indian groups with no medical services."[8]

Nelson's Latin American Junta

As the conference proceeded, it became apparent that a small group of Latin Americans were acting regularly in consort with Rockefeller. Mexican Foreign Minister Padilla was the most prominent. Backed by the United States, Padilla's election as president of the conference was unanimous. Ecuador's Galo Plaza was another helping hand, along with Colombia's Alberto Lleras Camargo. Both men were destined for even closer collaboration with Nelson as the presidents of their countries and secretaries-general of the Organization of American States (OAS); Lleras Camargo would even become a trustee of the Rockefeller Foundation. Both men would likewise help William Cameron Townsend establish the Summer Institute of Linguistics in South America.

Adolf Berle was also there. After Nelson's appointment as assistant secretary of state, Berle was given Ambassador Jefferson Caffery's job in Brazil. On taking over the embassy in Rio de Janeiro, Berle initiated a shake-up of personnel with Rockefeller's "full support."[9]

At Chapultepec, Berle joined Lleras Camargo and Rockefeller in drafting a resolution designed to bring Argentina back into the fold.

Perón's popular base was unshakable, and any inter-American meeting or economic pact would be severely weakened by the absence of Latin America's most industrialized nation. Moreover, there was always the threat of Britain reestablishing an economic beachhead in South America through Argentina if Washington did not restore relations. Using Britain's war plight to take over her holdings in Latin America had been a Rockefeller strategy for years. There were "good properties in the British portfolio," a CIAA aide noted. "We might as well pick them up now."[10]

Argentina's enduring nationalism was another consideration. Without U.S. restraint, it might get out of hand, inspiring similar declarations of economic independence throughout the hemisphere.

The resolution was almost an open invitation. All Perón had to do was declare war on a practically defeated Germany and demonstrate that he was eliminating Axis influence.

Still, Berle was worried. He steered Nelson out of the hotel, away from any of the delegates, and walked him to a small park. He then offered some wise advice.

"The war is almost over and we don't need them," he said of Perón's government. "They are still pro-Nazi and public opinion in the United States is not going to accept them. This conference has been a great success. You're now sitting on top of the world, so don't do anything to change that situation. Your desire for a united front in the hemisphere is sound and it is right to try to achieve it. But I think it would be a political error to rush into any negotiations with Perón."

Nelson mulled over Berle's words. But the temptation for a great diplomatic victory was too great. "Thanks," he replied, "I'll think about it."[11] But he had already made up his mind. He would take the risk.

He believed that he had already trounced the State Department's International Division in the battle over the conference's most important resolution, the one authorizing a regional military pact and a conference to implement it. Knowing small countries could not meet the onslaught of modern armies like those of Germany, Nelson's CIAA had already concluded that the purpose of U.S. military aid was to help "maintain internal order against revolutionary disturbance."

The U.S. generals at Chapultepec were adamant in their demands for an inter-American exchange of weapons. They were confident that distributing surplus U.S. arms through the military aid program would make Latin America's armed forces dependent on the United States. With military training programs came additional benefits that fell more properly within the purview of psychological warfare—and they were good business for a burgeoning war industry. As Secretary of War Henry Stimson commented on Army Air Force General "Hap" Arnold's plan to send warplanes to Latin America, the program "seemed wise and helpful and would tend to cultivate good relations with the South Americans which might prove very profitable to our aviation industry in the future."[12]

Nelson seized the moment offered by the Pentagon to confront the State Department's misgivings about creating a military pact that considered an attack against any American state an attack against all. Such a pact would violate the recent agreement at Dumbarton Oaks to refer all international disputes first to the proposed United Nations organization. The Soviet Union had signed the accord and would undoubtedly feel betrayed. Rockefeller's regional military pact might inspire the Soviets to do likewise, undermining the effectiveness of the United Nations; worse, it might destroy the U.N. founding conference itself, set for April in San Francisco. "If you're going to work against the agreed position of our delegation and the agreed position of the State Department, you better go on back to

Washington," Nelson thundered at a State Department representative in front of Stettinius, just back from Yalta. The State Department representative remained silent.

To add insult to injury, Rockefeller insisted upon a unanimous vote of approval by the U.S. delegation. He then signed the Act of Chapultepec for the United States.

On the night of March 6, two days before the end of the conference, Nelson showed up at Padilla's home. Through Rockefeller's support, Padilla had been unanimously elected chairman of the conference, giving Nelson effective control of the chair. Now he wanted Padilla to endorse the drafted invitation to Argentina. Padilla made a few changes and signed it. The resolution swept through the conference the next day. Nelson had fired one of the first shots of the Cold War.

Mexico's ex-president Lázaro Cárdenas was beside himself. He roared his disapproval of Rockefeller's inter-American system, calling instead for solely Latin American economic collaboration. He was convinced that the United States would dominate the system economically and draw Latin America into its military adventures abroad.

Cárdenas was not alone. Other veterans of confrontations with prewar Washington also were alarmed. Mexican labor leader Lombardo Toledano charged his government with "subordinating the Latin American bloc to the aims of the United States State Department." He called Rockefeller's regional pact "the final adoption of the Monroe Doctrine which would leave the Latin American republics at the mercy of the United States."[13]

Washington reacted differently. Secretary of War Stimson promptly authorized negotiations for postwar arms sales and training programs.

ROOSEVELT'S CRUCIAL DECISION

Franklin Roosevelt was obviously dying when Nelson showed up at the Oval Office for lunch on March 16. The president's trip to Yalta had drained his last stubborn energies.

But Roosevelt had shown surprising vigor during the Yalta negotiations. He got Stalin's assent to Chiang Kai-shek's leadership of China, abandoning Mao Tse-tung, on whom Stalin had little influence. He obtained a Soviet commitment to allow free elections in Eastern Europe, to meet in San Francisco to draw up a charter for the United Nations, to declare war on Japan as soon as Germany capitulated, and to reaffirm the principles of the Atlantic Charter that called for the formation of provisional governments in Eastern Europe with broad political representation.

Besides losing territory, Germany would be de-Nazified and disarmed, war crimes trials would be set up, and harsh reparations would be paid, Roosevelt agreeing to the Soviet Union's estimate of $20 billion worth of damage to its own territory and people.

There was also the familiar Anglophile motive for imposing a harsh peace treaty on Germany. Roosevelt wanted a wider Open Door and appealed to Churchill to end the closed British trade system of the Commonwealth. Opening the dominions' markets to "healthy competition" could be done only if Britain were spared competition from German industrial might. Britain also needed to maintain—at least temporarily—its strong trade with Argentina, a prospect put in constant jeopardy by Argentina's refusal to declare war on the Axis. Something had to be done by the Western powers to allay Soviet suspicions of an accommodation with fascism. Roosevelt and Churchill, therefore, went along with Russia and agreed that any government that had not joined the United Nations' war against the Axis powers by March 1, 1945, would not be invited to the San Francisco Conference to draw up the formal U.N. charter. Nor could it be eligible for charter membership in the United Nations.

Nelson was particularly unhappy with this aspect of the Yalta accord. The March 1 deadline was past. But Nelson believed it was possible to persuade Argentina to join the Allies, as long as that country's attendance at the U.N. conference was not foreclosed. "The important thing," he told Roosevelt, "is to get the Argentine government to reorient its policies, and join in cooperation with the other republics and, if that is done in good faith, it will be natural to want her in the world organization."[14]

Indeed, Nelson had already gotten the Latin American ambassadors in Washington and Secretary Stettinius to pledge U.S. recognition of the Perón regime and to recommend that Argentina be invited to the U.N. founding conference if it declared war on the Axis and signed the Act of Chapultepec.

Roosevelt was confronted with a tough decision. He was aware of the importance of Argentine exports to Britain. But he also believed that future relations with the Russians had been promising at Yalta. Ultimately, one thing stood in the way of postwar cooperation through the United Nations with the Soviet Union: rejection of the Yalta accords by Republicans in Congress. Roosevelt needed Rockefeller allies in the Republican party to ensure congressional support for the Yalta accords and the U.N. organization. He reluctantly initialed Nelson's memorandum recognizing Perón's Argentina.

The decision exhausted him. He collapsed in his seat as Nelson left with paper in hand. The next night, Nelson and Tod saw the president at a White House dinner. He seemed his old, strong self. But such public gestures could not hide the fact that his health no longer permitted him a full day's work.

Nelson never saw Franklin Roosevelt again.

Rekindling the Cold War

As official Washington learned of the new terms for Argentina's entry into the United Nations, a debate broke out over whether this was Roosevelt's policy or Rockefeller's. Even before Chapultepec, rumors had been circulating over Nicolo Tucci's resignation as head of the Bureau of Latin American Research. Tucci had asked that the bureau be dismantled because although it "was supposed to undo the Nazi and fascist propaganda in South America . . . Rockefeller was inviting the worst fascists and Nazis to Washington."

"Everybody is useful," Nelson had told him, "and we're going to convert these people to friendliness to the United States." Nelson's legal counsel explained what conversion meant. "Don't worry," he told Tucci, "we'll buy those people."[15]

The last week in March, with only six weeks of life left for the Third Reich, Argentina declared war on Germany "as an ally of Japan" and gave unguaranteed pledges of action against Axis influence.

Perón's change of heart after the Chapultepec conference gladdened Nelson, and he had no trouble claiming it as one of his war trophies. He then approached an old friend, Leo Rowe, who presided over the Pan American Union, the precursor of the OAS. Nelson wanted the Pan American Union to pass a U.S.-sponsored resolution inviting Perón to sign the Act of Chapultepec. Rowe, who had an esteemed record of service in Latin America, was happy to oblige.

The motion sailed through the next meeting of the Pan American Union, despite the unwillingness of any other nation to act as a sponsor. Once again, Nelson had his way.

It was also his undoing. Argentina quickly signed the act. Probably tipped off to the contents of the Rockefeller memorandum with Roosevelt's initials, Argentina then promptly requested that the United States support its bid to become a charter member of the United Nations.

Nelson now shifted his steamroller into high gear. On April 9, five days after Stettinius restored formal diplomatic relations with Argentina, Rockefeller tried to push Perón's case through a meeting of a committee of the State Department's top staff. To his surprise, he was hit from all sides. Even diehard conservatives were worried about this violation of the Yalta Agreement.

Twice at Yalta, Roosevelt had pledged to Stalin that Argentina would not be invited to the initial U.N. conference if Perón did not live up to the March 1 deadline to declare war. Argentina's presence at San Francisco would tarnish the Latin American bloc's image and reduce its propaganda value to the United States. There were already enough votes; Perón's was not needed.

Nelson insisted that his commitments to Argentina had the full knowledge of the president, the secretary of state, and the staff committee. He warned darkly of "political troubles" at San Francisco. "If we don't act, I do not believe we can persuade the other American republics to refrain from proposing Argentina for membership."[16]

No one bought it.

Nor could Nelson pull out his usual White House trump card. Three days later, on April 12, Franklin Roosevelt collapsed at his retreat in Warm Springs, Georgia, and died that afternoon. The president's last official act had been to agree to buy the first sheet of U.N. stamps on April 25, on his expected arrival at San Francisco.

Three days after Roosevelt's burial, Rockefeller aide Avra Warren flew to Argentina on a special mission. The newly installed President Harry S. Truman was inexperienced in foreign affairs; Nelson guessed that he had to act quickly on Perón's request for an invitation to San Francisco.

Most political analysts had studied Perón carefully and were not convinced that his regime was cleaned of fascist influences. Warren was—in two days. Business leaders assured him that Argentine markets were eager again for American industrial exports; generals said that their army and navy were hungry for U.S. weapons. Warren flew back on April 20 and recommended military aid.[17] Nelson embraced Warren's report with glee.

The same day, Nelson was summoned to Secretary Stettinius's office. "In view of the unhappy feelings between you and members of the International Division," Stettinius suggested that Nelson not go to San Francisco.

"You had a free hand in Mexico City," the secretary continued. "They want the same now in San Francisco."[18]

But within a few hours Stettinius began to question his own judgment. He told Nelson to go "talk to the Latin Americans and get the ball rolling." Then he was to come home.

Nelson stayed for two months. When he left, the Cold War was on the brink of becoming hot.

Charging Up Nob Hill

The Rockefeller road show rolled off Washington Airport's runway the following day, Nelson's chartered airliner again packed with his Latin American friends. Arriving in San Francisco, he dived into the parliamentary fray. "He jumped energetically from one thing to another," Alger Hiss, who was one of State's International Department representatives at the conference, later recalled. "He was the perennial adolescent."[19] Corralling votes, Nelson had learned in Washington, meant providing off-hour pleasures as well, and he threw banquets for the Latin Americans at such posh sites as Trader Vic's and the Bohemian Club. At the St. Francis Yacht Club, Nelson even had Carmen Miranda perform her Chiquita Banana dance for the delighted delegates.

Nelson, himself, was not an official delegate to the conference, but his staff—twenty-seven members in all—was larger than that of most nations.

Arraying these deputies across the conference floor like pieces on a chess board, Nelson became the United States' parliamentary whip over Latin America. Among the Latin American leaders whom Nelson also brought into play were Colombia's Lleras Camargo (recently appointed foreign minister), Ecuador's Galo Plaza, Mexico's Ezéquiel Padilla, and Bolivia's Victor Andrade.

Through these men, Rockefeller's crowd controlled representatives' votes cast in the name of millions of Latin Americans.

The opening days of the conference had all the makings of contemporary theater. Like a forced family reunion of estranged and disgruntled relatives, the conference of wartime allies began with squabbling over who should sit where at the negotiating table.

Soviet Foreign Minister Vyacheslav Molotov, fearing a U.S.-dominated conference, proposed revolving chairs.

Mexico's Padilla answered him by seconding the nomination of the U.S. secretary of state for chairman.

Molotov exploded, denouncing the proud Padilla as a tool of the U.S. delegation. Then he fired away at Colombia's Lleras Camargo for obstructing a resolution intended to seat the Ukraine and Byelorussia as agreed at Yalta.

Nelson stirred the resulting Latin American resentment toward Molotov into a fierce determination to seat Argentina and then, seeing that the Yalta accords gave Molotov the upper hand, suggested a three-week delay in seating *any* new members.

Finally, at a delegation meeting, Averell Harriman, ambassador to the Soviet Union, looked Rockefeller straight in the eye with the air of a disapproving uncle.

"Nelson," he asked, "are you the ambassador to the Argentine or the ambassador of the Argentine?"[20]

Stettinius made one last effort at reconciliation, convening a Big Four meeting with three representatives of the Latin American bloc at his penthouse suite atop the Fairmont Hotel. Led by Padilla, Nelson's friends repeated their demand for Perón. Molotov's patience was gone. He simply ended the meeting, turning the matter over to the conference's executive committee.

Nelson had no qualms about acting like an irrepressible family gossip, whispering first to his harassed secretary of state and then giving Cuban Ambassador Guillermo Belt the outline of points he should make in a speech. Ecuador's Galo Plaza, ever compliant, shuttled his aide back and forth to Rockefeller for instructions to give to the other Latin American delegations. Nelson's domination was shamelessly blatant, but it got results.

Less than a week after the conference had begun, the weary delegates were ready for anything called compromise. The time had come for the Americans to offer the seating of the Ukraine and Byelorussia in exchange for the admission of Argentina. Molotov again argued against the Perón regime and denounced the admission as a violation of the Yalta Agreement. His objections were futile. The thirty-two votes gathered by the United States, Britain, and France easily overrode the four votes his arguments attracted, although a number of small nations noticeably abstained. Molotov was furious, but there was nothing he could do. Nelson had guessed correctly that the Soviets would not storm out of the conference; nor could they stop the seating of Argentina with a veto, since the conference had not yet established the Security Council.

Yet to many it was a hollow victory. The American delegates were "riding roughshod through a world conference with a bloc of twenty votes," Walter Lippmann grimly assessed, with possible "disastrous consequences."[21] This founding session did not bode well for the future practical effectiveness of the United Nations as a peacekeeping body. If the organization could not cope with the behavior of one man, how could it restrain entire nations?

THE FUSE IS LIT

When Nelson arrived back in Washington for appropriations hearings, the attacks against him in Congress were immediate, widespread, and pitiless. The press, in an excess of political self-interest, ignored the Soviets' stated concerns and concentrated its criticism not on Nelson's manipulation of the Latin American bloc, but on his and Stettinius's alleged "knuckling under" to Latin American "blackjacking" over Argentina.

Nelson tried desperately to set the record—or at least his interpretation of it—straight. No, he insisted, he was not a friend of fascism or an enemy of peace and Allied unity. But he could not get through. Nelson went to the White House to explain why the press and Congress were wrong to criticize his advocacy of Argentina. But Truman's grasp of the issues was limited to a superficial distrust of both Russians and Rockefellers. Rockefeller continued to take the heat.

On May 5, Nelson Rockefeller arrived back in San Francisco. He had decided to leave to Undersecretary of State Joseph Grew the task of convincing Washington about Perón. It was a wise move. Grew called an anguished Cordell Hull, whose opinion was still respected by those opposing Perón's entry into the U.N., and persuaded him that "there was nothing to do but go along with the wishes of the Latin American republics." They "wanted Argentina in," he explained, and "if we had not done so there was the risk of their withdrawing and ruining the conference."[22]

With Argentina's entry secured, Nelson now turned his exuberant energies on preventing the Dumbarton Oaks and Yalta agreements from interfering with the U.S.-dominated military pact he projected for Latin America. He invited

Senator Arthur Vandenberg, chairman of the U.S. delegation, to a private dinner. Before long, Colombia's Lleras Camargo and Cuba's Guillermo Belt were summoned to join them. A letter was drafted for Vandenberg's signature that would have instant repercussions. Raising the specter of another political defeat like the one that the Republicans wreaked on Wilson's League of Nations, Vandenberg threatened Senate rejection of the United Nations charter unless the military pact in the Act of Chapultepec and the Monroe Doctrine were specifically exempted from any suggestion that they required approval by the United Nations. The U.S. delegation exploded when they read Vandenberg's ultimatum. The United States had already agreed that the United Nations would exempt only the anti-Axis military alliances from U.N. approval. Rockefeller was trying to change U.S. policy.

Now that the war was almost won, John Foster Dulles, a leader in the U.S. delegation, was adamant that the Wilsonian ideal of an ordered world be realized. "That letter might wreck the conference!" he told Nelson in a hastily convened meeting in Stettinius's penthouse.

Dulles's anger shook Nelson. A powerful Wall Street lawyer, Dulles was a pillar of the Republican party. Moreover, since defending Rev. Harry Emerson Fosdick during the Fundamentalist Controversy of the 1920s, Dulles had emerged as a leader of Presbyterian modernists and now served on the Rockefeller-backed Federal Council of Churches' influential Commission on a Just and Durable Peace. Being criticized for doing "a most dangerous and damaging thing" by a man Nelson's father trusted and respected almost shattered Nelson's confidence.

"I didn't write it," he whined. "Van wrote it."

"It makes no difference. It was extremely unwise."[23]

A battle erupted among the American delegates at their regular Monday meeting. Harold Stassen, a Republican, spoke to the heart of the issue. The proposal "would gut the international power by emphasizing regional authority." The first U.N. negotiations at Dumbarton Oaks had emphasized Roosevelt's conception of a U.N. General Assembly backed by "Four Policemen"—the Great Powers—to prevent regional trade alliances from crystallizing into aggressive military pacts.

For Nelson, U.N. oversight was an intolerable restraint on the United States'—and his—freedom of action. The military alliance he envisioned coming out of the Chapultepec conference had to be unhindered if it was to maintain the stability of governments with which he was friendly. Now that the United States' war boom was about to end, he was anxious about "unsettled conditions in Latin America."

Dulles would have none of it.

But Vandenberg was adamant, raising again the prospect of Senate rejection of the U.N. Charter. At an impasse, Stettinius looked over his shoulder at the ghost of Woodrow Wilson and requested a six-day recess to allow the United States time to resolve its internal crisis.

Washington, meanwhile, was in a furor. On the day before, VE Day no less, Truman had suddenly suspended all lend-lease aid to the Allies, including the Soviets. This, too, was the work of Nelson's ally, Joseph Grew. Grew had prepared the order, and the new president had signed it without even reading its contents.[24] It was an obvious grab for power. Grew was conducting a Cold War against the Russians on three fronts: in Latin America through Rockefeller, in the Far East, and in Eastern Europe through a cutoff of supplies. Grew hoped this cutoff of supplies would discourage the Soviet presence in Eastern Europe and any Soviet move against Japanese forces in Manchuria and Korea.

As it turned out, Grew's suspension of lend-lease aid was viewed as overkill and would lead to his ouster before the year was out. The gaffe also hurt Nelson. Grew had been Nelson's sponsor with Truman. The erosion of Grew's position put added pressure on Nelson to find some solution to the impasse over the Act of Chapultepec. Realizing that he "was the one everybody was sore at,"[25] Nelson used the interim to seek help. In desperation, he invited Harold Stassen to dinner.

After long hours, they worked out a twist. The "right of self defense," accepted at Dumbarton Oaks, was embraced as the rationale for including, not excluding, the Monroe Doctrine and Act of Chapultepec in Vandenberg's proposal.

Everyone was happy, so Truman had little choice but to accept, although this reversal of a previous agreement not to set up regional military pacts would surely mean Soviet objections—if not a walk-out—to any United Nations' blessing of the Monroe Doctrine. Britain realized this fact and told the U.S. delegation that it was firmly opposed. With Western unity crumbling, Rockefeller and Vandenberg finally conceded. The specific references to the Monroe Doctrine and the Act of Chapultepec were struck from what became Article 51 of the U.N. Charter, although "collective self-defense" was left in, buttressed later with key clauses permitting "regional action," opening the door for both sides of the Cold War.

The irony of the United States having to explain to Latin Americans why the interventionist doctrine they had historically resented could not specifically be included in the U.N. Charter was apparently lost on Nelson; the Cold War seemed to iron out all such wrinkles of the past. But he did note the Latin Americans' bitterness at the exclusion of the Act of Chapultepec. Only Truman's pledge to meet with them in Rio de Janeiro in August to finalize a military pact won them over to a unanimous vote of approval.

The Fall

Nelson was an isolated man when he returned to Washington in late June. He had to content himself with a voice from the past. "They make us very proud and humble," his father wrote of the praises he had received from some of the

Latin American diplomats and some newspaper clippings. Junior had issued a press statement in April urging people to pray for the success of the conference. The old man believed that his prayers had been answered.

Ezéquiel Padilla, Mexico's foreign minister, had similar delusions of success. But he paid highly for his friendship with Rockefeller. On his return to Mexico City, he was fired in disgrace, the Mexicans feeling that he had sold out his country to the United States.

Closer to the Rockefellers' hearth and office, Nelson's boss, Secretary of State Stettinius, was also replaced. Truman had decided to appoint his trusted old friend from South Carolina, James Byrnes.

In August, Nelson finally got his first audience with Byrnes. The real issue now was the Soviet Union and Argentine communists. With Germany's defeat and Hull's resignation, the focus of Nelson's concern had shifted from Perón to Argentine leftists. Nelson saw Perón as a means of controlling them.

To Rockefeller's horror, the new U.S. ambassador to Argentina, copper heir Spruille Braden, disagreed. As far as he was concerned, Perón was a menace to business. Braden had arrived in Argentina in May just as Perón was seeking labor's support in the free elections he had promised Rockefeller. Perón pledged never to use the army to crush strikes. As a result, all but a handful of Argentina's local business, industrial, and banking associations signed a denunciation against him. That was enough for Braden. To him, where labor marched, communism would follow.

Nelson decided that a conciliatory speech criticizing Perón might allow him to slip through the noose. He arranged to give a talk to Boston's Pan American Society, an audience of conservative heirs of banking and mining fortunes and a few young liberals. He sent a draft of his speech to Byrnes for approval with a note urging that they discuss it.

"What is it you want?" Byrnes crisply asked Nelson.

"I want to talk about Argentina," Nelson said, but Byrnes cut him off.

"Frankly, there's no use talking. The President is going to accept your resignation."

Nelson had just been fired, yet he insisted that he was going to speak on Argentina anyway.

"You'll no longer be Assistant Secretary."

Nelson was angry. In that case, he announced, he could make any speech he wanted to as a private citizen and "tell the whole story."

Byrnes did not need a scandal the first thing in office. He decided that "the President wouldn't accept Rockefeller's resignation until after the speech."[26] Nelson delivered his prepared text and got the rave reviews he expected from the *New York Times*. But it was too late. Nelson had to go, despite a personal visit to Truman. "I told him I didn't want to resign," he later recalled. "I said South America was too important."[27]

But that was precisely why Nelson had to go. The Democratic administration actually agreed with Rockefeller's policy toward Argentina and would continue it. The military pact envisioned by Rockefeller came into being at the promised Rio conference, although delayed for two years. Eventually, after the hemisphere was ushered toward the founding conference of the Organization of American States in 1948, it became clear that Rockefeller had been sacrificed to preserve his own policy. Disliked in the State Department, mistrusted by the public, and a Republican to boot, Nelson was expelled from Washington at a time when his departure would be widely misinterpreted as a stiffening of U.S. policy toward Perón.

Nelson never got over it. The thought that he, too, could be expendable seemed unbelievable. Almost twenty years later, he would still remember his meeting with Truman as something of a shock, repeating quizzically to friends, "He fired me!"[28]

13

LATIN AMERICA'S FIRST COLD WAR COUP

The Junta Regroups

Nelson thought of his firing as a temporary exile from Washington. The next day he returned to the Manhattan seat of his family's empire and convened a meeting of the prewar Junta. The wise old men answered the call. But it was the Junta's new members from the CIAA who had the most impact.

The CIAA's lawyer, John Lockwood, became Nelson's personal legal counsel, serving in much the same capacity as Thomas Debevoise had done for Nelson's father. Lockwood was conservative, a voice of caution that balanced Nelson's persistent ambition and enthusiasm for adventures.

Frank Jamieson, however, was the most influential, mainly because his journalist's ear was well tuned to public opinion, and he shared Nelson's ambition for himself. The former Pulitzer Prize–winning reporter of the Lindbergh baby kidnapping had been Nelson's propaganda czar at CIAA during the war, overseeing the radio broadcasts and magazines that CIAA's Publications and Information Division produced for Latin America. Under Jamieson's watchful eye, CIAA became the first official propaganda unit of the U.S. government, before the State Department's Office of Facts and Figures and, of course, long before the CIA's Voice of America.

He was also a seasoned political operator, having managed Charles Edison's successful campaign for governor in New Jersey. By the end of the war, Jamieson had, in effect, become Nelson's campaign manager, a role he would play until his untimely death in 1960. Jamieson viewed Latin America as Nelson's personal asset in politics; hewn to the nation's mounting concern over communism, the Americas could be turned into stepping stones for Rockefeller's triumphant return to Washington. If Nelson could no longer act officially, his wealth put him in a unique position to act in a private capacity, perhaps even regain some of the phil-anthropic luster that his power plays in Washington had tarnished.

Berent Friele was the third new luminary in the group. During the war, he had been Nelson's most important field general, overseeing the CIAA's largest operation in Latin America: Brazil. Now he represented the focus of Nelson's development program for the hemisphere: again, Brazil. A stalwart ally of the war effort, Brazil offered none of the political liabilities associated with Perón's Argentina. Its comparatively lower level of development could be turned to Nelson's benefit. Brazil held enormous industrial potential, with untapped resources in the Amazon states and in Minas Gerais. São Paulo offered a solid and familiar financial base on which to build. It was the perfect site for a model demonstration program. The largest country in South America could hold sway over the future of the entire continent. It was a measure of the great Rockefeller power that Friele, an influen-tial voice in his own right in Latin America's business world, was willing to give up his seats on the boards of the Atlantic and Pacific Tea Company (A&P) and A&P's subsidiary, the American Coffee Corporation, to follow Nelson.

Making Brazil the springboard for renewing Rockefeller's fame would not be easy. Nelson had enjoyed great prestige in Brazil during the middle years of the war. His efficient, effective sanitation and health programs were the only real U.S. successes in the Amazon basin. In contrast to the U.S. Rubber Development Corporation, which was made inept by sluggish transportation and a top-heavy wage structure that offered little incentive to labor, the Rockefeller name had sym-bolized wealth and economic progress in Brazil, even national pride, as Nelson's Museum of Modern Art gave world acclaim to Brazilian artists. But then the CIAA's operations and U.S. wartime purchases began to wind down, just when Nelson started to champion Perón.

That was hard to take. Brazilians had fought with the Allied armies in Italy. Their ships had been sunk by U-boats, often directed by clandestine German radios functioning out of Argentina. They had allowed Pan American Airways to replace German airlines and dominate their skyways. The CIAA's "industrial development" projects had helped funnel large sums of U.S. government funds to subsidiaries of American firms. Brazilians supplied the U.S. war machine with a large percentage of its quartz, manganese, iron, coffee, and rubber needs. Their government had allowed thousands of Brazilian peasants to be indoctrinated by CIAA films and be transported to the Amazon to harvest rubber for American factories. As Friele had predicted to Nelson two years earlier, Brazilian confidence in Americans plummeted when U.S. plans for Brazil's development were gradually abandoned as the war ebbed. A wave of indignation swept through the country. By the summer of 1944, the anger had not subsided; it was growing throughout Latin America. Washington's honeymoon with Brazilian President Getúlio Vargas was over.

Fortunately for Nelson, he still had two great assets in Brazil in August 1945. One was an economic asset: Standard Oil, which controlled the distribution of petroleum in Brazil. And access to oil, the Brazilians knew, was the foundation of industrialization.

But even more important was a political asset: his close friendship with the new U.S. ambassador, Adolf Berle.

Oil on the Mind

Nelson Rockefeller had owed much of his one great success as assistant secretary of state—the Chapultepec conference—to Adolf Berle's skillful diplomacy. Berle, in fact, played a central role in the conference's outcome.

Berle had one great bargaining chip: oil. Brazil's thirst for oil had been at the bottom of Vargas's eagerness to see Rockefeller's Orinoco Inland Waterways project come into being. That project would have enabled the vast Amazonian interior to tap the rich Oficina oil fields of Rockefeller's Creole Petroleum without running the gauntlet of the German submarines that were waiting off the coast. When that plan was scrapped by the Americans, Brazilian hopes centered on an oil strike at Lobato, in the state of Bahia, and reports of oil seepages in the lower Madeira River region of the Amazon basin. But the wartime shortage of spare parts and the dense jungle had made exploration impossible. Now that the war was over, there was only one source for such a large capital investment—the United States—and only one company that already had a stake in Brazil: Standard Oil of New Jersey.

Until the war, Standard Oil had little interest in exploring for oil in Brazil. It had been happily refining and processing Venezuelan and Colombian crude and selling it to Brazil at inflated prices. After the war, however, Standard Oil began taking a harder look at Brazil. Various reports by the CIAA—and even one by the Office of Strategic Services (OSS)—declared that Brazil had huge oil potential. The CIAA had received reports of "seepages" throughout the Amazon basin. Along Brazil's Madeira River, the land literally smelled of oil.[1]

Following the Chapultepec conference, Brazilian oil preoccupied Berle. "The oil thing is on my mind," he noted. "There is a good small field located in Bahia, there may be more oil up in the San Francisco Valley. There is undoubtedly a field in Paraná, but it will be long to explore. There is probably a great deal of oil in Amazonas, but a terrible job both of finding and getting it out. . . ."

There was a catch. Berle knew that "if the Brazilians wanted oil fast they could simply open the country to exploitation by the private companies. . . . But that does something else besides get oil—and that something else is not too nice."[2] If a nation lost control over its oil, it would also lose control over its destiny.

This was the dilemma confronting President Vargas: Should he depend on American capital and expertise to develop Brazil's oil at the risk of relinquishing Brazil's control over its most precious natural resource?

Vargas's nationalist officials were deeply suspicious of American oil companies, and for good reason. The presence of a Standard Oil man on the Rubber Development Corporation's staff and Berle's visit to him in Belém were no accidents. Dr. Harvey Bressler was known to Nelson Rockefeller. He was an oil geologist who knew "more about the Amazon Basin than any American," the CIAA's John McClintock had told Nelson in 1942.

Berle's arrival as Brazil's ambassador also was clearly no accident. Not only Brazil's oil, but also state-owned enterprises came under the ambassador's close scrutiny. Berle met with President Vargas and urged him to replace the Brazilian managing director of the Companhia Vale do Rio Doce, the company that ran the state-owned government iron-ore complex at Itabira, Minas Gerais, with an American. It was hard for Vargas to refuse. American banks had a lien on the complex's financial structure through Export-Import Bank loans arranged by Rockefeller's Inter-American Development Commission.[3]

Vargas did not want a confrontation. He agreed to replace the manager and have Finance Minister Souza Costa go over Berle's charges of financial mismanagement. In return for these concessions and the promise of crude oil from Itabira, Berle agreed to try to get more refined oil and coal to Brazil, promising to see about using ships that had been requisitioned for Perón's Argentina.[4]

But Vargas remained opposed to any foreign control over exploitation of any of the Amazon's resources. Preserving Brazil's economic autonomy had always been a priority. But now, even his hand-picked successor, General Eurico Gaspar Dutra, seemed to have fallen under the Rockefeller spell. As minister of war, Dutra had secured Rockefeller's loans and lend-lease military aid, and with them the power and prestige that came with the Pentagon's buildup of Brazil's armed forces.

As the 1945 Brazilian presidential elections approached, Dutra was showing a disarming willingness to allow foreign penetration of basic sectors of the economy that Vargas had preserved for public and private Brazilian entities.

Vargas began to have second thoughts about surrendering the presidency to this man. Ambassador Berle, meanwhile, kept in regular touch with Brazil's feuding political factions, ears perked for even the slightest rumblings of a challenge to Vargas's power. In February 1945, he got a signal. Major Juracy Magalhães, a rising star in Brazilian politics, visited him at the embassy. Magalhães had gained a reputation for fiery nationalism as a young lieutenant, and his meteoric career had many of the older generals, including the more conservative Dutra, worried. And with good reason.

Magalhães was the intervenor in Bahia. The intervenor was a powerful federal post, combining the duties of comptroller, supervisor, and inspector; anyone who occupied that post had a great deal of information, in this case in the one state in Brazil where commercial quantities of oil had been found.

Juracy Magalhães also led a secret life: Despite his proclaimed patriotism, he was an informant for the FBI. He had been reporting on the Vargas government to the FBI since at least 1942, when J. Edgar Hoover first identified him to the OSS as one of the FBI's key informants.[5]

The Brazilian officer pursued his penchant for intrigue with Berle. Vargas had offered him a variety of cabinet seats, Magalhães reported, but he had kept his independence. "He stated that he did not have any confidence in President Vargas, and that he and his group wanted a change of regime. He said that by this they meant a true revision to democratic government, and not a mere change of men."

Magalhães was talking about prospects for a coup. Berle cautiously approached an explanation of what U.S. policy would be. "I said he realized, of course, that the United States Government could not intervene in local politics, nor could the Ambassador." With that out of the way, Berle gave Magalhães cause for hope. Nonintervention, he hinted, could just as easily support those who wanted Vargas out. "I referred to a current story that the United States Government would intervene to prevent a change in government, and said that, of course, it was absolutely untrue; the non-intervention policy of the United States was well-established and would be scrupulously adhered to . . . we parted with expressions of mutual esteem."[6]

Meanwhile, everyone in Brazil was concerned about the upcoming presidential elections. Urban professionals and shop owners feared a victory by organized labor and formed the União Democrática Nacional (UDN), choosing an air force general as its candidate.

Bankers and merchants, who saw themselves as modernists, formed another group to defend law and electoral order and backed General Dutra's Social Democrat Party (PDS). They feared that Vargas might build a new political party that would unify the 800 labor unions that were prohibited by law from uniting into national labor confederations like the AFL or CIO in the United States. This concern was particularly important to UDN's base of professionals and shop owners, who feared challenges from organized labor.

And over all these fears, of course, hung the specter of communism. Since Vargas had declared his intention to end the dictatorship and had restored elected constitutional government, political prisoners, including Communist party leaders, had been released. The legalized Communist party moved onto the electoral stage to win the support of industrial workers.

Latent fears erupted into hysteria when Vargas founded the Brazilian Labor Party (PTB). The PTB quickly attracted industrialists who were equally fearful of the Communist party and American corporate penetration; nationalist intellectuals; workers in the new urban industries; and Vargas's fellow cattle ranchers, who believed that agrarian reform and a rise in industrial wages would increase meat consumption among the impoverished peasantry and workers.

Berle watched this new development with mounting anxiety. The PTB could stiffen the government's opposition to concessions for American companies in mining and oil.

Berle's Diplomatic Coup

In September, as the debate over the scheduling of elections for the presidency reached the boiling point, Berle received a stern warning from President Harry S. Truman: "I think it would be disastrous to interfere with the internal affairs of Brazil at the present time."[7] Yet that was precisely what Berle decided to do.

On September 18, Berle, responding to the rising clamor, sent Washington a telegram. He painted a picture of democracy in tatters and the emergence of a Brazilian government that would be "so antidemocratic as to be bracketed with that of the Argentine."[8] There were legitimate fears that Vargas would seize power or declare himself a candidate.

Berle had a solution: to send Vargas a loud message that Washington would not tolerate any postponement of the presidential elections—in effect, to bar his candidacy.

Berle hurriedly drafted a speech and sent off a wire to Washington, announcing that he would proceed unless ordered not to.

On September 29, Berle dropped his bomb on the presidential palace. Before the Brazilian journalists union, an audience chosen to give his remarks the widest possible circulation, Berle drew an analogy between George Washington's devotion to inaugurating a democratic system in the young North American republic as its first president and the scheduled December 2 date for national elections insisted on by Vargas's opponents, which Vargas was said to be resisting to give his new Labor party more time to organize.

"No true friend of Brazil or of the Brazilian people will interrupt that process. No true friend of the people of Brazil will be afraid of that process. No true friend of progress will accuse it of being reactionary. Opportunism, not practice of democratic institutions such as elections, is the real breeder of fascism and reaction."[9]

Berle gave a provocative performance. At the heart of his arguments, of course, was the fear that Vargas, Brazil's symbol of Latin America nationalism, would, as elected president, remain an obstacle to the Chapultepec conference's extension of the Open Door policy to South America. "Brazil, the United States, and the other great nations are now engaged in a titanic attempt to unify the world," Berle lectured reporters. Among the rights of "internal freedom" were "the right to access to the economic resources of the world."

Beyond the paeans to abstract ideals, Berle made no promise that there would ever be an end to the one-way street that brought most of the benefits of trade and investment to the northern half of the hemisphere. But he did mention "the right to be free from fear of invasion," even as a U.S. flotilla of six destroyers and two battleships began a goodwill tour of Latin America that planned to arrive in Rio de Janeiro on the eve of the scheduled elections.

Berle's speech caused a sensation. He happily cabled Washington that it "was widely printed and well-received by substantially all papers in Rio."[10] This wide coverage was predictable. Rio's newspapers had been financed during the war by advertising from American corporations doing business in Brazil. Much of the flow of this revenue had been directed by the J. Walter Thompson advertising firm, working in cooperation with Rockefeller's CIAA, for which it also directly placed advertisements for CIAA radio broadcasts.

The Brazilian public, however, was vociferous in its criticism. Berle's speech indicated that Washington was taking sides in Brazil's internal debate.

THE COUP TURNS VIOLENT

President Vargas was getting worried. Brazil's generals, now supplemented with the crack brigade of combat veterans from the Expeditionary Force that had fought under American command in Italy and with the renewal of U.S. military supplies to the air force, were mobilizing against him. On the evening of October 30, the principal barracks near Rio moved U.S.-trained troops in American-made tanks and armored vehicles into the city. Machine guns were set up in front of the Ministry of War. Soon they would be mounted throughout a quarter of Rio, trained on the streets.

Vargas was desperate. He had misjudged the consequences of his wartime alliance with the United States. As Berle later cabled Washington, the "army itself has acquired a far wider viewpoint. Rather than being local affair, its men have travelled, they have been in close contact with [the] U.S. Army, have had experience in Europe and are extremely impressed with democratic institutions of which previously they were unaware. Thus practically all officers and not inconsiderable numbers of common soldiers, instead of being merely instruments in [the hands] of anyone in power, have begun to think for themselves politically."[11]

This mobilization by a politicized army paralyzed the civilian government and made the police useless—at least, to President Vargas. His ministers of interior and labor found their homes surrounded by troops. The leader of the Communist party was arrested. No one who had supported Vargas was safe.

After conferring with his military attaché on the progress of the coup, Berle attended a dinner party. At one point, one of the host's sons slipped out to the street to see what was happening. He soon returned with the news everyone was expecting: A radio station was broadcasting that the president had resigned.

The deathwatch was over for Berle, "and I drank my coffee and cognac in relative calm."[12]

SHARING NELSON'S FATE

The next day, as the Brazilian army strengthened its hold over the nation, President Vargas and his wife were flown out of Rio de Janeiro to exile. With the eyes of the world upon them, the Vargases returned unharmed to their ranch in the southern state of Rio Grande do Sul. Meanwhile, the capital's citizens, isolated overnight by the army's interruption of all international cable and telegraph lines, slowly crept back into the streets to find press censorship and tank crews resting on the grass. The soldiers had been up all night waiting for any signs of resistance from the unarmed population. It never came.

Now Ambassador Berle's goal was to help the new regime consolidate its power through international recognition. He ran about town "trying to convey word delicately" that the new regime, nominally headed by Supreme Court president José Linhares, should improve its international image by ending censorship and ensuring political liberties to all parties, including the Communists. Berle's instincts were correct. France had withheld recognition until the new regime gave assurances that the Communists would not suffer persecution.[13]

There were some, however, who disapproved of the coup and Berle's role in it. Brazil's ambassador in Washington, Carlos Martins, was particularly distraught. He called Berle's speech "an inexcusable interference in local political matters."[14]

Former Undersecretary of State Sumner Welles agreed. In a letter to the *Washington Post* and later in a radio broadcast, Welles warned that the State Department's new policy was "radically undermining" the friendship between the American and Brazilian people. He criticized Berle for intervening in "an issue which solely affected the Brazilians themselves. It was a question which, as a sovereign people, they should have determined without outside interference."[15]

It was Welles's greatest crusade out of office, and his last. For speaking out, he would be sentenced to political exile.

Berle, meanwhile, began casting about for rationales for the coup. First he blamed the fascists, then a conspiracy between Vargas and Perón, and finally the Communists. In his own way, he was contributing to the ugly climate of fear growing in Washington, where critics of the new administration were accused of disloyalty to the United States and to democracy.

For the first time in American history, traditional skepticism about those in power was abandoned. The war against the Nazi evil had convinced most Americans that Washington's policies were altruistic. A wrong or unjust policy was seen only as a mistake, something accidental, with no ulterior purpose or gain involved.

In the weeks following Vargas's fall, Brazil's economic concessions came hard and furious. Six days after Vargas was sent back to his home state, Rio Grande do Sul, Berle sent Washington a "basic report" on Brazil's national iron industry, recommending American corporate penetration of the government firm, Companhia Vale do Rio Doce, as well as of its iron-ore deposits at Itabira, Minas Gerais. He made no mention of M. A. Hanna Company's lobbying of his superiors in Washington on September 28 for State Department assistance in getting Brazilian permission to investigate iron-ore deposits in the Amazonian territory of Amapá; but his urging of American penetration of the Minas Gerais deposits implied approval of Hanna's desire to enter Brazil, a desire he was apprised of by Washington. A week later, after the new regime graciously canceled rubber agreements that had required the U.S. Rubber Reserve Corporation to purchase rubber at fixed prices and minimum volumes for another year, Berle met with President Linhares. The ambassador reviewed a laundry list of economic issues that had remained unresolved under Vargas, among them the all-important issue of oil. But on this subject Berle was on shaky ground.

On the day of the coup, representatives of Rockefeller's Creole Petroleum and its parent, Standard Oil of New Jersey, had pressed their case with Assistant Secretary of State Spruille Braden, who had succeeded Nelson Rockefeller. Vargas had granted concessions to two Brazilian syndicates to build refineries in Rio and São Paulo. Since Brazilian law allowed only citizens to operate in the industry and refining offered "the only substantial profit in the petroleum business in Brazil, they considered this a monopoly." Standard wanted "to move in" and join the monopoly, it being understood that all the American companies, as well as a British company, Anglo-Mexican, "would be given an equal opportunity." The problem was that this participation in a monopoly, locking out other American companies in the future, might be seen by the Justice Department as a restraint on trade. Braden had agreed to back the oil companies, admitting that "this might be a technical violation of United States anti-trust laws, but that it was justified . . . to prevent the creation of a closely held Brazilian monopoly."[16] If there was to be a monopoly on Brazilian refining, it should not be a Brazilian monopoly.

Could United States' antitrust law be broken in order to apply its principles against a sovereign nation? Berle sensed the absurdity of his position: Big business and Washington, seizing the opportunities that this "coup for democracy" had given them, had put him in an untenable position with his own public statements. Postwar Washington was flooded with special interests fighting over the fruits of victory. Lacking Roosevelt's purposeful leadership, Washington was adrift, without a clear sense of mission. Its vision had narrowed to that of the self-seeking syndicalist; the broader, more farsighted view Berle believed he and people like Nelson Rockefeller offered was ignored.

Berle refused to surrender to irrelevance. He would not make any suggestion to President Linhares about the Brazilian oil refinery, except that "he might want to look into the situation."

Three days later, Berle met with representatives of the four American oil companies doing business in Brazil: Standard Oil of Brazil, Gulf Oil, Atlantic Refining Company (ARCO), and Texas Oil Company (Texaco). He argued that Brazil was a sovereign nation; that the refineries would be built in the future anyway to meet the country's needs; that they would leave at least 40 percent (by 1940 market standards) of the market to the Americans; and, finally, that any demands would have to include British companies, too, since Washington was pressing for an Open Door to the Commonwealth.

"There were social movements building against 'colonizing capital,'" he warned, "and the experience in other parts of Latin America with complete American control of vital national interests had not been reassuring, leading frequently to agitation and expropriation."[17]

Berle's words sounded like Nelson Rockefeller's earlier futile plea for reforms before Standard Oil's executives. But now the war was over, and it was back to business as usual in Latin America.

Berle got the final word from the State Department on November 23. Over the phone, he was ordered formally to protest the refinery concessions.

This order violated his political beliefs that local capitalists were the only viable means of inoculating a country against Soviet subversion. In this case, his friendships were being violated to boot.

The UDN's Drault Ernani headed Refinaria de Petróleo de Distrito Federal, the syndicate for the proposed Rio refinery; railroad magnate Albert Soares Sampaio led Refinaria e Exploração de Petroleo União, the syndicate backed by São Paulo banks that planned the second refinery.[18]

Berle made it clear to Washington that he wished "to have no part of it. . . . The Brazilians had a right to go into the refinery business in their own country and that any efforts on our part to oppose such a development would be construed by the Brazilians as an unwarranted interference with an internal matter."

But that was precisely the point that Washington wanted to challenge, insisting that the issue "was not the relative size of the market but the theory of operations restricted only to the nationals of a given country."[19]

At last it had been said. The Open Door policy was now being applied to South America. There would be no more peaceful accommodation with the Cárdenases of the world. Nationalizations were verboten; even reserving an industry for private enterprise by local nationals was now unacceptable. The Truman administration was effectively decreeing that all economies, resources, industries, trades, and markets in the world must be open to penetration by American corporations.

The coup did give Berle one boon: On November 23, 1945, Linhares decreed that the Congress elected on December 2 (which was expected to be

PSD/UDN-dominated) would replace the Constituent Assembly and have full constitutional powers. With this in mind, Berle got the National Petroleum Council to insert provisions in the refinery concessions making all terms subject to any new constitution or congressional laws.[20] Since voting was restricted to literates, about 60 percent of Brazil's people, most of the laboring population, were disfranchised. To diminish the likelihood of organized opposition in Congress even from those who were able to vote, no party was allowed on the ballot that did not have at least 10,000 votes in each of a minimum of five states.

But no one had counted on the surprisingly strong showings of Vargas's party, the PTB, and the Communist party. They captured a sizable congressional bloc, which could become larger by mobilizing popular resentment against Braden's make-the-world-American policies. And Vargas was soon back in Rio as the newly elected senator from his home state.

Berle tried to push matters forward before it was too late. Brazil's Ambassador Martins had been summoned to the White House after Welles's blast appeared in the *Washington Post* and had reportedly told Truman that relations between Brazil and the United States had deteriorated ever since Berle arrived as ambassador. He urged Truman to recall Berle before the situation became "practically irreparable."[21]

Berle, weary of the controversy, was thinking of quitting anyway. He dutifully prepared comprehensive memorandums on major economic issues confronting U.S.-Brazilian relations. They were premised on Berle's belief that Brazil needed American capital and trade to develop and that he had better try to give Truman's people some perspective on how to improve relations for the sake of the business interests of both countries. But they still read like a Christmas shopping list for the Fortune 500: the "amendment" of Vargas's taxes on imports, the removal of certain taxes on the earnings of American subsidiaries, the elimination of licensing controls on imports of American machinery and other manufactured goods, the purchase of "a large share" of the government's iron industry by "an American steel company," the American takeover of the operation of the Victoria-Minas Railway, and the revocation of the Constitutional prohibition against foreign-owned banks and insurance companies from operating in Brazil.

The First National Bank of Boston, long the financial bulwark of United Fruit and Boston's investors in Latin American sugar, coffee, and railroads, had already applied to the Linhares regime for permission to operate. Berle's comments were telling: "The Embassy has been informed in *strict confidence* that this application is receiving favorable consideration and that it probably will be approved by the President before the interim Government leaves office." Approval, he added, would "make it possible for any bank with head offices in the American republics, outside of Brazil, to operate in Brazil."[22]

With American bankers in place, Berle believed, Brazil's development had a glowing future, if only the Communists did not get in the way.

On February 6, 1946, Berle attended the opening session of the newly elected Brazilian Congress. Then he returned to his office to write his letter of resignation to Truman.

Six weeks after Berle's resignation, Nelson Rockefeller introduced Berle to the Council on Foreign Relations as "someone whom I'm sure you all know." The former ambassador had taken up Nelson's offer and returned to the place that Nelson had "reserved" for him. It was an impressive place, indeed. The council was the most influential organization on U.S. foreign policy in the corporate world. It also reflected Rockefeller influence. Nelson's father had bought the old mansion of Standard Oil Trust partner Charles Pratt and donated it to the council. Raymond Fosdick, president of the Rockefeller Foundation for the past ten years, had been one of its guiding lights, building its membership out of some of New York's top bankers, lawyers, and executives. Now Berle would join their prestigious ranks as chairman of the Taussig family's American Molasses Company, whose major creditor was the Rockefellers' Chase National Bank.

Yet Berle, like Rockefeller, would never acknowledge this business role or that his political philosophy was in any way influenced by it. Before the year was out, on the first anniversary of the Brazilian coup, Berle's assertion that he had been influenced by only the highest of motives would be challenged by an old nemesis. Vargas, breaking his silence, would blame Berle for inspiring his downfall and denying he had given Berle's speech his prior approval; he had told Berle, in fact, that he disagreed with it. "Ridiculous," Berle would respond,[23] and he never changed his line.

But Berle was uncomfortable. Like Rockefeller, he realized that some balance had to be struck between the nationalism of a Vargas and the narrow concerns of American corporate investors now championed by the Truman administration. He identified with Nelson's concern that U.S. foreign policy should not be seen as a crude, heavy-handed proponent of selfish business interests. A new theory of democracy would have to be worked out, one truly worthy of the United States' new global responsibility as leader of "the Free World."

Nelson was excited by the challenge. But he typically viewed his role as more of a doer than of a thinker. With his access to vast financing, his contacts among the powerful, and his top CIAA personnel turned into his private staff, Nelson believed that he could provide concrete demonstrations of the capitalist theory of development for the Third World. The problem was to find a theory.

Thus began one of the most remarkable and secret collaborations of the Cold War—and one that would have devastating results for the Indians of the Amazon.

Adjusting the Valves of Development

One of the great challenges facing Nelson and Berle in the postwar years was the need to revive Western Europe, even at the expense of Latin America. Both men remained convinced that Latin America, too, needed an inoculation of capital to ward off creeping socialism, but they accepted the Truman administration's emphasis on Europe. Nelson's family, in fact, played a key role in shaping this policy.

As Europe swung to the left after the Nazi collapse, the opening of the giant Arabian oil fields took on political urgency. Most of Europe's prewar industry used coal for fuel, and the coal miners' unions were among the most powerful Communist-led unions in France and Britain. Soviet ties to Europe's Communist parties could hamper industrial recovery under U.S. leadership; miners' strikes could cripple Europe and create the conditions for social unrest and possibly even revolution. Saudi oil was nearer than Latin American oil and under unquestioned American control. The importance of gaining control over Europe's energy supplies was foremost in the mind of the Rockefellers. As Nelson's father explained to the chairman of the Senate Commerce Committee, Maine's Owen Brewster, "In the next ten years Europe may shift from a coal to an oil economy, and therefore whoever sits on the valve of Middle East oil may control the destiny of Europe."[24]

If the Middle Eastern valve were to be opened, however, the Latin American valve would have to be closed. An oil glut would lower prices and profits and make the opening of the Middle Eastern fields commercially unfeasible. This required not only slowing down the production of oil in Latin America, but also controlling exploration for new fields.

The State-War-Navy Coordinating Committee (SWNCC), soon to become the National Security Council, had already found a solution: Oil deposits in South America should be secured through American oil companies as "petroleum reserves for [U.S.] government use," ostensibly in case of another war. Washington's auspices were needed to draw the Latin American governments into secret oil pacts as part of the inter-American military alliance. But there was an additional corporate goal. Involving Latin America's governments would offer "a hidden benefit," the SWNCC itself pointed out, of "diverting their attention from the general tendency to nationalizing their present petroleum industries."[25] Nelson's brother, John D. Rockefeller III, was a senior navy staff member of SWNCC when this proposal was first bandied about by the Office of Naval Petroleum Reserves.

SWNCC was to establish, through American oil companies, petroleum reserves along the eastern edge of the Andes Mountains in South America. "The area under discussion lies along the fringe of the Amazon jungle and western Savanna of Venezuela and includes areas in Bolivia, Peru, Brazil, Ecuador and Venezuela. It is believed to be one of the last underdeveloped petroleum fields in the Western Hemisphere."[26]

Since Venezuela and Bolivia were politically unstable and Brazil's nationalists were still holding General Dutra and the UDN at bay, it was not surprising that the navy plan gave special attention to the relatively unexplored Amazon of Peru and Ecuador.

The Peruvian Amazon was particularly attractive because of its "oil seeps and other evidences of the presence of oil" for "several hundred miles along the Rio Ucayali." Peru also had a "number of structures" suggesting oil "further north on the Rio Huallaga" and, of course, the "Agua Caliente oil field. It is estimated that this field alone, with further exploration, might be capable of producing approximately 30,000 bbls a day."

The Agua Caliente oil field, better known by the name of the company that had drilled the first test well in 1937, Ganso Azul (Blue Goose), was located near the Ucayali River port of Pucallpa.[27]

There was no mention of the Indians who lived there. Nor of the American missionaries who were just arriving, under a contract funded by Rockefeller's Inter-American Institute, to pacify them.

III

ARCHITECTS OF EMPIRE

Who will open Tibet, or claim the last acre of the Amazon, the hills of central India, the jungles of Borneo, the steppes of Siberia—the merchant or the missionary? When the war is over, let us take up the Sword of the Spirit and march.

—WILLIAM CAMERON TOWNSEND, 1942

14

AMERICAN WINGS OVER THE AMAZON

God's Beachhead

All his years of struggle against sin and pestilence had not prepared William Cameron Townsend for this. Like Heaven's Gates, the solid wall of snowcapped mountains suddenly parted before his plane's advance, revealing secret passes carpeted by clouds. Then the sharp peaks fell away into mist as he plunged into the miasma of a darker, primordial world. He was now on the eastern side of the Andes. For days the Amazon's dank breath had pinned his plane to earth until, as if by command, the weather cleared on the Lord's birthday, Christmas Day 1946. Buoyed, the small American plane climbed into the skies to resume its mission of redemption. At last the land flattened out into a luxuriant tropical green with gleaming lakes and rivers. But it was not a virgin forest Cam saw spreading out toward the horizon. He saw the realm of Satan, a Green Hell where the souls of lost tribes wandered hopeless and unseen beneath the jungle canopy.

Cam had been awed by the mere thought of his task when he arrived in Peru a year before. The Amazon, the greatest river on earth, stretched like a giant yellow-green boa across 3,600 miles of jungle and plains. And Cam was already staggered by the sight of just the western edge of it, in Peru. "No one organization, nor a single group of workers, no matter how concentrated, well supported and gifted they may be, can cope with the situation,"[1] he had written. Yet he did not hesitate the very next day to offer up his young followers to the jungle, pledging their labors to pacify forty tribes as he signed a contract with Peru's Prado government as head of "the Summer Institute of Linguistics Inc. of the University of the State of Oklahoma, USA."[2]

The logistical obstacles to delivering on the contract's terms would be enormous. But Cam rested his case on his faith in Jesus and his belief in his own divine calling. He interpreted the contract not as a burden, but as a solution: its promise to "service the government of Peru" and "all who want to help the Indians"[3] would necessarily involve SIL in a close collaboration with government agencies whose resources were immensely superior to his. There would be duties beyond the call of Fundamentalism, such as flying Catholic monks and nuns, beyond even the call of linguistic science, such as flying the government's political prisoners to jungle penal colonies or gathering data for the government on the jungle's economic resources. But these duties were justified in the name of God and country. The seeds of a bilingual education program in the jungle, arranged in cooperation with the U.S. Embassy, were being planted for a rich harvest of souls in the future.

This relationship with the U.S. Embassy provided continuity with the work of the recent past. In fact, Cam's new wife, Elaine, obtained her first job in Peru as a translator of primers for Indians through a program sponsored by an offshoot of Nelson Rockefeller's CIAA, the Peruvian-American Committee on Cultural Cooperation.

Elaine. Years later, her name alone would suffice for a chapter title in Cam's authorized biography, signifying the importance of this quiet-spoken woman in the missionary's life. Elaine Mielke had been a devout supporter of Christian missions since a local Chicago newspaper had awarded her a trip around the world as the windy city's "Outstanding Young Protestant." She caught Cam's eye soon after she arrived in Tetelcingo in 1943 to teach the children of SIL translators.

She was the opposite of Elvira. Whereas Elvira was frail, young Elaine radiated energy. She mastered Cam's "psycho-phonetic" translation techniques as easily as she made friends. And she brought badly needed administrative skills to the SIL field mission, having been supervisor of special education for handicapped children in some 300 Chicago schools before joining Cam's group. Few SILers were surprised when Cam and Elaine announced their engagement.

Nor were many surprised that Cam, ever watchful for every opportunity to advance his goals, turned their marriage into a diplomatic coup. He asked Lázaro Cárdenas to be his best man and Cárdenas's wife, Amalia, to be Elaine's matron of honor. Ever gracious, the Cárdenases had accepted. Holding the ceremony in Cárdenas's home at Lake Pátzcuaro ensured a large turnout of prominent Mexican officials, including six generals and the head of the Inter-American Indian Institute, Manuel Gamio.

Now, as the newlyweds ventured into Peru, they found their mission tailor-made to the needs of U.S. policymakers. Peru possessed large copper, zinc, and oil resources, as well as the hemisphere's longest frontier with the Brazilian Amazon.

American missionaries had always accompanied American businesses abroad, but the political climate in postwar Latin America gave Townsend's new crop of missionary translators and educators a special appeal to U.S. ambassadors who were charged with securing markets and resources for the American economy. If the drift toward the nationalization of resources in Latin America was to be arrested, economic development through a massive infusion of U.S. capital, accompanied by the expansion of American aid and cultural influences such as that represented by SIL, was vital.

So was the integration of the Peruvian armed forces within the U.S. Southern Command, based in the Panama Canal Zone. William Pawley had earned worldwide acclaim during the war for helping to create the "Flying Tigers" squadron that hunted down Japanese pilots in China. Now, as ambassador, Pawley backed the War Department's efforts to enlarge the U.S. military mission in Peru,* establishing a close relationship between the mission and Colonel Manuel Odría.

Odría was to have a major influence on Cam's success in Peru. He had been the hero of Peru's triumphant war with Ecuador in 1942 over the oil-rich borderlands of the Amazon. Odría was now a general and director of Lima's elite Superior War College, the training ground of scores of student officers from other Latin American countries that were tied to the Pentagon's wartime hemispheric defense network. Assisting General Odría in aviation training were U.S. Army advisers, which meant the further integration of Peru's land-based air force into the supply network of the U.S. Army Air Force, thereby assisting the standardization of Latin America's military equipment promoted by the Pentagon and American armaments contractors. Out of this enlarged U.S. military mission would emerge SIL's first director of aviation.

The Lieutenant Finds His Mission

Over all this, with a presence unseen but felt, loomed the promise of the Amazon. Aviation was to the Amazon what railroads were to the American West in the 1800s.

In the summer of 1946, Cam had received a phone call in Lima from Lieutenant Lawrence Montgomery, a member of the new U.S. Army Air Corps Mission.

"Would SIL be interested in purchasing a Duck for three thousand dollars?"[4]

The U.S. Embassy was offering a Grumman Duck, a single-propeller amphibian biplane used by the navy. Cam fired off three telegrams to the United States. Herbert Rankin, bow-tied fishing companion of citrus king–evangelist

* The U.S. military officers involved in the negotiations with Peru had been two of Rockefeller's strongest allies at Chapultepec and San Francisco on the question of regional military pacts, General George Brett and General Robert V. Strong.

Charles Fuller, had been so grateful to the Lord for preventing a threatened strike by employees of his Santa Ana department store that he sent Cam $3,000 he had reserved to fight the strike.

An airplane meant expenses above and beyond the purchase price. If SIL was to have an ongoing jungle aviation service, a network of two-way radios would be needed, along with money for maintenance and the construction of a hangar and a runway. Full-time pilots and mechanics would also be necessary.

Montgomery agreed to become SIL's first full-time aviator. The airman and his wife were Christians who shared Cam's vision of conquering the Amazon for Jesus, but it would be a while before he could leave the U.S. Air Mission. To fill the gap, Cam prevailed upon the Missionary Aviation Fellowship to lend one of its best pilots, former Women's Air Corps pilot Betty Greene.

The Peruvian government provided the balance. The occasion that resulted in this happy circumstance was unusual for Fundamentalist missionaries—a cocktail party honoring Peru's reputedly "communist" minister of education, Luis Valcarel. Cam's offer of the plane's services to the government inspired the ministers of health and education to reciprocate with a quarter of the plane's cost.

The U.S. Embassy was the linchpin holding together SIL's shaky success in these early years in Peru. It provided a jeep and a radio transmitter from Panama. It helped Elaine get a translation job with the Peruvian-American Committee on Cultural Cooperation. Montgomery acquired a surplus engine for the Duck for a mere $380. And the new U.S. ambassador, Prentice Cooper, even helped negotiate the purchase of the Duck from the U.S. Marines.

Cooper's arrival was another big break for Cam. Cam needed a friend in this strange land, and his courtship of the bachelor ambassador and his mother was fast and furious. His approach was vintage Cárdenas, composing a poem of praise to the ambassador and "Mother Cooper's winning smile" and "Queenlike charm,"[5] just as he had done for the Mexican president. He even sent flowers.

It worked. Mrs. Cooper took Cam's young translators under her wing. Cam did likewise with her son.

Cooper, a former governor of Tennessee familiar with the TVA-like dams envisioned by American mining companies and agribusinesses for Peru, was nevertheless a novice when it came to Latin America. He needed advice on how to sensitively implement the U.S. policy on foreign aid to Peru. The missionary was pragmatic about underlying American military and economic interests. "Expenditures made in line with the selfish reasons should be carefully directed into channels that will best serve our selfish ends," Cam wrote Cooper. "Close ties of friendship with Latin America, and especially cooperative enterprises such as our Government's participation in Peru and elsewhere open the doors for more American citizens . . . not only as business men but also as teachers, technicians, etc."[6]

And as Bible translators.

With the embassy's backing, Cam felt confident as his translators moved into the jungle to take their places among the tribes. A temporary base was set up at Aguaytia, just north of the former CIAA agricultural station at Tingo Maria at the foot of the Andes. The Peruvian government even gave them an abandoned hotel to use, but the location, with a suspension bridge spanning the Aguaytia River, made amphibious landings difficult for SIL's Duck.

At an elaborate ceremony highlighted by an aerial demonstration by Montgomery, the Duck had been rechristened *Amauta*, Inca for "wise man serving the people." In a significant gesture to the growing ties between SIL and the Peruvian military, Cam dedicated the plane's gas tanks to the Peruvian air force, which thereafter kept them full with free gasoline.

The *Amauta* was SIL's only real asset in the jungle, and Cam was eager to find it a safer harbor, especially after he almost drowned in the Aguaytia River's swift current while trying to scout local islands for a runway. Like Nelson Rockefeller, Cameron Townsend owed his life to Indians, who saved him from being swept downriver.

Betty Greene became the first woman to fly over the Andes when she flew Cam into oil-rich Pucallpa that December of 1946. Nearby Lake Yarina was perfect for SIL's purposes. The lake was half-wrapped around an island that could serve as the home base with a runway, and it had a stretch long enough to handle the Duck and other amphibious planes. A road could be built to Pucallpa, and one of Peru's most colorful tribes, the Shipibos, were close at hand for study, with most of the other tribes along the rivers within easy flying distance. Cam had found his jungle base, the first link in an SIL chain that would string God's love along the Amazon like Christmas lights into five countries.

The Birth of JAARS

The Townsends, with newborn Grace named after one of his benefactors, the wife of citrus king Charles Fuller, headed back to the United States on a fundraising drive.

SIL's jungle camp in Chiapas, Mexico, was the Townsends' first stop. In the romance of the campfire's flicker, Cam regaled the young wide-eyed recruits with tales of the Amazon. After a happy week, the Townsends boarded a rented Piper airplane. As the Mexican pilot pushed open the throttle, the plane bounced down the runway and lifted off sharply—too sharply in the humid air. The campers were still waving when the Piper suddenly lost altitude and, to their horror, crashed.

For a moment Cam could hear nothing but the sound of dripping gasoline. The pilot was unconscious. Both Cam and Elaine were trapped in the wreckage.

Again, as so often, it was an Indian who appeared as the savior. Cam quickly handed him Gracie through a broken window. "Take her quick," Cam said in Spanish, "before the plane explodes!"[7] By then the campers had scurried down the field and reached the plane.

As the ignition switch was safely turned off, Cam's mind switched on.

"Get your movie camera," he yelled to one young translator, Dale Kietzman, "and take pictures before they move us. People need to see how badly we need safe aviation in pioneering in the jungle."[8]

Cam, of course, was one of those who turned obstacles into advantages. The gory details captured on film worked miracles for fund-raising.

Arriving safely back in the United States, he knew just who to see. Despite the disagreement of his linguists, who wanted to rely on the more-experienced Missionary Aviation Fellowship, Cam recruited two evangelical elders, Dawson Trotman, founder of the veterans-based Navigators, and Torrey Johnson, head of Youth for Christ and, like Trotman, a backer of that organization's bright young hope, Rev. Billy Graham. Together, they formed a new corporation called the Jungle Aviation and Radio Service (JAARS). Next, Cam recruited onto the JAARS committee Clarence Erickson, pastor of Chicago's powerful Moody Church. SIL's translators, confronted by a fait accompli, gave in. The only question remaining was money, and here, too, Cam had an angel.

Cherub-faced Henry Coleman Crowell had one claim to fame and power: He was the son of the renowned "breakfast table autocrat," Henry P. Crowell, the founder of Quaker Oats. Like the Rockefellers, the Crowells had started out in Cleveland as wholesale merchants and grocers to the westward expansion. Inspired by a sermon by Rev. Dwight L. Moody, the elder Crowell had fallen to his knees with a prayer and a business deal for the Lord: "Oh God, if you will allow me to make money to be used in Your service, I will keep my name out of it so You will have the glory."[9]

God kept His end of the bargain. Crowell amassed a small fortune by speculating in Dakota lands seized from the Sioux and by manufacturing and selling kerosene stoves with the help of Rockefeller's Standard Oil salesmen. Crowell reneged. After Moody went to the Lord, a great cathedrallike hall rose above the campus of his Bible Institute; it was named not for the evangelist, but for Henry P. Crowell.

Henry P. died in 1946, but he left the bulk of his cereal fortune to a family trust headed by his only son, Henry Coleman Crowell.

Despite a Yale education, the younger Crowell had followed his father into the comforting certainties of Fundamentalism. Like many shy sons of the Robber Barons, including Rockefeller, Junior, Crowell took up the cross of religious philanthropy at the urging of his mother. When introduced to Cameron Townsend in 1945, Crowell was fifty-one years old and vice president of the Moody Bible Institute.

The heir to a great fortune was just what Cam needed. Cam persuaded the scion to share with JAARS some of the surplus government equipment that

Moody had gotten from Washington. A few days later, Crowell mailed off the first of what would become regular checks for $10,000. The following year he visited Cam in Peru and came away so impressed that he donated money and equipment for JAARS's first hangar in the Amazon at "Yarinacocha," the Quechua word for Lake Yarina that SIL had adopted for its jungle base. Returning to Chicago, Crowell followed up Cam's suggestion that he set up a Missionary Equipment Service (MES). Over the next ten years, MES served JAARS as a conduit for what effectively became a government-subsidy program of surplus equipment from the U.S. armed forces and other agencies.[10]

No one then, or afterward, questioned whether this program violated the separation of church and state mandated by the Constitution. In the emotional exigencies of the Cold War, both institutions, no matter what the law of the land, had use for each other.

MARSHALLING THE AMERICAS

Nelson Rockefeller learned during the war that President Roosevelt's army chief of staff, George Marshall, was not the kind of man to let adversity stand in his way. When Nelson needed pressure to be put on Argentina to join the war effort in 1942, Marshall did not hesitate to back Nelson's meddling in Argentina's internal political life. Three years later Marshall supported Nelson's efforts at the Chapultepec conference to lay the legal foundation for a U.S.-dominated military pact in the Western Hemisphere. Now, as delegates gathered under Bogotá's chilly clouds in April 1948 for the Ninth Inter-American Conference of Foreign Ministers, Nelson watched anxiously from New York to see if Marshall, now Truman's secretary of state, could carry through what had been started at Chapultepec.

Marshall, like Nelson, had a big stake in the conference's success. It was supposed to be his crowning achievement in Latin American policy. Here, the diplomatic keystone would be inserted in the arch of trade treaties supporting Europe's traditional conduit of supplies and raw materials from the Western Hemisphere— only with American, not European, banks controlling the flow. Bogotá, however, had suddenly become the scene of murder and mayhem, rocked by assassination and riots in the streets. But Marshall had not traveled all the way to the northern Andes only to turn tail and run at the first signs of revolt. The conference must take place as planned. At stake was no less than the founding of the Organization of American States (OAS), godchild of Nelson's diplomatic success at the Chapultepec conference.

Marshall's first task was to rally his Latin American colleagues, who were as wary of him as they were frightened of the rioters. The Latin American delegates had arrived in Bogotá with hopes that a new era in U.S.–Latin American relations was about to begin. They had heard talk of a Marshall Plan for the Americas, of long-overdue economic assistance to their neglected continent, of peaceful development and escape from the nightmare of military coups. These dreams, however, turned to despair with the speed of an assassin's bullet. Jorge Gaitán, former presidential candidate of the Liberal party and its greatest hope for a modern postwar Colombia, was on his way to political triumph when a gunman struck him down. Colombia, and possibly the entire continent, lost one of its most charismatic liberal leaders.

Rioting swept the capital, destroying much of the downtown business section; even the War Ministry was under siege. Students who had come from surrounding countries to petition the conference for economic reforms joined in the disorders. One was a young Cuban law student named Fidel Castro.

Marshall remained calm. He ordered the Southern Command in the U.S. Canal Zone in Panama to fly in raincoats and blankets for the shivering Colombian army units that were rushed in from the warm lowland provinces. Then he demanded that the conference reconvene under armed guard. The other delegations, however, wanted more reassurances. Frightened and confused, some even suggested a U.S. invasion to save their hides.

It took the ever-resourceful William Pawley, now Adolf Berle's successor as ambassador to Brazil, to come up with a typically American solution. He reached in his pocket and pulled out a wad of bills. Peeling off $5,000, he handed the money to one of his pilots, Grady Matthews, and commanded him to fly Pawley's private DC-3 to the Canal Zone.

"General," he said, turning to Marshall, "these delegations are living on army rations. They think they are in a state of siege. If I can get them some of the luxuries of life, they will settle back and vote to keep the conference here."[11]

They did. Grady returned, and Pawley drove to each delegation, leaving pots of caviar, foie gras, turkeys, and picnic hams. Heartened by their return to the good life, the delegates voted unanimously to brave on in a schoolhouse far from the center of town.

Through it all, delegate Averell Harriman, Nelson's arch rival at the State Department, maintained a regal poise equal to that of any Rockefeller. He was about to leave for Europe to oversee the Marshall Plan and regarded the violence in Colombia as a mere dress rehearsal for future confrontations with the Soviets. Joining him in this perspective was Major Vernon Walters, military intelligence officer at Pawley's Rio embassy and Marshall's interpreter. Together, Walters and Harriman easily persuaded Marshall that communists were to blame for the revolt.

The conference itself proved that more was at the core of Latin America's instability than any specter of international communist conspiracy. Most government leaders in Latin America knew only too well that instability reflected unmet needs. And unlike State Department diplomats who dealt mostly with government and business leaders, Americans who lived abroad, who were closer to the local people and who saw these unmet needs firsthand, understood the peril of continued neglect.

No single group of such Americans was closer to these local needs than missionaries. And no missionary in Latin America more fully grasped the potential for both disaster and opportunity in the United States' corporate expansion or had a better field record of sensitivity toward Latin American concerns for national sovereignty, than did William Cameron Townsend.

Cam had called for a "Marshall Plan for Latin America." He also had warned of Latin American resentment over the massive program of U.S. aid to Europe and Japan.

At Bogotá, Marshall had demonstrated his profound ignorance of Latin American relations by using precisely this European aid program as an excuse for the United States' failure to commit large funds to its Latin American allies. "The United States is helping Europe and Asia," Cam had written Ambassador Cooper in 1946:

> The papers tell constantly of food supplies and money being sent to the people of those lands, often at considerable inconvenience to ourselves. Everyone knows that millions and millions of dollars of what is being loaned to Europe will never be repaid, and that the inconvenience that Americans are being put to at the request of the UNRRA in order to feed Europe and Asia will not be rewarded with abiding appreciation on the part of many, should emergencies arise when we would need the help of those peoples. Latin Americans who are closer to us and have always stood by us in emergencies, can't help but wonder why we aren't as concerned about the undernourished poor of these lands, many of whom have less to eat and wear than do the people whom we are feeding in Europe.[12]

Such warnings had little effect on the outcome of the conference. Alleviating the causes of social unrest was subsumed under the more immediate U.S. objective of bringing Latin America, politically, economically, and militarily, under the American eagle's wings. With passage of the OAS charter, Marshall secured acceptance of a resolution that "looked [to many Latin American liberals] like the green light for power-hungry generals."[13] Like a self-fulfilling prophecy, Resolution 35 of the OAS charter hinted at something terrible beyond a pledge of respect for national sovereignty: future alliances between the U.S. government and Latin American dictators. Diplomatic relations with a government, it stated, did not imply any judgment of the domestic policy of that government.

CAPPING WELLS AND DREAMS

Cam watched helplessly from the sidelines as his own dreams for SIL's future in Latin America crumbled beneath the weight of high-powered politics. Only in hindsight would he understand the enormous role that oil played in fueling America's postwar advance through the Third World, spreading hope in one region as it sowed discord in another. For Cam's missionaries, as well as for Latin American governments, the primary obstacle to advancement was the Middle

East: As American companies tapped the great oil fields of distant deserts, they curtailed production and exploration throughout Latin America.

Peru, in particular, was in turmoil. The country endured two years of political, social, and economic instability, until in October 1948, the minister of government and police, General Manuel Odría, seized power through a military coup. Troops fanned out across Peru, making arrests that quickly filled the jungle penal colony of Sepa.

Through all this, Cam maintained discreet contact with the worried U.S. Embassy. Montgomery knew many of Odría's air force officers; some had been his students when he was part of the U.S. military mission. Cam's translators, meanwhile, kept a low profile in the jungle, where they worked among a dozen tribes. Striving to breach the barriers of culture through linguistics, they endured the hardships of the jungle and the defiance of Indians defending their lands from Lima's colonization. Montgomery's airflights kept SILers supplied with a steady stream of miracles from modern medicine. Intestinal flus and other diseases brought by the white man could now be conquered, proving the Lord's power over Satan and the feebleness—if not complicity—of hostile shamans. Unknown to Lima, Cam's linguists were now openly proselytizing the ways of midwestern America, challenging the Indians' communal traditions and their jungle-shaped cosmology with the rarefied spirit of an evangelical culture that stressed possessive individualism and exclusive property holding.

SILers seemed to have little difficulty accepting the Odría dictatorship, although they had some misgivings about his repressive policies. Odría was certainly no Cárdenas, and SIL's continued service to Odría's troops as translators and pilots while the dictator tightened his grip on the nation stretched the meaning of Christian service. Ferrying Odría's political prisoners to the Sepa penal colony eventually took its toll. Cam mastered the inner turmoil by finding passages from the Bible to use as rationales. His favorite was Paul's stoic instructions to the martyred Christians in Rome: "Obey the government, for all authority comes from God." In return for this Hail Caesar theology, Odría's regime increased SIL's supplies of aviation fuel and medicines.[14]

In 1949, Odría convened the Second Inter-American Indian Congress at Cuzco.

The politicization of the congress was apparent. If there were any doubts about the political meaning behind placing the congress's interim body, the Inter-American Indian Institute, under the auspices of the new OAS, they were put to rest by both the Odría regime and the U.S. delegation. "We want the Indian population of the different American states to be part of free nations, and not continue as a foreign population in its own country," the head of Peru's National Indian Institute told the assemblage. "We must not forget that he who has nothing to lose has nothing to defend."[15]

Odría, addressing the conference as its honorary president, emphasized the importance of the Indians' assimilation and "their appropriate responsibility to contribute to the nation's development and progress."[16]

It was left to the blunt North Americans to explain what this statement meant. "We can see no well-being for [the Indians] unless they be persuaded to mingle with us," summarized the chairman of the U.S. delegation, Assistant Interior Secretary William E. Warne, "and to share with us the riches yielded by the good American earth."[17]

If this idea ran contrary to the original philosophy of the Pátzcuaro conference's sponsors—Cárdenas, John Collier, Moisés Sáenz, and Manuel Gamio—no one pointed it out. Of the four men, Gamio and Collier were sick; Sáenz was dead; and although Cárdenas's spirit may have been present in the resolution pleading for an inter-American conference of Indian youths, spirit was not substance. The proposal was crushed by the U.S. delegation. It was "communist-inspired," someone said, and that was enough.

The legacy of Collier and Gamio was reduced to eulogies to their services, as if both were already dead. No one made the death of their ideas more clear than the Honorable William E. Warne: "We believe deeply that ours is a true and lasting way of life and we believe that the Indian way, valid though it may have been for the times in which it flourished unchallenged, will not suffice."[18]

The Pentagon's Plan for the Philippines

John Collier's failure to attend the Cuzco conference was due to more than the "sickness" alluded to in the U.S. delegation's official report. Marshall's State Department had refused him travel funds because of hostility to him from the Pentagon. Support from tribal people had made it impossible openly to purge him, but it also put him in direct conflict with the Truman administration's policies toward European, Japanese, and U.S. colonies, particularly in the Pacific.

By the time the Cuzco conference convened, Collier had also locked horns with the Truman administration over the Philippines. Central to Collier's concerns was the appointment of a former fascist sympathizer, Manuel Roxas, to the staff of the Supreme Allied Commander, General Douglas MacArthur. MacArthur subsequently backed Roxas's bid to become the first president of the newly independent republic, whereupon Roxas promptly surrendered 200,000 acres to the Pentagon for ninety-nine years for use as military bases.[19]

Roxas also amended the Philippine Constitution to guarantee parity rights for American companies to exploit natural resources and own utilities. In return for these guarantees, Roxas got $620 million in war damages and a Joint U.S. Military Advisory Group to help his Rural Constabulary repress landless peasants who had not given up their arms since World War II ended. During the war, many of these peasants had joined the communist-led Anti-Japanese People's Army, or Hukbalahap in Tagalog, the Philippines's major indigenous language. They expected agrarian reform and a share in political power for having fought on the Americans' side.

When they did not get either by 1948, the Huks, as the Americans called them, were in full revolt, capturing large areas of the rural Philippines—and the attention of a new secret agency operating out of wartime barracks flanking the reflecting pool between the Washington and Lincoln monuments: the CIA.

That year, the CIA set up a covert operating arm, the innocuous sounding Office of Policy Coordination (OPC). A CIA component, OPC nevertheless reported directly to Secretary of State Marshall. One of its first tasks was to send a military adviser back to the Philippines to organize "civic action" as part of the war against the Huks. The man chosen was Lieutenant Colonel Edward G. Lansdale, architect of the United States's entry almost ten years later into French Indochina's political cauldron.

Cam, too, became fixated on the Philippines.

The world press provided a daily parade of headlines spelling trouble for Western interests in that part of the world, including the "Moscow-inspired" rebellion, the "loss" of China to the communist revolution led by Mao Tse-tung, and the mounting tensions in Korea between Soviet-armed communists in the north and a new U.S.-backed regime in the south.

Emboldened by the sudden influx of $250,000 in 1949, including $41,000 for JAARS, Cam decided that the Pacific might offer more open doors for SIL's advancement into Bibleless hinterlands than did suspicious Latin America. By February 1950, Kenneth Pike was already in Australia, teaching linguistics to missionaries and making plans for SIL's entry into the Australian-ruled eastern half of New Guinea and the Philippines.

In June, SIL was given a fateful boost with the outbreak of the Korean War. MacArthur's goal was to push Kim Il-Sung's communist army north, not only back across the 38th parallel, but out of Korea altogether. His ambitions extended beyond the Yalu River, Korea's border with China, into China itself. What had been described as a U.N. "police action" was quickly escalating into a major war. With the French fighting Ho Chi Minh to retain their empire in Indochina and British support limited by its own war against communist-led peasants in Malaya, Washington was looking to Latin America for troop replacements. And Cam knew it.

Taking his newly completed film on SIL, *O, For a Thousand Tongues*, Cam headed for Washington. On September 22, he met with the State Department's Willard F. Barber and proposed an armed "volunteer inter-American brigade." One hundred men could be recruited in each capital of Latin America and flown to the United States for military training. Then they could be sent to Korea. Whatever Barber may have thought about the risk of angering governments by recruiting their own citizens into a foreign war, he noted that the "official result" would be "to show the world that the Latin American peoples want to take part in the struggle against communist imperialism."[20]

Cam had taken SIL beyond the Good Neighbor policy à la Cárdenas. He was joining the Cold War and helping it turn hot. By 1954, Barber's endeavors would include the CIA coup in Guatemala.[21]

Eager for the renewed opportunities Washington presented for SIL's expansion, Cam worked feverishly on final revisions of a biography of Cárdenas. The book would be evidence of SIL's close relationship with one of the strongest supporters of the wartime military alliance between the United States and Latin America. Indeed, he would soon use it as his calling card to OAS chief Lleras Camargo, Ecuadorian President Galo Plaza, and even the CIA-sponsored president of the Philippines. It would also, by its tone, demonstrate his sympathy for nationalist aspirations in the Third World, which would be necessary to fend off accusations of being the cultural vanguard of some American imperialism.

But he was uneasy about retaining Washington's support. The trip to Washington had seemed to go well, but politics is a fickle lover, subject to sudden changes of heart. Cam was painfully aware of the importance of an enlightened policy toward Latin America. Certainly a better strategy was needed than what had so far prevailed under the Europhile Truman administration. If he was to regain the momentum SIL had enjoyed during the war, Cam needed a breakthrough.

It came just a month after his Washington visit. President Truman had finally appointed someone to design the foreign aid program for the underdeveloped nations that he had promised as Point IV in his 1949 inaugural address. The new Point IV chairman with the familiar name boded well for SIL's future. "If the highly successful Rockefeller methods continue, and the budding Point IV program comes into full bloom," Cam wrote with conviction in his Cárdenas biography, "we shall become truly 'good neighbors.'"[22]

15

THE PRETENDER AT BAY

THE MISSIONARY IMPULSE

In the years between World War II and the Korean War, Nelson Rockefeller's face lost much of its youthful exuberance. Eyes that had shined in even the most arduous days of the war now seemed smaller and dimmer. His smile was drawn and thin, and his shoulders often appeared stooped, reflecting less the wear of time (for he was just entering his forties) than the strain of a frustrating political exile. During these years, Nelson learned that there were limits to what wealth, even Rockefeller wealth, could achieve in this world.

His family's support for former New York Governor Thomas Dewey's second drive for the White House had seemed a sure bet in 1948. Dewey's defeat by Truman dashed Nelson's hopes for an early return to Washington. On top of that, his mother, Abby Rockefeller, had been ill for several years. She had taken to wintering with Junior in Tucson, Arizona, where, in April, she died from a massive stroke. Nelson's bridge to his father was now gone.

Exiled from political power, Nelson had been putting his energies into the one power base he knew he could control: his family. Well before Abby's death, Nelson and his brothers took over Junior's offices in Room 5600 at Rockefeller Center and gradually brought in their own staffs, Nelson dominating the selections. The most important change was the replacement of Junior's old friend, Thomas Debevoise, by CIAA veteran John Lockwood as family counsel. Even the name on the door was changed. It now read "Rockefeller: Office of the Messrs."

Nelson next assaulted another citadel of his father's power: Rockefeller Center. The family's largest asset, the Center influenced New York City's economic and social life. It was not only a forum for a political aspirant, but a lever for influencing the city's economic—and thereby political—direction. The chance to merge Rockefeller financial power with Nelson's budding political career in New York came in 1946, when Mayor Paul O'Dwyer appointed Nelson to a committee charged with making sure United Nations headquarters was located in New York. Nelson impulsively offered Rockefeller Center's huge theater; Junior, just as quickly, insisted that he withdraw the offer.

Nelson refused to give up. On December 10, he came up with another site: Pocantico. To Junior's immense relief, however, some of the delegates balked; Pocantico was too far away. It was architect Wallace Harrison who finally found the solution. He was about to begin designing a rival to Rockefeller Center, "X City," for William Zeckendorf. The $200 million project was to be huge, stretching seven blocks along the East River from Forty-second Street to Forty-ninth Street, seventeen acres in all. Harrison had inside information that the heavily indebted Zeckendorf would be willing to sell out for a mere $8.5 million. Junior, glad to hear that his beloved Pocantico and Rockefeller Center could be spared the U.N. and competition, offered the entire sum.

Two days later, with the deal accepted by Zeckendorf and endorsed by the U.N. delegates, Nelson breakfasted with his father. After signing the papers, Nelson rose quickly to leave with his prize when Junior tugged at his coat. "Will this make up for the Center Theater?" the old man asked gently.

It did not. If anything, Nelson's embarrassment over Junior's withdrawal of Rockefeller Center Theater convinced him that his father's grip over the Rockefeller empire had to be broken. After Junior's chief Praetorian guard, Thomas Debevoise, was gone, it did not take much for Nelson to rally his brothers and sister Babs for the final onslaught. Stressing the tax benefits for the family by transferring title before his death, the younger generation persuaded Junior to sign over ownership of Rockefeller Center. Nelson, of course, remained president.

Pocantico was not spared either. It would take longer, but in the end, Junior would deed over his home to a holding company, Hills Realty. Nelson was president of Hills, too, waiting patiently as the old man continued in his role as lord of the manor.

Only the Rockefeller Foundation, Junior's greatest achievement, seemed sacrosanct. His eldest son, staid and reliable John 3rd, appeared committed to allowing the foundation a life of its own, separate from the brothers' individual pursuits. The rest of the brothers accepted John's well-established role, just as they embraced roles for themselves in other parts of the Rockefeller empire.

Winthrop had returned to Standard Oil of New York, but he yearned to cut his own path. He ended up in Arkansas, becoming its governor.

Nelson's closest brothers, on the other hand, thrived in his shadow. Laurance continued his prewar role as silent accomplice in business and politics. He became the leading force of Rockefeller Brothers, Inc., the brothers' profit-making complement to their philanthropic Rockefeller Brothers Fund. RBI provided financial support for Laurance's various ventures into the military-industrial complex.[1]

David, by 1948, was a senior vice president at Chase National Bank. At Nelson's urging, his specialty had become Latin America. He traveled with Nelson to see firsthand the opportunities his brother assured him were there for the taking. He then convinced his uncle, Chase National Chairman Winthrop Aldrich, to found a Latin American Department with him at its helm. David began *Latin American Business Highlights*, Chase's quarterly on the joys of Latin American financing, and pursued an aggressive campaign of branch openings in Latin America.

"Unfortunately, the trend toward nationalism and all that it connotes is on the rise in Latin America," David wrote his Uncle Winthrop after returning from his first Latin America tour with Nelson in 1948.

> The day has passed when our Latin American neighbors will tolerate American institutions on their soil unless those institutions are willing to take an interest in the local economy. I believe that it is in our own interests, therefore, as well as others' that Chase should rethink its policies. . . . I cannot see that the other North American branches have made much of a move in that direction, so we have an opportunity to be pioneers in the field.[2]

David's tutor in Latin American politics, of course, was Nelson. The brothers had already joined Nelson in his latest Latin American venture, whose motive was both economic and political: the Cold War.

In 1946, Nelson had convinced his brothers to sponsor a series of studies to pinpoint which nations in Latin America, Southeast Asia, the Middle East, and Africa were likely to become soft on communism or targets for subversion by the presumed monolithic world communist conspiracy. Two Latin America countries were selected for special treatment: Brazil, because of its size and influence on the entire South American continent and its enormous untapped potential wealth, and Venezuela, which, "particularly interested the Rockefellers because of their previous experience and their oil holdings in the country."[3]

Nelson persuaded his brothers, Babs, and even Junior to help him found the American International Association for Economic and Social Development (AIA). Six months later, in January 1947, Nelson set up a profit-making corollary, the International Basic Economy Corporation (IBEC). Its name was inspired by the CIAA's Basic Economy Division, but more than the name was borrowed. Much of the CIAA's top staff also reappeared on the boards of AIA and IBEC.[4]

The missionary impulse was evident. "The third generation of Rockefellers is still exporting the missionary idea," remarked a friend, "just as their grandfather did through his large contributions to foreign missions of the church."[5]

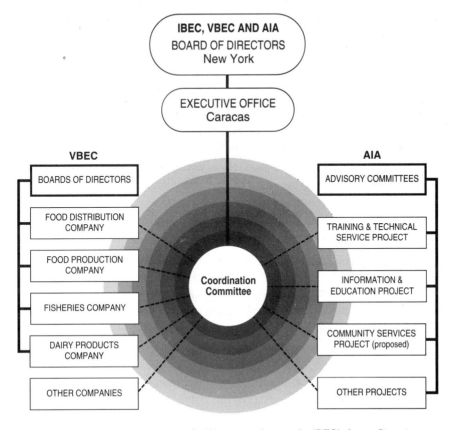

Venezuela Basic Economy Corporation
American International Association
IBEC Technical Services Corporation

IBEC, VBEC AND AIA
BOARD OF DIRECTORS
New York

EXECUTIVE OFFICE
Caracas

VBEC

BOARDS OF DIRECTORS

FOOD DISTRIBUTION
COMPANY

FOOD PRODUCTION
COMPANY

FISHERIES COMPANY

DAIRY PRODUCTS
COMPANY

OTHER COMPANIES

Coordination
Committee

AIA

ADVISORY COMMITTEES

TRAINING & TECHNICAL
SERVICE PROJECT

INFORMATION &
EDUCATION PROJECT

COMMUNITY SERVICES
PROJECT (proposed)

OTHER PROJECTS

Nelson Rockefeller used the nonprofit AIA to pave the way for IBEC's for-profit ventures.
This chart shows Venezuelan operations.
Source: Organizational chart, AIA Archives, Rockefeller Archive Center

Nelson agreed with that analysis, even urging his father to become AIA's chairman because, "You more than anyone have become a symbol to people throughout the world that democracy and the capitalistic system are interested in their well-being. The people must increasingly have reason to feel that their best interests and opportunity for the future are identified with our country and our way of life." Beyond Cold War politics, he stressed, lay family honor and tradition. "Now more than ever before it is important that we as a family carry on with the courage and vision that led you and Grandfather to pioneer new fields and blaze new trails."[6] Junior declined.

To Nelson, capitalism was the most revolutionary social force known to history, and his grandfather had been one of its great pioneers. The United States was then at the peak of its power. It was the only major power with its industrial plant intact, the only country capable of confronting communism as the leader of world capitalism. In such a world, the Rockefellers had to respond to destiny.

To Nelson and allies like Adolf Berle, only communists threatened this *Weltanschauung* of certainty and predictability by daring to stop the inevitable. The possibility of another path toward economic development than that which led toward the modern corporation, à la Standard Oil, could never be admitted. Herein lay the kernel of the "containment theory" proposed by author George Kennan. The theory claimed that communism, having bureaucratically centralized power under a party of ideologues purporting to speak for a working class, could never survive on its own because it lacked capitalism's internal dynamic of growth: freedom to accumulate great wealth and to tame, channel, and institutionalize human greed as private ownership of the means of economic production.

In this scenario, communism, dampening human initiative through overregulation and outright prohibition of great wealth in private hands, could gain resources only from abroad and was thereby inherently expansionist at other countries' expense. War, however, could be avoided through Western preparedness that would discourage aggression. Deprived of resources, contained, and isolated, the huge bureaucracy and its expensive armed forces and police apparatus would fall under its own weight. Nelson easily agreed that containment necessitated the Cold War, but to him, the successful prosecution of this war required more than armaments for military containment. Also needed were ideological containment and foreign aid for the promotion of capitalism in developing countries. And no one could demonstrate that better than himself, drawing on the enormous resources of the Rockefellers.

Some Brazilian nationalists did not agree. On hearing that the Rockefellers were interested in development projects in their country, they expressed bitter resentment over Standard Oil's renewed effort to control the refining of Brazil's oil. Nelson was branded as "the puppet-master who puts pressure on Brazil for surrender of its black gold."[7]

The Brazilians underestimated Nelson. He was interested in far more than their oil. He wanted their destiny.

THE LAND OF BEAUTIFUL HORIZONS

For his first postwar experiment in Latin America, Nelson chose the state of Minas Gerais, in Brazil's central plateau directly south of oil-rich Bahia. It was a wise choice. Somewhat larger than France, Minas Gerais was a rural mining and cotton stronghold of the conservative exporter wing of the Social Democratic party. This was the party that had broken with President Vargas in 1945 and supported the coup of General Eurico Gaspar Dutra.

In November 1946, Nelson had visited Rio. His offer of AIA's services—and his cocktail party for some 300 guests—were widely regarded as evidence of continued U.S. support for the Dutra regime, and Dutra reciprocated by awarding him Brazil's highest honor for foreigners, the Order of the Southern Cross. During his stay, Nelson learned that many of the poor who lived in the restless slums around Rio had been farmers who had migrated from Minas Gerais, the state directly north of the city whose small farms had been devastated by the reckless abuse of land resources. This migration to Rio had resulted in overcrowding and mounting political unrest. Nelson decided to address this problem by making small farming work in Minas Gerais.

Minas Gerais had been a mining center since the late seventeenth century, when the Portuguese had mined gold there using African slaves. The state had known deposits of limestone, beryllium, zinc, silver, lead, fluorite, titanium, sulphur, potassium, rock salt, and molybdenum. Most important, it had iron, developed by the government-owned Companhia Vale do Rio Doce, and manganese, the steel-hardening alloy mined and exported to the United States by Bethlehem Steel, the largest builder of U.S. Navy warships. Following the iron and manganese boom of the 1920s, the exporters who ruled the state had decided to build a new state capital in the interior. Perched 2,700 feet above sea level, the city was called Belo Horizonte, Beautiful Horizon. A symbol of the new era in mining and of the conquest of the interior, the city's construction was a dress rehearsal for the later creation of a new national capital, Brasília.

Indians, of course, had lived in Minas Gerais. The Botocudos had called the woodlands between the Rio Doce valley and the Rio Jequitinhonha their home; most of them were killed, the survivors pacified by Rondon's Service for the Protection of the Indian (SPI) in 1911–1914 and resettled at SPI posts in the state, where they quickly despaired and disappeared into graves. The Kayapó do Sul Indians had lived along the state's eastern border with São Paulo. Pacified and integrated into Brazilian society, they also were now extinct. Only the Maxakalí remained, some 200 survivors struggling peacefully to maintain their culture.

Minas Gerais was a prime example that most of the Indians who suffered extinction in the twentieth century were not the victims of European settlers. Rather, they stood in the way of extractive industries—rubber, nuts, diamonds, and other valued resources—operating mostly for export to Europe and the United States.[8]

At first, Nelson, too, looked at Brazil from an extractive industrial perspective. By January 1947, his engineers had already completed a survey of Brazil's phosphate deposits. Nelson was hoping to start a fertilizer industry as part of his grander scheme to bring midwestern farming to Brazil.

The only problem for Nelson was that there was yet no large market for chemical fertilizer anywhere in Brazil. Few Brazilian farmers had any knowledge of its use, nor could they afford it if they did. Nelson would have to create a market himself.

Nelson's financial wizards at Room 5600 whirred into action. Just two weeks later, on February 6, Laurance received a report proposing a three-step program for increasing consumption: Educate the farmers on how to increase their yields, organize the means of buying the farmers' surplus at attractive prices, and improve the means of transportation in Brazil to deliver fertilizers to the farmers at appealing terms.[9]

To overcome the individual farmer's reluctance to use fertilizer and his poor creditworthiness for both the fertilizer dealership and the factory (both of which were foreseen as at least partly Rockefeller owned), local farmers' cooperatives would be established.

Neanderthal right-wingers in the United States might think this was socialism, but Nelson knew better. It was in the Standard Oil Trust tradition to seek economies of scale, including lowering the cost of credit, through consolidation.

Rockefeller's men devised a strategy that was decidedly political. This would be a joint venture by three partners: the Rockefellers, "a powerful and reliable Brazilian group" to enable the Rockefellers to circumvent Brazil's prohibition of foreign ownership of mining concessions, and "an American group with capital" to participate in financing the factory. Meanwhile, the group would supply U.S.-produced fertilizers to stir Brazilian farmers' interest and test the market for future orders.

In 1948, Nelson and Milton Campos, the governor of Minas Gerais, signed a joint agreement to establish a farm-credit agency, ACAR (Associação de Crédito e Assistência Rural). Rockefeller's AIA managed the agency, which was given control over farmers' access to 8 percent loans from a state bank. Even the farmers' spending was controlled by technical teams from a local agency, who were given countersigning authority over farmers' checks.[10] Where some of this money went was predictable: Rockefeller agribusinesses. IBEC set up a hog-production company to raise and sell hogs from an imported breed that was resistant to cholera.

As AIA teams promoted poultry raising, Nelson set up an IBEC chicken-feed enterprise. As AIA teams pushed the virtues of chemical fertilizers, IBEC sold fertilizer. As AIA encouraged better-yielding seeds, IBEC raised and sold hybrid seeds.

As AIA spread the gospel of pesticides and herbicides, IBEC set up a crop-dusting company. The western plains of Paraná state offered suitable land for extensive mechanized farming. Here, AIA's gospel of the American tractor in the fruited plains of the Midwest found eager listeners. IBEC's Mechanized Agriculture Services Company (known as EMA) found ready sales as dealers for an American company with a large Rockefeller holding, International Harvester. More than $1 million worth of machinery was imported into Brazil within four years, and EMA cleared over 100,000 acres of forest under contract.

It seemed like old times. Nelson's AIA was replicating in South America what his father's General Education Board and the Rockefeller Sanitary Board had done in the American South and Midwest: promoting fertilizer, crop rotation, irri-

gation, sanitation, and mechanized agriculture, all the ingredients of a social formula that brought agribusiness to the United States at the expense of small farming. Besides what International Harvester paid the Rockefellers in continuing
dividends on their original $30 million investment, Nelson, through his EMA sub-
sidiary, was able to get a direct cut from Harvester's sales. He actually went much
further than his elders in pursuing vertical integration in agribusiness, setting up a
grain-storage company with the United States' largest privately owned grain company, Cargill. Cargill Agricola e Comercial, S.A., bought and stored grain throughout northern Paraná and in the fertile region just west of São Paulo.

These areas were all strongholds of the Brazilian Establishment that had
forced President Vargas's removal from office in 1945.

Brazil's Coup Spreads

Hearing of Nelson's first visit to Rio and of his agricultural proposals,
Rómulo Betancourt, Venezuela's new president, decided in 1947 to invite
Rockefeller to Caracas. He wanted to talk about Nelson setting up projects similar
to those proposed for Brazil.

When Nelson landed in Caracas, he was greeted by government aides and
driven to the yellow-walled Miraflores Palace. It took some nerve on both men's
part to shake hands. Betancourt had been a severe critic of Nelson's activities as an
oil man in Venezuela before the war. Moreover, he had come to power just over a
year ago by overthrowing a corrupt general staff and government controlled by
former president General Eleázar López Contreras, heir of the old Gomez dictatorship. López Contreras, in the heady days of democratic rights restored by popular
demand after Gomez's death, had inspired the building of Caracas's Ávila Hotel,
which Nelson had just completed; it was fast proving to be one of Nelson's greatest financial successes.

But Betancourt was now prepared to let bygones be bygones. He was planning a breathless series of economic and social reforms, as well as Venezuela's first
honest presidential election in this century. Nelson's former nemesis was now trying to run a government saddled with debts to foreign, mostly American, banks.
To raise capital to pay these debts and to diversify Venezuela's industrial growth
beyond oil, Betancourt had adopted a policy of *sembrando el petroleo*, or sowing
the oil. He pledged that 40 percent of government oil revenues would be reinvested in the country.

It was not really a new pledge. Every regime in the past decade had made an
identical promise. But Betancourt seemed to mean it. He imposed a 50 percent tax
on oil-company profits to ensure that the companies lived up to the 50–50 partnership that had been decreed ineffectually during World War II.

At first, Nelson seemed happy to cooperate. One of his promises when he founded IBEC in January 1947 was to give aid to Venezuela, and his development proposals had been endorsed by the Caracas press. He showed up in Caracas in June, glowing with confidence and good cheer, and signed a pact for agrarian and industrial development with the government's Venezuelan Production Development Corporation. To much press fanfare, Nelson announced the founding of three IBEC subsidiaries to promote development in fish and dairy production and food distribution. All were to be controlled by a holding company, the Venezuelan Basic Economy Corporation (VBEC).

Betancourt still had reason to worry. His 50 percent tax on oil profits and support for the oil workers' unions had raised the hackles of Creole, Gulf, and Sinclair Oil. Even before Nelson's arrival on the scene, American businessmen had petitioned the U.S. ambassador to save their holdings from the specter of international communism.[11] Three attempts at military coups had followed in rapid succession. Betancourt survived each only by his tenuous alliance with junior army officers who had helped overthrow the old regime. To keep these officers' loyalty, he had signed an agreement with Washington that brought a new U.S. military mission into Venezuela as their adviser.

This agreement proved to be his undoing. Although the military uprisings ended with the arrival of the Pentagon mission, it was merely a temporary calm before a greater storm. As relations with the U.S. Embassy began to deteriorate under pressure from the oil lobby, the young officers developed close relations with the embassy's new military attaché.

Shortly after the presidential candidate of Betancourt's Acción Democrática party, novelist Rómulo Gallegos, was elected in December 1947 by a three-to-one margin, the first signs of foreign intervention appeared. Over Venezuela's protests, Brazil, with no objection from Ambassador Pawley, shipped arms to the anti-Betancourt Trujillo dictatorship in the Dominican Republic. Two months later, Betancourt formally protested that the Somoza dictatorship in Nicaragua also was aiding a plot to disrupt President-elect Gallegos's inauguration by bombing Caracas on the day he was to take office. Betancourt revealed that the planes to be used in the bombing were American, as were the pilots.

Betancourt's revelations blew the cover off the conspiracy, and Gallegos's inauguration went off without a hitch.

There was an ominous portent of the coming new era when Nelson officiated at a meeting later that day in his Hotel Ávila. Reorganizing VBEC, Nelson decreed the termination of all its service activities, assigning all its engineering to a new profit-making subsidiary, IBEC Technical Service Corporation. He trimmed AIA down to demonstration projects, making them little more than a symbol of good works.

In much the same way that Townsend's Summer Institute of Linguistics served as the scientific face for a religious mission called the Wycliffe Bible

Translators, so Rockefeller's AIA had become the philanthropic face for what was basically a profit-making operation, IBEC. The distinction was not lost on American oil companies. They gave IBEC $15 million in pledged donations; AIA was given only $3 million.[12]

Gallegos's new government, lacking a loyal army, was doomed from the start. After his inauguration, Gallegos was wined and dined on a whirlwind tour of the United States as President Truman's guest. In retrospect, he would consider the tour the kiss of the Godfather. Three months later, in November 1948, he was overthrown by a military coup led by Lieutenant Colonel Marcos Pérez Jiménez, leader of the young officers who had supported Betancourt's movement but had gradually come under the influence of the U.S. military mission.

Fleeing into exile, Gallegos charged that U.S. Military Attaché Colonel Edward F. Adams and American oil companies, including Creole Petroleum, were involved in the coup. He blamed his downfall on military coups occurring all over Latin America.[13] Creole joined the State Department and Adams in issuing firm denials.

Pérez Jiménez assumed complete control within two years, his two fellow junta members dead by sudden illness or more sudden bullets. By 1950, he would ignore charges of human rights violations before the United Nations by having an investigation requested by Guatemala and Uruguay shelved under U.S. pressure.[14] He reciprocated by breaking up the oil workers' union, stifling all talk of a national petroleum company, and reopening the national oil reserves to the highest American bidder (eventually done in 1956). Colonel Adams, meanwhile, was elevated to the U.S. Command Staff of the OAS's Inter-American Defense Board.

CHILLING THE ROSE

With his ties to the oil companies, Nelson's operations survived the fall of the Acción Democrática government. But within two years, his operations in Venezuela and Brazil were developing serious financial troubles. His father had warned him to start small. That was never Nelson's way. He believed he could change the world almost single-handedly by demonstrating the superiority of the "American Way." A big splash was needed to make big waves.

Nature responded to the invasion of Rockefeller technology in disarmingly simple ways. Bulldozers scraped the land clear at his 18,000-acre Agua Blanca farm in Venezuela, and corn and rice were planted under clouds of insecticides. But the weeds grew faster than the corn, and Nelson's spraying machines did not arrive in time to save the crop. The same happened to his rice; what the weeds did not destroy, the heavy rains did.

It was no better with his fish company there. He poured $1.5 million into the company and built an $800,000 refrigeration and ice-making plant at Puerto La Cruz. But the Caribbean stubbornly hid its sea life from his fishermen, and when fish were found, prices at the fish market had gone up and the fishermen were unwilling to sell at lower rates.

His 7,800-acre cattle farm at the southern end of Lake Maracaibo came under criticism from local labor organizers and farmers. "With modern methods the North Americans may increase production a hundred times and prices will fall so low that we will be ruined," one farmer lamented. "Yes," shouted another, "and they'll buy up our bankrupt farms and turn the whole area into a mechanized operation!"[15]

Nelson tried to point to the relatively small size of his operations compared to Venezuela's output. But the fact that he himself called his farms pilot demonstrations for wide-scale operations in the future left many Venezuelans unconvinced.

His plantation at Monte Sacro, where Simón Bolívar had once lived, could produce citrus with superphosphate fertilizers and herbicides and pesticides, and his food-distribution company could build five warehouses and scatter them around the country to scoop up the farmers' output. But if wages were too low to purchase the food, the larger inventories would not generate profits. Frustrated, Nelson shifted from wholesale to more profitable retail operations, opening a modern supermarket at Maracaibo that catered to the American oil managers and their better-heeled retainers.

From store owners and employees, his criticism moved on to Mother Nature. He blamed his difficulties in Brazil on the weather. Drought, for instance, raised the cost of feed for his hogs, preventing his breeding farms from making a profit.

No one outside Room 5600 knew anything about these problems. Nelson touted his programs around Washington as success stories that demanded replication on a global scale. His self-promotion continued to go nowhere. Truman showed no inclination to end Nelson's exile from the nation's capital.

Cold-shouldered by Washington and discouraged by failures in Latin America, Nelson chose again to concentrate on the one arena of power where no one, not even his father, could stop him: Room 5600. He was now the dominant force there, easily outracing his shy older brother for the tireless loyalty of its staff. Although John 3rd had been president of the Rockefeller Brothers Fund since its inception, it was Nelson who really ran the show. And now even the Rockefeller Foundation, with John replacing Ray Fosdick as president, increasingly fell under Nelson's Cold Warrior eye.

Junior sensed the peril that would come if the foundation's carefully cultivated reputation for professional independence was lost. Yet it was precisely the part that Junior, and Senior before him, wanted the foundation to play in American corporate society—a leading role capable of creating a broad consensus—that undermined any chance the foundation had of ever being above Cold War goals.

The Cold War was seen as the defense of democracy. "Americans in Europe appear unanimous in the feeling that every possible step must be taken to combat communism," a foundation internal memorandum stated, but "the U.S. program should not be anti-communist but all out for democracy." Defending democracy meant helping Europe "get their economies going again—raise their standard of living—and to give them an understanding of democracy and the U.S. so that they can make their own decision between communism and democracy."[16] Out of this grew a concern for shaping mass opinion not only in Europe, but worldwide, even in the United States.

Policymaking—particularly toward Asia—became another imperative of the foundation. In the summer of 1949, the Truman administration appointed Fosdick to a secret fact-finding committee in Asia. Fosdick's retirement from the foundation the previous year did not negate the foundation's role in guiding government policy. Fosdick had been chosen precisely because of his career at the foundation and his ongoing ties with the Rockefellers.

By now the foundation's Cold War destiny was set in stone. A new crop of trustees, with decidedly political careers and personal ties to Nelson, John, or Laurance's wartime activities, appeared.

John J. McCloy had been appointed to the board in 1946. He had previously been assistant secretary of war and a senior member of John 3rd's intelligence group, the State-War-Navy Coordinating Committee (SWNCC).

Robert H. Lovett joined the foundation's board in 1949. Formerly Roosevelt's assistant secretary of war for air, he was Truman's undersecretary of state from 1947 to 1949. Lovett did not resign when he returned to Washington in 1950 as deputy secretary of defense. Neither he nor anyone else on the board accepted that there might be any conflict of interest between the mission of the foundation and the mission of the Pentagon. Indeed, by then there was none.

Also in 1949, Charles B. Fahs became head of the foundation's division of humanities. He was a former OSS officer and had worked for the State Department in the Far East. For his assistant, Fahs chose another OSS veteran and former staff officer of the Board of Economic Warfare, Chadbourne Gilpatrick. Gilpatrick's ties to the intelligence community were impeccable. He moved to the foundation directly from the CIA.[17]

Finally, as if to seal the foundation's marriage with the State Department, 1950 marked the election of the assistant secretary of state for Far Eastern affairs, Dean Rusk, to the board. Rusk's sponsor, State Department Special Consultant John Foster Dulles, was elected chairman of the board.

The Intelligence Factor

In the summer of 1950, there were few men in political life who had the independence of mind and the fortune to counter the prevailing wisdom of budget restraint and Atlanticist strategy and to advocate an aid program for the Third World.

Nelson Rockefeller was one of those few. Of all who testified for the International Development Act, no one had more experience running health, education, and cultural programs as an intelligence-gathering operation and psychological warfare than he. Moreover, he had just returned from helping now-President Galo Plaza with an IBEC planning survey in turbulent Ecuador. However, the timing was bad. The American position in Korea was in a state of emergency. Despite the CIA's warning of impending hostilities, General MacArthur had not taken precautions. Troops of the People's Republic of Korea, exiled in the north since 1946, were defeating Syngman Rhee's army. After Seoul fell, no one wanted to listen to Rockefeller talk about aid to Latin America—not congressmen; not the president; not the press; and, therefore, not the American people.

Nelson was despondent. He would have remained so, had Latin Americans not inadvertently intervened, in the most shocking way, on his behalf.

16

THE LATIN ROAD TO POWER

REVOLUTION RESURRECTS A CAREER

Washington was unseasonably warm on the afternoon of November 1 as Harry Truman stripped to his underwear and crawled between the sheets of his bed in Blair House for a nap. The president had moved into the vice presidential residence two years before while the White House was being remodeled, and the Secret Service was not happy about it. The house was on a busy street, its ground-floor windows exposed to passing pedestrians, cars, and trucks. Despite uniformed White House guards in sentry booths and two agents with submachine guns behind the front doors, the house was a Secret Serviceman's nightmare.

That day, two neatly dressed men approached the house. Both carried weapons.

Oscar Collazo, the taller of the two, had never fired a gun in his life. But that did not matter to him. He was ready to die if that was what it took to draw attention to what was happening in his homeland, Puerto Rico.

Collazo was one of the thousands of Puerto Ricans who had come to the United States in the 1940s in search of a better life. Their island was not a happy place. Since 1898, Puerto Ricans had lived under the colonial domination of the Colossus of the North, the United States. Every aspect of their life—social, political, economic, and legal—came under the purview of North American colonial administrators. Judges were appointed by the White House; courts were conducted in English; and all appeals were relegated to the federal court in Boston, home of the earliest American investors in Caribbean fruit, sugar, and tobacco.

By the late 1930s, fifty-one corporations, mostly American, controlled 249,000 acres, or 11.3 percent, of the island's land. By World War II, another 13 percent of Puerto Rico's arable land was under the control of the Pentagon for use as military bases. Meanwhile the CIAA-backed Puerto Rican Industrial Development Corporation, organized in 1942 under a bright young man named Teodoro Moscoso, tried feebly to reduce unemployment by building a few small factories to produce cement, paper, glass, and shoes.

With peace and cutbacks in U.S. funding came economic ruin and political unrest. More than 400,000 Puerto Ricans had fought in World War II in U.S. uniforms; in return, many hoped for independence. In 1945, responding to this sentiment, the Puerto Rican legislature formally requested that "the colonial system of government be ended" and that "free and democratic elections" be held. The following year, as the State Department pressured its European allies to end formal colonial rule and erect a Free World as a bulwark against Communist criticisms, President Truman named a Puerto Rican as governor of Puerto Rico for the first time; the next year he signed a law permitting the first popular election of that office.

Luis Muñoz Marín handily won the governorship, promising prosperity from a renewed economic alliance with the United States called Operation Bootstrap.

Many Puerto Ricans were not convinced the new industries would find jobs for displaced farmers, seasonal sugar plantation workers, and ruined craftsmen, and voted with their feet. The migration to New York became a flood; in 1940, fewer than 70,000 Puerto Ricans lived on the U.S. mainland; by 1950, the number was 300,000. One of the Nationalists who had left was Oscar Collazo.

Collazo had been elected president of the Nationalist party's branch in New York City, when, in late April 1950, as the Korean crisis was mounting, an urgent message arrived from Nationalist headquarters in San Juan. The secretary of defense had just visited U.S. base commanders on the island. The Nationalist headquarters claimed that the secretary had instructed the commanders to insist that Governor Muñoz Marín repress the Nationalist party and arrest its leaders or, if that was politically unfeasible, assassinate them. Whether true or not, Collazo took this as a real possibility. The immediate stakes were high for the United States in Korea, and American lives—and objectives in Asia—hung in the balance. Troops from Latin America would be needed, and resistance in Puerto Rico was no example to set for the hemispheric alliance.

Over the next six months, tensions rose steadily on the island. The Nationalists charged that while Muñoz Marín was shedding the trappings of political colonialism, Moscoso's Operation Bootstrap was taking Puerto Rico into deeper economic neocolonialism; Muñoz Marín's proposed commonwealth status, they believed, would end all hopes for national sovereignty.

If low wages and fewer labor rights were too high a price to pay for continued political domination by the United States, the drafting of Puerto Rican youths to fight in Korea seemed intolerable. The Nationalists had succeeded in getting Puerto Rico's legal status placed on the agenda of the scheduled 1951 meeting of the Organization of American States (OAS), the inter-American alliance on which the Pentagon was hoping for reinforcements for the Korean War. In doing so, they also succeeded in rousing Washington's wrath.

On October 27, just as Washington learned that Chinese troops had entered the Korean War, police began arresting Nationalist leaders in Puerto Rico. Demonstrations and armed revolts erupted in cities and villages across the island following a police raid on the farm of the mother of Nationalist party leader Albízu Campos that left three leaders dead.

In response, battalions of U.S.-trained National Guardsmen led by tanks thundered through villages and towns, easily blasting away Nationalist resistance with bazookas, cannon, and machine guns. The fighting would rage for six more days, the casualties reaching into the hundreds, before the revolt was crushed.

In Manhattan, Collazo resolved to act. Angry that the U.S. press ignored the mass arrests and blandly repeated the White House's claim that the revolt was "civil war," rather than an anticolonialist revolt, Collazo thought that only a direct action could expose the U.S. role and stop a slaughter.

With another Nationalist, Griselio Torresola, he bought railroad tickets to Washington. The tickets were one-way; neither man expected to return alive.

President Truman was napping upstairs when he heard gunshots in the street below. Collazo had taken the lead in drawing the guards' fire by launching the assault. As he did, Torresola attacked the west sentry booth, unloading his gun into two guards and racing up the steps to the front door of Blair House. But a guard, dying, squeezed off a shot, killing Torresola. A volley of gunfire cut down Collazo. Truman watched it all from an upstairs window.

As soon as Nelson Rockefeller heard of the assassination attempt, he wired the White House of his concern for Truman's safety. It was the kind of personal touch Harry Truman appreciated.

Truman now took another look at Nelson. On the day the insurrection had begun, Nelson had been recommended for appointment as chairman of the mandated Public Advisory Council for the Point IV Program.[1] The recommendation languished in the limbo of the State Department's bureaucracy. But on November 22, Undersecretary of State James Webb, by 1952 a director of Laurance Rockefeller's favorite jet-fighter manufacturer, McDonnell Aircraft, advised Truman to appoint Nelson chairman of the International Development Advisory Board (IDAB). This time, Truman agreed.

For once, Nelson played a cool hand. Even though this was his first chance in five years to come out of the cold, he did not immediately accept the appointment. He wanted more; he wanted a mandate to make a broad study of foreign aid, beyond technical aid and beyond Latin America.

Nelson's experience as a successful foreign-aid entrepreneur was too valuable to risk losing. With the Korean War raging and the insurrection in Puerto Rico still smoldering, Truman needed the Republican heir on board. He agreed to the study, permitting Nelson to select his own staff so a report could be ready by the following February.

Nelson knew just the people to put together the report, and just the place: Grandfather's old town house on West Fifty-third Street.

The Architect of Foreign Aid

It was like a homecoming. Many of Nelson's cronies were back, along with some new blood. Louis Strauss, Laurance's new adviser in Room 5600, was the most important face in the group. He filled the vacuum left by many of Junior's deposed Old Guard, charting an investment course that led beyond oil to arms and energy industries, particularly nuclear energy.

Nelson benefited directly from Strauss's expertise. He used Strauss to negotiate a renewal of Rockefeller Center's lease with Columbia University. He also drew on Strauss's knowledge of banking for his IDAB report. In Strauss, Nelson found the vision to move the family fortune away from oil and banking into the new high-tech industries, and he hoped to integrate this move into the global scheme IDAB was formulating. It was simply Nelson's way of putting capital to "good use."

In this larger sense, Nelson was searching for meaning. He hoped to strike a balance between the private and public sector in foreign aid, the private sector taking what was profitable, the public, what was necessary. He strove to find an approach toward development that integrated capital, government, and labor into a unified Cold War strategy.

Nelson's report for the IDAB, *Partners in Progress*, gave the technical-aid people what they wanted—a recommendation for $500 million. Predictably, Nelson wanted more, including a doubling of the $1 billion then invested each year by American corporations in the Third World, U.S. taxpayers' assumption of losses incurred by American businessmen when foreign currencies fell in value, an International Finance Corporation to modernize methods of marketing securities to local elites and facilitate corporate investments, bilateral tax and commercial treaties, and exemptions from income taxes on all corporate earnings abroad.

Finally, Nelson wanted all foreign-aid programs, including the Marshall Plan, centralized under a single agency, which he called the Overseas Economic Administration. He defended all these proposals by beating the drum of the Cold War. "The issue really is . . . economic development versus economic subversion."[2]

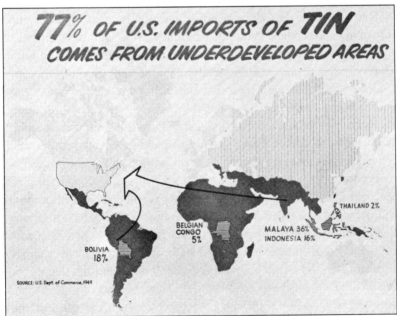

These maps in *Partners in Progress*, the presidential report issued in 1951 by IDAB under Rockefeller's leadership, emphasized the importance of Latin America and other underdeveloped areas as sources of resources for U.S. corporations during peacetime as well as during crises such as the Korean War.

Source: Nelson Rockefeller, *Partners in Progress: A Report to President Truman by the International Development Advisory Board* (Salem, N.H.: Ayer Company Publishers, 1951).

Linking all these proposals was Nelson's renewed drive for regional military pacts. Countries' receipt of U.S. aid would be conditional on their joining Washington's local military alliance: "We should also expect the Administrator to give priority to those nations cooperating with the other free peoples in mutual defense against aggression."[3]

This administrator would rule over a new International Development Authority that would centralize all foreign aid programs. The central administration in Washington would operate under contract with the World Bank.

It would have made Grandfather's head spin. No one doubted whom Nelson had in mind for the administrator.

Nelson's blueprint reached across oceans, even to the oil-rich Middle East. Iraq's Tigris-Euphrates Valley, properly irrigated and fertilized, could "absorb the 750,000 Arab refugees from Palestine, at present the gravest source of unrest in the Middle East."

The Amazon was claimed to have a "2,000 mile long stretch of fertile valleys and plateau land," which could "open up a new major source of food for the entire Continent, as well as a home for settlers from the most densely populated areas of Western Europe."[4]

Many Democrats recognized in Nelson's proposal for another superagency an attempt to reincarnate the CIAA, only worse: independent of the State Department and with global economic authority. It would even absorb Averell Harriman's Economic Cooperation Administration, the famous Marshall Plan in Europe. Harriman would not even let Nelson personally hand in the report to Truman. He delivered it himself, looking every bit like an undertaker bearing his wares.

Nelson was cheered by a note from the president a few days later stating how impressed he was and summarizing the report's salient points. But Nelson could not shake off the suspicion that Truman had not even read the report, much less drafted the letter. He knew how easy it was to get an overworked president's signature.

His later suggestions that Harriman sabotaged any serious consideration of the report were unfair.[5] The report was circulated widely within the administration. The problem was that *no one* liked it. Many took it as another Rockefeller grab for power.

Confronted by stony silence from the Administration, Nelson was frantic at the possibility of another exile. He swung to the right, putting more emphasis on the military aspect of foreign aid. He decided to testify before the House Foreign Affairs Committee, which was considering the Mutual Security Act. It was his last chance, and he came to the Hill with a platoon of aides and a prepared statement. His performance was vintage Rockefeller. He spoke authoritatively as aides propped up huge charts showing a growing gap since 1899 between the U.S. share of the world's production of industrial goods and its share of the world's known raw materials.

In the postwar era, he explained, with the Soviet Union still rebuilding and

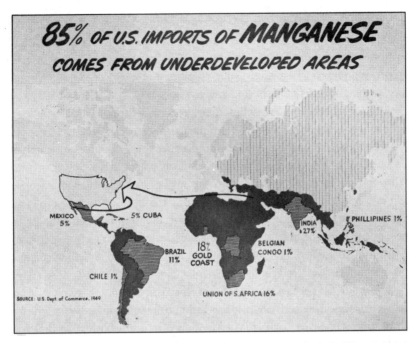

85% OF U.S. IMPORTS OF MANGANESE COMES FROM UNDERDEVELOPED AREAS

MEXICO 5%
5% CUBA
BRAZIL 11%
18% GOLD COAST
CHILE 1%
INDIA 27%
PHILLIPINES 1%
BELGIAN CONGO 1%
UNION OF S. AFRICA 16%
SOURCE: U.S. Dept. of Commerce, 1949

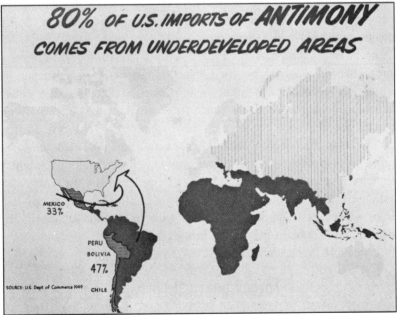

80% OF U.S. IMPORTS OF ANTIMONY COMES FROM UNDERDEVELOPED AREAS

MEXICO 33%
PERU BOLIVIA 47%
CHILE
SOURCE: U.S. Dept. of Commerce 1949

Rockefeller identified the Third World as the source for most of the manganese and antimony used by American companies to, respectively, toughen steel and manufacture medicines. Latin America alone supplied all the antimony imported into the United States and 22 percent of the manganese, a percentage that would soon grow as huge manganese deposits in Brazil's Amazon and western Mato Grosso frontier were mined by Bethlehem Steel and U.S. Steel.

Source: *Partners in Progress.*

the industrial strength of Europe not yet recovered (despite the Marshall Plan), the United States was producing 50 percent of the world's industrial goods, but only 33 percent of its raw materials. "The question is from where do we get the raw materials we import? The answer is that 73 percent of our needs for strategic and critical materials comes from the underdeveloped areas."[6]

Military alliances, such as those that grew out of the Act of Chapultepec, offered only one side of the United States' ability to wage war, he noted. The other side faces within, toward the people who produce these resources for export to the United States. And here was where the human side of the face of Mars had to be shown. Nelson turned to the Amazon for his key example. "For instance, you could not get rubber out of the Amazon during the last war because of disease, sickness and lack of food. . . . There is an interrelationship between all these factors, particularly in the underdeveloped areas of the world."[7]

And to coordinate the necessary aid projects, you need an administrator to oversee a unified Overseas Economic Administration.

It was his last appearance on the mutual-security bill. Nelson's pitch for his own agency was at loggerheads with the administration's plans. Worse, no one with memories of Nelson's maverick style wanted to deal with him again. By the end of October, he realized the fight was over. He would not be appointed to head the new aid agency. To save face and to claim that his job was done, he made an appointment to hand in his resignation.

In the Oval Office, he found Harry Truman serenely disposed to the news. Truman intended to incorporate the Economic Cooperative Administration into the proposed Mutual Security Agency, and, perhaps to deemphasize its military edge, would appoint Averell Harriman its chief. Harriman, after all, was a Democrat. Why don't you become one, too? he asked Nelson. Nelson refused.

The presidential elections were only a year away, and the Democrats were in trouble. Nelson's Uncle Winthrop and his father were behind Dwight D. Eisenhower's preparations to run. The popular general's election would allow Nelson to return to Washington in proper style and really shake things up—to do what he wanted. He could perhaps even move the ranks of the Republican party into the modern era associated with his family's endeavors.

It would be his biggest mistake.

FOLLOWING THE GENERAL

The Rockefellers were not prepared to be forced out of the party of their forebears by ultra-rightists. The GOP was still the party of the Eastern Establishment, and the Rockefellers were now that Establishment's First Family.

Chase National Bank's pioneering of American banking in postwar Germany and Standard Oil's control over much of the Middle East's oil had placed the Rockefellers at the financial and industrial nexus of European reconstruction. Their dominance over trans-Atlantic finance—with all that was implied in an Atlanticist-based foreign policy in Washington—was unassailable. Few financiers would miss the meaning of John J. McCloy's transfer from Germany as U.S. military governor and high commissioner to New York as chairman of Chase National Bank. And no one doubted that it was a promotion.

This deepening Rockefeller involvement in the fate of Europe, not the Third World, led to Nelson Rockefeller's return to Washington under Eisenhower. It was Latin America, however, that would return him to power.

By October 1951, all eyes of the Republican Eastern Establishment had settled on Eisenhower as the candidate. Eisenhower's loyalty to corporate prerogatives on gaining foreign markets and resources was in no doubt, and all hoped that he would take up the banner of internationalism for a wider NATO alliance that would include Turkey and Greece and a rearmed Germany. They saw in the general someone with enough prestige to override Taft's fiscal conservatism and his constitutionalist apprehensions about presidential usurpation of Congress's power to declare war.*

The Rockefellers in particular hoped the war hero could arrest the deterioration of the more moderate central faction of the Republican party. They wanted Eisenhower to rescue the party from the extreme nationalism espoused by General Douglas MacArthur and Wisconsin's junior senator, Joseph R. McCarthy.

By mid-1951, McCarthy's witch-hunt had consumed the careers of leftists and liberals who were never to Rockefeller's liking. But now his fires were spreading out of control, lapping at the doors of the very institutions that were the bedrock of the Rockefeller political empire, including the Rockefeller-financed Institute of Pacific Relations and the Rockefeller-funded Walter Hines Page School of International Relations at Johns Hopkins University.

To steady Washington's keel as the ship of state carried the American people through the McCarthyite storm would take a captain of unimpeachable reputation, yet one who was responsive to higher direction. Nelson's uncle, Winthrop Aldrich, led the way in recruiting Eisenhower as the Republican candidate.

Nelson, however, was kept in the background during the campaign. His penchant for attracting media attention would have tarnished Eisenhower's name with conservative Republicans. He displayed self-discipline by confining his help to backstage. He set up a team of economists to work on position

* Taft had been critical of Truman's sending troops into the Korean conflict without Congress's authorization, although he weakened the constitutional thrust of his argument considerably by backing the war once the troops were engaged in battle.

papers for the campaign and found Eisenhower's principal speechwriters. To cap it all off, Nelson joined his family in quietly slipping Eisenhower his largest campaign donation: $94,000.[8]

As the campaign rolled toward its landslide victory, Nelson was preoccupied with the Cold War. He grappled with how best to fight the holy crusade, exploring everything from the details of reorganizing Washington's bureaucracies, to the broader philosophical questions involved in constructing a popular argument that would link the cause of democracy and freedom with the ideology of capitalism. His ideas were not new, but they would make a deep impact on the lives of millions of people in the United States, as well as in the Third World.

THE COLD WAR'S NEW FRONTIERS

The "Shining Dream" of the Amazon returned. IBEC's John Camp wrote to Nelson from Venezuela, recommending that the new Republican administration open up South America's interior.

> I would propose a vast land development scheme for a belt of undeveloped area, extending from Venezuela through Colombia, Ecuador, Peru, Bolivia, Paraguay and Argentina; mostly on the east side of the Andes in the headwaters of the Orinoco, Amazon and Paraguay-Parana Rivers. This is the largest undeveloped land area available for settlement remaining in the Western World.
>
> Probably the first big need is a principal railroad and highway from Venezuela to Argentina through the heart of this area.[9]

Camp proposed what ultimately became the Trans-Amazonian Highway.

The death knell for the Amazonian Indian had just tolled.

The development of capitalism in the Third World was not moving rapidly enough to meet popular demands for land reform and industry. The settlement of Amazonia was an intriguing alternative to rupturing alliances with Latin American regimes by insisting that these regimes redistribute land—the very source of their monopoly on economic and political power.

Nowhere was the danger of this latter course more evident than in Guatemala, where a revolution was getting out of hand, and in the Philippines, where one had almost done so.

In Guatemala, the elected government of agrarian reformer President Jacobo Arbenz had embarked on a program of land redistribution that included expropriating uncultivated land. The largest owner of uncultivated land in Guatemala was Boston's United Fruit Company, a firm with ties to the inner circle of Eisenhower's campaign. United Fruit's continued success was vital to a host of Rockefeller's friends in business and government.[10]

In October 1952, these forces coalesced in a Council on Foreign Relations study group on "Political Unrest in Latin America." Several people voiced their opinions, but as usual Adolf Berle had the last word. Let's characterize the Arbenz government as not merely communist, Berle suggested, but as "a Russian-controlled dictatorship." It followed—somehow—that an elected government that displeased American corporate interests like United Fruit was actually "a clear-cut intervention by a foreign power, in this case, the Soviet Union."

That fork taken, Berle raced down a well-trod path: "It seemed to me that there was perfectly good ground for the United States to invoke the Act of Chapultepec and the Treaty of Rio de Janeiro, pledging all hands to defend against domination from without the hemisphere. . . . Certainly the Council on Foreign Relations the other night agreed generally that the Guatemalan government was communist."

The next step required no conspiracy. It was as natural as breathing.

"I am arranging to see Nelson Rockefeller. He knows the situation and can work a little with General Eisenhower on it."[11]

Shortly after Eisenhower's election, Berle also brought the machinations in Guatemala to the attention of Deputy CIA Director Allen Dulles and another old friend of Nelson's, J. C. King.

He was now Colonel King, having won promotion through sensitive intelligence work in Argentina, one of Latin America's most volatile posts during King's tenure there as a military attaché. Nazi scientists and Gestapo officers were being recruited by the U.S. Army Command in Germany for work against local communists; many of these men were then allowed to pass through the "rat pipeline" with Vatican passports from Italy and Spain to Argentina, where King, who had gained access to seized records[12] on secret German holdings in Argentina and other Latin American countries, was monitoring the corporate investments of the fugitives. At least a dozen of these Nazi fugitives remained CIA assets in countries like Bolivia and Chile.

The success of King's operations in Argentina was evident by his meteoric rise to the equivalent rank of a lieutenant general as the CIA's first Chief of Clandestine Services in the Western Hemisphere. For intelligence gathering, he relied on former FBI agents (J. Edgar Hoover having shared control with Rockefeller of intelligence operations in Latin America during World War II), using as their main sources American businessmen who were overseeing subsidiaries of major American corporations, as well as local police chiefs in Latin American cities.

King owed his rise in the CIA, therefore, to a network of operatives who were severely limited in their capacity to provide accurate and broad political intelligence. Most had little experience in the countryside, where most of Latin America's population still lived, and certainly not with the Indian miners and peasants.

Other sources of information were needed, people who, if not members of the targeted population themselves, had the trust of those who were: people whose presence in the rural areas would not be threatening or lacking in reason, who were academically trained enough to give insightful analysis into mores, if not political developments.

Adolf Berle had the answer. Berle had been helpful to Allen Dulles in the CIA's recent campaign against the Philippine Huks. The Free Asia Committee was formally established in 1952, just as the CIA was grooming Ramón Magsaysay to turn the Philippines into the American showcase for democracy in Asia. The Free Asia Committee, Berle advised Dulles, could engage in "pamphlet and infiltration work. Furthermore, there is a supply of personnel, chiefly men from the mission colleges."[13]

17

IN THE WAKE OF WAR–AND THE CIA

THE MIRACLE OF M-A-G-S-A-Y-S-A-Y

Lieutenant Colonel Edward Lansdale, Ramón Magsaysay's closest CIA adviser, had worked for years for this day. Magsaysay had just been nominated for the presidency of the Philippines, the strategic former U.S. colony of 7,000 islands stretching between Indonesia in the south and the Chinese mainland in the north.

Lansdale's counterinsurgency goals against the Hukbalahap (Huk) rebellion had been frustrated by the current president of the Philippines, Elpido Querino, who had been assuming an increasingly independent posture and distancing himself from the U.S. Embassy and Lansdale's campaign for limited economic and political reforms. By the summer of 1952, Washington had decided to give Lansdale the green light to make Magsaysay, the defense minister, president.

Lansdale launched the Magsaysay for President Movement as a broad-based coalition, building Magsaysay's name as a symbol against corruption. Meanwhile, he initiated psychological warfare against rural villagers who were sympathetic to the Huks. Troops dressed in Huk uniforms attacked hamlets. Then regular army units, scaled down to the self-sufficient light-battalion size that was more appropriate for high mobility in guerrilla warfare, descended on the confused villagers with a "program of attraction" directed by Magsaysay's Civil Affairs Office (CAO). While the soldiers dispensed candy and gum to children and built 4,000 prefabricated schools to show concern for the peasants, CAO-directed psychological warfare (psywar) teams spread rumors and propaganda and offered rewards for informers. Such "civic action" to assist villagers was standard fare, raising the morale of recruits who were often unaware that the propaganda against the Huks was "black," that is, false.

Religious beliefs were a key part of Lansdale's psywar operations. Sometimes families who were fingered as Huk sympathizers would wake in the morning to find the "Eye of God"—a painting of a giant eye—facing their front door. It was one of the harmonica-playing Lansdale's favorite ruses. Another was snatching the last man in a Huk patrol, killing him, puncturing his neck with two holes, and hanging him upside down until his blood drained out. Then his corpse would be put back on the trail to be mistaken as a victim of the *asuang*, the vampire of Philippine lore.[1]

Linguistics was also incorporated into the CIA's operation. Using a small aircraft with a mounted loudspeaker, Lansdale would fly in dense clouds over villagers who were suspected of being Huk sympathizers. Speaking in the Tagalog language, he would broadcast curses drawn from the CIA's and anthropologists' studies of local taboos and myths.

On the very day that Magsaysay was nominated as a coalition candidate for the presidency, a new American agency was brought into the pacification program. Headlines announcing his nomination were just hitting the Manila streets when Magsaysay ordered his secretary to drive to the docks. He wanted the secretary to meet a couple of Americans just arriving. Magsaysay considered these Americans so important that he had intended to meet their ship himself; because of the publicity surrounding his nomination, however, he changed his mind. The Philippines was a Catholic country, and he was already too closely identified with the U.S. Embassy to risk being seen greeting American Protestant missionaries as they stepped ashore. But Magsaysay was happy that the missionaries from the Summer Institute of Linguistics (SIL) had arrived. He needed them.

When Richard Pittman arrived in Manila, he was not aware of Colonel Lansdale or that the CIA had just completed its first investigation of SIL.[2] To the missionary, Magsaysay was an "instrument in the hand of God"[3] to launch SIL in the Philippines.

This was not Pittman's first visit to Manila. In April 1951, stopping en route to California from a Bible-translation seminar in Australia, he found Manila an armed camp. He spent six weeks surveying the islands' languages and dialects, estimating a number somewhere between 100 and 200. When he reported back to Cam in California, Cam's eyes lit up. As soon as Cam received copies of his biography of Cárdenas from the publisher, he forwarded one to Pittman to send to Magsaysay.

One day, the phone rang with a call from the Philippines. "Thank you," a voice said, "book . . . important for my people." Then he hung up. Pittman asked the operator the name of the caller.

"It was a Mr. M-A-G-S-A-Y-S-A-Y,"[4] she spelled.

Cam ordered SIL to begin preparations for an advance into the Pacific. Pittman was given the royal treatment, meeting with top Magsaysay aides and future cabinet members, college presidents, the current secretary of education,

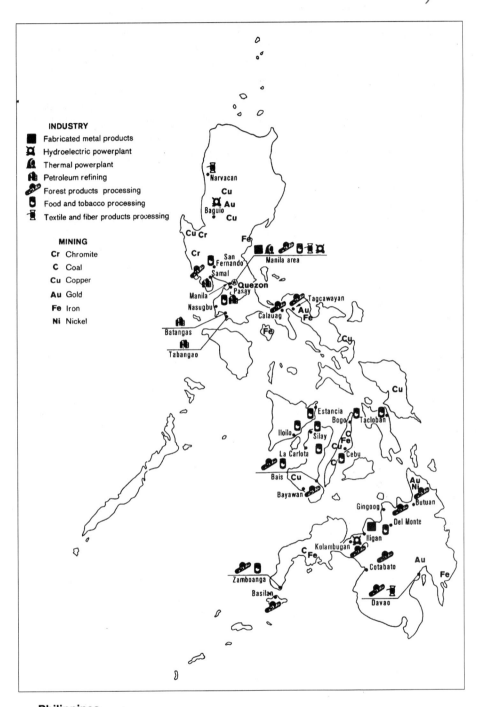

INDUSTRY

- ⬛ Fabricated metal products
- ⬛ Hydroelectric powerplant
- ⬛ Thermal powerplant
- ⬛ Petroleum refining
- ⬛ Forest products processing
- ⬛ Food and tobacco processing
- ⬛ Textile and fiber products processing

MINING

- **Cr** Chromite
- **C** Coal
- **Cu** Copper
- **Au** Gold
- **Fe** Iron
- **Ni** Nickel

Narvacan

Cu

Au

Baguio

Cu

Cu Cr

Cr

Fe

San Fernando

Manila area

Samal

Quezon

Pasay

Manila

Tagcawayan

Nasugbu

Calauag

Au

Fe

Batangas

Fe

Tabangao

Cu

Cu

Estancia

Bogo

Tacloban

Iloilo

Silay

Cu

Fe

La Carlota

Cu

Cebu

Bais

Cu

Bayawan

Au

Ni

Gingoog

Butuan

Del Monte

Iligan

Kolambugan

C Fe

Au

Cotabato

Fe

Zamboanga

Basilan

Davao

Philippines

Besides being home to Dole and Del Monte plantations and the Subic Bay U.S. Navy base, the Philippines was the site of mining activities by American-owned companies.

Source: Central Intelligence Agency, 1973.

and the director of the Institute of National Languages. Pittman found Magsaysay an awesome figure: Standing six feet tall, Magsaysay looked like a linebacker for the Chicago Bears. He ran an American-style campaign with the help of Lansdale and the CIA, complete with "Magsaysay's My Guy" buttons.

He won by a landslide. He was now hailed as Washington's alternative to the more neutral-minded anticolonial leaders of Asia, Nehru of India and Sukarno of Indonesia. Senate Majority Leader William F. Knowland of California invited Magsaysay to organize a military and economic alliance with Chiang Kai-shek and other anticommunist leaders in South Korea, Vietnam, Laos, Cambodia, and Thailand. This alliance would crystallize in 1956 as the Southeast Asia Treaty Organization (SEATO), a direct offshoot of the regional pact sanctioned at Chapultepec and San Francisco a decade earlier through the efforts of Nelson Rockefeller and Adolf Berle.

Lansdale was already way ahead of Knowland. As early as 1952, he secretly flew his Filipino counterinsurgency operatives into Vietnam to advise Ngo Dinh Diem, the CIA's heir apparent to the throne of France's puppet emperor, Bao Dai.[5] In 1954, with the French defeat at Dien Bien Phu, Lansdale would move his operation into Vietnam. In his wake would come SIL's Pittman, with a letter of introduction to Diem from Magsaysay.[6]

Cam greeted Pittman's contract with Magsaysay with the cry of a Cold Warrior, relishing the thought of translating the Bible "for scores and scores of tribes almost under the nose of communism; and someday on into tribal areas that exist behind the Iron Curtain."[7]

CAM'S MISSIONARY HOMECOMING

At about the same time Pittman wrote Cam for money to do more tribal surveys in the Philippines, Cam received an urgent letter from Guatemala. Donald Burns, his newest protégé, needed help. SIL had entered Guatemala in 1952 to provide translations to American Protestant missionary organizations, including his old friends at the Central American Mission (C.A.M.). The missionaries wanted to extend their work among the smaller Indian tribes. But the Protestants were confronted by a serious rival for the Indians' loyalty: the new democratically elected government headed by President Jacobo Arbenz Guzmán. The government's nationalistic program of improved wages and land reform had threatened one of the wellsprings of conversions for the C.A.M.: the United Fruit Company, the largest landowner in Guatemala.

After assuming office in 1951, Arbenz had initiated his land-distribution plan against foreign-owned United Fruit. C.A.M. missionaries were unhappy to see United Fruit singled out, believing that was the first step toward the expulsion of all American interests, including the C.A.M. The C.A.M. had marked "Red

Russia" as the outside agitator responsible for Guatemala's unrest. It had four intercessors pray daily that "the door of Guatemala and other Central American Republics . . . remain open in spite of Communist[s] . . . that Satanic opposition in the form of Communism be broken."[8]

Cam caught the first plane out of Lima. He seemed obsessed with gaining a foothold in Guatemala at the height of the crisis. He flew back and forth to the country four times in 1953 to break through each logjam in the negotiations. The U.S. Embassy was now deeply involved in CIA covert operations to undermine the Arbenz government. Ironically, the only point that the embassy and the government seemed to have agreed on that year was the usefulness of SIL, but for different reasons.

The embassy's biggest concern was for United Fruit. Arbenz's chief worry was the smaller coffee growers in the highlands and their allies among other rural landlords, the clergy, and the military. The growers dominated most of the best lands, which left the mass of the Indians landless, forcing them to work as seasonal laborers on the coffee fincas or on cotton and sugar plantations on the coast. The coffee growers had been an important base of support for the revolution that had overthrown the Ubico dictatorship in 1944. But strikes by Indian workers and land seizures by peasants—sometimes led by Guatemalan communists, but most often not*—alarmed the coffee growers. Arbenz's officials responded by trying to keep the highlands relatively undisturbed. Rather than initiate the kind of radical agrarian reform program that had already thrown the coastlands into turmoil, they sponsored programs initiated by the Guatemalan branch of the Inter-American Indian Institute—projects in archaeology, ethnography, bilingual education, and soil reclamation and surveys of health conditions, labor, and trade. None of these programs posed an immediate threat to the status quo. If anything, they all were a continuation of similar projects originally funded by Nelson Rockefeller's CIAA and the State Department.

Arbenz was convinced that roads, education, and fairer prices for goods and services would end the "backwardness" of the highland Indians. To carry out his plan, he relied on two old hands in Indian assimilation: the National Indian Institute and SIL.

Cam called down Ethel Wallis, an SILer from Mexico's Mezquital valley whom he would later choose as SIL's official historian, and assigned her to work on the Guatemalan government's new education and language program among the 300,000 Kikchí Indians of Alta Verapaz, a hilly, semitropical coffee region. Like most of the Indian highlands, the Kikchí villages would remain relatively silent when Guatemala City came under attack by a CIA-sponsored invasion in 1954.

---

* Few rural leaders of those jailed after the CIA-backed coup were found to understand, much less support, communist theories. See Stokes Newbold (Richard Adams), "Receptivity to Communist Fomented Agitation in Rural Guatemala," *Economic Development and Cultural Change* 5, no. 4 (1957).

Most of the poorer Indians could not be inspired to defend the Arbenz government because the core of their economic needs had not been reached by the revolution.

The same was true for the mining state of Huehuetenango, an area rich with Mayan ruins. Cam sent an SIL couple to the Aguatatec Mayas in that region. Not surprisingly, their Protestantism was appealing to some young garlic growers who were challenging the Ladino-dominated *cargo* system of their elders. But the vast majority of these landless Indians, their economic needs also untouched by Guatemala City, would not defend Arbenz when the crisis came.

Cam needed no introduction to the Cakchiquels, whom he visited earlier in the year. More than a thousand of these Indians turned out to hear the American speak to them in their own tongue of God's Will.

But the Black Carib tribe of the Caribbean coast were new to Cam. Some of them worked as seasonal laborers alongside blacks brought in from Jamaica to cultivate the banana plantations of United Fruit. Arbenz had recently penetrated the United Fruit stronghold with a long-promised road linking the Pacific Coast to Puerto Barrios on the Caribbean coast. The road provided an alternative to the high freight fares charged by the only railroad, owned by United Fruit. Just south of Puerto Barrios, Arbenz also built a new port connected to the road, to compete with United Fruit's docking monopoly.

Into this smoldering economic conflict, Cam sent two SIL women, who set up shop in Livingston, a Ladino-controlled town north of Puerto Barrios where landless peasants and United Fruit's agricultural workers were pressing for reforms. The peasants had legitimate grievances against the American company: discriminatory policies, high-priced company stores, low wages, poor housing, lack of safe working conditions or workers' compensation, hospital fees set at 2 percent of their salaries, and hundreds of thousands of acres of fallow land. The coffee growers had originally backed the revolution against Ubico to end United Fruit's domination of freight charges and its distortion of economic development. Now, fearful of the lower classes, they were closing ranks with the conservatives.

It was apparently too much for the two politically unprepared American women. At the close of 1953, as the political climate tightened with peasants seizing land and Arbenz agreeing to expropriate and distribute unused lands owned by United Fruit, they returned home.*

During their absence, the Arbenz government expropriated 173,000 acres from United Fruit's Banassera plantation on the Caribbean. This brought the total loss for United Fruit to more than 400,000 acres.[9] Through United Fruit's fallow

---

*They sat out the coup in a classroom in Oklahoma, and did not return until Arbenz was gone and United Fruit's land and order were restored.

landholding alone, Guatemala's peasantry had recovered one-seventh of their country's arable land.

The Final Break with the Cárdenas Legacy

While Arbenz acted, friends and associates of Nelson Rockefeller met secretly to bring Arbenz to his knees. They branded Arbenz in the hemisphere's press as a Soviet agent. Friends in the State Department informed Guatemala's ambassador that agrarian reform bills like Arbenz's were actually "secondary problems" of a much broader communist problem. United Fruit was breezily dismissed. The problem was communism. Communism was "not any economic, doctrinal or even military matter. It was a political one."[10]

Adolf Berle drew on the legacy of Nelson's work at the Chapultepec conference to urge the Eisenhower administration to use the OAS as the auspices through which Arbenz could be overthrown. After three weeks of intensive lobbying among Latin American diplomats in Washington failed, the State Department's political action officer in Guatemala suggested economic warfare "to keep Guatemala off balance" until Washington could line up votes for the "proposed OAS meeting." His list of economic weapons included diverting oil tankers to create a gasoline crisis, suspending credit for coffee growers, and spreading a CIA rumor about impending U.S. economic sanctions to stimulate a business panic and "flight of capital."[11]

Nelson's old friend J. C. King became the first field general in the CIA's plot to overthrow Arbenz. King, relying on the military and United Fruit, had tried twice before and failed.

CIA Director Allen Dulles and Deputy Director Frank Wisner decided that this time King needed troops who were more familiar with paramilitary operations and psychological warfare.

The CIA's station chief in South Korea, Colonel Albert Haney, was tapped for the job. Haney's plan was for a multimillion-dollar "Guatemalan exile" invasion backed by U.S. Marines, helicopters, and C-47 transports, if necessary. The problem was that it was too big to be a covert operation with plausible deniability for the United States. King suggested military aid to bribe the Guatemalan army. "J. C., you've had four years to try that approach," replied Wisner. "Now the situation is worse than ever."[12]

The CIA ended up applying many of the psychological warfare tactics it had used against the Huks to convince Arbenz he had lost the support of his country and that he was facing a formidable armed enemy. (Both were untrue, but Arbenz did not know it until he had already resigned.) The CIA's "Voice of Liberation" beamed to the country a painstakingly edited version of a drunken "call for desertion" by a Guatemalan pilot who had fled. Frightened, Arbenz grounded his air force. It was his first serious error.

This left the skies to CIA pilots. Flying out of clandestine airstrips in Honduras, the bombers pounded Guatemala.[13]

Unable to silence the CIA's radio broadcasts, Arbenz contributed to the panic by shutting off Guatemala City's electricity. This left the CIA's radio as the only source of "developing news" of mythical rebel columns approaching the city. The capital's residents promptly set up portable generators to listen—and began to flee. With the CIA's explosions flashing over the darkened city, the residents of Guatemala City became convinced that they were experiencing something like wartime London during the blitz.

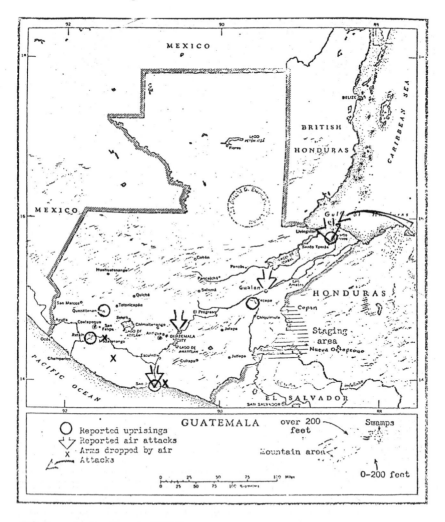

CIA Coup in Guatemala (1954)
This map, which the Agency presented to President Eisenhower, falsely reported popular uprisings in support of the CIA's coup.

Source: Central Intelligence Agency; map provided by the Dwight D. Eisenhower Library.

Meanwhile, the CIA's Colonel Carlos Castillo Armas, who had already been interviewed by King and chosen as "the Liberator,"[14] was making official history. The Liberator led a hastily trained "army" of fewer than 300 men, armed by United Fruit, across the Honduran border. After advancing only a few miles into Guatemala, he camped at the national shrine of the Church of the Black Christ. There, symbolically ensconced next to a Mecca for Catholics throughout Central America, he waited.

As bombs fell on Guatemala City, Allen Dulles coordinated CIA operations with his brother's State Department officials in Washington and New York. The U.S. delegation at the United Nations, led now by Nelson's friend and ally from Massachusetts, Henry Cabot Lodge, fought against the Security Council taking up Arbenz's complaint. This was an internal Guatemalan dispute, Lodge argued, which would be referred instead to the OAS.

John Foster Dulles used threats of economic reprisals to ram through a resolution condemning Guatemala.

Between June 18 and June 22, news flashed around the world of the invasion and of protests and riots in Mexico, Chile, Uruguay, Bolivia, Argentina, and even Honduras. The mission was condemned by the government of Ecuador and by the congresses of Argentina, Chile, and Uruguay. King had been right. An invasion was much too big an operation to conceal from the world.

Guatemala's request for a U.N. observer team to confirm the invasion was rejected by a vote of 10 to 1 in the Security Council, the Soviet delegation casting the one opposing vote (the misgivings of Britain and France were muffled by Dulles's warning about their need for U.S. support against Nasser over the Suez Canal). Instead, the Security Council declared that this was not a U.S. invasion, but an "internal dispute" that must be referred to the OAS. The president of the Security Council was U.S. Ambassador Henry Cabot Lodge. The Secretary General of the OAS was Nelson's good friend from the Chapultepec conference, Carlos Davila of Chile.

The end quickly came when the army balked on taking to the field to crush the leader of the coup, Castillo Armas. When Arbenz then asked the generals to distribute arms to the populace, they demanded his resignation. Arbenz, betrayed by his former military colleagues, lost confidence and surrendered.

The missionaries celebrated the fall of the Arbenz government, even as many of their Protestant converts were swept up in the massive arrests that followed. Protestant Indians—including nineteen in Cam's original mission—"suffered the judgment of God" for being "involved in communism."[15] A woman whom the Townsends had helped become the country's first female doctor had to flee after her husband was arrested as an Arbenz supporter.[16] Over 500 Ixil Maya Indians who participated in the land reform in northern Quiché were exiled to the jungles of Petén. Pocoman Maya Indians who led the local peasants' union were also jailed.

One Cakchiquel pastor could watch his people die only so long before he took to the hills to lead a Cakchiquel guerrilla unit; eventually, he, too, would be killed.

Ironically, a foreign physician, who was thought to have sympathies with Arbenz, was released by the CIA's E. Howard Hunt as one of his last acts before leaving Guatemala. Perhaps the young man was spared because he had applied for a job with United Fruit or because he came from a respected family in Argentina, with relatives in the United States. Whatever the reason, Hunt would regret letting Dr. Ernesto Lynch Guevara go. Citing the lessons he had learned from Arbenz's reliance on elections and the standing army, the physician would return to confront the CIA in Cuba as "Che" Guevara.

All lands distributed to the peasantry were returned to their former owners, predominantly United Fruit. More than 500 union locals lost their legal registration, which effectively destroyed the banana workers' federation.

Guatemala's lands, its Indians, its plantations, and its mines were now open again to American investment.

Castillo Armas also threw open the country to American oil companies. Dulles's State Department designed a new petroleum law for Guatemala, restricting Guatemala's share of profits to a maximum of 50 percent. In addition, the companies were granted a 27.5 percent oil-depletion allowance and were allowed to deduct any losses incurred since the 1945 revolution from any year's profits.[17]

By 1956, twenty oil companies had taken out forty-year concessions on over half of Guatemala. Barbed wire went up around oil derricks that were drilling on Indian lands. In 1959, oil was struck in the tropical state of Petén just above the coffee estates of Alta Verapaz. That was the year that William Cameron Townsend, attending an Inter-American Indian Conference in Guatemala City, secretly aided the efforts of the U.S. delegation to muffle the protests of Guatemalan Indians over the rollback of Arbenz's agrarian reform. In return, SIL would get land from the government for a new headquarters. Behind the rhetoric of God and bilingual democracies, oil and land whispered between the lines of government contracts with SIL. They were the secret of SIL's power and of Cam's unique ability to help the United States as an official delegate of Peru at Inter-American Indian Congresses. Cam owed that, too, to a dictator who ruled over a predominantly Indian people: Peru's General Manuel Odría.

NIBBLING AT THE AMAZON

General Odría had ridden the horse of the Apocalypse to the height of his power in the summer of 1953, when he took an unusual journey into the Peruvian Amazon jungle with two Cold Warriors from the United States. Appropriately "sheep-dipped" (as the CIA put it for military men wearing civilian clothes), the barrel-chested general arrived in Pucallpa in a muddy Chevrolet truck at the head of an armed caravan. With him were William Cameron Townsend and Robert Le Tourneau, a millionaire manufacturer of earth-moving machines from Texas.

After a short speech to the residents, the men drove to the airport, boarded a waiting DC-3, and took off south toward the largest-known oil field in the Amazon. Passing over the domelike ridge that outlined the underground oil pool, Odría pressed his nose to the window. Here, at Ganso Azul and in these Americans, he hoped he had found the panacea for his many problems.

Time was running out for him. Since he formally assumed the presidency three years before, Peru's economy—and his political fortunes—had boomed off the Korean War. In his first year of office, Peruvian exports to the United States, mostly strategic minerals clawed out of the Andes by Indian miners, had skyrocketed 50 percent. The bonanza in tax revenues had allowed him to resume paying off Peru's debts in full to anxious New York bankers, and Washington had shown its appreciation by arranging another $60 million loan for his ambitious array of highways, irrigation projects, port renovations, and other public works.

Now, all that was about to end. According to reports from the United States, President Eisenhower would soon end the Korean War. Odría would have to cut his budget drastically if he was to keep the almighty New York banks, and Washington, happy. Unless, that is, he could find some way of convincing foreign oil companies to develop that dome and any others like it down there that were hidden beneath the forest canopy.

Odría already had tried to entice the oilmen. He had summoned Peru's lawmakers to a special session of Congress and forced through a new petroleum law that gave generous terms to foreign oil companies: forty- to fifty-year concessions, a hefty depletion allowance, and 50 percent of the remaining profits. He ignored the outrage from nationalists on both the left and the right while officials of a dozen foreign firms descended on Lima in January 1953 for five days of bidding.

The companies included Union Oil of California, the fount of donations to Townsend's Church of the Open Door in Los Angeles. But it was Standard Oil of New Jersey's subsidiary, International Petroleum, that flew off with most of the prey. The prey, however, would prove gritty eating. Sechura Desert, where large oil pools were thought to exist, cost the oil companies $2.5 million for their concessions; they would spend $27 million more before realizing that it was not going to pay off like the Arabian desert had. For Odría, however, the Amazon bids were the greatest immediate disappointment. Although oil was already known to exist at the Ganso Azul dome near Pucallpa, Odría collected a total of only a little over $1,000 in bids. The general had special reasons to be dismayed. His closest business associate, Hernando de Lavalle, was a director of the Ganso Azul Petroleum Company. After the curtain fell on Odría's auction of the Peruvian Amazon, de Lavalle and the Americans on Ganso Azul's board decided to sell out. The buyer was an American consortium led by Texas Gulf, an independent oil company based in Houston. Texas Gulf's reach extended straight to the center of power in the American Northeast. Its principal investors, the Reeds of New York, had intimate ties with the Pentagon and the Rockefellers' trans-Atlantic financial networks.

Other powerful foreign investors were already in the area. Socony held concessions in four Amazonian states. Another 1,816,185-acre concession in the Amazon was held by the Gildemeisters, the powerful German-Peruvian sugar dynasty; still another 929,000 acres were controlled by Canadian investors.

All these holdings, no matter how promising, would languish without a transportation infrastructure. Pucallpa, with Ganso Azul bubbling happily nearby, seemed the most promising site for a trans-Andean pipeline terminus. Now, thanks to Townsend, Odría also had the prospect of a colony of settlers that could alleviate the pressure for land reform in the Andes and along the Pacific Coast while providing a profitable local market for his friends in the oil companies.

As Odría's plane circled Ganso Azul, the general looked up from the dome and eyed the American sitting next to Townsend who was also peering down at the oil field. This man, Townsend had promised, could help the regime. Robert Le Tourneau had flown down from Texas in his private plane to put a startling proposition to Odría. He would sponsor the development of a colony in the Pucallpa region. He would put up all the houses and install all the water-treatment and sewerage facilities, even a fifty-mile-long paved road linking the colony to the Trans-Andean highway that the United States had built during the war. All he wanted were two things: 1 million acres of land near the Ganso Azul field to harvest tropical hardwood and graze some 5,000 head of cattle, and the designation that the colony could be peopled by North American and Peruvian "Christians."

"Mr. President," Cam explained, "Le Tourneau is very much in love with his Lord and Savior, Jesus Christ. He wants to please his Lord. He realizes that his Lord does not need servants, but to serve his Lord he must serve his fellow men. So he wants to serve the people of Peru. He wants to lay up treasure in heaven so that when he goes up there he will have a fortune. Down here he has all he needs. He wants to have his treasure in heaven."[18]

Le Tourneau indeed had all he needed on earth. He was a multimillionaire. His name was synonymous with the world's largest earth-moving machines. Cam, as usual, had not told the whole story. Le Tourneau had just sold most of his company to Westinghouse Air Brake, the giant train brakes and signaling combine controlled by Pittsburgh's Richard K. Mellon and his son-in-law, Herbert A. May. The Mellons paid Le Tourneau over $26 million for his company, in exchange for his promise to stay out of the earth-moving business for five years.

Le Tourneau's deal with Odría, worked out in the middle of the jungle with Cam's translating help, was for a colony in one of the most remote places on earth. It was not likely to draw much attention in the United States. His working through a subsidiary of a tax-free evangelical school he had founded (ingeniously named Le Tourneau College) should also have been helpful. Headlines made by outraged Catholic leaders, however, were not.

A "Protestant nucleus" on the eastern side of the Andes "can have grave repercussions on the unity of the nation," challenged the group. The controversy became so heated that it made a headline in the *New York Times*: "CATHOLICS PROTEST TEXAN'S PERU PLANS. Fear Protestant Proselytizing in Jungle Reclamation Project of Le Tourneau."[19]

"This is a business deal," Le Tourneau retorted, but quickly added a qualification: "However, I'm a man that mixes business and religion. The President knows that."[20]

Seeing a crack in Odría's armor, his opponents zeroed in on his whole relationship with the Americans, lambasting Odría's vast concessions to Standard Oil. As the storm gathered in nationalist circles against growing U.S. influence in the Peruvian Amazon, it threatened to engulf SIL. Cam could not deny the economic implications of "Tournavista," as Le Tourneau called his planned colony in emulation of his Lord's humility. Cam had written about the coming economic miracle in the U.S. community's Lima daily, and, with Oscar Vasquez Benavides, former president of the board of the Inter-American Indian Institute, had surveyed the route of a proposed railway that would link Pucallpa with the rail network that served the American-owned copper mines in the Andes.

Proudly, Cam described how deforestation of the Peruvian Amazon "could be doubled as soon as the [Le Tourneau] highway has been paved, and it could be trebled if Mr. R.G. Le Tourneau put his Diesel-Electric Rubber-Tired Tournatrain to work on the highway, hauling in lumber at half the present cost of transportation."[21] As trees disappeared from the Amazon's delicate ecosystem, cattle ranches would appear in their place, Cam promised, again by Le Tourneau's design. Cam reported how impressed Le Tourneau was by his visit to the cattle ranch set up by the food supply service (SCIPA), established by Rockefeller's CIAA and since funded with Point IV money. Then there was the development of what might prove to be as big an oil field as Venezuela's, even a pipeline over the Andes to tap the oil fields along the Ecuadorian border, where Cam's missionaries battled the Prince of Darkness and the mysteries of strange tongues.

Peruvian eyes now focused on the man who had brought Le Tourneau to Peru and acted as his interpreter. Who was this man? How had he achieved such power to act as a broker for Peru's future? Was SIL really part of an American plot to undermine Peru's national sovereignty, as the Catholic engineers charged, perhaps to sever the oil-rich Amazon as an independent colony controlled by the United States? Suspicions fanned by Odría's opponents centered on SIL's contract with the general to start a bilingual school system for Indians in the Amazon. Cam tried to lessen dissent against SIL's bilingual schools by offering his Jungle

Aviation and Radio Service (JAARS) as a sacrificial goat. JAARS's four airplanes (eventually six) in Peru would become a subsidiary of General Odría's Military Air Transport, he pledged, and become a worthy civilian complement to the jet fighters Odría received from the Eisenhower administration. The missionary air fleet would cheerily haul government mail, baggage, and passengers—even Catholic priests and nuns—at commercial rates.

It was a masterly stroke. With the blessings of the powerful U.S. Embassy, Cam was making Odría an offer he could not refuse: a U.S.-backed aviation and radio service stretching across the borderless jungle. Odría, in accepting, also helped resolve JAARS's growing operating deficit. By 1958, the SIL line would gross as much as $35,000 a year from charters;[22] in one case it operated an oil company's Catalina for several months when the company's pilots could not handle the hazardous flights over jungles and mountains.[23]

Peru's Catholic hierarchy was not mollified. SIL admittedly was staffed by only evangelical Protestants. Worse, at SIL's recent first teacher training course only Protestant Indians or SIL sympathizers were taught.[24]

Cam again proved his capacity for the miraculous. He simply denied that SIL was really a Protestant missionary front. "We do not carry out evangelist work because the Institute has a mission of scientific character and not a religious end," he told the press.[25]

Peru's Apostolic Vicar was skeptical and within a week was able to produce a University of Oklahoma bulletin affirming SIL's ties to the Wycliffe Bible Translators; he also directly accused Cam of plotting with his "millionaire friend and financial backer . . . to Protestantize our jungle."[26]

Cam reeled in retreat. He wrote El Comercio a 4,000-word statement confessing that the Wycliffe Bible Translators "has absolutely no life apart from the Summer Institute of Linguistics." He still insisted, however, that it was "non-sectarian." As for Le Tourneau, "we have no other connection than a recent friendship."[27]

The friendship included money donated by Le Tourneau's tax-free foundation,[28] which controlled both his business and his college (including its Peruvian "development" subsidiary).

Nor was the friendship so recent.

"God's Partner"

Robert Gilman Le Tourneau was a born-again Christian businessman long known in Fundamentalist circles. During the 1920s, while making a small fortune off the public construction boom in California, he came to believe that he was specially blessed by the Lord of his childhood. He contributed regularly to the Christian Missionary Alliance. When the Great Depression hit, he plugged his company into the giant public works projects the Hoover administration had started to relieve unemployment. During the New Deal, he built irrigation systems and roads. Le Tourneau and his wife attributed their success to divine blessing, not Washington's public works programs, their previous business associations, or even Le Tourneau's inventive genius for designing bigger and more efficient machines. To thank Jesus, they set up the Le Tourneau Foundation under their control, pledging 50 percent of their company's profits and 50 percent of their personal income to "The Lord's Treasury."

The foundation became the conduit for hefty tax deductions for both the company and the family. This tax shelter also sponsored a technical school in Peoria, Illinois, near the site of the Le Tourneau factory, where workers were proselytized by Le Tourneau's Fundamentalist magazine, NOW. "God is chairman of my board of directors," he claimed, with some legal accuracy. The millionaire soon joined the board of John Brown Academy, where Paul Townsend (Cam's brother) taught, and Cam found his first support for nearby Camp Wycliffe.

By the end of World War II, God and war profits had boosted his company's sales 400 percent. His company supplied 70 percent of the earth-moving equipment used by the Pentagon. Thousands of mammoth Le Tourneau bulldozers, scrapers, rooters, dump carts, and sheepfoot rollers were used by U.S. forces in North Africa, India, Burma, China, and every major island in the South Pacific.[29]

In postwar Peru, the Catholic church soon found that it was no match for Le Tourneau or Townsend. Combined, the two men represented American wealth, colonization of the jungle, and the powerful U.S. Embassy, which saw "Tournavista" as an extension of its Point IV program.

In September 1953, Odría approved SIL's contract. To end public debate, Odría then decorated Cam for "distinguished service to Peru."

In December, Le Tourneau's contract was also sanctioned. Two months later, the Peruvian Senate ratified the agreement as Le Tourneau watched from the gallery. Within two years, even Nelson Rockefeller would be commenting on Le Tourneau's venture in the Peruvian Amazon. In October 1955, a "news clip" from the International Basic Economy Corporation (IBEC) crossed his desk noting that the Peruvian government had accepted a bid by Robert G. Le Tourneau to develop a "large tropical zone" and that Peru was seeking a $15 million loan to finance the development, along with a new highway connecting the Trans-Andes highway with the "Amazonas Valley." Nelson scribbled in the margins "we ought to take a look" and promptly fired off a memo to IBEC's Louise Boyer: "I would like to include this area in the discussion of new lands to be studied. . . ."[30]

At Brazil's Borders

Cam's next stop on his Latin American itinerary was Quito. High in the Ecuadorian Andes, Cam hurried through the ancient cobblestone streets of the capital of the Incas and the conquistadores to a crucial meeting with SIL's Robert Schneider and a young translator from the Peru branch named Rachel Saint.

Schneider had become Cam's top government relations aide in the South American advance. He had pioneered in Peru and had helped in the unsuccessful attempt to enter Venezuela. Now he had taken on the directorship of the Ecuadorian Amazon. Slowly, SIL was nibbling away at the outer edges of the western Amazon. If the Inter-American Indian Conference in La Paz in August proved fruitful, they would have a toehold in Bolivia, too. The Andean countries were the back door to the Brazilian Amazon. Success was imperative.

In Rachel Saint, Cam had found the ideal visionary to lead the dangerous advance into the unknown Ecuadorian jungle. As a girl in 1932, she had dreamed of a brown tribe surrounded by green jungle. She finally arrived in SIL's Peru branch in 1949, having spent a dozen years trying to convince New Jersey alcoholics to take the Lord's cure. The Indians should have proved easier. They didn't.

Rachel started her vision-quest with the Piro Indians along the Urubamba River, then moved on to the Shapra, in the oil-rich lands above the Marañon River. By 1953, she had settled on yet another tribe even farther north, across the border with Ecuador near the next large river, the Napo.

This tribe, in a fashion common among isolated hunting and gathering groups, called themselves simply "the people," or Huaorani. The Ecuadorians called them Auca, Quechua for "savage." Hunted by rubber slavers, the Auca had been reduced to about 400 souls scattered in four mutually warring groups by the time Robert Schneider arrived with the first SIL team in 1952. No one in the party entertained any illusion about conquering the Aucas for Christ. No one volunteered. They all accepted the wisdom of other missionaries that the hundred Auca spearmen who had held up civilization's advance would have no compunction sending white foreigners quickly to their God of Love.

Rachel accepted the challenge as her fate. The Lord had willed that the Auca were the "brown-skinned tribe" of her vision.

Cam and Schneider took Rachel to meet President José María Velasco Ibarra. Rachel's extraordinary offer was presented by Cam to the president. Velasco tried to warn her off. The Auca were "very dangerous. I once flew over them and they threw spears at the plane."[31]

Rachel would not be deterred. At last, Velasco sighed his assent.

One of those who received the news with some misgivings was her thirty-two-year-old brother, Nate, a pilot for the Missionary Aviation Fellowship (MAF). Nate's small yellow Piper Cub served Protestant missionaries scattered throughout the jungle. It was through Rachel's visits with him that she had heard of the Auca. Now he was beginning to wish she never had. Rachel's ambitions stood in the way.

While all this was happening, a Shell oil airplane was touring Latin America.

Its most interesting passenger was General James Doolittle, the famous army pilot who had flown raids over Tokyo. Doolittle's inspection of the MAF base at Shell Mera delighted Nate.

"How's our little air force?"[32] Doolittle asked with a twinkle in his eye.

Doolittle was now a director of Shell, though this mission, at President Eisenhower's request, was to conduct a secret investigation of the CIA's covert operations.

Doolittle presented his findings to Eisenhower in October 1954. The president now had a reliable report on the CIA and the "assets," including people, it used. He gave the study to Allen Dulles with instructions to "show it to no one else, but to get back to him about the report's conclusions and recommendations."[33]

Doolittle's recommendations were in keeping with the CIA's penchant for avoiding congressional oversight. They encouraged Eisenhower to endorse more covert operations, even, ominously, illegal ones beyond "the acceptable norms of human conduct."

> Hitherto acceptable norms of human conduct do not apply. If the United States is to survive, long-standing American concepts of "fair play" must be reconsidered. We must develop effective espionage and counterespionage services and must learn to subvert, sabotage and destroy our enemies by more clever, more sophisticated, and more effective methods than those used against us. It may become necessary that the American people be made acquainted with, understand and support this fundamentally repugnant philosophy.[34]

Eisenhower was enthusiastic about Doolittle's "Anticommunist Manifesto." Two months later, he appointed a new special assistant on Cold War strategy and psychological warfare. As the president's personal representative on the National Security Council, this man would oversee the global escalation of CIA covert warfare.

A Planning Coordination Group, which came to be called simply the "Special Group," was established. In a position of authority over policy second only to the president himself and actually exercising much more power than he did, three men—CIA Director Allen Dulles, Undersecretary of State Herbert Hoover, Jr., and Undersecretary of Defense Roger Kyes—would be in command, chaired by the president's new special assistant: Nelson Rockefeller.

IV

PROPHETS OF ARMEGEDDON

Fortunately, Brazil has a great vacant frontier area that offers the prospect of developing a new rural economy. . . . It should be emphasized that what is contemplated here is a program of opening up this new "west" in Brazil, in the manner our own "west" was opened up under the Homestead law after the Civil War.

—JOHN R. CAMP, Rockefeller AIA employee
*Proposal to the federal International
Cooperative Administration,
November 1960*

18

IKE'S COLD WAR GENERAL

A Pledge of Allegiance

Washington's fashionable Foxhall Road was dark when Ann Whitman, the president's personal secretary, left the large house. A single light burned, silent testimony to continued work in the library where she had dined alone that night with Nelson Rockefeller. Nelson might work into the wee hours, the fate of a middle-aged man seeking refuge from a marriage going sour and a career in doubt.

After Ike's election, Nelson had been made chairman of the President's Advisory Committee on Government Organization. His job held neither excitement nor prestige, but at least he was back in Washington, where his influence could be felt, if not feared.

He started off by confronting New Deal Democrats with typical vengeance. His grandfather would have been proud. Someone, after all, had to have enough credibility and gall to shake up Washington's bureaucracy and refit it to meet its new global opportunities.[1]

Within six months, with the approval of the president and the Republican-led Congress, Rockefeller had centralized the U.S. government into a modern corporate state. He tightened corporate control over the Defense Department, bringing the whole operation more into conformity with corporate streamlining.

He abolished the Export-Import Bank's four-man board, centralizing all power in the hands of a managing director. Control over the bank was crucial if American corporations were to penetrate the Third World trade of Western European powers, expand American investment in the Third World, and stave off the twin evils of nationalism and communism.

He abolished the State Department's International Information Agency, already mortally wounded by Senator Joseph McCarthy's witch-hunts, and set up the United States Information Agency (USIA). Virtually independent of the State Department and free of its diplomatic responsibilities, the USIA would prove more amenable to covert operations by the CIA, including disinformation news "feedback" into the United States.

Nelson also destroyed the Mutual Security Agency, merging its operations and those of three other foreign-aid agencies into the Foreign Operations Administration. FOA at last brought to fruition the proposal that Nelson, as chairman of Truman's International Development Advisory Board, had made for a centralized foreign-aid agency.

He merged the Federal Security Agency (and its $4.6 billion budget, ten operating units, and three federal corporations) into a single new cabinet-level department, Health, Education, and Welfare. (He managed to get himself appointed the first undersecretary of HEW to boot.) This was Nelson's best hope for salvaging some of the CIAA's legacy of education, public health, and vocational rehabilitation programs.

If not totally in substance, certainly in style, it was the CIAA mode of operation all over again. Nelson set up another chart room and ordered all agency heads to give weekly command performances. HEW became involved in intelligence matters that included not only the integration of the educational, health, sanitation, and technical assistance programs into overall foreign policy goals, but HEW serving as the CIA's first conduit for its "mind control" experiments.

Code-named Project ARTICHOKE and subsequently MKULTRA, the CIA's search for ways of modifying and controlling human behavior was given cover by both HEW and its subagency, the National Institute of Mental Health.[2] The CIA was anxious to learn why some American prisoners of war refused to be repatriated after the Korean War. Convinced that the GIs had been brainwashed, Allen Dulles, who was himself the father of a badly wounded GI, authorized the CIA to investigate mind-altering drugs and hypnosis, allegedly as a defense against the Soviet Union, but actually for the CIA's own use. The mind-control experiments would continue for twenty years, involving over 750 subjects.[3]

While HEW lent its facilities for CIA purposes, Nelson dismissed some 1,200 HEW employees. The Bureau of Indian Affairs also fell under the axe. An aging John Collier, still head of the Institute of Ethnic Affairs, fought back against federal efforts to "terminate" government protection of Indian land and services.[4] His efforts were in vain. Eisenhower soon authorized states to replace the federal government in Indian matters to override tribal constitutions, abolish tribal authorities, and distribute Indian assets, including lands that held oil deposits.

John Collier once again came under attack as a "radical," just as he had thirty years before. His defense of Samoan indigenous rights against the navy's testing of the atomic bomb on Bikini was the last straw. Conservative colleagues at City College of New York castigated him for stirring "violent controversies," and he was forced to resign. Collier, now seventy, left New York, his spirit broken. He ended up in Taos, New Mexico, decrying that Eisenhower's Public Law 280 was delivering the Indians into "a kind of social, cultural, and spiritual self-genocide."

Nelson, of course, was keenly aware of the witch-hunt against Collier. One of his aides, Victor Borella, brought it to his attention in 1955. But there was little that Nelson was willing to do for anyone in the prevailing atmosphere of loyalty oaths and witch-hunting.

There was, however, something he could do when tensions began to rise in South America in the wake of budget cuts in foreign aid.

Nelson's Brazilian Problem

Nelson's biggest private worry was Brazil. He was depending on that country's great economic potential to boost the fortunes of his ailing International Basic Economy Corporation (IBEC). In Venezuela, the American oil companies, including his own Creole Petroleum, and the Pérez Jiménez dictatorship had withdrawn their financial participation in IBEC's schemes by 1952, as did seven Venezuelan state governments from programs sponsored by IBEC's philanthropic arm, the American International Association for Economic and Social Development (AIA); within four years, three more state governments would desert AIA, along with the oil companies. The dictatorship had so deteriorated political conditions that it was impossible to carry on any supervised credit program.[5]

Already desperate in 1952, Nelson had swallowed his pride and turned to his father for help. He asked for $1 million to save IBEC. The president had enough confidence in Nelson to give him the task of reorganizing the United States government, but Junior would not lend him a penny unless he agreed to close up shop.

Nelson went to seek the money elsewhere.[6] He found it with his brother David at Chase National Bank. David was the bank's major proponent of increased investment in South America. Laurance was also on the Chase board.

Nelson liquidated his more troubled companies in Venezuela and Brazil and focused on making what *Fortune* magazine called "the normal Latin American profits" of anywhere from 30 percent to 100 percent.[7]

But Nelson still had a familiar problem in Brazil, Getúlio Vargas. Five years after the 1945 coup that had removed him from office, Vargas was once again president of Brazil. He had run an emotional campaign in 1950 on the theme "O petróleo é nosso" ("the oil is ours") and had blamed Adolf Berle and American oil companies for his overthrow. Now the sixty-eight-year-old nationalist had returned to his old mission of keeping Brazil's energy resources Brazilian. In 1952,

Vargas succeeded in having the Brazilian Chamber of Deputies, by almost a unanimous vote, establish the government-owned Brazilian Petroleum Company (known popularly as Petrobrás). The following year, Vargas, confronted by an angry Senate dominated by export businesses, sought to reserve for Petrobrás all rights to oil exploration, exploitation, and new refining.

The American companies, led by Standard Oil, fought back. Brazil was one of the hemisphere's largest oil markets, and Standard, Shell, Gulf, Texaco, and Atlantic controlled it all. If Vargas expanded Brazil's small refining capacity under Petrobrás, the companies would be locked out of all growth in this crucial market.

More than 100,000 motor vehicles were imported into Brazil in 1951. Vargas was planning to introduce diesel locomotives to "modernize" the railroads. Basic industrial expansion would also draw on oil. Fuel imports, accordingly, had risen 20 percent each year since 1949, costing $200 million in 1951, all of which, on the insistence of the oil companies, had to be paid in U.S. dollars. This "dollar drain" policy by the oil companies hemorrhaged Brazil's foreign-exchange reserves, of which 70 percent were earned each year by a single export, coffee, whose largest market was the United States.[8]

Probably none of Eisenhower's top officials understood the role that American coffee importers played in Brazil's economy better than Nelson Rockefeller. The former CIAA chief in Brazil, Berent Friele, now one of Nelson's closest IBEC aides, had been president of the American Coffee Company and a director of A&P, one of the largest buyers of Brazilian coffee.

So when the Vargas government raised Brazilian coffee prices after storms damaged crops in 1952–1953, Room 5600 was quick to take advantage of the howls from A&P and other American importers who feared that Vargas was pricing them out of the American housewives' market.[9] During the Korean War, Nelson had set up a powdered coffee company in El Salvador to exploit the market that had been stimulated among GIs. Now, as a more frugal alternative to fill coffeepots and as a manufacturing process that allowed the mixing of less expensive beans from other lands, powdered (instant) coffee took root in the marketplace. And as profits from IBEC's instant-coffee subsidiary grew during the Brazilian coffee crisis, Nelson's contributions through AIA to small Brazilian coffee growers and ranchers steadily declined.[10]

This cutback was also the result of Nelson's new conservative fiscal policies that dictated belt-tightening in the non-profit-making sector of his operations. Brazil's credit squeeze was another problem. The coffee squeeze on Brazilian earnings threatened Nelson's profit-making operations, too. His hybrid seed company was promising to score 3,000 metric tons in sales by 1955, a huge increase over the 35 tons sold in 1947, its first year of business. Likewise, Nelson's Inter-American Finance and Investment Corporation (IFI), IBEC's joint venture with Chase National and fourteen leading commercial banks in Brazil, was crippled by limited borrowing capacity. Brazilian bankers, feeling that IFI was competing for scarce investment capital, limited their willingness to underwrite IFI's loans.

Nelson grew frantic over the credit crunch after Brazil's ambassador, Walther Moreira Salles, visited him in Washington in February 1953. A loan to Brazil had been arranged, but the Eisenhower administration was thinking of canceling it.

Nelson caught a flight to New York, conferred with family members and advisers, and then called Adolf Berle. He hoped Berle could influence the Jackson Committee, Ike's special review board on intelligence operations chaired by former CIA Deputy Director William Jackson. Berle agreed to try.

Berle took Brazil's deepening financial crisis before the committee. He described the disastrous predictions for the coffee crop and the pressure these predictions put on the Brazilians' ability to finance their imports, debt payments, and industrial expansion. Within two months, psychological warfare adviser C. D. Jackson, another member of the committee, came up with a plan to send Milton Eisenhower, the president's brother, to Brazil to talk with "responsible Brazilians" about the country's deteriorating economic situation and President Vargas's handling of it.

Nelson Rockefeller, it was noted, "would have extreme difficulties in carrying on these exploratory conversations, but he could be extremely valuable once the situation was crystallized in liaison activities with the major oil companies." Milton Eisenhower, on the other hand, "has all the requisites, i.e. is a trusted and responsible member of the White House staff who can speak with authority, and also has no connections with the major oil companies."[11]

Milton Eisenhower's trip to Brazil turned out to be a great success as far as the oil companies were concerned, albeit a delayed one. He arrived in late July in the midst of an uproar in the United States over rising Brazilian coffee prices. Rumors were circulating that high Brazilian officials were speculating in the coffee-futures market.[12] Therefore, the Brazilian government was on the defensive when Eisenhower discussed trade relations.

Milton Eisenhower ended up infuriating the Brazilians by refusing to honor loans for high-priority projects. He even denied that the United States had ever made any commitments. (In fact, final decisions *had* been made—years earlier— by the Joint Brazil-U.S. Development Commission on a $1 billion program that required $300 million in promised U.S. loans and politically risky tax increases already introduced by Vargas to finance the cruzeiro portion of the program. But that was *before* Vargas pressed ahead for the Petrobrás oil monopoly.)

A month after Milton Eisenhower left Brazil, Vargas was still in a state of shock over the freeze on American loans. Desperate now for capital, he was more committed than ever to recovering the revenues Brazil spent on imported oil. To strengthen his base among nationalists, he appointed Juracy Magalhães as Petrobrás's first president.

It was his first serious mistake. Juracy Magalhães had been an FBI informer during the last Vargas administration and had confided to Adolf Berle that he had plotted against Vargas in 1945. Now, almost a decade later, having just completed a stint as Brazilian military attaché in Washington, he was being handed one of the most sensitive offices in the Vargas government.

VARGAS'S UNIFORMED FRANKENSTEIN

At this point, Vargas's Frankenstein monster from World War II rose up again. Veterans of the Brazilian Expeditionary Force who had fought under U.S. command in Italy had a wide following in the army, navy, and air force owing to U.S. military aid. These officers had gained additional prestige when the Pentagon helped them establish a replica of the U.S. National War College, the Higher War College. In 1949, the Brazilian military established a secret military protocol with the Pentagon, pending Washington's review of a formal military pact proposed by the Brazilians. Vargas was able to delay implementation of this pact until 1953 and to prevent the military from sending the infantry division to Korea that Truman had requested. More important, public outcries held up a U.S. survey authorized by the treaty even after it was signed. This survey aimed at "preparing topographic maps and air charts of Brazil," and ruled that original negatives and field observations "by the technical organs of the U.S. will be kept in their own files."[13]

The Brazilian generals seethed over the delays. Standard Oil, meanwhile, fretted over Petrobrás's inroads in supplying Brazil's internal market with state-controlled oil. In Manaus, the former rubber capital on the Amazon, Petrobrás even planned a new oil refinery. Though small, the refinery would within a year carry the seed of Petrobrás's potential for the Amazon basin, tapping Peru's Ganso Azul field for crude. Here also was the focus of Vargas's hope that the Amazon forest hid a great pool of oil. Petrobrás's geologists were directed to study the area carefully and, indeed, in April 1954, they reported finding indications of oil near Manaus at Nova Olinda; they would actually strike oil there, again within a year.

This was not good news to Standard Oil, which controlled refining and used Brazil as a consumer for Venezuelan crude exported by its Creole Petroleum subsidiary, Nelson Rockefeller's old haunt. Nor did it please the generals and admirals who used Standard Oil's crude. They had depended on Washington's largesse to fuel their ascent to power and had argued that Petrobrás's founding condemned Brazil's oil to stay in the ground. (In fact, Petrobrás would boost production more than tenfold by 1960.) In June 1954, General Juárez Távora attacked Petrobrás in a speech at the Higher War College, calling again for the participation of foreign capital.

Unfortunately for Vargas, Távora's attack coincided with an uproar in Brazil's business community over Vargas's pressuring the state government of Mato Grasso to nullify private titles to 21 million acres of Indian lands, which it had illegally sold to real estate companies and land speculators.[14] These lands, Vargas insisted, had been set aside for the Indians. The slash-and-burn techniques used by settlers had already been the source of Indian misery in similar colonization schemes east of Belém, transforming the zone's forests into the semidesert described by one Brazilian scientist as a "ghost landscape." Unlike the Indians' shifting cultivation system, the settlers' intense land-use system destroyed the canopy forest and with it, the source of most of the nutrients and protective cover used by the Amazon basin's poor soil base.

Equally restrictive was Vargas's 1954 Mineral Code, which separated soil rights from subsoil rights, the latter requiring federal licenses. The code left the exploitation of any subsoil riches, whether oil or solid minerals, to Brazilian companies.

In June, General Távora, eyeing his future presidential candidacy, called for the reversal of Vargas's policies. Carlos Lacerda, leader of the Democratic National Union (UDN) that had allied with Adolf Berle to unseat Vargas from his last presidency in 1945, went further, leading an impeachment drive against Vargas. Lacerda charged (falsely) the president with misappropriating funds and secretly collaborating with Argentina's Juan Perón to set up a Peronist labor syndicate type of government. At the same time, with U.S. credits suspended until Vargas surrendered on the oil issue and income from coffee exports diminished, the financial situation deteriorated. Prices rose. The opposition blamed it on incompetence and corruption in the Vargas administration. The impeachment effort failed, but Lacerda did succeed in forcing Vargas's labor minister, João Goulart, to resign.

On the night of August 5, 1954, shots were fired in front of Lacerda's Copacabana apartment just as he was returning home. Lacerda was wounded in the foot. Vargas's son, a federal deputy, was held responsible for the incident, along with the head of the presidential guard. More charges of corruption emerged, and Vice President Café Filho, an opponent of Petrobrás, suggested to Vargas that they should both resign.

"From here I'll leave dead," Vargas replied.

Rio's air force general and half the generals of the army then demanded his resignation. Naval and air units stood at alert, and army police surrounded the palace. The war minister warned Vargas of the likelihood of "much blood, a lot of bloodshed." After a two-hour meeting with the cabinet on August 24, Vargas agreed to ask Congress for a leave of absence to allow the pressures to cool. But the war minister told the generals the following morning that Vargas's leave was to be immediate and permanent. Vargas had been betrayed.

"This means I'm deposed?" Vargas asked his brother Benjamin on learning the news. Vargas's family had armed themselves, ready to face death.

"I don't know," Benjamin said. "But this is the end."[15]

Just before 8 A.M., Vargas appeared outside his bedroom, still in pajamas. He walked to the presidential office and then returned, closing the bedroom door behind him. Fifteen minutes later, a shot rang out. He had chosen the familiar option of the doomed gauchos of his homeland: suicide. On the bed stand, his family found his last letter to the Brazilian people:

> Once again, anti-national forces and interests, coordinated, have become infuriated with me. . . . After decades of domination and exploitation by international economic-financial groups, I made myself the chief of a revolution, and I won. I initiated the work of liberation and I inaugurated a regime of social liberty. . . .
>
> I returned to the government on the arms of the people. The underground campaign of the international groups allied with national groups revolted against the regime of guarantee to the worker. . . . They do not want the workers to be free. . . . I wanted to create national freedom in realizing oil wealth through Petrobrás. . . . They do not want the people to be independent.
>
> . . . I choose this means to be with you always. When they humiliate you, you shall feel my soul suffering at your side. When hunger beats at your door, you shall feel in your breasts the energy for the struggle for yourselves and your sons. When they slander you, you shall feel in my thoughts the strength for reaction. My sacrifice will maintain you united and my blood shall be your banner of struggle.[16]

The damage to Washington's propaganda goals against Petrobrás was irreparable. As Vargas's body lay in state, his letter was released to the world press. Cuba declared a three-day mourning period. So did Argentina. The United Nations flag was flown at half staff in New York. Thousands of Brazilians followed Vargas's coffin to Rio's airport, where it was flown to the president's home in Rio Grande do Sul for burial.

An era had ended, not only for Brazil, but for Washington's prestige in Latin America. Coming on the heels of the CIA's overthrow of Arbenz in Guatemala, Vargas's suicide gave official Washington reason to pause and ask how the damage might be controlled. Despite dark reports from intelligence sources that the Communist party had grown since Vargas's return to power, there was no way that Vargas could be painted as another Communist sympathizer as Arbenz had been. With Vargas, the issue was clear: The struggle for economic independence and national sovereignty was the fundamental problem Washington was facing in Latin America.

When the Brazilian people gave Vargas's party a resounding victory in Congress that November, the Eisenhower administration looked for someone to replace C. D. Jackson, someone with his experience in psychological warfare, who could be trusted with the knowledge of secret assets and operations, and someone who, unlike Jackson, had enough prestige—and raw power—in Latin America to restore the luster to the Eisenhower name.

There was really no competition for the job. Only Nelson Rockefeller would do.

IKE'S SECRET TEAM

To the general public, Nelson's new job as special assistant to the president for Cold War affairs was shadowy. *Newsweek* editors, when told he was to attend the Cabinet, the National Security Council, the Council on Foreign Economic Policy, and the Operations Coordinating Board, came closest to the truth by describing Nelson as Ike's "Cold War General." The president's press secretary, James Hagerty, would admit only that Nelson's tasks would be "much broader" than Jackson's. Nelson would add to that job "consideration of how to coordinate work of all government agencies toward the President's program for peace."[17]

"Dulles," Berle recalled in his diary, "had asked Nelson to take this new job . . . because . . . he is on the defensive everywhere. He . . . feels something is lacking, and expects Nelson to supply the miraculous element."[18]

The Third World, Berle intimated, was becoming dangerously restless, and Dulles felt ill equipped to handle it. Dulles also wanted to eliminate any Soviet doubts about the West's will to preserve its sphere of influence. But critics suggested that Dulles went too far, expanding that sphere to encompass most of the non-Communist world (and, if Radio Free Europe could be believed, most of the Communist world, too). Dulles was also accused of relying too heavily on nuclear weapons.[19] Nor did his plans to include a rearmed West Germany— including many ex-Nazis and SS spies in NATO—ease the misgivings of Africans and Asians about the United States' anti-communist zeal. No matter how skillfully argued or infused with moral "law," Dulles's claims rang hollow on Third World ears. Memories of the shame of colonial insult had never left the developing countries, nor did the bitterness over an average life expectancy of forty years and the world's highest incidence of untreated curable diseases and malnutrition.

Still, in the face of this reality, Berle and Rockefeller could believe that the problem Dulles was having with the Third World was fundamentally "philosophical." "Nelson felt and I cordially stimulated that the real trouble here was philosophical and spiritual more than economic, material and political. There is no guide line to any political policy. Another dimension was needed."[20]

With Nelson taking on the role of Cold War adviser, a new dimension *did* develop, but its thrust was decidedly more political than philosophical and spiritual. Its goal was control over all covert operations abroad, with Nelson in the cockpit.

On March 12, the CIA learned that all covert operations had to be approved first by the National Security Council's Operations Coordinating Board (OCB), on which Nelson was the president's representative. Under Eisenhower's instructions, the National Security Council authorized the CIA to "develop underground resistance and facilitate covert and guerrilla operations."

> Specifically, such operations shall include any covert activities related to propaganda, political action, economic warfare; preventive direct action, including sabotage . . . subversion against hostile states and groups including assistance to underground resistance movements, guerrillas and refugee liberations groups, support of indigenous and anti-communist elements . . . deception plans and operations . . . all protected by the new doctrine of "plausible" deniability.[21]

Nelson's Special Group was to oversee all these activities. If there was a philosophical underpinning to this group, it was Machiavelli.

Nelson's capacity as chairman of the Special Group allowed him to act as Eisenhower's "circuit breaker," informing the president of CIA covert operations while protecting the president's "plausible deniability" before Congress, since some operations ran afoul of American or international law and even of John Foster Dulles's much touted moral law.

Of all the CIA's secret activities, the most sensitive were called the "Family Jewels." That month, CIA Director Allen Dulles gave Nelson and other OCB members a Family Jewels briefing.

Dulles described all the CIA's covert operations,[22] past and present, including those having the most doubtful legality. By 1955, they included the following:

The CIA's penetration of the National Student Association.
The CIA's penetration of the news media as intelligence sources, using reporters as spies, planting spies, and spreading false stories ("black propaganda") in the foreign media that were "replayed" in domestic news sources.[23]
The CIA's penetration of the American book publishing industry.
The CIA's support for Ramón Magsaysay in the Philippines and George Papadopoulos in Greece.[24]
The CIA's instigation of coups in Iran and Guatemala.
The CIA's interception and reading, at New York's and San Francisco's post offices, of the private mail of American citizens sent to and received from the Soviet Union and China.[25]
The CIA's financing of Radio Free Europe and Radio Liberation (subsequently renamed Radio Liberty) broadcasts to, respectively, Eastern Europe and the Soviet Union.[26]
The CIA's establishment of a Domestic Operations Division, whose organization and functions were similar to a field station abroad, to conduct covert operations against U.S. citizens in American cities. This action violated the CIA's charter, which forbade the agency from spying on American citizens at home.
The CIA's "Operation Bloodstone," which protected and used Nazis in Europe and the Americas.[27]

Three other CIA operations, however, would have the most far-reaching implication for Nelson Rockefeller, American missionaries, and the Indians of Latin America: the CIA's expansion of its MKULTRA mind-control experiments, the use of Edward Lansdale's Filipinos to recruit Montagnard tribes in a war against Ho Chi Minh's Vietminh, and to build a new regime in Saigon to create a Korea-like partition of Vietnam, and its growing covert involvement in aviation.

BENDING MINDS WITH MKULTRA

Nelson needed little introduction to MKULTRA. The CIA's use of HEW for mind-control experiments had been initiated during his tenure as undersecretary. The Rockefeller Foundation was also no stranger to this field of research. In 1943, it had set up Allen Memorial Institute at McGill University in Montreal. The institute's articles attracted the attention of the Pentagon and the CIA, and Pentagon grants for research on brainwashing grew steadily.[28]

It was not long before Adolf Berle agreed to serve on the board of the Society for the Investigation of Human Ecology, a foundation the CIA created as a cover for MKULTRA. "I am frightened about this one," Berle wrote in his diary. "If the scientists do what they have laid out for themselves, men will become manageable ants. But I don't think it will happen."[29]

There were eminent physicians and scientists on the board of the society. But lurking behind the sterile formal reports of the researchers was violence. Unaware of their being guinea pigs for the CIA, patients were given a "sleep cocktail" of 100 mg. Thorazine, 100 mg. Nembutal, 100 mg. Seconal, 150 mg. Veronal, and 10 mg. Phenergan and then subjected to 150 volts of electroshock for periods twenty to ninety times longer than normally applied by physicians, two to three times a day for fifteen to thirty days, and sometimes as long as sixty-five days.[30] The CIA was interested in creating a blank mind that could be reprogrammed.

The Rockefeller Foundation funded the sensory deprivation research. The technique involved strapping people down in a large box and cutting them off from light, sound, smells, or touching. In March 1955, HEW's National Institutes of Health began CIA-funded experiments using the standard technique, *minus* the practice of freeing subjects when they wanted to be freed. Soon mind-control experiments spread throughout the country, nurtured by funding directed by Dr. Sidney Gottlieb, the head of the Chemical Division of the CIA Technical Services Staff and, according to one former CIA officer, part of the old-boy network in the CIA that included Nelson Rockefeller's former CIAA associate in Brazil, J. C. King, now CIA chief of clandestine activities in the Western Hemisphere.[31]

In May 1955, the CIA received a startling proposal to "provide for Agency-Sponsored Research Involving Covert Biological and Chemical Warfare."[32] Dr. Charles Geschickter asked the CIA to contribute $375,000 toward the construction of a special cancer research building at Georgetown University Hospital. He promised a "hospital safehouse" with one-sixth of the building's beds dedicated to the CIA, complete with cover for three CIA scientists and "human patients and volunteers for experimental use," including the severely mentally retarded and terminal cancer patients.

Allen Dulles approved, but the CIA money, passed through private channels, would allow Geschickter to get matching funds from HEW for the hospital's construction. This use of private foundations to pass on government (CIA) money, so HEW's matching grant requirements could be met, would mean deliberate misleading of at least one other executive department of the U.S. government (HEW), and probably the Treasury Department's Internal Revenue Service as well. Dulles decided to play it safe and get higher approval. He knew just the man.

Nelson Rockefeller, as chairman of the Special Group, listened attentively as Dulles laid out his case for the MKULTRA hospital. His only question was whether Geschickter could offer "a reasonable expectation" that the CIA scientists would have the space he promised. Given Dulles's assurance, Nelson gave his approval.[33]

During Nelson's chairmanship of the Special Group, the CIA also searched for some means to program assassins. The CIA had discovered that a man "could be surreptitiously drugged through the medium of an alcoholic cocktail at a social party . . . and the subject induced to perform the act of attempting assassination" of an official in a government in which he was "well established socially and politically."[34] The CIA officer in charge of security for the operation was Sheffield Edwards.[35] Edwards later worked under Edward Lansdale in Operation MONGOOSE, the assassination attempts against Cuba's Fidel Castro.

THE ROCKEFELLER FOUNDATION EMBRACES THE COLD WAR

In 1952, when John Foster Dulles was getting ready to become Eisenhower's secretary of state, Dulles turned over the chair of the Rockefeller Foundation to the family's "Mr. Asia," John 3rd. For the foundation's presidency, Dulles tapped his friend Dean Rusk.

In the transfer of one of the State Department's top Far East intelligence operators to the foundation lay the origin of Nelson's expectation of unreserved cooperation from the foundation in his own intelligence mission. Given the central roles that the Dulles brothers and Nelson now played in Washington, it was not an unreasonable expectation.

Rusk did not let the Rockefellers down. "We have the officers and staff with long experience in underdeveloped areas," he assured the trustees. "We can recruit for such service somewhat more readily than other types of organizations. We have earned a reputation for political disinterestedness; we are not widely regarded as the tool of any particular foreign policy; we are welcomed in politically sensitive situations."[36]

Rusk's new mission was accompanied by a shake-up in his first line of command. In 1955, the foundation took on new directors for five out of six of its programs: Public Health, Social Sciences, Agricultural Sciences, Medical Sciences, and Natural Sciences. Only Humanities was left untouched.

The Humanities Division, under ex-CIA officer Chadbourne Gilpatrick, gave $68,000 in 1955 to the University of Philippines's Institute of Public Administration to train selected students from Southeast Asia in the fine art of running Western-backed governments efficiently without appearing to be colonial appendages. One of the division's primary missions was to foster "community development," part of the "leadership training" component of Lansdale's "nation-building" concept. While the institute trained students from Thailand, Burma, and Indonesia in the complement to the grittier "community development" work in the barrios and hamlets of Southeast Asia, the university's Agricultural College at Los Baños prepared community organizers under the aegis of the CIA-controlled Office of the Presidential Assistant for Community Development.[37]

Community development organizers required a grounding in the psychology of group dynamics. They had to be able to "steer the conversation [of villagers] around to the needs of the barrio they thought should be attended," the CIA's Joseph Smith explained, "and they would get the barrio folk to discuss the characteristics of their ideal leader. It turned out the man they had in mind for the job fit these characteristics perfectly. The villagers would 'discover' that their ideal leader was in fact already in their midst."[38]

"Leadership training" required not only identifying and recruiting local leadership talent, but getting the CIA's chosen leader to be accepted by the people as their own choice.

In Vietnam, the chosen leader was Diem. At Lansdale's urging, in April 1955, Diem launched a successful military offensive against opium gangs in Saigon that were an obstacle to Diem's taking power. Secretary of State Dulles reversed his previous misgivings about Diem. From 1950 to 1954, Diem had been safely tucked away in Maryknoll monasteries in New York and New Jersey that were filled with missionaries who were exiled from China. There, he awaited Washington's call as the independent, nationalist "alternative" to Ho Chi Minh. Senator John F. Kennedy had predicted that such a leader would be needed to forestall the election of the popular Communist leader.[39] Now, with Diem's demonstration of military strength and Dulles's backing, the way was clear for Diem's claim to absolute power.

Enter Nelson Rockefeller in August 1955. He reminded the members of the Special Group that it was charged with finding "ways effectively to utilize U.S. and foreign individuals and groups and foreign public and private organizations" in covert operations.[40] These organizations included universities, which were used as "manpower reservoirs." Professors from Michigan State University (MSU) had flown to Saigon in May and they soon were joined by CIA officers. MSU's inventory request that year included grenade launchers, riot-gun ammunition, tear-gas projectiles, grenades, and mortars.[41] American academe was training Diem's police and Civil Guards in the dark side of Cold War democracy.

As it turned out, Diem was soon to be Washington's last hope for stemming communism in Southeast Asia. On March 17, 1957, Philippine President Ramón Magsaysay died in a plane crash.

The CIA picked the wrong candidate to succeed Magsaysay and was soon without a power base for its Southeast Asia operations. Nelson saw the crisis in leadership immediately. He contacted John 3rd about immortalizing the memory of Magsaysay throughout the region.

Nelson had an idea for a Rockefeller version of the Nobel Prize, with $25,000 to be awarded each year to someone in the Far East who exemplified Magsaysay's willingness to "stand up and be counted." Magsaysay, despite death— or because of it—could serve perpetually as Washington's "spirit of democracy" in Asia. Lansdale wrote a long memo describing Magsaysay's leadership qualities. He claimed that Magsaysay had had a profound impact on Diem and through Diem and his "civic action" soldiers, on Burma's prime minister and even on soldiers in Laos. Those who "found it amusing to tease Americans that he was an ignorant puppet of ours" were a "fringe smart-aleck set" that was "of little importance in Asia, even when quoted by Radio Peking."[42]

Cautious bureaucrats were overruled. The Rockefellers were definitely not of the "smart-aleck" set. The Magsaysay Foundation was open for business.

The foundation gave Operation Brotherhood, the CIA's program to assist Catholic Vietnamese who moved south of the 11th parallel to join Diem's regime, one of its first awards. "Our propaganda job was to emphasize that . . . people were rejecting Communist rule in Vietnam," the CIA's Smith later recalled. ". . . Operation Brotherhood [appeared] like another legitimate effort of humanitarian concern for brother Asians."[43] Catholic missions were not the only ones recruited in the effort to legitimate Diem's regime. Another Magsaysay Award would go to the Summer Institute of Linguistics, and be accepted by Richard Pittman, the top man in SIL's advance into the Philippines and the newly created South Vietnam.[44]

Central to U.S. strategy in the war in Vietnam, both in its initial covert stage and later in its massive overt stage, was aviation. As President Eisenhower's representative to the Special Group, Nelson Rockefeller had oversight responsibilities for the CIA's development of its clandestine aviation capacities.

Nelson's closest contact in the aviation industry was his brother Laurance. During Nelson's tenure as chairman of the Special Group in 1955, Laurance's top aide, Harper Woodward, joined the board of the CIA's Civil Aviation Transport (CAT), the Agency's major air freight carrier in Southeast Asia.[45]

Increasing covert operations in the steep forested valleys of Indochina forced the CIA to begin searching for a lightweight STOL (short-take-off-and-landing) plane to supplement CAT's fleet of larger planes.

A small aircraft firm in the peaceful Boston suburb of Norwood had developed an aeronautical marvel: the Helio Courier. Capable of taking off from a landing strip as short as a tennis court, soaring at speeds well over 100 miles per hour or hovering silently at 30 miles per hour, the Helio Courier could range as far as 842 miles.

It was perfect for the CIA's operations in remote areas where landing strips—if they existed at all—were clearings chiseled out of the side of a mountain.

19

DISARMING DISARMAMENT

LAST CALL AT QUANTICO

On the night of Sunday, June 5, 1955, guards snapped repeatedly to attention as a long line of automobiles pulled into the Marine Corps School at Quantico, Virginia. Against the opposition of the State Department, Nelson Rockefeller had convened a secret conference to prepare recommendations for strategies for the Cold War.

It was a historic gathering. The top foreign policy analysts, propagandists, and arms experts of the United States closeted themselves for four days and nights with men at the core of the Rockefeller brain trust.

Decades later, many of the recommendations that came out of Quantico would still be classified, their influence on U.S. government policy persisting through administrations without any public airing of the scope and content of what had been discussed or drafted. With Nelson Rockefeller, the "secret government" had truly arrived in the United States.

One proposal that would eventually come to light was the "Open Skies" plan. It suggested that at the summit conference in Geneva in July 1955, Eisenhower should parry the Soviets' call for a general disarmament and its unprecedented acceptance of inspectors at permanent stations on both sides of the Iron Curtain. If the Soviet Union would provide blueprints of all its military installations, allow U.S. teams to enter these bases and weapons production facilities, and, most important of all, permit U.S. military planes to penetrate Soviet airspace to photograph these installations, the United States would do likewise and restore the trade and cultural exchange that had been drastically curtailed since the end of World War II.

Nelson outlined the plan in the terse one-page military style to which Eisenhower was accustomed and then took it to the White House.

Eisenhower was interested. Both he and Nelson knew what others did not: The U-2, supported by the CIA's new photographic center, made Soviet permission for aerial inspection unnecessary. Flying at an altitude of 70,000 feet, beyond the reach of any Soviet missile in 1955, the plane's pictures revolutionized intelligence gathering.

The real value of Open Skies was its psychological warfare potential as propaganda to offset the Soviet's "peace offensive" and to convince the world—especially the American people as the 1956 elections approached—of the Republican administration's sincerity. The Soviets, moreover, could be expected to refuse to surrender their defense secrets and sovereignty over their airspace, giving Open Skies a double-fisted propaganda punch.

"Foster," the president phoned Secretary of State John Foster Dulles, "here's an idea."[1] But Dulles explained that the State Department had already seen the proposal and rejected it as a "public relations stunt"[2] that could undermine the serious work of the Summit and its potential—and particularly the department's own disarmament proposal that was being drafted by Harold Stassen. "We don't want to make this meeting a propaganda battlefield."[3]

Like Roosevelt and Truman before him, Eisenhower, when faced with a confrontation between Nelson and the State Department, usually deferred to the department. And he did this time, too. Nelson, true to his nature, persisted. Invited to a pre-Summit meeting between Eisenhower and John Foster Dulles two days later, Nelson hammered away at Dulles's position, emphasizing that unless the president took the initiative, the Soviets' "peace propaganda" would score big with the neutral nations of the Third World. "You may be certain that the Russians will attempt to make themselves important at this juncture in the Cold War," Rockefeller argued.[4]

Dulles was furious. He had been warned that Nelson might try to pull something like this. His staff had objected to Nelson's holding the Quantico seminar precisely for this reason. "The general attitude here is one of irritation," the CIA's Frank Wisner told C. D. Jackson, "at the idea that some smart outside one-shot kibitzers will be able to suck out of their thumbs something that the professionals who work 365 days a year won't already have thought of, and probably discarded."[5]

Finally, Dulles pulled rank, laying his job on the line. The president, he reminded Eisenhower, cannot have two secretaries of state, and statesmanship should not be reduced to propaganda shows.

Nelson pushed, but Eisenhower had had enough. "Damn it, Nelson," he snapped, "I've already told you we don't want to make this meeting a propaganda battlefield!"[6] In the end, he came up with a compromise. Over the State Department's objections, Nelson was permitted to fly to Paris on the condition that he would "stay out of sight" and wait for instructions from Geneva should he be needed.

As Nelson expected, the Soviet Union's peace proposals at Geneva went further than even Eisenhower had anticipated, including the complete outlawing of the manufacture and use of all nuclear weapons. Eisenhower and Dulles tried to respond by reviewing the issues of the Cold War, but no one was interested. The issue now was peace in the nuclear age. On Tuesday, the second day of the conference, Dulles ran out of steam, and Eisenhower was only too glad to receive the coded wire from Nelson in Paris suggesting other options. The president sent back orders to Nelson and Harold Stassen, Eisenhower's special assistant on disarmament and the drafter of the State Department's proposals, to advance to Geneva, and come up with new statements for Eisenhower to use.

After many versions ("Stassen insisting on plugging his [disarmament] line, Nelson editing it out"), Eisenhower ended the debate by writing his own version, based on Nelson's viewpoint. At the last moment, it was decided to keep the Open Skies proposal out of the text.[7] "All agreed to keep this top secret," Nelson said, "even from lower rank Americans."[8]

On Thursday, July 21, Eisenhower rode under cloudy skies from his lakeside villa to the old League of Nations building for the Summit's climactic session.

When it was his turn to speak, Eisenhower rose from the giant square conference table and began reading from a dry position paper. The Russians, British, and French listened politely. Some of them noticed for the first time a new face watching them from directly behind the president. A few of them recognized Nelson Rockefeller.

Then the dramatic moment arrived. Eisenhower was midway through his speech when he suddenly took off his glasses, summoned all his Kansas candor, and looked Soviet Premier Nikolai Bulganin squarely in the eye. Speaking as if extemporaneously, he proposed exchanging "a blueprint of our military establishments" and providing

> within our countries facilities for aerial photography to the other country to convince the world that we are providing, as between ourselves, against the possibility of great surprise attack. . . .
>
> I do not know how I could convince you of our sincerity in the matter and that we mean you no harm. I only wish that God would give me some means of convincing you of our sincerity and loyalty in making this proposal. . . . The time has come to end the Cold War. And I propose that we take practical steps to that end; that we begin an arrangement very quickly, as between ourselves—immediately.

At that very moment, lightning flashed, thunder clapped, and the hall's lights flickered. "To this day," chuckled U.S. interpreter Vernon Walters years later, "I am told the Russians are still trying to figure out how we did it."[9]

One Soviet delegate was particularly furious. His official rank was only that

John D. Rockefeller, Sr. (*left*), converses with his closest confidant and only son, John D. Rockefeller, Jr., while walking along Manhattan's streets, c. 1915. (Courtesy of the Rockefeller Archive Center)

Rockefeller, Jr. (*fifth from right*), with business leaders during a fund-raising drive for the Interchurch World Movement, 1920. Rockefeller, Jr., was the major funder of the movement "to Christianize the world" as an antidote to revolutions like the recent one in Russia. (Courtesy of the Rockefeller Archive Center)

Pocantico, the 3,600-acre Rockefeller family estate overlooking the Hudson in Tarrytown, New York, c. 1940. Main mansion, Kikjuit (Dutch for "the lookout"), is in left center of photo; a huge playhouse for children is at top center; Rockefeller, Jr.'s, mansion is to its left. (Courtesy of the Rockefeller Archive Center)

Bacone College for Indians. Its first building was Rockefeller Hall, donated by John D. Rockefeller, who began contributions after Rev. Almon A. Bacone provided information on Indian unrest in Oklahoma previous to Standard Oil's entry into the territory. (Courtesy of University of Oklahoma Library, Western History Collection)

Young Nelson Rockefeller in cowboy outfit, 1924. Nelson had his first experience with Spanish-speaking Indians during this trip to the West with his father and brothers John and Laurance. Standard Oil was then moving into Navajo lands.
(Courtesy of the Rockefeller Archive Center)

Rockefeller, Jr. (*center*), pats the shoulder of a Taos Pueblo Indian while giving out candy to Indian children, 1924. Unknown to the Indians, Rockefeller was funding Fundamentalist Christian missionaries who were then trying to stamp out their Indian religious traditions as "immoral."
(Courtesy of the Rockefeller Archive Center)

William Cameron Townsend (*center*), soon to become the Central American Mission's greatest success story, with his missionary wife, Elvira (*far left*), and Guatemalan Indian schoolchildren, 1922–1923. Townsend, impressed by the achievements of Rockefeller-funded scientists in health, sanitation, and linguistics, adopted their methods as well as Indian dress. (Courtesy of Wycliffe Bible Translators)

In April 1946, a year and a half after Elvira died, widower Cam Townsend married Elaine Mielke, an educator and member of Chicago's powerful Moody Memorial Church. Posing with the newlyweds are Lázaro Cárdenas, the former president of Mexico, and his wife, Amalia, at whose home the ceremony took place. Townsend had backed Cárdenas's nationalization of Standard Oil's properties in 1937. (Courtesy of Wycliffe Bible Translators)

The U.S. Coordinator of Inter-American Affairs during World War II, Nelson Rockefeller (*right*) is seen here with his chief of finance and industry, Joseph Rovensky. Earlier, as vice president of Chase National Bank, Rovensky steered Rockefeller toward his first investment in Latin America, Standard Oil's Creole Petroleum subsidiary in Venezuela. (Courtesy of U.S. National Archives)

Swastika over South America. Rockefeller's wartime propaganda featured South America under dire threat of a Nazi takeover. His small agency, the office of the Coordinator of Inter-American Affairs (CIAA), soon grew to become one of Washington's largest and most glamorous operations. (Courtesy of the U.S. National Archives)

The Coordinator, Nelson Rockefeller, and U.S. Chamber of Commerce president Eric Johnston (*left*), chair of the U.S. Committee of the Inter-American Development Commission, look over a map of South America showing human resources. Indian labor was vital for U.S. access to Latin America's natural resources. (Courtesy of the U.S. National Archives)

Rockefeller and Nicaragua's dictator, General Anastasio Somoza *(right)*, who provided access to Miskito Indians as labor for taking rubber out of Nicaragua's Atlantic coast. (Courtesy of the U.S. National Archives)

Colorado Indian tapping rubber tree in Ecuador for export to the U.S. during wartime shortages. Rockefeller rebuffed the efforts of Charles Collier and his father, John Collier, the reform-minded U.S. Commissioner of Indian Affairs, to extend protections over Indian laborers to prevent abuse by rubber companies. (Courtesy of the U.S. National Archives)

CIAA launch *Rockefeller*, named after the head of its governmental sponsor, arrives at a jungle port in the Peruvian Amazon to carry out medical operations in support of the U.S. rubber collection program. (Courtesy of the U.S. National Archives)

Rockefeller meets Brazil's nationalist president, Getúlio Vargas (*left*), 1942. Vargas opposed Rockefeller's scheme for a U.S.-dominated Amazon Development Corporation, preferring Brazilian sovereignty over development beyond rubber extraction in its territory. Overthrown in 1945 and reelected in 1950, he set up Brazil's national oil company, Petrobrás, to break the American monopoly over oil refining in Brazil. His suicide during a military revolt in 1954 saved Petrobrás from being dismantled. (Courtesy of the U.S. National Archives)

Peru's president, Manuel Prado, on a visit to the United States, waves to a crowd as his son, Manuel, Jr., looks on. Prado, a banker, was a friend of the Rockefellers and a classmate of Nelson's brother David at the London School of Economics. His son worked for Nelson at the CIAA; after the war the son worked for David at the Chase bank. (Courtesy of the U.S. National Archives)

Alberto Lleras Camargo (*left*), Colombia's ambassador to the United States during the war and foreign minister when this photograph was taken in 1945, became one of Rockefeller's closest allies among Latin America's elite. Later, as Colombia's president, he was given a ticker-tape parade in Manhattan by Governor Rockefeller and eventually served as a trustee of the Rockefeller Foundation. (Courtesy of the U.S. National Archives)

Galo Plaza (*right*) was a close friend and Nelson Rockefeller's parliamentary whip during the United Nations' San Francisco conference in 1945. In 1952, as president of Ecuador, he invited Rockefeller's IBEC and Townsend's SIL missionaries into the Ecuadorian Amazon. In 1967, when the Ecuadorian Amazon was confirmed to be awash with oil, Galo Plaza, at Rockefeller's urging, accepted election as secretary-general of the OAS. (Courtesy of the U.S. Department of State and the Harry S. Truman Library)

World War II gave Nelson Rockefeller his first opportunity to meet Brazil's most powerful businessmen. In this picture, he is barely visible at the head table in the top right, being hosted by Rio de Janeiro's chamber of commerce in September 1942. (Courtesy of the U.S. National Archives)

During his 1942 visit to Brazil, Rockefeller also developed a relationship with Brazil's military high command. He is pictured here reviewing a map of Brazil with General Pedro Góes Monteiro (left) and General Eurico Gaspar Dutra. To the far right is a senior U.S. military attaché. Three years later, the generals overthrew President Vargas. (Courtesy of the U.S. National Archives)

U.S. Ambassador Jefferson Caffery (*left*), an opponent of Rockefeller's Amazon development plans, failed to keep Rockefeller from visiting Brazil. Then he tried to disrupt the guest of honor's speech by loudly calling for cigarettes, only to be embarrassed by five minutes of Rockefeller's withering praise. A startled Oswaldo Aranha, Vargas's pro-U.S. foreign minister, sits between the two feuding American officials. (Courtesy of the U.S. National Archives)

Nelson Rockefeller, after being sworn in as assistant secretary of state in December 1945, had Ambassador Caffery moved to Paris, replacing him with Adolf Berle, Rockefeller's predecessor. Berle had been removed as assistant secretary by Roosevelt after showing unwillingness to cooperate in the wartime alliance between the United States and the Soviet Union. (Courtesy of the U.S. National Archives)

Rockefeller lands at Mexico City with his first wife, Mary "Tod" *(fore-ground)*, and a planeload of Latin American ambassadors and aides to attend the historic Chapultepec Inter-American Conference in February 1945. Rockefeller pushed through a regional military treaty that became the legal basis for the Organization of American States (OAS). (Courtesy of the U.S. National Archives)

At the United Nations' founding conference in San Francisco, Rockefeller *(fifth from right in back row along wall)* and his Latin allies pressed for the admission of Argentina's previously pro-Axis Péron dictatorship as key to the smooth integration of the hemispheric military alliance into the new international order. Secretary of State Edward Stettinius (with white hair) is at the center of the table, Soviet foreign minister Vyacheslav Molotov is six seats to the right. (Courtesy of the Rockefeller Archive Center)

The new U.S. ambassador to Brazil, Adolf Berle, and his wife, Beatrice, arrive in Rio de Janeiro, January 1945. Before the year was out, Berle had interfered with Brazil's internal politics, convincing many that he had encouraged the military to overthrow President Vargas in the first postwar coup of the Cold War in Latin America.
(Courtesy of the U.S. National Archives)

Brazil's new president, General Dutra, who along with General Góes Monteiro was the chief conspirator of the 1945 coup against Vargas, enjoyed a lighter moment trying out a gun during a previous visit to the United States.
(Courtesy of the U.S. National Archives)

Rockefeller with Berent Friele (*left*), his closest aide on Latin America, plans the expansion of Rockefeller operations into Venezuela with Venezuelan government officials. Friele gave up a seat on the board of directors of A & P to work full-time for Rockefeller.
(Courtesy of the Rockefeller Archive Center)

Monte Sacro, Nelson Rockefeller's 5,000-acre ranch in Venezuela, contained an estate that had once belonged to Símon Bolívar, leader of South America's war for independence from Spain. (Courtesy of the Rockefeller Archive Center)

Rockefeller experimented in hybrid seeds for corn and pasture grass in Brazil and Venezuela, set up demonstration projects and credit operations, and sold seeds and land-clearing equipment to advance the cattle frontier into the continent's interior. Here he inspects a variety of corn at one of his farms in Venezuela. (Courtesy of the Rockefeller Archive Center)

As successor to the investment company set up in 1952 by Nelson Rockefeller's IBEC and David Rockefeller's Chase National Bank, Crescinco was Brazil's largest mutual fund by 1959, with holdings in more than 100 Brazilian companies. (Courtesy of National Planning Association)

William Cameron Townsend regales recruits of the Wycliffe Bible Translators at jungle training camp in Chiapas, Mexico, near the Guatemalan border. (Courtesy of Wycliffe Bible Translators; photo by Cornell Capa)

Kenneth Pike (*below*) was indispensable for turning missionaries into linguists for bilingual education, as well as Bible translation, as members of Wycliffe's alter ego abroad, the Summer Institute of Linguistics (SIL). (Courtesy of Wycliffe Bible Translators) *Right:* An Indian listens to a recording of his language by an SIL linguist (c. 1964), the key to unlocking the secrets of an Indian culture. Breaking down a tribe's isolation is the necessary first step to its absorption and domination by the national marketplace's culture. SIL now uses advanced computer technology to speed up translations. (Courtesy of *La Prensa*)

Nelson Rockefeller (*center, directly behind President Truman*), chairman of the International Development Advisory Board (IDAB), with IDAB members. Rockefeller's IDAB report, *Partners in Progress*, called for a doubling of the $1 billion invested each year by American corporations in the Third World, acting in concert with the World Bank, as well as the forging of regional military pacts. (Courtesy of UPI/Bettmann Archive)

General Dwight Eisenhower, then president of Columbia University, flanked by Nelson Rockefeller's father, John D. Rockefeller, Jr. (*left*), and Nelson's uncle, Nelson Aldrich, former chairman of the Chase bank and later Eisenhower's ambassador to Great Britain. Rockefellers played a major role in Eisenhower's rise to the White House. (Courtesy of the Rockefeller Archive Center)

The payoff. Nelson Rockefeller is sworn in as President Eisenhower's special assistant in charge of Cold War strategy and psychological warfare, December 1954. Rockefeller chaired the supersecret Special Group, which oversaw all CIA covert operations, including mind-control experiments funded through the Department of Health, Education and Welfare when Rockefeller was its first undersecretary. (Courtesy of the Dwight D. Eisenhower Library)

Rockefeller brothers, Laurance (*center*) and John 3rd (*right*), receive the Magsaysay Award from the Magsaysay Foundation, which they set up at the urging of Nelson and the CIA. The foundation later gave the same award to the SIL. (Courtesy of the Rockefeller Archive Center)

Nelson Rockefeller in a jeep with aides during a 1956 tour of holdings in Venezuela and Brazil.
(Courtesy of the Rockefeller Archive Center)

Left: Rockefeller enjoys a laugh with his cousin Richard Aldrich, his top aide in Brazil, during a 1956 plane tour. In 1974, during the congressional confirmation hearings on his nomination to be vice president, Rockefeller revealed Aldrich's ties to the CIA. *Right:* Rockefeller with his major Brazilian business partner, banker Walther Moreira Salles (*left*), during the same flight. Rockefeller decided to become Moreira Salles's partner in the largest privately owned tract of land along the Brazil-Bolivia border, the 1-million-acre Fazenda Bodoquena. (Both photos courtesy of the Rockefeller Archive Center)

Rockefeller herds cattle on one of his ranches, 1959. Rockefeller's experiments in grasses and legumes were designed to encourage large Brazilian ranchers to expand their investments in the frontier. Cattle ranching soon became the greatest single threat to the survival of the Amazon rain forest and its Indian peoples. Less obvious, however, were Rockefeller-allied mining interests.
(Courtesy of Associated Press/Wide World Photos)

Indian boys watch missionaries land their Helio Courier on jungle airstrip, Ecuadorian Amazon, 1961. (Courtesy of Magnum Photos; photo by Cornell Capa)

Rachel Saint (rear) succeeded in converting some of the Huaorani (Auca) who killed her missionary brother, Nate; she then wowed U.S. audiences during a national tour with her Huaorani, language informant, Dayuma, including an appearance on Ralph Edwards's *This Is Your Life!* television show. (Courtesy of Wycliffe Bible Translators)

Billy Graham, who joined Wycliffe's board of directors, hosted Rachel Saint and Dayuma at his Madison Square Garden Crusade in New York City in 1957. Behind the scenes, John D. Rockefeller, Jr., was persuaded by Nelson's aides and mainline Protestant leaders to donate $50,000 to Graham's crusade. (Courtesy of Associated Press/Wide World Photos)

of a political observer on Bulganin's staff, but Walters, an intelligence officer with experience going back to Berle's Rio Embassy and the 1948 Organization of American States (OAS) conference in Bogotá, had already sized him up as the real leader of the Soviet delegation. As Rockefeller accompanied Eisenhower out of the hall, the short, bald man abandoned Bulganin's diplomatic niceties and personally confronted them.

"Khrushchev knew who I was," Nelson remembered, "but he just looked at me and went on talking to the President."[10] Walters's translation could barely keep up as the powerful secretary general of the Communist Party of the Soviet Union accused the Eisenhower administration of trying to sabotage the Summit with grandstanding gestures that could never be accepted by the Soviet Union. The arguments flew back and forth. Eisenhower tried to assure Nikita Khrushchev of his sincerity and challenged the Soviets to accept open skies; Khrushchev, knowing that his party hardliners and the Soviet military would never allow its provisions, bitterly denounced the speech. Then he abruptly turned away and left. "We knew the Soviets wouldn't accept it," Eisenhower admitted. "We were sure of that. But we took a look and thought it was a good move."[11]

GUNS AND BUTTER FOR THE THIRD WORLD

Back in Washington, Nelson's victory had produced unforeseen problems. The Soviets did not publicly reject Open Skies. And Eisenhower's speech raised false hopes among misguided Europeans and Americans alike that the "Spirit of Geneva" meant that military confrontation with the Soviets was less likely.

This expectation of lessened tensions disturbed Nelson. It was the threat of war that had forged into being not only NATO, but also the only major U.S. military pact in the Third World, the OAS in Latin America. War would also be the basic argument for setting up SEATO that September along Asia's Pacific Rim. To meet the challenge of this outbreak of peace, Nelson got Eisenhower's approval to reconvene the Special Group's brain trust at Quantico.

The first time, the State Department had been worried. "He seems to be building up a big staff," Dulles had complained. "He's got them down at Quantico, and nobody knows what they're doing."[12] Dulles and other Cabinet members had even more cause to worry about Quantico II. Although Nelson sold the second gathering to Eisenhower as an effort to "consider the psychological aspect of U.S. strategy" after Geneva, Nelson's interest was now more economic in nature and grander in scale. He wanted a new "world economic policy" for the United States.

Nelson's forty-one-page Quantico II report called for an $18 billion conventional arms buildup, coupled with a massive increase in foreign aid to help Third World governments finance the infrastructure needed for a huge infusion of American corporate investment. The latter included integrating nuclear power into overall power programs that rested mainly on coal and hydroelectric power. The report was mindful that "the American national conviction that 'colonialism' is bad under all circumstances . . . overlooks the fact that many peoples are incapable of self-government."[13]

To prevent the Soviets' publicly owned and subsidized socialist enterprises from competing "unfairly" against privately owned profit-seeking enterprises, the arms race would offer "the prospect of inducing strains in the Soviet economy." There would be "the added virtue of offering the type of production competition [high technology, capital intensive] that is comparatively most costly for the USSR to match."[14]

An arms race just might bankrupt the Soviet Union, or at least cripple its capacity to compete in world markets with Western private corporations. And an arms race was bound to curtail production of consumer goods, continuing consumer frustrations and fears that increased the strength of conservatives in the Soviet military; any plans by Khrushchev to dismantle Stalin's garrison state and introduce democratic reforms would have to give way before the perceived threat of imminent nuclear war. The United States, on the other hand, could "afford to survive" through an arms race. To rally the nation behind its new arms race, the report called for a presidential initiative in "explaining to the people of the United States the gravity of the world situation."[15]

Not everyone was impressed by Nelson or his Cold War intellectuals. And by the time his classified report was circulating among some 600 cleared government officials, the one man Nelson had most hoped to influence—the president— had been removed from action.

On September 24, the day before Quantico II convened, Dwight Eisenhower suffered a heart attack. Hospitalized until November 11, he was replaced at the helm titularly by Vice President Richard M. Nixon, but actually by Secretary of State Dulles. Suddenly, Nelson was confronted with the "sick president" syndrome that he had experienced with Roosevelt and had almost ended his career in government: a hostile vice president, a secretary of state who was jealous of his power, and a praetorian guard that considered him an outsider. With the loss of direct access to the president, Nelson was stripped of power and isolated.

Eisenhower was not in complete command even after his release from the hospital; he spent only four days in Washington before going to his Gettysburg farm to convalesce. Nelson next saw him at a National Security Council (NSC) meeting on November 21. It was not clear whether Eisenhower could run again in 1956, which left the field open. Lacking a bureaucratic base like the CIAA to enable him to remain a contender, Nelson tried to get appointed deputy secretary of the most powerful bureaucracy of all—the Defense Department. He did not get the job.

Nelson had to concede that his stint at the White House was turning out to be a failure, but he could claim success in one arena of the Cold War: Latin America. During Nelson's tenure as presidential coordinator of the CIA's covert operations in 1955, "Latin America began to emerge as an area of the Cold War," the CIA's Harry Rositzke wrote later. "The CIA became involved in a broad front of covert action: building news services and local outlets for distributing propaganda, supporting non-Communist student congresses, sponsoring or subsidizing anti-Communist publications, extending the activities of its intellectual front organizations into the youth, student and labor groups from Mexico to Brazil."[16]

Nelson's stint as the chief of psychological warfare coincided with a face-lift for the American business ethic for foreign appearances. The United States Information Agency, through a campaign called "People's Capitalism," was about to rechristen U.S. corporations as models of responsible behavior and democracy. People's Capitalism was an attempt to foster the image of a capitalism no longer predatory or abusive, but matured into a responsible corporate citizen, democratically owned and controlled. This argument for democracy through stock ownership ignored the central point of American democracy—the inherent right of enfranchisement, the right not to have to pay for a vote—and breezily overlooked the reality that in a stockholders' meeting in the United States the many can be outvoted by the few. People's Capitalism had one redeeming value: propaganda. Americans, convinced that anyone could get rich through hard work and luck, had also accepted the arbitrary prerogative of wealth as a right, as long as corporations at least appeared to be trying to act in a socially responsible manner. Fostering such an image always had been at the core of the Rockefeller family ethic.

"People's Capitalism" became the ideological soul of the CIA-funded People-to-People Program[17] promoted by the American Municipal Association's Committee on International Municipal Cooperation. The Washington-based committee sponsored "Sister City" projects between Chamber of Commerce types in the United States and abroad, including cities and towns in Amazon-basin countries, where prospects for American capital for development were often tied to the subject of oil.

Opening Doors for Oil Wars

Perhaps no one in Eisenhower's NSC understood more intimately the political sensitivities surrounding oil than did Nelson Rockefeller. He was certainly more sensitive than most NSC members to Egyptian national pride. He also had both the background and high position in the intelligence community to be able to see how the frustration of Egyptian President Gamal Abdel Nasser over his country's underdevelopment could affect Latin America through Egypt's control over oil supplied to Europe and the United States. In 1955, the continued flow of Middle Eastern oil through the Suez Canal to Western Europe was far from certain. The Pentagon had long been concerned about the paucity of tapped oil reserves in Latin America.[18]

The Pentagon's fretting dated back to 1944. The State-War-Navy Coordinating Committee, the wartime precursor to the National Security Council, had identified oil pools in the Amazon basin. These reserves had remained mostly untapped, precisely because of the availability of Middle Eastern oil. But now Soviet penetration of British, French, and American control over Middle Eastern oil seemed a definite possibility, with Nasser's arms accord with Czechoslovakia and the Soviet offer of financial and technical aid. Latin America's oil suddenly took on new significance.

Brazil's Amazon was out of bounds to American oil companies. With his suicide, President Vargas had achieved his most important political goal: The army had supported Petrobrás's monopoly over oil exploration.[19] Petrobrás's strike in March 1955 near Manaus had occurred despite the earlier-stated "disinterest" in the Amazon by exploration consultants from Geophysical Service, Inc. (GSI), a subsidiary of Texas Instruments (TI).

Since 1953, Texas Instruments had owned the Intercontinental Rubber Company, the old rubber firm associated with the family of Nelson Rockefeller's grandfather, Senator Nelson Aldrich, during the turn-of-the-century heyday of the Green Hell in the Belgian Congo and the Amazon. Whether the Brazilians were aware of Texas Instruments' close ties to the Rockefellers,[20] their rejection of GSI's advice paid off. Moreover, the Brazilian army was enthusiastic about cashing in on Brazil's 1938 treaty with Bolivia. That treaty provided that Brazil, in return for completing a railroad outlet for Bolivia's rubber and cattle in the jungle hills and lowlands east of the Andes, would receive joint rights in the region's Camirí district to develop oil. The railroad was completed in 1954, but neither the government in La Paz nor the one in Washington had any intention of allowing Petrobrás's holdings to extend into Bolivia.

The year 1955 marked a sudden turn for the worse in Brazil's relations with Bolivia. It also marked a concurrent boost in fortunes for American oil companies that were seeking some way of dealing with the new government that had come to power with the Indian Revolution of 1952. After oil was struck east of the Andes at Camirí in early 1954, Bolivian President Victor Paz Estenssoro's eagerness to see Petrobrás live up to its treaty obligations rapidly disintegrated. By the end of Nelson's White House tenure in December 1955, Paz Estenssoro announced that he was opening the region and almost all national territory—to foreign oil concessions. Petrobrás suddenly found itself competing with Standard Oil, Texaco, and Gulf, all of which now had Paz Estenssoro's favor.[21]

As Brazil's Petrobrás suffered quietly under Washington's "containment policy" (now extended beyond communism to any national oil entities, which were barred from U.S. aid), American interest focused on other countries in Latin America.

In the Caribbean basin, Standard Oil of New Jersey and Standard Oil of Indiana moved into Cuba and Jamaica. Guatemala's tropical Petén region was opened to Standard Oil of Ohio, Texaco, and Standard Oil of New Jersey.

In Venezuela, dictator Marcos Pérez Jiménez began negotiations for new concessions that would net him another $500 million by 1956. Colombia allowed oil teams to penetrate the last virgin forests around Lake Maracaibo along the border with Venezuela, provoking attacks by Matillone Indians defending their sole refuge.

But it was the Amazon, particularly the Ecuadorian Amazon, that excited the most concern in Washington. In 1942, all eyes were focused on the Marañon River. The Marañon was more than a river—it was a symbol of Ecuadorian pride turned sour when, under the U.S.-brokered Rio Protocol, portions of its oil reserves were ceded to neighboring Peru. Now, more than a decade later, Texaco's ships plowed up the Amazon River to deliver drilling rigs to the company's new concessions along the Marañon. Ecuador reacted sharply. Its president, José María Velasco Ibarra, was an ardent nationalist and deeply resented the loss of the oil region.

Not every Ecuadorian was upset, however: José Chiriboga, who actually helped negotiate the concession as a member of the Ecuadorian delegation to the Rio Conference, and fellow liberal Galo Plaza, who, as postwar president of

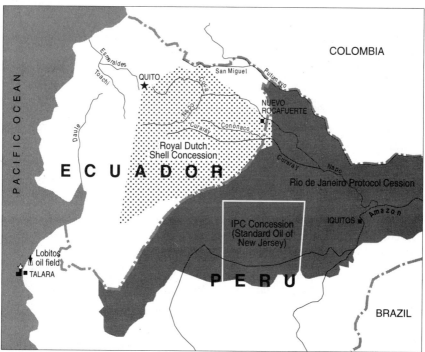

Ecuador Loses Access to the Amazon—and Potential Oil Lands (1941–1942)

As a result of Peru's invasion in 1941 and the U.S.-brokered Rio de Janeiro Protocol of 1942, Ecuador lost about half its territory (shaded area) to Peru, a portion of which Peru then leased to Standard Oil of New Jersey's International Petroleum Company (IPC), which already controlled the Lobitos oil field and the refinery at Talara, Peru.

Ecuador, had accepted it. Now, as Velasco's ambassador to the United States, Chiriboga received orders from Quito to protest an alleged Peruvian troop buildup along the border by Peru's president, Manuel Odría. Velasco reportedly feared that Peruvian troops moving along the border, coupled with the arrival of Texaco's ships, heralded the seizure of more of Ecuador's Amazonian lands.

Velasco ordered Chiriboga to demand OAS intervention. He got it. The OAS sent inspection teams. But when the teams denied that any Peruvian buildup was occurring, Velasco became suspicious. He promptly declared Ecuador's concession to the Canadian-based Peruvian Oil and Minerals Company null and "arbitrary."[22]

Velasco had good cause to worry. Two years before, at Odría's 1953 auction, the Canadian company had successfully bid for exploration rights to 135,000 acres of Amazonian oil lands just across Ecuador's border with Peru and had won exploration rights to another 17,000 acres. So had Standard Oil of New Jersey, which would soon replace the Peruvian Oil and Minerals Company. Yet another Canadian player, Ventures Limited, had also joined Jersey Standard in buying oil rights in northern Peru's Sechura Desert. By September 1955, three out of the four Special Group members who had overseen the CIA's covert operations in Ecuador and Peru that year had ties to American oil companies[23] operating across the border in Peru. The fourth member, Allen Dulles, was director of the same CIA that had overthrown the Iranian government two years before over the nagging question of oil.

Concern over renewed maneuvering by foreign oil companies in Latin America spread throughout the continent. And watching it all was the CIA, which sent reports to Washington. There, Nelson Rockefeller, as chairman of the Special Group and vice chairman of the larger Operations Coordinating Board, was responsible for monitoring covert operations throughout the Western Hemisphere. He controlled an apparatus that could spot problems—and opportunities—wherever they erupted in Latin America. In 1955, two developments must have seemed portentous. One was the election to the Brazilian presidency of the friend of the International Basic Economy Corporation from Minas Gerais, Governor Juscelino Kubitschek; the other was the fall of Nelson's most embarrassing client from the Roosevelt era, Juan Perón, as president of Argentina.

A week before Nelson convened Quantico II, the Argentine air force and navy staged a successful revolt against Perón. No longer guided by his wife's savvy—Eva had died in 1953—Perón had abandoned himself to personal and political excesses. He outraged Eva's followers by taking a fourteen-year-old girl as his mistress. Then he lost the support of the Roman Catholic Church by ending compulsory Catholic education and paid Catholic holidays for government workers. But what most undermined the morale of Perón's base of loyalists was his decision to allow Standard Oil of California to take over exploration in a huge portion of Santa Cruz province.

As Perón faced the likelihood of exile, George E. Allen was winging his way toward the Middle East. It was Allen's Atlas Corporation that had triggered Perón's decline by following Milton Eisenhower's visit two years before with a bid to drill 400 oil wells near the Argentine Andes. Now Allen was on his way to Egypt.

This mission, urged on a reluctant State Department by Nelson Rockefeller,[24] was to offer credit for the Aswan Dam if Nasser would stop talking about Soviet trade and Czech arms. Nelson had no reason to be optimistic. Nasser controlled the Suez choke point of the Persian Gulf oil flow; his Syrian allies controlled the pumping stations of Iraq Petroleum Company's pipeline. (Indeed, the Syrians would blow up the stations during the Suez Crisis the following year.) On top of that, Nasser promoted the spread of Arab nationalism in the Middle East, making the Pentagon's and oil companies' need to identify and secure Latin American oil reserves for future tapping a strategic necessity.

Nelson knew from experience that in cases of unrest in the Third World, military aid to compliant regimes could stem the tide of rising expectations only so long. As he had with Standard Oil's board twenty years before, he now argued strenuously that time was running out for American intervention in the developing world's political process.

Small wonder that Nelson was disheartened by the administration's failure to respond to Quantico II's warnings on Latin America's strategic importance.

If this were ever to change, Nelson needed more power, more than what appointed office offered and especially more than four secretaries of state in three administrations had been willing to allow. Even in a top-level White House job, his staff, with funds restricted by the Treasury Department, had never grown beyond twenty people, a far cry from his CIAA empire of thousands.

He decided to resign.

Before he left, he sent the recuperating Eisenhower two Christmas presents. One was traditional Americana: a nineteenth-century silk embroidery of a bald eagle. The other was traditional Rockefeller: a parting shot at his enemies. In a two-page memorandum, he argued that the time-honored approach of the secretary of state controlling foreign affairs no longer sufficed at a time when the United States was a global power.

His recommendation was startling: Centralized efficiency should replace the contending agencies of cabinet rule appropriate to an earlier laissez faire age. "You need an organization which can adequately coordinate the development of strategy, the carrying out of actions, the analysis and evaluation of programs to achieve stated objectives."

In other words, an appointed supergovernment, above and outside the departments and agencies known to the press and the people, acting in secrecy out of the White House, responsible to only one man, the president.

Eisenhower, however, was not ready to enter a dark age of executive power and take the nation on the path that would lead to the Nixon administration's Houston Plan for a centralized police state, to Watergate, and then to the Reagan administration's Iran-contra arms deal.

The president responded to Nelson's tough letter only with personal regrets about losing daily contact with the Rockefeller heir, "one of the sad developments of an otherwise happy holiday season."[25]

Nelson packed up his office.

"I'm convinced of one thing," he told one of his aides, while stopping by to say good-bye. "You can't have a voice in your party unless you've proved that you know how to get votes."[26]

Then he turned and left, closing the door behind him.

20

MESSENGERS OF THE SUN

LAUNCHING THE FLEET

A week before Nelson Rockefeller resigned as presidential assistant for psychological warfare and Cold War strategy, one of the Cold War's least-known but significant events took place outside a hangar in a Chicago airport. Braving a frigid wind blowing in from Lake Michigan, a group of men and women gathered on December 17, 1955, for what was supposed to be a celebration of American Christian charity toward less developed nations. But the two star celebrities of the occasion gave hint of another, more political purpose.

Richard J. Daley, looking the model of the stocky Irish American big-city politician, was a conservative but devout Roman Catholic. The newly elected mayor of Chicago was absolute ruler of arguably the most powerful Democratic machine in the United States. Daley had not risen to power championing the ambition of Fundamentalist Protestants in Catholic countries like Ecuador. Yet here he was, officially welcoming the crowd, including members of the press, to the dedication of an airplane that would bring the Wycliffe Bible Translators into the heart of the Ecuadorian Amazon. Standing beside Daley was Ecuador's ambassador José Chiriboga, who had earned a reputation for shrewdness as mayor of Quito equal to Daley's in Chicago. Only twelve years before, he had confounded his countrymen by signing over half of Ecuador's Amazon to Peru at Washington's behest. Pearl Harbor had made hemispheric unity essential, Chiriboga had explained, and the war between Ecuador and Peru had to end, even if that meant that Ecuador would lose land rumored to be coveted by Standard Oil's Peruvian subsidiary, International Petroleum Company. And now here was Chiriboga again, as ambassador of a self-described radical nationalist government, sanctioning the penetration of Ecuador's remaining Amazonian lands by a well-connected American missionary organization.

Perhaps the greatest enigma of the day was the thin, balding man who had led the dignitaries out of the hangar to watch the new airplaine in a demonstration flight. William Cameron Townsend was a paradox of naïveté and hard-nosed diplomacy, as innocent in purpose yet deliberately aimed as any "arrow of love" sent to Bibleless tribes by the unseen force he called Jesus. At fifty-nine, he retained his youthful exuberance and grace, smiling easily as he helped assemble the dignitaries and reporters before the plane Larry Montgomery was about to demonstrate. Only those closest to him knew his steely resolve and how it had led him across the United States' Rubicon of church-state separation to embrace the world of politics unlike any Fundamentalist missionary before him. This day marked the beginning of the Inter-American Friendship Fleet he was promoting in Washington's corridors and of the Jungle Aviation and Radio Service (JAARS) as an important instrument of the Cold War.

Pilot Larry Montgomery climbed aboard the small plane and taxied it away for the takeoff. It was an odd-looking craft, with a roaring, large twin-bladed propeller and a giant overhead wing with flaps so wide it seemed to hang over everything else, dwarfing the cabin. Six months before, another unusually long-winged airplane had zoomed into the stratosphere before startled onlookers, but it would be another half year before the CIA's U-2 would make its secret maiden voyage into Soviet skies. This plane, however, was ready now, and although its design came out of the same aeronautical origins as did the U-2, the Helio Courier was no secret. It could not be, for it was designed to be flown at low altitudes and speeds, not in the heavens beyond sight and sound. Both planes would make history for the CIA. But the U-2's mission would be exposed to the world within five years; the Helio's use as a CIA asset would remain virtually unknown for three more decades.[1]

At first, the board of the Summer Institute of Linguistics (SIL) had an attack of anxiety over the expense of Cam's vision of an airborne SIL. No one could argue that the Helio Courier was a bush pilot's dream. Even the name was intriguing: *Helio* is the Greek word for "sun," and *courier* is the Latin word for "messenger." There was something romantic about evangelical linguists bringing tribes the Light of God's Word in Helio Couriers, "Messengers of the Sun." But where would they ever get another $150,000?

"Uncle Cam has always been a step ahead of us," Ken Pike had insisted. "He may be again."[2]

He was. Cam used his tested formula for success, St. Paul's advice to "honor the King." To attract recognition from U.S. officialdom, Cam called on liberals in the Rockefeller sphere of influence. He contacted a corporate-backed group of

Good Neighbors he had been cultivating for years, the same Pan American Council of Chicago that Nelson Rockefeller's CIAA had supported during the war.[3]

Cam arranged for the Pan American Council to participate in the Helio ceremony by hosting a luncheon for Ambassador Chiriboga, to be presided over by Mayor Daley and to include guests from all the city's Good Neighbor committees that were working for closer ties with Latin America.[4]

Now more than ever, SIL's future was tied to aviation as much as to linguistics. Planes were becoming the most important means for governments involved in "nation-building" in the Third World to secure, penetrate, and colonize frontiers with landless peasants. As JAARS's dedication of its air fleet to the Peruvian military had demonstrated, through Cam's negotiated contracts, SIL's most important assets—airplanes—became *their* assets. Airplanes were much more versatile than translators, and skilled pilots, maintenance crews, and radios were even rarer in the oil-rich jungles of the Amazon than were airplanes. In just the past year, Cam had been given the green light from two governments that were searching for oil in the jungles east of the Andes: Bolivia and Ecuador.

But all these opportunities depended, in turn, on making the Inter-American Friendship Fleet a reality. Cam had spent most of this furlough year in the United States in a fruitless effort to convince the oilmen of Tulsa that JAARS was the answer to *their* prayers, not just his. He needed a publicity coup to win them over and to persuade businessmen in other cities to buy the Helios he had ordered.

He tried his best in Chicago. So did Ambassador Chiriboga, who helped arrange a wiregram of support from Ecuador's President Velasco Ibarra, which Don Burns read proudly to Mayor Daley and the other attenders of the "Friendship of Chicago" dedication. But when the ceremony was over and Larry Montgomery had finished his aerial acrobatics with the Helio and gone on his way to Quito for a similar ceremony there with Velasco, Cam knew it was not enough. The *Chicago Tribune*'s small column in the back pages the next day made that fact painfully clear. He needed something bigger, something inspiring, to encourage the participation of more famous politicians to draw the crowds that donors appreciated and to cheer the donors on to write checks in recognition of JAARS's unique potential.

He returned to Arkansas, to Wycliffe's home at Sulphur Springs, from where he wrote pleas for money to unheeding Fundamentalists. Then, as if from the Hand of God, lightning struck in the glint of spears.

Behind Operation Auca

Deep in Ecuador's Amazon jungle, at Shell Oil's abandoned base camp, a young SIL Bible translator named Betty Elliot sat with four other missionary wives, their eyes riveted on the silent radio receiver, their thoughts seized by dread. Hours had passed since their husbands had radioed from an unchartered beach on the Curaray River even deeper in the jungle. This was the river that lent its name to the famous poison used by Amazonian Indians to paralyze their prey—the same curare that Rockefeller-funded Dr. D. Ewen Cameron would soon be testing for the CIA at the Allen Memorial Institute in Montreal, Canada. Other than airplanes, the Curaray River was also the only means of transportation through an area where Shell's work crews had once fallen to Indian spears and poisoned darts from blow guns. These were the same Indians that the five American missionaries were trying to contact for the Lord, and their wives knew the risk was great. Since surviving enslavement and massacres by rubber barons, the elusive Huaorani Indians gained fame by the name given them by the terrified Quichua who lived in the area: the Auca, the Savage.

Nate Saint, the missionaries' leader, had told his wife, Marjorie, that he would call at 4:35. But that time was past, and the women were frantic. Marjorie kept calling. The jungle answered with an awful silence.

Of the five men, the lean thirty-two-year-old Nate was the oldest and most experienced. A pilot with the Missionary Aviation Fellowship (MAF), he had the most knowledge of the region and its people. His bright yellow Piper was a familiar sight throughout the Oriente or "East," as Ecuador's Amazon region east of the Andes was called. Nate was a welcome source of diesel fuel for missionary generators, mail from home, and medicine, the greatest weapon against the tribes' traditional religious leaders. For seven years, Nate had operated out of Shell Mera, the oil company's old base. There, in 1954, he met Shell director Jimmy Doolittle during the general's secret fact-finding tour of CIA covert assets for President Eisenhower. In September 1955, the same month that Ambassador Chiriboga announced that the Ecuadorian government no longer recognized the Oriente concessions of a Canadian-owned company, Peruvian Oils and Minerals Company, Nate suddenly launched Operation Auca.

It did not take much for Nate to convince the Elliots to join Operation Auca. Jim, aged twenty-eight, like many Fundamentalist missionaries who preceded him, had given up on the United States, where Christians "sold their lives to the service of Mammon," and had come to Romanist and heathen Latin America to save it from itself. He joined two other young recruits of the Plymouth Brethren mission, Ed McCully and Peter Fleming, in trying to bring the Fundamentalist Jesus to the Andes lowlands. After three years of inglorious service under Dr. Wilfrid Tidmarsh, strategically poised at the edge of the forbidding Auca jungle, the men were more than ready for Saint's adventure. So was a former paratrooper, Roger Youderian, who was on the verge of throwing in his missionary towel. A two-year bout for the Gospel Missionary Union trying to convert head-hunting Shuar Indians to the south had left him desperate for some victory for Christ somewhere, anywhere. Nate Saint offered a way out of defeat. There was no dispute when Nate urged a bond of secrecy, shared only with their wives.

Betty Elliot, the daughter of missionaries, was passionately evangelical. In fact, she agreed to marry Jim only after she was assured it would not interfere with her own missionary work. Betty had been part of SIL's first advance into Ecuador in 1952, when she settled among SIL's first tribe, the Colorados. When she joined Jim's work among the Quichua the following year, she apparently left behind any loyalty to SIL. She agreed not to mention Operation Auca to anyone, even Dr. Tidmarsh—and especially not to Nate Saint's sister, Rachel.

Rachel had invaded Nate's turf to study the "brown tribe in the green forest" of her vision: the Auca. Whatever Betty understood of Nate's rivalry with his older sister or of JAARS's rivalry with MAF over the future of missionary aviation in the Amazon was subsumed under more powerful, unseen forces that had placed her with both the Colorados and the Auca. The immediate economic issue in both cases was oil. The political forces included Nelson Rockefeller.

In 1948, the year Betty Elliot graduated from college and began her linguistic studies, Nelson Rockefeller's close friend from CIAA days, Galo Plaza, was elected president of Ecuador. Galo Plaza took office just when Standard Oil and Shell Oil had decided to suspend exploration in Ecuador's Oriente. Though no one would admit it, Middle Eastern oil was to take precedence. Caught between protests by his own Congress and the demands of the visiting chief of the U.S. Caribbean Command, Galo Plaza chose to tell his people, "The Oriente is a myth." No one in Ecuador believed it. Nor did many Americans who were familiar with the Oriente. Only two years before, Colonel Leonard Clark, a U.S. Army officer with much experience in the Oriente, had revealed that Ecuador's Amazonian oil reserves were similar to those in the Middle East.[5]

Despite mounting protests, Galo Plaza discouraged even agricultural colonization in the Ecuadorian Amazon, arguing "Ecuador must concentrate on the coastal lands" instead. And for good reason. His former legal client, United Fruit Company, was focusing on Ecuador's tropical coast to replace its disease-ravaged plantations in Central America.

To help convince his people, Galo Plaza turned to an old friend and expert in psychological warfare, Nelson Rockefeller. Nelson was already in close contact with United Fruit officials,[6] having consulted with them on their new agricultural techniques and accounting practices for his International Basic Economy Corporation (IBEC).* One of United Fruit's top executives had been a division chief for the CIAA.

*In 1948, Nelson had taken his eldest son, Rodman, with him to visit United Fruit's agricultural school in Honduras and was apparently considering asking the Boston firm to lend an expert to inspect IBEC's operations. The Rockefellers' Chase National Bank, with his brother David in charge of Latin American operations, was already involved in Ecuador's banana plantations through its client, Standard Fruit Company. Chase also had an interest in United Fruit and was represented on United Fruit's board by Chase's chairman, John J. McCloy.

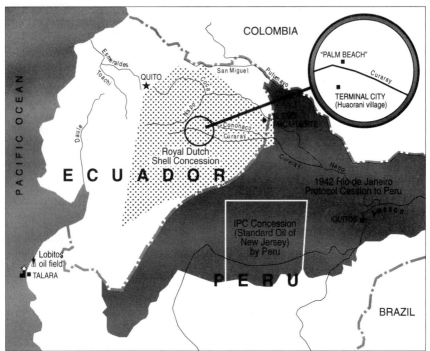

Ecuador's Oil and Operation Auca
Inset: "Palm Beach" site of Huaorani (Auca) Indians' massacre of American
Protestant missionaries

When Nelson got Galo Plaza's call for help, he responded immediately, sending in an IBEC survey team. IBEC recommended intensifying export production with new technology, particularly in agriculture. Ecuador should diversify its cash products beyond cacao and coffee and expand cattle ranches in the Andean highlands. Investments, financed by foreign loans and local capital, should be made in building roads into the coastal interior and the highlands to reach resources and serve commercial interests. A food industry should be developed to help replace the Indians' subsistence farming with a distribution system that was more appropriate to wage labor.

All these projects would be implemented by Point IV technicians who came on the heels of Galo Plaza's triumphant June 1951 visit to Washington. The visit reached its grand finale at the Rockefellers' Pocantico Hills estate, where Nelson, as chairman of Point IV's International Development Advisory Board (IDAB), threw a luncheon in his honor. The initial bills and the longer-term bonded debt with Chase and other New York banks would be underwritten, of course, by the banana boom inspired by United Fruit's massive purchases. Banana zones would spread from the southern state of El Oro up the tropical Guayas River Basin north of Guayaquil, pushing up the Daule River and toward virgin lands of the Colorado Indians.

PROPHETS OF ARMAGEDDON

It was not long before Galo Plaza concluded that the old-time Spanish-speaking American missionaries were not enough. The exotic-tongued Colorados, named by the Spanish for the brilliant red-orange luster in their annatto seed-dyed hair, needed a unique approach. They had never been subjugated. Looking over the Cárdenas biography Cam had sent him, Galo Plaza decided that SIL could provide the special touch. Cam signed the contract in 1952, just before Galo Plaza turned over the reins not to his designated heir, Chiriboga, but to his bitter opponent, Velasco Ibarra.

Velasco had always been sure that there was indeed oil in the Oriente. In 1953, his government had passed new petroleum laws and signed new exploration contracts with Canada's Peruvian Oils and Minerals Company. By 1955, when Velasco's patience with Peruvian Oils ended, SIL had dutifully shifted its focus to the Amazon and brought in Rachel Saint. The Chicago dedication of the Helio Courier for Ecuador signaled that Nate Saint's reign over the Oriente skies was about to end.

Nate had spent the past three months flying over an Auca village he called Terminal City, showering it with candy, pots, combs, tools, machetes, and even photos of the smiling men holding the same gifts to familiarize the Indians with the faces of their suitors. He had made fourteen drops in all. If he did not occupy Auca territory soon, Rachel would. She was making rapid progress in the Auca language with Dayuma, an Auca woman who had fled the tribe's internecine warfare for a life of peonage on a local plantation.

Nate had last seen Rachel just before he flew his expedition to "Palm Beach," his code name for a strip of beach on the Curaray that could serve as a landing strip for his Piper. He made no mention of his plans. Nor did he ask Rachel for help, knowing that his sister "was very possessive over the Aucas," Betty later recalled, "and was convinced that God had intended her to be the *only* one to work with the Aucas."[7] Nate feared that his sister would set up obstacles or "feel obligated to divulge this information to save me the risks involved."

Now, Betty and the other wives listened in vain for some signs of life from the radio in Nate's plane. Unable to bear the silence any longer, they broke the vow of secrecy and called for help.

The next day, after a missionary flight spotted Nate's wrecked plane on the beach, JAARS sprang into action. Larry Montgomery contacted the U.S. Caribbean Command at the Panama Canal, which immediately dispatched an air force commando to head up a helicopter and overland rescue. In New York, Henry Luce at Time-Life dispatched photographer Cornell Capa, who captured the eerie, fog-shrouded scene for *Life's* millions of readers.

The commando team, armed with carbines, landed at Palm Beach and found the five men floating in the Curaray River, Auca spears protruding from their bodies, some of which had been angrily hacked with the same machetes that had been given as gifts. The commandos managed to recover four of the bodies and hastily buried them under the driving rain of a sudden tropical storm. Early the next morning, they marched through the dawn mist down the beach to their motorized canoes and helicopter, leaving the Auca to their jungle and their oil.

Back at Shell Mera, a missionary reported the grim news to the wives. Operation Auca was over, he said.

In fact, it had just begun.

Rachel's Martyrs

Two weeks later, Henry Luce published Capa's photos, along with those the five men had taken at Palm Beach before their deaths. The photos and their diaries told a sorry tale of evangelical high hopes that were fatally flawed by linguistic ignorance.

At an initial meeting with three friendly Auca, Nate's group had found they could not understand a word the Indians said. They tried to compensate with gifts and tried to be as polite as possible in rejecting what they believed was a reciprocal peace offering—one of the two Indian women. Nate even gave the man a flight over Terminal City; he "shouted all the way over and back," noted Nate, who thought the Indian "thoroughly enjoyed the trip."[8] Still, when the Indians left and did not return the next day, Nate wondered if he and the other men had done something wrong. Two days later, shortly after scribbling "heart heavy that they fear us," in his diary, he got his answer. Reconnoitering over the area in his yellow Piper, Nate spotted a large group of Indians moving along the beach in the direction of the missionaries' camp. These were the Indians he thought would join the missionaries for Sunday afternoon service when he radioed Shell Mera the good news of an expected 2:30 visit and promised to call back at 4:35. His estimate of the Indians' arrival was not far off. Five days later, when his body was pulled from the river, his watch had stopped at 3:12.

It was assumed that the missionaries fired their rifles into the air and, when that did not work, chose death rather than kill the Indians.

Life magazine published a gripping account of Christian martyrdom, which caused a worldwide sensation. The doors of nationally known politicians, such as Vice President Nixon and former president Harry Truman, now opened to Cam's Helio promotions.

Planes were given to the governments of Latin American and Southeast Asian nations, but they were operated by SIL. The *Spirit of Kansas City,* accepted formally by ex-President Galo Plaza and by Chiriboga in Truman's presence, went to Ecuador; the *Friendship of Oklahoma* was given to Bolivia; and the *Friendship of Orange County*, dedicated by Nixon, now belonged to Peru.

President Magsaysay sent his warm endorsement of two Helios that would be operated by SIL "under the supervision of the Philippine Air Force." He would also support Cam's ambition to help out in the holy war in Vietnam. Magsaysay wrote letters of introduction for SIL's Richard Pittman to take to Diem. Pittman arrived in Saigon in January 1956 just after the Auca murders hit the headlines. "I was apprehensive," Pittman recalled of his first meeting with Diem, "but . . . he gave me a very friendly reception. His only caution was that we would 'have to be careful of infiltrators.'"[9]

A year later, U.S. Embassy officials welcomed the first SIL team's participation in intensive language classes at Saigon. SIL's incorporation into Edward Lansdale's "nation-building" for Diem had begun.

As SIL's vistas began to expand to these tropical horizons of the Cold War, Cam was anxious to strike the anvil of publicity while it was hot. Public interest in missionaries ebbed and flowed with political tides.

He contacted Rachel Saint and told her how he prayed "that the time would come when you would be able to introduce your brother's killer to the president of Ecuador."[10] Could she come back to the United States for a speaking tour?

Rachel was sure that she could testify that the Auca's destiny did belong to her brother's sacrifice. It merely confirmed her prophetic visions. The shedding of Nate's blood atoned for the sins of the Auca (as she insisted on calling the Huaorani, even after learning their language), sanctifying her own calling to bring them out of Satan's realm. To Rachel, the portrait of tribal life rendered by Dayuma, her informant on the Huaorani language, verified her own belief in a universe molded by the struggle between Good and Evil. Dayuma spoke in a trembling voice of her grandfather's tales of *Winae*, the small vampire of the forest night. In these stories Rachel saw not the normal human fear of a jungle full of predators and rubber slavers, but the power of Satan himself. In her mind, there was no question that the tribe's traditional shaman was a witch doctor doing Satan's bidding. Likewise, she was sure that the Indians' polygamy had dark metaphysical, not cultural, roots. The fact that her own brother had suffered martyrdom at the hands of at least one of Dayuma's brothers was another intimate sign of deep Christian meaning in the Auca destiny of salvation through blood atonement.

In June 1957, Dayuma and Rachel began Cam's whirlwind tour of twenty-seven American cities. A legend was being born.

Ralph Edwards's television show, *This Is Your Life*, made Rachel Saint the most famous missionary in the United States and, next to Albert Schweitzer, probably in the world. Overnight 30 million Americans could recognize the woman with intense eyes who had dedicated her life to converting her brother's killers. Television cameras focused on the startled Dayuma, her ears distended by wooden plugs.

A month later, on Sunday, July 7, Rachel and Dayuma stood in the spotlight before thousands of people who were packed into New York's Madison Square Garden for the Billy Graham Crusade.

Rachel and Dayuma's appearance at the Graham Crusade, filmed by the Billy Graham Evangelistic Corporation for sale and distribution as part of the $60,000 movie *Miracle in Manhattan,* netted SIL only $4,230 when the hat was passed.[11] But the exposure before millions on television—and before thousands of Fundamentalists who were bused in each night from around the country to fill 7,000 reserved seats out of a 20,000-seat capacity—was worth much more. *Reader's Digest* owner DeWitt Wallace, who gave a $25,000 tax-deductible donation to the crusade, wired Cam that his top editor would soon be flying down to Peru to do a story on SIL.

All was not easy, however. During the tour, Dayuma received audiotapes from Betty Elliot of greetings and news from her aunts in Ecuador. The news included a report that her older brother, Wawae, had been killed and the stunning revelation that her younger brother, Nampa, had died too—from a gunshot wound inflicted by one of the martyrs.[12] But Dayuma's rage was kept under wraps during her extended leave.

If the true account of Nampa's death nullified at least one American candidate for sainthood, Rachel never admitted it. The possibility that it had been her brother who had done the shooting would have tainted, if not canceled out, the blood debt owed her by the Huaorani. Nate's death would be seen as an atonement not for the tribe's sins, but, rather, for his own. Killing an Indian was bad enough. Killing someone who believed he was only defending his land from invasion was a curious way for a missionary to demonstrate Christ's life of love and self-sacrifice. If such failure of will to follow Christ to Calvary was admitted, much less excused as an understandable bending to the instinct for survival, then how could Rachel or any other missionary demand that the Huaorani not do likewise—against whites at Palm Beach or even each other?

The decision of the SIL board in September 1957 to name the jungle base it was building at Limoncocha just north of Huaorani territory not after Nate Saint, Jim Elliot, and the other Brethren martyrs, but after Cam's friend, Dawson Trotman, who had drowned the previous summer while saving a young swimmer, spared SIL public embarrassment in the future when doubts about Rachel's martyrs would grow. Trotman had been a consistent and loyal backer of JAARS and SIL, serving on both boards and supplying recruits from his own evangelical organization among sailors, the Navigators.

Trotman also had been Cam's liaison with the growing Billy Graham organization. He had worked for Graham since the early crusades and had just finished helping him with follow-up for the Oklahoma Crusade when he died. Graham, like Cam, appreciated the congruence of oil wealth and evangelism in the Bible Belt. Soon Cam would invite the evangelist to join Wycliffe's board, and Graham would accept.

But first Cam had a JAARS board member get in touch with Ed Darling, one of Graham's top lieutenants, to help with a problem. With all the Helios and now a DC-3 for Ecuador, the JAARS fleet was getting too big for any of the overseas jungle bases to handle. Spare parts were difficult to get in Latin America. Brazil was calling. So was Africa. Cam needed a JAARS home base in the United States for repairs and flight and mechanical training. It would also have to have international radio communications with jungle bases abroad.

Darling contacted Henderson Belk of Charlotte, North Carolina, where Billy Graham, an area resident, had just completed his latest crusade. Belk had converted from Presbyterianism to Southern Baptism and had become an arch Fundamentalist in the process. More important, he came from one of the most powerful families in the South.

The Belks had once owned slaves. Now they owned department stores, hundreds of them, all over the Southeast. They were on their way to a billion-dollar fortune, helping transform an underdeveloped, export-oriented South through internal commercial growth. The new interstate highway system being built by the Eisenhower administration would spur that growth, helping commercial and industrial development. So would the new airline link with the Northeast and the southeastern cities provided by Laurance Rockefeller's Eastern Airlines.

The Belks were also courting financing from Chase Manhattan Bank in New York, where they had a buying office in midtown Manhattan's garment district, even hosting a visit by David Rockefeller in 1956. But if the Rockefellers' money was welcome, their Yankee liberalism, with all its talk about evolution, modernizing God's religion with science, and integrating churches, schools, and workplaces, was not. An international aviation center for Fundamentalist missionaries would complement Charlotte, North Carolina's claim to be a growing commercial center, while reminding visitors and home folk alike that this was still God's country.

Belk arranged for JAARS to use a warehouse at an old U.S. Army base and Charlotte's Carpenter Airport. Eventually, in 1960, Belk donated an abandoned plantation south of Charlotte, 256 acres, complete with a columned antebellum manor house, to JAARS. JAARS's new air base was only thirty-five minutes Helio airtime from Fort Bragg, the new headquarters of the Green Berets who were protecting SIL translators in the hills of Vietnam.

Rachel and Dayuma's appearance at Graham's Crusade had paid off well for Cam. And for Graham—his second largest donation ($50,000) had come from a surprising source: the Rockefellers' Room 5600.

21

THE HIDDEN PERSUADERS

THE NEW CRUSADES

High above midtown Manhattan, in the hushed nerve center of the Rockefeller financial empire in Room 5600, the decision to quietly support Billy Graham had not been reached without apprehension. Prominent mainline pastors were worried that Graham's appearance would help a revived Fundamentalist movement lay siege to the country's media capital and largest city. Christian churches feared that the crusade would "reinforce and deepen a reactionary period in American life, moving us toward greater conformity and more coercive religion. . . . Fear is the largest factor in evangelistic conversion, and fear is no basis for creative religion."[1]

Christian Century magazine warned that

> the narrow and divisive creed which the churches rejected a generation ago is staging a comeback. Through skillful manipulation of means and persons, including a well publicized association with the President of the United States, fundamentalist forces are now in position aggressively to exploit the churches. If their effort succeeds, it will make mincemeat of the ecumenical movement, will divide congregations and denominations, will set back Protestant Christianity a half century.[2]

Liberal theologian Reinhold Niebuhr, vice president of Union Theological Seminary, struck a similar, but deeper historical chord:

> Graham's evangelism is in the tradition of America's frontier evangelical piety.
> . . . What makes it potent is that the gifts of a very personable young man and

gifted public speaker, representing a very charming embodiment of an old tradition, are related to all the high-pressure techniques of modern salesmanship. . . . All the arts of "Madison Avenue" (the advertising center of America) are practiced by the Graham entourage in the "Billy Graham Crusade."[3]

But it was precisely these arts that made Graham attractive to the hierarchy of New York's mainline Protestant denominations. And it was to these men that Junior listened. Key support for Graham came from Robert J. McCracken, Rev. Harry Fosdick's successor at Riverside Church; Union Theological Seminary President Henry Pitney Van Dusen, a trustee of the Rockefeller Foundation; and mining scion Cleveland E. Dodge. Junior had backed a similar ten-week "campaign" conducted by evangelist Billy Sunday forty years earlier, at the dawn of the United States' entry into World War I. Then, like now, New York's modernist Protestant leaders sought to use the appearance of a famed evangelist to restock the flocks of their own churches. Even earlier, in 1876, they had done likewise with Dwight Moody's "preaching missions." In each case, it was Fundamentalism, not a science-informed faith, that gained.

Rockefeller aides, despite the grimmest modernist prophecies, could not resist attending Graham's grand-opening dinner in New York. Lindsley Kimball, Dana Creel's predecessor at the Rockefeller Brothers Fund and now an executive of the Rockefeller Foundation, asked Creel if he had "a sufficiently hardy constitution" to help fill two tables he was "stuck" with at Graham's opening dinner, offering cocktails as a bracer. "I feel sure Billy will not provide cocktails, but I would like to. . . . How about it?"[4]

John Rockefeller 3rd attended the dinner, even though he rejected Chase chairman George Champion's request that he join the Crusade Committee.* Nelson, his mind set on winning some elected office in New York, declined any association with Graham—financial or otherwise—that might become public. He could not ignore the anti-Fundamentalist convictions of downstate Catholic and Jewish voters and upstate mainline Protestants. But who could argue with the support for the United States' influence in Southeast Asia given by Graham's film, *Eastward to Asia*, or his assertion at a University Club luncheon thrown by Champion in February 1957 that the revival of religion was necessary to assert the United States' moral leadership in the Free World?[5]

Nothing prevented Room 5600, again under Nelson's control, from silently

---

* Trusted Rockefeller allies in New York responded with enthusiasm, even joining Champion on the crusade's executive committee: R. H. Macy Company's Edwin Chinlund (treasurer), Phelp's Dodge heir Cleveland Dodge, and Mutual Life Insurance's J. Roger Hull (as chairman). Others joining the General Crusade Committee were Jeremiah Milbank, director of Chase Manhattan Bank; Henry Luce, of Time, Inc.; Thomas Watson, Jr., of IBM; and Eddie Rickenbacker, Laurance's partner in Eastern Airlines. In such company, who could doubt the sincerity of Chairman Hull, when he proclaimed, on behalf of the crusade, that "we believe in the free enterprise system." See Thomas C. Campbell, Jr., "Capitalism and Christianity," *Harvard Business Review* (July–August 1957).

throwing its weight behind Graham. Since returning from Washington, Nelson had resumed the presidency of the Rockefeller Brothers Fund. This prominent connection of his name ruled out any donation from the fund. But it did not rule out Nelson's top aide at the fund, Dana Creel, from encouraging Junior to contribute.

A vision of global missions persuaded Junior to OK a $50,000 donation. It was done quietly, without press releases or fanfare, a secret affirmation that helped make the New York Crusade "a turning point in Graham's American ministry."[6] It also was a turning point for Fundamentalism, ending its isolation on the fringe of American religious life and giving the movement the second wind it needed to make its postwar revival a durable mass phenomenon.

Nelson kept silent throughout Graham's appearances in Manhattan. John 3rd donated $1,500, and Laurance sent fifty shares of one of his favorite defense holdings, Airborne Instruments Laboratory, worth about $2,500. Graham's receipts totaled $2.8 million, more than $1 million of which was spent on television. The crusade generated a $217,000 profit; the Protestant Council of New York City gave Graham's organization $150,000 and kept the rest.[7]

Six "special offerings" had been collected. One was for the Wycliffe Bible Translators.[8]

Billy Graham's enormous success with Manhattan's business elite in 1957 signified that the U.S. Christian Fundamentalist movement, like the United States herself, was at the edge of a major transition. Graham's organization gave the movement a new corporate cohesiveness; his moderate evangelizing of modernist Protestants set the tone for the movement's future success. This success, in turn, fed upon a United States that was in cultural discontinuity with the old order. In the 1950s, the era of small-business ethics finally gave way in mainstream America to the march of the modern corporation and its big-business ethic of efficiency and conformity within a mass culture.

Billy Graham's New Testament of a living, forgiving God, now projected on television screens in millions of homes, offered solace to the lonely, the alienated, the guilt stricken, and the powerless. His predecessor, Dwight Moody, had attacked satanly labor unrest and sinful cities and stoked millenarian hopes among hard-pressed smallholders for the Second Coming and an end of the world that was ruining them; in so doing, he had married his career to the solid citizens of the industrial trusts who were bringing this corporate world into being—families like the Rockefellers. His own son-in-law, Rev. Arthur Packard, even ended up working for Nelson's father in Room 5600. Eight decades after Moody's first triumphant "campaign" in New York, it was left to Billy Graham to usher into the corporate culture the last vestiges of the rural population that had migrated to the new corporate suburbias.

For those who did not have to face the bulldozer or eviction, the changing face of Manhattan itself, from grimy brick to gleaming steel, seemed to reflect the promise of endless bounty. Corporate growth was now accepted as "the American way." Whole neighborhoods of ethnic communities that were revered in earlier melting-pot theories were being demolished, sleek glass and modernist arches sprouting in their place.* It was as if the creators of these buildings—the supremely wealthy men who commissioned these structures—needed to transubstantiate their power into something more tangible, something bigger than one man's lone ambition, something that could command respect.

Buying into the Shining Dream

The Waldorf-Astoria, Manhattan's most famous hotel, was glowing with New York's confidence in January 1956, when the president of Brazil arrived amid a flurry of excitement. Inside the grand ballroom, scores of dignitaries, led by New York's aristocratic governor, Averell Harriman, greeted Juscelino Kubitschek with the dignity due the new leader of the largest nation south of the Rio Grande. But one man offered a specially warm welcome, joining the president at his table with the familiar ease of someone who is used to rubbing shoulders with the powerful.

Kubitschek was no stranger to Nelson Rockefeller. As Governor of Minas Gerais, he had inherited a successful supervised credit program set up by Nelson's American International Association for Economic and Social Development (AIA) in 1948. Now he was seeking loans and investments, including financing for the realization of Nelson's "shining dream," the conquest of the Amazon. Unlike Vargas, Kubitschek had no qualms about taking in American corporations as partners. "The Vargas group, which Kubitschek succeeds, left Brazil in bad shape, chiefly because it inflated the currency violently," Adolf Berle briefed Governor Harriman before the banquet that night. "At the same time it refused to permit foreign companies to develop Brazil's oil resources and was unable to develop them itself. The issue is 'hot.' Kubitschek is looking for a viable compromise."[9]

---

*Nelson and his brothers were at the vanguard of this change. Resuming the presidency of Rockefeller Center, Nelson followed up on Rockefeller Center's recent successful negotiations with Adolf Berle for the purchase of prime midtown Manhattan real estate owned by the estate of the Bishop family, Berle's in-laws. He struck a deal with Henry Luce and C. D. Jackson that evicted tenants, razed buildings, and erected a new 70-story headquarters for Time-Life, across the Avenue of the Americas from RCA's Radio City.

On Manhattan's West Side, John 3rd took the lead in overseeing construction of a new cultural complex for the city, which came to be called the Lincoln Center for the Performing Arts. Wallace Harrison's firm did the design, assisted by MOMA associates and Gordon Bemshaft, architect of Chase's new downtown headquarters.

Farther uptown, David's Morningside Heights Association completed its eviction of 3,000 families and its demolition of ten acres; modern apartment buildings were erected, serving effectively as a buffer, critics later charged, between Harlem and the Rockefeller-funded educational-religious complex anchored by Columbia University, International House, Union Theological Seminary, and Riverside Church, the last three representing a $50 million investment by Rockefeller philanthropies. At the other end of the island, where Chase had $40 million in real estate investments, David led the Downtown Lower Manhattan Association's effort to revitalize the financial district. Plans to build ever taller skyscrapers to house America's largest and most profitable banks led eventually to the twin 110-story towers of the World Trade Center.

IBEC's Operations in Brazil (Late 1954)

Source: Wayne G. Broehl, *United States Business Performance Abroad: The Case Study of the International Basic Economy Corporation.*

Everyone knew why. Kubitschek had just barely survived a coup plot and was seeking desperately to reassure American investors of his good intentions toward them—particularly Standard Oil and U.S. Steel, whose officials were reportedly participants in the plot.[10] The inspiration for this plot, it was said, was the election of Kubitschek's left-leaning vice president, João Goulart, who had been Vargas's labor minister until conservative generals forced his ouster. Kubitschek was anxious to avoid a similar fate by demonstrating that his administration would not be in the Vargas vein of nationalism.

Nelson was impressed with the new president's vision of Brazilian-

PROPHETS OF ARMAGEDDON

Rockefeller Credit Network in Minas Gerais (1948–1961)

After successful demonstration projects (O) for a farm extension service were set up in São Paulo state, Rockefeller's AIA sponsored a network (☆) of rural credit agencies, ACAR, in collaboration with the state government in Minas Gerais. ACAR tried to stem farm failures and politically volatile migrations to coastal cities. During the Kubitschek presidency (1956–1960), AIA's rural credit and assistance system spread throughout rural Brazil, spurring commercial farming's advance into the Brazilian frontier.

Source: Map of AIA–ACAR operations, AIA Archives, Rockefeller Archive Center.

American relations, so much so that when Kubitschek had approached two of Nelson's AIA aides in Rio about expanding Minas Gerais's supervised credit program throughout rural Brazil, Nelson decided to fly to Brazil in April for further talks. Rockefeller arrived at Belo Horizonte on April 12 to meet with Kubitschek at the nearby farm of the credit program's director. At the last minute, however, Kubitschek canceled, chafing under critical queries by the Brazilian press about why he had arranged an "undercover meeting in Minas and above all on a secluded farm" instead of at the presidential palace. The next day, Nelson obliged, reaching an accord with Kubitschek while lunching at the presidential palace. Nelson pledged a $525,000 Rockefeller Brothers Fund grant to the AIA, reserving $100,000 per year for four years for the national program and

$50,000 a year to continue the credit program in Minas Gerais. The press, unable to take issue with such a worthy project as low-interest loans to farmers, was disarmed. The AIA's official history would later ridicule Brazilian editors for their suspicions.[11]

If they had known what Rockefeller officials knew, however, their concerns would not have been so easily laid to rest. During his visit, Nelson had decided to invest in what one official of the International Basic Economy Corporation (IBEC) secretly acknowledged was "the largest single tract of private property on the frontier between Brazil and Bolivia."[12] On more than one million acres of land in western Mato Grosso, Nelson now planned to build one of the world's largest cattle herds. The ranch already had 50,000 head of cattle, but Nelson had bigger plans, as much as five times bigger. Airplanes would soon arrive carrying Santa Gertrudis bulls from his brother Winthrop's prize herds at Winrock Farms in Arkansas.

The AIA's and IBEC's agricultural experts would also appear to begin cattle breeding and feeding experiments. Their goal was to reduce to two years the length of time required to raise and fatten a full-grown steer for market.

The plans called for a modern slaughterhouse and distribution of packaged meat in São Paulo and Rio, in competition with large processors like Anglo, Swift, Armour, and Wilson, as well as smaller ranches.

Beyond profits from beef was another possibility: mining. If Nelson had learned anything from Standard Oil's involvement with the Kleberg family's King Ranch in Texas, it was that giant ranches often contain valuable minerals or oil. U.S. Steel had recently bought a large manganese concession to the north of the ranch near Mato Grosso's commercial capital, Corumbá; the deposits would prove to be one of the world's richest reserves of manganese. Corumbá was also the Brazilian gateway to Bolivia's oil. A railway from São Paulo passed through Corumbá on its way to the Santa Cruz fields.

A recent poll indicated that Brazilians were swinging away from Vargas's oil policy. Encouraged by Berent Friele's interpretation that this was "the forerunner to a new economic era,"[13] Nelson insisted upon an amendment to the ranch's corporate bylaws that would allow him to participate if mineral wealth was found. Twenty years would pass before American readers of the *Engineering and Mining Journal* would learn, through the magazine's reprint of radar aerial maps, that Bodoquena contained significant deposits of copper, a rare metal in Brazil.[14] But they would have to look carefully, checking the keys to the maps for symbols and the size of deposits. And the Rockefeller ownership would remain a secret.

Bodoquena was the culmination of almost a decade of planning. Nelson's aides had targeted western Brazil for investment as early as March 1947, only three months after IBEC was founded and its philanthropic arm, the AIA, had set up shop in Brazil. The government had already projected Goiás, the frontier state west of Minas Gerais, as the site for a new federal capital; Rockefeller aides had noted that the construction of this capital was sure to stimulate economic development in the whole western frontier.

The CIAA's former agricultural chief in Brazil, working then for IBEC, had reported to Nelson and Friele that the "high plateau of southern and central Goiás and western Minas Gerais . . . has some of the finest land and timber and mineral resources in all Brazil." The aide recommended the immediate purchase of up to half a million acres of land, its colonization with Brazilians and foreigners, and its modernization and industrialization. The Rockefellers could "spearhead a movement into the area" by investing "considerable money" to "realize its investment potential to us" instead of others. The "others" were Brazilians, namely São Paulo coffee growers "who have purchased large estates" and English land speculators.[15]

Nelson, however, had been wary of doing anything that could trigger adverse publicity. Room 5600 had carefully monitored the Brazilian press as IBEC and the AIA set up operations that focused more on retail services and technical assistance than on the outright ownership of land. Unlike Venezuela, where a dictatorship stifled anti-U.S. fervor sufficiently to convince Nelson that owning large ranches was a safe investment, Brazil still had a strong nationalist movement and a leader, Vargas, who, by 1950, had returned to power. Nelson had attended his inauguration as Truman's special emissary. He had kept track of Vargas's personal career through Friele's friendship with the president's daughter Alzira and her husband, Ernani do Amaral Peixoto. During the postwar interregnum between Vargas's presidential terms, Peixoto had even attempted to become Nelson's sales agent in Brazil. In 1950, he rode the coattails of Vargas's successful presidential campaign to become governor of the state of Rio de Janeiro. In 1953, when Governor Peixoto and his wife arrived in Washington seeking U.S. aid, Nelson took time from his duties as a member of Eisenhower's transition team to throw a luncheon for the couple. Their visit gave him the opportunity for an important preparatory meeting with the Brazilian ambassador, Walther Moreira Salles.

From that time forward, Brazil would never be the same.

The ambassador was the son of João Moreira Salles, one of Brazil's most successful merchant bankers for the coffee growers of São Paulo state. Since World War II, the elder Moreira Salles had expanded into other areas of commercial banking, including cattle, real estate speculation, and oil refining, grooming his son for a leadership role in the industrial Brazil of the future. As producers of the largest export to the United States, São Paulo's coffee kings were powerful figures in any Brazilian government, and it was not surprising that when Vargas needed an intermediary with Washington, he chose a prince of that realm.

When Ambassador Moreira Salles and Rockefeller met in 1953, Brazil was plagued by debt and eager for assistance. Nelson, not shy about mixing government and personal business, discussed IBEC's Brazilian investment possibilities. He also lobbied Moreira Salles on behalf of J. C. King's old firm, Johnson &

Johnson of Brazil, for relief from Vargas's restrictions on profits leaving Brazil. He even probed to see if Vargas was willing to change proposed legislation that would give Petrobrás a monopoly over oil prospecting, development, refining, and transportation.[16] Vargas's refusal eventually earned him a financially destabilized government, Moreira Salles's resignation, and a military coup. But his suicide over Brazil's oil also chilled the goodwill atmosphere for investments associated with the Rockefeller name.

Traditionally a conservative lot anyway, Brazilian bankers would not give more than token support for the stock issues sponsored by Nelson's investment bank, Inter-American Finance Corporation (IFI). Of the fourteen Brazilian banks that owned 48 percent of IFI's stock, only two held any promise of being close collaborators and consistent underwriters of IFI's stock offerings. When Nelson conducted his own field investigation in Brazil the following spring, he narrowed the field to one: Banco Moreira Salles was the only bank that represented the kind of clout Nelson needed. It was Moreira Salles, in fact, who interested Nelson in the huge ranch in western Mato Grosso.

The Secrets of Bodoquena

Dwarfing the nearest large town, Aquidauana, Fazenda Bodoquena sprawled over 1,030,000 acres of forests, grasslands, and wetlands that had once been the lands of the Kadiwéu and their vassals, the Terêna Indians.

Situated south of the Amazon River Basin's floodplain, in southwestern Mato Grasso, the ranch took its name from the Bodoquena Mountains, home of the Kadiwéu. The only Indians in South America who made thorough use of horses, the nomadic Kadiwéu earned a reputation as the best light cavalry on the continent, successfully resisting all invaders for centuries. European colonization of their hunting lands was held up until modern weapons decimated the tribe's horsemen at the beginning of the twentieth century, massacres reducing their numbers to about 250 by the time Rockefeller moved into the area. The tribe's resistance, however, had won them a 1.7 million-acre reserve west of the mountains up to the Rio Nabileque on the left bank of the Paraguaí River, granted in perpetuity, but with no technical aid or resources to develop it or to create markets for their traditional artifacts. Almost half the Kadiwéu lands, some 842,000 acres, would be taken after the 1964 military coup by ranchers, land speculators, and settlers.[17]

Most of the Terêna lands east of the mountains, on the other hand, had already been expropriated through centuries of contact with Europeans. The tribe tilled what lands remained and hired themselves out as ranch hands and low-wage laborers in Aquidauana and other towns. Although literate and registered as army reservists, the Terêna were prevented from exercising their voting rights on the false ground that since Indians could not be drafted into military service, they could not vote. In fact, the Service for the Protection of the Indian feared conflict with local politicians over the Indians voting.[18] Politically disfranchised, the Indians had little means of influencing official policies or even illegal practices that affected land tenure.

In 1956, these Indians found themselves facing one of the world's richest land speculators. Nelson Rockefeller had had his sights on the Bodoquena ranch even before he arrived, writing Moreira Salles a month before that he had "several ideas about your big cattle property in Mato Grosso that I would like to discuss with you."[19] Nelson wanted in, and Moreira Salles was willing. The Brazilian banker at first offered to sell 20 percent of Bodoquena, or 18,000 shares for 4,000 cruzeiros ($60) per share. This was a price that Berent Friele thought was "extremely fair."[20] He then settled on 30 percent, or 27,000 shares, for a total of $1,620,000.

But Moreira Salles had made two mistakes. Hoping to inspire a Rockefeller investment, he had told Nelson earlier about his plans to divide and sell off part of another property he had invested in, the 137,000-acre Cambuhy Coffee and Cotton Estates, Ltd., owner of Fazendas Paulistas, in São Paulo State.[21] He also had been too quick in his willingness to sell 30 percent of Bodoquena.

Nelson caught the scent of desperation. He realized that Moreira Salles needed cash to develop his real estate ventures and improve his remaining coffee estates. And now Nelson knew the exact amount his friend wanted—$1,620,000. He decided to put on the squeeze. The Bodoquena ranch was remote, he wrote Friele, and that meant the property and its cattle were worth a whopping 25 percent less.

Nelson's argument was not strong. Much of the ranch's 50,000 head of cattle would have to be sold for slaughter anyway to make way for the better breeding stock Nelson planned to import from the United States. This sale would bring Nelson immediate cash-flow benefits. It was also obvious that Rockefeller planned to reduce the ranch's need for feed by improving the pasture's winter grass; that would reduce purchase and freight costs for grain. Finally, one of the ranch's attractions was the recently completed Santa Cruz–São Paulo railroad that passed directly north of the ranch, with a freight station at the nearest town. This station eliminated much of the losses in numbers and weight that are incurred when cattle must be driven to distant rail terminals, as in the United States' Old West.

Nelson buttressed his case for a better deal by reminding Moreira Salles of a more tangible asset of his own: the research resources Nelson would bring to the ranch through his two nonprofit organizations, IBEC Research and the AIA.[22]

Using nonprofits as a bargaining chip for personal gain was a violation of U.S. federal income tax laws that prohibit a director or trustee of a tax-exempt nonprofit corporation or foundation from any inurement from the nonprofit's operations. But Moreira Salles was not about to blow the whistle on a Rockefeller. He wanted "the opportunity of closer association" with the Rockefellers that

Nelson had offered when he sent Friele down to negotiate the Bodoquena purchase.[23] Moreira Salles had already made a down payment on that possibility with a donation of 2 million cruzeiros (about $30,000) to IBEC Research the previous year.[24] The Rockefeller name would bring prestige to his ventures in Brazil, making it easier to attract other partners and raise capital. Besides, he was Brazilian, and this was Brazil. U.S. law was unenforceable. The negotiations were confidential. The Rockefellers expected discretion. If they were exploiting that confidence, he could not break it without injury to his own interests.

Nelson, like his grandfather, had sized up his competition. He had Friele relay to Moreira Salles that he could recommend only 3,000 cruzeiros ($45) per share to IBEC for 30 percent of Bodoquena. But he also offered to sweeten the deal by having brothers David and Laurance join him in taking another 10 percent. That would give Moreira Salles the same $1,620,000. He had read the Brazilian right. Moreira Salles accepted.

The Rockefellers' purchase of 40 percent of Fazenda Bodoquena gave them a big stake in other developments in the 94-mile-wide corridor along Bolivia's border. This corridor was considered so politically sensitive that its development was governed by Brazil's Federal Border Zone Commission under national security laws. Nelson's aides feared that "nationalists . . . might try to connect our purchase of Bodoquena stock with oil in Bolivia and U.S. Steel's manganese concession in Mato Grosso."[25]

Their fear was not without foundation. Before serving as ambassador, Moreira Salles had been the chief negotiator of the bilateral accord that set the trade terms for U.S. access to Brazilian manganese during the Korean War. As for "oil in Bolivia," IBEC's Richard Aldrich had been monitoring a growing controversy over a 1938 treaty that gave Brazil a 50 percent stake in the development of Standard Oil's expropriated field in Santa Cruz. According to the treaty, Brazil's stake would go into effect just as soon as it fulfilled its commitment to build the railroad that would give eastern Bolivia duty-free access to the Atlantic. "The Brazilian-Bolivian railroad has been extended westward beyond the potentially rich oil field of eastern Bolivia," Aldrich reported in 1950. "Industrial urban growth of western Brazil should gain speed with the installation of the equipment to exploit these fields."[26]

Now the railroad's construction was completed, and the Bolivians were refusing to allow Petrobrás in, on the grounds that its status as a Brazilian government entity would threaten Bolivia's national sovereignty. At the same time, an old friend of Nelson, Bolivia's ambassador to the United States, Victor Andrade, insisted that Brazil forgo shipping the oil by rail and instead ship by pipeline, which, under Brazilian law, had to be owned by Petrobrás. The Brazilians, well aware of the enormous cost of building a pipeline, correctly suspected that the Bolivians were trying to break the agreement and were secretly negotiating with American oil companies to develop the field. The advantage to the Bolivians was

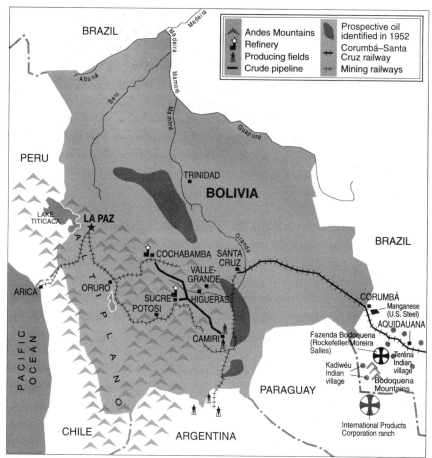

Brazil's Railroad Reaches Santa Cruz (1956)

The Corumbá–Santa Cruz railway linked Bolivia's oil lands to the Brazilian railroad passing north of the million-acre ranch owned by Rockefellers and Walther Moreira Salles, a São Paulo banker and principal stockholder in an oil firm prospecting in Santa Cruz.

Sources: *New York Times*, January 6, 1955, and September 13, 1958; *Ultima Hora*, September 13, 1958; Peter Seaborn Smith, *Oil and Politics in Modern Brazil*, pp. 119–21.

clear: Whereas Brazil was not obligated by the treaty to pay taxes on Bolivia's oil, the foreign oil companies were.

Kubitschek refused to be provoked or to back out. Since private Brazilian companies were not allowed to develop Brazil's oil, but faced no such restrictions outside their own country, he opened up bids for the Bolivian oil to private Brazilian companies. One of the companies that bid, indeed the only Brazilian company that would actually drill for oil in Santa Cruz, was Refinaria Exploração de Petrólio União, S.A. This firm already had a controversial history. Standard Oil of New Jersey had been its partner in a planned refinery until adverse publicity from nationalists forced Standard Oil's withdrawal in 1946. União had to go it alone, using Brazilian capital organized by railroad builder Alberto Soares de Sampaio to build a refinery at Capuava between São Paulo and the port of Santos. The refinery relied on Gulf Oil to supply it with Saudi Arabian crude. Now, with Gulf shortly to be given a large concession in Bolivia, União's crude source would be much closer to home, in Santa Cruz. But there was more involved here than convenience or cheaper oil: União's bank was none other than Banco Moreira Salles, with Walther's father, João Moreira Salles, overseeing the oil firm's finances as a member of its administrative council.[27] Walther Moreira Salles, in fact, was then the principal stockholder of União.

The Brazilian people, many of whom backed Petrobrás and suspected private oil companies of being fronts for Standard Oil, Gulf, and other foreign interests, did not know this; they, the media, and even historians later believed that the oil company was controlled by its founder, Alberto Soares. But the Rockefellers had been informed otherwise by the head of IFI's Rio office in November 1955, when Moreira Salles proposed two deals to the Rockefellers. The first was a capital increase of the Moreira Salles bank's stock by 168 million cruzeiros with "the underwriting headed by Interamericana [IFI]." The second deal involved the União refinery, proposing "a secondary distribution of the União stock subscribed by the controlling group—probably CR$100MM [100 million cruzeiros]—the principal shareholder being Moreira Salles."

Moreira Salles was the hidden force behind the União oil company, and now Moreira Salles was turning to the Rockefellers to act as a silent partner in arranging more money for his oil company to expand his refinery's capacity and to provide funds for exploration in Bolivia. Because Kubitschek was opening Bolivian oil to private Brazilian companies, and União was making a strong bid, União's stock would be attractive to investors. His bank's resources would not have to be tapped and, moreover, the additional capital for the bank would permit it to continue spreading throughout central Brazil. It was the chance of a lifetime, allowing a rapid growth in power for the Moreira Salles financial group. For the Rockefellers, it meant profitable fees for IFI as the lead investment bank handling the stock offerings and opened the possibility of a wider alliance with a major Brazilian bank, perhaps as partners in secondary stock sales to the public, a much larger, untapped source of capital, through a mutual fund.

The Rockefellers decided to test the prospects for this alliance. IFI offered a deal to Moreira Salles: to set up an investment company of 500 million to 2 billion cruzeiros "to settle Brazil's long defaulted French railroad and port improvement bonds." This deal would require "Walther Moreira Salles' liaison and connections with the government." Through the government's guarantee of new securities, money could be raised to pay off the French bonds. As the lead investment bank, control of the government-owned railroad's debt would pass to the

Rockefellers and the Moreira Salles group and their investors. This would be the opening wedge of a new financial era in Brazil in which the Rockefellers, in alliance with Moreira Salles, would gain a powerful influence over Brazil's finances; development plans; financial laws; and, ultimately, the government itself.

Nelson's men were clear about the role that Moreira Salles's bank and oil company could play in spreading the influence of the Rockefeller investment firm, IFI, throughout Brazil: "The capital increase of the bank stock, followed up by a secondary distribution of the oil refinery stock might well be the key to solving one of the basic problems [for IFI]—distribution of securities through a network of branch banks.

"Walther Moreira Salles is one of the closest collaborators with the newly elected [Kubitschek] administration and should have a great deal of influence. This could be of invaluable assistance to Interamericana." Moreira Salles had participated in all of IFI's recent underwritings and had pledged a 20 to 30 million cruzeiro standby loan, the kind of valuable local bank support the Rockefellers needed if they were to compete with the leading American investment firm in Brazil, Deltec, S.A., which was backed by the powerful Banco Mercantil de São Paulo, Moreira Salles's principal competitor.

"Moreira Salles is deal-minded and is anxious to share his bank in a leading position, which he feels can be in part accomplished through investment banking activities. . . . Based upon the verbal proposals of Moreira Salles, as well as growing actual participation and giving deals—União—Interamericana may have its best vehicle to develop and grow with the assistance of a commercial bank."[28] The IFI's underwriting of Banco Moreira Salles's stock increase was scheduled for distribution in March–April 1956, exactly when Nelson chose to strike the anvil with a visit.

These ties of the Moreira Salles group to railroad bonds and Bolivian oil could help Nelson develop Bodoquena, but they could also backfire on him. Indeed, in May 1957, the same month Nelson would announce his purchase of Bodoquena, IBEC would be accused by Brazilian congressmen and Rio's *Jornal do Comercio* of handling, through Walther Moreira Salles, the offering rights to stockholders for União's capital increase. The charge would be denied, but suspicions of Rockefeller–Moreira Salles ties to União's interest in Bolivian oil would linger.

Nelson's aides knew that Nelson's insistence on changing the Bodoquena company's bylaws to allow mining could inflame Brazilian public opinion, especially since the Santa Cruz–São Paulo railroad passed not only near U.S. Steel's mining concession north of Bodoquena, but also through Aquidauana, near Nelson's ranch. Any request for a change in the ranch's corporate bylaws that would permit foreign participation in "extractive industries" would require approval by Brazil's National Security Council, warned IBEC lawyers. In spite of the danger, the option was so important to Nelson that he was willing to risk the whole purchase by insisting upon the change in the bylaws.

To avoid "nationalist objections," the Rockefeller group got Moreira Salles's agreement to keep the purchase secret, at least until the Border Zone Commission approved the change in the bylaws. In early January 1957, however, Rockefeller aides became alarmed when "someone leaked" the news to two Brazilian newspapers. Their worst fears were realized when the *New York Times* called. The IBEC office at Rockefeller Plaza went into crisis mode. Frank Jamieson advised Nelson to keep a steady course and to continue to hold up any press release, despite the fear that silence from the Rockefellers could only increase Brazilian suspicions. Jamieson bought time by securing the cooperation of *Times* reporter Frank Garcia, an old friend, by promising him a scoop. On February 20, Jamieson met with Nelson on whether to disclose the size of the million-acre ranch. Nelson decided not to.[29]

Nelson's main worry was how much control Moreira Salles actually had. IBEC's press release would point out that 20 percent was held by Bodoquena's manager, Mauricio Verdier, allowing IBEC to reassure Brazilians that "the management and majority of the shares" were in Brazilian hands.[30] But in the real world beyond public relations, the Rockefeller group's goal was control.

"We hope that [Verdier] is not just a Moreira Salles stooge," an IBEC officer wrote Jamieson, "for we have had much unhappy experience in companies where our minority position kept us from having a strong voice."[31]

After the Bodoquena land purchase was approved, Nelson deepened his commitment to Kubitschek's economic expansion program. In mid-1957, while he and Winthrop guaranteed a $4.5 million loan from David's Chase National Bank, Nelson strengthened IBEC's access to capital in two ways, by reaching back to Washington and by reaching deeper into the savings of South America's largest country. IBEC acquired a substantial interest in a new leader in medium-term overseas venture finance, American Overseas Finance Company, setting up a parent holding company, American Overseas Investing Company, in partnership with CIT Financial Corporation of New York, a Chase holding company.[32]

That year, Nelson also began his most serious penetration yet of the Brazilian economy. IBEC replaced IFI with a mutual fund called Crescinco, offering shares to the Brazilian public in an initial portfolio of Brazilian stocks worth 40 million cruzeiros. In one year, Crescinco could announce in its 1958 annual report, it had made "a spectacular gain" in the sales of its participating certificates, leaping from 90 million to 400 million cruzeiros. How did it happen? Nelson's methods were as deceptively simple as they were quiet and unobtrusive. Working through a São Paulo–based subsidiary, Companhia Distribuidora de Valores, Crescinco "sold [its shares] from Belém on the Amazon to Port Alegro in the south" at a price based on the fund's current asset value; the money collected from the sales was then "invested in the stock of leading Brazilian companies." IBEC made more money as Crescinco's portfolio grew by having its management subsidiary, Emprendimentos ("Undertaking") charge an annual fee of 2 percent of Crescinco's total value.

As IBEC's mutual fund invested in more companies, the price of its stock rose. IBEC explained in its 1958 annual report that "the growth of Crescinco has served to broaden ownership in Brazilian industry," but IBEC's policy of increasing Crescinco's stock price as its portfolio got larger meant that fewer average Brazilians would be able to pay their way into that ownership, leaving the field to the better-heeled investor. As the Brazilian boom expanded with President Kubitschek's spending policies, São Paulo and Rio's wealthier crowd flooded through Crescinco's doors, doubling investors to 8,355 by the end of 1959; sales doubled with them, to 981 million cruzeiros. On January 9, 1960, Crescinco's sales passed the 1 billion cruzeiro mark. IBEC's mutual fund now had a holding in more than 100 Brazilian companies.

Beside its Crescinco investing arm, Nelson's IBEC directly owned the following: 99 percent of IBEC-Rollins Burdick Hunter, a general insurance brokerage with offices in São Paulo, Rio de Janeiro, and Porto Alegre; 15 percent of Avicultura, Comercio e Industria, S.A. (AVISCO), a São Paulo poultry feed plant with sales throughout Brazil; 13.86 percent of Industria Metalúrgica Forjaço, the drop-forging plant in São Paulo; and 66.15 percent of Sementes Agroceres, S.A. (SASA), Nelson's hybrid seed company with research and production centers in five of Brazil's most important states.

In 1957, Nelson also brought in a new American partner, Continental Grain, to replace Cargill in his grain storage company, with elevators in Paraná and São Paulo states. IBEC retained 45.4 percent. That year, he also liquidated EMA, IBEC's agricultural machinery firm, settling for 40 percent of Thela Comercial, S.A., the Barbosa family's importer of agricultural materials, supplies, and construction equipment. Thela's mission, however, remained identical to what Reader's Digest had praised EMA for: "clearing the jungle" for "the "Amazon farmers" with "mechanized land-clearing units which clear as much land in five minutes as a farmer can clear in five weeks."[33]

The frontier region received new emphasis. Crescinco invested in Itaú/Portland Cement, which controlled Mato Grosso's largest cement plant in Corumbá; COBRASMA, which was building Brasília with U.S. loans; and Cia. Brasileira de Construção Fichet & Schwartz-Hautmont, which supplied overhead cranes, metallic structures, and window frames for Brasília's construction.

In Mato Grosso, Nelson expanded his cattle ranching, experimenting with artificial insemination to increase the size and quality of his herds, and with rice production. But Nelson was not interested merely in cattle and rice. He also wanted colonizers, people who could provide agricultural skills and settle his huge landholdings. In the 1940s, his CIAA had earmarked the Amazon for postwar settlement by refugees from the war. After deciding to buy into the

Bodoquena ranch, he explored the possibility of bringing in Japanese settlers. Kubitschek's regime was willing, but the Japanese government's enthusiasm waned as nationalist sentiments rose in both countries.

In February 1959, Nelson turned to his brother, the American head of the influential Japan Society, for help. John 3rd received a letter from cousin Richard Aldrich, now Nelson's IBEC overseer in Brazil.

> As you may or may not know, Nelson, David and Laurance own 40% of a large tract of land in Mato Grosso. The remaining 60% is owned by Walther Moreira Salles, prominent Brazilian banker and diplomat, together with Mauricio Verdier. During the past three years they have been negotiating with the Japanese embassy to acquire about 100 families (for settlement and farming on the land). At the outset the embassy was extremely enthusiastic and promised 100 families. Subsequent to this, numbers of families promised have been reduced . . . and to this date the farm area has not received any. . . . Thinking of your interest in Japan . . . Verdier approached me the other day asking for your assistance. . . . I realize that any direct interest on your part, given Nelson's ownership of the farm, could involve certain public relations problems . . . but I hope that in some way you can be helpful to us.[34]

John 3rd, despite misgivings, obliged, removing his Japan Society hat and putting on his Population Council hat. "It would hardly seem to me that this was the type of thing in which either the Japan Society or myself personally should get involved. On the other hand, Japan does have a population problem." Ten years later, Brazil would host half a million Japanese, one of the largest Japanese populations in South America. But most settlers spurned western Brazil's backlands, favoring the already cultivated cotton lands and rolling coffee hills of the south. For labor in the Amazon, the Brazilian government would have to rely on migrants from the impoverished, politically turbulent Northeast; for capital, it would rely on Nelson's friends in New York and Washington.

22

THE BROTHERHOOD

GRABBING POWER

Nelson Rockefeller's reach for power between 1957 and 1960 was so transparent that it startled the nation.

First, he assembled the Rockefeller Brothers Panels to chart the nation's future and work up a Rockefeller platform on all the vital issues.

He recruited more than 100 distinguished Americans from every corridor of power through which he had marched in the past twenty years. Shepherding the flock was Henry Kissinger, on leave from Harvard.

They all knew why they were there: not just because of the Soviet threat, but because of the Rockefeller promise. "Many who joined the overall panel of the Special Studies Project were aware they were in the presence of someone who might be the President of the United States in the 1960's or 1970's," recalled a friend of Kissinger. "Their decision to join the group was not unaffected by that awareness."[1]

Nelson, of course, took most of the credit for the panel's work. On January 6, 1958, he appeared on the *Today* show to promote the national security panel report, *International Security: The Military Aspect.* He had rushed it to print to take advantage of the national hysteria over the Soviet launching of *Sputnik,* the first satellite, the previous October. Almost 200,000 viewers wrote in asking for copies. By the end of 1960, over half a million copies had been distributed, most at cost or free, all carrying Nelson's dire preamble: "At issue is nothing less than the future of America and the freedom of the world."

On January 10, he was again in front of the national cameras, this time testifying before Senator Lyndon B. Johnson's Senate Armed Services Committee. "Ever since World War II, the United States has suffered from a tendency to underestimate the military technology of the USSR," he warned. ". . . Unless present trends are reversed, the world balance of power will shift in favor of the Soviet bloc. If that should happen, we are not likely to be given another chance to remedy our failings."[2]

Five months later, wiser American political analysts found out what this was all about: Riding on the national furor and exploiting Governor Averell Harriman's strategic error in naming him chairman of a bipartisan commission to rewrite New York's Constitution, Nelson summoned reporters to Room 5600. Standing beside a bronze bust of his grandfather, he announced that he was running for office of the governor of the richest and most populous state in the union. Few doubted that New York was only a stepping-stone to his real ambition, the White House.

By August he was already contacting at least one foreign head of state whom he counted as a friend. "I have entered the political arena here in the State of New York and am leaving no stone unturned to obtain the nomination in the Gubernatorial race this fall," he wrote Alberto Lleras Camargo, who had just been elected Colombia's president. "If I get the nomination, the race will be a tough one but I think there's an outside chance."[3]

That month, the Republicans gave him the nomination no one else really wanted. Nelson logged 8,500 miles, wolfing down Manhattan knishes and sausages and upstate apple pies. He used his fluency in Spanish among Puerto Rican voters and Count Basie's band in Harlem. He charged Averell Harriman, another millionaire, with being controlled by Tammany Hall boss Carmine De Sapio. Finally, after enjoying a big boost from friendly articles in the *New York Post*, the all-but-official organ of Adolf Berle's Liberal party, Nelson won the governorship by a landslide.

It was dubbed the "Multimillionaire Sweepstakes" and "the battle of the billionaires." Rockefeller spent $1.87 million; Harriman, $1.1 million. Nelson's secret weapon, however, was not money, nor the much-vaunted difference in style between the stiff, aristocratic Harriman and the outgoing "Rocky." Neither was it just the Dewey machine that the Rockefellers had funded and now claimed for Nelson's own use. Ultimately, it was Rockefeller's twenty years of experience in psychological warfare, painting an image of himself in the public mind that won the day. Organized by the ever-able Frank Jamieson, Nelson's propaganda machine chewed up 40 percent of the campaign's budget for television alone. Everywhere that Nelson went, his movie crew was sure to go; every day, daily reports and short movie reels were distributed free to twenty-three television stations. Intelligence briefings on local communities were compiled and bound in the thick binders Nelson was seen carrying around with him everywhere; they gave his campaign a local flavor, showing that he was concerned about each community and better informed about local matters than were most of its citizens. And at the core of it all, overseeing all field operations, were Nelson's CIAA veterans.

Throughout the race, despite the international caliber of his advisory stable, Nelson stressed local issues, using them as an excuse to keep Eisenhower and Nixon out of the campaign. Yet everyone in the campaign leadership knew that the White House was the real target. When Nelson, grinning broadly and flanked by Tod and his favorite son, Michael, claimed victory on election night, the crowd broke out in chants of "Rocky for President!" But Nelson kept up the face of party unity. "His boyish grin faded," reported the Associated Press. "A well-bred frown flitted across his pale face. He shook his head, emphatically, turned away from the microphones and made toward the door. . . . 'I haven't given it a thought,' he told reporters as he left."[4] He then flew to South America to rest, inspect his ranches and agricultural research in Brazil, and discuss the implications of his election with his friends and allies.

On New Year's Eve, Nelson placed his hand on Great-Grandmother Eliza's Bible and repeated the New York governor's oath of office. He was now one of the most powerful politicians in the United States.

The following morning, eschewing tradition, he appeared at Albany's official inauguration ceremony in the state assembly chamber dressed in a plain business suit and delivered a speech meant more for a president than a governor. He spoke of "a world divided," with "weapons of war perfected to deadly extremes." His tone was religious, and missionary.

"The World . . . is divided, essentially, between those who believe in the brotherhood of men under the fatherhood of God—and those who scorn this as pious myth. . . .

"The division of the world—and this time of decision—leave no corner of the earth, no fraction of humanity, untouched. From this basic struggle, there can be no refuge nor escape."[5]

As he spoke, his greatest fear had been realized ninety miles off Florida's Key West. Fulgencio Batista, the dictator, had fled Cuba, and the streets of Havana were filled with Cubans welcoming the bereted revolutionaries led by Fidel Castro.

Investing in Preferred Revolutions

Adolf Berle had seen it coming. The wall of dictators that imprisoned Latin Americans had been crumbling since 1956. At first, the kind of Latin American democracies that both Berle and Nelson Rockefeller had hoped to see since the end of World War II emerged in their place.

Dictator General Manuel Odría of Peru was one of the first to go, wisely deciding to step down a year after the Iquitos garrison revolted in the Amazon.

Succeeding him was banker and ex-President Manuel Prado, an old friend of David Rockefeller's since their days at the London School of Economics.

General Gustavo Rojas Pinilla of Colombia fell next, in 1957, after his failure to quell a revolution of Indians and *mestizo* peasants in the hills. Riots had broken out against his forced "reelection." To carry out the coup, Colombia's U.S.-trained-and-supplied air force and army demanded his resignation. He, like Odría, hopped a plane into exile, choosing Franco's fascist Spain.

His successor, Alberto Lleras Camargo, took office after a year of transitional military rule and brought to bear the fruits of his friendship with Nelson Rockefeller while serving as Colombia's ambassador to the United States. He quickly decorated David Rockefeller, cousin James Stillman Rockefeller (president of First National City Bank of New York), J. Peter Grace (of W. R. Grace & Company), and ex-Undersecretary of State Henry Holland for renegotiating Colombia's huge debt. Trusted by Nelson and well known by New York business-men and Washington officialdom, Lleras Camargo was viewed as a good invest-ment: Holding his government's bonds was like holding preferred stock in Colombia's future; it gave you first rights to Colombia's treasury. There was more than symbolic meaning in the ticker-tape parade Wall Street and Governor Rockefeller gave Lleras Camargo in 1960.

The Pérez Jiménez dictatorship of Venezuela, so mired in corruption that the Roman Catholic Church publicly took issue with his regime, fell on January 23, 1958. The outcome was exactly as ex-President Rómulo Betancourt had predicted six months before, prompting Adolf Berle to remark: "He was right, almost to the day."[6] Pérez Jiménez was put on a plane to Trujillo's Dominican Republic. Three days later, Argentina's ex-President Juan Perón, whom Rojas Pinilla had been har-boring, joined him. Venezuelans then elected Rómulo Betancourt president.

Carlos Castillo Armas of Guatemala was also eliminated after a year of student demonstrations, in July 1957. Like Nicaraguan dictator Anastasio Somoza García the previous year, he was shot by an assassin. The CIA tried to prevent Castillo Armas's rival, Colonel Miguel Ydígoras Fuentes, from being elected president. When Ydígoras was elected anyway, a deal was worked out by the U.S. Embassy allowing him to take office, but at a price: In 1959, a Philippine CIA operative named Napoleon Valeriano arrived under the auspices of Colonel Edward Lansdale to begin training Cuban exiles at a Guatemalan ranch for the Bay of Pigs invasion.[7]

When neighboring Honduras faced elections, the CIA's Colonel J. C. King scrutinized the country's favored presidential candidate, Ramón Villeda. King gave Villeda the green light only after a meeting with Villeda at Berle's town house, where Villeda convinced him he was no communist. Berle could barely contain his delight, noting that "between Colombia, Venezuela, Costa Rica, and Honduras, with friends elsewhere, we have a fairly good galaxy of governments composed of exiles who at one time had few friends except Beatrice and me."[8]

One country, however, worried both Berle and King: Cuba. Revolution was spreading among the sugarcane workers and rolling toward Havana. Both men believed the young lawyer-turned-guerrilla-leader, Fidel Castro, was controlled by the Kremlin; they desperately sought a more happy, if less heroic alternative to Batista. Berle and Puerto Rican Governor Luis Muñoz Marín drafted a proposal for the State Department outlining a plan for Batista to step down and hold elections.[9] Batista refused. Berle submitted a candidate proposed by his friend President Figueres of Costa Rica.[10] That suggestion was also rejected. Colonel King and ex-Ambassador to Peru and Brazil William Pawley, who owned Havana's streetcar system, tried to find a conservative Cuban more amenable to Batista. They, too, failed.[11]

Time had run out. Castro's guerrillas entered Havana and took power as the Berles were dancing the night away to Cab Calloway's band at Nelson Rockefeller's inaugural ball. Merrymakers leaving the ball in the snowy wee hours in their dinner jackets, furs, and jewels joked that not such an evening had been seen since the balls at the czar's Winter Palace.[12] If Berle saw any irony in their comments, he did not record it in his diary.

Nelson was angry about Cuba. The island had long held Rockefeller investments, not the least of which were Standard Oil of New Jersey's refinery and Chase's holding of Batista's notes. Castro had given no assurances to the United States that his government would honor the proprietary rights of either, and Chase was not about to write off Batista's profitable bonds. Nelson's brother, David, was also on the board of Punta Alegre Sugar, the second largest sugar company in Cuba.

Sugar had dominated and unbalanced Cuba's economic development, creating unequal landownership and inefficient idleness in a hungry country. Castro's plans to distribute the sugar estates in whole to cooperatives or in sixty-six-acre "vital minimum" plots to family farmers was not what David or other Chase bankers had in mind when they thought of Cuba's development or Punta Alegre's annual report. Now the company, along with all the other great sugar plantations, was threatened with nationalization by Castro's proposed agrarian reform. Nationalization could affect the price of sugar imported into the United States as well, especially if the supply from Cuba was disrupted or made otherwise unreliable for American refiners. And one of the largest refiners on the East Coast was SuCrest. SuCrest's chairman was Adolf Berle.

The Cuban revolution represented what Nelson had always feared about Latin America since he had first articulated his worry about "losing our property" twenty years earlier to Standard Oil's directors. He had spent most of his political life working to avoid a Cuba. Since leaving Washington, he had addressed the problem of development with a sense of urgency atypical of American businessmen and politicians. His activities in the International Basic Economy Corporation (IBEC) and the American International Association for Economic and Social Development (AIA) reflected that urgency.

The Cuban revolution, building an army that was capable of toppling a U.S.-backed military dictator against all odds by seizing plantations and distributing the land to their farmworkers and peasants, stirred the imaginations of much of Latin America's educated youths. Brazil, approaching a presidential election, was no exception.

Four months after Castro's campesino army marched into Havana, Governor Nelson Rockefeller received an important message from IBEC's Berent Friele, Room 5600's top aide for Latin America. Friele was worried about political rumblings in his native land. Brazil's Vice President João Goulart had announced ten days before that he would campaign against "North American trusts which are exploiting Brazil's wealth."[13]

This was disturbing news. Nelson had underestimated Goulart. He had met him in May 1956, when President Juscelino Kubitschek, anxious for American capital, had sent him to the United States to reassure American businessmen and politicians. Nelson invited Goulart to lunch and asked Berle to join them. "I am watching Jango [João Goulart's nickname] with some interest," Berle wrote afterward. "He is a young man and can go far but I don't know how heavily committed he is to other interests." By "other interests," Berle meant Brazil's Communist party.[14] He was suspicious, but it was hard to discern if Goulart was just a Brazilian patriot who favored the rights of labor or if he was willing to go so far as to challenge American business interests, in which case he would have to be judged a tool of the Kremlin.

To the State Department, however, Goulart was simply "a complete opportunist" who had "neither ideology nor ideals" and was instead "possessed by consuming personal ambition."[15] They knew how to deal with his type; there was no reason for his presence in Brazil's cabinet to become an obstacle to American participation in Kubitschek's development plans for the Amazon.

Now it looked like everyone had miscalculated. Goulart, Berent Friele reported, "wants 'a fundamental change in the social, economic and political structure of Brazil to liberate ourselves from the exploitation of international economic groups.' This opening gun by the labor leader is disturbing, especially as discontent is spreading with the increased cost of living and the failure of government to come to grips with the inflation." Friele dreaded Goulart's succeeding the very man whose policies were responsible for the inflation, President Kubitschek. Kubitschek's vast borrowing and spending programs, without a commensurate growth in revenues from exports, had worsened the inflation that the military's overthrow of his predecessor, President Getúlio Vargas, was supposed to arrest. But Friele saw Kubitschek as an asset for both the United States and the Rockefellers.

"At no time in recent history has Brazil had a president and a government so friendly toward the United States," Friele reminded Nelson.[16]

Kubitschek had broken the embarrassing silence in Latin America that followed the stoning of Vice President Richard M. Nixon in Venezuela in 1958, writing President Dwight D. Eisenhower of his concern and making the improvement of relations between the United States and the rest of the hemisphere—"Operation Pan American"—the cornerstone of his foreign policy. He wanted the United States to broaden its economic assistance to Latin America. This foreign policy initiative, however, only followed his domestic economic policy of trying to lure American capital to help in the development of Brazil, particularly the Amazon.

THE EYE OF THE COMING STORM

Kubitschek had hoped to raise $200 million for Amazonian development from the United States by 1957. Instead, Eisenhower authorized $400 million by 1958, when Kubitschek hosted an international investment conference at his old haunt, Belo Horizonte.

The centerpiece of Kubitschek's economic strategy was his campaign to humble the mighty Amazon jungle. To dramatize his government's willingness to commit the Brazilian people to this conquest, he flew to the edge of the wilderness in the state of Goiás and began construction of the long-planned new national capital. He called it Brasília, in honor of his dream of the Brazil of the future, and recruited architect Oscar Niemeyer, the man who had helped Rockefeller aide Wally Harrison design the United Nations headquarters in New York and had built Kubitschek's last frontier capital, Belo Horizonte. Shining white buildings of marble and glass soon rose on a dusty red plain; so did prices, since Brasília's buildings began passing through feverish hands many times. Pushing south from Belém, swarms of road crews buzzed their way through hundreds of miles of rain forest. Behind them, a long brown highway snaked through the jungle. Its name augured the soulless, deadly efficiency to come: BR-010. Contrary to past Amazonian road failures, the serpent's progress toward Brasília was remarkably swift, fed with fat World Bank loans and shielded from the jungle's malarial counterattacks by needle-armed scientists from the Rockefeller Foundation-funded Belém Virus Laboratory.

Only a dozen years before, the mighty Xavante and other less formidable Indian tribes had called these lands between the Xingu and Tocantins rivers their own. But in 1946, the Brazilian Service for the Protection of the Indian (SPI) pacified the Xavante, the largest tribe.[17] Now the highway was arriving, bringing the first of the 1 million people who would settle along the road in the next decade. Nelson's IBEC Research Institute had already provided evidence that this scrub-brush area could be turned into productive pastureland. Trees would fall, land would be cleared, and the number of cattle in the area would grow to over 5 million head, accelerating the westward migration of the cattle-ranching frontier into the Mato Grosso. The Rockefeller brothers' large landholdings in Mato Grosso could only increase in value as a result. Unfortunately, another consequence would be soil erosion, with some areas, according to the Brazilian Institute of Forestry Development, "turning into desert."

Nothing like this was anticipated by either Nelson or Adolf Berle when they championed the cause of Amazonian development. Convinced of the might of the marketplace and American technology, they were more concerned with removing obstacles to that development. "Misguided" nationalists and recalcitrant Indian warriors were greater obstacles than the Amazon's environment.

In 1956, after Nelson's visit to Brazil and his meeting with Goulart that spring, Berle had followed up with his own trip to Brasília to get some idea of Kubitschek's development plans and the prospects for stability. Goulart, Kubitschek told him, "would stay in line." Heartened, Berle accepted the Brazilian army's offer of a plane trip to Goiás, then aflame with speculation sparked by Brasília's construction. "The country is so blazingly rich in internal resources and is growing so fast that they may be able to overcome inflation by sheer growth. The fascinating part is the growth of the west. All the way from Amapá to the border of Paraguay, you see new cities rising."[18]

Berle's last visit to the Amazon had been when he was ambassador in 1945. Flying over the jungle at that time, he had thought "it would be the last region to be tamed by man; the forest is unmaliciously impregnable. . . . What is inside of it no one yet knows."[19]

Now he knew. Like the Rockefellers, he had invested in land both in Mato Grosso and in Goiás.[20] He did not worry about the Indians of the frontier. SPI was doing a fine job, and he had no hesitation joining the chorus of human rights advocates who nominated SPI's dying founder, Colonel Rondon, for the Nobel Peace Prize in 1957, just as SPI was entering its terminal stage of corruption.

São Paulo financial syndicates were as anxious as North Americans to take advantage of the inflation in land values caused by the influx of settlers from the destitute northeastern states. This inflation was spurred to new heights after 1957, when Kubitschek allowed Chase Manhattan-backed Bethlehem Steel and Rockefeller ally Augusto Antunes to begin mining the huge manganese deposits in the state of Amapá, north of the mouth of the Amazon. The governor of Amapá, who had helped Bethlehem Steel gain its concession, now Kubitschek's president of Petrobrás, brought the oil refinery at Manaus fully on line that year, feeding the rumors of an impending oil boom that had been started by an oil strike on the Madeira River south of Manaus in 1955. Kubitschek made the Amazon River an international waterway to create the Free Trade Zone of Manaus. Thousands of foreign tourists and businessmen flooded into the Amazon, causing prices for consumer goods to skyrocket. Following the establishment of the "free trade" route from the Amazon River's mouth to the great jungle capital of Manaus, smuggling, black-market rackets, and political corruption erupted on a mammoth scale.

The SPI was one of the first victims of Brazil's runaway development. SPI had been originally set up not as a bureau of Indian affairs, but as a pacifier and protector of the Indians from encroachment. For years SPI's unarmed agents were billed as the world's lone example of how Europeans could have growth through capitalism without resorting to genocide. In the frontier state of Goiás, lands inhabited since time immemorial were gently conquered by SPI's policy of love: "Die if need be. Never kill." Most SPI agents practiced what they preached, and the besieged Indians, impressed by such quiet moral courage and disdain for violence, surrendered to what they thought might be their last chance: a modus vivendi with the encroaching whites.

In the process, however, SPI was overwhelmed by the developmental forces its success had unleashed on the frontier. Governor Ludovico of Goiás, an old crony of Vargas, oversaw the corruption of SPI in his state. In 1941, claiming to succumb to entreaties from "Indian-lovers," he set up a safe haven for the state's Indians. Restricted to a small zone of seventy-six square miles, the Indians found their haven turned into their prison. "Ludovico had buried the Indians alive," wrote French author Lucie Bodard, who interviewed the governor. "He had handled them in such a way that they died on their own, like sick animals, without assassins. This was the so-called policy of 'mildness,' in other words, the policy of hidden violence. In 1941 he had started, with the experts of the SPI, his generous policy which wiped out the problem of the Indians at the same time as it did the Indians. No more than a few remnants were left. Success."[21]

In Mato Grosso, where Nelson dreamed of immigrants working his land for him, land speculators cheated settlers out of their land titles. The speculators were often local politicians, a phenomenon not unknown in the United States. Once the settlers improved the land, the politicians used corrupted SPI agents to assert Indian land rights and then to move Indians onto remote parts of the land. The Indians, ironically, were the only people in Brazil who had constitutional first rights to untitled land they occupied.[22] Once the Indians were "discovered," the settlers were promptly denounced as "stealers" of Indian land and fleeced of their titles. Then the SPI removed the Indians to "safer" reserves and gave the titles to friends.

This use of the "Indian trick," as it became known, reached its height in 1958. In a sudden gush of enthusiasm for justice for the Indians, Mato Grosso's legislators passed a law returning hundreds of thousands of acres to the Indians.

There was one problem: No one knew about the law's terms of compensation to settlers and landowners except the legislators. Only two copies of the text were published, one sent to the eventual oblivion of SPI's archives, the other to the town of Campo Grande, where the federal Office for the Repatriation of Land was located. By the time word leaked out to the general public, the money allocated for land buy-backs was gone. The legislators had laid claim to it in their own names and those of their relatives.[23]

Such were the hallmarks of progress in the Amazon. But for the Indians of Mato Grosso, corruption was preferable to what was to come. Pressure was building on them from the Northeast, where low wages paid to European and African workers had produced economic growth for exporting corporations but not for a home market of consumers. The mass poverty and growing radicalism of the Northeast's population prompted the government to plan migrations into the Amazonian interior to turn "unproductive" and "surplus" populations into cheap-wage "production" workers and agricultural tenant farmers for export-oriented agribusiness processors and ranchers. This policy only further entrenched the export sector and deepened Brazil's dependence on exports for an economic growth that never reached the huge and growing population of average Brazilians. The Indians who still occupied the Amazonian interior lost their lands, susceptible to the spread of European diseases.

In 1957, as Nelson Rockefeller took possession of Fazenda Bodoquena and moved his technicians onto the former lands of the Terêna Indians, another American organization arrived to work among the Terêna. Dale Kietzman, the future director of the Summer Institute of Linguistics (SIL) in Brazil, led the first SIL teams invited by SPI to begin field operations in Brazil; he assigned one team to the Terêna Indians that year and another translator in 1959 and would himself author SIL's first linguistic study of the Terêna language in 1961.[24] No American would have more influence over the conquest of the Amazon than would Nelson Rockefeller. No American missionary would have more influence on the Brazilian tribes affected by that conquest than would Kietzman as SIL's first Brazil branch director. Ironically, both Rockefeller and Kietzman started their operations in the Brazilian Indian frontier in the same year, and in the same location, the land of the Terêna Indians.

Anthropologist Darcy Ribeiro thought he had found in William Cameron Townsend's missionaries an alternative to SPI's growing corruption and militarization by the Brazilian army. He had met SIL linguist Kenneth Pike at the Rio Conference of Americanists shortly after Vargas's death. Coached by Cam, Pike had offered SIL's assistance in a survey of the estimated 186 tribes that Ribeiro was preparing to do for SPI. SIL's missionary-linguists seemed sincere and eager to work under difficult circumstances. And, Ribeiro reckoned, time was running out for Brazil's Indians. More than 70 tribes had perished since 1900.

Ribeiro looked at the projected Amazonian highway system, the export-oriented mining companies it inspired, the settlers used as rain-forest burners and ultimately cheap laborers, and the European diseases and violence and concluded that he had no choice. The first SIL translators, Dale and Harriet Kietzman, had arrived in 1956 and spent a year in Rio de Janeiro. In 1957, two teams were sent into western Brazil, one to the SPI post among the Terêna,[25] the other to a center near an SPI post among the Kaiwá, a tribe of some 3,000 Indians directly south of the Bodoquena mountains. The next year another SIL team "occupied" the Terênas' former rulers on the other side of the Bodoquena mountains, the Kadiwéu.

By January 1959, Cam had placed eleven SIL teams in the Brazilian Amazon, all working closely with SPI, some even living at SPI's Indian posts. This collaboration apparently won the confidence of Kubitschek's officials, who that year approved a contract between SIL and the University of Brazil's National Museum, an institution associated with Cam's new friend, Darcy Ribeiro.

Cam discovered 106 tribes spread over an area two-thirds the size of the United States. SIL's teams in western Brazil formed a crescent from Paraná in the south, curving northwest into Mato Grosso, where most of the teams were concentrated, then turning northeast through Xavante country west of Brasília, and finally into the Karajá tribe north of the capital. SIL's second focus was on two tribes to the north, the Apinayé and the Guajajara. SIL's third eye was on two remaining tribes southeast and northeast of the Manaus Free Trade Zone, the Sataré and the Hixkaryána.

Linking all this together was left to the Jungle Aviation and Radio Service. That year, Guatemala's new president, General Ydígoras, provided the opportunity for Cam to make an important U.S. government contact for JAARS in Brazil. Ydígoras was known for his cruelty and had been charged by Rev. Samuel Guy Inman of the Committee on Cooperation in Latin America with having on at least one occasion ordered the rape of Indian women and the capture of their children.[26] Nevertheless, he was asked to host the Fourth Inter-American Indian Congress by Manuel Gamio, Mexico's famed anthropologist and director of the Inter-American Indian Institute. SIL sent a large delegation, led by Cam. To the dictator's dismay, Guatemalan Indians also showed up as official observers of the Guatemalan Ministry of Education, petitioning the conference for help in relieving the oppression they had suffered since Arbenz's overthrow.[27]

The U.S. delegation, led by Interior Undersecretary Elmer F. Bennett, sought to silence the Indians by invoking the prohibition against nondelegates speaking at the plenary session. The Americans' wrath extended to other delegates and even Ydígoras's own officials for failing to follow the Eisenhower administration's line on Latin America's development. Guatemalan participants who dared to mention the agrarian reforms of the Arbenz years were branded as "commie liners"[28] by the deputy chief of the U.S. delegation. The conference's executive secretary, Jorge Louis Arriola of the Guatemalan Ministry of Education, was dismissed by Bennett in his classified report as "a collaborator with communist front groups." Bennett based his case on the opinions of "our Embassy personnel."[29]

When the conference's Economics Committee (of which Bennett was co-chair), passed a resolution calling for agrarian reform, Bennett refused to support it. Then he had it changed to his liking in the steering committee. "In this way, we succeeded in modifying every important resolution to conform more closely to American interests."[30]

When another resolution calling for a minimum agricultural wage arrived at the steering committee, it too was amended "to take into account expressly the productivity of labor." Previous Inter-American Indian Congresses had adopted such resolutions, with U.S. support, on the basis of Indians' needs, not how fast or much they worked. "The precedent established this time may be helpful in future Congresses," Bennett reported to Christian Herter, Dulles's successor as secretary of state.

Bennett reported that he was helped by some of Latin America's most respected names in *indigenismo*. "In particular, I would like to mention the assistance we received from Dr. Walter Dupouy of Venezuela, Alfredo Fuentes Roldan of Ecuador, and Professor Darcy Ribeiro of Brazil."[31] The last two had developed a close working relationship with SIL in recent years.

Nor was that all. A well-known American anthropologist had joined with an American missionary in collaborating secretly with the U.S. government's delegation. "We also were assisted by two Americans who served on delegations from the Latin American nations," Bennett informed Herter. "These two were Mrs. Doris Stone of Costa Rica and Dr. William Townsend of the Peruvian delegation.

"We made every effort," he added, "to keep our cooperation with these two as inconspicuous as possible."[32]

For good reason. Doris Stone was the daughter of Samuel "Sam the Banana Man" Zemurray, former chairman of the United Fruit Company, which dominated Costa Rica's economy and much of Central America's as well. Because of her father's largesse and her work among the Indians of Honduras and Costa Rica, the United Fruit heiress was a power at Tulane's Middle America Research Institute and at Harvard's Peabody Museum, as well as a director of United Fruit–endowed Escuela Agricola Panamericana (Panamerican School of Agriculture). Stone's collaboration with Bennett revealed she was far from the usual apolitical social scientist. Angry over the attempt of the Guatemalan Indians and their allies in the Guatemalan Ministry of Education to sway "my Indians" in the Costa Rican delegation, Stone continued to provide political intelligence on her Guatemalan colleagues after the conference. She informed on Guatemalan delegate Joaquin Noval, who had been so upset by American dominance at the conference he had told her, "I am going to use everything in my power to see that this is the last Congreso Indigenista Interamericano. It has been a complete farce. The resolutions have been dictated by the United States and the Commission of Economy was ruined by Bennett."

"I thought you might be interested in hearing this," she wrote Bennett. "Just what Noval can do I am not sure. He belongs to the young intellectual group that has many connections in Mexico. I just site [sic] this to make it clear the kind of people with whom we are dealing."[33]

Cam, for his part, was supposed to be representing Peru, not the U.S. government. Revelations of the missionary's secret efforts on Bennett's behalf might jeopardize SIL contracts with governments throughout Latin America and Southeast Asia, undermining SIL's usefulness in the future.

Like Stone, Cam contacted Bennett after the conference; a month later, he tapped the undersecretary for a return favor, when Bennett helped Cam dedicate JAARS's Catalina amphibian airplane to service in "the five Amazonian nations of South America"—Brazil, Ecuador, Colombia, Peru, and Bolivia.

Putting JAARS in the air over the Brazilian Amazon was the job of not just Cam, but also the U.S. government. According to Cam himself, the idea of Orlando, Florida, giving SIL's Brazil branch a Catalina airplane named after the founder of SPI, General Cândido Rondon, originated with Christian Ravndal, the U.S. ambassador to Ecuador[34] and a top Cold War operative. Ravndal came to Washington from Eastern Europe in 1954 at the request of Nelson's friend and predecessor as presidential special assistant on Cold War propaganda, C. D. Jackson. Ravndal "understands and uses psychological warfare better than practically any other Ambassador I have ever met," said Jackson. "He has been particularly helpful to Radio Free Europe,"[35] the CIA's radio propaganda operation. Now he was being helpful to Cam. Ravndal's brother led the successful fund drive that enabled JAARS to buy the Catalina amphibian.

The dedication ceremony was a huge publicity success for Cam. It was attended by Bennett, an honor guard from McCoy Air Force Base, U.S. Senators John Baker and Spessard Holland, Orlando's mayor, and representatives from the five Amazon basin governments, including José Chiriboga Villagomez, the Colombian ambassador who had helped Cam dedicate the *Spirit of Kansas City* Helio with former presidents Galo Plaza and Harry Truman. Mrs. Bennett christened the plane with water from the Amazon River sweetened with Florida orange juice by Orlando's mayor, naming it *Cândido Rondon—The Spirit of Orlando.* Then Cam, the mayor, and a party of Orlando's first citizens were off on a "brotherly loop around the heart of South America" in the Catalina. This trip gave Cam his first knowledge of gold mines and U.S. Steel's iron mountain in Venezuela's Orinoco basin and the Brazilian Amazon's vast potential to become an "inland cattle empire."[36]

The following year, many of the same CIA operatives that had overthrown the Arbenz government returned to Guatemala to begin preparations for another CIA invasion. With startling historical insight—or lack of it—the CIA codenamed the operation after an Indian peasant revolutionary who once had troubled Washington with an agrarian reform plan for Mexico much more fundamental and far-reaching than Arbenz's. Operation Zapata's target was the new Cuban government of Fidel Castro.

SILers in Guatemala City, meanwhile, were enjoying their new headquarters in the capital on government-donated land. Just before the Inter-American Indian Congress closed in 1959, Cam paid a visit to General Ydígoras to express SIL's desires. The grateful dictator simply picked up the phone and called his minister of education. "I'm sending Townsend and his assistant over. They need land."[37] SIL's continued cooperation with Guatemala's military dictatorships would earn Cam the Order of the Quetzal, Guatemala's highest decoration.

In the United States, JAARS had much success, buoyed by a new federal law. Originally called "Townsend's Bill" because of SIL's lobbying effort, the law allowed religious missions to take abroad the surplus U.S. military apparatus the government sold or donated.[38] The U.S. Constitution notwithstanding, Cam even got the U.S. Army to turn over an abandoned warehouse for JAARS's plane repairs until a larger JAARS base could be built on one of Henderson Belk's old antebellum cotton plantations outside Charlotte, North Carolina.

Cam could see only a bright future. Even Lázaro Cárdenas, whom he visited in Mexico while getting a government land grant for a new SIL headquarters, could not shake his confidence. Cárdenas publicly supported the Cuban revolution and Fidel Castro. But to Cam, Cárdenas was still an old friend to whom he owed much of his early success. Cam listened for hours as Cárdenas poured out his heart about the warlike climate between the United States and the Soviet Union, the push for a new arms race, and the growing threat of nuclear war. To Cárdenas, who yearned for peace, Cam had only the Second Coming to offer. "The Bible tells us the Prince of Peace will return to earth and end all injustices. He will give everlasting peace," Cam said. Then he attempted once more to convert the ex-president. The old politician was touched. "You're the only one who talks to me about my soul," he told Cam as they parted with an embrace.[39]

Leaving Cárdenas behind with his worries, Cam flew back home and into the future that seemed so promising. More than anything, more than the new Mexican headquarters that symbolized the power SIL had gained in twenty-five years of service, more than the church crowds that turned out to hear Cam during a hectic speaking tour across the nation, JAARS represented that future. Yet even as he recruited the Belks and the Grahams to help him build a JAARS base in North Carolina, he was confronted by the contradiction of SIL's—and America's—origins.

23

ASCENT OF THE HAWK

The Fruits of Intolerance

Nothing like it had ever been seen before by the business leaders of Charlotte, North Carolina. The quiet commercial hub of the Piedmont textile belt and local big city of the billionaire Belks, the evangelical Grahams, and now Cam's missionary air force was shaken in February 1960 by civil rights demonstrations. Hundreds of African American students seeking an end to discrimination began sit-down demonstrations at segregated lunch counters in the Belks' new $4 million department store,[1] the same one whose opening four years before David Rockefeller had celebrated as a "shining example" of "the dynamic growth of the South."[2]

Southern intolerance toward African Americans, Jews, and Catholics was growing, recharging the Fundamentalist movement with renewed invective. Cam himself became a target. JAARS's service to Catholic clergy in Latin America was viewed as close to heresy. Cam found himself once again pleading for more broadmindedness in his own camp. "It's possible to know Christ as Lord and Savior and to continue in the Roman Church," he argued to the Evangelical Foreign Missionary Association. Anonymous charges against JAARS within the Interdenominational Foreign Missionary Association (IFMA) had become so strong in 1959 that the Summer Linguistic Institute (SIL) was forced to resign as a member. "We feel very strongly," Cam wrote IFMA headquarters, "that the way our critics want us to treat the monks and nuns is unscriptural."[3]

It was also strategically impractical. Anti-Catholicism would limit severely

SIL's expansion in Latin America, especially in Ecuador, Peru, and Cam's next goal, Colombia, where the new presidency of Alberto Lleras Camargo offered hope that a way might soon be found to enter that Catholic fortress.

As Cam began to see the future JAARS base in North Carolina as a springboard for SIL's entrée into West Africa and Colombia, the civil rights demonstrations at the Belk store in Charlotte and the growing anti-Catholicism in the South threatened the Fundamentalist base he relied on to fulfill his vision.

Even Billy Graham, who would soon join the Wycliffe board, was not immune to the pressures of racism among his supporters. Despite his earlier move to desegregate his crusades, Graham counted the Belks among his most powerful backers. Graham had personally commended the Belk managers of the segregated Charlotte store in 1958 during the Charlotte Crusade. He ignored the management's upholding of an American apartheid, focusing instead on its willingness to hold prayer meetings and on his admiration for family patriarch Henry Belk, who once shook his hand while Graham sold shoes at a Belk store in Tennessee. "I didn't wash my hand for a week," Graham said.[4]

Another threat to the ethnoreligious tightrope Cam was walking between the United States and the Third World was the pastor of the Dallas church in which Graham held membership. Rev. William Criswell of the First Baptist Church attacked the presidential ambitions of Massachusetts Senator John F. Kennedy because of his Catholicism. Cam had known Criswell since World War II, when Criswell was the pastor of the First Baptist Church in Muskogee, Oklahoma. Criswell was called to Dallas in 1944 to take over the 1,000-member congregation of George W. Truett, a supporter of Cam. Now Criswell's anti-Catholic sermons were making headlines.[5] But worse was to come: Some 100,000 copies of one of them would soon be distributed through the mails anonymously by oil tycoon H. L. Hunt, millionaire backer of Kennedy's rival, Texas Senator Lyndon B. Johnson. Senate investigators would later charge that, by its anonymity, the anti-Kennedy mailing had violated federal law.

The pastor of the largest Southern Baptist church in the world, a leader of Fundamentalism, attacking the only Catholic presidential candidate in thirty years and having his sermon distributed by one of the largest funders of Fundamentalist missions was in direct contradiction to the image Cam was trying to convey for his missionaries in Latin America.

It was also not the picture of the United States that Washington wanted to present to the world during the Cold War, especially to Africa. Africa's independence movements inspired young African American students, and the antics of the Criswells and Hunts were sure only to convince the nationalist leaders of Africa that the similarity between apartheid in South Africa and mandated segregation in the American South was no accident of history, but a social phenomenon—racism—rooted in European colonialism. The death of John Foster Dulles from cancer seemed to symbolize the failure of a foreign policy that overemphasized military alliances and nuclear brinkmanship to the point of making the United States almost irrelevant in the Third World.

Already, Fidel Castro in Cuba and Patrice Lumumba in the Belgian Congo were demonstrating that irrelevance by asserting, in the face of Washington's hostility, a dangerous economic and political independence. Washington responded with murder plots.

Castro was targeted for assassination as early as December 11, 1959, by Nelson's old friend from the CIAA days, J. C. King, now the CIA's Chief of Clandestine Services in the Western Hemisphere. Even before Castro had forced Fulgencio Batista to flee Havana, King and Adolf Berle had met to ponder the fate of Freeport Sulphur Company's mining project at Nicaro, in Oriente province. Now the Nicaro deposits and sugar plantations in Cuba were facing nationalization. It was clear to King that a "far left" government existed in Cuba. "If permitted to stand," he wrote CIA Director Allen Dulles, it would encourage similar actions against American companies elsewhere in Latin America. One of King's "recommended actions" was explicit:

> Thorough consideration [should] be given to the elimination of Fidel Castro. None of those close to Fidel, such as his brother Raul or his companion Che Guevara, have the same mesmeric appeal to the masses. Many informed people believe that the disappearance of Fidel would greatly accelerate the fall of the present Government.[6]

By July 1960, King would cable the CIA station in Havana informing it that "possible removal of top three leaders is receiving serious consideration at HQS." Some $10,000 was authorized for "arranging an accident" for Raúl Castro before King would fire off another cable ordering the station "to drop [the] matter." The CIA had decided instead to turn to Dr. Sidney Gottlieb's Technical Services Division for poison.[7]

The same recipe was prescribed for Patrice Lumumba. The Congo's independence leader had made the mistake of informing a group of visiting New York businessmen in 1959 that he meant to put his own country first when he became prime minister. "The exploitation of the mineral riches of the Congo should be primarily for the profit of our own people and other Africans," he declared. "We have decided to open the gates of the Congo to any foreign investors prepared to help us get the fullest and most immediate value from mineral resources and energy, so that we may achieve full employment, an improved standard of living for our people, and a stable currency for our young country. Belgium will no longer have a monopoly in the country."

A New York banker put the question of American access to uranium directly to Lumumba: "Do you know, for instance, that Congolese uranium is sold in the

United States as Belgian uranium, according to a legal and formal agreement between ourselves and Belgium?"

"As I have said, Belgium won't have a monopoly in the Congo now," Lumumba replied. "From now on we are an independent and sovereign state. Belgium doesn't produce any uranium; it would be to the advantage of both our countries if the Congo and the U.S. worked out their own agreements in the future."

The Americans, "all of whom represented powerful financial interests, looked at one another and exchanged meaningful smiles."[8]

Lumumba did not know that American corporations already had a big stake in Belgium's powerful copper and uranium monopoly in the Congo's Katanga province through Tanganyika Concessions, Limited. The Rockefellers were shareholders in this company;[9] in addition, the Rockefeller and Guggenheim groups held stock in Forminière, the Belgian diamond-mining operation in Kasai province, directly northwest of Katanga. The total American investment was about $20 million; that of their Belgian partners, $2 billion.

Lumumba's naïveté would be evident during his visit to Washington in late July 1960, one month after the Congo declared independence from Belgium and Katanga province seceded under a rich Congolese collaborator, Moise Tshombe. Prime Minister Lumumba and President Joseph Kasavubu, faced with Belgian troop landings, had appealed to the United Nations and the Soviet Union for assistance. U.S. Air Force planes hurried troops in, and Lumumba, upset at the unwillingness of the U.N. troops to move against the Belgian-inspired secession in Katanga, flew to the United States to appeal to the United Nations and to the Eisenhower administration.

The State Department Lumumba visited was then deeply divided between those who were worried about losing face with African nationalists and those Atlanticists who did not want to rupture relations with a NATO ally, Belgium. In his meeting with Christian Herter, John Foster Dulles's successor as secretary of state, and Undersecretary of State for Economic Affairs C. Douglas Dillon, Prime Minister Lumumba spoke about his government's concerns, not theirs. Dillon, a former ambassador to France and a firm Atlanticist, recalled that "his words didn't ever have any relation to the particular things that we wanted to discuss."[10]

And that was Lumumba's fatal mistake. Both men were not just American government officials; they had personal ties to powerful and growing interests in Africa. Dillon, in fact, was an investor with the Belgians in Laurance Rockefeller's textile mill in the Congo, Filatures et Tissage Africains, and in another of Laurance's holdings, Cegeac, which imported automobiles into the Congo.[11]

Perhaps Lumumba did not know of Dillon's investments, or perhaps he was simply imprudent. In any case, he refused to equivocate on an end to Belgian control. For him, that was the bottom line. It would cost him his life.

"The impression that was left was . . . very bad," noted Dillon. In fact, as he explained years later to Senate investigators who were looking into possible CIA involvement in Lumumba's murder, the impression was "that this was an individual whom it was impossible to deal with. And the feelings of the Government as a result of this sharpened very considerably at that time. . . . We [had] hoped to . . . see what we could do to come to a better understanding with him."[12] Belgium, after all, was a close ally, host of NATO's headquarters in Brussels.

"The concern with Lumumba was not really the concern with Lumumba as a person," the CIA's Bronson Tweedy explained to the Senate in 1975. "It was concern at this very pregnant point in the new African development . . . the Congo, after all, was the largest geographical expression. Contained within it were enormously important mineral resources. . . . "[13] And the highest percentage of those mineral resources then known lay in the Congolese province of Katanga, which was still dominated by Belgian colonial rule.

Within a few weeks, Lumumba's assassination was proposed by staff of the Joint Chiefs of Staff* at an "informal" interdepartmental meeting at the Pentagon with the State Department, the Defense Department, and the CIA. Shortly thereafter, at an August meeting of the National Security Council (NSC), Dillon reported that Lumumba had demanded the withdrawal of European U.N. troops from his country, charging that they were interfering with his government. This demand could undermine the efforts of U.N. Undersecretary General Ralph Bunche, a former Rockefeller Foundation grantee and current trustee of the foundation, to cut a deal with Moise Tshombe, the Belgian-backed leader of the Congo's mineral-rich Katanga province. The plan was for a token U.N. troop presence at Tshombe's capital in Elizabethville. In return, Katanga would not be invaded, and the U.N. troops could focus on pressuring for a new government to replace Lumumba. Sensing this plan, Lumumba recognized that subversion of his government was afoot and now demanded the withdrawal of all U.N. troops and threatened to ask for Soviet assistance. President Eisenhower, presiding over the meeting, exploded. According to a shocked NSC staff member, Eisenhower "said something—I can no longer remember his words, that came across to me as an order for the assassination of Lumumba."[14]

The CIA swung into high gear, ordering its Chief of Station in the Congo, Laurance Devlin, "to proceed with operation," in other words, to replace Lumumba and his government with a pro-Western group. At the same time, the CIA made plans to send the Belgian-backed regime in Katanga logistical support, which would eventually include Helio Courier airplanes—and JAARS's top pilot.

Once the Special Group agreed on August 25 "that planning for the Congo would not necessarily rule out 'consideration' of any particular kind of activity which might contribute to getting rid of Lumumba,"[15] the next step seemed preor-

*The top long-range planning assistant to the Army Chief of Staff at that time was Nelson Rockefeller's former counterinsurgency aide from the CIA, Colonel William Kintner.

dained. On September 26 CIA scientist "Joseph Schneider" arrived in Leopoldville, the Congolese capital, and delivered deadly biological materials, including tularemia (rabbit fever), tuberculosis, anthrax, smallpox, brucellosis (indolent fever), and Venezuelan equine encephalitis (sleeping sickness). One material "was supposed to produce a disease that was . . . indigenous to that area [of Africa] and that could be fatal."[16] "Schneider" was actually Dr. Gottlieb of MKULTRA.

A Military-Industrial Candidate

President Eisenhower himself was aware that real social and economic needs were driving the Third World's political revolutions. But unlike Rockefeller, he sought a way to use foreign aid to *reduce* competition with the Soviets, not to increase it. He considered offering Nikita Khrushchev during his 1959 visit a joint U.S.-USSR aid program to underdeveloped countries through the World Bank and the International Development Association; the idea was shot down by Treasury Secretary Robert B. Anderson on the grounds that the Soviet ruble was not as sound as the dollar and, thus, that the United States would get the worst end of the deal. Eisenhower proposed greater trade, only to be told that it would disrupt existing trade relations. He proposed a massive 10,000-students-per-year exchange program, again getting put off by the State Department. His talks with Khrushchev at Camp David remained, therefore, more spirit than substance, but the fact that there was even some goodwill was enough for him to press for "peaceful coexistence."

Eisenhower knew that economic competition was a "wasteful" drain on the American economy and that trade wars for markets and resources had led to real war in the past. The very intensity of trade relations and the interconnectedness of the world market in the twentieth century had already forced global military alliances that fought two world wars. Eisenhower was convinced that with the advent of atomic weapons in the last war, and now intercontinental ballistic missiles, humanity could not survive a third world war. Confronted by "serious talk of possible war," he was aghast. "You might as well go out and shoot everyone you see and then shoot yourself."[17]

Nelson's campaign for a crash spending program on fallout shelters did not impress Eisenhower as fiscally or politically responsible. Nelson kept pestering the president with studies. Eisenhower rejected them all.

In July 1959, after just six months in office as governor, Nelson Rockefeller organized a White House conference on fallout protection and used the conference to launch his drive for the White House. Eisenhower looked on helplessly as Nelson convened the Special Commission on Civil Defense and invited the press. Some commentators, feigning wisdom, mistook Nelson's campaign for shelters as merely a personal "preoccupation" or "obsession"; more savvy politicians understood it as a cynical attempt to stoke basic fears for survival to fire up the engine of his *real* campaign. Nelson himself ended all doubts on that matter after the annual governors' conference in Puerto Rico the next month gave him a more dignified launching pad (and the governors some posh accommodations at brother Laurance's El Dorado hotel).

He embarked on a speaking tour in the states where Republican leaders were most conservative. The strategy was obvious: By calling for increased conventional arms expenditures, he hoped to woo the party's powerful conservative wing away from the front-runner, Vice President Richard M. Nixon. The tour was the litmus test of his ability to shuck off his liberal image.

He failed. Twenty years of memories could not be erased: of Rockefeller, the New Dealer; of Truman's architect of foreign aid; of the Department of Health, Education, and Welfare's promoter of national medical insurance programs for catastrophic illnesses; of the millionaire philanthropist; of the governor of an eastern liberal state.

In November, a year before the election, the Rockefeller road show arrived on Nixon's home ground in California. Standing beneath a giant picture of Nixon at the Western States Republican Conference was not likely to win him much; the crowds were unenthusiastic, and donors said no.

By the time he reached Texas, Nelson was desperate. His reception in eight other states had ranged from lukewarm to frigid. He gambled that Texans, ever wary of the Spanish-speaking lands south of the Rio Grande, would respond to him talking about what he knew best: Latin America and the revolution of rising expectations.

Before a large crowd, he warned of the "very serious" situation in Cuba and about widespread disturbances throughout Latin America, a subtle reminder of the riots that turned Nixon's tour into an international embarrassment the previous year. He spoke knowledgeably and forcefully, emphasizing that Latin Americans did not control their own economies, but were dependent on the export prices of coffee, copper, tin, sugar, and bananas.

"A drop in the price of any of these commodities can cause havoc with the countries that export them. . . . The Soviets are just beginning to exploit the situation by offering trade agreements and promising aid on a large scale. If we are not successful in preserving and developing a strategy and vital free association of free peoples . . . it will cast doubt on our ability as a leader in the free world."[18]

The speech was a huge publicity success, appealing to conservative Democrats as well as Republicans. Democratic House Speaker Sam Rayburn drove 100 miles to be seen publicly embracing a Republican rising star, Nelson Rockefeller. "I didn't want you to leave Texas without seeing you," Rayburn said. "We have been friends under three presidents." Rayburn did not mention the $300,000 grant Nelson approved as Rockefeller Brothers Fund president for Rayburn's library a couple of years back.[19]

In the end, after futilely urging "big thinking" in Houston and espousing "the Brotherhood of Man under the Fatherhood of God,"[20] he got his most spirited welcome in Miami—from vacationing New Yorkers.

He had failed in his effort to show he was not just a maverick millionaire who was using the inherited money to win the White House.

Back in New York, Nelson convened his council of advisers. The advisers had sounded out Wall Street early in the campaign; to Nelson's surprise, the financiers trusted demonstrably controllable Nixon more than wealthy, uncontrollable Rockefeller. The day after Christmas, reporters were summoned to the Capitol in Albany for what most thought would be the governor's announcement of plans to enter the New Hampshire Republican primary that February. Instead, they were handed a statement that he was withdrawing from a race he had never formally entered.

His decision was "definite and final."[21]

Eisenhower kept a discreet silence. He wondered if Nelson's decision really was definite and final.

It was not. By April 1960, John F. Kennedy was on the way to winning primaries that the Democratic bosses, including Berle, said a Catholic could not win. It was a sign that the nation was in the mood for a change. That month Nelson published an article in *Foreign Affairs*, hinting that the Eisenhower administration was not doing enough in foreign aid to combat Soviet economic competition in the Third World or spending enough on defense. The article's publication coincided with two speeches.

In one speech in Philadelphia, Nelson mentioned missionaries to distant lands as examples of the kind of "concern for humanity at large" shown by Americans that should be matched with economic and military aid. "If we attempt to stand still, the world and its destiny will leave us and our destiny behind—perhaps in the dust." Again, he called for a Western Hemispheric "economic union."[22]

On the same day, Nelson, now plainly appealing to liberals and moderates of all parties, delivered a second speech at the University of Chicago's John D. Rockefeller Memorial Chapel. The subject was the Christian heritage in American law. It was a stirring address on the nation's moral purpose.

"This chapel in which we assemble today bears the name of my grandfather. One of the ruling axioms of his life was—in the words of my father—the conviction that 'every right implies a responsibility; every opportunity, an obligation; every possession, a duty. I believe that love is the greatest thing in the world, that it alone can overcome hate; that right can and will triumph over might.'"[23] The same words were carved on a bronze plaque at Rockefeller Center, the very embodiment of Rockefeller financial might.

Ten days later, Nelson received word that his father was dying at his winter retreat in Tucson, Arizona. Junior, no longer the Lord of Pocantico but a feeble eighty-six-year-old, had withdrawn from his sons, leaving them to their appointed tasks in the world.

Nelson and Laurance were by Junior's side when death came in his sleep. Nelson was moved, but not to the personal degree he felt when his mother had died. What made Junior's death so powerful was its timing, coming so soon on the heels of the death of Frank Jamieson, his closest political adviser. Jamieson's succumbing to the cancerous result of a lifetime of cigarette smoking was a terrible blow to Nelson, greater than Junior's death. Yet it had been Junior who played a deeper note in Nelson's soul. As long as Junior was alive, a firm grip of family duty and honor held Nelson under rein. Junior's traditions permeated the family's private lives, imbuing the very prayers Nelson led over his children's breakfast table and running unseen but felt through the labyrinth of Rockefeller Center, right into Room 5600 itself. Jamieson's advice may have saved Nelson's career more than once, but Junior's looming presence had always served to back Jamieson's wisdom.

Now, as Nelson stood at the family plot at Pocantico with the rest of the clan to bury the ashes he had brought back from Tucson, the last restraint on Nelson's ambitions was gone.

Descent of the Dove

On May 1, 1960, Premier Khrushchev was observing the annual May Day festivities in Moscow's Red Square, when Air Marshall Vershinin, arriving late and in duty uniform rather than the customary parade uniform, took him aside. Something had happened, something that would shock the world, end Eisenhower's last crusade for peace, and launch Nelson Rockefeller on a concerted drive to shape the selection of Eisenhower's successor.

A U-2 had crashed deep inside Soviet territory. Francis Gary Powers had broken standard operating procedure for CIA secret air flights by carrying on his person nineteen items proving his identity, including U.S. Air Force identification cards and his social security card. Someone was violating the NSC's directive requiring plausible deniability for clandestine operations.

Powers had decided to fly the falling U-2 down to 30,000 feet, forgo the CIA's standard poisoned needle for such situations, and use his parachute. Arrested and interrogated, he promptly admitted he was a spy.

The timing of Powers's flight was ominous. It occurred two weeks before the scheduled U.S.-Soviet Summit in Paris. Eisenhower had been impressed by the Soviets' unilateral decision to demobilize more than 1 million men from their armed forces. They also had proposed to negotiate disarmament and were willing to continue their unilateral suspension since 1958 of nuclear testing, as long as the United States did likewise. To ensure that nothing on the United States' part inadvertently sabotaged the summit, the president had Secretary of State Herter pledge that U.S. high-altitude flights in the tense Berlin Corridor would remain suspended indefinitely.

The State Department denied that Powers was a spy. "There was absolutely no-no-no deliberate attempt to violate Soviet air space and there never has been."[24] The flight was innocent. A "disabled" NASA pilot had been victimized.

This cover story, almost as much as the downing of the U-2, put both Eisenhower and Khrushchev in an impossible position. Eisenhower was neck-deep in a lie created by the State Department, and Khrushchev was being asked to swallow the lie at the risk of his own position in the Kremlin. Yet the Soviet pre-mier tried to save the summit by giving Eisenhower the plausible deniability that CIA's Powers had denied him. "I am prepared to grant that the President had no knowledge of a plane being dispatched to the Soviet Union and failing to return," he said, "but that should alert us still more."[25] The American president might not be in control of his generals.

The flight, however, *had* received presidential authorization—or at least had received authorization from someone in the White House. CIA Director Allen Dulles would admit to the Senate Foreign Relations Committee only that the flight had been authorized by "a group" that oversaw all covert operations. He refused to name names, but the NSC's Special Group at the time included the same men who recently had authorized an assassination plot against Lumumba. The Special Group included Allen Dulles, National Security Adviser Gordon Gray, and Assistant Secretary of Defense John Irwin II. Dulles "assumed" that Gray had Eisenhower's approval.

Ike's course of action—or more properly, inaction—had left him with an untenable choice: lying again in the face of Khrushchev's proof or admitting, as his critics charged, that he was not in control of his own administration.

On May 9, Eisenhower authorized Secretary of State Herter to acknowledge that the president had allowed U-2 flights over the Soviet Union. The president himself then announced that he had known about the flights and was taking full responsibility. He and Nixon excused the flights in the interest of preventing another Pearl Harbor. Few bought it.

The U-2 cost Eisenhower—and the world—the best opportunity for a disar-mament accord since the 1955 Geneva Summit. And Nelson Rockefeller, as the first chairman of the NSC's Special Group, had played a key role in destroying that opportunity.

Nelson listened to the administration's desperate allusion to the need for "open skies" with knowing appreciation. "Open Skies" had been his formulation to turn a peace agenda into a propaganda sideshow at Geneva in July 1955, the same month the new U-2, whose birth he had overseen as the Special Group's first chairman, was to make its maiden flight. Now that the "Spirit of Camp David" was going the way of the "Spirit of Geneva," and Vice President Nixon was obliged to make a lame televised "Pearl Harbor" defense of the administration's fumbling, Nelson saw his chance.

On May 23, he made his first formal statement on foreign affairs since withdrawing from the presidential race five months before. He praised Eisenhower's integrity and warned Democrats not to exploit the president's embarrassment. Then he did just that.

In blaming everyone but the president, Nelson was making no friends among Republican or Democratic leaders; he was, however, articulating the sense of frustration and confusion raging among the electorate. As anti-American riots broke out in Korea, Turkey, and Japan, Nelson used his speaking engagements in New York to push for increased arms expenditures.

On June 8 he announced his intention to lead the state's huge delegation to the Republican National Convention in July. He then exploited the front-runner's typical fear of controversy before obtaining the nomination: He challenged Vice President Nixon to speak out on the issues. He listed a "number of problems," including the missile gap, the need for a $3 billion per year defense spending increase and another $500 million for fallout shelters, a "more tightly organized Department of Defense," and "international inspection and control of arms."[26]

"I am deeply convinced, and deeply concerned, that those now assuming control of the Republican party have failed to make clear where this party is heading and where it proposes to lead the nation. . . .

"Once the Vice President has made his position clear on the specific issues . . . I shall be glad to debate these issues with him."[27]

Before startled Rotarians in upstate Binghamton, New York, he raised again the proposal Eisenhower had rejected for the creation of a "first secretary" or superassistant, who would assume the de facto powers of a premier. In Washington, he argued for centralization of the Defense Department and attacked the State Department for undermining his role as the first chairman of the Special Group.

He upped the ante in an appearance before downstate Young Republicans. He charged that Khrushchev's planned visit to Cuba "may be accompanied by the announcement of a military pact giving Russia air bases, missile bases and submarine bases in Cuba." This, he declared, would shift the balance of power against the United States. The country's "vulnerability to nuclear devastation" would be enhanced.

It would be a year before Khrushchev would place intermediate missiles in Cuba, and then only at Castro's request after the CIA's Bay of Pigs invasion. But Nelson's speech helped stir the war hysteria sweeping the nation. Nelson then used these fears to promote a cause that had been the cornerstone of his political career: counterinsurgency in Latin America. Revolution might spread, he warned. Through the use of Cuba as a base, the Soviets were moving "men, money and propaganda" into Latin America "on an unprecedented scale."

The solutions were familiar: industrialization and agrarian reform as the cornerstones of a broad program of economic and social development; a Western Hemisphere economic union, backed by a Marshall Plan for Latin America; and, of course, joint military and economic action against Cuba. But there was also a new, startling Rockefeller twist in the formula: a political confederation of the Western Hemisphere.[28]

Republican leaders were furious. But the Rockefeller onslaught continued. He rejected Republican platform drafts prepared by Nixon's handpicked chairman of the platform committee. He proposed his own program for increased defense spending, enhanced powers for a national security adviser, and civil rights enforcement, the last being the key to the African American vote without which no Republican candidate could hope to carry the big cities. Nelson indicated that he was prepared to fight for his own program on the convention floor.

But suddenly Nelson found himself trapped by his own ambition. His rashness had put him on the march toward a confrontation he could not win. If Nixon ignored him and was nominated, Nelson's power in the party would suffer immensely. If he engaged Nixon in an open floor fight, he would win over many independents who were crucial for any Republican's future presidential aspirations, but he would be forever damned by party regulars as a spoiler. His only hope was that Nixon, needing party unity, would bail him out.

Nixon did just that. Days before the convention opened, Nixon requested a meeting. It was his worst mistake. Nelson insisted that the vice president should call on him personally, and if Nixon wanted to meet, he would have to come to him, in New York.

The vice president arrived, weary and beaten, at Nelson's Fifth Avenue apartment on the evening of July 23. Over a quiet dinner, Nixon tried to give his humiliating trip some justification by seeking the governor of New York as his running mate. Had he succeeded, he would have turned a bad scene into a personal triumph: Between California and New York, with a unified party and Nelson's liberal big city constituency, Nixon could not lose.

Nelson flatly turned him down. Instead, he wanted Nixon to adopt his program for the United States and formally incorporate it into the Republican platform. It took until 3:00 A.M., but when Nelson was finished, Nixon had given in to almost all his demands. Only strict civil rights enforcement, which Nixon feared would lose him the segregationist South, went into the dustbin. This decision probably doomed Nixon in November.

Over a special trunk line Nelson had installed for this occasion, Nixon dictated their draft to the Republican Platform Committee in Chicago, which accepted the decision with grim resolution. The president, as titular leader of the party, had approved the old draft; he would not be happy about not being consulted.

Eisenhower's grumbling, however, was nothing compared to the furor of the conservatives. Arizona's Senator Barry Goldwater thundered that it was "the Munich of the Republican Party." Mindless of the bitterness he was stirring, Nelson arrived in Chicago with the largest staff at the convention and jubilantly waved his "Compact of Fifth Avenue" in front of reporters. "If you don't think this represents my views," he told them, "you're crazy."[29] Then, as if to rub salt in the wounds he had inflicted, he refused to nominate Nixon. He consented only to introduce him to the convention—and the nation, of course—after the nomination was over. To everyone's horror, even that introduction ended in humiliation for Nixon. Winding up his speech, Nelson called forward the "man who will succeed Dwight D. Eisenhower next January—Richard E. Nixon!"[30]

"Nelson has taken himself off the hook," a bemused Adolf Berle wrote in his diary. ". . . If Nixon wins, Rockefeller can claim he has at last pushed things in the right direction; if Nixon loses, Rockefeller is the logical candidate for '64. It was a good hand, well played."[31]

And well acted. Campaigning for Nixon gave Nelson more national exposure. But by October, Nixon was beaten. Nelson's closest aides were already working for Kennedy, shaping the issues of the campaign and the policies of the future administration. Henry Kissinger was on board, as were Berle and a score of other veterans of the Rockefeller Brothers Fund's Special Studies Project panels.

THE MATING DANCE

John F. Kennedy became a devotee of the Rockefeller Brothers Fund panel reports during the 1960 campaign. "When some foreign policy question came up, Kennedy yelled to Salinger, 'Hey, Pierre, get the Rockefeller Brothers Studies. It's all there.' "[32] Top Rockefeller aides were also there, right at Kennedy's ear, helping to shape the campaign's issues—and the future administration.

Roswell Gilpatric worked on reorganizing the Pentagon along the lines Nelson had advocated.[33] Nelson's "missile gap" became Kennedy's "missile gap." Almost a year after the election, Gilpatric would announce that there never had been a missile gap, or if there was, it was on the Soviet side. But in 1960, Rockefeller themes triumphed as Kennedy themes.

Nelson's demand that Nixon support greater government intervention to stimulate "economic growth" became Kennedy's call for greater "economic growth."

Nelson's call for more research in nuclear energy became Kennedy's call. "Our research in the peaceful uses of atomic energy has fallen far short of expectation."

Henry Kissinger, too, had joined the Kennedy "brain trust," advising the campaign while working out of both Harvard and a Manhattan town house on West Fifty-fifth Street as Nelson's adviser.

This cross-pollination of ideas between the Rockefeller and Kennedy camps—or, more precisely, the tutoring of the Kennedy campaign by the Rockefeller camp—reached its natural outcome in October, after the first Kennedy-Nixon debate, when it was clear that Kennedy was going to win.

Nelson decided he had better begin preparing for 1964, when he expected to run against Kennedy. On the day that the *New York Post* endorsed Kennedy, Nelson had Kissinger speak to Berle, who was by then assisting Kennedy as a speechwriter, to ask him to help draft a five-year program for regional confederations between the United States and its allies.[34]

Berle, in his loyalty to Rockefeller, was long past sensing any conflict of interest in advising a future opponent of the presidential candidate he was expecting would appoint him to a top-level job. Berle's only concern was for Nelson's political success.

Nelson eventually came to his senses and decided to defer discussing Berle's paper until after the campaign.[35] By December, the matter had been shunted over to the Rockefeller Foundation, which initiated a new program for young scholars in research on international relations.[36] And Berle had begun his new job as head of the president-elect's Task Force on Latin America.

Nixon had succumbed to the missile gap, the bomber gap, and, ultimately, the Cuba gap. Kennedy had pressed for tough measures against Cuba, expressing the same apprehension about communists "eight jet minutes from the coast of Florida" that Nelson had shown. Nixon, too, had called for surgery to remove the Castro "cancer" from the hemisphere "to prevent further Soviet penetration." Kennedy's staff, however, went further, issuing a statement calling for U.S. aid to Cuban "fighters of freedom."

Nixon again felt betrayed by Kennedy, never believing Allen Dulles's later claim that he had not briefed Kennedy on the plan for the Bay of Pigs invasion until after the election. Nixon was trapped by his knowledge of government secrets. He was not only aware of the coming CIA invasion, but he had had a hand in initiating it in 1959, and as de facto overseer of covert operations during 1960 had shifted the emphasis from the guerrilla campaign to a D-Day-type full-scale amphibious invasion.

Ultimately, however, it was Nixon's own indecisiveness and lack of commitment to enforcing the civil rights laws that brought him down. In the last three weeks of the campaign, as African American students demonstrated throughout the South, word flashed over the wires that Rev. Martin Luther King had been thrown into a Mississippi jail. Many feared for his life. While Nixon remained silent, Kennedy telephoned Coretta King to express his concern and support and had his campaign manager, brother Robert, wire Mississippi's governor urging King's release. Whether his motives were generous or self-serving, Kennedy had the courage to ignore the dire warnings of Southern white governors and defend what Nelson had said Nixon must defend if he wished to win the northern cities—civil rights. The African American vote gave Kennedy the slim margin he needed to win.

"I want to repeat my deep regret at the outcome of the elections," Nelson told reporters after the close election. "But I don't believe in post mortems."[37] Then he warned that "the party has got to get closer to the people." That was the road to power.

It was not, however, the means of exercising power. That, Nelson had learned early in his career, was best done without the knowledge of the people, with power centralized in a few hands.

The sweet irony for Nelson was that the defeat of his own party brought him closer to the citadel of power, the White House.

NELSON'S SECRET VICTORY

Within a month of Kennedy's election, some of Nelson's closest allies from the Special Group and the Rockefeller Brothers Fund's studies panels were meeting in the White House's Cabinet Room or heading key offices in the new administration. Swiftly and quietly, they began implementing many of the changes in government structure and policy that Nelson advocated.

This secret victory was the outcome of the young president-elect's administrative inexperience. Kennedy had spent the past five years running for office. He knew politicians, but not men who could run the government of a world power. He asked Robert Lovett, a former undersecretary of state and defense secretary in the Truman administration, for advice.

Kennedy firmly believed in the Establishment. He had no cause to doubt the wisdom of a man like Lovett, a power in the Democratic party. Lovett was the quintessential *consigliere* to the rich and powerful. He was also a trustee of the Rockefeller Foundation.

Lovett was not interested in heading the departments of State, Defense, or Treasury and turned down Kennedy's offer of each. He recommended Dean Rusk, the president of the Rockefeller Foundation, for secretary of state. On December 4, while attending a meeting of the Rockefeller Foundation's board, Rusk got a call from the president-elect. He was in Washington the next day.[38] He was soon joined by another Rockefeller Foundation trustee, Chester Bowles, as his undersecretary of state.

For the secretary of defense, Lovett recommended Robert McNamara, the recently appointed president of the Ford Motor Company and a former systems analyst of strategic bombing during World War II. McNamara's deputy secretary would be another trusted Rockefeller aviation associate, former Air Force Undersecretary Roswell Gilpatric.

For the secretary of the treasury, Lovett suggested C. Douglas Dillon, a Rockefeller business partner in the Congo and a scion of the Dillon Read investment bank. Dillon was also a Rockefeller Foundation trustee.

High Kennedy Appointments from the Rockefeller Network

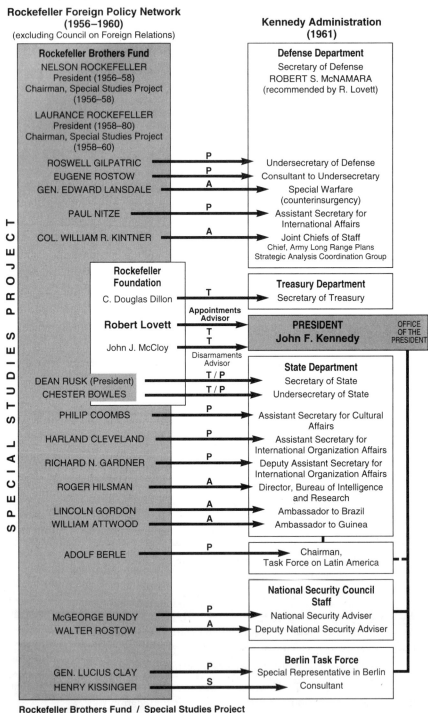

**Rockefeller Foreign Policy Network
(1956–1960)**
(excluding Council on Foreign Relations)

**Kennedy Administration
(1961)**

SPECIAL STUDIES PROJECT

Rockefeller Brothers Fund

NELSON ROCKEFELLER
President (1956–58)
Chairman, Special Studies Project
(1956–58)

LAURANCE ROCKEFELLER
President (1958–80)
Chairman, Special Studies Project
(1958–60)

ROSWELL GILPATRIC — P →
EUGENE ROSTOW — P →
GEN. EDWARD LANSDALE — A →

PAUL NITZE — P →

COL. WILLIAM R. KINTNER — A →

Defense Department

Secretary of Defense
ROBERT S. McNAMARA
(recommended by R. Lovett)

Undersecretary of Defense
Consultant to Undersecretary
Special Warfare
(counterinsurgency)
Assistant Secretary for
International Affairs
Joint Chiefs of Staff
Chief, Army Long Range Plans
Strategic Analysis Coordination Group

**Rockefeller
Foundation**

C. Douglas Dillon — T →

Robert Lovett — Appointments Advisor
— T →
John J. McCloy — T →
— Disarmaments Advisor

Treasury Department
Secretary of Treasury

**PRESIDENT
John F. Kennedy** — OFFICE OF THE PRESIDENT

DEAN RUSK (President) — T / P →
CHESTER BOWLES — T / P →

PHILIP COOMBS — P →

HARLAND CLEVELAND — P →

RICHARD N. GARDNER — P →

ROGER HILSMAN — A →

LINCOLN GORDON — A →
WILLIAM ATTWOOD — A →

ADOLF BERLE — P →

State Department
Secretary of State
Undersecretary of State

Assistant Secretary for Cultural
Affairs
Assistant Secretary for
International Organization Affairs
Deputy Assistant Secretary for
International Organization Affairs
Director, Bureau of Intelligence
and Research
Ambassador to Brazil
Ambassador to Guinea

Chairman,
Task Force on Latin America

**National Security Council
Staff**

McGEORGE BUNDY — P →
WALTER ROSTOW — A →

National Security Adviser
Deputy National Security Adviser

Berlin Task Force

GEN. LUCIUS CLAY — P →
HENRY KISSINGER — S →

Special Representative in Berlin
Consultant

Rockefeller Brothers Fund / Special Studies Project
P Panel members   **S** Staff   **A** Advisers

Rockefeller Foundation
T Trustees

Harvard's dean of the Faculty of Arts and Sciences, McGeorge Bundy, a member of the Rockefeller Brothers Fund's Special Studies panel, became special assistant to the president for national security affairs. Bundy shaped the NSC into the administration's major initiator of action on foreign policy. In doing so, he enhanced the powers of the presidential assistant for national security affairs along the lines originally proposed in 1955 by Nelson Rockefeller.

This change left Kennedy relying on Bundy for information on covert operations by intelligence agencies of the Pentagon and the CIA. And Bundy, in turn, relied on the CIA, where his brother Bill had worked before moving over to the Department of Defense to help Walt Rostow in "counterinsurgency planning."

With an allied covert-operations network inside the Defense Department and the CIA, Bundy's staff soon became a hidden government, accountable only to the president and unaccountable to Congress or the American people, a harbinger of Colonel Oliver North's operation twenty years later.

Eugene G. Fubini, another Rockefeller associate, became a top official in the National Security Agency (NSA), the Pentagon's supersecret electronics eavesdropper. Fubini was a vice president of Airborne Instruments Laboratory, a company controlled by Laurance Rockefeller that helped originate the "missile gap" thesis. In 1963, Fubini would be put in charge of the NSA as assistant secretary of defense.

Kenneth Holland, yet another Rockefeller associate, was also placed in the Kennedy foreign policy network. Holland had been Nelson Rockefeller's CIAA educational director during World War II and then headed CIAA's spin-off, the Inter-American Educational Foundation. He was appointed to the president's Task Force on International Education and the Task Force on Education of the Organization of American States. Holland was now president of the Institute of International Education, a conduit for CIA funds, including those used to sponsor young Africans who were identified by the African American Institute (now headed by David Rockefeller's closest aide, Dana Creel) as promising alternatives to the militant, anticolonialists symbolized by the former Belgian Congo's first premier, Patrice Lumumba.

KENNEDY'S BAPTISM BY BLOOD

On November 27, 1960, Patrice Lumumba, his family, and loyal government officials slipped away from their home in Leopoldville and drove into the African night. Lumumba had just been deposed as prime minister of the Congo in a CIA-backed coup. Threatened by the new ruler, Colonel Joseph Mobutu, he had only one hope: to try to reach safety in the friendly providence of Kivu, far to the east. It was a slim hope.

Mobutu's troops, assisted by the CIA in setting up road blocks,[39] caught up with Lumumba's caravan in Kivu. Since U.N. troops in the area had decided not to intervene, Lumumba and two of his colleagues were delivered to the Belgian-controlled Tshombe regime in Katanga.

Rockefeller Foundation trustee Ralph Bunche, working on behalf of the United Nations in the summer of 1959, had negotiated an agreement that U.S. forces were to share control with Belgian troops over the airport of Katanga's capital, Elizabethville. But when the Air Congo DC-4 carrying Lumumba arrived, the European-manned control tower merely telephoned the Belgian chief staff officer of the Katangese police, relaying the pilot's message that "three big packages" had arrived. In full view of U.N. officials, Lumumba and his companions were thrown out of the plane, beaten by Katangese soldiers commanded by Belgian officers, and trucked in a military convoy to a secluded house. There they were murdered.

Two months later, in March 1961, a small airplane hovered over the same Elizabethville airport and then floated down on unusually wide wings. From the cockpit emerged Larry Montgomery. The superintendent of SIL's missionary air fleet (JAARS) was now also a pioneer of the CIA-inspired advance of Helio Couriers into Africa.

The Helio Corporation originally had planned to enter the Third World via India, but as Helio president Lynn Bollinger later reported, "U.S. governmental officials with substantial international responsibilities" urged him to give Africa his top priority.[40] Since the CIA was then one of Helio's largest potential buyers and a secret backer, the agency's request could hardly be refused.

Early in 1961, Montgomery was recruited to fly a CIA-owned Helio Courier to Africa for demonstrations to local governments.[41] Bollinger had known Montgomery well. SIL purchased Helio Couriers for JAARS and, on at least one occasion, helped Bollinger sell four Couriers[42] to the Peruvian air force. Now it was the CIA who took up Montgomery's services, paying him $1,000 per month as salary and using Bollinger's Helio Corporation spin-off, General Aircraft, as a conduit.[43]

Montgomery had not resigned as JAARS's top pilot; instead, he took an unpaid leave of absence while serving on the CIA's payroll.*

The Elizabethville Larry Montgomery found was haunted by the CIA. Seven

---

*Cam's biographers explained Montgomery's new assignment by claiming that "his support had been dropping," with Cam noting regretfully that "I don't blame him for asking for a leave. But it's a hard blow when a partner, on whom you've depended for years, leaves you." Quoted in James Hefley and Marti Hefley, *Uncle Cam* (Waco, Tex.: Word Books, 1974), p. 223.

According to this 1971 account, Cam learned of Montgomery's desire to work for Helio sometime after May 1961, when Cam returned to Peru from his visit to Brazil. Thus when Montgomery first flew to Katanga in March 1961, he was still officially serving as JAARS's chief pilot even though he was on the CIA's payroll. However, in 1977, a year after the CIA's involvement with missionaries and its plot to murder Lumumba became public knowledge through U.S. Senate hearings, JAARS's attorney sought to dispel the impression of overlapping ties. He claimed that Montgomery took his leave at least three months earlier, on February 27, 1961. Whichever the case, Montgomery would remain JAARS's superintendent and chief pilot (on leave) for well over another year, not officially resigning until March 15, 1962.

Seas Airlines, a CIA proprietary airline, was making regular landings, bringing in badly needed supplies to Katanga from Europe, including fuel that Montgomery used for his own Courier. The Courier's maintenance at the airport was done by a CIA officer. The CIA had provided the Courier so that Montgomery could demonstrate its remarkable bush-warfare capacities to Katanga's Moise Tshombe and Interior Minister Godefroid Munongo, the officials responsible for Lumumba's murder.* What the CIA got in return was the placing of one of their airplanes, Montgomery's Courier, under a civilian cover (General Aircraft) in Katanga. They also got a CIA officer, Malcolm "Mac" Heckathorne, under cover as Montgomery's fellow General Aviation employee.

Heckathorne turned out to be a terrible embarrassment for Bollinger. His mercurial temper and cruel penchant for jokes at the expense of Africans, insulting them in public restaurants and once threatening a waiter with a loaded pistol, drew attention—and anger. His involvement with pilots of Seven Seas Airlines soon branded Heckathorne—and General Aircraft—as CIA. By the time Montgomery flew Heckathorne to Ethiopia allegedly as part of General Aircraft's marketing, their reputation had preceded them. African U.N. troops stationed at Addis Ababa's airport searched and impounded their Courier. Montgomery and Heckathorne were kept prisoners for three days before being expelled with the Courier.

Trips to other East African capitals produced less spectacular but similar results. No one was buying. Bollinger's dream of using Washington to establish an African market for Couriers had turned into a nightmare: The CIA affiliation made General Aircraft politically untouchable.

Still, despite these commercial failures, Montgomery continued to use the notorious Katanga province as his base of operations in Africa. He remained with Heckathorne, even after he found him snapping pictures of company documents with a miniature camera.† Together, they visited Moise Tshombe. Montgomery struck up a warm personal friendship with the dictator, a closeness he would speak proudly of for years.⁴⁴ But by August Tshombe's days were numbered. The Kennedy administration was keeping a close watch on the newly independent African governments and their sensitivity to issues of national sovereignty. The administration concluded that it had no choice but to pressure its NATO allies to abandon

*The United Nations Commission of Inquiry placed the blame on Katanga officials Tshombe, Munongo, and Jean-Baptiste Kibwe, Tshombe's finance minister. Reports differ as to who actually executed Lumumba; one report had Munongo knifing Lumumba, followed by a coup de grâce bullet to the head by a Belgian mercenary. Other reports named other Belgian mercenaries at the scene. One U.N. official, Conor Cruise O'Brien, later wrote that it was common belief in Elizabethville that Munongo was believed to have been the most directly responsible for the murders. See O'Brien's *To Katanga and Back: A U.N. Case History* (New York: Grosset & Dunlap, 1962), p. 129.

†Whether or not Montgomery knew at that time that he was working for the CIA is unknown. He has denied knowing that Heckathorne was with the CIA. His employer at the time, Helio president Lynn Bollinger, disputes his ignorance of this fact.

Belgium's secessionist Katanga and back a new central government in Leopoldville. In that climate, Montgomery's presence in Katanga became untenable. Finally, in August, Bollinger ordered Montgomery to return to the United States.

Arriving home, Montgomery found his services immediately requested by SIL's Robert Schneider, Cam's top liaison with the government. Schneider wanted Montgomery's help for JAARS's own Helio Courier program, then gearing up for Brazil and Southeast Asia. "If I don't have to participate, I would prefer not to," Montgomery wrote Bollinger.[45] Bollinger obliged, sending Montgomery to Eglin Air Force Base in Florida on another Helio assignment.

Eglin was then exploding with activity. It was now the CIA's special air-warfare center, a massive CIA-directed operation using secret air force units. These same units were involved in support missions for the Bay of Pigs invasion. Montgomery's work at the base under a secret Helio contract with the air force was merely one cog in a vast clandestine machine directed by a few men in Washington. In just a little over a year, with the crashing of President Eisenhower's hopes for a successful summit and his eclipse by the rise of John F. Kennedy, these men finally had come to almost absolute power over the nation's de facto foreign policy.

And they had a use for missionaries.

In March 1961, Cameron Townsend's and Lynn Bollinger's names were circulating around the Pentagon among counterinsurgency experts. Bollinger had proposed using JAARS's Peruvian Amazon operation as a model for an expanded foreign-aid program in transportation and communications in Africa: "The JAARS service pattern makes a tremendous contribution," he noted in a memo to the International Cooperation Administration, "to the political stability and communication network which must exist as a foundation for the civilization of these tribal groups." Bollinger went on to describe Cameron Townsend.

Bollinger's memorandum was boosted in the Pentagon by a companion memorandum prepared by Colonel Fletcher Prouty, entitled "Project Eagle—A Plan for the Development of the Continent of Africa."

Prouty's scheme for development, although focusing exclusively on aviation, was ambitious. Prouty envisioned using the Military Air Transport Service (MATS) to link U.S. embassies across Africa. The MATS network would provide a continentwide framework for local governments to develop national and regional air transportation services. These services would include, of course, STOL (short take-off and landing) aircraft like the Helio Courier. "Because most of these countries have almost no road or railroad system, they have little national unity," he wrote. STOLs would enable government officials to travel more widely, incorporate local personnel into the maintenance network, and break down isolation. "It [Project Eagle] will also phase in airfield and air facilities development sufficient to accommodate larger aircraft." What kind? Commercial airlines. And military aircraft. Here was the final phase of the program: "the establishment of an Air Force. For most of these countries an Air Transport Service sufficient to meet troop carrier and perhaps paratroop requirements should be adequate to assure internal security."[46]

If Prouty's proposal had only envisioned U.S. control over an entire continent's future transportation and communication, it would have been audacious. But that was just part of a grand theory of economic and political development formulated most articulately by a member of the Rockefeller Brothers Special Studies Panel, Walt Whitman Rostow.

It was Rostow who had come up with Kennedy's campaign phrase, "Let's get the country moving again." Having followed McGeorge Bundy to the White House as his deputy, Rostow was also author of the administration's bible on Third World national developments, *The Stages of Economic Growth*. He made counterinsurgency seem profound, reasonable, and eminently just. Prouty's Project Eagle fit right in to the holy war against insurgents. The idea was to prevent them from interfering with the "nation-building" process of economic development offered by Berle's Modern American Corporation and its "People's Capitalism."

Prouty and Bollinger's proposals went directly to the NSC's Special Group. There was a certain historical continuity, therefore, in the fact that the man who authorized their distribution was Edward Lansdale, Nelson Rockefeller's clandestine associate in Southeast Asian propaganda activities. Lansdale was Prouty's new superior.

Actually, he and Prouty were assigned to the new counterinsurgency office headed up by the Defense Department's representative to the Special Group, Deputy Secretary Roswell Gilpatric, one of the twenty-six men on the Rockefeller Brothers Fund panels who took top positions in the Kennedy administration.[47]

Beyond Rostow, Gilpatric, and other members of the Special Group, there was no one to advise the young president on the wisdom and efficacy of such covert operations as the Bay of Pigs invasion, the CIA's secret war in Indochina, Project Eagle, or Lumumba's murder.

According to members of his staff, news of Lumumba's murder stunned Kennedy. He did not know that the CIA had plotted for Lumumba's death or that Treasury Secretary C. Douglas Dillon had been involved in the decision to get rid of him.

Ignorant of these machinations, the new president, faced with rapidly evolving insurgences in the Third World, decided to focus on Cuba, where, during the campaign, he had pledged to do something about communism. But he was growing apprehensive about the CIA's invasion plan. The CIA's February offensive against a new military regime in Laos had broken up under fire on the Plain of Jars, and the CIA's secret army had been smashed.

Could the CIA also be wrong about the Cuban operation?

V

THE DAY OF THE WATCHMAN

The godly man has perished from the earth, and there is none upright among men; they all lie in wait for blood, and each hunts his brother with a net. Their hands are upon what is evil, to do it diligently; the prince and the judge ask for a bribe, and the great man utters the evil desire of his soul; thus they weave it together. The best of them is like a brier, the most upright of them a thorn hedge. The day of their watchmen, of their punishment, has come; now their confusion is at hand.

—MICAH 7:2–4

24

DEADLY INHERITANCE

LINING UP THE HEMISPHERE

On March 28, 1961, John F. Kennedy, looking tired and anxious, emerged from a war-plans briefing in the White House's ultrasecure Joint War Room. He was troubled by the many fronts on which he was expected to fight: Berlin, Laos, Vietnam, Cuba—hot spots in a broader Cold War being fought across most of Europe, Africa, Asia, and Latin America. What was left? The next day Kennedy expressed his worry that the CIA's planned invasion of Cuba might kill the chance for a settlement with the Soviet Union on Laos. He also worried about the invasion's "noise level"; the whole operation was clandestine in name only.

"Do you really have to have the air strikes?" he asked CIA's Richard Bissell, the mastermind of the invasion. Would there really be enough Cubans in the expected uprising? Could not the exiles' leadership be broadened to include members of the Left opposition who might attract more of a following?

To reduce the noise level, Kennedy insisted on moving the invasion site from heavily populated Trinidad Beach, just south of the Escambray Mountains, where anti-Castro guerrillas still operated. "This is too much like a World War II invasion," he protested.[1] Assistant Secretary of State Thomas Mann concurred, but in a way that made eyebrows rise. Noting that he was "gravely concerned" and "exhausted," Mann angled himself out of responsibilities by taking the ambassador's post in Mexico. The CIA's Richard Helms, meanwhile, was reprimanded by his boss, Allen Dulles, for protesting against the conventional amphibious nature of the invasion, now moved east to the more remote Bay of Pigs, a site not exactly optimal for CIA propaganda purposes, as Guatemala coup veteran David Atlee

Phillips grimly noted. Helms took it upon himself to advise his friends not to get enmeshed in Bissell's plans. Bissell, the orchestrator of the CIA's coup in Guatemala seven years earlier, needed another success in Cuba if he was to succeed Dulles as CIA director; Kennedy had intimated to Undersecretary of State Chester Bowles that he planned to appoint Bissell in July, only three months after the expected victory over Castro.

As Operation Zapata's D-Day thundered over the horizon, Kennedy grew more apprehensive. A critical Helms-inspired report complained about the stifling way Bissell had organized the project. The report had originated in the State Department.[2] Kennedy, faced with conflicts between the State Department and the CIA and within the CIA itself, was at best confused, at worst, seriously uninformed. There was much that the CIA did not tell him: That Colonel J. C. King, though a CIA officer, had offered $50,000 to the Mafia's John Roselli and Santos Trafficante to have a Cuban agent poison Castro, that a colleague of King had set up another "Executive Action" capability, and that the arms drops to the Cuban resistance promised by Bissell had been failing for months.[3]

Adolf Berle, witnessing Kennedy's anguish, was sympathetic. Yet, despite his long experience in intelligence matters since setting up the State Department's Bureau of Intelligence and Research during the Roosevelt years, Berle tried to steer the president toward invasion. Berle had been influenced by the opinion of his chief CIA contact, Colonel King, "that much of Latin America is lost: the combination of hotheads with quietly organized Communists waiting to take over may be invincible." To avoid "a growing catastrophe in foreign affairs," Berle concluded that the United States should "behave like a great power" and "defend the hemisphere" not only with the Marshall Plan for Latin America that he had championed in the past, but with military interventions he had earlier approached with some trepidation.[4]

Berle extended his prescription for the ailing United States—a vigorous flexing of muscles—to the needs of his own career. He had not agreed to become chief of the Latin America Task Force in order to be powerless. Before the inauguration, he had met with Dean Rusk at the Rockefeller Foundation and turned down offers of the ambassadorship to the Organization of American States (OAS) and White House special assistant. "Extraneous jobs, however bespangled with titles, didn't do the job," he noted, "and no one knows that better than Latin America. Nelson Rockefeller had that job and it didn't work."[5]

He knew what had happened to Nelson as Coordinator of Inter-American Affairs during World War II and special assistant under Eisenhower; although he would enjoy access to the president, real power over foreign policy would remain institutionalized within the State Department.

Berle therefore pressed Kennedy to upgrade Latin American affairs to the subcabinet level of an undersecretary of state. Kennedy, however, did not want

Latin America to upstage other continents, particularly Africa, where matters were sensitive enough. The Latin America Task Force, appointed by the president but formally stationed in the State Department, was the compromise. As the invasion plans were stepped up, the president had turned increasingly to Berle for advice. Berle, as a living symbol of the administration's continuity of Roosevelt's Good Neighbor Policy, could provide the personal touch in lining up hemispheric support for the invasion. It was the kind of mission Berle liked best. A great believer in the power of his own personality, Berle leaped at the chance to display his diplomatic skills. Considering the crisis he believed the United States was in, a successful tour of old haunts would be his greatest challenge, requiring him to draw upon all his diplomatic experience and the network of friendships with the powerful that he had so carefully cultivated over forty years. It could have been his greatest triumph; instead, it became his Waterloo.

After asking Colonel King for information on "anything communist" in the background of Venezuela's Rómulo Betancourt, Berle flew to Caracas in February to talk to the ex-radical, now the president of Venezuela. Betancourt was easy to convince. He needed money to rehire 300,000 men who were recently laid off from public works projects. He offered arms and the Venezuelan navy for action against Cuba. Berle, in turn, offered to handle his requests for money.[6]

Colombian president Alberto Lleras Camargo had a more pressing shopping list. For years he had been worried about the peasant "red republics" of Marquetalia, Sumapaz, and El Pato that had been set up along the valleys and hills running northeast between Cali and Bogotá. Armed refugees of the decade-long *La Violencia* civil war had retained the lands they had moved onto, set up municipal governments, and been able to turn their territory into experimental "peasant republics" that challenged the legitimacy of the central regime in Bogotá.

The Eisenhower administration had secretly sent a team of antiguerrilla warfare experts to Colombia. This CIA-Pentagon Survey Team, all veterans of similar programs in areas such as the Philippines and Vietnam, advised Lleras Camargo to develop an antiguerrilla force and "establish effective intelligence and information services" and propaganda operations "to restore popular confidence in the Armed Forces."[7]

But the State Department worried how it could justify giving military aid to attack the peasant republics when such aid was specifically prohibited by law. In an attempt to curtail U.S. support for dictatorships or taking sides in civil wars, the Morse Amendment to the Mutual Securities Act prohibited the United States from granting aid to Latin American countries for internal security purposes. The republics could be denigrated as "outlaw guerrilla bands," but unless some tie was made to the Soviet Union, the United States could not invoke the Monroe Doctrine or the Act of Chapultepec, especially when even the diplomats at Foggy Bottom admitted that "the remaining guerrilla bands cannot be said as a whole to be Communist controlled."[8] The only solution was for the president to issue a secret "determination" with operations monitored not by Congress, but by Nelson's legacy to the White House, the National Security Council's Special Group.

Cuba's turn to the Soviets for aid provided a solution for both Washington and Bogotá. When Berle arrived in Bogotá to line up support for U.S. policy against Cuba, Lleras Camargo was ready with a quid pro quo. He wanted small arms and helicopter gunships, as well as some practical U.S. help. Berle noted from his conversation with Lleras Camargo:

> The danger to Colombia is not, he said, formal invasion but guerrilla attacks. . . . We talked of the enclave cities—the bandit-held towns. . . . It was a situation wide open for Communist infiltration—easy from the Cuban side—and he [Camargo] was worried. . . . His army was being trained by the American mission to study the invasion on the Normandy Beach, but this had nothing whatever to do with meeting bandits in the high hills.[9]

Berle left Colombia with the impression that "if we had to confront the [Cuban] situation," Lleras Camargo could be counted on for at least sympathy. "But he said he was in no position to head a movement to deal with the situation—if the OAS would go along, or a consultation of foreign ministers evidenced substantial support, something could be done." This would depend on Brazil, where President Quadros was "a mystery."

The Brazilian Cog

Brazil should have been Berle's strongest card in this diplomatic game. In no other country besides his own did Berle feel more at home. He moved easily through the Brazilian businessmen's network that Nelson Rockefeller had organized into joint Brazilian-American advisory councils. He depended on his friends. They had served him well in past confrontations with independent-minded nationalists like former president Getúlio Vargas. He had always won, and he expected he would win now, too.

Berle showed up at the Brazilian Foreign Ministry, initiating discussions in a now-familiar pattern: first money, then Cuba. The new foreign minister had his own shopping list ready in the form of a memorandum of what he needed, which was considerable. Berle moved on to the Caribbean crisis. "I made the same presentation I had in Colombia and Venezuela," Berle said, adding local punch with the claim that "much of Uruguay had become Communist and was about to take over Paraguay." But Brazil was not flushed out by Berle's claim of a threat on its border. "It really added up that they did not feel they wanted to do anything [about Cuba] though they were in agreement that something had to be done."[10]

Berle next met with Jânio Quadros, president of Brazil for only a few months, who had won the largest vote ever accorded a presidential candidate.

Berle later denied press reports that he and Quadros quarreled during their meeting, but he noted in his diary that they "sparred a bit" at the beginning of their talks. Quadros was aware that most Brazilians wanted no part of the Cold War. A public opinion poll taken before Quadros took office reported that 63 percent of the Brazilians who were questioned favored neutrality. Over 83 percent of the legislators who were questioned in another poll at that time favored increased trade with the Soviets. Moreover, Quadros did not share most American investors' enthusiasm for the Kubitschek years. Quadros "said he had inherited Brazil in a shocking condition; the government was insolvent. Worse, it was demoralized. There was corruption everywhere you looked. . . . He was prepared to sacrifice everything to get this situation turned around.[11] But he wanted U.S. financing without the political tar of lining up behind U.S. foreign policy to Cuba.

Berle later said he offered $100 million in loans. Ambassador John Moors Cabot, who was present at the meeting with Quadros, reportedly said that the offer actually went as high as $300 million; he even termed it a "bribe."[12]

Quadros rejected it all and begged off from signing up against Cuba, claiming that the Brazilian Left "could put on an opposition which would paralyze his government. He therefore could not do very much," Berle recorded. "I said that I hoped we could count on his sympathy." According to Berle, Quadros pledged cooperation, said he was sending banker Walther Moreira Salles to Washington "to break ground" on aid, and bade his Americans farewell "on the most friendly terms."[13] But when Berle went to the airport, he went alone, without the customary send-off by Brazilian officials.

Berle arrived in New York in time to catch headlines in the *New York Times* announcing that Brazil had invited Yugoslav Communist leader Josip Tito to visit, hinting of a neutral foreign policy in the making. Moreira Salles arrived for a meeting, and Berle resolved to help him with the State Department. Then rumors that Berle had had a row with Quadros also hit the news. All the bad press about Brazil began to get to him.

A month later, Berle, eager to tell Kennedy his overall judgment on whether the invasion should proceed, took the step that would end his career. The CIA had abandoned the "noisy" heavily populated Trinidad invasion site in Cuba and delayed the attack until the Bay of Pigs was selected from 70,000 feet of film from U-2 flights. Everything was set to go. Berle said to the president, "Let 'er rip!"[14]

Betrayal at Bay

President Kennedy gave the final go-ahead for the Bay of Pigs invasion after being convinced by U.S. Marine Corps Colonel Jack Hawkins and the CIA's Richard Bissell that "the exiled brigade did not expect U.S. armed forces support."

"The Castro regime," they further assured him, "is steadily losing popularity . . . the Cuban army has been successfully penetrated . . . it will not fight in a showdown."[15]

Kennedy's approval included the fateful proviso that the CIA's first air strike against Castro's air force must be with a "minimal" number of planes. Bissell did more than offer the president reassurances. He reduced the invasion's air force, from sixteen to an inadequate six planes. Colonel Stan Beerli, the CIA air operations chief who had overseen the CIA's use of Helio Couriers in Cuba and Montgomery's mission in the Congo, telexed the targets, selected from U-2 photographs, to Nicaragua.

On April 17, 1961, these six specially modified, heavily armed B-26s, flown over from Puerto Cabezas on Nicaragua's Atlantic coast with Somoza's blessing and personal send-off, bombed and strafed Cuban military airfields. But they failed to knock out some of Castro's rocket-firing Sea Furies and the T-33 jet trainers stationed at another air base near Santiago. The element of surprise was now lost. Meanwhile, the ruse of a Cuban exile pilot flying a B-26 into Miami Airport posing as a Cuban air force defector was quickly exposed. His plane had a steel nose; all Castro's planes had plastic noses. U.N. Ambassador Adlai Stevenson, tricked into using a picture of the plane released from Washington as proof that the United States was not involved, had claimed that the raid on Cuban airfields was by defectors from the Cuban air force; now he began to worry about his own credibility. Stevenson's worrying, in turn, caused Kennedy to worry about *his* credibility. On Rusk's suggestion, he canceled the CIA's second air strike until a beachhead could be secured and the local airstrip taken, so that it could at least appear to be the launch site for the B-26 raids, unless "overriding circumstances" developed.

The fact that Castro with his jets still had air superiority over the invasion force was just such an overriding circumstance. The B-26s were supposed to bomb and strafe any of Castro's ground forces that attempted to use the causeways to reach the beaches of the Bay of Pigs. The success of the invasion hinged on taking out Castro's jets.

CIA Deputy Director Charles Cabell, suddenly taking responsibility for the prestigious operation while Director Allen Dulles was in Puerto Rico, shared his anguish with invasion planner Richard Bissell. Despite protests from CIA operations officers, Cabell had waited too long to get the president's authorization to send the first air strike from Nicaragua to hit Castro's plans *before* the invasion brigade was to reach the beaches of the Bay of Pigs at dawn. Cabell, known more for grunts than articulation, also made the bad decision of channeling the CIA's protests over the invasion's inadequate air support through Secretary of State Dean Rusk. If Cabell was grandstanding, as some claimed, it backfired. Rusk was known more for being a good listener and consensus reporter than for moving quickly into action. Now, with the first raid having failed and Cabell asking for the second raid, Rusk called Kennedy's weekend Virginia estate, Glen Ora, and reported the CIA's protests to the president. "But I am still recommending in view of what is going on [at the United Nations] in New York that we cancel," Rusk advised Kennedy. Cabell, also not known for making waves, shrugged off Rusk's offer that he state his case directly to the president over the phone; he knew that Kennedy did not like him. Bissell, whom Kennedy did like, wondered if the president was aware that he, too, was worried. But he let the matter pass.

The military were aghast when they were informed of the canceled second strike. Their reactions ranged from "criminally negligent" to "absolutely reprehensible, almost criminal." J. C. King, the CIA's chief of Western Hemisphere Operations, had been bypassed. The old spy watched from the sidelines as Bissell, having gotten the Cuban exiles into a jam, expected Kennedy to bail them out with U.S. armed forces.

Kennedy was awakened sometime after 4 A.M. on April 18, by the CIA's request for direct U.S. intervention. The Agency had expected that the president, faced with the fait accompli of an inadequately equipped invasion force, would acquiesce. But Kennedy refused. He would not break his public pledge at a press conference to keep U.S. forces out of any invasion of Cuba. The CIA's covert operation was one thing. It had promised deniability. U.S. jets did not. World opinion did not agree with arguments by Cold War hardliners like Berle that Castro was just a Soviet puppet. Although he was a communist of some sort, international law on the sovereignty of nations fell on his side. Kennedy hoped that the CIA's own pledge to him that the Cuban people would arise, stripping Castro of his legitimacy as the leader of a popular revolution, would be fulfilled.

The CIA's pledge proved false. The Cuban armed forces did not revolt. In Cuba, unlike in Guatemala, the revolution had been against the army, not by it. It was not just government that had changed, but the old state apparatus. Batista's army, air force, judges, and police had been smashed by a popular armed revolution. The new state apparatus, including the local citizenry's 200,000-man militia that replaced it, was loyal to the new regime that had created it. As Naval Intelligence could have told Kennedy had they been asked, the Cuban people were more concerned about the poverty Batista had imposed than the political democracy that Washington now suddenly claimed it was willing to bring them.[16]

Unknown to Bissell's computers or King's rightist network, the impoverished local population at the Bay of Pigs had been helped by Castro's reforms. And unlike the U-2 cameras that hovered above and the CIA operatives who chose the Bay of Pigs, Fidel Castro knew every detail, every back road, every path of that area's terrain. The invaders' landing crafts were ripped apart by reefs the CIA did not know about. But Castro knew. It was his favorite fishing spot.

Pounded on the beaches by what remained of Castro's air force, members of the brigade watched their supplies sink with the ships that carried them into the Bay of Pigs. They also found themselves surrounded by swamps. The only routes out were by three causeways that Castro, personally leading his forces into battle, had already captured. News of the brigade's entrapment soon reached Washington and the Cuban exile community's Revolutionary Council in Miami. At the White House, the Pentagon and Bissell insisted that Kennedy should send in the air force. But he had warned them he would not engage in a direct U.S. military intervention, and he remained adamant. The option of turning the operation into a guerrilla action by escaping into the hills was mentioned. Only then did Kennedy learn from Bissell that "they were not prepared to go guerrilla."[17]

Kennedy kept his composure. Walt Rostow realized then that the president had not been given "a very good visual picture of the whole thing." No one had told him that the Escambray Mountains were too far away or that the brigade would be surrounded by impassable swamps. Faced with the gory details in dispatches from the beach and with news that the Revolutionary Council was in revolt, Kennedy finally acted. He believed that he had no choice but to order the *Essex,* hovering off the coast of Cuba, to send six jets to fly cover for another B-26 strike from Nicaragua. The jets were not to bomb ground targets and would have to fly without U.S. insignias. Plausible deniability was incredibly still in effect. Presidential Assistant Arthur Schlesinger worried that the restriction was "a somewhat tricky instruction." Rusk, on the other hand, backed the CIA and the Pentagon. The mission, he argued, required a deeper commitment.

Kennedy would be pushed in no deeper. "We're already in it up to here," he said with his hand raised to just below his nose.[18]

To calm the Cuban exile leaders, Kennedy sent for Berle. Berle had worked with Schlesinger in selecting the group of Cubans who were expected to take over the reins of "New Cuba" once Castro was overthrown. Kennedy did not know that Berle had pledged that 15,000 troops would back the invasion.[19] This pledge stood in direct contradiction to what Bissell had told the president, that no U.S. support was expected. The president was also unaware that King's original suggestion that Castro should be assassinated[20] had been included in the CIA's invasion plans.[21] Florida Mafia chieftain Santos Trafficante, who hoped to regain the gambling, narcotics, and prostitution rings he had created in Havana during the Batista regime, had given a top Cuban exile some of Dr. Sidney Gottlieb's poison pills for use at Castro's favorite restaurant at the same time as the invasion.[22] Castro was supposed to have been dead by now. But like so much the CIA planned for Cuba that year, this plan failed as well. Castro had stopped eating at the restaurant. Eventually, after the invasion failed, the exile leader had to return the $10,000 advance from the $50,000 King had allocated for a successful murder.[23]

Arriving at the White House, Berle encountered a wake in the Oval Office. Kennedy told him the bad news about the exiles' Revolutionary Council. "All are furious with CIA. They do not know how dismal things are. You must go down and talk to them."

Seeing that Berle needed shoring up himself, Kennedy turned to Schlesinger. "You ought to go with Berle," he said. Visibly upset, Kennedy abruptly left to walk alone and coatless on the White House grounds. Later, he told his brother Robert that he would have done more if he had known "what was going on."[24]

By the time Berle and Schlesinger arrived the next morning at the CIA's secret base at Opa-Locka, Florida, the six authorized U.S. Navy jets had lifted off from the *Essex* and flown to their scheduled rendezvous at the Bay of Pigs with the CIA's B-26s from Nicaragua. They found the B-26s not there, waited, then left. An hour later, the B-26s arrived, flown (without presidential authorization) by Alabama National Guard pilots recruited by the CIA. Lacking air cover for their bombing and strafing runs, four of them were quickly shot down by Cuban Sea Furies and antiaircraft fire. The others limped back to Nicaragua. Radio Havana announced that the downed American pilots were proof of U.S. involvement. Meanwhile, the brigade's ships had either been sunk or had fled to sea.

Berle found the Cuban exile leaders in tears and inconsolable. They were being held incommunicado and unconsulted by the CIA. "We don't know whether we are your allies or your prisoners." They begged for more pilots; if not, at least let them die on the beaches with the troops. Hearing of their despair from Schlesinger, Kennedy asked that the exile leaders be flown to the White House. He assured them of his resolve to remove Castro and expressed compassion for three of their sons in the brigade. Schlesinger believed that the Cubans were impressed with Kennedy's gracious performance—at least, *he* was.

After accepting full responsibility for the disaster at a press conference, Kennedy phoned retired Army General Maxwell Taylor, like Nelson Rockefeller, an advocate of "limited war," who was then serving as Laurance Rockefeller's successor as head of the Lincoln Center for the Performing Arts. Yes, Taylor told Kennedy, he could come to Washington to help. The president had admitted he was in "deep trouble," and Taylor always answered his commander in chief's call to duty.

In the Oval Office the next day, Taylor accepted Kennedy's appointment as chairman of a special commission to investigate the Bay of Pigs failure. Kennedy also appointed Allen Dulles; Admiral Arleigh Burke (who had advocated sending the air force to back the invasion); and his brother Robert, the attorney general. But everyone knew it would be Taylor's show.

Kennedy next phoned Eisenhower, Senator Barry Goldwater, and Governor Nelson Rockefeller.[25] Of the three, Rockefeller was the most powerful office holder in the opposition party. The president wanted him to understand what had gone wrong. Nelson pledged his public support during the crisis, but if Nelson shared the views of his own adviser, Henry Kissinger, he undoubtedly thought that Kennedy should have invaded Cuba with U.S. forces. Queried by his Harvard students when news arrived of the invasion, Kissinger had thought long. Then he said, "Well, as long as we're there, I don't think it would do us any good to lose."[26]

In these early months after the Bay of Pigs invasion, Kennedy was blaming the Eisenhower legacy, not the military-industrial complex or the "technological elite" that Eisenhower had warned about in his Farewell Address. Even before the Bay of Pigs, the president had planned to replace the aging sage of intelligence, Allen Dulles, with the less legendary and thus more controllable Richard Bissell. Now it looked like Bissell, too, would have to go, as well as those top advisers who had been so enthusiastic about the Bay of Pigs: the amiable chairman of the Joint Chiefs of Staff, General Lyman Lemnitzer, and the chief of the Latin America Task Force, Adolf Berle.

But not right away. The connection between the dismissals and the Bay of Pigs defeat should not be so obvious. A facade of confidence and stability was crucial.

THE RISE OF COUNTERINSURGENCY

On March 31, President Kennedy had given a speech designed, in part, to soften the blow of the impending Bay of Pigs invasion. He outlined a broadened Good Neighbor Policy called the Alliance for Progress. The Alliance pledged liberal economic, social, and political development for the hemisphere that went far beyond the noninterventionist theme of Roosevelt's Good Neighbor Policy. To head the Alliance, the next year Kennedy would appoint another former Rockefeller associate from the CIAA days, Puerto Rico's Teodoro Moscoso, who had overseen Operation Bootstrap as the island's devlopment undersecretary and then had served on Berle's Latin America Task Force and been Kennedy's first ambassador to Venezuela.

After the Bay of Pigs, J. C. King, who had the good fortune of not being directly responsible for the debacle, enjoyed a rebound in baronial power over covert operations in Latin America. But he feared it was only a temporary respite from creeping liberalism. Moreover, the CIA was viewed with unprecedented skepticism.

King liked right-wing liberals like Berle, who understood the blood and thunder behind the Cold War. He had little use for Harvard intellectuals like White House aides Richard Goodwin and Arthur Schlesinger, who were insisting on more liberal approaches to Latin America's mounting economic and social problems.* These do-gooders believed that U.S.-funded government planning was

---

*As a speechwriter during the 1960 Kennedy campaign, Goodwin had invaded King's turf, citing Latin America as proof of Republican incompetence. It was he who crafted the phrase *Alliance for Progress* to signal support for land reform and opposition to dictatorship. Goodwin's friend and fellow task force member, Robert Alexander of Rutgers, had gone so far as to point out American corporate ties to Argentina's Perón, Santo Domingo's Trujillo, and Venezuela's Pérez Jiménez in his book, *The Struggle for Democracy in Latin America.*

the key to Latin America's development, not simply the arbitrary decisions of private investment (particularly American investment). That kind of thinking was anathema to a former entrepreneur like King, who had opened Brazil's first condom factory and risen to become Johnson & Johnson's top executive in Brazil and Argentina.

King's people in the Western Hemisphere Division worried that these views on the CIA would gain ascendance in the aftermath of the Bay of Pigs. They were especially concerned that Cord Meyer's International Organizations Division in the CIA would throw its labor contacts behind the liberal approach. "I've told J.C. that his old crowd has let him down," a liberal-minded officer said. "The day is over when contact with the police chief can be called a CIA station in our area. We've given away all the important contacts with the new leadership group in every country to Cord's people. Now it looks like the White House will finish the job. If Cord Meyer and they get together on something like this proposal, they'll put old WH [Western Hemisphere] out of business."[27]

King decided he would rise to the challenge. The mysterious Western Hemisphere chief had left his mark on every administration since Truman's, and the Kennedy administration would be no exception.

At the same time, Kennedy's commitment to beefing up limited war capabilities deepened. The young president had mistaken Eisenhower's wisdom and restraint as the inertia of an old man who played too much golf. Eisenhower, questioning the viability of financing endless wars that being the world's policeman would entail, had resisted the military-industrial complex. Kennedy, lacking Eisenhower's experience, did not.

After the Bay of Pigs, Kennedy felt more vulnerable than ever from pressures from the right. He worried that "if there were another Bay of Pigs . . . the military would almost feel it was their patriotic obligation to stand ready to protect the integrity of the nation, and only God knows just what segment of democracy they would be defending if they overthrew the elected establishment."[28] Kennedy resented the CIA's efforts at the Bay of Pigs to manipulate him into launching a U.S. armed-forces attack against Cuba and toyed with the idea of breaking the CIA "into a thousand pieces." But he held off because of the lure of presidential covert operations. He settled for appointing his brother Robert to the Special Group as his watchdog.

These were the days of the "junior officers of the Second World War finally come to responsibility,"[29] as Walt Rostow's wife put it, young men who saw themselves as superior in substance and style to the New Deal's supposed sentimentalists. Their tough, pragmatic air would reign over the New Frontier until the missile crisis of October 1962. Then, when confronted by "preemptive first strike" recommendations from their own National Security Council (NSC) for a nuclear attack on the Soviet Union, the Kennedy brothers were jarred into concluding, as the president whispered to Bobby, "the military is mad." Until then, the NSC's Special Group had girded Camelot for an endless series of Armageddons in remote areas of the world, where the Forces of Darkness, it was feared, were busy turning peasants and tribesmen into communist guerrillas.

The importance of covert operations grew after the Bay of Pigs. And as it did, so did the influence of the new counterinsurgency office at the Pentagon. The office was headed by two close allies of Nelson Rockefeller, Deputy Defense Secretary Roswell Gilpatric and General Edward Lansdale.

Quietly and purposefully, Gilpatric emerged as the one member of the Special Group whose covert-operation capacities were enhanced, not diminished. In April, the first Green Beret teams were sent into the Central Highlands of Vietnam to teach Montagnard tribesmen, then learning to read and write from Wycliffe Bible Translators, how to blow up bridges and fire M-16 rifles.[30] More than 400 Green Berets were sent in, and Gilpatric wanted to send in 3,000 to 4,000 more U.S. personnel. Kennedy refused. He did agree, however, to send Green Beret teams to Ecuador and Guatemala to teach the local military how to defeat the hit-and-run tactics of revolutionary peasants who were living off the land.[31] The Green Berets' Special Forces Headquarters at Fort Bragg, North Carolina, were upgraded to a Special Warfare Center, and their mission was expanded beyond a guerrilla force modeled after OSS teams that had operated behind German lines during World War II; they now became a *counter*guerrilla force.[32]

This change meant a whole new kind of warfare. Instead of the traditional concentration of forces and armaments for a push through identifiable enemy lines, counterinsurgency warfare emphasized the use of small mobile units with light arms for decentralized search-and-destroy operations. By dividing a "hostile territory" into smaller sections, surrounding and quarantining the area, and then sending in units to make contact with enemy guerrillas and backing up these antiguerrilla units with heavily armed and concentrated air-mobile reinforcements, Gilpatric hoped to "clean out" sections, one by one. The purported goal of all these actions, of course, was to take people, not territory. "Body counts" of the enemy were to be complemented with Lansdale's projected victories over the minds and hearts of the people. Rescued from guerrilla terror, the grateful indigenous population was expected to be won over by Philippine-style limited land reform and "civic action" projects by the "native" army, government agencies, and voluntary civilian organizations—domestic and foreign.

MISSION: TOWARD GENOCIDE

Arthur Schlesinger would one day recall Kennedy entertaining his wife on country weekends "by inventing aphorisms in the manner of Mao's 'Guerrillas must move among the people as fish swim in the sea.'" By winning over the civilian population—or removing them to fenced-in "strategic hamlets"—allied governments could dam the flow of recruits. The Pentagon's social engineers hoped to dry up the seas, leaving the guerrillas deprived of supplies and cover. No one asked if Asia's vast human sea could be dammed like the Colorado River, and no one thought that the Vietnamese sea might prefer the local Communist Party's Ho Chi Minh to a good Catholic patriot like Diem or one of his pro-U.S. generals.

And no one in Camelot, apparently, thought to consider the implications of counterinsurgency warfare if they were wrong: If the indigenous people could not be won over, the stress on American troops would grow. The line between the enemy and the people, between those who were to be killed and those who were to be rescued, would fade. The "rules of engagement" would become intolerable; "free-fire" zones would become wider and more arbitrarily declared. No one at the State Department's Bureau of Intelligence, at the Pentagon, or at the Special Group dared to take the logic of counterinsurgency to its inevitable end: Unless the people were won over, there were really only two options—withdrawal or genocide.

No one conceived, much less admitted, these options, even as Fort Bragg's instructors summoned ghosts from the American Plains to reenact lessons from the Indian Wars. Then, too, the U.S. Army's cavalry had carried out highly mobile, lightly armed search-and-destroy missions. Then, too, missionaries served as both the well-intentioned vanguard of the coming conquest and later as cultural administrators of the precursor of the strategic hamlet, the reservation. And then, too, the result had been genocidal, notwithstanding survivors.

Nelson Rockefeller's former NSC aide, William Kintner, grasped the strategic meaning of civilian, including missionary, involvement in the new counterinsurgency. Kintner had moved up the ladder from merely advising Nelson on counterguerrilla strategy; now he implemented the new doctrine as chief of long-range planning for General Lemnitzer, the army chief of staff. He believed in incorporating religious organizations into counterinsurgency strategy.[33] Coincidentally, it was during this year that plans moved rapidly ahead for Wycliffe Bible Translators to build a JAARS air base only thirty-five minutes by air from Fort Bragg.

Wycliffe was the fastest growing missionary organization in the United States. In the glow of counterinsurgency planning radiating from Washington, William Cameron Townsend found troubled Latin America warming to his touch. Ecuador's President José María Velasco Ibarra, who at first criticized the Bay of Pigs and refused to condemn Castro, had triggered a CIA campaign to undermine his government.[34] He acquiesced to the demands of his generals to accept Washington's offer of Green Berets and to expel the Cuban ambassador. CIA agents in Ecuador's police circulated fake reports charging that guerrillas were being trained in secret sites throughout the country.[35] Pro-Castro Cubans, they charged, had been seen visiting "Auca" (Huaorani) Indian territory in the Ecuadorian Amazon.[36] Oil had been seen there, too, and two North American companies were asking for a 4.35 million hectare concession.[37] Velasco Ibarra now visited Rachel Saint, of the Summer Institute of Linguistics (SIL), and her Auca wards at SIL's Limoncocha jungle base, accompanied by Cam. The president stated that he was concerned about the Indians' welfare.

So was Brazilian president Jânio Quadros when Cam, escorted by Velasco's ambassador, visited Brasília in May. Cam thought that Quadros's concern for Indians was genuine. "I know the Terêna tribe," Quadros said when shown a Terêna language primer. "I lived near them as a boy."[38] Quadros endorsed Cam's requests for government assistance to SIL's work among nineteen Amazonian tribes.

Quadros, like his predecessors and like Velasco in Ecuador, was in favor of settling the Amazon and saw SIL as a pacifier of the Indians. But he had been disturbed by reports of invasions of Indian lands by settlers and of murders of Indians. Epidemics brought by road builders and colonists raged through the tribes. SPI's new military leaders seemed unable or unwilling to stop it. In April, Quadros had established legal boundaries for the first Indian land reserve in Brazil, the 21,600-square-kilometer Xingu National Park.

But unlike Ecuador's Velasco, Quadros was also fighting the prerogatives of American interests. He began an investigation into how Hanna Mining had gotten control of the iron-mining rights in Minas Gerais during the Kubitschek regime. He also broke his campaign pledge to move the administrative seat of Petrobrás to Bahia. According to Petrobrás's director of exploration, former Standard Oil geologist Walter Link, the only commercially feasible oil deposits in Brazil were in Bahia.[39] Instead, Petrobrás continued its search in the Amazon basin, keeping its headquarters in Rio; worse, it continued Brazil's growing tendency to swap Soviet crude for unsold Brazilian coffee and to buy Soviet crude for its refineries instead of Creole's Venezuelan oil. Finally, although Nelson's friend and business partner, Walther Moreira Salles, had worked out a financial deal with Chase and other banks to help Brazil pay its debt, Quadros's refusal to condemn Castro still angered Washington. "I think we are right in not letting Brazil go bankrupt irrespective of its current attitude in foreign affairs," Berle wrote. "It does not buy friendship. But Brazilian politicians can create enmity and this is what they are doing. If they cannot be helpful, they ought to quit."[40]

Quadros, hammered by criticism from the right, did just that. In August he made a series of political blunders. First, he introduced a bill to the Brazilian Congress that would tax all corporate earnings by 30 percent. According to this bill, American companies, whose exported profits were already taxed 20 percent, would face a 50 percent total tax on earnings sent back to the United States. Although this rate was far below what American companies then paid in U.S. income taxes at home, the tax won Quadros no new friends on Wall Street or in Washington.

Quadros added insult to injury by awarding Cuba's foreign minister, Ernesto

"Che" Guevara, the same Southern Cross medal that had been given to Rockefeller and Berle. Guevara had stopped in Brasília on his way home from the Inter-American Foreign Ministers Conference at Punta del Este, Uruguay. The conference became a turning point in relations between the North American business community and the Kennedy administration.

It was a turn for the worse.

Punta del Este: The Price of Disloyalty

For one week in August 1961, balmy Punta del Este captured the attention of the world by hosting two people whose very appearance symbolized the conflict between the conservative United States and revolutionary Cuba.

On one side stood the dignified, blue-eyed C. Douglas Dillon, in his blue pin-striped suit looking just like the Wall Street banker-turned-treasury-secretary he was. Facing him was the black-bereted Che Guevara, described by the U.S. ambassador to the OAS as "handsome, dashing in his olive green uniform with scarf tied ascot fashion," with "dark flashing eyes, distinctive black mutton chop beard and an infectious smile."[41] Dillon was surrounded by Washington diplomats and civilian-clothed security officers. Guevara wore combat boots and was accompanied by four comrades who had fought beside him in Cuba's mountains and served now as his bodyguards.

Guevara mocked Dillon's offer of $20 billion in U.S. aid for the Alliance for Progress over the next decade. It was the Cuban revolution, he maintained, not Kennedy's Alliance, that was the hallmark of the coming "new age" and the reason that Washington was offering this money. Suddenly, Guevara startled his audience by holding up classified documents taken from the car of U.S. Ambassador to Venezuela Teodoro Moscoso. The documents, he said, were evidence of the administration's duplicity. The papers showed that the United States had little confidence in Venezuela's agrarian reformers and technicians. Instead, it viewed the Betancourt government as "corrupt." Guevara called the United States "that monster of intervention" offering only "schemes to give latrines to the poor."[42] He invited the other Latin American delegates to reassemble in 1980 to compare Cuba's progress in meeting the needs of its people with that of the rest of Latin America. The Alliance for Progress was doomed, he claimed, by its ties to the "American imperialism" of American banks and corporations. Cuba agreed with many of the Alliance's goals, but would abstain rather than vote for a doomed program.

Guevara's challenge infuriated the American businessmen in attendance, a delegation already peeved by Kennedy's last-minute invitation for them to attend, and then only as observers.

The situation was more delicate for Kennedy. Berle's Latin American allies had warned Kennedy in March that the Alliance for Progress must not be seen as the spearhead for a new investment drive by American corporations. Only three days before the conference, Kennedy finally decided not to risk corporate ire. He had an aide call Nelson Rockefeller's cousin, IBEC Vice President Richard Aldrich, for help in organizing an "unofficial business delegation."[43]

Kennedy recognized the paramount role of the Rockefellers among American activities in Latin America, which is why he authorized Aldrich to select the American business delegation. Not surprisingly, the delegation was top-heavy with representatives of companies within the Rockefeller sphere of influence. These delegates were dismayed by the way Guevara stole the media's limelight. They were also put off by the unwillingness of the Latin American delegates to follow up on their offer to help formulate national-development proposals to the Inter-American Development Bank. Brazil's and Argentina's delegations were eager to talk, but not to bargain away their national sovereignty. Smaller nations like Ecuador simply lacked the technical skills required for nationwide developmental planning.

Even so wise a business hand as Dillon had underestimated the businessmen's negative reaction to Kennedy's late solicitation of their participation. He also had not appreciated fully their hostility to Kennedy's recent reversal of the Republican policy of giving aid only through private banks and companies. Kennedy now offered direct government-to-government aid. As Guevara predicted, they flatly rejected the administration's $20 billion goal for American private investment in the draft charter of the Alliance. The Cuban revolution meant that all bets were off. The businessmen wanted the U.S. government to guarantee their investments from expropriation or undercompensated nationalization. They also wanted guarantees from the Latin American governments that profits or royalties from the Latin American operations would be returned to the United States without currency-exchange restrictions. The businessmen left Punta del Este unsatisfied with the conference—and with Kennedy.

The Rockefellers had cause for alarm. They had lost much in Cuba to the revolution. David sat on the board of Punta Alegre Sugar Corporation, owner of plantations, mills, railroads, shipping ports, barges, and tugboats. Che Guevara had led an attack against Batista's forces near one of the company's key ports, Boca Grande, during the revolution. As minister of finance, Che later oversaw the company's expropriation after the Eisenhower administration (its foreign economic policy at the State Department being overseen by Undersecretary Dillon) imposed a cut in its quota for purchases of Cuban sugar. This cut, in turn, was triggered by the refusal of Standard Oil of New Jersey and other Dutch and American companies to refine low-priced oil that Cuba imported from the Soviet Union, in order to improve its balance of payments. Such outcomes of the Cuban revolution lent a personal, bitter quality to confrontations with Che at Punta del Este.

David Rockefeller's Chase Bank, of course, had long backed dictatorial reigns in Cuba, both Batista's and that of his predecessor, Gerardo Machado. When the revolution came, there went the value of notes issued by these regimes, one of the largest holders of which was Chase.

Finally—and for one Rockefeller, fatally—there were the holdings of Freeport Sulphur in Cuba, one of the largest and richest nickel deposits in all the world. On Freeport's board a number of Rockefeller allies and Rockefeller family members had sat.[44]

In 1959, on the heels of Cuba's new tax laws (which effectively nationalized the country's mineral resources, including Freeport's rich Nicaro deposits), Freeport had initiated a search for a new, equally lucrative investment. The company found it in Dutch New Guinea, unleashing a chain of events that brought personal tragedy into Nelson Rockefeller's life.

Copper Mountain

Don Gregory was worried. The tropical night sea had turned ugly. Wind lashed his face with water from the twenty-foot tide swelling the black waters beneath him. His small boat no longer obeyed its rudder and bounced helplessly to and fro atop the wave. Time was running out.

The tide would rush up along the banks of the Eilanden River and then reverse itself, pouring back down toward him at the river's mouth in a crashing wave. It was just such a wave that had swamped Michael Rockefeller's catamaran, stalling its outboard engines and pushing Rockefeller and his companions out into the vast Arafura Sea. This south coastland of Dutch New Guinea, Holland's last colonial possession in the South Pacific, was infamous for its treacherous waters.

The fuel gauge was low. Gregory informed the Dutch colonial policeman sitting at the other end of the boat. Both of them, hearing over the radio that Rockefeller's party was lost at sea, had grabbed a boat and took a tribesman along as a guide through the mangroved coastland. They were the first to search the area. Gregory hoped to be useful as an interpreter. He belonged to the Evangelical Alliance Mission, whose members received excellent linguistic training in Australia from SIL. He was studying the language of former headhunters who lived along the Asmat coast where Rockefeller would have to come ashore. But now, after hours of searching in the dark, it was getting too dangerous. "There's not much point in losing three more lives too," Gregory said to his companions.[45] He turned the boat around and headed for shore, leaving Michael Rockefeller to God.

At the other side of the globe, 10,000 miles away, Nelson Rockefeller was lunching with David at Pocantico, when the phone rang. Over a scratchy radio telephone transmission, Nelson heard a Dutch official garble the ominous news: Michael was missing at sea. That night, Nelson boarded a plane for the South Pacific with Michael's twin sister, Mary.

Of Nelson's three sons, his second—impetuous, adventuresome Michael—

was his favorite, probably because he most reminded Nelson of himself. Like Nelson when he was young, Michael had tried to please his father by working in various Rockefeller enterprises. He did his best at Nelson's vast ranch in Venezuela and at an IBEC-owned supermarket in Puerto Rico. But a taste of Latin America only whetted his appetite for adventure.

Like Nelson before him, Michael rebelled at the thought of entering the family business. He preferred to leave the great weight of family responsibilities to his more staid eldest brother Rodman, much as Nelson had left the burden of administering Junior's charities to his elder brother, John 3rd.

Michael, too, was probably unaware of the Rockefeller forces that shaped the circumstances of his own search for meaning and identity in Dutch New Guinea. His adventure in the South Pacific began a year after he graduated cum laude from Harvard. His interest peaked when his former Harvard roommate, photographer Sam Putnam, asked him if he would like to come as his assistant on the Peabody Museum's anthropological expedition. Michael did not hesitate. "It's the desire to do something romantic and adventurous," Michael explained to his father, "at a time when frontiers in the real sense of the word are disappearing."[46]

Nelson could not resist his son's request to join the expedition. Michael offered to collect tribal art in New Guinea for Nelson's new Museum of Primitive Art. It had been exactly thirty years before, while honeymooning in Asia, that Nelson had bought his first piece of primitive art on the island of Sumatra, then a Dutch East Indies colony. It was his first indulgence in what became a lifelong passion. Now his son, made a director of the Museum of Primitive Art, wanted to carry on the tradition.

To Westerners, New Guinea was like a gifted child pulled in opposite directions by covetous guardians. The Dutch clung to the western half as the sole remnant of their once-vast East Indies empire. Their longtime British allies, acting through Australia, controlled the eastern half. Neighboring Indonesians, on the other hand, thought that all New Guinea was part of their national territory, even if it was still colonized by Europeans.

In 1955, when nationalist Prime Minister Sukarno coined the term *Third World* at the first Conference of Non-Aligned Nations at Bandung, it was obvious that Indonesia, a mostly Muslim, Buddhist, and Hindu nation of almost 82 million people, would oppose the expansion of Western cultural influence not only in its own territory, but in nearby New Guinea.

In 1959, Freeport Sulphur, mindful of possible revenue losses from anticipated Cuban nickel expropriations, sent scientists to Amsterdam to blow the dust off a 1936 report on a rich copper outcrop found by a Royal Dutch Shell geologist deep in the central mountains of New Guinea, where Royal Dutch Shell and Standard Oil of New Jersey had joint exploration rights through a jointly held subsidiary. The Dutch were more than willing to assist. They had longstanding business ties to American financiers, including the Rockefellers. A team of American geologists went to Dutch New Guinea in 1960 to conduct a field survey. After consulting with evangelical missionaries about native traits, they plunged into the tribal highlands, traveling by dugout canoes and overland into the central highland's Baliem Valley and the Ertsberg, the "Copper Mountain" discovered a quarter century before. When they emerged, they happily conveyed their secret to

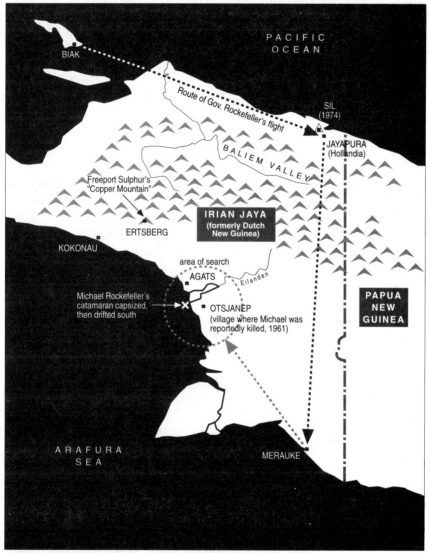

Copper Mountain and the Death of Michael Rockefeller

Sources: Forbes Wilson, *The Conquest of Copper Mountain*; Milt Machlin, *Search for Michael Rockefeller*; various contemporaneous news services.

Freeport's New York headquarters: They had discovered one of the world's richest deposits of copper, indeed a whole mountain of almost pure copper.

There was only one problem: The mountain tribes were stubbornly independent and protective of their lands. Likewise, the tribes along the remote coastland to the south had only recently been persuaded to give up head-hunting for religious ceremonies.

Ten years of Dutch missionary efforts to pacify the tribes had failed to eradicate older tribal gods as powerful symbols of an indigenous culture. More missionaries were needed, especially linguistically trained American ones. Such recruitment goals required greater public interest in New Guinea in the United States. To win acceptance by American academe, however, and to pave the way for massive injections of U.S. foreign aid, the Dutch needed more prestigious American social scientists in New Guinea.

To both Freeport Sulphur and the Dutch, that meant social scientists from Harvard.

COLLECTING DEATH

In the early 1960s, just before Freeport Sulphur's expedition got under way, the Dutch director of the Bureau of Native Affairs in New Guinea traveled to the United States to make the necessary arrangements. An experienced intelligence officer, Dr. Victor De Bruyn[47] knew that Dutch control over New Guinea was facing a challenge: Indonesian nationalism.

In New York, he advised Freeport's top geologist on how best to reach the Ertsberg Mountain with as little commotion as possible. Then he urged the Film Study Center at Harvard's Peabody Museum to mount an anthropological expedition to the Baliem Valley. The center's founder, thirty-five-year-old Robert Gardner, quickly mounted the expedition. To research New Guinea's tribes he traveled to the New York headquarters of the Christian and Missionary Alliance (C&MA), SIL's closest collaborators. C&MA's evangelical missionaries gave the unmistakable impression that the tribesmen were "deceitful and barbaric pagans, driven by the devil to loot and kill as they fancied."

Arriving with the Harvard expedition in New Guinea in March 1961, Michael dove into his work with gusto. He had no airs. His natural curiosity worked wonders with the children of the Kurulu tribe, who were eager to have this friendly white man try to explain the marvel of a wristwatch or the miracle of tape recordings. His scientific interest grew. He taped the tribesmen's strange means of making music by grinding their teeth with the same zeal he showed in recording their drums and war chants.

On a side trip to the Asmat, the southern coastal lowlands, in mid-August, he decried the violence done tribal psyches when the Euro-American economic hurricane ripped up the roots of an indigenous culture. "The Asmat is filled with a kind of tragedy," he wrote his parents,

> for many of the villages have reached the point where they are beginning to doubt their own culture and crave things Western. There is everywhere a depressing respect for white man's shirt and pants, no matter how tattered and dirty, even though these doubtful symbols of another world seem to hide a proud form and replace a far finer . . . form of dress. . . . Like every other corner of the world [the Asmat] is being sucked into a world economy and a world culture which insists on economic plenty as a primary ideal.[48]

But he also found himself being drawn into this very process of destruction after he discovered the power and beauty of the art of the Asmat tribes. The Asmat villages brimmed with treasures. Michael started collecting all he could, trading steel hatchets, which the Asmat tribesmen found most useful.

Asmat art became important to Michael because it was a bond between the world of his father, whom he revered, and his own world of aesthetics and science. In the end, he amassed one of the largest collections of Southwest Pacific primitive art in the world.

Michael decided to stay when the Harvard expedition ended in September. After a brief visit home, where he encountered the upsetting news of his parents' imminent divorce, he flew back to New Guinea and made preparations for a second trip to the coast, losing himself in his work.

There was a dark side to Michael's work, however. He collected beautifully painted human skulls, rare in recent years, since missionaries had persuaded the tribes to give up head-hunting. "A single axehead in some areas could buy the labor of a small village for a day," commented one investigator.[49] Michael was offering ten steel hatchets for each skull.

The Dutch authorities were aghast. They tried to warn him off because "he was creating a demand that could not be met without bloodshed."[50]

In two months, he had collected more than fifty pieces of Asmat art, including figurines, shields, and skulls. With two Papuan paddlers and a Dutch ethnologist who were collecting primitive art for Rotterdam's museum, Michael set out in a catamaran and headed through the Arafura Sea to barter for skulls and elaborately carved totemlike *bisj* poles in villages along the coast. His simple craft was fashioned out of two dugout canoes lashed together with a support deck and an eighteen-horsepower outboard motor. Dutch missionaries warned him that the Arafura was treacherous; the twenty-foot tides would surge seventy-five miles up the river's banks, rush back down, and collide with incoming tides, creating huge waves that overpowered the best Papuan oarsmen.

And that is what happened. A "rolling sea" swamped Michael's catamaran, stalling its engine and pushing the boat farther out to sea. The two Papuans swam toward shore for help. They alerted the colonial authorities, prompting the radio news that inspired missionary Don Gregory's futile effort to rescue Michael and the scratchy phone call that interrupted Nelson's lunch with David.

Michael's companion had been rescued. He had seen Michael alive twenty-four hours earlier, but only as a small speck in an angry sea, trying to reach the shore some three miles away. He saw Michael for half an hour, swimming for the shore. Then all he could see were three dots: Michael's hat and the two bright red gasoline cans he had been using as buoys.[51]

Michael's problem was that the tribe on that coast—the very tribe he hoped would save him—had a hatred of white men. Their war chief, Ajam, had sworn revenge for his kin who had been slain a few years before, when the Dutch military raided the coast in a punitive expedition that used submachine guns. In fact, the bisj poles, recorded by French filmmakers in *The Sky Above, the Mud Below*, were erected as *revenge* poles, their human figures appearing to be Europeans. In the film, Ajam is seen overseeing warriors carving the very poles that inspired Michael's visit to Otsjanep. Later, when Michael finally emerged from the sea after his long swim, he found not rescue, but death from Ajam's party. He was speared just below his left collarbone as he came ashore. He was still alive when taken upriver; killed with an axe; and, in the religious manner of cannibals seeking the strength of their victims, cooked with sago palm and eaten.[52]

A Shroud of Deceit

The Dutch governor dared not admit anything that would give credence to Indonesia's claim for Dutch New Guinea. Any mistreatment of native Papuans had to be covered up.

Nelson had cause to blame the Dutch. Despite Foreign Minister Luns's personal assurances, the Dutch had not ensured Michael's safety. They had appointed an ethnographer as Michael's escort, not a patrol officer. The ethnographer had offered no protection for Michael in an area known by Dutch authorities to be potentially dangerous because of the 1958 killings. Moreover, he did nothing to prevent Michael's fateful trade in human skulls and bisj poles.

Yet Nelson, in front of the press, had only praise for the Dutch colonial regime. Criticism would have given Indonesia's President Sukarno ammunition. And Nelson, like the Dutch, had every reason to avoid that.

Standard Oil had been drilling in Indonesia since 1914. Because of large oil fields, mineral resources, and vast rubber plantations, the 2,000-mile-long archipelago had been considered one of the great prizes of the Pacific theater of World War II. Sukarno's newly independent republic refused to grant any further concessions after 1948, and in 1960, two years after the CIA tried to overthrow him, he prohibited all exploration for oil by foreign companies.

The economic stakes were too high for Nelson to risk a personal vendetta against the Dutch officials for Michael's death. He would only have undermined Holland's argument that it had pacified the tribes of West New Guinea and was more qualified than Sukarno, the most outspoken proponent of Third World neutralism in the Cold War. Nelson showed exactly where he stood by staying at the Dutch district commissioner's home during his entire visit.

On their return trip to the United States, Nelson and daughter Mary found his sons Rodman and Steven, Steven's wife, Anne-Marie, and his brother David waiting at the airport. Turning to the reporters, Nelson quietly offered a brief eulogy to Michael. "Even as a little boy, he was always aware of people, their feelings, their thoughts. He always loved people, and was loved in turn."[53] Then he climbed into a waiting limousine and began the long, lonely drive to Pocantico through the night.

25

BUILDING THE WARFARE STATE

Pocantico's Arms Bazaar

Since leaving the Eisenhower White House, Nelson had emerged as the nation's leading advocate of bomb shelters. He had a massive $4 million bunker built in Albany that could allow 700 top officials to sit quietly through a minimum of two weeks of nuclear hell.[1] To lend the issue personal drama, he had a storeroom converted into a shelter under his home at Pocantico[2] and had other ones constructed in the basement of his Manhattan town house and his estate house in Washington, D.C. And he encouraged New York's families to build the $200 bargain-basement models advocated by Edward Teller, father of the H-bomb, by pushing tax exemptions in the legislature.

In the governor's mansion, his passion became macabre: He covered the walls of the red room with maps displaying nuclear bombs exploding in living color.[3] His pleadings for shelters became evangelical, whether with legislators or foreign leaders. "He talked to me about nothing but bomb shelters," complained India's Prime Minister Jawaharlal Nehru in 1960. "Why does he think I am interested in bomb shelters? He gave me a pamphlet on how to build my own shelter."[4]

President John F. Kennedy worried about this aspect of Nelson's politics, if only because it gave Nelson an entering wedge into the issue of national defense. Nelson's chairmanship of the Governors' Conference Committee on Civil Defense lent his maneuverings a troubling nonpartisan cover. Moreover, Nelson used this position to maintain old friendships at the Pentagon, where the efficacy of "lim-

ited" nuclear war had its supporters. Rockefeller, like Kissinger and other participants of the Rockefeller Brothers Fund Special Studies Project, accepted this efficacy; Kennedy did not.

It was hard enough for Kennedy to have as his political opponent a liberal,
urban-based multimillionaire whose family had longer ties to union leaders (like
George Meany) and African American leaders (like Whitney Young), to say nothing of a level of wealth that made the Kennedy fortune seem puny by comparison.
But when such economic and political power was allied with top military and
civilian officials at the Pentagon, Kennedy's nervousness had a more realistic foundation than that of an average politician's paranoia.

One Rockefeller associate at the Pentagon was CIA veteran William R.
Kintner. Here was the epitome of the intelligence operative, a "spook" who filtered
easily into all social and political levels, moving in and out of a labyrinth of clandestine circles. Kintner owed his rise at the Pentagon to Nelson Rockefeller, first
as a member of Nelson's White House staff, serving as his chief aide at the top-
secret Quantico seminars, then as a participant in the Rockefeller Brothers Fund
Special Studies Project, and finally as an aide to the Joint Chiefs of Staff, where he
headed long-range planning for the army. In 1961, Kintner left the Joint Chiefs to
become deputy director of the Foreign Policy Research Institute, a CIA-associated
think tank based in Philadelphia. There he began advocating the use of private
voluntary organizations, including religious personnel, in Cold War operations.

From the beginning, Kintner argued for the adoption of the counterinsurgency doctrine at all levels of government, military and civilian. He rejected
"peaceful coexistence" as illusory; "violent coexistence" was his reality.[5] Local elite
military officers, trained "to assume not only military duties but also 'civilian' roles
in government," were his preferred weapons in fighting the Cold War. Only the
military would provide "the indispensable base for proper economic development" in the Third World. This militarized development thesis gave a theoretical
foundation to the "civic action" programs of unconventional warfare previously
tested in the Philippines by General Edward Lansdale. Kintner's emphasis on the
military for counterinsurgency strategy and economic development was elevated
to a new status in the National Security Council (when the president, smarting
from the Bay of Pigs defeat, created the Special Group-C.I. [counterinsurgency] in
August 1961). Kennedy's appointment of General Maxwell Taylor as its chair
crowned the new doctrine with administrative competence. Robert Kennedy, as
cochair, was only a presidential watchdog. Taylor ran the show, focusing attention
on Vietnam and on the Pentagon's "flexible response" ability to wage counterinsurgency war, not just nuclear war.

Nelson was pleased with this reorganization of the Pentagon around counterinsurgency. Better yet was Kennedy's willingness to raise the policymaking sta-

tus of the office of the national security adviser, adopting much of the substance, without the title, of Nelson's previous proposal for a presidential assistant with "first secretary" premierlike powers.

From his Foxhall Road estate in Washington and visits to the Pentagon, Nelson could keep abreast of foreign developments and the Kennedy administration's reactions to them. When he spoke publicly, however, Nelson tended to beat the drums of his favorite subject, nuclear war. No matter what the Soviets did, he told 346 journalists at Miami's Fontainebleau Hotel, the United States should not only continue underground nuclear testing, but resume testing in the atmosphere as well.

More research, he insisted, was needed: research and development of lighter nuclear warheads; new weapons, such as the neutron bomb; antimissile defense systems (more missiles), and tactical nuclear weapons "so needed for local and limited military action."[6]

He did not mention that his International Basic Economy Corporation (IBEC) was now moving rapidly into the production of missile components. IBEC's rubber, plastics, and plywood division had expanded to include fluid power systems for satellite launches; air compressor units to start jet aircraft; valves in nuclear reactors; and, by 1963, direct Pentagon orders for Titan II ICBM skirt assemblies.[7]

Neither did Nelson mention Airborne Instruments Laboratory, one of Laurance's favorite ventures, whose Eugene Fubini was a recent full-time addition to the Pentagon and subsequently the National Security Agency's top official. Or Reaction Motors, another of Laurance's holdings, maker of liquid fuel rockets and now part of the rapidly growing Thiokol Chemical Corporation, developer and producer of motors for the Minuteman ICBM since 1961 and much later the producer of the faulty O-rings that doomed the *Challenger* spacecraft.

Nor did he mention Rockwell Manufacturing Company, a major air force contractor, which had IBEC director and Room 5600 financial director J. Richardson Dilworth as a board member. Or Vitro Corporation, a defense contractor controlled by Nelson's close friend and CIA collaborator, John Hay "Jock" Whitney, which had first Laurance and then Nelson's IBEC chairman Robert Purcell on the board. Or Itek, the maker of the U-2's ultrapowerful camera lens, which had Laurance as a major investor and his aides Harper Woodward and Theodore F. Walkowicz as directors.* Or Marquardt Aircraft, another of Laurance's "risk" investments. Or Vertrol Aircraft, maker of Piasecki helicopters, which Laurance and Treasury Secretary C. Douglas Dillon had helped, at the behest of the Pentagon, giving it the financial launching pad to take off toward more lucrative "limited war" horizons by demonstrating the helicopter's utility during the Korean War.

---

*In 1962, Colonel Frank Lindsay, former deputy chief of the CIA's Office of Policy Coordination, was made Itek's president.

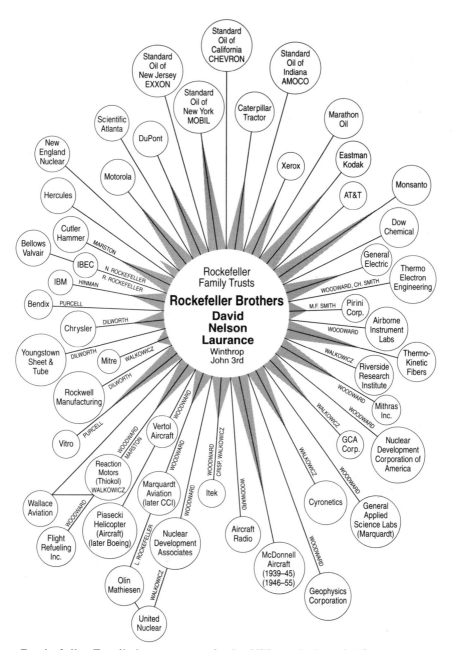

Rockefeller Family Investments in the Military-Industrial Complex (1950–1974)

Of the five Rockefeller brothers, David, Nelson, and Laurance were the most active in this area. (Names of individuals are of Rockefeller family representatives on boards of directors of companies with defense contracts.)

Sources: Nelson Rockefeller vice presidential confirmation hearings; *New York Times*, December 4, 1974, p. 29; U.S. Department of Defense, *100 Companies and Their Subsidiary Corporations, Listed According to Net Value of Military Prime Contract Awards* (annual, various years); U.S. Department of Defense, *500 Contractors Receiving the Largest Dollar Volume of Military Prime Contract Awards for Research, Development, Test and Evaluation Work* (annual, various years); company annual reports; *Moody's Industrials Manual*; and *Who's Who in America*.

Dependence on the Pentagon for, effectively, a public subsidy of many of the largest private employers in the United States grew enormously during the Kennedy era. And out of this public subsidy came an escalated arms race. It mattered little that the much-touted "missile gap" did not, according to Secretary of Defense Robert McNamara, exist;[8] contracting for missiles, the Pentagon convinced Kennedy, was an easy way to buy off corporate proponents of the already outdated B-70 bombers. Through the arms race, the Pentagon was taking Kennedy and the American people on their first fateful step to the Cuban Missile Crisis of October 1962.

Kennedy's rapid missile buildup supplemented an already overwhelmingly superior U.S. nuclear strike force of ICBMs, bombers, intermediate-range missiles in Western Europe and Turkey, and unmatched data on Soviet strength from Richard Bissell's U-2s and satellite reconnaissance. For the Soviets to conclude that their own nuclear deterrence force was no longer credible, all that remained was the defection in April 1961 of Colonel Oleg Penkovsky, one of the KGB's top missile intelligence officers. It took another year for the Soviets to learn that Penkovsky had passed some 5,000 frames of microfilm of top-secret information to the CIA.

With some political voices in the United States calling loudly for a "first strike" on the Soviet Union and Kennedy's buildup proceeding at breakneck pace, the Soviets became willing to gamble on Fidel Castro's request for "defensive" intermediate-range missiles to deter an expected U.S. invasion.

Cuba, only ninety miles from U.S. shores, put major metropolitan cities in the Southeast within range of Soviet intermediate missiles. (Soviet submarines capable of firing Polaris-type missiles like the U.S. Polaris submarines were still years away.) Using Cuba as a base would circumvent the bulk of the U.S.'s early-warning radar system aimed at the polar cap. Here was an opportunity for the Soviets, under standard nuclear deterrence doctrine, to restore the credibility of their defense system.[9] As in the United States, fear and desperation played too important a role in shaping defense strategies in the Soviet Union; unlike Nelson Rockefeller, however, both Nikita Khrushchev and Kennedy had enough sense to know that fallout shelters bought little hope of survival if nuclear war broke out. But also unlike Rockefeller, they underestimated how easily Latin America could be turned into Armageddon.

The Education Offensive

As the nuclear deterrence strategies of the United States and the Soviet Union were leading both nations at the end of 1961 toward nuclear confrontation in Latin America, one of the Democratic party's most experienced Latin America hands, Adolf Berle, was still chafing over having been pushed out of the Kennedy administration. The president had done it gracefully, leaving his options open to use Berle's talents in the future. But all the praise and smiles for the cameras could not hide Berle's unhappiness at being made the first scapegoat for the Bay of Pigs failure. Berle believed that the invasion, though a "fiasco," was "entirely lawful and consistent with international law and with our treaties . . . probably one of the few intelligent things we did. It was noted in the Soviet Union and possibly in China that they had met the threshold of armed action and overtly at least pulled in their horns."

Berle's hatred of the traditionalists in the State Department was stronger than ever. He called the department's bureaucracy for Latin America, the Bureau of Latin American Affairs, "unready, inefficient, even in its own way corrupt."[10] His bitterness was directed less at the president than at the "views and delaying tactics of a State Department Bureaucracy" whose "tenacity is not justified by its record of success."[11]

Berle believed that the State Department had singled out Kennedy's Alliance for Progress policy for attack. Kennedy was well aware of the bureau's opposition. "These fellows really object to my being President," Kennedy told Berle.[12]

A bond, though weak, still remained between Kennedy and Berle, sealed by a mutual belief that democratic reforms and imaginative counterinsurgency programs could dampen revolutionary fervor, prevent the spread of communism, and usher in a new prosperous epoch of American-led capitalist growth in the Third World. And both men knew that some of the brightest architects of this strategy had worked above and apart from the State Department, drawn instead into orbits more influenced by Rockefeller power than by the more diffused, unfocused, and often contradictory policies of a federal government filled with the laissez-faire advocates in the Republican administration.

Kennedy had been fully persuaded by veterans of the Rockefeller Brothers Fund's Special Studies Project like McGeorge Bundy, Walt Rostow, Roswell Gilpatric, and Edward Lansdale to rely on their counterinsurgency doctrine to prevent World War III. With the help of the Green Berets, the CIA, and the Agency for International Development, Kennedy had been told, allied governments could carry out successful antiguerrilla military operations and initiate social and political reforms and economic progress that could "contain" communist-led revolutions as "limited wars" and prevent their growing into major wars and sparks for nuclear conflagration. In this way, counterinsurgency and its limited wars remarkably became both a global and an internal quest for peace.

The whole strategy depended, of course, on the willingness of the "host" government to initiate social reforms, especially in the countryside. It was there, according to Walt Rostow's theory of economic growth, that economic development could take place along general capitalist lines. The formula was ingenuously simple: Small title-holding farmers could use crop rotation, hybrid seeds, fertilizer, and machinery to increase productivity and lower food prices in urban areas. Lower food prices would reduce inflation, contribute to political and market stability, and lower the cost of hiring workers. The upper class would be more encouraged to invest in other manufacturing and home-market ventures instead of sending its money abroad or investing in the traditional export sector. All these economic developments, in turn, would increase the volume of goods and services for the domestic mass market, which would grow as credit and the better-paid wage-earning middle class grew. Rockefeller well understood and shared this thesis.

Kennedy worried about Rockefeller. Whereas a governor can build his track record on domestic affairs, a U.S. president ultimately is judged by his accomplishments in foreign affairs. And it was not Vietnam that had become the embarrassment of Kennedy's presidency, but Rockefeller's claimed domain of expertise: Latin America.

So it had come to pass that at the same time that Kennedy endorsed an escalation of counterinsurgency forces in South Vietnam, he did likewise in Latin America. And rather than avoid Nelson Rockefeller's influence south of the border, Kennedy decided to tap it, seeking access to Nelson through Berle.

Berle was an old master at psychological warfare, a skill honed and developed while working with Nelson's CIAA during World War II. Now, to counter the State Department's perceived resistance to the Alliance for Progress, Kennedy asked Berle to "work out a good propaganda education program" for Latin America.

Berle was happy to oblige. Kennedy's assignment allowed him to work out his frustrations by drafting a twenty-four-page "Psychological Offensive in Latin America." He argued that the State Department's lack of clear democratic objectives and methods had allowed movements for social change in Latin America to relapse into dictatorships. These dictatorships, in turn, only set the stage for more disorder.[13] The State Department's cultural officers, he went on, were not up to the task of effectively spreading propaganda because of their fear of offending the host governments. "As a great Power, we are entitled to have propaganda," he insisted. " 'Cold Wars' are no less serious than 'Hot Wars' in this respect."[14] The intellectual effort, he argued, "ranks in importance and scale with our economic offensive and with our measures for military defense."

"Contrary to most impressions," he went on, in Latin America "the battlefield is not for the 'minds of the masses.' Essentially the objective is control of the relatively small stratum of intellectuals, the educated and the semi-educated. The strategy is to achieve domination of Latin American intellectual life now, and to assure indefinite perpetuation of that domination by controlling educational processes."

Berle laid out a strategy of U.S. government control of Latin America's educational processes, covertly carried out through private agencies. Books would be selected, promoted, and distributed by "a philosophical and intellectual staff." These efforts would be backed by a director of educational activities who would "assure that in all the departments of instruction in the various universities of

Latin America, professors who expound the American philosophy have support and encouragement." His proposed Directorate of Information would "own or control in each Latin American country and through citizens of it, at least one newspaper of general circulation and, if feasible, at least one substantial radio chain. In fact, he recommended establishing a central radio station modeled on Radio Havana, capable of broadcasting regularly to the entire Latin American area. "There is no reason why we should not have our own 'Tass.'"[15]

If all this sounded like Nelson Rockefeller's CIAA operation during World War II, it also dovetailed with Kennedy's interest in breaking down the feudal bureaucracies that Eisenhower's hierarchical style had fostered and replacing them with his own centralized command and loyal lieutenants.

Berle also wanted to get the Alliance for Progress, a key element of counterinsurgency, off the ground. He introduced White House aide Richard Goodwin, who had helped design the Alliance for Progress, to Rockefeller. "I think all the White House wants is to exchange ideas [about the Cold War]," Berle told Nelson, "because matters are getting tight."[16]

Berle knew, however, that Nelson Rockefeller had more than ideas and experience when it came to propaganda in Latin America. Nelson controlled access to a private network of business and political contacts, in Latin America and the United States, that was not readily accessible to the bureaucrats in the State Department's Latin America Division.

Nelson's network reached not only high but deep and far, touching everything in the world of the Rockefellers, from Nelson's own political and business connections to the vast business and philanthropic empire sired by Grandfather's fortune. At certain times and in certain companies, markets, or geographic areas, the interests of political and business contacts in this network met. These mutual points of interest held the potential for making history.

Such mutual points of interest during the Kennedy era were the seemingly disparate cases of North Carolina and Colombia. North Carolina, a state with Rockefeller ties since Grandfather had done business in Charlotte in the nineteenth century, would have a profound impact on the development of counterinsurgency policy through the Alliance for Progress in Latin America. And Colombia, a nation that had played host to Standard Oil for almost forty years, would be the doctrine's laboratory.

North Carolina and the Colombian Experiment

Sixty years had passed since Nelson's father had toured North Carolina on the Southern Railway's "Millionaire's Special" with other northern financiers to inspect that state's potential for school funds and industrial development. Rockefeller's Sanitary Commission and General Education Board, having used

North Carolina as their medical and social laboratory, had taken their programs abroad to Latin America and Asia, eventually merging as the giant of American philanthropy, the Rockefeller Foundation.

North Carolina was still a poor state in desperate need of development. To satisfy that need, its leaders again courted northern capital. And once again, North Carolina would be used as a launching pad for social engineering in Latin America. But this time both the Cold War and economics conspired against maintaining the status quo of white supremacy.

North Carolina's development of a home market was hampered by the servitude imposed on its African American population, whose low wages, backed by Klan terror, put downward pressure on the price of all labor. Although low wages could attract northern industries, they also retarded the growth of a home market of consumers. And from Washington's viewpoint, the South's version of apartheid was not the image needed for the self-proclaimed leader of the Free World. Could North Carolina break the segregationist mold and become the model of development and trade for the Alliance for Progress as it had for the health and sanitation programs that accompanied U.S. corporate investment in Latin America sixty years before?

North Carolina's governor in the late 1950s was Luther Hodges, the former top manager of Marshall Field and Company's textile mills. Hodges's genteel corporate liberalism toward racial integration had won the admiration of northern liberals. Hodges realized that to attract northern industry and to promote stable development in the South, the rural reactionaries' stranglehold on the region's economy and politics had to be broken. As in Latin America, a huge migration of whites and blacks from the countryside had occurred; for the first time in the South, cities with populations of over 10,000 were growing faster than were towns with fewer than 10,000 people. Pressure for social and political reforms was mounting from disfranchised African Americans. If social stability that was conducive to long-term investment was to be achieved, reform had better come soon. If it came too late, the South's instability might be even greater, from either violence by white reactionaries or from social changes more fundamental than business leaders could accept. Jobs had to be found for black as well as white workers, and Hodges looked to the federal government, as well as to northern businesses, to provide them, giving added impetus to the civil rights movement. North Carolina industry, with a growing labor surplus, would become more eligible for Pentagon contracts under the Pentagon's "set-aside" procurement contracts for areas with persistent labor surpluses.

During Hodges's tenure as governor, North Carolina received a large slice of the Pentagon pie. After Kennedy came into office, the state enjoyed substantial increases in Defense Department purchases, and military wages and salaries increased more than in any other state in the South Atlantic region.[17] But the state lacked the industrial infrastructure to really cash in or to grow the way its leaders, including the Belk family of Charlotte, wanted.

To attract northern defense contractors, including Rockefeller ones, Hodges pushed for the desegregation of workplaces, the rational integration of the country-side into urban industrial needs, and an upgrading of the higher educational system.

Hodges's image as a genteel older Southerner who took a moderate course on desegregation, coupled with his success, convinced Kennedy that Hodges's appointment as secretary of commerce would reassure both business and the Senate that the new Democratic administration was neither rash nor antibusiness. With Hodges on his team, Kennedy hoped to get support for reforms in foreign as well as domestic policy, for it would be by the Cold War—particularly his performance in Latin America—that he would be judged.

Kennedy still preferred elected governments in the Third World that offered some hope for land reform and economic progress beyond the stagnation of the old landed aristocracies' dictatorships. Elected governments were not only more palatable to his tastes; they also offered a benefit any psychological warfare expert would covet: legitimacy. Hodges, who, as governor, had also faced landed aristo-crats opposed to mobile and free labor markets, was enlisted in the cause.

Like Nelson Rockefeller, Hodges urged support for Kennedy's first foreign aid bill. The Alliance for Progress, Hodges argued, could help fulfill corporate objectives in Latin America. It could also help achieve the aims of North Carolina's textile industries, especially in dealing with foreign competitors like Colombia. There was only one problem, the same problem that had confronted American businessmen for a century: Latin American nationalism, whether political or eco-nomic, had its own agenda for development.

One objective of the American textile industry was to restrict foreign imports, a goal dear to Hodges's heart. The problem was that it ran counter to the desires of foreign exporters like Colombia to broaden their markets, especially in the United States. Somehow, Hodges had to resolve this fundamental contradiction.

Complicating his task were Colombia's growing economic woes. President Alberto Lleras Camargo was particularly anxious because prices for coffee—Colombia's major export—had fallen during 1960, thanks to the recession in the United States, Colombia's biggest coffee market. As export earnings declined, Colombia's continued high debt payments to American and European banks and bond holders triggered inflation in that country. Lleras Camargo feared that this economic situation would give impetus to rural guerrillas who were sympathetic to the Cuban revolutionary example and bolster the stature of the "peasant republics" that still survived in Colombia's central Andes. What Lleras Camargo needed—besides friendly American markets for exports—was immediate assis-tance. A comprehensive economic confederation with U.S. allies in the hemi-sphere, along the lines outlined by his friend Nelson Rockefeller in 1960—backed by U.S. arms, Green Berets, agricultural technicians, engineers, and money—seemed like the answer.

And here lay the solution to Hodges's political dilemma. There was one American family he knew he could count on to help deliver what they wanted for Colombia, just as this same family had helped deliver for North Carolina: the Rockefellers.

By the middle of 1961, the Rockefeller interests had big plans for Colombia. Since the 1950s, Nelson's IBEC had been exploring the potential of Colombia's Cauca Valley, directly west of the peasant republics. IBEC's profit-making ventures would be complemented by programs operated by its nonprofit arm, the American International Association for Economic and Social Development (AIA).[18]

IBEC had brought together twenty companies and banks shortly after Nelson's 1958 election, to form the Colombian Finance Corporation to invest in Colombian companies. In 1959, IBEC had set up industrial-development offices and insurance brokerages in Bogotá, as well as a Colombian investment company. It also expanded its poultry operations in the Cauca Valley, which was the source of much of the cotton used by mills in Medellín, Colombia's fastest-growing city in the central Andes. Medellín had once been a major coffee exporter and now was a major site of textile manufacturing, ironically putting the city on a collision course with North Carolina's textile plants. In the absence of a significant lowering of the U.S. tariff wall, some of the city's troubled entrepreneurs would invest in a new, more lucrative export: cocaine.

The Rockefeller brothers could not have anticipated this new cash crop or the tragic violence it would bring to Medellín—and both Colombia and the United States. But they had always maintained that industrial growth was impossible for Latin America unless impediments to more trade with the United States and Europe were removed. Colombia's economic well-being depended on access to the giant U.S. market. Although they encouraged diversification beyond traditional exports, Rockefeller investments nevertheless had to take these exports into account in calculating Colombia's debt-carrying capacity for financing this diversification.

For this reason, Nelson and David continued to promote freer trade between Colombia and the United States, Nelson, through a proposal for an economic confederation for the entire hemisphere, and David, through his idea of a Latin American Common Market that would include the United States and Canada. Such a trade bloc could help force European and Japanese competitors to accept terms of trade more favorable to American exporters and investors, or threaten to lock them out. But achieving it meant applying pressure not only on Washington, but on Latin America. And pressure meant not only overt force, but its subtler, covert form that the Rockefeller brothers had used with such skill abroad—propaganda. This time, however, their target was not intellectuals, but businessmen.

Nelson's cousin, Richard Aldrich, IBEC's vice president who sometimes did undercover work for the CIA,[19] joined eight other men to plan assistance to Latin American business allies in the field of propaganda. Representatives of fifteen companies met with the State Department and the U.S. Information Agency in October 1960 to discuss "an organized counterattack" against the arguments of both communists and nationalists who were opposed to more U.S. holdings in Latin America. Out of these deliberations came an organizing group that set up the Latin American Information Committee (LAIC), which was formally introduced to the business world at a dinner on the following May 1. LAIC's executive director was Enno Hobbing, who switched back and forth between the CIA and Time/Life assignments.

Colombia, LAIC found, had a "large, well organized and experienced group of [American] private businessmen" working there. The country was also representative of the rest of South America. It had industrial cities; its export income relied primarily on one crop; and, of course, it had "in recent times been the scene of unrest and of considerable communist infiltration."[20]

In search of a model laboratory for "nation-building" in Latin America, the Kennedy administration focused the twin eyes of counterinsurgency—liberal reforms and military operations—on Colombia. Here, unlike Ydígoras's Guatemala, was a government unsullied with the reputation of being a CIA creation. Here, unlike Somoza's Nicaragua, was an elected government billed as a democratic alternative to both a dictatorial past and a communist future. And most important, unlike Brazil or Argentina, here was a reliable ally, Nelson Rockefeller's old friend Alberto Lleras Camargo, who had backed the invasion of Cuba and challenged his neighbors to do likewise.

Kennedy planned to visit Lleras Camargo that December. At the same time, Hodges, whose Commerce Department saw the Alliance for Progress as a vehicle for exports by American businesses, was eager to have Colombia as a customer for the goods of his home state. With Rockefeller interests already on line to facilitate "freer" trade between the two countries, everything seemed to fall into place.

More than goods would be offered from North Carolina, however. Green Berets and William Cameron Townsend's missionaries were also ready for service.

26

MIRACLES DÉJÀ VU

Behind the Lord's Call from North Carolina

William Cameron Townsend was in Mexico in the fall of 1961 preparing for a banquet to honor the biggest Mexican benefactor of the Summer Linguistic Institute (SIL), Aarón Sáenz, when he received the Lord's call from North Carolina.

The Colombian ambassador would be in Charlotte over the weekend as the guest of honor at the state's first international trade fair. He was staying with Henderson and Ann Belk.

Cam's sixty-five years had not dimmed his zeal for opportunity. He had learned long ago, since his first "miraculous" encounter with Mexico's President Lázaro Cárdenas a quarter century ago, not to hesitate when the Lord intervened on his behalf.

"I'll be on the next flight out!" he said. "Tell the Belks and pray!"[1]

The Alliance for Progress was proving fertile ground for Cam's efforts to spread SIL throughout the tribal world. Since President John F. Kennedy took office, Cam had been shuttling back and forth between SIL's Peruvian jungle base and Latin American capitals that were signing on, in some cases reluctantly, with the Alliance for Progress: Lima, Quito, Brasília, and Mexico City. Next would be Bogotá.

When Cam arrived in Charlotte, he found a bustling new financial domain, one increasingly dominated by Rockefeller banking ties and marked by the conspicuous presence of a new arrival, Laurance Rockefeller's Eastern Airlines.[2]

Charlotte was Luther Hodges's selection as the site for a much-needed public relations boost for the state and for his position as secretary of commerce.

Through this fair, Hodges hoped to use the Alliance for Progress to promote North Carolina's products in Latin America. His tenure as secretary of commerce certainly needed some face-lifting. Since his return from promoting the Alliance in Mexico, Hodges's attempts to restore government control over the business-dominated Commerce Department and to steer economic aid to depressed areas like his own state had gotten him and Kennedy into trouble. Wall Street had enough concerns about the administration's massive aid program to Latin America; it did not need a domestic Alliance for Progress as well. From the beginning, Hodges's maverick style had worried financial interests who had dominated the Eisenhower administration's business policies. "You will never hear from me," Hodges said at the outset, "that this country should do this or that simply because business wants it. What is good for General Motors may, or may not, be good for the country."

Two of the business community's leading lobbies—the U.S. Chamber of Commerce and the National Association of Manufacturers—likewise frowned on Hodges's preference for federal aid to depressed areas and for federal involvement in investment planning. They viewed investment of capital and the planning of it as the businessman's prerogative. But if there had to be such ideological heresy, they preferred having the program under the old Commerce Department, where they might expect to exercise traditional influence and gained information on the government's plans through the department's Business Advisory Council (BAC).

Above all, they wanted to avoid a separate government agency dedicated to economic development, as preferred by Kennedy's more liberal social planners and by minorities, who traditionally were kept out of the loop of information and decision making. Hodges was put in the difficult position of trying to assure big business that Kennedy was not antibusiness, while trying to allay suspicions within the administration that the Department of Commerce would continue to be the instrument of corporate executives in the BAC. This was a delicate balancing act, with the future of the Commerce Department and the question of its autonomy as an ostensibly nonpartisan government agency teetering first one way and then the other.

First, Secretary Hodges challenged the self-perpetuating leadership of the council. The BAC was made up of 174 executives of the bluest blue-chip corporations. Hodges challenged the BAC's access to the federal government's economic secrets. With Kennedy's blessings, he asserted his right to appoint new members to the BAC and demanded a change in its rule barring the press from meetings.

New York's Morgan-dominated financial establishment had looked on Kennedy's candidacy with as much suspicion as it did Nelson Rockefeller's, and for much the same reason: fear of the rich maverick who played outside established rules. Memories were still painfully fresh of a similar financial squire who had been imbued with noblesse oblige: Franklin D. Roosevelt. They saw Hodges's power move as Kennedy's.

. The BAC did eventually agree to meet under more liberalized press rules and to allow more small-business representation. But that was as far as it would go. Hodges's attempt to prove the integrity of the Department of Commerce only united big business in opposition. The BAC deserted Hodges en masse over the summer of 1961, severing formal ties with the department and renaming itself simply the Business Council.

It was left to Rockefeller ally C. Douglas Dillon to try his hand at damage control. The treasury secretary urged Kennedy publicly to distance himself from Hodges's position and to seek a reconciliation. By September 2, the president was having dinner with the BAC. On October 13, he lunched with members again. A week later he addressed the BAC still again. But he remained unsatisfied with the New York establishment. According to Arthur Schlesinger, he mused on the paradox that American labor leaders, who he thought were often individually mediocre and selfish, belonged to a movement that usually took the responsible side of great public issues, while American businessmen, though better educated and more often individually enlightened, seemed almost backward as a group on public policy. He understood better Roosevelt's attitude toward business and wished the Cold War were out of the way so he could openly debate business on the future of the country.[3] Neither Kennedy nor Hodges could anticipate that their attempted reforms would stir such animosity within the Eastern Establishment or that Kennedy's long-awaited opportunity to debate business openly would never occur.

The president's visit to North Carolina and Secretary Hodges's imminent arrival for the trade fair were the talk of Charlotte by the time Cam Townsend arrived. But Cam had not come to see a fair. He was, as ever, SIL's roving ambassador, the proverbial seeker of open doors and heaven-sent opportunities. On his first night in town, he dined at a local country club with Colombia's ambassador, Carlos Sanz de Santamaría.

Sanz was no stranger to the United States or to the Helio Couriers used by Cam's Jungle Aviation and Radio Service (JAARS). In 1960, he had accompanied Lleras Camargo to the United States, backing his president's request for arms, advisers, and military helicopters. A U.S. military survey team that was sent to Colombia had recommended Helio Couriers as cheaper, "versatile light aircraft useful for anti-guerrilla activities." But it was illegal to use U.S. grants to Latin American countries for domestic police or army internal security. Therefore, the U.S. Department of State recommended that Lleras Camargo purchase the Helio Couriers outright.[4] In those pre-Vietnam days of the Cold War, the United States was sensitive to any suggestion that it was backing Latin American dictators or carrying out military interventions by proxy.

No Couriers were ever sold directly to the Colombian government by Helio Aircraft, according to the company's records.[5] That did not, however, rule out sales to Colombia through a CIA proprietary company like King Hurley or Air Asia or leasing Helio Couriers through a private American third party like JAARS. And the goal of the Helio Couriers' projected use—repression of rural revolts—required that any transaction be clandestine.

Sanz de Santamaría at first listened to Cam talk about SIL's work only as a courtesy to the Belks. He was more concerned about winning the goodwill of this powerful family and their friends in textiles than he was about missionaries.

"We import tobacco now from North Carolina and some other products," Sanz had told a breakfast party thrown for him by Irwin Belk, "but we were invited here to see what else you have. Eighty percent of Colombia's imports are from the U.S. . . . Right now, we and other South American countries are not importing as much from this country as possible."[6] And if he could not get tariffs reciprocally lowered (Colombia exported a lot of coffee to the United States), perhaps he could get investments and capital.

The Belks had access to both. They were a key force behind Charlotte's courting of New York capital and the city's bid to host the state's first International Trade Fair.[7]

As in the Rockefeller family, one Belk son, Irwin, dwelled in the higher realm of finance. He shared with his oldest brother, John, responsibility as financial overseer of a retail empire of 300 stores stretching from Ohio to Texas.

Like the Rockefellers, the Belks had a Brothers Investment Corporation, of which Irwin was president. Irwin also sat on the boards of a bank (First Union National), local insurance and telephone companies, the family foundation, and nine textile mills.

Like the Rockefellers, the Belks took seriously their social and financial status. They recognized the importance of economically integrating the countryside into the national mainstream to carry out industrialization and the huge profits to be made from millions of better-paid consumers, including African Americans.

And like the Rockefellers, the Belks were not afraid to involve themselves in political intrigues.[8] In December 1961 the Belks would host the two most prominent Cold Warriors of the Rockefeller camp, Secretary of State Dean Rusk, addressing the Chamber of Commerce, and Governor of New York Nelson Rockefeller, speaking to the Republican State Executive Committee. Charlotte, it was clear to Sanz, was a city at the crossroads of power.

As JAARS's presence symbolized, it was also a city at the crossroads of Fundamentalism. Charlotte retained its cultural insularity. Recent arrivals from the countryside used zoning much as they did throughout the South, allowing suburbs to resemble small towns and retaining a rural character. These people brought with them the rural culture of the South, including racial segregation and Protestant Fundamentalism, both practiced in the Charlotte area with zeal. In Charlotte, as in other southern cities, business looked to the white suburban church as a precious market; the growth of church memberships complemented the local government objectives of growth.[9] It was no accident that a former Bible salesman named Luther Hodges could rise through textiles to become North Carolina's governor. Or that former Bible salesman Billy Graham had preceded another ex-Bible salesman, William Cameron Townsend, in finding support for setting up operations in the Charlotte area. Or that both would be followed by Pat Robertson's Christian Television Network and the more sensational scam of Jim and Tammy Bakker. Charlotte, the commercial hub of the Piedmont, seemed made for selling, with a characteristic lack of self-reflection—or self-consciousness—when goods and services were offered with a strong dose of local Christian culture. What was good for Charlotte was good not only for the United States, but also for the world.

Therefore, if Ambassador Sanz was in Charlotte to sell Colombia to North Carolinians, Cam Townsend was in Charlotte to sell SIL to Colombians. And as Cam laid out his wares, Sanz became intrigued. The missionary offered Sanz two things that Lleras Camargo badly needed: a tested bilingual education program that could help Colombia's national economy integrate rural Indians who were susceptible to guerrilla insurgencies, and Helio Couriers, serviced by a Belk-sponsored JAARS base in the heart of Belk country.

Partners of the Alliance

The decidedly military overtone of federal blessing at the trade fair's opening indicated the importance the Pentagon placed on North Carolina as a strategic home base for its counterinsurgency doctrine. Luther Hodges arrived, flanked by two deputy assistant secretaries of defense for installations and logistics, a deputy assistant secretary of the air force, a major general of the army's Procurement and Distribution Division, a brigadier general of the army's Signal Supply Agency, a rear admiral who served as a deputy with NATO, and an assistant secretary of the navy for installations and logistics.

As if to underscore the counterinsurgency buildup at Fort Bragg as a new growth industry for North Carolina, the fair was symbolically opened at the Raleigh-Durham Airport by President Kennedy while en route to Fort Bragg. Praising North Carolina's "most vigorous" industrial and business development, Kennedy characterized his symbolic role as a "high honor" and the fair as a way "to show the world" what the United States had to offer. Then the president flew to Fort Bragg to watch the army demonstrate its prowess.

Surrounded by aides, Defense Secretary Robert McNamara, army brass, and Latin American and South Vietnamese military officers, Kennedy was treated to a fiery, earth-shattering display of jet bombings, helicopters firing rockets, a 55-10 guided missile blasting tank targets, a giant howitzer shooting projectiles twenty miles, and a "Red Eye" shoulder missile exploding aircraft out of the sky. The demonstration "made me want to join the Army,"[10] gushed McNamara.

But what made the president lean forward in his chair were the Green Berets. The Green Berets passed in review in full battle gear, their young faces blackened in camouflage except for white eyes turned right and looking straight at him. Aircraft swooped overhead, dropping leaflets. Kennedy inspected one. It had a picture of him as he had arrived only a few hours before; the other side read: "You call the tune and we'll play it . . . in any theater, cold or hot . . . to any audience, favorable or not." It was psychological warfare in the best Lansdalean tradition. Kennedy, one reporter noted, "nodded and smiled when some of the men explained they were trained to speak two or more foreign languages."[11]

Cam knew, as he flew from Charlotte to Washington with Ambassador Sanz after the fair's opening, that SILers working in Vietnam under Green Beret protection were making great headway in unraveling the mysteries of Montagnard tribal dialects. Bilingual education of tribesmen had many applications, not the least of which was to inculcate in them political loyalty to SIL's host government. Cam hoped he could extend SIL's work into Colombia. Kennedy's intervention in Lleras Camargo's political and economic crisis would need an educational component in tribal areas like the *Llanos*, where oil had been found.

While in Washington, the ambassador took the missionary to lunch. Sanz gave Cam three letters. One was for President Lleras Camargo; the others were for the minister of education and the secretary of the archbishop.

Cam was holding the keys to the kingdom. He immediately flew south and met with Colombia's director of Indian affairs, Gregorio Hernández de Alba. An anthropologist, Hernández de Alba was delighted to help. Lleras Camargo's Liberal government wanted to parcel out the church's mission lands to Indians with individual title-deeds, not unlike what misguided American reformers had done in the United States through the infamous Allotment Act of 1887.

In Colombia, this struggle against the church's power was centered in the province of Putumayo, where the church's Capuchin Mission had turned most of the Sibundoy Indians landless. It was also where Gulf Oil had joined New York–based Texaco in test drilling that would soon be announced as successful.[12]

Hernández de Alba took Cam to see Lleras Camargo. Nine years had passed since Cam had last seen the thin, frail president when Lleras Camargo was visiting Chicago's Pan American Council as secretary general of the Organization of American States. Cam had lobbied futilely for SIL's entry into Colombia. But now Lleras Camargo was in need of U.S. aid and some flexibility on tariffs from North Carolina's textile magnates. "We'll be glad to give you a contract,"[13] he said after reading Sanz's letter.

Then came Cam's biggest test. It was not with the education minister or even the Roman Catholic archbishop, but with the apostolic vicar of the Caquetá region, ruler of all lands of Colombia's Amazonian Indians.

The vicar was Father Eduardo Canyes, a refugee of the Spanish Civil War. As

Territory Under Bishop Canyes's Vicariate in Colombia

SIL's closest ally in Colombia's Catholic hierarchy, Bishop Marceliano Canyes, was the subject of criticism for his treatment of Indians in the Putumayo region. Later, he was given a vast territory (shaded on the map) as his vicariate, stretching south from the Caquetá River to Colombia's only port on the Amazon, Leticia.

Source: Walter Dostal, ed., *The Situation of the Indian in South America.*

a priest in "red" Barcelona, Canyes had found his sympathy for General Francisco Franco's uprising against the Spanish Republic unwelcome. Renaming himself Father Marceliano de Vilafranca, he prudently fled Spain with his brother, also a priest, and immigrated to more hospitable Colombia. Here, through the Capuchin Friars Mission, he rose to power as Father Marceliano Canyes. Appointed apostolic vicar of the Putumayo region, Canyes operated huge dairy farms on ancestral Sibundoy Indian lands while the Indians, regarded traditionally as wards of the church, went undernourished. According to charges by anthropologist Victor Daniel Borilla, Canyes took the fertile lands and gave the Indians the Sibundoy swamp in exchange. He quickly sold the untitled lands to private interests, mostly important families from the interior.[14]

In 1951, the Vatican split his vicariate. Losing Cauca and the Putumayo, Bishop Canyes had to settle for the southeastern half, a vast tropical territory running from the Caquetá River region down to the Amazon River itself. Canyes placed the seat of his bishopric at strategic Leticia, Colombia's only port on the Amazon, and continued to rule in the manner that already had earned him the name "Fray Manga," Brother Strongman.

Facing the fierce, bearded Canyes, Cam tried to strike a common chord: "I remember in 1937 your brother and I both had articles in the same linguistic magazine in Mexico. He was well known in linguistic circles."

"Yes," said Canyes, "he always wanted to help the Indians." Canyes's brother, Marcelino, had also been a sympathizer of Franco when both fled Barcelona and came to Colombia. Marcelino turned a blind eye toward his brother's dispossession of the Sibundoy, occupying his mind instead with an insatiable scientific curiosity about Amazonian flora and Indian languages, as if both were already relics. But unlike the bishop, Marcelino showed a genuine, if patronizing, regard for Indian culture, and many inhabitants of the Sibundoy valley responded to this unusual white man by loving him as a living saint. When Marcelino died in 1953, Bishop Canyes insisted that the government pay for the upkeep of his brother's botanical laboratory and large scientific archives. When the government refused, Canyes placed the papers under lock and key, forbidding anyone to use them.

"I have his manuscripts and books in my residence," Canyes told Cam, "but they've never been put in order."

Cam explained that SIL's translations were available to Catholics and evangelicals alike. Canyes's face dropped into a frown. "This is a Catholic state," he said, "although Protestant missionaries are allowed in the Spanish speaking areas. But the Church has an agreement with the government forbidding the Protestants to propagate their sects in the Indian territories." Cam offered help, favors, and even planes "at a moderate price."

That seemed to do the trick. "Well, perhaps we can work together," said Canyes.[15]

"I'll take it from here," Hernández de Alba told Cam. Returning to Yarinacocha in Peru, Cam wrote SILers, warning that the organization needed to be ready to enter Colombia within six months. He also laid down the law on sectarianism. "Don't apply unless you are willing to go an extra mile in serving the monks and nuns."[16] He almost sounded like a liberal.

To get the Kennedy White House further involved in SIL's cause, Cam would have to enlist SIL in the holy war against Castroism. That meant meeting with Kennedy's new assistant secretary of state for Latin America, Robert Forbes Woodward. Cam brought with him two men who were skilled in public relations with high-ranking government leaders. One was Dr. Torrey Johnson, Billy Graham's aging former leader of Youth for Christ and an original member of the JAARS board. The other was Robert Schneider, his top government liaison official over the years. Schneider had negotiated SIL's advance into the Peruvian and Ecuadorian Amazon, making them SIL's first beachheads in the Amazon basin. Now he was concentrating on Cam's planned advances into western Africa and Colombia.

Woodward was sympathetic. Cam's bilingual educators and JAARS's Helio Couriers were just what the State Department needed. SIL could help the United States respond to Cuba's much-heralded literacy campaign by integrating the hemisphere's guerrilla-prone rural areas into a cultural and political, if not economic, "American solidarity."

Cam was ready for more than words, however. The meeting at the State Department inspired him to a much broader proposal, "An Idea for Inter-American Friendship" that embraced Christ and literacy as instruments of psychological warfare.

The CIA's William Kintner, who had been Nelson Rockefeller's top assistant during his Special Group assignment, was a friend of Schneider. So Cam and Schneider turned to him.

To SILers and Kintner, Indians' political allegiances were worrisome. "These groups, often living in isolated areas, are special targets of communism," warned Schneider. This project would discourage communism by equipping the people to read and write and by supplying literature of the Free World.[17]

Kintner passed the proposal on to Arthur Schlesinger, the White House's link between the liberal intelligentsia and the CIA's covert operations.

Schlesinger listened to SIL's case and subsequently got Kennedy to endorse JAARS's new Helio Courier for Brazil, the *Spirit of Philadelphia,* at a dedication ceremony hosted by Mayor Richardson Dilworth, cousin of Rockefeller aide J. Richardson Dilworth. Once again, Cam's instinct was right. SIL, like the Helio Courier, could make a name for itself as an indispensable component of the Cold War.

The Special Group-C.I. (counterinsurgency) meanwhile made plans for its own secret mission in Brazil. Green Berets would shortly be sent to assist elite Brazilian military units in honing their skills for jungle warfare against insurgents.

Plans were also made to send Green Berets to help the Ecuadorian military beef up its counterinsurgency units.[18] The Ecuadorian generals, prompted by false CIA reports of a mounting Cuban-trained guerrilla insurgency in the Ecuadorian Andes,[19] were already plotting their own coup.

But the highest priority was given to Colombia. There, insurgency had been a reality for over a decade, complete with a self-administered rebel territory liberated from the old dictatorship of General Gustavo Rojas Pinilla. The military was also growing restless. On October 11, army units linked to Rojas Pinilla revolted. Other units who were loyal to President Lleras Camargo crushed the rebellion.

Lleras Camargo insisted that elections would take place as scheduled in 1962. He also muffled the opposition by banning rallies and censoring the news.

Lleras Camargo had survived these confrontations with the U.S.-armed military because he was no Quadros of Brazil or Velasco Ibarra of Ecuador; he was a loyal friend of Washington and New York's power brokers, including Nelson Rockefeller. Green Berets would be sent down, not to back coup plotters but to shore up his relationship with the military by assisting the generals' war against the "Red republics."

To demonstrate U.S. commitment to Lleras Camargo and his new Ten-Year Plan for Colombia as a pilot project for the Alliance for Progress, the Green Berets soon would appear in rural Colombia—but only after their commander in chief, President Kennedy, had laid the psychological-warfare groundwork with a personal visit.

THE YARBOROUGH REPORT: A POLICE STATE FOR DEMOCRACY

Arriving in Bogotá on December 17, 1961, the glamorous first couple of the United States were the perfect touch for inaugurating the Alliance for Progress in Colombia. Greeted by President Lleras Camargo and Ambassador Sanz de Santamaría, the Kennedy party traveled under surprisingly little security in a nation living under a declared state of siege. A coup attempt by right-wing generals had just been thwarted, but Lleras Camargo, in the spirit of openness, insisted that the elections should take place as scheduled the next year. This announcement would please the visiting American president.

Kennedy was loved in Latin America. His motorcade passed by cheering throngs of more than 500,000 Colombians. "Do you know why those workers and *campesinos* are cheering you like that?" Lleras Camargo asked Kennedy. "It's because they believe you are on their side."[20]

To encourage that belief, Kennedy gave a speech at the laying of a cornerstone for a new housing project, and Jacqueline visited a children's hospital.

That night, at the San Carlos Palace, Kennedy impressed Colombians with a humility that was rare in American presidents. "We in the United States have made many mistakes in our relations with Latin America," he said. "We have not always understood the magnitude of your problems, or accepted our share of responsibility for the welfare of the hemisphere. But we are committed in the United States—our will and our energy—to an untiring pursuit of that welfare and I have come to this country to reaffirm that dedication."

He then went further to solidarize himself with the workers and campesinos than many in Colombia and the State Department would have liked. He apologized for the United States' traditional allies. "The leaders of Latin America, the industrialists and the landowners, are, I am sure, also ready to admit past mistakes and accept new responsibilities."[21] It was a brave moment, and to some in Colombia and in the United States, rash.

But it was Mrs. Kennedy who stole the show. Her speech was short, less visionary, and less inspired, but it had a single, powerful sign of respect: it was in Spanish.

Kennedy returned to Washington in triumph.

Colombian rightists among the military and the landowners, however, remained unconvinced that fundamental reforms were necessary. They were fixated on a military solution: removing the peasant republics that offered too fundamental an alternative to what Kennedy had called the "ancient institutions which perpetuate privilege."[22] They viewed Washington's concern over a continental spreading of the Cuban revolution as their opportunity for encouraging U.S. intervention; the intervention would be on behalf of their civil war against the left wing of the Liberal party that the assassinated Jorge Gaitán had once led.

Two events occurred that same month that gave the Colombian military what it wanted. The first was a letter allegedly written by Colombian guerrillas to the already legendary Cuba-based Che Guevara. An army unit operating in Colombia's Llanos Orientales near the Venezuelan border produced a letter it claimed to have captured. Addressed to Che Guevara in Havana, it was purportedly written by an intellectual named Ramón La Rotta, who had joined Liberal settlers who had responded to Conservative persecution by becoming guerrillas. The letter linked Che, if tenuously, to the left Liberals' attempt to form a united National Guerrilla Command. The December 1 letter was accepted as genuine, precipitating a break in diplomatic relations with Cuba a week later. (In Ecuador, similar letters implying Cuban interference had actually been forged by the CIA.[23] Those letters were believed by a gullible press and helped cause the fall of then-President Velasco Arosemena, who had already been forced to break diplomatic relations with Cuba by a bombing of the Catholic cardinal's home, attributed falsely to communists, but actually done by CIA-financed Ecuadorians.[24] This was precisely the CIA's goal.)

The second event boding well for the military occurred a week after Kennedy's departure. In the town of Buga, a bomb exploded amid a Christmas procession; 51 people were killed, and more than 100 wounded. This was the pretext the Pentagon needed to send top U.S. counterinsurgency experts from Fort Bragg, led by Brigadier General William P. Yarborough, commanding general of Fort Bragg's Special Warfare Center. (Later in the decade, as assistant chief of staff for intelligence, Yarborough would bring home his counterinsurgency skills and direct a domestic intelligence program, in collaboration with the FBI's COINTELPRO program and then Deputy Attorney General Warren Christopher, against American civilians identified as "dissident elements." Yarborough specifically targeted the civil rights movement and the "anti-Vietnam/anti-draft movements," extending the army's intelligence gathering beyond "subversion" and "dissident groups" to "prominent persons" who were "friendly" with "leaders of the disturbance or sympathetic with their plans."[25])

Yarborough's team arrived in Colombia on February 2, 1962. Lleras Camargo's press censorship worked smoothly. The chief of staff for the Colombian army turned out the entire officer corps staffing the Colombian army headquarters, but no press account appeared in Bogotá's newspapers. Yarborough's team next consulted U.S. Embassy consul Henry Dearborn,[26] the former de facto CIA chief of station in the Dominican Republic.[27]

Dearborn, a veteran operative in Latin America, was an old acquaintance of the CIA's J. C. King; both had operated in Peronist Argentina after World War II. Recently, Dearborn had been transferred to Colombia from the Dominican Republic, where he and King engineered the CIA's delivery of weapons that were used to assassinate dictator Rafael Trujillo in 1961.[28]

Now Dearborn was conferring with the commander of the Green Berets and arranging for his briefing by CIA station officers. Yarborough apparently was not persuaded that Colombia's communists were "inept bumblers and posed no real threat to the government."[29] He wanted to see for himself. First, he flew to Medellín to inspect the Colombian IV Brigade's antiguerrilla intelligence-gathering capabilities. Then his team moved on to the VI Brigade, which had responsibility for the southern part of the country, and to units spread out over the vast eastern plains. The focus of his attention, however, was the VII Brigade at the cattle town of Villavicencio, gateway to the southern plains that slope gradually into the tropical Amazon basin. Here, in the Department of Meta, was where the action was. Refugees from army attacks on the peasant republics had settled here and turned to guerrilla warfare when attacked.

The VII Brigade kept most of its twenty-two outposts in this region, supplemented by many more police outposts and a paramilitary nonuniformed cavalry, modeled after the Texas Rangers and called "Rurales." The Rurales were controlled by DAS, Colombia's secret police and, like the Rangers, were not known for kindness to Indians. Yarborough took notice that a local battalion commander had "made a successful attempt to win the confidence of the Indians" by assisting them with problems and setting up an army-sponsored store. As a consequence, "the Indians have assisted Lt. Col. Valencia in his internal security mission."[30]

Yarborough was impressed. To help Valencia maintain control over the battalion's "enormous area," the general suggested airplanes.

Specifically, Yarborough recommended Helio Couriers.

Yarborough drafted a long, inclusive set of recommendations for the Special Group in Washington. Besides Green Beret units, he stressed the value of psychological warfare in terrorizing the countryside. Where high-tech solar-powered film projectors did not work, sodium Pentothal would. "Polygraph operators should be trained by the Army and DAS and should habitually interrogate villagers who are believed to be knowledgeable of guerrilla activities. . . . Exhaustive interrogation of bandits, to include sodium pentothal and polygraph, should be used to elicit every shred of information."[31]

Yarborough envisioned setting up a vast police state. "The intensive civilian registration program must be undertaken in order that every resident of Colombia be eventually registered in government files with fingerprints and photographs. Government registration personnel with cameras and fingerprint apparatus must accompany military patrols."[32]

The Inter-American Geographic Survey would be enlisted to make aerial maps of guerrilla-affected areas. "Villages and areas known to harbor bandits should be alleged by the government to be feeding information to the government. Polygraph teams should elicit such information as is needed for this operation."

Troops in civilian clothes would ride armored buses. "Government propaganda should allege certain groups gave evidence against others, and should fabricate evidence to include picture of gang member receiving award. . . . Government success against bandits should be blown up to great proportion. Bandit attacks should be universally described as amateurish, stupid, unsuccessful due to caliber of bandit leadership."[33]

Cordoning off areas; questioning every man, woman, and child twelve years or older; tracking with dogs; shooting the enemy on sight; using helicopters for highly mobile strikes—shades of Vietnam and the Philippines.

It was all vintage Lansdale, to whom, after all, Yarborough ultimately reported at the top of the chain of counterinsurgency command.[34] Lleras Camargo's army chief of staff, General Nova Ruíz, accepted every recommendation except bringing in the Green Beret combat units.[35] That was going too far.

Yarborough was not put off by Nova Ruíz's hesitancy. In a "secret supplement" to his report, he recommended establishing a covert apparatus that "should be charged with clandestine execution of plans developed by the United States Government toward objectives in the political, economic and military fields," rather than depending on the Colombians to find their own solutions. Yarborough justified this summary dismissal of the inter-American principle of mutual respect for national sovereignty on the grounds of "the propensity of most of the leaders in both political and economic fields to ignore their national responsibilities and to seek personal aggrandizement instead. . . .

"It is the considered opinion of the survey team," he concluded, "that a concerted country team effort should be made now to select civilian and military personnel for clandestine training in resistance operations in case they are needed later. This should be done with a view toward development of a civil and military structure for exploitation in the event the Colombians' internal security system deteriorates further. This structure should be used to pressure toward reforms known to be needed, perform counteragent and counterpropaganda functions and as necessary execute paramilitary sabotage and/or terrorist activities against known communist proponents. It should be backed by the United States."[36]

This covert U.S.-backed civilian and military apparatus would supplement the "Army-sponsored nation building or 'civic action' programs." At the same time, the Colombian air force would be urged "to acquire a higher percentage of helicopters and light aircraft, such as the helio courier, in order to support Army anti-guerrilla operations."[37]

A few days before General Yarborough's survey team returned to Fort Bragg, Cam was summoned to Bogotá. SIL's contract had been approved, a smiling Hernández de Alba announced. If SIL would pledge to "respect the prerogatives of the Catholic Church according to the terms of the Concordat"[38] between the Vatican and Colombia, the Conservatives who would soon succeed Lleras Camargo's Liberal government would allow Cam's American Protestants into the Indian tribes. Cam agreed without hesitation.

The Colombian air force's General Armando Urrego Bernal provided Cam with land for SIL's base near the town of Puerto Lleras in Meta department, south of Villavicencio. The base was called Lomalinda, "Pretty Place."*

Shortly after Cam signed the contract and General Yarborough's report was read at a March meeting of the Special Group in Washington, Colombians near Villavicencio watched a long column of army trucks bearing U.S. insignias pass through. The column headed south, toward the Macarena Mountains, just east of where SIL's base would be located. No troops ever came out, they claimed. Explosions were heard rumbling from the Macarena Mountains, however. Soon afterward, the Colombian military ruled that airspace over the mountains was off-limits for all commercial airplanes. Over the years, reports would appear sporadically of planes being lost. Some pilots who strayed overhead and did come out reported seeing air runways and telecommunications antennas. In the early 1970s, the Colombian military would deny any foreign base or presence in the Macarena. Only American stockholders of the Loeb family-owned APCO Oil company and those who read APCO's annual reports knew better. APCO entered the Macarena in 1967. In 1976, an APCO map showed that the Macarena had been honeycombed with clandestine runways.[39]

By then, Standard Oil of New Jersey, Texaco, and Gulf had joined other oil companies in drilling for oil in the Llanos. JAARS's Helio Couriers were taking off for Villavicencio from Lomalinda, the gray-misted Macarena Mountains hovering in the distance like a mirage.

With SIL's entry into Colombia, the final assault on the Amazon—and the Indians—had begun.

---

*Celanese Corporation (of Charlotte, North Carolina, and Bogotá) would donate the first new plane; Quaker Oats would be asked by heir Henry Crowell to provide a radio; and Cam would help Robert Schneider in the advance, living with Elaine and their children in two trailers donated by Standard Oil of New Jersey.

27

CAMELOT VERSUS POCANTICO: THE DECLINE AND FALL OF JOHN F. KENNEDY

Fractures in the Dream

On July 18, 1962, guards at the presidential palace in Lima, Peru, watched helplessly as a U.S.-supplied Sherman tank suddenly appeared out of the night and smashed through the palace's tall iron gates. U.S.-trained Rangers poured through and quickly seized the building. Inside, President Manuel Prado y Ugarteche woke in his bed to find a Ranger officer standing over him, announcing that he was under arrest. Peru, the original showcase for both SIL- and U.S.-sponsored development in the Amazon basin, was placed under martial law.

Informed of the coup, the Kennedy White House was worried, but not surprised. Peru in the last year had become a cauldron of conflicting ideologies, and recent elections had done nothing to resolve the internal tension that threatened to engulf the country in violence. The indefatigable leader of Peru's Indians, Haya de la Torre, head of the reformist APRA party, had just won a plurality in a three-way presidential race. But the army had refused to accept Haya—an enemy of thirty years—as president. Desperate to hold on to the power he had sought for so

---

long, Haya tried to cut a deal: He would give former dictator Manuel Odría the presidency if APRA were given a cabinet majority. Haya's proposal only inflamed the generals.

APRA's power base was the rural and urban labor force. As a result of Peru's large foreign debts, low wages at foreign-owned mines, and an almost feudal system of land tenure, the Andes' huge Indian population had remained impoverished, illiterate, and unassimilated. As Indians migrated from poor mountain villages, great shantytowns began to ring Andean cities and Lima, gradually encroaching on Peru's upper-class urban enclaves.

Haya's program of nationalization and "Indo-American" unity, meanwhile, threatened industrialists, the military, and the more conservative covert operatives in J. C. King's Western Hemisphere Division of the CIA. Haya's APRA was the only popular-based alternative to the growing influence of Marxism and Castroism, but King's operatives did not see it that way. When the generals decided to act, the local CIA station did nothing to deter them.

With the military coup, the immediate threat of APRA coming to power was removed. President Kennedy, however, was unhappy about the coup's damage to the democratic image and social goals of the Alliance for Progress.

Kennedy sensed that the Alliance's democratic ideology was on the verge of being surrendered to the tired cynicism of Realpolitik. He could no longer sit on the sidelines. He broke diplomatic relations with Lima and suspended $80 million in credits and all military aid.

"The declaration of the peoples of America adopted at Punta del Este," Kennedy declared, "set forth the aim to improve and strengthen democratic institutions through the application of the principle of self determination within a framework of developing democratic institutions. In the case of Peru this great cause has suffered a severe setback." Kennedy called for a return to civilian rule. "We feel that this hemisphere can only be secure and free with democratic governments."[1]

Such a strong statement against a ruling military junta by an American president was unprecedented. Kennedy was gambling his administration's prestige on APRA's ability to mobilize a popular protest against the coup. When APRA's call for a national strike failed, so did Kennedy's resolve.

It was left to David's and Nelson's friend, J. Peter Grace of W. R. Grace & Company, to deliver the coup de grace to the Alliance's reforms in Peru. Leading a delegation of executives from American mining companies that were doing business in Peru, Grace descended upon the White House like an avenging angel. His delegation told Kennedy that his actions might provoke the Peruvian military to expropriate their properties.[2]

Kennedy listened carefully. Men like Grace were ignored only at great peril. Within a month, accepting the junta's release of prisoners and promise to hold elections in 1963, Kennedy restored full diplomatic relations and all economic assistance to the Peruvian junta. Nine Latin American governments that had followed Kennedy's lead had to swallow their pride and do likewise. The prestige of the United States suffered, and the influence of Marxism among frustrated young Peruvian intellectuals soon grew into plans for guerrilla war.

If Kennedy was concerned that U.S. military aid was being used to prop up military dictatorships in Latin America, he was even more worried about communist insurgencies. In January, staff members of the National Security Council (NSC) had persuaded him to reverse his earlier decision to separate the economic programs of the Agency for International Development (AID) from the CIA's police training programs. He quietly set up a task force to study the usefulness of the police program. The result was retrenchment: the creation of an Office of Public Safety within AID. Soon an International Police Academy sprouted in Washington, sponsored by AID but actually run by the CIA.[3] In the years ahead, the academy's students would include trainers of tribal police in Brazil. Once again, Kennedy's desire for at least the rudiments of democracy in Latin America fell beneath the wheels of the United States' powerful military-industrial juggernaut.

At the same time, Rockefeller allies consolidated their hold on the new counterinsurgency infrastructure by expanding it. General Maxwell Taylor, who now chaired the Special Group-C.I., joined Roswell Gilpatric in founding a new counterinsurgency school for foreign service officers, to be operated under the auspices of the State Department's Foreign Service Institute. Billed as the National Interdepartmental Seminar, the school began in June 1962. Lecturers included General Edward Lansdale, then in charge of a new ultrasecret effort to assassinate Fidel Castro, code-named Operation MONGOOSE.

Attorney General Robert Kennedy enthusiastically served as the president's eyes and ears in the C.I. infrastructure. But as he prodded this apparatus to greater efforts against Cuba, this only prodded Cuba, in turn, to seek greater security from invasion.

On October 15, the president was presented with U-2 photographic evidence that the Soviets, contrary to their previous pledges, were placing surface-to-surface missiles in Cuba with a 2,000-mile range. These missiles could reach the entire United States up to the Rocky Mountains.

That afternoon, Kennedy convened the NSC Executive Committee. It would meet, with intermission, for the rest of the week.

The ExCom, as the press called the committee, had a heavy representation of veterans of the Rockefeller network of influence. They all supported an action proposed by the Joint Chiefs of Staff that probably would have triggered World War III: a first-strike by jets to "take out" the missile sites. Robert Kennedy was appalled. "I now know how Tojo felt when he was planning Pearl Harbor," he said.[4] He and Defense Secretary Robert McNamara pushed for a naval quarantine to buy time for negotiations. This proposal provided a middle ground between unacceptable acquiescence and nuclear war.

Meanwhile, the Pentagon assembled the largest invasion force since World War II. More than 100,000 combat-ready troops gathered in Florida, an amphibious task force steamed in the area with 40,000 marines, and tactical fighters and 14,000 reservists were brought into Florida to provide airborne transfer support for the Green Berets. Only Robert Kennedy's direct intervention prevented one of Colonel King's CIA colleagues from sending CIA hit teams into Cuba against Castro at the height of the crisis.[5]

As Soviet ships and submarines steamed toward the U.S. naval blockade, religious services were held throughout the world. In Buenos Aires, Billy Graham preached about "The End of the World."

Running though John Kennedy's deliberations about the planet's life and death was his concern about New York's Republican leaders, Governor Nelson Rockefeller and Senator Kenneth Keating. Rockefeller had launched a salvo of criticism against the administration during a speaking tour that spring.

More ominous, Keating, whose own chances for reelection in 1964 would be greatly influenced by Rockefeller's presidential race that same year, had been challenging Kennedy since August on the Senate floor with reports about the presence of Soviet missiles in Cuba.

In July, the head of the Veterans of Foreign Wars had made a similar claim, citing the CIA's U-2 flights as the source.[6] The White House had begun to suspect that Keating's source was someone high in the CIA who had been asked to undermine the president.[7] (In fact, Keating was getting his information from the conservative network of Cuban refugees that was tied to King.) On October 10, Senator Keating upped the ante. Leaving his sources mysterious, Keating charged that he had confirmed reports that Soviet offensive missiles were in Cuba. Kennedy's advisers were alarmed. Keating was publicly disclosing astounding facts that they themselves were not aware of until October 14, when the CIA's Richard Helms informed McGeorge Bundy of the U-2 findings.

A week later, on October 22, Adolf Berle was waiting to go on public television with the Rockefeller Foundation's Kenneth Thompson when President Kennedy made his dramatic announcement of a U.S. blockade of Cuba. "I was supporting [Kennedy] for all in sight," Berle recorded in his diary, ". . . and this time there will be no charges that somebody weakened at the crucial moment."

To Berle, the U.S. military blockade was simply a matter of self-defense and therefore legal under Article 51 of the U.N. Charter. Kennedy's mentioning that Latin American cities could also be targeted by the missiles in Cuba was "technically beautiful," judged Berle, giving members of the Organization of American States the ammunition they needed to back the blockade.

However, legal gymnastics could not prevent war or hold the U.S. military in line. "The President is in a grave situation, and he does not know how to get out of it. We are under very severe stress," Robert Kennedy informed the Soviets at the height of the crisis, according to Nikita Khrushchev. "In fact, we are under pressure from our military to use force against Cuba. . . . If the situation continues much longer, the President is not sure that the military will not overthrow him and seize power. The American Army could get out of control."[8] Even after the Soviets capitulated, Robert Kennedy later reported that at least one high-ranking military official (probably Air Force General Curtis LeMay) advised President Kennedy to proceed with air strikes on Cuba anyway.[9]

Later, after Khrushchev agreed to dismantle the missile bases in return for Kennedy's calling off a planned U.S. invasion of Cuba, Berle could not resist giving his friend Nelson Rockefeller some credit for Kennedy's success. "I never was fonder in my life of Article 51, nor gladder that it was there (Nelson Rockefeller's personal achievement) and that exactly similar language is in the Treaty of Rio: 'The inherent right of individual or collective self defense.'"[10]

Nelson's contribution to Kennedy's success, if bitterly ironic, was also unrecognized outside Nelson's circle. Nelson won reelection in November, but by a smaller margin than in 1958. Berle suffered, too. "Having split my ticket and supported Rockefeller, I am in political isolation again. . . . The White House would like to destroy Rockefeller as a possible rival."[11]

The sixty-seven-year-old Berle's long career was all but over. Four days after the election, beneath a storm-tossed gray sky, he saw Kennedy and Rockefeller again at Eleanor Roosevelt's funeral. Walking with mourners from the little church at Hyde Park, New York, down to Eleanor's grave beside her husband's in the rose garden of the old Roosevelt mansion, Berle remembered that he had first seen that house in May 1932, when he joined Franklin D. Roosevelt's brain trust as one of its more conservative members. Eleanor's funeral "was distinctly the end of an era," he wrote, observing that the original New Dealers were "now old and white haired . . . and perhaps I with them, visibly going over the horizon line which divides politics and history. . . ."[12]

The Berles shared their pew with Roosevelt's second vice president, Henry Wallace, as if the deep differences over the social direction of the nation were now also relegated to the grave. For in the postwar generation led by Rockefeller and Kennedy, the new gospel was not redistribution of the nation's wealth, but unending growth. Arguments about the need for income distribution to bolster consumer demand were sent into exile. What now ruled was the "trickle-down" theory of an economy fueled by tax cuts and increasing amounts of credit commanded by governments willing to go ever deeper into debt, control over cheap oil, and widening markets in the Third World.

Yet the Rockefellers and Berle were unhappy. The Cuban missile crisis, once publicly supported and past, seemed a bitter victory to Berle. Castro, though humiliated by the Soviets' unilateral decision to withdraw the missiles, won survival for his revolution. Kennedy, by calling off an invasion by armed forces and avoiding the risk of nuclear war, had removed the only real possibility of reversing Cuba's nationalization of American corporate properties within Berle's lifetime.

Behind the doors of the boardrooms of many of the nation's largest corporations, Kennedy's greatest victory quickly developed into his greatest defeat.

The Pyrrhic Victory

For some business interests, leaving Castro in Cuba was the final straw. Kennedy already had earned their wrath when he took to national television in April 1962 to announce his opposition to U.S. Steel's price hikes. Fearing inflation, the administration had also leaned on the steelworkers' unions not to strike, but instead to defer a wage increase for the first time in a generation. But business resisted the guidelines; maximizing profits was its raison d'être. "My father always told me that all businessmen were sons-of-bitches," Kennedy said privately after being told by U.S. Steel chairman Roger Blough of the coming price increase, "but I never believed it till now."[13]

The president's statement was leaked to the press, infuriating corporate America. Confronted with Bethlehem Steel and four other companies joining the price increase, Kennedy used a televised press conference to say that with all the sacrifices and changes the nation was enduring, "the American people will find it hard, as I do, to accept a situation in which a tiny handful of steel executives, whose pursuit of private power and profit exceeds their sense of public responsibility, can show such utter contempt for the interest of one hundred and eighty five million Americans."[14]

Kennedy mustered the vast federal resources at his disposal. The administration shifted defense contracts from the Morgan-controlled steel giant, threatened legislation, used a grand jury investigation of possible antitrust violations of price-fixing collusion, and even sent FBI agents to question a newsman about a report that U.S. Steel had pressured Bethlehem into collusion.

Within days, Inland Steel and Bethlehem Steel abandoned the fight. U.S. Steel then surrendered with a price rollback. Kennedy had proved just who was president of the United States. But he paid a price: corporate enmity.

Now, with Cuba, the domestic dispute over who should hold the ultimate legal power—corporations or the elected government—became an issue of foreign policy. On the face of it, Kennedy's foreign policy looked like a businessman's formula for success. The president persuaded foreign governments to buy more military equipment from the United States arms industry to reduce the deficit in the balance of payments. At home, he encouraged domestic savings with tax cuts benefiting corporations. He reduced the deficit in the balance of payments abroad by tying 80 percent of foreign aid to purchases in the United States. He encouraged restraint of tourist spending abroad. He reduced tariffs (except for those on textiles and chemicals) to promote sales of U.S. goods.

To those who followed U.S. trade, the Trade Expansion Act of 1962 served only those large corporations that could afford a "free trade" policy. The pressing need was not for increased trade, at least not yet. The balance of trade was already favorable, amounting to nearly $5 billion a year. The problem was the balance-of-payments deficit. And that deficit was caused not by unfavorable trade, but by government spending in Europe and Asia on military installations and servicemen's salaries and by corporate investments in foreign factories, mines, and agribusinesses.[15] Foreign earnings, "parked" in Swiss and Caribbean banks serving as tax havens, were never repatriated.

If Kennedy's restraining of spending abroad contradicted his encouraging American corporations to invest in the Third World as a bulwark against communism, U.S. corporations resolved the contradiction. In the wake of the Cuban Missile Crisis in turbulent Latin America, Teodoro Moscoso and other administrators of the Alliance for Progress read with dismay a *New York Times* report in November that American corporate investment in Latin America was "drying up." Business leaders demanded that the U.S. Treasury guarantee their private investments from losses from nationalization. Otherwise, they would not invest.

David Rockefeller led the most sophisticated wing of the business critics. On May 11, he was a guest at a state dinner for France's cultural minister, André Malraux. Kennedy, eager to win over business, sought David's views on the economy in a private conversation. David had been Kennedy's first choice for treasury secretary, and Kennedy's suggestion that he write his views in a letter seemed innocent enough. David responded with a long letter calling for a reduction in government spending and a cut in corporate income taxes to stimulate domestic investment, bolster economic growth, and restore the United States' competitive edge against the European Common Market.

Kennedy's answer to David, while confident in tone, was defensive in substance. The president insisted that the economy's basic position was strong. He ticked off his administration's efforts to cut business taxes, increase trade, reduce tariffs, keep the dollar strong, and hold increases in the cost of labor within the confines of productivity increases—all points that David already had acknowledged and did not need repeating except for their publicity value. But where Kennedy, perhaps inadvertently, touched a raw nerve was in the area of corporate America's hidden wealth abroad. While reassuring the United States' foremost international banker that he had no plans to restrict the flight of private capital,

Kennedy insisted that "our tax laws should surely not encourage the export of dollars by permitting 'tax havens' and other undue preferences."[16]

The president had struck home. The Rockefellers had many such tax havens abroad. Small Caribbean "brass plate" banks, large Swiss commercial banks, and vaguely named private investment firms in small countries like Luxembourg overflowed with American cash, precious metals, and, most important for tax purposes, portfolios of stock holdings in foreign companies. Most large American corporations doing business overseas also "parked" their profits in foreign commercial banks under the names of wholly owned subsidiaries or limited partnerships, and often in foreign subsidiaries of megabanks like David's Chase Manhattan. The Rockefellers' top financial aide, J. Richardson Dilworth, was a director of two Luxembourg holding companies with investments in Latin America and oversaw the investment firms of the International Basic Economy Corporation (IBEC) in Colombia, Brazil, Peru, and other countries. In addition, IBEC's American Overseas Finance Company held over $26 million worth of holdings in twenty-nine countries.[17]

Kennedy's 1962 tax bill directly challenged these tax benefits by removing the distinction between repatriated profits and profits reinvested abroad, making both taxable. It also brought under the scrutiny of the Internal Revenue Service revenues "parked" in overseas tax havens by subsidiary companies.

Eager to show some support from business, Kennedy released his correspondence with David to *Life* magazine. Kennedy had concluded his letter by stating that "I am gratified that we agree so widely on basic problems and goals." If this statement appeared disingenuous to those privy to the Kennedy-Rockefeller disagreements, it at least had the saving grace of ignoring means—including the value the Kennedys placed on social reform. To *Life's* editor, Kennedy praised Rockefeller's letter as the kind of serious "dialogue" he enjoyed with business leaders. But for David, this would be the last time Kennedy would use the Rockefeller name for public relations purposes—and the last time David would try publicly to persuade Kennedy to change course. From now on, if anything, the Rockefellers would attack.

Nelson, buoyed by his 1962 reelection, attempted to leap into the breach between Kennedy and business. He was sure he could beat Kennedy in 1964, he said,[18] and many believed him.

David helped in his capacity as chairman of a key subcommittee of the Commerce Committee for the Alliance for Progress, a group of business executives of companies active in Latin America. Chase Manhattan Bank, on the anniversary of the first Punta del Este conference, had already warned that Kennedy's willingness to lend funds for government-owned projects would sour corporate America on the Alliance for Progress.

Kennedy had extended credit for development in Brazil's impoverished

Northeast in April, only months after President João Goulart nationalized ITT and issued an expropriation decree against Hanna Mining's rich iron concession in Minas Gerais. Kennedy's loan won him little love on Wall Street. Hanna Mining was part of an industrial troika that involved National Steel and Chrysler, and the Rockefellers had just bought a large interest in Chrysler.

Kennedy's acknowledgment of Brazil's rights under national sovereignty and his granting of yet another AID loan for $398.5 million in 1963 were judged foolhardy and dangerous, despite Robert Kennedy's wringing a handsome settlement for ITT out of Goulart. Now, with American investment in Latin America heading for a net *withdrawal* of $38 million, a far cry from the $300 million yearly *investment* Kennedy had pledged at Punta del Este, David's Commerce Department subcommittee demanded that Kennedy abandon his government-to-government loan policy and his emphasis on social reforms and concentrate instead on loans to businesses and social policies favored by businessmen. Only this policy reversal could dampen the tidal wave of rising expectations that Latin American conservative landholders and businessmen feared. "The first requirement is that the governments—and as far as possible, the people—of Latin America know that the U.S. has changed its policy to put primary stress on improvement in the general business climate as a prerequisite for social development and reform. . . .

"A second requirement concerns a change in the criteria for granting aid. . . . The U.S. should concentrate its economic aid program in countries that show the greatest inclination to adopt measures to improve the investment climate, and withhold aid from others until satisfactory performance has been demonstrated."[19] It was the type of all-or-nothing ultimatum that would end up keeping most of South America in line up to the present day.

The CIA's Loose Cannon

In the last year of the Kennedy administration, communism—and those in Washington who were alleged to be "soft" on it—emerged as the major theme of Nelson Rockefeller's campaign to replace John F. Kennedy as president of the United States.

Nelson returned to what he considered Kennedy's Achilles heel, Cuba, the chief outpost of the Evil Empire overseas. Following the domino theory in reverse, he traced the mounting revolution in the hemisphere back to Cuba. Castro's daring nationalization of American properties encouraged similar sentiments that had been simmering in Latin America since the Bolivian and Mexican expropriations of Standard Oil in the 1930s. Those expropriations had been Nelson's schoolhouse in foreign affairs. Now Kennedy, by agreeing not to invade Cuba in order to end the Cuban missile crisis peaceably, had allowed the task to remain uncompleted.

Cuba was only "a half done job," wrote Berle, because the Soviets were still in Cuba in "control of the territory." Most important, Castro would be allowed to survive.

The Kennedy administration had ordered the CIA to end its raids on Cuba and close down its secret training base in Louisiana. It told General Lansdale to stop the MONGOOSE assassination attempts on Castro. Invasion plans were scuttled. Nothing, certainly not pledges by Kennedy to veterans of the Bay of Pigs that their flag would be flown again over "a free Havana," could soothe the feelings of betrayal. The hopeful exiles had answered Kennedy's promise by chanting "War! War! War!" and war they would have, if only by proxy. Flying CIA warplanes against the followers of the deceased Patrice Lumumba in the Congo and hunting down guerrillas for the CIA throughout Latin America, they would be the CIA's loose cannons, the unresolved "disposal problem" that Allen Dulles had used to persuade Kennedy to approve the invasion.[20]

In Latin America, Kennedy was the most popular American president since Roosevelt. Even before the missile crisis, in June 1962, Mexicans had thrown confetti and given him a hero's welcome as he laid a wreath at the monument to the fallen cadets of Chapultepec Hill. In the United States, however, hatred was growing.

Mafia chieftains, who had been recruited by the CIA to kill Castro, now found themselves the target of investigations launched by Attorney General Robert Kennedy. "Here I am helping the government, helping the country," said John Roselli, "and that little sonofabitch is breaking my balls. Let the little bastard do what he wants. There isn't anything he can do to me. . . . I got important friends in important places in Washington that'll cut his water off."[21]

Santos Trafficante, owner of casinos and prostitution and narcotics rings in prerevolutionary Havana, told Cuban exile leader José Alemán, "Mark my word, this man [Robert] Kennedy is in trouble and he will get what is coming to him." New Orleans's Carlos Marcello, having illegally returned from El Salvador after being deported by Kennedy to Guatemala, drew his bead higher. "The dog will keep biting you if you only cut off its tail," he said of the president, comparing the attorney general to the tail; "but if you cut off the dog's head it will die."[22]

The Mafia and Cuban exiles were not the only breeders of hatred. Southern segregationists were furious over Kennedy's desegregation of federal housing after the November 1962 election and his subsequent introduction of a civil rights bill that had only one major supporter in the administration: Robert Kennedy.[23]

And the military and the CIA were furious over Kennedy's plan to have Undersecretary of State Averell Harriman negotiate a nuclear test ban with the Soviets.

By the spring, when Senator John Stennis of Texas responded to leaks from the CIA and held hearings on a test ban, the conspiracy against the treaty had reached up to the office of the director of the CIA at Langley, Virginia. Dean Rusk had been less than enthusiastic about the test ban. But no one expected the new CIA director, John McCone, former director of Standard Oil of California, actually to help Stennis make his case against a treaty by secretly lending him CIA advisers on nuclear weapons. But McCone did.[24]

In September, just before the election, Nelson had asked Berle what he thought of Kennedy. "I said I thought Kennedy thought and worried too much," Berle recalled, "and too deeply—thus impairing capacity for action. . . . He wondered whether Kennedy did think."[25] Now Nelson publicly wondered if Kennedy was following a policy of appeasement.

Nelson took this theme of White House trickery before the press in January 1963, accusing Kennedy of withholding facts before the blockade and then doing the same with regard to the "Cuban war-making build-up. This, as the first, probably is just the starter."[26] Two weeks later, Nelson hosted a formal lunch at his Pocantico estate for Venezuela's Rómulo Betancourt, who was hoping to persuade U.S. Steel to mine ore in the Orinoco area for the state-owned Venezuelan Steel Company, not just export ore to the States and Japan in ships owned by D. K. Ludwig. Berle was among the guests.

"He [Betancourt] apparently had a good talk with Kennedy. . . . Increasingly it is clear that Kennedy did negotiate with the Russians about Cuba; did get a half agreement to withdraw some troops; did impliedly at least accept a Russian force of greater or less strength in Cuba—in a word, was jockeyed into the position of agreeing to permit a Russian force in Cuba. This will raise hell as it increasingly comes out."[27] Nelson made sure it did, taking his charges of appeasement to Houston in April.

"There has been a sharp change of policy of which the public has not been advised," he told Texas Republican congressmen. Nelson had no trouble suggesting that the president was getting soft on communism. He found the suspension of raids on Cuba "very hard to understand. I hope it is not an arrangement to appease Khrushchev."[28] Nelson was making an obvious bid for the conservative wing of the Republican party, which was backing his major rival for the nomination, Senator Barry Goldwater.

It was beginning to look like Nelson was unstoppable. He was the only Republican who could win the large industrial cities of the North, as well as attract some of the more conservative votes of the West and Southwest. If the white South disliked the Rockefellers, they disliked the Kennedys even more.

The president was worried. Roswell Gilpatric, who knew the Rockefeller brothers personally, noted Kennedy's obsession with his most dangerous rival. "JFK regarded Nelson Rockefeller as his probable opposition in 1964. He had both a fascination and a fear of Rockefeller"—fascination because Nelson was a liberal; fear because Kennedy did not know a lot about political power in New York.

"Whenever I was with the President alone, whether it was on the *Enterprise* or on the *Northampton* or down in Palm Beach or at the Army-Navy football game, he endlessly questioned me about every phase of the Rockefeller family. . . . You know, their marriages, their children, their wealth. It just absorbed him. . . . I think he felt that it would be a close contest between the two of them, as he saw it, and he wanted to have a good feel for what he was going to encounter."[29]

But then Nelson, whom Tod had divorced a year earlier, made one of his characteristic impulsive moves that he relished and his family dreaded. He decided to marry the woman he had loved since 1958.

For the Woman He Loved

She was called "Happy" for her bright disposition, but Margaretta Murphy was taking a terrible risk. So was Nelson. Happy had divorced her husband just a month before. To be free for Nelson, she gave up her four children. Nelson, feeling that he had paid his dues by his own divorce, gambled that voters would accept true love.

His family was stunned. Junior had tried to press upon all his sons the burden of social responsibility that came with wealth. A Rockefeller would be wise to subject himself to the laws of a Protestant heaven and the limits of mortal men. But for Nelson, only the first half of Junior's lesson stuck.

Now, both Junior and family adviser Frank Jamieson were gone. Nelson could not be constrained from following his heart. And as the wedding approached, there was much tugging at his heart. The woman he had loved for five years had given up everything for him. She was eager for the official consecration of their love.

So was he. At fifty-four, Nelson was eighteen years older than Happy, but the attractive woman made him look and feel younger. United in marriage at Laurance's home on the Pocantico estate, they smiled bravely, ignoring the absence of Nelson's children—Rodman, Steven, and Mary—and of his brothers John 3rd, David, and Winthrop.

The quiet event at Pocantico exploded in the headlines when it was announced four hours after the ceremony. Nelson was besieged by reporters. As he had done so often in the past, he retreated to Latin America. He jetted south with Happy into the welcoming arms of Venezuela.

At Monte Sacro, Nelson's vast 18,000-acre ranch, the couple posed for honeymoon pictures, then flew north to Laurance's resort in the Virgin Islands. When the honeymoon was over and Nelson returned with his now-pregnant wife, he found that his lead over Goldwater had evaporated. He now was 30 to 35 percent behind.

An old enemy of the Rockefellers, not seen since the Fundamentalist Controversy of the 1920s, was aroused. Forty years had not weakened Fundamentalism. If anything, the Great Depression, World War II, and the renewed destruction of parity between agricultural prices and the costs of production since 1953 had nourished it. As the fabric of rural society continued to unravel, migration to the cities spread its unrest, resentment, and Fundamentalist culture to the new working-class suburbs. These bedroom communities retained the character of isolated small towns. With the exception of the national media, exposure to outside cultural influences was contained through local school boards and zoning. Fundamentalism thrived, immune from challenge by science until *Sputnik* forced the federal government to provide funds for the sciences through grants and a massive student-loan program. And even then, the influence of science often was restricted to the technological and seldom allowed into the social realm and discourse on philosophical foundations.

Fundamentalism had been beaten before, and Nelson, insulated from the provincialism that still held sway over much of American life, did not consider it a great threat. He and his brothers had gloried in their self-appointed roles as the vanguard of the last drive of urban modernity upon not only rural America, but a predominantly rural world. As Nelson championed higher educational standards, a state university system, racial integration, and a science-based faith, the old battle with Fundamentalism was joined.

Only now, Fundamentalism had corporate angels like the Pews of Philadelphia and the Hunts of Texas, men whose wealth offered Fundamentalism unprecedented financial means to enter politics on a more sophisticated level. Through the modern corporation and the armed forces, Fundamentalism had experienced men and women who had seen the world and learned modern organizational, fund-raising, communication, and transportation skills. So armed, all the furies of the Religious Right focused their hatred on the one man standing in the way of the Republican nomination of ultraconservative Barry Goldwater: the quintessential liberal of the Eastern Establishment, Nelson Rockefeller.

Scorn came down in cascades of "two broken homes" and "children deprived of their mother," pounding away at the rock of reputation Junior had laid as a foundation for the family. For the first time since the turn of the century, when the Congregational elders rejected a $100,000 Rockefeller gift to their missionaries as "tainted money," the name Rockefeller had become synonymous with immorality in the press. It was as if all that his father had tried to bury under good works was now being unearthed by Nelson's ambition.

If Nelson was surprised by the conservatives' reaction, criticism from the liberal camp stunned him. Reinhold Niebuhr, the outstanding resident theorist of the Rockefeller-funded Union Theological Seminary, thought his cleaning woman right when she judged the governor's remarriage "too quick."[30] The local Pocantico minister who had presided over the ceremony was rebuked by his own presbytery.

Stung, Nelson tried to recapture his reputation and his liberal base by attacking the conservative wing he now had no hope of winning over. In July, he ended his truce with Goldwater. Releasing a manifesto entitled "A Matter of Principle," he charged that "the Republican Party is in real danger of subversion by a radical, well financed and highly disciplined minority." Using the recent Young Republicans convention in San Francisco as his sole example, he denounced "vociferous and well-drilled extremist elements boring within the party."[31] On November 7, Nelson called a press conference in the Red Room of the State Capitol, an imposing hall with plush red carpets and drapes and Honduran mahogany wainscotted walls—a place where history in the Empire State had been made many times. Surrounded by such regal splendor, Nelson had no qualms about asking ordinary Americans to support his quest for the presidency.

A CLASH OF WILLS

Nelson pointedly attacked the Right's proposal that the Republican Party "write off the Negro and other minority states . . . write off the big cities, and that it direct its appeal primarily to the electoral votes of the South, plus the West . . . to erect political power on the outlawed and immoral base of segregation."[32] Wooing the African American vote had the dual value of enlisting liberal support against Goldwater's followers from the John Birch Society while offering frustrated civil rights activists an alternative to a cautious Kennedy.

Kennedy, who once confessed that Rockefeller could have beaten him in 1960, thought that Nelson would be a greater threat than Goldwater in 1964. Nelson's speeches in September scored Kennedy for his caution on civil rights despite the president's introduction of a civil rights bill.

The international balance of payments, likewise, had "actually gotten worse," he charged. Unless corporate and personal income taxes were cut further to stimulate investment and spending overseas was reduced, the national debt would cause such a hemorrhage of gold to foreign investors who were worried about the dollar that it "could cause a worldwide financial collapse similar to that which made the depression of the 1930s so severe."[33]

Similar apocalyptic visions filled Nelson's criticisms of Kennedy's nuclear arms policies. Kennedy's insistence on keeping U.S. control over nuclear weapons in Europe was a "delusion" that "keeps us from exercising leadership in the crucial area of strategic doctrine." This, he told the American Newspaper Publishers Association, was a "prescription for chaos."[34]

By October, Nelson struck the anvil of anticommunism again. He could barely give lukewarm support to Kennedy's test-ban treaty with the Soviets, advocating "a strong and aggressive program of underground testing" backed up with "preparation of a series of stand-by atmospheric tests for the contingency of cancellation of the treaty."[35]

Finally, after criticizing Kennedy for allowing President Sukarno of Indonesia to regain West New Guinea from the Dutch, he tackled the question of Vietnam. Here, on the question of U.S. withdrawal, Rockefeller and Goldwater could agree. "Pulling out cannot ever be considered," said Nelson in October[36] after the president authorized Defense Secretary McNamara to announce plans to pull 1,000 U.S. Marines out of Vietnam by the end of the year. Nelson was sharply critical of Kennedy's suspension of U.S. military aid to Ngo Dinh Diem after Diem used troops to raid Buddhist temples and repress the legal opposition to his rule.

"We have witnessed the extraordinary spectacle of the U.S. Government apparently encouraging a military revolt and otherwise undermining the existing government in a way that can only further the objectives of the communist campaign."[37] Nelson was hinting, as Kenneth Keating had done a year before with regard to the presence of Cuban missiles, that he had knowledge of government secrets: A coup was in the making.

The military coup—urged on the president by Averell Harriman, the NSC, and the CIA—took place on November 1. Kennedy was in a meeting in the Cabinet Room when word arrived that President Diem and his brother-in-law, Ngo Dinh Nhu, had been murdered.

The president was stunned. He had wanted Diem out of the way so that a more popular government around General Duong Van "Big" Minh would allow him to disengage U.S. combat troops after the 1964 election. But he had not wanted Diem dead. He had ordered Harriman to send explicit instructions to Ambassador Henry Cabot Lodge in Saigon to warn the CIA station that the United States could not be involved in assassination. The death of an allied head of state in a U.S.-backed coup was terrible news for other U.S. allies. It was also terrible news for Kennedy: His twenty-eight-month-long effort to regain the president's constitutional authority over the CIA had failed.

"Kennedy leaped to his feet and rushed from the room with a look of shock and dismay on his face which I had never seen before," General Maxwell Taylor recalled.[38] When he was gone, some NSC members amused themselves by mulling over the president's naïveté in encouraging a coup without realizing that assassination was always a likely prospect.

No one understood this likelihood better than Nelson's old friend, J. C. King. Although Cuba had been taken out of his hands after CIA Director Allen Dulles's fall and been given to Deputy Director of Plans Richard Helms, King had tried to reassert control over Cuban affairs after the Bay of Pigs failure caused a power vacuum in the CIA's Cuban operations. King's original proposal to assassinate Cuba's leaders was being followed up with vigor by the CIA. Despite the president's explicit order that assassinations were not to be U.S. policy, despite Robert Kennedy's termination of General Lansdale's MONGOOSE assassination plots after the Cuban missile crisis, and despite the president's authorization of the

Department of State's William Atwood to open negotiations with Cuba about normalizing relations, the CIA was pursuing Fidel Castro's death.

Years later, the CIA's new director, John McCone, would deny any knowledge of what was under way, but he clearly had grave differences with his commander in chief. He had lent CIA analysts to Senator John Stennis's effort to kill Kennedy's nuclear test-ban treaty.[39] And as a former large stockholder and director of Standard Oil of California, he may have differed with Kennedy on the president's recent threat to reduce the oil-depletion allowance, a move that would cost oil companies an estimated $280 million a year. He certainly had not liked the president's July 1961 recommendation to the Foreign Intelligence Advisory Board to dismember the CIA. He had been unhappy with Kennedy's directives making the military responsible for all large covert operations like the Bay of Pigs and the CIA's "Secret Army" in Indochina. And, of course, he had favored Diem in Vietnam.

But he always followed the president's orders. Had he not removed J. C. King from any control over Cuban affairs as his first act after taking over as director of the CIA?[40] And had he not given the intelligence division more oversight over covert operations, setting up a special study group to restructure the CIA, appointing as one of its members General Cortlandt Van Rensselaer Schuyler, executive assistant to Governor Rockefeller?[41]

THE BROKEN CROWN

In November, two days after his brother declared himself the candidate for John Kennedy's job, David Rockefeller announced the formation of the Business Group on Latin America. The president, who had encouraged David to organize the Business Group, graciously put out a statement congratulating David on its founding. He was hoping that the Business Group might signal a rapprochement between himself and business over the Alliance for Progress.

It did not. David was still opposed to rapid social reforms in Latin America and government-to-government loans. This sentiment was strong in the corporate world, and Kennedy was the object of increasing criticism from that quarter. The missile showdown had restored his popular support, and he was looking forward to taking on Barry Goldwater. But not Nelson Rockefeller. His candidacy remained Kennedy's greatest fear. "I never saw more concentrated attention given to any political subject,"said Roswell Gilpatric.[42]

It was understandable. On November 17, 1963, Nelson delivered his first major speech since formally announcing his candidacy. Kennedy, he said, was "jeopardizing the peace and demoralizing America's allies with a weak, indecisive foreign policy."[43]

Nelson's criticisms struck home precisely because they exploited a series of reversals in Kennedy's Latin American policies. Military coups had badly rocked

Latin America that year, shaking the administration's confidence in the prodemocracy ideological foundation of its Alliance for Progress. The blows came in rapid, violent succession: Argentina and Guatemala in March, Peru and Ecuador in July, the Dominican Republic in September, and finally Honduras in October. Patterns were discernible. With the CIA's nodding, if not prodding, the military had prevailed in Argentina and Ecuador.[44] In Honduras, President Ramón Villeda Morales vacillated too long on Cuba. That, and his inability to crush Cuban-trained Nicaraguans who were passing across the Honduran border to fight dictator Luis Somoza, cost him his job.

In Guatemala, the U.S. military mission made no secret of its favoring the generals who had overthrown President Ydígoras in March. Ydígoras was considered unreliable and too corrupt to crush a new guerrilla insurgency. The elections slated for November, which Jacobo Arbenz's predecessor, ex-President Juan Arévalo, was expected to win, were never held. Three years later, when escalation of violence in Guatemala and Vietnam was being justified as a Kennedy-originated response to communist subversion, columnist Georgie Anne Geyer, who enjoyed access to the intelligence community, reported that "top sources within the Kennedy administration" had told her that Kennedy authorized the coup after a majority of the Latin American experts he consulted recommended it.[45] But the purported participants not only denied Kennedy's giving any green light, they insisted that the meeting never took place.[46] Some experts believed that an Arévalo government, perhaps including Ydígoras's ally Roberto Alegos, brother of the ambassador to the United States and host of the CIA training camp for the Bay of Pigs, was Kennedy's preferred option to avoid greater unrest and prevent guerrilla war from spreading.[47]

Other patterns in the coups, including beneficiaries, were not so obvious. One of the beneficiaries was the New Orleans-based Standard Fruit and Steamship Company. Standard Fruit and United Fruit were the major figures in the "banana boom" in Ecuador that Nelson's friend, President Galo Plaza, sponsored (with the advice of IBEC) as a substitute for lost oil revenues when Standard Oil and Shell withdrew from Ecuador in the late 1940s.

David Rockefeller's Latin American Division of Chase Bank was Standard Fruit's transfer agent for its stock. Standard Fruit owned more than 600,000 acres in the Caribbean-basin countries, not counting Cuban lands expropriated by the Castro government in 1960.

Standard kept offices in New York to oversee marketing. Its central offices, however, were in New Orleans. There, some directors and executives vented their rage against Castro by supporting CIA-sponsored Cuban exiles led by Manuel Artime.[48]

Artime, at the CIA's insistence,[49] had been selected head of the exiles' brigade by the Cuban Revolutionary Council (CRC), the official sponsor of the Bay of Pigs invasion. "His youth, his military experience, his political inexperience and his personal tractability," Arthur Schlesinger wrote of Artime, "all recommended him to the CIA field operatives."[50] After the Bay of Pigs invasion failed, Artime became the CIA's instrument for continued raids on Cuba. He was directly tied to the Agency's "executive action" assassination plots against Castro through his association with mobster Santos Trafficante and Castro's deputy intelligence chief, Rolando Cubela, an assassin code-named by the CIA as AM/LASH. Artime set up a CIA-backed guerrilla training camp at Lake Pontchartrain, north of New Orleans. Standard Fruit employee Manuel Gil, a veteran of the CRC, was a key supporter of the camp through another CIA front, the Information Council of the Americas. CRC's New Orleans office at 544 Camp Street, in turn, was in a building owned by the local longshoremen's union controlled by mobster Carlos Marcello (who shared in the proceeds of Havana's gambling empire and lost it all when came the revolution). Standard Fruit, which reportedly acquiesced in the Mob's control over New York's Pier 13, had long collaborated with the CIA in countries where it did business; like most American companies in the Third World, it put order at a high premium.[51]

The Somoza dictatorship in Nicaragua was a key financial backer of the Lake Pontchartrain camp. Somoza's secret agents were active throughout Central America, particularly in Mexico City, and collaborated regularly with the clandestine activities branch of the CIA, headed by J. C. King, and with the intelligence-gathering activities of American corporations in Central America.

In 1963, the Somoza clan hosted Manuel Artime as he began to organize a second invasion of Cuba. This second invasion, like the CIA's renewed assassination plots through AM/LASH, was never authorized by Kennedy and was in direct violation of the presidential ban on assassinations. Nevertheless, the Somozas provided Artime with a base in Nicaragua to which the Lake Pontchartrain trainees were to be sent. As late as October 1963, ignoring Kennedy's ban against raids on Cuba "launched, manned or equipped from U.S. territory," Artime launched a raid from Florida using the *Rex*, a Florida-based ship owned by the Somozas and skippered by Eugenio R. Martínez, a CIA operative and Bay of Pigs veteran who would later earn fame as one of President Richard M. Nixon's Watergate burglars.

Although Kennedy secretly had authorized the Special Group to mount a CIA sabotage program against Cuba "to nourish the spirit of resistance" and pressure Castro to move Cuba's foreign policy away from the Soviet Union's, Artime's raid was not among the approved projects.

The continued unauthorized raids on Cuba frustrated the Kennedy White House, and in October the culmination in Honduras of the great wave of military coups forced the administration to recognize that it had better change its policy if it wished to avoid embarrassment.

The net effect of these coups was the administration's serious reevaluation of its emphasis on democratic governments, social reforms, and civilian authority as the bedrock for economic growth in Latin America. In October, Assistant

Secretary of State Edwin Martin acknowledged that civilian rule could not be maintained by "keeping a man in office by use of [U.S.] economic pressure or even military force, when his own people are not willing to fight to defend him." If the military did go beyond "the most constructive peacetime role of maintaining internal security and working on civil action programs" and carry out coups, then "we must use our leverage to keep these new [military] regimes as liberal and considerate of the welfare of the people as possible."

Many would consider this policy a return to traditional U.S. acceptance of dictatorships in the region. Martin tried to mollify concerns by denying that Kennedy had abandoned democratic ideals. At the same time, he also defended the value of a more cynical Realpolitik that spared the administration defeats as the 1964 elections approached. "I fear that there are some who will accuse me of having written an apology for coups. I have not. They are to be fought with all the means we have available. Rather, I would protest that I am urging the rejection of the thesis of the French philosophers that democracy can be legislated—established by constitutional fiat."[52]

Despite the sobering series of coups, Kennedy felt more confident about his chances for reelection. The Cuban missile crisis had given him such popularity that he now thought a thaw in the Cold War might be politically feasible for the first time since the CIA's U-2 affair wrecked the 1960 Summit. In western states, the president found the normally conservative audiences surprisingly enthusiastic when he talked about peace and the test ban. He took this theme right into the supposed heart of Goldwater country, at the Mormon Tabernacle in Salt Lake City, Utah, and got a five-minute standing ovation. It convinced him that the Far Right was overrated and that he could easily beat Goldwater.

Kennedy was convinced that he also could hold his liberal base against any Rockefeller raid; in fact, his trip west showed that he could widen his appeal for peace without fear. He had come to terms with himself, the Russians, and the American people. His suggestion in August that peaceful coexistence was possible had been hailed. His decision in October to sell wheat to the Soviet Union was accepted by most Americans as a profitable gesture of goodwill. His quiet reduction of the CIA's budget in 1962 and 1963, which had been twice the size of the State Department's when he arrived, had been achieved without flack, and he hoped for a 20 percent reduction by 1966.[53] Although shaken by the murders of Diem and Nhu, Kennedy thought that the more liberal General Minh seemed to be taking control.

He felt confident. Too confident.

In the interest of Democratic party unity in Texas, a state that was crucial for a big victory over any Rockefeller or Goldwater southern strategy, he agreed to Governor John Connally's plea that he go to Dallas.

The Dallas trip was vintage Kennedy, a far cry from Rockefeller's tendency to be overcautious when confronted by controversy. Nelson, hit by the issue that could cripple his candidacy—his divorce and remarriage—chose evasion. Rather than seize the issue and shape it by calling for liberal reforms of the state's divorce laws, Nelson took shelter by calling the issue "a personal matter." It won him no credit, especially when he took his pregnant wife on the campaign trail, as if his insisting that voters accept her presence was an effective way to address the issue. It was not.

Kennedy, on the other hand, had not hidden behind the "personal" when his 1960 campaign was threatened by the issue of papal edicts on Catholic behavior in civil life. He defined the issue as a political one, but on his own terms: the separation of church and state. Resting his case on solid constitutional grounds, he settled for most Americans the issue of religion in the campaign.

Now Kennedy would try to do the same with the issue of peace. He ignored the warnings from U.N. Ambassador Adlai Stevenson, who had been physically attacked in Dallas in September, and from Senator William Fulbright, who also had encountered ugly crowds. He also ignored the fact that the Secret Service had investigated thirty-four threats on his life from Texas alone since 1961.

Dallas was clear and sunny on November 22, when the *Dallas Morning News* appeared with a full-page advertisement charging Kennedy with having "scrapped the Monroe Doctrine in favor of the 'Spirit of Moscow.'"[54] The advertisement, which listed a series of provocative charges that all but indicted the president for treason, had secretly been paid for by a group that included the local John Birch Society leader and Nelson Bunker Hunt, H. L. Hunt's son.[55] "How can people write such things?" Kennedy asked after seeing the ad.[56]

If Texas was the newest of the new-wealth states, Dallas was its capital in the raw, a booming oil city of white shirts with string ties and Stetsons, where the Stennis family set the example for real estate speculators by making a fortune off land deals and nonunion industrial parks, where the myth of machismo ran wild and the murder rate was twice the national average. It was in Dallas where a recently uprooted rural population, which had doubled the city's citizenry since World War II, were besieged by a barrage of right-wing hysteria and Fundamentalist absolutism.

Kennedy shrugged off concerns, telling Jacqueline and aide Kenneth O'Donnell that there was little the Secret Service could do if a man wanted to get on a high building with a telescopic rifle. And any way, Dallas Mayor Earl Cabell had promised a cheerful reception.

The president planned to deliver a speech at Trammel Crow's Trade Mart on the need for balancing a strong defense with a recognition of the world's craving for social justice. Here, in the heart of the Dallas–Fort Worth military-industrial complex, he would make a plea for strength tempered by reason in a nuclear age.

Mayor Cabell greeted the president warmly, even though Kennedy had fired his brother, General Charles Cabell, as the CIA's deputy director after the Bay of Pigs.

Secretary of State Rusk was flying to Japan for negotiations, when *Air Force*

II suddenly lost all communication with Washington. At that moment bullets raced beyond sound in Dallas's Dealey Plaza.

French journalist Jean Daniel, acting as Kennedy's secret envoy to Havana, was with Fidel Castro when the news reached Cuba. Castro considered it a bad turn for his country. He had been eager to establish communication with the United States, using journalist Lisa Howard to pass the word on to the administration's special U.N. adviser, William Atwood. Kennedy had cut the CIA out of the information loop, not wanting the Agency to know.[57]

"Did the CIA kill my brother?"[58] Robert Kennedy confronted John McCone after the assassination. No, McCone assured him, ignorant of the CIA's assassination plots after the Bay of Pigs, or so McCone would claim. But the attorney general remained skeptical. Right after the assassination, he had called the CIA to ask a startled duty officer, "Did your outfit have anything to do with this horror?"[59]

Years later, when he heard that New Orleans District Attorney Jim Garrison was about to bring indictments against CIA operatives whom Garrison claimed had known Lee Harvey Oswald, he sent an aide to investigate. Garrison charged that he had uncovered evidence that Oswald had been in league with three CIA operatives: Clay Shaw, a director of the New Orleans Trade Mart; George de Mohrenschildt, a Dallas oil geologist and White Russian émigré who befriended Oswald's Russian wife; and David Ferrie, an instructor at the Lake Pontchartrain training camp when it was raided by the FBI and closed in September, in compliance with the Cuban Missile deal. Ferrie was also the pilot who had been hired to return Carlos Marcello illegally from El Salvador after the New Orleans Mafia chief's deportation to Guatemala by Attorney General Robert Kennedy. The younger Kennedy, skeptical of Garrison but intrigued by the possibility that his brother was a victim of conspiracy, asked press secretary Frank Mankiewicz if Garrison "had anything." "No, but I think there is something," said Mankiewicz. "So do I," said Kennedy, nodding. "You stay on it."[60] But after Robert Kennedy's own assassination in 1968, Mankiewicz had had enough.

Nelson Rockefeller was lunching with Thomas Dewey, preparing for a campaign trip to New Hampshire where the first presidential primary was scheduled for March, when he got word of Kennedy's murder. He immediately ordered all flags on state buildings flown at half mast and canceled speeches for a month of mourning. Three days later, Rockefeller walked solemnly amid the crowd of dignitaries that followed the funeral procession escorting the young president to his grave.

Nelson called the loss a "terrible tragedy." He left eloquence, however, to his friend, Alberto Lleras Camargo: "For Latin America, Kennedy's passing is a blackening, a tunnel, a gust of cloud and smoke."[61]

Only a few days after the funeral, Jacqueline Kennedy, the children, and the late president's personal effects were gone, spirited out of the White House with such haste that the attorney general had snapped at the new president, Lyndon B. Johnson, "Can't you wait?"[62]

Johnson was now firmly in power, accepting offers of help on Latin America from Adolf Berle and David Rockefeller. The new president, acting on the advice of CIA Director McCone, quickly replaced both Assistant Secretary of State Edward Martin and AID Director Teodoro Moscoso with Ambassador to Mexico Thomas Mann, who had announced earlier, after rumors circulated that he had been involved in the planning of the coup in Guatemala, that he was retiring.

Johnson brought his fellow Texan in from the cold to combine both the Department of State and AID into one mailed fist for American business abroad. As Johnson quietly reversed Kennedy's plan to withdraw from Vietnam, Mann focused on Brazil. Both countries would become milestones in American history, Vietnam as a disaster, Brazil as a triumph. And with Brazil's military coup, J. C. King would at last return to the shining dream of thirty years past: the Amazon.

VI

THE SLAUGHTER OF THE INNOCENTS

Then Herod, when he saw that he had been tricked by the wise men, was in a furious rage, and he sent and killed all the male children in Bethlehem and in all that region who were two years old or under, according to the time which he had ascertained from the wise men. Then was fulfilled what was spoken by the prophet Jeremiah:

A voice was heard in Ramah, wailing and loud lamentation, Rachel weeping for her children; she refused to be consoled, because they were no more.

—MATTHEW 2:16–18

28

TO TURN A CONTINENT

THE HARDENED FACE

News of John Kennedy's murder sent a shudder through Brazil. Then came grief such as had not been shown for the death of any foreign leader since President Franklin D. Roosevelt. As then, Brazilians sensed that the world had taken a dramatic turn. A shroud had been hung over the face of the future, making the loss of Kennedy so unexpectedly personal. In Rio de Janeiro, rivers of grief swept through the streets as lines of people converged to mourn at the U.S. Embassy.

Ambassador Lincoln Gordon was startled by the emotional crowds and what they could mean for President Lyndon B. Johnson in Latin America. "The experience we had that Friday afternoon and evening and the following weekend, I suppose, was repeated all over the world," he later recalled. "But in Rio it was a most dramatic thing. We opened a book at the chancery and another one at our residence, and over that weekend we had a line of people stretching for three or four blocks. It was continuous, day and night, of every class of person, every type, poor, rich, middle class, most of them weeping. It was a most extraordinary outpouring of emotion. So as a reaction to that, there would inevitably be some doubts about Kennedy's successor."[1]

There was no doubt in Washington's higher circles, however, about Lyndon Johnson. The former Senate majority leader was no maverick like Kennedy. He was the classic insider among Washington's power brokers. Ironically, Vice President Johnson was an outsider within the Kennedy administration, not only to the Kennedys, but even to conservative Texans who believed that he had betrayed them. He had not. But he could not tell them his true feelings without betraying President Kennedy and isolating himself further.

Nelson Rockefeller saw Johnson's agony at the 1963 Governors Conference. Johnson "was a mighty discouraged man," Nelson recalled. "I knew him pretty well and I really felt for him. . . . He was making a speech . . . that no more reflected his thinking than the man in the moon. He was given a speech which he had to give because it was the Administration's position."[2] White House aide Arthur Schlesinger wrote of the differences: "The Vice President disagreed with administration tactics in 1963 on a number of points—on the civil rights bill, on the Committee on Equal Employment Opportunity, on selling wheat to the Soviet Union, on Vietnam."[3]

Now, after three years of suffering in silence, Johnson wanted to show his own worth. And to do that, he did what came naturally: He listened to the wise men in the central core of Washington's unelected state apparatus, men of wealth and influence and armies, who were accustomed to ruling while others merely held office.

One unfinished project that required the new president's immediate attention was the transformation of the United States' foreign-aid policies. Kennedy's emphasis on direct government-to-government assistance through the Alliance for Progress and AID had never been popular with the business community, and now it was incumbent on the Johnson administration to provide a transition that would more readily promote private corporate investments under the rubric of U.S. government aid.

CIA Director John McCone had someone in mind to achieve that transition. He urged Johnson to return Robert B. Anderson, a fellow Rockefeller associate from the Eisenhower era, to Washington. Nelson Rockefeller's former ally in business and the Special Group's counterinsurgency operations would be the perfect person to head the Alliance for Progress.

McCone recommended a host of other Rockefeller allies, all of whom were attuned to the prerogatives of American business, to assist Anderson's work for the Alliance. In particular, he persuaded Johnson to bring Thomas Mann back from Mexico, to replace Puerto Rico's Teodoro Moscoso as administrator of the Alliance.[4]

Mann's return to Washington as assistant secretary of state, head of the Alliance for Progress, and White House special assistant ("to emphasize his control," Johnson explained to Berle[5]) was viewed with trepidation by many Latin Americans.

Mann's experience included running the Bolivian desk at the State Department during the grim days of Indian tin miners' strikes in 1942, heading up the Platte River development program in Uruguay, overseeing American interests during the Perónist threat from the Argentine south, helping Nelson Rockefeller and the FBI draw up a blacklist of suspected Axis sympathizers, heading up petroleum affairs at the postwar embassy in the Venezuela of Creole

Petroleum and other oil companies, assisting the CIA's new dictatorship in Guatemala as U.S. consul in 1954, and promoting U.S. big business in Latin America first as assistant secretary for economic affairs and then as acting assistant secretary for Latin America. Mann was the quintessential leader of the Old Guard in Latin American affairs.

Experience often breeds cynicism. Some Latin Americans worried that the idealism that had promoted the Alliance for Progress had died with Kennedy. Some Brazilians would later blame Mann for the coming military coup. But they were wrong, Gordon would argue. "The Brazilian revolution, or coup . . . was already in the making."[6]

Islands of Treachery

Preparations for that option had begun as early as 1961, when Vice President João Goulart managed to succeed President Jânio Quadros despite opposition from Brazilian generals.

A stocky, handsome man with a large popular following, Goulart viewed himself as Getúlio Vargas's spiritual successor in the struggle to rid Brazil of foreign domination. For that reason alone, he made Washington nervous at every step in his rise to power. As Vargas's minister of labor, he had built himself a base among Brazil's growing, restless working class. In gestures all too reminiscent of Argentina's Juan Perón, he found every opportunity to deliver rousing, populist speeches to the masses. As Brazil's vice president, he showed no hesitation in cultivating friendly ties with Communist regimes. He was, in fact, on a diplomatic visit to China in 1961 when Quadros was deposed.

To the dismay of the Brazilian right, no amount of secret plotting could prevent Goulart from returning from China and assuming the presidency of Brazil. He was simply too popular with the people. To have stopped him would have meant risking civil war. The Kennedy administration's avowed stake in promoting constitutional governments for the Alliance for Progress was an additional consideration. Brazil's generals finally came up with an unconstitutional compromise: Goulart would be allowed to return if he accepted a presidency with only titular powers. Unwilling to test the army's power, Goulart had reluctantly agreed.

Adolf Berle kept careful track of Brazilian developments from his personal command post in Manhattan. Like an eagle flying high above its perch, scouting for trouble, Berle scanned his list of Brazilian friends and then invited them to his townhouse. Though powerless now to act in any official capacity, Nelson's old "Brazil hand" could not resist one of his favorite political pastimes: gathering intelligence.

One visitor that fall was his old friend and confidant on Brazilian rightist intrigue: Carlos Lacerda. Lacerda was now governor of the influential state of Guanabara, created in 1960 as political compensation to Rio when the overcrowded "Fabulous City" lost the seat of national government to Brasília.

The same man who had successfully conspired against Vargas and then Quadros was now telling Berle, over drinks, that Goulart was not expected to last.

"Lacerda thought the situation was in transition," Berle wrote in his diary. "Goulart would hardly accept a position as figure-head President. He [Lacerda] himself was joining with several other Governors . . . to make a 'Governors' block.'"[7]

For a while, official Washington had watched Goulart warily but did not intervene. To head the U.S. Embassy, Kennedy had appointed Lincoln Gordon, a Harvard economist who had worked in the Marshall Plan under Averell Harriman and was completing a major book on U.S. manufacturing investment's impact on postwar Brazilian government policies. Gordon had been a consultant to the Rockefeller Brothers Fund's Special Studies Project. Goulart's people at first were glad to see Gordon in place of the vexing John Moors Cabot, a member of the Boston clan whose Cabot Corporation exported black carbon out of Brazil. Before he left Washington, Gordon was briefed on the American International Association for Economic and Social Development (AIA) in Brazil by Nelson Rockefeller's top aide, Berent Friele, who then arranged some briefings in Brazil by AIA's Brazil director, Walter Crawford, and Minas Gerais's governor, José Magalhães Pinto.[8]

Washington seemed even friendly when Goulart visited Kennedy in April 1962, to court U.S. opinion and financial aid. When he left Washington, Goulart had an agreement from the Agency for International Development (AID) for $398.5 million in loans, including $131 million in assistance to Brazil's impoverished and potentially unstable Northeast.

AID attached so much importance to Brazil's Northeast, in fact, that it set up the only AID mission especially devoted to a region within one country. Recife, the region's commercial capital, became the U.S. administrative seat for AID, Washington beefing up not only its consular staff, but its CIA "security" operations there. What Goulart did not know was that the CIA had an additional objective. Its Recife-based operations were overseen in Washington by Colonel J. C. King. The CIA spent anywhere from $5 million (Gordon's estimate) to $20 million (former CIA officer Philip Agee's claim, citing a Brazilian congressional investigation[9]) to support anti-Goulart activities in 1962 alone.

The Brazilian Congress, unaware of these intrigues, was jubilant over Goulart's successful trip to Washington and restored him to full presidential powers following a January 1963 national plebiscite. The generals looked outflanked. Goulart's populist speeches, however, only triggered more secret meetings between Brazilian military and business leaders and top U.S. officials, including Washington's newly posted military attaché, Vernon Walters. Walters was the perfect man to keep an eye on Goulart. He was a top intelligence officer and veteran of the U.S. Embassy in Brazil in the days of Adolf Berle and William Pawley. He had also been a close friend of Brazil's powerful General Humberto de Castelo Branco since both had served in the invasion of Italy during World War II. When Walters arrived at Rio's airport, he was met by fourteen old friends, all of them now generals. One of them, Castelo Branco, would replace Goulart as the next president of Brazil.

Goulart's undoing began the day his brother-in-law, Governor Leonel Brizola of Rio Grande do Sul, expropriated a subsidiary of International Telephone & Telegraph (ITT) in Pôrto Alegre and assigned its broken-down properties a value of $6 million for compensation purposes. The response from American business leaders was swift and merciless. ITT President Harold Geneen led the charge, lobbying for an amendment to the 1962 foreign-aid bill that would suspend all aid to any country that nationalized an American company. Even if a country merely repudiated a contract with an American company or specially taxed or regulated an American company, the results would be the same: no aid.

Such a Big Stick approach appalled President Kennedy, who worried that it would further enflame Third World nationalism, appear to corroborate Soviet propaganda about "U.S. imperialism," and force the United States to take the side of American companies more often than was merited. He frantically worked behind the scenes, including lobbying Governor Rockefeller, to try to defeat the amendment. He sent his brother Robert to Brazil to urge Goulart to settle. Either settle or face the cutoff of aid, Robert Kennedy warned. To add to the pressure, the president directed AID to fund projects that would benefit potential political rivals of Goulart—Brazilian gubernatorial candidates identified by the State Department and the CIA as reliable.[10]

Goulart came around. He agreed to pay ITT $8 million. ITT, in turn, agreed to reinvest 15 percent of that amount in Brazilian nonutility interests. In April 1963, Goulart, seeking to control inflation by capping energy rates, then offered to buy out all American-owned utilities. He offered American and Foreign Power Company, for example, $70 million for its Brazilian telephone subsidiary, with the condition that 75 percent of this amount would be reinvested in Brazilian nonutility interests. The company accepted.

Kennedy endorsed the idea. He wanted to avoid Brazilian anger at rising electric bills. "It's that damned U.S. company,"[11] he thought Brazilians would say when their monthly bill arrived.

Carlos Lacerda was not happy. Charging that the company's equipment was obsolete, Lacerda led a right-wing nationalist attack that soon had Goulart reeling. More than $450 million would be needed, Lacerda argued, to upgrade the company to meet telephone orders. Goulart eventually canceled the deal. Four cabinet members—the ministers of finance, war, justice, and foreign affairs—were sacrificed in the turmoil and forced to resign.

From then on, the noose tightened around Goulart. All U.S. aid to the Brazilian government was cut off. Instead, Washington focused its largess on governors who were opposed to Goulart, hailing their states as "islands of sanity."

Lacerda's state of Guanabara was one such island. Guanabara, made up essentially of the city of Rio de Janeiro, had only 4 million citizens and had the highest standard of living of any state in Brazil. It had received $71 million in U.S. aid from the end of 1961 to 1963. In comparison, the impoverished seven state governments of the Northeast, with 20 million people trapped in one of the world's lowest standards of living, received only $13 million.[12]

AID officials, defending themselves against criticism by the General Accounting Office in the mid-1960s, explained why: "The governor of the state of Guanabara was then Carlos Lacerda, who had an active development plan for the state, was an able administrator, and was favorably disposed to the U.S."

Lacerda was also a shrewd politician. He placed signs on AID's projects reading "Works of the Government of Carlos Lacerda."[13]

The states of Minas Gerais and São Paulo, both governed by critics of Goulart, also were favored.

Meanwhile, Goulart was left out to dry. Brazil's per capita gross national product, which had reached a postwar high of 7.2 percent in 1961, collapsed to 2.3 percent the following year. By 1963, it registered at -1.3 percent.[14]

To stem Brazil's hemorrhage of capital, Goulart ordered his new finance minister to apply "rigorously" a 10 percent ceiling on the remittance of foreign profits.[15] Then, in a bold attempt to restore federal authority over foreign-aid policy, he insisted that all states that wanted U.S. aid must channel their requests through the federal government. To Governor Lacerda, that requirement meant a budget paralysis on his home state.

Foreign development projects came under equally harsh scrutiny. Hanna Mining's rich iron-ore holdings in Minas Gerais were targeted for nationalization, a reversal of Hanna's fortunes that could not go unnoticed in Room 5600, given recent Rockefeller investments in the Hanna–National Steel–Chrysler industrial complex.*

The Rockefellers' AIA† also became vulnerable, including its colonization plan in Minas Gerais, aimed at "providing new settlement opportunities for rural families from the over crowded . . . dry northeast zone."[16]

---

*Hanna Mining was the financial linchpin that held together an interdependent, industrial triplex: Hanna, National Steel, and Chrysler. Hanna's iron and coal were crucial raw materials for National Steel; National Steel, in turn, supplied 40 percent of Chrysler's steel needs.

George Love, National Steel's head, had recently placed Paul C. Cabot, cousin of the former ambassador to Brazil, on the board of M. A. Hanna Company. He also invited Nelson's top financial aide, J. Richardson Dilworth, to be a member of Chrysler's board.

†AIA, Nelson's nonprofit, "philanthropic" arm, was often used in conjunction with his for-profit International Basic Economy Corporation (IBEC).

THE SLAUGHTER OF THE INNOCENTS

Planning Planalto: Phase I of the Shining Dream

Goulart's Ministry of Agriculture wanted to gain control over AIA's rural credit association. Over the years, AIA had launched seventeen branches of the credit association, expanding the AIA's credit program and colonizing unsettled lands with peasants from the turbulent Northeast.[17] AIA also had negotiated for the colonization schemes with the Inter-American Development Bank—and the World Bank.[18] AIA's original proposal was made the month Kennedy was elected. It called for the United States to lend Brazil $10 million to develop the west-central region, encompassing the states of Goiás and Mato Grosso, including the area where Nelson had his million-acre property.[19]

The Goulart government was not opposed to colonization schemes in principle. Its regional agency for the Northeast, SUDENE, had earmarked highway construction into the Amazon as one of the top priorities of its colonization plans to drain off peasant unrest. The problem was that Goulart now favored development of the Brazilian Amazon by Brazilians.

AIA successfully thwarted Brazil's efforts to control its credit associations,[20] but not without learning a valuable lesson about Brazilian nationalism. If AIA was to continue unimpeded in its plans to develop the frontier, it would have to submerge its identity behind a "Brazilian Foundation." The foundation could be both the recipient of, and conduit for, American aid. It would further remove any Brazilian suspicions that American corporations were pushing their own agendas in the Amazon. "It is my feeling that the Foundation should be entirely a Brazilian organization," AIA's Walter Crawford wrote Nelson's longtime confidant, Berent Friele. "I would hope it is still possible to get some of Brazil's leading citizens [involved]."[21]

By 1962, AIA had scaled back its proposed project area for developing the Brazilian interior, but its plans remained ambitious, starting with large-scale cattle ranching. IBEC had already conducted a soil survey to determine the feasibility of using grass seeds for pastureland. The Planalto, as Brazil's vast central plain was called, encompassed a huge piece of territory the size of Texas. It included most of western and northwestern Minas Gerais, southern Goiás, and eastern Mato Grosso.

This was the edge of the frontier. Indians had already been pushed into the tropical Xingu valley or met death on the plains or the swamps of the Planalto. The region was also long known to IBEC, with holdings in deposits of phosphates and newly discovered deposits of nickel. Later, projects would be launched to mine vanadium, lead, silver, diamonds, and niobium as well.[22] By 1962, an AIA survey team identified the Planalto as "a prime candidate for large scale economic development."

Part of the area's attractiveness, according to a preliminary report, was its strategic location "near the principal industrial and consumer centers of Brazil."

As such, it was the "natural gateway for extending the more technologically advanced agriculture in the south to the still unsettled reaches of northern Goiás, Mato Grosso and southern Pará." Roads to the area had already been built, and more were on the way. The Rockefeller survey concluded that the area could absorb "appreciable numbers of new people"—350,000 "new farm families," an equal number of "non farm families" providing support services, and another 100,000 families "employed by a fully developed forest products industry." Development of the area would also require "the establishment of a domestic fertilizer industry" that could "supply the demands of an industrialized agriculture."[23]

And here, on the crucial question of how to develop a fertilizer industry, "an infrastructure investment comparable to roads, electric energy, etc.," the report finally arrived at the subject of oil, specifically the Bolivian oil lands to the west of Rockefeller's and Moreira Salles's Bodoquena ranch in Mato Grosso—the very oil lands in the Santa Cruz region that had been targeted by Moreira Salles's União oil firm for development: "Bolivian oil . . . could have agricultural impacts as well as industrial aspects. . . . A refinery for Bolivian crude oil located in Mato Grasso could have an accelerating effect on the westward expansion of agriculture, both as a source of tractor and truck fuel and as a source of agricultural nitrogen."[24]

The report brimmed with specific recommendations, including "a search for fertilizer raw materials"; a survey of all the resources in 220,000 square miles, requiring extensive mapmaking based on 250,000 aerial photos; educational programs for farmers; development of a professional and semiprofessional labor force specializing in banking, agricultural planning, and management; and the "relocation of people from surplus population areas."

It was like settling the Wild West in a decade, with the value of hindsight and large sums of money to carry it out. Concern for winning the Cold War also lent the colonization scheme an air of urgency and political purpose. The impoverished Northeast offered the necessary pool of surplus labor. "Time is of the essence and we ought to get moving before it is too late," Berent Friele wrote Berle. "The Castro forces are very active in this area."[25]

In anticipation of nationalist rumblings over U.S. exploitation of Brazil's natural resources, AIA's Walter Crawford had already approached "a number of influential people—both Brazilian and American"—to discuss the AIA's concept of creating a Brazilian foundation. His listeners, carefully chosen from among a Rockefeller network of allied businessmen, reacted favorably to the idea.

Crawford eventually found the perfect sponsor for the foundation—a Brazilian mining conglomerate, called Companhia Auxilar de Emprésas Mineração (CAEMI), that had been founded by Augusto T. A. Antunes. The Antunes complex mined manganese in partnership with Bethlehem Steel in Amapá, site of some of the largest manganese and bauxite deposits in the world.

The new foundation would be called the Antunes Foundation. AIA's balancing act was not over, however. Having lined up its Brazilian friends on one end, the Rockefeller team was still faced with hostility on the other end, from none other than foreign-aid officials in the Kennedy administration. The whole Planalto Survey could come crashing down in defeat at any moment because it did not have the full support of Kennedy's AID administrators.

Kennedy's first AID director, Fowler Hamilton, had been persuaded by a staff report that AID should not be pressured by U.S. corporations into guaranteeing their portfolio investments in foreign companies if the companies became slated for nationalization. This attitude reflected a certain leeriness toward the role of big business in directing U.S. aid policy, and it showed up in AID's preference for giving immediate assistance to Brazil's drought-ridden Northeast, rather than supporting the Rockefeller people's emphasis on migration to Goiás and Mato Grosso.

AID was skeptical about AIA's vast Planalto project, and provided enough money for only a small, preliminary survey of the region, as far west as 55 degrees longitude, just east of Nelson's Bodoquena ranch—with strings attached to boot. The contract departed from the usual policy in that it ran "directly between AID and AIA," AIA lawyer Philip Glick noted to AIA's top administrator, John Camp, and was "cost reimbursable rather than at a fixed price." The fixed price was set too low by AID, so AIA had to settle for doing the work almost at cost. Worse, this arrangement gave AID the right to audit AIA's overhead expenditures.

AIA officials did not like the arrangement, which threatened to "put AIA at the mercy of AID and make it impossible for us to operate with any degree of autonomy."[26] Rockefeller's organization did not appreciate being regulated by the Kennedy administration on a project that had taken almost two decades to break ground.

The only reason that AIA had gone ahead and accepted the contract was that the work had to be "initiated immediately or wait for a whole year."[27] Besides, AIA had hoped that the limited survey would lead to a much larger survey and colonization project in the future. But by March 1963, even after the exploratory survey, AID was not willing to commit to the larger survey.

The Planalto proposal was put on hold. Crawford was advised to look elsewhere than Brazil.

Crawford agreed. In the absence of a Brazilian foundation acting as a conduit (the Antunes Foundation had not as yet gotten off the ground), the problem would continue to be "the Brazilians."[28] Therefore, AIA found itself squeezed on both ends: by the Brazilian government, headed by Goulart, and by the U.S. government, headed by Kennedy. With Kennedy gone by December 1963, the problem of how U.S. aid would be administered began to clear up with the appointment of Thomas Mann as assistant secretary of state for Latin America. The "Brazilian problem" under Goulart, however, remained.

Stalking the Reformer

AIA's Walter Crawford viewed Goulart's new land-reform law as being "rather extreme."[29] Although it did emphasize individual ownership of family farm units, the means of achieving more equitable landownership set Goulart squarely against Brazilian and foreign land speculators; among the latter, some twenty U.S. firms had been counted by Rockefeller aides. Only family farms and some large, well-managed plantations were exempted from purchase by the government for redistribution to landless peasants.

Rockefeller's AIA officials knew that most of the land in the Planalto was privately owned, the state governments having sold most of the "public" lands. Former Indian lands in Goiás that had been sold by the state for $5 per twelve acres only a few years before now sold for twelve times as much. In fact, "most of it is in rather large holdings . . . [and] held almost entirely for speculation purposes." Rather than see the land broken up and distributed, thereby upsetting the status quo, AIA officials had intended to accommodate AID with private landowning interests, making "full use of private initiative" and confining its role to lending technical assistance to "individual owners, land developers and colonization companies," as well as to "farm owned and controlled cooperatives." Their idea had been to "colonize and develop the presently existing non-productive large land holdings" through a "special type of credit." But ownership of the land would remain unchanged.[30]

The landowners, whether Brazilian or American, were not impressed by Brazilian government statistics showing how land reform would redress the unequal distribution of wealth. Nor did the landowners and speculators see how the concentration of income in the upper brackets would limit the growth of a broader consumer home market for business. Nor, finally, were they moved by moral arguments about responsibility for the poor or patriotic arguments about sharing the wealth of the nation to build it through wider participation in the economy. Instead, they thought that Goulart's concentration of authority over Brazil's agrarian reform agency was undermining their own traditional prerogatives and was therefore a step toward dictatorship.

Nelson's top lieutenants at Room 5600, for their part, had been pleased with Brazil's progress before Goulart and his land-reform schemes got in the way. They had only to look at Nelson's Brazilian mutual fund, Crescinco, for proof that investors were helping Brazil build its own industries to substitute for imports. Crescinco's fabulous success in attracting money from urban upper- and middle-income families that concentrated Brazil's wealth had allowed Nelson's firm to invest in more than 100 Brazilian companies, encouraging the growth of Brazil's stock exchange.

When this success was arrested by currency depletion and inflation in 1962–1963, the Rockefellers blamed Goulart's policies, which they regarded as so spendthrift that investors' confidence had collapsed.

In fact, Goulart's policies were no more extravagant than were those of his predecessors. Inflation during his administration was caused not so much by demand, as by rising costs. Since Quadros's fall, Washington had demanded more "fiscal responsibility" in exchange for U.S. loans for industrialization and debt service. Goulart was forced to devalue the Brazilian cruzeiro, causing prices to soar and making capital the most expensive item for businessmen next to labor costs. If private profits were to be taken, little room was left over for compromise with the wage demands of Goulart's labor constituency, who suffered most from this new form of inflation. Adding pressure was the fact that the capital-intensive investments involved in the heavy industrialization of chemicals, durable goods, and machinery were incapable of employing the 1 million new workers who arrived in cities every year from the rural areas. Caught between the industrialists and the workers, Goulart's administration vacillated, trying to placate one and then the other, until neither side could be satisfied. Goulart's grip on the wheels of state weakened. His enemies moved in with ever-louder calls for cuts in services and wages for his working-class constituency and its only real bastion of defense: the organized labor movement.

Beneath these claims for fiscal prudence, however, was a distinct distaste for the shifts in power that Goulart's officials were initiating, shifts that gave more economic power to Goulart's labor and peasant constituencies and thereby greater political power to the officials who implemented the policies. It did not take long for these officials to be branded as communists, first, by Governor Lacerda, and then, by the CIA station in the U.S. Embassy.

In 1963, the CIA generated three reports on Brazilian politics that argued that communists were steering Goulart toward dictatorship. One of the reports sounded a familiar theme for U.S. intervention: saving a country from an international communist conspiracy. If some in Washington argued that Brazil's economic woes really had more to do with relations with Washington and New York than with Moscow, it no longer mattered. For President João Goulart, the die was cast.[31]

Pentagon ties to the Brazilian military already had an obvious intelligence focal point in the U.S. Embassy's military attaché, Vernon Walters, future assistant director of the CIA. Quieter forces, capable of manipulating Brazilian public opinion, were also at play. And as they worked, Goulart was not the only one caught between the military and their opponents: so also was a group of American Fundamentalist missionaries led by William Cameron Townsend.

THE AMAZON CONNECTION: "PULLING THE WHOLE THING TOGETHER"

By 1963, the destruction of the Amazonian Indians had grown in direct proportion to the military's increasing control over a corrupted Service for the

Protection of the Indian (SPI). The organization, founded to ensure the Indians' survival, had become the instrument of their death.

"In principle the Service for the Protection of the Indian is supposed to provide for their security and facilitate [the Indians'] integration into modern Brazil," wrote French anthropologist Alfred Métraux. "In fact the [SPI] 'postos' are not only centers of demoralization and exploitation, but veritable traps. Once caught in them, the Indians are condemned to rapid extinction."[32]

Darcy Ribeiro was more blunt about the militarized condition of the SPI with which he had worked.

> The last four years of military administrations . . . led the Service for the Protection of the Indian to the lowest point of its history, bringing it down in certain regions to the degrading condition of an agent and prop of the despoilers and murderers of the Indians. The work of assistance, on the other hand, is most definitely concerned with the specific needs of the Indians. Nevertheless, the SPI frequently failed even in the domain of aid and protection. Pacification carried out at the cost of many lives, of heroic endeavor to lead more tribes to peace, brought nothing but frustration to those involved when they realized that their victory ultimately meant the defeat of their ideas, that not even the possession of the land was assured to the Indians, for whom peaceful coexistence was to mean hunger, disease and disillusion.[33]

Similar reports were made of the Kayapó in southwest Pará,[34] the Ticúna in Amazonas, and the Tapirapé and Terêna in Mato Grosso.[35] This last region, rapidly being developed by cattle companies and colonization identical to what the Rockefellers and Berle urged, was overwhelmed by measles, smallpox, influenza, and tuberculosis, which were deliberately introduced among the Indians by land speculators, according to Brazilian government files.[36] Only in the Xingu National Park, northwest of Brasília, the sole legacy of Quadros's short reign, were the epidemics brought under control. In fact, the Indian population there rose.[37]

Conditions were also perilous for the Apalaí in Amapá, north of the Amazon delta, which contained some of the largest manganese and bauxite deposits in the world. The bauxite may not have been known of during the Goulart era, but the manganese had been mined since 1957 by Bethlehem Steel and Augusto Antunes's CAEMI.

With pressures on the Indians of Mato Grosso and the northern Amazon basin increasing, it is not surprising that Darcy Ribeiro should have sought a way to counterbalance the influence on SPI of the Brazilian military and land speculators. Outside the Xingu Park, where the Villas Boas brothers held sway as protectionists, the only serious alternative was the American Bible translators of the Summer Institute of Linguistics (SIL).

SIL's linguists were more educated than most Protestant missionaries from the United States, and Cam and his people had shown an unusual sensitivity

THE SLAUGHTER OF THE INNOCENTS

toward Indian language as an integral part of Indian culture. Townsend's missionaries had lived among the tribes since 1957, a year after Ribeiro brought them in to the country, but their work had been limited by SPI's protocols. Now, with Goulart appointing him the rector of the new University of Brasília, Ribeiro saw his chance to use SIL to set up a new structure of linguistically trained field anthropologists to augment, if not replace, the corrupted SPI.

What Ribeiro did not know was that SIL had ties to the American right wing. Nor could he have known of SIL's history of moving within a course set by even more powerful forces: the Rockefellers, U.S. intelligence agencies, and, ironically, the U.S. military. At the very time Ribeiro was looking to the missionaries as innocent protectors of Brazil's embattled tribes, SIL was reinforcing its ties with these more powerful forces in the Amazon region of Brazil's western neighbor, Ecuador.

At its expanding Ecuadorian jungle base in Limoncocha, SIL played host to a party of Rockefeller Foundation officials in the spring of 1962. These men sought SIL's assistance in tropical agricultural experiments for colonizing the Amazon. They wanted to move in a group of technicians to study the area's suitability for the classic first stages of colonization: raising cattle and planting seeds, both of which, if successful, would accelerate the razing of the rain forest. It was the beginning of SIL's active collaboration with the Rockefeller Foundation at Limoncocha, a collaboration that continued up to the base's abandonment in 1982.

Whether coincidence or not, both the Rockefeller team and the Ecuadorian army were especially interested in the Pioneer 530, a powerful short-wave-radio communications system developed by the Jungle Aviation and Radio Service (JAARS).

The Rockefeller team had barely departed when Limoncocha hosted a Green Beret counterinsurgency team, consisting of five men, who called themselves the Civic Action Team. The men were led by Colonel Joseph A. McChristian.

McChristian was a true believer, and not only about the Cold War. He believed in the Bible. As special assistant to the Joint U.S. Military Advisory Group in Greece from 1949 to 1950 at the end of the Greek civil war, he had Protestant Bibles distributed to every Greek soldier. He was also one of the army's top intelligence officers, a man who earned his spurs in postwar Germany and would turn them in after service in Vietnam.[38] McChristian understood the value of religious war in Cold War strategy. Acting for God, he believed, lent confidence to acting for one's country.

By April 1962, McChristian's rank of colonel at Limoncocha was also a cover; he was actually a major general, working in army intelligence as chief of the Western Hemisphere Division. His counterpart in the CIA was Colonel J. C. King. McChristian was only forty-seven years old when he visited Limoncocha, but there was no mistaking his mastery of counterinsurgency command. Moreover, he was well connected to conservative networks, being the son-in-law of General James A. Van Fleet, who had recently violated military law by publicly challenging

President Kennedy's handling of the Bay of Pigs.[39] Van Fleet was then a top counterinsurgency consultant to Kennedy's army secretary on guerrilla warfare. His son-in-law did him proud. McChristian was persuasive on the guerrilla threat, helped by doctored interrogation reports to the Ecuadorian military that falsely linked the Ecuadorian Communist party to a group of young intellectuals who were arrested while training to defend the government of President Carlos Julio Arósemena from a rebellion by the CIA-advised Cuenca garrison.[40] Arósemena, forced to break relations with Cuba, would soon announce that Ecuador was launching the first civic action program of its kind in Latin America, combining $1.5 million in U.S. military assistance with another $500,000 in AID funds for public works projects. Collaborating with McChristian's local mission officer, an army major who trained the tank crews for the Bay of Pigs, would be the CIA.[41]

McChristian clearly understood the soft-spoken clandestine side of persuasion. "He was one of the most impressive officers that I have ever met," SIL's Donald Johnson said of McChristian. "If all of our top commanders and diplomats were of his caliber, we could be proud and there would not be any 'ugly Americans.'"[42] McChristian's team used JAARS's Helio Couriers to survey the entire Ecuadorian Amazon.[43] The Green Berets stayed in Ecuador for three months while McChristian continued his tour of Amazon-basin countries. He was probably the colorful "general" referred to by General Lansdale's boss, Undersecretary of Defense Roswell Gilpatric, when he recalled, years later, that "we had this general who was of rather broad gauge; he sensed all the psychological, political and other than military aspects of the thing and really got around Latin America much more than any other men had done. Through this Southern Command we began to pull the whole thing together and get some priorities instead of having it done on sort of a country by country basis and just between top military establishments. . . . I remember Colombia, Peru, Ecuador, Brazil particularly."[44]

This transnational approach to counterinsurgency in "remote areas" was uniquely reflected in the missionary realm by the activities of SIL, then the only truly transnational presence in almost all the Amazon-basin countries. From Peru, SIL's Jerry Elder sent Cam a clipping from Lima's *La Prensa* that reported on a conference between Ecuadorian and Peruvian army commanders on the border. "The high point was the fact that they should unite to fight the common enemy, Communism," wrote Elder. "I think this is particularly significant in light of the fact that one of the reasons that Commander Melger went out there was to give a report to the military on the possibility of our doing espionage along the border."[45]

According to Elder, Melger was going to show him his report to the military before giving a fuller report to the minister of education. SIL's willingness to collaborate extended beyond the primers for the Ministry of Education; apparently, espionage also might come under the missionary rubric.

SIL's traditional support of Washington's counterinsurgency doctrine by deferring to regimes that were allied with Washington had been successful in some countries. But it would prove counterproductive in Brazil. There the Goulart government had been targeted by Washington not for stability, but for destabilization.

Cam Townsend, overlooking this difference, failed to recognize how SIL could be trapped by his eagerness to seize the opportunity offered by his most important Brazilian contact, Darcy Ribeiro. Appointed to steer the new University of Brasília to safe haven, Ribeiro was himself lost in these turbulent political seas. The ceremony in Brasília in May 1963 for the *Spirit of Philadelphia* demonstrated the conflicting currents.

Ribeiro officiated, breaking protocol to put his arm around Cam in praise, while an air force officer representing President Goulart and the ministers of foreign affairs and aeronautics looked on, along with a U.S. Embassy official and a film crew of the U.S. Information Agency, headed by Charles Mertz, a veteran of Lansdale's psychological warfare operations in the Philippines and South Vietnam.

The Helio Courier itself symbolized the political and cultural contradictions that Cam had used to build SIL, explosive contradictions that he now brought into the long-sought Brazilian Amazon. At that time, the Helio Corporation was deeply involved with the same CIA that was seeking the downfall of Goulart's and Ribeiro's government.

The plane had been christened in Philadelphia by Mayor Richardson Dilworth, a cousin of J. Richardson Dilworth, Nelson Rockefeller's top financial aide. The latter was the key representative of the Rockefeller family in the Hanna Mining–Chrysler–National Steel financial complex that Ribeiro's government was fighting in the Brazilian courts. The Helio Courier had been purchased from a Cuban American in Miami with a $5,000 down payment donated by Sam Milbank, one of Cam's most influential contacts on Wall Street and a key corporate link between SIL and Brazil.[46] Until recently an investor in sugar plantations and cattle ranches in Cuba, Milbank was eager to preserve American influence in Latin America. The Milbank family's law firm had presidential adviser and former Chase Manhattan chairman John J. McCloy as one of its senior partners. The firm had been retained by Hanna Mining; McCloy was in charge of Hanna's suit against Brazil's nationalization of its iron resources. Later, McCloy would represent Hanna successfully before the generals who would overthrow Goulart's government.

The plane's other major donor was the Pew Memorial Fund,[47] controlled by J. Howard Pew, Sun Oil Company (Sunoco) competitor of the Rockefellers' oil interests and a man so profoundly distrustful of everything to the left of Barry Goldwater that he thought Nelson Rockefeller was soft on communism. More to the point, Sun Oil was, after Texaco, the second-largest seller of crude oil to Brazil, most of it from Venezuela's Lake Maracaibo.[48]

None of this was known to Ribeiro, and it might not have made any difference anyway. Ribeiro was eager for SIL to help him set up a linguistics department at the new University of Brasília to train anthropologists for work among the Indians. And Townsend, in turn, was eager to reach the Bibleless tribes of Brazil. These Indians had been Cam's goal for forty years, since the day his Presbyterian inspirer from Philadelphia, L. L. Legters, had sent him pictures of a "fine, stalwart, naked Indian" along the Amazon and Xingu rivers and awakened Cam to the dream of reaching "a thousand tribes without the Bible."[49] In Brazil, SIL was already suffering from the suspicions of foreigners operating airplanes in the undefended Amazon. According to Jim Wilson, SIL's new branch director in Brazil, "support for our use of planes and radio must come from the top. . . . As far as I can see, the Indian Protective Service and the University of Brasília are the two most probable opportunities at present for underwriting our JAARS service."[50]

Wilson, therefore, courted SPI's new military director, using a document giving SIL authorization to set up and operate a radio and transport service in collaboration with the SPI. It was designed to help both SPI and SIL "give emergency help to the Indians," as well as "for the benefit of whatever government services require collaboration."[51] The document was unsigned, but Wilson insisted that former President Quadros had given his OK. SIL informed the Brazilian ambassador in Washington, Roberto Campos, of this document to get his support.

Campos offered more than support. An active proponent of U.S. corporate investment in Brazil, particularly in the Amazon, Campos had originated the idea of SIL using the University of Brasília as a legal ownership cover for SIL's Helios.[52] Like the Rockefeller's AIA, with which he frequently consulted, Campos understood the importance of brushing American enterprises with a Brazilian veneer.

For his own reasons, Darcy Ribeiro liked the idea of SIL's affiliation with the University of Brasília. Ribeiro, in fact, had become so enamored with SIL that he offered its members the use of a tourist hotel in Goiás on the Ilha do Bananal, a huge tract of dry land jutting out of the Araguaia River that marks the border between the states of Mato Grosso and Goiás.[53]

The hotel, built to allow guests "a view of the Indians,"[54] was the latest of the steps that were already bringing an end to the Karajá Indians' rule over their own lands. SIL had sent a team into the tribe in 1958. In the 1930s, there were some 4,000 Karajás; by 1967, there were only about 400.[55] The Karajás' lands were rapidly being taken over by cattle ranchers. All this had been overseen by SPI agents.

The SPI had great hopes of using JAARS to expand its control over the tribes. Wilson reported that Colonel Moacyr, SPI's director, had SIL's proposal for a contract between SPI and SIL that would allow SIL to work directly with the

Indians, with no intermediary Brazilian sponsors. Moacyr had given reason for hope. He was taking a personal hand in helping SIL import a new Helio Courier and was interested in having SPI use SIL's Pioneer 530 radio transmitters in order to "amplify the SPI network."[56]

From Washington, Ambassador Campos continued to urge SIL on. He had discussions with AIA over the various colonization schemes and realized the potential usefulness of these resourceful Americans for conquering Brazil's newest frontiers.[57]

The Campos Connection

Roberto Campos was an active promoter of SIL. It was he who, after attending the 1961 Philadelphia dedication of *The Spirit of Philadelphia,* suggested that SIL's Robert Schneider and JAARS's Lawrence Routh come to the Brazilian Embassy to work out a tentative contract, assuring that "he would see that such a plan got into the right hands in Brasília," Schneider wrote Wilson, urging him, Dale Kietzman, and Cam to send ideas.

Campos, however, had wider plans for the Amazon than saving the tribes for Jesus.

Campos was a clever U.S.-educated economist who had met Nelson Rockefeller while serving in Brazil's embassy in Washington during World War II. He had worked closely with New York financiers during his years as director of Kubitschek's National Bank for Economic Development, which promoted Amazonian development. He saw SIL as another tool for prying open the Amazon. If this perspective brought him into an alliance with Goulart supporters like Ribeiro, he accepted it only as a temporary pact of convenience. Campos was an internationalist when it came to development theories. He was no friend of Goulart and his nationalist policies.

Campos's political loyalties were known in Washington, where the National Security Council (NSC) had embarked on a pressure campaign against Goulart. Unfortunately for Campos, despite his sympathy for U.S. corporate goals, he was caught between Goulart and the NSC's desire for a "political confrontation" with Goulart that could "bring our influence to bear on important near future political decisions (e.g., appointments to the new cabinet)." There was no doubt in the NSC about the ultimate goal: removal of Goulart or Goulart's retreat on policies that obstructed "the climate for private investment."[58]

By December 1963, the pressure had become too great for Campos. He resigned as Goulart's ambassador with the stated intention of engaging in politics when he returned home. The Johnson White House knew his number. The State Department noted to NSC's McGeorge Bundy that Campos "is interested in financial success and sometimes regrets that to serve as ambassador, he had to give up his directorship of CONSULTEC, a profit-making consulting firm in Rio de Janeiro. . . . He has advocated the encouragement of private enterprise and foreign investments with specific reference to the participation of private foreign capital in the development of Brazil's petroleum resources."[59]

The departure of Campos was the last of a series of reversals for Cam in Brazil. Like Nelson Rockefeller's AIA, Cam's SIL had gotten only token support from AID during the Kennedy years. Only when the Johnson administration was in place did hope shine again. Cam made this fact clear in a cable he sent to President Johnson only weeks after Kennedy's death. "HERETOFORE, WE WERE NOT TREATED AS ALLIES BY OUR OWN GOVERNMENT, DUE PERHAPS TO THE EMPHASIS WE PLACE ON THE BIBLE AS A POWERFUL INSTRUMENT FOR FREEING INDIAN TRIBES FROM FEAR AND SUPERSTITION. YOUR GOAL, SO CLEARLY STATED, REPRESENTS INESCAPABLE DUTY [FOR] ALL OUR CITIZENS AGAIN. I CONGRATULATE YOU."[60]

Carlos Sanz de Santamaría, the former Colombian ambassador who had been instrumental in SIL's entry into Colombia, accepted the Johnson administration's nod to become chairman of the Alliance for Progress's executive advisory committee, the Inter-American Economic and Social Council. Since the council had a large technical secretariat to review national and regional development plans, Cam fired off a congratulatory letter to Sanz, loaded with proposals, and even visited Sanz to cement his relationship.

Cam urged essentially what was already well known as the new policy of AID Administrator Thomas Mann: The Alliance for Progress must become an alliance of businessmen. "How different it would be if business and professional men in the United States were encouraged to get together with their counterparts in Latin America and develop projects for whose success they would be responsible but for which they could secure financial backing from the Alliance for Progress. The American people have confidence in their business and professional men and would back them."[61]

Cam's specific proposal centered on transportation to move American tourists and machinery into Latin America. Use the U.S. Navy and Air Force to transport them free, he urged, and use private organizations, assisted by the Alliance for Progress and army surplus equipment, to airlift them over unfinished portions of the Pan American Highway and even to help "open up some important but isolated areas of commerce and colonization while roads that have been planned are being built."[62]

Cam, of course, offered the service of SIL's hundreds of linguists "and other technicians."

Sanz could not take Cam up on his offer, however. He had no real power, which was why Alberto Lleras Camargo had turned down the chairmanship of the council when Johnson offered it to him. Stunned by Sanz's unresponsiveness,

Cam had no choice now but to seek sources of assistance for SIL and JAARS in the private sector.

The Rockefellers were the obvious source of funds, and SIL petitioned the Rockefeller Foundation office in Rio. Unfortunately, all contributions from the Rockefeller Foundation were earmarked for the University of Brasília, headed by Darcy Ribeiro.[63]

Ribeiro's ties to Goulart may have hindered Cam's access to AID funds, but precisely because of these ties, Ribeiro was too valuable a card to ignore. However, in March 1964, his ace was removed with the overthrow of Goulart. With it, ironically, went the last barrier to the genocide of the Amazonian Indian.

29

OPERATION BROTHER SAM

SETTING THE CLOCK

Adolf Berle's Manhattan town house crackled with the sound of a short-wave radio on the evening of March 30, 1964, as Berle adjusted knobs, trying to hear the latest news on troop movements in Brazil. Listening with him was Alberto Byington, a Brazilian whose family had long linked the Amazon to the United States. Byington was a descendant of Confederate slaveholders who had migrated to the lower Amazon city of Santarém, where slavery was then still legal, rather than accept Abraham Lincoln's forced emancipation of African Americans. Surviving Brazil's own Emancipation in 1888, Byington's ancestors had done well in business. Byington himself tied his destiny to ALCOA's expansion in Brazil, which would soon include bauxite deposits in the Amazon. Since at least 1962, he had been passing U.S. funds to the rebels.[1] He was one of the chief plotters of the military coup now under way.

"He laid out the plan," said Berle. "Through the evening, we watched it work out with almost clock-work precision."[2]

In Rio, President João Goulart watched also, but in dismay, as army after army deserted Brazil's constitutional government and marched on Rio. Gone were the brave presidential words he used to answer the first news of the rebellion. Now Goulart was worried that he would not be able to get out of Rio alive.

He had expected the coup attempt. As long as John F. Kennedy was alive, he believed, he could expect restraint. Even so, Kennedy had been tough, sending his brother, Robert, the previous year to lay down a series of demands. The demands were so similar to those of Goulart's domestic opponents that the Brazilian president, astonished, had looked at the U.S. attorney general and asked, "How can it be that you are in contact with my enemies?"[3]

His enemies were legion, starting with the admirals and generals who had tried to prevent his succeeding to the presidency after Jânio Quadros had resigned. Then there were conservative state governors like Juracy Magalhães, the former FBI informant and confidant of U.S. ambassadors since Berle's wartime tenure, and now governor of Bahia; Governor Adhemar de Barros of São Paulo, a wealthy physician who had left the União Democratica National (UDN), which had helped overthrow Vargas in 1945, to form his own Social Progressive Party; and UDN governors José de Magalhães Pinto of Minas Gerais, a banker, and, of course, the ever-vengeful Carlos Lacerda of Rio's own Guanabara state. The generals had been preparing for this day for years. Moreover, they knew they had support from the new Johnson administration in Washington: tangible support—money, arms, the promise of diplomatic recognition, and even a U.S. Navy carrier task force ready to steam into the fray.

Goulart's long deathwatch over his credit-starved government was over. His fortunes had declined rapidly since Kennedy's death. In early January, shortly before the petroleum workers' strike, he had made the mistake of expressing his belief that the political crises he had faced during the previous year were even more dramatic in other countries in Latin America. He did not specifically mention the many CIA-backed military coups that had swept the hemisphere in 1963. He did not need to. Everyone knew to what he was referring. But he did note that "the phenomenon that generated these times was the same in all countries. It is that the popular masses are becoming more politically aware at each step; it is that popular hopes are becoming more forceful, leading society to conquer barriers so as to transform itself into the democracy of all for all."

The U.S. Embassy's political officers underlined that last phrase in reporting his speech to Washington. They also underlined two other sentences: "That we may be able to make Brazil overcome that phase of transition, emerging from an egoistic and capitalistic democracy into a Christian and social democracy, within a climate of understanding and brotherhood. That will be the great victory that history will record in favor of the government."[4]

The CIA had been active in Brazil since the 1962 elections. Brazilian agents controlled by J. C. King's Western Hemisphere Clandestine Services infiltrated the Peasant Leagues, it was later charged.[5] Following the passage of the Rural Workers Law in March 1963, detailing the rights of rural workers and unions, the CIA-funded American Institute for Free Labor Development (AIFLD) initiated attempts to penetrate the rural labor movement in the Northeast. AIFLD, with the support of Nelson Rockefeller's old labor ally from Rockefeller Center days, AFL-CIO president George Meany,[6] was quickly becoming an arm of the CIA.

By the autumn of 1963, São Paulo Governor Adhemar de Barros was telling AIFLD's executive director, former Rockefeller wartime associate Serafino Romualdi, of plans "to mobilize military and police contingents" against President Goulart. AIFLD then hurriedly set up a training session for thirty-three Brazilian unionists in the United States. "When they returned . . . some of them . . . became intimately involved in some of the clandestine operations of the revolution before it took place on April 1," explained Romualdi's successor as executive director, William Doherty, Jr., in a radio interview after the coup. "What happened in Brazil . . . did not just happen—it was planned—and planned months in advance."[7]

Part of the planning included the use of yet another front group, the Brazilian Institute of Democratic Action (IBAD). Like AIFLD, IBAD's money was assumed to come from American big business. Some 1.4 billion cruzeiros were passed to IBAD through the Brazilian branches of three North American banks. The North American banks refused to reveal the names of IBAD's depositors when subpoenaed by Brazilian congressional investigators, but all three were subsequently identified as CIA conduits by a former CIA officer.[8]

Nelson's International Basic Economy Corporation (IBEC) was also later named as one of IBAD's major benefactors,[9] as were Standard Oil of New Jersey, Hanna Mining, Bethlehem Steel, Texaco, Gulf Oil, U.S. Steel, and General Motors.[10] In 1975, former CIA officer Philip Agee confirmed that IBAD was "one of the Rio [CIA] Station's main political-action operations."[11]

But the CIA's most important asset was the Brazilian army. IBAD had hired retired senior officers in an attempt to influence the 1962 elections at the Club Militar against Goulart candidates. A congressional investigation ultimately led to Goulart's closing IBAD's offices in October 1963, but by then it was too late. IBAD's operators were in place, continuing to function in the labor movement, the Higher War College, and the powerful Fourth Army. The veterans of the Brazilian Expeditionary Force who had fought with military attaché Colonel Vernon Walters in Italy during World War II emerged triumphant in the Club Militar elections. This group, called the "Sorbonne" Group, branded all criticism of the United States as inspired by the Communist party and subversive.

Many members of the Sorbonne Group were sons of career officers. They were part of a military caste that saw itself as unique and different from the rest of Brazilian society.[12] They prided themselves on their technical training and looked with disdain on the inefficiency of civilian rule. Every individual abuse or incompetency in government was taken as a sign of general corruption. These officers rejected the traditional emphasis on maintaining a balance of power in a region of shifting alliances; instead, they now accepted the Pentagon's line that the Cold War required a permanent alliance with the United States and adoption of the Pentagon's doctrine of "internal warfare."[13]

The enemy now became the citizens of their own country—all Brazilians

THE SLAUGHTER OF THE INNOCENTS

allied with the Left and even conservatives and nationalists who were reluctant to allow American corporations to dominate sectors of the economy or regions like the Amazon. The stress placed on nation-building by American counterinsurgency doctrine was replicated in the Brazilian Army Command and General Staff School well before the coup. And key to nation-building were law and order. Studying the U.S. Army's basic manual, Brazilian and other Latin American officers learned that "stability and law and order are essential to the success of Cold War efforts."[14] Taken out of its American context of rule by the people through direct vote or vote by fairly elected representatives, "stability and law and order" could be redefined as martial law.

In those words were the seeds not only of Brazil's 1964 coup, but of its 1968 "Supercoup," and not only Brazil's coups, but many other coups in Latin America. It was only natural, therefore, that President Kennedy's $9 million reduction in U.S. military aid to Brazil in 1963 was viewed with alarm by the Sorbonne Group. The blame, of course, fell on Goulart. Goulart's unwillingness to surrender Brazil's national sovereignty over its own foreign policy was perceived as a Communist-inspired alliance with the Soviet Union and therefore treason. The minister of war was feeling enough heat from the generals to call Goulart's foreign ministry and complain. "He asked whether we were trying to abolish his ministry. He said that the United States military mission had told him it might be very difficult to get aid and supplies for the next year unless Brazil supported the United States."[15] That was just before the coup.

Goulart saw it coming. Plans were announced to hold a huge anti-Goulart rally in Rio on April 12. The rally was to have been the start of the coup, Alberto Byington admitted to Berle, but Goulart's efforts to mobilize the populace behind him forced their hand earlier.[16]

Goulart called for a counterrally by labor. Despite Governor Lacerda's declaration of a holiday to lessen the turnout, 150,000 people showed up on March 13. They cheered Goulart as he signed decrees expropriating land along rural highways for redistribution to landless peasants and nationalizing Brazil's private refineries. Goulart also announced that the marketing and distribution of petroleum products would be put in the hands of public agencies, not private companies like Standard Oil. This had been the demand of oil workers for years; they had been impatient with Goulart, who knew how nationalization of the refineries into Petrobrás would enrage Lacerda's UDN party leaders, some of whom were investors in the refineries. He also knew that American oil companies would be furious. Standard Oil of California and Texaco had helped finance the Duque de Caxias refinery in Rio; another American company helped finance the terminal and oil-tanker docks in Santos near São Paulo for the refinery at Cubatão, used by the Pews' Sun Oil Company. But he was heartened by the fact that now the oil workers cheered him despite his intervention against their strike in January. The workers cheered even louder when he called for amending the Constitution to permit payment for the expropriated lands and refineries with government bonds instead of scarce cash.

The generals, however, did not cheer. Three days later, Army Chief of Staff Humberto Castelo Branco approached U.S. Ambassador Lincoln Gordon with a "white paper" rationale for a military uprising. Brazil had to be saved from itself, or at least from Goulart. What would be Washington's reaction?

Gordon allegedly replied that President Johnson was prepared to recognize any rebel government on Brazilian territory that proclaimed itself in opposition to Goulart and communism and could hold out for forty-eight hours (a prescription similar to that given for the Bay of Pigs). He suggested that Minas Gerais, home of the Fourth Army, might be the best locale from which to launch such a rebellion.[17]

Encouraged by the U.S. ambassador's support, General Castelo Branco assembled his fellow generals. Adolf Berle later described what happened:

"Using units he knew had been unhappy about Goulart's probably projected dictatorship, he [the general] had worked out combined action with three of the four army groups . . . [and] was a little more than half certain that the other group . . . would go over to him. . . . He had also activated the political and other elements. A civilian demonstration of several hundred thousand was planned for Rio on April 2 as a preliminary but they could not wait for that."[18]

These "other elements" included AIFLD agents in the labor movement, who maintained vital telephone lines during the coup despite a union's call for a general strike,[19] and who fire-bombed the Rio headquarters of the Brazilian Communist party.[20] They also included the Research Group of retired military officers who had received several hundred thousand dollars from the Institute of Research and Social Studies (IPES).[21]

IPES, founded in 1961 by conservative businessmen with ties to American Power and Light and a São Paulo drug firm, was the major financial backer of and political guide to the principal overt sponsors of two huge anti-Goulart demonstrations that took place the last week of March, the Women's Campaign for Democracy and the Women's Civic Union.[22] Behind IPES was J. C. King's Clandestine Services, whose "Rio station and its larger bases," the CIA's Philip Agee noted in his diary, "were financing the mass urban demonstrations against the Goulart government, proving the old themes of God, country, family and liberty to be as effective as ever."[23] Marches were held in Belo Horizonte and São Paulo, the seats of government of two of the governors involved in the coup, banker Magalhães Pinto and Adhemar de Barros. American businessmen in close contact with the CIA were also involved.[24]

The head of this IPES network, General Golbery do Couto e Silva of IPES's Research Group, would become chief of Castelo Branco's intelligence service after the coup.

IPES was funded by U.S. subsidiaries, including American Light and Power and Rockefeller-affiliated DELTEC, which allegedly dipped into a $7 million cash reserve in the Bahamas.[25] Another funder, according to historian René Dreyfuss, was Moreira Salles's bank.[26] U.S. Chargé d'Affairs Niles Bond later suggested that U.S. funds for IPES had probably "been passed to IPES through a middleman: Alberto Byington."[27]

Back in Berle's Manhattan town house, Byington fretted over the safety of his wife, whom he had sent to Rio by plane on the previous afternoon. Mrs. Byington carried a secret message to the plotters that Byington had successfully "bought on his own credit a shipload of oil to make sure the Brazilian navy would be able to function."[28] Standard Oil of New Jersey, which provided the Brazilian navy with its oil supplies, would keep the flow coming.[29]

The plotters had good reason to worry that oil storage facilities and refineries would be seized or blown up by the oil workers to foil the coup. Brazil's oil workers had been at the forefront of the struggle to preserve Petrobrás, calling on Goulart to nationalize the private refineries, including those owned by Lacerda's UDN entrepreneurs. The navy was crucial to the coup's chances if the Northeast remained loyal to Goulart and army units were needed to be shipped there. Brazilian naval forces also would be needed to back up another option: a landing by U.S. Marines.

U.S. military intervention was considered in earnest following Ambassador Gordon's visit to Washington for consultations in mid-March. General Andrew O'Meara, commander of the U.S. Southern Command, reportedly flew from his Panama Canal headquarters to Rio a week before the coup to assure Castelo Branco of U.S. aid. The Brazilian general had given U.S. Military Attaché Vernon Walters a document describing a rationale for the coup on March 17. General O'Meara wanted Castelo Branco to know that the Johnson administration was willing to drop paratroopers in any area Goulart attempted to hold.[30]

Things fell into place quickly after that. On March 27, Ambassador Gordon, acting on CIA reports, cabled Secretary of State Dean Rusk that it was his impression and that of "some well informed Brazilians" that Goulart was definitely opting "to seize dictatorial power, accepting the active collaboration of the Brazilian Communist Party. . . . If he were to succeed it is more than likely that Brazil would come under full communist control."

Gordon noted that Petrobrás "is now taking over the five remaining oil refineries not already under its control." He applauded the recent anti-Goulart demonstrations as having provided "an important element of mass popular showing, which reacts favorably in turn on Congress and the Armed Forces." Gordon reported that five governors were now joined by a military group under Castelo Branco, who was assuming control "in all areas of the country."[31] Gordon asked that his report be passed on to top administration officials and higher-ups in the CIA, including J. C. King.

Two days later, Gordon sent Rusk another top-secret cable, warning that three hundred Brazilian marines had been unable or unwilling to break up a sit-in by sailors protesting the arrest of thirty other sailors who had spoken out in Goulart's defense during a rally. Goulart returned from an Easter holiday at his ranch in Rio Grande do Sul ready to grant amnesty to the marines and the sailors. The subsequent march of the freed sailors through the streets shouting "Long Live Jango" (Goulart's nickname) galvanized the military hierarchy into opposition against the government. To these men, Goulart was condoning mutiny against their own authority, an authority they believed predated the republic and was derived from the days of the Portuguese emperor when the armed forces were assumed to serve Brazil by being the state above politics and class interests. Twice before, during the general's attempts in 1955 and 1961 to overthrow constitutional succession by elected civilians, the refusal of noncommissioned officers to obey illegal orders for a putsch had proved decisive. The generals and admirals were determined not to have that resistance succeed again.

The generals now spoke out against Goulart's proposed constitutional reforms. "Resistance forces, both military and civilian [are] seeking [to] recover from unexpected setback and consulting feverishly on future courses of action,"[32] Gordon cabled. Again, King was listed among the select few to receive Gordon's cables.

King, however, was not content to remain so far from the action. He would not suffer being bypassed as he had in Guatemala and the Bay of Pigs. Brazil was his baby, his specialty since the days he headed Johnson & Johnson's subsidiary there and surveyed the Amazon for Nelson Rockefeller during World War II. His contacts among conservative businessmen, politicians, and military officers—once disdained by the CIA's fair-haired Ivy Leaguers—now found their place in the Brazilian sun. He secretly flew to Brazil to be on hand when the coup took place. He arrived just in time. "Actually, King had been very quietly in Rio through the recent April revolution there," Berle recorded a month later in his diary. "Some day we will get the story."[33]

In the Pentagon and the White House, the story already had a title: "Operation Brother Sam." Informants provided the CIA station on March 30 with news that the governors of São Paulo and Minas Gerais had "definitely reached accord" and that a coup was imminent "probably within the next few days. Revolution will not be resolved quickly and will be bloody. Fighting in North might continue for a long period."[34]

The drama reached its climax on March 30, when Goulart told the pardoned marine sergeants that many of the resources for the mobilization against the government had "come from the money of the businessmen who received the illicit remission of profits that were recently regulated by means of a law. It is the money provided by the enormous international petroleum interests and [Brazilian] companies which are against the law I also signed giving a monopoly on the importation of oil to Petrobrás."[35] This oil policy impacted negatively on the fortunes of

Refinaria Exploração de Petróleo União, whose principal stockholder, Rockefeller ally Walther Moreira Salles, would later be criticized for allegedly supporting the coup that was being planned.[36] When Goulart made a similar televised appeal to the Brazilian people that day, the conspirators knew they had to act fast.

The Alarm Rings

The Situation Room in the White House responded immediately with Operation Brother Sam, the contingency plan to land U.S. armed forces in Brazil. At 1:50 A.M. on March 31, a U.S. Navy task force, ostensibly conducting maneuvers in the South Atlantic, received orders from the Joint Chiefs to move secretly toward Brazil and stand by off Santos, a port south of São Paulo, for orders from the U.S. Embassy.[37]

The task force consisted of eleven tankers, six destroyers, an aircraft carrier with jet fighter-bombers, and a helicopter carrier ready to fly in a U.S. Marines strike force.[38] Six tons of small arms and ammunition were also readied at McGuire Air Force base in New Jersey for shipment by C-135 transports to the Brazilian governors and generals. State governors mobilized state militia units with officers trained by the CIA under the Agency for International Development's (AID's) "Public Safety" cover.

Ambassador Gordon and Vernon Walters knew that General Armoury Kruel was the key to success. He was the commander of the powerful Second Army in São Paulo. No coup could succeed in Rio or São Paulo without the Second Army. Under pressure from younger colonels who were in contact with King's CIA operatives,[39] Kruel demanded that Goulart break with the Brazilian Left. Goulart refused. At midnight, Kruel left São Paulo, and the Second Army was moving against Rio by 4 A.M.

It was a rout. Within a few hours, contingents of Castelo Branco's Fourth Army had completed their march from Minas Gerais and taken Rio. When Alberto Byington's wife arrived at the Rio airport from the United States, she found a large contingent of police waiting for her—not to arrest her, but as an escort under the command of her son-in-law.

Carlos Lacerda was triumphant. He had opted to hold out in the governor's mansion until the Second Army arrived, calling for his supporters to defend the palace. Organized by the management of American Light and Power, the group that surrounded the palace had only one problem: no ammunition. Until, that is, a long black limousine arrived, its back seats replaced by containers carrying ammunition, which was distributed by a man speaking English.[40]

On June 18, a beaming Lacerda would appear before the Council on Foreign Relations to the applause of New York's financial and academic elite; Adolf Berle would introduce him.

No such accolades would be given Pernambuco's governor in the Northeast. After troops from the Fourth Army surrounded the governor's mansion and fired on his supporters, killing two students, Governor Miguel Arraes was seized and imprisoned.

Meanwhile, Goulart disappeared from Rio. He flew to Brasília, where he immediately conferred with congressional leaders and denied reports he had resigned. At about 10 P.M., the White House learned that Goulart would not resign and would, if necessary, go to Rio Grande do Sul to lead the resistance.[41] Intelligence sources confirmed that the president's jet was fully fueled for a flight up to 5,500 miles and that no flight plan had been filed. The CIA was already on Goulart's trail.

Goulart signed the decree he had announced in Rio a few days earlier that nationalized the distribution of petroleum products. This legally put Standard Oil out of business in Brazil. It was also one of Goulart's last acts as president.

The Johnson administration's anxiety over whether Goulart intended to put up a fight ended when the Brazilian president, facing reports of troop movements against him from Minas Gerais, flew out of Brasília around midnight. This left the government in the hands of his chief domestic policy adviser, Darcy Ribeiro. Ribeiro officiated over the closing of the airport, pro-Goulart rallies at the University of Brasília, a failed general strike called by local unions,[42] and a radio call to arms. Against the oncoming Fourth Army, his efforts were feeble.

The Congress convened in an agitated joint session protected by local tanks and troops. Ribeiro's message that Goulart had not fled Brazil but had gone to Rio Grande do Sul was ignored. The presidency was declared "vacated." An hour and a half later, Speaker Ramieri Mazzilli took the oath of office as next in line of constitutional succession. The coup had effectively been endorsed by the time the Fourth Army's tanks arrived.

Ambassador Gordon signaled triumph with characteristic understatement. He had ordered the old Rio embassy's air conditioners shut off to prevent smoke spreading in case of fire. Learning from street runners (much as Berle had twenty years earlier) that the army was in control, he turned to his staff, who were expecting some comment on this historic moment, and simply said, "Turn on the air conditioners."

Outside, the CIA-financed "March of the Family with God for Liberty" became a huge million-strong victory parade complete with tons of ticker tape-like fluttering paper. Gordon observed that the "only unfortunate note was the obviously limited participation in the march of the lower classes." This, clearly, was a victory for the shopkeepers, the professionals, the landlords, and the upper classes, "a great victory for the free world," the only alternative to what otherwise would have been the "total loss to the West of all South American Republics." Gordon cautioned the Johnson administration, however, not to share his hyperbole; "avoidance of a jubilant posture"[43] was the watchword. Instead, Gordon advised that Johnson send a congratulatory telegram to the new acting president, Mazzilli, offering "America's warmest good wishes."[44]

The speed of Johnson's recognition pleased Brazil's new leaders, who had not been getting a good reception in Latin America's press. Johnson's congratulatory message, on the other hand, shocked many followers of John F. Kennedy. The late president's practice was to break diplomatic relations and pending aid when military coups, most often with CIA backing, took place. Kennedy had done so in Ecuador, Peru, Guatemala, Honduras, Argentina, the Dominican Republic, and Haiti.

The Johnson administration had given no cause for such illusions. It had already pronounced the Mann Doctrine of limited social reforms and toleration of military rule on March 18, when Assistant Secretary Mann called in Gordon and other ambassadors from Latin America to explain what *New York Times* reporter Tad Szulc described as "a radical modification of the policies of the Kennedy administration."[45] No clearer message needed to be sent to the generals of Brazil, other than speedy recognition, that is.

Later, both Gordon and Walters would deny any U.S. involvement in the coup.[46] "Neither the American Embassy nor I personally played any part in the process whatsoever,"[47] Gordon, under oath, told skeptical senators in 1966 during his confirmation hearings as Johnson's new assistant secretary of state for inter-American affairs.

Walters was with Castelo Branco at the general's home on April 6 when Governor Lacerda announced over the radio that Castelo Branco was to be the presidential candidate of the rebel coalition. Castelo Branco and the rebel governors had conferred that morning on the drafting of the first of a series of arbitrary Institutional Acts that established military rule by decree. The group had agreed to declare the de facto president, Castelo Branco, the legal president with wide powers of arrest, suspension of constitutional guarantees of due process and voting rights, and dismissal from office of all elected federal, state, and local officials who had supported the overthrown constitutional government. Such supporters were condemned to "political death," meaning they could neither act nor speak on public affairs.

The Johnson administration, apprised of these actions by the CIA,[48] quietly exercised the kind of sweeping transnational power that would have been the envy of imperial Rome. The CIA was ordered to conduct close surveillance of Goulart after he arrived in Uruguay. Secretary of State Rusk ordered the U.S. Embassy in Montevideo to insist that Goulart had voluntarily abandoned Brazil's presidency. Thus Rusk hoped to persuade the Uruguayan government to deny Goulart the refugee status that would have permitted him to organize politically more freely.[49]

At the same time, the CIA's Rio station sent some of its most prized Brazilian agents to Uruguay as, respectively, Brazil's new ambassador, first secretary, and military attaché to run penetration and propaganda operations against Goulart supporters in the exile community.[50]

The Brazilian generals moved quickly to consolidate their seizure of power.

On April 9, after Congress hesitated to give them authority, they issued their first Institutional Act, suspending the rights of 1,150 political leaders, including former President Juscelino Kubitschek, and abrogating the Constitution's direct election of the president, so the Congress, now purged of its Labor party-led majority coalition, could name Castelo Branco as Goulart's successor.

Castelo Branco then turned to filling his three most important posts. To oversee Petrobrás, he appointed General Adhemar de Queiróz, later the president of ALCOA's Brazilian subsidiary, who pledged to give Petrobrás a "total cleaning of extremist elements."[51]

It was an easy task. The entire staff of Petrobrás in Rio had already been imprisoned as alleged saboteurs;[52] when they were released, an air of terror hung over Petrobrás as thirty teams of investigators combed through employee files and financial records, producing the inevitable public report on corruption. Now came the purges, justified by precoup "financial irregularities."

These purges paved the way for the return of the refineries to their previous owners. Petrobrás made a perfunctory effort to uphold the nationalization decree, and the Supreme Court, now arbitrarily expanded by President Castelo Branco, quashed it. As for Goulart's nationalization of the marketing of oil products, it was ignored. Standard Oil of New Jersey's Esso was again in charge, leading a pack of companies that eventually included Shell, ARCO, and Texaco.[53]

For his intelligence agency, the National Information Service (SNI), Castelo Branco turned to General Golbery do Couto e Silva, later the president of Dow Chemical's Brazilian subsidiary. Under Golbery, SNI became the subject of controversy when two dozen cases of torture were documented by the press during the next six months. Some of the victims were Communist party members, some were socialists, and most were Catholic peasants and labor leaders. One was a Catholic priest. But the most flagrant atrocities went unprotested until 1967 because they were occurring in the jungle, and to Indians whose only crime was trying to defend their land.

For this, responsibility was shared by SPI, private developers who hired *pistoleiros* (hired guns), the military, and perhaps most important, the quiet, refined presence of Castelo Branco's third crucial appointee: Roberto Campos, former ambassador to the United States, as minister of finance and planning.

Campos saw development of the Amazon by American companies as a critical part of Brazil's economic growth. In July, he and Castelo Branco ended a ten-year suspension of plans by the U.S. Geological Survey to conduct aerial mapping of the Amazon to detect mineral deposits. Now the U.S. Air Force was invited in.

In October, Campos welcomed news that the World Bank was sending its largest-ever mission on a seven-week tour of Brazil's interior.[54] The Johnson administration had released $200 million in aid that was previously pledged to Goulart and delivered another $50 million AID loan shortly after Campos announced that he was reconsidering Goulart's 10 percent limit on profit repatriation.[55] In November, Campos's Ministry of Planning and Economic Coordination published his manifesto for Brazil's future. *Program of Economic Action of the Government* predicted that hundreds of millions of dollars in foreign investments would stimulate Brazil's stabilization and growth. His predictions rested on his "theory of constructive bankruptcy," a denationalization policy that turned petrochemical development, for example, away from Petrobrás and toward Union Carbide and Phillips Petroleum. It also placed Brazilian-owned firms at a competitive disadvantage by giving foreign firms investment guarantees, profits-repatriation rights, special exchange rates in case of the devaluation of the cruzeiro, and dollar-based duty and tax subsidies.[56]

Chase Manhattan Bank's former chairman, John J. McCloy, presided over the first concrete result of Campos's new policy. On November 6, McCloy, representing Hanna Mining and escorted by Ambassador Gordon, paid a visit to President Castelo Branco "to discuss company plans to develop iron ore deposits totalling an estimated 4 billion tons" and the company's "long-standing proposal to build an iron-ore shipping port at Sepetiba Bay." The port was essential to making Hanna's concession, earlier canceled by Quadros, profitable. McCloy argued his case, knowing that Governor Carlos Lacerda wanted to build his own state-owned steel plant in Guanabara and opposed the Sepetiba Bay project in favor of Rio.

McCloy also realized, as did Castelo Branco, that Minas Gerais's governor disputed the Hanna concession in his state, as did the chief of Castelo Branco's army. But none of these men was more important to the new regime than the United States, especially after Ambassador Gordon outlined the U.S. "financial and economic mission to Brazil."[57] Two weeks later, the Johnson administration leaked plans to provide Castelo Branco with another $400 million in aid.[58]

On December 15, the aid package was announced in Washington. In addition to the promised $400 million, it provided for $450 million more in loans from private banks guaranteed by the International Monetary Fund, the Inter-American Development Bank, and private investment firms.[59] All loans, of course, would have to be paid back; debt payments could be rescheduled, but only at the consent of the lending institutions actually making the loans, that is, the banks, including Chase Manhattan.

On December 23, a grateful Castelo Branco decreed a new mining code endorsing private development of Brazil's iron-ore reserves. This code triggered the release of $28.8 million from Washington's Inter-American Development Bank.[60] But Hanna, the test case for all potential American investors, still faced the Brazilian Supreme Court. The following October, McCloy, again escorted by Ambassador Gordon, would meet with Castelo Branco and the minister of mines to urge the restoration of Hanna Mining's contested concession.[61] Backed by Campos, who had served as Hanna's technical adviser, Castelo Branco issued the

Second Institutional Act. The act had two purposes: to respond to the stunning electoral defeat that month of the regime's gubernatorial candidates by banning all existing political parties and continuing the power to rule by decree and suspend Congress, and to pack the federal appeals courts and Supreme Court with military backers to outnumber judges who had been appointed by Kubitschek and Goulart. (Hanna won its case in June 1966 against token government opposition before an overhauled Court of Appeals.)

There were other paybacks.

The inflated purchase of American Power and Light's subsidiaries, negotiated at $70 million by Campos and canceled by Goulart, now went through at Campos's urging. Only now the price was $135 million, plus a $17.7 million penalty as "compensation" for the delay.[62]

In May 1964, a month after the coup, Brazil had broken off relations with Cuba; a year later, it joined the Johnson administration's resolution of condemnation of Cuba in the Organization of American States (OAS). The previous month, at General Vernon Walters's request, Castelo Branco had provided 1,500 of the OAS's 2,500 troops (as well as their nominal commander) that backed U.S. Marine intervention in the Dominican Republic.[63] The Brazilian foreign minister, who then toured South American capitals urging the creation of a permanent OAS strike force, was another old hand at intrigue, Petrobrás's first president, Juracy Magalhães.

The Rockefellers made no effort to hide their feelings about the coup in Brazil. Angry over declines in the stock market and therefore the net asset value of the Crescinco Fund, IBEC officials had privately charged Goulart with "governmental mismanagement."[64]

"The market is very unstable and weak, reacting violently to rumors of a political nature," one official had written Richard Aldrich in January. "The President is constantly being denounced for permitting communist infiltration, arming labor syndicates and preparing for a coup."[65] A week before the coup, Berent Friele analyzed Brazil's crisis for Nelson Rockefeller and Henry Kissinger. He dismissed as demagoguery Goulart's request for constitutional amendments to give illiterates and privates and noncommissioned officers the right to vote and to allow payments for nationalized properties to be made in bonds, rather than in cash, to speed up his agrarian reform program. "Goulart's real objective is to obtain an amendment . . . which will permit him to be a candidate for re-election in October 1965 or to find an excuse for perpetuating himself in office by force," Friele wrote.[66]

Friele continued this rationale to support the army after its coup. "Communists are being rounded up all over the country," he wrote. "In spite of criticism of high-handedness and over-zealousness in certain cases, the new regime enjoys universal respect and represents the will of the great masses of the Brazilian people. . . . It is my hope that the United States and the entire free world will be understanding and sympathetic."[67]

Nelson was. "Permit me to congratulate your excellency and the freedom loving people of your great country on having won a significant victory for democracy and constitutional rights without bloodshed and horrors of civil war," he cabled Brazil's interim president. "Brazil has set an outstanding example to the entire world and demonstrated its determination to reject communism and solve its problems as a free and independent nation. . . . Accept my very best wishes for continued success in your patriotic efforts."[68]

IBEC's 1964 annual report was filled with praise for the generals: "During 1964 a popular revolution in Brazil redirected the trend of the country's government by installing a new soundly-based administration under President Humberto Castelo Branco, dedicated to the improvement of the welfare of the Brazilian people through constitutional means. Many businesses in Brazil are going through a very difficult period because of the Government's effort to stem runaway inflation through a variety of means, including severe credit restrictions. However, your company and business generally are patriotically supporting the program and all have confidence in its eventual success."[69]

David, attending a conference on Latin America at West Point in the fall of 1964, revealed to a discussion group that "it had been decided quite early that Goulart was not acceptable to the United States."[70]

Nelson was more partisan. He blamed the coup on President Kennedy and the Democrats. "He argued," reported the New York Times, "that this nation under the Democrats had encouraged the Government headed by President João Goulart, which was overthrown yesterday. Encouragement was given although the Brazilian President had placed Communists in government positions in opposition to the wishes of many of Brazil's state governors."[71]

On the same page, the New York Times carried a small item noting that on Easter Sunday the waiting line at President Kennedy's grave site in Arlington National Cemetery was so long that there was a wait of more than an hour and a half to view the grave.

Pyrrhic Victories

For millions of Americans, the television image was riveting: Governor Nelson Rockefeller, waiting patiently to speak to the Republican Convention and the nation, while howling delegates, their faces skewed by hate, booed.

Nelson had just called for support for a resolution against extremism, and the Goldwaterites had taken the bait, exposing their fanaticism and intolerance on national television, all but killing any chance for their own candidate.

Nelson knew, as did much of the nation, that Barry Goldwater had refused to disavow support from the ultrarightist John Birch Society. He also knew, as most Americans did not, that Goldwater and the Birch Society were both heavily funded by

J. Howard Pew, owner of one of Standard Oil's major rivals, the Sun Oil Company.[72]

Nelson had not underestimated the Pews. They were part of a powerful, ultraconservative network of corporate leaders in the Republican party, who had made no secret of their preference for "Mr. Conservative." Nelson knew these enemies and judged them to be beatable, especially after Kennedy's death. The assassination had bred fear of extremes in the voters' hearts, or so Nelson thought.

Nelson had played the theme successfully in the Oregon primary, beating Goldwater handily. But California had a strong streak of conservatism, especially in the south, where Protestant Fundamentalism, Pentagon contracts, and the exploitation of Mexican farmhands shaped much of the region's politics.

Goldwater had forged a new alliance of suburban Roman Catholics and rural and suburban Protestant Fundamentalists, who were uneasy about Nelson's support for civil rights and so found it easier to set their case on the higher ground of private morals: opposing a wealthy liberal "home wrecker" who was also a political "wrecker" of the Republican party. To Nelson's surprise, nothing could stop this religious firestorm, not even the $3 million he spent on the primaries (including $250,000 from David and $100,000 from sister Babs).[73] Defeat seemed certain.

In July, as Nelson addressed a crowd of 40,000 who had gathered in San Francisco to show support for civil rights, young Goldwater delegates poured into the city's Cow Palace. It seemed obvious that Goldwater had won the Republican Convention where it mattered most, at the grass roots, electing delegates to the state conventions. Now, dominating the convention, the zealots would at last have their day. They would defeat the Eastern Establishment that had ruled the Republican party since John D. Rockefeller had helped put William McKinley in the White House in 1897. And they would mark the occasion for the world to see, by confronting Nelson Rockefeller, the liberal governor of the nation's richest state.

"This is still a free country, ladies and gentlemen," Nelson goaded the young Republicans before him. Stubbornly and patiently, he stood on the platform as a symbol of courage, exposing the booing to the glare of the world's television cameras for a full quarter of an hour. When it was over, he had extracted a final victory over them and Barry Goldwater. Some said it was his finest hour in the Republican party.

It was a Pyrrhic victory. When his shining hour had passed and his resolutions for civil rights and against extremism were duly stoned as heresy, Nelson was left with his party's enmity.

Goldwater's acceptance speech, declaring, "Extremism in defense of liberty is not a vice," did allow Nelson to issue a final indictment. He called the Republican candidate's views "dangerous, irresponsible and frightening."[74] Then he flew to the Rockefeller ranch at Jackson Hole, Wyoming, to join Happy, leaving mass defections to Lyndon Johnson in his wake.

Whereas Nelson had never been able to capture the moderate conservative mainstream of the Republican party, Johnson did, thanks partly to his own foreign-policy coup, Brazil. Ironically, the fall of Goulart that Nelson had cheered in April sealed both his and Goldwater's fate in the race for the presidency.

"In order to win all, or practically all, of the 50 American states next November," wrote a Goldwater backer two weeks after the coup, "Lyndon Johnson will have to convert millions of Republicans, Southerners, reactionaries and anti-Texas hate-mongers, a goal toward which he took a giant step by his instant recognition of the military coup in Brazil."[75]

Johnson did just that. He won the greatest landslide victory since Franklin D. Roosevelt's reelection in 1936.

Johnson began calling the Rockefellers to the White House as special advisers on Latin America, population control, and conservation. Yet the joy had gone out of politics for Nelson, perhaps long before the 1964 primaries. Norman Mailer had noticed the change in Nelson's face even while victory in California still looked possible. "He had a strong, decent face and something tough as a handball in his makeup, but his eyes had been punched out a long time ago—they had the distant lunar glow of the small sad eyes you see in a caged chimpanzee or a gorilla."[76]

Nelson's view of people and life had hardened since his last campaign, and not only because of the heavy political price he had paid for marrying Happy. In January 1964, Nelson had asked a judge in Westchester County, home of Pocantico, to declare his favorite son legally dead. The book on Michael Rockefeller's life was closed on February 3. Its solemn finality echoed in Nelson's soul like the closing of a tomb.

Nelson now viewed the world from behind a mask of iron cynicism. Despite power and riches that others could not even imagine (including a weekly dividend income of over $96,000),[77] his life had become an endless series of frustrations. Even his one great chance for personal happiness, his marriage to Happy, had been strained by a loss so great he could barely speak of it.

But if his view of people—all people, "civilized" or tribal—had hardened in the process, he did not admit it. Indeed, his liberal positions on domestic issues, so well groomed by the late Frank Jamieson, seemed unaffected. Only in foreign policy could the glint of a steel will be observed in the eyes' lunar glow.

30

BENEATH THE EYEBROWS
OF THE JUNGLE

Donning the Kennedy Mantle—Too Late

In 1964, the *Annual Report* of the International Basic Economy Corporation (IBEC) pictured Quechua Indian peasants applying weed killer in the Peruvian Andes. The same year, nearly 1,750 workers, most of Indian heritage, effectively toiled for Nelson Rockefeller on IBEC's sugar plantation on the coast in central Peru. Negociación Azucarera Nepeña, S.A., 61 percent of which was owned by IBEC, was one of Peru's largest producers of sugar. Thanks to the U.S. boycott on Cuban sugar, the Rockefellers were enjoying record sugar prices on the world market; Nepeña, in effect, had replaced Rockefeller profits that would otherwise have been made in Cuba through such expropriated firms as Punta Alegre Sugar, just as Adolf Berle's SuCrest hoped to score record profits through its mills in the Dominican Republic. But as in Cuba and the Dominican Republic, impatience was growing with the slow evolutionary schemes of Thomas Mann's revised Alliance for Progress. Social reforms were urgently needed, even at Nepeña, where thousands of sugar workers and their families had erected a crowded town surrounding the mill.

Two hundred and fifty miles to the south, in Lima, the social crisis was worse. Encircling the capital, like the camp of a besieging army of the poor, was a vast slum: homes tacked together from tin cans and packing crates, children exposed to raw sewage picking through garbage, and always the dreadful meaning behind ugly black clouds of vultures circling overhead.

Peruvians mordantly called it the "Ciudad de Dios," the City of God. But Peru now had a young liberal president who looked at these slums and knew that more than prayers were needed; otherwise it would be educated men like he, Peru's own best and the brightest, who would also be needing prayers. The desperation in God's City might soon bring its living hell right to the doorstep of Lima's fashionable commercial and residential district, demanding immediate relief, if not heads.

Yet Fernando Belaúnde Terry, an architect by training, took the long view. The immediate origins of the slums and the anger simmering among their half million residents lay in the mountains to the east, where another storm of far greater dimensions was building like the Wrath of God.

In the Andean highlands, millions of Indian peasants, called Quechua after the language imposed on them by the Incan lords, still tilled a land no longer their own. Legal title had been taken from the Incas by the Spanish conquistadors and passed, through the psychological and military power of property laws, to the conquistadors' wealthy descendants. Serfdom, abolished in the previous century by the laws of propertied liberal revolutionaries, still thrived in practice on highland manors and coastal plantations.

The enslavement of Indians under the Spaniards in the mines and plantations had led to the abandonment and collapse of Incan irrigation and terraced agriculture in the highlands. Overtilling what good land remained led to soil erosion, smaller crops, and larger debts. Fertile land became scarce, and starvation was common.

With conditions worsening, wave upon wave of Indians migrated down the mountain roads to the coastal cities that could neither feed nor house them. There, industry, dependent for capital on the ups and downs of world prices for Peru's exports, was growing in fits and starts, but not fast enough to provide enough jobs or the kind of wages that could pay for industrial expansion as a consumer market. Unrest, born in the highlands, now spread into the streets of Lima.

Belaúnde had vowed to avert impending disaster with modern technology when he campaigned for the presidency in 1963. He had lost twice before, campaigning around the country much like John F. Kennedy. A charismatic candidate in his forties, he projected youth, vigor, and the power of a good education. Everywhere he went, he brought a team of university experts for answers and modern advertising techniques for image. His calls for progress and change to get the country "on the move" bore a strong resemblance to Kennedy's pledge to "get this country moving again," stirring the hearts of newly enfranchised women voters and the social aspirations of young male professionals.

By borrowing from rival Haya de la Torre APRA's vague mystical nationalism but not its working-class ideology ("Peru is its own ideology," he insisted), he also attracted the hopes of patriotic young army officers.

Many of these officers had, like Belaúnde, been trained in the United States and had seen its technological development and material wealth as their own future. They also knew firsthand of the conditions in the highlands. They had been ordered by President Manuel Prado and his military successors to put down mounting revolts in the Andes in 1962–1963 that were unprecedented in their lifetimes. Moreover, they were obliged to use Indian soldiers who were forcibly conscripted from Quechua villages. Facing possible mutiny, these officers understood that the desperation and anger of the Indian peasantry had reached the breaking point.

They demanded reforms, and Belaúnde promised agrarian reforms in the highlands and Peru's recovery of its oil resources from Standard Oil's control. In both cases, Belaúnde would confront powerful enemies.

Standard Oil of New Jersey owned a huge refinery at Talara; it also controlled the pace of the extraction of oil beneath the sands of Peru's coast. To meet Peru's needs, Standard Oil was importing oil from its huge reserve in Venezuela, while conserving Peru's oil for its own future use. As a result, oil import charges were taking a huge cut out of Peru's export earnings, retarding the capital reserves the country needed to pay debts and finance improvements in the infrastructure, agrarian reforms, and industrial growth.

After his election in 1963, Belaúnde was forced to reconsider the initiation of many of the far-reaching reforms he had promised. He had anticipated assistance from President Kennedy's Alliance for Progress. But Teodoro Moscoso of the Agency for International Development made it clear, on a trip to Lima, that U.S. private and government loans could be suspended if Belaúnde did not comply with Standard Oil's wishes.

Kennedy's assassination became Belaúnde's tragedy as well. It effectively eliminated any chance of achieving the promised reforms without provoking a violent reaction from either the landed oligarchy or from their American allies in mining and oil.

No funds were available to the Peruvian government to pay the landlords what they demanded for their estates. Agrarian reform, without immediate cash payments, would provoke the ire of the powerful landed interests, previously tied to General Odría and ex-President Manuel Prado, an ally of the Rockefellers and Chase Bank. And even if Belaúnde wanted to assert state control over Peru's oil and other subsoil mineral resources, he was faced with the Hickenlooper Amendment, which required the United States to suspend aid to any country that expropriated U.S.-owned property without compensation. Not to mention the wrath of Standard Oil and, behind it, the Johnson administration's powerful assistant secretary of state for Latin America, Thomas Mann, a former petroleum lawyer.

Although perhaps not convinced that Moscoso's freeze on new loans had now been made permanent by Mann, Belaúnde certainly suspected it. For this reason, he continued to balk on his inaugural promise to submit a bill to Congress within ninety days that would lay the legal foundation for reclaiming Peru's control over its oil.

Instead, he took up the dream of his predecessors, the Amazon. It was not a new dream for him. Like Juscelino Kubitschek's use of Brasília as a symbol for Brazil's determination to conquer the Amazon, Belaúnde had held his party's national convention in Iquitos to signal his own intentions to do likewise. He hoped that the colonization of the Peruvian Amazon would provide the Andes with a pressure valve. Tapping its mineral and agricultural resources might even spur Peru's economic development.

"Peru's young president," the *New York Times's* Tad Szulc wrote, "whose great dream is an international highway running along the Andes, once told me that he hopes only to be able to do what his Indian [Inca] forefathers did. . . . The desert, the Andes and the jungle, he said, must be crisscrossed with penetration roads. Then the Indians and the *Cholos* [a title of contempt that is used for lower-class people of mixed Indian and European parentage], instead of crowding the high plateau cities and adding to the coastal cities' slums, could move out into the fertile jungle lands, clear them and colonize them."[1] Internal infrastructure, agrarian reform, and industrialization for an internal market might all be paid for by the Amazon's development.

There was another ingredient, too, one that made the lure of the Amazon even more inviting: newly discovered oil.

Belaúnde could smell it in the air when he flew to the Amazon in January 1964. Only a month before, oil had been struck in a new well at Ganso Azul.[2] Texas Gulf Producing Company used the find to springboard into a more lucrative concession in Libya, selling the Ganso Azul oil field to Sinclair Oil.

For Lima's financial and industrial promoters, this was good news. Sinclair was a large, powerful company. Its banking ties included David Rockefeller's Chase Manhattan Bank and James Stillman Rockefeller's First National City Bank.[3] Its experience in Latin America included a giant success in Venezuela and a hopeful recent excursion into the Llanos plains of eastern Colombia. And in recent years it finally had made the big leap into retail marketing abroad, requiring new sources of crude.[4]

Belaúnde was so eager for Amazonian oil and development that he signed into law a ten-year moratorium on taxes in the jungle provinces east of the Andes.[5] One of the beneficiaries was Texaco, which owned a huge concession in Peru's upper Marañon River Valley. Another was Texaco's Peruvian legal representative, Antonio Miró Quesada, whose enormously powerful family would prove crucial to the Summer Institute of Linguistics' prospects in the Peruvian Amazon and the Andes.

The Miró Quesadas shaped law, politics, and public opinion. They owned Lima's most influential paper, *El Comercio*. And despite patriarch Carlos Miró

Quesada's infatuation with Spanish fascism before the war, they now boasted a son, Francisco Miró Quesada, who was moderate enough to be chosen Belaúnde's minister of education. Francisco took charge of overseeing SIL in much the same way that air force generals commanded the resources of SIL's Jungle Aviation and Radio Service (JAARS). Both were integrated into Belaúnde's grand scheme to conquer the Amazon with roads and planes, for both highways and jungle aviation were common immediate goals of Cam Townsend and the new Peruvian president. If Cam did not see the connection immediately during Belaúnde's campaign, he did so after the election, when Francisco Miró Quesada inducted Cam into the Order of Distinguished Service, a high honor.

Counterinsurgency, if not the motive, was a useful rationale for Cam to act on Belaúnde's behalf. He now used it for Belaúnde in Washington, just as he had intervened for Lázaro Cárdenas a quarter century earlier. "Any help you may be able to give the [Peruvian] project in Congress would be an effective way of combatting communism in South America," Cam wrote Oklahoma's Senator Mike Monroney, chairman of the Senate Aeronautics Committee, "for it would give poverty stricken laborers on the coast and in the highlands a chance to start a new life in a new region with new hopes. The results of their getting such an opportunity would be, I believe, not unlike what happened in Oklahoma eighty years ago."[6]

Referring to Oklahoma as if it were an example of Indian opportunity was revealing. It underscored how much racial bias still penetrated Cam's and his missionaries' understanding of American Indian history.* Monroney's state, in fact, had originally been set aside by the federal government as Indian Territory for expropriated Cherokees and Creeks of the Southeast and the butchered tribes of the western Plains and Texas. Then, eighty years ago, came an onslaught of white settlers and oil companies of such huge dimension and official sanction that the Indians were overwhelmed in their last refuge. Carved up and parceled out, Indian Territory was turned into a white-dominated political state called Oklahoma, current academic home of Cam's grateful Summer Institute of Linguistics.

Now Cam wanted to replicate the "Oklahoma experience" in the Peruvian Amazon, using Belaúnde's architectural vision of roads as instruments of social engineering.

Cam wrote to the Helio Corporation offering to suggest to Belaúnde that he purchase Helios for a network of small airports strung across the jungle. Cam wrote Lynn Bollinger, attempting to renew SIL's brokerage relationship. He

---

*Apparently Cam and his Fundamentalist followers had never absorbed John Collier's writings on the plight of Oklahoma's Indians. Collier specifically referred to the period Cam praised (1880–1920) as an era of the "demolition of Indian rights" in Oklahoma. See John Collier, "Terminating the American Indians," p. 4. Unpublished manuscript, February 13, 1954, Institute of Ethnic Affairs, in Papers of Philleo Nash, Harry S. Truman Library.

assured Bollinger that together they could help Belaúnde's effort to colonize the Peruvian Amazon, hinting that Belaúnde was very friendly with SIL.[7]

Belaúnde's $2 million "peripheral road" scheme through the Amazon toward the Brazilian border was approved.

The first victims of Cam's promotion of road colonization were not, of course, communists, in either the highlands or the Amazon, but Amazonian Indians.

THE MAYORUNA MYSTERY

In March 1964, SIL's Harriet Fields was working hard at Yarinacocha with two Indian informants to prepare for SIL's first contact with the elusive Matses Indians. Developers at the time were taking a renewed interest in their territory, east of Pucallpa along the invisible border with Brazil.

The Matses had earned a reputation for fiercely resisting encroachment on their lands. Nature had conferred upon them the unhappy fate of living among some of the richest rubber forests in the world. Promised wages, goods, and medicine for their labor, they were often rewarded with massacres during the rubber boom of the 1900s. The Matses responded in kind, driving rubber hunters and settlers out of their homelands.

For defending the great rain forests between the Tapiche, Blanco, and Yavarí rivers, the fast-hitting Matses became a subject of fear and mystery among the settlers, who adopted the Quechuas' term for them, "Mayoruna," or "Man of the River."

While Harriet Fields got ready for the Lord's first peaceful contact with the Matses, preparations of a different kind were taking place at Requeña, a small town at the junction of the Tapiche and Ucayali rivers. Members of a road-survey expedition armed themselves with heavy weaponry before heading off into Matses territory. They expected trouble.

Now that Pucallpa was developing into a large timber exporter, the Matses' territory, long referred to as "the most productive region of the entire Peruvian jungle,"[8] was rediscovered. It contained not only the highest-grade rubber, not only vegetable oils and thirty-four different species of rose orchids (including from the genus *Cattleya*), but an immense forest of cedar—and possibly even oil.

Since the strike in Ganso Azul in December and Belaúnde's visit to Iquitos in January, oil fever had swept through the region. Then the *Peruvian Times* announced on January 31 that a consortium of German companies was joining Standard Oil of New York (Mobil) to investigate the possibility of huge natural gas deposits in the Aguaytia River region north of Pucallpa.[9] Although the Matses' potentially lucrative tropical hardwoods were the most immediate motivation for the road, the promise of oil hovered over the jungle like an evil spell.

As the expedition hacked its way for twenty days through the jungle, the

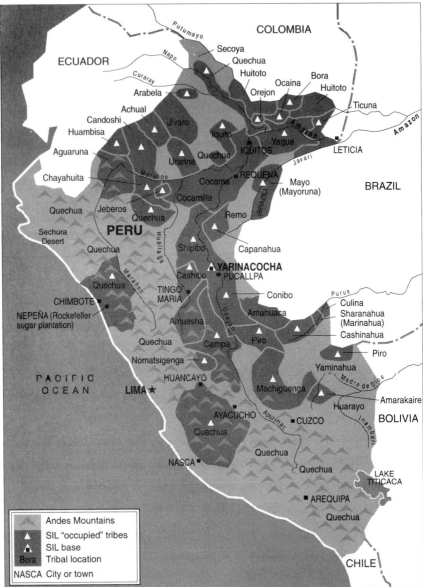

COLOMBIA

Putumayo

ECUADOR

Secoya
Quechua
Napo
Huitoto
Curaray
Ocaina
Bora
Arabela
Orejon
Huitoto
Achual
Ticuna
Candoshi
Jivaro
Amazon
Huambisa
Iquito
Amazon
Aguaruna
Quechua
Yagua
IQUITOS
Urarina
LETICIA
Chayahuita
Marañon
Javari
Cocama
REQUENA
Quechua
Jeberos
Cocamilla
Mayo
(Mayoruna)
Quechua
BRAZIL
Sechura
Desert
Quechua
Remo
PERU
Huallaga
(BRAZIL)
Quechua
Shipibo
Capanahua

YARINACOCHA
Cashibo
PUCALLPA
Quechua
Marañon
TINGO
MARIA
Conibo
Purus
CHIMBOTE
Culina
NEPEÑA (Rockefeller
Amuesha
Amahuaca
Culina
sugar plantation)
Sharanahua
(Marinahua)
Ucayali
Quechua
Campa
Piro
Cashinahua
Nomatsigenga
Piro
PACIFIC
OCEAN
Yaminahua
HUANCAYO
Machiguenga
Madre de Dios
LIMA ★
Huarayo
Amarakaire
AYACUCHO
Apurimac
CUZCO
BOLIVIA
Quechua
Inambari
Quechua
NASCA
Quechua
LAKE
TITICACA
AREQUIPA
Quechua
CHILE

⛰	Andes Mountains
▲	SIL "occupied" tribes
⌂	SIL base
Bora	Tribal location
NASCA	City or town

Peru's Indians and SIL

Sources: Hugo Pesce, *Mapa de Selvícolas del Peru*, Ministerio de Educacion Publica, 1969; Stefano Varese, "The Forest Indians in the Present Political Situation in Peru," pp. 14–15; IBEC annual reports.

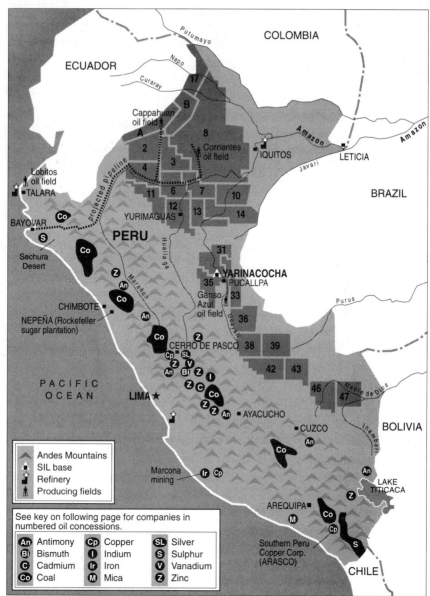

COLOMBIA

Putumayo

ECUADOR

Napo

Curaray

17

B

Cappahuari
oil field

A

2

8

3

Corrientes
oil field

IQUITOS

LETICIA

Amazon

Amazon

Javari

BRAZIL

Lobitos
oil field
TALARA

BAYOVAR

Co

S

Sechura
Desert

PERU

4

11

6

12

7

13

10

14

YURIMAGUAS

Marañon

Huallaga

31

Co

Co

Z

An

Co

An

Co

35

Ganso
Azul
oil field

33

36

YARINACOCHA

PUCALLPA

Ucayali

Purus

CHIMBOTE

NEPEÑA (Rockefeller
sugar plantation)

Z

CERRO DE PASCO

38

39

Cp SL

Z V

An Bi Z

Z C

Z

Z An

Co

AYACUCHO

42

43

46

47

Madre de Dios

PACIFIC
OCEAN

LIMA

CUZCO

An

BOLIVIA

Co

Inambari

An

LAKE
TITICACA

Marcona
mining

Ir Cp

AREQUIPA

M

Z

Co

Cp

Southern Peru
Copper Corp.
(ARASCO)

S

CHILE

Andes Mountains
SIL base
Refinery
Producing fields

See key on following page for companies in
numbered oil concessions.

An	Antimony	Cp	Copper	SL	Silver
Bi	Bismuth	I	Indium	S	Sulphur
C	Cadmium	Ir	Iron	V	Vanadium
Co	Coal	M	Mica	Z	Zinc

Peru Oil and Mining (1974)

Sources: *Latin America Economic Report*, May 9, 1975, pp. 20, 70; "Peru Petroleum
Survey 1974," *Andean Times*, September 20, 1974, pp. 69–74; *Peruvian Times*, June
1953; *The Andean Report*, December 1976, pp. 226–28; Shelton H. Davis and Robert O.
Mathews, *The Geological Imperative*, pp. 64, 66.

Key to "Companies in Peru Oil and Mining (1974)" (preceding page)

Contract Block	Companies Involved	Contract Block	Companies Involved
A	Occidental Petroleum	13	BP (British Petroleum)
B	Union Oil Tenneco Champlin Exploration	14	Arco [Atlantic Richfield Company] (70%) Andes Petroleum [subsidiary of 13 Japanese companies] (30%)
2	Petroperu		
3	Getty Oil (50%) Pan Ocean Oil (25%) Transworld (25%)	17	Petroperu
		31	Petroperu
4	El Paso Natural Gas Company (50%) Oceanic Exploration (37½%) Charter Oil (12½%)	33	Signal Oil & Gas (35%) Deminex (25%) Cities Service (22%) Superior (17%) Sumisho [Sumitomo, Japan] (1%)
6	Sun Oil Company (SUNOCO) Continental Oil Company (CONOCO) Champlin Oil	35	Petroperu
7	Phillips Petroleum	36	Deminex (33⅓%) Hispanoil (33⅓%) Total (33⅓%)
8	Petroperu	38	Petroperu
10	Amoco [Standard Oil of Indiana] (50%) Shell-Pecten (50%)	39	Total (45%) El Paso Natural Gas (20%) Hispanoil (20%) Deminex (15%)
11	Amerada Hess	42	Petroperu
12	Amoco [Standard Oil of Indiana] (20%) Deminex [Deutsche Erdoel, Germany] (20%) Hispanoil [Spain] (15%) Saga Petroleum (15%) Shenandoah Oil (15%) Total [Cie. Française des Peroles] (15%)	43	Petroperu
		46	Cities Service (70%) Andes Petroleum (30%)
		47	Andes Petroleum (70%) Cities Service (30%)

fleshy leaves and strangler vines seemed alive with danger. The suffocating heat and eerie silence that pervade the Amazon in daylight deepened the men's dread. The men were marching along a spine of land that ran from Requeña through the wetlands to the Matses villages. It was rainy season. They knew that the flooded rivers had covered the forest floor with water, driving the Indians up to the spine.

At any moment, the Mayoruna could attack, first silently with curare-poisoned blowguns and arrows, then loudly with shotguns and Winchester Repeaters smuggled in from Brazil.

When, at last, the great green vault of the rain forest opened and they emerged into a clearing near the Yavarí River, they found crops ready for harvest. The Matses were less nomadic and more settled than anyone in Requeña or Lima had cared to believe. The men of the expedition showed their intent by cutting down the crops, depriving the Indians not only of a vital food source, but of prima facie evidence of any claim for title to the land.

Now the Indians attacked, and with swift, precise fury. From all sides came arrows. Two Indian guides and three members of the expedition fell wounded. The Matses vanished again into the dense foliage.

In Requeña, excitement grew when local authorities lost radio contact with the expedition. The first press reports in Lima reflected the hysteria generated by local government officials: The expedition, besides the guides, had suffered 2 wounded, then 4, then 11 out of 38 men.[10] The Indians—numbered first at 8,000, then at 2,000, and then 500[11]—were armed with modern weapons; they fought like drilled units, they had radios, they intercepted radio transmissions from Requeña, they were led by whites.[12]

SIL missionaries inadvertently added fuel to the fire by assuring the press that the attackers were neither their "civilized" wards nor the Indians known to be currently living on the border.[13] Was this an incursion by Brazilians? Brazilian smugglers? Brazilian communists?[14]

What did Brazil have to say? The Brazilian ambassador in Lima kept his composure. No, he knew only what he read in the papers. No, he knew of no unusual activities on the Brazilian side of the border.[15]

It blew up into a national crisis with possible international repercussions. Belaúnde sent Requeña a wire of concern for the expedition. Peruvian air force units based at the U.S.-made airport in Iquitos were put on alert to repel any "new incursions."[16] The commander of Peru's air force flew to Iquitos to direct the operations personally. European and American reporters arrived. A rescue force, equipped with special arms for jungle warfare, was quickly assembled in Requeña and sent in to break the Indian circle surrounding the expedition.

The Matses, meanwhile, tried one more attack. Encountering heavy resistance, they gave it up. When planes were heard overhead, they melted into the jungle, leaving the whites wide-eyed and feverish behind their guns.

Peruvians suspected foreigners of arming Mayoruna Indians who defended their lands in March 1964. Suspects included communist guerrillas, cocaine smugglers, and the Brazilian government. Fear of foreign designs on the Peruvian Amazon inspired Lima's request for U.S. military assistance during the fighting, which the Johnson administration quickly granted.

Source: *La Prensa* (Lima), March 21, 1964.

Now came the bombs; shrapnel ripping through foliage; the rat-tat-tat of machine-gun fire raking the forest; and a new weapon, the one Standard Oil's local subsidiary reportedly had asked Washington for permission to produce for the Belaúnde regime of democracy—napalm[17]—making the tribe's thatched long communal homes, exposed in clearings, explode in flames. But the bombs and bullets could not penetrate the living roof of forest canopy. Again and again the old U.S.-surplus B-26 bombers unloaded their bombs as if this were again the Ecuador war over the Amazon, and again the Indians were protected by nature.* The Amazon jungle still had awesome powers.

For a reason that remained unexplained, Requeña's mayor had launched his expedition in the middle of the rainy season. If his purpose was to hunt down the Indians more easily, since they were more visible on the high ground, he got his wish. But the Amazon also extracted its own price: Its torrential rains kept the small Peruvian helicopters from rescuing the wounded members of his expedition. The Peruvian military blamed the weather and the difficulty of landing heli-

---

*William Cameron Townsend told the authors in 1977 of another possibility. A Peruvian general named Barbosa had recently visited him at his home near the JAARS base in Waxhaw, North Carolina, and claimed that he had deliberately disobeyed orders from his superiors while participating in the bombing of the Matses, dropping his bombs harmlessly in spots where he "knew" the Indians were not hiding.

copters amid canopy jungle. Then, without blinking an eye, they announced a solution: not only larger helicopters, but the U.S. Marines.[18]

An enterprising newsman from Lima took photographs of the marines arming the choppers. The photographs were never printed. They show bubble-headed marine helicopters that looked more like fragile dragonflies than the monster aerial ambulances mentioned in Lima's newspapers.[19] They were not large, certainly not capable of carrying the twenty people promised by Lima's press.[20] But the U.S. "rescue operation" (which was actually accomplished by the Peruvian army's relief column) served to lend "civic action" a humanitarian image to what would otherwise have been a questionable American presence for Peruvians—U.S. Marines in the Peruvian Amazon during a heated Standard Oil controversy.

The U.S. Southern Command could not afford it to be otherwise. A U.S. military presence in the Peruvian Amazon had to be secured for a reason other than humanitarian purposes: counterinsurgency. The CIA had information that arms were being smuggled from Manaus down the Amazon and across the Brazilian border to Peruvian leftists who were planning to launch a guerrilla war on the tropical eastern slopes of the Andes, along what Peruvians called "the eyebrows of the jungle."

The CIA knew about this plan because it had an informer inside the Peruvian group that was planning the guerrilla war, the Movimiento de Izquierda Revolucionaria (MIR), or Movement of the Revolutionary Left. This was the same name that young pro-Castro dissenters in Rómulo Betancourt's party in Venezuela had adopted after being jailed and expelled. CIA analysts were convinced, not inaccurately, that they were confronting an international guerrilla alliance. Their only mistake, as in Vietnam, was overestimating its coordination and control by Moscow and China and underestimating each guerrilla group's national origins and sense of patriotism as motives for its willingness to fight and die. But two things the CIA did not underestimate: the danger to U.S.-backed regimes in Colombia, Ecuador, Peru, and Bolivia posed by unrest spreading along the Andes among 11 million Quechua Indians and the potential of disciplined guerrillas to spark the Andean tinderbox into a continentwide revolution.

WAITING FOR MIR

In the White House, alarm was growing. President Johnson had been briefed at a meeting with Peru's ambassador that the unrest by Indian peasants in the Andes was "communist-inspired."

"Communist subversive activity in Peru has been increasing," Johnson learned, "particularly in communist-inspired peasant 'invasions' of land-holdings in the Sierra, resulting in recent bloody clashes." Assistant Secretary Thomas Mann had been impatient with Belaúnde's coolheaded reaction. Now, however, he was getting a response more to his liking, thanks to press hysteria in Peru. Police claimed to have seized a cache of weapons in a raid in Miraflores, a suburb of Lima, in January. The raid caused a sensation, backing the government's charges that a "terrorist" plot was under way.[21] In fact, the weapons had been "planted by police," the U.S. Air Force attaché in Lima later cabled the Pentagon, "in order [to] help alert high government officials and the general public to [the] danger of communist subversive activities."[22]

The ruse worked on both the American and Peruvian presidents. Belaúnde's government had been "at first inclined to belittle the problem, but is now showing signs of taking more forceful action," Johnson was told. "A number of Communist and Castroist leaders have been arrested, a large arms cache has been found in the Lima area, and constitutional guarantees have just been suspended in the Department of Cuzco where the land invasion problem is more serious." Johnson was advised to "express our concern and sympathy over the problem of Castro-Communist subversion and violence, and to express satisfaction over the recent measures taken by the Government to cope with the problem."[23]

But the State Department was, in fact, not satisfied with the pace of agrarian and educational reform. The CIA noted that Peru had maintained a "noteworthy record of financial stability" during the conservative regime of Manuel Prado, with balanced budgets, a favorable trade balance, a stable currency, and a growth in the gross national product of close to 6 percent per year. "However, the economic benefits have accrued to only a small minority of Peru's 11 million inhabitants." The CIA memo continued:

> The sprawling slums of Lima are also a fertile breeding ground for violence and subversion. The continuous influx of Indians from the highlands has swollen the slum population to close to 500,000. Thus far, extremist elements have not had much success in exploiting the situation in the "barriadas"; the security police have been able to bring sporadic, unorganized riots under control. Given leadership and organization or a provocative enough incident, however, the potential does exist for systematic disorder in this key metropolitan area.[24]

The root of the crisis was the landed aristocracy in the highlands, "where many landlords and overseers are determined to keep the Indian population in a state of peonage." And, the CIA added ominously, "the MIR is only the most recent organization to seek to exploit these grievances."

To the CIA, however, and to most officials of the Johnson administration, the MIR's acceptance of aid from Cuba and China precluded its being an authentic Peruvian political phenomenon; it was instead looked upon as one more arm of the International Communist Conspiracy that Washington was fighting from the Berlin Wall to the rice paddies of Vietnam. Therefore, if Peru was to become a model for Mann's new Alliance for Progress, its handling of the MIR would have to

THE SLAUGHTER OF THE INNOCENTS

become an example to the rest of Latin America. The Alliance's military would have to be able to defend itself against insurgences that, although appearing to be native, were actually directed from dark powers outside the hemisphere.

The MIR was no match for the determined military might arrayed against it. If anything, its opponents—the CIA, AID, and the Pentagon, allied with Belaúnde and the Peruvian military—were more truly an international alliance than was the MIR, whose ties to Cuba and China were much weaker politically and militarily in both kind and degree.

The MIR was composed, for the most part, of young APRA intellectuals. Inspired by the Cuban revolution against the Batista dictatorship and the sweeping social and agrarian reforms that followed, they had challenged Haya de la Torre's increasingly conservative dominion over APRA and had been expelled. After the military abruptly canceled APRA's hairbreadth victory over Belaúnde in the 1962 elections, the MIR decided to follow the path of the guerrilla.

CIA officer Philip Agee's March 1963 interrogation of Enrique Amaya Quintana, a MIR deserter, confirmed that the MIR had sent several hundred men to Cuba for three months of intensive training in guerrilla warfare. Amaya's desertion was the key to the MIR's destruction.

"He really is a case of nerves," Agee recorded in his diary. "What he wants is financial assistance to get his wife and child out of Peru and to resettle in some other country. He says he became disillusioned during the training in Cuba, but my guess is that he's lost his nerve now that he's almost on the battlefield." In return for his safety, Amaya provided addresses throughout Latin America and the key to a code system for communications with Havana. But Agee was not satisfied. He wanted an agent in place. "I finally got him to agree to spending at least a short period in Peru with his former friends."[25]

Amaya, at the heart of MIR's communications, provided the CIA with secret intelligence. By November 1963, Clark Simmons, deputy chief of the CIA station in Lima, was able to report to Agee that Amaya's information was "pure gold":

> He has pinpointed about ten base camps and caching sites plus identification of much of the urban infrastructure with full details of each phase of their training and planning. The Lima station has a notebook with maps, names and addresses, photographs and everything else of importance on the MIR, which the station considered to be the most important insurgency threat in Peru. The notebook is in Spanish and is constantly updated so that just at the right moment it can be turned over to the Peruvian military."[26]

Was this the right moment? Peasant unrest in the Andes had reached new heights in 1962 and 1963. In the valleys of Cuzco department, a spontaneous Quechua movement of peasant leagues and trade unions had been politicized by a young anti-Stalinist intellectual named Hugo Blanco.

The son of a peasant mother and a lawyer, Blanco had joined the Revolutionary Workers party after returning from college in Argentina. This was a Marxist party that accepted the analysis of Russia's Leon Trotsky. Lenin's former lieutenant, Trotsky had led the Left Opposition against Stalin and had been expelled and then murdered in Mexico in 1940 by Stalin's henchmen. Blanco, like many intellectuals, had been greatly influenced by the Mexican, Russian, and Cuban revolutions, as well as by the corruption of the Russian revolution by Stalin and antidemocratic elements in the Soviet Communist party. This last lesson cost Blanco the support of the Peruvian Communists, who isolated him and the peasant movement he had organized with Cuban financial support. That did not stop the Indians from seizing estates and setting up their own local governments or the CIA authorities from denouncing him as a Communist. By November 1962, after a clash with police, Blanco had became a fugitive; the self-defense zone in the Valley of La Convención proved unable to resist military repression; land seizures were brutally repressed.

In May 1963, following the shooting near the Bolivian border of Peruvian intellectuals (including one of the country's foremost young poets, Javier Heraud) returning from Cuba, the military junta charged that there were ties between the would-be guerrillas and Blanco's movement. It conducted mass arrests of leftists throughout Peru. Blanco was finally captured on May 29, tried, and sentenced to twenty years in prison.

Blanco's imprisonment and the repression of the peasant movement did not stop the MIR, but they did deprive the organization of its only indigenous leader of highland peasants when it began guerrilla operations.

By early February 1964, peasant unrest was again mounting in the valleys of Cuzco. The CIA had information that MIR operations were imminent. Campesinos had attacked and surrounded a police post in Huarocondo and stoned the police. Belaúnde had been prompted to order the military to fly in hundreds of assault police.[27]

A week later, the CIA learned that the MIR was gearing up for revolutionary action and would be receiving arms through Brazil's Amazon.[28] The Brazilian connection was seen as ominous; indeed, "Brazil is the most serious problem for us in Latin America," said the CIA.[29] Another source of arms, a gunrunner in Bolivia named Klaus Altmann, was less worrisome. Altmann was a CIA asset whose real name was Klaus Barbie, a Nazi fugitive. After helping U.S. intelligence during the postwar occupation of Germany, he was allowed to escape to Argentina, the old haunt of a former Nazi fugitive investigator from U.S. army intelligence and subsequent chief of the CIA's clandestine operations in Latin America, Colonel J. C. King. Barbie was loyal to his new masters. After his intermediary delivered the Mausers that MIR had purchased, MIR found that the firing pins were defective and the wrong kind of ammunition had been supplied. MIR's leaders shrugged it off, preferring to believe they could obtain arms from captured soldiers.[30] They did not see Barbie's defective shipment as an ominous sign, any more than they did the arrival of a U.S. general in Lima.

Air Force General Robert W. Breitweiser had been the Pentagon's director of intelligence. In 1963, however, he accepted a politically loaded field assignment, the kind that makes or breaks military careers. He was moved out of the Joint Chiefs office and assigned to Panama as commander of all U.S. air forces in Latin America. This command included the aviation mission to Peru commanded by Clark Simmons, a U.S. Air Force attaché (and CIA operative); Simmons's mission worked with Peruvian army pilots who were being trained by SIL's JAARS in the use of Helios for jungle flying.

On March 4, 1964, Breitweiser arrived in Lima. He conferred with several of his counterparts in the Peruvian air force, with members of the U.S. aviation mission to Peru, and undoubtedly with Ambassador James Wesley Jones and the top men in the CIA station, including Clark Simmons. When Breitweiser arrived back in Panama, it was normal procedure for him to report to his superior, the commander in chief of the Southern Command, General Andrew O'Meara, who was then reviewing contingency plans for a possible U.S. military intervention against Brazil. Tensions were high among intelligence officials over the Amazon-basin countries.

When word came from Peru's air force commander of the Matses' attack on the road-surveying expedition, Breitweiser and O'Meara did not hesitate.

Two transport planes carrying U.S. Marines and two H-43 assault helicopters were rushed to Iquitos. Weather prevented them from rescuing the wounded before the relief column reached them. But the helicopters remained in Iquitos, fully armed. They were waiting for the MIR.

On March 21, one day after the marines surveyed the Matses area by chopper, using new helipads erected in Requeña and Curuga, Belaúnde's government announced that it would study the possibility of establishing "military colonies" along the Blanco and Tapiche rivers near the Brazilian border.[31]

INTERNAL WARS AND "OCCUPIED" INDIANS

While they waited for the MIR, U.S. counterinsurgency experts were not idle. The CIA built one of its largest stations in Latin America at this time, in Pucallpa, buying information, loyalty, assets, and ultimately agents with distributor franchises for American companies like Coca-Cola. The CIA station kept lists of agents and assets, who were given preferential treatment when AID officers in the embassy were asked by American companies for recommendations on local representatives. The same applied to AID credit itself.[32]

At the same time, the "Mayoruna attack" provided the perfect cover for intervening in neighboring Bolivia. The CIA sent air shipments of small arms through Iquitos, across the Peruvian Amazon, and down to Cuzco and Lake Titicaca to the south. These arms were bound for the Bolivian military, which was planning to overthrow the civilian government of President Victor Paz Estenssoro.[33] The objective was to prevent the coming to power of the Indian miners' candidate, former Vice President Juan Lechín.

In November, the CIA station in La Paz worked closely with U.S. Air Force Attaché Colonel Edward Fox to install Bolivia's air force chief, General René Barrientos as the new president.

The coup had a profound impact on the future of Bolivia's Indians. Paz had allowed the traditional army, smashed by the Aymará Indian miners' revolution in 1952, to be rebuilt quietly by the U.S. military aid program; by 1964, 1,200 soldiers had been trained in the Panama Canal Zone or the United States.[34] Now it was the bedrock of the Barrientos dictatorship.

By the end of 1964, it was obvious that Brazil's military coup had been the bellwether for an end to civilian democracy in much of Latin America. Just as the Bolivian coup came in the wake of the Brazilian coup, so did the launching of a ferocious military offensive against the "red" peasant republics in the Andes of southern Colombia.

Shortly after President João Goulart had been removed in Brazil, Colombian President León Valencia gave his army the green light to move on the peasant republics. With CIA and Green Beret guidance, spies had already been sent in, informers recruited, and "civic action" initiated. The building of roads, bridges, and schools by the army was accompanied by the distribution of clothes and food from CARE, then under the control of the CIA[35] and its Latin adjunct, Caritas. The army then set up a blockade around the strongest of the peasant republics, Marquetalia, to isolate the area and control the civilian population. But with the forced relocation of peasants to barbed-wired "strategic hamlets," hostilities, as in Vietnam, ensued.

The Colombian generals felt obliged to speed things up. The air force was authorized to drop napalm on villages. Specially trained troops were whisked in at treetop level by machine-gun-firing helicopters; peasants were shot, and villages were razed. *Time* and other mainstream press sources were invited in to observe the victory. Sixteen thousand Colombian troops were airlifted in the first massive military use in Latin America of the Pentagon's new counterinsurgency "limited warfare" tactics, a pre-Vietnam experiment in McNamara's "systems" approach to integrating communications (command and control), rapid air mobility, concentrated firepower, and computer-assisted intelligence for finding and tracking an enemy.

The republic's radical social policies were replaced by a timid agrarian reform necessarily crippled by the Liberals' alliance with the landowning Conservatives. Roads came, but were fringed by shantytowns that defied the government's propaganda with their silent misery. Progress arrived, but it was a strange kind of progress, heralded by growing poverty and tainted by crime. For with speculators buying land and merchants selling imported foodstuffs, commercial agriculture—with all its expensive fertilizers, pesticides, herbicides, and machinery—eventually forced many peasants out of subsistence farming toward the only crop capable of commanding high prices on the world market: marijuana.

With the military's occupation of the Marquetalia stronghold, Colombia's other smaller peasant republics also soon fell. It was during this tumultuous period that Colombian Air Force General Armando Urrego Bernal donated land near Puerto Lleras, a contraband center in the state of Metá, to the American Bible translators of William Cameron Townsend.

With the endorsement of Catholic Bishop Marceliano Canyes, won by Cam's providing a librarian to help Canyes organize his late brother's ethnographic papers, SIL missionaries marched triumphantly into the liberated Indian tribes of the southern Andes and eastern plains they had recently surveyed. By March 1965, when the end of "the zones of peasant self-defense" came with the fall of the thirteen-year-old Independent Republic of El Pato, Cam was overseeing the "occupation for the Lord" of nineteen Indian language groups.

In May 1965, the Left's traditional strategy of self-defense zones suffered another blow in Bolivia. General Barrientos's U.S.-trained army attacked the Indian miners' "zone of worker self-defense" surrounding Oruro with bloody results. Thereafter the Communist parties' traditional approach of self-defense zones would be dismissed by a younger generation as passivity and a failure of will to take the offensive through guerrilla warfare.

At the White House, the Special Group was keenly aware of the attraction that guerrilla war held for younger Latin Americans. The Special Group continued its reviews of CIA initiatives in Colombia, Bolivia, and Brazil, as well as the Agency's preparations for the MIR in Peru. After the election in November, however, Johnson had no longer been willing to chafe under the advice of Kennedy's appointees, including CIA Director John McCone. He began to rely more on the advice of Thomas Mann, the new assistant secretary of state for Latin America and coordinator of the Alliance for Progress.

But what was even more important during this period was the ascendancy of the Rockefellers in shaping the post-Kennedy policy toward Latin America.

The Rockefeller Courtship

Nelson, smarting from his race against Goldwater for the Republican nomination, refrained from continuing his earlier campaign of criticism of Johnson's "unilateral" Latin policy. Johnson had put out feelers to the Rockefeller brothers for help, and the brothers responded. With Thomas Mann's appointment, Johnson had signaled that the Alliance for Progress was to change its goals from Kennedy's rapid social and political reforms to the traditional path of political evolution based on gradual private economic development funded by loans and investments by the largest American banks and corporations. For the effective chairmanship of the finance committee of a new support committee (called the National Committee for the Alliance for Progress), Johnson chose David Rockefeller.

The Rockefellers were preeminent in their influence on American businessmen over Latin American policy. In addition to Nelson's vast political networks, David was chairman of the Business Group on Latin America and the new International Executive Services Committee (essentially a Peace Corps for retired executives).

David was eager to speak for business's perspectives on the Alliance for Progress. He was also willing to take on assignments that were directly related to Rockefeller investments, including Peru's dispute with Standard Oil of New Jersey over subsoil mineral rights.

In March 1965, with Chase's associated bank, Banco Lar Brasileiro, S.A., standing at the ready, David traveled to Rio to see about the financial needs of the Brazilian junta's development plans. He reported to Johnson on his return. In April, Johnson appointed David to a new special review panel on AID, chaired by Cornell University's president, Dr. James Perkins, a Chase director—and by 1966 a director also of Nelson's IBEC and of the Cornell Aeronautical Laboratory, a Pentagon contractor for research and military aircraft, chemical and biological warfare, and "Project Heatwave," to study the effectiveness of napalm.

Called the General Advisory Committee on Foreign Assistance Programs, the AID review panel would provide the Rockefellers with a strong influence on policy deliberations. At the same time, David made plans to absorb Nelson's old Inter-American Council and the Latin American Information Committee into the Business Group for Latin America. What emerged was the Council for Latin America (now called the Council of the Americas), which united more than 200 corporations with more than 80 percent of U.S. investments in Latin America into a common business front.[36] David set up the council in a Manhattan town house across the street from the mansion Junior had given the Council on Foreign Relations (CFR). He used the CFR's influential magazine *Foreign Affairs* to explain what had happened to the Alliance for Progress, stressing that the "new concept of the Alliance for Progress with its emphasis on economic development" was restoring the confidence of companies that were considering investments in Latin America. This was a marked improvement from the "overly ambitious concepts of revolutionary change of the program's early years, because it created a climate more attractive to U.S. business." David also prescribed Nelson's old formula: Remove tariff protections for local industries and agriculture and replace them with free trade in a hemispheric community. Free trade, in turn, necessitated "modernization, diversification and expansion of agriculture" based not on the redistribution of land to the peasants who worked it, but on the transformation of the great landed estates into capital-intensive commercial farms that used modern machinery, fertilizers, and scientific techniques.[37]

David cited Chase's financing of a "scientific program of seeding, feeding and breeding" cattle in Panama for corporate exporters to the international market, including the American market. It was the same formula being prescribed by Nelson's American International Association for Economic and Social Development (AIA) and IBEC for the Amazon. This formula, of course, precluded the nationalization of resources held by foreign interests. In 1965, David visited Peru to make that point clear to Belaúnde's government. Standard Oil's subsoil properties must remain with Standard Oil, he intimated, or Peru would suffer the consequences.

It was left to Nelson's and David's older brother, the staid and serious John 3rd, to work out the Alliance's new strategy for the peasants of the Andes and Brazil's Northeast. In February 1965, John, as head of the Agricultural Development Council and the Population Council, gave the opening address to the Conference on Subsistence and Peasant Economies in Honolulu. He made no bones about what was at stake: the political status quo.

"If we cannot control population growth," he told the audience, "life as we know it, or—more important—life as we want it to be, shall surely, slowly waste away."[38] John had taken up the mantle of his father.

Junior had been influenced by eugenicists like Frederick Osborn, Henry Fairchild, and Warren Thompson, who, despite their conscious disdain for racism, still subscribed to Malthusian arguments about population growth causing poverty, with a curious focus on populations who were poor or in the Third World. That such arguments did not seem to apply to men like Junior, who had six children, never bothered John 3rd (who had four children), or Nelson (who had seven) or Laurance (who had four) or David (who had six).

What bothered the Rockefellers were the dangers created by social unrest and the fact that the world's majority seemed to be turning to native communists or nationalist leaders in their impatience with starvation. In the 1950s, as Nelson's IBEC expanded its investments in Teodoro Moscoso's Operation Bootstrap industrialization program in Puerto Rico, John's Population Council was actively encouraging sterilization as a means of birth control. By 1965, about 35 percent of Puerto Rico's women of childbearing age had been sterilized.[39]

Inadequate health care was the basis of the argument for sterilization as a means of promoting better health and protecting incomes from falling any lower than they already were.[40]

In early 1964, Thomas Mann had established an Office of Population within the Alliance for Progress and got Congress to fund the office through AID. Now

John 3rd wanted more. He urged that a presidential commission be formed to investigate the implications of population numbers for aid to Third World countries. He hoped that the intrauterine device might be the beginning of the "ultimate solution of the population problem." But that did not remove the immediate threat of starvation, as he explained in Honolulu.

> Until population is stabilized, every increase in food production is an important holding action. In effect, we are "buying time" until the scales of survival can be brought into lasting balance. How then can we best increase food production? I believe an important key to the answer is the subsistence farmer. . . . He is found wherever land is arable. . . . He almost always works close to the edge of poverty, seeking out a living as best he knows how, with implements that are often primitive.

The problem was how to persuade the subsistence farmers to increase their productivity, and to do so, they had to be able to afford and use modern techniques, machines, seeds, and insecticides. The problem was compounded by the First World's ignorance of Third World people. "Despite the importance of the subsistence farmer, little is known of him," Rockefeller complained. What knowledge existed suffered from "little coordination and exchange between disciplines. Anthropologists have studied the primitive tribes of Borneo and Congo while economists have tended to focus on the more commercialized farms."

John intended to change that situation with behavioral studies and cross-disciplinary approaches.

> The subsistence farmer is not merely an economic man; he has a psychological side, a social side, and a cultural side. Too little is known of his motivations and human responses, of his sociocultural environment, of his ability to change the age-old patterns of his life.
>
> . . . Then there are all the questions of individual motivation. How can he be induced to put aside centuries-old methods to experiment with the new and the foreign, when he is experimenting, literally, with the food his family must have to survive? How can one persuade an individual, self-reliant by nature, to work in intelligent concert with others, who are sometimes total strangers?

How, indeed?

THE FRONT IS EVERYWHERE—FROM VICOS TO CAMELOT

Allen Holmberg had come far from his days at Yale University, when he helped the Yale Cross Cultural Survey Program (the origin of Yale's Human Relations Areas Institute) set up the cross-cultural index that was so valuable to the intelligence activities of Nelson's CIAA. Now, an anthropologist at Cornell University and director of the experimental Vicos Project in Peru, he was at the height of his career.

Vicos was a model land-reform project in the highlands that offered Western development agencies like AID important lessons in how a community-owned and directed agricultural cooperative might be a model for peaceful change. Even with the backing of American technicians, it had taken Vicos more than ten years to earn enough money to purchase a local estate. In the process, the Indians had founded a credit union, communal workshops, and a forestry program and developed incomes and skills in democratically controlled and rotated self-management that preserved the family-owned community and ended outmigration. Vicos's success made AID officers in Lima green with envy, but they also realized that its success was a qualified one. It had relied on the project's ability to purchase land from local landlords; others, they knew, would not be so quick to sell out.[41]

Holmberg described his efforts to "modernize" agriculture to John D. Rockefeller 3rd and a specially selected audience meeting in Honolulu, Hawaii, at a subsistence agriculture conference party sponsored by Rockefeller's Agricultural Development Council. The key, Holmberg explained, lay in changing the cultural and social patterns of the Indians.

He did not describe, however, how his project had been financed by the Department of Defense, as well as AID, to the tune of $662,000.[42] Neither did he mention that he had given a similar accounting of his methods and their results in April 1963 to the first civic action course offered at the Army Civil Affairs School at Fort Gordon, Georgia.[43]

Americans' quest to mold indigenous people into their own image of success was not, of course, a new phenomenon. Missionaries and the Bureau of Indian Affairs had been trying for decades in the United States. Since World War II, social scientists knew that effective psychological warfare operations required in-depth knowledge of a population's culture. Researchers had to study and master a people's belief systems, expressed most truly through their language, and their social organization, the most significant means by which people can mediate successfully with nature and adapt to changes in their environment. They knew that culture is one of the great advantages *Homo sapiens* has in the struggle for survival: Through intelligent deliberate selection, culture allows people to adapt much more quickly than does genetic mutation through natural selection, which can take thousands of years. They also knew that culture allows a group of people—a tribe, even a nation—to adapt to changes in an environment initiated by another people's actions. Learning a culture's key components—its genetic structure and neurotransmitters, so to speak—could also give social engineers, whether armed or not, the tools to manipulate minds. In the quest for control, the CIA's counterinsurgency practitioners already had learned that there were weapons other than guns and gases, and that the path from the social sciences that engineered whole societies, to the physical sciences that engineered minds, was short indeed.

The Institute of Defense Analysis (IDA), founded in 1956 by the

Massachusetts Institute of Technology, Case Institute, Stanford University, the California Institute of Technology, and United Fruit's favorite university, Tulane, had led the way in an unprecedented marshaling of academic, social, and physical scientists to serve the Pentagon and the CIA in preparing for "remote area conflicts." After Kennedy's death, IDA's work expanded under the guidance of its new president, former Special Group-C.I. Chairman General Maxwell Taylor (now retired) and a board that included former Special Group members and Rockefeller allies such as C. Douglas Dillon and Roswell Gilpatric. Though focused mostly on the phased escalation in Vietnam, IDA's research also included special designs for weapons and vehicles to be tested and used in the jungles of Latin America, such as in eastern Bolivia. These weapons included infrared photography and heat-seeking devices for aerial reconnaissance and electronic sensors to track movements along jungle trails.[44]

Beyond the use of physical sciences to design such weapons was the application of social sciences as part of a "systems management" approach to judging the cost-effectiveness of the command and control of counterinsurgency programs. IDA was trying to develop "integrated, functionally-oriented counterinsurgency programs . . . wielding weapons and politics, mobility and social development, communications and economic progress into effective instruments for counterinsurgency . . . in present and incipient conflicts."[45]

Meanwhile, the work of anthropologists at Vicos, done under academic cover for a U.S. government-sponsored program, fit into the Pentagon's and CIA's efforts to neutralize the opposition of indigenous people in Latin America that raised the potential for "internal war."

Fear had been growing in Washington that the Andes could become the Sierra Maestra of South America. If Communist guerrillas were to be prevented from winning an indigenous base of support along the Andes the way Castro had done among peasants in the Sierra Maestra mountains, every effort had to be made as quickly as possible.

Peru was the center of the Andean spine. U.S. military strategists had long recognized the importance of the Peruvian military, training 3,000 Peruvian officers under the Military Assistance Program between 1950 and 1963.[46] In 1964, however, the second year counterinsurgency training and supplies were made available to Latin American armies, Washington gave more military aid to the Peruvian generals than to the military of any other country in Latin America. Aid to the Peruvian generals dropped to second place in fiscal year 1965, behind aid to the Brazilian generals, who by then had seized power.

AID's Public Safety Program, controlled by the CIA, made up the slack, providing Peruvian police with almost as much money, arms, vehicles, gases, radios, and paramilitary and police training as it gave to Brazil's rulers.[47] Many of these policemen were knowingly trained by the CIA at the AID-sponsored International

Police Academy in Washington, D.C., except for three intense days at the renamed "John F. Kennedy" Special Warfare Center at Fort Bragg, North Carolina. At Fort Bragg, between briefings on "civil-military relationships in counterinsurgency operations and police support in unconventional warfare,"[48] Peruvian police and military officers met some of the Green Berets who would help them destroy civilian rebellions, including that of the MIR.

The social sciences were the brains, what a computerized guidance system is to a deadly missile. In July 1964, the U.S. Army gave the Special Operations Research Office (SORO) at American University in Washington, D.C., the largest single grant ever awarded a social science project.[49] The project's targets for "field research" in Latin America were Peru, Ecuador, Paraguay, Venezuela, and Colombia.[50]

Its name was Project Camelot.

The project's purpose was described by the army as follows:

> Success in such tasks as equipping and training indigenous forces for an internal security mission, civic action, psychological warfare or other counterinsurgency action depends on a thorough understanding of the indigenous social structure, upon the accuracy with which changes within the indigenous culture, particularly violent changes, are anticipated, and the effects of various courses of action available to the military and other agencies of government upon the indigenous process of change.[51]

Rex Hopper, director of the $1.5 million project, tried to recruit the preeminent behavioral scientists in the United States. Project Camelot, he explained, hoped to develop a "social systems model" that would allow the Pentagon "to predict and influence significant aspects of social change in the developing nations of the world."

Hopper was more explicit in a working paper he wrote to orient the Pentagon about Camelot's military applications, which included

> forecasting the potential for internal war; . . . estimating the relative effectiveness of various military and quasi-military postures . . . over a wide range of environmental conditions; and means and procedures for rapid collection, storage and retrieval of data on internal war potential and effects of governmental action.[52]

Project Camelot was to be a broad sweep for local data collection, including everything from the language, social structure, and history of peoples to labor strikes, peasants' seizures of haciendas, and violence. Anthropologists, linguists, psychologists, sociologists, and economists would be joined by political scientists, mathematicians, and the military to produce a deliberate political objective of social control.

While Camelot was gearing up, recruiting more than fifty top social scientists as consultants, the SORO assisted in the production of the U.S. Army's field manual for Peru. Evaluating development projects and social communication, it took particular note of SIL's bilingual schools among the Indians living in the rain forests of the lower eastern slopes of the Andes. The Peruvian government was eager to develop this region economically.

The SORO also produced a "Psychological Operation Handbook." The title was changed to "Intercultural Communications Guide," which provided "appeals and symbols of persuasiveness for communicating messages to specific audiences in a given country." In addition,

> each study . . . seeks to identify various groupings in the population—ethnic, geographic, economic, social, etc.—and their attitudes and probable behavior toward the United States. The studies assess the susceptibility of the various audiences to persuasion and their effectiveness or influence in their own society.[53]

Cornell University, through its CIA-financed School of Industrial and Labor Relations,[54] in conjunction with six Peruvian universities, studied changes in Peruvian villages and industrial organization. It also sponsored the Cornell–San Marcos Project in Linguistics with the National University of San Marcos. One graduate was SIL's top Quechua translator, Donald Burns.

31

MISTAKEN IDENTITIES

THE PACIFICATION OF THE ANDES

In 1964, while Peru's Matses Indians still remained the unsolved problem for President Fernando Belaúnde Terry's road-building march to the Brazilian border, his minister of education, Francisco Miró Quesada, arrived at Yarinacocha, the jungle base of the Summer Linguistic Institute (SIL). He had come to attend a graduation ceremony for Indian bilingual teachers. Like so many others before him, he would be amazed at what he saw in the middle of the rain forest.

Yarinacocha seemed to be living proof of how ingenuity, dedication, and the spirit of the Lord could tame the Amazonian wilderness—and its people. Modern, low-slung bungalows, with screened porches, manicured lawns, and flowering shrubs, greeted visitors who landed on the river in a single-engine amphibious plane. Once on shore, the tour would proceed up dirt paths, past smiling missionaries on motorbikes, to a complex of classrooms, administrative offices, a church, a clinic, a soccer field, a dining hall, a hangar, an airfield, and finally, the nerve center of the base: a simple, two-story, one-room radio tower that connected Yarinacocha with all SIL's tribes scattered up and down the jungle for 1,000 miles. This radio tower, along with JAARS's Helios, was perhaps SIL's most important possession.

Visitors like Miró Quesada could get a taste of the daily life of the SIL missionaries by just listening to the squawking transmissions between Yarinacocha and its outposts. Field reports from remote areas ranged from the relatively mundane ("Bob needs a box of .22 rifle shells and requests that some Indians from the occupational course be hired to cut his lawn for the next two Saturdays") to the mildly unnerving ("The monkey that bit Mrs. Dunca did, repeat, did, have rabies") to what one amused SILer called "a riot," when a JAARS pilot was interpreted as announcing that he had a "pair of live Indians on board" when he had actually said, "I have a paralyzed Indian on board."[1] In exchange for such field reports three times a day, the isolated missionaries were treated to the latest gossip from Lima and "a bit of world news."

Not every visitor, however, would get the full lowdown on what crackled over the radio. "We are being a little mysterious, I'm afraid," admitted the radio transmitter. "We have the army's permission for all that we are doing up there, but we don't want everyone in the jungle to know about it. Many Peruvians might get upset over our trying to contact this hostile tribe. They wouldn't understand just what we are trying to do and that we have the government's blessings."[2]

Lima's blessings for the Matses' pacification and more originated in Miró Quesada's 1964 visit to Yarinacocha. During SIL's annual graduation ceremonies for its Indian bilingual teachers, SIL made it a habit of showing its guests how the linguists instilled pride and patriotism among their Indian students. Even out in the remote villages, linguists would have their students "line up in formation, salute the Peruvian flag, and sing the national anthem."[3] That year, as MIR dropped out of sight in Lima and rumors of an imminent guerrilla war spread, premilitary training of Indians had been introduced by SIL at Yarinacocha. Cam proudly reviewed the uniformed students parading before the visitors from Lima. The lesson was not lost on either Belaúnde or Miró Quesada. The education minister saw clearly that SIL offered a step toward greater national integration and thereby greater national security. Before he left, he would grant SIL the franchise for the pacification not only of the Matses, but of the Andes.

If the Andes were feared as the potential Sierra Maestra for South American revolutionaries, the Amazon was the Sierra Maestra's soft underbelly. With about 60 percent of Peru's territory, the Amazonian Oriente had only 623,000 people. Virtually unoccupied except by tribes and isolated towns of whites and mestizo traders, the area was considered vulnerable to both guerrilla insurgency and the claims of neighboring nations like Brazil. Indeed, one war had already been fought with Ecuador over oil. Now oil and gas had been found near the Brazilian border, and Brazil was a much stronger country than Ecuador or Peru.

Miró Quesada's approval of SIL's attempt to pacify the Matses was, therefore, not surprising. But it was not the Matses who were his greatest worry that day at Yarinacocha. It was the millions of landless peasants and miners in the Andes, most of them Quechua. The greatest obstacle to giving the Quechua some hope of relief from centuries of slavery and powerlessness in the Andes was, as in the Amazon, the *patrón*.

As he watched the Indians receive their teacher certificates, Miró Quesada understood that Cam's Bible translators offered at least some Indians an entrepreneurial alternative to the patrón's debts and wage slavery.

The American translators brought Western medicine more powerful than the herbs prepared by the traditional medicine men. They brought pots that did not break, nylon fishline and hooks, axheads and nails, matches, kerosene and flashlights, gasoline for water pumps and generators, and often an American wife who was a nurse.[4] From these Americans came education in the Indians' own languages, a bilingual program instituted by William Cameron Townsend's contact with the ministry in 1952. SIL's bilingual schools were a linguistic highway to the national language, Spanish, the prerequisite for commercial communications with the coastal cities and Peru's dominant mestizo culture.

SIL developed Indian-owned rubber cooperatives and stores, cutting out the local mestizo middleman. More often than not, it was SIL's local bilingual teacher who now played the role of middleman. Through him grew the desire for more cleared land, seedlings, insecticides, land titles, more schools, and more business.

This, then, was how SIL could unlock the spell that the centuries-old feudal manorial system had cast over the Andes. The key was bilingual education.

Belaúnde had only to look at Peru's recent economic history to see the link to language barriers. Where modern commercial relations had entered as a result of economic development, linguistic homogeneity had triumphed at the expense of Quechua and other Indian languages, but where they did not enter, Indian tongues continued to prevail. The result was a linguistic fragmentation that retarded commercial growth and the orthodox nation-building process.

SIL's method used bilingual education to erode traditional authority in the tribe, undermining the power of the chief and the shaman by replacing them with the native bilingual teacher—who, hopefully, was also a convert to Fundamentalist Protestantism. In at least one case, SIL translators were able to win over even the son of a chief. This man became a storekeeper, replacing the patrón, but he also brought the cash economy directly into the tribe's values, with all its unintended results: private hoarding of wealth, resentment, theft, locked doors, and the call for a jail.[5]

This erosion of community will to resist change was valuable to Lima's development officials who were planning for the Amazon and the Andes. SIL was a more immediate option than the small long-range experiments that the Vicos Project exemplified. In 1963, therefore, Belaúnde and Miró Quesada initiated the National Bilingual Education Program through a network of linguists, anthropologists, and educators.

SIL followed up in the summer of 1964 with a pilot project to promote bilingual education in the Sierras, with Donald Burns as director. The franchise for the pacification of the Matses had become a franchise for the pacification of the entire Andes.

The Quechua bilingual training center would become a springboard for

Quechua scholarships to Cornell University—and for a growing resentment against the conservative politics and Fundamentalist proselytizing practiced by Burns and his wife, Nadine.

Before launching his new career, Donald Burns acceded to an urgent request from Cam. SIL had opened an exhibit hall at the 1964–1965 World's Fair in New York, featuring the story of a Peruvian Indian convert. The exhibit hall had rapidly proved to be a financial disaster, threatening SIL's viability and undermining confidence in Cam's judgment within SIL.

"From Savage to Citizen"

Cam hoped that Peru would catapult SIL to world status among missions. He had coordinated the World's Fair exhibit with the publication of Matthew Huxley and Cornell Capa's *Farewell to Eden* about SIL's activities in Peru. But the real force behind SIL's promotion was New York financier Sam Milbank, owner of mines and plantations throughout the Caribbean basin.

Milbank had helped underwrite the book's first printing. Although Cam actually thought the book was "not the weighty presentation of the Indian problems we had hoped for,"[6] he hoped to sell 75,000 copies.[7] He was severely disappointed.

But the greatest mistake was SIL's pavilion at the World's Fair. To be sure, its simple style, modeled after a thatched hut with brand-new carved totem poles in front, offered welcome relief from some of the other religious exhibits, such as the ostentatious miniature of Salt Lake City's Mormon Temple and the forty-four-second spin past Michelangelo's *Pietà* on moving sidewalks offered by the Vatican.

There, however, the contrast ended. For beneath Wycliffe's global logo and the words "2,000 Tribes" hung a garish sign over the entrance, flanked by another stuck in the earth to catch the attention of fair goers:

See the
"From Savage to Citizen"
mural

At a cost of $20,000, Cam had commissioned painter Douglas Riseborough to paint five scenes on a 100-foot-long, 10-foot-high canvas supposedly depicting the life of Tariri, a Shapra (Candoshi) headhunter from the Peruvian Amazon who had been brought to peace in the Lord by SIL translators.

Cam instructed the hapless artist to increase his colors to resemble the special effects of Cecil B. DeMille's *The Ten Commandments*. Under Cam's advice, Riseborough produced a vision garish and horrifying: A wild Tariri at war, holding a weapon in one hand and a blood-dripping head in the other, became the model Christian. If the reality of Shapra headhunting was debatable according to anthropologists, and Tariri (except when prodded to brag) himself denied ever severing a head,[8] Cam was not to be put off.

Tariri was news, and had been used once before, in 1957, when he accompanied Rachel Saint and Dayuma on tour. A powerfully built man with shoulder-length black hair and a winning smile, Tariri had been a hit on Ralph Edwards's *This Is Your Life* television program for Rachel Saint and at the Billy Graham Crusade in New York. Tariri had enjoyed all the attention, and Hollywood's audiences liked the feathered and earringed chief as well. Now the publisher of *Farewell to Eden* was interested in having Tariri give his recollections of the good old days, as well as of the newer, holier ones. Cam's eyes widened when he realized the book would be sold at the fair. Then, just as the fair opened, word came from Peru that Tariri was about to ruin everything by going on a rampage.

Cam fired off his alarm to SIL's branch director in Peru, Eugene Loos.

"Tariri was drinking, seeing the witchdoctor, and talking of revenge killings in the Upriver group," Loos wrote back. "I immediately asked the group to pray for him, not only because of the ruination that would result if he destroyed his testimony, but because we know that the publicity and the strength of his testimony as it is given in the World's Fair will surely bring on renewed attacks from Satan upon him."

Meanwhile, an American physician had speculated that Tariri might be suffering from brain damage acquired from a bout of cerebral malaria the year before.

What Tariri needed, Loos concluded, was the Lord's Word, preferably from a man. Perhaps Cam could write him?[9] Cam sent a message.

But there *was* a problem. Tariri, having been introduced by SIL missionaries to the Protestant work ethic and associated notions of possessive individualism, seemed less the model Christian than he testified to being. Tariri's response was full of tenderness (he expressed his love for Cam), denials (stories told about him at Yarinacocha by children, he explained, were lies), and dreams of success (he wanted to hold on to land that had belonged to the family of a dead chief). He had big plans for this land: rubber, cedar, peanuts, beans, rice, sugar, and coffee. He did not desire a fight, and if SIL could help him, he would construct a church and a school. His conception of civil service for this community was classic nepotism: one of his children could be the health worker, another could be the mechanic, and his nephew could be his official aide. As for himself, he would settle for a large house.[10]

Cam was despondent. Tariri's behavior made it too dangerous for SIL's reputation to bring him to the United States right now to have the publishers tape him telling anecdotes, experiences, and impressions. But Cam had an idea to save the project: Perhaps he could send Ethel Wallis, SIL's trusted in-house writer, to Peru and meet Tariri in Yarinacocha. She could put the book together there. The only hitch was that the publisher would have to pay for her trip. "Wycliffe can't do it when we are in such a bind on our World's Fair project."[11]

"Bind" was the height of understatement. The entire cost of the World's Fair pavilion had been estimated at over $600,000. Cam had already appealed to everyone who had ever contributed to SIL. First, were the rocks on which he had built SIL, the American Fundamentalist preachers and prominent educators who gave Cam's vision both its religious foundation and its scientific legitimacy. Then there were the donors from big business who provided the heavy beams of finance on which all else rested.

Since Peru was being given top billing at SIL's exhibit, Cerro de Pasco Corporation sent SIL's Peruvian chapter a check for $8,500. Cerro de Pasco, which would later be nationalized in Peru, was then facing growing unrest by Quechua miners.[12]

The largest donation, $11,000, was from the Pew family of Sun Oil Company (Sunoco), which in the 1970s would drill for oil in the homelands of the Shapra-Candoshi Indians, Tariri's tribe. Sam Milbank, whose foundation journal would publish the Vicos Project's report on its AID-funded research on the Quechua Indians, gave $5,000. So did David Weyerhaeuser, whose family's lumber company did a huge business in extracting tropical woods from South and Central America. Quaker Oats heir Henry Crowell provided $10,000.

More than $150,000 had been raised in pledges, and a Charlotte, North Carolina, bank had set up a line of credit for over twice that amount.[13] But that was far from the $600,000 cost. Worse, Cam's projections of gate receipts had proved to be unrealistic; they would not overtake the costs by the end of the season in October. The board was worried about SIL's future fund-raising prospects.

Cam dismissed Wycliffe's thirty-year-old policy against solicitations as a "man-made rule." He invoked Henderson Belk's name as a supporter of his demand, insisting that the board "protect our backers from loss."

"It's our God-given duty," he thundered. "And a man-made rule is not going to stop me from protecting my friends from loss and the cause of Christ from shame and defeat."

He pulled out his ace. He offered his resignation, but insisted that he was going ahead in his appeals since he was receiving wonderful responses.[14]

He was seizing the prerogative of a founder, riding over democratic norms. Then he hit the board at its Achilles' heel: their own new building in California. "What appalls me is that the five of you didn't hit upon the obvious solution for paying our present unfunded bills: a mortgage on our Santa Ana property. Debtors shouldn't call themselves insolvent when they have unencumbered property."[15]

There were casualties. Billy Graham, who had been a member of Wycliffe's board since 1961, resigned. But an old friend came to the rescue.

Cam had kept in touch with Rev. William Criswell over the years, as Criswell's First Baptist Church of Dallas grew to become the largest Southern Baptist congregation in the United States. On almost any Sunday, more than 1,000 people packed the pews, including oil billionaire H. L. Hunt and his son

Nelson Bunker Hunt. Criswell's enmity for John F. Kennedy predated Hunt's, but by 1964 both were joined behind Barry Goldwater's struggle against Nelson Rockefeller. Texans, often sensitive to what goes on south of the Rio Grande, had already been impressed enough by SIL's work to donate a "Friendship of Texas" building for SIL's compound in Mexico City. Now Criswell wanted to see the fabled Amazon. Cam was only too happy to oblige. Luckily for Cam, the trip almost cost Criswell his life.

Cam accompanied Criswell as far as the Limoncocha base in Ecuador, then returned to the Lomalinda base in Colombia. Criswell proceeded on to Peru and the Yarinacocha base. From there, on a clear September morning, he flew out with JAARS's Floyd Lyon in a pontooned Helio Courier used by the Peruvian army,[16] heading northwest at 6,500 feet over the jungle. Criswell had seen the bloodcurdling mural of Tariri at the World's Fair and wanted to meet the Shapra headman personally.

Halfway there, the plane's engine failed.

"Tighten your seat belt, doctor," said Lyon. "We're going down!"

This Helio had floats, not wheels. So Lyon had to head for a stream and hope that if the plane nosed over when he hit the shallow stream, it would not catch fire.

It did not. The plane landed with a thud, stalled, and was stopped on a sandbar. Criswell and Lyon broke into jubilant prayer. Then Criswell lifted his head and his eyes widened. Indians, surrounding the plane, were peering in through the windows.

"It's okay, doctor," Lyon said. "They're friendly."[17]

So friendly, in fact, that Criswell did not even have to get his shoes wet. The village leader carried the beefy preacher on his back to the riverbank, even though the water was only ankle-high.

Criswell returned to Yarinacocha in another JAARS plane that afternoon. Two days later, after phoning in a story to the *Dallas Morning News* on his crash and assuring SIL that "this experience will bring in a lot more money for our work here in the jungle," he flew back to Dallas. Tariri would have to wait.

Hearing the news at Lomalinda, Cam was grateful to the Lord for good fortune delivered exactly when needed to beat back the Wycliffe board's challenge to the World's Fair pavilion.

Criswell, too, was so grateful to the Lord and JAARS that he opened his church's doors to SIL for a fund-raiser that netted more than $7,500 after Criswell told his tale to his congregation.

A group of Dallas businessmen, including the Hunts, began to gather in SIL's name, offering the promise of resources that far exceeded those of the Belks and Charlotte, North Carolina. In all this enthusiasm, Cam caught a glimpse of the future: a new international translation center in Dallas.

At the same time Cam was casting SIL's seed over Dallas, Dale Kietzman, the former Brazil branch director who was now extension director, and Lawrence

PEW Family
Sun Oil Company
(SUNOCO) Fortune
Philadelphia, Pa.

Irvine Foundation
(Citrus, Ranching, Real Estate)
California

Clark BREEDING
(Aztec Oil)
Dallas, Texas

Nelson Bunker HUNT
(Placid Oil)
Dallas, Texas

Herbert RANKIN
Dept. Store
Santa Ana, Calif.

PITCAIRN Family
Pittsburgh Plate Glass
Pittsburgh, Pa.

LeTOURNEAU Family
Earth Moving
Lumber
Cattle

Robert WELCH
(Real Estate)
Huntington Beach, Calif.

Earl MILLER
Grocery Stores
San Diego, Calif.

James EZELL
Dallas, Texas

Maxey JARMAN
(GENESCO) CORP.
Tennessee

WYCLIFFE BIBLE TRANSLATORS WBT

SIL SUMMER INSTITUTE OF LINGUISTICS

Weldon THOMAS

Frank SHERRILL
S & W (Cafeterias)
N.C.

Kejn Foundation

Lawrence ROUTH
(Construction)
N.C.

Services

BELK Family
(Department Stores)
Charlotte, N.C.

Henry C. CROWELL
and Henry P. and Susan Crowell Trust
(Quaker Oats) Fortune
Chicago, Ill.

Amos BAKER
(oil)
Tulsa, Okla.

Services

G.S. JONES
N.C.

Aaron SAENZ
Sugar, Banking
Mexico City

Albert Johnson
Insurance
Chicago, Ill.

Helio, Couriers · Airplane Parts · Radios · Helicopters

Trailers (Colombia) Boats · Madras (Peru)

Trammel CROW
Real Estate
Dallas, Tex.

Woodward Foundation
New York

David WEYERHAUSER
(Lumber)

Standard Oil OF New Jersey
Humble Oil (Colombia)
International Petroleum (Peru)

Cerro de Pasco Corporation
(Peru)

Samuel MILBANK
(Corn Products Corp.)
Ranching, Mining, Mutual Funds, Banking, Borden Corp., Railroads
New York

Surplus Military Equip.
Phoenix, Arizona
Harrisburg, Pa.

U.S. Agency for International Development (AID)

Asia Foundation
(1967-68)

U.S. Defense Department

U.S. State Department

Central Intelligence Agency (CIA)

→ Indicates specific contribution to Wycliffe Bible Translators (WBT), Summer Institute of Linguistics (SIL), or Jungle Aviation and Radio Service (JAARS)

- - - - Indicates funding relationship or governmental auspices and departmental relationship

Major Donors to SIL/WBT (includes Jungle Aviation and Radio Service [JAARS])

Sources: WBT/SIL Records, Foundation Center reports, and U.S. government records.

Routh, JAARS's fund-raising dynamo from North Carolina, began to organize testimonial dinners in cities across the country, using them as fund-raisers by selling $100 shares in the World's Fair pavilion. Called "Operation 2000" from Cam's "2000 Tribes to Go" slogan, these dinners became the means for establishing the Committee of Friends of Wycliffe, a network of businessmen and retirees of whom many would someday help Ronald Reagan win the White House.

Already, Cam could point to success for the pavilion that went beyond dollars: nationwide publicity. NBC's Huntley and Brinkley news show had interviewed Cam and talked about the mural. In just this first year, Cam told his rebellious board, 40,000 people had gone through SIL's main exhibit each week, and 20,000 had viewed the Tariri mural.[18] By the end of the 1964 season, over 312,000 people had seen Tariri's terrifying story.[19]

How many more could be attracted if Tariri were able to come to the United States? Tariri's biography, now completed by Ethel Wallis, would be ready by then for sale at the fair. Tariri could be put on tour throughout the nation, but only if kept on a tight rein.

Cam turned to Don Burns, who in September had just been appointed chair of the committee on bilingual education for the Peruvian Andes. Burns could not speak to Tariri in Shapra, but American audiences could not understand Tariri's words either. Besides, Burns was loyal to Cam and could be counted on to follow his orders explicitly. Could he come up with Tariri next summer?

Burns was only too happy to go as guerrilla war broke out that summer in the Andean highlands. The National Liberation Army led by Héctor Béjar was operating near his bilingual center in Ayacucho, and it was not a healthy time for an unarmed American working for the Belaúnde regime to be there. SIL's programs could be misconstrued as gathering intelligence on the Indians, and it admittedly ran a jungle-aviation subsidiary of the regime's air force.

In the lowlands to the east, Will Kindberg, SIL's translator among the Campa Indians, also withdrew from his village post. U.S. military action was heating up on the Andes' eastern slopes, the "eyebrows of the jungle." Green Berets were seen in the area with Peruvian Rangers. Rumors, which turned out to be true, had it that the CIA, under AID cover, was setting up a secret training camp to drill a new elite battalion of Rangers in jungle warfare. The Peruvians called the camp *Sinchi,* or Crossed Spears; others in the CIA would call it a "miniature Fort Bragg."[20]

PREPARING THE KILLING GROUND

In May 1965, as Peruvian intelligence chief General Armando Artola attended a meeting in Brazil of Latin America's intelligence chiefs,[21] the CIA station in Lima began sending a series of concerned reports to National Security Adviser McGeorge Bundy. The Moviemiento de Izquierda Revolucionaria (MIR), according to a CIA informant, was about to commence guerrilla operations in the Campa Indian area in the eastern Andes. More disturbing, however, were reports that among the guerrilla leaders was a man named Guevara.

Cuba's Che Guevara had recently disappeared from public view. Was he in Peru?

The Peruvian economy, spurred on by exports and increased European and American investments, had enjoyed a 7 percent growth rate during Belaúnde's first year in office. But these exports and investments, while benefiting the upper classes, also masked a continuing grim picture for the peasants. Everyone knew that the peasants' patience eventually would run out. The only question was timing: Would that happen during a guerrilla war?

Convinced that Peru was in a state of "latent insurgency," the military increased its civic action, employing students in a wide range of activities in the Andes.[22] At the same time, with the help of the CIA and the U.S. Military Mission, it prepared to deal with insurgency the way Winston Churchill had recommended the Western powers should deal with the Russian Revolution: "Strangle the infant in its crib."

The CIA's "miniature Fort Bragg" in the Peruvian jungle grew during the first six months of 1965. Classrooms were erected beside barracks and mess halls, and Green Berets were soon putting Peruvians through exercises at parachute-jump towers and amphibious-landing facilities. The official U.S. military aid program, ostensibly overseen by the air force attaché but actually by the CIA, provided assault helicopters for treetop raid mobility. Helipads and a runway were installed. Arms and other equipment were flown in clandestinely.[23]

SIL's James Wroughton later told author David Stoll that he thought JAARS had been called on by the Peruvian military to do a "bit of transport" and provide "some flights for the Army or Güardia Civil" during the 1965 operations against the MIR, a claim subsequently denied by another SIL official, Eugene Loos.[24] But there could be no denying that JAARS's Helios, after all, were part of the Peruvian air force and were available on command. JAARS pilots had been training Peruvian army pilots for years, and their use in the jungle was not new. The CIA was already leasing Helios in Peru at such a reasonable price that CIA Deputy Director Richard Bissell was said to have complained to Helio Corporation president Lynn Bollinger about Helio leasing costs in Laos, which were four times higher. Helios provided a longer range than did helicopters, and their use in the jungle was not new. Just the previous May, the CIA had cooperated with the Helio Corporation to sell more planes to Belaúnde, assigning a Helio owned by one of its fronts, King Hurley Company, to Larry Montgomery and Colonel L. Fletcher Prouty for a sales visit to Lima.[25]

Recruitment of the special strike force was more of a problem for the CIA. The Peruvian generals were "uneasy" about the presence of the CIA and the Green Berets in Peruvian military operations in the vast, unprotected Amazon. They also worried about the loyalty of Quechua Indian draftees, even to the point of declining to assign troops for training. So the CIA began to hire its own troops. "The CIA had been required to recruit its fighting manpower from among the available local populace. By paying higher wages than the army (and offering fringe benefits, better training, and 'esprit de corps') the agency soon developed a relatively efficient fighting force."[26]

The CIA's task was eased by a fundamental flaw in the MIR's planning. The MIR began working in the area only six months before it began its military operations, hardly enough time to develop ties to the local populace. The MIR's desire to begin guerrilla warfare as soon as possible, although designed to preempt Belaúnde's counterinsurgency operations, ironically dovetailed with the CIA's timetable. An American journalist who traveled through the Campa area after the MIR was defeated analyzed the problem confronting Guillermo Lobatón, the MIR field commander of the Túpac Amaru Front. Lobatón, a cultured Peruvian of African descent who understood what discrimination practiced by Lima's white elite felt like, "was apparently attempting to work with the warlike Campa the way General Vo Nguyen Giap worked with the mountain tribes of northeastern Vietnam during the Second World War. The difference, however, is that Giap worked *politically* with his tribesmen for two years before entering combat; the Peruvian guerrillas worked with the Campas for less than six months in a very desultory fashion."[27] Few of the Indians, despite sympathy for the MIR, joined the Túpac Amaru Front as either guerrillas or village cadre.

Tragically for the Indians, neither the CIA nor the Peruvian military made that distinction.

Gods of Wrath

The moon is a god, the Campa Indians believe, a kindly god who gives the people their food, manioc, and takes in return their dead. Like many Amazonian tribes, the Campa place their dead in the river, to float downstream, where the Moon-God turns the body to stone and swallows it. When the face of the moon turns dark, it is because the god has choked on a body. When the moon shines its eerie silver over their river and thatched homes, the god is content. The people can look forward to the morning sun.

But in August 1965, it was different. The gods brought not warmth from the heavens, but roaring, fiery death.

Peruvian air force pilots, following the winding Sonomoro River that drained the lower Andes, looked down upon the Campa village of Bustamente. Twenty years before, it would have been impossible to know which village was which. But now, with the help of the American flying missionaries, the maps were more accurate.

The Indians did not understand what the approaching planes meant. They did not know that some of their brethren had been seized a few days before by troops searching for leftist guerrillas. They knew only that the soldiers were angry with the bearded white men who had begun showing up in their villages six months before. The bearded ones were armed and had called themselves revolutionaries, using the old Inca name Túpac Amaru, the leader of the last great Inca revolt against the Spaniards. They had camped among the people and spoke of their willingness to help the Campa resist the land grabbers who came from across the mountains. And the Indians listened, impressed by the fact that no whites had ever spoken this way before.

Even when columns of army Rangers appeared, demanding answers, the quiet words of the Túpac Amaru group, not the soldiers' threats, lingered in the Indians' ears. Later, the Peruvian War Ministry argued that the Campa seldom cooperated with the troops. But the Indians never expected what came next.

Bombs exploded all around them, dismembering men, women, and children alike. Houses and people erupted in flames. Orange walls of fire rolled over the people, leaving behind flaming jelly that clung to their skin. Napalm, reportedly made for the Peruvian air force by Standard Oil's International Petroleum Company,[28] had come to the Amazon, courtesy of the Pentagon and some of the same Peruvian air force generals Larry Montgomery had once taught to fly. Hell had arrived on the wings of an angel, and to the Campa majority holding onto the old ways, both hell and the angel were Christian.

The MIR guerrillas were equally surprised at the ferocity of the aerial attacks. They had begun military operations two months earlier, in June, shortly after their leaders had gathered downstream from the Inca ruins of Machu-Picchu. There, they had drawn up a "Revolutionary Proclamation to the Peruvian People," emphasizing the need for "genuine agrarian reform," "recovery of full national sovereignty," a "living wage for the family," urban reform through homeownership, and "immediate recovery of Peru's oil."[29]

The issues were out, and the lines were drawn. After a few weeks of sacking estates and mines in the hills west of the Campa territory, the MIR guerrillas were hit by the CIA's new strike force. Green Beret-advised Rangers rushed east in trucks as far as the roads went, taking positions at the northern and southern perimeters of the combat zone. Naval units plowed up the Ucayali River from Iquitos, sweeping past Pucallpa into the Ucayali's local tributaries to seal off the area. After encountering guerrilla resistance, the northern column wheeled south in a classic pincer strategy to converge with the southern column at the town of Pucutá, which had been occupied by MIR and was being bombed with napalm and machine-gunned by the Peruvian air force. The combined army forces then moved north again and found that the MIR had withdrawn deeper into the eastern rain forest.

Fresh Ranger units were flown in for an attack on the Campa town of Satipo, in the north, where massacres of Indians took place. The Green Berets then marched troops south, setting up a command headquarters near Mazanari and seizing the village of Kubanti. Another column marched north to reinforce them for the final assault on the Campa village of Bustamente, Lobatón's headquarters. Again they bombed and machine-gunned, only to find that the guerrillas had moved east again, even deeper into the rain forest.

A month passed with no contact. The CIA tried to tighten its hold on the Campa villages with both civic action and interrogations. Then, in September, the Andes erupted. Quechua Indians rebelled near Don Burns's new bilingual school. MIR's allies, Héctor Béjar's National Liberation Army, gave armed support.

The army attack on MIR resumed, killing and wounding guerrillas, driving Lobatón north again toward the Green Berets' headquarters at Mazanari.

Hundreds of Campa were killed. Some Campa charged that JAARS pilots had flown Helios overhead with loudspeakers, urging them to cooperate in the army's campaign,[30] an aerial technique that SIL would soon use in its pacification efforts with the Mayoruna and the Auca in Ecuador. Some Americans reviewing the Campa charges would later question how the Indians could distinguish SIL's planes from others, although many SIL planes bear the distinctive SIL emblem, an Incan Indian within a triangle, and Helios have unparalleled wingspans. Finally, all SIL's planes, thanks to Cam's public relations, were officially part of the Peruvian air force and subject to its commands.

SIL claimed that it had no flights and no missionaries in the area at the time, although a journalist reported that "American missionaries working in the zone reported that the Peruvian air force had bombed a number of Campa villages."[31] The army, for its part, boasted of carrying out "an intensive information and warning campaign, giving out messages in the native language through loudspeakers on warplanes and helicopters."[32]

In Washington the CIA and the Special Group remained unsatisfied. The MIR had produced a Guevara, but it was Hector Cordero Guevara, principal coordinator of the MIR's central committee. Years later, Belaúnde claimed to have met Che Guevara in 1962 at Puerto Bermúdez, a remote village just north of the Túpac Amaru column's area of operations; he suspected that Guevara was scouting the area for guerrilla operations.[33] Was Guevara leading the MIR? But the *New York Times* report that the Cuban ex-minister had been captured was mistaken.[34]

Che Guevara was, in fact, then fighting for the followers of the slain Prime Minister Patrice Lumumba in the former Belgian Congo, but the CIA's Western Hemisphere Division had no way of confirming the reports. And anyway, the CIA assumed that Guevara would be fighting in Latin America, his homeland.

To mount an operation against the likes of Che, the CIA needed the best counterinsurgency experts with combat experiences in the jungle. That was no problem; the CIA simply turned to its ample stock of CIA officers in Vietnam. But the Agency needed more, one of its own field generals, a master of clandestine operations, who knew the backwoods of Latin America—especially the whole Amazon—like no other American; who had protected his Agency identity from all but the most privy; who had contacts from years in business as well as spying; and, most important, who knew about assassinations and had long ago fingered Che Guevara for death.

The CIA needed Colonel J. C. King.

32

POISONS OF THE AMAZON

The Sorcerer's Apprentice

While the CIA's war against leftist guerrillas raged in the Peruvian Amazon throughout 1965, an elderly American landed at Iquitos's sweltering airport. His arrival in the country's largest port on the Amazon River went unnoticed. Iquitos was by then a true small city, with buses, hotels, newspapers, and even a radio station. Foreign travelers were a common sight walking down the Malecón, the wide promenade along the river, enjoying the colorful tropical vistas. Although the guerrilla war had scared off some tourists, the nearest fighting was far to the southwest in the jungle, and Iquitos's white-shirted merchants still hoped for a tourist boom that might rival the rubber boom of a headier past. No one had any reason to offer an American stranger anything but a welcome, especially when he asked only about where he could find another American who was herself a local tourist attraction, Nicole Maxwell.

These days Maxwell never knew who might ring her doorbell. Her book, *Witch Doctor's Apprentice*, had made her a celebrity. It recounted her solo expedition to the Peruvian jungle in 1958 to gather Indian medicinal plants for a New York pharmaceutical company. That eight-month trip netted a publicity bonanza for her corporate sponsor, but only $1,000 for Maxwell. But in the course of Maxwell's television appearances, the media warmed to her and she to them. In her late fifties, Maxwell was still a handsome woman, with brown hair, bright blue eyes, and a slight, almost petite figure that seemed exotically at odds with the image of a jungle adventurer. Her book became a mild success. More important, it brought opportunity literally knocking on her door.

The gray-haired man standing at her door introduced himself in a manner she would later remember as correct, even courtly. He had read her book and been given her address by a mutual friend. He knew the jungle, he said, having served with the Rubber Production Board during World War II. He had learned then that the power of Indian medicinal plants was more than superstition. Now that he was retired from heading the South American division of Johnson & Johnson, he was free to investigate these remedies. Would she be interested in joining in the effort if he set up a firm on a solid scientific and financial basis?[1]

Maxwell accepted. This man, she learned from friends in New York, was an important industrialist. She could feel confident that he would know people who might invest some risk capital.[2]

He, on the other hand, knew that Maxwell was a person with some savvy on South America. During World War II, she had worked in Washington as director of the Latin American Institute, an organization associated with Nelson Rockefeller's CIAA. In 1948, she launched her first expedition into the Amazon, one that coincided with Standard Oil of New Jersey's first expedition into the Ecuadorian Amazon. Rumors that she was a spy could have proved more dangerous than the Jivaro headhunters. Despite it all, she survived her jungle adventure, but only because Standard Oil flew her out, rescuing her, she claimed, from a bad case of dysentery.

From Galo Plaza's Ecuador, she moved to Manuel Odría's Peru, when Odría was opening new tracts of the Amazon to American and other foreign oil companies. She updated an English-language guidebook to Peru and reported the goings-on in the Amazon for the American colony's English daily, the *Peruvian Times*, a major booster of Peru's oil sales and the Amazon's economic potential. From Peru, she moved to La Paz at the very time that Indian miners in Bolivia successfully led that nation in overthrowing the old oligarchy. The revolution cleared the way for the government's development of Standard Oil's nationalized oil fields near Camirí. Maxwell worked as a correspondent for *Vision* magazine, since revealed as financed by a CIA conduit.[3] (She would, however, always deny any ties to the Agency.) She stayed in Bolivia for the four years that were the Indians' heyday, perfecting her writing style and reportage. By 1958, the Indian revolution was over, and Maxwell returned to New York.

It was here that she met with the executives of a pharmaceutical company who were seeking medicinal plants of the Peruvian Amazon and took the assignment that made her famous.

Therefore, when she was approached by the courtly gentleman in Iquitos, Nicole Maxwell was already known in certain circles for being more than just an explorer and aficionada of jungle remedies. To this new business associate, who traveled easily in these circles, her knowledge of South America, not just its plants, could be very useful.

Years later, whenever she wrote about him, Maxwell never revealed his identity. He was always referred to as Mr. Arthur Jones.

J. C. King had officially retired from the CIA in 1964 after the overthrow of the government of João Goulart in Brazil. Decades would pass before the myth would be dispelled that King had been forced to retire because of the Bay of Pigs or because of his age, sixty being the supposed mandatory retirement age.[4] In fact, King was sixty-four when he officially retired and he remained on the CIA's payroll thereafter as a special consultant.[5]

It was common knowledge that King was involved in chemical and biological warfare after he retired as chief of Clandestine Services in Latin America.

"I was pretty sure he was on a CBW [chemical and biological warfare] contract," a former CIA official recalled. "Every year he had a project worth $100,000 to $150,000 a year. Everybody laughed, but he always got approval. I was always curious why, with King, no one wanted to take any responsibility. Not even the Director, John [Clarke, Jr.], signed off on King's things. All this bullshit on mushrooms and flowers and herbs and gobbledlygook . . . I had all these visions of Hitchcock."[6]

With charm unburdened by fanfare, King easily recruited Nicole Maxwell. She was flattered by his praise for her book and she needed money. Maxwell agreed to enter into a contract that required her to collect plants and to set up a field office in Iquitos.

Next, King flew to the Boston area and approached Georgia Persinos, a young botanist at the Massachusetts College of Pharmacy, on whom he used the same technique as he used with Nicole Maxwell: He had seen her picture in a recent book on native remedies, Margaret Kreig's *Green Medicine*. He did not tell Persinos, of course, that one of the famed mycologists featured by Kreig, R. Gordon Wasson, had unwittingly helped the CIA's hunt for mind-controlling drugs by taking an MKULTRA scientist, the University of Delaware's James Moore, on a CIA-funded expedition to Oaxaca, Mexico, to learn the secrets of "God's flesh," the hallucinogenic mushroom the local Mazatec Indians considered sacred.[7]

A registered pharmacist, Persinos was then only in her twenties and naive. It was her job to analyze plants used in Indian remedies collected by Nicole Maxwell.

In March 1966, King was ready. He had lawyers register incorporation papers in New Jersey, calling his new venture the Amazon Natural Drug Company (ANDCO). ANDCO's stated objective was to develop, manufacture, and sell drugs and to "explore the commercial uses of natural plants and chemical derivatives thereof." King named himself president.

It all sounded quite proper to Persinos and Maxwell. King set up a lab for Persinos at Rockville, Maryland, and later opened an office in Washington. It was really only a room, but neither Persinos nor Maxwell was bothered about why it was even necessary. All Maxwell knew was that King sent her a check to cover her travel expenses to the United States. He wanted her to come immediately and to bring with her an Indian remedy that she had discovered during her 1958–1959 expedition. Called *sangre de drago*, "dragon's blood," the remedy was drawn from the sap of a tree and accelerated the healing of wounds without leaving scars. She filled five bottles with the sap and caught a flight north.

King met Maxwell at the airport and whisked her away to his estate in Oakton, Virginia. King's family was impressed by the results of her application of sangre de drago to a cut on the foot of their family dog: The improvement was immediate. The next morning King took the remedy to his lab. Five days later he returned "in a state of excitement I would never have believed possible in such a cool, rather poker-faced individual," she later recalled. "He positively leapt up the stairs."

"'It's absolutely incredible,' he said before even taking off his topcoat. . . . 'We need a bottle of champagne for a toast. My research director suspects we may have discovered a healing principle hitherto unknown to medical science.'"[8]

He asked Maxwell to return to Iquitos as soon as possible and to send a steady supply of the remedy for further lab experiments. She would also have to rent a house in Iquitos to serve as ANDCO's field headquarters. Plants would be stored and initially tested there, he explained, using animals that would be held in an air-conditioned building. Would she accept a modest salary, a $1,000 bonus for each plant found to be of value, plus a small royalty from each product sold?

Starry-eyed, she flew back to Iquitos to set up operations.

King's interest was more than "dragon's blood," however; it was, as usual, counterinsurgency. King was still an adviser to the CIA, and the Agency was interested in things other than tropical ointments. Population control was becoming a major focus of the Johnson administration's policy toward the Third World, with John D. Rockefeller 3rd pushing for the creation of a special assistant to the president to oversee birth control programs.

King saw fortune beckoning. Indian contraceptive plants had been sought since anthropologists reported more than twenty years earlier that Indian women knew plants that could control their fertility. Maxwell, in fact, had made her name promoting native contraceptives.

King asked Maxwell to grow Indian contraceptive sedges in her garden. He even provided her with a supply of eager rabbits. Through an Indian shaman's son she hired, Maxwell also located medicines that were new to her. The drying, grinding, and pinching continued for ten months. The demands of King's biochemists in the United States for more plants and sangre de drago seemed insatiable. Maxwell's staff, grown to five men, could barely keep up, and Maxwell was driven to exhaustion.

King's frequent trips to Iquitos that year did not help matters. He often brought a botanist or pharmacologist with him and always threw a large dinner party for thirty or forty people. King was obviously well connected. Sometimes he would have Maxwell organize a "river expedition" up the tributaries of the Amazon to gather plants. The expeditions included CIA officers who were veterans of jungle warfare in Vietnam.[9]

Armed with mortars and grenades, their assignment was obviously not to collect plants. They were to kill any Indians who judged King's encroachments into their territory to be unfriendly and attacked.[10] By 1965, "wild Indian" scouting had become a priority for the CIA in the Amazon, not just in Peru, and not just by undercover agents.

"Targeting the Hostiles"

In late 1964, following the coup in Brazil, William Cameron Townsend had asked Dale Kietzman, the director of the Summer Linguistic Institute (SIL) in Brazil, to study the feasibility of setting up a series of SIL bases in southern Amazonas and Acre Territory. Acre formed the westernmost boundary of the Brazilian Amazon and jutted into Peru between Iquitos and Pucallpa.

More important (and probably unknown to Cam), Acre was reported to have the richest oil reserves in the area. As far back as 1948, the CIA had pinpointed five regions in Brazil where petroleum was believed to exist. Acre was the most promising. "The same geological formation as those found in the abundant oil fields of Peru and Bolivia extend all throughout this area." But it was also the most remote. Transportation was required.[11]

By late 1964 and early 1965, SIL was ready and eager to help Brazil's new military dictatorship solve these transportation problems. Always thinking ahead, Cam had laid the groundwork at the beginning of 1964, before the coup had even taken place. Despite the Goulart government's widespread suspicion and resentment of growing American influence in Brazil, Cam had encouraged the Jungle Aviation and Radio Service (JAARS) to shift resources from Peru to Brazil for the big push ahead into the Amazon.[12]

In "formal conversations" at SIL's June 1964 board meeting, Cam and the director of SIL's Peru branch, Eugene Loos, came to an agreement that the big Catalina (Cat) amphibian that had been donated in 1959 by Orlando, Florida, businessmen for use throughout the Amazon basin "probably was excess to the Peru program and could be transferred to Brazil as soon as a crew might be available and the need established for a plane."[13] Named *Marshall Rondon* in memory of the founder of Brazil's Service for the Protection of the Indian (SPI), the World War II–vintage Cat had helped SIL advance into the jungles of Peru, Ecuador, and

Bolivia. Now it would supply SIL's penetration of the Brazilian Amazon, the wings of Fundamentalist Christianity bearing home, ironically, the name of the positivist Rondon.

This agreement was a key factor in the decision of SIL's Brazil branch to study the feasibility of establishing other SIL/JAARS bases in the Brazilian Amazon. Because the territory was so immense, Dale Kietzman suggested that the tribes north of the Amazon River should be effectively ceded to allied Fundamentalist Protestant missions (the New Tribes Mission and the Unevangelized Fields Mission) that were already there, and that SIL concentrate instead on "beginning our major aviation operation out of a point such as Pôrto Velho."[14]

It turned out to be a choice location. Pôrto Velho, the biggest town on the Madeira River, was the projected terminus of Brazil's first all-weather road in the trans-Amazonian highway system. The road was being built with $1 million worth of heavy equipment donated by the U.S. Army and $2.6 million in loans from the Agency for International Development.[15] The road plowed west from Brasília through Cuiabá, Mato Grosso's captial, and was expected to reach Pôrto Velho, the capital of Rondonia territory some 900 miles west, by 1968.

Kietzman sent Cam a copy of his report, specifying tribes and distances between proposed subbases, as well as a map of "occupied" tribes showing his strategy of using Pôrto Velho as a jumping-off point and linking SIL's bases in Amazonas and Acre by air with the Catalina. He noted that "the heaviest concentration" of tribes not yet reached by American Fundamentalist missionaries was "west of the Madeira River," which included much of Amazonas and all of Acre. In fact, there could be as many as 100 tribes in this vast area. But "the exact situation will be known only after completion of the present CNPI survey."[16]

The CNPI was the National Council for the Protection of the Indian, the official overseer of the SPI. But even before the coup, the CNPI was under the thumbs of the military officers who dominated the SPI. Following the agenda for development of the Amazon, particularly road building, just before March 1964, the CNPI ordered a survey of Indian tribes in the Brazilian Amazon. To cover the tribes of the southern Amazon valley, it turned to SIL.

"Think of it!" Kietzman exclaimed. "The small surveys we had planned, limited because of the costs of travel, had been expanded over the territory we knew least about, with travel expenses provided.

"Our teams were soon in the field, penetrating into remote river valleys."[17]

SIL teams moved along the Juruá and Purus rivers, scoured the state of Goiás, crossed the state of Acre from east to west, and pushed west along the lower tributaries of the Amazon all the way to Peru. When the task was done, Kietzman compiled the data from SILers and other surveyors into a document that was remarkable for both its scope and its potential for horror.

The most striking innovation was his demarcation on maps of many Indian homelands as an "area of potentially hostile Indians." These words, as well as "warlike" and "wild groups,"[18] conveyed an image of aggressive Indians straight out of Hollywood's version of the American West.

Kietzman pinpointed the "hostile" areas on maps that broke down the Amazon into Indian "culture areas." The maps, in turn, were incorporated into an English-language book, entitled *Indians of Brazil in the Twentieth Century,* which seemed designated more for American readers than for Brazilians. Academic in form and content and designed specifically for "field workers," the book appeared to be a harmless cataloguing of tribes—their location, their culture, their population size, and their acceptance of Brazilian domination. But it also offered a road map for American penetration into the Brazilian interior, much like that which occurred a century earlier in the American West, including warnings about "hostile" areas.

The book was all the more potent because of its impressive scientific credentials. Kietzman's editor, Janice Hopper of Washington, D.C.'s Institute for Cross Cultural Research, backed up Kietzman's methodology by revealing its roots: Brazilian anthropologist Eduardo Galvão's monumental paper, "Indigenous Culture Areas of Brazil, 1900–1959," which refined for Brazil the "culture area" classification first brought to the Americas from Germany by the renowned Franz Boas, the father of modern anthropology. The book also contained a bibliography of Brazilian ethnology up to 1960 by Herbert Baldus and, most important, an earlier demographic study of the tribes based on SPI's archives by SIL's chief Brazilian benefactor before the coup, Darcy Ribeiro. Entitled "Indigenous Cultures and Languages of Brazil," Ribeiro's remarkable study classified tribes on the basis of their degree of integration into the national Brazilian culture.

But SIL's survey was the book's centerpiece. Kietzman's report contained mild praise for the SPI three years after Darcy Ribeiro had denounced it for corruption and abuse of the Indians it was supposed to protect.[19] Kietzman repeatedly described tribes as being "aided by the SPI,"[20] despite Ribeiro's conclusion that military control over the SPI since 1958 had led it to "the lowest point of its history, bringing it down in certain regions to the degrading condition of an agent and prop of the despoilers and murderers of Indians."[21] Instead, Kietzman portrayed the SPI in its official guise as savior of the Indian, offering "protection"[22] from attacks by colonists. Not once in his survey of all Brazil's tribes was there even a hint that something was rotten in the halls of the SPI.

Nor was there a hint anywhere in the book that its publisher had ties to any U.S. government agency, much less the CIA. The Institute for Cross Cultural Research was a division of Operations and Policy Research, a private group that, in turn, received CIA money in 1963, 1964, and 1965.[23] The 1965 CIA grant was for another study on Brazil that explained trends in voting that could be useful in

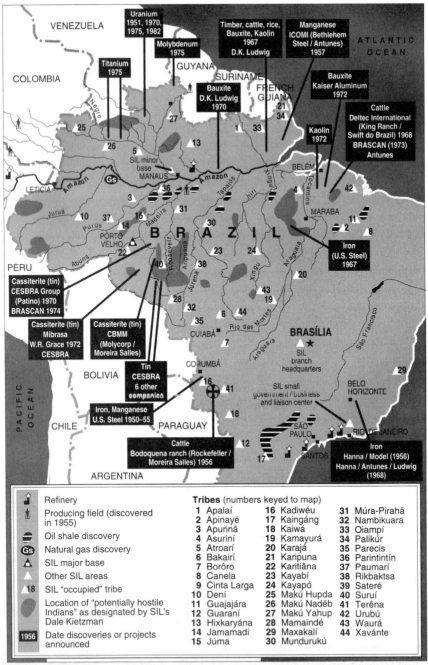

Tribes (numbers keyed to map)

1	Apalaí	16	Kadiwéu	31	Múra-Pirahã
2	Apinayé	17	Kaingáng	32	Nambikuara
3	Apurinã	18	Kaiwá	33	Oiampí
4	Asuriní	19	Kamayurá	34	Palikúr
5	Atroarí	20	Karajá	35	Parecis
6	Bakairí	21	Karipuna	36	Parintintín
7	Boróro	22	Karitiâna	37	Paumarí
8	Canela	23	Kayabí	38	Rikbaktsa
9	Cinta Larga	24	Kayapó	39	Sateré
10	Dení	25	Makú Hupda	40	Suruí
11	Guajajára	26	Makú Nadëb	41	Terêna
12	Guaraní	27	Makú Yahup	42	Urubú
13	Hixkaryána	28	Mamaindé	43	Waurá
14	Jamamadí	29	Maxakalí	44	Xavánte
15	Júma	30	Mundurukú		

Legend:
- Refinery
- Producing field (discovered in 1955)
- Oil shale discovery
- **Gs** Natural gas discovery
- SIL major base
- Other SIL areas
- **18** SIL "occupied" tribe
- Location of "potentially hostile Indians" as designated by SIL's Dale Kietzman
- **1956** Date discoveries or projects announced

SIL's "Hostile Tribes" and Rockefeller-Allied Companies in Brazilian Amazon

In 1966, two years after the military coup in Brazil and following a survey of the Indian frontier by SIL missionaries for the Brazilian government, Dale Kietzman identified areas of "potentially hostile Indians" in maps prepared for *Indians of Brazil in the Twentieth Century*.

Sources: Dale Kietzman, "Indians and Culture Areas," in Janice H. Hopper, ed., *Indians of Brazil in the Twentieth Century*; "Wycliffe Bible Translators in Brazil" (Huntington Beach, Calif.: Wycliffe Bible Translators, c. 1976); *Annual Report of the Work of the Summer Institute of Linguistics* (Brasília: SIL, 1976); *Engineering and Mining Journal* (November 1975), pp. 159, 170–71; Shelton H. Davis, *Victims of the Miracle*, pp. 94–95; "Rondônia, Capital do Estanho," *Visão*, August 28, 1972; "La Politica de Genocidio Contra los Indios de Brasil," report to the 41st Congress of Americanists, 1974, p. 19; *International Petroleum Encyclopedia, 1983* (Tulsa, Okla.: PennWell Publishing Company, 1983), p. 105.

trying to measure the Brazilian people's political interests and loyalties, including their willingness to participate in the elections under the generals' new political regime. The book was written by Ronald Schneider, who, using CIA documents, had earlier written a book vindicating the CIA's 1954 coup in Guatemala. That book had been commissioned by the Foreign Policy Research Institute, whose assistant director was a former CIA officer and Rockefeller aide, William Kintner, a friend of SIL's Robert Schneider.

Ronald Schneider's *Brazilian Election Factbook* had been published by another division of Operations and Policy Research, the Institute for Comparative Study of Political Systems. From a strategic perspective, *Indians of Brazil in the Twentieth Century* was a sociological companion to Schneider's political study of Brazilian society. It surveyed the social conditions of indigenous populations that occupied the Amazonian frontier, the escape valve for the pressure cooker that Brazilian society had become. In the minds of many generals and the political and economic interests behind them in Rio de Janeiro and São Paulo—and in Washington and New York—the Indians of Brazil, by defending their land against road builders, corporations, cattlemen, and destitute peasants brought in from the Northeast, stood in the way of prosperity and the diffusing of a dangerous political powder keg.

Janice Hopper, Kietzman's editor, was the recent widow of Rex Hopper, a behind-the-scenes collaborator in her book, acknowledged in her preface for his "encouragement, criticisms and suggestions." Rex Hopper had earned his own measure of infamy in 1965 as director of Project Camelot, the counterinsurgency operation par excellence. Hopper himself defined Camelot's purpose as a study designed to assess the potential for "internal war" in South America, as well as "the effects of government action on such potential."[24]

Rex Hopper had studied how "indigenous groups" could be trained and used by the U.S. military to control change in South American society, politics, and economics. Project Camelot's goal, however, was not just to "use" indigenous groups, but to spy on them for potential unrest that could lead to revolts and internal civil war. The strategy of divide and conquer had been practiced since the Romans. In Central and South America, Spaniards had used Indian tribes to conquer their former Aztec and Incan overlords. In North America, the British, French, and U.S. military had used Indians to fight for opposing colonial powers. Now, in his zeal for God and SIL's mission to reach the Bibleless tribes, Dale Kietzman inadvertently had shown the modern enemies of the Indians of Brazil precisely where the indigenous groups could be found, not to avoid them, but to "reach" them.

Brazilian generals had their own reasons for locating the tribes. The Jungle Warfare Training Center outside Manaus had recently been set up with support from the CIA and the Green Berets. The CIA had reports that arms were being shipped up the Amazon and its tributaries to guerrillas across the Brazilian border, in Peru definitely, and quite possibly in Colombia, Ecuador, and Bolivia. Moreover, there was always the threat—real or perceived—of a guerrilla insurgency within Brazil itself. Indeed, by the early 1970s, Surui Indians would be used to hunt down followers of former Brazilian Communist Party leader and congressman Carlos Marighella in the Araguaia River region of the Amazon; Aché Indians would be similarly deployed in Paraguay against rebels near the Brazilian border, as were Indians in the Caquetá River region of southern Colombia.

Tribal peoples, as the inhabitants of remote areas where rebels of governments usually launched guerrilla wars, had to be reached for military, as well as economic reasons. Potential allies of the government's enemies had to be identified and located. Even if guerrilla allies could not be invented, as they had been among the Mayorunas along the Peru-Brazil border in 1964, "hostiles" by their very designation were a "danger to society."

Among the regime's American advisers, this was a concern that dated back to the conquest of the American West. Whether they were missionaries reporting on "hostiles" for John D. Rockefeller or the U.S. Cavalry in the 1880s or SIL's naive linguists in the 1960s, the result was the same: trouble spots were identified for those who wanted the Indians' lands and the riches beneath them.

Shamans of the Cold War

One of the CIA officers who teamed up with King in the Amazon was William Buckley, a seasoned MKULTRA operative and the jungle warfare expert who, as the future chief of station in Beirut, would die in 1985 as a hostage of the Hizballah ("Army of God") fundamentalist Muslim guerrillas.

Both Buckley and King knew that the Amazon was a virtual reservoir of deadly poisons. One such poison, curare, which some Indians put on their arrows and blowgun darts, had been stored by the CIA for simulating heart attacks in people who were targeted for assassination. Another was a leaf that killed cattle. Still another leaf caused hair to fall out. Some plants killed fish. One sap rendered victims temporarily blind.[25]

Much of this research had been carried out by scientists at pharmaceutical companies or at academic centers with chemical-industry affiliations. But by 1965 the CIA was forced to change some of its specific fronts and code names. Studies of the CIA's operations that Kennedy ordered after the Bay of Pigs finally produced a critical report by CIA Inspector General Lyman Kirkpatrick. As a result of Kirkpatrick's report, Deputy Director Helms in 1965 agreed to a change: MKULTRA was henceforth called MKSEARCH. But its goal remained the same: to "develop, test and evaluate capabilities in the covert use of biological, chemical and radioactive material systems."[26]

By January 1967, Buckley had left the Amazon and returned to Vietnam; that month, Nicole Maxwell also left King's Amazonian adventure. With her departure, ANDCO plunged into darker, more sinister missions. Maxwell had already suspected that something was amiss, since King kept putting off the royalty contract he had promised her. She had given him all her notes on the plants, and after ten months, she had nothing to show for her work but a small salary. So she insisted that she had to know the status of the contract. His reply was crisp and evasive. Marketing was for a "nebulous future." He found it "distressing" that she should be "worrying about anything so remote and undefined." She should be content with her work as "the realization of your dreams of many years."[27]

In that case, she decided she would quit. Besides, her health had deteriorated.

King showed up at her door and whisked her off to a small hospital in Maryland. There, doctors claimed that she had become infected by a small parasite named "Providence."

King settled her accounts and gave her severance pay and compensation for her furniture. He wanted her out of Iquitos. Maxwell never got her contract from King or any royalties from the patent ANDCO took on sangre de drago.

With Maxwell gone, ANDCO's collaboration with the CIA's MKSEARCH specialists proceeded at a brisk pace. ANDCO botanists sent hallucinogenic plants back to the CIA's Dr. Sidney Gottlieb for testing on apes and monkeys.[28] Gottlieb's scientists at Georgetown University Hospital, led by Dr. Charles Geschickter, had already bombarded the animals' brains with radio-frequency energy waves until they fell unconscious; autopsies revealed that their brains had fried in their skulls.[29] Then Gottlieb's scientists fed simians food that was laced with dust from pulverized Amazonian magic plants to see if they could be induced to kill one another. This experiment, which drove the animals insane, succeeded.

ANDCO's purported mission of funding jungle medicines provided the perfect cover for MKSEARCH and other covert operations along the Amazon.

King had already begun to recruit unwitting students. To do so, he solicited and got the cooperation of the United States' leading economic botanist, Richard Evans Schultes of Harvard University.

Schultes's star had risen high since World War II, when he worked briefly for the Rockefeller Agricultural Mission to Mexico and then joined the U.S. effort to get rubber out of the Amazon-basin countries. An assignment in Colombia with the Department of Agriculture continued after the war and his reports included descriptions of the politics of various individual Colombians during the civil war. When the end of the Korean War quelled fears of another rubber emergency, he returned to Harvard's Peabody Museum, where he soon imparted his knowledge of the Aztec Indians' magic mushrooms to R. Gordon Wasson before the banker-turned-mycologist left for Mexico. Over subsequent years, Schultes's scientific papers had built his reputation as the United States leading expert on Amazonian

Amazon River Basin (1960–1970)

Legend:
- ▲ Andes Mountains
- Refinery
- Producing field
- Oil shale
- **B** Bauxite mine
- **Gs** Natural gas
- **Ir** Iron mine
- **Mg** Manganese mine
- **T** Tin mine
- ♀ Wild rubber
- △ SIL base
- ⊗ Jungle warfare training base (CIA/Green Beret assistance)
- ★ Area of guerrilla war battle
- ⬚ War zones
- Areas proposed for flooding by Hudson Institute's "Great Lakes" scheme
- ╫ Railway

Map labels:
Communist-led peasant republics attacked 1962 conquered 1964–65
BOGOTÁ
VILLAVICENCIO
CALI
LOMALINDA
COLOMBIA
VENEZUELA
Orinoco
Negro
Casiquiare
LLANOS
Meta
Vaupés
Apaporis
Caquetá
Putumayo
Caquetá
Japurá
QUITO
LIMONCOCHA
ECUADOR
Napo
Napo
Amazon
Icá
Amazon
Amazon
Uaupés
IQUITOS
LETICIA
TALARA
PERU
Marañón
Huallaga
Ucayali
Juruá
Purús
B R
PÔRTO VELHO
PUCALLPA
YARINACOCHA
TINGO MARIA
RIO BRANCO
Abuná
TUMI CHUCUA
RIBERALTA
Defeat of MIR 1965
SATIPO
1965
HUANCAYO
LIMA
AYACUCHO
ELN 1965
Machupicchu ruins
CUZCO
MIR 1965
Madre de Dios
Beni
Guaporé
Mamoré
TRINIDAD
CIA Green Beret base 1967
PACIFIC OCEAN
Lake Titicaca
AREQUIPA
LA PAZ
BOLIVIA
COCHABAMBA
A L T I P L A N O
SANTA CRUZ
VALLEGRANDE
SUCRE
Defeat of Che Guevara 1967
CAMIRI
Grande
CHILE
ARGENTINA

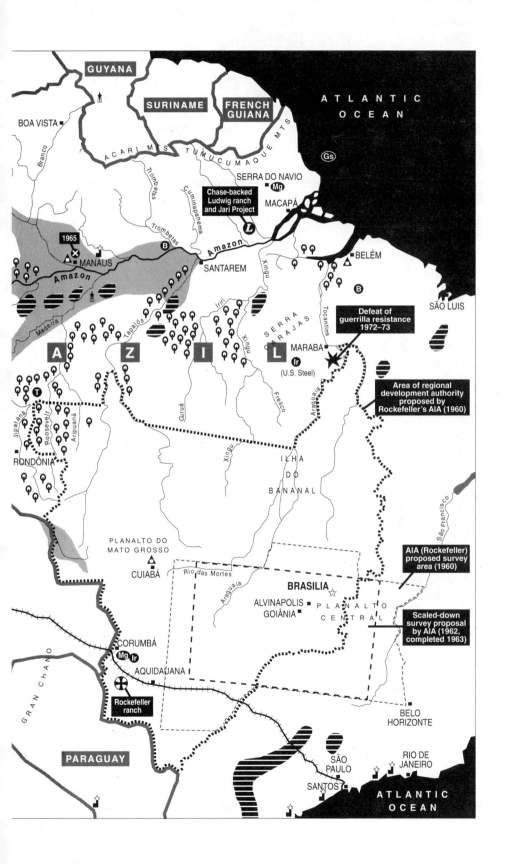

GUYANA

SURINAME

FRENCH GUIANA

BOA VISTA

ATLANTIC OCEAN

ACARI MTS TUMUCUMAQUE MTS

Gs

SERRA DO NAVIO

Mg

MACAPÁ

Chase-backed Ludwig ranch and Jari Project

L

1965

MANAUS

B

SANTAREM

Amazon

Amazon

Madeira

BELÉM

B

SÃO LUIS

Trombetas

Trombetas

Cuminapanema

Xingu

Iriri

Tocantins

SERRA DOS CARAJAS

Defeat of guerrilla resistance 1972–73

A   Z   I   L

Tapajós

MARABA

Ir

(U.S. Steel)

Area of regional development authority proposed by Rockefeller's AIA (1960)

Curuá

Xingu

Fresco

Araguaia

T

Jiparaná

Roosevelt

Aripuanã

RONDÔNIA

ILHA

DO

BANANAL

São Francisco

PLANALTO DO MATO GROSSO

CUIABÁ

Rio das Mortes

Araguaia

BRASILIA

ALVINÁPOLIS

GOIÂNIA

PLANALTO

CENTRAL

AIA (Rockefeller) proposed survey area (1960)

Scaled-down survey proposal by AIA (1962, completed 1963)

CORUMBÁ

Mg Ir

AQUIDAUANA

Rockefeller ranch

GRAN CHANO

BELO HORIZONTE

SÃO PAULO

SANTOS

RIO DE JANEIRO

PARAGUAY

ATLANTIC OCEAN

rubber varieties, hallucinogens, and Indian herbal medicines. He founded *Economic Botany*, a magazine that published his scientific findings and promoted the commercial exploitation of Amazonian flora.

The CIA kept abreast of all these discoveries through the magazine and a network that included informants at the Department of Agriculture.[30] Schultes's professional network included some of the most prestigious ethnobotanists and botanists in the world, including the discoverer of LSD, Albert Hoffman. For years, the Agency had been tracking disbursements of LSD from Sandoz laboratories in Basle, Switzerland, where Hoffman worked. It also bought Eli Lilly's entire supply of its own newly synthesized LSD. Sidney Gottlieb hoped to corner the mind-altering drug for CIA covert operations.[31]

Whether Schultes himself knew of CIA's MKULTRA experiments, some of Harvard's top officials did. They were aware of CIA contracts in the university and exercised at least some degree of oversight.[32]

On special collecting expeditions, Schultes continued to hack his way through the rain forests of Ecuador, Colombia, Peru, and Brazil, pursuing the secrets of the magical plants that soon, he often explained matter-of-factly to students, would die with the Indians.

Stories abounded of his marching up to his waist in water through the jungle during the rainy season while balancing a portage pack on his head, going for days without food when game was scarce—all to find the botanical treasures of the jungle. Indian plants became an obsession, with the Indians themselves merely a means toward that end.

One of Schultes's favorite stories was of his search during the Korean War for a rare dwarf variety of the *Havea* rubber tree. They grew only in the "lost world" atop one of the sandstone mountains that rear up from the flat grasslands at the headwaters of the Apáporis River in southeast Colombia. The trick was to get the Indians to take him there. The local shaman warned that trespassers met certain death from hordes of elflike men who suddenly appeared to defend the hill at the approach of people.

"I don't know what you will think," he wrote the Department of Agriculture, "when I tell you that I have been dancing, chewing coca, drinking *Chicha de Chontaduro* for two days as part of my Point IV work!"

> By entering the festivities and dancing in the mask and palm skirt that the natives made for me, I have finally convinced the medicine man that I am the type of person who would do his trolls no harm. For last night, when we were smoking a three foot communal cigar . . . Marakayooreena told me that he had thought about the trip to the mountain, and that he would take me there. He said that, as I was not an Indian, I would not be able to see the dwarf people but that they would be there nevertheless. He would practice his magic and tell them my mission was to collect plants, not to molest them. I would hear them, he assured me, but I would think it is the wind rustling the tree tops.

So, tomorrow, the dancers rest after their three day and night ordeal. Then, I shall send ahead to cut a small path to the Cerro de la Gente Chiquita. When it is ready, we shall see what botanical treasures be there for me.[33]

By 1966, Schultes was a legend. Some of his colleagues were already on the CIA or Pentagon payroll, probing the mysteries of native medicines and poisons. It did not seem out of place for King, a former drug company executive, to approach Schultes for his help or for Schultes to assent. Some of the professor's young protégés soon found themselves in the Amazon, working for King.

William Buckley, ANDCO's first paramilitary guard, remembered King sitting in a canvas chair on a large houseboat he used for collecting expeditions. He would sit there for hours, sipping scotch, while his botanists hacked away at the jungle, most of them stoned on *yagé*, one of the hallucinogens ANDCO sent back to the United States.

The ANDCO experience seemed to cast a veil of conformity over everyone who took part in it, creating an ambience of plausible deniability. Like Nicole Maxwell, student Timothy Plowman would deny knowledge of King's CIA sponsorship, insisting that ANDCO collected only medicinal plants, never hallucinogens, never poisons.[34] Later confronted by investigators using declassified MKULTRA and MKSEARCH documents, Plowman changed his story. Yes, he admitted, ANDCO shipped back a paralytic agent named *Chondodendron toxicoferum*, which was "absolutely lethal in high doses."[35]

SIL was drawn into aiding the botanists simply by its pervasive presence among the jungle's tribes. SIL missionaries were stationed among tribes throughout the Amazon. They had collected a vast store of data on Indian cultures through their Bible-translation efforts. When one of Schultes's botanists, Homer Pinkley, needed help collecting linguistic data to identify hallucinogenic plants used in tribal ceremonial drinks, he turned to Limoncocha. SIL was willing and able to help.[36]

Another collaboration between SIL and Schultes's network was more ominous. This one took place in Ecuador and Peru, when Dr. Dermot B. Taylor, chairman of UCLA's Pharmacology Department, used Limoncocha and Yarinacocha to collect plants for the U.S. Army. Taylor did not try to hide his purpose. His study, "Medical Aspects of Chemical Warfare," was published by the Pentagon. Its goal was "to determine through clinical research the effect of selected toxic compounds and of drugs antagonistic thereto. . . . Also, to advise and assist in the search for more effective toxic compounds." Taylor's three-man expedition to the Amazon rain forests was a great success; more than 2,500 plants were collected. Extracts of the plants were prepared "and screened for biological activity."[37]

Another expedition that swung through SIL's Peruvian base was composed of former U.S. Marine-turned-author, Margaret Kreig, who was compiling data for her book, *Green Medicine,* and Bruce Halstead, M.D., a former Loma Linda

University trainer of Fundamentalist Christian medical missionaries. Although Halstead was an expert on marine poisons and then under contract with the Pentagon, his purported mission on this 1962 trip with Kreig was to collect information on medicinal plants from Indians and Protestant missionaries for the Pfizer chemical company. However, he was not interested only in Indian medicines; hallucinogens were definitely on his mind. "Halstead naturally was alert whenever we went for new methods of preparing *ayahuasca* and for botanical specimens of the vine," Kreig wrote at the time. "I recorded on tape a number of . . . native recipes, all highly contradictory, and wondered whether the Pfizer researchers would make any use of them."[38] Later, she discovered that they did not. But Halstead nevertheless was anxious to get his plants back to his own new $15 million World Life Research Institute for preliminary studies. "We have no secrets," he told an American missionary among the Campa Indians. "If any of these plants prove out, we will relay the information to you so that the natives can use them more efficiently in care of themselves."[39] The Indians, however, had little need of American efficiency in using their own tribal medicines.

Back at his institute in California's San Bernardino Mountains, the devout Christian worked feverishly to complete a monumental work, not on the jungle's medicines, but on the sea's poisons—and not for God, but for the Pentagon. "Russia is exceedingly interested in nerve drugs such as this," Halstead once told a reporter, "so I can't disclose the name of the fish or the poison. But just think of the psychological effect it would have on a political prisoner—perhaps even on an entire population."[40]

Biological and chemical warfare had reached new heights of prestige among counterinsurgency experts. Former Rockefeller aide and SIL associate William R. Kintner and his colleagues at the University of Pennsylvania's Foreign Policy Research Institute conducted a study entitled, "The Role of Biological and Chemical Weapons in the Defense Strategy of the United States." To Cold Warriors like Kintner, local insurgencies were part of the global struggle waged by the Soviet Union, and their suppression—by any means—was necessary to prevent a nuclear war.

"The capability to engage in offensive and defensive biological and chemical operations gives a nation a much stronger position in the struggle for power and provides a powerful deterrent force to bridge the gap between continental and nuclear weapons capabilities," Kintner and his colleagues wrote in the abstract for their army contract. "B/C weapons could provide capabilities for covert and overt strategic and tactical operations of any required intensity in any type of power struggle or warfare without imposing a logistics load beyond the capacities of many of the smaller nations."[41]

Were chemical and biological weapons now being considered for inclusion in foreign-aid packages to "smaller" countries like Iraq or Israel or Peru? The

Department of Defense already was conducting feasibility studies on the use of chemical and biological agents in counterinsurgency, combined with "the development of mathematical models for computation of weapons effects."[42]

Schultes traveled regularly to Washington to consult with the Agricultural Research Service, which was studying the effectiveness of Agent Orange defoliation in Vietnam for the Pentagon. The project required "classification of tropical forests" in Vietnam, Cambodia, and Laos and a report on tests of chemical defoliants in Thailand.[43]

King, meanwhile, continued to take boat trips down the Amazon into Brazil on ANDCO's large houseboat, *Fennewood II*, named after his Virginia estate. He collected plants, but he also visited sources of intelligence in towns along the way, including a Roman Catholic bishop from the United States who was posted by the Vatican at a small city on the Amazon. It was in the middle of the night, an ANDCO plant collector recalled years later, and the secretary to the bishop who greeted King at the bishop's residence thought it was too late.

"The Bishop cannot see anyone," said the priest. "He is very tired."

"Tell him J. C. King is here," the colonel said.

"I'll go upstairs and see what he says," said the priest, an effeminate, thin American with dark hair. He was soon back in high spirits.

"Oh, the Bishop will see you!" said the priest. "Oh, he says you're from the CIA!"[44]

Here was the first confirmation of the collector's growing suspicions about King. And here was the collector's Donnybrook with Colonel King. Casually repeating what had happened the next evening over dinner, she was fired the next day.*

A regular stop was Manaus, the free-port capital of Brazil's largest state, Amazonas. Besides containing intelligence resources on Amazonian Indians and plants, the region also was host to the Brazilian junta's new Jungle Warfare Training Center. If some Brazilian intelligence officers at first questioned its purpose in a jungle more known for Indians with blowguns than leftists with AK-47s, any skepticism melted when they learned that their training center was only one of many set up recently throughout the Amazon basin with advisers from the CIA and the U.S. Special Forces. Reports persisted of a secret antiguerrilla base and a U.S. satellite-tracking station built in the isolated Macarena Mountains of Colombia during the 1962–1964 offensive against the peasant republics; all commercial flights over the 120-kilometer-long mountain chain were prohibited and would continue to be for the next decade.

Peru, of course, had had a jungle warfare training center since the CIA's

---

* Curiously, despite her knowledge of King's CIA ties and despite the well-known leftist views of her husband, she tried to get back her job with ANDCO the following year—to no avail.

1965 offensive against the Movimiento de Izquierda Revolucionaria (MIR) in the Campa Indians' territory. And in 1967, still another special warfare base was set up at an abandoned sugar mill north of Santa Cruz, at the foot of the jungle *montaña* of eastern Bolivia. Here, at La Esperanza (Spanish for "hope"), Green Berets and CIA Cuban exiles began training Rangers of the new military regime of General René Barrientos in the relentless science of hunting down guerrillas.

As the United States' hidden war in the Amazon basin was reaching its final stages of preparation, the last deepwater port on the Amazon emerged as a clandestine central command station: Iquitos, boomtown of the Peruvian Amazon's oil industry and home base of J. C. King.

33

DEATH OF A CONTINENTAL REVOLUTION

Mr. Pilsner's Deadly Friends

Two worlds vied for J. C. King's attention when he stepped outside ANDCO's lab in Iquitos and walked down the hill to his boat on the Amazon. One was noisy, the clamor of motorbikes mingling with the rattle of new construction to lend an air of progress and excitement. Tourists actually competed for taxis, although vultures as large as turkeys still stalked the streets.

The second world was quieter, a floating shantytown of makeshift huts built on rafts. This waterfront slum, called Belén and invariably described as "colorful" in tourist guides, was growing. And it was growing not in contradiction to the first world, but because of it: What was progress for some, was misery for others.

Every time King took his houseboat out of port, he had to pass by Belén and the sullen, sometimes bitter stares of its residents. Here were the displaced Indians of the jungle who had ended up at a watery edge of world commerce.

Oil was responsible for both worlds. The question was, Which would outrace the other: prosperity or despair in the system? In Washington, King had watched counterinsurgency theorist Walt Rostow wrestle with that question in the White House. Rostow's economics saw both worlds ultimately as mutually contradictory, dismissing their confluence in the river of time as only a temporary aberration of development. The two worlds symbolized growing pains in a society that was passing through a necessary, albeit potentially messy, stage toward the modern new order. And the new order just happened, as history would have it, to be dominated by northern metropolitan centers of finance and trade, like the New York Stock Exchange and the oil industry.

By the time King set up shop in Iquitos, competition was hot to find oil in Peru, sometimes as hot as lead bullets whistling through the rain forest. In 1967, a Standard Oil of New Jersey mapping and exploration crew cut down twenty Amahuaca Indians northeast of the Campas' territory.[1] Sinclair Oil's Ganso Azul oil field near Pucallpa was more secure. Peruvian colonists had replaced forest-dwelling Indians in that area, and protection of the proved oil field was a national security priority for both the Peruvian military and the CIA's jungle warfare training center. Closer to Iquitos, AMOCO and Royal Dutch Shell were looking forward to moving into the Mayorunas' territory once SIL translators had completed their pacification of that tribe. Texaco was still in the Marañon River basin in the north; Standard Oil of New York (Mobil) and California Fundamentalism's original oil angel, Union Oil, were spending $10 million exploring the nearby Santiago River. With war raging in Southeast Asia and OPEC's challenge rising in the Middle East, Latin America's oil was not to be taken for granted.

The pacified Indians, however, were. Faced with the loss of their land to settlers and road crews, along with food shortages following the introduction of firearms into their hunting lands, they had only two options: work for the oil companies or follow newly built roads out of the jungle and into the boomtowns along the Amazon. In either case, their lives were transformed; hunters and gatherers became landless laborers. And when jobs ran short, they flooded into Iquitos, many becoming beggars and prostitutes, some even agreeing to help drug smugglers.

It was the laborers who worried the Peruvians—and the Americans—most. Lima's press reported charges that Standard Oil of New Jersey, fearing nationalization of its Peruvian subsidiary, was overworking its crews to increase production.[2] Meanwhile, Peruvian nationalists of all political stripes were getting angry over the depletion of their oil reserves. Some of their antigringo feelings spilled over to other American enterprises in the Pucallpa area, including the logging operations of William Cameron Townsend's millionaire associate from Texas, Robert Le Tourneau.

As protests widened and the political crisis deepened for President Fernando Belaúnde Terry despite his crushing of the pro-Castro guerrillas and communists of various persuasions (pro-Stalin, pro-Mao, and pro-Trotsky currents were given the same broad brush), Peru's generals began to give serious thought to taking matters into their own hands. The CIA worried that a military takeover might be inevitable.[3]

CIA officers in the U.S. Embassy in Lima monitored developments in the military. And as they did, the activities of at least one of King's ANDCO operatives expanded beyond collecting plants and intelligence.

The arrival in Iquitos of King's new ANDCO director was greeted with joy by some shadier circles. In temperament, Garland "Dee" Williams was quite unlike his predecessor, William Buckley. Although both men were CIA veterans from

THE SLAUGHTER OF THE INNOCENTS

Vietnam, Buckley was reserved, almost professorial, perfect for ANDCO's scholarly cover. Williams, on the other hand, was an extrovert. He made friends by throwing wild parties at the ANDCO compound. Alcohol and sex seemed always there for the taking. To keep Peruvian military officers happy, Williams maintained a young woman in residence, earning him the disdain of other ANDCO botanists and anthropologists who too easily dismissed him as "Mr. Pilsner."

Behind this exterior, however, lurked a more serious nature. Williams was a top paramilitary officer with an extensive counterinsurgency background who also knew the ways of drug smugglers.

Williams soon began training Peruvian military officers in how to make parachute jumps into the jungle. These officers were serving under General Armando Artola, who had been commander of the Iquitos garrison. Artola, however, had long since moved up. His men actually were attached to Peru's National Intelligence Service, which Artola now headed.

Beefy and bald, Artola was as fierce as he looked. Working closely with the CIA paramilitary experts, he scored Latin America's first unqualified antiguerrilla success by wiping out the Movimiento de Izquierda Revolucionario (MIR) in the Campa Indian region and in the Quechua highlands near Machu-Picchu in the south.

This success came hot on the heels of Artola's visit in May 1965 to Rio de Janeiro, where the newly installed junta hosted a conference of chiefs of South American intelligence services. Brazil's generals were now playing a major role in politicizing other Latin American military chiefs with the CIA's Cold War ideology. They had been told of a vast conspiracy directed by Moscow and Cuba against Argentina, Bolivia, Brazil, Colombia, Chile, Ecuador, Paraguay, Peru, Uruguay, and Venezuela—virtually the entire continent.[4] Whatever the reality of Cuba's military threat to the vastly superior armed forces of these nations, the political threat of Fidel Castro's example was keenly felt by these generals.

Castro and Che Guevara had shown that it was possible, given the right terrain and political circumstances, to win a guerrilla war in Latin America. By demystifying the power of a better armed and equipped regular army, they had raised the expectations of Cuba's peasants and urban allies and inspired a coordinated popular uprising in the cities and countryside. This victory terrified traditional military leaders, who were used to having their way in plantations, mines, and villages, as well as in government palaces. But the generals did not grasp Che's central lesson: All guerrilla actions should be aimed at swaying mass political opinion.[5]

Generals like Artola and many of their American military advisers mistook their task as merely one of military strategy: better police techniques, followed by arrests and the forced relocation of the local rural population, quarantine of the "infected" area, and search-and-destroy missions by elite antiguerrilla units. Civic action by the army was rarely embraced with enthusiasm. Basic reforms in government and land tenure that redistributed political power and the more fertile lands were not really on the agenda. Instead, in the face of mounting demands and growing unrest, massacres of villages and death squads roaming urban streets at night were becoming more common.

King's operation in Iquitos was seen as so important that Artola, renowned for his fierce political ambition,[6] was in constant touch with Dee Williams.[7] Mistakenly dismissed by many liberal Americans and Peruvians as a political Neanderthal, Artola shrewdly positioned himself at the forefront of the right wing of the restless Peruvian army command through his collaboration with the CIA. Understandably, in Latin America, as in most of the Third World, waging war in the jungle was not as attractive to aspiring military careerists as was commanding jets or tanks. To sweeten the pot, the CIA often held out the promise of political power to those who would do the down-and-dirty job of counterinsurgency. And in Peru, as in most of Latin America, the U.S. Embassy could deliver because it controlled the military pursestrings. The U.S. Embassy was in a strong position to choose which generals would play major roles in the national government.

Artola had never had much sympathy for the current president of Peru, Fernando Belaúnde Terry, the rich, Kennedy-type liberal who had joined the attack against the dictatorship of General Manuel Odría. Artola took comfort in the turmoil that had raged within Belaúnde's party since its poor showing in the 1966 local elections. The growing split within Belaúnde's party meant, however, that Haya de la Torre's APRA would hold the balance of power in the scheduled 1969 elections.

APRA was an unacceptable alternative. Haya de la Torre had been hated by older, conservative officers since the 1930s and was distrusted by younger officers for having acquiesced in 1956 to the landed oligarchy's candidates, Manuel Prado and Pedro Beltrán. The prospect of an APRA victory forged a temporary alliance among the military factions. The younger colonels were impatient with Belaúnde's vacillations and lack of courage; and the generals were worried that spreading corruption in the army might lead them to a fate similar to Batista's army in Cuba. As the elections approached, rumors began circulating of plans for a coup. "Plan Inca" was carried out in October 1968 following a scandal over the failure of security forces to stop smugglers from flying over the border from Bolivia, and charges that Belaúnde was compromising the nation with a secret protocol with Standard Oil. There was also a feeling that the existing constitutional structure was unable to integrate the rural peasants and urban poor into the national political and economic mainstream.

The coup put Artola in control of Peru's national police and intelligence services as minister of the interior. Artola became the leading rightist in the new junta headed by General Juan Velasco Alvarado.

Artola owed this extraordinary achievement not only to his own ambition, but also to three foreign forces that converged on Peru in the 1960s, each associated with the career of Dee Williams's boss, J. C. King: Nazi refugees who were involved in contraband and the drug trade with Latin American military officers in the Andean countries, the CIA's hunt for Che Guevara, and the resistance of the Rockefellers to Peru's claim against Standard Oil of New Jersey.

Rat Line to the Amazon

Peru was the first stop in a cocaine-smuggling route that started in Bolivia, where most of the world's supply of coca leaves were grown, and ended on the streets of the United States. Smugglers moved the coca out of the Bolivian Altiplano across Lake Titicaca or from the Beni region into southern Peru, using trucks, boats, or, more often, airplanes. In Peru, the coca was processed into paste or sent on to processing plants in Guayaquil in southern Ecuador; from Ecuador, the paste or its dried crystallized powder was smuggled through Panama. There it was listed on freight manifests as a legal commodity and sent on to Miami or New Orleans or, less often, to Tampa, the domains of Mafia chiefs Meyer Lansky, Carlos Marcello, and Santos Trafficante.

An alternative route out of Peru was across the jungle east of the Andes and then down the Amazon. Iquitos was the first deepwater port for oceangoing boats heading east to the Atlantic. It was also the host of the largest airport in that part of the Amazon, thanks to the U.S. Rubber Procurement Program during World War II. Therefore, Iquitos became a favorite rendezvous for smugglers and Interpol agents, outmatched only by Leticia, Colombia's river port farther downriver. Strategically located just where the borders of Colombia, Peru, and Brazil converge, Leticia became notorious for a while as the cocaine-smuggling capital of the world. The town's police force was too small and its customs officers were unprepared for the influx of cocaine being shipped to points east and north by river and air.

From ports along the Amazon route, a unique improvement over the airplane emerged for smuggling huge amounts of cocaine: shiploads of Amazonian cedar and mahogany. Hollowed out and stuffed with wrapped cocaine, the boards were mixed with regular planks. Emerging into the open sea, the ships headed north to Panama, where money was exchanged and laundered, or they sailed farther north into the Caribbean, where "brass-plate" banks, one-office affairs, flourished. Sometimes, the tropical hardwoods were shipped directly to Miami, the new "Little Havana," since Fidel Castro chased Florida mobsters Meyer Lansky and Santos Trafficante out of Cuba in 1958.

The influx of thousands of refugees into Miami was difficult enough, but the added influx of mobsters and the CIA, huge amounts of money and material for anti-Castro raids, and now drug smugglers was too much for Miami's political infrastructure to cope with. Real estate prices soared, corruption became rampant, and in the midst of the social crisis, the birth of the "Amazon connection" to Miami drug smuggling passed unnoticed.

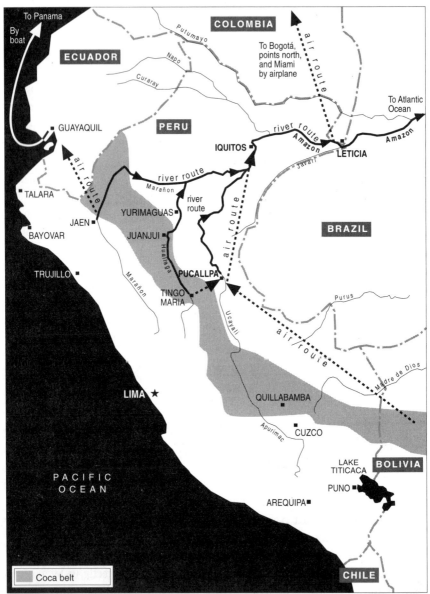

Amazon's River Routes for Cocaine Smuggling

During the 1960s, cocaine smuggling found a new route down the Amazon toward Leticia, where U.S. Consul Mike Tsalickis built a fortune in tourism and the exporting of exotic fish, animals, and cocaine.

Sources: Smuggling routes–Authors' interviews; Coca leaf belt–Edmundo Morales, *Cocaine: White Gold Rush in Peru*; James Painter, *Bolivia and Coca: A Study in Dependency* (Boulder, Colo.: Lynne Reinner, 1994).

In 1963, a mysterious middle-aged German appeared in Leticia. He planned to purchase the region's only large sawmill, he explained. He called himself Rafael von Steinbeck, but actually he had many names. He had entered South America after World War II through Peronist Argentina, exactly when King was serving in Buenos Aires as the assistant military attaché charged with monitoring Nazi corporate assets and spy networks. It would be three decades before the world would learn of the protection provided by U.S. intelligence agencies for Nazi war criminals who were willing to collaborate in the Cold War against communism.[8]

Von Steinbeck had escaped from Poland via the Vatican "rat line" run by a Croatian priest, Father Dragonovic. Apparently well connected and financed, he went from Argentina to Panama, where he was given Panamanian citizenship by dictator Simón Vallarino. But Vallarino's fascist leanings did not sit well in Washington, and Vallarino's subsequent fall forced von Steinbeck to seek protection next from Peru's right-wing dictator, General Odría.

Using the alias José Marie Still Georges, he became well known as Peru's premier smuggler of *oro blanco*, the "white gold." In 1958, following Odría's fall, 7½ kilos of cocaine discovered en route to Panama were traced back to Still Georges. Fleeing to remote Iquitos, he was given false identity papers by a sympathetic Capuchin superior and continued north through the jungle that fueled the rubber boom of half a century earlier, working his way up to the Putumayo River and west to Brazil.[9]

Still Georges found refuge downriver in another Capuchin mission at Manaus. After a decent interval, he returned to Leticia. There, yet another Capuchin friar with a pro-Franco Falangist background awaited. Bishop Marceliano Canyes was the same Catalan Capuchin who, charged anthropologist Victor Daniel Bonilla, had won infamy in the Putumayo region for fleecing the Sibundoy valley tribes of their lands.[10] He was now apostolic vicar of the Amazonas commissariat. Canyes appointed Still Georges the engineer of the apostolic prefect and let him acquire an identity card in the name of Rafael von Steinbeck.[11]

Von Steinbeck obtained a loan from a local government bank of which Canyes was a director. Then, in 1963, he joined two of Canyes's friends in forming a company to sell fish and hides and to export mahogany, cedar, and rosewood from Santa Clara, north of Leticia.

This region offered von Steinbeck some ethnic conviviality. It had been frequented by Germans since 1905, and after World War II, Leticia was the source of reported sightings of Nazi refugees.

Von Steinbeck named his firm the Amazon Rosewood and Commerce Society. Well financed, he took over Santa Clara's abandoned sawmill and made plans to hire over 400 men, including Indians, to provide wood and hides. He was buying supplies to begin operations, when into the Santa Clara picture walked a thin, dark-haired American whom *Life* magazine called "The Tarzan of the Amazon."

The Tarzan of the Amazon

Mike Tsalickis was a native of Tarpon Springs, Florida, a community on the Gulf coast north of Tampa that was famous for its sponge industry. Mike reveled in his self-cultivated reputation as the All-American Boy Scout. He had earned more than 100 merit badges. Love of the outdoors, he explained, had led him to the Amazon and adventure in the jungle. Following a hitch in the navy, so the story goes, in 1946 he helped set up the Tarpon Springs Zoo to import animals from Latin America.

Mike Tsalickis followed the route of a fledgling St. Petersburg airline, Aerovias Sud Americana (ASA), as it built the first air-freight line between Central America and the United States. He sent back live animals to his partner, Gertrude Jerkins, for resale to pet shops and zoos. Eventually finding himself in Barranquilla, Colombia's major Caribbean harbor, he heard stories about vast untapped animal resources along the Amazon.

In 1953, he decided to investigate. Traveling by boat through Caribbean ports in Venezuela and Guyana, he finally arrived in Belém, Brazil, at the Amazon's mouth. He worked his way up the Amazon until, in August of that year, he came upon Leticia, then a sleepy river town with no hot water or electricity. But he saw an animal exporter's paradise. He convinced ASA to try a freight line between Leticia, Bogotá, and Panama. He would bring in commercial goods and export natural rubber, hides, tropical fish, and exotic animals. The regularity of flights made ASA's new route—and ASA agent Mike Tsalickis—a success. He was soon exporting big Amazon fish to restaurants in Bogotá and providing free ASA passes to both buyers and sellers of his animals.

But even he could not monopolize the depletion of Amazonian fauna. Other American exporters operating out of Iquitos undercut his prices, so Tsalickis made two fateful business moves around 1957. He decided to go into the exporting of research animals, especially the white-lipped marmoset and the squirrel monkey. And, after investigating the lumber industry, he also invested in the export of rosewood used in extracting perfume. Rosewood trees were cut down in the vast rain forest to the north, and the logs were floated down the Putumayo to the region's only large sawmill, owned by von Steinbeck.

In Santa Clara, then, converged three of the most notorious figures of the Colombian Amazon: Tsalickis, Bishop Canyes, and von Steinbeck. The mix was explosive, and it did not take long for Colombia's Liberals to light the match. Bogotá's *El Espectador* began a series of articles exposing von Steinbeck's past smuggling activities. Von Steinbeck's ownership of the only large sawmill in Colombia's Amazon smacked of corruption. Von Steinbeck had contacted several local politicians to lock up public-works contracts for his enterprise, including projects sponsored by the Alliance for Progress. His commercial reach extended

THE SLAUGHTER OF THE INNOCENTS

back to Iquitos, whose refinery, tapping Sinclair Oil's Ganso Azul field, would give his riverboats all the fuel he needed to dominate the region. But most important was the revelation that his cocaine operations in Peru had been located next to a sawmill.[12] Did he plan to export more than rosewood?

Von Steinbeck disappeared. In February 1964, after having disguised himself as a Capuchin monk while living in Manaus, he resurfaced in Leticia. He tried to reorganize his company, drawing on a $35,000 loan provided by Canyes's bank. But in 1966, at about the time when King set up ANDCO, he vanished again, never to return. He took up residence in Guayaquil, home of a bevy of cocaine-processing plants thriving under a CIA-backed military dictatorship.

The collapse of von Steinbeck's company removed the only sawmill in Colombia's Amazonas commissariat. Mike Tsalickis had to write off his investment in his Santa Clara rosewood operation. But it would not be the last time he would be tied to business deals with Bishop Canyes's network or have a close brush with the other side of the law.

That year King opened shop in Iquitos and hired Mike Tsalickis as ANDCO's supply agent in Leticia. In May, the State Department also opened shop in Leticia, setting up a U.S. consulate with some fanfare and appointing Tsalickis as unofficial U.S. consul. The party thrown by the Bogotá embassy included Tsalickis and Bishop Canyes as guests. Tsalickis even took U.S. Ambassador Covey Oliver, fresh from his victory over Colombia's "red" peasant republics and soon to become assistant secretary for Latin America, on a nighttime alligator hunt, complete with armed security guards. The following year Tsalickis was named U.S. consular agent. "He was doing the job anyway," said Oliver, "so we decided to make it official."[13] Tsalickis was an old Amazon hand for the U.S. Embassy by then. When Leticia's doctor had wanted to set up a hospital in this remote region, the U.S. military mission, which was advising the government of Alberto Lleras Camargo on antiguerilla operations, stepped in at Tsalickis's request. A U.S. Marine colonel arranged for the U.S. Navy to fly in an unused mobile clinic from the Panama Canal Zone. The embassy arranged a $25,000 U.S. donation to this "Project Halo."

This was not the only feat that made Mike a local celebrity. Back in 1959, the Colombian government had discovered that ASA had been using Colombian air permits to control the freight business between Leticia and Bogotá. The Lleras Camargo government canceled the permits, and Colombians moved in to replace ASA. Tsalickis did not fight it. Instead, he bought his own DC-3, invested in Leticia real estate, and launched a brick factory and a tourist hotel. He became the most prominent American in the region, billing himself as the Tarzan of the Amazon to visiting journalists. His appointment as U.S. consul in Leticia, then, came as no surprise.

Tsalickis's involvement with ANDCO's notorious Dee Williams, however, raised some eyebrows. Williams hired Tsalickis just as the Amazon's Tarzan was expanding the research side of his animal export business. In 1967, Tsalickis bought an island in one of the Amazon's remote tributaries between Leticia and Iquitos. The purpose, he explained, was to experiment in letting monkeys run wild to see if their breeding habits improved. This experiment would allow him to restock the surrounding jungle out of which he took as many as 6,000 monkeys a year. The experiment worked. Starting with 3,691 monkeys, the island would hold over 20,000 by 1971; of those, 5,690 had been deposited by Tsalickis, thanks to the labor of hundreds of hired native trappers.[14]

Yet the extraordinary security measures Tsalickis took inspired rumors. A staff of eighteen men armed with walkie-talkies patrolled the island, keeping out intruders and maintaining the island's isolation. Tsalickis's customers in the United States included the U.S. Naval Toxicology Unit, the U.S. Army, and many research institutions where scientists had been involved in MKULTRA experiments. The monkeys were used in a wide range of experiments, including tests for cancer viruses, brain tumors, poisons, and psychoactive drugs.

King occasionally stayed at Tsalickis's Ticuna Hotel, but he never allowed himself to be seen as having the kind of relations with Tsalickis that Dee Williams did. King's operational style was quiet. Tsalickis's modus operandi was brash and crudely commercial, sporting everything from round glass paperweights encasing an overhead profile sketch of his head to picture postcards bearing his signature over the photographs. The photographs inadvertently painted an image of an Amazon besieged. One had the Tarzan of the Amazon wrestling knee deep in mud with a huge (and reportedly drugged) anaconda, a scene he repeated for the "Wild Kingdom" television show. Another showed him in a Tarpon Zoo sweatshirt grinning between two shy, bare-breasted Yagua Indian girls, his arms around their shoulders. *National Geographic* and *True* magazines ran feature stories about him. He was always seeking publicity for his Ticuna Hotel, his tourist services (which included hunting expeditions), and, of course, himself.

Yet he was useful. Since he knew everyone, he was a valuable source of information. He helped plant collector Nicole Maxwell during her first expedition and later provided plants and supplies for ANDCO. When King took his floating lab, the *Fennewood II*, on an expedition into the backwaters, Mike was always available to arrange equipment, fuel, and provisions. He seemed willing to do anything for the U.S. government.

And for friends.

Like the American missionaries, including SIL translators and JAARS pilots, who occasionally stayed at his hotel and enjoyed his famed hospitality.

Like oil companies, such as AMOCO, which, after two SIL women had conquered the Mayoruna with trinkets and love, employed his aerial services and SIL friend Jerry Cobb's piloting skills to penetrate the tribe's forbidding forest with drilling supplies.

Like Bishop Canyes, who used Tsalickis's air taxi service to descend like an avenging angel on sinners in his vicariate.

Besides hides and animals, Mike's most coveted export was cocaine. And it was cocaine that would cause his arrests in 1975 and 1988. The latter date marked one of the largest cocaine seizures in American history, 3,270 kilograms (over 7,000 pounds) of cocaine at Tsalickis's warehouse in Tarpon Springs, Florida. The cocaine, worth an estimated $1.4 billion, was shipped from Colombia to St. Petersburg, Florida, by Tsalickis's freighter, *Amazon Sky,* in 700 hollowed-out cedar boards, which were then trucked north to Tarpon Springs. More than 1,000 people, it was estimated, were involved in the packing and smuggling. Tsalickis, who owned lumber mills in Leticia and Brazil, was believed by the Drug Enforcement Agency to have been linked to the Mafia in Cali since 1984.[15]

But it was the 1975 arrest that revealed that more was at stake than drug smuggling. Between the arrival of Dee Williams in 1967 and Tsalickis's first arrest eight years later, the CIA's counterinsurgency operations in Bolivia, particularly—but also in Peru and Ecuador—greatly enhanced the power of drug-smuggling uniformed warlords and Nazi refugees. The springboard for these operations and their onerous result was the search for J. C. King's old prey, Che Guevara.

TILLERS OF THE GRAVEYARD

Felix Rodriguez hoped that his arrival in La Paz was the beginning of better days. He had worked since 1963 running communications for CIA-funded raids out of Anastasio Somoza's Nicaragua to Cuba. The raids were designed to sabotage Cuba's socialist economy, increase shortages of goods and services, and weaken its image as an economic alternative to the "people's capitalism" exemplified by the American corporation. Although such attacks could only stimulate the Soviet-style garrison state that could tarnish Cuba's image abroad, the raids were meant to punish Cuba for that very dependence on the Soviet Union for survival.

Rodriguez began this work after President Kennedy's assassination, when the CIA, nervous about all the Secret Service agents who descended on the Agency's South Florida headquarters on November 22 looking for files on Cuban exile organizations,[16] shut down its Florida base and moved its operations to more secure bases abroad. All went well until 1965, when his commandos mistakenly attacked a Spanish freighter, killing the captain and injuring the crew. In the ensuing international uproar, the CIA closed down the operation and moved ships and some of the Cuban exiles to the Congo. Che Guevara had been spotted there, leading followers of assassinated premier Patrice Lumumba against the army of Colonel Joseph Mobutu.

Now, two years later, Rodriguez was getting another crack at Cuba's former foreign minister. Che had been sighted in a remote area south of Santa Cruz, known mostly for Indians, American missionaries, oil, and cocaine.

As in Southeast Asia and later in Southwestern Asia (Afghanistan and Pakistan), the CIA's secret war in South America led it into conflict with official U.S. policy. The CIA provided arms and equipment (including air transportation) for uniformed warlords who were financed by revenues from cash crops grown by peasants and processed into narcotics. Such operations created a network for clandestine international arms deals that could finance illegal CIA wars without congressional knowledge, much less oversight.

Behind this entanglement of the CIA with drug traffickers, ironically, were a handful of economic forces of more respectable appearance: multinational conglomerates that had increasing domination over the world's commercial agriculture. The problems posed to subsistence farmers in the Third World by the growth of well-financed commercial agriculture were overwhelming: the buying up of fertile lands; the use of pesticides and herbicides that poisoned the waters; and the use of expensive fertilizers, techniques, and harvesting machinery to generate high volumes of products that, in turn, drove down the prices of farm products in the national and world markets.

On the brink of losing their lands, peasants and small farmers increasingly turned to cash crops that commanded higher prices and better income: poppy in Asia, marijuana and coca in the Americas. Laws against marijuana, cocaine, and heroin did not stem the demand or, therefore, the supply. Local warlords or military and police officials, using arms and equipment provided by the CIA and the Pentagon "to fight communism," established protection rackets that often mushroomed into full-scale trafficking, including processing plants and laundering money through banks. As with Air America in Southeast Asia, the CIA's aviation contractors in Latin America became indirectly involved in the trade by asking few questions about the cargo of CIA clients or became directly involved as participants in drug runs.

In 1967, the center of both the German community in Bolivia and of the country's growing illicit cocaine trade was the Santa Cruz region, east of the Andes. One of the most powerful Germans in Bolivia at that time was a middle-aged merchant named Klaus Altmann. His real name was Klaus Barbie, the "Butcher of Lyons," who had escaped prosecution for mass murder in France through the assistance of the CIA, which used him as an "asset" in the Cold War.[17] (It was one of Barbie's intermediaries, according to one report, who helped doom MIR guerrillas in Peru in 1965 by supplying them with defective weapons and wrong ammunition on behalf of a Bolivian gunrunner known to MIR as Klaus Altmann.[18]) Barbie's partner in "business" affairs in Lima was Friedrich Schwend, formerly Hitler's official SS counterfeiter, and now the self-appointed minister of finance of Nazi funds smuggled out of Germany and used to finance the German

THE SLAUGHTER OF THE INNOCENTS

exile network's often illegal ventures, including gunrunning and cocaine trafficking.[19] Like most German communities in the big cities, Santa Cruz's Germans had supported the CIA-backed military coup of Air Force General René Barrientos in 1964. Few places could have been more hostile to the presence of the Argentine revolutionary and guerrilla ally of Fidel Castro, Che Guevara.

Guevara's presence in the area was not suspected until March 1967, when his group of guerrillas first engaged Bolivian soldiers in combat. The fight was premature. Originally, Guevara had planned to use Bolivia as a training base and staging ground for guerrilla operations in neighboring Argentina, Peru, and possibly Brazil. His vision was a continentwide revolution. The Bolivian Amazon, particularly the Beni region, was chosen because it was remote from roads, yet straddled the Peruvian and Brazilian borders. Mario Monje, leader of the Central Committee of the Bolivian Communist party, was supposed to coordinate "the matter of Brazil with [Lionel] Brizola, the brother-in-law of deposed Brazilian president João Goulart."[20] Peruvian leadership was to be provided by Juan Pablo Chang, a Peruvian of Chinese lineage called "El Chino," who had participated in the planning of the 1965 guerrilla campaign of Héctor Béjar's National Liberation Army in the Andes, but not its ill-starred execution. Of the three, only El Chino actually ended up involved in Guevara's campaign, first as an observer and trainee and then as a fighter.

Monje withdrew after learning that Guevara was to lead the guerrilla war without being subject to Monje's political control. The same formula—independent leadership of the guerrillas by the guerrillas—had worked in Cuba. But there, Fidel Castro was already a famed rebel, if not national hero, the young lawyer who had stormed Batista's Moncada Barracks. Guevara, although a legend in his own time, was not Bolivian. The older Bolivian Communists felt offended, and Monje would not follow up on his earlier pledge to participate; rather, young Communists who elected to join Guevara were expelled from the party. From then on, Guevara was doomed. Monje's rejection effectively isolated Guevara from his closest political base of support in Bolivia's cities and mines, where the Communist party was the most efficiently organized political force on the Left. The arms-supply link with Peru across Lake Titicaca never materialized. Neither did any link to the restless Indian miners in the mountains, despite their suffering that June some of the worst massacres by the army since the 1952 revolution.

But the greatest disaster for Guevara was his own second and final choice for an area of operations: a rugged range of hills located between Santa Cruz, the eastern capital of Bolivia, and the oil town of Camirí to the south. The area was penetrated by two familiar American interests. Gulf Oil had a large concession near Camirí. American Protestant Fundamentalists had a concession there, too, but theirs was of souls and minds. The area was home to 15,000 Guaraní Indians,

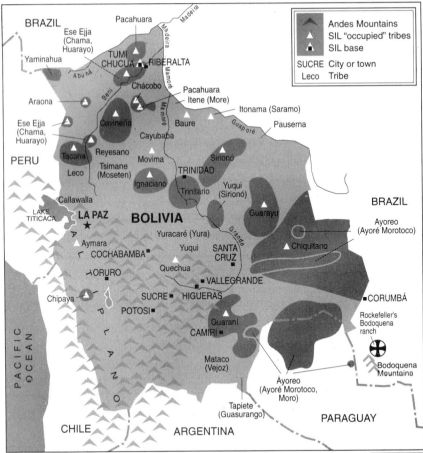

Bolivia's Indians and SIL (1978)

Sources: *Forjando un Mañana Mejor, 1955–1975* (La Paz: Ministerio de Educacion y Cultura and Instituto Linguistico de Verano, 1975); Walter Dostal, ed., *The Situation of the Indian in South America*, pp. 417–19.

who were long acculturated to oil wars since the 1932–1935 Chaco War drove many of them to flee to Argentina. Any armed revolt in an area where American oil companies had interests was bound to draw the local CIA station's early attention—and Washington's concern. Guevara must have known this and, indeed, seemed to relish Barrientos's admission in July that the legendary Che was leading the fight.[21] And Che also should have known that the Indians probably had grown accustomed to the presence of Bolivian soldiers (mostly also Indians) in their midst and would not see troops as a shocking invasion to be resisted. But he could not have known that another force was aggravating the fear and suspicion of local Indian peasants: the German-Bolivian community in nearby Santa Cruz.

THE SLAUGHTER OF THE INNOCENTS

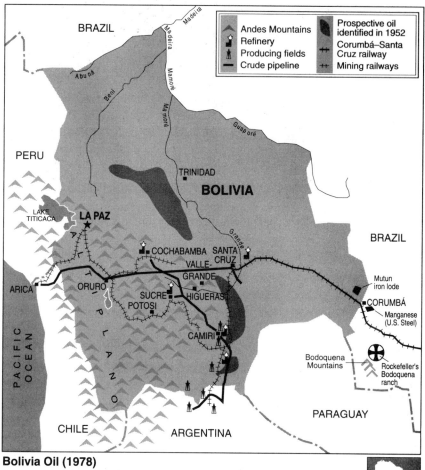

Bolivia Oil (1978)

Sources: *International Petroleum Encyclopedia*, 1983 (Tulsa, Okla.: PennWell Publishing Company, 1983); *Peruvian Times*, 1952.

Vehemently right wing, and probably the most powerful influence on La Paz's military high command, the German Bolivians were becoming deeply involved in turning the Indians' peaceful coca-leaf trade into a plague of violence through the processing and trafficking of cocaine.

The cocaine trade, in fact, was already so widespread in the guerrillas' area of operations that Guevara's training camp was first discovered by police looking for a cocaine-processing plant, not for revolutionaries.

"They only looked over the house and observed some strange things, such as calcium carbide bought for our lamps, which had not been taken to the caves," Guevara wrote in his diary. The policemen, mistaking the camp for the factory, collected a few jars of chemicals "and withdrew with the warning that they knew everything and [we] had better take them into account."[22]

In Bolivia, as anywhere, drug smuggling quickly corrupted all levels of society. The $450,000 that Gulf Oil admitted giving as "political contributions," mostly to El Presidente Barrientos between 1966 and 1969,[23] played its role, but left few roots in local villages. Cocaine did, making for networks of informers everywhere.

Cam Townsend's SIL missionaries had entered the area in 1957, just as Gulf Oil was also moving in to exploit a huge 1.1-million-acre concession granted by the government of Victor Paz Estenssoro. Three years later, Gulf struck oil and gas at Caranda, west of Santa Cruz and just north of where Che Guevara's guerrillas would end up making their last stand. SIL remained farther south, near Camirí, where Guevara's march to his death began.

THE STING OF ISOLATION

On May 28, 1967, Che occupied the village of SIL's Guaraní translator, Harry Rosbottom, but found no American presence, at least not physically. SIL's translator and his family had been withdrawn "on furlough."

Called Caraqatarenda, Guaraní for "place of the cactus," the village lived up to its name: Guevara got no recruits. The Guaraní did not appreciate the usual military practice of detaining civilians to prevent them from warning that a village was being advanced upon. The town was taken without much difficulty, but not the Indians' evangelized hearts. Using commandeered oil trucks, Guevara then moved north from one Indian town to the next, writing IOUs for store merchandise he seized and distributed to the peasants. But still there were no recruits.

Advancing north along the "oil road" that connects Santa Cruz with the Camirí oil field, Guevara defeated an army detachment that was sent to stop him. Then, when his vehicles failed and planes appeared overhead, he decided to swing west toward the mountains and melt into the forest.

Despite these bold early victories, the political war was going badly. The Guaraní proved more conservative than Guevara had anticipated. "Complete lack of incorporation of the peasants," he wrote in his diary, "although they are losing their fear of us, and we are succeeding in winning their admiration. It's a slow and patient task."[24]

The army was doing everything it could to make the task impossible. Unable to rout Che's guerrillas, it turned on the Indians. "The army issued the communication about the detention of all the peasants who collaborated with us in the zone. Now comes the period when both sides shall exert pressure upon the peasants but in different ways; our triumph will mean the qualitative change for a leap in development."[25]

But it was not to be. Part of the reason Guevara himself discovered in the town of Espino: "It is a Guaraní community whose members are very shy and speak or pretend to speak very little Spanish."[26] The Indians were unwilling to join a revolution that was not yet their own. And Che lacked the linguistic talents of SIL's Harry Rosbottom to give them more confidence in him; Quechua lessons taken in training proved useless.

Military victories, Che had written in Cuba, were not enough to ensure success; political victories were needed. Politically isolated, military victory, aside from a few local skirmishes, was fleeting. "The army goes on without being organized and its technique does not improve substantially,"[27] he noted after defeating an army detachment in Guaraní country, but even then, so early in the campaign, powerful forces from the Colossus of the North were descending to remedy the problem.

Already, thanks to Bolivian deserters, his training camp had been located "with absolute precision,"[28] Che fumed. A week after his first clash with Barrientos's troops on March 23, the *Times* of London's Murray Sayle arrived. One of the first reporters on the scene, Sayle was also spying for the United States. He had accepted "an unofficial assignment by the Americans who wanted to know whether these rebels really existed." Sayle confirmed that they did and gave another startling piece of information: "Among the rubbish neatly raked from the [training camp's] dormitory area, I found a picture of Dr. Che Guevara taken in a jungle and a copy of a speech by General Vo Nguyen Giap, the North Vietnamese victor at Dien Bien Phu, translated into Spanish."[29] Only the previous year, Che had sent a message to Third World revolutionaries gathered in Havana for the Tricontinental Conference, pledging "two, three, many Vietnams." If Vietnam had become a horror to the Vietnamese, it also had become Washington's nightmare.

Alarm bells rang in Washington's inner sanctum. Barrientos already had dispatched his air force chief of staff to the Brazilian junta and to the regimes of neighboring Paraguay, Argentina, and Peru, to ask for their cooperation in sealing off Bolivia's border. Peru's President Belaúnde pledged his support, as did the military rulers of Brazil and Paraguay; Argentina did more, offering to intervene with troops if necessary.

It was not necessary. Washington's counterinsurgency machinery sprang into action. Twelve years had passed since C. D. Jackson, who had emphasized psychological warfare, was replaced by a man more sympathetic to covert military solutions, Nelson Rockefeller. Those dozen years had been wasted.

Santa Cruz soon had visitors: Aurelio Hernandez, one of the Cuban exiles the CIA had placed in Bolivia's Ministry of the Interior, arrived with four military attachés from the U.S. Embassy in La Paz.[30] C-130 transports from the Panama Canal Zone also began landing at Santa Cruz. They unloaded napalm; weapons; radios; and that most important mainstay of jungle patrols, medical supplies, something Guevara, a chronic asthmatic, would be denied after his supply caves were unearthed in August. A few miles south of Guevara's abandoned training camp, two Green Berets were photographed training Barrientos's soldiers.

In Washington, on April 8, the secretary of state's limousine pulled up to the Pentagon. Dean Rusk, his face tired from daily encounters over the Vietnam War, was meeting with counterinsurgency experts Walt Rostow and William Bowdler of Johnson's National Security Council. This meeting, however, was not about Vietnam. It was a secret strategy session about Bolivia. Attending were CIA Director Richard Helms; General Robert Porter, chief of the Southern (Latin American) Command; and other top officials.

These men pored over their options and ruled out massive U.S. military intervention. Che Guevara must not be given the "two, three, many Vietnams" he sought in his message "from somewhere in the world" to the Tricontinental Conference. Instead, covert action, the kind of strategy that would not rouse new concerns among an American public already alarmed by the increasing violence in the Vietnam adventure, was the chosen road.

Yet the plan was straight Vietnam: isolate the guerrilla zone, offer a price on Che's head to gain informants, use "interrogation" to force prisoners and suspected sympathizers to talk, employ sophisticated aerial surveillance to locate the guerrilla camps, and send in shock troops that were especially trained in jungle warfare on search-and-destroy missions. It had worked in Peru. It was supposed to be working in Vietnam. So why should it not work in Bolivia?

And the propaganda value of Guevara's presence outside Cuba could be enormous. From the start, it could be denounced to Bolivians and the world as a foreign invasion. In September, at the Punta del Este conference, Rusk would charge just that. He did not mention that the Green Beret leading the battle in Bolivia, Major "Poppy" Shelton, was a veteran of similar U.S. search-and-destroy missions in Vietnam. On April 12, 1967, the first group of what would be a sixteen-man Green Beret task force left Panama for Bolivia. By the end of the month, the embassy's senior military attaché and the Berets' leader had scouted the Santa Cruz area and picked out a sugar mill north of the city. The mill was called La Esperanza, Spanish for "Hope." Shortly thereafter, 600 freshly drafted Indians arrived for the first drills that would teach them the pride of being "El Ranger."

In the years ahead, charges would abound of SIL's complicity in the CIA's hunt for Che. None would be proved. The closest were claims that an SIL agronomist in Colombia boasted of helping locate Che through Indian informants while he was in Bolivia. SIL denied these, as well as the claim that a JAARS pilot had participated in the CIA's aerial search for the guerrillas. For many critics, it was not impossible, or even out of character, given charges of JAARS's "transport" and mapping role during the CIA campaign against the MIR in Peru (a claim subsequently denied by one SIL official), or SIL's own pride in being of service to governments, maintaining military Helios, leasing Helios, even SIL's own uncritical

　　　　　　　　THE SLAUGHTER OF THE INNOCENTS

reference in 1961 to the Peruvian military's assuming SIL was willing to engage in "espionage" along the Peru-Ecuador border.[31] But it was not necessary, either, for the CIA to recruit JAARS to hunt Che. Because of the presence of oil and mining companies in the area, there were plenty of bush planes and military planes. These planes were not very effective, though. Guevara was unconcerned about the frequent bombing and strafing by Bolivian propeller fighters. As Vietnam was demonstrating, such attacks were fruitless against guerrillas who were on the move beneath the jungle canopy.

On September 18, Che grew worried when "at dusk a small plane and the mustang [a propeller fighter] flew over the zone suspiciously."[32] The planes did not bomb or strafe, which bothered him. What were they doing?

His instincts were right. The planes were "pinpointing every single heat source on miles and miles of winding infrared superfilm," reporter Andrew St. George later explained.[33] These heat sources were matched against small grids of the area's rugged terrain mapped earlier by U-2-like camera operations. With the aid of informers, Guevara's new area of operations was located, and the planes homed in on his group's campfires. The planes easily tracked the men's movements in the jungle because, contrary to many later reports, guerrillas who are innocent of such high-tech surveillance do cook; at least Che's did, according to his diary.

Guevara continued moving toward the more populated area, to the western mountains, hoping to recruit more politicized peasants and miners and to find medical aid for his group's wounded doctor. Reaching Pichacho, "the peasants treated us very well," he noted with relief. But at the next town, La Higuera, "everything had changed: the men had disappeared and there were only a few women." An old man was questioned, and a merchant arrived "very nervous"; but "despite the lies they told us," Che let them go, a trademark of the guerrilla strategy to win people over.

The merchant was actually an army spy, one of many sown throughout the area as part of the CIA strategy, and the army had the town surrounded. Suspicious, Che had just gone out toward the summit of the hill to inspect the area when "shots from all over . . . announced that our men had fallen into an ambush."[34]

Murder in a Schoolhouse Jail

Disaster struck with a hailstorm of lead, killing some of Che Guevara's most experienced men. Gathering his wounded, Guevara retreated into a narrow forested canyon that led down to one of the great tributaries to the Amazon, the Rio Grande. He hoped to move down the river valley and escape from the canyon after nightfall. But the U.S.-supplied helicopters had moved the 600 Rangers who had been trained by the Green Berets to strategic locations. The Rangers closed the knot. There was no escape. During the battle, Che was wounded in the leg, his rifle barrel smashed by a bullet, allowing the Rangers to take him alive. Other wounded guerrillas, including El Chino, were also captured and returned to La Higuera. In La Paz's presidential palace that night, the lights stayed on. Barrientos and top officers of the junta, reportedly including Minister of Education General Hugo Banzer, deliberated over Che's fate. Was he more dangerous dead or alive?

In the darkness, the 400 Indians of La Higuera shared the military quarantine that descended like a pall over Che and his comrades. The town would remain quarantined for months, a futile effort to hide the decision the regime would make about Guevara's fate. Inside the town's two-room earthen-floored schoolhouse, Che, bound and seated, smoked a pipe lit for him and watched soldiers divide his belongings among themselves. His requests that his cuff links be given to his son were ignored; he remained calm. But when an officer grabbed his hair and tried to take his pipe, shouting "Ha! You are the famous Che Guevara!" he sprang to life. "Yes, I am Che. A minister of State too! And you're not going to treat me like that!" and he kicked the officer into the benches. The Rangers' commander intervened. Instead of being shot, Che won respect. A medic was brought in to examine his leg wound.

When morning came, Guevara asked to speak to the schoolmistress. "I was afraid to go there," the twenty-two-year-old teacher told a Catholic priest, "afraid he would be a brute. But instead I found an agreeable-looking man, with a soft and ironic glance. . . . It was impossible for me to look him in the eye."

As an introduction, Che mildly pointed out a grammatical error on one of the drawings on the wall, then spoke of the alternative he championed. He looked at the school's dirt floor, its partly collapsed roof, its dim light. "You know that in Cuba there are no schools like this one. We would call this a prison. How can children of the *campesino* study here . . . it's antipedagogical."

"We live in a poor country," she answered.

"But the government officials and the generals have Mercedes cars and plenty of things. . . . Verdad? That's what we are fighting against."

"You have come a long way to fight in Bolivia."

"I am a revolutionary and I've been in a lot of places."

"You have come to kill our soldiers."

"You know, a war is either won or lost," he said with a gaze she later described as "unbearable. Piercing . . . and so tranquil."[35]

A helicopter arrived bearing high-ranking officers. The mayor of the village later insisted that junta members tried to interrogate Che and that Che spat in their faces. He knew that the decision to kill him had already been made, and he refused to give them any moral victory.

The mayor also remembered an American.

The CIA's Felix Rodriguez had reached Bolivia in August. Rodriguez had spent the last two months improving communications between army units on the ground and the air force surveillance planes overhead. More important, he stressed the necessity of coordination among intelligence agencies for the success of a counterinsurgency operation. Rodriguez and Gonzales built up psychological profiles on the guerrillas that were designed to help the Bolivian commanders identify individuals in the command structure and anticipate how the guerrillas would act under a situation and where they would move.

When Rodriguez arrived with Colonel Zenteno at La Higuera, the Bolivians had already killed El Chino. A survivor of Héctor Béjar's National Liberation Army, El Chino would never lead a revived Peruvian guerrilla movement. Another of Che's wounded companions was brought in, shot in the face, and placed next to El Chino's body. After Zenteno gave up trying to get Che to answer his questions and left, Rodriguez began photographing Che's diary and other documents. Then he set up his R5-48 portable communications system, made radio contact with the CIA, and began pounding the keyboards, sending out his cipher groups, oblivious to all but his coded report. At 10 A.M. he received a phone message allegedly from the Bolivian command at Vallegrande: "You are authorized by the Superior Command to conduct operation Five Hundred and Six Hundred."[36] Five hundred was the code for "Che," and six hundred was the code for "dead."

Rodriguez later claimed that he begged Colonel Zenteno to try to get Barrientos to change his mind. The CIA wanted Che alive for interrogation in Panama, he explained. "But if you cannot get the counterorder, I give you my word as a man that at two P.M. I will bring you back the dead body of Che Guevara."[37]

Rodriguez had talked with Guevara and surprised himself by coming to respect not only Che's refusal to discuss his specific operations, but his courage as he faced certain death. Che had already heard two of his companions being shot in the next room. "He did not say anything about the shooting, but his face reflected sadness and he shook his head slowly from left to right several times."[38]

Rodriguez left the actual murder to a lower-ranking Bolivian soldier whose courage had to be fortified by alcohol. "Sit down!" the soldier ordered Che. The prisoner refused. "Why bother? You are going to kill me." The soldier turned as if to leave, then spun about, firing off a burst of his automatic rifle. Che crumpled to the floor, still alive. Only then did the Rangers enter the room and fire into the body, carefully avoiding Che's face. Rodriguez had left strict orders that there must be no question about Che's identity for the world press.

Che's body was strapped to the runner of a helicopter. The chopper looked like a giant wasp carrying prey in its feet when it descended on Vallegrande's airport. The eerie scene created chaos among the throng of waiting reporters and soldiers. Rodriguez turned the body over to a CIA partner. He left with two souvenirs: Che's Rolex watch and a chronic shortness of breath. Rodriguez would see Che's ghost for the rest of his life. "Che may have been dead, but somehow his asthma—a condition I had never had in my life—had attached itself to me. To this day, my chronic shortness of breath is a constant reminder of Che and his last hours alive in the tiny town of La Higuera."[39]

News of Che's death, repeating the regime's claim that he had been killed in combat, swept across Latin America. General Barrientos and the commander-in-chief of the armed forces, General Alfredo Ovando, obsessed with being able to prove that Che was indeed dead, ordered Che's hands cut off and preserved in alcohol before having the body burned. The ferocious Ovando actually wanted Che's head, Rodriguez later admitted. "Fortunately, he was subsequently convinced that such an act would go beyond propriety."[40] The man who oversaw the disposal of Che's remains, Barrientos's Minister of Interior, Antonio Argueadas Mendieta, eventually was so moved by guilt—and fear of the Bolivian fascists around him—that he fled Bolivia, made a public confession of his CIA ties, and defected to Cuba, bringing with him Che's diary, his death mask, and his hands.

As for Barrientos, in April 1968 the Gulf Oil helicopter he was riding exploded. Within six months, his vice president was deposed by General Ovando.

Meanwhile, the repression of Indian miners continued, and the legend of Che Guevara grew to saintly proportions, his face a picture of martyrdom often seen propped on the dashboards of buses throughout the Andes, right next to the portrait of a bleeding, enthroned Christ. Che Guevara, atheist, had been absorbed like so many gods of the past into the religious cosmos of Indian need.

The Birth of Dissent

Felix Rodriguez's work did not end with the death of Che in Bolivia. His next CIA assignments led him to Peru via Ecuador in 1968. In Ecuador, he spent several months training military personnel in secure communications and interrogation techniques.

The Ecuadorians listened eagerly. They were part of the new breed of junior officers who had been trained in the United States or through military aid and FBI programs for leadership—in the civilian sector, as well as the military.[41] A little over a year would pass before their ambitions would be given official U.S. sanction by presidential envoy Nelson Rockefeller, champion of "the new military" in Latin America.

Rodriguez moved on to the Campa Indian region of Peru to accomplish the same ends. One of the CIA officers who had overseen the operation against Che in Bolivia had also been transferred to Peru.[42] Something big was about to happen, but not an antiguerrilla campaign. With the MIR and Héctor Béjar's National Liberation Army destroyed and El Chino dead, there was no immediate guerrilla threat left.

Rodriguez was assigned to train the same unit that the CIA and the Special Forces had set up to hunt down the MIR. The unit, now called *Los Sinchis*, although officially under Peru's national police, was actually part of the CIA-trained network controlled by the chief of national intelligence, General Armando Artola.

The nature of their training by U.S. Special Forces instructors gave clues to the Sinchis' future use: parachute jumping. Rodriguez, a communications and intelligence officer, was, of course, no paratrooper, but King's new ANDCO director, Dee Williams, the former Green Beret in Vietnam, was. Williams helped Artola's troops master the art.

The purpose beneath all this training exploded to the surface in October 1968. In a series of coordinated lightning moves, including the mobilization of the Sinchis, the military overthrew President Belaúnde Terry. Belaúnde had been worried about the CIA force, preventing it from visiting Lima and eventually moving to dismantle it.[43] But he had moved too late. With the installation of a military junta, the Sinchis fell under the control of the new minister of the interior, General Artola.

The new regime, seeking to consolidate its base of popular support, immediately moved to nationalize Standard Oil's holdings.

Later, when trying to account for Peru's nationalization of Standard Oil and the subsequent "drift to the left" that would lead to Artola's dismissal as minister of the interior, some would blame liberals like Senator Robert Kennedy, who tolerated dissent and rebelliousness in the provinces. Artola's loss as a CIA asset was a blow to the conservative wing of the Agency that had been identified with King. They never forgot that it had been Kennedy's comments during a tour in Peru in 1965 that gave the Peruvians their first ally among prominent Americans over the most fundamental challenge to their national sovereignty—Standard Oil. To Agency veterans like King, the danger posed to vital American interests like Standard Oil by men such as Kennedy was unthinkable. The enemy was not just outside. Bobby Kennedy had said it himself: The enemy was also within.

34

THE ENEMY WITHIN

THE SECRET ALLIANCE

Robert Kennedy was everything Nelson Rockefeller was fast not becoming: young, energetic, and liberal, the professed champion of the disaffected, the poor, and the angry. Above all, despite his family's wealth, his political banner's egalitarian message was persuasive. His scrappy concern for the forgotten was more believable to millions than was any lofty Rockefeller sincerity about the rights of the poor. Yet there were two sides to Robert Kennedy's personality: a compassionate side, earnestly searching for justice and equal rights, and a competitive side, sometimes so ruthless that it could stun the unsuspecting.

It was the strength of character in both sides that made Robert Kennedy attractive to some and dangerous to others.

By 1967, his popular following was obvious, especially to Kennedy's arch foes in the political arena: President Lyndon Johnson and Johnson's major Republican rivals for the American presidency, Richard Nixon and Nelson Rockefeller. The aura of the Kennedy name hung like a pall over the presidential aspirations of each man.

By early 1965, having emerged from mourning his brother, Robert Kennedy was carrying on with his life as senator from New York. He had turned into something of an iconoclast, speaking for those who disapproved of U.S. government policy at home and abroad. Years later, it would be revealed that the CIA considered spying on Senator Kennedy almost as important as gathering intelligence on the Soviet Union.[1]

The move toward open criticism of "Johnson's war" was difficult for Kennedy. Yet it was only the last of a number of disputes he had with Johnson and Rockefeller, both of whom had opposed Kennedy's decision in 1964 to unseat New York's Republican senator, Kenneth Keating. Keating was an ally of Nelson and the Cuban exile community and had been a sharp critic of President Kennedy's handling of the Cuban Missile Crisis. Robert Kennedy had played a key role in urging the negotiated settlement. Both Rockefeller and Johnson also knew that Kennedy's bid for a seat in the U.S. Senate was really the beginning of his campaign for the White House. Robert Kennedy, like Richard Nixon, became their common political foe, creating a surreptitious political alliance that soon deepened into personal friendship.

Outside Johnson's and Rockefeller's families and closest aides, no one knew that this bond existed. Johnson had too much to fear from his own party if word got out. Nelson's 1966 reelection as governor had made him a viable contender for the 1968 Republican presidential nomination. But the 1964 disaster had left him gun-shy, a behavior so uncharacteristic of him that Johnson could not have missed it. Nelson was less of a threat to the president than was Robert Kennedy, and would remain so as long as Nelson had Kennedy to worry about in his own backyard. Kennedy was now a contender for Nelson's own base among downstate minorities and the upstate poor, the latter still following a Republican rural tradition at the polls.

The political war for that base had begun almost as soon as Kennedy took office. Kennedy's first speech on the Senate floor offered an amendment to the Appalachian aid bill to include thirteen upstate New York counties in the War on Poverty that his brother had planned. Those counties had been overlooked by "shortsighted," state officials, he said, in a stinging criticism of the governor. Nelson reacted angrily, claiming that twelve of the thirteen counties had no need for federal aid to their poor and that the thirteenth would have benefited more from a federal highway to open it up to more industry and commerce for business investors. But even Nelson's ally, Republican Senator Jacob Javits, saw Nelson's excuses as politically lame and signed on to Kennedy's amendment, voting with the majority to pass it.

Kennedy's pronouncements about U.S. policy toward the Third World likewise were tinged with sympathy for the poor. Following the April 1965 U.S. invasion of the Dominican Republic, Kennedy had questioned the unilateral character of Johnson's decision to intervene and the message that it sent to Third World people who were suffering under repressive regimes. "Our determination to stop Communist revolution in the Hemisphere must not be construed as opposition to popular uprisings against injustice and oppression just because the targets of such popular uprisings say they are Communist-inspired or Communist-led or even because known Communists take part in them."[2] Johnson had justified sending in more than 22,000 "neutral" troops on the basis of CIA reports alleging that local Communist party members were involved in the popular revolt that demanded the return of former President Juan Bosch, a victim of a military coup in 1963. Kennedy was not impressed by the CIA's claims or by the election staged the following year to ratify the regime that was in power.

Nelson, on the other hand, was impressed, along with his ally in the Liberal party, Adolf Berle,* and gave support to the grateful President Johnson.

Backdrop to Tragedy: Eating Rockefellers for Breakfast

Two months later, during a trip to Latin America, Kennedy's differences with Rockefeller on foreign affairs became more direct. Kennedy had a bitter argument with the U.S. deputy chargé d'affaires in Peru over Standard Oil's and the embassy's equating Standard Oil's interest with those of the United States.[3] Fortunately, the explosive Standard Oil controversy did not specifically come up at Kennedy's press conference. "He did receive [a] general question on nationalization," Ambassador J. Wesley Jones reported to Secretary of State Dean Rusk, "to which he responded that [the] question of nationalization [was] to be decided by [the] country concerned and would be respected by us so long as there is just and fair compensation."[4]

If Kennedy's comment gave oil executives and embassy officials the jitters, it was still only official U.S. policy and probably the best that could be expected from the liberal senator. As Kennedy left Lima for Santiago, the capital of Chile, and a tour of conditions in American-owned mines, the embassy was relieved it had been spared controversy.

However, Kennedy had had a "frank and free" discussion that did not get reported to the ambassador, or to Rusk, until a story appeared in the local press. He had met with Peruvian artists and intellectuals, who immediately asked about Standard Oil. "Are you aware of the problem of IPC [International Petroleum Company, Standard's subsidiary in Peru]?" one of the artists asked.

"I understand President Belaúnde is trying to get an acceptable solution from the company," said Kennedy.

"Perhaps. But first it should be established what is understood as acceptable and then, what is more serious, that such [a] solution will not be accepted by IPC."[5]

The Peruvians were only repeating what was commonly understood in both Lima and Washington. Johnson had already sent to Peru fellow Texan Robert B.

---

*An earlier U.S. Marine intervention had given Berle his start as a lawyer for sugar interests represented by the law firm of Nelson's father's legal counsel, Thomas Debevoise. He had opposed the marines' occupation. Now, as chairman of one of the largest importers of black-strap molasses from the Dominican Republic, the American Molasses Company, he supported it.

THE SLAUGHTER OF THE INNOCENTS

Anderson, Eisenhower's former deputy defense secretary and treasury secretary and a man who knew the Rockefellers, having worked with Nelson in the Special Group and having been involved in subsequent business ties between Texas oil interests and Nelson's International Basic Economy Corporation. Anderson had called on President Belaúnde in mid-July "to explain to him that his demands [were] beyond anything an international oil company could accept."[6]

Then David Rockefeller made a trip to Lima, arriving a week ahead of Kennedy, to persuade the Belaúnde government to back down. Belaúnde's officials listened closely, for here was an unparalleled combination of financial and political power in the flesh of one man. David was not just the brother of one of the best-known Americans in Latin America, and not just president of the Chase bank. He also represented the Council for Latin America, the enlarged offspring of the Business Group, which now numbered over 200 companies, 85 percent of all American firms conducting business in Latin America.[7] Furthermore, as if to make the change of fortune since Dallas absolutely clear, David Rockefeller now had official status in the Johnson administration as chairman of the finance committee of the U.S. Business Advisory Council of the Alliance for Progress.

But whatever Rockefeller gained for Standard Oil was undermined when Senator Kennedy arrived. Kennedy's comments about Standard Oil's recalcitrance were published in the Peruvian press.

"So then, why don't you act?" Kennedy reportedly asked the Peruvians.

"Because pressures exist which involve the power of IPC and the problems of credit badly needed by the country," one of them replied. "In some way, if you will pardon the expression, it could be said to be blackmail."

Kennedy stayed on the offensive, challenging the Peruvians to act for themselves:

> In the conversation I had with the students at the Peruvian-American Cultural Institute, I heard many complaints and criticisms, but not once was I told about what they thought or what they supposed should be done in this or that problem. I think that the action is up to you people. President Kennedy had to act against some large American firms; Argentina has cancelled its oil contracts; years ago Mexico nationalized its oil, and what happened? It is up to you not to get overwhelmed and to act according to your interests and according with what you consider is more convenient. And nothing can happen, as nothing happened before.

Kennedy then asked for views on "the most difficult and urgent problem that your country is facing": assimilation of the Indians into the rest of the population. Kennedy had touched on a central dynamic in the hemisphere's history. But he had not grasped that if it was left to private entrepreneurs allied to U.S. corporations, development would continue to take place at a cost to Indian peoples that far outweighed any benefits. Kennedy saw the problem in the traditional sense— "integration" of the indigenous population—which could be addressed as a civil rights issue. Indian rights was a cause that would hold his interest to his last days, in the United States, in Peru, and later, during this tour, in Brazil, where he would slog through Amazonian mud stripped to his waist to push a dugout canoe through the backwaters to visit the Hixkaryána Indians, a tribe already "occupied" by missionaries from the Summer Institute of Linguistics. But Kennedy's interpretation of the problem was basically a legal one of ensuring civil rights for non-whites. His failure to address more fundamental questions about a society that perpetuated institutionalized inequities rang hollow in the ears of his listeners.

"I don't agree," one Peruvian reportedly had told Kennedy. "What does indigenous mean? Has this word any pejorative meaning?"

Peruvians were proud of their Indian ancestry.

"The problem lays in the need of change or the structure of the government. As things are in this moment, decisions are not truly taken by the [Belaúnde] government. . . . The power lays, at least for the most important decisions, in the oligarchy of the exporter groups, which in the last instance are representatives of foreign economic powers of the large enterprises and companies."

Kennedy's belief that in the United States democratic government already prevailed over privilege was unshaken. "Do you really believe," he asked, "that the enterprises and companies have so large a political influence here and so much political influence over the U.S. Government? During President Kennedy's administration, businessmen did not enter the White House. My trip to Latin America was certainly not looked on with favor by the State Department. But from what you people tell me, I can say again that it is up to you to change things if they are as you said."

"And how about the Marines?" asked one man, referring to the recent Dominican intervention.

"Surely you are not aware, Mr. Kennedy," said another, "that not long ago Mr. Rockefeller said in Lima that future financing is conditional to the favorable solution to the problems of the IPC and the International Telephone Company."[8]

Kennedy's face tensed. "And what importance do you give to this kind of threat? We Kennedys, we eat Rockefellers for breakfast."[9]

The U.S. Embassy in Lima asked Kennedy "for a statement clarifying" his view. Kennedy refused either to denounce the Peruvians or to retract his statements. "Someone at the gathering leaked the incident to the press," Kennedy aide Richard Goodwin later told Rockefeller family historians Peter Collier and David Horowitz, "and it got around. When we stopped in Argentina, a reporter rushed up to Bobby and said [in a mistranslation that nonetheless managed to capture a sense of the way Latin American policy was made in the Johnson administration]: 'Senator, is it true that you have breakfast with Rockefeller every morning?'"[10]

The Johnson White House was not amused. "The stories have him in effect saying: 'Go ahead and nationalize. Others (Argentina, Brazil, Mexico) have done this. In the end, things work out,'" William Bowdler reported to National Security Adviser McGeorge Bundy. "I don't see that there is anything that we can do about the episode," Bowdler concluded.[11]

Lyndon Johnson disagreed. Something could be done.

Kennedy's views on the Dominican Republic and on Peru won him no praise in Room 5600. Neither did his damning of apartheid in South Africa as an evil comparable to "discrimination in New York, serfdom in Peru, starvation in India, mass slaughter in Indonesia, and the jailing of intellectuals in the Soviet Union."[12] David Rockefeller was the most active American banker promoting financial ties with South Africa.*

The summer of 1966, Kennedy locked horns with the Rockefellers over Brooklyn's Bedford-Stuyvesant area. Moved by the riots there and in Los Angeles's Watts district, Kennedy had decided to address the despair in the ghettos with a demonstration project. While his staff walked the streets to interest community leaders, he approached a number of corporate leaders to join in a nonprofit community development corporation in Bedford-Stuyvesant. Despite an exodus of whites encouraged by real estate speculators and declining essential services, a stable home-owning middle class still existed to offer leadership for reforms. Rockefeller had done little to help them. He had cut funds for the community's Youth-in-Action programs and, as a result, job training and college preparatory courses suffered.

Of all the business leaders Kennedy approached, only one refused to join his board: David Rockefeller.[13]

The list of conflicts continued to grow, ranging from preserving the Hudson River Valley from Rockefeller's energy and highway schemes to Kennedy's aborted effort to form a Democratic reform coalition to rob Rockefeller of his favorite campaign target, Tammany Hall "bossism." More than anything he did in New York, however, Kennedy's attack on Rockefeller's mental health care system hit a raw nerve. Senator Kennedy was especially critical of Rockefeller's draconian Addict Treatment Act, which considered addiction a crime to be punished, not an illness to be treated. He conducted an unannounced inspection of Rockland State Hospital.

At this institution, Kennedy protested that children were kept tranquilized and ignored. Patients were put in "cells," he charged, where, "amidst brutality and human excrement and intestinal disease," they were forced to live in conditions "worse off than in a zoo."[14]

Nelson was furious. He countered that New York's programs had been "the blueprint for the federal program presented to the Congress by the late President Kennedy." When it was revealed that the New York legislature had received similar

---

*Chase had recently purchased a major holding of South Africa's second biggest bank, Standard Banks, Ltd.

critical reports, Nelson turned on the legislators. They had not appropriated the funds he wanted, he insisted.

Kennedy acted as if Rockefeller simply was not informed by the state bureaucracy, which itself was a subtle condemnation of the Rockefeller administration. "I am sure that when you are aware of the extent of unused federal assistance available, you will wish to make the appropriate changes in the relevant state machinery to insure that you will be properly informed in the future."[15]

Nelson turned defensive, which only made matters worse. "I trust that . . . the obtaining of assistance for the mentally retarded," he wired back, "will not depend on your acting as the political broker."

"He is jeopardizing the future of children and others for the benefit of his own political administration," Kennedy told reporters at a press conference. "Evidently, he . . . doesn't want to cooperate at all in any matter in which I am involved."[16]

Kennedy also requested a state investigation of the deplorable health conditions at camps set up for migrant workers, most of whom were Hispanic, African American, and Native American. He urged trade unions to organize the migrants. "I guess I'm very gloomy about things," he once told journalist Jack Newfield. "I don't expect much anymore. But you have to make yourself keep trying. Whenever I see a Cesar Chavez, or a Marian Wright, or a VISTA volunteer, then I get reconvinced that maybe one person can actually make some difference. But mostly I expect the worst."[17]

For Kennedy, "the worst" had already begun to reveal itself abroad, in "the inhuman slaughter in Indonesia, where over 100,000 alleged Communists have been not perpetrators, but victims," and where "the New Order" of CIA-backed generals granted huge oil concessions to Standard Oil of New York (Mobil) and offered the copper of Irian Jaya, the former Dutch New Guinea, to another Rockefeller family holding, Freeport Sulphur.

But the very *worst* was Vietnam. And it was over this issue that Robert Kennedy engaged in his greatest confrontation with Lyndon Johnson and Nelson Rockefeller.

SHOWDOWN OVER VIETNAM

A true believer in counterinsurgency, Bobby Kennedy had agreed with his brother's deployment of U.S. Marines to back the Saigon regime. Yet by July 1965, he had noted with dismay the ascendancy of Dean Rusk and Walt Rostow, both advocates of escalation and both veterans of the Rockefeller Brothers Fund's Special Studies Project that had called for increased arms spending for counterinsurgency warfare.

That month Kennedy released to the press a speech he planned to deliver to the CIA's International Police Academy. "Victory in a revolutionary war is not won by escalation, but by de-escalation. . . . Air attacks by a government of its own villages are likely to be far more dangerous and costly to the people than is the individual and selective terrorism of an insurgent movement."[18] He did not include these words when he actually gave the speech, although they were widely quoted. He simply was not yet ready to break with Johnson. But he was convinced that conventional warfare and indiscriminate carpet bombing would not win the hearts and minds of anyone. "If we regard bombing as the answer to Vietnam, we are headed for disaster," he finally said in January 1966.

Kennedy was moved further against the president's policy by Johnson's subsequent renewal of the bombing of North Vietnam; by Johnson's snubs of the Senate's constitutional right to advise on foreign affairs; and, finally, by the February 1966 televised debate at the Senate Foreign Relations Committee hearings between its chairman, Senator William Fulbright, and Dean Rusk. Thinking that Fulbright was too intellectual to be effective, Kennedy answered with his own proposal for a negotiated compromise with Ho Chi Minh.

The attacks on him were immediate, from Vice President Hubert Humphrey, from McGeorge Bundy, and, behind the scenes, from Johnson. Stunned, Kennedy remained silent for almost a year. "I'm afraid that by speaking out I just make Lyndon do the opposite, out of spite. He hates me so much that if I asked for snow, he would make rain, just because it was me. But, maybe I will have to say something. The bombing is getting worse all the time now,"[19] he said in December.

On March 2, 1967, Kennedy broke his silence. A week earlier, U.S. artillery had shelled across the Demilitarized Zone into North Vietnam for the first time. Then U.S. warships initiated twenty-four-hour firing on sea routes into North Vietnam, and warplanes began indiscriminately mining North Vietnam's rivers.

Kennedy delivered a 6,000-word speech on the Senate floor. By most accounts, it was a remarkable moment in American history. Kennedy accepted part of the blame for how far things had gotten out of control. "Three Presidents have taken action in Vietnam. As one who was involved in those decisions, I can testify that if fault is to be found or responsibility assessed, there is enough to go round for all—including myself." Then he urged Americans to accept their own responsibility as citizens for the actions of their government. "All we say and do must be informed by our awareness that this horror is partly our responsibility. . . . It is our chemicals that scorch the children and our bombs that level the villages. We are all participants . . . we must also feel as men the anguish of what it is we are doing."[20]

Then, after transparently hollow praise for Johnson's "restraint," he called on the president to accept Soviet Premier Aleksei Kosygin's recent assertion that a halt to bombing would allow negotiations to begin.

Johnson reacted quickly. He invited all fifty governors to the White House for consultations. He had Secretary of State Rusk and General William

Westmoreland announce their disagreement with Kennedy. Both actions paved the way for Johnson's formal rejection of Kennedy's proposal on March 9.

For all his posturing, however, Johnson fretted that peace—in Vietnam or the United States—was not in sight. So, like most men of rural America, Johnson turned to the God of his Texas forebears or, at least, to God's self-appointed spokesmen.

BLESSINGS FROM BILLY

The Fundamentalists gave Johnson their support without hesitation. This battle was part of God's test of Americans as the Chosen People of this age, destined to defeat Satan's godless legions and lead the world into a holy new order.

Billy Graham was the most visible Protestant preacher who rallied to Johnson's side. Between patriotic exhortations at crusades in cities across the Sunbelt, he held formal prayer breakfasts at the White House, offered reports from crusades overseas, and generally tried to soothe the president's worried brow. He had been doing so since the first frightening days after John Kennedy's death, when he compared Johnson's task to that of Joshua after Moses' death. Such assertions, in the light of hindsight on Vietnam, should have been a testament to Graham's gift of prophecy, considering Joshua's own scorched-earth policy when he led the host of Israel down the hills to conquer the people living in the land of Canaan. But Graham could not contain himself to that vision; he moved rapidly to more American, democratic examples: "As God was with Washington at Valley Forge and with Lincoln in the darkest hours of the Civil War, so God will be with you."[21]

Johnson loved the analogy, asking Graham to keep writing him letters like that one. Graham obliged. Johnson became "not only the choice of the American people, but of God. You are as truly a servant of God as was your great grandfather Baines when he preached the gospel."[22] No one was surprised when the Grahams stood beside Johnson in the president's reviewing stand for the inaugural parade or when Johnson had Graham lead an interfaith service or when Johnson presented Graham with the Big Brothers of America Man of the Year Award, a prestigious recognition usually bestowed on corporate liberals like Nelson Rockefeller.

Finally, as he had done with so many before, Johnson called in his IOUs. He wanted Graham to visit Vietnam for Christmas.[23] No one knew of the president's request for this command performance; Graham sent out Christmas cards that year, saying that the invitation came from General Westmoreland. Almost half a million American GIs were in Vietnam by then, and thousands more would follow. Graham spoke glowingly of his trip to Vietnam and of Johnson as a "deeply religious" man. He called for the "success of soldiers in the pacification program." Vietnam, he explained, was "wealthy enough to feed all of India and China."[24]

Shortly afterward, the White House received an unusual request from one of

Graham's fellow preachers in his hometown, Montreat, North Carolina. The preacher had joined the U.S. Navy Chaplain Corps and served a stint as a White House chaplain. Rev. Calvin Thielman, an enthusiastic supporter of the president and Presbyterian pastor to Graham's wife, wanted to go to Vietnam.

"He wants to observe the effectiveness of civic action in which the military is involved, with special attention and emphasis on the Montagnard tribes," a White House aide noted. "Wishes to study literacy work by AID. To assist, he wants to take with him William Cameron Townsend."[25]

35

APOCALYPSE NOW: THE TRIBES OF INDOCHINA

Battling the Hordes of Satan

Vietnam begins with a blast of hot air. The land takes your breath away as soon as you step out of the air-conditioned jet, as if already demanding your surrender to its climate, its ways, its ancient national will.

Calvin Thielman could not see the mountains from Saigon's airport, but he knew that a hundred or so miles away were the Central Highlands where missionaries of the Summer Institute of Linguistics (SIL) did most of their work. There, surrounded by tropical forest that hid the enemy, SIL translators labored over the linguistic secrets of some dozen hill tribes. Every time Thielman came to Vietnam, he made a point of visiting these brave bearers of the Word. He could not, however, see the full scope of the impact of Bible translation work, which extended to tribes farther north, in the highlands of Laos and Thailand. For Thielman, as for most Americans in those years, it was quite enough to see Vietnam.

This land was the front line of the U.S. war in Southeast Asia. Beyond the flatlands of coastal Vietnam, the Central Highlands climbed up to the steep Annam mountain chain that divided Vietnam from the Asian interior. Here tribal peoples, who centuries before had been pushed out of the fertile flatlands by the Vietnamese, scratched a living out of stony soil and hunted the great forests. They lived without regard for the legal formalities of borders that obsessed the

Vietnamese authorities. They crossed at will into the hills of Cambodia and Laos, where poppies had been grown since the previous century, when the British used gunboats and modern armies to force its lucrative opium trade upon a resistant but weak China; now, thanks to the CIA's secret war, opium bound for the European and U.S. markets was becoming the major cash crop.

Cambodia and Laos were both officially neutral in this war, Cambodia by the design of its ruler, Prince Norodom Sihanouk, and Laos by the 1962 Geneva Accord negotiated by Averell Harriman with China and the Soviet Union. But Laos's neutrality was fiction, and not just legally, as in the case of Cambodia (whose territory was also used as a supply line to the Communist-led National Liberation Front [NLF] in South Vietnam), but militarily as well. Caught between efforts of North Vietnam's Ho Chi Minh to ship supplies and reinforcements to his NLF allies in the south, and U.S. determination to stop this aid while it armed its own client regime in Saigon, Laos for a time would become the target for more U.S. bombs than North Vietnam. Most of these bombs were dropped by U.S. planes flying from bases in neighboring Thailand, the projected industrial heartland of the subcontinent and inspiration of the most grandiose of dreams of Western investors for Southeast Asia.

During this period, Nelson Rockefeller and his brothers had invested in a number of companies through IBEC in Thailand: Siam Fibrecement, one of Thailand's major industries; Thai Coconut Industries, which used coconut husks to manufacture upholstery fiber for European markets; Thai Celadon, Ltd., which produced high-fired stoneware for American and European markets; and the Thai Industrial Development Corporation, a joint venture with Denmark's East Asiatic Company. In addition, John D. Rockefeller 3rd's importing firm, Products of Asia, had led IBEC into Bangkok Industries and his Design Thai operations, which provided Thai textiles for Lord and Taylor's racks of expensive clothes in Manhattan.[1]

IBEC's Thaibec Investment Service steered investors toward Thai opportunities for profits, including IBEC's own associated companies: Star of Siam, Silk of Siam, and Arbor Acres Thailand. IBEC's Chicago-based insurance firm, ROLIBEC, had moved into IBEC's office in Bangkok in 1961 and used its Thai subsidiary to score commissions as general agents for reinsurance and life insurance companies doing business in the Pacific Rim countries. ROLIBEC provided in-house insurance for these IBEC firms, as well as for the Rockefeller Foundation and such U.S. financed nonprofit and international agencies as Planned Parenthood and the Southeast Asia Treaty Organization. Its corporate clients included some of the largest American companies doing business in Thailand: Shell Oil, Colgate Palmolive, Kraft Paper, Eli Lilly, Upjohn, IBM, John Deere, 3M Corporation, and Far East Mining. Using Bangkok as the regional base, ROLIBEC made "quite handsome profits" between 1967 and 1971 by tripling its portfolio in Japan and writing off over 50 percent of the purchase price as "goodwill."[2]

ROLIBEC expanded into Hong Kong, Seoul, Tokyo and Yokohama, and

Vientiane (Laos). It was also a war profiteer, "Vietnam business"[3] generating much of its income. Its clients included Bird & Sons,[4] which flew supplies from Thailand to the CIA's Hmong army in Laos, supplementing the CIA's Air America, which also was a ROLIBEC client.[5]

By 1971, when the vice president of ROLIBEC had hopeful words for the Thai generals who had overthrown the government ("There is sort of an air of expectancy . . . as many people believe that the generals mean business. . . . We can be mildly optimistic"),[6] IBEC would be using the guaranty of the State Department's taxpayer-funded Overseas Private Investment Corporation to insure its poultry farms in Thailand against possible losses.

Nelson was aware of the economic stake. As far back as his involvement in the Truman and Eisenhower administrations, the United States was interested in Southeast Asia. Eisenhower had justified U.S. support for France's efforts to hold on to her colonies as "the cheapest way that we can . . . to get certain things we need from the riches of the Indochinese territory and from Southeast Asia."[7]

Vietnam was "the controlling hub," as Secretary of State John Foster Dulles put it, of an area rich in tin, tungsten, oil, rubber, and iron ore. As communist-led nationalist revolutions against Western domination spread from China into Vietnam, Laos, and Thailand, the war in South Vietnam became a war for the entire Southeast Asian mainland. In this war, Thailand was not only a staging base for attacks on the Ho Chi Minh Trail in Laos and North Vietnam; it was also Southeast Asia's industrial heartland, the hydroelectric foundation for the development of the entire 236,000-square-mile Mekong River Basin, and the strategic gateway below the Himalayas to Burma and ultimately to the jewel of the former British Empire, India.

By 1967, the war had made Thailand, the largest Southeast Asian country, host to U.S. bombers, 20,000 U.S. troops, and teams of Green Berets and CIA officers. It also hosted the largest U.S. corporate investment in the region. Thailand had become the Brazil of Southeast Asia. U.S. mining and hydroelectric projects in Thailand were financed by such banks as David Rockefeller's Chase. The country's giant Mekong River had become the object of vast development schemes, rivaled in the Third World only by those proposed for the Amazon.

Calvin Thielman, who knew the president of the United States, understood why a Texas politician like Lyndon Johnson could not bend to Ho Chi Minh. The war was simply a test of wills. On one side stood all that seemed righteous: a Christian, Bible-quoting fellow Southerner leading the Western world's superpower in defense of a beleaguered ally. On the other side hid the hordes of Satan, stalking the jungle to murder and frighten peasants into submission, all directed by the inscrutable Ho hundreds of miles to the north, who, in turn, was controlled by other Evil Emperors thousands of miles away in Peking and Moscow. There was no wondering why Vietnamese peasants should be willing to take on such incredible odds against so powerful an enemy as America and to suffer and die, simply because someone hundreds of miles away ordered them to do so: communist brainwashing techniques were legend. There were also the lack of the Western respect for human life and the fatalism of the Asian mind, both alleged traits long detected by Western scholars and missionaries. It was all so Oriental, so difficult for the Calvinist folks back home to understand, so different from what Rev. Thielman's congregation could feel: a patriotic outrage against foreign intrigue and threatened conquest of the "little guy" who, being a member of our "free world," was—as Lansdale said of Magsaysay—"*our* guy."

Some Protestant missionaries felt little hesitation about describing the war as a great "opportunity" to harvest souls for the Lord, giving out gospel readings to grim-faced Vietnamese draftees at Saigon's induction center. After his first visit to Vietnam, in 1965, Thielman told a reporter that "some of our military people are almost like missionaries," and the missionaries were almost like the military. "I talked with twenty-one missionaries—Catholic and Protestant—out there. Not one of them thought we should withdraw."[8]

Nothing he saw two years later changed his mind. "I spoke in free conversation (with no military personnel present) with approximately 50 missionaries of at least a dozen religious groups in Vietnam and Thailand," he reported to President Johnson on his return. "I found no missionary who felt we should pull out of Vietnam."[9] The communist-led NLF had to be defeated.

Johnson's intensified bombing of North Vietnam was another matter. During his visits to U.S. Civic Action projects among the hill tribes, Thielman found missionaries and "at least three colonels engaged in pacification . . . who felt the bombing was an error and should be phased out."[10] More troops should be sent instead, the colonels advised.

This was the kind of advice Johnson's top White House advisers did not want to hear, and it went nowhere but to the files. A condition of Thielman's visit was that there should be no advance publicity. To ensure that there were no leaks, the White House refused Thielman's request to take Cam Townsend along to help him study the effectiveness of AID's literacy work among the Montagnards.[11]

Cam's reservations about sending SIL recruits to Vietnam dated back to 1962, when Christian and Missionary Alliance missionaries were seized by NLF soldiers after defying a warning not to repair a bridge the NLF had burned. Around the same time, a Central Highlands village housing an SIL team, Hank and Evangeline Blood, came under Viet Cong attack for a second time.[12] The Bloods had been away, but the NLF had come looking for them, perhaps mistaking them for U.S. government "advisers" or believing that they were part of the American intervention symbolized by the Green Beret fort forty miles away at Banmethuot.

But the Cold War momentum sweeping Americans toward their destiny in Vietnam was too great to resist. By 1963, SIL's Fundamentalist affiliate, the

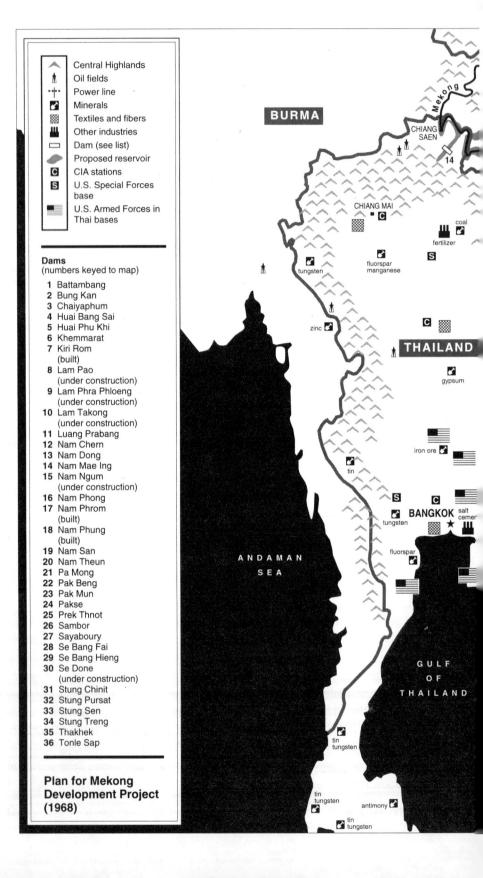

Legend

- Central Highlands
- Oil fields
- Power line
- Minerals
- Textiles and fibers
- Other industries
- Dam (see list)
- Proposed reservoir
- **C** CIA stations
- **S** U.S. Special Forces base
- U.S. Armed Forces in Thai bases

Dams
(numbers keyed to map)

1 Battambang
2 Bung Kan
3 Chaiyaphum
4 Huai Bang Sai
5 Huai Phu Khi
6 Khemmarat
7 Kiri Rom
   (built)
8 Lam Pao
   (under construction)
9 Lam Phra Phloeng
   (under construction)
10 Lam Takong
   (under construction)
11 Luang Prabang
12 Nam Chern
13 Nam Dong
14 Nam Mae Ing
15 Nam Ngum
   (under construction)
16 Nam Phong
17 Nam Phrom
   (built)
18 Nam Phung
   (built)
19 Nam San
20 Nam Theun
21 Pa Mong
22 Pak Beng
23 Pak Mun
24 Pakse
25 Prek Thnot
26 Sambor
27 Sayaboury
28 Se Bang Fai
29 Se Bang Hieng
30 Se Done
   (under construction)
31 Stung Chinit
32 Stung Pursat
33 Stung Sen
34 Stung Treng
35 Thakhek
36 Tonle Sap

**Plan for Mekong
Development Project
(1968)**

BURMA

CHIANG SAEN

14

CHIANG MAI

coal

fertilizer

fluorspar
manganese

tungsten

S

zinc

THAILAND

gypsum

iron ore

tin

S

C BANGKOK

salt
cement

tungsten

fluorspar

ANDAMAN
SEA

GULF
OF
THAILAND

tin
tungsten

tin
tungsten

antimony

tin
tungsten

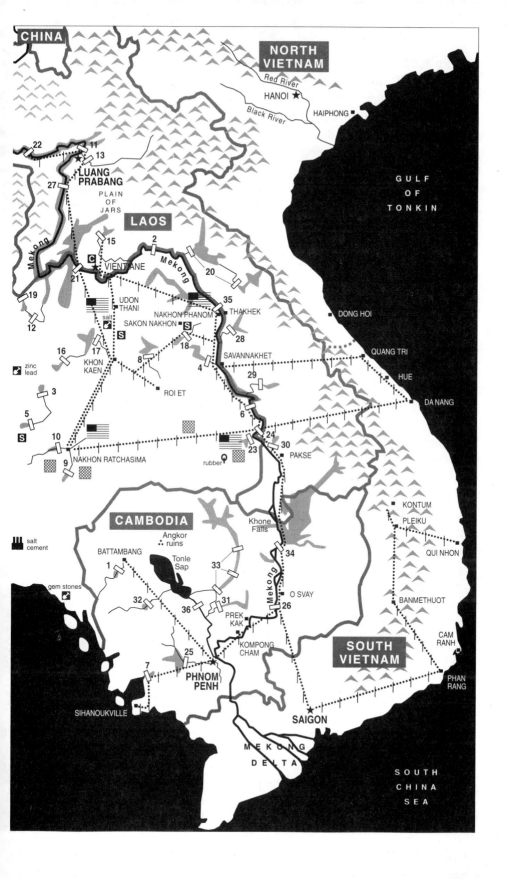

Christian and Missionary Alliance, had 125 missionaries in twenty cities and villages in South Vietnam; SIL, with 41 translators, was right behind, working among fourteen tribes. That year SIL suffered its first violent deaths since Cam founded the organization thirty years earlier. Two SIL families were caught in a crossfire when the Army of the Republic of South Vietnam (ARVN) came upon armed black-pajama-clad peasants of the NLF conducting a roadblock and search for medicine. Two SIL men and one child were killed.

Cam eulogized the missionaries as "Wycliffe's first martyrs: We believe that a host of new recruits will pick up the task that fell from the limp hands of our martyred colleagues." Yet he was uneasy. The Cold War that had propelled SIL's expansion was now extracting a price in blood.

Cam used the deaths to encourage recruitment for the new Colombian and West African mission fields, not for Vietnam.[13] However, SIL's enthusiastic leader in Vietnam, Hank Blood, wanted more recruits. Cam responded, "I don't feel that I should put pressure on recruits to go to a certain field."[14]

He did not have to. Billy Graham's and Calvin Thielman's championing of the Indochina mission fields was accomplishing more for Hank Blood's cause than anything Cam could have done. SIL's former top pilot, Larry Montgomery, also was providing the CIA's Casirio "Chick" Barquin, the Agency's top air operations officer and liaison with the Helio Aircraft Corporation, with the names of key officials of the Missionary Aviation Fellowship (including his old friend, director Betty Greene) and the director of the Christian and Missionary Alliance in Vientiane, Rev. T. J. Andrianoff, in 1964, during the time that the CIA was building its secret army in Laos.[15]

In 1967, as B-52s carpet-bombed North Vietnamese villages and rumors abounded in South Vietnam of massacres of civilians in rice paddies and as millions of Americans found it increasingly difficult to accept "His will" as coming from the Prince of Peace, SIL signed its first bilingual education contract with the Saigon regime and USAID's Office of Education. AID provided the money—more than $160,000—and CIA-directed Montagnard "Rural Reconnaissance Patrols" assisted by Green Berets provided the protection. From the seventeen tribal groups it eventually "occupied," SIL recruited and trained some 800 Montagnard teachers.[16] In March, workshops for the Highlander Education Project were held in four local languages. SIL helped set up the Linguistic Circle of Saigon, just as it had done in Mexico decades earlier. To aid the war effort more directly, SIL also provided information on these same tribes to the U.S. Marines for compilation into a "trans-cultural" area handbook on Montagnard cultures.[17]

Just how deeply SIL had become involved in the war was revealed in 1968 by *National Geographic* magazine. Howard Sochurek was a veteran reporter who had written favorable accounts of the war in 1964 and 1965.[18]

On his 1967 trip, Sochurek had a guide: Patrick Cohen, SIL's translator

THE SLAUGHTER OF THE INNOCENTS

among the Jeh tribesmen. To the journalist, Cohen was living "in the great Christian missionary tradition that in Vietnam goes back to January 18, 1615, when Father Francesco Buzomi, a Neapolitan, landed in Hue." Confounded by animism, the European Catholics found a little better luck among the Vietnamese along the coastal lowlands. But in 1967, with the influx of American guns, medicine, and food to fight the holy war, the highland tribes experienced an unprecedented fervor for the Protestant God brought by the Americans. The Christian and Missionary Alliance built churches, SIL supplied translations of the Bible, and AID supplied the food and farming techniques. And the Green Berets provided the training that turned young tribesmen into "strikers" (the name the CIA gave to the CIDGs, the Civil Irregular Defense Groups). "They tried to break up infiltration routes from North Vietnam,"[19] a U.S. helicopter crewman explained. To boost morale, the Green Berets composed a marching song for strikers from the village of An Loc that was sung to the tune of "Onward Christian Soldiers." Still, the U.S. command at An Loc estimated that one local village's Viet Cong sympathies were probably as high as 25 percent.[20]

And the NLF forces around An Loc continued to grow, led by a Montagnard tribesman who was reported to be a major general in the North Vietnamese army. The NLF promised the Montagnards a degree of autonomy in postwar Vietnam. The Saigon regime, in contrast, had been jailing the leaders of the Montagnard autonomy movement since 1958. After ruthlessly suppressing Montagnard revolts in 1964 and 1965, the regime hastily redrafted its constitution to grant Montagnard representation in an all but impotent legislature. But the constitution and a decree promising the tribes land titles remained little more than paper. The regime offered only absorption into a South Vietnam ruled by a military clique and bloodshed in a CIA-directed war.

As the Montagnards' manhood was marched into the holocaust, their replacements became younger and younger. By 1967, Sochurek found boys under arms, "the proud possessors of transistor radios and aspirin tablets."[21] They were paid $12.71 a month. This was a cheap war for the CIA. It would continue despite enormous losses and long after the realization that the CIA's Montagnard army could not win.

Cam's translators, of course, did not see it that way. They were true believers in the war, as well as in the Word. They listened appreciatively to the American officials who explained the Montagnards' place in God's celestial plan: "Because they occupy a strategic position on the outer rim of China, they have an influence on the balance of power in Asia between China and the Western World. They most certainly can upset that balance in spite of their backwardness."[22]

And, after all, as Walt Rostow argued in the White House, was not China behind the Viet Cong and the Soviet Union, in turn, behind China?

To lift tribes out of such backwardness with the Light of the Word had

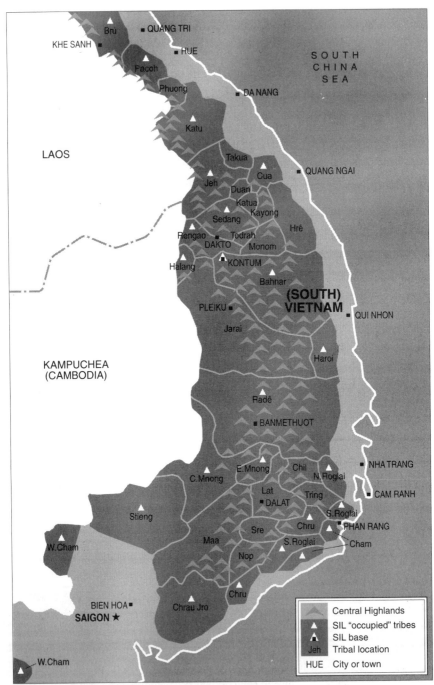

Tribes "Occupied" by SIL During Vietnam War

Sources: Nguyen Ngoc Bich, *An Annotated Atlas of the Republic of Viet-nam* (Washington, D.C.: Embassy of Viet-Nam, 1972), p. 40; Gerald C. Hickey, *The Highland People of South Vietnam: Social and Economic Development* (Santa Monica, Calif.: Rand Corporation, 1967), p. xv; Marilyn Gregerson et al., *Tales from Indochina* (Dallas: International Museum of Cultures, 1987); *Bibliography of the Summer Institute of Linguistics, Volume One: 1935–1975* (Dallas: Summer Institute of Linguistics, 1979).

always been SIL's mission. Why should Vietnam be any different? The Saigon government wanted SIL, the U.S. government wanted SIL, and so God must want SIL. The Montagnards, almost 2 million people in villages strung across 1,500 miles of mountains stretching from South Vietnam to the Himalayas, waited for deliverance from Satan.

They constituted 15 percent of the population of South Vietnam, 50 percent of the population of Laos, and 20 percent of the population of Burma. More important to the CIA devisers of the Montagnard "trip-wire" strategy to foil communist infiltration from the north was the land these tribes occupied: half of Burma, four-fifths of Laos, two-thirds of South Vietnam, and a good chunk of northeastern Cambodia.

Thailand, too, had hill tribes numbering some 200,000 people. Previously ignored by the U.S.-backed government in Bangkok, the tribes became important by 1967, when U.S. warplanes were flying daily out of some of the world's newest and largest air bases in Thailand. The largest base was in northeastern Thailand at Udorn, where the CIA had a huge helicopter, Helio, and DC-3 base-within-a-base to support its secret war in Laos.

The Udorn air base gave the surrounding area a priority in 1967 for Rockefeller funding of a study done in collaboration with the Rural Affairs Division of the United States Operation Mission (USOM) in Thailand. The study was conducted by Michigan State University's Nicolaas G. M. Luykx II (head of MSU's Pakistan Project), at the request of Clifton R. Wharton, director of the American Universities Research Program of John 3rd's Agricultural Development Council;[23] it involved interviews with regional and local government officials and village leaders to gather impressions on how well the Thai military regime's American-advised development projects and government infrastructure were progressing and how they were regarded by the local villagers.[24] As a Cornell graduate student, Luykx had done a similar Rockefeller-funded study of local government effectiveness in Vietnam, the Philippines, and Thailand in 1956, the year Diem proclaimed the independence of South Vietnam; Wharton called this new study "Udorn Revisited." The largest change, of course, was the presence of thousands of Americans and the economic domination of the area by the huge U.S. air base. But for many villagers, poverty remained, and the new American presence was symbolized by the constant procession of giant Air Force bombers roaring their domination of the skies to oxen and farmer alike.

The warplanes headed northeast, their mission to bomb Laos and North Vietnam. They were guided by the CIA's mountaintop directional beacons that were strung across Thailand and Laos's tribal highlands. In Laos, as the CIA's secret army of the Hmong tribesmen retreated steadily west toward the Thai border, Thai troops were being called into the fight in Laos's poppy-growing highlands. They were part of a strategy that relied on tribes that were financed partly by the opium trade.

It was then that the government in Bangkok suddenly took an interest in the schooling of Thailand's own mountain tribes. Assisted by the Asia Foundation (which had origins as a CIA conduit), the U.S. Information Agency, and the USOM, eleven Protestant missionary groups and several Catholic orders joined programs sponsored by the regime. These programs included civic action carried out by the Thai Border Patrol Police,[25] the very police organization that was involved in illegal opium smuggling.[26]

Unknown to the missionaries, the Border Patrol Police and Thailand's hill tribes were being drawn into a financial web[27] with threads that stretched back to the CIA station in Miami—the same station that recruited the Cuban exiles for the Bay of Pigs invasion.

At Chiang Mai, northern Thailand's most important trade center, the CIA set up one of its largest stations. AID's Accelerated Rural Development program in Thailand built roads, but the roads became more of a boon for heroin smugglers than for the Thai army, whose clumsy armored units found the highlands rough going. Thailand's largest tribe, the Lahu, and another large tribe, the Yao, had followed William and Harold Young, Baptist missionaries turned CIA agents,[28] in cross-border raids from Burma into China, the supposed evil force behind the revolution in South Vietnam. They reported by radio to a third missionary, Harold's son Gordon Young, who translated their reports and turned them over to the CIA chief of station, who doubled as the U.S. vice consul in Chiang Mai. To supply the Lahu warriors with arms without risking American helicopters so deep in enemy territory, the CIA struck deals with Shan tribal rebels in Burma. The Shan ran opium caravans southeast to Thailand and Laos and returned with weapons. A few extra weapons for CIA's Lahu strike forces along the Burma-China border could easily be accommodated in these caravans. Like the Shan, the Lahu were a dispersed people. They grew poppies as their principal cash crop and were involved in the opium trade.

Yet the missionaries kept their silence. Only the sheer ferocity of U.S. military operations in Southeast Asia forced Americans publicly to raise questions about what was happening in Chiang Mai.[29]

DEPOLITICIZING POLITICAL SURVEILLANCE

Nestled in the mountains of northern Thailand, Chiang Mai gave Americans stationed there a welcome relief from hot, humid Bangkok. Thais had been noticing an increasing number of Americans arriving in Chiang Mai since 1962, when CIA missionary William Young began his Lahu raids into Laos, as well as China. Chiang Mai's status as the last rail terminal in northern Thailand ensured its growth into a bustling little city with even a new university. But there was an older trade, opium. By 1967, competition for the opium trade forced the CIA-allied

　　　　　　　　　　　　THE SLAUGHTER OF THE INNOCENTS

Chinese Nationalist exiles, who had dominated the trade since 1947, to intervene.

Thai troops now flooded Chiang Mai to defend the north from the CIA allies they had always known were there. They were also there to back up "communist suppression operations" along the Laos border, where indiscriminate napalm bombing and massacres had provoked Hmong tribesmen to revolt. To supplement the widening counterinsurgency operations, the Lahu were again called up in the hills, along with draftees from Thailand's two other poppy-growing tribes, the Akha and the Lisu.

This was the backdrop for the CIA's and Pentagon's interest in the hill tribes of Thailand and in Chiang Mai as the base of operations for studying them. At stake were not only the air strikes launched against Hanoi from bases in northeastern Thailand, but the opium trade that paid for many of the arms used by the CIA's tribal and military allies in Southeast Asia's opium corridor. The opium trade moved southeast from Burma, through Thailand and Laos, and into South Vietnam, bringing money, corruption, addiction, and weapons. The lands it passed through were tribal lands, poor and potentially revolutionary, all of them requiring the careful collection of intelligence, all of them remote yet requiring constant surveillance.

Resting in the cool mountain air above the Ping River, Chiang Mai, with only 75,000 people, was famous for its old houses made of teak from nearby forests. It also sported four new hotels to accommodate throngs of tourists, who were attracted by the local tribal crafts. Beyond these mostly Hmong hamlets, deeper in the mountains, dwelled tribes whose isolation was seen as a breeding ground for subversion and revolution. To correct that situation, and to efficiently exploit the tungsten, manganese, and fluorspar lodes in the mountains south of Chiang Mai,[30] the regime was rushing an Accelerated Rural Development program to tie Bangkok to the backlands with modern roads built by the U.S. Army Corps of Engineers.

Lyndon Johnson had descended on Thailand in *Air Force One* in 1966 to seal an accord that gave him six air bases to bomb North Vietnam; in exchange, he pledged money, arms, and technical assistance. "Technical assistance" was a catchall; it included arms, as well as the Tribal Research Center in Chiang Mai, engineers, as well as anthropologists and linguists.

In the name of the United States and the Cold War, AID and Pentagon grants were given to discover why people in foreign lands were willing to join guerrilla groups and risk their lives, what local "sociopolitical structure and dynamics as well as the aspect of leadership resources would be of significance to military operations,"[31] and how ethnic minorities could be mobilized instead to support U.S. intervention. Subsequent investigation by the American Anthropological Association's Ethics Committee uncovered the fact that anthropologists had been given a priority in the project precisely because their work required them to know the area and win the trust of its people. Social scientists soon began churning out studies on the hill tribes of Southeast Asia, extending their usefulness to the American war effort. "Minority Groups in the Republic of Vietnam," for instance, was completed in 1966 by the Pentagon-funded Center for Research in Social Sciences (CRESS)[32] of American University, the same group that did similar studies for the Pentagon in Latin America.*

Tribal peoples became the focus of yet another social science think tank in northern Virginia called the Research Analysis Corp., whose studies included "The Mobilization and Utilization of Minority Groups for Counterinsurgency"; "Brief Notes on the Tahoi, Pocoh and Phuong Tribes of the Republic of Vietnam"; "The Customs and Taboos of Selected Tribes Residing Along the Western [Cambodian and Laotian] Borders of the Republic of Vietnam";[33] and "The Major Ethnic Groups of the South Vietnamese Highlands" and their "settlement pattern, social organization, and religious practices."[34]

The study on "Mobilization and Utilization of Minority Groups for Counterinsurgency" could have offered SIL's Dale Kietzman a few lessons on what the Pentagon and the CIA were looking for, assuming that a knowledge of CIA misuse of anthropological and linguistic data might have persuaded Kietzman to be less enthusiastic about identifying "potentially hostile" tribes and their locations on a map of the Brazilian Amazon. The Pentagon-funded study's stated concern was to target those tribal groups judged susceptible to "subversion in future communist wars of 'national liberation'" because of (1) the "history of hostility between them and the dominant ethnic group; (2) their location in remote areas and consequently their lack of close contact with the national government and its representatives; (3) the fact that they occupy terrain of strategic importance both to insurgent and government forces; or (4) a combination of these reasons."[35]

World War II's legacy of the social sciences at the service of political power, pioneered in the cultural and intelligence operations of Nelson Rockefeller's CIAA, had come to full, horrifying bloom.

In the summer of 1967, the Pentagon-sponsored Jason Division of the Institute for Defense Analysis (IDA) convened a Thailand Study Group to see how it could quietly enlist the aid of academics in counterinsurgency without causing a scandal like Project Camelot.

One of IDA's twelve member universities, the University of Michigan, was already deeply involved in Thailand, seeding the jungle with microphones and seis-

---

* CRESS had been set up to carry out research for the Pentagon under a more military-sounding name, the Special Operation Research Office. Following revelations of its sponsorship of Project Camelot's planned counterinsurgency study in Chile, it had to change its name. CRESS's classified area handbooks showed how to conduct psychological warfare that might complement low-intensity warfare. In 1967, to escape growing student protests, CRESS moved off American University's campus and disappeared into the folds of another Pentagon think tank, American Institute for Research, known charmingly as AIR. Based in Pittsburgh, it had only one foreign office: in Bangkok, Thailand.

mic devices to distinguish natural varieties of background noise (created by insects and animals) from human movements, so that troops, artillery, or bombers could be alerted.[36] That university also trained Thai officers in aerial surveillance technology and the analysis of imagery at its Infrared Physics laboratory at Willow Run.

To facilitate using the Tribal Research Center's resources and contacts (including its associated American anthropologists, linguists, and missionaries), the American Advisory Council for Thailand joined the Thai National Police in signing a contract with UCLA. The council's work was understood explicitly to be organized as "part of the operation of the U.S. Overseas Mission."[37]

Operating behind the advisory council was another organization with a larger regional vision: the Southeast Asia Development Advisory Group (SEADAG). In fact, the Advisory Council for Thailand was the creation of SEADAG.[38]

With SEADAG, the chain of manipulation in the Southeast Asian war, running from tribal recruits to missionaries and anthropologists to AID and the CIA, finally ended. It ended where it usually did, at the top, where purse strings were held by policymakers who just happened to control larger purses, literally the deposits and debts of whole nations. These were powerful businessmen, and among their leaders were the Rockefellers.

The Force Behind the War

SEADAG had been set up in the early 1960s as an Asian counterpart to David Rockefeller's Business Group for Latin America. Its membership included Rockefeller Brothers, Inc., Chase Manhattan Bank, the Rockefeller Foundation, Standard Oil of California, Standard Oil of New Jersey, Standard Oil of Indiana, and IBEC (which invested heavily in Thailand).

Ironically, of the five Rockefeller brothers, the one who became the most associated in the public eye with SEADAG was the least political: John 3rd. Unlike Nelson with IBEC, David with Chase Bank, and Laurance with Eastern Airlines, John 3rd had no great personal business interest, much less one in Vietnam. He was the quintessential naive philanthropist. He was "Mr. Asia," the leader of the Japan Society and the founder of the Asia Society. Yet it was this status and this last organization that tainted the Rockefeller name.

The man who, however inadvertently, pulled the Rockefeller name into the sordid spotlight the family had been trained to avoid was one of the Rockefeller family's most astute political operatives in Southeast Asia. The son of missionaries, Kenneth Todd Young had weathered a nationalist upheaval at Ling Nam University in China and escaped to the Sorbonne in the mid-1930s. Thanks to a teaching scholarship at Harvard, he became one of the best-connected economic thinkers at wartime Washington's Natural Resources Planning Board and the War Production Board. Then

Young became a political intelligence officer in the State Department and later vice president of Standard Oil of New York (Mobil). It was Young who paved the way for American backing of Diem during the Eisenhower Administration, when he was acting director of the State Department's Office of Philippine and Southeast Asian Affairs; in fact, it was he who drafted Eisenhower's fateful letter to Diem in 1954 committing U.S. support to replace the French colonialists.

In the late 1950s, Young went to work for Mobil's subsidiary in the Far East. With his rarefied background among missionaries and oil executives, his credentials were attractive to President Kennedy's counterinsurgency experts at a time when the CIA's "secret war" was being launched in Laos. In 1961, Roswell Gilpatric, Edward Lansdale, and Chester Bowles quietly nudged him into accepting the ambassadorship to Thailand.

With the stoic resolve of a professional, Young accepted Washington's orders to direct his own staff in Thailand to back the losing effort in South Vietnam. But he was unconvinced of the capacities of the U.S. Embassy in Saigon or of Washington's resolve to back Diem as long as Diem's troublesome in-laws, the Nhus, were dominant figures in Saigon.

By 1963, Ambassador Young had had enough. He decided to retire. By doing so, he averted personal political disaster in the short run, only to ensure it later.

His first stateside job was on John 3rd's personal staff. Then John 3rd took another fateful step: He made Young president of the Asia Society. This was not John's inspiration; Dean Rusk's State Department had suggested it.

Rumors of U.S. government direction of the Asia Society were already afloat when Young moved SEADAG into the Asia Society's four-story headquarters in Manhattan. John approved this relocation, despite SEADAG's obvious sponsorship by the U.S. government, the involvement of the CIA-funded Asia Foundation, and overt funding by AID. It was a sign of just how far the Rockefellers were willing to go in committing the United States—as well as their own name—to back the Saigon regime. This was not merely a matter of the Rockefellers patriotically doing what the U.S. government wanted; they wanted the U.S. government to do what *they* wanted: prevent the NLF from coming to power in South Vietnam, by war if necessary. Responding affirmatively to Rusk's people at State was essentially a matter of responding affirmatively to the implementation of a policy that was a reflection of their own ideological orientation. Packaged sincerely as patriotism, State's request could hardly be refused. Rockefellers, too, must be prepared to share the nation's risks during war.

The son who had been charged with defending the family's honor, who had taken pains to preserve a humanitarian, politically gray image of the Rockefeller Foundation, was now risking it all for the sake of victory in a war that was destroying the very art and culture he had championed as Mr. Asia. By 1967, the

Evangelist Billy Graham listens to former Rockefeller Foundation chairman and current secretary of state John Foster Dulles in 1956 after conferring in Dulles's home. Graham was about to leave on a tour of the Far East, where Dulles and his brother, CIA director Allen Dulles, had recently installed Ngo Dinh Diem as president of a newly declared South Vietnam, ignoring the Geneva accord calling for Vietnam-wide elections. (Courtesy of Associated Press/Wide World Photos)

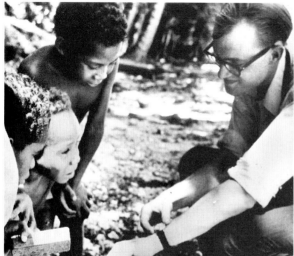

Michael Rockefeller, son of Nelson and Tod Rockefeller, shows his watch to children of the New Guinea tribe he was studying as a member of a Harvard expedition. Michael's search for artifacts for his father's Museum of Primitive Art revitalized the headhunting that took his own life in 1961. (Courtesy of UPI/Bettmann Archive)

Nelson Rockefeller stands in the family-donated wing of New York's Metropolitan Museum of Art, next to the *bisj* (revenge) poles that Michael collected from New Guinea's Asmat tribesmen. Some of the poles depict men wearing European-style hats, possibly the Dutch officers who shot up their village in 1958. (Courtesy of UPI/ Bettmann Archive)

The brothers Rockefeller in 1967. *From left:* David, Winthrop, John 3rd, Nelson, and Laurance. Each played a role in the current state of Latin America's economy: David in banking, Winthrop in cattle breeding, John 3rd in population control and agricultural development, Nelson in championing conquest of the frontier and "New Military" dictatorships, and Laurance in the development of resorts and venture-capital investments, sometimes as Nelson's silent partner. (Courtesy of UPI/Bettmann Archive)

IBEC garment sweatshop in 1966 in Bangkok, Thailand. This low-wage labor pool was the site of most IBEC investments in Southeast Asia before the escalation of the war in neighboring Vietnam. (Courtesy of the National Planning Association)

Two rivals for the 1964 presidential election. The Rockefeller Brothers Fund's Special Studies Reports, overseen by Henry Kissinger, had a major impact on the 1960 Kennedy campaign and the early administration. Many of the reports' authors went on to serve in key posts in the Kennedy administration, including the cabinet and the Pentagon's counterinsurgency command. Later, Rockefeller opposed Kennedy's policies, especially in Latin America. (Courtesy of the John F. Kennedy Library)

Rockefeller *(center)* continued influencing defense policies during the Kennedy years as chairman of the Governors' Civil Defense Committee, advocating "winnable nuclear war" and a massive fallout shelter program. (Courtesy of Associated Press/Wide World Photos and the John F. Kennedy Library)

General William P. Yarborough greets President Kennedy during Fort Bragg visit, 1961. A few months later Yarborough made a counterinsurgency survey in Colombia, returning with recommendations to set up a police state in rural areas where insurgents were active, including the registration, fingerprinting, and photographing of every man, woman, and child over the age of twelve and the use of drugs during interrogations. Later, Yarborough oversaw U.S. Army illegal surveillance of American civilians active in civil rights and antiwar movements. (Courtesy of the John F. Kennedy Library)

Aerial view of counterinsurgency forces arrayed for President Kennedy's visit to Fort Bragg, 1961. (Courtesy of the John F. Kennedy Library)

President Kennedy lays brick for a housing project in Bogotá, while Jacqueline Kennedy and Colombia's President Alberto Lleras Camargo, friend of Nelson Rockefeller, look on. Within two months, as Yarborough's Green Berets arrived, Lleras Camargo had authorized SIL's entry into Colombia's tribes. (Courtesy of the John F. Kennedy Library)

As in other countries, SIL's airplanes, airstrips, and communications tower (pictured here) at Lomalinda jungle base in Colombia were pledged to serve local government needs when called upon. Land for Lomalinda base was donated by a Colombian air force general. (Author photo)

Surplus military equipment was key to the early growth of Wycliffe's Jungle Aviation and Radio Service (JAARS). This Navy Catalina, pictured landing at SIL's Yarinacocha jungle base, was flown to Peru by former U.S. military mission member Larry Montgomery. During Montgomery's tenure as JAARS's chief pilot, JAARS trained the Peruvian air force in jungle flying. Montgomery took a leave of absence in 1961 to sell Helio Couriers, JAARS's favorite planes, to CIA-client regimes in Africa; the CIA contracted with the Helios' manufacturer for his services. Counterinsurgency planners used JAARS as their model for jungle communications and transportation systems throughout the Third World. (Courtesy of Wycliffe Bible Translators)

In 1963, a year after the Peruvian military, at the urging of candidate Fernando Belaúnde Terry, aborted the presidential election of Haya de la Torre, the new Belaúnde government awards William Cameron Townsend the Order of Distinguished Service upon his departure for Colombia to begin SIL's work there. (Courtesy of Wycliffe Bible Translators)

Townsend reviews Indian teacher recruits arrayed before SIL school in the Peruvian Amazon in 1964, premilitary instruction having been introduced at SIL's Yarinacocha jungle base as the army geared up for an expected counterinsurgency campaign against leftist guerrillas in the jungle. (Courtesy of *La Prensa*)

U.S.-supplied Venezuelan troops guard a food warehouse owned by Rockefeller's IBEC supermarket chain, CADA, c. 1963–1964. (Courtesy of the National Planning Association)

1964 was also the year that U.S. Marines were sent into the Peruvian Amazon in support of a Peruvian air force attack, including napalming, against feared "Mayoruna" (Matses) Indians defending their lands near the Brazilian border. The assault proved ineffective in the canopied rain forest, and the Belaúnde government turned instead to SIL. (Courtesy of *La Prensa*)

Conquest by love, 1969. This first photograph of Matses Indians was taken by SIL missionaries who "pacified" the tribe by learning their language from a captured Matses. SIL flew over their village and used wing-mounted loud-speakers to shout offers to help the Indians trade their pigskins for "valuable goods." Soon, despite SIL's efforts, instead of government demarcation of Matses lands, oil exploration crews arrived. (Courtesy of Wycliffe Bible Translators)

Green Berets lead Peruvian commandos into battle against leftist guerrillas and Campa Indians in the Peruvian Amazon, 1965. The commandos were trained at a "miniature Fort Bragg" set up by the CIA in the jungle. Hundreds of Campa Indians were killed by napalm dropped by the Peruvian air force. Some Campa Indians charged SIL with collaborating with the military in the attack. (Courtesy of the U.S. State Department)

Amazon Natural Drug Company president Colonel J. C. King (*left*), here receiving Distinguished Intelligence Award from CIA Director Richard Helms in 1967, was chief of the CIA's Clandestine Services in the Western Hemisphere. During World War II, King surveyed the Brazilian Amazon for Nelson Rockefeller. An associate of Adolf Berle, King was, in 1959, the first U.S. official to finger Fidel Castro and Che Guevara for assassination, and was present at the 1964 military coup in Brazil. *Inset:* King at his Virginia estate in 1963. (Courtesy of Eloise King Ricciardelli)

Mike Tsalickis, self-styled "Tarzan of the Amazon," was the host of SIL missionaries and other travelers through Leticia, Colombia's only port on the Amazon. Tsalickis also used Indians to boost his tourist trade. The Amazon's biggest exporter of animals, Tsalickis was also supply agent for Colonel King's CIA front, the Amazon Natural Drug Company. (Courtesy of James Holland)

After overseeing successful U.S. participation in the counterinsurgency campaign in Colombia, Ambassador Covey Oliver (*rear*) joined Tsalickis (in black shirt) in gator hunting in the Amazon in 1966. Shortly thereafter, Oliver appointed Tsalickis U.S. consul and was himself elevated to assistant secretary of state for Inter-American Affairs. (Courtesy of United States Information Service)

Tsalickis in handcuffs (*left*) after his 1988 arrest in Tarpon Springs, Florida, for attempting to smuggle the second-largest cache of cocaine in American history, over 7,000 pounds worth more than $1 billion, in hollow tropical lumber boards on his ship, *Amazon Sky*. (Courtesy of *St. Petersburg Times*; photo by Victor Junco)

While Rockefeller ally and treasury secretary C. Douglas Dillon listens (*right*), Cuba's foreign minister Ernesto "Che" Guevara defends the Cuban revolution and denounces Latin American governments' dependency on U.S. loans and arms. Foreign ministers conference at Punta del Este, Uruguay, 1961. (Courtesy of UPI/Bettmann Archive)

Nelson Rockefeller expresses his support to Cuban exiles protesting a CBS television appearance by Guevara during a visit to the United Nations, 1964. (Courtesy of UPI/Bettmann Archive)

Che Guevara (right), after his capture in the Bolivian jungle by Green Beret–trained rangers. The man in the Bolivian military uniform was actually the CIA's Felix Rodriguez, a Cuban exile who subsequently taught counterinsurgency in the jungles of Peru and Vietnam. Guevara was executed shortly afterward. (Courtesy of Felix Rodriguez)

Che Guevara in death. Guevara's body, after being displayed to reporters, was buried in secret to prevent its location from becoming a shrine. A decade later, however, his picture could still be found in homes and buses throughout the Andes, as many peasants considered him a martyr. (Courtesy of José Luis Alcazan/Edicion Era)

Construction of the first major highway in the Brazilian Amazon was partly made possible by Rockefeller Foundation support of antimalarial inoculations for construction workers. (Courtesy of the Rockefeller Archive Center)

John F. Kennedy hosts Brazil's President João Goulart at the White House, April 1962. Goulart's defense of Petrobrás, nationalization of Hanna Mining properties, and Brazilian control of Amazonian development was costly: After Kennedy's assassination, he was overthrown by a military coup backed by the Johnson administration. (Courtesy of the John F. Kennedy Library)

Senator Robert F. Kennedy visited Amazonian Indians in Brazil during a 1965 tour of Latin America that caused consternation in the Johnson administration, particularly the State Department under Secretary Dean Rusk, former Rockefeller Foundation president. Kennedy refused to accept State's argument that the interests of the United States and Standard Oil in Peru were synonymous. (Courtesy of the John F. Kennedy Library)

President Lyndon Johnson urged Nelson Rockefeller to run for the presidency in 1968, despite the candidacy of his own vice president, Hubert Humphrey. Unlike their shared enmity for Robert Kennedy, Johnson's close friendship with Rockefeller was one of Pocantico's best-kept secrets. The two are pictured here in conference one week after Senator Kennedy's murder. (Courtesy of Lyndon Baines Johnson Library; photo by Frank Wolfe)

Governor Nelson Rockefeller, during his riot-plagued tour of Latin America for President Richard Nixon, arrives at Rio de Janeiro's airport guarded by Brazilian soldiers carrying automatic weapons, 1969. Tranquility was assured by the arrest of thousands before his arrival. During his meeting with the head of the Brazilian junta, Rockefeller was handed a report by the Brazilian secret police to relay to Nixon and National Security Adviser Henry Kissinger. (Courtesy of UPI/Bettmann Archive)

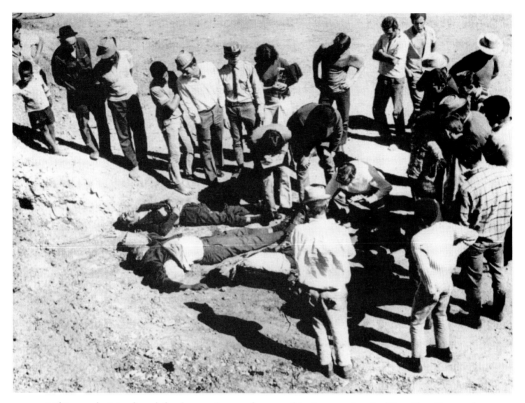

Military rule introduced death squads as enforcers of its laws under the "Brazilian Economic Miracle"; starting with criminals, then dissenters, soon students and common citizens were kidnapped and murdered, their bodies dumped on city outskirts or garbage heaps. (Courtesy of Associated Press/Wide World Photos)

Rockefeller's ROLIBEC brokerage insured CIA's Air America in Thailand. Here, a ROLIBEC salesman uses a sampan to visit a client in Bangkok. (Courtesy of the National Planning Association)

Protecting the family jewels. Commission member C. Douglas Dillon smiles as Vice President Rockefeller laughs as he peeks at the report of the presidential commission he chaired to look into CIA abuses, some of which occurred during his stint as President Eisenhower's liaison with the CIA. (Courtesy of UPI/Bettmann Archive)

The board of directors of Nelson Rockefeller's International Basic Economy Corporation (IBEC) at the height of its power, early 1970s. IBEC controlled Brazil's largest mutual fund and its largest hybrid seed company, and shared control over its eighth-largest agribusiness and one of the country's largest ranches. Richard Aldrich is fifth from the left; Nelson's eldest son, Rodman, is at the head of the table, on the left. (Courtesy of the Rockefeller Archive Center)

Vice President Nelson Rockefeller shares a light moment
with his longtime friend,
Secretary of State Henry
Kissinger, Rockefeller's foreign
policy adviser since 1955,
when the Harvard professor
attended White House Special
Assistant Rockefeller's top-
secret Cold War strategy meetings at the Quantico Marine
Corps base. (Courtesy of the Rockefeller Archive Center)

The memorial service for Nelson Rockefeller, 1979, was held at New York's Riverside
Church, once denounced by Fundamentalist Christian leaders as the "cathedral of modernism." President Jimmy Carter joined mourners to hear eulogies by David Rockefeller
(shown in pulpit), Henry Kissinger, and others. (Courtesy of UPI/Bettmann Archive)

Oil pipeline in Roirama, northern Brazil. Slowly and insidiously, leaks from capped oil wells and pipelines are killing the Amazon rain forest. American oil companies disclaim responsibility for the pollution. (Courtesy of Associated Press/Wide World Photos)

Indigenous peoples convened in Rio de Janeiro in 1992. Here, Brazilian Indians from the Mato Grosso and Amazon rain forests leave the Global Forum of the United Nation's nongovernmental organizations after meeting on issues concerning the environment, hunger, land rights, and invasions. (Courtesy of Associated Press/Wide World Photos)

U.S. military adviser George Maynes *(right)* at Nebaj, El Quiché, Guatemala, April 1982, during the counterinsurgency offensive launched against predominantly Indian people's Army of the Poor by "born-again" evangelical dictator, General Efraín Ríos Montt. SIL cooperated with successive military regimes between 1977 and 1982 as Guatemala's holocaust displaced over 1 million people and claimed over 75,000 lives, mostly Indians. (Courtesy of Jean Marie Simon). *Inset:* Ríos Montt, here with Ronald Reagan during meeting in Honduras, sought and received U.S. military aid previously suspended because of human rights violations. Oil strikes by American oil companies had sparked speculation by military officers in Indian lands. (Courtesy of UPI/Bettmann Archive)

Bodies of Indians presumed to be members of the Zapatista Army of National Liberation, 1994. Some U.S. congressmen have speculated that the CIA had covered up earlier predictions of growing dissent in Mexico to bolster its own testimony in favor of the North American Free Trade Agreement (NAFTA) and now was involved in another cover-up of army atrocities in Chiapas. (Courtesy of Cuartoscuro/Impact Visuals)

head of SEADAG's Council of Vietnamese Studies, Samuel P. Huntington, had devised a rationalization for Johnson's massive bombing of rural South Vietnam: "forced urbanization."

SEADAG, of which Young became chairman, had grandiose plans for Southeast Asia. Oil and natural gas reserves were known to exist in Thailand and off the coast of Vietnam.* More immediately promising, however, was the hydroelectric energy that could be harvested by building dams along the upper Mekong River.

The Mekong River Delta's 5,500 miles of interlaced waterways already provided drainage, irrigation, and transportation across a tangle of swamps. Because the region lacked roads, the delta had always been a difficult area for Saigon to control—until Johnson's massive U.S. military intervention. Following the recommendations of Pentagon-financed aerial research studies,[39] the United States transformed the delta's languid calm into a clattering hothouse of death. The U.S. Army's Ninth Infantry Division arrived to provide troops for a Mekong Delta Mobile Riverine Force to help the U.S. Navy's River Assault Flotillas keep the rice flowing up the Cho Gao Canal to Saigon. Swarms of U.S. Army helicopter gunships and U.S. Marine Corps riverboats descended upon the delta. Ironically, but predictably, rice production in the area—which previously had earned the delta its fame as "the Rice Bowl of Asia"—plummeted. To Asians, the word *paddy* meant rice; to young American GIs, it meant a quick death. The enemy remained mostly invisible, revealed only at the point of crippling spikes submerged in muddy water or by bullets fired by local peasants, who belonged to the NLF by night and to Saigon by day.

But there was more at stake along the Mekong River Delta than the lives of GIs, even if death was what the American media focused on. Military control over the Mekong made strategic sense to U.S. generals concerned about maintaining the river as the lifeline to Saigon and the Cambodian and Laotian capitals on its banks to the north; to American businessmen associated with SEADAG, U.S. occupation of the Mekong River basin meant some of the world's largest dams, financed by AID and the World Bank, all designed to produce cheap hydroenergy for industrialization in Thailand and South Vietnam. It meant the cheap labor of peasants flee-

---

*Besides the huge Arawakan fields in Burma, northwestern Thailand in fact did have three oil fields east of Burma's Irrawaddy River, knowledge of which was made public in the American press as early as 1967. Natural gas reserves were also locked beneath the sea in the Gulf of Thailand. Years later, Union Oil of California—whose founding family had underwritten Fundamentalist Christian missionaries, including Cameron Townsend—would discover gas there, as would Texas Pacific. But the major discovery would be by Standard Oil of New Jersey (Exxon) at Channabot, again in northwestern Thailand, where Standard Oil had a 50,000-square-mile concession. Oil was also believed to exist (and has since been confirmed) beneath the Gulf of Tonkin (claimed by the People's Republic of China, as it was then called) between Hanoi and China's Hainan Island, and gas was believed to exist off the Red River Delta.

The biggest hopes, of course, were placed in South Vietnam's vast Mekong River Delta. Oil existed south of the delta, in an offshore field named Dua-IX by the oil companies (see *International Petroleum Encyclopedia,* 1983, p. 234).

ing the increasingly indiscriminate U.S. bombings and search-and-destroy sweeps across the countryside. And it meant cheap commercial food production, not only for South Vietnam, but for exports to the much vaster cheap labor pool in India.

India, in fact, was the Asian home base for Rockefeller Foundation operations in Southern Asia. At the capital in New Delhi, the Rockefeller Foundation maintained its last remaining office abroad, headed by former Defense Undersecretary Roswell Gilpatric's brother, Chadbourne Gilpatric, himself a former CIA officer and a current member of John 3rd's Asia Society. This office directed funds into New Delhi's Indian Agricultural Research Institute, making India a host for training Southeast Asian agronomists.[40] The idea was to develop, as in the Philippines, "training facilities in agriculture, medicine and administration in the expectation that their influence will radiate throughout South Asia."[41]

The vision of Nelson and his brothers went far beyond the immediate war profiteering enjoyed by some of Johnson's closest friends among Texas's nouveau riche. The Rockefellers were talking about bigger things, like changing the landscape of entire subcontinents.

There were, to be sure, short-term profits to be made. Rockefeller-family investments scored well in blue-chip defense contractors, such as Standard Oil of California, Standard Oil of New Jersey, Boeing, and General Motors—which took in more than $1.3 billion in military contracts in 1968 alone.[42]

Expecting the United States to win the war, U.S. banks began to open branches in Saigon. "Afterwards, you'll have a major job of reconstruction on your hands that will take financing," said a vice president of J. Stillman Rockefeller's First National City Bank, "and financing means banks."[43]

David Rockefeller understood that fact. In 1965, Chase announced that it, too, was opening a branch in downtown Saigon. The Chase building stood like a giant fortress dwarfing the GI bars and small shops that surrounded it. There were no windows, just thick glass blocks. The stone walls were built to withstand mortar attacks. It was as if David Rockefeller was making a point in the face of the Viet Cong threat: Here was *real power*. It was the kind of blunt challenge liked by his colleagues in the most ironically named prowar group of the Vietnam era: the Committee for an Effective and Desirable Peace in Asia.

Chase was indeed an effective and durable force in the world, but that was to be expected; it was, after all, the Pentagon that asked David to open the branch in Saigon.[44]

In July 1966, David flew to Saigon. He came, he explained, officially to inaugurate Chase's new branch. But he also was there to show his support for Johnson's war, and he paid a call on Premier General Nguyen Cao Ky. Ky was not only head of Saigon's government; he also commanded officers who controlled much of Saigon's drug trade.[45] According to CIA contract employee Sam Mustard,

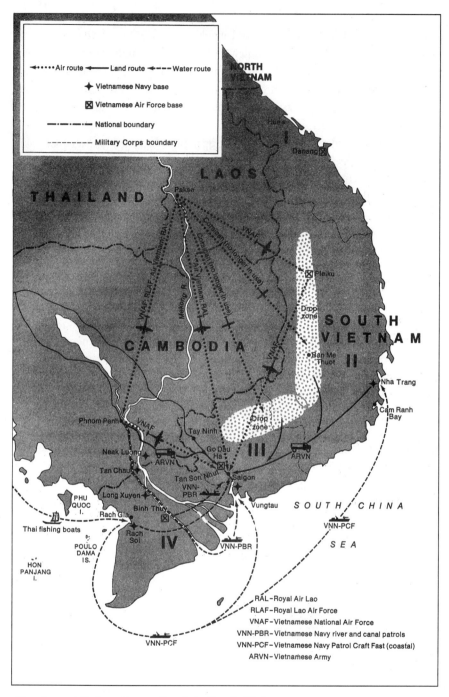

Heroin and Opium Smuggling into South Vietnam

Helio Couriers helped the CIA's Air America, the transporter of opium for Indochinese drug lords.

Source: Alfred W. McCoy and Cathleen B. Read, *The Politics of Heroin in Southeast Asia*, p. 155. Copyright © 1972 by Alfred W. McCoy and Cathleen B. Read. Reprinted by permission of HarperCollins Publishers, Inc.

an associate of SIL's former chief pilot Larry Montgomery,* Ky's involvement went back to the early 1960s, when he flew CIA commandos into North Vietnam via Laos.[46] The substance of David's talks with Ky were kept confidential, but David's mere presence in Ky's war-torn capital spoke for itself: Ky and his rival, General Nguyen Van Thieu, could rest assured that the Rockefellers and the investors they represented were here to stay.[47]

David's president of Chase's Far East operations had tried to make that point the previous year, shortly after Johnson escalated U.S. military involvement: "I must say . . . that the U.S. actions in Vietnam this year—which have demonstrated that the U.S. will continue to give effective protection to the free nations of the region—have considerably reassured both Asian and Western investors." He predicted a level of economic growth similar to that achieved in postwar Europe under the Marshall Plan.[48] If anyone had doubted the bank officer's word, David Rockefeller's chauffeured car whisking through the streets of Saigon testified to the Rockefellers' commitment to SEADAG's vision.

The theories of SEADAG's Samuel P. Huntington provided the grimmer reality behind these dramas: cheap labor created by forced relocation from a terrorized countryside. Anthropologist Jules Henry, who had witnessed tribal decimation in Brazil, explained to a numbed American people what this entailed: "The establishment throughout Southeast Asia of industrial complexes backed by American capital is sure to have a salutary effect on the development of our foreign investment. The vast land's cheap labor pool will permit competition with the lower productive costs of Chinese and Japanese industry, which have immobilized our trading capabilities in Asia for many years. . . . The destruction of the Vietnamese countryside is the first, and necessary, step to the industrialization of Vietnam and the nationalization of its agriculture."[49]

But if anthropologists like Henry were seriously questioning the war's purported sole anticommunist motive in a nation with a $27 per month average wage, there were few doubts among American missionaries.

In the heat of war, some American missionaries shed their clerical neutrality and picked up the gun. The most famous missionary soldiers were the Youngs of Burma. They were recruited by the CIA to gain compliance from the tribesmen in northwestern Burma in gathering intelligence on political activities in their own countries, southern China, and Thailand.

*Sam Mustard wrote to Senator Ernest Gruening on March 9, 1968 (see New York Times, April 19, 1968, p. 1). The association between Mustard and Montgomery was as fellow CIA contract employees who had as their mission the setting up of a more effective maintenance and communications system in Laos similar to the JAARS model described by Helio Corporation president Lynn Bollinger and Colonel L. Fletcher Prouty in 1961. Montgomery's participation in the mission overseas was scrubbed after two months of preparations, and Mustard, trained by Montgomery, went to Southeast Asia alone in March 1962. Montgomery's association with Mustard is described in a memorandum from Nathan Fitts, a Helio employee secretly placed in the company by the CIA, and CIA general counsel Lawrence R. Houston. A copy of this memorandum, dated June 5, 1962, is in the authors' possession.

Using Chiang Mai as their listening post and base of operations, the Youngs directed military raids by the CIA's tribal recruits against suspected "communist" villages in eastern Thailand and Laos, as well as into China's Yunan Province. Another pistol-packing missionary, Joseph Flipse, assisted the Youngs in leading commando raids by Yao tribesmen on Laotian villages that were identified as sympathetic to the Pathet Lao communists.[50] Flipse was a member of the International Volunteer Service (IVS), Christian Fundamentalism's answer to the secular Peace Corps. IVS's Saigon office was headed by Don Luce, a prominent member of SEADAG's advisory panels.

Another IVS volunteer, the folksy Edgar ("Pop") Buell, was the classic grandfatherly American missionary. Buell trained Hmong tribesmen in demolition and organized the dynamiting of bridges and passes through the Laotian mountains. He also arranged the first contact with the poppy-growing Hmong for the CIA and got the tribesmen to carve landing strips out of the mountainside for the CIA's wide-winged Helio Couriers. In 1961, General Edward Lansdale reported to Washington that 9,000 Hmong had been "recruited" for guerrilla warfare. The recruitment was actually a draft system by elders of young men; the CIA's weapons, clothes, and rice encouraged clan rivalries to express themselves through violence against clans allied with the Pathet Lao. AID provided cover for CIA operations and agents, who directed at its peak an army of 40,000 men from the Hmong and other tribes. Pop Buell joined them in AID's ranks. Rice was cut off by the CIA to villages that did not want to keep sending their men to war or did not want to move on CIA orders; forced migrations often caused villages a 20 percent casualty rate, mostly children and elders. Buell defended the use of humanitarian relief to support the CIA's war. By 1970, this Indiana farmer would be cajoling the polygamist general of the CIA's secret army, Vang Pao, to "hold on," to keep fighting, despite 30,000 Hmong dead, the drafting of twelve-year-old boys, and Vang Pao's pleas that "the good ones are all dead, my Father. Dead."[51]

As souls ascended to heaven in the fight against Satan, many clergy became direct collaborators with the CIA. One member of the Christian and Missionary Alliance (C&MA) was proud of this collaboration. William Carlsen, a missionary in northeastern Thailand, considered it "a privilege to share information with responsible agencies of the government where they seek us out." Carlsen gave an eight-hour briefing to the CIA on Thailand's tribal areas when he returned home for a furlough. Most C&MA missionaries did likewise, according to a CIA source. Most of the information gleaned was about people, their actions, opinions, and grievances.[52]

Yet the full implications of the missionaries' complicity in the CIA and military intelligence operations would not hit home until stories began to surface about a massacre in a village named My Lai and a CIA program of mass assassinations called Operation Phoenix.

36
"NATION-BUILDING" THROUGH WAR

Riding the Phoenix

By the end of the 1960s, only a few Washington insiders knew that Nelson Rockefeller's institutional legacy from his days as Eisenhower's special assistant for Cold War strategy—the National Security Council's Special Group—was responsible for a massive campaign of arrest, torture, and murder in Vietnam. Named appropriately after the mythical bird that rises reborn from the ashes, Phoenix was the last great effort at a counterinsurgency victory that the Special Group would attempt in Vietnam.

Hatched by the CIA in the fall of 1967, Phoenix was directly responsible for the deaths of some 26,000 Vietnamese by official U.S. count, or almost 41,000 if Saigon's estimate is to be believed. Phoenix rose to these heights of terror under a genteel, God-fearing, Princeton-educated Catholic named William Colby. As CIA station chief in Saigon during the Eisenhower-Kennedy transition years between 1959 and 1962, Colby had directed clandestine operations in support of the dictatorship of Diem, a fellow Catholic in a mostly Buddhist nation. Subsequently chief of the Far East Division of the CIA's clandestine services, Colby also oversaw the CIA's secret war in Laos from the Agency's headquarters in Langley, Virginia. He did so with such little expense ($20 million to $30 million per year) that the war in Laos was considered a great success, despite the battering his 36,000 tribal soldiers received and despite the continuing deterioration in neighboring South Vietnam. In 1966, he was back in Saigon, assisting one of the Special Group's top counterinsurgency aides, Robert Komer, in directing Civil Operations and Rural Development Support (CORDS), the overall pacification program that had

Phoenix as its terrorizing component. CORDS also had responsibility for CIA officers who were using the Agency for International Development (AID) as a cover and for cultivation of CORDS's AID cover with American civilians in the countryside, including missionaries.

By 1968, when Colby was elevated to the rank of special ambassador, Phoenix was forcing 250,000 civilians through South Vietnam's prison system, often relying on no more than the word of paid informers. This was at a time when the CIA estimated that the communist-led National Liberation Front (NLF) totaled at most 150,000 people. Moreover, this flow of 250,000 suspects continued annually until 1972, when the operation was shut down.

The spine of Phoenix was a series of Provincial Interrogation Centers stretching across South Vietnam's forty-four provinces, but Phoenix's muscle was the CIA's Provincial Reconnaissance Units (PRU). "CIA representatives recruited, organized, supplied, and directly paid CT [counter-terror] teams," whose function was to use Viet Cong techniques of terror, assassination, abuses, kidnappings, and intimidation—against the Viet Cong leadership."[1] Under Phoenix, however, the "leadership" became anyone a paid informer chose to accuse, multiplied by hundreds of thousands of people.

The CIA's William Buckley, as early as May 1967, had warned the Agency's top scientist, Sidney Gottlieb, that such abuses of civilians—including raping and pillaging by American soldiers—as well as indiscriminate carpet bombing and chemical defoliation of the countryside were giving the NLF ammunition for propaganda operations and indoctrination of recruits. But others at CIA headquarters in Langley disagreed. Gottlieb sent Buckley's report to CIA Director Richard Helms, who rewarded Buckley by recalling him to Langley and demoting him to "Agency drudge."[2] Felix Rodriguez, on the other hand, who had recently arrived in Vietnam from his adventures against Che Guevara in Bolivia, continued recruiting NLF war prisoners for PRU hunts against their former compatriots, deliberately releasing their identities to the NLF to remove any hope of reconciliation.

For NLF prisoners who did not cooperate, the CIA had an efficient procedure: They were tortured until they died. CIA doctors conducted medical experiments, including those on prisoners held in a compound behind the Bien Hoa hospital, all in violation of international law. Slowly, methodically, the Agency's psychiatrists tortured prisoners classified by local CIA officers as "typical examples of communist indoctrination." When their attempts to shake the prisoners' beliefs met with frustration, the scientists decided to continue electrically shocking the prisoners. The torture went on for three weeks, until the last prisoner died.[3]

That was the "hard" side of "reeducation" under Komer's and Colby's pacification program. The "soft" side was where Cam Townsend's missionaries came in. The SIL's bilingual education program worked well in meeting the U.S. mission's technical needs among the Montagnard tribes. English had replaced French as Vietnam's second language in the upper classes of secondary schools, contributing to Saigon's drive to assimilate the fiercely independent people of the Central Highlands.

These forested mountains, actually a continuation of the Annam chain separating Vietnam from Cambodia and Laos, were the weak backbone of South Vietnam, subject to easy penetration by soldiers from the north and feeble local support for the regime in Saigon. To promoters of U.S. intervention, however, they were strategically valuable for more than military reasons. As early as February 1958, a conference in New York organized by the Vietnam Lobby ("American Friends of Vietnam") and attended by scores of representatives of business—including representatives of the International Basic Economy Corporation (IBEC), Chase Manhattan Bank, Standard-Vacuum Oil, Chase International Investment Corporation, and the Asia Society—had identified the high plateau in the Central Highlands as offering "rich possibilities of investment for new capital,"[4] with coal reserves and molybdenite. In these sections, "one can draw on the mountaineer Mois [French Vietnamese for the Montagnard or mountain peoples, meaning "Savage"] for a labor supply, but the mountain people are not yet accustomed to holding regular jobs."[5]

The job of AID and other Christian missionaries was to change all that and instill in the Montagnard tribes the discipline of the Protestant work ethic. Whatever earlier misgivings Uncle Cam had about channeling SIL recruits into the war zone were now overwhelmed by the enthusiasm of his field missionaries. These missionaries, like Cam, were caught up in the fray by their own Cold War ideological proclivities and ultimately by the pull of powerful forces in the U.S. government and in the corporate world.

The growing apprehension among some reporters and GIs about the summary executions by CIA-directed PRUs did not deter SILers from the swift completion of their appointed rounds in the villages. The SILers continued to gather words, vowels, and syntaxes and to learn the names of sympathizers and opponents in the villages. SILers were supposed to protect the confidentiality of their linguistic informants and to avoid involvement with anything—including intelligence operations—that could compromise their relationship with their tribe or their Bible translation mission. But sometimes there could be a conflict between their professed neutrality and their mission under the auspices of a government that had expectations. Sometimes this resulted in pressures by the CIA for interviews, which, Townsend claimed, had to be refused.[6] But at least one time, SIL did collaborate in a linguistic survey conducted by a Pentagon-funded researcher from RAND, Gerald C. Hickey of the U.S. Embassy staff in Saigon, under contract with the Advanced Research Projects Agency. SIL even turned over its linguistic informants to Hickey for his questioning. In fact, Hickey specifically thanked SIL in his acknowledgments, along with "MAC/V [U.S. Military Assistance Command/Vietnam] advisory groups," U.S. AID representatives, "the Advanced Research Projects Agency Field Unit in

Saigon," and the Saigon government's Special Commission for Highland Affairs, SIL's contractor.[7]

The ties were too deep, and the strings led high, from Vietnam—where the head of U.S. Army Intelligence, General Joseph McChristian, had known SIL since visiting Limoncocha while conducting a counterinsurgency survey in Ecuador during the early Kennedy years—to Washington itself.

After forty years of futilely trying to scale the heights of Washington's power, SIL found that the White House was at last accessible. Cam had even gotten so far as to cross the White House threshold. Through the good offices of Rev. Calvin Thielman and Nebraska's Senator Carl Curtis, Cam gained access to Lyndon Johnson's outer office. Meeting with a presidential aide, Cam lobbied hard (and eventually successfully) for the president to proclaim an official national day for Bible translation. Over and above it all, unspoken but discernible to any politician, loomed the promise of SIL's large donors, including those from Johnson's home state. This was no idle dream. Reality had already arrived in the form of gifts "upwards to $100,000 from a couple that divide their time between Dallas and Mexico City," Cam wrote Rev. Thielman in 1967.[8] This letter, ironically enough, was in response to a claim filed by Billy Graham's father-in-law, *Christianity Today* editor Nelson Bell, that SIL's American alias, the Wycliffe Bible Translators (WBT), "was receiving large sums from foundations." Cam denied this claim to Thielman, although in doing so he confirmed that SIL/WBT had received $450,000 from six sources, four of them private foundations,* with only $10,000 from the liberal Ford Foundation and nearly $50,000 "from a U.S. Government agency for a special research project in Africa," which went unnamed.

Texan Lures, New York Strings

Dallas was growing like an incubus in Cam's dreams for SIL's expansion. Cam's ties to Dallas had developed out of his friendship with William Criswell and a supporting group of Texas businessmen.

In the public eye, the center of financial gravity of this group was the Hunt family, longtime supporters of SIL and Texas's most notorious oilmen. By 1967–1968, when the Hunts' rightward rush led them away from Johnson and toward the third-party effort headed by Alabama segregationist Governor George Wallace and General "Bomb Them Back to the Stone Age" Curtis LeMay, Cam's base of support among Dallas businessmen had widened to include oilmen, ranchers, an executive in United Fidelity Union Life Insurance Company, the chairman and a director of Texas Instruments, a director of the Dallas Trust Company, and the chairman of the First National Bank of Dallas. The core group came from Texas Instruments (TI), the giant

---

*The foundations, besides Ford, were the Crowell Trust (based on the Crowell family's Quaker Oats fortune in Chicago), the Glenmeade Trust (based on the Pew family's Sun Oil Company fortune in Philadelphia), and the Lilly Foundation (based on the Lilly pharmaceutical company).

electronics conglomerate that had absorbed Intercontinental Rubber of past infamy in the Congo and Geophysical Service, Inc., a major oil surveyor in the Peruvian Amazon. In 1974 the Rockefellers would reveal, in the course of Nelson's confirmation hearings for the vice presidency, that they and their family trusts owned over $17 million worth of TI's common stock. The trust department of David's Chase bank also held a large block of stock in TI's bank, First National, the largest holding being controlled by the registrar, Stillman Rockefeller's First National City Bank.[9]

In 1967, Cam used his newfound Dallas friends to leverage additional support from his old funding base in southern California. He threatened to move SIL's international headquarters from Santa Ana to Dallas unless money was raised for a larger building. "This city may be deprived of a twenty-year-old business employing 1900 persons," reported the *Santa Ana Register*, mistaking SIL's global enrollment for employees in the area. "We are now processing applications to add 200 employees and will be adding at least that many each year into the future," SIL's extension director, Dale Kietzman, told the *Register*. "As a result a new location would need to be donated to us entirely, and we found nothing here," adding that "we would still prefer to relocate right here in Orange County."[10]

While thus arming his Orange County supporters for a fund-raising appeal for a new administrative headquarters, Cam plunged ahead with plans to expand into Dallas with a new international translation center. Right-wing oilman Nelson Bunker Hunt had made an offer Cam could not refuse: 100 acres abutting Hunt's other properties near the Southwest Center for Advanced Studies, or money toward buying any other site in the Dallas area. Hunt's offer, along with $200,000 in contributions, bolstered Cam's ambitions for SIL in Texas.[11] Cam planned to build a $5 million complex of classrooms, libraries, an auditorium, a museum to house tribal artifacts, housing, and a large administrative headquarters, he told the press in September.[12] Cam was given the key to the city by the mayor, Erik Jonsson, TI's former top executive.

With all this excitement, something more significant than Bibles seemed afoot, but the press could not grasp it. In the end, Cam had his cake and ate it, too: He built the International Linguistics Center that Dallas's oilmen and electronics bigwigs wanted. He got southern California businessmen to donate land and raise funds for a new SIL headquarters in Orange County's oil-rich Huntington Beach, the future home in exile of South Vietnam's Nguyen Cao Ky.

Cam was now moving in different, more mainstream financial circles than from those he was accustomed to. Hunt notwithstanding, Cam's business allies in Dallas were part of a corporate network whose financial lines ran north to New York's financial establishment and south and west to oil exploration in the Amazon and Southeast Asia.

The Dallas–New York connection had a direct impact on SIL. Cam's ambitions for SIL had led him into financial dependence on backers of Lyndon Johnson's deepening commitment to a war now spreading across all Southeast Asia.

REVOLT OF THE MONTAGNARDS

As the war escalated, the American press generally remained loyal to the presidency, rather than to its constitutional mission under the First Amendment. Truth was once more the first casualty. British author Philip Knightly correctly noted that American journalists were not trained to question basic national beliefs, including a Cold War turned hot. He pointed out that "the correspondents were not questioning the American intervention itself, but only its effectiveness." Atrocities were ignored, not because they were unbelievable, but because they had become commonplace and therefore unnewsworthy.[13] Anticipating censorship by military authorities or editors, some reporters became self-censors.

It took political earthquakes to break this trance. The highland rebellions of 1965 were one such seismic warning.

In September of that year, more than 3,000 heavily armed tribesmen in five Green Beret camps revolted against the military regime in Saigon. Raising a black, red, and green flag with three white stars that represented the largest of the thirty-three highland tribes, the Montagnards killed twenty-nine members of the Vietnamese Special Forces and seized hundreds of prisoners, including twenty Americans. The revolt of one-third of the 10,000-man Montagnard army threatened to sever General Edward D. Lansdale's "trip wire" for Vietnam's vulnerable lowlands. The lives of SIL translators and their associates in the Christian and Missionary Alliance and the International Voluntary Service were put at risk. The mountain people were angry and provided the rebels with a popular base of support. Lowland Vietnamese migrations into the highlands had been sponsored by Saigon and the developers of AID. The U.S. Command had participated in securing Vietnamese control over U.S. aid to the tribes, and Vietnamese had been appointed province district chiefs and commanders over tribal soldiers, much to the resentment of tribal leaders.

By pledging loyalty to the Radê tribe in their desire for reforms by Saigon and by exercising a timely display of General Ky's airpower, the Green Berets' coolheaded approach ended the revolt. But the economic origins of the revolt—AID's colonization schemes for the highlands—remained generally ignored. Only a month later, Cam's translators held their first Translation Workshop in Kontum,[14] oblivious of almost all but their millennial vision.

Nevertheless, much more was influencing SIL than millennial visions. In the neighboring Philippines, long the United States' armed forces' stepping-stone to the Asian mainland, the CIA-funded Asia Foundation granted $1,500 to SIL to finance the production of primers for hill tribes. The strategic importance of the Asia Foundation in the region and the possibility that this grant could lead to the financing of SIL operations elsewhere was not lost on SIL officials. "We have been cultivating them for quite some time," branch leader Les Troyer wrote Cam, "and feel this has great potential for Wycliffe in the Orient."[15]

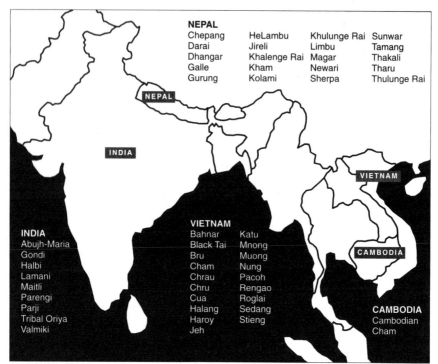

Tribes in Southern Asia "Occupied" by SIL or Languages Under Study by SIL in 1972 During Vietnam War
Source: SIL.

The Asia Foundation was one of AID's top technical service contractors.[16] The Asia Foundation was also involved in the economic planning for Vietnam's highlands being conducted by the South East Asia Development Advisory Group (SEADAG). Working out of Asia House, the Manhattan headquarters of John D. Rockefeller 3rd's Asia Society, SEADAG's planners worked on the very nation-building development schemes for the Saigon regime that had inspired the Montagnard tribesmen to revolt twice in the mid-1960s. SEADAG's use of linguists, anthropologists, and other social scientists was part of the government's "expanding effort aimed at co-optation of the academic community and its more general intention to use academics as a cover for covert activities in Southeast Asia."[17] Like Ho Chi Minh, SEADAG's corporate sponsors were "nation-building" through war; a major difference, however, was for whom.

Behind SEADAG was AID, and behind AID was David Rockefeller, Rockefeller Foundation president J. George Harrar, Chase Manhattan Bank director Eugene Black (former head of the World Bank), and Cornell University president James Perkins (another Chase Bank director, as well as a director of Nelson's IBEC). These men led Johnson's General Advisory Committee on the Foreign Assistance Program. It was David Rockefeller who chaired the group's Subcommittee on Private Enterprise and who recommended in 1966 the deletion of President Kennedy's prohibition against transferring U.S. foreign-aid funds to the World Bank to pay off Third World debts to private banks such as Chase.

By then, Nelson's IBEC also had financial links to lucrative credit operations in Southeast Asia. On IBEC's board since 1964 sat Christian Cardin, executive vice president and then president of Paribas Corporation and its parent, Banque de Paris et des Pays-Bas, France's largest privately owned bank and a major backer of IBEC's ventures in Europe, as well as an important IBEC stockholder.[18] Paribas representatives sat on the boards of French companies with investments in the former French Indochina. Carrying out the directives of David Rockefeller and his colleagues on the Foreign Aid Advisory Committee was the committee's fifty-four-year-old executive director, Howard Kresge. Kresge was SIL's liaison, and Cam made it a point to visit the committee's offices when Cam was in Washington.[19]

Yet, even though he had a sixth sense about who held power, Cam rarely looked further to see what those people did with their power. Nor was he immune to manipulation within the grander schemes. For Cam, and for most Americans imbued with a similar Cold War ideology, it was enough to identify with the Christian West, in general, and with the U.S. military presence in Vietnam, in particular. And that self-identity by SIL translators was not lost on Vietnamese communists.

Local NLF organizers might have looked upon Cam's translators with unexpected tolerance, having learned the religious predomination of their work from villagers. But this experience was to be shared by regular army troops from the North who were moving across the demilitarized zone or down the Ho Chi Minh trail along the western borders of Vietnam.

These units were the army of Ho's Democratic Republic of Vietnam (DRV), which was at war with the United States and its allied regime in Saigon, the Republic of Vietnam. They were imbued more with nationalist than with communist ideals. To confront the Americans and Saigon's troops, General Giap and the DRV leaders chose the mountains surrounding the village of Khe Sanh for their battleground.

The Battle of Khe Sanh

It was from this area that the CIA had directed the Green Berets to lead Brú tribesmen in ambushing DRV soldiers and their supply caravans heading south to aid the communist-led NLF.

Khe Sanh was also the base from which the U.S. commander in Vietnam, General William Westmoreland, hoped to launch an invasion into Laos to cut the Ho

Chi Minh Trail. Border violations on all sides were rampant. The commander of "unconventional warfare" in the Khe Sanh area, Colonel John K. Singlaub, was not unknown to the Vietnamese opposition. Singlaub, who would be exposed years later for his part in the Iran-Contra arms scandal, had helped set up the "Eagles Nest" head-quarters at Phou Phi Thi in Laos for the CIA's secret war using Hmong tribesmen.[20]

Cam was aware that Khe Sanh was coming under increasing pressure. SIL's *Translation* magazine reported as early as January 1966 that two SIL women trans-lators among the Brú had been forced by a mortar attack to retreat to the U.S. Special Forces camp nearby. Two years later, the camp had grown into a fortress with an all-weather runway as U.S. Marine units were hurried up from the low-lands. Harassment from CIA's Montagnard strike forces was now being answered by well-trained regular North Vietnamese Army units. The SIL translators had their own responses, handing out Old Testament Bible stories in the Brú language to the Khe Sanh village's district chief.

General Westmoreland was convinced that the long-awaited Korea-type invasion from the north was finally about to happen and intended to meet it at Khe Sanh. A true believer in technology, Westmoreland was a promoter of inte-grated air-land combat systems. He was convinced that Khe Sanh's mountainous terrain would make it impossible for North Vietnam's General Giap to move in the necessary forces and artillery to surround and entrap the marines. The Joint Chiefs of Staff and President Johnson, needing a victory to persuade American voters that progress was being made, concurred.[21]

Even as the Khe Sanh area was heating up, neither Cam nor Vietnam branch leader Hank Blood ordered the withdrawal of local missionaries. SIL's two transla-tors continued their work among the Brú while U.S. Marines kept arriving in greater numbers. And in the hills surrounding Khe Sanh, more and more North Vietnamese units kept arriving, building up their forces, moving up artillery, and doing exactly what the omniscient U.S. Military Command in Saigon believed was impossible. Here at sensor-sowed Khe Sanh, Westmoreland assured the Joint Chiefs of Staff that a target was emerging for massive American firepower that was more tangible than body counts.

And yet Westmoreland's body counts also continued to grow, often inflated beyond any totals the CIA estimated for the Viet Cong. Civilian massacres in the lowlands resulting from vanguard aerial bombings followed by "free fire-zone" sweeps by U.S. forces were, just as CIA's William Buckley warned, driving the desperate peasantry into the ranks of the NLF.

In the highlands of Laos, the retreat southward and westward of Hmong tribesmen also grew, especially after a January 1968 offensive by the Pathet Lao and North Vietnamese regulars. In South Vietnam's highlands, too, the tribes were being bloodied. But Lansdale's "trip wire" against North Vietnamese troop and supply movements southward remained intact, even if it took a terrible toll on the

Montagnards. In fact, the trip wire now was stretched south through the heart of the Annam Mountains, studded with Special Forces forts from which spurs of the Green Beret-led Civil Irregular Defense Groups (CIDG) struck westward, with local tribesmen recruited for cross-border patrols.

The SILers, like the missionaries of the Christian and Missionary Alliance and AID's agronomists, played an important part in erecting this trip wire and keeping it intact. The compassion shown Montagnard villagers by American missionaries lessened traditional tribal mistrust of outsiders and eased the task of recruitment. Like the Green Berets who fought alongside the tribesmen, SIL translators saw themselves as helping an embattled country and its threatened tribes. More objective observations were left to less involved visitors. "Pawns in a war of surprise and ambush," wrote *National Geographic's* Howard Sochurek, "the primitive villagers often change loyalties to survive."[22] But surviving to become cannon fodder was never promising in any war, whether the victims were Scottish Highlanders at Culloden or Brú highlanders at Khe Sanh.

Reporters began to chronicle the war's ugly racial undertone. Green Berets, leading SIL-evangelized Jeh tribesmen toward the Laotian border to ambush North Vietnamese supply lines, still used a tactical guide card made up of orders attributed to Major Robert Rogers, organizer in 1759 of the Rangers, the British Empire's first antiguerrilla strike force and the most notorious Indian killers of the French and Indian War.[23] And although a 1940 *Small Wars Manual's* account of Custer's nineteenth-century defeat by the Plains tribes was no longer required reading for eager young U.S. Marines, American soldiers were still calling the foes they hunted in Vietnam's rain forests "Indians." British mathematician and philosopher Bertrand Russell, appalled by the indiscriminate "carpet bombing" and use of chemical weapons like Agent Orange, branded the relentless slaughter "genocide."

For the Johnson administration, this label was particularly embarrassing, especially since the United States was one of only a few governments in the West that had failed to ratify the 1925 Geneva Convention banning the use of poison gases and the United Nations Human Rights Covenants that had come out of the Nuremberg trials. Yet, despite a rising chorus of alarm from the United States' allies, intelligence officials inside the White House still missed Russell's historic allusion. A veteran's proposal to celebrate the Indian wars on the heels of the 100th anniversary of Custer's massacre of the southern Cheyenne had even gotten as far as presidential aide Douglas Cater, a former CIA operative, before it was derailed.

"It seems to me," warned former Rockefeller Foundation fellow and political scientist John P. Roche, "that this is a rather bad time to celebrate the Indian wars. Bertrand Russell might, after all, enlarge his genocide charge.

"Why not ship this off to the Commission on Indian Affairs? Bureaucratically yours . . . "[24]

37

TET: THE YEAR OF THE MONKEY

THE GREAT WHITE WAR CHIEF

Far from the domestic problems plaguing Lyndon Johnson, Americans in Saigon celebrated New Year's Eve at the impressive U.S. Embassy with the air of optimism expected of them. Ambassador Ellsworth Bunker's invitations had set the tone: "Come see the light at the end of the tunnel." But after the Christian New Year of 1968 had passed, and with it the cease-fire that had been intermittently broken, the war resumed in all its fury. There would not be another truce until Tet, the Vietnamese New Year, at the end of the month. By then hundreds of Americans and thousands of Vietnamese would become casualties.

Ten thousand miles to the east, a caravan of cars sped through the snowy Shoshone-Bannock Indian reservation in southern Idaho carrying government officials, reporters, and the chairman of the Senate Subcommittee on Indian Education. Senator Robert Kennedy had interrupted his ski holiday at Sun Valley to carry out a surprise inspection of the reservation. It was part of his committee's oversight responsibilities to review the work of Johnson's reorganized Bureau of Indian Affairs and its new Division of Education. But the reporters who accompanied him speculated that this trip was also the beginning of Kennedy's presidential campaign.

Many Indians hoped it was. "The Kennedys increased the normal margin which minority groups gave to the Democrats because of their apparent interest in minority groups," observed Indian historian Vine Deloria, Jr., a critic of the Kennedys' record in office. "Indian people loved the idea of Robert Kennedy replacing Jack. For them it was an affirmation of the great war chief from the great family leading his people in his brother's place."[1]

The Shoshone welcomed Robert Kennedy as if he were a godsend. They considered New York's junior senator one of their few friends in Washington. Just a month before, after Pueblo and Oglala Sioux tribal leaders had testified at hearings on the BIA's boarding schools before Kennedy's subcommittee, Kennedy had called the BIA's policy of forcibly separating school-aged Indian children from their families "barbaric." Now Kennedy had come to Idaho's Fort Hall reservation to see for himself. "Kennedy presented himself as a person who could move from world to world and never be a stranger anywhere," Deloria explained. "His genius was that he personified the best traits of his Irish heritage and made an attempt to define white in a different way."[2]

Kennedy's focusing on the BIA was not welcomed by Interior Secretary Stewart Udall, a member of the Mormon Church, which preached the racial inferiority of American Indians and had colluded with the BIA to "save" Indian schoolchildren by legally adopting them without their parents' knowledge or consent.[3] President Johnson also was not happy with Kennedy. All the polls indicated that he would have a tough time getting reelected this year because of the Vietnam War and domestic unrest. Already suspicious of Kennedy's every move, Johnson did not need Kennedy's spotlighting of BIA policies under his administration, especially ones that demonstrated racial and cultural insensitivity on top of Washington's traditional negligence.

"Why don't Indians riot?" Kennedy had asked a Navajo during the hearings, wondering about a seeming difference between Indians on rural reservations and African Americans in urban ghettos. "It isn't in their nature to demonstrate," explained the executive director of the National Congress of American Indians.[4] But anger among Indians over deplorable conditions, including Vietnam veterans returning to job discrimination and police violence at home, was building. It would soon explode in demonstrations at BIA headquarters and a shoot-out at Wounded Knee, the site of a historic massacre of Indians some seventy-five years earlier.

During the presidential campaign, Kennedy would try to awaken Euro-Americans to the plight of Native Americans, but the smugness of middle America was hard to shake. To a sullen audience at Purdue University, he tried to explain what Indian children faced on a reservation, "where suicide is the most frequent form of death among adolescents." Reporter Jack Newfield saw him later on the campaign plane, sitting "alone by the window for a half hour, tears in the corner of his eyes, the familiar ravaged look on his face, unapproachable."[5]

If Lyndon Johnson was troubled by having such a sensitive rival, so, too, was one of his strongest supporters on Vietnam, Governor Nelson Rockefeller. Nelson also had felt Bobby Kennedy's sting. Migrant laborers—whether Indians, African Americans, or Mexican Americans—were one of Kennedy's special concerns. The orchards of Rockefeller's New York were no more spared Kennedy's senatorial investigations than were the vineyards of Governor Ronald Reagan's California.

Rockefeller did not appreciate Kennedy's calling for a state investigation of health conditions at migrant labor camps. Reagan had even less use for Kennedy's urging labor leaders to unionize migrant farmworkers.

Kennedy supported Cesar Chavez's striking grape pickers and sponsored legislation to grant migrant farmworkers collective bargaining rights. This struck at the foundation of the cheap-labor code of agribusinesses.

If all this were not bad enough for business, Martin Luther King, Jr., had begun to see wealth and poverty as being interrelated phenomena rather than separate, contradictory ones. His projected Poor People's March to Washington struck terror in the hearts of FBI Director J. Edgar Hoover and his admiring superior, President Johnson. King was speaking about hypocrisy in the United States, including the goals and methods of the Vietnam War, exactly when the Johnson White House was suffering from a growing "credibility gap."

Still, Nelson Rockefeller was reluctant to take on Johnson. For one thing, he was still licking his wounds from 1964. Rockefeller also feared appearing "soft" on Vietnam, especially after his stalking horse candidate, Governor George Romney, was brutalized by the press for suggesting after a tour to Vietnam that he had been "brainwashed" by the Pentagon.

Besides, Nelson genuinely liked Lyndon Johnson. Nelson and Happy often visited the president and Lady Bird at their West Texas ranch on the Perdernales River. It seemed a strange match between an old-wealth Manhattan sophisticate and a nouveau riche cowboy.

But that difference missed the essential point of agreement: Both were glad-handing politicians, who, beneath it all, had never given up their New Deal belief that government could make a positive difference in society and advance private enterprise, including big business, at the same time. They were just what the conservative right wings of their respective parties called them: corporate liberals. For those who understood the historic role of foreign economic policy in promoting the prosperity that passed for domestic reform, there was no mystery to corporate liberals like Rockefeller and Johnson accepting dictatorship in Latin America as easily as a war against communist nationalists in Vietnam.

With Nelson vacillating and Kennedy still unannounced, only one man seemed certain about his future: Richard M. Nixon.

The Return of Richard Nixon

High above New York's Fifth Avenue, in an apartment just a few floors beneath Nelson Rockefeller's luxurious three-story penthouse, Richard Nixon was making a decision about 1968. He had been carefully laying the foundation for this campaign ever since he moved to New York in 1963 to join the Mudge, Rose law firm. He had become involved with a new financial group, organized around the mutual funds and railroad fortune of Alan and Fred Kirby of Texas and their allies, including Donald Kendall, head of PepsiCo. Nixon was now on the boards of six companies, where he rubbed shoulders for the first time with the Eastern Establishment in its own lair.

Even though he had lost his races for the presidency in 1960 and California's governorship in 1962, Nixon continued to play the loyal Republican. Even during the 1964 Goldwater debacle, he traveled the rubber-chicken circuit, boosting local candidates and collecting IOUs in the process. He did the same in 1966. Now he was ready.

So were a large number of Republican moneymen.

Nixon's globe-trotting in the Kendalls' jet on behalf of PepsiCo's international sales expansion and his success in promoting Pepsi franchises—including those in Saigon and Bangkok—earned him high marks on Wall Street and a regular six-figure income. It also convinced many business leaders that Nixon was a suitable safe alternative to the besieged Lyndon Johnson.

Nixon was not only a political alternative to Johnson; he was also a means of escape from the scandals and indiscretions surrounding Johnson. Foremost was the famous Bobby Baker scandal, which had erupted during the Kennedy administration when Attorney General Robert Kennedy conducted a bribery investigation against Johnson's former Senate aide. Baker's ties to land-development schemes involving Texas oil moneymen surfaced during the investigation. In October 1963, the U.S. Senate began holding hearings on the scandal. Some of the same Texans had been named in Senate Rules Committee hearings in connection with payoffs and loans to Baker in a land-development scheme tied to Jimmy Hoffa's Teamster Pension Fund. Johnson had cause to worry that his name would be smeared, and he was not the only one. Years later, it was revealed that one of the Texas real estate firms active in the Dallas–Fort Worth area in 1963—a firm that was partly owned by the family of Bedford Wynne, one of the named "Bobby Baker set"—had a second controlling interest: the Rockefeller family. Through Rockefeller Center, Inc., the Manhattan real estate firm now owned by Nelson and his brothers, the Rockefellers had become partners with the Wynne family in the Great Southwest Corporation.[6]

Should Robert Kennedy run for president and be elected, there was the likelihood of renewed federal investigations of organized crime and of Baker and those linked to him. Who knew where this could lead? Lyndon Johnson, his power wrecked on the shoals of Vietnam, could not protect his friends or even himself.

The movement of conservative Texas money toward Richard Nixon took on the appearance of a stampede. Some leading figures, like Governor John Connally, eventually would follow the herd right out of the Democratic party.

Of great importance to Nixon was the backing of Barry Goldwater, rendered publicly as early as 1965. This backing brought in Christian Fundamentalists and the money behind Fundamentalism. Both the new money and the old money had a symbolic center in Billy Graham. Graham's ministry, in turn, offered Nixon a mass base of conservative, middle-of-the-road voters.

In January 1968, Richard Nixon decided to move beyond his preoccupation with courting the Goldwater ultraconservative wing and to begin capturing the moderately conservative center by inviting Billy Graham to his Florida home. Nixon asked for Graham's help in deciding whether to run. Graham had known Nixon since the 1950s. They were golfing buddies. Both were hawkish on Vietnam, although Nixon hoped that those who were tired of the war would support him over Johnson. An endorsement from Billy Graham, a registered conservative Democrat, would be a hard blow to Johnson.

Graham prayed, and Nixon joined in. Graham read the Bible, and Nixon read it, too. They watched football. But still no word from Graham about the race. Finally, as Graham prepared to depart, Nixon's patience ran out.

"You still haven't told me what I ought to do," he said.

Graham turned back, a smile on his face. "Well, if you don't run, you'll always wonder," he said.[7]

Nixon had no intention of wondering. With Graham's support, God would appear to be on his side.

A thousand miles to the north, Robert Kennedy's mind was also on Nixon and Johnson. He had decided to enter the race. But when North Korea suddenly seized the U.S.S. *Pueblo* and its crew during an electronic spying mission off the Korean coast, Kennedy thought it could only benefit Johnson: A wave of sympathy for the crew and patriotic fervor would overwhelm any efforts to launch a challenge to the president.

A week later, suppressing his anguish, he announced that he "would not oppose Lyndon Johnson under any foreseeable circumstances."

That same night, as Kennedy slept, coffins were being unearthed in Saigon's cemeteries and guns were being taken out and distributed. Throughout Vietnam, the scene was being repeated. The Tet Offensive, which would dramatically change the course of the war and throw Robert Kennedy back into the fray, was about to begin.

Tet

The New Year's firecrackers kept SILers awake. Radê tribesmen living nearby had warned the American missionaries that they had better leave Banmethuot. Rumors about a big attack during Tet had been circulating for weeks, and far to the north, the village of Khe Sanh was already overrun by North Vietnamese troops.

But the Fundamentalist missionaries at Banmethuot were unmoved. "Don't you know we are immortal until our work is done?" one wrote her children.

Another, nurse Betty Olsen, told a journalist, "I have no fear because I am in the will of God."[8]

The Saigon military regime had built an army base just behind the Christian and Missionary Alliance compound nearby, and on the northern outskirts of Banmethuot the U.S. Military Command had established bases for Green Berets and the 155th Helicopter Company. SIL's Hank Blood felt safe.

In the middle of the night, the Christian and Missionary Alliance compound was caught in a crossfire between Saigon's troops and guerrilla forces of the communist-led National Liberation Front (NLF). Four missionaries were killed; several were wounded; and two, Hank Blood and Betty Olsen, were taken prisoner by the NLF, along with an AID official.* Only the AID officer would survive the long march north through the jungle.

At the Bible translation center at Kontum, SIL missionaries fared better. Twelve fled in U.S. helicopters while a C-47 "dragon" spewed down a hailstorm of bullets to cover their escape. The fighting between the Americans and their Vietnamese enemy was often at close range. "The Americans cranked their big guns down to zero and aimed them point bank at the waves of shrieking soldiers," one evangelical wrote, as if reporting a scene out of the American West. "The missionaries inside the bunkers could clearly hear the screams of the wounded and dying."[9] When, after two days and nights of fighting, the attack ended with 960 Vietnamese bodies counted by the Americans, the missionaries sang hymns.

In Saigon, a group of NLF guerrillas tried to storm Diem's National Palace, demanding "Open the Gates! We are the Liberation Army!" But the palace, perhaps because of the ever-present possibility of coups, was prepared for attackers. The assault failed.

But the attack on "Bunker's Bunker," the fortified new six-story white U.S. Embassy, was more effective. Blasting a hole through the nine-foot-high wall surrounding the embassy compound, nineteen guerrillas charged toward the main chancery building. A marine guard managed to slam and bolt the building's giant Thai teak doors just in time.

By early morning, General Westmoreland's MPs had stormed the embassy grounds and overwhelmed the attackers. Shortly afterward, Ambassador Ellsworth Bunker arrived with reporters and joined in Westmoreland's declaration of victory.

---

*The missionaries' open admiration for AID's Mike Benge was precarious. A tough ex-Marine, Benge's close ties to the U.S. Embassy as a worker for the International Volunteer Service (IVS) among the 100,000 Radê Montagnards around Banmethuot had made him a special prize for his captors. In Fundamentalist accounts of the Tet Offensive, Benge never denied ties to the CIA when questioned by the Vietnamese, answering accusations instead with countercharges that his captors were really North Vietnamese soldiers. Years later, after Benge helped launch the MIA (Missing-in-Action) movement in the States, former CIA Director William Colby would reveal that a Radê-speaking IVS worker had helped the CIA set up the Green Beret and AID program among the Radê and then joined the CIA itself. See William Colby, *Honorable Men: My Life in the CIA* (New York: Simon & Schuster, 1978).

But to the reporters and the world that saw their photographs, the attack on the embassy had shattered the illusion of U.S. invulnerability. For millions, the picture of Premier Ky's power broker and National Police director, General Nguyen Ngoc Loan, coldbloodedly executing an NLF suspect with a gunshot to the head shattered the carefully orchestrated image of the Saigon regime as a guardian of democracy, due process, and human rights. The regime's worth in American blood plummeted in U.S. opinion polls. For above it all was the stark fact that more than a hundred cities and villages throughout South Vietnam had been struck at once, and with the obvious sympathy, if not collaboration, of a sizable proportion of the Vietnamese population.

For the next four months, the attacks would continue, with two major offensives, including one enormous one in May, proving that Westmoreland's gleeful claims about an exhausted enemy were really wishful thinking. Instead, the destruction that accompanied the American counterattack, the killing of thousands of civilians caught in the cross fires, bombings, and assassinations by both sides, appalled the American people and undermined their confidence that this war could be won, or that it was even worth winning. A young American major's Orwellian doublethink explanation for the U.S. destruction of Ben Tri, a major commercial center in the Mekong Delta, with napalm and 5,000-pound bombs, seemed to sum up where it was all leading to: "It became necessary to destroy the town to save it."

If the genocidal nature of the war was not clear yet to the American public, it was to the Vietnamese civilians of My Lai hamlet. The frightened GIs of Charlie Company had already learned to despise the Vietnamese with racist slurs like "gook" when they were given orders to massacre civilians. It took less than two hours, but when it was over, 347 men, women, and children, including babies, were dead. Although news of the massacre would not leak out for another year, the moral force of the American intervention had been fatally wounded. From then on, its symbol would not be the GI with candy for kids, but My Lai and the assassins of CIA's Operation Phoenix.

The Tet Offensive proved the folly of General Westmoreland's insistence that the real battle would be at Khe Sanh, that the mounting conflicts in the cities were only a planned diversion from the long-anticipated invasion from the north. In fact, the real diversion was in such highland strongholds as Khe Sanh. British General Robert T. Thompson, the antiguerrilla expert who had masterminded the successful British counterinsurgency campaign in Malaysia, warned just that: "These battles within the cities are the decisive ones, and the larger scale battles which have, and are, being fought in the Annamite Mountains chain are the diversion." To Thompson, the U.S. tendency to believe that Tet was a desperate "go for broke" tactic demonstrated "a complete lack of understanding of the war and the stage it has now reached."[10]

By allowing Westmoreland to withdraw troops from the countryside at Khe

Sanh's rear, Johnson and the Joint Chiefs of Staff had opened the door to the NLF's reemergence in the villages, where the CIA's own arrests, assassinations, and installation of collaborators in official posts inadvertently had identified Saigon's network of supporters.

The NLF now struck back, executing collaborators and destroying the social infrastructure of the CIA's pacification program. Johnson's obsession with the highlands as the barrier to the war's being brought to the cities ironically had ensured that the final staging ground would, in fact, be the cities. Trapped by their own Cold War ideology into thinking that they were fighting a proxy Soviet and Chinese foreign invasion of Vietnam, Johnson, Walt Rostow, and the Joint Chiefs could not admit they were deeply involved in a civil war in Vietnam.

General Thompson, on the other hand, was not confused; he, as President Kennedy had said before him, knew that the regime in Saigon could not be saved if it did not gain popular support. And popular support could not be gained by U.S. military escalation. That was why Kennedy had begun the withdrawal of U.S. Marines just before his death. "Now obviously withdrawal means losing," Thompson explained, "but massive escalation equally means losing. . . . If you escalate massively, it would mean that the rest of the world would want to have very little to do with you as a people. And I think that, quite possibly, the United States as a result of all this would have lost its soul and would tear itself apart."[11]

Even SIL's Asia director, Richard Pittman, was unnerved by Tet: "The devastation of our center is like a scene of judgment day," he wrote Cam from Kontum.

But his faith was not shaken. The Hand of God was in evidence even in body counts. The low number of SIL casualties seemed to indicate that God's thumb was on the scales of justice.

Reassuring Cam that all SIL teams had moved "near American military facilities," Pittman was "happy to say that morale is high."[12]

In Washington, however, it was more difficult to see the Lord at work in anything in Vietnam. The North Vietnamese siege of Khe Sanh had not yet been broken, and despite massive bombings of North Vietnam, General Giap's buildup around Khe Sanh had not been hindered. If anything, "on balance, North Vietnam's a stronger military power today than before the bombing began," aide Townsend Hoopes reported to the new defense secretary, Clark Clifford. In the south, meanwhile, the Americans now had lost much of the countryside to the NLF.

"Johnson can't get away with saying it [Tet] is really a victory for us," Robert Kennedy said in a speech. "The Viet Cong . . . have demonstrated despite all our reports of progress . . . that half a million American soldiers with 700,000 Vietnamese allies, with total command of the air [and] sea, backed by huge resources and the most modern weapons, are unable to secure even a single city from the attack of an enemy whose total strength is about 250,000."

Then Kennedy struck the chords of the past, echoing his dead brother:

We have misconceived the nature of the war. . . . We have sought to resolve by military might a conflict whose issue depends upon the will and conviction of the South Vietnamese people. . . . This misconception rests on a second illusion—the illusion that we can win a war which the South Vietnamese cannot win for themselves. . . . Government corruption [in Saigon] is the source of the enemy's strength. . . . The third illusion is that the unswerving pursuit of military victory, whatever its cost, is in the interest of either ourselves or the people of Vietnam. . . . Their tiny land has been devastated by a weight of bombs and shells greater than Nazi Germany knew. . . . More than 2 million South Vietnamese are now homeless refugees. . . . Whatever the outcome of these battles, it is the people we seek to defend who are the great losers. The fourth illusion is that the American national interest is identical with—or should be subordinated to—the selfish interest of an incompetent military regime. . . . The fifth illusion is that this war can be settled in our own way and in our own time on our own terms.

To Kennedy, the choice was clear: "Our nation must be told the truth about this war, in all its terrible reality." There was a domestic price with that reality, as well: "We cannot build a Great Society there if we cannot build one in our own country."[13]

Never before had the credibility of an American president been so undermined by his own policies at home and abroad.

"Declare now," Richard Goodwin urged Kennedy clandestinely from the McCarthy campaign in New Hampshire.

On March 5, a full week before the New Hampshire primary, Kennedy decided to do just that.[14] On March 7, he asked his brother Ted to inform Eugene McCarthy that he would probably enter the race after the Wisconsin primary in early April. Ted, unhappy, procrastinated until March 11 and then passed the responsibility to Richard Goodwin, who told McCarthy the next day, March 12, on the evening before the New Hampshire primary. McCarthy, anticipating a victory after weathering red-baiting by conservative Democrats, was understandably bitter.

The Ides of March

The country was going through a sea-change in opinion. Even SIL's board, meeting in early March, expressed reservations about the war. "We are much concerned that we could have very strong criticism even affecting the work if another tragedy occurred."[15]

The next day, New Hampshire held its primary. Voters showed their disenchantment with the war by giving McCarthy 42 percent of the votes. Even at this late date, an air of unreality surrounded the Johnson administration. Dean Rusk testified before the Senate Foreign Relations Committee on foreign aid to South Vietnam as if Tet had never happened. Kennedy made Johnson an offer he was convinced no one but Lyndon Johnson could refuse: He would not enter the race if Johnson would appoint a presidential task force, with Kennedy included, to review

Vietnam policy with the intention of recommending a change. Clark Clifford reported back on March 14 that Johnson immediately rejected the proposal.

Meanwhile, Clark Clifford had more than a Kennedy candidacy or South Vietnam's viability to worry about: When does counterinsurgency become genocide, and what was the war costing Americans? His aide, Townsend Hoopes, touched the nerve of the matter: "Anything resembling a clear-cut military victory in this appears possible only at the price of literally destroying South Vietnam, tearing apart the social and political fabric of our own country, alienating our European friends, and gravely weakening the whole free world structure of relations and alliances."[16]

Clifford noted grimly that with the exception of the Marcos regime in the Philippines and the client regime in South Korea, the United States' traditional allies had failed to back U.S. intervention in Indochina; even nearby Australia and New Zealand sent only token forces into the battlefield. Latin America, despite Johnson's entreaties, remained aloof; only the Brazilian junta sent men, but they were medics, not troops. And Europe was becoming openly critical.

In addition, European banks and other foreign investors holding U.S. dollars were increasingly worried about what the war's inflation was doing to the value of the dollar. Not only did the declining value of the dollar give U.S. companies' exports a competitive advantage in Europe and other markets that they probably did not deserve, but it also undermined the dollar-based assets of European balance sheets. Not the least of these assets were dollars that had been left in Europe from Marshall Plan loans, as well as direct U.S. corporate investments and dollars brought in by U.S servicemen and tourists. All created deficits in the balance of payments that reached $40 billion by 1968. Even gold, the reference point for all noncommunist currencies, was pegged to the dollar's value, at $35 per ounce.

In late 1967 and early 1968, as a wave of imports hit American markets, as inflation and the U.S. budget deficit grew with the Vietnam War, and as an end to the war that would be favorable to the United States looked further away than ever, European confidence in the dollar collapsed. Dollars were cashed in for gold in European money markets, and the flight of gold from the U.S. Treasury reached a crisis stage.[17] This "Gold Crisis" came to the steps of the Johnson White House, in the form of a delegation of powerful bankers.

The Tet Offensive had convinced much of the international business community that the war would take too long and therefore would be too costly to win. On March 13, the day after his defeat in New Hampshire, Johnson suffered the indignity of hearing Rockefeller ally C. Douglas Dillon and other members of a presidential advisory panel warn him of "the grave consequences to the United States' international trade and financial position" if he did not raise taxes to increase treasury revenues.[18]

Johnson called British Prime Minister Harold Wilson on the Hot Line that was usually reserved for nuclear threats, asking him to suspend gold payments.

That night Queen Elizabeth made a proclamation that closed Britain's stock exchanges, its foreign-exchange markets, all the foreign departments of banks, and, of course, the London Gold Exchange.

Nelson Rockefeller remained aloof, but watchful. He refused to join the chorus of budget-conscious critics of foreign aid. He was still convinced of the necessity of foreign aid for U.S. corporate investment abroad, both as the promoter of Third World development and the bulwark against revolution and Soviet infiltration. Just the previous year, his brother David had pressured congressmen against cuts in aid to Latin America and had rallied corporate leaders in the Council of the Americas to do likewise. This accord on Third World policy extended to Vietnam. The Rockefellers continued to back Johnson. George Romney's campaign, hobbled by Rockefeller aides crafting prowar speeches for the Michigan governor, had succumbed on February 28. A bitter Romney explained privately that he withdrew because "he found out he was being used by Rockefeller as a stalking horse."[19] On March 12, a write-in campaign for Nelson gathered 11 percent of the votes in the New Hampshire Republican primary. A Gallup poll showed him beating Johnson handily.

On March 16, Robert Kennedy's announcement, televised from the same Senate Caucus Room from which John Kennedy had announced his bid for the White House, helped Nelson make up his mind. Kennedy's candidacy, Nelson realized, would draw from his own traditional constituency: moderates, liberals, and minorities. On March 21, after concluding that he could not win over Nixon's supporters, he again withdrew from a race he had never formally entered.

What Rockefeller could not have known was how a small battle in the tribal highlands of Laos, even more than the massive air strikes around Khe Sanh, was playing a crucial part in the American domestic drama leading to the resignation of Lyndon Johnson. Johnson's announcement that the United States would halt the bombing of North Vietnam and open negotiations in Paris came just three weeks after the CIA's "Eagle's Nest," a mile up in the mountains of Laos, had fallen to the Pathet Lao. With the capture of Phon Pha Thi on March 11, the U.S. Command had lost its key radar guidance center for B-52s that were flying from Thailand across Laos to bomb Hanoi and the Red River Delta in the east. By the time this bombing campaign was halted, it was already electronically blind.

Johnson had mentioned not running again as early as August 1967, but few had taken him seriously. Lady Bird, always worried about his health, attributed several factors to his retreat: the Gold Crisis, the shift in sentiment against the war among Johnson's "wise men" advisory panel, and, finally, the prospect of electoral defeat by that "pipsqueak" Robert Kennedy.

Johnson himself later confirmed the fears about his psychological state. "I felt that I was being dared on all sides by a giant stampede coming at me from all directions."[20] He had succumbed to tirades in front of both the Cabinet and the public.

"Let's get one thing clear," he told the Cabinet on March 16. "I'm not going to stop the bombing. . . . I am not interested in further discussion."[21] Speeches became a tantrum against "moving the battlefield into cities where people lived." Better to bomb Khe Sanh to keep the Montagnard hills' "trip wire" in place, if it could still be found. By then, after forty days of siege, the jungle hills around Khe Sanh had been turned into a scorched desert, having received more bombs, according to Townsend Hoopes, than "any target in the history of warfare, including Hiroshima."[22]

But there *was* more discussion, strong dissent, in fact, from the very "wise men" he had chosen to advise him. When Clark Clifford finally insisted that the draft of a speech drop defiant analogies to the Alamo, the hawks were stunned. "The President cannot give that speech. It would be a disaster." What "seems not to be understood," he added, "is that major elements of the national constituency—the business community, the press, the churches, professional groups, college presidents, students, most of the intellectual community—have turned against the war."[23] Johnson got the message. On March 31, just before the Wisconsin primary could bring decisive embarrassment, he went on national television and told the divided nation that he would not seek a second term.

No sooner had Johnson made his announcement than he received a call from Nelson at the White House. "Tell him that Happy and I watched him," Nelson told a White House aide. "We thought that he was fabulous. His friends are with him one hundred percent. He's a great patriot. We're both devoted to him and just want to reach out to him at this time."[24]

At one minute to midnight, the White House received another call from Rockefeller. This time Johnson took it, though alone in his bedroom. When he emerged ten minutes later, he looked relieved, chuckling "Now Nelson Rockefeller is reassessing things."[25]

The Power of Personal Loyalty

Over the next few weeks, Nelson watched cautiously as events in Vietnam unfolded: Ho Chi Minh's quick acceptance of Johnson's offer of peace talks, Rusk and Rostow's discord on accepting, the breaking of the siege of Khe Sanh, the continued rocket attacks on Saigon, and the persistent refusal of the alleged "dominos" surrounding South Vietnam to respond to the call for troops.

Harvard professor Henry Kissinger, infuriated by Hanoi's obvious decision in July 1967 to launch the Tet Offensive and to take a hard line against concessions to the Ky-Thieu regime, had moved away from the peace proposal he had brought secretly to Paris on Johnson's behalf in August 1967. In so doing, he was rejecting the very outlines of a peace plan that Clark Clifford and Johnson's top negotiator, Averell Harriman, were now embracing: an end to bombing in the North and the strategic withdrawal of U.S. troops from the highlands to the demilitarized zone, the lowland Vietnamese cities, and the highways and the important Mekong Delta.

Nelson, for his part, had to offer some kind of peace plan if he were to become a viable candidate. He turned to Kissinger. The two worked out a proposed disengagement based on a model already discredited by Saigon and U.S. violations: the 1954 Geneva Agreement of free elections, coupled with North Vietnamese withdrawal, the NLF's surrender of arms, and the continued reign of the Saigon regime's deadly security forces.[26]

Meanwhile, as the war raged on, Nelson pondered his chances if he reentered the race. He could not break Nixon's hold over the Republican party's regulars. The only way to win would be, once again, to take the convention by storm through an appeal directly to the voters and the delegates. However, this was the strategy that had failed in 1960 and 1964.

Ironically, it was not Republicans who finally persuaded Rockefeller to take the plunge; it was the titular head of the Democratic party and the president of the United States, Lyndon Johnson.

After his withdrawal speech, Johnson had invited the Rockefellers for a "very secret"[27] private dinner at the White House. Johnson chose April 23, when the White House would be hosting a black-tie diplomatic reception in honor of Johnson's signing the U.S. ratification of amendments to the Charter of the Organization of American States. Nelson's appearance at the White House would not cause undue speculation by the press. But Nelson was not a guest at that reception. The affair was already breaking up when he and Happy arrived at the White House's basement entrance. Nelson was probably expecting a quiet evening with an old friend, perhaps to console the president confidentially as he had over the phone on March 31. Happy, at least, did not expect what came next: Johnson wanted Nelson to declare for the presidency.

"He told me he could not sleep at night if Nixon were president," Nelson recalled years later, "and he wasn't sure about Hubert [Humphrey] either."

"I told him I'd made a promise to Happy that I would not run again."

"Let me talk to Happy," said Johnson, and he took her down the hall for a dose of his famous personal persuasion.

Happy and Johnson had a special relationship based on Happy's ability to make men feel important. By almost all accounts, Lyndon Johnson was the kind of man who needed such stroking.

The conversation lasted half an hour. Happy was swayed by Johnson's arguments about how important Nelson's campaign was to the country; to the presidency; to Lyndon Johnson; and, ultimately, to Nelson.

"I've talked her into letting you run," Johnson reported.[28]

A week later, Rockefeller once more convened reporters in the opulent Red Room of Albany's State Capitol to announce that his candidacy was now "active."

38

NELSON'S LAST CHARGE

Through the Valley of Death

As early as 1964, Nelson Rockefeller had been aware of the FBI's slander campaign against Rev. Martin Luther King, Jr., having secretly been briefed by the FBI during its attempts to discourage participation in receptions held to honor King's return from Sweden with the Nobel Peace Prize.[1] By 1968, King was speaking out against the war in Vietnam, threatening to widen the civil rights movement to include those who were opposed to the war. At the same time, he began to strike at the economic inequities by allying his movement with the struggles of African American workers in the cities, further widening the movement and deepening its roots within the urban working class.

Lyndon Johnson understood the threat posed to the political establishment by King's new emphasis on economics and the war. "That goddamn nigger preacher may drive me out of the White House,"[2] he told cabinet members after King's April 4, 1967, speech against the war. A year later to the day, in Memphis, Tennessee, to support predominantly black sanitation workers striking for collective bargaining rights supposedly guaranteed by federal law, King was assassinated. Riots erupted throughout the nation.

Nelson Rockefeller and Lyndon Johnson attended King's funeral in Atlanta. So did their leading rival for the loyalty of African American voters, Robert Kennedy.

In the aftermath of King's death, Rockefeller was criticized for his membership in the discriminatory Knickerbocker Club and heckled by African American students at Spelman College, long funded by his family. Kennedy, in contrast, won praise from African American students. During his tour of Washington's riot-torn neighborhoods right after the King assassination, Kennedy was riding a swell of revulsion against injustice and death, in Vietnam and in the agrifields and ghettos of the United States. The revulsion reached even into the ranks of the normally conservative leadership of white Protestant Fundamentalism.

"Americans everywhere must be searching their hearts. I am mine," Cam Townsend wrote to SIL's membership the day before King's funeral:

> What have I done to help my fellow citizen whose complexion is darker than my own? . . . I maintained that I loved them, but where was the practical demonstration of that love? I lied. . . . Dear fellow worker, we need to search our souls. Are we living a lie?
>
> . . . We have gone along with certain prevalent attitudes even though they were obnoxious to us. Another question. Are we doing all we can to get Negro members? Shouldn't we assign someone to visit their colleges with the challenge of Bible translation work and assure them that we would welcome more Negro members. Yours in memory of Martin Luther King.[3]

Nevertheless, SIL would remain overwhelmingly white, even in Africa. Not even Catholics would be welcome. The board of SIL/Wycliffe Bible Translators had specifically ruled against admitting Catholics the previous year, when a young Catholic, Paul Witte, sought membership. Cam responded by arranging for Witte's association with the Colombian branch through Bishop Canyes, for which he was rewarded with official criticism of the Colombia branch by the board and hints that perhaps Cam was getting too old for the job of general director.

Kennedy, too, came under attack from Fundamentalists who were sympathetic to Governor George Wallace's candidacy on the American Independent party ticket. SIL backer Nelson Bunker Hunt set up a $1 million trust fund to lure General Curtis LeMay into the campaign as Wallace's running mate.[4]

Rockefeller watched enviously as Kennedy crossed effortlessly from one political world to another, courting white farmers in Indiana and suburban "white-backlash" blue-collar workers with the same courage he showed among Mexican American farmworkers in California and African American workers in Washington.

And through it all, Kennedy was being monitored, like Martin Luther King, Jr., before him, by the FBI and targeted by ultrarightists. After being humbled in Oregon with second place, following victories in the Indiana and Washington, D.C., primaries, he entered southern California with the knowledge that the home of Richard Nixon and Ronald Reagan, a hotbed of Fundamentalist reaction, would be his greatest challenge. He never conceived that it would be his doom.

Sirhan Sirhan had been a Kennedy supporter until he saw a news photo of Kennedy wearing a yarmulke, appealing to Jewish voters in Oregon with his support for selling fifty Phantom jet bombers to Israel. Sirhan was a refugee from Palestine, having immigrated to the United States with his family in the mid-

1950s. Kennedy's remarks came only seven months after Jordan, Sirhan's legal homeland, and other Arab states had been defeated in the June 1967 War. June 5 was the first anniversary of the war; Sirhan had written in his diary of his resolve to kill Kennedy before that date. His words were repetitive, compulsive.

Sirhan Sirhan made his way to the hotel kitchen and waited with a gun. The place was packed. Senator Kennedy, after a grueling campaign and having held his own in a televised debate with Senator Eugene McCarthy, had won the California Democratic primary. He had just made his victory statement in the ballroom, calling for national unity to heal the wounds of war and division. Now he was on his way to a press conference. He detoured through the kitchen. Suddenly, shots were fired and Kennedy fell with a head wound. He died the next day. A major contender had been removed from the American political arena.

Nelson Rockefeller, acting in his capacity as governor, met the Kennedys and the senator's body at New York's La Guardia Airport. As he had for the family of Martin Luther King, Jr., Nelson provided Pocantico's major domo, Joseph Canzeri, to help the Kennedys with funeral arrangements. He spent the next day of mourning in New York, attending Kennedy's service with 2,500 foreign dignitaries in St. Patrick's Cathedral. He rode the funeral train the following day to Washington, and he watched thousands of mourners sing a last farewell at the Lincoln Memorial, then follow the funeral procession across the bridge into Arlington National Cemetery and up the hill overlooking the Potomac, where Bobby was buried next to his brother. Then Nelson met at the State Department in the office of his family foundation's former president, Secretary Dean Rusk. He needed a briefing immediately. He was, after all, now a leading presidential candidate.

It was natural that the poor and disfranchised should mourn Bobby Kennedy more than did the rest of the nation. His loss was felt particularly by minorities, who believed he was their last hope in American national politics.

Rockefeller sensed the vacuum in leadership among these people and immediately tried to fill it. He knew he was no Kennedy to them. But he also knew there was no one else they could turn to, with Hubert Humphrey still the candidate of the war and Eugene McCarthy still the candidate of the discomfited comfortable in educated white suburbia. And he also could see that the hard questions that might have made his own candidacy—or Humphrey's or Nixon's—less viable, would not be asked by the molders of mass opinion after the assassination. Wrote journalist Jack Newfield, "Sociologists, politicians, and religious leaders [were] blaming movies, comic strips, and television. No one seemed to think that Vietnam, or poverty, or lynchings, or our genocide against Indians had anything to do with it. Just popular culture like *Bonnie and Clyde*, never political institutions, or our own tortured history."

"I got home about 2 A.M. New York time," Newfield continued, "and put on the television to see a tape of President Johnson announcing a new commission to study the causes of violence in America. One of the members of the commission, he said, would be Roman Hruska, the Republican Senator from Nebraska who was the major Congressional spokesmen for the National Rifle Association. I could imagine Bobby wincing as he heard the absurd views."[5]

Nelson did not wince. Instead, he met with the president at the White House immediately after Johnson announced the commission's charges.

Rockefeller's conversation with Johnson that day in the Oval Office was kept "off the record," but Nelson had a press conference afterward in the White House's West Lobby. He was the first candidate to resume campaigning after Kennedy's death, and the White House setting gave every indication of the president's blessing. "I requested a meeting with the President so that, as a result of last week's tragedy, we discussed the role of a candidate in assisting to bring the kind of stability and healing of wounds and division which exist in this country." Having proclaimed himself a national healer, he already spoke like a president-elect. "I spent quite a lot of time with the President alone. Then Secretary Rusk, General Wheeler [chairman of the Joint Chiefs of Staff], and Mr. Rostow came in. We spent two hours on the situation at home and abroad."

Asked if there would be any changes in his campaign, Nelson managed to tie personal courage to support for the war in Vietnam. "No. . . . If democracy is to stay alive and strong, then there can be no timidity. . . . There are some 500,000 Americans fighting on the front in Southeast Asia, some 20,000 have given their lives, and I don't think it is for us at home who are trying to represent the forces of democracy in the heart of the nation to cringe from risks."

Then he revealed his campaign strategy. Asked if Kennedy's death had changed the political picture for the Republicans, Nelson nodded. "I think . . . the shock and sorrow will be reflected in a changed mood, that the bridges which he built to our groups who have not shared largely in the American way of life are going to be bridges which will influence both those who are in these groups and the rest of this country."[6]

Nelson offered Kennedy's Senate seat to two liberals, albeit Republican liberals, in the Kennedy maverick vein: New York Mayor John Lindsay, who declined, and then Rep. Charles Goodell, who accepted. He then appointed the former California chair of "People for Kennedy" and a close friend of the Kennedys, Mrs. Thomas Braden, to lead a national "People for Rockefeller" organization. "Most of the people I know who were for Robert F. Kennedy are now for Nelson A. Rockefeller," she explained. "Some are still too stunned to do much but those who can will help Governor Rockefeller." She was not quoted as mentioning her husband's debt to Nelson for a loan that helped him buy a California newspaper.

To launch his 66,000-mile blitzkrieg around the country, Nelson headed for

Braden country, Los Angeles. For the first time he included Watts in his itinerary. "I think the people who supported Bobby Kennedy are going to come to me now," he told his staff, and he instructed them to begin all speeches on the West Coast with a tribute to Kennedy. But the speeches should not be too introspective. "I don't want any of that sick society stuff. A few nuts don't reflect the state of the country," he insisted. The United States had better stop "looking backward" on past tragedies and mistakes and get beyond such "negative thinking."[7] California Governor Ronald Reagan's claim that the assassination was the result of a growing attitude of permissiveness by the nation's courts and leaders might have contained a kernel of truth for New York's "Get Tough on Crime" governor. Nelson could not accept Billy Graham's belief that the shooting was symbolic of world moral and spiritual decline or Eugene McCarthy's belief that the United States bore too great a burden of guilt for the kind of neglect that had allowed the disposition of violence to grow in the country. Nelson Rockefeller was bullish about America and still the perennial optimist about his own political ambitions.

He could pull together minorities, liberals, and youths into a new Rockefeller coalition, he confided to his antiwar son, Steven. He believed he could "get the nomination by a great public outcry." Steven explained later. "Going to the people is his thing; he loves the applause. Going to the delegates was not his thing."[8] And in the end, that was his undoing. If average Republican delegates were anything in 1968, they were not minorities, not liberals, not youths.

And Nelson Rockefeller was not Robert Kennedy. Henry Kissinger's plan for withdrawal from Vietnam and his constant efforts to make Nelson's confusing statements come out sounding right did not create the excitement that Kennedy's clean break with Johnson had.

Rockefeller by now had adopted the Kennedy style of plunging recklessly into crowds, pumping hands, and losing cuff links. Desperate to win over Kennedy's Latino supporters in Texas, Florida, and California, he played his Latin American ties to the hilt. He often spoke in Spanish at such events. But by the end of July, it was clear to the country that Rockefeller's Kennedy style was not Kennedy substance.

His "New Leadership versus Old Politics" theme fell flat with both voters and delegates, especially when they looked at who was backing him. These backers were no populist mavericks like those who had backed Kennedy. These were millionaire businessmen, men like David and Winthrop's real estate partner, Trammel Crow; luxury department store owner Stanley Marcus; Du Pont family in-law Baron Kidd; and chemical scion A. Felix du Pont, Jr.

In the waning days of the campaign, with the Republican Convention in Miami just a week away, the *Miami Herald* prematurely released a Gallup poll showing that Nixon could do better than Rockefeller against Humphrey or McCarthy.

"Nixon or John Mitchell must have gotten to Gallup," Rockefeller said. He knew all about the use of polls in psychological warfare, and Gallup was suspect as a "born-again Christian." So he responded in kind, leaking a Harris poll that showed himself the victor. Then he repeated this maneuver by releasing a poll taken by his own campaign staff after the convention had begun. But it did no good.

Rockefeller lost on the first ballot, 277 votes to Nixon's 692. His last campaign to win the White House he coveted all his life was over.

It was a terrible shock to his sense of self-worth. He flew back to New York, comforting his backers with a typical self-effacing apology. "You were fine. I just wasn't good enough. I let you down."[9] Even Humphrey's offer later that month to share the Democratic ticket as the vice presidential nominee did not soften the blow. "Franklin Roosevelt wanted me to be a Democrat (back in the 1940s). It was too late."[10] He had cast his lot: Win or lose, Nelson Rockefeller would die a member of the Republican Party.

Nelson spent the months up to election day quietly betraying Lyndon Johnson. After Nixon's nomination, he had offered the services of his top foreign policy aide, Henry Kissinger, to the Nixon camp. Kissinger, for his part, remained privately bitter about Nixon, but to Nixon's face the Rockefeller camp stayed on the track of party loyalty, even to the point of betraying Lyndon Johnson's trust.

THE FIRST OCTOBER SURPRISE

Nelson Rockefeller wanted a seat in Nixon's cabinet. And Nixon wanted to be president. Building a bridge between the two goals was Kissinger's job.

Kissinger had had Johnson's confidence since 1967, when Kissinger approached Defense Secretary Robert McNamara, offering to engage in secret shuttle diplomacy to Paris to see if the North Vietnamese were ready to talk. Because they were planning the Tet Offensive, they were not. Nevertheless, Kissinger's hard work and discretion convinced Secretary McNamara and Deputy Secretary Cyrus Vance that he could be trusted. That trust would cost the Democrats the White House.

In the weeks immediately following the Democratic and Republican conventions, the Paris peace talks were on hold. Saigon refused to consider the participation of the National Liberation Front (NLF) in a new coalition government in exchange for peace. Johnson's continued bombing of Vietnam, meanwhile, only deepened Hanoi's resolve to keep fighting. After much discussion, McNamara's replacement as defense secretary, Clark Clifford, came up with a new, two-track approach: the United States would deal directly with North Vietnam and let the Saigon-NLF dispute be approached on a separate track of negotiations. Johnson thought it over.

On September 17, the same day Johnson OK'd Clifford's approach, Henry

Kissinger arrived in Paris. Two days later, Averell Harriman arrived, with the news that he had a breakthrough in the peace talks: Johnson had agreed to halt the bombing without Hanoi's having to commit itself first to stopping the war. Serious negotiations could now begin. What was crucial was to keep the Republicans from getting wind of this new stance and any agreement with Hanoi to prevent them from urging the Saigon regime to resist.

It was at this time that Kissinger visited Harriman's aide in Paris, Daniel Davidson, and dined with Harriman's deputy, Cyrus Vance. Davidson, who knew only that "something was going on" with Harriman and Vance, spoke freely with Kissinger, encouraged by Kissinger's confiding that "six days a week I'm for Hubert, but on the seventh day, I think they're both awful."[11] Kissinger promised to make Davidson his deputy if he got any post in Humphrey's administration or in Nixon's.

What he did not tell Davidson was that he was secretly informing on the negotiations to the Nixon campaign staff.

"I knew that Rockefeller had been offering Kissinger's assistance and urging that I make use of it ever since the convention," Nixon later wrote in his memoirs. "I told [H. R.] Haldeman that [campaign manager John] Mitchell should continue as liaison with Kissinger and that we should honor his desire to keep his role completely confidential."[12]

Mitchell, too, was sure that Nelson Rockefeller was the prime mover: "I thought Henry was doing it because Nelson wanted him to. Nelson asked Henry to help and he did."[13]

In late September, Kissinger, now back from Paris, reported the dreaded news that "there is a better than even chance that Johnson will order a bombing halt at approximately mid-October."

"Our source," Haldeman cryptically told Nixon, "is extremely concerned about the moves Johnson may take and expects that he will take some action before the election." On October 12, three days after Harriman made another breakthrough in Paris, Kissinger called Nixon staffer Richard Allen to warn of a likely development before October 23 and that there was "more to this than meets the eye."[14]

This was exactly the kind of ominous impression that Harriman and Clifford did not want to convey to Saigon. And that was exactly what the Nixon campaign passed on to Saigon through an old political friend of Richard Nixon and Nelson Rockefeller, Anna Chennault.*

By passing on state secrets that involved the lives of American soldiers, Kissinger was risking possible federal prosecution. He had also compromised any future Nixon administration. "My attitude was that it was inevitable that Kissinger

---

*Mrs. Chennault, a founder of the "China Lobby" that had backed Chiang Kai-shek, was the widow of General Claire Chennault, the founder of Civil Air Transport (CAT), the CIA's airline in Southeast Asia. CAT was the CIA airline that Harper Woodward, a top Rockefeller aide, was a director of during the year Nelson oversaw covert operations as Eisenhower's special assistant on Cold War strategy.

would have to be part of our administration," Richard Allen later concluded. The Nixon staff knew that it was "a pretty dangerous thing for him to be screwing around with the national security."[15]

The same could have been said for the Nixon campaign. Warned by an excited Kissinger just twelve hours before the announcement of the bombing halt that Harriman and Vance had "broken open the champagne," believing they had gotten Saigon's approval to participate in the negotiations, the Nixon campaign leaked the news to Saigon hardliners.[16] That day, General Thieu, the president in Saigon, announced he would not participate in the talks. The agreement collapsed. The war would go on for six more years; as many Americans would die in Vietnam during this period as had died there before.

Hubert Humphrey's campaign, riding the crest of the negotiations' progress and sustained now by his belated break with Johnson's escalation, had come to within one point of overtaking Nixon, thanks to Nixon's own intransigence on Vietnam. But the collapse of the negotiations hurt him.

Johnson had received CIA reports that pointed to a security leak in Paris through the Nixon camp and Mrs. Chennault to Saigon. But Johnson could not get proof and feared exposing intelligence sources or discrediting his administration with unsubstantiated charges. Besides, angry with Humphrey's defection from his war policies, Johnson had lost any interest in helping him.

Rockefeller expected his reward: perhaps a seat in the new Nixon cabinet. To the press he had speculated that he was interested in only the State Department or the Defense Department; the Departments of Health, Education, and Welfare, Housing and Urban Development, or even the Treasury had little attraction for him. On September 25, he convened his aides, including Kissinger, for a luncheon meeting in Manhattan to ponder the question of which seat he should take if one was offered. There was a phone call from Dwight Chapin, Nixon's appointments secretary.

But the call was for Kissinger, not for Rockefeller. When Kissinger returned, the group took up Rockefeller's role in a Nixon cabinet "as if nothing had happened. No one at the lunch," Kissinger later recalled, "could conceive that the purpose of the call would be to offer me a major position in the new Administration."[17]

No one, that is, except Kissinger, who had discussed the possibility of the position of national security adviser shortly after the Republican Convention.

And Richard Nixon. The idea of looking across the Cabinet Room table at Nelson Rockefeller did not appeal to him at all.

"At Treasury, what about David Rockefeller?" William Safire asked Nixon when the cabinet was being selected. "No, you can't have two Rockefellers in the Cabinet," Safire concluded.

"Is there a law," asked Nixon, "that you have to have one?"[18]

In the end, Rockefeller was told by Nixon that he would be of better service to the country as a governor than as a cabinet member.

Yet, even Richard Nixon would finally have to bend before the Rockefellers' special place in U.S. relations with Latin America. In confronting the vast market potential and the mounting rebellions south of the Rio Grande, there simply was no way to avoid Nelson Rockefeller.

VII

A NEW WORLD ORDER

A new type of military man is coming to the fore and often becoming a major force for constructive social change in the American republics. Motivated by increasing impatience with corruption, inefficiency, and a stagnant political order, the new military man is prepared to adapt his authoritarian tradition to the goals of social and economic progress.

This new role by the military, however, is not free from perils and dilemmas. There is always the risk that the authoritarian style will result in repression. The temptation to expand measures for security or discipline or efficiency to the point of curtailing individual liberties, beyond what is required for the restoration of order and social progress, is not easy to resist.

—NELSON ROCKEFELLER,
The Rockefeller Report on the Americas:
The Official Report of a United States
Presidential Mission for the Western Hemisphere (1969)

39

INVASION OF THE AMAZON

The Rise of Galo Plaza

This was not the first time that the tall, distinguished, gray-haired man had been to the White House. During his forty years of public life, Ecuador's Galo Plaza had often appeared in Washington as the representative of one of South America's smaller countries, either as ambassador or as its visiting head of state. But never before had he been invited to a reception for a newly inaugurated U.S. president as representative of all Latin America, the secretary general of the Organization of American States (OAS). And never with such influential friends as Nelson Rockefeller so close to the pinnacle of power in the hemisphere—or so it seemed in January 1969.

As the new head of the OAS, Galo Plaza had much to look forward to with the Nixon administration. Rockefeller's top foreign policy aide, Henry Kissinger, was now in charge of the powerful National Security Council. At the urging of David Rockefeller, Charles Meyer of the Latin American division of Sears, Roebuck was now head of the State Department's Latin American branch. Both men could be assumed to share many of the views of Nelson Rockefeller and, therefore, of Galo Plaza.

This was the happy end of a series of events that had started less than a year before, on April 23, 1968, when Galo Plaza had attended his first White House dinner for OAS delegates as their newly elected secretary general. That evening, neither he nor any of his fellow guests could have fathomed the reasons or surmised the lengths that Lyndon Johnson had gone to ensure a future for Latin American friends of Republican Nelson Rockefeller. When President Johnson had slipped out of the dinner hall that night, it was to meet secretly with the man who had done more than any other since World War II to shape U.S.–Latin American relations, and to urge him to run for president.

But no one could have missed the meaning of Johnson's parting speech to the OAS delegates that night. Johnson spoke of the Amazon basin as if another Mekong Basin Development Program were in the works. "Locked behind the high mountain ranges and rain forests . . . we find many unknown resources. The new frontiers of South America's heartland beckon."[1] It seemed that the Amazon was at last at hand. And with Galo Plaza as the new head of the OAS, both Rockefeller and Johnson knew they had a dependable hand on the rudder of U.S.–Latin American diplomatic relations.

In 1967, the Johnson administration had learned of attempts by Latin Americans to take control of their organization or, more precisely, of its finances. Five American officers in the OAS Treasury suddenly found themselves scheduled for reassignment.[2] The Johnson administration moved quickly to forestall this development. Its purported task was to breathe "new life" into the OAS. Internal power struggles had developed over Johnson's use of the OAS as a thin cover for the U.S. invasion of the Dominican Republic. And there was also the vexing problem of Cuba's continuing defiance of U.S. power over the hemisphere's economic future.

Galo Plaza seemed perfect for restoring the OAS's internal stability and improving the organization's image. Rockefeller circles likened him to an "international troubleshooter." Loyal to his roots as a major Ecuadorian landowner, lawyer for the United Fruit Company, and former student at the Georgetown University School of Foreign Service, Galo Plaza could be counted on to maintain order within the organization while ensuring OAS support for CIA subversion of leftist-minded governments, not only in Ecuador (where the Velasco and Arósemena governments had both fallen to CIA-backed coups), but throughout Latin America. He had also endorsed the efforts of Nelson's brother, John 3rd, to introduce birth control among Ecuador's Indians through the Agency for International Development, a major new policy initiative. In addition, Galo Plaza could ensure the hemispherewide transfer of rural development programs from Rockefeller's American International Association for Economic and Social Development (AIA) to the OAS. Most important, all this would give Rockefeller, through his influence on Galo Plaza, added weight not only in the OAS, but also in any White House deliberation over using the OAS.

Galo Plaza's recruitment had not come easily. He had been courted by Rockefeller, Lincoln Gordon (who had been rewarded for his ambassadorial performance in Brazil with appointment as assistant secretary of state), and U.S. Ambassador to Ecuador Wymberly Coerr. But the Ecuadorian was reluctant to sit in the hot seat of the hemisphere, acting as a foil for unilateral decisions by

Washington. David Rockefeller's friend, former Xerox Corporation chairman and current OAS Ambassador Sol Linowitz, had to phone Washington's assurance "that we are eager to make the OAS one of the truly significant international organizations of our time."

Flattered, Galo Plaza agreed to a lunch at which Linowitz assured him that Washington would not divulge their conversation to Galo Plaza's OAS colleagues.[3] Linowitz conferred again with Rockefeller, and when he met Galo Plaza later, he found the Ecuadorian more amenable. "He told me—and later repeated to Nelson Rockefeller," Linowitz reported to Secretary of State Dean Rusk, "that if he felt there is an opportunity for him to render important service he would not refuse it."[4]

Galo Plaza was elected by OAS member states in February 1968 almost by acclamation; only Fernando Belaúnde Terry's representative from Peru, Ecuador's rival for Amazonian oil lands, abstained.

News of the election of this known Rockefeller friend roused cheers from an unexpected quarter. William Cameron Townsend immediately sent a letter of congratulations to the man who had welcomed the missionaries of the Summer Institute of Linguistics into Ecuador's Amazon jungle. Galo Plaza answered that "the Inter-American system is about to reach the most decisive moment in its history."[5] Only those who were privy to Townsend's five decades of successful maneuvering within the outer orbit of Rockefeller power could have guessed why Ecuador's former president provided common ground for the interests of Cam and Nelson Rockefeller to converge.

Binding them, like so many others, was that magical subterranean substance called oil.

Significant quantities of petroleum had been rediscovered in the very region of Ecuador, the Amazonian Oriente, where Galo Plaza had argued two decades earlier that there was no oil. The 1967 oil discovery at Lago Agrio had been aided by SIL's presence in the jungle; Limoncocha's airstrip was used by the oilmen and on at least one occasion JAARS ferried Texaco oil geologists in and out of the jungle. The pace of exploration was feverish because OPEC was becoming bolder in its arguments for higher prices for Middle East oil. Ecuador's 6 percent royalty was eight times less than the lowest royalty received in the Middle East, and Arab-Israeli conflicts threatened to disrupt oil supplies. (Indeed, the Amazon discovery beat out the 1967 Arab-Israeli War by only two months.) In addition, Texaco-Gulf's five-year exploration contract with Ecuador and its 1.65-million-hectare concession was due to expire in 1969. Accordingly, Ecuador's Amazon jungle was now discovered to be awash with oil; of 78 test wells drilled by 1971, Texaco reported that 74 were productive.[6] Oil crews drilled wells and built a pipeline through the lands of the Kofán, Siona, and Secoya Indians; other crews pushed into the jungles south of the Napo River, home of Rachel Saint's feared "Auca," the Huaorani Indians.

SIL's missionaries took on the role of vanguard for the oil companies, flying ahead to warn the Huaorani away from oil crews advancing through the jungle and trying to persuade the Indians to surrender to the inevitability of Rachel Saint's love. SIL's tactics succeeded in avoiding confrontations, but through fear more than love. Swooping down with loudspeakers mounted on wings, JAARS planes, though speaking Huao, terrified the Huaorani. The Indians kept burning their thatched houses and fleeing into the forest. The breakthrough for the Lord came in 1968, when SIL switched to air-dropping baskets containing hidden radio transmitters. Hearing a brother of a captured Huaorani demand an ax, a plane supplied the miracle from the sky. Exhausted, sick, and faced with an evi-

Ecuador's Indians and SIL

Sources: Scott S. Robinson, "Numbers, Distribution and Present State of the Indigenous Groups of the Coastal and Amazonian Regions of Ecuador," in Walter Dostal, ed., *The Situation of the Indian in South America*, p. 398; Angel Barriga B., *Mapas de Grupos Indigenas* (Quito: Instituto Ecuatoriano de Antropologia y Geografia, 1961); Wycliffe Bible Translators, *Middle of the World: Wycliffe Bible Translators in Ecuador* (Santa Ana, Calif.: Wycliffe Bible Translators, 1972).

dently greater power, ninety-two Huaorani delivered themselves to Rachel's care at a specified village site near SIL's jungle base, Limoncocha.

For six weeks, the village, now suddenly doubled in size to more than 200 Huaorani, tried to cope with hunger, malnutrition, and disease. Worried about exposing the newcomers to diseases they had no immunity against, Rachel halted JAARS landings and had supplies air-dropped. As resources dwindled and disputes deteriorated into threats of spearing, some of the newcomers tried to leave, only to be forced back by Rachel's followers.[7] Christian guilt grew over "illegitimate" babies, leaving one pregnant convert a suicide and babies near-victims of drowning.[8]

Ecuador Oil

Sources: *International Petroleum Encyclopedia, 1983* (Tulsa, Okla.: PennWell Publishing Company, 1983), p. 111; *New Orleans Times-Picayune*, October 16, 1977; *Wall Street Journal*, February 25, 1969; *Journal of Commerce*, November 18, 1970; *Oil and Gas Journal*, November 30, 1970.

Meanwhile, the oil crews pressed on against the territory of the last Huaorani still in the jungle; helicopters arrived and, with them, ultimatums. In August 1969, one of the two remaining bands straggled into Rachel's village seeking refuge. "How can they assume good will when we ferret them out so relentlessly," SIL's Catherine Peeke later asked in her diary, "approaching from the very sky, the sphere which they do not control? They are desperate to hide from forces which they do not understand—but how much more desperate they would be if they really did understand!"[9]

Enlightenment came in the form of a polio epidemic that struck two weeks after the latest band of Indians arrived. It hit so fast that by the time polio was diagnosed, scores of Indians were sick, and two had died. Missionary physicians prescribed immediate vaccination. But Rachel decided that the new arrivals might flee or mistake a male doctor's puncturing their skins with needles for an attack, becoming violent and resorting to spears. She refused, waiting until both she and the Huaorani were too sick to resist. By that time, all the Huaorani were infected; sixteen deaths would be recorded, and another sixteen Indians were left crippled.

All this occurred in the land of Galo Plaza, the friend of Cam Townsend and Nelson Rockefeller, who brought SIL and Nelson's International Basic Economy Corporation into Ecuador to prompt development in Indian lands. Now, as head of the OAS, he would further that goal to include Johnson's new frontiers in the Amazon.

Galo Plaza was shrewd enough to call for a sharing of power over financing and planning. The OAS, he said, "in order to recover the confidence of Latin America as an instrument of relationships among the countries, should play a decisive role in the [economic] integration effort. The image of the Alliance will continue to be distorted if the fallacy that this is a bilateral action is allowed to persist. As a matter of dignity, the concept of donation must be destroyed and cast out from the hemisphere. Aid must be furnished with severity, as an investment in stability." The alternative, "unilateral political intervention" by the United States, was "contrary to the very idea of the Organization." Galo Plaza argued instead for "collective measures that will reflect the clear will of the peoples."[10] The concept really did not abandon economic sanctions or military interventions, such as those used against Cuba and the Dominican Republic; it merely shifted the auspices to the OAS. Galo Plaza preferred genuine inter-American actions to the United States' use of the OAS as a fig leaf. If his approach was to succeed, however, the United States would have to restrain itself from the temptation of using its economic and military power unilaterally.

Adolf Berle echoed this theme more urgently as cochairman of the OAS Association, but placed more of the onus on Latin Americans. Speaking at a special "summit" luncheon of U.S. inter-American and foreign affairs leaders held by the association just before Richard Nixon's inauguration, Berle urged public support for the OAS as the Western Hemisphere's "substitute for empire."

In attendance, Galo Plaza listened as Berle, in what became the swan song of his long career, issued a blunt ultimatum. He warned some eighty association guests that "unless the Organization of American States succeeds, I see no escape from empire. . . . This is a frightening statement but I think true. For the past generation, the U.S. has been doing its best to avoid becoming an empire." The problem was "how we can avoid it."

His solution was even more startling: He called upon the OAS to discuss Nelson's suggestion regarding "huge deposits of oil and other resources under the high seas of the Caribbean and the Gulf of Mexico."

"Governor Rockefeller has proposed that under common agreement these resources be exploited for the benefit of the capital-hungry American states. Here is a task *par excellence* for the OAS."[11]

Some of the revenues paid by oil companies, mostly U.S. firms, would be passed on to the OAS to finance its policing and other tasks in the hemisphere. Another chunk of oil royalties would be passed on to banks, again mostly U.S. banks, to help pay for debt service. By then, foreign debts consumed 65 percent of Latin America's foreign income and left OAS member countries in arrears averaging 10 percent.

Such "extranational" financing of the OAS would also take financial pressure off member states to adopt protectionism in inter-American trade. Banks with heavy loan performance in Latin America, including David Rockefeller's Chase, would have little to gain by currency restrictions or tariffs that stemmed the flow of capital or direct-investment earnings from Latin America back to the United States. Free trade, it was argued, was the way to avoid tariff wars, declining trade, world economic depression, and world wars.

Now, at the White House for his first meeting with President Nixon, Galo Plaza pressed the matter. When Nixon asked him what should be done first to develop policy for Latin America, Galo Plaza seized the moment:

"Send Nelson Rockefeller to Latin America. His name is magic."[12]

That's what Galo Plaza thought. And so, obviously, did Nelson. There was little reason to think otherwise, especially in Brazil.

An American Bonanza: Ranching in Brazil

Of all Nelson's friends in Brazil, no one had been more helpful than Walther Moreira Salles, former Brazilian ambassador to the United States. Salles's connections to Brazilian banking and ranching interests had achieved for Nelson a bonanza of opportunities in his efforts to conquer the prairies and forests of Brazil's frontiers.

Back in the mid-1950s, during the euphoria following the fall of Getúlio Vargas, Nelson, David, and IBEC had joined Moreira Salles in investing in the million-acre Bodoquena cattle ranch in Mato Grosso. Besides cattle raising and possibly mining, Nelson was interested in developing a coffee plantation on the slopes of the Bodoquena mountains. Moreira Salles helped Nelson explore the possibilities of both cattle ranching and coffee growing by making available a large tract of his 5 million coffee-tree Fazendas Paulistas to IBEC Research, Inc. (IRI). IRI was headed by a former president of Standard Oil of New Jersey's research division and a top-notch staff of ex-employees of the Hawaiian Pineapple Company. Working with the OAS's Inter-American Institute of Agricultural Sciences in Costa Rica, it was among the best agricultural research groups in Latin America.

Using Moreira Salles's plantation and land offered by other large ranchers in the states of São Paulo, Goiás, Minas Gerais, and Paraná,[13] IRI experimented with chemical pesticides and defoliants (Dow's Dalapón and Shell Chemical's Dieldren were favorites) nitrogen-rich legumes to increase the fertility of pasturelands (and therefore pounds of beef per acre), irrigation techniques for coffee trees, chemical stimulation of coffee flowering for uniform harvesting times, standardized measuring techniques for coffee beans, the regulation of temperatures for bean drying, and the application of more processing and storage techniques. Large non-Brazilian meat processors like Armour Packing, Wilson Packing, and Anglo Frigorífico consulted IRI to benefit from its research, as did Fazenda Cambuhy, the large cattle ranch that controlled Fazendas Paulistas and was 40 percent owned by Moreira Salles.

Nelson was kept abreast of how IRI's experiments were going and how well the new techniques were being accepted by Brazilian ranchers. In just one IRI test area in 1956, some 150 ranchers visited to observe the experiments of the Rockefeller men; 22 of them adopted IRI-recommended chemical defoliants to remove native brush from 20,000 acres.[14] American chemical companies reciprocated with donations to IRI. Olin Mathieson, which had Laurance Rockefeller as a director, gave IRI $10,000.[15] American Export Potash Associates contributed $3,000.[16] Pfizer, which sold a hormone used to fatten cattle, gave also, as did Anderson Clayton (cotton), Stauffer Chemical, the Sulphur Institute, and Standard Oil's Brazilian Esso subsidiary. Point IV officials from the U.S. Embassy spent days at IRI's labs and pastures and came away impressed. But the Rockefeller men did not simply wait for Muhammed to come to the mountain; they brought mountains of research to the Brazilian ranchers through talks before groups of farmers and ranchers and through courses at Brazilian agricultural institutes.

Thousands of copies of IRI's technical reports were distributed as extension bulletins and pamphlets by government officials. As early as 1957, IRI's mailing list included 5,000 Brazilians.

The underlying theme of all these efforts was that Brazil's agrarian crisis was not a political crisis—of who held power over the government and fertile land, and who did not—but a crisis of agricultural method and location that was solvable by instruction, demonstrations, and migration. The problems of Brazilian agriculture could be solved by relocating farmers to "virgin" land in the Amazonian West; consolidating small farms into more efficient, mechanized large farms; and modernizing techniques, all serviced by roads to markets, chemical companies, and adequate credit from private bank loans and government agencies subsidized by taxes. The existing institutions of the status quo—the banks controlled by the large coffee landholders of São Paulo; the government dominated by their political parties, and the wealthy ranchers, factory owners, mining companies, and their allied American and European corporations and banks—were sufficient means to solve the social crisis over which they presided, with the help of an "enlightened" military.

Beneath it all was a cornerstone of prejudice among the Americans, a belief that, as AIA's Walter Crawford had argued in his "comprehensive" report *Agriculture in Brazil* (1961), the problem in Brazil was in Brazilian genes. "They are not born farmers. They are descended from the Portuguese who were famous explorers and traders, not men of the land."[17] Although Brazil had always been an agriculturally based country, Crawford cited as proof of his assertion a comment Brazil's "discoverer," Pedro Alvares Cabral, had made to King Manuel of Portugal on Brazil's agricultural potential: "Plant, and it will grow." A similarly misguided assumption about the New World's "inexhaustible" soil fertility actually had been made by Crawford's own British forebears in the antebellum South of North America, until they, too, had to seek virgin lands in Western "territories" taken from the Indians. But a broad grasp of history was never a strong point with American technicians or with their pragmatic overseers in business or politics. Nor was questioning the viability of U.S. technical-aid programs for sustainable small-scale farming in the Third World, such as Rockefeller's IRI-sponsored lectures by imported American agriculturalists that were attended mostly by owners of large farms, ranchers, and government technicians.

If this emphasis on large-scale ranching was in sharp contrast with Nelson's professed concern for owners of small farms, so the backgrounds of Nelson and David's fellow IRI trustees were in contrast with IRI's and AIA's purported mission of replicating small farming in the United States: Hartley Rowe was a former vice president of United Fruit Company, and Glenn E. Rogers had been responsible for Metropolitan Life Insurance Company's successful farm-management operations after Metropolitan foreclosed on some 10,000 American farms in the early 1930s during the depression.[18]

By mid-1963, Nelson's IRI and AIA bonanza was in danger. Moreira Salles's efforts to keep Presidents Quadros and Goulart on Juscelino Kubitschek's internationalist course through currency devaluations, tight budgets, and other austerity measures as Goulart's home secretary had failed. Meanwhile, David's proposed U.S. government guarantees for investments abroad were still not endorsed by the Kennedy administration (they would be enacted by Congress later that year as a condition of passing a foreign aid bill), and national economic sovereignty was again a major issue in Venezuela under President Rómulo Betancourt and in Brazil under President Goulart. Seeking to limit the risk and strengthen his holding at the same time, Nelson sought partners with capital and experience in beef marketing, negotiating with the Swifts to explore merging both Bodoquena and his five NAR (Nelson A. Rockefeller) Farms in Venezuela with the Swifts' International Packers.[19] The merger did not occur. But thanks to the military coup of 1964, even more of Brazil's Amazonian interior could be purchased by American interests, including those associated with IBEC. Having Moreira Salles, now one of Rio de Janeiro's most powerful bankers, on the board certainly helped. So did having a politically savvy cousin like Richard Aldrich.

The Banking Advantage

Aldrich was well placed to work behind the scenes, whether in the United States or in Brazil. While he was IBEC's vice president in New York, Aldrich was also an agent for the CIA.[20]

In January 1965, ten months after the coup, Aldrich had written President Castelo Branco, urging greater restrictions on speculative, short-term loans to Brazilians called *letras de cambios*.[21] These loans allowed Brazilian businessmen suffering from skyrocketing inflation to get higher earnings through short-term speculation than they were getting from their shares in the Rockefeller mutual fund, Crescinco. The letras had the extra advantage of allowing investors anonymity and evasion from income taxes.

The drain on Crescinco, however, could not be tolerated. By March 1965, the IBEC office in Brazil learned that the regime was ready to listen because it was "very much under the influence of U.S. financial and economic advisers and . . . their recommendations are usually taken seriously and followed."[22] Aldrich wrote immediately to Minister of Planning Roberto Campos, pointing out that the letras contributed to a loss of tax revenues for the regime through tax evasion and to Brazil's high domestic interest rates. Such "inflationary effects" could not "be helpful to the objectives which I know you are seeking."[23]

Campos took the hint. A banking law was drafted that not only required all letras to be registered, but eliminated taxes on stock transfers and gave tax incentives to companies that were selling stock on the open market and to investors. The predictable result was a boom in Brazil's stock market—and salvation for Crescinco. Whereupon Aldrich was rewarded with a seat on IBEC's board.

The next step was to forge an alliance with Crescinco's major competitor, the Bahamas-based holding company, Deltec International. During the Kubitschek years, Deltec had played a prominent role in the commercial expansion of Brazil's western frontier, speculating in a real estate boom in Anápolis caused by the construction of Brasília sixty miles away.[24] During the 1950s, Deltec's investment firm,

Deltec Banking, was Brazil's leading securities underwriter and distribution organization. This dominance ended with the economic hardships of the early Quadros-Goulart years; Deltec's investment banking in Brazil contracted, while the Rockefellers' Crescinco grew, including the steady increase in its 5-million-cruzeiro investment in timber operations in the Amazon, Madeiros Compendas do Amazonia Cia (COMPENSA). In 1966, Crescinco unloaded its COMPENSA holdings (by then worth 76.7 million cruzeiros, although much of it was the result of inflation) and increased its holdings in electronics, metallurgy, cement, and, of course, banks. IBEC's position with banks in Brazil was considerably strengthened that year when Moreira Salles came on IBEC's board. Following the military coup, Moreira Salles had focused his attention on making money, seizing opportunities presented by the international investment climate and the difficulties suffered by local banks from inflation and Brazilian business loan defaults. He absorbed two banks, Agrícola Mercantil and Predial. Backed by IBEC and Deltec Banking, Moreira Salles's own hold on Brazilian banking was strengthened in 1967 by his takeover of União de Bancos Brasileiros, which had more than 330 branches and agencies.

In 1967, Moreira Salles's bank and Nelson's IBEC teamed up with Deltec Banking and other Canadian and European investors to form Banco de Investimento do Brazil, the Brazilian Investment Bank (BIB), which was set up to arrange hard-currency loans to Brazilian borrowers, including Export-Import Bank credit lines to finance imports of U.S. capital goods. BIB was given the management contract for Crescinco, by then South America's largest mutual fund. The following year, when Moreira Salles succeeded his father as formal head of BIB, Nelson sold Crescinco outright to BIB for 19 percent of BIB's stock.

For those who looked closely at IBEC's board, the implications of BIB's founding were obvious. In 1966, IBEC had added four new directors: Moreira Salles; Alberto Ferrari, general manager of Rome's Banco Nazionale del Lavoro, one of Italy's largest commercial banks with a New York branch and South American offices (two decades later, executives of the Atlanta branch of the Lavoro bank would be indicted for making secret illegal loans to Saddam Hussein's Iraq during its war against Ayatollah Khomeini's Iran; the bank also had dealings with the Bank of Credit and Commerce International [BCCI], a CIA conduit for covert operations, including the Iran-Contra arms-sales financial network[25]); James Perkins, trustee of the Air Force's think tank, the RAND Corporation, and president of Cornell University, a leading sponsor of Rockefeller-funded agricultural and social surveys in Brazil's rural areas; and Richard Aldrich, who by 1972 would become the leader of the Brazilian-American Chamber of Commerce.

By now, the Rockefeller interests in Room 5600 had been well-enough primed by outbursts of Brazilian nationalism to seek ways of disguising American control over Brazilian economic affairs.

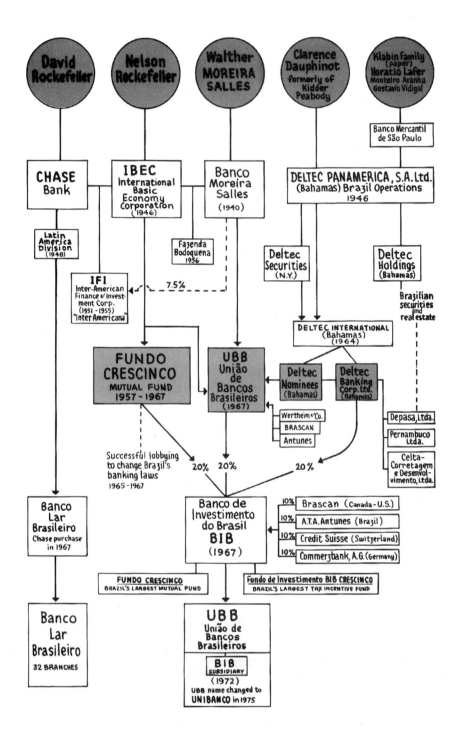

The Rockefellers and Brazilian Finance (1951–1972)

Nelson's lieutenants in IBEC's philanthropic arm, AIA, had completed their efforts to launch a Brazilian foundation that would obscure AIA's obvious American—and Rockefeller—affiliation.

The Antunes Shield

Nelson Rockefeller's aides originally conceived a Brazilian foundation as a local conduit for funds to support the resettlement of impoverished tenant farmers from the Northeast on the prairies around Brasília. In the Northeast, 30 million peasants had shown the kind of desperate impatience that could lead to a Cuban-style revolution. This growing radicalism had been monitored in Room 5600. Its AIA and IBEC files contained press accounts and gravely worded memorandums from IBEC's Berent Friele and others about the political turmoil. "Time is of the essence and we ought to get moving before it is too late," Friele had written Adolf Berle back in 1961. "The Castro forces are very active in the area."[26]

AIA had previously zeroed in on Planalto Central, Brazil's vast central plains that, during the Kennedy years, Nelson looked on as a gateway to the interior from the industrial south.

Originally, AIA's proposal to U.S. foreign-aid officials for a new regional development agency for Brazil encompassed a huge area, Brazil's entire west-central region of Goiás and Mato Grosso, including the territory where Nelson's own ranch, Fazenda Bodoquena, was located.[27] Later, the proposed survey area was scaled down, and AIA developed a strategy of using a Brazilian foundation to sponsor a demonstration colony on almost one million state-owned acres at Jaíba, a dry and isolated part of the São Francisco River Valley northeast of Brasília, "and then spreading to the Planalto."[28] But when the Jaíba project stalled and Kennedy's AID would not bend to the Rockefeller agency's ambitious colonization plans for the Planalto or provide the compensation that AIA expected, AIA withdrew after completing preliminary surveys. AIA's geographic attention then switched to Amapá, a territory north of the Amazon River delta that is about the size of France and is known more for the haunting beauty of its malarial rubber jungle than for cattle ranching. Yet this new frontier for AIA was not surprising, considering that Amapá was also the focus of new investments in the Amazon by the man whom the Rockefeller office chose to head the new Brazilian foundation, Augusto T. A. Antunes.

The prosperous Antunes had his own reasons for a foundation. He had been involved in a joint mining venture, called ICOMI, with Bethlehem Steel in Amapá since the Kubitschek years. In December 1964, just months after the coup, he visited New York with the new minister of planning, Roberto Campos, and with other officials of the new military regime. They were seeking corporate investments from the Rockefellers and their allies, including shipping magnate Daniel K. Ludwig. "He was very enthusiastic about his work and particularly appreciative of your contribution to the success of his foundation," IBEC's Berent Friele wrote AIA's Walter Crawford from Room 5600. ". . . Unfortunately, he could not stay over to attend a luncheon to be given by David Rockefeller on Monday for [Foreign Minister] Vasco Leitão da Cunha. Antunes has never met David and I am sure it would be most helpful for them to become acquainted. David is planning a trip to Brazil early in March.

"We are following with keen interest developments in Brazil which, everything considered, are very encouraging. Politics will always be a problem. However, it is fortunate that President Castelo Branco has the wisdom and courage to stick to his guns and follow the course which has been charted by his economic advisors."[29]

Castelo Branco did stick to his guns—literally—and so did Crawford in his belief that the new foundation conduit for AIA's programs "should get as much money donated privately as possible."[30] Antunes's ability to pay the piper, starting with a donation of 20 million cruzeiros in July 1965, made it inevitable that AIA would shift its attention to Antunes's focus on his holdings in Amapá.

Within months, AIA was assisting the Antunes Foundation in setting up a Regional Development Institute in Amapá, a project Crawford had earlier proposed to Antunes for the Planalto.[31] By 1967, the Antunes Foundation's activities had expanded into the promotion of agricultural development to support colonization by northeasterners. "Recent discoveries of manganese deposits," AIA's official historian wrote in 1968, "have brought a measure of prosperity to the region, but there is great need for the development of agricultural resources."[32] Local food production was essential if labor costs for Antunes's mining colony were to be reduced.

As AIA was now being phased out in favor of the Antunes Foundation and agencies of the military regime, IBEC, working through alliances with Deltec, Antunes, Moreira Salles, and European creditors, seemed poised on the brink of a great expansion into Brazil's Amazonian interior.[33]

There was only one problem—the nagging protests of smaller business interests and nationalist military officers, led by Carlos Lacerda and the interior minister, General Albuquerque Lima.

"The Amazon Is Ours"

What neither Galo Plaza nor Nixon nor Nelson himself realized was that, by 1969, the Rockefeller name was not magic to everyone. In Brazil, where the Rockefeller family's influence among the international business elite was indeed formidable, nationalist feelings, promoted by the military regime to consolidate its power, had not dissipated since the coup. In an ironic twist, the coup that had brought such sighs of relief to corporate circles in the United States had engendered passions that now threatened to backfire on Nelson's and his allies' two-decades-old plans to develop the Amazon.

Foreign control over many of Brazil's largest companies had become a serious issue under President Goulart. In 1962, responding to a study that showed that twenty of Brazil's largest fifty-five economic groups were controlled by foreign companies, Goulart had launched an economic program to promote Brazilian ownership. The image of the Amazon as the Great Frontier made foreign—especially American—control particularly grating to many Brazilian businessmen, who feared they would be squeezed out by larger foreign companies or by their large subsidiaries and allies from southern Brazil.

The first cries of protest over control of the Amazon were raised as early as June 1965, when news leaked that a delegation of Americans from the U.S. National Academy of Science had visited the military regime's minister of agriculture and the National Research Council. The delegation proposed setting up research centers to study forestry and farming in the Amazon basin. The centers would be run exclusively by Americans, instead of the traditional joint U.S.-Brazilian administration. The proposal enjoyed the backing of Rusk's State Department, which sent two representatives to the meeting to show its blessing for the project. Hearing the proposal, Amazonas state Governor Arthur Ferreira Reis walked out and denounced the project as a threat to Brazil's sovereignty.

"The Amazon is ours," he told the press. Reis also charged that Roberto Campos, minister of planning and a friend of Nelson Rockefeller, supported the scheme as a step toward "internationalization" of the Amazon basin. Reis accused two Pentagon think tanks, New York's Hudson Institute and California's RAND Corporation, of conducting research in the Amazon without proper authorization.[34]

The regime and Campos issued prompt denials, Campos adding that Brazilians who opposed cooperation with foreign scientists were displaying intellectual underdevelopment. The U.S. Embassy also denied any U.S. consideration of a plan to internationalize the Amazon. So did the Hudson Institute: "Hudson Institute personnel have not been conducting any studies or even visits in the Brazilian Amazon. Certainly, we have never advocated internationalizing the region."[35]

What was not admitted to the press, however, was the obvious: The State Department had been involved in backing the research proposals. Nor did Herman Kahn, the director of the Hudson Institute, subsequently acknowledge his own involvement in proposing to the State Department a series of "Aswan Dams" for Latin America. In fact, by July 1965, the State Department's approval of Kahn's dams had reached the National Security Council of the Johnson White House.[36]

This was not Kahn's first interest in the Amazon. Almost twenty years before, he had prepared a study on the Amazon basin for RAND, the air force's think tank. But his newest scheme was more grandiose: a series of dams and locks that would flood huge areas of the Amazon and Orinoco basins.

The idea actually had a Rockefeller origin. During World War II, Nelson, in his capacity as Coordinator of Inter-American Affairs, had authorized his staff to prepare proposals for improving South America's inland waterways to "link the

Amazon Valley with the oil fields of Eastern Venezuela."[37] These oil fields included those owned by Standard Oil's Creole Petroleum, of which Nelson was a major stockholder and former director.* Even months before Pearl Harbor, Nelson, using the rubric of "economic defense" of the hemisphere, pushed for development of the *entire* Amazon basin area, with the inland waterways acting as connective tissue. In November 1942, Venezuela's foreign minister announced a Brazilian-Venezuelan accord setting up a commission to develop an inter-American waterway linking the Orinoco and Amazon rivers through two tributaries, the Casiquiare and the Negro.[38]

Kahn's scheme resurrected this earlier plan and went even further. When revealed in two Hudson Institute reports by Robert Panero, the "South American Great Lakes System" would have consisted of a series of *five* artificial lakes, the first and most important one linking Venezuela's upper Orinoco River with Brazil's Negro River along the Colombian border.

Kahn's "Great Lakes" system focused on commercial and industrial development of the Amazon basin, ignoring the potential ecological havoc of such an approach on a complex, vulnerable ecosystem. Indeed, the widening of the Amazon was not being proposed primarily to improve navigability, but to eliminate the swampy wetlands and rapids that impeded development of the higher, supposedly more fertile, plains and blocked access to newly discovered mineral resources.

Thanks to the generals' granting of subsoil rights to foreign companies through their new constitution, the mineral resources promised to provide the inflation-plagued regime with foreign currency through exports. Some of the dams used to create the lakes would generate enough electricity to run not only mines but processing plants, while the lakes themselves would allow ore-bearing deep-draft ships to link the mines and plants to foreign markets.

Yet, it was precisely this promise of the exploitation of the Amazon that inspired Brazilian anger instead of praise. By ignoring questions of control and ownership, Kahn's technical feasibility study inspired Brazilians to take these issues up.

Between 1965 and 1967, the Brazilians learned for the first time that aerial surveys by the U.S. Air Force—previously suspended by President Vargas—had been resumed after the 1964 coup, under the auspices of the Inter-American Geodetic Survey. The overflights had been granted without approval by Brazil's Congress,[39] and they covered areas of suspected valuable mineral lodes. Under the

---

*Brazil and Venezuela were the linchpins of Nelson's and J. C. King's proposed Amazon Development Project—Brazil, because most of the Amazon basin was within its territory, and Venezuela, because its developed oil resources (something Brazil lacked and needed) could fuel the basin's commercial and industrial development. One of Nelson's advisers on the basin, in fact, was Dr. Harvey Bassler, a former geologist for Standard Oil of New Jersey. See John McClintock to Nelson Rockefeller, April 1, 1942, Central Files, Box 1, Coordinator of Inter-American Affairs files, National Archives (Federal Records Center, Suitland, Maryland).

original contract with Vargas's government, all film negatives, after processing in the United States, were supposed to have been shipped back to Brazil and held in confidence. But by the end of 1967, leaks from the Brazilian military and, later, the staff of the U.S. Senate Foreign Relations Committee indicated that U.S. and Canadian corporations had used the photographic surveys to locate for themselves rich mineral outcroppings in Minas Gerais. After site investigations, these companies successfully applied to the military regime for concessions,[40] long before the mineral deposits were acknowledged to Brazilians by their own government.

News of the surveys, unauthorized flights, and clandestine airports caused a series of uproars in Brazil. Carlos Lacerda, previously an informant to Adolf Berle and a promoter of the demise of earlier nationalist governments, suddenly spoke out with his own version of nationalism, charging that the military regime had introduced the "politics of technocrats" that fostered "a neo-colonialist concept in Brazil," that is, dependence on the United States.[41] In 1966, he dropped a bombshell, revealing that U.S. Ambassador Lincoln Gordon had said he was grateful that Goulart's government had been overthrown so the United States did not have to intervene directly with its own military operations.[42] Gordon denied the statement, but that did not stop Lacerda from making accusations to the press that the Johnson administration had been "indiscreet" in "interfering in Brazilian political affairs and unwise in business and aid relationships." Then he proclaimed, as if he had recently discovered what he had secretly known all along: "I am convinced that the U.S. helped with the 1964 revolution."[43]

Now *Lacerda* was being indiscreet. But he was playing for high stakes: He hoped to lead a right-wing nationalist revolt in the scheduled coming elections that would unseat General Costa e Silva, President Castelo Branco's chosen successor.

Lacerda was banking on a growing conviction among many Brazilians that the regime's austerity measures hurt not only labor, but business. The regime's tightening of credit and narrow lending policies were forcing Brazilian firms to sell their assets for as little as 40 percent of their value. As early as December 1966, *Time* magazine reported that 50 percent of Brazil's industries had passed into foreign hands since the coup.[44]

Wealthy Brazilians who were tied to such foreign interests, like the Antunes mining magnates, benefited through joint ventures with American and Canadian companies, including firms with ties to the Rockefellers. So it was ironic that Lacerda, a nationalist, traveled to New York in October 1968 to visit internationalists Nelson Rockefeller and Adolf Berle to solicit American neutrality, if not help, in his bid for power.[45]

If the results of Lacerda's campaign seemed preordained to men like Berle, they were not obvious to Brazilians. Most Brazilians assumed that the generals needed the support of conservative political leaders like Governor Lacerda and Governor Magalhães Pinto to rule. There was also strong nationalist sentiment in the military's own ranks, particularly among its junior officers, to consider.

Finally, there was the growing scandal of the Amazon. Foreign companies were moving in at an unprecedented rate. U.S. Steel's entry into Pará, where geologists were said to have discovered "by accident" one of the world's largest deposits of iron in the Carajás Mountains, aroused suspicions. Had the company gained access to secret aerial surveys? Not according to one version of the lucrative find: A company geologist had just happened to pick the mountain out of tens of thousands of acres of jungle because he had to make a forced helicopter landing and lucked upon a bald spot in the green jungle.[46] After landing, he found that the reason the area lacked trees was that the ground consisted of high-grade iron ore, 18 billion tons of it, it turned out.

U.S. Steel's own report in the *Engineering and Mining Journal*, on the other hand, admitted that the discovery was anything but an accident: "The discovery was made during a systematic exploration program in the southern part of Pará State, between the Xingu and Tocantins Rivers."[47] How did the American companies know where to look? Expensive explorations "using boats, single-engine aircraft and helicopters" would not have been launched without reasonable expectations. The search had begun in early 1967, a year after a similar Union Carbide survey came back with manganese from a location only forty-three miles away. U.S. Steel, like Union Carbide, employed experienced geologists. By August, U.S. Steel had struck pay dirt in the same region.

The fact that the Carajás mountain range was also the home of the Xikrín Indians, a Kayapó tribe marked by SIL as "potentially hostile," did not diminish U.S. Steel's enthusiasm for staking its claim. Nor did the presence of three other tribes, the Mudjetíre, the Parakanân, and the mysterious Kréen-Akaróre, all of whom should have enjoyed land rights under Brazil's constitution.

Ranching with Kings

Whatever doubts existed that the military regime in Brasília was beginning to abandon its stated reliance on small-farmer colonists to develop the Amazon ended when the Superintendency for the Development of the Amazon (SUDAM) announced tax incentives in late 1966 to encourage larger corporate firms. Any company set up by 1974 and judged to have a regional economic impact would be granted a ten-year exemption from all taxes; parent companies of the Amazonian subsidiaries would be given a 50 percent cut in the corporate income tax; and imported farm machinery would be free of all duties. To back up the financing of investments, the regime established the Bank of the Amazon.

The Klebergs of Texas, allies of Standard Oil of New Jersey and the Rockefellers for more than thirty years, were among the first Americans to take advantage of the military regime's new law. In 1968, the Klebergs' King Ranch joined Swift-Armour

Company of Brazil in winning Brasília's approval for a 180,000-acre ranch in Pará state. Located near Paragominas, the ranch was supposed to realize the dream of transplanting to South America's vast Amazonian interior the cattle-breeding and grazing techniques perfected in the dry grasslands of Texas and New Zealand.[48]

Equally promising, the land in Pará was immediately south of where Rio Tinto Zinc, the British mining company, was staking claims for what would turn out to be a 1.1-billion-ton reserve of bauxite, three times what the government estimated.[49] It was not surprising that the well-drained land was the ancestral home of two Indian tribes, the Tembé and the Urubús-Kaapor. The tribes had been pacified by the Service for the Protection of the Indian (SPI), and the Urubus had subsequently been "occupied" by SIL missionaries. The government of Pará had even recognized the tribes' title to these lands as part of a projected reserve for the Indians.

In 1968, however, SPI's successor, FUNAI (the Portuguese acronym for the National Indian Foundation) issued King Ranch and Swift a certificate declaring that the 180,000 acres wanted by the companies were not occupied by Indians. This certificate was a necessary legal prerequisite for the companies to begin operations in the area with investment tax credits from SUDAM. According to various reports, King/Swift then petitioned Pará to annul the Indians' land tenure titles altogether. The Pará government resisted, as did FUNAI,[50] but Interior Minister General Costa Cavalcante and the federal government's mining company, Cia. Vale do Rio Doce, intervened on the side of Rio Tinto as a minority shareholder in a new joint venture with the British company, forcing FUNAI into an accord that would begin the systematic dismembering of the Indians' reserve.

Meanwhile, by July 1969, King and Swift were boasting to *Fortune* magazine not only that they had gotten title to the 180,000 acres, but that they had negotiated with Pará for another 120,000 acres.[51] By then, the Swifts and the Klebergs had new partners: the Rockefellers. Deltec International had swallowed up International Packers, Ltd., Swift's holding company for its herds and global meat-packing operations, in a single gulp.[52]

That the "New Brazil" under the generals should become the meeting ground for the Rockefellers, Klebergs, and Swifts was no historical accident. Harold Swift had been a friend of Nelson years before, when the Swifts and the Armours were already the beef kings of the American West. In 1957, the Rockefellers had sent cousin Richard Aldrich to inspect the Swift-Armour property in Brazil, which attracted them because its water rights were valuable for ranching during Brazil's dry winter season.[53] The Klebergs' ties to Nelson, on the other hand, went back to the early 1930s, when Nelson, Uncle Winthrop Aldrich, and officials of the Chase bank visited King Ranch, site of newly found oil by Standard Oil of New Jersey's Texas subsidiary, Esso. It was these oil revenues, in fact, that had given King Ranch the means to expand abroad. Now, in Brazil, a new "West" had brought these same families together for similar economic conquest. As if to underscore the importance of their financial alliance, International Packers chairman A. Thomas Taylor, husband of Geraldine Swift, was made chairman of Deltec International.

Deltec, once the major competitor of IBEC's investment bank, Crescinco, had become a Rockefeller financial powerhouse. The Rockefellers had summoned to Deltec's side powerful financial furies from the past: David's Chase Manhattan; Irving Trust; J. Henry Schroder Banking Corporation; and First National Bank of Chicago, the favorite bank of Standard Oil of Indiana, parent of Nelson's first and only oil directorship, Creole Petroleum of Venezuela.[54] Deltec's board reflected this financial clout, with Nelson represented by his major partner in Brazil, Walther Moreira Salles, a director of IBEC.

Championing the Untouchables

In the heat of Brazilian expectations for developing the Amazon, a strange transformation took place among the country's right-wing nationalists. The same people who had shown no concern for the inhabitants of the lands they ravaged now spoke out for those they previously regarded only as obstacles to human greed. The Indians of the jungle, the Untouchables of Brazil, suddenly found an unexpected champion. It was a shameless metamorphosis, but for those, like the Villas Boas brothers, who feared worse horrors, an embraceable one.

It came about just as the celebrated SPI bubble burst, exploding the myth of a society protecting its Indians. The issue that precipitated SPI's crisis was a 1966 article in an international anthropological journal about the 1963 massacre of a village of Cintas Largas Indians. The author, Georg Grünberg, had the audacity to brand the massacre as genocide.[55] His timing was fortunate, for now political conditions were ripe for exposure.

The article reported what was happening in that part of northwest Mato Grosso where American Caterpillar bulldozers were plowing through the jungle to construct a link of the trans-Amazonian highway system from Cuiabá, Mato Grosso's capital, to Pôrto Velho, capital of Rondônia. Fourteen bridges were built along the 900-mile route with $52.6 million in AID loans. The U.S. Army donated another $1 million worth of heavy equipment. The Brazilian army did the actual work. Clearly, here was a project involving a national security issue for both the Brazilian and American governments.

A new source of wealth had been discovered in the area: cassiterite, the essential ore in the production of tin. It was this rare mineral that had inspired Arruda and Junqueira Company to launch an expedition in the Cintas Largas territory in 1963 that resulted in mass murder.

The expedition had "cleared" people like trees. Using one of the many airstrips cut out of the jungle since World War II, a Cessna flew in, armed with two weapons: sugar, to lure the Indians out of hiding and to calm their fears, and

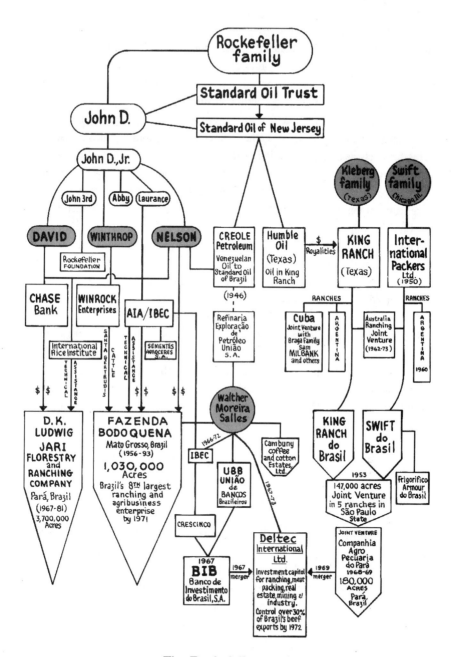

**The Rockefellers and
Ranching/Agribusiness in Brazil (1946–1970)**

then dynamite. Aerial reconnaissance found the few survivors of the village bombed, and they were killed, too.

This massacre would never have come to light had not one of the murderers, Ataide Pereira, told his Catholic confessor about the attack. Father Edgar Smith persuaded the man to repeat his story on tape, which the priest then delivered to the SPI. The involvement of the Catholic Church and the fact that Pereira's account of the murders was so graphic, ensured that the attacks would not be ignored. "It is not the first time that the firm of Arruda and Junqueira has committed crimes against the Indians," Father Valdemar Veber told a police investigator. "This firm acts as a cover for other undertakings who are interested in acquiring land, or who plan to exploit the rich mineral deposits existing in the area." Cassiterite was just the latest craze.[56] But there were rumors that powerful American companies were interested in Rondônia's potential as a source for tin. No one knew how many Cintas Largas had been killed so far, and how many more stood in the way. Later, some 3,000 to 5,000 Indians were found in villages scattered between the headwaters of the Aripuanã and Jipapana rivers, north of SIL's new base at Vilhena and along the very river first explored in 1913 by former president Theodore Roosevelt and General Cândido Rondon.

Three years later, after being passed through four reluctant prosecutors, the case of the Cintas Largas massacre was still languishing in the provincial court system. There had been no formal charges, and no trial, and at least four of the defendants were absent. Two had drowned "while on fishing trips." The pilot of the plane used to dynamite the Indians' village was reportedly dead also, the victim of a plane crash. The leader of the expedition died at the hands of revolting rubber tappers. Father Smith, a critical witness, disappeared; later, it was discovered that he had been killed in an auto accident.

Grünberg's article recounted the attempted genocide not only of the Cintas Largas, but of their neighbors, the Beiço-de-Pau Indians. The article set the stage for the nationalist interior minister, General Albuquerque Lima, to take up the case when it was referred to Attorney General Jader Figueiredo in September 1967. Albuquerque Lima launched a full investigation not only of the Cintas Largas incident, but of what SPI was doing to protect all the tribes entrusted to its care.

The attorney general's investigators traveled 10,000 miles and visited some 130 SPI posts around the country. When they were through, they had amassed twenty volumes of evidence of crimes, ranging from embezzlement to murder. In March 1968, Albuquerque Lima released the attorney general's official 5,115-page report. In a calm, understated tone, the report cited case after case of atrocities that had been committed against Indians with the collaboration of the SPI that could be described only as systematic: clothing infected with smallpox, food supplies poisoned, children forced into slavery, and women forced into prostitution. Yes, the SPI suffered from cutbacks in funding and had to contend with "the disastrous impact of missionary activity." But the SPI itself had relegated to missionaries, many of them American Fundamentalists with little sympathy for native religion, responsibilities for pacification and services that were actually its duty. This situation could no longer be tolerated. SPI had to be abolished, the interior minister decreed, and 134 of its 700 functionaries would face formal judicial inquiries for crimes that, when published in the press, took up a full newspaper page in small print.

Major Luis Neves, the head of the SPI, alone was accused of forty-two crimes, including the embezzlement of $300,000, the illegal sale of Indian lands, and complicity in a series of murders.

Attorney General Figueiredo offered terrifying details to reporters. Since 1958, when the military took over the SPI and Kubitschek began the construction of Brasília in earnest, some $62 million worth of Indian property had been stolen. But that was the least of it. "It is not only the embezzlement of funds, but by the admission of sexual perversions, murders and all other crimes listed in the penal code against Indians and their property, that one can see that the Indian Protection Service was for years a den of corruption and indiscriminate killings."[57]

The Guaranís, of southern Mato Grosso, western Paraná, and northwestern Rio Grande do Sul, had been numbered at 3,000 to 4,000 by Darcy Ribeiro in 1957;[58] now there were only 300 left.[59] The Borôros had many of their cattle illegally sold off by SPI agents at Teresa Cristina, the reserve in southern Mato Grosso given to them supposedly in perpetuity to honor of the memory of SPI's compassionate founder, General Cândido Rondon, whose mother was part Borôro.

"There were two fazendas [estates], one called Teresa, where the Indians worked as slaves," a Borôro Indian girl had testified.

> They took me from my mother when I was a child. Afterwards I heard that they hung my mother up all night. . . . She was very ill and I wanted to see her before she died. . . . When I got back they thrashed me with a raw-hide whip. They prostituted the Indian girls. . . . The Indians were used for target practice.[60]

The Borôros were in such a state of despair that the women took a secret plant that temporarily rendered them sterile.[61]

The litany of murdered Indians seemed endless. The Nambiquára had been mowed down by machine-gun fire, the Patachós had been injected with smallpox when they thought they were being given a vaccine, the Canelas had been massacred by hired guns, and the Maxakalís had been given firewater and often shot when drunk. "To exterminate the tribe Beiços de Pau . . . an expedition was formed which went up the River Arinos carrying presents and a great quantity of foodstuffs for the Indians. These were mixed with arsenic and formicides."[62]

Of the 100,000 to 200,000 Indians who were estimated to be living in Brazil in

1957,[63] fewer than 50,000, some anthropologists claimed, had survived. Albuquerque Lima and Figueiredo promised justice. First, the FUNAI was created, and a civilian, José de Queiroz Campos, was named its first president. Second, the Xingu National Park was expanded from 22,000 to 30,000 square kilometers. Third, three new Indian parks were established: the Aripuanã Park in western Mato Grosso and Rondônia, the Araguaia Park in the Ilha do Bananal, and Tumucumaque Park in Pará.

New Indian reserves were also recognized for single tribes. The Beiços-de-Pau were to be protected with a 3,000-square-mile reservation, and a FUNAI team was readied to enter the area to pacify them.

As for the besieged Cintas Largas, Francisco Meirelles, pacifier of the Xavánte tribe, and his son Apoena were dispatched to the new Aripuanã Park to convince the bark-belted Indians that all was now safe; they could trust their new FUNAI friends and settle near a new FUNAI post. For nine months, the Indians would resist the initial "flirtation" stage of Meirelles's pacification campaign, ignoring his gifts of trinkets and tools. Finally, they also succumbed to love.

It was harder to trap their killers. In March 1968, Attorney General Figueiredo ordered charges pressed against members of the 1963 expedition against the Cintas Largas. "Since August 1966, the papers relating to this case have been shuffled about in an endless game of farcical excuses and pretexts," Figueiredo stated, "to the grave detriment of the prestige of justice."[64] Tough words like these were unusual. The newest prosecutor, the eighth in the call of duty on this case, filed formal charges. The owners of the Arruda and Junqueira firm, Sebastiano Arruda and Antonio Junqueira, were not charged "as their assent to the massacre of the Indians has never been established." But the sadistic leader of the expedition—de Brito—who was now dead and the three others who had drowned in fishing accidents or died by other means were indicted, along with two survivors. A trial would not take place, however, until another four years had passed amid growing international protests.

REMOVING THE LAST RESTRAINT

Albuquerque Lima and his nationalist allies pressed on with their campaign to reclaim Amazonian land from foreign companies. In April 1968, Brazil was startled by the news that much of the land at the mouth of the Amazon River was owned by foreigners.

Albuquerque Lima had backed a congressional investigation of foreign ownership of Amazon land, triggered by a 1967 report to Congress sent by the Brazilian Institute of Agrarian Reform. The report listed eighty of Brazil's largest foreign landowners, now in charge of the country's richest mineral deposits. Albuquerque Lima also favored President Costa e Silva's decree that would restrict further purchases of Amazonia by foreign interests. At about the same time, the voice of Lacerda's nationalist wing, *Jornal do Brasil*, called for Petrobrás to increase its exploration efforts to make Brazil self-sufficient in crude oil. Petrobrás officials clearly saw the Amazon connection and testily responded that some groups wanted to waste millions of dollars drilling "dry holes in the Amazon Region."[65]

The issue of American Bible translators collaborating with the SPI was also raised: "In reality, those in command of these Indian Protection posts are North American missionaries—they are all in the posts—and they disfigure the original Indian culture and enforce the acceptance of Protestantism."[66]

Ironically, the nationalists, with all their fervor against North American penetration of the Amazon and Lacerda's claims that the military regime had become a tool of the CIA, missed the fact that SIL's 1965 survey of Indian tribes for SPI's agency overseer, the National Council for the Protection of the Indian, had been published by a division of an American research institute with known CIA ties, and that the book's translator and editor, Janice Hopper, was the recent widow of the head of Project Camelot, Rex Hopper, whose help she acknowledged in her preface.

Operations and Policy Research, Inc., was identified as early as February 19, 1967, by the *New York Times* as a recipient of CIA funds. This oversight was all the more remarkable, since the survey's publication coincided with both the publicity about the CIA's connections and the Brazilian uproar over American corporate penetration of Brazil, including the Amazon. No questions were raised about the fact that nine of the Indian tribes reported to have been subjected to genocidal practices or outright attacks while under SPI's custody were "occupied" by SIL:

Indian Tribes Subjected to Genocidal Attacks[67]	*Year "Occupied" by SIL*
Xavánte	1958
Karajá	1958
Kadiwéu	1958
Parukotó-Charúma (including Hixkaryána)	1958
Borôro	1959
Guaraní	1959
Maxakalí	1959
Canela	1968
Ticúna	1959

Nor were any questions raised then or afterward about SIL's use of the words *hostile* and *warlike* to describe Indians who were attempting to defend their traditional land from invasions, including three tribes then being subjected to genocidal attacks: the Cintas Largas, the Beiços-de-Pau, and the Xikrín. Even the sheer number of tribes—twenty-four—who were placed in mapped areas that SIL had designated as "potentially hostile"[68] might have raised some eyebrows.*

Tribes Placed Inside "Potentially Hostile" Areas

Júma

Cintas Largas (this "warlike" tribe was placed just below the "potentially hostile" area of the upper Aripuanã, where most of them could actually be found)

Parukotó-Charúma (SIL had begun work with one group, the Hixkaryána)

Apalaí (Aparaí)

Kayabí

Aiwatéri

Guaharibo

Kámpa (Campa in Peru)

Máya (Mayoruna in Peru)

Mandawáka

Beiços-de-Pau

Ipewí

Itagopúk

Mudjetíre

Apurinã

Bôca Negra

Suruí

Gavião

Txikão

Dioré

Xikrín

Kréen-Akaróre

Arara

Pakidái

In fact, of the 140 tribes listed in the survey, only 2, the Canela of the Tocantins River Valley and the Júma of the Mucuim River, were specifically acknowledged as having their survival endangered by current violent attacks, and then only by "local Brazilians," not as the result of the development policy set in Brasília. In other negative reports, tribes instead were depicted as "losing the will

---

*Dale Kietzman, SIL's Brazil branch director, did report a few cases of invasions of Indian lands in the 1950s and the "recent past," particularly in the Northeast, by "colonists" and "landowners"; with only a few exceptions—notably the taking of lands of the Xokléng of Santa Catarina and the Bororo of Mato Grosso—past invasions were still referred as being part of a vague "integration" process that produced "survivors" or "extinct" tribes.

to live" or "disintegrating" as a result of "contact" with Brazilians. And even in the Canela case, the SPI was pictured as offering "the only possible protection against further attacks."[69] Into this "confused" contemporary situation, SIL entered in 1966, the same year the survey was published, to hurry the translation of the Bible into the Canela tongue before it disappeared with the Indians.

One area where SIL *did* come under scrutiny was its aviation program. More than enough Brazilians were trained pilots. "There is also lurking in the background the question of national security and foreign pilots,"[70] Jim Wilson, the publicity officer of SIL's Brazil branch, wrote Cam Townsend in April 1968.

This was a potentially explosive issue for SIL. Americans not related to SIL had recently been arrested for allegedly smuggling mineral samples out of the Brazilian Amazon, and the press was full of protests by Brazilian nationalists about Americans flying ore samples out of Indian areas, including the lands of the Cintas Largas, for American companies.

Cam moved quickly. While attending another Inter-American Indian Conference in Mexico, he met the new head of FUNAI. Next, he visited the Brazilian ambassador to lobby for a draft contract between SIL and FUNAI.

Cam spent two weeks in Rio and Brasília, building SIL's image through a carefully planned series of public relations events, including a formal reception at the Indian Museum in Rio that Darcy Ribeiro had founded. Cam's goal remained unchanged: to reach the people who were in power.

Success came on September 1, when Cam rode the crest of this public relations wave into the office of Brazil's president. General Costa e Silva was not adverse to Cam's proposals for a ministerial-level contract and sent him to his interior minister. The president's backing outweighed any reluctance on the part of Albuquerque Lima's staff. When Cam left the ministry, he had Albuquerque Lima's agreement in principle to provide gasoline, as in Peru, to let JAARS fly and to provide SIL with a contract with the assent of FUNAI's president. Cam departed Brazil for Peru, confident that "our pilots will doubtless get to fly again."[71] They did, but only after Albuquerque Lima was gone from office.

At first, it appeared that the minister was trying to back out of the accord. The ministry balked at signing an agreement with a U.S.-based organization over which there could be little legal control. For a government that was licensing an organization to operate airplanes over a vast stretch of isolated territory, the poor prospects of exercising even informal control over SIL's activities were unsettling; using a contract to exercise legal power over its local functionaries was the only recourse. Albuquerque Lima insisted that the agreement could be signed only with the Brazil branch of SIL, not with Cam as general director of the U.S.-based parent organization. It was another example of the struggle against foreign influence that soon led to the minister's fall from power.

Albuquerque Lima was making many enemies. While his army units built roads, railways, and bridges and established thirteen colonies to encourage development in the Amazon,[72] he also seemed bent upon protecting Amazonian Indians. He set aside a 3,000-square-mile reservation in October 1968 for Mato Grosso's Beiços-de-Pau.

At the same time, the Villas Boas brothers, founders of the Xingu Indian Park, were authorized to try to contact the Kréen-Akaróre, the mysterious group made famous as the "tribe that hides from man," by author and expedition member Adrian Crowell. The tribe's fierce defense of their lands just northwest of the park had, with its "no prisoners" policy toward white intruders, understandably been effective. The tribe's territory was at the heart of an old gold mining district. The undeveloped rectangle, 350 miles by 200 miles of jungle valleys and cliffs between the Xingu and Tapajós rivers, had been left blank on SIL's 1964 map of tribes, as if inadvertently prophesying the tribe's destiny.

Watching the way bulldozers so easily toppled the shallow-rooted trees of the rain forest, Claudio and Orlando Villas Boas could foresee that terrible end as well. They asked only that they be funded to outfit an expedition of peaceful contact with the Indians before Operation Amazon's road crews sparked a holocaust from Brazil's military firepower. Already in July 1967, an incident had occurred when a band of about 100 Kréen-Akaróre decided to visit Cachimbo, one of the airstrips built by the Villas Boas brothers in 1951, which was later expanded into an Amazonian air base.

Although the peaceful intent of the Indian men was indicated by their approaching without weapons (having left them at one end of the base) and their being accompanied by women and children, their appearance out of the jungle nevertheless inspired such panic at the air base that jet fighters and troops were flown in from Belém, Manaus, and even Bananal. The troops were trained in jungle combat, presumably graduates of the new CIA- and Green Beret–inspired Jungle Warfare Training Center north of Manaus. But the local general, attempting to land, had seen the Indians near the runway, and he dived and swooped over the Indians' heads. The Kréen-Akaróre fled back into the rain forest.[73]

Rather than create Indian attacks where none had occurred, the new FUNAI under Albuquerque Lima hoped that none would be provoked. Instead, it authorized peaceful expeditions to the Kréen-Akaróre and other tribes in the north, while moving to create parks and reserves to protect the Indians. To prove his sincerity and to dissipate a worldwide outcry, Albuquerque Lima invited several international human rights organizations to send their own investigators into the tribes. To the horror of the regime, several accepted.

If that were not bad enough for an interior minister's political career in post-coup Brazil, Albuquerque Lima was probably the most outspoken member of the cabinet who supported efforts in the Brazilian Congress to restore democracy and to curtail the acquisition of Brazilian lands and companies by foreign interests, most of whom were powerful American corporations. By December 1968, this campaign had built up such a momentum that it appeared that the opposition would sweep the scheduled coming congressional elections. Fear spread that another coup was in the making. The death of former president Castelo Branco the previous year had removed the only significant restraint on the generals. When the coup finally came, it was almost an anticlimax. In 1964, it had been the left wing of Brazil's nationalists that was smashed; this time, it was the right wing, including former Governor Carlos Lacerda, the opponent of Hanna Mining's planned ore-export terminal in his state of Guanabara, and Albuquerque Lima. Lacerda was placed under arrest; Albuquerque Lima was politically marginalized and soon lost his job.

40

ROCKY HORROR ROAD SHOW

"WALKING" INTO THE NIGHT

High above Manhattan's Rockefeller Plaza, Rockefeller family agents in Room 5600 watched in stony silence as repression, savagely modern, tightened over Brazil, decreeing by day, hunting by night. Associates of the family's financial empire had kept them apprised in graphic detail of what was happening. Cornell University's Presbyterian chaplain, William W. Rogers, the former director of the now-defunct Brazil-Cornell Project in the Brazilian Northeast (a victim of fear of the CIA), brought the kind of news that few American journalists, including those outside Brazil and free of the regime's censorship, either cared to report or were allowed to.

"One thousand leaders of the outlawed National Union [of] Students were arrested and jailed in São Paulo over the weekend," he wrote from Rio in October 1968, two months before Brazil's second coup of the decade. Students responded with demonstrations in every major city, but they were no match for armed soldiers. Rogers's report was vivid:

> The military police, for the most part, are swift, tough and efficient. They can also be destructive and deadly. . . . Some students have been shot to death in the last three months. There are times when downtown Rio is like an occupied city. The streets are regularly patrolled by elite, well-disciplined riot squads—and as occasion demands these are reinforced by mounted cavalry, water cannons and tanks.
> . . . It is clear that the government regards these students as a threat to the "national security." In this case, "national security" probably should read "the security of the present government," since it seems highly unlikely that these students could actually subvert and take over Brazil. . . .

Talk of a potential right-wing coup is common, and is openly discussed in the congress. . . . The present government [is not expected] to last beyond December.[1]

Despite dictatorial rule, the will of the students had not yet been broken. At the nationally televised International Festival of Popular Songs in Rio de Janeiro's huge sports arena, young Geraldo Vandre sang a powerful protest song called "Caminhando" ("Walking"). He "sang of hunger and protest, of soldiers and guns, of living and dying without reason," Rogers informed the Rockefeller office. "The crowd, mostly students . . . cheered and sang every word with Vandre. 'Caminhando' was their song and Vandre their hero."[2]

Brazil's picture magazine, *O Cruzeiro*, called the occasion "Vandre's Festival." Rogers noted the military government's extreme reaction, quoting from Rio's English-language *Brazil Herald*:

RIO DE JANEIRO (October 15)—Stores selling records were notified by the political police yesterday that they must not play for the public the song "Caminhando" by Geraldo Vandre. . . .

The Guanabara (Rio) police chief . . . described the text of the song as offensive to the armed forces because it includes a passage which says that soldiers in the barracks "learn to kill and lead a meaningless life. . . ."

Steps are being taken to ban sales of the record . . . and all performances. . . . Police in Rio also arrested people who allegedly carried copies of the text.

Rogers wrote of riots between pro-U.S. students at Mackenzie College, "apparently the headquarters of a rightist organization called the CCC (the Portuguese acronym for Commandos to Hunt Communists) who pledged to "kill five communists for every democrat killed," and leftist students at the University of São Paulo. "The conflict is sharp and serious, and still another newspaper speaks of a 'pre-Nazi' atmosphere of fear and violence in the country."[3]

Henry W. Bagley, public relations director for the International Basic Economy Corporation, dismissed this news with businesslike Realpolitik and a crisp philosophical air. "Rogers's report seems accurate," he wrote, "and is certainly interesting. But I doubt—as he does—that the students or others can oust the military right. . . . I can't forecast what will develop, but personally, I would feel a little more secure in Brazil than New York City right now. I spent 8 days in São Paulo this month and really enjoyed it. But in that short time I obviously couldn't get close to the political and economic trends."[4] Among these trends was the arrival of U.S. military officers, including an army captain fresh from Vietnam who was assassinated in the streets of Rio for allegedly helping the Brazilian military's repression. The U.S. Embassy insisted that the captain was only a student at the University of São Paulo.

Two weeks later, Rogers wrote home again. The targets of the Brazilian police were now the same people who were being encouraged to move into Indian lands in the Amazon: poor families from the Northeast and other rural areas. "There seems to be little doubt that as cities like Rio and São Paulo experience the impact of migration from the countryside, urban life becomes more and more difficult for many thousands of the marginally poor, and crime rates rise to alarming proportions. It is principally in response to urban crime, and the inability of municipal governments to control it, that acts of the most brutal and deadly violence occur."[5]

This level of violence by Brazilians against Brazilians was a new phenomenon—if one did not count violence against the Indians, who seldom were counted; since 1900, an estimated 800,000 people, including eighty whole tribes, had just "disappeared" into "extinction."[6]

In Rio and its suburbs, as well as in São Paulo, local death squads murdered with impunity. Many leftists were murdered as "criminals"; newspapers were bombed; and in the Northeast, the home of an outspoken defender of human rights—the Catholic archbishop of Recife—was machine-gunned by CCC terrorists. Soon the sweep widened to include not only "respectable" opponents of the regime, but an increasing number of Rio's migrant poor from the countryside; homeless and crammed into shantytowns, they had committed the crime of turning the beautiful mountains surrounding Rio into an eyesore of human misery. Eventually, with money from the U.S. Agency for International Development (AID), the regime would save Rio's status as a tourist mecca by tearing down many *favelas* (slums) and replacing them with public housing or a one-way ticket to the Amazon. But in the years right after the coup, as the regime struggled for its political and economic life, discouraging immigrants from choosing the cities over the jungle often meant inspiring terror with mutilated corpses.

Swift and Rockefeller: Alliance in the Amazon

Despite knowledge of this state of affairs, the Rockefeller office overlooked the link between terror in the urban slums and Operation Amazon's hoped-for colonies while it made business decisions in Brazil. No sooner had the generals' so-called supercoup taken place in December 1968 than Deltec International further consolidated its power in Brazil, buying up International Packers, Ltd. The purchase of this huge meat-packing conglomerate brought not only members of the Swift family and most of the Swift family's international meat-packing empire into an alliance with the Rockefeller camp, but the Milbank interests through Deltec director Arthur Oakley Brooks, a longtime executive of mutual funds controlled by Sam Milbank,[7] friend of Cam Townsend and contributor to the Summer Institute of Linguistics (SIL). Milbank's largesse spanned the theological gap that separated the Townsends and the Rockefellers; he was chairman of the Milbank Memorial Fund, one of Wall Street's richest foundations, which contributed funds to Nelson's AIA.[8]

Through IBEC's holdings in Deltec's Brazilian Investment Bank (BIB), this alliance offered an unprecedented consolidation of foreign power in Brazil, with great expectations for the Amazon. International Packers chairman A. Thomas Taylor, husband of Geraldine Swift, was made chairman of Deltec International; Milbank executive A. Oakley Brooks was made vice chairman; Walther Moreira Salles, director of both IBEC and Deltec, continued as president of BIB, with IBEC's Fulton Boyd also a BIB director; and David Rockefeller's Chase Manhattan Bank continued as Deltec's transfer agent.

Rockefeller interests were now, through Deltec, interlocked with one of Brazil's largest processors of frozen meats and one of the largest ranching concessions in the Amazon, Swift do Brasíl, S.A. Deltec also began preparations to construct a meat-packing plant north of Pará at the mouth of the Amazon, at Ilha de Marajó, an island the size of Switzerland.

With Deltec's purchase of the Swift and Armour beef operations, the twenty-year-old "shining dream" of developing South America's interior seemed within reach. Within two years, Deltec would begin cutting down the rain forest at its 180,000-acre ranch straddling Maranhão and Pará. Shipping billionaire Daniel Ludwig, long backed by Chase Manhattan Bank, had decided to do his own cutting in the Brazilian Amazon, but on a far grander scale. He had plans for a giant project that would startle the world. Mining would be included, along with dams. The "Great Lakes" proposal for South America by Herman Kahn, the director of the Hudson Institute, also remained alive and well. In fact, Nelson's good friend and trustee of the Rockefeller Foundation, former Colombian president Alberto Lleras Camargo, was to head a special commission to investigate the Colombian part of that proposal: a series of low dams, or dikes, to flood western Colombia's Chocó Valley, creating two huge lakes that would be linked by a canal excavated by nuclear blasts, creating a new waterway between the Atlantic and Pacific oceans. As *Fortune* explained, this plan would "open up the vast quantities of high-grade, fast growing timber that are known to be there, plus a variety of minerals, including gold, platinum, copper, zinc, bauxite, and oil, that are either known or believed to be there."[9] (Among the more active gold-mining companies in the region, coincidentally, was a subsidiary of the International Mining Corporation, chaired by Lewis B. Harder, a partner with Rockefeller ally Moreira Salles in the Brazilian mining company CBMM.[10]) The Chocó dams would provide electricity to power the industrialization of the Cauca Valley, fifty miles to the east, and its major cities, Medellín, Manizales, and Cali. No comment was made on how flooding the Chocó Valley would impact on the 13,000 to 20,000 Indians of the Catio, Embera, and Noanama tribes in the vicinity, but SIL did make the decision to send in translators among the Noanama in 1969, having already "occupied" the Catio since 1966.

That Kahn's proposals received serious consideration was alone a triumph of will, and not just Kahn's. Nelson's CIAA had developed the plan in Washington as a proposed inland waterways project. That project proposed using the same rivers in Brazil and Venezuela as Kahn did a quarter century later—the Orinoco, the Casiquiare, the Negro, and, of course, the Amazon; then as now the object was to link oil, mining, and forest resources inside the Orinoco and Amazon basins for extraction to the war industries and markets of the United States and her allies.

For Nelson, the triumph of his ideals for growth—symbolized by IBEC's own growth—was also personal. At IBEC's April 1969 annual meeting, he had the satisfaction of seeing his eldest son, Rodman, installed as president of IBEC. Rockefeller family financial interests now shared control over Brazil's largest mutual fund, Crescinco, through one of Brazil's largest investment banks, BIB. They controlled outright one of Brazil's largest commercial banks, Banco Lar Brasileiro, S.A. (through David's Chase Manhattan Bank); its largest hybrid seed company, SASA, producing 45 percent of all hybrid seeds planted in Brazil; one of its largest manufacturers of CMC (carboxyl-methyl-cellulose, a vital moisture-control agent in detergents, paints, adhesives, ceramics, and oil-well drilling); and one of its largest drop-forging plants. Through Crescinco, they controlled stock holdings in more than 100 Brazilian firms; through Rockefeller Brothers, Inc.'s holding in Chrysler, they held a stake in one of Brazil's largest car manufacturers. They owned a large share in one of Brazil's largest ranches (Fazenda Bodoquena); and now, through Deltec, they had a stake in one of Brazil's (and the world's) largest beef-processing operations, which was about to launch another huge cattle ranch in the Amazon. With Rodman as president of IBEC and cousin Richard Aldrich on IBEC's board as effective vice president of IBEC for Brazil, Nelson's commitment to Brazil's future seemed beyond dispute. And as his arch rival, Richard Nixon, would soon put it, as Brazil went, so did all South America. With Latin American leaders worried about their own future with the newly elected Republican administration in Washington, it made perfect sense to the new president to take the advice of Galo Plaza, secretary general of the Organization of American States (OAS): tap Nelson Rockefeller to head a fact-finding mission to Latin America that would be designed to reassure its leaders. Such a mission would also give Rockefeller a consolation prize. No one anticipated that it would become, for all concerned, a nightmare.

"ROCKY'S SIDESHOW"

It was difficult for Nelson to see his former adversary sitting behind the president's desk in the Oval Office on his first day on the job. But after an hour of discussion, Nelson emerged with a new job: chief of the Presidential Mission to Latin America. The title was Nelson's idea. So was the size of his mission. "Keep it small. Keep it small," Secretary of State William Rogers warned Nelson. Nelson settled for an entourage of sixty, including twenty-seven experts on everything from counterguerrilla operations to women's rights, some of whom were veterans of Nelson's CIAA.* Before it was over, it would cost

*See Appendix A for the names of some of the most interesting members of the mission.

him $760,000 in personal funds above what the government would allow.[11]

No matter how expert Nelson's delegation was, however, nothing could prepare it for the chaos that greeted their leader at each stop over the next months in Latin America.

In Honduras, Nelson was met by rioters shouting "Rockefeller, go home!" And in Managua, Nicaragua, he was again greeted by students chanting "Rocky, go home!" The students burned a U.S. flag to protest the visit. In Costa Rica, thousands of pro- and anti-Rockefeller demonstrators clashed.

Nelson was shocked. For decades, he had devoted time, energy, and capital to Latin America's problems and potentials. He expected respect, admiration, and even love. He was not alone in this expectation. Indeed, that was the reason Galo Plaza felt confident in urging Nixon to send Nelson down. And the "magic" of the Rockefeller name still did work with Latin America's elite; it was only with the rest of the hemisphere's population, most visibly with its students and workers, that there seemed to be some insurmountable problems.

Nelson tried to blame it all on communists, and there was no doubt that they were agitating against him. But when Peru's new military leaders declared that it would be "inopportune" to host him as scheduled, it was obvious that the opposition ran deeper than Nelson was willing to admit. Peru's February 13 seizure of American tuna boats operating off that country's Pacific coast demonstrated that more was involved in the anti-Rockefeller protests than communist agitators or the Cold War. IBEC's own tuna boat and cannery in Puerto Rico may not have been threatened directly, but the issue of national sovereignty in Latin America stuck like a craw in the throats of multinational businessmen like the Rockefellers.

Adolf Berle had seen it coming the month before, after the Peruvian military's seizure of Standard Oil of New Jersey's oil refinery in Talara. "Practically all local sentiment is against the United States," he noted in his diary, "and might be stirred to violent action if the [Hickenlooper] amendment is used [to intervene in Peruvian affairs]. The Peru government talks about throwing all Americans out within forty-eight hours. Given the sentiment elsewhere in the continent—Chile, Bolivia, possibly Brazil—we may see a clear breakdown of inter-American relations."[12] The Nixon administration had responded by halting arms sales to the Peruvian government. The Peruvians then canceled Nelson's visit in the same official communiqué that declared that the U.S. Army, Navy, and Air Force missions in Peru were without further purpose.

"Rocky's Road Show," as the American press had dubbed it, now threatened to become a sideshow. After more protest-marred stops in Costa Rica and Panama, Nelson returned home to rest and confer with Nixon and Henry Kissinger. Then, despite Peru's rebuff in May, he was off again to Latin America.

Nelson landed first in the home of his old friend, ex-president Lleras

Camargo. But Colombia, long the site of Standard Oil operations and currently the host of Texaco-Gulf's expansion in the Putumayo region, gave Nelson no relief. Rioting broke out in Bogotá. U.S. flags were again burned, and the student council at the National University declared a twenty-four-hour strike. Over 100 persons were reported injured. Liberals, Conservatives, and various leftist parties, including communists, had a common foe: him.

Worse awaited him in Galo Plaza's Ecuador. Club-swinging police had to battle through Quito's narrow streets to cut a path for the Rockefeller motorcade. Rocks pelted the cars, smashing windows and injuring three American reporters. Rockefeller's men feared for their lives, but not Nelson. "I didn't see a thing, not a thing," he told reporters when he pulled up to the presidential palace.

Throughout this violence-plagued tour, Nelson never lacked courage. In Guatemala it was the CIA, not Nelson, that insisted he restrict his movements. In Honduras, after the killing of a student by the police, he had dismissed warnings by his Secret Service detail and waded into the crowd to argue with the youths in Spanish. "See, nobody laid a hand on me," he said later, "but somebody lifted my wallet."[13] In Ecuador, where Nelson owned a coffee plantation north of Guayaquil, ten students were killed at Guayaquil's university by army troops, but Nelson was not dissuaded from offering a hand of friendship. "We have come to listen, not to fight,"[14] he told a news conference while police beat students at Quito's Central University. His offer to talk with student leaders was rejected.

Even his visit to Bolivia, "where we have come as Good Neighbors," was reduced to a three-hour meeting because of his concerns over possible bloodshed between soldiers and students. Meeting with President Adolfo Siles Salinas at the heavily guarded John F. Kennedy Airport outside La Paz, he found Siles urging the United States to refrain from dumping tin from its strategic stockpile to force down prices. Meanwhile, thousands of students, prevented by troops from accepting Nelson's challenge to come and talk instead of throw stones, carried placards against U.S. "imperialism" in front of La Paz's presidential palace. Nelson turned their marginalization into his own political asset.

"I'm not going to take responsibility," he explained to reporters, "for bringing about an incident that would cause loss of lives if the armed forces had to act against demonstrators to provide security."[15]

Reporters next found him resting with Happy beside a pool in Trinidad, awaiting news from Venezuela, his next scheduled stop. The Venezuelans were understandably nervous. So far, the Caracas government and Nelson had not been disturbed enough to scratch Venezuela from his itinerary. Venezuela was, after all, Nelson's second home, the site of his huge Monte Sacro ranch (which had briefly been seized by guerrillas in September, just six months after Adolf Berle had visited "for three days loafing"[16]). Venezuela was the place where he discovered South America's oil as a personal investment, the place where he had put IBEC and AIA to the test, the place he even had chosen to bring his wife for their honeymoon. Venezuela had been special. Until now.

Students announced plans to hold sit-in demonstrations at IBEC-owned supermarkets. Strong objections to Nelson's visit by opposition parties put the Venezuelan cabinet in a crisis. The Venezuelan government begged Nelson off, explaining that it could not guarantee his safety, even if he spent most of his visit, as planned, behind a heavy security guard at the swank Club Militar built by former dictator Marcos Pérez Jiménez.

"In all the years I worked for him, the hardest thing I ever had to do was deliver the word on Venezuela," one of his top aides, James Cannon, said later. "They were uninviting him."

Nelson was having lunch when he heard the bad news. He stopped and looked up at Cannon, stunned and pained. "After all that country has meant to me. And all I've done for them?" His head shook sadly. "This is a terrible blow."[17]

Nelson's immediate reaction was defensive. "Extremists are out to destroy the unity between the United States and her Latin American neighbors," he explained to the press troupe. "We must recognize what our friends are up against."[18]

He was saved further gaffes by the very man who had urged Nixon to send Nelson on the mission: Galo Plaza. Flying into Trinidad from Washington to confer with Nelson between sessions of an inter-American educational conference, the OAS secretary general urged his old friend to change course from such simplistic explanations.

"Whatever interest outside groups may have," he told the Rockefeller party, "there is a genuine national resentment that doesn't need much outside influence." Instead, look to the discontent over the slowness of the Alliance for Progress to achieve its stated goals, he advised, and to the feeling that the United States regards Latin America as merely a backwater.[19]

Galo Plaza's counsel hit home. In the future, Nelson would caution against blaming "outside forces" for disrupting his mission. "There is strong evidence that there is some popular support for these demonstrations," he explained.[20]

In Valencia, an industrial city 100 miles west of Caracas, hundreds of students stormed an IBEC supermarket, stoned First National City Bank's offices, attacked a Mobil gasoline station, and battled police and the Venezuelan National Guard.

But Nelson was optimistic. He looked forward to his next scheduled stop. In Brazil, at last, he was certain to get a respectful hearing and good headlines, even if they were censored.

HOUSES OF GLASS

The long silver jet that flew toward the edge of the Amazon frontier with Nelson Rockefeller on board seemed to be casting a mirror image of itself as it descended over Brasília, the ultramodern city of glass. A long fusillade of govern-ment ministries stretched across a red-earth plateau, ending with huge fins of resi-dential blocks jutting out like wings, as if wanting to take off into the future.[21]

Brasília had grown remarkably since the 1964 coup. If the city's cathedral looked from the air like a crown of thorns surrounding the simple cross perched high on its belfry, Nelson did not see it as a sign of Brazil's suffering. Rather, the country was now liberated, at least in his mind. Symbolized by the cathedral, Christ's crucifixion had been reduced to a bloodless essence by modern architec-ture. Artificial cascades flowing among the columns of government buildings now signified a nation washed of its original sins as the last country in the Western Hemisphere to abandon slavery—and as the largest green hell for the Amazon's native inhabitants. Brazil's record in the Amazon had been sanitized by mysterious fires that swept through the archives of the Service for the Protection of the Indian shortly after the completion of Brasília at the gateway to the Amazon.

In the summer of 1969, Nelson did not ask about Indians. But he knew there were victims of repression in Brazil. One, in fact, was the creator of Brasília: the architect Oscar Niemeyer. Twenty years earlier, Niemeyer had joined forces with Nelson's close friend Wallace Harrison to design the artifice for another great humanitarian dream, the United Nations. Now, his beloved Brasília had fallen into the hands of military chiefs who watched his every move. Niemeyer was allowed to go on designing the city, but Brasília belonged to the generals. The dream of an open, democratic government, symbolized by long transparent government min-istries with polyglass walls, remained simply that: a dream.

In July 1969, the Rockefeller mission found Brasília locked under a political chill. Brasília's deserted congressional halls spoke with an appalling, eloquent silence as Nelson walked through the chambers with Brazilian legislators and journalists. Only a dozen senators and deputies dared to be present: five dozen of their colleagues were under arrest. So were journalists, mayors, and 3,000 other political leaders and students, many of them subjected to torture.

Walking beside Nelson was Vice President Pedro Alexio. Before the year was out, he would be denied his constitutional right of succession to the presidency. Brazil's Supreme Court could not help him, any more than it could help itself: After three of its justices were summarily removed from the bench by the generals in January, the president of the Supreme Court resigned in protest. The junta responded by simply announcing the reduction of seats on the Supreme Court from fifteen to eleven. Five state legislatures, after first suffering a 30 percent cut in federal funds, had been closed by military decree, and all municipal, state, and federal elections were suspended. Censorship was imposed, and movie theaters were required to show government-supplied "educational material."

But perhaps the most poignant abuse, at least for Americans who were pre-viously supportive of the 1964 coup, was the military's purge of the universities.

More than sixty-eight professors at São Paulo University and the federal universities in Rio and Brasília were "retired" in May. When thousands of students boycotted classes in protest, the military issued a decree outlawing all student strikes and demonstrations, removed eight judges who disagreed, and began kidnapping and torturing student-government leaders.

The Brazilian generals had decided to use Nelson's mission to create the impression of an official U.S. blessing of the regime by decorating Nelson's top military adviser, General Robert Porter, the hero of the Bolivian campaign against Che Guevara. Nelson sidestepped the regime's request that he attend the award ceremony. But he also refused to call for Brazil's return to democracy, ordering aides to expunge such a reference from his arrival speech. He would speak privately to President Arthur Costa e Silva, not publicly, and not about specific victims of repression. That would be insulting to the general, who only two years before had been greeted with such high hopes as president-elect when honored at a luncheon of the Council for Latin America hosted by Nelson's brother, David.

Instead, Nelson accepted a lecture on national security from Costa e Silva and a report written by the SNI, the regime's secret police. Nelson would dutifully take the report to President Nixon, keeping its contents secret. He would rely on his closest political advisers on Brazil, Walther Moreira Salles and Berent Friele, to keep in touch with the SNI. His trust was not misguided. In September, while Nelson fretted that his own report was being held up by Nixon, Friele would reassure him that Moreira Salles had been "with the same young dedicated army officer in the SNI with whom I have been in contact and who wrote the report given to you by President Costa e Silva. Walther tells me that the influence of this group is increasing and that their confidence in you is unshaken. They understand the cause of President Nixon's delay in releasing your report and recommendations."[22] Apparently, Brazil's secret police had a better idea of what Nelson would recommend to the president of the United States than did the American people.

The power of SNI was indeed increasing. Within months, its chief, General Emílio Garrastazú Médici, would become president. "He reflects the thinking in the 'secret' report presented to you by President Costa e Silva," Friele would write Nelson.[23] That thinking included "agricultural development" in the Amazon at the expense of the Indians and a stifling authoritarian rule by decree.

Nelson was keenly aware, however, that beyond the generals' ceremonial greetings, the band music and guards' snapping salute, was hidden the fear and frustrations of Brazil's future elite, its students. So Nelson's limousine rolled out of the government complex as soon as protocol would permit and headed for the bow-shaped highway that bordered Brasília's artificial lake and its airports, to visit the university that Darcy Ribeiro had founded.

They were there, young men and women, angry despite their fear, but hopeful, like so many before in the Rockefeller story, that here, perhaps, was a powerful ally against the repression. And he listened, his famous square jaw jutting, his rugged good looks masking the priggish displeasure that only his aides recognized when he pursed his lips. Some of what the students said was challenging, almost defiant, of the regime whose "revolution" he hailed. Many of their friends had disappeared in the labyrinth of military prisons, some forever. Others had simply been jailed and tortured without charges or hearings, much less trials. Nelson seemed sympathetic.

On his second day in Brasília, Nelson met at the ultramodern U.S. Embassy with another group of students, but this time, ones who were carefully chosen by the embassy staff. These students, too, were upset, and again he listened. But he did nothing, then or later, that could compromise his relations with the dictatorship.

He rode through a Brasília gripped in a tomblike calm. The tranquility had been ensured by mass arrests and a huge security force. The contrast with the 1965 visit by Bobby Kennedy, who had infuriated both the generals and the U.S. Embassy by his call for elections, stood in bold relief. "When Robert Kennedy came here three years ago, I was able to shake his hand at the airport," said one man waiting to see Rockefeller after the small group he was in was herded by police far from the airport gates. "Now, I can't even see Rockefeller," he said, and he walked away in disgust.[24]

One group was thoroughly pleased with Nelson's visit. The economic achievements of São Paulo businessmen were "the most tangible, inescapable evidence of the power of responsible private initiative to elevate man's standard of life,"[25] Nelson told the city's Chamber of Commerce. Brazil's economy was now growing more than 6 percent a year, he said, outpacing by two times the percentage of population growth that gave the Rockefellers nightmares about the Third World's revolution of rising needs and expectations.

"Over the Hump"

Collecting General Porter, now sporting his new Brazilian medal, Nelson flew off to Paraguay, where force of arms assured another undisturbed welcome by Latin America's longest reigning dictator, General Alfredo Stroessner. A crowd of 3,000 carefully chosen Paraguayans welcomed him cordially. Photographs of Nelson shaking their hands at the Asunción airport also revealed the strain on his face; his ambitious trip was exacting a price.

A price was also exacted by Stroessner: He wanted $108 million in long-term U.S. loans for roads, railroads, and even a satellite communications station. It seemed a small price to pay in a country where, as early as 1963, AID had admitted to AIA's Walter Crawford that the "rural situation seems quite serious, almost to the stage of crisis."[26]

In the absence of serious land reform by Stroessner, AID was already considering relocating landless peasants who were crowded into the area around Asunción to colonies in the Alto Paraná region and the savanna lands in the Chaco to the north. There they could work on cattle ranches or establish small farms with AID-sponsored loans.[27] Crawford, as he had done in Brazil, made no mention in his reports to Room 5600 of the land rights of Indian tribes in Alto Paraná or the Chaco.

After the counterfeit peace of militarized Brazil and Paraguay, Nelson proceeded to unruly, democratic Uruguay, where students battled police in the streets while a General Motors plant erupted in flames. Nelson prudently shifted his visit to the resort town of Punta del Este, whose beaches and limited access controlled by a single highway had long made it a favorite of OAS conferees. Behind a shield of troops and guard dogs, he met with Uruguayan leaders, who two years earlier, backed by the local CIA station and the pro-Brazilian wing of the military, outlawed the Uruguayan Labor Confederation.[28]

"We are over the hump," Nelson told reporters afterward. "People are beginning to recognize the real potential of this mission."[29]

The potential was seen a week later in the streets of Argentina, where Nelson was surrounded by 10,000 troops with machine guns and police dogs. The smell of tear gas still wafted through Buenos Aires. Earlier that day, the police had attacked an impromptu demonstration of mourners at the funeral of a communist trade union leader, who, although he had opposed a recent general strike, had been machine-gunned by police during an attempted anti-Rockefeller demonstration two nights before.

The good news at Room 5600 was that Nelson had arrived safely. He had again eluded protesters by avoiding a car caravan from the international airport, taking a small U.S. Air Force plane into the heavily guarded downtown airport only a dozen blocks from his hotel.

The bad news was that he did not escape financial injury. Seventeen IBEC supermarkets in cities across the country were firebombed.

This was the worst, but Nelson was determined to extract some political victory. He swung back to his old tactic of confronting his opposition, to disarm them with his presence, and to live up to his pledge to skeptical American reporters that his visits would not be limited to meeting Latin America's Establishment. He wanted to meet his critics, he said. Argentine officials objected. The Secret Service said no. But Nelson, grabbing some aides, slipped out of his hotel for an hour with six young students at a prearranged meeting. "They studied him with disbelief," recalled aide Joseph Persico, "as though unable to accept that the living symbol of all they abhorred was actually with them in a small middle-class living room. He spoke in Spanish, which helped dissolve the tension, as he answered their politely phrased but increasingly probing questions. He and the students parted as philosophically distant as ever, but with friendly handshakes.

Outside, this great city of three million lay under a pall. Streets were dark and deserted, and the atmosphere was of a nation on the brink of civil war."[30]

It was. Before long, once the "compromise" ghost of a returned aged Juan Perón and spouse was exorcised by a military coup, many of Argentina's dissenting youths would "disappear," much like the Indians of the frankly termed "Wars of Extermination" of a century before.

Nelson flew home via the Caribbean, where he mortified State Department officials by appearing before cameras smiling with his arm draped around Haitian "President-for-Life" François "Papa Doc" Duvalier. In Haiti, however, Nelson's wish to meet the opposition was not granted. "In Haiti," the U.S. ambassador said dryly, "he'll have to do it in the cemetery."[31]

His last stop was the Dominican Republic, the sugar kingdom in which Nelson's friend, Adolf Berle, began his Latin American career. The U.S. Marines were still there, a remnant of the 20,000 marines who stormed the beaches allegedly to fight fifty-six identified communists and to restore the "democracy" of a military-backed regime. Now, despite four bodies removed by the police after demonstrations, "democracy" prevailed along Nelson's path. He was safe as long as armored carriers escorted his bus to and from the capital, ignoring the 450-year-old cathedral where Christopher Columbus was believed buried and where striking metalworkers had hung a banner over the entrance the previous week: "OUT WITH ROCKEFELLER."

Nelson Rockefeller would never be the same after this trip.

Neither would Latin America.

41

FORGING THE DOLLAR ZONE

THE "NEW MILITARY"

Three months after his last trip, without having any of the experts who accompanied him review the last draft, Nelson submitted *The Rockefeller Report on the Americas* to President Nixon. In this, his last public attempt officially to shape U.S. policy toward Latin America, Nelson pushed for greater centralized power in Washington over the Western Hemisphere's economic and political developments.

For two decades, he had urged that there be an undersecretary of state for Latin America; now he raised the stakes. Nelson called for *two* undersecretaries, one each for economic and political affairs, and again argued for his cherished all-powerful "first secretary" position. This time, however, he scaled down the proposed office's global scope of authority to the Americas. He called for a secretary of "Western Hemisphere Affairs," to be directly under the secretary of state to "coordinate all United States government activities in the Western Hemisphere."[1] This secretary would represent both the secretary of state and the president and presumably would have direct contact with the Oval Office. He would also command a Western Hemisphere policy staff in the National Security Council (NSC). Those above the hemisphere secretary (the president and the secretary of state) and other departments and agencies that were involved in the NSC would also be served, but there was little doubt that the hemisphere secretary would be in charge of all U.S. policy toward Latin America and probably Canada as well. Nor was there much doubt who Nelson thought might best hold this powerful new post.

Nelson's goal was not merely the centralization of power for its own sake, but the marshaling of U.S. power to achieve a long-desired objective he shared with his brother, David: the creation of a Western Hemisphere Free Trade Zone. This "Dollar Zone," as it would later be called, anticipated the future emergence of the Pacific Rim, dominated by Japan's yen, and the European Currency Zone, dominated by Germany's deutsche mark.

Both Rockefellers recognized the practical problems of dealing in a real world of powerful competitors. In the late nineteenth century, the United States had been joined by three other newcomers in the struggle for markets, colonies, and political influence in the world: Germany, Japan, and Russia. After World War II, the Soviet Union had been the U.S.'s only serious competitor, contending on an ideological level, as well as in the more traditional economic, political, and military spheres. In the late 1960s, however, reconstructed Japan and West Germany were reemerging as world powers with new factories and higher productivity. Although not yet competing militarily or politically, their economic competition was not to be ignored.

In the face of the traditional Soviet commitment to back insurgent movements even when Soviet national interests were not threatened, some U.S. strategists like Zbigniew Brzezinski of the Rockefeller-funded Russian Research Institute at

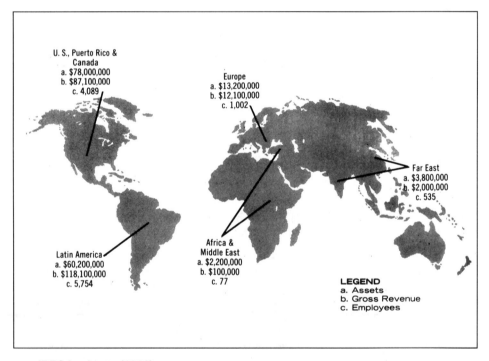

IBEC by Areas (1966)
Latin America was IBEC's biggest moneymaker.
Source: Wayne G. Broehl, Jr., *United States Business Performance Abroad.*

Columbia University reasoned that Japan and Germany had to be kept within the postwar alliance. As long as the Cold War demanded unity among capitalist great powers, the United States would have to concede a sharing of power with governments of powerful economies. If some "free traders" earnestly believed that free trade prevented trade wars that became world wars, it was still the Cold War that was the immediate imperative for sharing power with former enemies. But if that concession was not to become merely a stopgap tactic, it would have to be a political corollary to a broader economic strategy. For the United States to maintain its political domination in the long run, it had to retain economic domination. To overcome the country's growing trade problems in overseas markets, it was essential for American corporations to develop a wider home market: a strong trade zone in their own hemisphere where "free trade" would mean domination by American companies and local allies sweeping over national boundaries as "multinational" corporations.

Nelson did not spell this all out in his *Report on the Americas*. And since he was not such a reflective man to be guided by past historical trends, he would not predict the probable failure of the "New World Order" of free trade that David's future Trilateral Commission would struggle to achieve in the decades to come. But in 1969, he was projecting victory in the Cold War at least through an arms race too expensive for the Soviets (a strategy since his Quantico seminars in 1955) and the creation of a Dollar Zone, presaged by such regional developments as the Central American Common Market, the Caribbean Free Trade Association, the Latin American Free Trade Association, and the Andean Group and River Platte hydroelectric development negotiations then under way in South America. And the prediction that Latin America's population would grow in the next thirty years from 250 million to 643 million people meant time was running out. To speed the free-trade process along, Nelson recommended that the Nixon administration should work through the Organization of American States (OAS) and the Inter-American Council for the Alliance for Progress (CIAP).

The fact that both organizations were headed by allies of Nelson, Galo Plaza and Carlos Sanz de Santamaría, would probably have been enough to doom Nelson's suggestions in a Nixon White House. But there was more to Nixon's decision to let Nelson's report wither on the Rose Garden's vines. Nixon perceived that most of his financial backers were not members of the tweed-and-pin-striped Eastern Establishment who thought along Nelson's lines and already had the inside track in Latin America's markets. Nixon's backers were the nouveau riche of the postwar era, who still had markets to conquer from others, including older American companies and their Latin allies. Nor would Henry Kissinger's ego take lightly the idea of a competitor in his NSC, even if that competitor might be a friend and mentor. Kissinger enjoyed his obvious domination of foreign policy over Secretary of State William Rogers; he did not relish the idea of Nelson's experience and commanding influence overreaching him. Neither, of course, did Richard Nixon.

In the end, thanks to the Constitution, it was the president who counted in Washington, not Kissinger, and not Nelson Rockefeller. And Nixon was more concerned about the hot war in Asia and Vietnam than the Cold War in Latin America. Nixon was prepared to let Kissinger's NSC aide, Viron Vaky, the acting assistant secretary of state for Latin America, keep house in Latin America. Affairs would drift as they had done before, in their natural corporate way, while Nelson's Latin American tour would be relegated to the status of a public relations stunt to

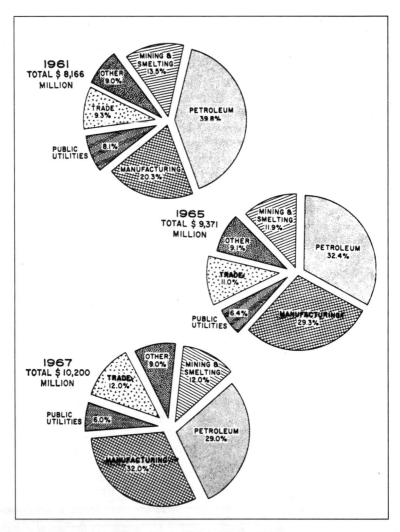

U.S. Private Investment in Latin America (1961–1967)

Manufacturing investment by American corporations in Latin America became the largest sector of investment during this six-year period. These "runaway shops" meant a loss of jobs in the United States to sources of low-wage labor in Latin America.

Source: U.S. Department of Commerce, as cited in Nelson Rockefeller, *The Rockefeller Report on the Americas*, p. 92.

show unity between the liberal and conservative factions of the Republican party.[2]

Lacking substance in economic policy, this unity coalesced around an unimaginative preservation of the status quo. For many Latin American countries in the aftermath of John Kennedy's doomed push for social reform, this political policy meant accommodation with military dictatorships, whether nationalist (as in Peru) or internationalist (pro-U.S.), as in Brazil.

Members of the "new military," Nelson insisted, were "deeply motivated" by the need for social and economic progress. "They are searching for ways to bring education and better standards of living to their people while avoiding anarchy or violent revolution. In many cases, it will be more useful for the United States to try to work with them, rather than to abandon or insult them because we are conditioned by arbitrary ideological stereotype."[3]

Undoubtedly, Nelson's attitude was taken in Brasília as a green light for more repression in Brazil. A month before the *Rockefeller Report* was released, the *New York Times* reported a shift in guerrilla tactics to urban countermeasures by the ideological heirs of Che Guevara.[4] A week later, the newspaper reported that the Brazilian generals were rewriting Brazil's constitution along the outlines of their "national security state."

On September 1, 1969, President Costa e Silva suffered a stroke, giving his succeeding triumvirate the excuse to cut short the beginnings of political and economic reforms, like restrictions on foreign land ownership in the Amazon. Instead, his successors would tighten censorship and postpone indefinitely a return to civilian democracy. Then, while the generals were in the thick of negotiations over choosing their next presidential candidate, U.S. Ambassador Charles Elbrick was kidnapped. Under U.S. pressure, the generals had to endure the humiliation of allowing newspapers to print the rebels' manifesto and flying fourteen political prisoners—most of whom had been tortured—to Mexico and then watch the freed ambassador describe his captors as misguided idealists.

But once Elbrick was released, vengeance came swiftly: The death penalty was officially restored in Brazil for the first time since 1891, and former Congressman Carlos Marighella, a folk hero among leftist students for organizing a guerrilla group, was killed on November 4 in an ambush laid by the military with the assistance of an agent of the CIA. The CIA had infiltrated the group in order to kill Marighella; with the approval of Henry Kissinger, it had even allowed an airliner to be hijacked by members of the group and the guerrillas to escape to Cuba, rather than risk exposing its penetration.[5] To the CIA and Kissinger, more was at stake than the safety of innocent passengers: Marighella's death succeeded in breaking the Brazilian Left's morale. It demonstrated exactly what the police could do if, in Rockefeller's words, they were provided with assistance and "the essential tools to do their job."[6]

Yet, despite the attention Nelson attracted with his call for more arms sales to Latin America's military, the darkest side of his report was economic, not military.

The Economics of Denial

For decades, it had been argued that radical land reform could end the stifling monopoly over the most fertile lands by exporters, return the land to a more stable balance between export and domestic agriculture, and build a home market with cheaper food that could *peaceably* lower the price of labor and fuel industrialization. In the absence of such basic reform, credit, the supposed elixir for every generation of Latin Americans, always turned into a poisonous cancer that engendered a huge debt. Nelson's prescription was more of the same, extending the life of the patient (or account) by extracting fewer pounds of flesh each year and by offering the bedside manner of Pollyanna prognoses. In studying Latin America's debt, CIAP (which Nelson would rename the Western Hemisphere Development Committee) would discover credit problems early, so that rescheduling negotiations could begin to stretch out payments. This strategy effectively would put a public inter-American agency in charge of monitoring and ensuring debt payments to private banks—banks like Chase, a leader in loans to Latin America.

If the *Rockefeller Report's* section on debt payments sounded self-serving, its emphasis on beef exports was even more blatant. Although not specifically addressed in the report's text, beef received more attention in the report's tables and charts than did any other single commodity, including sugar, coffee, or cotton. Oil, a source of contention over ownership and high import costs in Latin America, was not even mentioned.

Nelson's commissioned charts argued that the United States should remove restrictions on imports of processed beef from Latin America. Low-income families, he argued, would suffer if restrictions on imported supplies continued to force up the price of processed beef.[7]

Such humanitarian appeals notwithstanding, Nelson had a hidden conflict of interest as a major stockholder in the International Basic Economy Corporation (IBEC), a company with a large stake in Latin American beef production and exports of canned and frozen beef to the United States. Nelson, his brothers, and Walther Moreira Salles owned the eighth-largest ranching operation in Brazil (Fazenda Bodoquena) and, through IBEC's holding in Deltec International's Brazilian Investment Bank and its direct board interlock with Deltec, were involved in overseeing Deltec's vast Swift-Armour beef-processing operations in Argentina and Brazil.[8]

After the official release of the *Rockefeller Report* in October 1969, the nationalists' floodgates that had held back American investment in the Amazon opened wide. General Emílio Garrastazú Médici, the generals' hand-picked successor to Costa e Silva, welcomed U.S. investment to Brazil in his first statement as president.[9] In response, the State Department, its Latin American division now headed by Sears, Roebuck's Latin America chief, Charles Appleton Meyer (who had been appointed at the urging of David Rockefeller[10]), announced the granting of an export license for

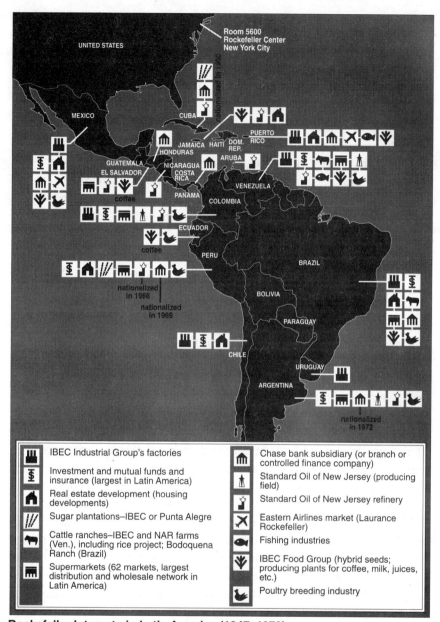

Rockefeller Interests in Latin America (1947–1972)

Includes minimum admitted Rockefeller family holding in Exxon (Standard Oil of New Jersey) of 2.2 million shares worth $156 million in 1975. Does not include Rockefeller interests (among top 10 stockholdings) in Standard Oil of California (Chevron), 3.3 million shares, and Standard Oil of New York (Mobil), 1.7 million shares, worth respectively $85 million and $63 million. (For verification of Rockefellers among top 10 stockholdings in oil companies, compare 1974 Metcalf Report to admitted Rockefeller holdings in 1974.)

Sources: IBEC annual reports; *New York Times*, December 4, 1974, p. 29; Standard Oil of New Jersey and Chase (National) Manhattan Bank property and branch listings in *Moody's Industrial Manual*, annual, 1947–1972; *Disclosure of Corporate Ownership* (Metcalf Report), Subcommittees on Intergovernmental Relations, and Budgeting, Management and Expenditures, Committee on Government Operations.

10,000 M-16 assault rifles that had been held up by the Johnson administration since 1966. The *New York Times* immediately saw a connection, noting that Nelson's report had recommended allowing the commercial sale of all modern weapons to Latin American governments for use against internal subversion.[11] On December 7, one day after the Brazilian air force disclaimed any intention of purchasing the rifles, Brazilian military and police units swept across Rio de Janeiro, arresting 1,500 people in an effort to rid the city of "undesirable elements."[12]

"We military men today see Brazil with new eyes," a general in Rio told a reporter. "The military can no longer separate itself from politics." Another officer was more blunt: "Let's not play games. We are not living in a democracy. Ours is a government of force and authority. Democracy is a word that fills the mouth. What we need is social and economic justice. And to achieve these goals, I wouldn't be surprised if the military had to keep running things in Brazil for another decade."[13] Actually, it would be another fifteen years.

The general's comments should not have come as a surprise. Nelson had been equally candid in his report: "Democracy is a very subtle and difficult problem for most of the other countries in the hemisphere. The authoritarian and hierarchical tradition which has conditioned and formed the cultures of most of these societies does not lend itself to the particular kind of popular government we are used to. Few of these countries, moreover, have achieved the sufficiently advanced economic and social systems required to support a consistently democratic system. For many of these societies, therefore, the question is less one of democracy or lack of it than it is simply of orderly ways of getting along."[14]

In his introduction to the published edition of the *Rockefeller Report*, *New York Times* reporter Tad Szulc argued that Nelson was merely proposing a "pragmatic concept that diplomatic relations should not constitute moral approval, and that our dislike of a regime must not deprive the people of that country of the economic aid they need. He admits that the Kennedy-initiated Alliance for Progress raised expectations that could not be met, but he recognizes that through the Alliance valuable lessons were learned that can now serve as the basis for new policies."[15] If rule by terror was not what Kennedy had envisioned or what Nelson enunciated as one of the "new policies," it became, nevertheless, the pervasive governing force that kept an entire continent in line, with Brazilian military officers playing key roles as backers of coups.

In Brasília, the new policies were taking shape. Médici's predecessor, Costa e Silva, had parried Nelson's politically required query about democracy by upbraiding the United States for failing to appreciate Brazil's "sacrifices." Nelson, impressed, had pulled out a yellow pad and begun taking notes like a schoolboy. He did not mention the charges of human rights abuses against Amazonian Indians. The omission, and Nelson's subsequent praise for the good intentions of "many new military leaders,"[16] was not lost on the new regime. Six months later,

Médici's new Interior Ministry turned General Albuquerque Lima's legacy on its head, announcing that it was preparing a dossier to refute charges in the European press that Brazilians moving westward were slaughtering Indians for their land.[17]

Gone was the moral outrage expressed by Albuquerque Lima when he denounced the Service for the Protection of the Indian to the press as the "Service for the Prostitution of the Indian." There was no genocide, explained Deputy Interior Minister Manuel Sampaio, only isolated murders resulting from the nation's natural expansion into her frontiers. Accusations such as those of Norman Lewis of the London *Sunday Times* stemmed from the government's own probe, he noted, and no government employees had yet had to stand trial.[18]

The Summer Institute of Linguistics, perhaps emboldened by the regime's denials, was equally indignant. SIL's Dale Kietzman responded to one letter of concern from an SIL supporter in 1970 by calling the reports on genocide from European investigators "pure bunk" and dismissed the killings as isolated incidents. "There have been killings in some areas, carried out by commercial interests generally. . . ."

The dictatorship was earnestly attempting to stop abuses, and was guilty at worst of only being tardy. "The government has reacted within its capability, but the army patrols have arrived after the fact and have not been all that helpful," Kietzman said.

A "wide investigation" into SPI had resulted in thorough reform, Kietzman went on. "The whole system has been revamped, with the organization of an Indian Foundation [FUNAI]." As proof, he offered that "within the past year [1969], the foundation called in all missionary organizations to consult on ways in which the missions could help with the administration of education and welfare in areas where the government could not be active." He concluded by recommending that the SIL supporter should read *Indians of Brazil in the Twentieth Century.*[19]

The SIL supporter was so impressed that he sent Kietzman's letter to New York's *Atlas* magazine, where he had first read the charges of genocide. "I now have some doubt as to the truth behind your article,"[20] he wrote the editors.

The editors were not impressed. "Since the Brazilian Government itself admitted the complicity of 134 of its Indian agents, the crimes ranging from embezzlement to murder, in a March 1968 report, it is probably premature on the part of the Wycliffe Bible Translators to state that 'government officials have never been involved in any sort of mass murder.'"[21] The point the European journalists were making was that there was no indication that the accused agents had actually been brought to trial. In fact, very few were ever punished.

Instead, FUNAI's civilian president, Dr. José de Queiroz Campos, besieged by charges that his sister had stolen material from Indian hospitals, was forced to resign.[22] His successor, General Oscar Bandeira de Mello, was expansive on the rights of developers. He ran the agency with the goal of generating the highest return on its legal 10 percent cut of the income for the Indian tribal estates it managed. This modus operandi was intentionally modeled after the U.S. Bureau of Indian Affairs (BIA). Part of FUNAI's mission, according to the congressional intent behind the 1967 law that created it, was to turn "tribal patrimony into productive assets [so that] it will be able to support them, as happens in the U.S.A."[23] This orientation, of course, only replicated in Brazil the essential weakness of the BIA in the United States, whose tribal royalties came from corporate mining, logging, and agricultural concessions approved by the big business–oriented Department of the Interior. (In 1976, Bandeira de Mello would leave FUNAI to become a director of Sanchez Galdeano, a firm actively pursuing cassiterite deposits in the lands of Surui Indians in Rondônia.)

The regime's mandate to FUNAI became clearer with the National Integration Plan, which resurrected the Amazon highway network proposed by the Hudson Institute. Branching west from two north–south roads—the Brasília–Belém highway (nearing completion) and the 1,000-mile Cuiabá–Santarém highway (under construction)—the 5,000-mile network envisioned by the regime would form a loop around the Amazon. This loop would be intersected by two roads, one running across the middle of the Amazon via the 3,400-mile-long Trans-Amazon Highway and the other, in the west, running south–north.

More than 50,000 families, mostly from the Northeast, were scheduled to be settled along the trans-Amazon highway system. As in the United States, the settlements were not the cause of commercial arteries, but their result. The real object of the arteries was to take minerals, lumber, and other natural resources out of the west and transport them to the east coast for foreign export or domestic manufacturing. The highways were also designed to vent social pressure mounting in the eastern states and cities that were overcrowded with landless peasants and immigrants. The historical analogy to the nineteenth-century United States was useful for the regime to light up the imaginations of investors.

Railroads and ports were also part of this plan. In Pará, a 400-mile railroad was planned to carry iron ore from U.S. Steel's new Sierra dos Carajás mines to a new port south of Belém, at Itaqui on the island of São Luis. Likewise, Hanna Mining's plan to build a 400-mile railway from the Agua Clara iron mines in Minas Gerais and expand terminal and port facilities at Sepetiba Bay south of Rio was revitalized. New oceangoing ports were planned for Santarém on the Amazon River, Imperatriz on the Tocantins, Altamira on the Xingu, Itaituba on the Tapajós, and Pôrto Velho on the Madeira. The selected port sites indicated a knowledge of the valuable mineral deposits nearby: bauxite near Santarém; manganese, iron, and diamonds near Imperatriz; lead and copper near Altamira; and cassiterite, an

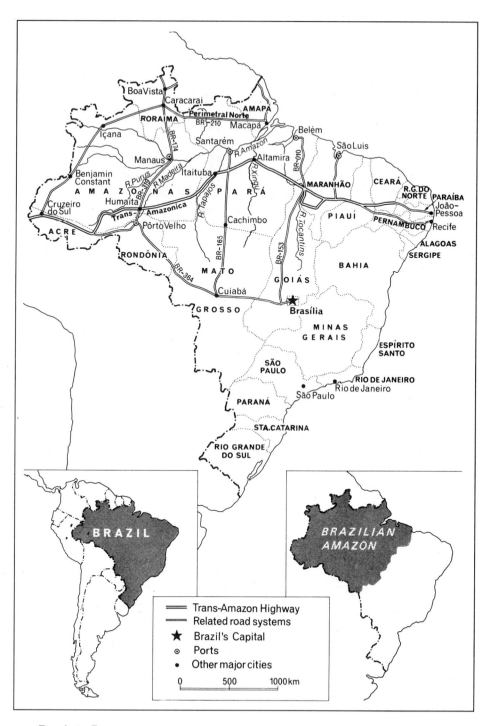

Roads to Resources

Source: Shelton H. Davis, *Victims of the Miracle.*

essential element in the production of tin, near Pôrto Velho and Itaituba.

North American companies staked their claims immediately.[24] But the most dramatic arrival in the area was New York's mysterious billionaire, Daniel K. Ludwig.

LUDWIG'S WILD KINGDOM

Before long, the world would be stunned by reports of the world's biggest lumbering operation, the world's largest rice paddy, some of the world's richest kaolin and bauxite mines, and even a floating sawmill towed overseas from Japan. Only later did it hear of vast deforestation of the rain forest, strip-mining, ecological disaster, and slave labor. And never—until Jerry Shields's 1986 book, *The Invisible Billionaire*—did the world learn of the Rockefeller banks and allies behind Daniel K. Ludwig.

"Do come to our country, Mr. Ludwig," General Castelo Branco greeted the billionaire when he accepted Roberto Campos's invitation to visit Brasília in 1966. "These days, Brazil is a safe country!"[25]

Ludwig was no stranger to Castelo Branco. He had been buying land in the Jari River Valley north of the Amazon, in Amapá state, since just before the 1964 coup. At that time, President João Goulart's minister of war, Henrique Lott, sent Castelo Branco to Belém to investigate rumors of a mysterious American who was buying up land. Those times were dangerous for American holdings in Brazil because of nationalist challenges from both the Left and Right. Even after the coup removed the Left from positions of power, the Right, led by Governor Carlos Lacerda, were still strong. Ludwig lay low.

Three years later, with the blessing of President Castelo Branco, Ludwig bought a 4,560-square-mile tract along the Jari and Parú rivers. This purchase raised his total holding to some 3.7 million acres. Complicating the identity of his ownership were "170 land titles of various types, acquired from 52 different sellers."[26]

The next year Ludwig's Universe Tankships quietly bought a small sixty-year-old exporting firm specializing in rain-forest products—rubber, nuts, and hides—along the Jari. He renamed it Jari Forestry and Ranching, Ltd., with the goal of using a projected pulp shortage to corner the world's paper market.

Then Ludwig moved in his first Caterpillar tractors, toppling the rain forest and planting seeds of two fast-growing trees, the *Gmelina arborea* from Africa (which can grow sixteen feet in less than a year) and the Honduran *Pinus carybea*, projected as a suitable replacement for the depleted soils left behind after the African tree was harvested. By 1970, hundreds of mostly uneducated northeasterners, rounded up by tough subcontractors, had arrived to work on the estate and live at Ludwig's self-contained small city, Dourado, named after his first manager, Rodolfo Dourado.

He might just as well have named the Jari project after his major financial backers: David Rockefeller's Chase Manhattan Bank and other Rockefeller-allied banks that had long been underwriters of Ludwig's corporate expansion.[27] In the mid-1960s, a boom in tanker profits brought about by the Vietnam War swelled Ludwig's liquid capital resources, making him a billionaire by 1969. After the Brazilian military's "supercoup" in 1968, he began pouring money into the Amazon. His plan: to turn his 3.7 million-acre jungle kingdom into a world-class lumbering operation. The Amazon rain forest, although dense, contains far too many different species of trees—more than 300 in a single acre—to make lumbering commercially feasible. So Ludwig decided to solve the problem by denuding 189,000 acres of forest, an area ten times the size of Manhattan, and replanting them with his African and Honduran trees. Soon crews driving giant Caterpillar "jungle crushers"— imported at $250,000 apiece—were smashing down trees with abandon.

As his kingdom took shape, partly financed by World Bank loans and eventually requiring more loans from Chase Manhattan, Ludwig's dreams expanded: a 120,000-herd of hump-backed cattle, imported from India, and a $25 million meat-processing plant; the world's largest rice paddy (overseen by former agronomists from the Rockefeller-funded International Rice Research Institute in the Philippines); and mining rights along the Trombetas River in neighboring Pará.

Ludwig's mining venture was the result of the military regime's National Integration Plan for a deep-draught port on the Trombetas River near the bauxite deposits. The bauxite had been discovered in 1962 by ALCAN. After the coup, Ludwig had vied with ALCAN and ALCOA over overlapping requests for concessions to the military regime. But Albuquerque Lima, then interior minister, had refused to grant concessions to foreign companies for more than 500 hectares per plot. In 1968, under pressure from the pro-U.S. wing of the military, he doubled this limitation to 1,000 hectares, which still would have left enough for Brazilian companies. But Ludwig, ALCOA, and ALCAN hoped for more. Albuquerque Lima's fall from power in 1969 granted their wish: In 1970, the Médici regime raised the limit to 10,000 hectares, or 24,700 acres per plot, far beyond the means of almost all Brazilian investors, effectively giving the largest American and Brazilian companies a monopoly.

The following year Ludwig visited the governor of Pará and walked away with approved plans for both processing and mining bauxite. His plan included a city between the Trombetas valley and his Jari headquarters, Monte Dourado, and an aluminum-processing plant capable of turning out 250,000 tons of aluminum bars per year. Both would be powered by a 500,000-kilowatt dam across a tributary of the Trombetas. To make the Amazon dream even more vivid, Ludwig also located one of the world's largest deposits (an estimated 50 million metric tons) of kaolin, a mineral used to make fine china and high-quality paper. By 1972, Jari was strip-mining and exporting 5,000 tons of kaolin, worth as much as $70 a ton on the world market. That was the year Ludwig felt enough confidence in his Amazon operations to borrow $150 million from David Rockefeller's Chase

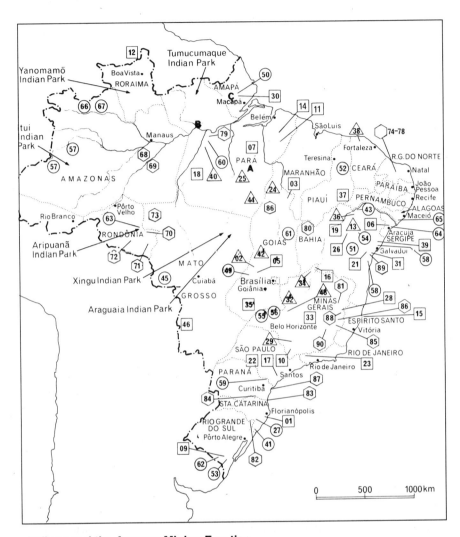

Indians and the Amazon Mining Frontier

Backed by a $400 million World Bank loan in 1972, Brazil's military dictatorship built highways that opened the Brazilian Amazon, including Indian lands, to unprecedented penetration by mining companies during the 1970s. A government-owned exploration company, Cia. de Pesquisas de Recursos Minerais (CPRM), working with the U.S. Geological Survey under a contract with the U.S. Agency for International Development, used Brazilian tax revenues to employ more than 500 technicians to absorb much of the initial costs of twenty-one mineral exploration projects in the Amazon that CPRM was involved in by 1973.

Sources: Shelton H. Davis, *Victims of the Miracle*, pp. 94–95; Shelton H. Davis and Robert O. Mathews, *The Geological Imperative*, p. 34; "CPRM: A Catalyst in Brazilian Exploration Programs," *Engineering and Mining Journal*, November 1975, pp. 169–71.

Multinational mining projects in the Amazon Basin:

A   *Amazonia Mineração* (iron ore, Serra dos Carajas); $3 billion (American) project of U.S. Steel Corporation and Companhia Vale do Rio Doce to begin in 1980.

B   *Mineração Rio do Norte* (bauxite, Trombetas River): $260 million project of Alcan Aluminum Company and Companhia Vale do Rio Doce to begin in 1977.

C   *Industria e Comercio de Minerios* (manganese, Serra do Navio): large manganese mining and processing project of Bethlehem Steel Corporation and Cia. Auxiliar de Empresas Mineração began in 1957.

Mineral exploration projects carried out by CPRM:

☐ **Finished projects**
1. Morro da Fumaça (fluorite)
3. Serra da Gangalha (diamonds)
5. Santa Fé (nickel)
6. Carmopolis (potassium, rock salt)
7. Transamazonica
9. Bagé (copper)
10. Poços de Caldas (molybdenum)
11. Paragominas (bauxite)
12. Serra do Mel (molybdenum)
14. Rio Capim (kaolin)
15. Plat. Continental (rock salt, potassium, sulphur)
16. Montalvania (silver, zinc, lead, fluorite)
17. Morro do Serrote (phosphate)
18. Rio Jamanxim (silver, zinc, copper, lead)
19. Xique Xique (lead)
21. Brasileia (copper)
22. Cerro Azul (niobium)
23. Morro Redondo (bauxite)
26. Sacaiba (chrome)
28. Aimores (titanium)
30. Rio Falsino (copper)
31. Itaparica (limestone)
33. Alterosa (limestone, beryllium)
35. Paraúna (phosphate)
37. Massape (vermiculite)
39. Araçás (coal)
46. Corumbá (iron)

△ **Projects under way**
2. Morro do Engenho (nickel)
13. Andorinha (chrome)
24. Arapoema (nickel, copper)
25. São Felix do Xingu (lead)
29. Catalão (chrome)
32. Chaminés Alcalinas (phosphate, diamonds, titanium, niobium)
34. Januaria-Itacarambi (vanadium, silver, lead)
36. Curaçá (copper)

38. Aprazivel (copper)
40. Itamaguari (gypsum)
42. Canadá (copper)
44. Gradaus (iron)
48. Patos de Minas (phosphate)

◯ **Projects awaiting a decision from DNPM**
27. Orleães (coal)
41. Ararangua (coal)
43. Tombador (syenite)
45. Santa Barbara (copper, chrome)
49. Bom Jardim (lead, zinc)
50. Ita (silver)
51. Ipirá (chrome)
52. Pimenteiras (phosphate)
53. Candiota (coal)
54. Coite (copper)
55. Três Ranchos (niobium)
56. Ouvidor (niobium)
57. Rio Jutai (lignite, peat, saprolite)
58. Ilheus (phosphate)
59. Barra do Mendes (nickel)
60. Aveiro (limestone)
61. Dianópolis (zinc)
62. Irui-Butia (lignite)
63. Presidente Hermes (iron)
64. São Cristovão (phosphate, limestone, gypsum)
65. Propriá (phosphate)
66. Uaupés (titanium)
67. Tapuruquara (titanium)

◯ **1975 projects financed through CPRM**
68. Mineração Angelim, S.A. (cassiterite)
69. Concisa—Construção Civil e Industrial Ltda. (cassiterite)
70. Progresso da Rondônia Mineração (cassiterite)
71. Tin Brasil Mineração Ltda. (cassiterite)
72. Mineração Aracazeiros Ltda. (cassiterite)
73. Mineração Rio das Garças Ltda. (cassiterite)
74. Mineração Amarante (scheelite)
75. Mineração Tijuca Ltda. (scheelite)
76. Mineração Acquarius (scheelite)
77. Zangarelhas Mineração Ltda. (scheelite)
78. Mineração Nordeste do Brasil Ltda. (scheelite)
79. Camita, S.A. (rock salt)
80. Serrasa—Serra do Ramalho Mineração Ltda. (fluorite)
81. Operadora de Equipamentos, S.A. (chromite)
82. Emp. Min. Imarui e Salomão Mineração Ltda. (fluorite)
83. Leprovost e Cia. (gold)
84. Mineração Morretes (gold)
85. Minas del Rei D. Pedro, S.A. (gold)
86. Mineração Morro Velho, S.A. (gold)
87. Eneel (nickel)
88. C.R. Almeida, S.A. (ilmenite)
89. Somicol, S.A. (manganese)
90. Cia. Bozano Simonsen (iron)

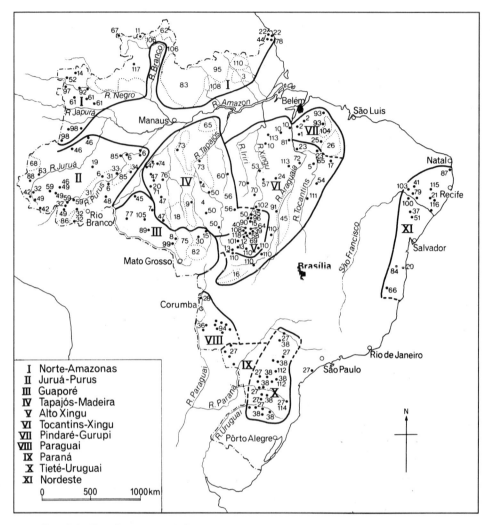

Brazil Indian Groups and Culture Areas

Source: Walter Dostal, ed., *The Situation of the Indian in South America.*, pp. 434–42, as cited in Shelton H. Davis, *Victims of the Miracle*, pp. 8–9.

1. Amaneyé	12. Awéti	22. Galibí
2. Anambe	13. Bakairí	23. Gavião
3. Aparaí (Apalaí)	14. Baníwa	24. Gorotíre
4. Apiaká	15. Beiço-de-Pau	25. Guajá
5. Apinayé	16. Borôro	26. Guajajára
6. Apurinã (Ipuriná)	17. Canela	27. Guaraní
7. Arara	18. Cintas Largas	28. Guató
8. Arikapú	(Cinta-Larga)	29. Gueren
9. Aripaktsá	19. Deni (Daní)	30. Irantxe
10. Asuriní	20. Diarrói	31. Jamamadí
11. Awake	21. Fulniô	32. Jamináwa

Legend on map:

I Norte-Amazonas
II Juruá-Purus
III Guaporé
IV Tapajós-Madeira
V Alto Xingu
VI Tocantins-Xingu
VII Pindaré-Gurupi
VIII Paraguai
IX Paraná
X Tieté-Uruguai
XI Nordeste

0   500   1000km

33. Jaruára	63. Marúbo	94. Têrena
34. Júma	64. Matipuhy	95. Tiriyo-Pianokoto
35. Jurúna	65. Mawé (Sataré)	96. Trumái
36. Kadiwéu (Cadureo)	66. Maxakalí	97. Tukána (Tukano)
37. Kaimbé	67. Mayongóng	98. Tukúna (Ticúna)
38. Kaingáng	68. Mayoruna	99. Tupari
39. Kalapálo	69. Mehináku	100. Tuxá
40. Kamayurá	70. Menkranotire	101. Txikão
41. Kambiwá	71. Morerébi	102. Txukahamẽi
42. Kámpa (Kampá, Campa)	72. Mudjetíre	(Txukahamaẽ)
43. Karajá (Carajá)	73. Mundurukú	103. Uamué (Aticum)
44. Karipúna	74. Mura	104. Urubú (Urubús-Kaapor)
45. Karitiã	75. Nambikuára	105. Urupá
46. Katukína	76. Numbiaí	106. Wapitxana
47. Kawahib	77. Pakahanova (Uómo, Jaru)	107. Waríkyana
48. Kaxararí	78. Palikúr	108. Waurá
49. Kaxináwa (Kaxanáwa, Cashinua)	79. Pankarare	109. Wayâna
50. Kayabí	80. Pankararú	110. Xavante (Chavante, Shavante)
51. Kirirí	81. Parakanán	111. Xerénte (Sherente)
52. Kobéwa	82. Paresí	112. Xetá (Aré)
53. Kokraimoro	83. Parukotó-Xarúma	113. Xikrín
54. Krahó	84. Pataxó	114. Xokléng (Botocudos, Aweikoma)
55. Krikatí	85. Paumarí	115. Xukurú
56. Kréen-Akaróre	86. Piro	116. Xukurú-Karirí
57. Kubén-Kran-Kegn	87. Potiguára	117. Yanomami (Yanomamö)
58. Kuikúru	88. Poyanáwa	118. Yawalapiti
59. Kulína	89. Puruborá	
60. Kuruáya	90. Suyá (Suiá)	
61. Makú	91. Tapirapé	
62. Makuxí	92. Tariána	
	93. Tembé	

Manhattan Bank.[28] By 1977, he would be back for more, Chase rounding up a syndicate that lent him another $400 million.

Ludwig, of course, was not alone in sharing the Rockefellers' dreams for Brazil. Also prominent was the Antunes family. The Antuneses were advisers to Chase's Brazilian subsidiary and partners with Ludwig and Hanna Mining in Minas Gerais's huge iron deposit. The clan also had been getting technical assistance from the IBEC Research Institute since the early 1960s to analyze soil prospects for an Amazonian colonization project in Amapá near the manganese mine they operated jointly as ICOMI with Bethlehem Steel. In fact, the Antunes Foundation had replaced the Rockefellers' American International Association for Economic and Social Development (AIA) in 1967 as a major philanthropic conduit for research on development in the Amazonian frontier. The research included "crop and livestock production and exploring future possibilities of fisheries, forestry and small business to service the [Antunes manganese] mining*

*The Amapá Development Institute, for example, was set up with funding by Antunes's ICOMI to carry out recommendations prepared by AIA's Walter Crawford based on an AIA field survey conducted under the auspices of the Antunes Foundation

enterprises organized under ICOMI," by 1972 the twenty-second-largest corporation in Brazil.[29] Apparently, the fact that 49 percent of ICOMI's stock was held by Bethlehem Steel, a company with long-standing ties to James Stillman Rockefeller's First National City Bank, did not discourage Nelson's wing of the Rockefellers from pursuing an alliance with Antunes. The potential for profit and influence over Brazil's future required partnerships with Brazilian families who opposed the nationalist current represented by Albuquerque Lima.

Accordingly, Antunes was brought on to the board of the Brazilian Investment Bank (BIB), the investment bank set up by IBEC, the Rockefellers' Walther Moreira Salles, and Deltec Banking, just as Juracy Magalhães, former ambassador to the United States and foreign minister in the Castelo Branco regime, was made a director of Crescinco's firm in Anápolis near Brasília, Companhia City de Desenvolvimento, now controlled by BIB.

Other powerful Brazilians on BIB's board completed the portrait of the Rockefeller alliance in South America's largest country:

*Paulo Fontainha Geyer, president of Refinaria e Exploracão de Petróleo União, the oil firm controlled by Moreira Salles that had its ambition to exploit Bolivia's Santa Cruz oil thwarted when the Goulart government refused to allow União's subsidiary to go to its shareholders for more capital.[30] Now prospects looked better, the firm having entered into a $100 million joint venture with its crude-oil supplier, Gulf Oil, to produce chemicals used in fertilizers.

*Paulo Reis de Magalhães, head of Industrias Quimicas e Texteis, S.A., and Dunlop do Brasil, a tire manufacturer with rubber plantations in Bahia and an old Crescinco investment. He was later president of the Brazilian subsidiary of Champion International, one of the largest paper manufacturers in the world and a major spoiler of the Amazon rain forest.

*Antonio Gallotti, president of Light Companies of Brazil, the latest name for the Brazilian Traction Light and Power Company. Gallotti was also vice president of Light's parent company, Brascan, Ltd., an investment firm involved in both Brazil and Canada (hence, its name) and controlled 75 percent by Canadian investors and 25 percent by U.S. investors, including a group represented by a Rockefeller ally, J. Peter Grace, of W. R. Grace & Company.

Of all of these firms, Light was the giant. The largest private company in Brazil, Light provided Brascan with 77 percent of its net income.[31] In 1972, when Light's net utility income increased by 24 percent ($87 million) in one year, Brascan took all that it could from Light under the military regime's profits-remittance law. This lucrative relationship underscored the vested interest of Brascan's major stockholders in Brazil's industrialization and in increasing Brazil's hydroelectric-power capacity.

Besides Gallotti, Augusto T. A. Antunes was Brascan's only Brazilian director.

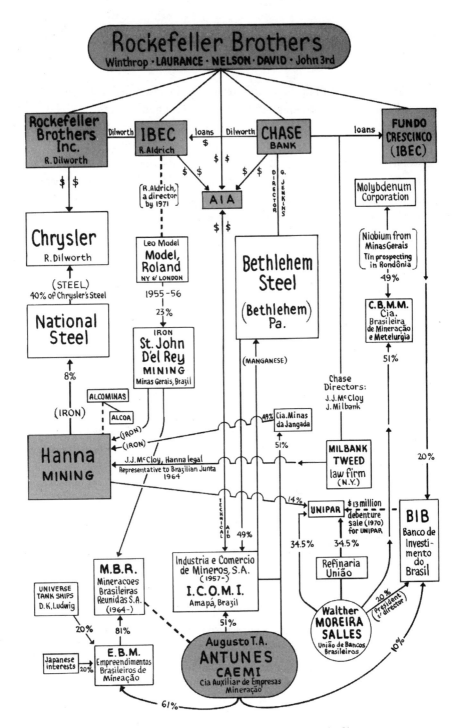

Rockefeller–Hanna Mining Ties in Brazil (1960–1972)

Sources: Jean Bernet, *Interinvest Guide – Brazil and International Capital* (Rio de Janeiro: Interinvest Editora e Distribuidora Ltda., 1973), cited in Shelton H. Davis and Robert O. Mathews, *The Geological Imperative*, p. 31; various annual reports of companies on chart; Edie Black and Fred Goff, "The Hanna Industrial Complex," *Latin America Report*, North American Congress on Latin America, 1969.

Six Americans, however, sat on Brascan's board, four of whom represented firms with a stake in Brazil.[32]

The targeting of Brazil's Amazon region by American multinational corporations became more obvious after April 1971, when the regime's National Department of Mineral Production outlawed all individual prospecting in Rondônia. More than 2,000 Brazilian prospectors were expelled, while 1,500 others opted for jobs with large companies. American firms moved into Rondônia, using Brazilian fronts, like MISBA, a joint venture of Companhia Espirito Santo de Mineração (owned by the Patiño family of Bolivia and their Brazilian ally Antonio Sanchez Galdeano) and J. Peter Grace's W. R. Grace & Company, and Companhia Brasileira de Metalurgía e Mineração (CBMM), owned jointly by Lewis Harder's Molybdenum Corporation[33] and União Banco, controlled by Rockefeller ally Moreira Salles.[34]

By now, South America's frontier meant almost as much to Nelson and David as the American West did to their grandfather. John, Senior, had also been enamored by the myth of the endless frontier, with its promise of rare minerals, oil, and vast grazing lands for cattle. This myth had much to do with Americans' traditional presumptions about a symbiosis between their prosperity and their democracy, and of each being tied to their ability to expand into new frontiers, to freely trade and invest in the world, to exploit natural resources and develop the land, and to demand "open doors" to all markets. This was the essence of the frontier thesis in American history, linking practical economic need to a sense of national purpose: promoting democracy and pursuing happiness through the American ideal of a genocide-less frontier that never actually existed.

Of all Senior's grandsons, Nelson had caught this pioneering fever for frontier development the most. Nelson's initial postwar investments in Brazil had grown into a financial, industrial, commercial, real estate, mining, and ranching empire. IBEC now had more than 130 wholly owned or partially owned subsidiaries, and more of them were in Brazil than in any other country. Nelson's shared control over Deltec International's BIB was accompanied by the appearance on Deltec's board of Richard J. Kleberg, Jr., a friend of Nelson and a supporter of the 1964 coup[35] whose King Ranch ran a huge cattle operation in Brazil jointly with Deltec, and Augustín E. Edwards, publisher of Chile's *El Mercurio* newspaper chain. Edwards was the Chilean connection to Rockefeller and CIA operations in Brazil. His newspapers had been covertly funded by the CIA and ITT since 1964, when the Johnson administration decided to intervene in Chile to prevent the election of Senator Salvador Allende as president. The Special Group set up a special Chile electoral committee that included then-Assistant Secretary of State Thomas Mann and J. C. King's successor as the chief of the CIA's Western Hemisphere Division, Desmond Fitzgerald. "CIA money represented as private money was passed to the Christian Democrats through a private businessman," the U.S. Senate Intelligence Committee later reported, to defame Allende and to help the Christian Democrats' candidate, Eduardo Frei, get elected. The businessman was Augustín Edwards.[36]

Four years later, Edwards was at it again. John McCone, having left the CIA for ITT, offered the CIA $2 million to finance another effort to stop Allende's election. To undermine Allende's support in the countryside, the field of rural education had been sowed by Nelson through an earlier overhaul of Chile's rural school system. After an initial survey for AIA by Galo Plaza, the Rockefeller Brothers Fund financed, from 1962 to 1965, model schools to demonstrate what a "modern" curriculum taught in new schools could do for the next generation of Chile's Indian peasants. This prevocational program, called Plan Victoria, was adopted by the new Frei government in 1965 with AID money and continued AIA oversight.[37] Its purpose was billed by AIA as a humanitarian response to the 1960 earthquake in Chile, but the participation of the Chilean Development Corporation and a specific instruction to AID revealed years later by U.S. Ambassador Edward Korry was more telling: ending the economic and political isolation of Indian villages and absorbing them into Chile's urban-based corporate-dominated national economy and state, while strengthening Christian Democratic support among peasants and undermining support for critics like Allende.[38]

At the same time, AIA promoted the founding of Rural Youth Clubs, backed by the government and the Inter-American Rural Youth Committee. Nelson sat on this committee with OAS Agricultural Chief Armando Samper and four former presidential collaborators with the Rockefellers: Galo Plaza (Ecuador and now OAS), Kubitschek (Brazil), Figueres (Costa Rica), and Gonzalez Videla (Chile).[39]

But by 1970, time had run out in Chile for slow reforms; CIA and AID "labor and 'community development' projects were deemed [by the CIA] rather unsuccessful in countering the growth of strong leftist sentiment and organization among workers, peasants and slum-dwellers," the Senate Intelligence Committee later reported.[40]

The Chilean Connection

Allende's impending victory at the ballot box inspired Augustín Edwards to fly to Washington for a meeting with Nixon officials arranged by PepsiCo's Donald Kendall. Besides owning Chile's largest newspaper chain, largest granary, and largest chicken farm, Edwards owned Pepsi's bottling operation in Chile.

Equally important were Edwards's ties to the Rockefellers. In 1964, David Rockefeller had hosted Edwards and other top corporate executives at his Fifth Avenue office, where the first anti-Allende plot was hatched.[41] By the late 1960s, Edwards was president of the Chilean branch of IBEC. Not surprisingly, it was Nelson's former adviser, Henry Kissinger, who met with Edwards and Kendall on September 15, 1970, just a week after Allende won a plurality in the election.[42] Edwards had good reason to be worried: Foreign-dominated consumer-goods industries, in which IBEC was a leader, would be one of the first areas nationalized by Allende's government.

Nelson, as a member of the Nixon's Foreign Intelligence Advisory Board, was aware of the anti-Allende policy in the Nixon White House. The National Security Council's Special Group (called the 40 Committee during the Nixon administration) was chaired by Kissinger. This committee had overseen the CIA's use of journalist-agents at *El Mercurio* to place almost daily anti-Allende editorials and disinformation in Edwards's newspapers.

"I don't see why we need to stand by and watch a country go Communist due to the irresponsibility of its own people," Kissinger told a June 1970 meeting of the Special Group. On September 14, the National Security Council resolved to take action. The next day, as Kissinger breakfasted with Edwards, Nixon ordered CIA Director Richard Helms to organize a military coup to prevent Allende's accession to the presidency.[43] "Make the economy scream," Nixon told Helms. An anti-Allende campaign in Edwards's newspapers* would be complemented by a Brazil-like women's March of Empty Pots, strikes, cutbacks in U.S. economic aid, and the lowering of Chile's bond rating in global financial markets.

To precipitate the coup that would cost Allende and thousands of Chileans (including Mapuche Indians) their lives, Kissinger rebuilt the "country team" in Chile. Ray Warren, a former crony of J. C. King and a veteran of CIA operations in Guatemala (during the year of the coup of 1954), Colombia (where he was embassy consul during the military campaign against the peasant republics), Bolivia, and Chile itself, was made CIA station chief in the U.S. Embassy in Santiago.

Nathaniel M. Davis, who presided over the CIA's "pacification" campaigns in Guatemala during the late 1960s as ambassador, became the new ambassador. Black (false) propaganda, identical to that used in Brazil to frighten and mobilize the military, alleged a plot by Allende to behead the army high command, notwithstanding the fact that it was the CIA that encouraged the assassination of Chile's chief of staff, General René Schneider, a supporter of Chile's constitutional succession.

In 1973, leaving behind a postcoup Chile gripped by murder and terror, Davis would return to Washington to head the U.S. Foreign Service, while his predecessor, Edward Korry, would later charge that some of the business leaders of David Rockefeller's Council of the Americas had collaborated with the CIA in covert political action in Chile. "We have never been," answered a council officer, "nor will we ever be, involved in covert or political action in any country."[44]

The Brazilian junta, meanwhile, would strengthen its ties to the Chilean military. Even before the coup that killed Allende, Brazil's military regime would leave its

*Edwards's papers were supported against Allende's criticisms by money and by orchestrated cables of protest about freedom of the press from foreign newspapers and the Inter-American Press Association (run for years by J. C. King's old friend, Joshua Powers. Edwards was president of IAPA in the early 1970s) and by CIA "agent"-journalists from ten countries who were sent into Chile.

imprint on other coups in the region. In August 1971, Brazil's Second Air Land Brigade was stationed in Mato Grosso, allegedly to back up the CIA's smuggling of arms and equipment into Bolivia's neighboring Santa Cruz state. There the Brazilian consulate would be charged with helping coordinate the coup that toppled Bolivia's left-leaning nationalist president, General Juan José Torres. Brazilian generals were also reportedly in close contact with the Uruguayan military leaders before their overthrow of the civilian government in Montevideo in June 1973. Three months later, rumors persisted of Brazilian troops having been stationed along Bolivia's border with Chile during the coup against Allende; there, too, Brazilian troops were said to be part of a contingency plan for intervention if the Chilean military had faltered.

To Brazil's military, it seemed, had fallen the task of policing a piece of a new world order that reached continental scale.

THE COLD WAR: SPEARHEAD OF UNRESTRAINED IDEOLOGY

The Cold War doctrine of counterinsurgency had brought U.S. policy full circle, blurring means and ends: Development was necessary for order, and order was necessary for development.

David Rockefeller had explained the first half of this thesis from an exclusively corporate interpretation of development in 1963. He had called upon President Kennedy to shift foreign economic aid away from government-to-government aid. Such aid allowed governments in underdeveloped countries to fund publicly owned enterprises that competed with privately owned (often American-controlled) companies. Local government aid, in turn, encouraged political independence from Washington and greater national sovereignty—including nationalization of American holdings.

David wanted Kennedy to proclaim a shift in foreign-aid policy toward private entrepreneurs, both American and allied local investors, on the grounds that private enterprise per se was the basis of political freedom:

"The first requirement is that the governments—and, as far as possible, the people—of Latin America know that the U.S. has changed its policy, so as to put primary stress on improvement in the general business climate as a prerequisite for social development and reform."[45]

But David went beyond the classical liberal argument of the market basis for individual liberty. He extended it to suggest that U.S. policy should not merely prefer private enterprise, but should oppose public enterprise and its creation out of private corporations, no matter what the public's grievances or the corporation's crimes. David wanted a general U.S. policy that discouraged all nationalizations. He wanted to set up rules that not only extended to corporations abroad an extraterritorial imperial right to assert the U.S. Constitution's guarantee of fair compensation to persons when property is seized, but also included "indemnification," a much broader legal term that encompassed legal exemption from liabilities or penalties incurred by one's actions.[46]

David and his corporate allies feared "possible changes in the rules of the game." To soothe corporate jitters in corporate boardrooms and securities exchanges, the "obstacles" that a developing nation usually erected to protect its infant industries, small farms, and working-class's buying power had to be done away with. These obstacles included, in David's words, "over valued and multi-valued exchange systems, complex import controls with high and highly variable tariffs, quotas and other forms of trade restriction, price controls and highly unpredictable budgetary practice." Multinational corporate ideology had not yet advanced to the point of asserting that these protections were "outmoded" in their global marketplace, but this would be the next step.

Six years later, after Kennedy's skepticism was history and the Republicans had won back the White House they would occupy for all but four years during the next quarter century, it was left to Nelson Rockefeller to explain what this new world order would require in Latin America: accepting U.S.-trained or U.S.-allied military rulers as the agents of change. "A new type of military man is coming to the fore," Nelson wrote in his *Report on the Americas*, "and often becoming a major force for constructive social change in the American republics. Motivated by increasing impatience with corruption, inefficiency, and a stagnant political order, the new military man is prepared to adapt his authoritarian tradition to the goals of social and economic progress."[47]

If Brazil set the example on the right side of the question of how the Nixon administration should deal with the Third World's militarized nationalism, Peru set the example on the left side. And again it was the Rockefeller brothers who provided the lesson and guided policy. In June 1969, while Nelson was in Brazil, Humberto Cortina, a Cuban exile and veteran of the Bay of Pigs, finished behind-doors negotiations with the Peruvian generals over their nationalization of Standard Oil's refinery and oil holdings. Nelson's IBEC, which had investments in about twenty firms in Peru, had taken the initiative to urge the Nixon administration to hold off enforcing the Hickenlooper Amendment to cut off aid to Peru. During the Cold War, when the Soviet Union was poised as an alternative source of aid, such a cutoff was subtly threatened, rather than actually implemented. The Peruvian junta led by General Velasco Alvarado should not be goaded, Nelson's aides had warned; Cortina, the Peruvian representative of David Rockefeller's Council for Latin America, should be given time to work out "new rules" for negotiating compensation. The Rockefeller strategy proved wise. In June, Cortina relayed the good news of "very satisfactory" results to David, who thanked him for "saving Peru."[48]

Four months later, both sides of the nationalization question—the Brazilian model and the Peruvian model—were encompassed within Nelson's concept of a "new military." It mattered little that Nelson's claim for the "progressive" character of these regimes rested on a false assertion: that Latin American officer corps were no longer an elite but a "middle class," the supposed bedrock of capitalist development and democracy championed in American political science textbooks. In fact, the percentage of lower-class youths entering army careers had actually declined between 1941 and 1966. And there was little that was "new" about the class origin of most officers: In 1941, 80 percent of all military cadets came from middle-class families; by 1966, the figure was 85 percent, only a 5 percent increase over twenty-five years.[49] With fewer men from poor backgrounds, the military of Latin America was even less representative of Brazil's vast majority of poor peasants. What was new were the social engineering concepts that these men had learned from U.S.-sponsored "civic action" courses in the United States, the Panama Canal Zone's schools, and Brazil's Escola Superior de Guerra, the Higher War College. The latter was founded in 1949 with Pentagon assistance to teach the higher sciences of counterinsurgency, strong centralized government, and "national planning."[50]

To Nelson, military aid was part of the more general concept of foreign aid that advanced "nation-building." This was not a new idea. Rockefeller Brothers Fund reports had been urging this approach since the late 1950s, and many of their recommendations had been adopted by the Kennedy and Johnson administrations. But Kennedy's leaning toward basic social reforms and political liberalism had sent counterinsurgency down a different—and to the Rockefeller brothers, wrong—path, leaving a legacy of democratic baggage in the Johnson administration that even Thomas Mann's Realpolitik could not throw off. Now, however, Nelson had put things back on track, parrying charges of cynicism by elevating Realpolitik as a new theory of development. He answered claims that he had been frightened to the Right by the riots that confronted him during his Latin American tour by writing his report in a calm tone, channeling his sense of urgency into firm, tough prose.

The policy goal was the same one he had pursued for three decades: the incorporation of Latin America into an economic "unity" of the Western Hemisphere with the United States as its leader. Development would take place within this broader continental scheme, rather than nationally or bilaterally. Order would be along the model of Indirect Rule that Britain used in the Commonwealth. The developed nations, as Adolf Berle had warned the OAS Association, should not be forced to defend their control over the destinies of "developing" nations through the direct rule of a colonial "empire." Both Senior and Junior had taught Nelson that power was most efficiently exercised quietly and out of sight through subtle, indirect means. And, as the Vietnam War had taught belatedly, if economic power was not enough to control the pace and direction of progress of peoples suffering from the pains of debt and poverty, hunger and disease, and marines were needed, it was better that these marines were indigenous than American.

Here, on the question of force, the value of regional junior partners could not be underestimated. In Latin America, as the invasion of the Dominican Republic demonstrated, only one country had both the means and ideological bent to play the role of regional policeman: Brazil.

Was it coincidental that many of the generals who now ruled Argentina, Bolivia, Brazil, Guatemala, Honduras, Panama, Paraguay, and Peru had been the recipients of U.S. arms and training? Or that the most influential of Latin America's war colleges, Brazil's Higher War College, was modeled on the National War College in Washington? Or that two of the three members of the military triumvirate that ruled Brazil between Costa e Silva's stroke and Médici's assumption of the presidency were veterans of military collaboration with U.S. armed forces during World War II?[51] Or that lecturers at the Higher War College inculcated officers with the concept of the "Brazilian model" for development of all Latin America? Or that these lecturers insisted, as the price for Brazil's willingness to play junior partner in an American corporate and military strategy toward the Pacific Rim and Europe, that "free trade" doctrines like those espoused by David Rockefeller would have to be "imposed" not only on Europe, but on the United States as well? "The developed nations depend on us as markets for their exports," explained one lecturer. "If we can bring about a more unified approach, then the nations of Latin America—with Brazil as their leader—will be able to impose conditions."[52]

Should the United States wish to avoid such a North-South hemispheric economic schism, it would have to develop an alliance like that long envisioned by the Rockefellers; Washington would have to lower its own regulatory protections—and with them, over time, probably many of its environmental, health, and wage standards—to allow Latin American goods (including goods made by U.S. companies that had moved factories to the cheaper wage markets imposed by military regimes) to compete freely in the United States against not only Japanese, Pacific Rim, and European products, but American goods and jobs.

This, not mere continental strategy, was the global meaning behind Nixon's startling toast to visiting General Médici that, "As Brazil goes, so will the rest of that Latin American continent." But for the tribal peoples of Brazil in the early 1970s, corporate development in a new world order offered no more promise than it had for the tribal peoples of Southeast Asia.

David Lilienthal, who had been an architect of the Mekong Basin Development Project as cochairman of Johnson's Joint Post-War Development Group for Vietnam, went to Brazil in 1971 to examine the U.S. aid program for Nixon. He returned with rumors of great dams in the mode of Herman Kahn. Lilienthal's visit to the Amazon was at the invitation of the Médici regime, which was impressed by Lilienthal's background as former director of the Tennessee Valley Authority and the Atomic Energy Commission.

Lilienthal, who had also been ambassador to the OAS and to the Inter-American Council for the Alliance for Progress, was now an IBEC director and head of a wholly owned IBEC subsidiary, Development and Resources Corporation, which had a long history of being able to get U.S. foreign aid money for regional planning.

In 1970, Brazil's rulers did not foresee the social and ecological furies that could be unleashed by rapid development. They saw only the promise of replicating the U.S. conquest of its own West and the historic link between that conquest and its current power and prosperity.

Peasants had grown desperate after a drought in the Northeast in 1970. Fearful that this situation could affect the stability of Brazil, the rulers saw colonization along the trans-Amazon highway system—providing cheap labor for ranchers and jobs for peasants—as the solution. The generals did not want to listen to Lilienthal's warnings that, given the Amazon's delicate ecology and poor soil fertility, current farming practices would overgraze pastures and reduce their usefulness to at most five to ten years.[53]

This ecological disaster, of course, was not expected to affect the well-financed technically sophisticated ranches of the big corporations, like Deltec and King Ranch's planned Swift-Armour 186,000-acre operation in Pará. Nor supposedly, would it affect the Amazonian mining operations serviced by the trans-Amazonian highways. As J. Stillman Rockefeller's First National City Bank, one of Brazil's largest creditors, would shortly acknowledge in a survey of the Brazilian economy: "The building of roads into the remote interior does not mean . . . substantial colonization of the area but rather . . . interest in finding and exploiting resources in the Amazon basin and the Central-West. Already, cattle raisers have extended their grazing land deep into Goiás and Mato Grosso, utilizing the Brasília-Belém highway to bring their produce to market. The Trans-Amazon highway may prove a deciding factor in the development of new mineral wealth."[54]

The generals simply put on blinders as they focused on reviving the "Great Lakes" proposal of the Hudson Institute, which coincidentally the Rockefeller Foundation had recently begun joining Nelson in funding.[55]

Some years before, an unnamed American corporate group that was exploring for carbon along the Fresco River, a tributary of the lower Xingu, discovered not only the probability of carbon gas, manganese, and iron, but an ideal site for a dam, just where the Xingu joins with the La Paz between two mountain ranges. The dam would be able to flood nearby valleys to create the largest artificial lake in the world. The lake would be a natural system for penetrating the interior, allowing ships access to the nickel reserves, gas, iron, manganese, lead, diamonds, and gold and providing a fluvial tie binding Brasília with the rest of the Amazon, including U.S. Steel's rich iron lode in the Carajás Mountains. The electricity generated for the mines would be enormous. The generals projected a dam 12 kilometers long and 50 meters high, confining a body of water four times greater than that created by Egypt's Aswan Dam—in effect, a giant canal into the Amazon's interior. This one project, they hoped, would bridge the gap of 100 years of development that separated Brazil from the United States.[56]

There was, as always, a human problem. The artificial lake could affect four Kayapó tribes of the Xingu valley: The Gorotíre, the Kubén-Kran-Kegn, the Tapirapé, and the Karajá. Most of these tribes had been pacified by the SPI, and one—the Karajá Indians—had been "occupied" by SIL since 1958.

Brazilian law had long recognized Indian land rights, even if Brazilian developers did not. Now FUNAI's lease policies were opening Indian lands to American companies. Eleven companies were prospecting inside or near the Aripuanã Indian Park. Deltec's Swift/King Ranch in Pará was jeopardizing the future of the Tembé/Urubús-Kaapor Indian Reserve.[57] Daniel Ludwig's Jari jungle kingdom in northern Pará was reported to be doing likewise to the Tumucumaque Indian Park and nine Apalaí villages, while Ludwig's bauxite operation in the Trombetas River region, along with those of ALCAN and ALCOA, endangered the future of the Arikiéna tribe.[58] SIL's translators, who had worked and lived among the Urubús-Kaapor and Apalaí Indians, remained silent.

U.S. Steel's giant Carajás iron-ore project in southern Pará put Xikrín-Kayapó tribal lands under peril; SIL had "occupied" the Kayapó, too, since 1965. And Augusto Antunes's manganese project in Amapá's Serra do Navio was slated to be served by the trans-Amazon highway system's Northern Perimeter Road.* The road would cut through Tumucumaque Indian Park.

None of these projects or the trans-Amazon road system that would service them was opposed by FUNAI. Instead, in October 1970, President Médici announced the impending agreement between FUNAI and SUDAM, the Superintendency for the Development of the Amazon, to pacify some thirty tribes who were known from an SIL survey to be living along the projected route of the system's central road, the Trans-Amazon Highway. At the same time, Médici revealed that a new Indian Law was being written that would empower him to relocate tribes for six reasons: intertribal fighting, epidemics, national security, public works of national development, disorder, and "to work valuable subsoil deposits of outstanding interest for national security and development."[59]

A Caravelle jet owned by Texas's Litton Industries began flights 4,000 feet over the Amazon at 500 miles per hour. Using spectral cameras, infrared scanners,

---

*The trans-Amazon highway system includes a number of interconnected roads, the longest of which is the central highway running east to west, the Trans-Amazon Highway.

and side-winding radar, snapping side-angle radar images, it revealed topographical contours beneath the jungle canopy, including geological anomalies that suggested mineral deposits. Project RADAM (for Radar Amazon) was off and running. When the mapping was through six years later, the Amazon had lost many of its last secrets. For $7 million, Litton had provided a cartographic detail of minerals, density, and kinds of vegetation of an area covering over 4 to 5 million square kilometers, right down to the soil of the jungle floor and even to the minerals beneath it. Significant copper deposits were found at Mato Grosso's Bodoquena hills, where Moreira Salles and Nelson Rockefeller owned their million-acre ranch.

Nelson Rockefeller could take pride in his Brazilian accomplishments when he accepted the Man of the Year Award from the Brazilian-American Chamber of Commerce in 1971. Most of the equipment used in Project RADAM was provided by a new affiliate of IBEC, Westinghouse Electric. That year, Westinghouse's senior vice president for Latin America, José de Cubas, had joined IBEC's board. Also that year, Nelson's cousin, Richard Aldrich, was elected president of the Brazilian-American Chamber of Commerce.

Aldrich was now overseeing IBEC's growing stake in Brazil's economic expansion, leaving behind, he would later confess, sleuthing for the CIA. His new mission was an indication of just how important Brazil's success—and the trans-Amazon highways—had become to the heavily indebted IBEC. Despite losses in other countries, IBEC's interests in Brazil were solid moneymakers with premium value as salable assets. Its 19 percent stake in the Brazilian Investment Bank alone was reaping rewards, and BIB had almost doubled its stockholders' equity in the preceding year.[60]

Aldrich embraced his position with the Brazilian-American Chamber of Commerce with gusto, promoting the trans-Amazon highway system with a zeal worthy of his cousin's trust. "This highway is terrifically important to the development of the hinterland," he told journalist Robert Hummerstone, who was preparing an article for the New York Times Magazine. "It's already drawing people in, and it will make raw materials far more available to the outside world." Aldrich asserted that Caterpillar and John Deere had done extensive studies, "showing that properly cleared and fertilized, the Amazon soil can support ranching and certain crops."

Hummerstone was skeptical, noting that Aldrich was "a relative of the Rockefeller brothers, who have vast cattle ranch holdings in the western Amazon basin."[61] He wrote of the danger in the military regime's haste to build the highways, of the worry that the Amazon forest supplied one-fifth of the world's oxygen, of the failure of past attempts at Amazonian agriculture, and of the predictions of dirt roads collapsing under the heavy pounding of the tropics' rainy season.

And he wrote of the Indians. "This road could be fatal for the Brazilian

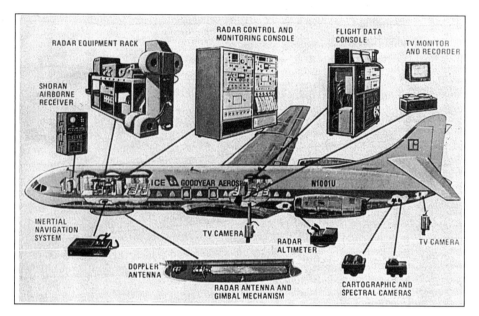

Project RADAM used specially equipped jet aircraft to map the Amazon basin.

Source: *Engineering and Mining Journal*, November 1975.

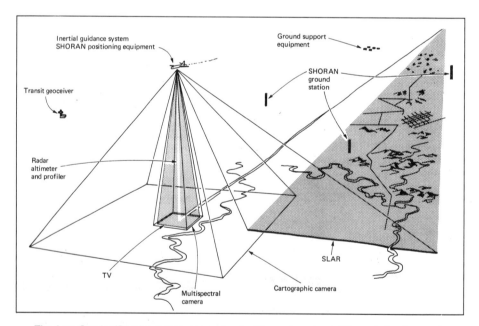

The Aero Service/Goodyear mapping system's side-angle radar cut through the Amazon's dense jungle to reveal its mineral riches.

Source: *Engineering and Mining Journal*, November 1975.

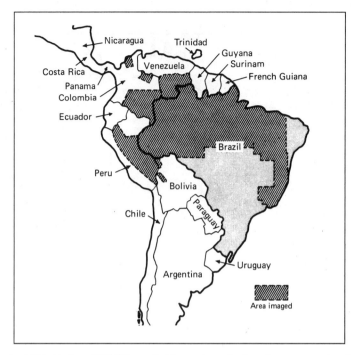

Starting in 1971, Project RADAM used side-angle radar imaging to map the Amazon basin, providing important data on the soil and water conditions as well as pinpointing areas with significant lodes of minerals.

Source: *Engineering and Mining Journal*, November 1975.

Indian. . . . FUNAI, charged with the Indian problem, is basically a military-run organization. The agency's main purpose is to get the Indians out of the way of colonization and onto the four reservations that have been set up for them."[62]

Yet the territorial integrity of even these reservations was under attack, not only by mining companies and ranchers but by FUNAI. In 1971, FUNAI had allowed the Cuiabá-Santarém highway to slice off a forty-kilometer northern section of the Xingu National Park. "You cannot stop the development of Brazil on account of the Xingu Park," FUNAI's director General Bandeira de Mello explained.[63] The Txukahamēi tribe, whom Senator Robert Kennedy had visited in 1965, would end up decimated by measles and bronchial pneumonia that were brought in by the highway crews.[64]

"We want to integrate the Indians into Brazilian society," Bandeira de Mello continued, "to make them Brazilians, like we are."[65] But FUNAI was no model. Corruption was rife among its top command and within much of the government. SIL, which had "occupied" both the Cintas Largas and the Txukahamēi Indians for the Lord, said nothing. The Rockefellers, whose close ally, J. Peter Grace, was chairman of a company (W. R. Grace & Company) that was named as having participated in surveys of the Cintas Largas lands for tin and would indeed mine tin

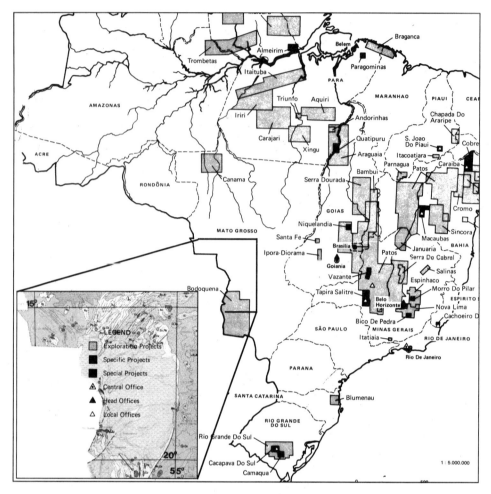

Project RADAM found "significant" copper deposits in Bodoquena area (inset map). Other resources in the area of Rockefeller's ranch included uranium, zinc, lead, and quartz.

Source: Engineering and Mining Journal, November 1975

in Rondônia,[66] said nothing. Nelson's closest Brazilian business partner, IBEC director Walther Moreira Salles, and Molybdenum Corporation chairman Lewis B. Harder (like Grace, a director of Brascan, which would buy the Jacundá tin mines in Rondônia within a few years), said nothing; Moreira Salles's and Harder's joint venture in mining, Companhia Brasiliera de Metalurgía e Mineração (CBMM), was named by a group of Brazilian anthropologists as one of ten companies having been authorized by FUNAI to prospect for tin in the Aripuanã Indian Park.[67] And Aldrich said nothing, save praise for the regime's effort to conquer the hinterland.

Meanwhile, despite evidence of "death squads" of "off-duty" policemen prowling through the Brazilian night, Nelson characteristically never looked back.

He would not contribute to doubts about the wisdom of his recommendation to Nixon that "the United States should meet reasonable requests from other hemispheric nationals for trucks, jeeps, helicopters, and like equipment to provide mobility and logistical support for these forces, for radios, and other command control equipment for proper telecommunications among the forces, and for small arms for security forces."[68]

Policing the Amazon

Within a year, Nelson's recommendations were translated into action. The U.S. Senate reported that the number of Brazilian policemen brought to the United States for training, mostly at the CIA's International Police Academy in Washington, had tripled in one year and that the number of Brazilian military officers being trained in the United States had reached the highest level since World War II.[69]

Nelson's search for Realpolitik support for the new military gave this U.S. trend toward militarizing Brazil a shot in the arm, reversing the fever of guilt and embarrassment that had swept the U.S. Congress after the regime closed down Brazil's Congress and forced Kissinger and Secretary of State Rogers to suspend economic aid for a few months.

For fiscal year 1969, five years after the coup, U.S. military aid to Brazil was cut to $800,000; a public outcry over abuses and death squads following on the heels of the regime's supercoup had prompted Congress to put a halt to the steadily increasing military grants and sales on credit, which had reached over $36 million in fiscal year 1968 (approved before the supercoup). In 1969, Congress still held the line at $800,000 for fiscal year 1970. But after the release of the *Rockefeller Report on the Americas*, it was raised to $12 million; in 1972, after Nixon arbitrarily waived Congress's four-year-old annual ceiling of $75 million in arms assistance to Latin America, military aid and sales to Brazil soared to $20.8 million.[70]

In October 1970, the same month the Interior Ministry and other agencies of the military regime launched Project RADAM, the magazine of the CIA's International Police Academy, acting under the cover of AID's Office of Public Safety, reported that one of its Brazilian graduates, Colonel José Ortiga, was setting up an Indian police force to enforce the regime's laws. Ortiga was commander of Minas Gerais's feared military police.

Ortiga had been asked by the Interior Ministry to use his military police to train a Rural Indian Guard selected from five tribes in the states of Pará, Goiás, Maranhão, and Minas Gerais. And soon eighty-five Indians arrived at Ortiga's Military Police Academy in Belo Horizonte, ready to receive training in arrests, search and seizure, crowd control, firearms, unarmed defense, civics, and the regime's Indian laws. The academy's *IPA Review* billed the Indian Guard, modeled after the BIA's tribal police, as a means of defending Indian lands from unauthorized prospectors, settlers, and other intruders. The example given for the Indian Guard's effectiveness, however, was how the guard had defended a mestizo trespasser and murderer from the anger of Indians and spirited him away to the safety of federal authorities.[71]

It took two years before the full story of this experiment got out. The Indian Guard was seizing recalcitrant Indians, including tribesmen who were resisting the military regime's laws and development projects. Amazonian Indians were taken far from their villages to Crenaque in Minas Gerais, where they were subjected to imprisonment, hard labor, and forced indoctrination. The commander of Crenaque was Manuel dos Santos Pinheiro, a captain in the federal military police who had been commissioned by General Bandeira de Mello himself when the FUNAI president was still a functionary of the military intelligence division, an arm of the regime infamous for its use of torture during interrogation. Captain Pinheiro had gained special attention from his superiors for putting down a revolt by Maxakalí Indians against land invasions by squatters in Jequitinhonha Valley in northeastern Minas Gerais. Pinheiro seized the Indian leaders, imposing order and charging the squatters rent, and then used the funds to build three irrigation dams and other development projects. "My work was considered excellent, and I was therefore invited by the President of FUNAI to work with Indians in the state of Minas Gerais," Pinheiro later explained.[72] He helped Captain Ortiga set up the Indian Guard and, in 1971, was put in charge of Crenaque, to deal with "bad" Indians who were rounded up for "rehabilitation."

"We are not dealing out punishment here at Crenaque," Pinheiro said. "The Indian, by his behavior, determines the length of time he remains in the camp. . . . I understand how sad and hard it is for the Indian to be separated from his family. . . . but it is necessary to get erroneous ideas out of his head." Such as resisting "integration."

All this repression was supposed to have ended with the end of the SPI in 1968. "The Indian Protection Service investigation will wind up in the United Nations," Rio's *Jornal do Brasil* had speculated at the time of Albuquerque Lima's revelations. "The crime is genocide and violation of the rights of man. It is better that crimes like this be exposed so that our shame may be seen in daylight."[73]

But the regime had other ideas. FUNAI and Crenaque were two of them. A trans-Amazon highway system was another, along with expanded exports of Amazonian beef and minerals to pay for an "economic miracle" with foreign earnings.

Denial of genocide was still another.

The regime tried various ways to deny that genocide had occurred. One of its more artful attempts was General Bandeira de Mello's use of the nomination of

Claudio Villas Boas, Brazil's famed Indian protector, for the Nobel Peace Prize as a means of vindicating Brazil's Indian policies, even though the nomination had been organized not by FUNAI, but by Robin Hanbury-Tenison of London's Survival International. The general's opportunism was shameless: "The fact that Claudio has been nominated by men of such repute in the scientific world represents a positive reply to those who for ulterior motives try to denigrate the Indian policy of the Brazilian government."[74] A year later, the leader of these men of scientific repute, after visiting the Mato Grosso tribes for London's Primitive People's Fund, would condemn the hunger and disease he found resulting from cattle ranchers' invasion of the Indian hunting grounds.

The regime's most important means for international propaganda was an old one, the Inter-American Indian Institute. The way had been cleared by government representatives to the Sixth Inter-American Indian Conference in 1968. The conference was held, ironically, at Pátzcuaro, Mexico, where the rights of Indians throughout the Americas had first been proclaimed in 1940 in the days of Lázaro Cárdenas and John Collier. The Second Pátzcuaro conference, which reaffirmed the goal of absorbing the Indian into the national economies, had asked the OAS to evaluate the efforts of the Inter-American Indian Institute toward accomplishing this goal since the first Pátzcuaro conference and confirmed the principle of equality among member governments by accepting the invitation of Brazil to hold the next Inter-American Conference in Brasília.

Nelson Rockefeller, as Coordinator of Inter-American Affairs, had looked warily at the Inter-American Indian Institute in its early years during World War II. He had released funds for American participation in the institute's programs only after protests by BIA Commissioner John Collier, and only after he was sure the inter-American programs of Collier's U.S. branch, the National Indian Institute, would facilitate, not get in the way of, his wartime mission of getting rubber out of the Amazon. He incorporated Collier's top agent in Latin America, Ernest Maes, into the Rockefeller fold. And he left a record bereft of knowledge or concern when Collier's and Colonel Cândido Rondon's fear that Indians would again suffer exploitation from the revived rubber boom was borne out when Brazilian troops had to intervene against at least one rubber company for enslaving Indians and cutting off their ears for failing to meet daily quotas; chased across the Peruvian border, the company simply opened shop there.[75] Now, twenty-eight years later, as the Amazon was being tapped for riches far greater than rubber, Maes was finishing his career in Nelson's AIA, and Nelson's Ecuadorian friend since the war, Galo Plaza, was in charge of the OAS, keeping a close eye on the Inter-American Indian Institute.

In August 1968, to emphasize the importance the OAS placed on the institute's influence on Indian integration policies, Galo Plaza visited the institute's headquarters in Mexico City. Pledging financial support, he called for urgent work in Guatemala (where the CIA-backed military regime was fighting a guerrilla insurgency it feared would spread to the Indian hills in the west) and cited the institute's efforts in Ecuador, Peru, and Bolivia "to defend certain basic principles."[76] Brazil's besieged Indians, however, were ignored.

William Cameron Townsend's missionaries, meanwhile, were not ignored. In 1969, among its last round of grants, New York's Woodward Foundation, founded and run by the brother of Rockefeller aide Harper Woodward, gave the Wycliffe Bible Translators $25,000.[77]

In 1971, when the World Council of Churches' Program to Combat Racism sponsored a conference on Indian conditions, anthropologists from throughout Latin America responded. These anthropologists were ready to risk their careers to speak out for Indians—against colleagues, against missionaries, against companies, even against governments and the Inter-American Indian Institute.

And what they said would stun the world.

42

IN THE AGE OF GENOCIDE

The Turning Point: Barbados

Of all places for anthropologists to convene on the horrors of the Amazon, Barbados in January 1971 may have offered the most historical irony. Once a British colony of sugar plantations known for the crack of the slave master's whip and a visit by fellow planter George Washington, Barbados was now a tourist mecca. The plantations and rum distilleries were still there, but much of the human labor of the past had been replaced by machines. Blacks were still there, too, descendants of slaves, constituting 70 percent of the electorate. But despite an almost 100 percent literacy rate among the island's 850,000 people, Barbados was still ruled by a minority of white and Creole property holders who kept the island clean and prosperous looking for resident movie stars and wealthy expatriates. Blacks still lived in poverty, working for low wages in the service sector, supplying the needs of the island's eighty hotels and guest houses.

A modern jet airport brought a steady flow of white tourists. And who would not be charmed by the fashionable boutiques, sophisticated entertainment, convenient check-cashing facilities offered by branch offices of the Barclay, Royal, and Chase banks, and, of course, the island's quaint flowered beauty? To those uninitiated in the continuing economic legacies of colonialism, Barbados was the model tropical paradise of the corporate age: The streets were safe, the shops were plentiful, and the servants were courteous and refreshingly literate and spoke with a delightful Caribbean lilt to the King's English. For most Americans, this kind of setting was the only Latin America they ever would see.

Even for some of the anthropologists, Barbados's limbo dancers, steel bands, and cricket and polo matches seemed light-years from the mounting horror just a thousand miles radius to the south. Yet here the University of the West Indies also housed the Center for Multi-Racial Studies that financially enabled the World Council of Churches (WCC) to bring together anthropologists and ethnologists who were willing to report on what was really happening to the Indians of South America.

Faced with riots and revolutions worldwide, the WCC had set up the Program to Combat Racism to gather information that would alert member churches and secular agencies to the task of "helping to prevent the growth of tensions arising from racism." For its first region for study, the program chose South America. Some of the participants were titans in anthropology; others were young scholars just becoming known for their work. But all had been driven by their fieldwork into fearless advocacy for the rights of the people they studied. They rejected the norm of most of their colleagues and dared to publish their findings on the "collective crimes" committed against the South American Indians, despite "the risk of incurring discrimination and repression at the hands of government or missionary institutions."

The reports were excruciatingly detailed and morally devastating. They described the condition of Indians in the interior regions of South America, where the least had been written and where the indigenous groups' "very existence" was "seriously threatened." Specifically, the anthropologists focused on three areas for their reports: the Chaco grasslands of Argentina and Paraguay, the vast plains, or Llanos, of Colombia, and the jungles of the Amazon.

Professor Miguel Alberto Bartolomé of Mexico told of the torture of Indians by police in El Gran Chaco, a huge grassy plain that straddles northern Argentina and much of western Paraguay. The region, used mostly by cattle ranchers, began to attract oil companies in the late 1960s. By 1969, the Trans-Chaco Highway was being built for the same purposes as its trans-Amazonian counterpart in Brazil: to connect extractive industries to their world markets. Settlements began to spring up along the road, just as settlements had accompanied railroads a century earlier in North and South America, with similar results for indigenous peoples. At the conference in Barbados, the name Chaco drew charges of degradation, despoliation, and, ultimately, genocide.

Bartolomé spoke of hospitals refusing to admit Indians; of efforts to drive out Indians who were seeking work in towns; of the growth of ghetto shantytowns on the outskirts of towns and cities; and of hunger, malnutrition, and disease.

Professor Miguel Chase Sardi told of worse conditions in the Paraguayan part of the Gran Chaco. Ayoreo (Moro) and Tomarxa Indians were forced to choose between surrender and peonage or fighting the advance of the frontier of General Alfredo Stroessner's dictatorship, which boasted census figures showing that 52 percent of the country's arable land belonged to 145 owners. There were Indian raids on settlements along the Trans-Chaco Highway (financed with U.S. money under sponsorship of the Inter-American Development Bank).[1] Here was a history of dispossession of Indian lands by the Mennonite Colonies and coercive methods of promoting birth control with dangerous IUD coils among Chulupí Indians by Mennonite missionaries from Pennsylvania. Indian cooperatives were defrauded of aid sent by the West German government for the development of the Chaco.[2] Paraguayan and German cattlemen organized slave hunts and massacres of Indian people, particularly the Aché Indians of the Yvytyrusú hills in eastern Paraguay. In the 1960s, the military used the Aché to hunt down and destroy rebels in the area who were fighting the dictatorship. Racism toward the Aché was self-evident not only in deeds, but in words: Paraguayans referred to the Indians as *"Guayakí,"* Guaraní for "rabid rats."

The news from Colombia was equally grim. A series of attacks on Colombia's Guajibo, Arauca, and Sibundoy Indians in 1969 had prompted clerics and anthropologists to appeal to the Vatican and the WCC. Some 7,000 Guajibos were said to be hiding from army hunts in the forests of the *Planas* region of northern Meta, a department west of Bogotá in the vast grasslands the Colombians call the Llanos. Sixty percent of the Guajibos were suffering from tuberculosis; 100 percent were malnourished.[3] When Colombian anthropologist Victor Daniel Bonilla described the systematic oppression and killing of Colombia's Indians, he called it "colonialist genocide."[4]

As elsewhere, the Guajibo story began as a conflict between ranchers and Indians over land. The Llanos grasslands always had been a source of conflict, but in recent years, as world beef prices rose with demand, cattle interests, including American ranchers, had been moving onto Indian lands. In December 1967, this conflict led to the massacre of a band of Cuiva Indians who lived along the Colombia-Venezuela border.[5] The killers were arrested, but "Indian hunts" continued.

The hunts centered on three Guajibo Indian reserves—San Rafael de Planas, Ibibi, and Abariba—just south of the huge American oil concessions recently obtained from the Colombian government.[6] These Indian reserves had been the creation of Rafael Jaramillo Ulloa, a government malaria inspector. Ranchers had staked claims for as much as 98,000 acres, in blatant violation of the 7,413-acre limit in the Llanos set by Colombian law.[7] Working his network of contacts in the government, Jaramillo persuaded INCORA, the government colonization agency, to provide loans to start a farm cooperative, an electricity-generating plant, a health clinic, and reserves totaling 34,594 acres, which was not much for 7,000 Indians. To protect the Indians' land, Jaramillo got himself appointed police inspector. But as the rice cooperative began to succeed and more Indians became involved, the ranchers and farmers found themselves deprived of their source of cheap labor and cheap food. They accused Jaramillo of being a communist and began setting fire to villages.

In February 1970, in the face of escalating attacks on Jaramillo and his community and the death of an American rancher, he and 200 Guajibos withdrew into the forests for protection, determined to start another self-sustaining community.

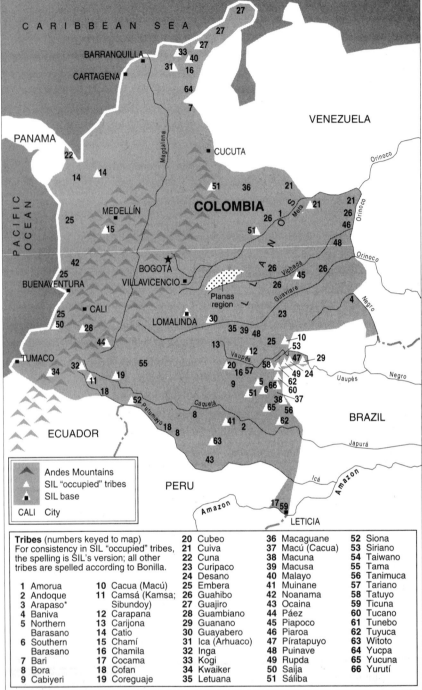

Legend

- Andes Mountains
- SIL "occupied" tribes
- SIL base
- CALI City

Colombia's Indians and SIL

*An Eastern Tucano tribe in Vaupés; no population data available

Sources: Victor Daniel Bonilla, Map of Colombia and Its Indian Groups, in Walter Dostal, ed., *The Situation of the Indian in South America*, p. 392; *Anales del Congreso*, Republica de Colombia, November 14, 1975, p. 1170; Richard Evans Schultes, *Where the Gods Reign: Plants and Peoples of the Colombian Amazon* (Oracle, Ariz.: Synergetics Press, 1988); Center for Folklore Studies, National University of Colombia.

Tribes (numbers keyed to map)
For consistency in SIL "occupied" tribes, the spelling is SIL's version; all other tribes are spelled according to Bonilla.

1	Amorua	20	Cubeo	36	Macaguane	52	Siona
2	Andoque	21	Cuiva	37	Macú (Cacua)	53	Siriano
3	Arapaso*	22	Cuna	38	Macuna	54	Taiwano
4	Baniva	23	Curipaco	39	Macusa	55	Tama
5	Northern Barasano	24	Desano	40	Malayo	56	Tanimuca
6	Southern Barasano	25	Embera	41	Muinane	57	Tariano
7	Bari	26	Guahibo	42	Noanama	58	Ticuna
8	Bora	27	Guajiro	43	Ocaina	59	Tucano
9	Cabiyeri	28	Guambiano	44	Páez	60	Tunebo
10	Cacua (Macú)	29	Guanano	45	Piapoco	61	Tuyuca
11	Camsá (Kamsa; Sibundoy)	30	Guayabero	46	Piaroa	62	Witoto
12	Carapana	31	Ica (Arhuaco)	47	Píratapuyo	63	Yucpa
13	Carijona	32	Inga	48	Puinave	64	Yucuna
14	Catio	33	Kogi	49	Rupda	65	Yurutí
15	Chamí	34	Kwaiker	50	Saija	66	
16	Chamila	35	Letuana	51	Sáliba		
17	Cocama						
18	Cofan						
19	Coreguaje						

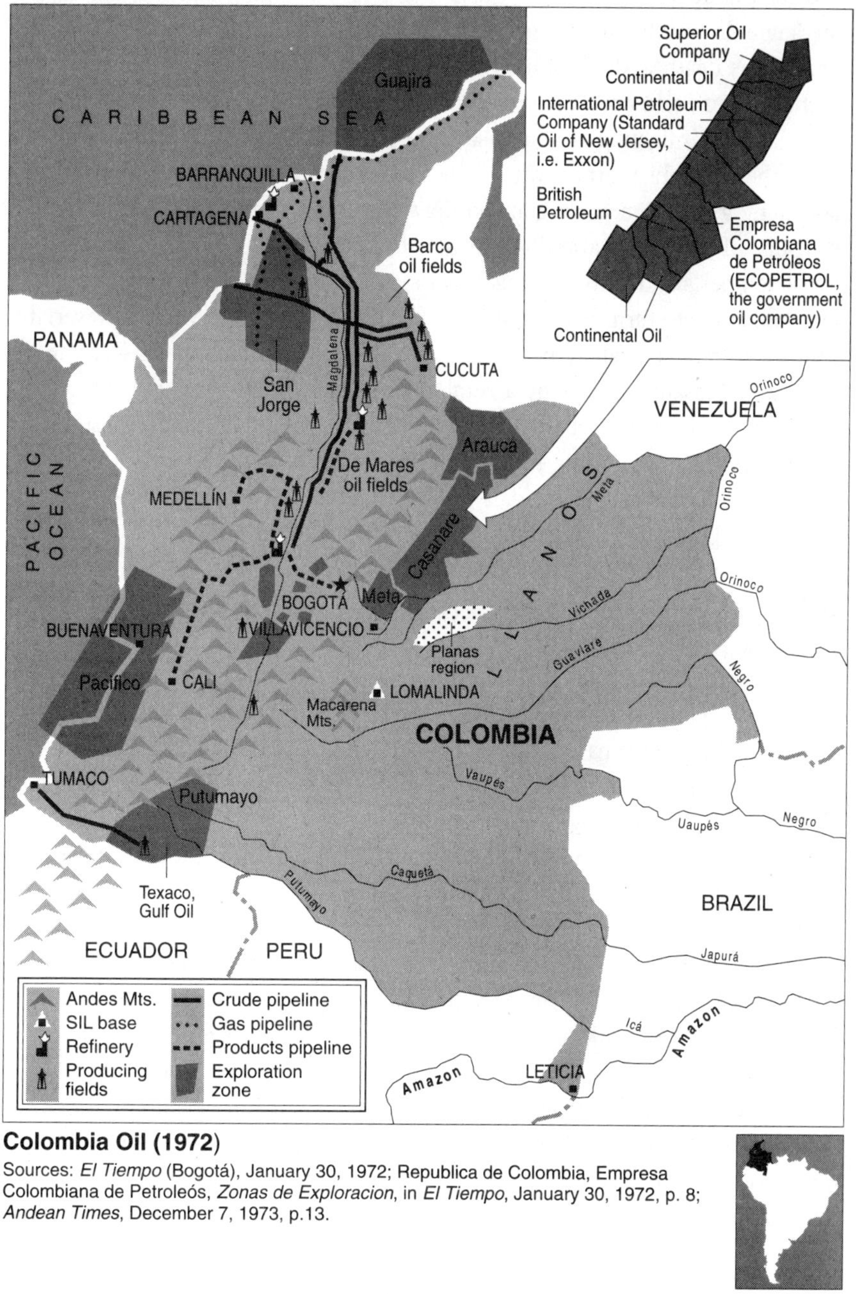
CARIBBEAN SEA
Guajira
BARRANQUILLA
CARTAGENA
Barco oil fields
PANAMA
San Jorge
Magdalena
CUCUTA
PACIFIC OCEAN
De Mares oil fields
Arauca
MEDELLÍN
Casanare
LLANOS
Meta
BOGOTÁ
BUENAVENTURA
VILLAVICENCIO
Vichada
Planas region
Guaviare
Pacífico
CALI
LOMALINDA
Macarena Mts.
COLOMBIA
TUMACO
Putumayo
Vaupés
Uaupés
Negro
Texaco, Gulf Oil
Caquetá
Putumayo
BRAZIL
ECUADOR
PERU
Japurá
VENEZUELA
Orinoco
Orinoco
Orinoco
Negro
Içá
Amazon
Amazon
LETICIA
Superior Oil Company
Continental Oil
International Petroleum Company (Standard Oil of New Jersey, i.e. Exxon)
British Petroleum
Empresa Colombiana de Petróleos (ECOPETROL, the government oil company)
Continental Oil
Andes Mts.
SIL base
Refinery
Producing fields
Crude pipeline
Gas pipeline
Products pipeline
Exploration zone

Colombia Oil (1972)

Sources: *El Tiempo* (Bogotá), January 30, 1972; Republica de Colombia, Empresa Colombiana de Petroleós, *Zonas de Exploracion*, in *El Tiempo*, January 30, 1972, p. 8; *Andean Times*, December 7, 1973, p.13.

Colombian authorities sent in the army. Indians were arrested, many were tortured, and some were killed, including Guajibo leaders. The army claimed to be looking for Jaramillo and his followers, who were accused of being responsible for the American's death and of joining communist guerrillas in the vogue of Father Camilo Torres Restrepo, a Catholic priest and advocate of peasants' rights who died five years earlier fighting as a guerrilla in the ELN, the National Liberation Army.

The Colombian army switched to more modern counterinsurgency tactics, launching a civic action program to draw the Indians out of the forests for the purpose of isolating Jaramillo's armed Indians. Well-publicized protests of Catholic priests and anthropologists had focused attention on the Guajibos, making it impolitic to turn their forests into "free fire" zones. Otherwise, however, the counterinsurgency strategy perfected by Lansdale in the Philippines—drying up the sea of peasants needed by a rural guerrilla movement—was put into effect. The same methods were used—including translators of the Summer Institute of Linguistics (SIL), according to one report—as those used by the U.S. forces in Vietnam. Bogotá's respected daily, *El Espectador,* reported that "the Summer Institute of Linguistics entered into collaboration with the civic action program of the Planas government . . . its purpose was to serve as direct mediator with the Indians" to persuade them "in the proper language and dialect" to surrender under the guarantee that "they will not be punished. . . . The Linguistic Institute also was prepared to offer radio equipment to establish direct communication between the police station in Planas and the Department capital," Villavicencio.[8]

SIL's Lomalinda base was situated between Villavicencio and Planas and had the most powerful telecommunications tower east of the Andes, quite capable of daily reports to the Jungle Aviation and Radio Services (JAARS) base in Waxhaw, North Carolina, never mind Villavicencio. But from this news report sprang charges that SIL was giving the military logistical support, including aerial maps to help locate Guajibo settlements in the forest, in much the same manner that they were alleged to have done during the attacks on the Campa Indians in Peru in 1965. All charges were denied by SIL officials.

Whatever the truth of these allegations, the anthropologists who gathered at Barbados began to notice that SIL was a common factor in their reports. Whether in Peru or Bolivia, Ecuador or Brazil or Colombia, there was SIL, operating out of huge jungle bases strategically located throughout the Amazon basin. SIL seemed to have easy access to high government officials; it employed a fleet of airplanes and powerful radio transmitters, flew across borders like they did not exist, and knew more about the location and cultures of tribes of the Amazon than local governments did.

To some degree, many of Latin America's anthropologists had only themselves to blame for being passive bystanders; most of them lived in comfortable academic surroundings. Often from privileged backgrounds, they were simply unwilling to endure the hardships of the jungle the way missionaries were. When it came to motivation, the will of science was not as strong as the Will of God. That was nothing new. But the sudden appearance of foreign capital in the wilderness—development loans for roads, cattle ranches, and colonization schemes billed as "agrarian reform," bulldozers and jungle crushers paving the way to open pit mines and oil wells—*was* new in the Amazon.

The simultaneous forced "integration" of Indians—with increasing use of Bible translators by governments to carry out the first stage of contact that often led to degradation, ethnocide, and even extinction—could no longer be ignored. Guiding the anthropologists at Barbados was not only a strong humanitarian concern for Indians, but the nagging fear that what was happening to the Indians of South America's interior was the first stage in the extinction of national sovereignty itself. Multinational corporations had arrived in the Amazon more often with missionaries than with soldiers, driven by competition and their own struggles with debts to dominate nature's last refuges. Their domination of resources and their "free-trade" exchange of products threatened to sweep away national barriers and in so doing, to establish a new world order where cultural homogeneity, rather than diversity, would rule.

Cultural diversity is not only humanity's hallmark of progress, but an insurance policy against extinction as a species. Diversity gives not only cultural and economic riches derived from different perspectives on natural resources and what it means to be human, but options to problem solving that are stifled in a homogenized society. When such a society is organized around economic goals that are measured by profit margins for private gain by powerful elites, where the demands of those who bear cash as the ticket of admission to the marketplace rule rather than the needs of people, then those who are deprived—and those who have never been part of such a global economy—must necessarily suffer. The genocide of tribal peoples, therefore, is symptomatic of a deep malaise in the world's metropolises. Indigenous peoples will suffer the most, but humanity as a whole will suffer the loss of some of its memory, not only of a unique knowledge of the natural world, but of its ability to cope with the future in various, diverse ways. Unless scientists can persuade their colleagues and other important constituencies in society to intervene.

This was the meaning of Scott Robinson's report on Texaco and on SIL's collaboration in the penetration of Kofán Indian lands in Ecuador's rain forest;[9] of Victor Daniel Bonilla's report on the same oil company moving into Colombia's Putumayo River Valley, where the Sibundoy and other tribes lived, and into the lands of the Guajibo as part of a cultural penetration again facilitated by SIL; and of Miguel Chase Sardi's report on European Mennonites marketing cotton produced by Indian Mennonites to world markets. It was also the meaning of Nelly Arvelo de Jiménez's plea for enforcement of Indian land guarantees in President Betancourt's 1960 Agrarian Reform Law (a toothless law without rules for implementation) in

Venezuela, and of Esteban Mosonyi's report on the massacre of forty Guajibos by ranchers in Venezuela's Apure state on the Colombian frontier; of Guillermo Bonfíl Batalla's analysis of the Indians suffering under South America's "internal colonialism," including the detachment and careerism of the "indigenist" school of anthropologists in the face of a $60 million U.S. grant for development of the Chocó Valley, including studies on Herman Kahn's proposals for giant dams and canals; of Georg Grünberg's searing bibliography for the study of discrimination against the Indians in Brazil; of Jürgen Riester's report on Indians enslaved in eastern Bolivia, where rubber, sugar, and, clandestinely, cocaine were shipped by Santa Cruz's railway to Brazil and then overseas; of Gonzalo Castillo-Cárdenas's accounts of the struggle in Colombia of the Motilone Indians against the oil towns of Standard Oil's Barco concession, and of the similar struggle waged by the Guajibo against oil-crazed land speculators and ranchers; of Miguel Alberto Bartolomé's analysis of the impact of the timber and cotton industries on the Indians of northern Argentina and of the Indians' susceptibility to "millenarian and messianic elements present in Protestant teaching"; of Bartolomé's criticism of anthropologists who, trained as "specialists completely cut off from the actual national reality," seldom concerned themselves with the "socioeconomic situation of the aborigines in their conflict with the national society"; and of Stefano Varese's report on the expansion of ranches and plantations into Indian lands in Peru, including the colonization of the oil-rich upper Marañon River, and of SIL's success in creating dependence among the Indians, while excluding Peruvian linguists and anthropologists from decisions that ended up introducing SIL's Bible-based bilingual education into 146 schools with more than 260 teachers who were trained at SIL's base in Yarinacocha.

As Scott Robinson explained, "A global market system links the society that produces missionaries with those regions and communities where they work. What is too often overlooked, however, are the set of social relations and economic transactions born of industrialism that evoked changes in rural America as significant as those occurring presently in the strategic, back-country portions of nations such as Ecuador."

This "global reach," coupled with SIL's millennial vision of the Second Coming, gave meaning to SIL's silence in the face of the official repression of Indians. It explained the secrecy of SIL's new contract with the Colombian government to carry out a pilot program of bilingual instructions of the Guajibo;[10] it explained SIL's 99 personnel, 3 airplanes, and 40 runways in Colombia alone; it explained why, with more than 1,500 missionaries in Latin America and some 2,200 missionaries in 22 countries throughout the world, SIL seemed everywhere.

To the anthropologists, this was not a sign of blessing from an omnipotent God. On the contrary, they concluded that SIL's presence was more destructive than helpful to the Indians. Darcy Ribeiro, notwithstanding his previous role in bringing SIL into Brazil, signed the conference's call for the expulsion of missionaries from Indian lands.

The Declaration of Barbados charged that

> there occur both active interventions to "protect" Indian society as well as massacres and forced migration from homelands. These acts and policies are not unknown to the armed forces and other governmental agencies in several countries. Even the official "Indian policies" of the Latin American states are explicitly directed toward the destruction of aboriginal culture. These polices are employed to manipulate and control Indian populations in order to consolidate the status of existing social groups and classes, and only diminish the possibility that Indian society may free itself from colonial domination and settle its own future.
>
> As a consequence, we feel the several states, the religious missions and social scientists, primarily anthropologists, must assume the unavoidable responsibilities for immediate action to halt this aggression and contribute significantly to the process of Indian liberation.

The declaration charged the state with "direct responsibility for and connivance with its many armies of genocide and ethnocide that we have been able to verify." Furthermore, it called for guarantees and protection of Indian lives, of tribal land "as perpetual, inalienable collective property," for Indian rights to their own traditions and self-governance, and for "recognition that Indian groups possess rights prior to those of other national constituencies."

The anthropologists had even more to say about the responsibility of religious missions: "The missionary presence has always implied the imposition of criteria and patterns of thought and behavior alien to the colonized Indian societies. A religious pretext has too often justified the economic and human exploitation of the aboriginal population." They criticized "the inherent ethnocentric aspect of the evangelization process" as "a component of the colonialist ideology." They insisted that missionaries must end the "essentially discriminatory nature implicit in the hostile relationship to Indian cultures conceived as pagan and heretical." Instead, they argued that "true respect for Indian culture" was needed to end "the long and shameful history of despotism and intolerance characteristic of missionary work, which rarely manifests sensitivity to aboriginal religious sentiments and values."

They demanded that the missions "halt both the theft of Indian property by religious missionaries who appropriate labor, lands and natural resources as their own" and "the indifference in the face of Indian expropriation by third parties." They condemned the missions' practice of sending Indians to "long-term boarding schools where Indian children are inculcated with alien values." They called on missions to suspend immediately all practices of population displacement done "in order to evangelize and assimilate more effectively" and described the process as provoking "an increase in morbidity, mortality, and family disorganization among Indian communities."

"To the degree that religious missions do not assume these minimal obligations," the anthropologists concluded, "they, too, must be held responsible by default for crimes of ethnocide and connivance with genocide."

Never had social scientists so taken missionaries to task. But the anthropologists saved their strongest criticisms for their own profession. "Anthropology took form within and became an instrument of colonial domination, openly or surreptitiously," they confessed. "It has often rationalized and justified in scientific language the domination of some people by others. The discipline has continued to supply information and methods of action useful for maintaining, reaffirming and disguising social relations of a colonial nature."

Anthropologists, they maintained, must join the struggle for Indian liberation by correcting stereotypes of Indians in the national culture, providing Indians with data on their colonizers, and "denouncing systematically by any and all means cases of genocide and those practices conducive to ethnocide."

Finally, the Barbados Conference rejected any patronizing "right" to interfere in Indian traditional forms of self-governance, including "development and defense programs." The transformation of national society, they said, was "not possible if there remain groups, such as Indians, who do not feel free to command their own destiny."[11]

This last point not only struck at the heart of Euro-American ethnocentrism, but echoed the very basis of evolutionary science: Diversity is the most successful means of ensuring the survival of species. In the human species, this means cultural diversity.

Ethnologist Betty Megers had warned about the potential environmental disaster that could happen in the Amazon if its treasure of diverse botanical and fauna species was no longer protected. The airplane runways cut out of the jungle by the likes of SIL missionaries and the Villas Boas brothers had been mere beachheads for a larger invasion of tribal lands. The trans-Amazon highway system would make that invasion irrevocable and would break through the geographic barriers that enabled flora, fauna, and human cultural diversity to resist destruction.

Meanwhile, SIL's flying translators would break down the last linguistic barriers, language having long been recognized as one of the most effective means humans have to save a culture from absorption by a more aggressive culture.[12] However sincere SIL linguists may have been about their work, many of the anthropologists who worked among the same tribes saw a different reality: one of Indian languages being "reduced" to writing, not with the purpose of empowering the tribe with communication skills to protect the existing tribal culture, but to destroy the culture's core belief system, its pre-Christian religion, and replace it with an American version of Fundamentalist Protestantism. This penetration and "occupation," linguistic and religious, economic and cultural, led to the Indians' absorption by the national economy and often the rapid extinction of the language and the tribe.[13] With game depleted, the forests burned for pasture, and the Indians reduced to a source of cheap labor, poverty—the kind that can be measured not in naked communes of well-fed tribesmen but in the rags worn by malnourished people infected with disease and despair—took root. As income disparities and debts grew, the dream of capitalist development became the nightmare of under-development.

The reaction from mainline Fundamentalism toward the Declaration of Barbados was immediate and predictable. "A highly biased and inaccurate report," charged Wade Coggins, associate director of the Evangelical Foreign Missions Association. ". . . It promotes a neo-racism similar to 'black power' and 'black nationalism' in the U.S."[14] An editorial in *Christianity Today*, the Pew-funded magazine founded by Billy Graham's father-in-law, urged the WCC to "promptly disassociate itself" from the conference's findings. "At best [the findings] are gross oversimplification, at worst a calculated attempt to undermine biblical Christianity."[15] And Fuller Theological Seminary's professor of missionary anthropology, A. R. Tippett, blasted the declaration as "thoroughly racist. . . . The Declaration of Barbados is not a scientific document, but a radical opinion statement. Its credibility lies in the current secular situation, the permissive mood, the general hostility toward the establishment."[16]

THE RETURN OF BILLY GRAHAM

The Establishment, on the other hand, was not hostile to Fundamentalist missions. Only two years before, Billy Graham had returned to the spotlight at Madison Square Garden, twelve years since his last New York Crusade. John D. Rockefeller, Jr., was not there this time to give another $50,000. But David contributed, and Chase Manhattan Bank chairman George Champion again helped lead the fund-raising drive.

Richard Nixon was there, too, returning Graham's favors during the previous year's presidential campaign, when the minister bestowed blessings on Nixon at the Republican Convention, preached at the funeral of Nixon's mother, and then appeared with Nixon in church after the election. It was 1957 all over again: the reserved block of seats for evangelical churches and the enthusiastic response of the already converted to Graham's exhausting exhortations to come forth and "make a decision for Christ."

Graham's attacks on sin focused on symbols. "The Bible teaches that the policeman is the agent of God," Graham told the St. George Association, New York's organization of Protestant policemen, gathered at the swank Waldorf-Astoria Hotel for a communion breakfast. "And the authority that he has is given to him not only by the city and the state but . . . by Almighty God. So you have a tremendous responsibility at this hour of revolution and anarchy and rebellion against all authority that is sweeping across our nation."[17]

Graham's message, presented in the context of "law and order" during growing public dissent over the Vietnam War and racism, had a decidedly political content that was in sync with the Nixon White House's war drums. Social action and suffering for justice were not at the heart of the Gospel, Graham insisted. Social problems like racism were signs of man's fall from Grace and would not be solved "until Christ comes back again and rules as a benevolent monarch."[18]

This argument set Graham at loggerheads with the views of both the WCC and the Barbados Conference. Catholic bishops, too, had recently gathered in Medellín, Colombia, and espoused the belief that Christ was found in the poor and the struggle for peace and justice, inspiring a "Theology of Liberation" that spread among liberal Christians, Catholic and Protestant alike. This belief that personal salvation was found through the struggle for virtue in social behavior, not just individual piety, was vehemently derided as "humanist" by Graham and his more conservative followers.

Graham's vision of Fundamentalism, like Cam's, could embrace Catholics who unquestioningly accepted every word of the Bible as literal truth; since individual piety outweighed social behavior, Graham could even accept a former torturer from Uruguay's Death Squad, Nelson Bardesio, as an advance man for his Mexico Crusade in 1977, when Graham made a big push to attract *carismáticos*.[19] Bardesio had been the chauffeur in Montevideo for William Cantrell, the CIA operations officer who, acting under cover as the AID Public Safety adviser, helped establish Uruguay's dreaded secret police.[20] Bardesio had bombed the homes of teachers and lawyers with gelignite that was passed through Sidney Gottlieb's CIA Technical Services Department office in Argentina.[21] The darker implications of Nelson Rockefeller's policy recommendations to Nixon to support the "new military" had entered directly into the evangelical crusades of Billy Graham.

In the years that followed, Nelson Rockefeller and Billy Graham would have a peculiar common point of contact in Nixon's national security adviser, Henry Kissinger. Nelson would be made privy to state secrets by Kissinger as a member of the President's Foreign Intelligence Advisory Board. And Nixon would insist that Kissinger listen to Billy Graham about what was happening in the world and give briefings to conservative evangelical Christian leaders like Graham and Dallas's Rev. William Criswell, publisher Pat Zondervan, Holiday Inn's president William Walton, and the publishers of magazines like *Christianity Today*.[22]

The sessions were only one more price that Kissinger, the urbane Harvard professor and Rockefeller confidant, had to pay for power. "Mr. Nixon always considered me somewhat of an authority on world affairs," Graham later recalled. "He wanted to know what missionaries were thinking in certain countries because he felt that they knew more, many times, than the embassy knew about what was going on because they were much closer to the people."[23] And of all the missionary organizations that Graham had come in contact with over the years, few were better known to him than SIL. "I meet the ambassadors, I meet the heads of state and I meet different people and talk to them," said Graham, "and sometimes they'll tell me things they'll never tell a visiting political leader—they'd never tell Kissinger, for example." Only after the disgrace of Richard Nixon and the damage done to Graham's public image by accompanying Nixon to a prayer breakfast during the Watergate investigation would Graham realize how dangerous it was to give political information to the White House. "I don't think I would now [be an informant] because of the CIA revelations . . . that they have used missionaries [to get foreign political information]. . . . I would shy away now from giving counsel and advice to a President [that is] purely secular. Mine would be of a spiritual nature now. I had to learn that lesson the hard way."[24]

So, apparently, did SIL. After charges appeared in the Colombian press alleging SIL's collaboration in the repression of the Guajibo Indians, SIL came under increasing scrutiny. Indians in the eastern Vaupés region expelled teams of translators from two tribes,[25] and Catholic clerics, led by Bishop Gerardo Valencia Cano, a proponent of the Theology of Liberation, attacked first the domination of rubber *patrónes* and then the missionaries of the "independent republic" within Colombia, SIL's Lomalinda.

The young priests claimed that the translators were really missionaries who failed to train Colombians as linguists. The atrocities in the Planas region had inspired warnings about the possibility that SILers were gathering political intelligence. Before long, an official commission recommended that a new contract be negotiated, striking the clause giving SIL the mission of the Indians' "moral improvement," since that mission violated the Colombian Constitution's guarantee of freedom of conscience. Proselytizing under government contract must end, the priests declared, and SIL would have to share linguistic and educational responsibility with Colombians.

Similar thunder was heard over SIL's Peru branch. In 1970, Indian teachers and students at the Andean bilingual school in Ayacucho revolted against the authoritarian rule of Nadine and Don Burns. In 1968, Nadine had publicly humiliated the general administrator of the Andes bilingual education project for hanging up a poster in the Ayacucho training school from a Lima newspaper expressing patriotic approval of the government's nationalizing Standard Oil's properties. Two years more, and the teaching staff had had enough. Risking divine wrath and the Cornell scholarships the Burnses offered, the staff petitioned the Ministry of Education for relief.[26] Within weeks, the Velasco government sent the Burnses packing. SIL's Peru branch was then given a more restrictive contract that limited translation work to only the thirty-two tribes already "occupied" by SIL. The contract required incorporating more Peruvian linguists and, for the first time, imposed an expiration date on SIL's charter, five years away.

SIL's leaders responded to these troubles with confidence in the Lord and in the knowledge that their services would be in even greater demand now that American oil companies were rushing into South America's interior, spurring a new wave of speculative development. Two months after the Barbados Conference,

International Petroleum Company, the South American subsidiary of Standard Oil of New Jersey (Exxon), entered into an agreement with the Colombian National Oil Company to explore for oil in the Llanos. Continental Oil, another spin-off of the old Standard Oil Trust, did likewise. The new concessions covered more than 2.4 million acres, a huge tract stretching northeast between the Meta and Casanare rivers in Boyacá Department[27] just north of the lands of the Sáliba and Guajibo Indians.[28]

This region was also designated by INCORA as a zone for colonization.[29] By January 1972, International Petroleum and Continental would be joined in the same concession area by Superior Oil. At the end of the month, Phillips Petroleum and Standard Oil of California's subsidiary, Chevron, joined the hunt for oil in the Llanos.[30] By 1973, the year of the Middle East oil embargo, fifteen new exploration contracts would be signed in Colombia. The Llanos exploration zone would be stretched northeast toward the Venezuelan border[31] and right through the lands of the Guajibo-speaking Macaguane Indians.[32]

In Peru, Petroperu and Occidental struck oil in the Amazon in 1972. The Velasco government plunged ahead with plans for the Trans-Andean pipeline, drawing down international loans to pay three Tulsa-based firms to build it. The engineering was left to the respected Bechtel Corporation, which estimated that the cost would be $250 million—a figure that would grow to $650 million by 1976. With feeder lines and a terminal, the estimated $1 billion total cost would make the Peruvian pipeline, mile for mile, the most expensive on earth.[33] The Amazonian pipeline would become an Amazonian pipe dream.

The Brazilian-Bolivian Connection

SIL's branch in Bolivia was worried. Gulf Oil's restored properties had been nationalized, and the new government of General Juan José Torres had national-ized the properties of the International Metals Processing Company, a firm based in Dallas, where Cam and his fund-raisers, the Wycliffe Associates, were depend-ing on local corporate support for SIL's projected new International Linguistic Center. Torres also nationalized the Matilde zinc mine, a majority of whose shares were owned by two Rockefeller-allied firms, U.S. Steel and Engelhard Minerals. But perhaps most alarming from SIL's perspective was the cutoff of SIL's access to the Brazilian Cabinet, something it had enjoyed since it had entered the country in the mid-1950s. Then came a scandal over charges that the Peace Corps had carried out a birth control program among Indians in the Lake Titicaca region that had included the sterilization of women. Though the U.S. Embassy denied the charges, a documentary film entitled *Blood of the Condor* made it impossible for Torres to ignore the allegations and their widespread acceptance. Birth control had long been resisted by Bolivia, a country with a population density of only four inhabitants per square kilometer, when the United States first proposed it as a condition of loans after the 1952 Indian miners' revolution and the Paz Estenssoro government's nationalization of Gulf Oil holdings. The Peace Corps was expelled. Would SIL, facing similar rumors in Colombia, be next?

There were greater stakes in Bolivia for the Nixon administration. Torres's independence in foreign affairs, including his lack of enthusiasm for the U.S. campaign to isolate Cuba, threatened to give credence to what Che Guevara had fought against. Despite military defeat, Guevara's guerrilla band had a profound political impact on Bolivia. The army's massacre of eighty-seven men, women, and children at the Catavi mine in July 1967 may have discouraged miners from following up on their vote of support for Guevara's guerrillas at a subsequent miners' conference, but Guevara's courage and death had left them inspired rather than defeated. In just a few years, Guevara's public defiance of U.S. power and corporate property rights was given new life by Torres in Bolivia, Salvador Allende in Chile, and Juan Velasco Alvarado in Peru. Such formerly stalwart U.S. allies as Guyana and Ecuador were seizing, respectively, ALCAN's bauxite mines and American tuna-fishing boats. In Suriname, suggestions were being aired in government circles that ALCOA's huge bauxite mines should go the way of ALCAN's in neighboring Guyana. Venezuela was moving toward pressuring American companies to sell majority holdings in key profitable ventures to Venezuelan nationals; only Brazil, thanks to the 1964 military coup, resisted this trend, instead opening the Amazon, including rich bauxite lodes, to ALCOA's and ALCAN's roving eyes.

And it was here, at the Brazilian border, that Torres met his Waterloo. A branch of Brazil's trans-Amazon highways, which served as both commercial and military roads, was pushing steadily toward Corumbá, Brazil's southeastern border with Bolivia. Iron and manganese deposits recently found by U.S. Steel in Mato Grosso, just south of Corumbá (and north of the Rockefellers' Bodoquena ranch), stretched across the Bolivian border into the isolated region of Mutun. Mutun's 40 billion tons of iron made it the largest estimated lode in Latin America and the third largest on earth. Brazil, with U.S. Steel's immense Serra dos Carajás deposits in the Amazon and Hanna's rich mines in Minas Gerais, did not need iron. But Argentina, Brazil's traditional rival for dominance in the "southern cone" of the South American continent, did. In January 1971, former Brazilian ambassador General Hugo Bethelen was caught in La Paz financing a conspiracy against the Torres government. Bethelen was convicted of passing about $60,000 to Bolivian plotters, whose leader was Colonel Hugo Banzer Suarez, a graduate of Green Beret counterinsurgency training at Fort Bragg and former military attaché to Washington.[34] Banzer's close ties to the U.S. Embassy and the support offered by the Santa Cruz–based Falange party emboldened him not only to attempt the coup, but not to be discouraged by its failure. Indian miners, armed with only machetes, picks, and dynamite from the mines, mobilized in trucks in defense of the government, persuading the army to continue to back Torres.[35]

Torres's survival now depended on maintaining his own support among the Indian miners and peasants. In June, he allowed them to convene a Popular Assembly. This assembly and the press coverage that resulted inspired Indians to seize mines and plantations where they worked. It was as if the spirit of the Indian Revolution of 1952 had reappeared to sweep through the Andes and appeal once more to the Indians in the army rank and file. Confrontation with the U.S.-trained officer corps was inevitable. By early August, when rumors spread of another military plot being organized in Santa Cruz, there was a call for arms to be distributed to the populace to "defend their revolution and the positive steps toward socialism."[36] This call only convinced the generals that the Falange party was right: A communist conspiracy was afoot.

Inflamed by Cold War ideology, the generals accelerated their preparations for the coup. General Bethelen had already proposed to Brazil's *Visão* magazine that countries like Bolivia might have to be taken over as protectorates if they maintained relations with countries (such as Cuba) that were outside the Organization of American States (OAS) and were, therefore, deemed a threat to internal security.[37] Denunciations of his statements by Torres's foreign minister as "provocative and imperialist" only encouraged Bethelen to repeat his demand for "a form of intervention which the Brazilian imagination, creative in developing new forms of co-existence among men, can discover in the realm of international relations, principally among Latin American nations which I consider one family."[38]

The junta's "Brazilian imagination" had come up with a strategy as old as the CIA coup in Guatemala: an invasion of "volunteers" from neighboring Brazil, Paraguay, and Argentina to back a move for power by the neo-fascist Falange party and its army coconspirators. CIA money was said to be involved. That same month, Nelson Rockefeller's friend, Victor Andrade, former Bolivian minister of labor and of foreign affairs and ambassador to the OAS, arrived in Brasília as a special envoy of OAS Secretary General Galo Plaza. (Three years later, during Nelson's confirmation hearings for the vice presidency, congressional investigators not only would reveal that Andrade had received gifts totaling $38,000 from Nelson, but would secretly identify him as a conduit "for CIA funds for the purposes of manipulating elections in Bolivia.")[39]

A delegation of Brazilian businessmen failed to convince Torres to accept Brazilian control over the Mutun iron deposits. Torres could not acquiesce to their demands; he had decided to accept $200 million in Soviet loans to develop Mutun through the construction of a metallurgical processing plant. His hesitation removed all doubts about what was to be done. Two days later, the first planes of the Brazilian air force arrived at Santa Cruz airport, bearing machine guns for the Falange party.

Torres's interior minister issued a formal protest to Brazil. La Paz's *Jornada* described the appearance of mercenaries from Brazil and Paraguay. How much of this was true, how much inadvertently contributed to fears, and how much was fabricated to create hysteria would never be known. But the resemblance to the CIA's "black propaganda" operation against the government of Jacobo Arbenz in Guatemala twenty years before was striking: an invasion from neighboring countries by "liberating" troops, foreign bombers with freshly painted national insignias, and a U.S. Air Force radio transmitter lent to the rebels by the U.S. military attaché in Santa Cruz.[40] There were even scratchy radio broadcasts of an appeal allegedly by former president Paz Estenssoro to the armed miners of Siglo XX mine, urging them to surrender the airport at the key mining capital, Oruro. When the miners later tried to rescue the airport from the coup, they encountered a hail of automatic gunfire from U.S.-trained Rangers who had been flown in from Santa Cruz.

If the coup's success was helped by international conspiracy, it was just as much the result of Torres's own vacillation at critical moments. On August 14, Santa Cruz's labor union leaders warned Torres that subversion was under way in their city, but Torres did not respond to their request for arms. Only after the negotiations over Mutun's iron had collapsed and Brazilian planes had begun landing in Santa Cruz did he arrest Banzer and thirty-eight other conspirators, then only to release them after a day in prison because of Falangist demonstrations. Ironically, the lessons of Torres's hesitation to distribute arms against a military coup were not learned by Allende's government either, which met a similar fate for similar reasons. In Chile, like Bolivia, Brazil, Guatemala, and Peru, there were no Minutemen ready to defend their government.

Within twenty-four hours, Torres was seeking asylum in the Chilean Embassy. The Indian peasants and miners, mostly armed with only machetes and dynamite, and unarmed students were left to face Banzer's fascists and Rangers alone; their resistance was met with massacre. Some 120 were killed, and more than 700 wounded.[41] In 1974, more than 100 peasants would be murdered in the Cochabamba Valley, as would dozens of miners in 1976; and that July Torres would be gunned down in Argentina, where he lived in exile.

On August 22, General Emílio Garrastazú Médici's Brazilian junta rushed to recognize the new Bolivian cabinet headed by Banzer. Practically all the important ministries were held by the Santa Cruz Establishment. The important post of interior minister was given to Colonel Andrés Selich, field commander of the Rangers who had hunted down Che Guevara.[42] As president, Banzer conceded that Bolivia now had an "interest in Brazilian investment." A week later, the Brazilian Investexport gave a $5 million credit to the Bolivian Agricultural Bank for loans to allow larger landowners in the Santa Cruz region to purchase heavy machinery from Brazil, most of which was sold by American corporations like International Harvester, Deere, and Caterpillar.

Banco do Brasil chipped in another $5 million. In September, the link between the coup and Brazil's economic interests became clearer: $10 million in credits was provided to allow the Banzer regime to import more machinery for completing the rail line between Santa Cruz and Corumbá in Brazil and to construct a highway along the route to connect with Brazil's trans-Amazon highway system.

In the following month, the Brazilian construction giant ALFONSECA agreed to build a $50 million, 558-mile paved highway between Bolivia's interior and Brazil's Mato Grosso. Meanwhile, the Nixon administration offered a $2.5 million loan for cotton growers (many of whom were in the state of Santa Cruz); a grant of $2 million for Banzer's *Plan de Emergencia* for schools, hospitals, and commercial infrastructure; $20 million in additional credits; and increases in military aid.

Mounting unrest in the highlands was answered, as elsewhere, with Inter-American Development Bank (IDB) loans "for maximum occupation of the Amazon Basin" where fertile lands were falsely promised to those who would join some 100,000 Andean peasants who had moved there since 1960. A massive birth control program, promoted by the World Bank and John D. Rockefeller 3rd's Population Council, was unleashed in the highlands to curb what an IDB consultant had termed the "incredible rate of fertility" among the "primitive" Andean people.[43]

The price Bolivians would pay would be high: a 15 percent increase in their debt in one year; devaluation of their currency; a dramatic shift in their trade reliance from Argentina to Brazil; and, for Banzer, a rupture of his ruling coalition with Paz Estenssoro's MNR party. Banzer would also have to borrow from the First National City Bank and other creditors to pay $13.5 million to U.S. Steel and the other former owners of the Matilde Mines and another $1.5 million for the nationalized holdings of Texas's International Metals Processing Company. On April 4, 1972, Banzer met with Brazil's president, General Médici, at the Brazilian border town of Corumbá. Médici pledged aid for the Banzer government, including $1 million to help plan development in the lowlands around Santa Cruz. That week arrests swept through La Paz as the army seized arms caches of leftist guerrillas. Among those arrested was Loyola Guzmán, who had been purged from the Bolivian Communist party for acting as courier and treasurer for Che Guevara. Now her capture was used by Banzer as an excuse to show his pro-U.S. loyalty by expelling sixty-nine Soviet diplomats and embassy staff.

In June 1972, Treasury Secretary John Connally visited La Paz to extend Nixon's "warmest wishes" and praise for Banzer's "great courage." Bolivia was now a junior partner of Washington's alliance with the junta in Brasília; within the next few years, as Henry Kissinger took over the State Department, Nelson Rockefeller took over the vice presidency, and George Bush took over the CIA, Banzer would be joined by military rulers in Chile, Peru, and Ecuador.

Che Guevara had believed that the popular struggle in Bolivia would cause the United States and its client allies to internationalize the conflict in the Andes, just as U.S. intervention against the revolution in Vietnam had ignited all

Indochina. He had been proved correct. But the outcome had not been as he expected. He had underestimated the depth of U.S. penetration of South America's rural interior and overestimated the capacities of his own ideological compatriots to unite. Many Vietnams would not be created, but many dictatorships would. The regimes of Nelson Rockefeller's New Military, not successful revolutions, would be South America's destiny for the next quarter of a century.

Now that the Lord's Will had come upon Bolivia, SIL was restored to its former respected status. Its leaders again were given access to government on a high level. Banzer, in turn, was given access to SIL's jungle base in the eastern lowlands, Tumi Chucua.

A year after the coup, in 1972, SIL's Bolivia branch published a yearbook of students' activities at the base called "Jungle Gems," showing their American children "listening to the Presidential Prayer Breakfast," presumably Banzer's celebration with a Graham protégé from Argentina. If the presidential prayer breakfast had been Billy Graham's and Nixon's, the effect would have been no different. "Is God's time your time?" wrote "Best Groomed" Calvin Shoemaker. "If it is, use it wisely. Christ is coming soon."

Banzer came sooner. A section called "President's Visit" was a pictorial account of the warm reception offered the dictator. "We welcome the Banzer family with flowers, then up to the Main Building for refreshments and a program" before assembled Indians, including the presentation of SIL's bilingual primers. Banzer took such a shine to Tumi Chucua that it became his favorite vacation spot for escape and relaxation from the rigors of dictatorship. SIL sanctified the use of the base with Romans 13:1 in Spanish and eight Indian languages. The translation was a multilingual wonder: "Obey legal superiors, because God is one who has granted the office. There is no government on earth which God has not permitted to come to power."[44]

Banzer must have agreed. He had posters plastered throughout the city of La Paz bearing a hand with the index finger pointing heavenward, as if to say, "Obey this government, for all authority does indeed come from God."

SIL's strict adherence to Romans 13 and its stoic code of obedience were at the political core of William Cameron Townsend's success in building SIL into the Christian world's largest nondenominational missionary organization. Through forty years it had taken him far, from Guatemala to Mexico, then to Peru, then to Ecuador, and on and on, marching as to war, riding the horse of nuclear apocalypse, the Cold War, in a race against time and a millennial prophecy, until now, at last, he had reached his original goal: L. L. Legter's "naked savages," the Bibleless tribes of the Brazilian Amazon.

And now, in August 1972, at Brasília, the city of dreams and host of the Seventh Inter-American Indian Congress, he had even lived to see himself applauded by the heirs of John Collier.

The Junta's Salute to Human Rights

Under the cold eye of Brazil's junta and its secret police, this conference could speak only official truth. Most scientists who disagreed with that version, including most of the signers of the Barbados Declaration, chose to stay home. "Those of us, both here and in Europe, who have been concerned about the critical situation of Indian peoples in Brazil, were outraged by the VIIth Inter-American Indianist Congress," explained Harvard anthropologist Shelton Davis. "We had been following the situation closely through newspaper clippings and reports of observers, and knew that what was actually occurring had been clouded by secrecy, rhetoric, and lies. We knew that many others shared our beliefs within Brazil, but were silenced by a military government bordering on fascism and maintained by political repression and torture."[45] Davis joined other colleagues in refusing to attend.

The road to Brasília had already been sanitized. The previous September, *National Geographic* inadvertently did its part by publishing W. Jesco Von Puttkamer's photographs and article on FUNAI's first contact with the besieged Cintas Largas Indians—two years after the fact. In a story entitled "Brazil Protects Her Cintas Largas," FUNAI was described in heroic terms, and its predecessor, the Service for the Protection of the Indian, was mentioned only once, in a single sentence, its crimes reduced to manageable proportions: "Over the years the old service had grown cumbersome and tangled in red tape."[46]

Opening the Brazilian conference, FUNAI president General Oscar Bandeira de Mello proudly pointed to the hero of Brazil's independence, José Bonifácio de Andrada e Silva, as the real spiritual founder of Brazil's celebrated Indian policy. The director of the OAS's Inter-American Indian Institute, Gonzalo Rubio Orbe, asked for compassion by scientists for the "delicate and complex problem of forest Indians" in the general's country.

The Chilean delegate had the audacity to report on the Allende government's new agrarian reform among the Mapuche Indians, but otherwise, the dining at the elegant presidential palace went undisturbed, and future programs for anthropologists were explored, along with Indian malnutrition, music, and integration.

Brazil's Interior Minister José Costa Cavalcante's claims that his government was "making a great effort to create a humane and objective Indian policy" was not challenged, even though his son was widely rumored to be the co-owner of one of Brazil's largest land companies. Neither was Minister of Exterior Gibson Barbosa's assurances that "your travels [around Brazil] will demonstrate that all we possess and are realizing is not only for the Indian, but for the nation as a whole."[47] Both men were warmly applauded. The delegates were looking forward to FUNAI's tour of the Xingu Park and the Ilha do Bananal. Both Indian reserves were under severe attack by the regime's development schemes, but the delegates knew how to behave. All was right in the Brazilian Indian world; most of the peoples of the thirteen nations represented by these delegates would never know what had been hidden from them. Fundamentalist Christians in the United States would learn, rather, that the conference, by resolution, and OAS Secretary General Galo Plaza, by decree, had officially proclaimed "Uncle Cam" Townsend "Benefactor of the Linguistically Isolated Human Groups of the Americas."

It should have been the crowning achievement of Cam's career. For most men over seventy-five, it would have been. Yet for Cam it carried a bittersweet message: He was already being treated as if he were history. The previous year, after a series of disagreements with the Wycliffe/SIL board, he was elevated out of SIL's general directorship to the ethereal status of "Founder." He had argued for the inclusion of Catholics, African Americans, and national languages within SIL's lily-white Anglo-Saxon mainstream—and gotten nowhere. "Our folks were just too narrow,"[48] he had told a colleague. But the final blow was the way he and his wife, Elaine, were treated after their return from a visit to the Soviet Union.

The Townsends had been impressed by Soviet bilingual programs for minorities in the Caucasus.[49] They had been "taken in by the communists," one financial backer told Elaine. "We didn't go to the USSR to find fault," she lamely replied. "We went to see how we could serve and pave the way for the Bible to be translated into more languages."[50] If SIL's version of Romans 13:1 was good enough for colonels, it was good enough for commissars—at least in their own land. Cam saw nothing inconsistent about praising a country's bilingual education programs in its and U.S. newspapers, just as he had done in the days of Cárdenas's Mexico. He strolled about Red Square in his Texan fedora at peace with himself. Was not Russia just like any other new frontier for the Lord?

Even Cam's allies began talking about his age and ailments often enough to give him a picture of what was desired. In 1971, he resigned as SIL's general director, but not without some stinging last words. SIL, he warned, was guilty of "incomplete adherence to our non-sectarian policy." It had shown intolerance of alcohol-drinking Lutherans from Germany and of American Pentecostalists who believed that the Holy Spirit's possession gave one the power to speak in alien or dead tongues. It had exhibited an "almost unconscious going along with racist attitudes"; showed an "over independence" from national cultures; and what was perhaps most ironic, engaged in "missionary type activities" that could cost SIL contracts and retard the advance of the Lord's Word among the Bibleless tribes.[51]

Now, a year later, the most prestigious Indianist organization in the world was paying his accomplishments and abilities the deference his own colleagues refused. Yet he knew that the Lord's Will was still unfolding. Tribes were still waiting for the Word, and governments and anthropologists were increasingly in the way. His services and humble manner would be needed again.

43

CRITICAL CHOICES

Navigating the Rapids—Rightward

For Nelson Rockefeller, 1972 was the watershed in the United States'—and his—political life. At the zenith of its power, the presidency of Richard Nixon was self-destructing.

This time, there would be no Checkers speech, only tapes revealing the seamier side of big-league politics in the United States. The first revelation of criminal behavior came with a simple piece of adhesive tape affixed across the lock of an office door, not in the way expected of professional burglars—not vertically, so it would be invisible with the door closed—but horizontally, producing just the kind of telltale sign of intrusion that raw recruits at CIA's Camp Peary learned not to do in Break-In 101. Yet, inexplicably, this was what the CIA's former chief of security, James McCord, did at the entrance to the office of the Democratic National Committee at the Watergate complex. Predictably, after a guard found, for the second time that night, that the door to the Watergate basement garage had been taped open and called the police, plainclothes officers entered the complex; they searched their way to the Democratic headquarters, immediately noticed the tapes, and advanced on the burglars with guns drawn. They never expected to bag such illustrious lights of the Cold War's underworld, men with records of accomplishment in CIA service in Latin America going back to the Bay of Pigs and before, to Colonel J. C. King's Western Hemisphere barony. But once the perpetrators were brought in, for those in the know in Washington, it was obvious that the clock was ticking on the presidency of Richard Nixon.

For Nelson, it had been difficult watching Nixon's heady ride from Capitol

Hill to the White House on inauguration day almost four years ago. Nixon had outtoughed the party regulars from the Eastern Establishment, including Rockefeller. All Nixon had to do was move steadily forward as the central candidate, steering carefully between Rockefeller on the left and Goldwaterites on the right, to the nomination. Once the nomination was secured, all else followed: Rockefeller's endorsement, Kissinger's clandestine informing on the Paris Peace talks, and Nixon's pledge of having a "secret plan" to end the war and return law and order to American streets and campuses.

Most recently, Nixon had outmaneuvered the Rockefeller camp on economic and trade issues as well. At first, David Rockefeller did not object to PepsiCo's Donald Kendell being named chairman of the Emergency Committee for American Trade. But then Nixon did something highly unorthodox in an effort to reverse the first U.S. trade deficit in a century. To stem the flow of gold to overseas dollar creditors, he unilaterally suspended the convertibility of dollars to gold. Then he allowed the dollar's exchange value to "float" in world markets, rather than to be anchored at a fixed value (previously $35 per ounce of gold).

This action came as a great shock to Wall Street. It ended the international monetary agreements that had provided stability for world currencies and for long-range corporate planning, which included such vital items on a balance sheet as the dollar-value of assets (like factories) and liabilities (like bonds).

It was a crude effort by Nixon and Treasury Secretary John Connally to reverse the deficit through a simplistic monetary manipulation: devaluing the dollar. Nixon followed up the devaluation in the fall of 1971 by forcing Japan and other Pacific Rim countries "voluntarily" to reduce their own textile exports to the United States and to allow more U.S. imports into their markets at favorable prices. He took the same audacious stance with Europe, causing West Germany's foreign minister to warn, "By its decisions on trade policy, the United States may bring about the disintegration of the Western world."[1]

The Eastern Establishment was appalled. *Foreign Affairs* magazine, published by the Rockefeller-funded Council on Foreign Relations, issued a blistering indictment on Nixon's "disastrous isolationist trend." Nixon had "terminated the convertibility of the dollar, shattering the linchpin of the international monetary system on whose smooth functioning the world economy depends." He had "imposed an import surcharge, proposed both the most sweeping U.S. export subsidy in history and discriminated against foreign machinery by making it ineligible for the Job Development Credit," a tax break for companies that upgraded their factories. He had "bludgeoned East Asia into 'voluntary' restraint agreements on textiles," the article continued (without explicitly stating that this practice would also hurt Asian subsidiaries owned by American corporations that were often controlled by Old Wealth, like the Thai textile firm owned by Nelson Rockefeller's International Basic Economy Corporation (IBEC).

Finally, Nixon had "sought to extend and tighten the existing 'voluntary' agreement on steel—completely revising the traditional position of U.S. administrations in resisting protectionism and leading the world toward ever freer trade"—even if that trade was dominated by giant corporations. In short, Nixon had "violated the letter and the spirit of the reigning international law in both the monetary and trade fields."[2]

To the older American corporations who called themselves "multinational" companies (even though by and large they were still American-controlled transnational corporations operating across borders), Nixon's policy was a body blow. If unintentional, it was stupid; if intentional, it was treachery. The State Department suffered a hemorrhage of foreign-trade experts and investment bankers, who fled to think tanks, such as the Council on Foreign Relations or the Brookings Institution.

Nixon's protectionism could not have come at a worse time for IBEC. The company had extended its investments to every continent, overstretching its capital capacities. More trade, not less, was what IBEC needed to make its assets abroad yield revenues for debt service at home. Some investments, like the Brazilian Investment Bank, were paying off; BIB almost doubled its stockholder equity from 1970 to 1971, from 59 million cruzeiros to 101 million cruzeiros, increasing the value of IBEC's share in BIB from $2.4 million to $3.7 million. But other IBEC holdings, such as its hydraulics plant in West Berlin, sapped the capital of its parent, leaving Nelson's pride and joy $138 million in the red in 1972.

And then there were the political blows as Rockefeller holdings were caught between the protectionist crossfire from Latin American governments and Richard Nixon. In Argentina, BIB's parent company, Deltec International, was denied government loans for its huge Swift-Plata ranching and meat-processing operations, because it was not Argentine majority owned. It eventually closed its plants when cattle deliveries dwindled and cattle prices rose. Finally, failing to find Argentine buyers, Swift sought bankruptcy protection from its creditors.[3]

In June 1971, Deltec had secured an $18 million credit line in Eurodollars, only to see its value undermined by Nixon's devaluation of the dollar. Investment banks (like New York's Model, Roland, of which IBEC's top Brazil overseer, Richard Aldrich, was vice president) dealing in Eurodollars for American and foreign borrowers were aghast at the instability in the European financial markets caused by Nixon's suspension of gold payments and devaluation of the dollar.*

IBEC itself had suffered huge losses in South America for reasons ranging from the environmental to the political.

---

*The uncertainty about the dollar in the European money markets worried U.S. companies with longstanding investments and financial ties abroad. These companies were dependent on Eurodollars to finance investments and imports of capital goods into developing countries like Brazil. BIB, for instance, arranged Eurodollar loans to Brazilian borrowers on behalf of Deltec International's Bahamas-based offshore bank, Deltec Banking. See Deltec 1970 10-K form, p. 10.

In Brazil, the entire 1971 crop of IBEC's hybrid corn seed was destroyed by leaf blight, severely lowering the earnings of its most dramatic success story, Sementes Agroceres, S.A., now the fourth-largest seed company in the world, with research and production centers in five Brazilian states.

In Argentina, IBEC was left with large debts as a result of Nelson's 1969 visit, when thirteen of the Minimax supermarkets were burned.

In Chile, workers seized IBEC's ready-mix concrete plant, despite the opposition of the government of Salvador Allende. The plant would not be returned until after the military coup in 1973 displaced the workers at gunpoint.

In Venezuela, IBEC's thirty-nine CADA supermarkets were still being criticized for favoring imported items over locally produced products, with critics charging that IBEC had reversed the 80:20 ratio in discriminatory purchases simply by buying from U.S. subsidiaries in Venezuela.[4]

In Peru, IBEC executives were still worried over the penchant of the government of Juan Velasco Alvarado for nationalization to bring foreign companies' investments into correspondence with the government's development agenda. Rockefeller Foundation trustee John Irwin's negotiations on behalf of Washington still had not produced the money Standard Oil wanted for properties seized allegedly in lieu of back taxes. In 1969, the government limited to 25 percent foreign capital holdings in Peru's banks, including Banco Continental, controlled by Chase Manhattan Bank. In July 1970, the government decreed that all industrial firms had to be Peruvian majority-owned, and followed that up the next year by nationalizing a mine owned by South Peru Copper Company, a subsidiary of one of Chase's closest clients in mining, the American Smelting and Refining Company (ASARCO). By 1975, a similar fate would befall the Peruvian holdings of Marcona Mining, Cerro [de Pasco] Corporation, International Telephone and Telegraph (ITT), and Standard Oil of California (which shared ownership of a refinery with a Peruvian banking group led by David Rockefeller's friend, Manuel Prado, and W. R. Grace & Company, chaired by another of David's friends, J. Peter Grace).

The Chase bank also had its 70 percent-owned Banco Argentino de Comercio nationalized in Argentina, and in Chile the Allende government nationalized the holdings of ITT and the three copper giants, Anaconda, Cerro, and Kennecott, regaining Chilean control over the source of 89 percent of Chile's exports earnings; Allende offered compensation based on the companies' own previous claims of the worth of the properties for tax purposes. Eleven banks were nationalized as well in 1971 to prevent denials of credits to the government's agrarian reform program and its state-owned industries.

These were also bad times for Nelson's political career. His reputation had suffered since the disastrous Latin American tour. There had even been demonstrations in the United States and bombings by American students of Rockefeller-

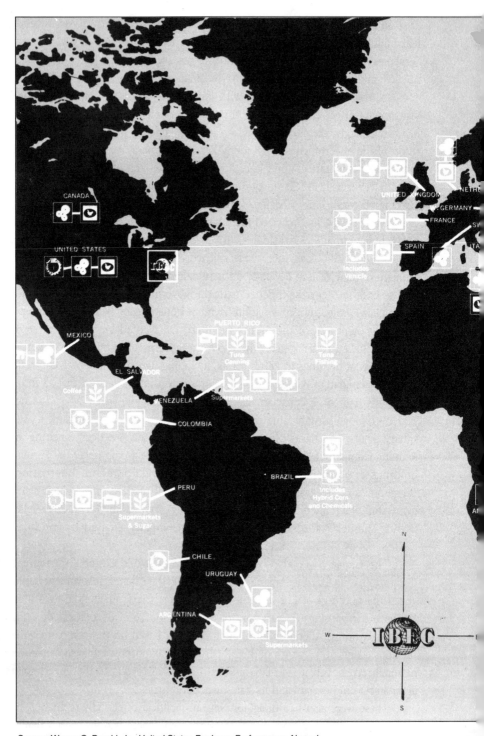

Source: Wayne G. Broehl, Jr., *United States Business Performance Abroad.*

**IBEC
Around
the
World**

LEBANON

PAKISTAN

INDIA

SOUTH
KOREA

JAPAN

HONG KONG

THAILAND

Includes
Textiles

SOUTH VIET NAM

PHILIPPINES

ZAMBIA

MOZAMBIQUE

RHODESIA

FOOD GROUP

POULTRY GROUP

HOUSING GROUP

INDUSTRIAL GROUP

FUNDS (F), INVESTMENT, and INSURANCE (I) GROUP

affiliated companies, including the RCA Building at Rockefeller Center and the Standard Oil refinery in Bayonne, New Jersey.

And then there was the nightmare of Attica. Nelson had been attending a meeting in Washington, D.C., of the Foreign Advisory Committee on International Intelligence when he got word of the rebellion at the state penitentiary at Attica, New York. Thirteen hundred, mostly African American, prisoners were holding 38 prison employees hostage. Their demands for safe transfer to a "nonimperialist" country were answered by his stony refusal even to come to hear their complaints about the brutality of their guards. After a five-day standoff, during which Nelson never visited the prison, a helicopter suddenly dropped pepper gas onto the yard.

When the gas had lifted and the six-minute volley from hundreds of police guns ended, 10 hostages and 29 inmates were dead, and 80 prisoners were wounded, some fatally. Nelson was "amazed" only that more had not been killed. He dismissed the medical examiner's report, which disclaimed reports by prison officials of atrocities committed against hostages. The governor's counsel's claim—that the examiner was a "known leftist"—attempted to pull a Cold War veil over the bodies.

"Sure, it all fits," said Nelson, elevating the worst prison riot in U.S. history to the status of an international conspiracy. "The prisoners' demands transcended prison reform and had political implications," he later explained.[5]

But the veil was too thin. The official investigating commission criticized Nelson's refusal to be present at the scene when critical decisions were made involving a potential great loss of life. Attica, it determined, was, "with the exception of Indian massacres in the late 19th century . . . the bloodiest one-day encounter between Americans since the Civil War."[6]

There were political rewards. President Nixon, with whom Nelson had been in touch throughout the crisis, praised Nelson's "courage." Nixon's rival had passed the test for many conservatives by answering definitively, if bloodily, the growing mood of revolt behind prison walls. "The assault on Attica was a moral disgrace," admitted Nixon aide William Safire, "but politically he did what our people wanted."[7]

Pocantico's Watergate Secrets

To the uninitiated, Republican politics seemed topsy-turvy. Nelson Rockefeller, the liberal, appeared to liberals to be the warmonger on Vietnam, even the executioner of African Americans in his own state, while Richard Nixon appeared to be the would-be peacemaker.

This change in the Republican political spectrum alone should have indicated that Nixon's choice of the New York governor to nominate him for a second term at the 1972 Republican convention was not merely the usual gesture of party unity. Thanks to Nelson's move to the right, there was little gap to close between the Right and liberal wings of the party—at least no obvious gap. Nelson had demonstrated his willingness to shed much of his liberalism and move to the right to join the new Republican mainstream.

The Rockefellers showered $260,700 on the Republican campaign that year.[8] Nelson personally ran Nixon's campaign in New York State to give the president the biggest victory of any state in the Union. He traveled more than 30,000 miles to deliver 44 speeches in 33 cities to help Nixon.

Nelson had been a loyal member of the President's Foreign Intelligence Advisory Board, not because he liked Nixon, but because he agreed with most of the administration's foreign policy initiatives—the invasion of Cambodia, the resumed bombings of North Vietnam, the mining of Haiphong Harbor, and the increased bombings in the countryside and police repression of Vietnamese civilian "suspects" despite the My Lai massacre.* After all, his protégé, Henry Kissinger, was overseeing that policy and effectively neutralizing arch conservatives who considered Rockefeller anathema.

Kissinger's ignorance of Latin America and Nixon's hatred of any Kennedy legacy like the Alliance for Progress did have their fallout on Nelson, however. Cutbacks in foreign aid had triggered the Chilean cancellation of Nelson's visit during his 1969 tour. The coincidental lecture at a June 1969 White House meeting of Latin American ministers by Chile's foreign minister, Gabriel Valdés, on North-South trade and financial inequities, left Nixon in a rage. When the minister explained that Latin America was sending back to the United States $3.80 for every dollar it received in U.S. aid, Nixon interrupted. The statistic must be wrong, the president said. The minister answered that his source was a study by a major American bank.

Kissinger seized the opportunity to appease his superior and to play on Nixon's intolerance of such "Communist-leaning" liberal nationalist governments as Eduardo Frei's in Chile. Nixon had taken Valdés's comments as a personal insult, and Kissinger was eager to answer in kind.

The next day, Kissinger was staring Valdés down at the Chilean embassy. "Mr. Minister, you made a strange speech," Kissinger opined. "Nothing important can come from the South. History has never been produced in the South. The axis of history starts in Moscow, goes to Bonn, crosses over to Washington, and then goes to Tokyo. What happens in the South is of no importance. You're wasting your time."

Valdés was astonished. "Mr. Kissinger, you know nothing of the South."

"No," Kissinger responded, "and I don't care."[9]

Nelson Rockefeller, however, did care. Frei had been a Rockefeller favorite,

---

*Nixon opposed cutting the budget of the CIA's local assassination teams for Colby's Operation Phoenix. "We got to have more assassinations. Killings. That's what they're doing [the other side]." Kissinger was equally callous. "I hold the strong view that human rights are not appropriate for discussion in a foreign policy context," he told Chilean dictator Augusto Pinochet's foreign minister on May 8, 1975, two years after the military coup that toppled President Salvador Allende and began the repression that would take an estimated 50,000 lives by 1976. See Seymour Hersh, The Price of Power (New York: Summit, 1983), pp. 135–36.

enjoying the backing of David's Business Group for Latin America, whose members were the principal conduit for corporate and CIA funding of Frei's 1964 presidential campaign against Salvador Allende.* Although he would back Nixon in overthrowing Frei's leftist successor, again Allende, in 1973, Nelson's loyalty to the president was being severely put to the test by the 1972 reelection campaign. Nixon did not, of course, dump his vice president and former Rockefeller-backer, Spiro Agnew. Agnew was useful to Nixon as a foil for attacks on his enemies, despite rumors that Agnew had been deeply involved in Maryland's corrupt graft-taking political machine. Agnew was more to Nixon's liking than was Nelson Rockefeller.

So were CIA veterans of the Guatemala and Bay of Pigs invasions for finding and plugging up leaks to the press and for carrying out illegal operations against Nixon's long list of "enemies." This "Plumbers Unit"—headed in the field by E. Howard Hunt—had as its first assignment the discovery of who was leaking intelligence documents revealing the hidden history of the Vietnam War. Wiretaps were placed on the phones of current and former staff members of the National Security Council (NSC). Break-ins were proposed to recover documents believed to be stored at the Rockefeller-funded Brookings Institution. When the *New York Times* was preparing to publish the Pentagon's top-secret study of the Vietnam War in 1971 (leaked to the newspaper by Daniel Ellsberg, a former Defense Department analyst), Nixon was desperate. He had the FBI place taps on the home phones of NSC staff members who had been privy to the report, even Kissinger, a notorious leaker and the only senior adviser not openly enthusiastic about the Plumbers Unit.

It was the Kissinger wiretaps that caused Nixon the most concern. He had been warned that FBI Director J. Edgar Hoover would respond to the Justice Department's request for evidence against Ellsberg by providing logs of the illegal wiretaps on Kissinger. Hoover might even use the wiretap summaries and documents to bribe Nixon to keep his job, as he had previous presidents. Therefore, Nixon wanted Hoover's assistant director and rival, William Sullivan, the FBI official in charge of transcripts of the phone taps, to destroy the evidence. Meanwhile, Hunt's team of Cuban CIA operatives was sent in to burglarize the office of Ellsberg's psychiatrist to try to get information that would damage Ellsberg's credibility. Ellsberg had learned of Nixon's secret B-54 bombing of Cambodia, nuclear threats against the Soviet Union over Hanoi's refusal to bend to his will, and Kissinger's studies on mining Haiphong Harbor; Nixon was worried that Ellsberg might be believed when he outlined Nixon's strategy of escalation, not peace, in Indochina.

Through all this, Nelson Rockefeller kept up his close relationship with Henry Kissinger. Kissinger provided free NSC office space for Nelson's assistant,

*The CIA's liaison to Rockefeller's Group, Enno Hobbing of Guatemala coup fame and Richard Aldrich's Latin American Information Committee, later became the Group's top operations officer under its new incarnation, the Council of the Americas. See Hersh, *The Price of Power*, p. 260.

Nancy Maginnes (Kissinger's future wife), in the Executive Office Building.[10] Nelson liked to keep a New York State Office in Washington. But never before had he such access to the inner sanctum of the NSC—at least, not since he had served on the NSC himself. In fact, according to one NSC official, Kissinger had such trust in his mentor that since 1970 he had been smuggling his most sensitive national security documents out of the White House to Pocantico, for Nelson's safekeeping.[11]

Kissinger had reason to violate normal security procedures. He had to protect himself from Nixon's orders to destroy evidence and to rewrite history. Kissinger, of course, had his own version of history, and he would use the documents to write his own memoirs. It was precisely Kissinger's penchant for keeping his own logs for such obvious purposes that inspired Nixon, in self-defense, to set up the less time-consuming audiotaping system that ultimately destroyed his career.

Nothing better illustrated the danger of Nixon's duplicity, however, than his backing off from Kissinger's negotiated and approved peace accord of October 1972. Kissinger had traveled to Saigon in August to manipulate South Vietnam's President Nguyen Van Thieu into silence during the election campaign by promising escalation of the war after the election; however, Kissinger was negotiating an agreement with North Vietnam's Le Duc Tho that secretly promised a coalition government. Withdrawals of U.S. ground troops continued, and an end to the U.S. draft by July 1973 was announced.

Nixon appeared to many Americans as a peacemaker who wanted détente rather than war with the Communist nuclear powers. His trip to China was seen by most as a gesture for world peace, when in fact it was an effort to widen the split between China and the Soviet Union, to increase Soviet insecurity about its relations with the United States, and to demonstrate to North Vietnam its isolation and the fickleness of its supposed Communist allies. Polls showed that the American people believed that their president was doing everything reasonable to end the war. But they also showed Nixon that 47 percent opposed any coalition government, the very thing Kissinger was secretly pushing for. Kissinger was pledging a de facto recognition of the Provisional Revolutionary Government of the National Liberation Front (NLF) as an equal player with Thieu. The North Vietnamese asked only for elections and an international election commission, something the Saigon regime had never accepted. Thus, after telling the world "peace is at hand" in late October, Kissinger found himself and his reputation out on a limb after Nixon's reelection: The president reneged, backing Thieu's rejection of the election commission and opting instead for the Christmas 1972 bombing campaign.

Nelson publicly backed the bombing that followed. But the public's distaste for the war (by now a majority of those polled) guaranteed that Congress would cut off funds for the war in early 1973. Nixon knew that it would, and he hoped to bring North Vietnam to its knees before then. Kissinger knew it also. So did Nelson Rockefeller. But when Hanoi did not surrender, Nixon opted to end the bombing before Congress acted, reopened negotiations in Paris, and declared victory.

The generals in Hanoi, Saigon, and the Pentagon were not fooled, especially when Nixon, announcing the end of the war, declared that the United States stood behind the Saigon regime as the only legitimate government in South Vietnam. Not only would Hanoi and the NLF in the South not accept that declaration, Saigon's soldiers either would not, or could not, fight well enough to protect Thieu's rule. North Vietnam and its NLF allies had no reason to surrender. The war would continue, and Nixon would not be able to keep his promise of continued U.S. military support to Thieu that his Christmas bombing had seemed to make credible.

Watergate had made it impossible for Nixon to do so. If his hush payments to Howard Hunt's Cuban team ever became public—and there was every likelihood that they would—he could not resume bombing without spurring Congress to open a full investigation of his possible misuse of presidential powers, including his authorization of illegal wiretaps, which, in turn, could have revealed his secret bombing of Cambodia and his role in Watergate itself (particularly his obstruction of justice by trying to use the CIA to get the FBI to drop its investigation of the Watergate burglary). Nixon's own secret wars and illegal activities doomed any chance he had of winning the Vietnam War. If the choice was between saving Thieu's presidency or his own, the decision was obvious.

Kissinger was certainly apprised of this situation, and given his close relationship to Rockefeller, Nelson probably was, too. Pocantico hid Kissinger's secrets, one of the gravest of which was Kissinger's knowledge of the Plumbers Unit and the White House tapes. Later, during Nelson's confirmation hearings as vice president, charges would be made that Rockefeller was aware of the tapes and their contents, but a key witness from Kissinger's NSC staff, who had earlier made such a claim, waffled before Congress, his memory failing. And Nelson denied everything.[12]

The Great Commissions

Richard Nixon was unusually acquiescent to Nelson Rockefeller after his reelection. Given the animosities between the two men in the past, this behavior was unexpected, even considering Nelson's help in the campaign. Yet, when Nelson (his excitement about the national arena rekindled by his involvement in a winning campaign and the warm support he at last received from Republican audiences) approached Nixon in December 1972, Nixon did not reject a request for a presidential endorsement of a vague National Commission on Critical Choices—chaired by Nelson, with members selected by Nelson. As governor, Nelson had started a Commission on the Role of a Modern State in a Changing World, but had "discovered" that New York's problems were really inseparable from the world's. A national commission was needed, he told the president.

White House aide John Ehrlichman immediately saw the political potential for

Nelson and suggested that the commission be a federal project, so that there could be some White House oversight. No, answered Nelson, a bipartisan commission would have more credibility and could command more resources if it were not part of the government.

Nixon acquiesced. The fall of John Connally as treasury secretary and architect of Nixon's "New Economic Policy" had already been forced by Rockefeller allies, Connally later charging that he had been "stabbed in the back" by Kissinger, who persuaded Nixon to abandon Connally's xenophobic trade and monetary policies.[13] With Watergate revelations looming, Nixon needed friends, not enemies, among the Rockefellers.

Lyndon Johnson was Nelson's first choice for cochair of the commission. The Rockefellers had kept up their friendship with the Johnsons. Nelson and Happy had spent the last weekend of Johnson's presidency with him at Camp David and "had a good time," Nelson recalled. "Happy conjectured as to whether everything said in the room was being recorded. She was fabulous."

Since Johnson's retirement, they often visited the LBJ Ranch, the last patch of the world Johnson could control, issuing orders to field hands like he had to White House officials. The Perdernales River Valley, a beautiful oasis filled with wild flowers that had once been the home of the Comanche Indians, had caught Nelson's fancy. He credited Happy with getting Lyndon to slow down, and the former president tried futilely to loosen up; he even grew his silver locks long like the peaceniks he loathed. But he agonized over the course of the war navigated by Kissinger and Nixon or over what Nixon's "New Federalism" was doing to his Great Society programs by requiring local antipoverty projects to be approved by local politicians.

The last time they had seen Johnson was in June 1972, when they joined him and Mrs. Johnson in a round of golf. When it came time to go, the two couples drove out together in a golf cart to the Rockefellers' plane. Nelson sat up front with Lady Bird and overheard Johnson's last remark. "Happy, I'll never see you again."[14]

On January 21, 1973, the day after Nixon took the oath of the presidency for a second term, a cease-fire was declared in Vietnam. Nixon finished the day of celebration by announcing his new plan to end the Great Society.

Nelson understood the political significance for his own future. He immediately set up a meeting at the LBJ Ranch for the evening of January 23, to ask Johnson to cochair his Critical Choices commission.

It would have been a brilliant move. Johnson would have provided a bipartisan alliance and an entry to the conservative Southern Democrats that John Connally was trying to deliver to Nixon. But on January 22, fate struck down Nelson's plan. Johnson, alone in his bedroom, suffered a fatal heart attack. Nelson's last great hope to rally Middle America behind him was dead.

Johnson's death was also a terrible personal blow, the worst since another stalwart ally, Adolf Berle, suffered a fatal massive cerebral hemorrhage at his East

Nineteenth Street home in February 1971. The town house in which Berle had entertained and counseled some of the world's most wealthy and powerful men for half a century closed its doors to history.

Then, in February 1973, Nelson's brother, Winthrop, died. Nelson and his brothers were confronted with the fact of their own mortality.

So now Nelson speeded up his efforts to achieve his lifelong goal: the presidency of the United States. Encumbered by Nixon's protectionism and no longer in the grip of his youthful passion for Latin America since his disastrous tour in 1969, he began to pull in IBEC's horns. Paring off losing subsidiaries and consolidating the winners became the order of the day. Faced with Nixon's import quotas on Far Eastern textiles, Nelson and brother John 3rd sold off IBEC's fabric factories in Thailand, not an imprudent move considering how badly the war was going. Patriotism in Latin America was also taking its toll, not to mention the potential for scandal in Brazil. IBEC sold its holding in Deltec International's Brazil Investment Bank (BIB).

The Amazon basin would still become one of the great cattle-raising and mining areas in the world—at the expense of the rain forest and its Indian people, but, besides retaining the million-acre Fazenda Bodoquena just south of the basin's watershed, the Rockefellers would leave that to Augusto Antunes, J. Peter Grace, and their associates on the board of Brascan, the Canadian holding company. Brascan bought Deltec's two ranching companies and the Swift-Armour Brazilian meat-packing subsidiary. IBEC's 19 percent holding in Deltec's BIB was sold to Walther Moreira Salles's group for a handsome profit: a $25,000 initial investment in 1957 to hire a staff for Fundo Crescinco's management firm had yielded a company that was sold for $10 million;[15] IBEC, even after discounting for later advances, marked up a net return of $2 million on its books.

Nelson lost nothing politically with these withdrawals, either. Old allies took up the slack and earned handsome profits, men like Moreira Salles, the Klebergs of Texas, Antunes, Grace, and Lewis B. Harder (Brascan director and head of Molybdenum Corporation, Moreira Salles's partner in a rare metals mining venture in Minas Gerais, Cia. Brasíliera de Metalurgía e Mineração [CBMM],[16] and in the search for cassiterite in Rondônia region[17] near the lands of the besieged Cintas Largas and Surui Indians). Deltec's chairman, Swift in-law A. Thomas Taylor, remained in leadership, along with Deltec president Clarence Dauphinot, the man who first gave D. K. Ludwig a stake in Brazil by selling him 25 percent of St. John d'el Rey, the owner of the massive Aguas Claras iron lode in Minas Gerais. Ludwig's holding in St. John d'el Rey, in turn, had by now given him 19 percent of MBR, the Brazilian firm that brought together still other Rockefeller associates—investment banker Leo Model (chairman of St. John d'el Rey), Antunes, and Hanna Mining—to lock up control of Minas Gerais's iron riches in 1971.

The Rockefellers were not withdrawing from IBEC or from Brazil, only from

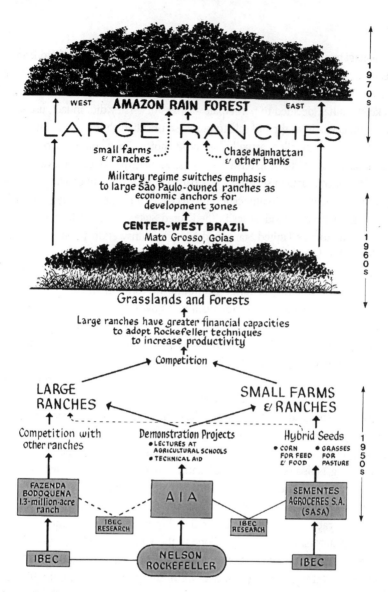

WEST **AMAZON RAIN FOREST** EAST

LARGE | RANCHES

small farms ⋯⋰ ⋱⋯ Chase Manhattan
& ranches &' other banks

Military regime switches emphasis
to large São Paulo-owned ranches as
economic anchors for
development zones

CENTER-WEST BRAZIL
Mato Grosso, Goias

1
9
6
0
s

Grasslands and Forests

Large ranches have greater financial capacities
to adopt Rockefeller techniques
to increase productivity

Competition

**LARGE
RANCHES**

**SMALL FARMS
&' RANCHES**

1
9
5
0
s

Competition with
other ranches

Demonstration Projects
● LECTURES AT
  AGRICULTURAL SCHOOLS
● TECHNICAL AID

Hybrid Seeds
● CORN   ● GRASSES
  FOR FEED   FOR
  &' FOOD   PASTURE

FAZENDA
BODOQUENA
1.3-million-acre
ranch

AIA

SEMENTES
AGROCERES S.A.
(SASA)

IBEC
RESEARCH

IBEC
RESEARCH

IBEC

NELSON
ROCKEFELLER

IBEC

Nelson Rockefeller and Brazil's Advancing Northern Frontier

Rockefeller's economic activities in Brazil's Center-West pushed the colonization of Goias
and southern Mato Grosso with migrants from the restless, impoverished Northeast, developing what one of the leaders of the 1964 military coup, General Golbery do Couta e Silva,
called the "central platform" for the conquest of the Amazon. Golbery explained that colonization would "advance from a forward base, developed in the central west and coordinated
with an east-west progression following the bed of the great [Amazon] river, [in order] to
protect certain frontier points and inundate the Amazon forest with civilization." Golbery
founded the dictatorship's dreaded secret police, the SNI, which kept close ties with Rockefeller allies. Rockefeller himself carried back from his 1969 visit a secret message from SNI
senior officers to President Nixon at a time when repression, Amazon development through
U.S. corporations, and Indian genocide were the top items of international concern about
U.S. aid to Brazil.

Sources: AIA Archives, IBEC Archives, and the Nelson A. Rockefeller Papers, Rockefeller Archive Center;
Jerry Shields, The Invisible Billionaire: Daniel Ludwig; Susan Branford and Oriel Glock, The Last Frontier:
Fighting over Land in the Amazon; Alexander Cockburn and Susanna B. Hecht, The Fate of the Forest:
Developers, Destroyers and Defenders of the Amazon.

the management side of the Brazilian securities market they had helped bring into existence. At first, this decision appeared to be based on a desire to keep the fruits of success. Now that Brazil's securities market was off and running, the Rockefellers had decided to participate as investors. They did, in fact, use some of IBEC's proceeds from the BIB sale to purchase Brazilian short-term securities.

But the Rockefellers actually had little choice. They could not risk tying up IBEC's liquid assets in long-term securities. Rather, their recent move out of the management of Brazilian securities was part of global shifts in capital flows resulting from Europe's and Japan's economic recovery and their growing productivity differentials with older industries in the United States. These shifts had resulted in trade deficits for the United States and Nixon's clumsy effort to cut this deficit by devaluing the dollar to lower the price of exports so they could win back foreign markets. In an earlier age, Nixon's arbitrary monetary policies might have served as a jump-start for longer-range economic investment in new technology in American industry. But world capitalism was now too integrated. West European holders of American dollars could not tolerate a devalued dollar that limited the financial horizons of their own rebuilt postwar industries. A devalued dollar also meant less buying power for Middle Eastern shahs and sheiks, whose oil revenues were based on oil prices pegged to the dollar, and less collateral for European investors in the face value of American bonds and notes. The Middle Eastern oil producers responded with oil price hikes that aggravated inflation in the West. Nixon's arbitrary monetary moves not only undermined a unified Western response, but threatened even more chaos in the financial markets.

During Nelson's 1969 tour of Latin America, not even the most cynical Rockefeller-baiters discerned that after the Gold Crisis of 1968, Nelson's shift in his public image—from an entrepreneur-philanthropist espousing development *with* democracy to one arguing for development *without* democracy ("New Military" dictatorships) in a Dollar Zone in the Western Hemisphere—might have been precipitated by anticipation of this shift in financial relations between the American Eurodollar and a revitalized North European capitalism. In 1973, David Rockefeller gave Nelson's case for putting the priority on political stability a stunningly bold financial rationale and broader interpretation, applying it now even to Communist states in Eastern Europe and socialist countries in the Third World. "In terms of straight credit risk," he explained, "the presumption is that there is greater continuity in government in certain socialist states than in nonsocialist states."[18]

Since Europe and Japan's rebuilt postwar industries had the technological edge and Japan had restrictions on foreign imports and foreign financial penetration of its companies, the Rockefeller brothers took preemptive action to stall hemispheric-level competition. In the post–World War II era, the United States had enjoyed enormous, almost exclusive, world power as the West's only superpower militarily and as controller of the all-important Middle Eastern oil. Now, the Rockefeller brothers offered to share the power.

In July 1972, one month after the Watergate burglary, David Rockefeller hosted a meeting at Pocantico. Some of the most influential foreign policy strategists in the United States, Japan, and Europe gathered to plan the founding of what David called an "International Commission for Peace and Prosperity": the Trilateral Commission.

The conference was designed to reassure major U.S. allies in the Cold War that Nixon's protectionism would not prevail, that wiser, more experienced, and more powerful forces were opposed to it and were prepared to offer Europe and Japan an alternative. Neither the nationalism that led to two world wars in this century nor the hemispheric walls that Nelson and David actually had championed in the Western Hemisphere was necessary—at least, not before mutually satisfactory roles could be worked out.

The commission would formally begin its work in July 1973. Columbia University's Zbigniew Brzezinski, promoter of a "community of developed nations" and professor at the Rockefeller Foundation-funded Russian Institute,[19] would soon be appointed the commission's first director. Under Brzezinski, the commission's dominant topics for deliberation would be consistent over the next two years: "global redistribution of power," the problems of building a "trilateral community," and the troublesome "governability of democracies."

Nelson kept a low profile. He did not attend any of the commission's meetings and never even joined the commission, thereby avoiding any appearance of working behind Nixon's back. But Nixon's "economic nationalism," as it was derided by the Trilateralists, ran squarely against IBEC's new activities in Brazil.*

In November 1972, Nelson visited Nixon at Camp David to get his own commission off the ground. The idea was for a more national version of the Trilateral Commission that would dovetail with many of David's goals on the international level. Membership would overlap in some cases, to promote a common Rockefeller-led agenda for a new world order that could ultimately include the Russians, although none of this agenda was ever explained to Nixon. The same willpower that had created the CIAA, laid the foundation of the OAS military alliance, launched the

---

*Plans were under way to draw European investors into the São Francisco River Valley. To follow up on investment potentials there that were identified by IBEC's Development and Resources Corporation, IBEC set up a consulting firm jointly owned by Europeans and called Disenvolvimento e Sistemas, S.A. At the same time, IBEC launched a huge 4,200-unit housing project near São Paulo and, with German and Dutch investors, opened two wholesale distributors in the city as part of a chain of MAKRO stores planned for other countries in Latin America. Other ventures revealed that more than political symbolism was behind the Rockefellers' choice of Nathaniel Samuels, Nixon's former deputy undersecretary of state for economic affairs, as IBEC's new chairman. Samuels had been a director of one of Belgium's largest companies, Sofina, and—besides his government tenure as an alternate U.S. representative to the International Monetary Fund, the World Bank, the Asian Development Bank, and the Inter-American Development Bank—had been a managing partner of Kuhn, Loeb, one of Wall Street's most active investment banks in Europe.

crucial study panels on winning the Cold War through bankrupting Russian Communists with an arms race and counterinsurgency warfare, and braved riots to lead the "fact-finding" mission to Latin America would again prevail.

In March 1973, Nelson announced his Commission on Critical Choices for Americans. To finance it, Nelson had a federal bill drafted allocating $20 million. By the time he began lobbying Congress in May, that figure had drifted down to a more reasonable $1 million. But even that amount was too much for the Senate, and the bill died. Nelson quickly came up with the kind of solution that had made the name Rockefeller unique in American politics: his own $1 million contribution to the commission's tax-exempt Third Century Corporation. Reliable Laurance kicked in a similar amount, and a few corporate foundations threw in the rest. Then, with himself as chairman, Nelson announced its panels of "prominent Americans." These were some of the most powerful men—and women—in government, big business, academia, law, banking, science, and the arts—as well as two CIA contractors and, of course, brother Laurance.

This was the kind of power that made Richard Nixon feel unsafe. Nelson had stacked his commission with the very Eastern Establishment types who had frowned on Nixon's own rise to power from southern California. The following October, Nixon surprised no one—except Nelson—when he passed over Nelson and chose House Minority Leader Gerald Ford to replace his disgraced vice president, Spiro Agnew. Agnew's plea of *nolo contendere* to accusations of financial misconduct while he was Maryland's governor was more damaging to the Nixon administration than was his actual resignation. It raised a cloud over the White House, suggesting occupancy by crooks, exactly when Nixon was trying to convince the nation that he was not one. Gerald Ford was the perfect antidote: hardworking, decent, unimpeachably conservative, and, it was rumored, not bright enough to prove a threat or succumb to intrigues that were disloyal to the president.

Nelson still managed to believe that Nixon might choose him as his successor. It was only the latest example of the headstrong attitude he had exhibited all his life, what his secretary Ann Whitman came to call his "I can do anything if I want to" air.[20]

Yet another trait that Nelson acquired in childhood proved a boon. The Rockefeller penchant for secrecy served Nelson well. As long as a goal was in sight and attainable, Nelson, like Senior and Junior, never lost control of himself in public over things that were out of his control; he shrugged them off and moved ahead. But even here, Nelson added his own fateful twist: He never looked back.

Two months later he resigned as governor of New York. He could now spend the next three years gaining national visibility and strengthening his power base with his Commission on Critical Choices.

The latest Arab-Israeli war and Arab oil embargo prompted him to focus the commission's search for solutions to oil and uranium shortages in two traditional

Rockefeller haunts: the American West and Latin America. The two regions had become mirror images of an entrenched development policy focused entirely on the extraction of wealth with little regard for the consequences.

THE MOST CRITICAL CHOICE: ENERGY AND WOUNDED KNEE

Nelson commissioned Edward Teller, the father of the hydrogen bomb, to report on the oil potential in the West, especially in its shale rock.[21] Teller's background in nuclear physics would have inclined him to look into potential sources of uranium as well. He played an important role in shaping the commission's interest in nuclear power and coal as supplements to increased oil development in the Southwest. Like Herman Kahn had prescribed for the Amazon, Teller initially advocated excavation by nuclear explosion.[22] Teller identified shale oil deposits in the Green River Formation of Colorado, Utah, and Wyoming that were capable of yielding an estimated 100 billion barrels of oil. "The federal government owns four fifths of the nation's oil shale-bearing land in the Western states,"[23] Nelson wrote, not mentioning that most of the uranium, coal, and oil in the West were located on Indian lands.

For instance, rich coal deposits on 58,000 acres of Hopi land in New Mexico had been strip-mined by Kennecott Company, the giant mining conglomerate that was owned, in part, by the Mormon church and that listed among its board members Rockefeller allies J. Peter Grace and John Schiff. Under Johnson's secretary of the interior, Stuart Udall, a member of a rich and powerful Mormon family, Kennecott's Peabody Coal had secured leases to mine coal on the Hopi Indian reservation from the Hopi Tribal Council, one of the elected Indian councils that John Collier's "Indian New Deal" had brought into being.[24] It was not long before ash-spewing coal-fired electricity plants sprouted up at Four Corners, New Mexico,* to provide energy to Phoenix, Las Vegas, and Los Angeles through a consortium of 223 utility companies.

The plants burned ten tons of coal every minute and pitted the Bureau of Indian Affairs (BIA)-controlled tribal councils against Navajo and Hopi tribal elders and environmentalists. Grass began to die near Shiprock, the same area to which Junior had brought young Nelson Rockefeller and his brothers some fifty-four years earlier. Sheep and people became sick, while the Black Mesa's precious aquifers were tapped and drained for the mining and power-plant operations.[25] This "development" program brought little to most Indians. The majority continued to live without electricity and many without running water. Meanwhile, the uranium miners among them began to come down with lung cancer. Shiprock

---

*In the Four Corners area, Kennecott's Peabody was joined by Tenneco, Climax Uranium, Standard Oil of New York (Mobil), and Standard Oil of New Jersey (Exxon).

Hospital admitted the first of seventeen Navajo men who would be diagnosed by 1979 as having lung cancer; fifteen of them had mined uranium[26] at the Shiprock uranium mine operated by Kerr-McGee.

"It was not our responsibility to warn them," one BIA official would assert years later. "That was the job of the landowner."[27] The landowner was the Navajo tribe, administered by the elected tribal council—the Western democratic structure that John Collier had championed to replace traditional tribal elders. If Collier had hoped that the tribal council would be a step forward in Indian self-rule, he was sadly mistaken. The elected leaders of the tribal council simply became middlemen for the oil and uranium companies.

Some of the largest concessions went to Exxon (Standard Oil of New Jersey), Mobil (Standard Oil of New York), and United Nuclear, a company that Laurance Rockefeller helped found in the 1950s.[28]

The BIA evaded responsibility for the deaths of Navajo miners and the poisoning of their ancestral lands. So did Kerr-McGee. Missionaries of the Summer Institute of Linguistics (SIL), who had been working among the Navajo since the 1940s, remained silent, too, even after the existence of lung cancer, a hitherto unknown disease among the Navajo, became public knowledge.

Meanwhile, one of SIL's largest contributors, the Pew family, was guiding its Sun Oil Company (SUNOCO) into strip-mining coal near Gillette, Wyoming, joining Exxon and Kerr-McGee in shifting from the largely unionized Appalachian region. The Pews' Cordero Mine in Wyoming was south of the Northern Cheyenne and Cree reservations in Montana, where the BIA had been urging the Indians to grant coal concessions to corporations since 1966.[29] The reservations, coincidentally, were subsequently identified by SIL as "urgent areas where Bible Translation needs to be undertaken."

As in Brazil, the government agency that was supposed to be dedicated to the Indians' welfare was collecting revenues by leasing out Indian lands to corporations. And as in Brazil, SIL missionaries were being sent into the same tribes. SIL went to work among the Apache, whose language had been translated centuries before by Catholic missionaries, but whose Jicarilla reservation in New Mexico was discovered to contain an estimated 154 million barrels of oil and 2 trillion cubic feet of gas. In Alaska, SIL's linguistic surveys soon brought teams into Inuit communities at St. Lawrence Island in the Yukon Delta; by 1975, SIL's Operation Deep Freeze had reached Barrow, just west of the giant Kuparuk and Prudhoe Bay oil fields. The fields had been discovered in 1969 by Sinclair Oil, the same firm that had bought up the Ganso Azul field in Peru near SIL's Yarinacocha jungle base, and by Sinclair's new owner, Atlantic Richfield Oil Company (ARCO), and Standard Oil of New Jersey (Exxon).

Still another "urgent area" was the land of New Mexico's Keres Indians, which was identified by the Energy Research and Development Administration as containing uranium. Other SIL-chosen tribes were the Havasupai-Walappai of northwestern Arizona and the Shoshone of Nevada, Utah, and Idaho, both of whom owned uranium-bearing lands; the Cree of Canada, who were soon confronted by the James Bay hydroelectric project backed by Chase Manhattan Bank; the Eastern Ojibwa of New York, who were resisting land encroachments near aluminum plants; the Tsimhian of Canada, whose lands were to be crossed by the Alaskan oil pipelines carrying oil from the Mackenzie Delta and Beaufort Sea, where both the Rockefellers' Exxon and the Pews' SUNOCO owned huge oil concessions; and, despite over a century of Euro-American acculturation, the Cherokee and Creek of Oklahoma, whose lands happened to lie on the route of a proposed coal-slurry pipeline to energy-hungry Baton Rouge, Louisiana.

This increasing pressure on Indian lands already had pushed Indians into confrontations, first with tribal council leaders; then with the BIA; then with the FBI; and, finally, with the entire power structure of the U.S. government. In November 1972, following the killings of Indian activists by police, Indians who participated in a "Trail of Broken Treaties" caravan to Washington, D.C., would no longer accept rebuffs by Nixon officials and occupied BIA headquarters. After a standoff with U.S. marshals under the glare of the news media, the Indians left peaceably. BIA officials, infuriated over the bad publicity and the release of captured BIA documents, brought charges against leaders of the American Indian Movement (AIM) who conducted negotiations on behalf of the protesters.

The following February, AIM responded to a call for help from Lakota and Oglala Sioux Indians in South Dakota, including two leading AIM members, Russell and Bill Means. Money due from BIA leases had not been paid, and the recently elected chairman of the Sioux Tribal Council, Richard "Dickie" Wilson, was suspected by some of the Indians.[30] Moreover, Wilson favored taking money from the Interior Department's Indian Claims Commission in exchange for all claims to the Sioux's sacred Black Hills. (There, gold had once lured General George Custer along with prospectors, prompting the Sioux to fight back to defend their rights to the hills guaranteed by the 1868 Treaty of Fort Laramie. The results, despite Custer's hopes for a military campaign that would earn him a presidential nomination and profits from a mining company he was involved in,[31] were disastrous for Custer and thousands of Indians.)

Now, as Standard Oil of California's Chevron Resources joined Anaconda, Phillips Uranium, and Union Carbide in negotiating for leases to explore for uranium in the Black Hills, and the National Park Service pressed the tribe to sell 133,000 acres of the Pine Ridge Reservation, the traditionalists worried that Dickie Wilson's willingness to sell the tribe's birthright would find its way through the legal grist mill set up to facilitate cash settlements by the Indian Claims Commission.

The traditionalists wanted to stop, not facilitate, the loss of Indian lands, and feared money would be provided to tribal council lawyers by the new Native

American Rights Fund. The fund had been established in 1971 with a $1.2 million donation announced by Ford Foundation president McGeorge Bundy, former national security adviser to presidents Kennedy and Johnson and a former member of the Rockefeller Brothers Fund's Special Studies Panel.

These fears of Wilson's intentions were confirmed when, despite the tribe's previous rejection in 1972, he reopened negotiations with the National Park Service. Wilson also refused to allow the traditionalists' request for higher rents from ranchers to be raised with the BIA in the tribe's name, banned meetings, hired his own security guards with tribal funds, and attempted to create a witch-hunt atmosphere against AIM supporters by showing a John Birch Society film, *Anarchy, USA*, depicting ghetto riots and burning buildings. An effort to impeach him resulted in the arrival of seventy counterinsurgency troops of the U.S. Marshal's Services, Special Operations Group patrols throughout the reservation, and an impeachment trial presided over by a tribal judge of Wilson's choice. The judge's conduct so upset the 600 Indians in attendance that most, including opposition members of the twenty-member tribal council, walked out.

It was the traditional Indian way of expressing no confidence, but the BIA accepted the report that Wilson was voted back into office by a council vote of 4 to 0.[32]

The next day, responding to demands and pleas expressed by elders at a meeting, AIM supporters drove fifteen miles in a fifty-four-car caravan to seize and occupy Wounded Knee, South Dakota. This site of the 1890 massacre of 300 Sioux men, women, and children by Custer's reorganized Seventh Regiment suddenly found itself surrounded by hundreds of armed state police, federal marshals, FBI agents, and armored units of the U.S. Sixth Army.

Operational command was at the Pentagon, FBI headquarters, and the Nixon White House, where Chief of Staff Alexander Haig presided. After taking fire for seventy-one days, the Indians were allowed to surrender peacefully. But the FBI stepped up arrests, the Justice Department brought down a hail of indictments, and killings of AIM supporters mounted; between March 1973 and March 1976, the Pine Ridge Reservation would suffer from a murder rate almost nine times higher than that of Denver, then the reputed "murder capital of the United States."[33]

In Latin America, such disturbances were less likely, thanks to the even freer hand given to Nelson's "New Military." Indians in the Amazon never came up in the report by the Commission on Critical Choices. But oil did. After reviewing the excellent prospects along Venezuela's Orinoco River, which was estimated to have 700 to 800 billion barrels of oil, the commission reported that "another area likely to yield substantial new oil supplies in the near future is the Upper Amazon basin of Brazil, Ecuador and Peru, and the adjacent Beni area in Bolivia, which is now being actively explored by foreign oil companies."[34]

The prospects of finding more oil underscored the important role that SIL played in the Amazonian fields of the Lord for American oil interests and why the State Department under Henry Kissinger, a member of both the Commission on Critical Choices and the Trilateral Commission, would seek to preserve SIL as an asset. But probably the man who would do the most to protect the role of missionaries as assets of the U.S. government, and particularly of the CIA, was the man chosen to head the official inquiry into the CIA's alleged abuses of power: Kissinger's mentor and patron, Nelson Rockefeller.

ONLY A HEARTBEAT AWAY

The Rockefellers did get one prize from Nixon after his reelection. Nixon reversed the Civil Aeronautics Board's ruling that had prevented Laurance's Eastern Airlines from taking over a coveted Caribbean route. But other than that and giving Nelson his Commission on Critical Choices, Nixon did not reward Rockefeller for his loyalty. After all, where was Rockefeller when aid was called for from behind the scenes, when Nixon was battling in the dark to hold his rattled staff in line? Nelson did not respond to letters from Nixon's former chief of staff, John Ehrlichman, asking for help to pay his legal bills. And he failed to offer consolation to Attorney General John Mitchell after his indictment.

During what turned out to be the final days of Nixon's presidency, Nelson never publicly spoke of his disdain for Nixon or his bitterness over being snubbed by Nixon's aides when he showed up at the Waldorf-Astoria Hotel in New York on election night 1968 to offer Nixon congratulations and was told that the president-elect was resting.

By July 1974, as impeachment articles were being prepared in Congress and the Supreme Court ordered Nixon to surrender the White House tapes, Nixon was drinking heavily. The insecurity of being a poor man trying to rise in, and eventually being in charge of, a rich man's party had grown into a paranoia over "enemies" that now was destroying his presidency. Kissinger advised Defense Secretary James Schlesinger to intercept any rash orders from the White House and to keep his generals at close rein. He then visited the White House to tell Nixon that history's memory and world peace required him to consider stepping down.

As Nixon collapsed into teary hysterics, insisting that Kissinger kneel with him in prayer for divine guidance, former Kissinger aide Alexander Haig, now White House chief of staff, set up a cot in the White House Situation Room to carry out a deathwatch over the Nixon presidency. Nixon's efforts to shift the blame for Watergate to the CIA had failed, just like his wider effort to assert control over the CIA had backfired.

That night, Nixon told his family it was all over. The next day, he gave a terse resignation note to Kissinger that was drafted by Haig. After giving speeches to the nation and his staff and another longer letter to Vice President Ford advising Haig's removal as chief of staff, he flew home to southern California, abandoning the White House to Gerald Ford and, it turned out, to Nelson Rockefeller.

The phone call offering Nelson the vice presidency came on Saturday morning, August 21, 1974, when Nelson and the family were at their estate in Mount Desert, Maine. Nelson said he was not sure that he could accept, that he would have to talk to Happy and the kids. He told President Ford that he would call back the next day.

It was a shrewd ploy. Raising the specter of an embarrassing refusal put Ford on the ropes. Nelson had built a credible background for a refusal through years of proclaiming no love for the vice presidency. He had known every miserable man who held that office since Henry Wallace, way back in 1941. There was really no question about his accepting. He was getting too old to wait for Jerry Ford to serve two terms before he would have another chance. He would be only a heartbeat away. Besides, he reminded everyone, the country was in the throes of a constitutional crisis, and his country was calling.

But patriotism, despite his public posture, had its limits. Nelson wanted power, a role for the vice presidency that would be more active than anything the country had seen before. Ford was too inexperienced to challenge Kissinger on the formulation of foreign policy. Nor could Ford match Nelson on domestic policy. And Ford knew it. "I'd like you to do in the domestic field what Henry's doing in the international field," he told Nelson.[35]

Nelson called back on Sunday and told Ford that he could not accept unless he was allowed to be an active vice president. Nelson had always said, "I am just not built for standby equipment."[36] Ford could not deny that Rockefeller would bring executive experience; it was one of his major assets. And Nelson's Eastern liberal image would help balance his own Midwest conservatism in the public's perception. But above all, he needed the Rockefeller name to give his presidency the appearance of wealth beyond corruption. Just like Nixon had done fifteen years earlier, he accepted Nelson's terms—and in writing.

Two days later, Nelson was in Washington for his first formal meeting with Ford. The president, for the first time, officially offered him the vice presidency and, upon hearing Nelson's formal acceptance, immediately called Richard Nixon. Nelson stood there, astonished, until Ford indicated that he should get on an extension. Nelson heard Nixon praise Ford for choosing a "big man for a big job." Then he was surprised to find himself alone on the line with Nixon. Ford, with characteristic naïveté, had taken another call and left the two foes alone in awkward silence.

"Hello," Nelson said.

"Congratulations and best wishes," said Nixon. "I think you are great to do it."

"And that was it," Nelson recalled later.[37]

　　　　　　　　　　　　　　　　　　A NEW WORLD ORDER

44

HIDING THE FAMILY JEWELS

THE MYTH OF ROCKEFELLER POWER

Nelson never expected his confirmation hearings to be so tough. His greatest strength—the influence and resources that came with his wealth—suddenly became the focus of controversy that almost destroyed his nomination. He arrived at the Senate caucus room on September 23 confident that his recent lobbying would produce results, attacking friendly hands with two-handed handshakes and spreading good cheer.

He began by reading his own seventy-two-page history of the Rockefeller family, its virtuous struggle against racism, from the abolitionist days of Grandmother Spelman; her husband's adventurousness and fearlessness as the inspiration for Grandfather John D.'s heroic construction of Standard Oil; and John D.'s compassionate nature setting the example for the "family ethic" that his own father, John D., Junior, extended through philanthropy "throughout the world." Nelson dismissed the power of the Rockefellers as myth.

"This myth about the power which my family exercises needs to be brought out into the light," he told the Senate. "It just does not exist." The senators glared in silence. What potential distortion of the constitutional republic could the nation suffer from this unparalleled marriage of wealth and political power? Little, Nelson assured them, asserting that his personal assets, including his $33 million art collection, totaled only $62 million. When his share of Junior's trusts was included, his grand total still was only $179 million. This, the senators knew, was far below that of some other Americans. And anyway, the Senate itself was known as the "millionaires club."

Nelson was hurt, however, by a recent Internal Revenue Service audit that showed that his worth was actually $218 million; moreover, the IRS had billed Nelson for more than $903,000 for five years of back taxes he owed, including $83,000 in gift taxes.[1] These gifts included a $50,000 "loan" to Henry Kissinger just a few days before he took office in the Nixon administration, and a combined total of $875,000 to two New York cronies he had put in charge of the Urban Development Corporation and the Metropolitan Transportation Authority.

Nelson responded by listing $24 million in contributions to nonprofit agencies and charities. He did not mention that he had given more than half that amount to institutions that were founded or controlled by the Rockefeller family.[2] Of those institutions, his or his family's own operations in Latin America took $2.6 million.[3] When other Latin American interests were added ($103,168),[4] the figure rose to $2.7 million, or 11.4 percent of all his admitted "charitable" contributions. Moreover, this figure did not include Nelson's donations to Latin American recipients that were passed through the Rockefeller Brothers Fund or the Latin American studies funded by donations to the Council on Foreign Relations.[5]

These revelations caused more eyebrows to raise in Congress about how much taxes he had avoided by funding nonprofit institutions that carried out operations to his liking. Nelson reported a total personal income of over $47 million between 1964, the year he first ran in earnest for the presidency, and 1973, when he resigned as governor. His payment of $12 million in income taxes during the same period would have been considerably more—$16 million more, in fact—had he not made his donations to "charity."

By mid-October, Nelson was in trouble. The controversy over his contributions to political figures and nonprofits and the scandal of his brother Laurance "investing" $60,000 in a 1970 book attacking Arthur Goldberg, Nelson's 1970 Democratic gubernatorial opponent, were threatening to get out of control. The House Judiciary Committee decided to broaden its investigation into the Goldberg biography. Nelson tried charm and obfuscation. When they did not work, he took a stab at honesty. Nelson reversed his earlier denials and admitted knowledge that the book would be published, wiring Goldberg an apology.

Worried that this admission could kill his nomination, he called President Gerald Ford, who blandly assured him, "There is no problem."[6]

Ford was not omniscient, only savvy. Behind the scenes, beyond the glare of television lights, there was a strange serenity in the proceedings, as if despite the ugly show, or, more accurately, because of it, the hearings would lead to the opposite of what many observers thought would happen: Nelson's confirmation. As attacks came down upon his nomination from the Left and the Right, Nelson smiled; he knew he had captured the vital center, appearing as the moderate between two political extremes. He was used to rolling with the punches in a ring where the rules were set by corporate parameters. Room 5600 had left little in

Nelson's business affairs that was not legally tidy. Tax deductions that were challenged by the IRS were easily adjusted; the Rockefeller family office fired off checks, defusing any legal arguments. Critics who based their case on the size of the Rockefeller wealth and the long reach of its influence met an unenthusiastic response by both Democratic and Republican congressmen and senators.

J. Richardson Dilworth, head of the family office, appeared before the committee to explain the world of trust accounts. He listed only "major stock holdings," although it was unclear if they were the largest in the sense of market values or of a percentage of a company's total outstanding shares. He gave amounts only in the aggregate and did not break them down for each of the eighty-four family members. Yet he insisted at the same time that each member had sharply different attitudes, that each one set down general guidelines for his or her portfolio managers, and he denied "that this family acts in concert when in fact this has never been the case."

The $262 million Rockefeller Brothers Fund was excluded, Dilworth explained, since the family office no longer managed its funds. So was the Rockefeller Family Fund, because that, too, had independent investment advisers. Laurance's controlling interest in Eastern Airlines was left out, as was the Rockefeller Foundation, since, as Dilworth asserted, "the [family] office has no connection whatsoever with the Rockefeller Foundation."[7]

No one dared question the credibility of Dilworth's accounting. No one seemed to know how. His list of major Rockefeller stock holdings included only the largest, and of those, only two besides IBEC and Rockefeller Center were near the 10 percent category he conceded as possibly giving the owner control: Coherent Radiation (19 percent), a laser-systems manufacturer, and Thermo Electron (9.79 percent), a thermionic research firm. Dilworth did not include Standard Oil of California, Exxon (Standard Oil of New Jersey), Mobil (Standard Oil of New York), and Chase Manhattan Bank in his 10 percent category, ignoring the fact that no single group of investors in any of these giant companies held as much as 10 percent, and yet all these corporations were controlled by a board of directors representing investors, if not themselves. If anything, Nelson's $1 billion figure for the family fortune was disappointing after estimates of $5–10 billion had been mentioned in earlier testimony. The family members had found even these revelations excruciating, Dilworth told the committee, and that comment seemed enough to satisfy everyone.

The only awkward moments for Dilworth came when New York Representative Elizabeth Holtzman questioned his statement that the Rockefellers and their investment adviser were "totally uninterested in controlling anything" and that the family's role was as passive investors, using the $60,000 financing of the derogatory Goldberg biography as an example of a financial, not a political, undertaking. It "defies credibility," said Maryland Republican Laurence J. Hogan, that this was a "straight investment."

ADMITTED ROCKEFELLER FAMILY STOCKHOLDINGS (1974)

Aggregate of Major Stock Holdings of 84 Members of the Rockefeller Family

Market value	Company	Total shares	Percentage of outstanding shares
$21,600,000	Exxon (Standard Oil of New Jersey)	315,507	.14
16,100,000	IBM	85,218	.06
14,900,000	Standard Oil of California	594,838	.35
12,000,000	Chase	429,959	1.34
12,000,000	Mobil	325,290	.33
5,800,000	Eastman Kodak	81,069	.11
5,400,000	AT&T	116,231	.02
5,200,000	General Electric	137,016	.08
4,700,000	Standard Oil of Indiana	53,784	.08
4,700,000	Dow	22,400	.08
4,200,000	IBEC	379,430	78.60
3,300,000	Aluminum Co. of America (ALCOA)	99,633	.30
2,800,000	Texas Instruments	37,644	.17
2,600,000	International Paper	63,470	.14
2,300,000	Coherent Radiation	316,805	19.08
2,200,000	Caterpillar Tractor	41,227	.07
2,200,000	Marathon Oil	58,783	.20
2,100,000	Motorola	47,000	.17
2,100,000	Thermo Electron	189,129	9.79
2,100,000	Allied Chemical	65,985	.24
2,000,000	Sears, Roebuck	38,584	.03
1,900,000	DuPont	17,533	.04
1,600,000	Lubrizol	39,283	.19
1,500,000	Daniel International	102,125	1.46
1,500,000	Archer Daniels Midland	89,404	.59
1,400,000	Weyerhaeuser	50,414	.04
$138,200,000	Total		

Aggregate of Major Stock Holdings in Trusts Created by John D. Rockefeller, Jr., for Benefit of His Descendants

Market value	Company	Total shares	Percentage of outstanding shares
$135,100,000	Exxon (Standard Oil of New Jersey)	1,972,664	.88
98,300,000[1]	Rockefeller Center	1,125,000	100.00
70,400,000	Standard Oil of California	2,815,000	1.66
56,500,000	IBM	298,824	.20
51,600,000	Mobil	1,436,916	1.41
32,600,000	Eastman Kodak	454,904	.28
30,000,000	Merck	455,100	.61
14,900,000	Texas Instruments	203,900	.90
14,200,000	General Electric	372,936	.21
13,700,000	Minnesota Mining & Manufacturing.	221,700	.20
10,900,000	Monsanto	213,273	.64
10,100,000	Aluminum Co. of America (ALCOA)	306,150	.92
9,200,000	Caterpillar Tractor	172,752	.30
8,700,000	Xerox	86,900	.15
8,300,000	Kresge	336,800	.28
7,600,000	Motorola	169,200	.60
7,000,000	Standard Oil of Indiana	80,868	.12
5,400,000	Johnson & Johnson	62,000	.11
5,100,000	Marathon Oil	135,434	.45
4,600,000	Hercules	130,000	.31
4,100,000	Allis Chalmers Pfd.	430,000	3.45
3,900,000	Coca-Cola	62,200	.10
3,600,000	Weyerhaeuser	130,000	.10
3,000,000	Upjohn	65,000	.22
2,000,000	Chesebrough Pond's	45,311	.29
1.700,000	J. C. Penney	40,596	.07
1,400,000	Dun & Bradstreet	73,400	.28

$613,900,000 **Total**

$752,100,000 **Grand Total**

Additional Holdings Not Specified By Dilworth

$224,600,000   Securities owned by 7 charities (particularly Colonial Williamsburg and Rockefeller University) whose investments were managed by finance committees advised by Rockefeller Family & Associates.

Additonal Holdings Not Included in Dilworth's Disclosure

Eastern Airlines: 216,000 shares (preferred, convertible at $63); Laurance Rockefeller held control of 100 percent of the preferred shares of Eastern Airlines, whose assets were then worth over $1 billion.

$229,976,000 in investments by the Rockefeller Brothers Fund (managed by the United States Trust Company).[2]

$13,000,000 in investments by the Rockefeller Family Fund (managed by two firms, Battery March and Franklin Cole).[2]

---

[1]This $98 million figure was a gross underestimate of the value of the fifteen-building Rockefeller Center complex. Merely a decade later, the Rockefellers paid Columbia University $400 million for the land beneath Rockefeller Center; then, after replacing their private holding company with the Rockefeller Group, a real estate investment trust company that publicly offered shares to outside investors, they were able to get $1.3 billion through a twenty-two-year mortgage on the Center's twelve original buildings. They expected to cash in on rising real estate values and higher rents from Manhattan's speculative boom during the Reagan era.

Fortunately for the family fortune, before the boom ended and the Center's rental leases took a price dive, reducing the property's value to less than $1 billion, the insistence of the Cousins (the fourth generation) for more access to their fortune forced the sale of 80 percent of the stock of the Rockefeller Group to Japan's Mitsubishi Estate Company for $1.4 billion. This left Mitsubishi with the $1.3 billion mortgage and the Rockefellers and other investors with 20 percent (worth about $200 million). Through these transactions, the Rockefellers reaped over $2 billion in cash for other investments; this was more than twenty times what J. Richardson Dilworth had told Congress was the worth of the family's holding in Rockefeller Center.

[2]Source: *The Foundation Directory* (New York: The Foundation Center, 1972), p. 272.

Sources: Charts presented by J. Richardson Dilworth of Rockefeller Family & Associates during testimony on the nomination of Nelson A. Rockefeller to be Vice President of the United States, December 3, 1974; financial records from the Rockefeller Archive Center.

"It was an underwriting, sir," Dilworth corrected, "not an investment," inadvertently contradicting his own point about the venture not being a political undertaking and confirming Hogan's.

But such gaffes did not really matter.

The Congress of the United States seemed grateful that the Rockefellers had merely complied with a partial disclosure before placing Nelson Rockefeller at the head of the line of presidential succession.

Years later, when many of the House Judiciary Committee's files were declassified and released by the Ford Presidential Library, historians could see that the congressmen had much more information on Nelson's family than they let on during the hearings. The focus of a good part of the Congressional Research Service's investigation was on Latin America. The CRS prepared detailed reports on Nelson's intelligence activities, his IBEC investments, and on development activities of the American International Association for Economic and Social Development (AIA), including David Lilienthal's survey in the Amazon and Nelson's extensive holdings in Brazil.

Yet, deprived of the meaning that these holdings had for their own lives, most Americans remained uninterested in Latin America, what Nelson was doing there, or what the U.S. government was doing there in their name. Nelson felt free bluntly to confess his support for the Kissinger-Nixon policy against the Salvador Allende government in Chile, which had led to the bloody military coup of the previous year and subsequent executions, terror, and dictatorship. The CRS report on Nelson's intelligence activities in Latin America, including his possible knowledge of CIA efforts to overthrow Allende and the purported CIA ties of one of the admitted recipients of Nelson's gifts, Bolivia's Victor Andrade, remained locked away in the committee's files. Most Americans would never read these reports, but Nelson's allies in the Ford White House would, and they would keep them from public exposure.

Finally, after eight days of hearings and forty-eight witnesses, Nelson was confirmed by the Senate on November 22. House confirmation followed on December 19. In January 1975—one month after receiving the Christmas present of his life, confirmation as the vice president—Nelson received his first assignment. It was, considering all that he had gone through in recent months and all that still remained secret, apropos: He was to chair the President's special investigation of the CIA's abuses.

The Latin Legacy

While Nelson had been battling his way into the White House, a strange undercurrent of intrigue had swept through Washington. The fall of Richard Nixon may have brought Nelson Rockefeller into the White House, but it also threatened to bring down a carefully constructed network of bureaucratic dikes that had been built over a quarter of a century to compartmentalize the flow of information in the executive branch and keep state secrets from the American people, including Congress. The architect of their design was the CIA. Nixon was no friend of the CIA. He believed, with some justification, that the Agency was run by the same pin-striped Eastern Establishment that had always looked on him with disdain. He believed that the CIA had given candidate John F. Kennedy false claims about a missile gap with the Soviets and tipped off Kennedy on plans for the Bay of Pigs invasion, prompting Kennedy to call for U.S. action against Fidel Castro exactly when Nixon could not for fear of compromising the mission.

But there was something else about the CIA and Cuba that Nixon knew, something he believed he could use against Richard Helms, the current director of the CIA appointed by Lyndon Johnson. Nixon knew that several people who were involved in the Watergate break-in had worked for the CIA, specifically in the operations surrounding the Bay of Pigs invasion. He also knew that several ex-FBI men had headed up "dirty tricks" operations in J. C. King's Western Hemisphere Division before and after the invasion.

Nixon ordered H. R. Haldeman and John D. Ehrlichman to meet with the CIA to pressure the FBI to curtail its investigation of the Watergate burglary.[8] "Just say [unintelligible] very bad to have this fellow [E. Howard] Hunt," Nixon instructed Haldeman, "he knows too damned much, if he was involved—you happen to know that? If it gets out that this is all involved, the Cuba thing would be a fiasco. It would make the CIA look bad, it's going to make Hunt look bad, and it is likely to blow the whole Bay of Pigs thing, which we think would be very unfortunate—both for the CIA, and for the country, at this time, and for American foreign policy."[9]

E. Howard Hunt, the man in charge of the Watergate plumbers, had been the CIA's overseer of the Cuban exile force in Guatemala and Nicaragua, the training and staging areas for the Bay of Pigs invasion. He had intimate knowledge of the invasion's strategy. Being a seasoned veteran of the 1954 Guatemala coup, he could not have been unaware that both the choice of location for the invasion (an isthmus far from mountain havens and cut off from the interior by swamps except by causeways) and the use of propeller planes to fight Castro's jet fighters meant that direct intervention by U.S. armed forces might very well be necessary to save the invasion from failure. Indeed, having put the men on the beach even after a poorly informed air strike had missed knocking out Castro's jets, the CIA did make such a last-minute effort to convince Kennedy officials to use U.S. armed forces to back the invasion. But Kennedy, besides the use of uninitialed jet fighters for a botched escort rendezvous with the exile brigade's bombers, would not allow himself to be manipulated, earning the hatred of the CIA officers who had been closest to the exiles while they were training in Guatemala. "If someone had gotten close to Kennedy, he'd have killed him," recalled Robert Davis, CIA station chief in Guatemala City at the time of the invasion. "Oh, they hated him."[10]

Was this risky manipulation of a president and its failure—with direct consequences for Cubans, Kennedy, and the world when Castro turned to the Soviet

Union for missiles for defense—"the whole Bay of Pigs thing," as Nixon called it? Or was it CIA plots to assassinate Castro just prior to and during the invasion? Or similar CIA plots after the invasion, even during the tense Cuban missile crisis? Or the unauthorized CIA assassination plots against Castro in 1963? Or the unauthorized CIA-backed sabotage raids of that year by Bay of Pigs veterans that forced Attorney General Robert Kennedy to order FBI raids against training camps for Cuban exiles outside New Orleans? Or links between these embittered exiles and people who were the subject of investigations of the assassination of President Kennedy? Or, finally, the role of Howard Hughes's agent, Robert Maheu, in the CIA-Mob-Cuban exile assassination plots against Castro and Hughes's secret $100,000 contribution to the Nixon presidential campaign?*

Any of these activities—especially when tied to Hunt's CIA background and his having been given listening devices and disguises by the CIA for the plumbers' use—could severely damage the CIA's reputation, if not jeopardize its very existence.

Nixon wanted the FBI to stop its investigation of Watergate. But he needed leverage with the successor to the deceased J. Edgar Hoover, the FBI's acting director, L. Patrick Gray. So he decided to blackmail the CIA into persuading the FBI to drop Watergate and, in the process, set up the CIA to take the fall for Watergate. He dictated what Haldeman, when meeting with Director Helms and Assistant Director General Vernon Walters, should advise the CIA to tell L. Patrick Gray: "Just tell him [Gray] to lay off."[11] By doing so, Nixon crossed the line of legality and entered the realm of crime: attempting to obstruct justice.

Nixon based his strategy of playing the FBI and the CIA against each other on his knowledge of J. Edgar Hoover's long-running dispute with Helms over turf. Hoover was reluctant to cooperate with the CIA's requests for the FBI to install electronic eavesdropping devices and use mail-opening operations. Hoover had also refused to agree to an unprecedented interagency Committee on Intelligence that would use illegal techniques to spy on Americans who were opposed to the Vietnam War and certain domestic policies. This plan would involve the CIA in domestic operations against citizens who clearly had no ties to foreign spies. This was a violation of the CIA's legal charter and an intrusion into the FBI's area of responsibility. Hoover was not opposed to such "dirty tricks"; he had authorized such activities by the FBI against Martin Luther King, Jr., and thousands of other Americans as part of the FBI's COINTELPRO program. He just wanted the CIA to stay out of his territory. Knowing the limits of the CIA's charter, Hoover had sought legal counsel from the Justice Department. Hearing of Hoover's breach of confidence, Helms had been furious.[12]

*Hughes's contribution may have been the cause of Hunt's Plumbers Unit breaking into the Democratic National Committee headquarters at Watergate to confirm or dispel fears that incriminating evidence of Hughes's illegal campaign donations had been leaked to Democratic National Chairman Lawrence O'Brien, the object of McCord's illegal wiretap.

Helms continued domestic surveillance anyway. He later fell back on the classic rationale of military hierarchy: He was only taking orders from his superior, the president. This rationale got the CIA into an enormous legal mess, for not only did Nixon approve of its engaging in domestic spying to obtain foreign policy objectives, he also approved of using the Agency in the realm of domestic politics. Nixon, after all, had obtained the CIA's cooperation in providing equipment from Dr. Sidney Gottlieb's Technical Services to the ex-CIA men, who, led by Hunt and former FBI agent G. Gordon Liddy, constituted the Watergate burglars.

The CIA's operations in Latin America, particularly those against Cuba, set into motion the forces that brought Nelson Rockefeller within a heartbeat of the presidency. Helms's resistance to Nixon's efforts to make the CIA responsible for Watergate forced Nixon to take desperate measures, warning the CIA about "the Bay of Pigs thing." The CIA was well aware that Hunt's burglary team had ties to the Bay of Pigs invasion. Hunt had even recruited Eugenio Martinez into the Plumbers Unit by arranging to meet him at a time and place loaded with symbolism: on April 16, 1971, the tenth anniversary of the Bay of Pigs invasion, and at Miami's Bay of Pigs Monument. "We talked about the liberation of Cuba, and he assured us that the 'whole thing is not over,'" Martinez, who reported the meeting to his CIA case officer in Miami, confessed later.[13]

By the end of 1972, the CIA backgrounds of Watergate burglars Martinez, James McCord, Hunt, and Bernard Barker had given Nixon the excuse to make Helms the sacrificial goat to the president's "CIA-dunnit" line. McCord, loyal to the CIA, had written Helms in July exposing the ploy. In December, McCord fired Gerald Alch, his lawyer from the Committee to Re-elect the President (CREEP). During the trial, a Nixon aide would offer McCord money to pay for his legal defense, if he would fall in line as the other members of the Plumbers Unit had done.

The following month, in January 1973, Helms learned of his imminent firing by Nixon. He had refused to turn over to Nixon a report ordered by Lyndon Johnson in 1967 by CIA's inspector general on all the CIA's attempts to assassinate Fidel Castro. Helms feared that Nixon would use the report to blackmail the CIA further into compliance on Watergate. Rumors would abound later that before his more stately resignation and reassignment to a plush ambassador's post, Helms struck a deal with Nixon. In fact, on January 22, 1973, Helms did order all the tapes destroyed in the CIA's central taping facility at Langley. The tapes related not only to McCord and Watergate, in direct violation of Senator Mike Mansfield's request that the CIA should retain all "evidentiary material" pertaining to Watergate, but to records of the CIA's illegal activities, including assassinations and Project MKULTRA, the CIA's mind-control experiments.[14]

Shortly thereafter, Nixon announced that Helms was leaving the CIA to become ambassador to the Shah of Iran, who literally owed his throne to a CIA coup.

Atomic Energy Commission chairman James Schlesinger was Helms's replacement. A well-respected outsider, he offered corporate management skills that Helms had little interest in developing.

Schlesinger started out by beefing up Clandestine Services, transferring to it one of the Intelligence Directorate's most coveted assets, the Domestic Contract Service (DCS). This CIA branch overtly collected intelligence from American businessmen, missionaries, and scholars who were returning from abroad; now travelers might not even be informed that they were dealing with the CIA, which would incorporate the DCS into a network of contacts in business, foundations, academia, and church missions. This was the kind of decompartmentalizing for efficiency's sake that Nixon expected of Schlesinger.

What Nixon never expected—or learned—was that Schlesinger also attempted to reconstruct the records that Helms had destroyed, including those on the CIA's involvement in Watergate. On May 2, 1973, Schlesinger sent a memorandum to CIA personnel inviting them to give him information on all past CIA operations they considered "questionable activities." More than 690 pages came in, a devastating inventory of the most secret secrets, evidence of high crimes and illegal operations. It came to be known within the Agency as "the Family Jewels."

The report based on these revelations covered "those activities that are or might be illegal or that could cause the Agency embarrassment if they were exposed,"[15] activities so sensitive that they should be "most closely held."

Schlesinger did not send the report to the White House. With Watergate growing, as White House Counsel John Dean later put it, "like a cancer on the presidency," Richard Nixon was not the type of man to be given a loaded gun. Instead, Schlesinger urged top leaders of the Operations Division's old-boy network to close down or limit programs that were in violation of the CIA's charter. These programs included CHAOS (the Agency's operations against dissenting American citizens), mail opening, and the National Security Agency's cable interceptions and military surveillance of civilians.

Schlesinger's new policy did not mean that covert operations were being scaled down, however. Schlesinger had not appointed William Colby, the former head of the Phoenix mass assassination program in Vietnam, as deputy director to oversee Clandestine Services for that to happen. CIA case officers who had penetrated the Chilean military, for example, continued monitoring and encouraging the progress of the military's plans for a coup, while providing financial support for strikers and other forms of destabilization of the government. That September, their efforts brought forth ghastly fruit when thousands of Chileans, including President Allende, were murdered.

In the cabinet reshuffling that accompanied the Watergate crisis and that incidentally coincided with charges of the CIA's involvement in the coup in Chile, Schlesinger was moved to the Department of Defense, vacating the director's seat for

Colby. Nixon had every reason to believe that Colby, who for the last six months had overseen CIA operations in Chile, would perform well for him in the current hot spots: Southeast Asia, Latin America, and even Watergate. Colby was outside the tweedy Eastern Establishment and was socially isolated from traditional networks of power in the intelligence community. Like Nixon, Colby was a connoisseur of the art of dirty tricks. Finally, he seemed a man more of action than of ideas.

At first, it appeared that Colby was exactly that, carrying forward the structural changes in the CIA started by Schlesinger that met Nixon's and Kissinger's need for the quick, concise intelligence analysis. But if Colby had a field officer's nearsightedness and a penchant for "sound bite" analyses, he also had a genuine concern for the survival of those under his command. With the Watergate scandal mushrooming, growing larger than the president himself, Colby grew increasingly worried that the CIA would be engulfed by revelations of government improprieties. He decided to brief the chairmen of the congressional oversight committees on the CIA's domestic spying. But he continued Schlesinger's policy of withholding the Family Jewels report from Nixon, battening down the hatches until Watergate's hurricane had passed. Then, after Ford was safely installed in the White House and after trying to placate Kissinger by forcing the former head of the CIA's Intelligence Directorate, Ray Cline, to resign in an effort to plug leaks, and after firing the CIA's longtime counterintelligence chief, James Angleton, for resisting détente with the Soviet Union, Colby took the offensive. His aim: to shape public opinion about the CIA with a series of unprecedented, ostensibly candid, interviews on the CIA's past covert operations and on its use of paid American journalists.

Colby knew that these stories were breaking, and he hoped he would have time to scale down the Agency's use of paid reporters before the story broke; by then he hoped to be able to preserve the most important of the Agency's propaganda assets by converting them into a network of freelancers, stringers, and editors at smaller news sources. This way he would also be able to deny plausibly to editors of major news sources that CIA operatives were on their staffs. Colby would succeed by the time his successor, George Bush, announced that the CIA would stop contracting with accredited correspondents, giving the appearance of reform without its substance. But to preempt congressional investigations, he also had to open the door to other queries. In the year of Watergate, this inevitably led back to the Plumbers Unit.

On December 18, 1974, E. Howard Hunt had testified before Senate investigators on his participation in CIA's Domestic Operations Division, including spying on Americans and CIA funding of publishers.

On December 22, 1974—only three days after Nelson took his oath of office on the same family Bible he had used four times before as governor, swearing to uphold the Constitution's covenant between the government and the people—

Seymour Hersh released the results of a two-year *New York Times* investigation.

The report created a furor. What the CIA did overseas was one thing; what it did in the homeland was quite another. The thought that dirty tricks were being brought home to roost caused an outcry. The nation's nerves were already raw from presidential abuses of authority.

Gerald Ford was jarred loose from his skis in Vail, Colorado, and pleaded ignorance. He would find out immediately, he pledged, and called Colby demanding information. Colby was ready. He merely affixed a cover letter to the Family Jewels report and handed it to Kissinger to give to the president. Ford read the cover letter that denied any current or massive illegal activities and reported likewise to the press. But Hersh had discovered too much for that denial to be believed.

In Hersh's New Year's Eve story, "the Bay of Pigs thing" resurfaced with potentially astounding implications: "The *Times* reported Sunday that the new domestic unit was formed in 1964 but Mr. Hunt recalled that it was assembled shortly after the failure of the Bay of Pigs operation in 1961. Many Agency men connected with that failure were shunted into the new domestic unit." Hunt placed the date of its founding in 1962, before, not after, the Kennedy assassination, and noted that Helms was strenuously opposed to its establishment.[16] Who, then, ran this secret operation of Bay of Pigs veterans? According to one source at the Defense Intelligence Agency, such operations fell within the domain of the Clandestine Services' chief of the Western Hemisphere Division: Nelson Rockefeller's old friend from CIAA days in the Brazilian Amazon, Colonel J. C. King.

Four days later, after an even more sensitive oral briefing by Colby in the White House, President Ford announced that he was appointing Nelson Rockefeller to head an eight-member "blue-ribbon" commission (including Nelson's old friend and coinvestor in Belgian Congo properties, C. Douglas Dillon) to probe the CIA's illegal operations in the United States.

The Day of the Foxes

The Rockefeller Commission on CIA Abuses* spent six months investigating. In June 1975 Nelson issued a report.

The report was clearly designed to protect the CIA by recommending changes that everyone already knew were needed, while defending certain secret practices (including keeping files on Americans) and, in so doing, raising the public's threshold of tolerance. Nelson's immediate problem was William Colby. Colby

---

* See Appendix B for the names of the commission's members.

believed that loyalty to the CIA required him to win over the media with more candor than Nelson thought appropriate. When Colby showed up on the first day of the hearings on January 13, Nelson warned him not to reveal all.[17]

He recommended keeping secret what in some cases even Colby thought unnecessary.

But Nelson had personal, not just official, reasons for secrecy. As Eisenhower's undersecretary of the Department of Health, Education, and Welfare (HEW) and then as his special assistant on Cold War strategy and psychological warfare, Nelson knew about many of the CIA's covert actions, including the mind-control experiments (which were funded partly through HEW) and assassination plots. Indeed, as chairman of the National Security Council's Special Group, he was briefed on *all* covert operations and would have had to approve some of the most questionable ones, including coups and assassinations abroad and continuing mind-control experiments at home.[18]

President Ford was particularly interested in having Nelson "look into this assassination business."[19] Nelson understood the implications immediately. He already knew about the attempts on Castro's life and the theory that such attempts had backfired on Kennedy in Dallas. "This was another way of chopping my head off and of getting me out there where I was the one who was putting the finger on the Kennedys, see, as chairman of the committee. Also getting me into an impossible hole because I happened to know this thing had been investigated a good many times and there was a lot of very interesting leads."

Faced with Nelson's threat to resign, Ford dropped his insistence on a written report on this specific subject. But the investigation would go forward. Nelson began assembling the case for a Castro-Kennedy assassination link. "We got this information and we put it together and it was hot." When he had enough, he decided to confront Senator Edward Kennedy with a classified document to see if he could shake more secrets loose.

"Look, Teddy, this is being looked into informally," he recalled telling the last Kennedy brother. "Can you remember your brother talking about this because this isn't meant to embarrass anybody, [but] it can be embarrassing. I want you to know what we are doing and what is going on so that it isn't being done behind your back."

Nelson's attempt at candor won him nothing. "I only have vague recollections about this document. I talked about this maybe once or twice up at Hyannis Port," Kennedy responded.

Unable to find any evidence that proved the Kennedys had ordered the CIA to try to kill Castro, Nelson gave up the investigation. Avoiding having to report "got the President off the hook, got me off the hook, got it right where it belonged: in the Congress."[20]

Despite Nelson's claim that he was sticking to the commission's original mandate to investigate only the CIA's domestic activities, some activities that bore on operations overseas were addressed in Nelson's report, but in a highly contained and selective manner.

The CIA's illegal cooperation with the NSA in monitoring phone conversations by narcotics traffickers between Latin America and the United States in 1973 was considered a worthy target for criticism; the CIA's ties to American cocaine traffickers operating between the United States and Colombia were not.

The CIA's support for the activities of the Cabinet Committee on Narcotics Control, including investigations abroad, was reported; the involvement of the CIA's Air America in the transport of the very Southeast Asian heroin that the committee was so concerned about (and ultimately reported the futility of trying to stop) was not.

The CIA's use of domestic police was discouraged; the CIA's training of Latin American police was not.

Nixon's abuse of the CIA on such matters as access to files and equipment, Watergate, and requisitioning more than $33,000 from the CIA to pay for White House responses to mail on the Cambodia invasion was fair game. The CIA's conspiring with mobsters and Cuban exiles in the United States to assassinate the Cuban head of state was not. Neither was the CIA's abuse of the names of President Kennedy and Attorney General Robert Kennedy after the missile crisis to continue these assassination attempts illegally and without authorization.

While taking a properly critical tone and making some sound structural and procedural recommendations to correct the most glaring errors of process and of the government's line of authority, Nelson, in most cases, projected confidence in the Agency's claim that the abuses had been stopped and reforms had already been enacted, including a prohibition against assassinations of foreign leaders. He did not mention the CIA's unauthorized storage of curare, cobra venom, shellfish poison, and other toxins and biological weapons, in direct violation of President Nixon's executive order of February 1970 to destroy the stockpiles. Among the scientists collaborating with the CIA in the illegal storage of these biological weapons were four scientists at Rockefeller University.[21]

The Rockefeller Commission's report on the CIA's mind-control experiments was allegedly limited by Helms's destruction of the records; however, some 1,600 documents would be found at the CIA within three years. Nelson's only hint of the scope of the mind-control programs was in two sentences: "The drug program was part of a much larger CIA program to study possible means of controlling human behavior. Other studies explored the effects of radiation, electric shock, psychology, psychiatry, sociology and harassment substances." Now, assured Nelson, HEW's guidelines were in place.

Because the Vietnam War had inspired questions about its escalation after John Kennedy's death and Ford was under pressure to reopen the investigation of

Kennedy's assassination, Nelson also had to confront allegations of the CIA's involvement in the Kennedy assassination. He handled it masterfully, rebutting only the most outlandish conspiracy theories and ignoring the substantive criticisms and allegations of the CIA's involvement in a postassassination cover-up of facts related to the assassination. His conclusion was predictable, given the presence of David Belin, former Warren Commission counsel, as staff director and the fact that President Ford had been a member of the Warren Commission: the Warren Commission, he affirmed, was right.

Just as Nelson was involved in containing revelations on the CIA's past violations of law, he was contemporaneously involved as vice president in a new cover-up of the CIA's actions during the final days of the Vietnam War—as well as of the Agency's launching of a new secret war in oil-rich Angola. The CIA was again utilizing tribal differences between contending sides to prosecute a bloody civil war. This effort to overthrow Angola's leftist government would continue for over a decade, leaving the country in ruins and its people facing famine.

Nelson tried to put his CIA investigation behind him, displeased as he was with Colby's candor before the congressional committees. Needless to say, his report did not seriously address the CIA's MKULTRA and MKSEARCH mind-control experiments or even mention the Agency's assassination attempts or the role played in both by one key witness: Colonel J. C. King.

The Untimely Demise of J. C. King et Al.

CIA Director Schlesinger's order in 1973 to cease the MKSEARCH program meant closing down the Amazon Natural Drug Company (ANDCO), including its plant-collection houseboat; its laboratory in Iquitos, Peru; and its Washington, D.C., office. Nevertheless, King took two years to comply with the order.

The laboratory compound where King had hosted his dinner parties and organized plant-collecting expeditions up the Amazon's tributaries was finally sold in 1975 to one of King's employees, Dr. Sidney McDaniel.[22] And ANDCO was dissolved that December.

King continued to haunt the Amazon, according to some reports. Residents of Leticia, the Colombian port on the Amazon where Mike Tsalickis had aided King's operation, remembered seeing King there in 1976; the register of a local hotel indeed recorded "Mr. and Mrs. King." But there was really no way of telling if this Mr. King was the elusive former chief of CIA's Clandestine Services in Latin America; King had seldom allowed himself to be photographed. What was known, however, was that he had been called before congressional investigators in July 1975 to answer questions about the CIA's assassination plots.

In 1967, King had been questioned by the CIA's inspector general. He insisted that he had only limited knowledge of a plan to assassinate Castro. By

1975, when he was questioned by Rockefeller's commission, he could remember nothing at all, even when confronted with documents confirming his part in the earliest National Security Council (NSC) and CIA deliberations and actions involving Castro and Rafaél Trujillo. Yes, an NSC document indicated that he had targeted Castro for assassination as early as 1959, but he had no recollection and "denied that the Castro underworld plots originated with him."[23] Yes, another document recorded him asking Assistant Secretary of State Roy Rubbottom if the United States would be willing to provide sniper rifles to kill Trujillo (Rubbottom had answered yes), but this question did not ring any bells either.[24]

Some witnesses in the assassinations investigation were too sick to testify. Others began to die, and not all by natural causes:

*In June 1975, before he could testify, Jack Ruby's old boss from Chicago, Sam Giancana, was shot to death. Giancana had arranged assassins for the CIA in collaboration with mobsters Santos Trafficante and John Roselli and CIA liaison Robert Maheu.

*In July, Bobby Kennedy's old foe, Jimmy Hoffa, disappeared.

*In April 1976, Robert Maheu died mysteriously.

*Three months later, following his testimony before the Senate Intelligence Committee, mobster John Roselli, who passed poison received from the CIA to would-be assassins in Havana in 1962, disappeared; ten days later his mutilated body was found floating in a fifty-eight-gallon oil drum in Biscayne Bay off Miami.

*In January 1977, William Pawley, who had worked with King trying to get an acceptable successor for Fulgencio Batista, was found dead of a gunshot wound to his chest in his home near Miami Beach. His death was ruled a suicide; he left behind a note complaining of neurological pain he had endured for a year.[25]

*In March 1977, the White Russian emigré who had been Lee Harvey Oswald's closest confidant in Dallas, oil geologist and CIA collaborator George de Mohrenschildt, was found in his home dead of a gunshot wound, just before he was scheduled to speak to an investigator for the House Assassinations Intelligence Committee. He had worried about being assassinated and had installed an alarm system wired to the house's windows. A tape recorder found near his body had inadvertently recorded the "suicide," as well as the sound of a bell going off just before the victim allegedly shot himself.

*A week later, Carlos Prio, the former president of Cuba and a leader in the CIA-financed anti-Castro movement, was shot to death before he was to talk to a congressional investigator.

*In November 1977, William Sullivan, once J. Edgar Hoover's top intelligence officer and head of the Domestic Intelligence Division that supervised the FBI investigation of Lee Harvey Oswald before the assassination, was also shot to death in a hunting accident.

In early 1977, King also died. He had been suffering for years from a neurological disorder, said to be Parkinson's disease. His death came a little over a year after the Senate Committee on Intelligence, against Colby's protests to have King's and nine other names omitted from its report,[26] identified King, Roselli, Trafficante, Maheu, and others as having been being involved in CIA assassination plots. When King died, the U.S. House of Representatives was about to begin its own investigation of President Kennedy's assassination. King, a key witness to the CIA's ties to a Cuban exile organization in New Orleans that Lee Harvey Oswald had tried to join, had taken his secrets to the grave.

Nelson, though supposedly the president's chief investigator of the CIA's activities, was almost as tight-lipped as King was in death. CIA domestic operations that involved covert deals with Mafia chieftains, assassins, cocaine smugglers in South America, heroin smugglers in Southeast Asia—none was mentioned in Nelson's report.

Neither was Nelson's own role as undersecretary of HEW in the early days, when the CIA was just beginning to make HEW and its subagency, the National Institute of Mental Health, its biggest conduits for mind-control experiments in more than eighty hospitals, universities, and psychiatric institutions.

Neither was Nelson's own contribution to the Pan American Foundation. Included in his list of charitable donations during his confirmation hearing, the foundation was acknowledged as a CIA front, the same CIA front that had been used by King.[27]

Neither was Nelson's role during the Eisenhower administration as chairman of the first NSC Special Group that oversaw CIA covert operations, including an assassination plot against China's premier, Chou En-lai.

And neither, of course, was the part played by Nelson's IBEC or other companies in coups that were inspired, if not planned, by the CIA in the United States or the undercover work done for the CIA by Nelson's top IBEC lieutenant, cousin Richard Aldrich.

Yet, surprisingly, Nelson included Indians (specifically members of the American Indian Movement) in his list of those citizens who had been subjected to the CIA's illegal operations. He did not, however, include missionaries. If he had, and reported on what the CIA was doing with missionaries who worked with tribal peoples, the impact might have forced a reconsideration not only of the purpose of the CIA, but its misuse for private, corporate, ends.

Missionaries, like assassinations, were too hot.

Then it all exploded.

VIII

DAYS OF JUDGMENT

We in this country are, by destiny rather than choice, the watchmen on the walls of world freedom. We ask, therefore, that we may be worthy of our power and responsibility, that we may exercise our strength with wisdom and restraint, and that we may achieve in our time and for all time the ancient version of "peace on earth, good will toward men." That must always be our goal—and the righteousness of our cause must always underlie our strength. For as was written long ago: "Except the Lord keep the city, the Watchman waketh but in vain."

—PRESIDENT JOHN F. KENNEDY
Undelivered speech,
Dallas, November 22, 1963

45

SIL UNDER SIEGE

Religious Cloaks, CIA Daggers

William Cameron Townsend watched the controversy over the CIA's use of missionaries with curiosity and growing alarm. The CIA's penetration of religious missions, an issue previously overlooked by the media, was now, in 1975, making international headlines.

The story had been building since 1970, when Dr. Eric Wolfe, chair of the American Anthropological Association's ethics committee, explained how anthropologists had been manipulated through the Chiang Mai Tribal Research Center in northern Thailand, which was funded through the Agency for International Development (AID). He also revealed that American missionary organizations had been drawn into this counterinsurgency operation as well.

That June, President Nixon's director of AID, John Hannah, had admitted publicly that AID had funded CIA operations in Laos, and subsequent revelations pointed to CIA-AID collaboration in Ecuador, Uruguay, Thailand, and the Philippines.

These revelations could hurt all missionary efforts, but the Summer Institute of Linguistics (SIL) was particularly vulnerable. Cam Townsend had been aggressively pursuing government funding for his Bible translators for decades, first from foreign governments and then from his own government. The amendment to the 1949 Federal Property and Administrative Services Act that allowed religious missions to take surplus U.S. government property abroad had even been called "Townsend's bill" in some congressional circles. By the 1960s, SIL was receiving a hefty income from AID indirectly through foreign governments that received U.S. foreign aid or directly through AID-funded programs in bilingual education and agricultural development cooperatives. This income was supplemented by surplus military equipment, including helicopters that were retired from Vietnam and donated to SIL. Evangelized pilots of these choppers became soldiers for Christ in the tradition of Dawson Trotman's Navigators. In Peru, after the nationalization of Standard Oil, the head of the U.S. Embassy's AID office even became a member of SIL.

Back in Washington, at the urging of Ed Boyer (an official in the Department of Health, Education, and Welfare's International Education Department and a future board member of SIL's Jungle Aviation and Radio Service [JAARS]), Cam set up a full-time SIL office to help the Lord get His due. On December 2, 1970, President Nixon gave his seal of approval to expanding Cam's proposed national Bible Translation Day into a full "Year of Minority Language Groups." Cam's nephew, Lorin Griset, used his influence as mayor of Santa Ana with fellow Orange County Republican John Finch, the head of HEW, to get Nixon on board. Billy Graham also helped. Years of lobbying had finally brought Cam a photo opportunity with the president of the United States, along with the gift of a Bible graced with Nixon's autograph.

But it had all gone downhill since then. Finch lost his job in a cabinet dispute, and SIL lost its inside track with the Oval Office. Then Nixon himself fell. The dam holding back knowledge of high crimes and misdemeanors collapsed, threatening to overwhelm Billy Graham and SIL with public disclosures about Nixon.

All publicists since John D. Rockefeller's Ivy Lee had known that the way to stop disclosures from happening was to discourage the temptation to probe by attacking unfounded charges. The more outlandish the charge, the easier to discredit, and the wider the chilling ripple factor.

In the heat of Watergate, it was not so easy to do so. Nothing seemed outlandish anymore. In the case of leftists' charges against missionaries, it became even more troublesome because now it was missionaries who were doing the disclosures. Church leaders, angry that their integrity had been undermined by missionaries' collaboration with the CIA, began to protest against the political corruption of the Lord's work and the manipulation by spies of naive clergy. There was a pragmatic aspect, too: Years of work to build trust among peoples abroad were being threatened with destruction. And there was also genuine horror of the violence that had been unleashed in Vietnam and Chile in the name of the Christian struggle for God against the godless.

When Rockefeller and President Ford both spoke of the coup in Chile as being good for the Chilean people, outrage echoed in churches across the United States. Cam remained silent, sticking with the tried and true Romans 13:1. But other missionaries, Protestant and Catholic alike, spoke out. Sixteen mission leaders issued a statement in October 1974 disassociating themselves from Ford's statement and calling for a full airing of the CIA's crimes, for prosecutions when these crimes were apparent, and for a stronger law prohibiting covert activities that were designed to destabilize the elected governments of other nations. Such "destabilizations" were condemned as "blatantly incompatible with the ideals we hold as Americans and as Christians. Gangster methods undermine world order and promote widespread hatred of the United States. Watergate has shown that such methods, once accepted, will eventually be turned against our own citizens."

"I have personally witnessed the aftermath of CIA intervention in more than one country," said one of the signatories, Father William Davis, national director of the Jesuit Social Ministries, "and know it to be a legacy of fear, hatred, oppression and even death."[1] Davis emphasized that at issue were national policy and its potential for corrupting goodwill and souls. "In addition to performing some useful function, the CIA contains many good and responsible people. I have known a few over the years. But, obviously, good people can be, and are, used for evil ends by those bent on retaining power, or Vietnam and Watergate have taught us nothing."

In New York, the Rockefeller-funded National Council of Churches convened a meeting to discuss the integrity of missions in the face of the CIA's covert actions. Allegations of the CIA's manipulation, and even infiltration, of missionary ranks now became detailed reports. John Marks, former State Department analyst, decided to investigate. In August 1975, articles began to appear in which Marks was quoted making startling revelations.[2] The stories from Vietnam of a Catholic Relief Services worker who was really a military intelligence officer and of a bishop who was on the CIA payroll were hot enough. But Marks also repeated a story told in 1970 of some $10 million funneled through AID, half of it from the CIA, to finance the anti-Allende work of a Jesuit in Chile, Roger Vekemans. Other CIA money went to a priest in Colombia, to turn a radio literacy campaign among the rural poor into a Cold War propaganda machine. And Catholic nuns, believing they were fighting illiteracy, unwittingly turned over to the CIA details on people's lives taken from census data they collected.[3]

The worst cases came from Bolivia. One Protestant missionary informed on labor unions, rural cooperatives, and the political activities of citizens to the CIA; another provided the CIA with names of people he suspected of being communists. His replacement in 1973 refused to cooperate, but the dictatorship of Hugo Banzer would not take no for an answer. Any missionaries who would not cooperate would join the list of suspects. The Bolivian government's "Plan of Action Against the Church" was leaked to the clergy, reportedly by an alarmed Catholic official in Banzer's own regime. The CIA had pledged to inform on American priests, and in forty-eight hours two CIA officers compiled complete dossiers on certain priests, including the names of their friends and contacts abroad.

Maryknoll Father Charles Curry sent a copy of the Banzer plan to the Senate Intelligence Committee. "Such alleged cooperation has ominous implications," he wrote the chairman, Frank Church, "especially when viewed in the light of widespread and violent repression taking place in Bolivia today."[4]

"Arrests [of priests]," the plan advised, "should be made preferably in the countryside, on deserted streets or late at night."

Big Brother in Bolivia

SIL took another stand in the name of Christ: collaboration. SIL's Donald Burns was working under an AID contract to design and facilitate data collection for CENACO, Banzer's national AID-financed computerized data agency.* Data collected from CENACO was not protected from abuse by Banzer's secret police the way U.S. census data are protected by privacy statutes in the United States.

SIL's official sponsor in La Paz, the Ministry of Education and Culture, set up an Academy of Educational Development with AID money to carry out "sociolinguistic and education research" under Burns's direction. The targeted populations were Quechua Indians who lived in the Andean valleys and Aymará Indians who lived in the Andean highlands. The politically sophisticated project noted the "great disparity in the distribution of the nation's income . . . and its relationship to the growing problem of migration from rural areas either to peripheral slum dwellings in the towns and cities or to neighboring countries, bringing social instability affecting the youth."[5]

This situation, of forced poverty in the Andes causing migration down to overcrowded coastal cities, was nothing new. What was new was how blatantly political intelligence was included in a project involving a top SIL official. The research in rural communities included "linguistic profiles" of "patterns of language usage and preference" with parameters defined by age, sex, and the "social category" of individuals, whether they had a formal education and were parents or children, as well as whether there were "social and political elements" inside or "outside" their community to which they had ties.[6]

Family and community aspirations, including "economic" aspirations, were incorporated into the study, a crucial piece of intelligence for the Banzer regime in developing its ability to gauge the political temperament of Aymará Indian

---

*This was not the first time that Burns worked with AID. Forced out of his Peru base by local students and teachers, Burns had moved to Ecuador to set up the National Bilingual Education Seminar. That seminar featured an AID official who had worked closely with SIL in Vietnam on behalf of the Saigon regime, Charles H. Reed. AID's plan for SIL included the collection of data from students and teachers and the subtle promotion of the military regime's network of local Committees of Family Elders, a network modeled after AID's work in Vietnam. The plan was defeated, however, by Ecuadorian anthropologists who were suspicious of SIL's role. See Charles H. Reed, "Linguaje y Educación Bilingüe en Vietnam," in *Shucniqui Tandanacuy Ishcay Shimipi Yachachingapac, Documento Final*, Primer Seminario Nacional ed Educación Bilingüe del Ecuador, Octubre 15–20, 1973 (Quito: Palacio Legislativo, 1974), pp. 33–38. See also Douglas Williams, ed., *Mission Supplement* (Huntington Beach, Calif.: Wycliffe Bible Translators, Mission Department, January 1976).

miners. Through such "psychology research" and "socio-economic research," the project was designed to "provide a basis for establishing specific policies and designing special rural community development and educational programs for national integration."

The data base on the Indians would then be directly keyed into CENACO's computer through a terminal at the AID-funded academy's offices. The distribution of the data and the resulting analyses would not necessarily be confined to Bolivia. The project envisioned consultation with non-Bolivian linguists outside the academy, "to assure compatibility of this proposed research with worldwide socio-linguistic research efforts." Among those specifically mentioned as offering such foreign expertise were Dr. Ted Haney ("Specialist in Audience Sampling") of the Far Eastern Broadcasting Company of Redwood City, California.[7] Haney, long a promoter of the advance of American Christian Fundamentalism into Southeast Asia, was the world's largest multilingual dispenser of Fundamentalist radio programs. His cofounder of Eastern Broadcast, John Broger, was now the Pentagon's director of information and education.[8]

Bolivia was the unlucky beneficiary of some of the deadliest lessons learned by the CIA in Vietnam. William Colby's Phoenix program had raised police surveillance, interrogations, assassination, and terror to a science in Vietnam's countryside. These techniques were being brought back to Latin America on a more systematic and refined computerized level by the CIA through the Pentagon's military aid program, AID's Office of Public Safety, and, after its abolishment in 1974, the Drug Enforcement Agency (DEA). Stability for investments in the hemispheric "Dollar Zone," promoted by David Rockefeller and other advocates of "free trade," required security from revolts through the melding of the intelligence services of Latin America's military regimes. With the CIA's help, Banzer expanded the powers of his police state. Having barely escaped ruin when a military revolt briefly put him in prison, Banzer was grateful to the CIA for helping him regain power in a counter-coup. He was also grateful to SIL's government liaison officer, David Farah, who visited him in prison to offer counsel, encouragement, and prayer. After Banzer's restoration, Farah was useful in improving the dictatorship's public image. Farah suggested that Banzer hold a presidential prayer breakfast modeled after Washington's.[9] It was this 1975 event that was monitored by SIL children at the Tumi Chucua jungle base.

SIL's base continued to be one of Banzer's favorite vacation haunts even after the CIA-funded Banzer "Plan for Action" against progressive church leaders became known to the public. The intimacy between SIL and Banzer quickly developed into a source of embarrassment when reports surfaced that the CIA used missionaries. Banzer's censorship of the media would not be complete until 1976, when his totalitarian "New Order" took full effect, aided by Bolivia's neo-fascist Falange party.

The implication of computerizing the dictatorships' police investigations was not lost on the National Council of Churches (NCC). The NCC attended IBM's 1975 annual meeting and voted 200,000 shares against sales of IBM computers to Latin American dictatorships that were violating human rights. "The question is not whether they would sell computers to Hitler," said Rev. William Wipfler, "but whether they would sell gas chambers to Hitler. Either way you're giving him weapons." IBM's director of information attempted to defend IBM's sales. "If General Motors sells you a car, and you use it to kill someone, that doesn't make General Motors responsible." Unless, perhaps, General Motors knew you were a killer who used cars as a weapon. "When you know who Hitler is," concluded Wipfler, "you can't pretend you don't know what he's doing with your equipment."[10]

SILers seldom mentioned how their work with AID in Vietnam's Central Highlands might have contributed to the Agency's collection of data on Montagnard tribesmen and the political profiles that were built up by the CIA's Operation Phoenix. Nor did SIL's *Translation* magazine reflect any pondering by SILers in Bolivia over the darker meaning of their organization's subsequent involvement in a scheme to resettle the CIA's Montagnard troops in Bolivia's northern Beni region, where SIL's Tumi Chucua jungle base was located.[11]

From Laos to Bolivia with Love

These Montagnards were the Hmong of Laos, the "Meo" tribes of international headlines. More than 40,000 survivors of missionary "Pop" Buel's and the CIA's secret war had ended their tragic retreat across Laos's mountains by fleeing into neighboring Thailand. Packed into overcrowded refugee camps, they were prey for extortion by corrupt officials or further cross-border adventures against the communist Pathet Lao. Despite their service to the CIA, the only assistance to the Hmong came from U.S. Christian missions and relief agencies. These agencies were coordinated out of the U.S. Embassy in Bangkok of Nixon's new ambassador to Thailand, William Kintner—former CIA officer, former aide to White House special assistant Nelson Rockefeller, former Pentagon official, advocate of using missionaries in counterinsurgency, and a friend of SIL's Robert Schneider.

In early 1975, as the Montagnard revolt spread in the Central Highlands and the Saigon army collapsed, Larry Ward, president of a private Christian relief agency called Food for the Hungry, abandoned his post as special adviser to the Saigon regime on rural minorities and fled to Thailand. Ward subsequently contacted SIL and arranged meetings between Hmong leaders and SIL in Bolivia. Ward's contact in Washington was Cleo Shook, a zealous Fundamentalist and associate director of AID's Office of Private and Voluntary Cooperation, the same office Cam had worked with. Shook's access to more than $240 million in foreign-aid funds resulted in cash grants to many Christian missionary groups that were doing relief work abroad, including those in Thailand.[12] Some of that money was targeted for the relocation of the Hmong to Bolivia, where SIL's David Farah helped coordinate the project. Farah saw no problem with the fact that Indians already lived in the Beni region, where the Banzer regime designated more than 37,000 acres for the Hmong. From his point of view, the Hmong's "facial characteristics would fit in very well with the American Indian of the Amazon basin."[13]

Left unanswered was the question of health. The Hmong, a mountainous people, were suffering from climatic adjustments and malaria in the Thai lowlands; the Amazon would be even worse. What they would grow in the fragile Amazon soil also was not adequately addressed, especially for a people whose only cash crop for decades had been opium. Finally, there was the larger question of why the Banzer regime, which encouraged birth control among the Indians, who made up 70 percent of Bolivia's population, was suddenly concerned about remedying Bolivia's newfound "population deficit" with foreign refugees.

Part of the answer may have been the Hmong's recent history as the CIA's largest fighting army. Isolated in a strange land, the Hmong would be dependent on the Banzer regime for survival. They would be susceptible once again to manipulation as a counterinsurgency force against politically rebellious Indian miners or a guerrilla movement in Beni, which had been Che Guevara's first choice for a guerrilla-training base. For much the same reason, Banzer was also considering another resettlement colony in Beni for Germans who were migrating from Southwest Africa (now Namibia).

There were already about 300,000 Bolivians of German descent, who often "adopted" Indian *criadas* (servants)—mostly girls—into the household to serve as virtual slaves. Slavery extended into the fields of estates as well.[14] Labor costs were one factor that four South African businessmen considered when they visited Bolivia in 1976: Indian labor could replace African labor. As one South African Boer who was considering immigration put it after visiting Bolivia, "Obviously, we are not altogether happy with the racial situation over there [in Bolivia]. I do not foresee any real problems, however, because, like us, they practice discrimination. The whole economy is ruled by a small minority of white immigrants from Europe who keep the Spanish and the local Indians well and truly in their place. The only difference is that they do it quietly and without advertising it to the outside world. From their point of view, white South Africans will feel very much at home there."[15]

THE BANZER PLAN FOR BOLIVIA'S OIL

A key reason for Banzer's new immigration policy was the concern among Santa Cruz's and La Paz's upper classes that the lands east of the Andes should be occupied by Bolivia before Brazilian settlers made them a de facto part of their own homeland. Banzer's regime emphasized Bolivia's need for commercial farmers in the virgin lands to expand agricultural production and to reduce the cost of importing expensive food. This was the ostensible reason for the preparation of a new immigration law. Decreed in January 1976, it offered fifty acres, a house, loans, technical support, and citizenship to every immigrant who stayed in Bolivia on the land for only one year. Larger concessions of land and support were available to those who set up cattle ranches. But the biggest dreams were of the potential mineral riches.

And here, as throughout the entire Amazon basin, oil carried away the most expansive imaginations. Banzer's German colony in Santa Cruz had seen what oil could buy. The city now hosted a new Holiday Inn for the baseball-capped American oilmen. The hope was that the field south of Santa Cruz might extend north of it as well, into the Beni.

Already, geologists employed by Union Oil of California were prowling through the eastern jungles in search of oil. Those from Texaco and Getty Oil were there, too, exploring a 2.59-million acre concession.[16] Banzer was finishing construction of a highway from La Paz through the jungles and pampean homelands of some 25,000 Movima and Mojo Indians to Trinidad, Beni's largest town. Here in the Beni River Basin, cattle herds as large as 17,000 head grazed on the pampas, controlled by large landowners who used Banzer's so-called agrarian reform to consolidate their holdings and hence to pauperize the Indians.[17] In the name of protecting Indian land rights, SIL lobbied La Paz and Washington to launch "leadership training" courses for its Indian students with Banzer's blessings and $100,000 from AID.

The program's community development projects included small-scale entrepreneurial pursuits like beekeeping and shopkeeping, the development of a client Protestant merchant class that would replace traditional tribal authority, and the building of airstrips and roads to hurry the passage of some 120,000 Amazonian Indians into Banzer's glorious "national integration." Funded by another $5 million from AID to Banzer's regime, SIL doubled the number of bilingual teachers, putting forty-five out of fifty on government salaries. SIL leaders were appreciative. "Banzer is a moral man," exclaimed Bolivia branch director Ronald D. Olson in 1976[18]—only a few months after Banzer's predecessor, former president Juan Torres, was assassinated in Argentina; Banzer's fellow conspirator in the 1971 coup, Colonel Andrés Selich, who had helped hunt down Che Guevara, died during an "interrogation" by Banzer's police; scores of Indian miners had been killed by Banzer's army during a strike, hundreds more had been imprisoned, over 50 of those exiled by Banzer, joining some 5,000 others in exile; and the Ayoreo and other Indians, despite the protest of Catholic priests, were being recruited to work in the Beni region (where SIL's Tumi Chucua base was located) on ranches and plantations that La Paz's daily *Excelsior* would later describe as "slave camps."[19]

But anthropologists were unhappy with SIL's "occupation" of the tribes. By forbidding converts to smoke, drink, and participate in non-Protestant religious festivals, the missionaries were excluding Indians from "the civic life of their communities," argued anthropologist Jürgen Riester. "Since their prohibition decreases their success among village Indians, the Protestants concentrate their main efforts on the conversion of native groups still living a traditional cultural life. Among these groups they generally implement a policy of isolation [working] . . . against the participation of the Indians in Bolivian society. Ideologically motivated, they produce in their converts a degree of alienation from the national society which is even more effective than a state of total isolation."[20]

As news of the CIA's use of missionaries reached the media in Latin America, SIL's collaboration with rightist regimes and the favors it received from AID made it a natural target for suspicions of collaboration with the CIA, too. These charges lacked proof. Nevertheless, many of those who raised the charges earnestly believed that there was some link between SIL and U.S. counterinsurgency programs, and more cynical nationalists of both the Right and Left hoped that the rules of perception in politics would carry the day.

They almost did. The international storm over the possible trans-Atlantic migration of apartheid converged in Bolivia, casting a dark cloud over the trans-Pacific migration of a defeated CIA tribal army. SIL's involvement in the exodus from Thailand to Bolivia was used to claim that SIL was involved in the plans to settle supporters of apartheid from southern Africa in Bolivia as well. Repeated denials by SIL's South Africa branch[21] only seemed to confirm the charge, by affirming the all-white branch's very existence in the heartland of apartheid. Was that not proof enough?

Clearly, it was not. But SIL was condemned by its very success. For a number of years, the Wycliffe Bible Translators had been the Protestant mission agency with the largest number of personnel (more than 2,500), although it was only seventh in reported income ($16 million). The difference was attributed to the low overhead of its translators' expenses; another factor was the hardware it received from AID and other government agencies, which entered SIL's books as undervalued discounted assets for the organization and JAARS, not income for its translators. U.S. government (AID) support was public record for those who took the time to look.

SIL officials' emphasis on the support given by local churches to its translators only heightened suspicions that SIL had something to hide. SIL's ownership of surplus U.S. military hardware was obvious to investigators, and SIL's effort to downplay the role of Caesar to broadcast the role of God spread the contagion of cynicism over the genuine motives of most of SIL's missionaries. An SIL official who called AID's gift of seven Hiller H-23 helicopters and the Pentagon's gift of matching spare parts a "miracle" appeared incredible to those who were not familiar with the simple political backgrounds of most of SIL's recruits.[22]

Cleo Shook resented and denied the accusation of SIL's collaboration with the CIA. The charges had been "trumped up from the opposition," he insisted. The major culprits were "anthropological scholars who say 'Don't disturb the natives.' There is a professional quarrel among those circles." Food for the Hungry's Larry Ward was equally indignant. SIL's Bolivia branch official David Farah only offered advice and "opened doors," he said.[23]

Farah himself had earlier gone so far as to denounce the CIA's efforts to recruit Bible translators. In January 1976, while serving as SIL's government liaison officer in Washington, D.C., he inadvertently admitted that SIL's top officials had been contacted by the CIA, but he denied any cooperation by SIL, at least with respect to recruiting linguists. "We have always refused to assist when CIA agents have been sent to our training camp at the various universities where we have training centers, especially at Norman, Oklahoma," he said.[24]

Some Bolivians were not convinced. After Food for the Hungry's bus was stoned in Bolivia, Ward had second thoughts about expanding the resettlement of the Hmong in Bolivia beyond the 550 who were initially scheduled to be brought over. "We're certainly ready to move on and help the Indians. If there's a place on the face of the earth better than Bolivia, then we'll go there."[25]

Because of revelations about the CIA's covert operations, it was becoming difficult for past CIA collaborators to go anywhere. The global scope of such activities, with their potential for counterinsurgency applications, invited charges against SIL, whose very success in expanding abroad with U.S. and local government (and often military) grants and contracts made its conservative missionaries targets of criticism from every political direction. In Peru alone, in a single four-week period in 1975, SIL was the subject of forty-four critical editorials and articles.[26]

Kissinger's State Department to the Rescue

Back in Waxhaw, North Carolina, at JAARS's growing base, SIL's retired general director, Cam Townsend, watched with dismay as the accusations seemed to snowball from one country to the next. In Washington, where SIL's office maintained liaison with government officials, the Kissinger State Department kept a wary eye on the anti-SIL campaigns, too.

In Colombia, criticism of SIL was particularly harsh, with charges ranging from the extreme (drug smuggling and uranium mining) to the serious (kidnapping Indian children and elders for extended fund-raising tours in the United States) to an approximation of reality (destroying the Indians' cultural values, creating religious divisions within Indian communities, deceiving the government about its evangelical goals, and indoctrinating Indians with loyalty to the United States).

In June 1975, an official report on the government's investigation of the charges was published. Although no evidence was found to support the more serious charges, linguists and anthropologists across Colombia called for the termination of SIL's contract, which was up for renewal. President Alfonso López Michelsen decided to preempt an investigation of SIL by the Colombian Congress.

His strategy was the same as that of the Ford administration, which had tried to preempt a U.S. congressional investigation of the CIA by appointing the Rockefeller Commission. López Michelsen, whose party, the Revolutionary Liberal Movement, was supported by the CIA's Bogotá station,[27] took control of SIL's fate with a brilliant tactic: Rather than wait for the results of a commission's investigation, he pledged outright nationalization of SIL's bilingual programs.

López Michelsen's co-optative tactic was admired by Kissinger's new ambassador, Viron Vaky. The appointment of Vaky, a top State Department expert on Latin America, to the U.S. Embassy in Bogotá indicated the importance that Kissinger placed on Colombia in his Latin American strategy. Vaky had helped oversee the American counterinsurgency buildup in Alberto Lleras Camargo's Colombia and in Guatemala during the 1960s. As Kissinger's top aide on Latin America in the National Security Council, Vaky had been involved in Kissinger's 1970 effort to stop Chile's President-elect Allende from taking office, acting, according to Nixon aide Charles Colson, as Kissinger's liaison to ITT chairman Harold Geneen when Geneen was "bragging about all the money he had given to the Agency."[28] Vaky arrived in Bogotá in 1974. López Michelsen's party, the Revolutionary Liberal Movement, which was backed by the Bogotá CIA station,[29] had taken over just as the SIL controversy was heating up over the Guajibo Indian scandal, and Vaky was impressed with how López was preventing it from becoming a major political crisis.

"The Lopez approach," Vaky cabled Kissinger, "gives the appearance of a unilateral, GOC [Government of Colombia] decision, while in effect implementing the basic terms of the long-standing proposal for a new government agreement with the SIL. The President's action will, we believe, eventually prove an effective way of removing the troublesome SIL question from the public eye."[30]

Vaky's concern was for SIL's survival as an American presence in Colombia. SIL's expulsion would damage the United States' reputation and the U.S. Embassy's ability to gather intelligence on Colombia's hinterlands.

SIL was in contact with the U.S. Embassy. An SIL spokesman, noted Vaky, "pointed out that Lopez set no time limit for the Colombian take-over. . . . In addition . . . Cornelio Reyes said that he would speak on behalf of the SIL programs."[31]

Cornelio Reyes, Lopez's interior minister, was a large landowner in the Planas region of the Guajibo Indians, near where exploration by American oil companies was taking place. He had also backed landlords in the fertile Cauca valley, where Indians who were active in the Regional Indian Council of the Cauca (CRIC), including those who were training their own bilingual teachers and organizing mass passive resistance to the theft of Indian lands, were being arrested, tortured, and murdered. Now Reyes was suddenly posing as the champion of Indian bilingual education—at least as carried out by SIL. He agreed with Cam's translators that "outside agitators" could be found everywhere there were "Indian problems." To SIL, these "agitators" were the agents of Satan. To Reyes, they were communists. The distinction blurred.

In November, besieged by congressional critics, SIL's Colombia branch called for help from beyond the U.S. Embassy. It turned to the man who had led SIL's advance to Lomalinda out of donated Standard Oil trailers and who had been "retired" from the field only four years earlier.

Cam to the Rescue

Cam Townsend flew into Bogotá and threw himself into organizing SIL's defense with the energy of a much younger man. Needed as more than just a legend, he found that he still had the old skills and hard drive. He worked the halls of government like a pro from Capitol Hill, making discreet calls on high officials, marshaling his old allies, and using whatever help Vaky's embassy could provide. When a congressman displayed U.S. military maps designating the Macarena Mountains as a security zone and charged that a secret U.S. base existed there equipped with missiles, Colombia's defense minister did a turn for the Lord. A former critic of SIL's alleged clandestine operations, he was now ready to defend SIL and publicly dismissed the claims as fabrications.

Ambassador Vaky cabled Kissinger with reassurances that "Colombianization . . . is essentially what the SIL has proposed for the new contract. The López move may, accordingly, provide an arrangement satisfactory to both parties while providing an appearance of [government] action that should placate most SIL critics here."[32]

The same was true in Peru, where the battle in Colombia was carefully monitored by SIL's friends and foes. "The reported [expulsion from Colombia] will complicate the scheduled February renewal of SIL's contract," U.S. Ambassador Robert Dean cabled Kissinger.[33] Dean was another old hand in intelligence circles, having worked closely with the CIA and the Pentagon on a number of missions in the past, including the 1964 coup in Brazil.[34] Now Dean was in volatile Peru, where SIL was not above criticism. SIL's Fundamentalists did not bring Peruvians into the organization or its decision-making process, reported anthropologist Stefano Varese of the Ministry of Agriculture in the government of Juan Velasco Alvarado.[35] Peruvian linguists and anthropologists charged that government dependence on SIL for bilingual education programs was not healthy for Latin America or Indians.[36] Moreover, SIL made arbitrary interventions in tribal affairs, entering tribes without permission and flying JAARS planes without regard for national borders.

Negotiations over SIL seemed to be going the way of the nationalization of Standard Oil, until a military coup came to the rescue once again.

President Velasco's revolution had been bankrupted by his trans-Andean

YARINACOCHA JUNGLE BASE
Summer Institute of Linguistics
Peru (1976)

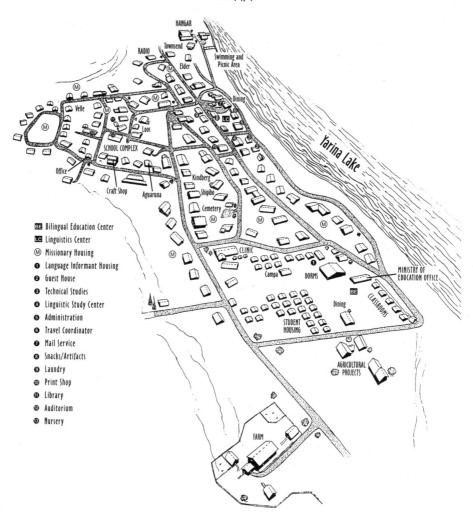

Bilingual Education Center
Linguistics Center
Missionary Housing
1 Language Informant Housing
2 Guest House
3 Technical Studies
4 Linguistic Study Center
5 Administration
6 Travel Coordinator
7 Mail Service
8 Snacks/Artifacts
9 Laundry
10 Print Shop
11 Library
12 Auditorium
13 Nursery

HANGAR
RADIO
Townsend
Elder
Swimming and
Picnic Area
Dining
Velle
Loos
SCHOOL COMPLEX
Office
Craft Shop
Aguaruna
Kindberg
Shipibo
Cemetery
CLINIC
Campa
DORMS
MINISTRY OF
EDUCATION OFFICE
CLASSROOMS
Dining
STUDENT
HOUSING
AGRICULTURAL
PROJECTS
FARM

Yarina Lake

pipeline to Amazonian oil fields that every American company but Armand Hammer's Occidental Petroleum had trouble finding. Forced out of office by his fellow officers in 1975, Velasco was replaced by a more conservative general, Francisco Morales Bermudez. The new president proved more amenable to Kissinger's regional designs, including the reversal of Velasco's nationalizations and agrarian reforms and acceptance of World Bank president Robert McNamara's demands for tightening already short Peruvian belts. In the midst of this reversal, Ambassador Dean paid his respects to SIL's Yarinacocha base. He discussed the renewal of contracts and applauded Cam Townsend at a banquet in his honor. Cam pushed for Peru's renewal of its contract with SIL before flying on to Bogotá to do the same there. In Colombia, he hosed down the last embers with an endorsement by López's education minister, Llanos landowner Hernando Duran Dusan.

Cam flew back to the United States to find that the CIA's use of missionaries had escalated into a major international scandal. The publicizing of Banzer's Plan of Action had prompted an ad hoc coalition of Protestant and Catholic missionaries to draft a suggested "Code of Ethics and Action" on involvement with the CIA. This code of ethics inspired Senator Mark Hatfield, a supporter of Protestant overseas missions in the past (including SIL), to ask William Colby to halt the CIA's use of missionaries. Colby rejected Hatfield's request. "I believe it would be neither necessary nor appropriate to bar any connection between CIA and the clergy and the churches." Colby wrote:

> In many countries of the world representatives of the clergy, foreign and local, play a significant role and can be of assistance to the United States through CIA with no reflection upon their integrity nor their mission. . . . Thus, I believe that any sweeping prohibition such as you suggest would be a mistake and impose a handicap on this Agency which would reduce its future effectiveness to a degree not warranted by the real facts of the situation.[37]

Hatfield then wrote President Ford, noting reports of the CIA's use of missionaries in Chile and in Mozambique and Angola. In the latter country, the chief of the CIA task force that was using tribal differences to foster a civil war was actually posing as a missionary.

If legislation was needed to put a stop to this practice, Hatfield was prepared to introduce it, he warned Ford. The integrity of American religious missions was not the only thing being threatened; missionaries' lives were at stake. Efforts to secure the release of missionaries who had been captured in Vietnam were being answered with charges that the missionaries were involved with the CIA.

THE BANMETHUOT FOURTEEN

SIL translators Jim and Carolyn Miller had been among the missionaries who were captured when the Saigon regime collapsed in April 1975. In fact, they had been caught at the beginning of the collapse, in March, when the CIA's Montagnard troops in the Central Highlands once again revolted against Saigon's rule. The Millers had been working with the same Brú tribe that the CIA used in cross-border attacks against North Vietnamese supply lines along the Ho Chi Minh Trail in neighboring Laos. When the Vietnamese struck back against the CIA base in the Brú town of Khe Sanh during the 1968 Tet Offensive, the Millers barely escaped.

In 1974, they had followed Brú refugees when they were relocated by the CIA to Banmethuot, a large town in the Central Highlands. It was here, a center of CIA activity among the Radê who dominated the area, that SIL and the Christian and Missionary Alliance (C&MA) had suffered severe losses during the Tet Offensive. Despite the prominence of the missionary compound near the Vietnamese army base and the fact that it had been the site of most of the deaths of missionaries during Tet, the Millers moved into a C&MA house there. As in 1968, when the missionaries were captured with a Radê-speaking AID official, the Millers took refuge from the fighting in the house of the local AID official, Paul Struharik, not knowing that the house had previously been occupied by the CIA.[38] Here, they found themselves with Jay Scarborough, a visiting member of the International Volunteer Service, and Enrique Tolentino, a Filipino community development specialist working with AID under the CIA-sponsored Operation Brotherhood. Peter Whitlock, an Australian who had just arrived from Chiang Mai, Thailand (where he had been setting up tribal-language radio broadcasts), was also with them. Struharik was frantically trying to contact the CIA's Air America with the missionaries' radio using a code name: "Any Air America station. Any Air American station. This is Foxtrot. This is Foxtrot."[39]

The presence of such AID-linked Americans among them, and the fact that the missionary International Voluntary Service in Vietnam and Laos was funded entirely by the U.S. government,[40] did not help the Millers convince the Vietnamese Communists that they were not CIA agents. The CIA had left officers and agents behind as "sheep-dipped" civilians when the Kissinger–Le Duc Tho cease-fire was finally signed in 1973, and Struharik suspected that his radio appeals had been monitored. "We know there are 24,000 American military men in Vietnam masquerading as civilians," was one of the first statements the Millers heard from their captors.[41]

Senator Hatfield's concerns were based on such realities. Jerry Ford was guided by the concern of Director Colby and probably other members of the National Security Council that the CIA should have access to missionaries' knowledge and contacts.

On November 5, Ford had his White House counsel, Philip Buchen, respond to Hatfield. Buchen argued that "the President does not feel it would be wise at present to prohibit the CIA from having any connection with the clergy. Clergymen throughout the world are often valuable sources of intelligence and many clergymen, motivated solely by patriotism, voluntarily and willingly aid the government by providing information of intelligence value."[42]

For all his legal experience, Buchen carelessly had conceded that the CIA's use of missionaries was standard procedure. That admission confirmed Hatfield's worst fears, and Ford's intransigence forced him to go public in the next month. By then, it was already all over for Colby. Rockefeller and Kissinger had been upset with Colby's candor early in the year before congressional committees. By sacrificing the CIA director, Ford was able to placate the Angleton Counter-Intelligence wing in the CIA and the Rockefeller wing of his party, while offering outraged clergy, congressional critics, the press, and the public a scapegoat for the CIA's abuses.

To replace Colby, Ford appointed a man close to Rockefeller's own views, Connecticut-Yankee-turned-Texan George Bush, former congressman and current ambassador to China (and the son of a prominent Wall Street investment banker and former United States senator). Bush was a presidential contender, but his appointment as the nation's top sleuth when the CIA's reputation was at an all-time low effectively killed his chances in 1976.[43]

SIL officials showed no displeasure at Ford's sacking of Colby. Colby's admission and defense of the CIA's use of missionaries could have jeopardized lives, including the Millers'. During interrogation in Hanoi, Paul Struharik had been pressured to state that the missionaries had collaborated with him in intelligence work. "They tried to get me to admit that the missionaries in Banmethuot were an intelligence gathering network which reported to me," he told the Millers. "They couldn't believe that we never met socially and that I didn't go to your houses or you to mine. I gave them a little talk on difference in life styles, and I think that helped them to understand."[44]

It did. The missionaries' sincerity about wanting to bring the Bible to tribes won over Hanoi's officials. After almost eight months in captivity, the "Banmethuot Fourteen," including Struharik and Tolentino, were going home. Exchanging gifts with the staff and commander of the prisoner-of-war camp, they were urged to "give a true report of what you have seen and experienced."[45]

The Millers and their friends were flown first to Vientiane, Laos, and then to Bangkok, Thailand, for a press conference and an interview with Far Eastern Broadcasting's Manila correspondent. After a short rest, they flew to the Philippines for debriefing by SIL officials and a reunion in Muslim Mindanao with the displaced Vietnam branch. Their compatriots were now calling themselves the Mainland Southeast Asia Branch, dreaming of "an expanded ministry." But that would not happen.

Laos remained closed to them. Nepal was considering SIL's expulsion for alleged religious conversions and "divisive" vernacular translations. Cambodia's Lon Nol government had fallen to the Khmer Rouge, who hated the Communist victors in Vietnam almost as much as they hated the Americans and their

Cambodian urban collaborators. Burma was still nervous about the CIA's use of tribes and the Nationalist Chinese troops in the separatist Shan states in the north, and negotiations with Thailand would not improve until the democracy was again overthrown by the military in 1977.

Most of SIL's Vietnam veterans ended up not in mainland Asia, but in Sabah, the Malaysian northern half of Borneo. Sabah was now open to missionaries and oil companies, which would soon be drilling offshore west of Mount Kinabalu.

The Lord's work among the Montagnards remained stymied, notwithstanding the transmission of SIL-translated gospels to the lost highlands by Far Eastern Broadcasting. Overall, by early 1976, some SILers had concluded that the CIA's use of missionaries had closed more doors for the Lord than it opened.

At SIL's Washington office, David Farah joined the chorus of church officials backing Senator Hatfield's legislation that would bar the CIA's contact with missionaries.[46] "I feel the bill has many aspects in it that would help us to be free from the stigma of the CIA," he said. "This degrades the entire profession of missionaries and it makes us all suspect because of the actions of a few. The missionaries that I have heard were operating have left their missions and their mission boards, which I think is the only honorable thing to do. I believe if they want to get into this type of cloak and dagger operation, they should do it under another guise. I believe the clergy should be free from this type of infiltration."[47]

In Waxhaw, North Carolina, Cam Townsend kept his silence. He was loyal to the organization he had founded.

46

THE BETRAYAL

DOMESTIC VIOLENCES

Although Gerald Ford had testified during his own confirmation hearings for the vice presidency in late 1973 that he would not run for reelection if he succeeded Nixon, by 1975, Ford's desire for election in his own right had grown. Nelson watched this development with concern. He had expected to succeed Ford; now he was not sure Ford would not bend to pressure from the right wing of the Republican party and seek a running mate more to their liking. Nelson knew that California's Ronald Reagan was busy building a challenge in the Bible Belt. However, he underestimated Reagan, considering him a "lightweight." Ford's political advisers took Reagan more seriously.

In the summer, Nelson took a swing through the South. He believed he was stronger there. Except with African Americans, he was wrong. Most white southern Democrats remembered Nelson's opposition to segregation and his friendship with Martin Luther King, Jr. If they had to choose between Rockefeller or even Ford and a fellow "born-again" Baptist like Jimmy Carter, the most conservative of the 1976 Democratic presidential candidates, there was really no contest. African Americans would also go for Carter, perhaps because they were attracted by his Baptist background and his pledge of an honest, caring government backed by a Democratic Congress that could pass the kind of legislation that Ford, a fiscal conservative, would never introduce.

Southern Republicans were not a base for Nelson, either. Many of them were of the Nixon variety. They had taken their small-town values to the booming sub-urbs of the New South's cheap-wage industrialization. They looked to business, not Nelson's liberal union friends, for progress and to Billy Graham for spiritual inspiration, not the Rockefeller-backed Union Theological Seminary and Riverside Church's liberal antiwar pastor, Dr. William Sloane Coffin.

Nelson had encountered this stone wall in Alabama, the home state of his "good friend" George Wallace. He found the same chilly reception in Dallas when he lunched with corporate bigwigs like Texas International executives Pat Haggerty and John Erik Johnson (the former mayor who had given William Cameron Townsend the key to the city), computer magnate Ross Perot, and devel-oper Trammel Crow. He thought he had friends here. When he had still been gov-ernor, he gave Perot a big contract to process New York's welfare rolls, even though Perot was not the low bidder. Crow was a business partner of his brothers Winthrop and David. His family owned more than $17 million worth of Texas Instruments stock.[1] He even bought 6,000 acres next to the Klebergs' King Ranch in Texas "for family outings" and Thanksgiving dinners.

But it did no good. What was sweeping the South and Southwest after the defeat in Vietnam and Nixon's fall was stronger than anything Nelson could stop: a profound feeling radiating out of the region's two strongest cultural forces—the socially conservative churches and military bases—that an Apocalyptic crisis was at hand.

Nelson left the South defeated. One South Carolina Republican summed up his achievement: "You might say he changed some of our minds from 'hell no' to just plain 'no.'"[2]

Ford had looked on with growing consternation as Reagan appealed to the Republican southern delegates. Anticipating this move by Reagan and taking Ford at his word that he would not seek election in 1976, Nelson had courted Barry Goldwater, assuring the 1964 Republican standard bearer of his basic conser-vatism. Goldwater was convinced: "Rocky and I see more eye to eye on foreign policy than I and Ford do," he said. "I think [Rockefeller] makes me look like a dove, to tell you the truth."[3]

Nelson was trying to use the Ford White House to gain the limelight. Ford had inadvertently given him the vehicle for achieving his ambition: oversight of the Domestic Council, an advisory organization that was the domestic equiva-lent of the foreign affairs-oriented National Security Council. Given Ford's lack of experience in executive administration, Nelson thought he would end up in charge of the government. "I'm going to run the White House," he said.[4]

But Nelson underestimated the men Ford had around him. One of the first conflicts was over Nelson's efforts to restore the office of the president's science adviser, which had been terminated by Nixon. This office had national-security implications that were tied to the sensitive issues of software for aerial guidance systems and other advanced computer technology, satellite communications and aerial photography, sea mining, the procurement of energy resources, and the development of nuclear weapons. It also had domestic implications, involving environmental and health regulations, artificial intelligence (computer technology), communications systems, and the increasingly lucrative field of biomedical technology.

The structure of the science adviser's office was important for it to work, and Nelson submitted his recommendations to Ford. His recommendations soon came back through the Domestic Council in altered form, as only one of three options for the president and dubbed "the Kennedy plan" to discredit it with Ford. Nelson knew who was blocking him: Donald Rumsfeld, Al Haig's replacement as White House chief of staff.

After a sharp exchange, Nelson took the proposal back to the Domestic Council, having redrafted it in option form that enhanced his own position. Three months later, Ford adopted the proposal—as a recommendation to Congress that carried Ford's, not Nelson's, name. Although that was a normal practice, it was difficult for Nelson Rockefeller to swallow.

Those three months gave Rumsfeld time to beat back Nelson's attempt to control the Domestic Council. Nelson tried and failed to fire two of Rumsfeld's allies. Worse, the council's executive director, James Cannon, who had been one of Nelson's most trusted aides in New York, deferred to Rumsfeld's leadership.

Desperate, Nelson turned to the president. His usefulness in the council was over, he warned Ford. But the president would not intervene. Rumsfeld remained in control of the staff.

Nelson then tried an end run. He set tasks for the council much like he had with the Rockefeller panels and the Commission on Critical Choices: Groups of experts worked on various problems and drafted recommendations for policies. Nelson decided to take the council on the road for a well-publicized series of town meetings around the country. Television and radio gave him publicity as an unusually active vice president grappling with the nation's problems. "It was a beautifully organized operation," he said.[5]

He pressed on in other fronts, as well. From the CIA hearings, Nelson produced a verbatim transcript, a digest, and a book of policy recommendations. He also rushed to print Edward Teller's energy report to the Commission on Critical Choices a full two years before the commission's own multivolume report would be released.

Teller's report left little doubt that the vice president's concerns over domestic issues went beyond the concerns of a political officeholder. As he did in South America, Nelson was carefully monitoring the development of North American energy policies covering oil, gas, uranium, and such hydroelectric projects as the James Bay dams on Cree Indian land in Quebec. And as with Latin America, Nelson's vision of an energy policy ran smack into opposition from indigenous forces.

Teller's report was really a blueprint for Nelson's energy program. Teller compared the threat OPEC posed to American business's access to oil with that posed by the Axis powers during World War II. Teller's proposals, which were adopted by Ford, replaced Nixon's voluntary conservation and price controls with deregulation of prices for natural gas moving interstate. The objective was to stimulate gas and oil production, increase nuclear power, and promote the strip-mining of coal. It also had the taxpayer share the oil companies' financial expenses for exploration and research.

One month after Nelson released Teller's report, 3,000 National Guardsmen occupied the Black Hills in South Dakota, where uranium exploration had reached the lands of the Sioux. Purportedly there for "maneuvers," the Guardsmen were followed by sixty FBI agents, who poured into the vicinity of the nearby Sioux Pine Ridge reservation. The following month, Richard Wilson, the tribal council chairman, signed away one-eighth of the reservation—mostly Black Hills land claims—to the National Park Service, aggravating a tense situation. The reservation had already been bloodied by murders of American Indian Movement (AIM) supporters following AIM member Russell Means's 1974 defeat by Wilson in an election replete with so many irregularities that the U.S. Civil Rights Commission had recommended, futilely, a new election. Then came the trials of AIM leaders for Wounded Knee, including a riot in the courtroom involving police beatings when the judge ordered the room cleared after spectators (including Lutheran bishops) refused to stand as he entered.

By June 26, 1975, as Wilson signed away 800,000 acres, the Tennessee Valley Authority (TVA) had drilled 6,000 test holes throughout 65,000 acres of recently leased land in the Black Hills, and had located an estimated five to six million pounds of uranium.[6]

That same day, an FBI attempt to carry out a warrantless arrest of one of Wilson's opponents triggered a shoot-out that left two agents and one Indian dead, 200 Guardsmen placed on alert, and what the chairman of the Civil Rights Commission later characterized as "a full-scale military-type invasion of the reservation" by 170 agents using armored personnel carriers, helicopters, and M-16 rifles. The FBI's investigation of the shooting turned into a nationwide dragnet of suspected AIM activists. A reign of terror gripped the 4,000-square-mile reservation of the Oglala Lakota Sioux nation as federal and state agencies put into effect coordinated "sweeps" through the reservation, similar to the Pentagon's "garden plot" domestic counterinsurgency plan effected two years before at Wounded Knee.[7] As vice president and vice chairman of the Domestic Council, Nelson shared responsibility in the administration's overseeing of the FBI's activities against AIM.

In September, Nelson Rockefeller came as close as he ever would to becoming president. Only two feet from President Ford in Sacramento, California, Lynette "Squeaky" Fromm, a member of the murderous Charles Manson gang, was arrested carrying a loaded Colt .45 she intended to use to kill the president. Nelson was in New York to make speeches when he suddenly found Secret Service agents hustling him out of reach of the public. "What is the Manson gang?" Nelson asked as his plane streaked back to Washington.* Nothing seemed to break his confident stride. Nothing, that is, until the fateful day in the Oval Office when President Ford decided to shift direction to placate the right wing of his party.

BENDING TO BIBLES

In late October, Nelson Rockefeller entered the Oval Office for his regular private meeting with the president. Nelson had suggested these weekly consultations when he took office. He did not need them to gain access to Ford; the president's door was always open to him, he said. He needed the meetings to offer the president his frank opinions about the nation and the world. Ford, he believed, valued their sessions. Now he learned otherwise.

Ford was feeling the heat. He was slipping badly in the polls, and the Right was putting the blame on Rockefeller, charging that his liberal image was losing the South's Bible Belt for Ford. Reagan, who was wooing the South, would be better for the ticket, they argued.

"I have been talking with my political advisers," Ford said after a long silence, "and I think it would be, as much as personally I feel badly about it, it would be better if you were not on the ticket and if you would withdraw."

If Nelson was shocked, he did not show it. "Fine," he said quietly. "I will write you a letter."

Ford said that would be wonderful.[8]

Nelson flew to Pocantico for the weekend. He needed the distance from Washington to put his political life into perspective. One thing was clear, however. The looming presence of the Republican right wing was edging him off center stage.

On Sunday, Nelson received a phone call. The president was on the line from Jacksonville, Florida. Was Ford reconsidering?

"Do you think you could have that letter by Monday?" Ford asked. "I have got some other changes I am making and the story has leaked."

"Well, of course it would leak," Nelson later told Ford speechwriter Robert Hartmann, "because those who were promoting it were bound to leak it fearing he might change his mind."[9]

Nelson called a press conference to announce his withdrawal from the ticket. Not elegant dinners, or wealth, or energy programs, or Domestic Council town meetings, or Commissions on Critical Choices or the CIA, or courting the South,

*There would be four other arrests of would-be assassins of Ford and Rockefeller in the next three months.

or even Barry Goldwater could have prevented this day. All he could do was pre-serve his dignity by maintaining control over at least the words of his own resignation letter, in exchange for agreeing to save Ford and himself embarrassment.

"The decision by Vice President Rockefeller was a decision on his own," Ford told the press. "Under no circumstances was it a request by me. It was a decision by him."[10]

After a decent but short interval, Ford carried out his purge of Rockefeller power from the Cabinet. Henry Kissinger was fired as national security adviser, James Schlesinger was fired as defense secretary, and William Colby was fired as CIA director, as Nelson and Kissinger had desired; but this action, too, involved a deft political weakening of another Rockefeller like-thinker, George Bush, by appointing him head of the scandal-ridden spy agency.

Kissinger accepted the coup on one condition: His aide, Brent Scowcroft, would have to be named his successor. Otherwise, he would resign as secretary of state, too.[11] Ford agreed.

Nelson would always claim that his removal from the 1976 Republican ticket was a deliberate effort to sabotage Gerald Ford's presidency. He saw Rumsfeld leading the Nixon wing and allying it with the Far Right, backing Reagan to stop the Rockefeller wing of the party and bring down Ford in the process. Rumsfeld's move to the Pentagon to take Schlesinger's place as defense secretary would not remove his influence on the White House; Rumsfeld kept in daily touch with his successor as White House chief of staff, Dick Cheney. The bureaucratic repression of Nelson's initiatives remained in force. Nelson's bound volume of policy recommendations from the Domestic Council, including welfare reform and national health insurance, succumbed to a conservative budget. Nelson had hoped Ford might use them to launch the 1976 campaign; instead, they gathered dust.

So Nelson pressed on the national security front. If he could not assert his leadership—and his right to be Ford's running mate—in domestic affairs, he would surely shine in foreign policy. In the National Security Council, where he was vice chairman, Nelson raised the existence of the Soviet navy to the level of an imminent threat to ocean and Caribbean shipping lanes for American oil companies. He implied that the Soviets had plans for a classic naval confrontation. Nelson posed the issue on elevated terms, moving it beyond the terms of corporate access to oil and other world resources, to the higher realm of an ideal that could rally the American people: "freedom of the seas." The sense of being heir to the British Empire and needing access to oil was never far from Nelson's mind. He later explained:

> In our studies on the Commission on Critical Choices, we came to the conclusion that the freedom of the seas . . . which the British preserved for how many hundreds of years, and which we preserved . . . was a position which could be chal-

lenged by the Soviet Navy's development. . . . This was a very serious matter for the future, particularly as we were becoming increasingly dependent on the foreign imports of oil and strategic materials.[12]

Nelson used this point to pressure Rumsfeld as Defense Secretary at National Security Council meetings. "I would speak, and speak very frankly . . . where I did not think he [President Ford] was being properly served."[13] Nelson wanted increased expenditures for naval arms.

He also wanted deeper resolve by the president for the CIA's secret war in oil-rich Angola. In 1975, Ford, on Kissinger's advice, had authorized $32 million for the CIA's covert war in Angola to overthrow the Soviet-backed MPLA government.[14] Once again, as in the Congo and Southeast Asia, the CIA used animosities among tribal peoples to accomplish this end. The rationale for the heavier U.S. commitment was that Castro had sent 2,800 Cuban volunteers to Angola on the MPLA's request in response to the intervention by the CIA and South African armed forces in support of the MPLA's rivals. Ford, however, was worried about being caught in a public flap over this deepening military and financial commitment in another Vietnam-like escalation, spreading a civil war that allied the CIA with apartheid South Africa. Exposure of this secret war on the side of South Africa, coming on the heels of revelations about how the CIA's "secret war" in Laos had contributed to U.S. entanglement in Southeast Asia and the Vietnam War, could cost him many votes. Besides, the CIA's Angolan forces did not fight well, and the South African attack in southern Angola had been met by an additional 10,000 well-armed Cubans who were hurriedly flown in. In January, the South Africans withdrew. The U.S. Senate, angry over Kissinger's defiance of its constitutional inquiries, passed the Tunney Amendment to the Defense Appropriations Bill, prohibiting the use of defense funds in Angola for anything but gathering intelligence. On February 9, Ford signed the bill into law.

It was hard for Nelson to take, serving under someone as inexperienced in exercising superpower muscle as Jerry Ford. Riding in his limousine from a White House meeting one morning, Nelson lamented, while gazing absently through the window, "He's sure no Roosevelt."[15]

By June 1976, the rest of the country suspected the same. Ford, despite feeding his vice president to the sharks, had not placated the Right or kept Reagan from winning the South. The economy was moving into a recession, and Rumsfeld had still not released $16 billion in defense contracts that could win votes. The campaign was suffering, as well as the government. The Republican party—his party—would suffer, too, if things were not straightened out. Still believing he was the best choice for Ford's running mate, if not for president, Nelson caught the glint of an opportunity: *He* would run the White House.

"I figured that he [Ford] was going to come around," he said later, "which politically, of course, he should have. I mean, it was obvious with Reagan on the other side that I was the best balance that he had and I got him the votes anyhow from our northeastern states. But by that time I had decided that it was impossible for me to continue in the administration the way the caliber of people was slipping. . . . There was tremendous unrest in the cabinet and he was going to lose most of the good people. . . . The only way this could be stopped would be for me to go in as his Chief of Staff."[16]

In short, Nelson was targeting Rumsfeld's old job, now occupied by Dick Cheney. His goal was to rejoin the ticket, and he believed that Ford was desperate enough to go for it. Nelson even made Cheney's removal his price. "The only condition I would stay and go on the ticket with him would be if I could run his organization for him." This condition, if accepted, effectively meant that Rockefeller would run the cabinet while Ford campaigned. "Mr. President," he said, "it is against my interest, but I offer my services to you to take over as Chief of Staff and organize your White House and organize your cabinet for you."[17]

Ford thanked Nelson, but said he did not plan to change the structure.[18] When Ford did not bring the matter up again, Nelson had the final answer. It was to be the last time he would act out the overconfidence of the rich and powerful.

COWBOY HUMILIATIONS

Once again, Republican leaders gathered at a historic site of the conquest of the American West: Kansas City, Missouri, a center of the cattle industry. Reagan had made a crucial error. He had announced that Pennsylvania's moderate Senator Richard Schweiker would be his running mate before the convention had assembled. Ford had some people in mind for his vice president, but he decided not to announce his choice until after the balloting for the presidential nomination.

In Kansas City, Reagan found his old nemesis, Rockefeller, waiting for him. Nelson commanded not only the large New York delegation, but the larger New England votes. "Reagan thought he had the nomination. I knew he didn't because we had a very good organization and our New York State Chairman [Richard Rosenbaum] was first elected Chairman of the New England Chairmen and then Chairman of all the Chairmen."[19] Rosenbaum kept the large Pennsylvania delegation, led by Schweiker's close friend, Drew Lewis, in Ford's camp. With moderates afraid of Reagan because of his Far Right backers and Southerners put off by Reagan's choice of Schweiker, Ford won. He then named Senator Robert Dole of Kansas as his running mate. Nelson was left with the humiliation of nominating Dole before the convention on national television with a microphone that went dead. When the same thing happened to Dole, Nelson again saw a Cheney-Rumsfeld conspiracy.

The final insult came at the convention finale. Even though the nominations had been completed, Nelson insisted he would follow Ford up to the podium instead of Ford's new running mate, Dole. Resting his case on the state protocol for the reigning vice president, he confronted Cheney, venting months of frustration:

"Look, you so and so, I know what has been going on and I have been taking this all the way through, and now it is over. You tell the President for me what has happened here. You tell him about turning down the mike when I made my speech, and you tell him I'm not going to Vail and I am not going to have anything further to do with his campaign. I have fulfilled my duties. He has now got a new Vice President. And I am finished. You can take full credit with Mr. Rumsfeld for what has happened."[20]

Cheney, visibly shaken by Rockefeller's fury, turned white.

Nelson repeated it all to the president later when he announced that he would not go to Vail, Colorado, for the traditional postconvention party-unity meeting. "I told you almost a year and a half ago that there were people around you who didn't want you to succeed, who didn't want to see you nominated, and who don't want to see you elected if you get nominated. I have got to tell you the truth, I have had it. These are the final insults tonight that have happened. I love you but I am finished."

So was Ford.

In spite of it all, Nelson went to Vail and worked hard for the ticket. He took Dole across New York, although he was unable to control his habit of condescension and upstaging. In Binghamton, a Republican rally became the source of scandal when Nelson confronted demonstrators with lewd behavior. Leaning forward, with a gargoyle-like, ear-to-ear grin, he joyfully offered students of his state university the finger. Captured on film by a news photographer, Nelson answered mailed protests and praise in his own unique way: He sent out over a hundred autographed copies.

Ford lost not only New York, but every large state in the Northeast except Connecticut. Yet the paradox of the election was the returns from the Bible Belt. Despite the best efforts of Dallas's Rev. William Criswell to hold his Fundamentalist flocks for the Republicans, social conservatives took up the banner of the self-proclaimed "born-again" Christian, Jimmy Carter. Little did they know it had been hoisted by David Rockefeller's Trilateral Commission, of which Carter had been a member for two years, using the commission's Zbigniew Brzezinski and Samuel Huntington as his top foreign policy advisers.

On January 20, 1977, shortly after Jimmy Carter took the oath of office, Nelson Rockefeller and Gerald Ford boarded *Air Force I* and *Air Force II* for their last official rides home. The two giant planes lifted off Andrews Air Force Base and circled, observing Washington in the distance. Then each went its way, Ford heading west into political oblivion, Nelson flying north toward New York and an uncertain future filled with bitterness, haunting memories, and habitual political intrigue.

More than anything else, Nelson now wanted to put the Rockefeller house in order for the next generation. That meant saving his own financial empire, including the International Basic Economy Corporation in Latin America, for his two sons and two daughters by Tod and his two sons by Happy. To the press, he had given family affairs as his reason for withdrawing from the vice presidency, but he had not meant it. Now, despite his continued yearning for the White House, he had a foreboding that he should. His hair had turned silver, and he was feeling and looking his sixty-eight years.

But the Rockefeller business legacy was intensely political, involving the affairs of state, not just hearth. Unsure of Jimmy Carter's ability to wage the Cold War or to control an oil-fired global inflation and revolutions in the "developing" Third World, he was equally worried about the New Right's promotion of Ronald Reagan and what the new alliance with the growing Fundamentalist movement held for the Republican party and for the United States. Exiled from Washington, a postelection offer to serve Carter in some capacity never taken up, he did not trust the future. But then, he never had.

47

THE GREAT TRIBULATION

Divine Interventions

There were signs of the coming Great Tribulation throughout the 1970s in Latin America, especially earthquakes in Peru, Nicaragua, and Guatemala.

Peru had suffered the first blow at the beginning of the decade, when a mountainside collapsed into a heavily populated Andean valley, killing more than 70,000 people. Resident translators of the Summer Institute of Linguistics thanked the Lord that none of them had been hurt and that they had been able to radio Yarinacocha's tower with the first disaster call to the outside world. The Charismatic Renewal championed by SIL's leading Pentecostalist, Jerry Elder, had already gained a foothold in Yarinacocha by then, but the symbolic swallowing of five branch members by the jungle on Christmas Eve, 1971, when a plane carrying ninety-five passengers disappeared, triggered a mass confession of mutual sins, followed by forgiveness and a calming love. The revival served as a vent and a balm for hysterics that were generated by pressure from Satan's agents in the government of Juan Velasco Alvarado in Lima.

Now, the Lord's anger had passed and Jesus had rewarded their patient suffering by bringing about President Velasco's overthrow in an August 1975 coup led by General Francisco Morales Bermudez. But some of Velasco's army allies were able to hold on to their government posts as the price the new president had to pay for army unity.

Satan made a last effort to inspire doubt when Education Minister Ramón Miranda Ampuero announced that SIL had a December 1976 deadline for finishing its work among the tribes. But Miranda's move came too late. The debts incurred by Velasco's construction of the trans-Andean pipeline to Amazonian oil had fatally weakened the government's strength to resist conservative forces in Lima and Washington. Former AID administrator Donald Lindholm, now director of the Yarinacocha jungle base, ignored the government's request to keep its decision to cancel SIL's contract confidential and leaked the news to the Lima daily newspaper, *El Comercio*. This newspaper had been owned by the family of former Education Minister Francisco Miró Quesada. In those days, SIL was given favorable review. This situation was reversed when the Velasco government expropriated Lima's dailies and appointed editors sympathetic to its goals. But now that Velasco had fallen, the editors had been replaced, and the pendulum had swung back in SIL's favor. The newspaper made the contract's cancellation front-page news on April 12, surprising even branch director Lambert Anderson, who relayed his worries to the U.S. Embassy about a government backlash. But Ambassador Robert Dean, trusted veteran of the Brazilian coup, was confident. He undertook a series of actions that would end all doubts about the Lord's Will.

Dean wired Henry Kissinger, stoking the secretary of state's Cold War suspicions by emphasizing that Miranda's announcement about SIL had been made during an interview at Lima's airport before Miranda had explained the purposes of an official visit to Cuba. Dean grimly noted that his Cuban counterpart on Lima's embassy row "was at Miranda's side during the interview," as if Cuba were behind the termination of SIL's contract. In contrast to this international communist conspiracy were SIL's God-fearing uniformed friends. "With possibility of postponing or reversing that policy, friends of SIL are continuing with plans to release more names of prominent Peruvians supporting SIL's retention, and several favorable press articles have been generated."[1] The absence of linguists from the two petitions' 119 names could have been an embarrassment had military power not compensated: 35 percent of the signers were senior officers, including 12 admirals and 21 generals.[2] Among the signatories were General Armando Artola, the hunter of MIR guerrillas in 1965, and Comandante Fernando Melgar Escute, the air force officer who in 1962 had been involved in discussions with SIL's Jerry Elder, with Cam's knowledge, on the possibility of SIL's doing espionage along the Peru-Ecuador border.[3] There were also five former ministers of education with close ties to SIL, including former President Manuel Odría's General Juan Mendoza and Fernando Belaúnde Terry's Francisco Miró Quesada.

The Cold War was hitched to SIL's wagon to pull it into the political limelight. Dean informed Kissinger of the signatories' concern: "A key SIL supporter [Miró Quesada] has warned [President] Morales Bermudez of the political danger of terminating SIL activities only to allow a leftist campesino organization to extend its operation among jungle Indians."[4]

Within months, SIL was treated to another seemingly divine intervention. Another military coup purged the last holdovers from the Velasco era, including Prime Minister Jorge Maldonado, whose political career had been fatally weakened by the failure to find enough Amazonian oil to pay for the pipeline he had constructed as Velasco's minister of energy. President Morales Bermudez installed a new rightist junta and closed down opposition newspapers. Austerity measures that had been demanded by Chase and other bank creditors, and resisted by Maldonado's ministers, were put into effect and backed by a curfew and troops in the streets. In this political cliimate, SIL's contract was extended for at least five more years. The Cabinet that had ordered SIL's expulsion was overthrown.

Despite the insistence of SIL's government liaison in Peru that it had maintained "no contact with the U.S. embassy," branch leader Lambert Anderson admitted a year later in a letter to President Jimmy Carter that "Ambassador Dean's professional correctness and precision, coupled with a warm personal interest and private words of support, without doubt contributed greatly to the happy outcome."[5]

Dean had known that the dispute would further undermine Prime Minister Maldonado's government, which, he had wired Kissinger on March 10, was trying "to avoid another political controversy." Rallying the generals, SIL would prevail. When it did, Dean conveyed the good news to Kissinger with military flair: "Mission Accomplished."[6]

SIL's version of its reprieve was more inspired: "God intervened."[7]

William Cameron Townsend arrived to confirm the Lord's Will in a celebratory visit the following year.

God was more tentative in other lands. National sovereignty, once the cry of Indian miners and leftists against foreign imperialism, was now taken up by their military dictatorships and used as a rallying cry to consolidate a popular base by expelling unnecessary foreigners.

In Ecuador, local resentments against the "Queen of the Auca," Rachel Saint, forced the SIL branch to order her evacuation from "her" Huaorani. Packed off to SIL's apartment house in Quito, Rachel would wait in vain for SIL's permission to reenter her beloved tribe, many of whom had discovered the sins of material goods from oil companies and tourists.

Nowhere was the sting of nationalism felt more painfully and with greater potential repercussions for SIL than in Brazil. The vaunted "Brazilian Miracle" had been brought to hard ground by oil debts. Standard Oil of New Jersey and its other Six Sisters had simply passed along the price increase imposed by sheik and shah to consumers, including Third World nations like Brazil.

The political rumblings began in 1976, two years after the Brazilian Miracle ended. Amazonian Indians, helped by Catholic priests of the Missionary Indigenist Council (CIMI), held national conferences on Indian rights. FUNAI struck back with a ban on CIMI in Indian reserves and then on all foreign anthropologists in "border" areas where most isolated tribes lived. The tribes were not so much the regime's concern as the ground beneath them. SIL, given the green light to enter the northwest, kept its traditional silence, eager to occupy the tribes scheduled to encounter the Northern Perimeter Highway, the northern loop of the trans-Amazon highway system, soon.[8]

On Brazil's border with Venezuela were uranium deposits that the regime had targeted for the development of nuclear energy and, some feared, nuclear bombs. The problem was that the uranium was in the traditional lands of the Yanomami Indians, the largest unacculturated tribe in the Brazilian Amazon. These Indians, numbering between 10,000 and 15,000 people, had been made infamous as "the fierce people" by Pennsylvania State University anthropologist Napoleon Chagnon,[9] who studied the tribe under a research grant from the U.S. Atomic Energy Commission.[10] SIL's Fundamentalist ally, the New Tribes Mission, was among the Yanomami in Venezuela and was studying the languages of the region with SIL translators at SIL's Pôrto Velho base in Brazil in preparation for working with the Yanomami on the Brazilian side of the border. The Evangelical Mission Society of Amazonia and the Unevangelized Field Mission (the UFM having provided Chagnon with his initial data on Yanomami infanticide) were already there. SIL had been invited by the Brazilian government and the U.S. Bureau of Indian Affairs[11] to occupy the Yanomami tribe's southwestern neighbors, the Wasiana and Taríana of the Uaupés River just east of Colombia (on the Colombian side, the river is called the Vaupés, and uranium prospectors were there, too). Anthropologists and ecologists had been trying to get relief for the tribes of northwest Brazil, particularly the Yanomami, from the growing contagion of river blindness, which was spread by the tiny black flies breeding in stagnant pools along the Northern Perimeter Highway.* The scientists' relief efforts were not appreciated by the region's military governor, who had complained in March 1975 about outside pressures to reform Brazil's Indian policy. "I am of the opinion," he told reporters, "that an area as rich as this—with gold, diamonds, and uranium—cannot afford the luxury of conserving half a dozen Indian tribes who are holding back the development of Brazil."[12] As rumors spread of the discovery also of cassiterite, the same ore for tin production that threatened to doom the Cintas Largas, the head of FUNAI, General Ismarth de Araújo Oliveira, explained that the medicine used to control river blindness was very expensive and that it killed the Indians because they lacked sufficient physical resistance.[13]

---

*The appearance of the disease in so remote an area and over such a wide range, far beyond the highway's vicinity and the flies' flight range, was as mysterious to some observers as the sudden disappearance over such a wide area of birds that had kept the fly population in check; for others, the noise accompanying the highway's construction and subsequent deforestation offered a solution to the birds' disappearance (at least in the road's vicinity), while the fact that a human—not just flies—can carry the disease's microscopic worms as a host offered a reason for the spread of the disease beyond the flies' flight range.

That November, ICOMI, Augusto Antunes's joint venture with Bethlehem Steel, began surveying. In 1976, the cassiterite discovery on Yanomami land was revealed in the Brazilian press, which reported that the governor gave Mineração Além-Equador an exclusive exploration concession.[14] That year the Brazilian military regime expelled all foreign anthropologists from Yanomami lands for "national security" reasons. The reason given was recent violence among shotgun-armed Yanomami bands and attacks by Indians on prospectors. The scenario was identical to claims against the Cintas Largas in Rondônia. There, the federal government had taken matters into its own hands to end the Indians' isolation and allow São Paulo companies access to mineral riches. As FUNAI's sheriff in Pôrto Velho explained to the authors in October 1976, "FUNAI's main philosophy is to integrate the Indians into civilization, so that someday there will be no Indians."[15]

Having entered the Cintas Largas territory in 1972, SIL was in agreement with FUNAI's philosophy—however, it posed the choice for Indians in more stark terms. "You have a choice," SIL's Dr. Ursula Wiesemann told thirty-five Kaingáng Indians taken unaware by the military government in 1972 and sent to a bilingual training center that she ran. "You can choose between your own way of life or the life of the *civilizado*; each has a price and a recompense. For your way, the price is lack of progress, hunger and death."

The recompense was supposedly being spared the pain of change. The alternative, according to Wiesemann, was full of promise. "For the *civilizado* way, the price is work and maintaining what you've achieved. Your recompense is that you will have more."[16]

In 1973, however, the Trans-Amazon Highway's expense caused cuts in the bilingual training program. In 1976, with the highway scheduled to reach the northwestern tribes, SIL was again given the nod. SIL was enthusiastic. "We work very closely with FUNAI," the business manager of SIL's Pôrto Velho base told the authors.[17] The paid work included pacification of tribes resisting incursions. "We have a few people trying to contact a wild Indian tribe, but that's purely a pacification contract." And what of the moral obligation to expose Brazilian abuses of Indian human rights? "Brazil is very conscious of articles of that sort. We knew someone else who planned to go home and tell some of the seamier side of it and we told him that the best way to help the Indians was to come back. He wrote articles and didn't get a visa to get back."[18] SILers would not make the same mistake.

The following year, however, Brazil's contract with West German companies to provide uranium in exchange for nuclear technology and nuclear power plants would help trigger President Jimmy Carter's new foreign policy initiative to limit nuclear proliferation and protect human rights in the Third World. General Médici's successor as president, the former intelligence chief General Ernesto Geisel, would be so bothered by Carter's new direction he would turn on SIL, ordering its missionaries expelled from the tribes by December 1977. But Cam would know who the enemy really was. He would blame SIL's declining fortunes in Brazil on the general political atmosphere stirred by anthropologists in other lands.[19]

GENOCIDE IN PARAGUAY

No event in 1976 proved more ominous for SIL and closely allied American groups like the New Tribes Mission than news about what Fundamentalist missionaries were doing in neighboring Paraguay. That year, anthropologists, human rights advocates, and social scientists contributed essays to *Genocide in Paraguay*. The book, which created an immediate sensation, was the response by the anthropological community to the repression of colleagues in Paraguay.

It appeared five years after Professor Miguel Chase Sardi revealed at the Barbados Conference the atrocities against the Aché and Ayoreo Indians and the policy of Pennsylvania's Mennonite Central Committee to make all economic aid to Indians of the Chaco conditional on their agreeing to practice birth control through submission of the women to fittings for intrauterine devices.[20] In 1976, he and his staff were arrested at an Indian self-help organization and imprisoned, and the police were said to have used torture. In May 1976, six Catholic priests, including the secretary of the Missions Department of the Paraguayan Bishops' Conference, were arrested and deported, and six Protestant missionaries were also seized. U.S. Senators James Abourezk and Thomas Eagleton voiced their concern, while the president of the Senate, Vice President Nelson Rockefeller, remained mute. Despite growing protests in Congress over the arrests and deportations, silence reigned supreme in the Kissinger State Department.

The State Department's official line had always been that the Aché were victims of only "harsh individual acts" by "isolated ranchers" and ranch hands "said to have been drunk." Jack B. Kubisch, Kissinger's assistant secretary for Inter-American Affairs, assured Congress in 1974 that "this situation has now changed with the appointment of a new and more suitable administration," New Tribes.

"We do not believe that there has been a planned or conscious effort on the part of the Government of Paraguay to exterminate, molest, or harm the Aché Indians in any way. The unfortunate acts in remote areas seem to have been individual ones."[21]

Nothing was mentioned about Paraguayan military trucks that were seen moving captured Aché to the New Tribes colony. Or about Standard Oil of New Jersey, Pennsylvania Oil (Pennzoil), and Texaco preparing to explore for oil in the homelands of the Ayoreos, who were also "occupied" by New Tribes Mission. Or about these companies' negotiations, with the regime of Alfredo Stroessner, of contracts that contained "some of the most generous clauses recently granted to foreign oil companies anywhere in the world."[22] Or about International Products Corporation, the American firm better known for its Ogden affiliate's Tillie Lewis brand names, which owned 2 million acres of land for cattle breeding around

Puerto Pinasco on the Paraguai River, about 150 miles southwest of Nelson Rockefeller's Bodoquena ranch in Brazil.

Nelson had been apprised of International Products' ranch when control of the firm was bought by Pamela Woolworth, an heiress of the F. W. Woolworth chain-store fortune in February 1956, just a few months before Nelson's purchase of Bodoquena. The *New York Times* story reporting the purchase, a clipping of which was found by the authors in Nelson's personal files years later,[23] noted that the firm had closed down its meat processing operation in 1950, when economic instability under President Juan Perón made it difficult to acquire Argentine cattle. By 1955, Perón had been overthrown and Paraguay's own cattle production was sufficient to assure ample supply. The firm shifted the ranch's focus from produc-

The shaded areas represent the location of Indian groups. The word *Guayaki* is another term for the Aché Indians.

Source: Richard Arens, ed., *Genocide in Paraguay*, p. 2, based in part on map contained in Norman Lewis, "Manhunt," *Sunday Times Magazine* (London), January 26, 1975.

ing tanning substances from quebracho trees back to producing cattle for slaughter and export. Neither the *New York Times* nor Kubisch mentioned the plight of thousands of Indians of the Angaité, Lengua, and Senapaná tribes who lived in the area. Dispossessed of most of their lands, the Indians had been reduced to the status of underpaid day laborers at Puerto Pinasco's tannin factories, until those were closed; then, the Indians were forced to seek what little work they could find on the area's revived cattle ranches. The ranches usually paid in kind rather than in wages, encouraged the use of credit that kept the Indians in peonage, and fenced all the fields and prohibited Indian agriculture.[24] The presence of two Fundamentalist missionaries among the Indians was not mentioned either in the *Times* story: the South American Missionary Society and the New Tribes Mission.

Nor did Kubisch mention that Rockefeller's American International Association had designed colonization schemes in Paraguay for the Agency for International Development and had gotten dictator Stroessner's "green light" to "proceed with studies and preparation of the prospectus for presentation to U.S. and Paraguayan investors," including the International Products Corporation, which wanted to expand its exports and had "shown interest in this proposal."[25] AIA's Walter Crawford gave AID's Paraguay Rural Development officers a tour of Brazilian institutions, which resulted in closer economic ties between the two dictatorships, including a host of cooperative research ventures and a visit by the manager of King Ranch of Brazil to an AID-affiliated experimental ranch in Paraguay.*

Kubisch also did not mention that the Itaipu and Acaray Dams were located near the forests inhabited by the Aché. These dams were part of a giant AID-backed development project designed to turn the Paraná River into a source of cheap hydroelectric energy for the mines and cities of Brazil to the east.

Kubisch was not ignorant of these links between AID's development plans in militarized Brazil and militarized Paraguay. He had headed AID's mission to Brazil from 1962 to 1965, when the agency was financing Brazilian state governors and politicians who were conspiring to overthrow the government of João Goulart. After the coup, Kubisch became chief of the Brazilian Desk of the State Department in Washington, arranging restoration of AID loans to the central government that kept the Brazilian

---

*Crawford had prepared a confidential report to the Stroessner regime entitled *Colonization in Paraguay* as early as 1964. By 1966, he had drawn in the Buenos Aires office of the International Committee for European Migration (ICEM), which had been hired as researchers by one of the AIA's top Venezuelan associates, Fernando Rondon. Rondon was assistant director of CBR (Consejo de Bienestar Rural, or Council of Rural Welfare), a colonization agency set up jointly by the AIA and Venezuela's Technical Institute for Immigration and Colonization and funded by Mobil, International Petroleum, Shell Oil, and Nelson's favorite, Creole Petroleum. CBR was engaged in a resource survey of Venezuela's Orinoco River Basin when Rondon switched over to ICEM in Buenos Aires; from there it did not take long for Crawford to draw ICEM into the Stroessner Colony Project of Alto Paraná and to bring Brazilians into consultations on setting up a rural credit system like Brazil's Associação Brasileira de Crédito e Assistência Rural (ABCAR), the national system that AIA set up for then President Kubitschek.

junta alive and launched the first development schemes for conquering the Amazon. This work had catapulted him to Kissinger's side as overseer of all Latin America.

Genocide in Paraguay filled in some of these information gaps—and others. The book contained a full accounting by German anthropologist Mark Münzel of his experience not only with the Aché between 1970 and 1972, but with the New Tribes Mission that took over the Achés' reservation after its administrator was forced to resign in disgrace for "killing, torture and slave-trading." Münzel was unsparing in his criticism of the New Tribes Mission, noting that "inhuman conditions" continued to persist on the reservation and that an American missionary associated with the group "has himself been observed participating in Indian hunts within the forest areas and, beyond that, in the lucrative sale of captives in his charge."[26] Dr. Eric Wolfe, the same anthropologist who had exposed the CIA's use of anthropologists and missionaries in Thailand, concluded that the reservation was nothing less than "an extermination camp" and that the New Tribes Mission was its "handmaiden, gun bearer and prison warden." Norman Lewis, the author who had blown the whistle on the Cintas Largas massacres, captured the full horror of the Aché experience with a summary of indictments against the Paraguayan government by the International League for the Rights of Man and the Inter-American Association for Democracy and Freedom in 1974:

> 1) enslavement, torture, and killing of the Guayakí [Aché] Indians in reservations in eastern Paraguay; 2) withholding of food and medicine from them resulting in their death by starvation and disease; 3) massacre of their members outside the reservations by hunters and slave traders with the toleration and even encouragement of members of the government and with the aid of the armed forces; 4) splitting up of families and selling into slavery of children, in particular girls for prostitution; and 5) denial and destruction of Guayakí cultural traditions, including use of their language, traditional music, and religious practices.[27]

Of all the 144 pages of *Genocide in Paraguay*, the implications of the horror were best conveyed in a single quote from Richard Rubenstein's 1975 essay, "After Auschwitz": "Perhaps we are at the beginning, not the end, of the age of genocide."[28]

With SIL, the word *genocide* was never uttered and never even considered. Instead, SIL had a conspiracy theory of its own to fall back on. Sometimes it took supposedly material form as the International Communist Conspiracy, but always lurking in the spiritual shadows was Satan, who could be felt to be working his evil ways with lies, confusion, violence.

In Indonesia's conquered Dutch West Guinea, renamed Irian Jaya by the Indonesians, evidence of the forces of Darkness—and Light—was seen in 1977 when the Baliem Valley "just blew up." By the early 1970s, President Suharto, the general who led the Indonesian occupation of the copper-rich Baliem Valley, allowed not only the Rockefellers' and Whitneys' Freeport Sulphur to occupy and steadily export the valley's legendary "Copper Mountain," but Cam's Christian missionaries to occupy the valley's Dani tribe spiritually.

SIL's officialdom, in its eagerness to show its devotion to Indonesian absorption of the Baliem, plunged to familiar depths. Ignatius Suharno and Ken Pike published *From Baudi to Indonesian* with Asia Foundation funds in 1976.[29] But SIL's field missionaries seemed to have cut their own path toward the Dani. It is some indication of the degree to which the missionaries shelved Cam's Hail, Caesar! doctrine that when the Papuans revolted against Indonesian rule in 1977, they spared SIL's missions. Nevertheless, the rebellion was ruthlessly crushed by Indonesian troops using U.S. weapons. The Dani language that Michael Rockefeller had once recorded with such wonder returned to SIL's base at Danau Bira (Lake Holmes) in the words of language informants and grounds keepers. By then, as Caltex (a joint venture of Standard Oil of California and Texaco) oil rigs sprouted in the seas off the Irian coast,[30] Copper Mountain had all but disappeared into the maw of American industry.

CRACKING AT THE SEAMS OF EMPIRE

The same year that the Papuans revolted in Baliem Valley, Nelson Rockefeller was preparing to sell images of their art and that of the coastal tribesmen who killed his son. He had already published an earlier book on the "primitive" art Michael had collected. It had been a private edition and had cost him money. Now Nelson intended to make money. He had been astounded to learn that publishers would actually pay *him* to print books of photographs of his art collection. It also occurred to him that a marvelously accurate method of making reproductions might also be a moneymaker; using his own art collection would require no royalty payments to artists or other collectors.

The Nelson Rockefeller Collection, Inc., could make a fortune, just as long as he ignored the art critics' disdain for such "tacky" behavior by a collector, and a Rockefeller at that. Nelson thought it all fun, potentially lucrative, and a way to share the art that he had enjoyed privately; he saw it as almost a profitable public service.

"Tacky" had also been hurled at him when he sold his Foxhall Road estate in Washington, D.C.—a stately relic of his CIAA days—to a developer for subdivision into house lots. The property was a rarity in Washington, D.C., in that it included twenty-five wooded acres along the Potomac and a large colonial house. More important to Nelson, it had been the symbol of over three decades of dreams of someday occupying another house in Washington. He had paid only $225,000 for it in the 1940s. Local assessors now placed a value for tax purposes at $2.1 million, the second highest in the capital. Now that he no longer needed it, Nelson quickly discarded this symbol of his dreams, offering it for sale before he even left Washington. He wanted $8.8 million.

Outraged neighbors wailed at the developers' plan to carve up the old property. Nelson shrugged, moving on, characteristically never looking back.

He sought similar liquidity from assets by selling part of his Fifth Avenue luxury duplex apartment in New York, pulling in his belt to the twenty-two-room notch. Furthermore, during his protracted absence while vice president, some of his father's Navajo Indian rugs from those early trips to New Mexico had been stolen from an unlocked building on his estate on Mount Desert Island, Maine. It was a sign of the times; never before in his adult life had such disrespect been shown. He concluded that it did no good to try to keep what was not used. So, he put that estate up for sale as well, asking $1 million for the property. Systematically, piece by piece, every tangible part of his past was being expelled from his life, as were his dreams.

Only Pocantico remained, precisely because it belonged not to him, but to the whole family as part of its heritage and legend, designated by outgoing President Ford as a national historic landmark at a special ceremony that brought Nelson, David, and Laurance together with other family members. Ironically, the ceremony was performed on the eve of the thirteenth anniversary of John F. Kennedy's assassination. Here, too, were bitter memories. Kennedy, who had disagreed strongly with the Rockefellers about the exclusive reliance on private enterprise in foreign-aid grants and loans, was the first president—and the last—who did not ask Nelson to help in his administration. Yet Kennedy's name was still revered in Latin America, while Nelson's was reviled. Kennedy had brought out cheering crowds; Nelson, jeering mobs and riots.

Kennedy's Alliance for Progress was remembered, more even than Franklin D. Roosevelt's Good Neighbor Policy, as a Camelotian "one great shining moment" in the United States' relations with its southern neighbors, yet Nelson's own philanthropic and business efforts in the development in Latin America, which had preceded Kennedy's by many years, had suffered under a twist of fate. Its philanthropic face had been sacrificed for its business side. It had been a vain forfeit. Because of Nelson's political ambitions, the overarching nature of Rockefeller investments throughout Latin America had been revealed during his vice presidential confirmation hearings. Nelson's philanthropic focus on Latin America, embodied in AIA, survived only in memory and in the government programs it spawned.

His model for private businesses, the International Basic Economy Corporation, was also dying, another victim of the ambitions of its founders. IBEC's growth had overextended its reach; there were simply not enough successes or enough of a track record to encourage private investors to provide the capital IBEC needed to reach out to its far-flung subsidiaries with nurturing finances, technology, and administrative skills.

IBEC would have been sustainable if its costs had remained tolerable and its

Geographic Distribution*

U.S., Puerto Rico and Canada

Revenue	$108,000,000
Income (loss**)	$ (7,600,000)
Assets	$118,800,000
Employees	4,300

Latin America

Revenue	$138,200,000
Income**	$ 2,200,000
Assets	$ 62,000,000
Employees	4,500

Europe

Revenue	$ 8,800,000
Income (loss**)	$ (400,000)
Assets	$ 12,700,000
Employees	400

Africa and Asia

Revenue	$ 2,500,000
Income**	$ 300,000
Assets	$ 7,700,000
Employees	200

*Includes data of continuing operations.
**Before extraordinary items and accounting change.

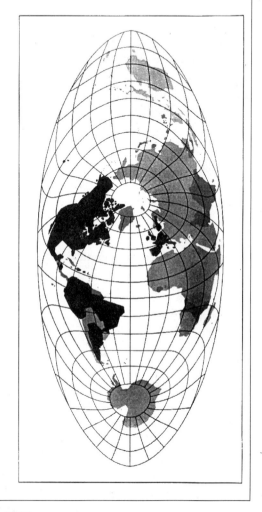

Rockefeller's IBEC World Holdings (1972)

In the six years between 1966 and 1972, Latin America continued to outpace all other areas of the world in return on investment for Rockefeller's IBEC. By 1972, IBEC's revenues from Latin America were $20 million more than in 1966, while its assets were only $2 million more.

Source: IBEC annual report, courtesy of the Rockefeller Archive Center.

revenues had showed promise of growing at a faster pace. But with the hike in oil prices increasing energy costs and sales hit by ensuing cutbacks, IBEC had racked up $98 million in debts by September 30, 1974.

Before his confirmation, Nelson had agreed to help his son, Rodman, save IBEC. The Rockefeller company was unable to meet its obligations to its biggest creditors, a banking group led by Chase Manhattan and two insurance companies. During the confirmation hearings, Nelson had assured senators that "I have no active part, no interest in business affairs." Three weeks after he took office, Room 5600's J. Richardson Dilworth sent a letter to IBEC confirming the tentative agreement of two unnamed Rockefeller family members (Nelson and Laurance) to provide IBEC with up to $3 million in credit in return for IBEC's major lenders extending their loans. Neither insurance company knew who the "principal interests" were, but the fact that the term indicated that the parties had a current investment in IBEC made a mockery of Nelson's claim to have put his holdings in a blind trust. Nelson was obviously not so blind.

Rodman worked to get IBEC's house in shape. He had already sold off over $50 million in assets in the previous two years. Some $20 million more were targeted for disposal in 1975, including stock holdings in IBEC's Arbor Acres chicken subsidiaries in Mexico and Venezuela and 51 percent of one of IBEC's most lucrative operations, its CADA supermarket chain.

In all, Rodman sold seventeen companies and merged or liquidated nine more, including IBEC's once-vaunted precast concrete housing project in Puerto Rico. Rodman succeeded in reducing IBEC's debt by $60 million, including Eurodollar notes. But former IBEC executives were not sure that Rodman could steer IBEC out of the storm. "To run a far-flung company like IBEC," one said, "you need imagination, a strong managerial talent and the ability to pick out profitable ventures. With regard to Rodman, the jury is still out."[31]

By 1978, the jury had come in, and the verdict was not good for IBEC. Despite Rodman's strong will and courage, IBEC's $16.6 million loss in 1976 had obliged him to borrow $10 million more from institutional investors.[32] The following year, he sold IBEC's Bellows International subsidiary for $26.5 million to Scovill Manufacturing, headed by Ronald Reagan's future secretary of commerce, Malcolm Baldrige.

But politics again intervened, this time the CIA's civil wars in southern Africa, where IBEC's Arbor Acres had subsidiaries in Angola, Mozambique, Rhodesia, South Africa, and Zambia. Currency fluctuations also had their impact. In Zambia, Arbor Acres was hit with a $500,000 fine for currency violations.[33]

To offset another $13.2 million loss suffered in 1977, Rodman spun off a housing project in Caguas, Puerto Rico, for $3.3 million. IBEC's prognosis was grave. Like the charitable mask that had covered it, Nelson's business empire was cracking apart.

Still hoping that IBEC could weather the storm, the Rockefellers continued to throw off dead wood. If it could not survive as a company, perhaps it could at least hold itself together long enough to find a safe harbor with a purchaser.

Revolt in the Provinces

News on other fronts was also grim. In 1978, General Anastasio Somoza of Nicaragua was besieged by a popular revolution led by the Sandinistas. Although Nelson had never liked Somoza's father, he had dealt with him during World War II. The Somozas subsequently got Nicaragua into debt to the tune of $580 million to some 100 banks, including Chase Manhattan. Now it was not clear that a revolutionary government would honor that debt. American corporations might lose assets, including gold mines owned by ASARCO, a mining concern with Rockefeller ties represented on ASARCO's board by Chase directors George Champion, Willard Butcher, and Charles Barber. The mines were worked by Miskito Indians who had been evangelized by the American Moravian Church, which was based in Bethlehem, Pennsylvania, home of Bethlehem Steel.

The news was equally bad from the Middle East, where both Chase and IBEC had been involved in development projects in Iran and Lebanon. The Palestinians, expelled in 1970 from Jordan by King Hussein's army, were becoming a serious force in Lebanon, and unrest was growing in the Shah's Iran. The Soviets had grown close to the independent-minded new strongman in Iraq, Saddam Hussein, the Shah's arch rival for control of the Persian Gulf. Thanks to U.S. support for the Shah's territorial ambition, the CIA was losing its influence to the Soviet KGB in neighboring Afghanistan.

Nelson had plans for the Shah and the other leaders in the Middle East. He had just launched Saraborn, a company he hoped would become the conduit for recycling OPEC's petrodollars back to the United States for investments. It would provide OPEC leaders like the Shah—especially the Shah—with a safe refuge for their wealth, tie them closer to U.S. policies, and fatten the coffers of banks like Chase that could hold their money as deposits and perhaps back up joint ventures suggested by Nelson's firm. The Saraborn conduit might even help lower the balance-of-payments deficit, a perfect example of a corporate merger of profits and patriotism.

In May 1978, just weeks after a coup in Afghanistan established a communist government, Nelson and Happy flew to Iran. The Shah was shaken by riots by fundamentalist Muslim followers of Ayatollah Khomeini, then living in exile. His policies for rapid development and its accompanying radical cultural and political changes challenged traditional Muslim values. He failed to see the looming threat of a Muslim fundamentalist backlash to the urban elite's adoption of Western lifestyles. He saw only communists and worried about their influence among the oil workers in the southwest, where Nelson's IBEC had been working on development.

ROCKEFELLER HOLDINGS IN BRAZIL

IBEC Holdings in Brazil (1976)

Desenvolvimento e Sistemas, S.A.—Real estate development at headwaters of the São Francisco River in Minas Gerais state

Fazenda Bodoquena (IBEC—30%; Nelson, David, and Laurance Rockefeller direct holding—10%; Rockefeller total—40%)—Eighth-largest agribusiness in Brazil, including ranching and beef processing on 1,030,000-acre estate in Mato Grosso

Arbor Acres Avicultura, S.A. (100%)—Poultry breeding stock for farmers and chicken industry

ROLIBEC S.A. Corretagem de Seguros e Participações (100%)—General insurance

IBEC Ltda. (100%)—IBEC central office in São Paulo, Brazil

Brazilian Investments, Inc. (100%)—Holding company based in Delaware

  ASSAI-Administração e Servicos S.A. (100%)

    Contabilidade Mecantzada e Participações (COMEPA) (89.57%)

    Agrobras Comercial e Industrial, S.A. (80.98%)

    IBEC-Representações, Administração e Servicos Ltda. (98%)

    Toledo-Bellows Equipamentos Pneumaticos S.A. (formerly Carrera Equipamenticos S.A.) (85.42%)—Pneumatic drills and hydraulic control equipment

  Sementes Agroceres, S.A. (SASA) (64%)—Fourth-largest seed company in the world; hybrid cornseeds and experimentation with pasture grass, legumes, and sorghum. Hog breeding farm. Owned 4,000 acres of agricultural land for experiments and 59,000 square feet of plant and office space.

    Agroceres Comercial, S.A. (99.95%)

    Agroceres de Nordeste, S.A. (54%)

  Sementes Norticeres, S.A.—Vegetable seed company

IBECASA Brasileira, S.A. (90%)—Subsidiary of IBEC Housing International, Inc.

San Jose dos Campos—4,200-unit IBEC housing project in São Paulo state by IBEC Housing International, Inc.

Makro Atacadista, S.A. (MAKRO) (34.13%)—Wholesale cash-and-carry distribution centers for small retailers

  Comercial Makro Ltda. (99.9%)

  Ulmak Corretagem de Seguros Ltda. (49.9%)

Brazilian Creditors and/or Stockholders in
Makro Atacadista, S.A., and/or IBEC (1976)

SHV Brasileira Participações Ltda.
Mepaso Participações Ltda.
Banco Bozzano Simonsen
Petrobrás Distribuidora S.A.
Banco de Minas Gerais
Banco Comercio e Industria de São Paulo
Banco Real

Source: IBEC 1976 10K filing with the U.S. Securities and Exchange Commission, filed April 1977.

Other Pre-1976 IBEC Holdings in Brazil

Avicultura, Comercio e Industria, S.A. (AVISCO) (20%)—Poultry breeder
Inter-American Finance and Investment Corporation (IFI, or "Interameri-cana") (20%) (1951–1955)—Joint venture with Chase National Bank (31.2%) and fourteen Brazilian banks (48%)
Crescinco (100%) (1957–1968)—South America's largest mutual fund, controlling over $200 million in assets. Investments in more than 100 Brazilian companies.
Cia. Carioca Industrial (5.3%)—Producer of vegetable oils, soap, and detergent
Cia. Empreendimentos e Administração IBEC (100%) (1957–1967)—Management firm for Crescinco
Cia. Distribuidora de Valores (CODIVAL) (100%) (1957–1967)—Sales company for Crescinco
Banco de Investimento do Brasil (BIB) (18.55%) (1967–1972)—Investment banking, underwriting, brokerage, and mutual funds (including IBEC's formerly owned Crescinco), controlling over $400 million in assets
Brazilian Investments, Inc. (Delaware) (100%) (1957–1967)—Earlier named Crescinco Investments, Inc. (Brazil), originally a U.S.-registered subsidiary for investments in U.S. corporations operating in Brazil. A relatively small fund designed to supplement Crescinco's Brazilian earnings with more predictable U.S. earnings and offset losses from Brazilian inflation and currency fluctuations.
Cargill Agricola e Comercial, S.A. (CACSA) (45% of common stock, 81% of preferred)—Grain-storage company joint venture with U.S.-based Cargill. In 1957 Cargill sold its interest to Continental Grain and CACSA's name

was changed to **Granar Agricola e Comercial, S.A. (GRANAR)** (45.41%).

IBEC-Rollins Burdick Hunter Ltda. (99%)—General insurance brokerage. Name later changed to **ROLIBEC S.A. Corretagem de Seguros e Participações**.

Industria Metalúrgica Forjaço, S.A. (13.86%)—Drop-forging plant in São Paulo

Regencia Companhia—Joint venture with Sears, Roebuck and Brazilian interests; men's clothing manufacturer in São Paulo

Thela Comercial, S.A. (40%)—Importer of U.S.-made agricultural materials, supplies, and construction equipment

Early IBEC Ventures Dissolved by 1957

Emprêsa de Mecanização Agricola (EMA) (82%)—Sales of U.S.-manufactured tractors, disk plows, disk harrowers, terracers, planters, cultivators, and harvesters. Land development, including forest clearance.

Emprêsa de Combate a Pragas Agricolas (100%)

Helicopter Crop Dusting Company (HELICO) (100%)

S.A. Fomento Agro-Pecuario (SAFAB) (100%)—Hog-production company

Companies in Which IBEC's Crescinco Mutual Fund Was a Self-described "Principal Shareholder"

Braspla, S.A., Indústria e Comèrcio de Matéria Plástica (15% of common stock, 66.66% of preferred shares)—Plastic products manufacturer, including thermoplastics, plastic bags, supplies for automotive industry, and toys under Walt Disney license agreements

Dunlop do Brasil, S.A. (preferred shares)—Tire manufacturer, with rubber plantations in Bahia.

Cia. Carioca Industrial (5.3% of common stock)—Producer of vegetable oils, with factories in São Luís (Maranhão) and São Paulo

Source: IBEC annual reports and 10K filings with the U.S. Securities and Exchange Commission; IBEC Archives, Rockefeller Archive Center.

Chase Manhattan Bank Holdings in Brazil

Banco Lar Brasileiro, S.A. (98%)—42 branches, subsidiaries, affiliates, and representative offices with activities in over 100 countries by 1982

Banco de Investimentos Lar Brasileiro, S.A. (100%)—Investment subsidiary

Fianceira Lar (100%)—Finance company

During their talks, the Shah asked his friend whether President Carter's unwillingness to go to war in Afghanistan meant that "the Americans and the Russians have divided the world between them."[34] Nelson assured him that nothing of the sort had happened, but the Shah continued to worry about some international conspiracy for resources. So while the Rockefellers dined with the Shah, Nelson's Pocantico manager and jack-of-all-trades, Joe Canzeri, dined with the chief of SAVAK, the Shah's secret police.

The Rockefellers returned home to celebrate Nelson's seventieth birthday with 400 guests at Pocantico. Shortly afterward, Nelson experienced another family tragedy. His brother John 3rd, the family's most dedicated philanthropist, was killed in an automobile accident on a road right outside the Pocantico estate.

The shock impressed on Nelson that not much time might be left to prepare the next generation for succession to Rockefeller power or to finish his own projects. He had already changed the policies of the $209 million Rockefeller Brothers Fund and stacked the board with his influence, getting his brothers to agree to put Henry Kissinger's aide, Nancy Hanks (a veteran of Nelson's staff in the Eisenhower White House), and Nelson's son Steven on the board. Nelson's new directors then pledged $50 million in commitments to twenty causes and institutions that the brothers had a personal tie to or had supported for many years.

Former Secretary of Health, Education, and Welfare John Gardner resigned in disgust, expressing disagreement with the "special status" enjoyed by the brothers.[35] The younger Rockefellers took offense, but Nelson once again had his way. This, Nelson explained, was all part of ensuring an orderly transition from one generation to the next,[36] as well as giving the brothers' special interests a final injection of capital. At the same time, he also moved to protect the family's largest single investment, Rockefeller Center. He rewarded Richard Rosenbaum, the man who had field generaled the Rockefeller charge at the 1976 convention to secure the nomination for Ford over Reagan, with a seat on the Center's board.

By August, the rebellion in Iran would be swelling and the Shah's troops wearying of firing volley after volley "point-blank" into unarmed crowds of demonstrators.

Nelson knew that the CIA station of the U.S. Embassy in Teheran was bound to be a target for demonstrations. The CIA had continued to support SAVAK's training and operations, even after SAVAK's brutality became public, and the CIA still relied on SAVAK for intelligence and cooperation. Then there was the link between terror against "communist" dissidents and U.S. taxpayers' money for the Shah; dead communists supposedly assured the continuing flow of oil revenues to pay for the Shah's debts and development schemes. David's Chase Manhattan Bank was the Shah's personal banker, as well as banker to the National Iranian Oil Company and joint owner of the Teheran-based International Bank of

Iran. In 1977, Chase had led the consortium that lent Iranian utilities $500 million; Chase's stake was $50 million.[37] It was not only money that mattered, but plans for the future—and Nelson's personal commitment to a man who, like himself, had a royal blood line that was only two generations old.

COLLAPSE OF THE PEACOCK THRONE

In January 1979, Nelson received a call from Henry Kissinger. His friend was worried that the Shah would perish in Khomeini's revolution because his situation had deteriorated beyond repair. Revolutionary ferment had halted the Karkheh River Basin development project in western Iran, for which IBEC's David Lilienthal had acted as a consultant. IBEC's work with the Khuzestan Water and Power Authority in western Iran near the Abadan oil fields was also coming to naught. The Shah's Industrial and Mining Development Bank reportedly had lent the Shah's family and enterprises of its Pahlavi Foundation more than $510 million, some of it unsecured, in violation of Iranian law.[38] The oil workers were on strike, and the Shah had sent in the navy to occupy the fields, reducing the country to running on less than a third of its normal oil output. Lower oil revenues meant that Iran's creditors would soon start to suffer. And once the Shah was absent from Teheran, Iran's substantial deposits in Chase Manhattan could be stopped and billions of dollars in assets withdrawn by a revolutionary government—unless the Shah's presence in the United States could add weight to a court contest over rightful custody. The Shah, after all, was not just Nelson's personal friend; he was a head of state and an ally of the United States.

Nelson called his troubleshooter, Joe Canzeri, and told him to find a home for the Shah in the United States. Near Warm Springs, Georgia, Canzeri found a hilltop mansion that could easily be secured with fencing and guards.

A week later, with the revolution raging, the Shah agreed to leave Iran, but not forever. He did not abdicate. He even decided to accept the offer of Anwar Sadat to "visit" Egypt en route to his new Rockefeller-procured home in the United States. He had been suspicious of Sadat's offer, fearing it was President Jimmy Carter's ploy to keep him at arm's length, but his brother-in-law and confidant, Ambassador to the United States Ardeshir Zahedi, argued that he should not seem to be fleeing into the arms of the Americans. On January 16, his 707 arrived at Aswan airport, the Shah flying it in himself. The Sadats gave him full honors, complete with a military band and a twenty-one-gun salute. He expected to stay only a short time before proceeding to Georgia. But his brother-in-law again urged restraint. Visit King Hassan, your old friend in Morocco, he urged. The Shah did. Then fate intervened in Manhattan.

CHASE MANHATTAN BANK: A MEETING GROUND OF THE ROCKEFELLER FINANCIAL NETWORK

Corporations marked with an asterisk (*) have investments or significant business in Brazil; corporations with a dagger (†) have invested in, or have done significant business (including oil exploration) in, South America's Amazon River basin.

Board of Directors

1970

With $11.8 billion to be invested by Chase's Trust Department, $8 billion was left to its sole discretion, $3.8 billion shared with other investment advisers.

David Rockefeller, chairman, Chase Manhattan Bank†
Robert O. Anderson, chairman, Atlantic Richfield Company (ARCO)†
C. Douglas Dillon, chairman, U.S. & International Securities
J. Richardson Dilworth, director, Rockefeller Family & Associates; director, Chrysler Corporation*
J. K. Jamieson, chairman, Standard Oil of New Jersey (Exxon)†
Frederick Kappel, chairman, International Paper
Robert Lilley, vice president, AT&T; director, Celanese Corporation*
Jeremiah Milbank, chairman, Commercial Solvents Corporation
Charles Myers, Jr., chairman, Burlington Industries; director, U.S. Steel†; director, R.J. Reynolds Industries
C. Jay Parkinson, chairman, Anaconda*
James Perkins, former president, Cornell University
Richard R. Shinn, president, Metropolitan Life Insurance Company; director, Allied Chemical Corporation*
J. Henry Smith, president, Equitable Life Assurance Society
Whitney Stone, chairman, Stone and Webster*
John A. Swearingen, chairman, Standard Oil of Indiana (AMOCO)†
Thomas A. Wood, president, TAW International Leasing Corporation

1972

Charles Barber, chairman, American Smelting & Refining Company (ASARCO); director, South Peru Copper Corporation

Chase Manhattan Bank: A Meeting Ground (*cont.*)

1976

James H. Binger, director, Honeywell, Inc.*; director, Minnesota Mining & Manufacturing*

Willard C. Butcher, director, American Smelting & Refining Company (ASARCO); director, Firestone Tire & Rubber Company*

John T. Connor, chairman, Allied Chemical*; director, General Electric*; director, General Motors*; director, Warner-Lambert Company*

C. G. Eklund, director, Bendix Corporation*

James L. Ferguson, director, Union Carbide Corporation*

Richard H. Furlaud, chairman, Squibb Corporation*

Patricia R. Harris, director, International Business Machines (IBM)*

Theodore M. Hesburgh, president, Notre Dame University; director, Utah (Mining) International*; director, International Business Machines (IBM)*

William R. Hewlett, director, Chrysler Corporation*

Ralph Lazarus, chairman, Federated Department Stores; director, General Electric*; director, Scott Paper*

Edward T. Pratt, Jr., director, International Paper Company

J. Stanford Smith, director, General Motors*; director, International Paper Company

1980

Alexander Haig, president, United Technologies (resigned to become secretary of state)

1982

Robert Floeree, chairman, Georgia-Pacific†

Howard Kauffmann, President, Exxon†

Richard Lyman, Rockefeller Foundation

John D. Macomber, chairman, Celanese Corporation*

Donald Trautlein, chairman, Bethlehem Steel†

Selected Members of Chase Manhattan Bank's International Advisory Board

Members from Brazil

1970   **Augusto T. A. Antunes**, CAEMI and ICOMI†

1977   **Antonio Gallotti**, president, Brazil Light and BRASCAN—Administração Investimentos Ltda.†

1982   **Paulo D. Villares**, Villares Group*

Members from the United States

1970   **Eugene Black**, former president, World Bank†

William Blackie, chairman, Caterpillar Tractor Company†

Donald C. Burnham, chairman, Westinghouse Electric*

George Champion, former Chase president and chairman

Harrison Dunning, chairman, Scott Paper*

Carl Gerstacker, chairman, Dow Chemical*

Patrick Haggerty, Chairman, Texas Instruments†

William A. Hewitt, chairman, Deere & Company†

John J. Powers, Jr., Pfizer*

Rawleigh Warner, Jr., chairman, Mobil (Standard Oil of New York)†

1977   **Henry Kissinger**, former secretary of state and national security adviser and former executive studies project consultant, Goldman Sachs

1978   **John Louden**, Chairman of Supervisory Board, Royal Dutch Petroleum†

1982   **David Rockefeller**

Chairmen of the boards of American Metal Climax (AMAX); Caterpillar†; Boise Cascade

Sources: Chase Manhattan Bank, annual reports, 1970-1982; *Directory of American Firms Operating in Foreign Countries* (New York: Simon & Schuster), annual, various years; *Engineering and Mining Journal*, November 1975; *Moody's Industrial Manual* (New York: Frederic Hatch & Company) annual, 1970–1982; *Who's Who in America* (Chicago: Marquis Who's Who, Inc., 1972 and 1982 editions); U. S. Senate, 95th Cong., 2d sess., Committee on Governmental Affairs, Subcommittee on Reports, Accounting and Management, *Interlocking Directorates Among the Major U.S. Corporations* (Washington, D.C.: Government Printing Office, 1978).

THE LAST HURRAH

Nelson Rockefeller was in good spirits when he arrived at Room 5600 on January 27. He was now the master of this realm, a hushed hive of scores of secretaries, accountants, and financial analysts busily working to preserve, protect, and defend the Rockefeller name and family empire. Here seventy-five family trusts, valued at more than $1 billion in 1974, were administered. But the family's wealth was much greater. Because of a recent real estate boom, Rockefeller Center alone was worth several hundred million dollars. Twelve other foundations were also under the Rockefellers' influence.

Greater than their money was their reach. David's rule was unquestioned over a bank whose assets had grown from $13.6 billion in 1969 to over $30 billion by 1979. Through Chase, the family not only had access to credit for their own ventures, like IBEC, but had influence on the boards of scores of corporations and private companies and nonprofit institutions, here and abroad. Governments, too, listened to David Rockefeller; Chase's huge trust department commanded a ready market for vital bond sales for everything from housing projects to hospitals, from nuclear power plants to hydroelectric dams, from computers to campuses. In Room 5600, insulated from Manhattan's sirens and roaring streets, Nelson moved through a world of whispered deference to the very mention of his name.

It was a name he had always been comfortable with, unlike his father and his children. Rodman was the exception, hiding his shyness behind a haughty exterior, eager to prove his worth to a doubting father. Despite IBEC's chronic failure to pay a dividend and losses in the tens of millions, Rodman was now drawing an annual salary of more than $100,000.[39] Nelson had not been impressed by Rodman's captaining of IBEC, but at least the company's most important and potential lucrative assets in Brazil had been saved. If the Brazilian Miracle reappeared and the conquest of the Amazon was renewed, IBEC, or whatever firm bought IBEC, would be positioned to make a killing, especially in real estate. The value of the 1,030,000-acre Bodoquena ranch alone would be enormous. The development projects planned or pioneered by IBEC and AIA in areas like the São Francisco River Valley, Mato Grosso, and the Central Planalto would come to fruition eventually, as would scores of downsized versions of the hydroelectric dams and Great Lakes that had been proposed for flooding Indian lands along the Amazon, Xingu, Araguaia, Tocantins, Tapajós, Negro, and—yes—Roosevelt rivers. The economic boom on the frontier, in turn, could only help IBEC's other ventures in the coastal metropolitan areas. Whether IBEC or its successor participated, all hinged on Rodman, which made Nelson uneasy. He and Rodman had never been close. Rodman was starved for affection, and Nelson, like his father before him, was unable to give it.

It had not been that way with Michael, and in these last years he had given the lost son much thought. Like his older brother Steven's reflective retreat from power into antiwar sentiments, philosophy, and the classroom, Michael's withdrawal into anthropology had puzzled his father. Michael had felt the need to step back—as far as New Guinea—to put the Rockefeller name into perspective within a broader human plane. Nelson had never felt such a need. He unquestioningly and eagerly accepted his legacy of power.

Only Laurance, of all of his generation, seemed to recognize the ideological fuel that fired Nelson's drive and backed off from the Manichaean Calvinism that had penetrated and taken over his family's early Baptist roots. With his characteristic sardonic smile, Laurance turned, instead, to his work in conservation and, ultimately, to the inner peace of Zen. His curiosity about venture capital adventures had grown into a belief that conservation and capitalism were not mutually exclusive, but, rather, were mutually dependent if both the planet and humanity were to thrive. It was as if a lifetime of investing in aviation (now extended into outer space through a holding company called National Aviation) had given him a U-2's view of the world, where green—not people or their borders—is seen.*

Laurance still commanded the conservation side of the realm, which Nelson respected. But while Laurance gave beauty to the world, Nelson took it or, rather, bought it for his own possession. Even his decision to share his art collection through reproductions was based on an anticipation of pecuniary return. It was this that gave him such cheer on the morning of January 27 when he entered his office in Room 5600 and began work with his twenty-five-year-old aide, Megan Marshack.

Yet there was also a haunting quality to this effort. His first book on his collection had been of the carvings of New Guinea tribesmen. Other men may have balked at creating a memorial to a dead son by using the carvings of the people who had taken his life, but Nelson had no such qualms. He saw these carvings, like all art, as objets d'art, separate from the people who created them. If he had any interest in the artists themselves, it was only to enhance his own enjoyment of what they had created.

There was nothing new here in Nelson's life. He had the same attitude when he thought he could destroy Diego Rivera's mural because he—or others he respected—found it politically offensive. Placing the Asmat tribesmen's art in a book or in a museum was not different from placing any "primitive" art for display; like pinned butterflies, they were beauty for the eye of the beholder. If anything, such practices were a time-honored tradition in the Americas, since Hernán Cortés dazzled Europe with the art of the slaughtered Aztec Indians and the descendants

*Even this perspective had its contradictions. National Aviation's portfolio was as consciously oriented toward the Pentagon and the industry's "struggling to adjust to the winddown of the Vietnam War" as it was to NASA's space program; see National Aviation's 1971 *Annual Report*, p. 7.

of European colonists in North America established the first museums to preserve the artifacts of the continent's Native American dead. Nelson's father, John, Jr., had collected Navajo rugs and exquisite pottery. John 3rd had collected George Catlin's stoical portraits of "vanishing" Indians, including Catlin's depiction of prairie Indians fleeing before nature's fire. Laurance enjoyed Indian animist myths that enhanced the wonder of nature's beauties. During a tour of South America, he was entranced by local Indian lore about the Iguaçu Falls between Paraguay and Brazil, which had "such obvious hydroelectrical potential,"[40] but in his story for *National Geographic* he did not mention the Indians themselves or ask what had happened to them. The sufferings of indigenous peoples, although lamentable, were never mentioned in Rockefeller accounts of their art. The myth of the essential goodness of a country was not open to question; you either "believed" in the United States or Brazil and were patriotic or risked seeming un-American or un-Brazilian or, in Michael's case, an ingrate before one's European hosts.

Yet, had Michael known the recent political history of the Asmat's clash with Dutch colonial authorities; had he known this origin of the *bisj* poles, the revenge poles that he craved for his father's Museum of Primitive Art; or, finally, had he been told and had he only *listened* to what he heard, he might have broken the acquisitive habits of his family, of his culture, if only for the more selfish reason of protecting his own life. Because he had chosen adventure and taken the risks to possess art he admired, he had perished.

Nelson honored this trait in Michael, much as he honored it in himself. When he published the first volume of his art collection, *Masterpieces of Primitive Art*, it included pieces collected by Michael and himself, dating back to his first acquisition, the Sumatran dagger with the handle shaped like a shrunken human skull, hair and all. Mindlessly, Nelson had included this piece in a book he meant as a tribute to the son who best carried forward his own spirit, at least in this corner of Nelson's capacity for love. He never questioned the more horrifying aspects of what the presence of such tribal art said about the advance of European civilization. Michael, near the end of his short life, did, showing more wisdom than his elders. "The West thinks in terms of bringing advance and opportunity to such a place," he had written his parents from the Dutch colony. "In actuality, we bring a cultural bankruptcy which will last for many years. The Asmat, like every other corner of the world, is being sucked into a world economy and a world culture which insists on economic plenty as a primary ideal."[41]

Now Nelson was preparing another book as a family memorial, this one to the person who had given him his love of art, his mother. He spent the day going over photographs of Abby's collection. Helping him was Megan Marshack, who buoyed his spirits with a good-natured bantering that only she seemed to get away with. Nelson obviously enjoyed her.

Later in the afternoon, Nelson excused himself and hurried over to the

Buckley School, a private elementary school on East Seventy-third Street. Henry Kissinger had agreed to address the student body, which included Nelson's sons by Happy, Nelson, Jr., and Mark. Nelson introduced the former secretary of state.

After the event, Nelson and the boys went to the Rockefeller apartment on Fifth Avenue. That evening after dinner, he said he was going to the office to work on the art project. Instead, he joined Marshack at Junior's old town house on West Fifty-fourth Street, around the corner from Abby's Museum of Modern Art. Nelson had used it as his office, governing the state from there rather than from the dreary Governor's Mansion in Albany, which he seldom shared with either Tod or Happy. He had always had a roving eye. Now, well past the autumn of his years, he had found someone who gave him the illusion of youth.

At about 10:15 P.M., Nelson suffered a massive heart attack. Two hours later, he was pronounced dead at the hospital.

Try as they might, his family and aides could not conceal the fact that Nelson had died in the company of a woman whose home across the street had been paid for by Nelson, as had the flowers he often sent her. Hoping to avoid any suggestion of adultery, Nelson's closest aide, Hugh Morrow, initially told the press that Nelson had been discovered by his bodyguard, slumped over his work at Room 5600. But within twenty-four hours, the cover-up unraveled. Witnesses had seen Megan at Nelson's town house and later at the hospital, still holding the oxygen bottle.

Steven Rockefeller, Jr., handled the matter with grace. Asked during a radio appearance what he would say if she walked in, he responded, "I would say to her, I hope you made Grandfather happy."[42]

On Sunday, January 28, 1979, Nelson's body was cremated. The next day, only his immediate family took part in the procession of limousines that accompanied his ashes to the small family cemetery at Pocantico. As the procession wound its way up a moss-covered road to the grassy hilltop overlooking the Hudson, a news helicopter hovered in the distance. For once in the Nelson Rockefeller story, the press was told to keep a distance.

Three days later, some 2,200 people poured into Riverside Church to attend an invitation-only memorial service. United Nations Secretary General Kurt Waldheim led princes, ambassadors, and other dignitaries from seventy-one nations. Chief Justice Warren Burger, Nixon's replacement for liberal Earl Warren, led the Supreme Court justices. Martin Luther King, Sr., prayed for Nelson's restless soul. Lady Bird Johnson lowered her head in memory of her late husband's friend as Dr. William Sloane Coffin, the liberal pastor who had opposed Nelson's support for "LBJ's War" in Vietnam, gave the invocation. Metropolitan Opera's Roberta Peters sent "Dear Lord and Father of Mankind" echoing through the vaulted Gothic cathedral Nelson's father had built as Christian modernism's answer to Fundamentalism.

While David Rockefeller eulogized his older brother, President Carter sat stiffly in the front pew with Happy, never anticipating how actions Nelson had already taken on behalf of the Shah of Iran would lead to his own fall from power within the year. Former President Jerry Ford was there, too, anticipating the coming Republican victory that might have been his—or Nelson's—had he kept Rockefeller and won the critical northeastern states in 1976. Ford's secretary of state and the next administration's chief of the Central American Task Force, Henry Kissinger, his voice breaking with emotion, recalled his old friend in all his contradictions, his outrageous demands, his perennial optimism, and his loneliness at the top.

Yet it was the least eloquent eulogy that captured the essence of what it meant to be a son of John D. Rockefeller, Jr. Rodman, IBEC's president, bearing a torch that now barely flickered, still staggered under the weight of the dream of what IBEC should have been and his father's expectations. His prose, like his voice, was numb. "I thank God that the world is a better place because Nelson Rockefeller passed by," he finally said, moving Happy to her only tears during the hour and a half ceremony. Rodman's loss, terrible and final, had preceded this day by many years. It was, in its own stilted way, Nelson's most telling legacy.

Except for another: 1,610 works of "primitive art" collected from indigenous peoples around the world. He left them all, valued conservatively at $5 million, to the Metropolitan Museum of Art to keep alive the name of the son whose memory haunted him to the end, Michael.

The day before Nelson's memorial service, 3 million Iranians filled the streets of Teheran to cheer the return of the Muslim priest who had called the Shah "the servant of the dollar." Ayatollah Khomeini, after years of exile, went immediately to his new home, a school on the poorer south side of the city in symbolic disdain for the posh homes that oil money had built in the northern sector. Khomeini was now denouncing American oil companies and the CIA with the same vehemence he had used to condemn the Shah's effort to enfranchise women as an attempt "to corrupt our chaste women" and the Shah's Literacy Corps as a plot to undermine the fundamentalist Muslim clergy in the countryside. Fewer than two weeks later, the Shah's army, reeling before assaults by Islamic militiamen and pro-Khomeini mutinies, collapsed. Within weeks, the Carter administration was reassessing its open-door policy toward the Shah. The monarch, on bad advice, had waited too long to come to the United States; now, without his most powerful advocate, Nelson Rockefeller, to keep them open, the gates were closed. It would take David Rockefeller and Kissinger months to pull them open again, triggering the overrunning of the U.S. Embassy and the taking of hostages that would allow the election of Nelson's arch foe, Ronald Reagan.

By then, a tide of religious fundamentalism had swept over not only Iran, but the United States as well. The Rockefellers' choice for president, George Bush, would have to settle, like Nelson, for second place. Again, it was the socially conservative born-again movement that had rejected the "womanizing divorcee" from New York in 1964 that played a key role. Jimmy Carter had awakened them four years before into political life; after Carter revealed his liberal agenda, they joined forces with the young Turks of the New Right that had backed Reagan in 1976. Together, these forces had swelled into a powerful movement behind Reagan by 1979.

Nelson, quietly backing George Bush, had seen the Reagan wave coming and been appalled. What Nelson never knew was that the principal players in that movement included leaders of the Fundamentalist missionary organization whose success had been shaped by his own career and by his personal allies in government and business: the Wycliffe Bible Translators.

48

THY WILL BE DONE

Retreat of the Chosen

William Cameron Townsend was not happy that one door after another in the Islamic world was slamming in the face of the Lord. Kenneth Pike, his top linguist, was about to visit Iran for consultations with the Shah's government when the Islamic revolution erupted. Translators from the Summer Institute of Linguistics (SIL) already were there; now their prayers were whether to stay. The U.S. Embassy, after all, was still a formidable presence in Teheran.

Muslim countries to the east were also off limits. Afghanistan had balked on a contract despite SIL's efforts that dated back to 1971; the recent communist coup made entry even less plausible. Pakistan's President Ali Bhutto, despite his defense of minorities and Cam's personal appeal, had also hesitated. When he was overthrown by General Zia, CIA-backed cross-border operations against the communist government in Afghanistan began in earnest, triggering the Soviet Union's own massive military intervention.

It looked like Indochina all over again, without the jungle and with the roles reversed. This time, it would be Soviet soldiers dying in a hopeless war against well-armed guerrillas enjoying local support. It would prove to be Leonid Brezhnev's worst mistake and the Soviet Union's fatal adventure, but the CIA's secret war—fought in the name of Allah—also barred Cam's Christian missionaries from having an official sponsor.

Cam's effort to get Bible translators into the Muslim world through its back door, the Soviet Union's southern republics, was no more successful. It was not for want of trying. He made eleven trips to the Soviet Union, mostly to the oil-rich

Caucasus. But the charges that SIL had had links to the CIA in Vietnam and Latin America were having their effect, *Pravda* calling SIL a "nest of spies."

For Cam personally, the worst casualty was not the loss of Vietnam, or even possibly Brazil. The worst was Mexico. He did not have Lázaro Cárdenas behind him now. The former president had died in October 1970, worried to the end about U.S. dominance of the hemisphere. Cam had tried to develop a closer relationship with the Cárdenas family through a museum memorializing his friendship with the "Great Commoner" and Cam's support of the president's Indian policies and confrontation with Standard Oil. In 1977, he invited the president's family—including his son, Senator Cuauhtémoc Cárdenas Solarzano, a rising leader in Mexican national politics—to North Carolina to attend the dedication of the Cárdenas Museum at the JAARS base.

It was a Townsend public relations coup. The Belk fortune was amply represented in the program by scion John Belk, now the mayor of Charlotte, North Carolina. Lieutenant Governor James Green, U.S. Senator Carl Curtis, and Mexican Ambassador Hugo Márgain were also on hand to remind Americans of the importance that Cárdenas and Uncle Cam had for inter-American friendship. But the real stars were the Cárdenas family: the deceased president's widow, who cut the ribbon, and the senator and his wife and two sons.

The Mexican blessing, publicized in the United States and abroad, signaled that all was well again in the world of the Wycliffe Bible Translators. In Peru, Cam's second oldest branch, the military regime deemed it timely to grant SIL a new contract. The process involved still another commission with a new set of recommendations and an offer to SIL of another twenty years. SIL wisely settled for ten. Social stability in Peru was tenuous, and the presence of Americans in sensitive positions could still arouse passions. For instance, teachers had recently gone on strike across the country except in the jungle, where most of SIL's bilingual teachers did not miss a beat. SIL's deference to those in power brought its rewards, first with the renewed contract and then with a medal for Cam from Fernando Belaúnde Terry, who took office again on the promise of Amazonian oil, more deforestation, and fifty new jungle cities.

Similar recognition occurred in the South Pacific. The Philippine Ministry of Education gave SIL a medal for helping dictator Ferdinand Marcos build his "New Society." In 1973, the regime had given SIL the Ramón Magsaysay Award, the prize that had its origins in Nelson Rockefeller's collaboration with Magsaysay's CIA mentor, Colonel Edward Lansdale, in Cold War propaganda. "We would like to erase the impression that there is a dictatorship," Marcos's ambassador had said upon arriving in Charlotte, North Carolina, for the award ceremonies.[1]

Marcos's "New Society" had slated dams and floods for the famous rice terraces of the tribes of Luzon to provide irrigation and electricity for coastal plantations. To build this Bicol River Basin Development Project, the Marcos regime had already received millions of dollars in loans from the Agency for International

Development and Eximbank to finance studies. Although modeled after the Mekong River Basin and the Volta River Basin projects, the Bicol project was billed as the forerunner. AID argued that "once the project is found to be successful it would be replicated in other underdeveloped countries in the world, notably Southeast Asian and African countries."[2]

The selling of all these projects, like Cam's pitches for SIL to Washington, was always couched in the context of their prophylactic benefits against communist insurgencies. Yet the real mobilization of peasants into rebellion, giving communists a local mass base, usually followed the development schemes and relocation plans and growing militarization in the countryside. This was certainly true in the Bicol project, which initiated AID fieldwork in 1972, with firefights between Marcos's constabulary and the New People's Army first recorded in the Camarines Sur in August 1973. Although the value of the projects as a substitute for agrarian reform was unquestionable, they were on the drawing boards before insurgency was serious. It was their implementation and threat of displacing 90,000 Igorot people that made the rebellion serious. The Cold War was a tried-and-true excuse for corporate planners to get money past congressional tightwads in foreign-aid hearings; once the projects were initiated and rebellion broke out, the self-fulfilling prophecy was perpetuated.

Despite counterinsurgency operations in the Philippines that were backed with U.S. helicopters, weapons, and Special Forces, the Kalinga and Bôntoc tribesmen of Luzon were holding their own. This situation worried the CIA station in Manila, especially the tribes' willingness to form a bloc with communist-led guerrillas from the New Peoples Army, the Huks reincarnated. In the Muslim south, on Mindanao and the Sulu Islands, the Moro National Liberation Front (MNLF) was doing the same with small farmers who were being pushed off their lands to make way for plantations that supplied bananas and pineapples to Del Monte (which had recently purchased United Fruit's infamous banana plantations in Guatemala, as well). The Marcos regime put a special emphasis on the Muslim islands; it was here that 80 percent of his army was stationed, having earned the wrath of the local population in February 1974 by indiscriminate use of U.S.-supplied naval firepower against MNLF rebels, almost leveling the city of Jolo, the historical center of Muslim culture. It was here that Marcos sent Christian settlers from the north as part of an "agrarian reform" that applied only to lands on which rice and corn were cultivated, thereby exempting two-thirds of the lands used by exporters like Del Monte. And, it is not surprising, it was here that SIL established its Philippines headquarters in an attempt to occupy local Muslim tribes with the power of the Christian Lord. By 1981, SIL had more personnel in the Philippines (287) than in Peru (262), all working under contracts with Marcos's Education and National Defense departments.

But even in these victories for the Lord, there were portents of change, some of them unsettling. In SIL's younger ranks, there was a growing recognition of the need for a less strident and more sensitive mission in that part of the world. These younger SILers also wanted to upscale SIL's linguistic skills and to embrace new anthropological ones. To earn respect as competent genuine contributors to the science of linguistics, SILers tried to integrate into their work the more recent study of the connection between theories of knowledge and language that interpreted grammar as the conceptualization of experience, including culture. It was precisely this deeper cultural probe that gave linguistics an added attraction to the intelligence community, including the CIA. And it was precisely this nonjudgmental, relativistic equaling of cultural planes and its capacity for self-reflection on one's own values that made it so challenging, even threatening, to those who believed they were the Chosen.

Anthropologist Jon Landaburu charged that there was a lack of professionalism among SIL's translators who, like most technicians, did not have the higher training needed to go beyond the same theory and method they had been learning almost by rote since the inception of SIL's summer sessions. "Is it possible that this attitude has something to do with religious models?" he asked. ". . . Why don't they carry out research aimed at a deeper understanding of the indigenous mentality? . . . In my opinion, the answer is obvious. SIL theory is that which is best adapted to its missionary practice. . . . The missionary tells the Indians 'Give us the form [of your language] so that we can take care of the content.'"[3]

A new voice rose in the debate, SIL's biggest nightmare: Indian critics. In the past, SIL only rarely had to deal with them. In 1959 at the Inter-American Indian Institute's conference in Guatemala, Cam and anthropologist Doris Stone (daughter of United Fruit's chairman "Sam the Banana Man" Zemurray) had helped the U.S. delegation marginalize as "Communist" Guatemalan Indian dissent over the reversal of land reform since the CIA overthrew the elected government of President Jacobo Arbenz.[4] In the past, conferences had been dominated by Anglos or *ladinos* who were delegates of governments; in some cases, Cam and other SILers actually spoke for the Indians as official delegates from Peru.

Now the Indians spoke for themselves. At the second Barbados Conference in 1977, Indian representatives insisted that "the use of language . . . ought to be governed by the Indian people themselves within their own channels of creativity."[5] The following year, Campa Indians in Peru held their first convention that was free of influence by the government's agrarian reform agency. They promptly affiliated with the besieged National Agrarian Confederation and discussed Lima's unwillingness to grant titles to land that lumber interests and foreign oil and other companies coveted. After approving laws on behalf of elders, women, and children, they endorsed the calling of a national Indian congress.

SIL's record had already come under scrutiny for the failure of its Peru branch to push for land titles or to intervene against Cities Service in 1974 for turning an SIL airstrip into a supply depot, then trying to destroy fruit trees to lengthen the airstrip—all without permission from the local Amarakaeri Indians.

In Mexico's southern state of Chiapas, the site of recently located oil deposits, journalists investigating U.S. missions in Chiapas began focusing on SIL's jungle training camp. Beleaguered by calls for protectionism, the government of José López Portillo distanced itself from SIL. Officials of the National Indian Institute launched investigations into SIL's practices and record of compliance with its contract with them.

As foreigners and opponents of many of the Indians' religious traditions, SILers were easy scapegoats. The smoke from SIL's sacrifice served as a screen for López Portillo's sale of oil and natural gas to the United States. Two weeks after the unpopular natural-gas negotiations with the Carter administration culminated in a deal, Mexico's Education Department announced that its contract with SIL was over. SIL members would no longer be able to receive student visas, a privilege enjoyed since the 1930s. Half the branch was obliged to retreat back to SIL's new International Linguistics Center in Dallas; SIL's fabled jungle training camp in Chiapas was closed. For SIL, the era of Cárdenas was over.

It had been over for the Mexican people for some forty years. South of the United States, environmental and labor conditions had deteriorated for Mexicans who were working in vegetable plantations of firms like Del Monte serving the U.S. winter market and in factories of American companies that had abandoned the American worker in search of low-wage labor. Out of this poverty amid foreign-dominated development, the name Cárdenas again emerged as a symbol of resistance. His family had watched the investigations around SIL. Persuaded by mounting charges of improprieties, they, too, began to distance themselves. For Cam, this was a hard blow.

The worst came in November 1980, when the Inter-American Indian Institute (III) sponsored the next Inter-American Indian conference in Mérida, Mexico, the country of its birth. Cam led SIL's traditional delegation. But for the first time in its history, the conference included many Indian representatives of governments. Cam listened, disbelieving, as delegate after delegate denounced his life's work. SIL was "an ideological and political institution,"[6] he heard, its scientific name concealing not only a religious agenda, but a worldview that was alien to Indian traditions and a U.S. political force that undermined national sovereignty. SIL's allies—notably the delegations from the military regimes of Chile, Bolivia, Brazil, Paraguay, and Honduras—fought back, but now they were a minority. The majority of the conference's delegates passed a resolution calling on member governments to scrutinize SIL's activities and, if necessary, to banish the organization.

To give their target a human face, the delegates focused on the man among them who most symbolized SIL: its founder, William Cameron Townsend. It was a chance for the Inter-American Indian Institute Conference to salvage its credibility and authenticity and to rescue the name of Cárdenas from gringo usurpers. For Cam, it may have been the worst day of his life.

A resolution was introduced to strip him of the title "Benefactor of the Linguistically Isolated Population of America," an honor given him at the previous conference in Brazil in 1972. The delegates rose and gave the resolution a standing ovation. When the applause finally ended, Cam left, never to return.

It was the culmination of a rise of national Indian organizations throughout the Western Hemisphere. In Brazil, Indian resistance had grown since progressive Catholic clerics, acting as the Indigenist Missionary Council, had sponsored Indian leadership conferences. In 1980, Indian leaders assembled at Campo Grande in Mato Grosso do Sul, Brazil, and formed the Union of Indian Nations (UNI), Brazil's first national Indian organization. One of the leaders of the Xavante tribe, Mário Juruna, was then denied his right to attend the Fourth Russell Tribunal on Human Rights in Rotterdam. FUNAI argued before the Brazilian court that Juruna was legally their ward and as a minor, he could not leave the country without FUNAI's permission; FUNAI lost. Juruna not only attended, but chaired some of the tribunal's sessions and went on to become the first Amazonian Indian elected to the Brazilian Congress. Under the watchful eye of the international press, bigots now had to suffer the challenges of an Indian fellow congressman.

Cam should have seen it coming. In 1976, when SIL was preparing to enter the Uaupés jungle in northwestern Brazil at the request of the military regime and the U.S. Bureau of Indian Affairs, the BIA's strongest Indian opponent, the American Indian Movement (AIM), was already moving into the international arena. SIL translators had seen them at the hearings in Geneva of the United Nations' international Human Rights Commission. After a dramatic entry beating drums, AIM leaders presented the cases of the seizure of the Sioux's Black Hills for gold and now uranium, of strip-mining in Colorado and Wyoming on Indian reservations, of the deaths of Navajo uranium miners in New Mexico, and on and on, joining the Indian chorus from other countries where charges ranged from theft and repression to systematic ethnocide and, in the case of the Aché of Paraguay, genocide.

THE RESURRECTION OF RONALD REAGAN—AND HOLOCAUST

In the face of such growing resistance and his own humiliation at the Inter-American Indian Conference, Cam consoled himself by knowing the Will of the Lord and seeing it expressed in the victory that month of Ronald Reagan. He had made himself part of Reagan's will to conquer the Rockefeller liberals of his party, the Lord's Will to let it happen, Americans' will to see that it did.

In 1979, after Nelson Rockefeller had passed from living humanity into history, Cam had gathered with other members of Christian Fundamentalism to form the Religious Roundtable. The choice of the name was not accidental.

The Business Roundtable, which had been formed earlier in the decade by corporate luminaries, had been at the heart of corporate reaction to the environmental, labor, and foreign policy reforms urged by the grass-roots consumer and political movements of the 1960s and 1970s. Disenchantment with Carter by social conservatives and born-again Christians convinced a sales executive from one corporate member, Colgate-Palmolive, that the time was ripe to organize Fundamentalism with corporate organizational techniques and money into a new political movement in the United States. The targets were politicians who did not pass the test of biblical purity. Such tests had first been used during the 1976 elections, when candidates in the primaries in Texas were confronted with a thirty-five-page questionnaire prepared by Fundamentalists; the primary winners were those who had been judged most biblically "correct."[7] By 1979, Virginia preacher Jerry Falwell's Moral Majority was targeting liberals like Frank Church, chairman of the Senate Intelligence Committee, for political oblivion. Falwell's goal was a Fundamentalist president and a Fundamentalist Congress ruling a Christian America. He had reason to hope for success. Pollsters estimated that more than 45 million Protestants considered themselves evangelicals, and although they did not vote as a bloc, most were conservative, white, and suburban and deeply upset by the social reform and protest movements. Like their rural forebears from small towns, they blamed cities for the sins of women's liberation, the Equal Rights Amendment, abortion, drugs, and wayward children.

Criminals, homosexuals, and socialists were grouped together in the litany of the damned, with liberals, biological scientists, and "secular humanists" a close second in the race to hell. Satan's commission was winning, they feared, and Carter's defense policy had left the South, the home of many of the nation's military bases, yearning for defense contracts on the scale of the prosperous war years. Ironically, the Vietnam War had left many Americans with a general decline of faith in science and rationality. Some, because it was fought at all, others, because they believed it was not fought hard enough. In both camps of dissenters, the blame was put on liberal policymakers. Millions of Americans felt frightened and were easy prey to apocalyptic visions.

Ronald Reagan appeared to share those visions and sought to appeal as a savior to those who held them. There were profound political differences within the evangelical movement, but all evangelicals had one common characteristic: They tended to be more conservative than their peers in every demographic group and were at least a large minority of each.[8] Carter's people, too, understood the importance of these voters. "We're working as if born-again were the crucial factor in this election," said an aide.[9] But it was Reagan who stole the show, helped by Jerry Falwell and his Texas-based colleague, Jim Robinson. "I'll do anything I can to see that Carter is not re-elected," Robinson said.[10]

Yet, of all the principles building the Religious Right into a cohesive political force, the most important was perhaps the least known. Edward McAteer was the

Colgate-Palmolive salesman who was the real organizing force behind the politi-cized Fundamentalist movement. McAteer had the glib tongue of his profession, substituting Christ for soap in his market analysis. He was more than a friend of Cam Townsend; he was a major figure on the board of Wycliffe Associates, which was now a powerhouse of resources for SIL, providing it and JAARS with con-struction skills, money, promotion, and overnight stays for furloughed translators on fund-raising tours. In return, testimonies from returned translators, films, books, and slide shows parlayed surrogate travels around the world for suburban believers. Special trips to the jungle bases allowed the more affluent faithful actu-ally to partake in adventure for God. The sheer human energy amassed by Wycliffe Associates was impressive, but the financial core was fueled by reliable wealthy SIL backers like North Carolina's James A. Jones, one of the largest con-tractors for military bases in Vietnam, and oilman Nelson Bunker Hunt of Texas. "Bunker Hunt had helped me considerably," McAteer freely offered.

Wycliffe Associates' "500 Club" was designed to offer the richer members a way out of service through cash; $500 or more each year was all it took to get a special certificate of membership. Some gave much more. Texas's corporate lead-ers were prominent in helping Cam build SIL's International Linguistics Center near Dallas; the Linguistics Center's board meeting was one of those special occa-sions where a Rockefeller business partner like Trammel Crow could rub shoul-ders with an ultrarightist like Nelson Bunker Hunt. But they were the old core of supporters. The real power in Wycliffe Associates was its thousands of newer members, spreading the influence of SIL across the country, and the influence of Wycliffe Associates in Cam's organization.

Promoting and leading this base of support into politics was McAteer's forte. During the Carter administration, his name began to appear among New Right circles in Washington, D.C., connected with North Carolina's Senator Jesse Helms. It was McAteer who brought Jerry Falwell into this crowd, helping Falwell build the Moral Majority. Then, in 1979, McAteer organized the Religious Roundtable. Well funded, McAteer pulled together many of the Fundamentalists leaders of the nation to back the candidacy of Ronald Reagan.

Cam was one of those who followed McAteer into the founding meeting of the Religious Roundtable. If he had any reservations about where this would lead SIL and how it would play in Latin America (where Reagan's name was anathema because of his condemnation of Carter's Panama Canal treaty), Cam's base of sup-port in the homeland and his top financial backers left him little choice. He was, at the end of his career, trapped by the Far Right Fundamentalist base on which he had built Wycliffe's success at home.

Cam explained his political metamorphosis as nonideological, the result of a service to God and Indian that led him into a different set of circumstances. He never recognized that his success abroad was the result of more earthly powers, not the least of whom was Nelson Rockefeller.

In 1980, while Ronald Reagan was riding fear and anger to the White House, Cam celebrated the dedication of SIL's new translation of the Cakchiquel New Testament in Guatemala. Cam's old translation, done fifty years before, had proved inadequate. Many of the Indians had found his celebrated psychophonemic translation too general to be understood by Indians speaking different Cakchiquel dialects. SIL accompanied its release with a new edition of *Tolo: The Volcano's Son,* Cam's tale of how Guatemalan Indians almost succumbed to the temptation of Russian-inspired Indian revolutions raging across the border in El Salvador. Only now, perhaps in deference to Cam's ambition to have SIL enter the Soviet Caucasus, the Russian was simply called a "foreigner."

In the Guatemalan hills that had launched his career, Cam could see the results of the Lord's Will. If they were not all he had hoped for, there was at least a great harvest of souls. If he was disturbed that many of these souls had been dispatched to their Maker by murder or that many of these murders now included Cakchiquel Protestants, he did not say, at least publicly. The seizure of Indian lands along highways leading to recent mineral and oil strikes had politicized the Christian highlanders. Most of these evangelized Maya tribes were the same Indians who had all but ignored the fall of Arbenz in 1954 and had shown little interest in the ladino guerrillas who had been hunted down by the army and the Green Berets in the 1960s. Now, however, they were learning firsthand about the army and its U.S. military and CIA advisers. In May 1978, more than 600 Kekchí Indians who were protesting eviction from the Polochí Valley were fired upon by the army in Panzós, Alta Verapaz, a new oil-exploration district about 125 miles north of Guatemala City.[11] The Panzós massacre of some 100 men, women, and children was a turning point; word raced through the highlands, radicalizing whole villages. Indians of the Guerrilla Army of the Poor entered Nebáj in El Quiché department on a Sunday market day in January 1979 and made speeches to some 3,000 Indian campesinos. The army responded with a brutal occupation.

In January 1980, a delegation of twenty-seven Ixil Indians and clerical supporters from villages in Quiché took their protest over seized lands and mounting army repression to the Spanish Embassy after they had been turned away from the Congress, the Presidential Palace, and the U.S. Embassy. Oil had been struck by France's Elf Aquitaine at Rubelsanto, north of the Ixil villages, in 1972. Since then, four other companies had moved in: Shenandoah Oil (which had Elliot Roosevelt, Jr., the late president's son, as a director); Texaco; Saga Petroleum, a Norwegian partner with Shenandoah in exploring off the coast of Ireland; and Elf's partner, Basic Resources International, on whose board sat Rockefeller associate Robert W. Purcell, director and past chairman of Nelson's International Basic Economy

Corporation and a director of Rockefeller Center.* Big money was at stake. In 1977, Basic Resources and Shenandoah announced plans to link the Rubelsanto oil field and the Atlantic coast of Guatemala with a $30 million, twelve-inch pipeline capable of carrying 50,000 barrels of oil a day.[12]

The Ixils of northern Quiché had never been passive about injustice from outsiders. They had twice revolted against the dictatorship of Jorge Ubico and had supported the revolution that overthrew him. When the Arbenz government, in turn, was overthrown by the CIA, the Ixils suffered persecution for having participated in land reform. Five hundred were sent into exile in the jungles of Petén; others were murdered or jailed.[13] In the ensuing decade, colonization projects promoted by the military regime—some involving Nelson Rockefeller's AIA as consultants to the Organization of American States' Inter-American Institute of Agricultural Services,[14] others organized as cooperatives by Catholic Action and American Maryknoll priests—began to move into northern Huehuetenango and northern Quiché.

The Ixil watched these developments carefully. For decades, they had resisted efforts by ladino landlords and the military to force them off their lands. In 1971, they revolted, and the regime had to send in troops. For the Ixils, it was a losing battle against a land-tenure system that absorbed the most fertile Ixil lands into large plantations for cash crops for export. This system consistently reduced the size of the Indians' small farms to below subsistence level and forced the Indians to work on the plantations for an average wage of $1.50 a day. Tied to the price fluctuations of the coffee markets of New York and London, this system left 80 to 90 percent of the Indian population illiterate and 75 percent of their children under the age of five malnourished. Life expectancy for non-Indians was sixty years; for Indians, forty-four years, tying neighboring Honduras, another banana republic, for the shortest life span in Central America.[15]

The Ixils' one fallback was their ancestral lands in the jungles of northern Quiché. Then in 1972 came the worst news yet: Oil had been struck in northern Quiché. A highway was cut into the region, which sent land values soaring. The pressure on both the Ixil and the Indian settlers in the northern colonies increased, as high ranking military officers laid claim to the jungle lands, displaying deeds granted earlier by the regime.[16]

These were the conditions that had prompted several Ixil villages to send a delegation to Guatemala City in 1980 and, ultimately, to peacefully occupy the Spanish Embassy when no one would hear their grievances.

Before anyone thought to ask why the Indians were there, and despite the Spanish ambassador's explicit request that the embassy's extraterritorial rights be respected by Guatemala's military regime, the building was promptly surrounded

*IBEC had already sold its coffee interests in Guatemala, but Basic Resources International, which was based in Luxembourg and the Bahamas, offered greater returns. Besides the one at Rubelsanto, Basic Resources and its French partner, Elf Aquitaine, also found oil fields at Caribe and at West Chinaja.

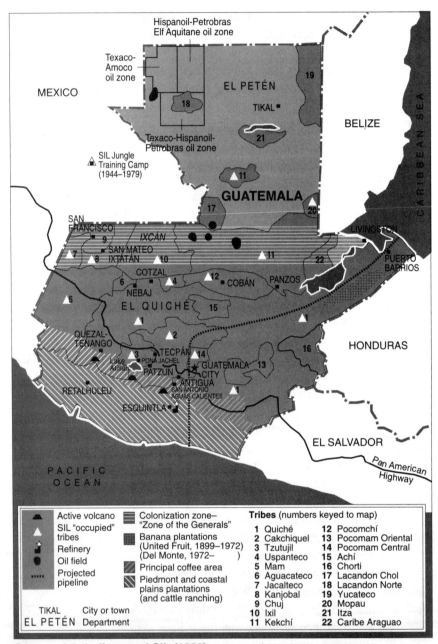

Guatemala's Indians and SIL (1980)

Legend:

- ▲ Active volcano
- △ SIL "occupied" tribes
- ◆ Refinery
- ● Oil field
- ▪▪▪▪▪ Projected pipeline
- ▦ Colonization zone— "Zone of the Generals"
- ▨ Banana plantations (United Fruit, 1899–1972) (Del Monte, 1972–)
- ▨ Principal coffee area
- ▨ Piedmont and coastal plains plantations (and cattle ranching)
- TIKAL City or town
- EL PETÉN Department

Tribes (numbers keyed to map)

1 Quiché	12 Pocomchí
2 Cakchiquel	13 Pocomam Oriental
3 Tzutujil	14 Pocomam Central
4 Uspanteco	15 Achí
5 Mam	16 Chorti
6 Aguacateco	17 Lacandon Chol
7 Jacalteco	18 Lacandon Norte
8 Kanjobal	19 Yucateco
9 Chuj	20 Mopau
10 Ixil	21 Itza
11 Kekchí	22 Caribe Araguao

Sources: Wycliffe Bible Translators, "Wycliffe Bible Translators in Central America" (1976); Summer Institute of Linguistics, *Bibliography of the Summer Institute of Linguistics, Volume One: 1935–1975* (Dallas: Summer Institute of Linguistics, 1979) and *Volume Two: 1976–1982* (Dallas: Summer Institute of Linguistics, 1985); *International Petroleum Encyclopedia, 1983* (Tulsa, Okla.: PennWell Publishing Company, 1983); "Lenguas Indígenas de Guatemala" (map), Instituto Geográfico Nacional, Guatemala, 1975; Beatriz Manz, *Refugees of a Hidden War: The Aftermath of Counterinsurgency in Guatemala*.

by troops and firebombed, killing almost everyone, including the embassy staff, inside. The one Indian survivor was subsequently kidnapped from his hospital bed; his mangled body was found a few days later on the university campus as a warning to students.

Spain immediately broke off relations with Guatemala. But by 1982, relations were back on track as Basic Resources International brought Spain's national oil company, Hispanoil, into plans to develop its 500,000-acre concession. The concession in the Ixil ancestral territory now had two producing oil fields and the 50,000-barrel-a-day pipeline to Puerto Barrios, United Fruit's old shipping terminal on the Caribbean coast.

Meanwhile, Guatemala was developing a reputation as a killing ground. Since the CIA's 1954 coup, the number of Guatemalans who were murdered and tortured to death by CIA-advised security forces, Green Beret–trained army troops, and night-stalking death squads had reached an estimated 80,000.[17] Indians who made up the Guerrilla Army of the Poor were expelling SIL translators and engaging the regime's troops in open battles that inspired evangelical conversions on an unprecedented scale. "It was during the guerrilla activity of the early 1980s that it really turned around," an SILer later explained. "So many people were killed. There was so much upheaval.* Their old [Mayan] way wasn't working."[18] Guatemala's official National Indian Institute kept peace with the military by ignoring the massacres in the hills; not one article on the atrocities appeared in its bulletin, although one did appear in 1982 honoring Cam, ironically, as an eminent "humanist."[19]

That year Cam's legacy to Guatemalan Protestantism also took a bloody turn. General Efraín Ríos Montt, converted after the 1976 earthquake to the Church of the Word by Gospel Outreach missionaries from California, seized power one month after the guerrilla groups politically united. Assassinations of the regime's political opponents in the cities by death squads and six months of Indian holocaust were creating a terrible image abroad of an army that had turned against its own people while mobilizing much of the population into the ranks of the revolution. Ríos Montt initiated a new approach to the war that actually looked quite old to the CIA counterinsurgency experts who were advising him. The new strategy involved a scaling down of violence in the cities, where reporters could confirm an improved climate, while in the countryside a grimmer drama was taking place behind the veil of military quarantine and censorship: the forced removal of Indian populations to strategic hamlets, an involuntary civilian militia, and "free-fire" zones for the army in supposedly evacuated areas. More than 400 Indian villages were destroyed or damaged,[20] and some 500,000 to 1 million people were uprooted. Thousands were forced into barbed-

*Susan Jewett's comment was similar to what SIL's Thomas Weisman told the authors in Zurich, Switzerland, in 1978 about the conversions won during the Biafra Civil War in Nigeria: "As the old systems cracked, people were open for new spiritual values," he explained. "It was similar to Vietnam." Interview with Thomas Weisman, Zurich, Switzerland, February 5, 1978.

wired reindoctrination camps that were commanded by army interrogators and served by SIL translators and Christian aid agencies, or put on deadly forced marches to the border. As the holocaust rolled northward, some 70,000 Indians fled into Mexico, worrying the Mexican government that Indian unrest would spread. Ríos Montt took to the airwaves amid the slaughter, preaching sermons to the nation, a born-again Christian dictator rapidly descending into what many believed was madness. In December, the general slipped quietly into Honduras (where the CIA was arming displaced Miskito Indians for attacks on the Sandinista government in Nicaragua) for a discreet rendezvous with President Ronald Reagan.

Reagan was near the end of a hemispheric tour that included a gaffe that astonished his Brazilian hosts (he invited the junta's president, with great flourish, to "join me in a toast to the people of Bolivia"), sharp criticism from Colombia's president over the U.S.-backed Contra war in Nicaragua, rioting in Bogotá, U.S. concessions in Brasília (dropping objections to Brazil's export subsidies, easing U.S. sugar quotas, a $1.2 billion loan to help the regime's austerity measures, and hints at renewed military ties and resumed sales of nuclear fuel to Brazil), and his own proclamations of El Salvador's "progress" in human rights (at least enough to warrant continued U.S. military aid). He had no problem granting Ríos Montt's simple request for a meeting. It would give his dictatorship a badly needed boost among Guatemala City's elite, who were nervous about the general's Fundamentalist evangelical fervor ("God gives power to whomever he wants, and he gave it to me.") and his demagogic raving that the country's battered, terrorized Indian majority "should be its rulers, not its slaves."[21]

Cam never publicly questioned his translators' presence behind army lines in Guatemala, any more than he questioned Ronald Reagan's leadership. Typically, Cam never seemed to doubt his own innocence when others, caught in the ambiguities of his Hail, Caesar policy, died in the inevitable crossfire, even when the victims were four American churchwomen who were murdered by an army death squad in El Salvador, and even when the victims included an SIL translator in Colombia.

The Fruits of Martyrdom

Chester Bitterman had wanted nothing more in life than to serve the Lord by translating the Word for people who had never read the Bible. A native of Lancaster, Pennsylvania, Bitterman was attracted to the dynamism of the Wycliffe Bible Translators. "Like his colleagues, Chester Bitterman left the United States as a missionary of the Wycliffe Bible Translators," commented anthropologist David Stoll, "but arrived in the field as something else, a scientific investigator of the Summer Institute of Linguistics."[22] Carrying this dual identity, Bitterman was trapped in the perception of SIL as something duplicitous, even clandestine.

Bitterman was only twenty-eight in 1981, a graduate of Billy Graham's alma mater, South Carolina's Columbia Bible College, and son-in-law of SIL's flight manager in Colombia. His post was among the 120 Carijona Indians of southern Colombia's Caquetá region, an area known to harbor both guerrillas and Indians whom the CIA used to hunt the guerrillas; in fact, in 1976, a Drug Enforcement Agency (DEA) agent was expelled for allegedly being a CIA officer who clandestinely trained Indians in Caquetá for just such a purpose.[23] During the year and a half Bitterman had tried to gain Colombian approval for his tribal work, SIL was again under intense scrutiny. In 1978, Cam had to intervene personally with President Julio Turbay Ayala to prevent SIL's expulsion. By 1980, marijuana and coca planters and armed rebels so frightened SIL's Lomalinda base that President Turbay sent in troops to protect it. Rumors still abounded that the Yankee translators were informers for the police, if not for the CIA station in the Bogotá embassy.*

On January 19, 1981, SIL's Bogotá residence, which had already been bombed in the summer of 1976, had unexpected visitors. Seven armed men burst in, looking for branch director Alvaro Wheeler. Learning he was not there, they seized instead the young translator. Chester Bitterman, suffering from a gall bladder ailment, had unluckily left the Carijona Indians to go to Bogotá for medical treatment.

The kidnappers sent a message to President Reagan: SIL must leave Colombia immediately; if not, the hostage would be executed.

The Reagan administration did not negotiate with hostage takers; that was what Reagan had said about Iran and Beirut. It was policy.

The kidnappers said they were M-19 guerrillas, the movement launched after the miraculous April 19, 1970, reelection of the incumbent National Front. The congressional opposition had called for SIL's expulsion. Was it not reasonable to believe that M-19 had decided on more drastic measures?

The leaders of M-19 denied it. They had everything to lose by this attack on unarmed missionaries. Only recently, *Cromos*, a magazine that had run the stories on the investigations of SIL, had released a poll that placed two M-19 leaders as the first and second in national popularity. President Turbay was tenth. Now, buoyed by the outcry over Bitterman's kidnapping, Turbay charged M-19 fighters with having been trained in Cuba. Such charges of outside intervention increased his standing among Colombian nationalists, disarmed his opposition, and pleased the Kissinger task

---

*SIL's Colombia branch leader Alvaro Wheeler could publicly deny any relationship between SIL and the CIA, insisting that the CIA was prohibited from querying missionaries. But U.S. Consul-General Richard Morefield reported secretly to Washington on March 12, 1979, that he knew of no such ban. William Colby's 1976 rulings apparently had never been taken seriously. Morefield also confided that SIL "would have no alternative but to provide the information requested" of it by Colombian authorities. "Failure to cooperate would only lead to great difficulty." Quoted in David Stoll, *Fishers of Men or Founders of Empire? The Wycliffe Bible Translators in Latin America* (London: Zed Press, 1982), p. 84.

force charged with combating the specter of "Castro terrorism." M-19 desperately blamed another faction. That faction also denied it. When the two groups conferred on February 14, they concluded that they had been set up. They blamed the intelligence service of the military, which had recently come under criticism by the OAS for torture and murder. Perhaps the real architect, said the groups, was the CIA. But no one in SIL bought it. The CIA did not abuse Americans' rights, much less deliberately put Americans in mortal danger; the CIA existed to protect American lives.

The Reagan administration continued to refuse to negotiate. SIL refused to consider withdrawal; it had plans to enter fifteen more tribes and to stay until 1995.

On March 7, Bitterman's body was found wrapped in an M-19 flag in a parked van. He had been shot through the heart. M-19 denied responsibility and condemned the murder. President Turbay condemned M-19 again and ordered the army to arrest 100 of his critics who he believed were M-19 supporters, including an official of the Council of Latin American Churches.

In Washington, Secretary of State Alexander Haig expressed shock and anger: Military aid was needed and counterinsurgency operations would be stepped up, killing more than 30,000 persons by the end of the decade.[24] The violence and public outcry would force the National Front to offer M-19 an amnesty. M-19, which had a more flexible strategy than Che Guevara's focus on the path of the guerrilla, accepted and entered the electoral arena, but at a high price: the assassination of their presidential candidate. In Lancaster, Pennsylvania, Bitterman's family buried their son. His mother had already expressed her belief that Chet had been destined by the Lord to minister to M-19.[25] Chet's widow found comfort in the same conclusion: "I know this was God's ministry for Chet. He was chosen!"[26]

Two months later, Cam was in the audience as Billy Graham made Chester Bitterman the focus of his sermon at Wycliffe's Golden Jubilee Rally at Anaheim, California. "To serve Him is costly, as the Bittermans have found out and as those five brave young men killed by the Aucas found out," Graham said.

> But the rewards are overwhelming in this life and the life to come. It's already been demonstrated time and time again that the death of those brave young men in Ecuador [in 1956] led to a whole new dimension of missions in other countries. And Chet Bitterman's going home to glory I believe was planned in the providence of God to open up a new chapter in missions. To call up the young men and young women to say, "I'll go and take his place so that Chet Bitterman will be multiplied hundreds and thousands of times over until his job is finished. . . ."
>
> There are three thousand languages yet to go. Wycliffe can now absorb about five hundred new translators and back up personnel a year. This means that every one of these language groups can be touched and occupied within this decade of the eighties. . . .
>
> I'm convinced that we're approaching the last days. We must work before the night comes and we come back to our text . . . the Good News About the

Kingdom will be preached throughout the whole world so that all nations will hear it, and *then*, and *then*, and *then*, the end will come!

I don't see but one thing standing in the way of the coming of the Lord. Now I believe He could come tonight. But there's one thing . . . that puzzles me in the signs: All nations must hear. And this is what Cameron Townsend has always believed.[27]

Years later, SIL leaders at the International Linguistics Center would try to play down the millennialism that drove Cam's vision of SIL's mission,[28] but Cam himself was not confused. For him, the evidence of the Lord's Will in this tragedy was in the 70 percent increase in SIL recruits during the next year, a 22 percent boost in contributions, and a sudden positive change in SIL's fortunes throughout Latin America that more cynical observers might have attributed to the equally dramatic change taking place in Washington with the triumph of Fundamentalism's candidate, Ronald Reagan.[29]

At Peace with the Lord

Ronald Reagan's election had been followed by a reprieve for SIL in Brazil. The military regime no longer thought SIL a threat to national security and opened negotiations for SIL to enter the uranium-rich northwestern Amazon. In Colombia's Congress, Alejandro Carrion also argued for SIL to remain, claiming that SIL's opponents were in league with the same Satanic forces directed by Moscow who had murdered Chester Bitterman.[30] In civilian-restored Ecuador, two days after President Jaime Roldos ordered SIL's branch to leave the country, he died in a plane crash.

The same fate hit Panama's General Omar Torrijos. In July 1981, Torrijos expelled SIL's branch on six days' notice. Shortly afterward, his plane, too, fell from the sky. SIL remained. As elsewhere, the Lord's hand was easier to see than that of the alleged real assassin: drug trafficker and then-CIA collaborator Manuel Noriega.

In Bolivia, General Ariel Coca eventually saved SIL from some difficulties under civilian President Lidea Guelier by arranging the bloody "cocaine coup" of 1980. Then he got SIL to accept his Education Ministry's award in February 1981,[31] just a few months before he was exposed as Bolivia's major cocaine trafficker. Cocaine now brought $1.6 billion a year into Bolivia, three times the amount received for tin, the leading legal export. Meanwhile, Indian miners continued to die from silicosis. In the state-owned tin mines, miners with ten years underground had an estimated 40 percent chance of contracting lung cancer and an average life expectancy of fewer than forty years.[32]

As murderous "clearances" razed the Mayan highlands of Guatemala and as veterans of CIA's CORDS program appeared in Guatemala and El Salvador (where the military and death squads would kill 50,000 people between 1981 and 1985[33] in a carnage rivaling the Pipil Indian massacres of Cam's *Tolo* days), along with much of the CIA's old secret air network from Southeast Asia, Cam Townsend continued to remain serene with the Lord. Not even his own deteriorating health seemed to affect him.

In August 1981, a month after observing his eighty-fifth birthday and the same month he had celebrated the Golden Jubilee of his translation of the Cakchiquel New Testament, Cam's physician told him he had borderline leukemia.

He took the news in stride. In October, he flew to Lima. Five years had passed since SIL had weathered the final storm of the 1968 "Revolution" of young colonels led by General Juan Velasco Alvarado. Among the senior officers who had stood by SIL was Admiral Luis Vargas Caballero, the former navy minister who had been fired by Velasco in 1974. Vargas's successor challenged the CIA's influence, expelled a CIA officer, and was rewarded with terrorist attacks that were later confirmed as having come from Peru's Naval Intelligence Service. All this came to a head in 1976 when Vargas and the other remaining Velasco ministers were purged in a coup directed by older admirals and generals, the same coup that saved SIL from expulsion. To meet the demands of American banks and the Washington-based International Monetary Fund, the new military regime cut government programs for peasants, workers, and Amazonian Indians; changed laws to remove obstacles to pillaging the Amazon; and curtailed Indian land rights. In 1979, while firing Indian bilingual teachers who joined the national teachers' strike, the minister of education attended SIL's ceremony announcing the completion of five New Testaments. This general's presence was proof of whose side God was on.

That point may have been lost on the Indians who suffered most from the "economic reforms" of the post-Velasco years. The per capita protein intake in Peru had been halved since 1974, to less than 50 percent of the minimum standard set by the United Nations' Food and Agriculture Organization. A Catholic missionary testifying before a U.S. Senate committee in 1980 said that Peru's infant mortality rate had climbed to over 80 percent, resulting in the deaths of at least 30,000 children who would not have died in 1974 under Velasco.[34]

But Cam was not in Peru to voice his concern. He was there because President Fernando Belaúnde, restored to office and still promising Peruvians escape from their international debts through the conquest of the Amazon, was giving him Peru's Order of the Sun. It was the highest award Peru could bestow on a foreigner; not even Nelson Rockefeller had been so honored.

That same month, in the mountains of Cam's beloved Cakchiquels, Guatemalan army columns arrived in full battle gear. General Benedicto Lucas had decided to move 5,000 troops into Chimaltenango, just west of Guatemala City, for a "final offensive" against Indian guerrillas. It was an offensive that, in fact, involved few confrontations with the guerrillas, but did achieve the systematic massacre of thousands of unarmed Indians, the Indian population having been targeted as the social base for the guerrillas. By 1986, a study by St. Anne's Parish in Chimaltenango reported that 8,000 to 10,000 people had disappeared, most of them believed killed, leaving behind 3,000 orphans (1,000 of these children had lost both parents).[35]

By January 1982, the army's offensive had pushed north into Quiché, home of the Ixil. The army's elite shock troops, the *kaibiles*, struck by night and from the air, using U.S.-made helicopters and Special Forces advisers. On January 4, Guatemalan troops descended on the town of San Bartolo; gathered some 300 Indian men, women, and children; and began slaughtering them, community after community. Children's throats were slit, men were crucified, and women were raped and cut open. The sheer horror was enough to send the countryside into a panic. But its impact on SIL's commitment to silence was negligible.

Later that month, Cam attended Wycliffe's board meeting. The reports were heartening. Chester Bitterman's martyrdom had had an impact unlike anything seen since the Auca slayings. Wycliffe was now the largest independent mission in history, with more than 4,500 members working in 735 indigenous language groups. There were still thousands of language groups to be reached. Wycliffe had long ago quietly dropped the slogan, "Every tribe by '85."

In Guatemala, however, there would be fewer Indians to reach. More than sixty massacres would take place in 1982. Villages targeted as "lost" to the Indian guerrillas were attacked without regard for the human rights of civilians. The army slaughters forced the dislocation of some 1 million out of the 4 million people who lived in the Mayan highlands, including 30,000 who fled across the border into the Lacondón jungle of Chiapas, Mexico, not far from SIL's recently abandoned jungle training camp. For them, and for the many more thousands who wandered the mountains of Guatemala without food or shelter, there was no need for missionaries to predict an apocalypse. It had already come—in bullets, in napalm, in knives and clubs, in death from exposure.[36]

Far to the north, for reasons unrelated, Cam Townsend also came down with pneumonia. When physicians checked his blood, they found that the leukemia was devouring his immune system. His hemoglobin count was collapsing.

Unlike Nelson Rockefeller, Cam had no sudden bolt of the heart to eternity. He suffered for three more months, sometimes enduring four transfusions in a single day. He never complained, said a nurse. "Every time I came in he had a sweet smile." Waiting for the Lord allowed him to remember the early years in Guatemala and the Golden Jubilee of the previous year and to see the line of triumphs that tied these two ends of his life together so neatly, as God's Will.

In Guatemala, the Lord's Will was being invoked by the country's rulers against their own people. At 11 P.M. on February 15, while Cam slept in his hospital bed, the Guatemalan army appeared at the Ixil village of Santo Tomás Ixcán and began firing automatic weapons into its homes. Families who were not killed outright were dragged outside and shot. Their bodies were then carried into the village church. The killings continued for two more days. The church was set afire, and then the entire village.

To achieve this military victory, the army used linguistic differences, deploying Indian soldiers to areas where the tribal languages were alien to them. This strategy made it easier to dehumanize the enemy, which, as in Vietnam, quickly became the local population. Sometimes, however, the army needed to communicate with the Indians to carry out its "civic action" and relief projects in occupied territory. For this more specialized task, it turned to American missionaries, including SIL.[37]

In March 1982, the CIA-backed counterinsurgency officers seized Guatemala's government. Romans 13:1 came back in the words of born-again General Ríos Montt, who declared himself "God's choice." That summer, Ríos Montt would order the army to transport SIL's veteran translators, Ray and Helen Elliot, to Nebáj, a tropical mountain village in the Ixil Indian region of Quiché. The Elliots translated for four American dentists from Eureka, California's, Gospel Outreach. Founded by James Degolyer, an ex-hippie who had roamed the drug-filled streets of San Francisco's Haight-Ashbury district for five years before being "saved" by Jesus,[38] Gospel Outreach was Ríos Montt's original evangelizer when the general's political fortunes were at low tide. His 1974 presidential election had reportedly been stolen by fraud; having recently returned from a thinly veiled exile in an overseas embassy to duties without any specific assignment, Ríos Montt was a general without an army. But he did find Jesus in 1978 and a new constituency through Gospel Outreach's American missionaries, who were dispensing private aid to victims of the disastrous 1976 earthquake. They helped found the general's Christian Church of the Word and now provided scriptural verses to help the general rule; the church even provided two elders as official aides to the new president and coordinated evangelical relief efforts through its Foundation for the Support of Indian Peoples.

The irony of the foundation's name was outranked only by the name of its fund-raising arm in the United States, which was endorsed by TV evangelist Pat Robertson: International Love Lift. Love was "the only solution" to the civil strife, Ríos Montt had explained to a New York Times reporter, amid animated praise for the $1 billion he said he was promised by Robertson's organization (Robertson confirmed only his hope to give "comparable assistance" to the $350,000 he said his group raised for earthquake relief). Fundamentalist missionaries would soon help him build "model villages" for the peasants, based on "communitarianism," a system of church-centered community ownership of property that vaguely would include private ownership of homes and land. International Love Lift was supposed to get it all off the ground, local church elders hoping to raise $20 million in the United States.[39] (They ended up with only $1.5 million,[40] despite the effort of Ríos Montt to take the advice of Reagan officials to improve his reputation abroad by emphasizing alleged abuses and killings by the Left.[41])

According to American Fundamentalists who attended a special State Department briefing for them on the alleged communist threat to Guatemala, the Reagan administration hoped Love Lift's proposed truck convoy of aid from Fundamentalist churches also "might be the vehicle that could get U.S. recognition for the Montt government."[42] During his first interview with the *New York Times*, Ríos Montt tried to evade questions on human rights. Atrocities had caused the Carter administration to suspend U.S. military aid in 1977 and were supposedly the cause of the Reagan administration's hesitancy to recognize the coup, among whose participants was Sandoval Alarcón, the alleged godfather of the death squads who called his movement "the party of violence."[43] But the reporter persisted against Ríos Montt's evasive tactics. What about reports of continued violations of human rights? "Yes," the general finally conceded; then he added, "as in all parts of the world." And what of local newspaper accounts of unarmed women and children being killed? "It is war," he answered, "a permanent war."[44] A few months later, Ríos Montt would be even more candid with a group of politicians: "We declared a state of siege so we could kill legally."[45]

Love was beginning to take on a strange look. Pat Robertson, who also attended another State Department briefing on Ríos Montt's behalf with Reverend Jerry Falwell, was so inspired by the general's counterinsurgency campaign that he had to share a quote from the Bible with fellow believers in the Word: "He who wields the sword does not wield it in vain."[46]

In Cunén, a central market town in El Quiché province, the message of love was similar, if less poetic. An army officer explained the government's "beans and bullets" program: "If you are with us, we'll feed you; if not we'll kill you." A preacher in the Church of God intoned the Wycliffe version of Romans 13:1 to several hundred Indians summoned to a progovernment rally at the town's soccer field: "He who resists the authorities is resisting the will of God."[47]

About a dozen miles northwest, at Nebáj, Gospel Outreach's American dentists were extracting teeth in the midst of the army's "search and destroy" campaign against the predominantly Indian Guerrilla Army of the Poor. "The President of Guatemala's people from the Iglesia del Verbo [the Church of the Word], and especially a missionary team of the Church, have been looking for a way in which help for the Ixil Area can be used as a base for doing more evangelical work there," Wycliffe's Ray Elliot wrote to supporters back home.

> . . . By 6 P.M., the boys had already pulled out 100 teeth. By Thursday, they had increased that number to 900. . . . As a workplace we chose an open corridor in front of the municipal entryroom. There was an empty room at the end of the [cor-

ridor to] the municipal offices. Afterward, we discovered that this was a morgue.

Bodies of Indians, sometimes piled on top of each other, were kept there. . . .

Tuesday morning, we saw and heard an exchange of fire between a helicopter and men on the ground. This is the first time we had seen the war live and it impressed me. . . . Helen and the dentists saw the bodies arrive, and how they were thrown from the truck and dragged to the morgue. That afternoon they were carried again to a pick-up and then thrown along the roadside, which will serve as a cemetery in cases like this. Afterwards, someone threw water in the room and with a broom swept out the blood. We were glad to have made the decision to work in the corridor and not in that room.[48]

Between 3,000 and 4,000 persons were killed in the Nebáj municipality; another 20,000 fled, leaving half the area's towns and villages abandoned. Several thousand fled to the mountains, another 5,000 were packed into a single plantation designed to normally employ 350 workers.[49] Traditional life had been shattered and replaced by the military regime's AID-advised development plans, which were dominated by Guatemala City's speculators and corporate agendas.

Within three months of Ríos Montt's self-declaration as "God's choice," in June 1982, Amnesty International would issue a special report, *Massive Extrajudicial Executions in Rural Areas Under the Government of General Efraín Ríos Montt.* Its "partial listing of massacres," totaling more than sixty, included one village where survivors witnessed soldiers beheading men, battering children's heads against rocks, and raping women. More than 500 Indian people were killed in three villages in the departments of Quiché and Huehuetenango on March 23. In addition, 100 people were slaughtered in three villages in Alta Verapaz between March 24 and March 27; 250 people, in three villages in Chimaltenango the first two weeks of April; 100, in the village of Nangal alone in Quiché on April 5; 193, in Río Negro on April 15; 54, in Macalbaj on April 18; and 100, in Josefinos on April 20.[50]

Machine guns, grenades, and machetes were used with sadistic abandon. Most of the victims were women and children.

In Alta Verapaz, home of the Kekchí Indians, more than 1,000 of the 2,500 communities in the province were abandoned or destroyed. Those communities that remained were decimated by losses. In one municipality, Santa Cristobal Verapaz, up to 10,000 of the 28,000 residents were believed by local authorities to have died.[51]

Some Catholic clerics had already stood by the Indians and shared their martyrdom. The diocese in Quiché was closed in July, and priests were withdrawn after the murder of priests and two attempts on the life of Bishop Juan Gerardi. Ten priests had already been murdered in two years, one man was kidnapped and killed, and sixty-four other clerics were forced to leave after being marked for death. Rectories were bombed, parish radio stations were destroyed, and parochial schools and twelve religious training centers and Christian leadership teaching centers were closed.

The traditionally conservative Catholic Bishops Conference, like bishops had

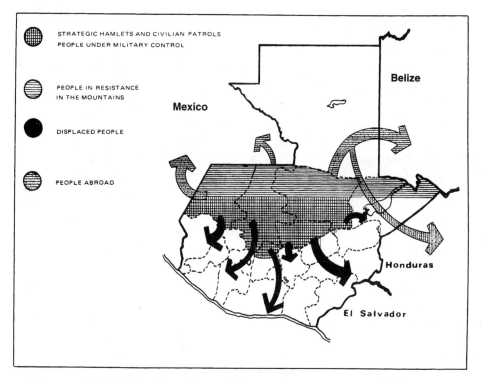

STRATEGIC HAMLETS AND CIVILIAN PATROLS
PEOPLE UNDER MILITARY CONTROL

PEOPLE IN RESISTANCE
IN THE MOUNTAINS

DISPLACED PEOPLE

PEOPLE ABROAD

Belize

Mexico

Honduras

El Salvador

Massacres by Efraín Ríos Montt, Guatemala's evangelical dictator, caused massive dislocation of more than 1 million Indians in 1982 and 1983.
Source: Luisa Frank and Philip Wheaton, *Indian Guatemala*, p. 97.

done in Brazil a decade earlier, denounced the government's policy as "genocide."[52] In December, an investigating commission of the U.S. National Council of Churches confirmed the Mayan holocaust was taking place, but, after meeting Ríos Montt in Honduras later that month, President Reagan insisted that the regime was "getting a bad deal"[53] from the accusations of massacres and deserved renewed military aid from the United States (which he granted the following month). Had not the White House received a flood of letters calling for renewed arms sales to Guatemala after Pat Robertson appealed on his *700 Club* television show for prayers and money for the regime? SIL's Ray Elliot, for his part, privately wrote leaders of the Church of the Word of his concern about the atrocities against the Indians, but the elders believed it was all the work of the Indian guerrillas; most Fundamentalists breezily dismissed the charges against the army as "totally wrong or totally perverted,"[54] echoing Ríos Montt. "We have no scorched-earth policy," the general explained at a news conference after conferring with Reagan. "We have a policy of scorched Communists."[55] A few months later, following Pope John Paul II's call for respect for Indians' human rights during a visit marred by attacks by Fundamentalist pastors on the pontiff as "the Beast" of the Apocalypse,[56] even Ríos Montt would admit that "We know and understand that we have sinned, that we have abused power."[57]

Yet, through all the massacres of Indians and murders of clerics, nothing seemed to penetrate the consciousness—or conscience—of SIL's leaders. In January 1982, the first civilian militia in the Ixil *altiplano* was organized in Cotzal with the help of an Ixil Pentecostal pastor who collaborated with SIL's Paul Townsend. When Ríos Montt drafted the Cotzal militia into his mandatory Civil Self-Defense Patrol, Townsend's only reaction was to actively support the dictator's stated desire to "humanize" the army's operations. And when this was demonstrated by the army's killing sixty-four Indians, including the pastor's brother, as a reprisal for guerrilla attacks on the occupation, the pastor blamed the guerrillas and helped the army hunt down the guerrillas' support network among the Indian villages; out of twenty-nine villages placed on the army's list, twenty-six were burned or depopulated within three months.[58]

That year Paul Townsend published the primer he had written in Cotzal, in the heart of Ixil country, without a word about the slaughter around him. It was as if a strange veil, blinding and deafening, had fallen over SIL's headquarters in Guatemala City and the United States, including North Carolina, where a different kind of deathwatch was taking place.

"It won't be long now until you're over there in Glory," Cam's physician told him on April 22.

"It'll be good to be over there," said Cam.

The next day, just after the sun set, he was.

More than a thousand people came to the funeral at Charlotte's Calvary Church. This church was no cathedral, but a simple church. The singing was not by a renowned opera star, but by a congregation who knew Cam's missionary hymn, "Bibleless Tribes," by heart. The personal tributes were warm, the grief genuine.

Ken Pike described Cam as "a giant under God, one of the greatest leaders since Paul." Yet not one of the national leaders Cam called friends in so many countries throughout the world came to his funeral. But a few did send messages. Peru's Belaúnde spoke of "an irreparable loss," and Colombia's Turbay, of "profound sadness." Billy Graham, unable to attend, sent a message describing Cam's death as "a great loss to the Christian world. I lost a great personal friend."[59]

But in the end, only his followers and closest collaborators were there to see him off to "the other side." On this side, his body was laid to rest in a grove of pines beside the Cárdenas Museum. Even in death, Cam was promoting his dream, serving the institution he created, which lived on after him. Chiseled in the simple headstone is the script of a last message, as if by Cam's own hand: "Dear ones, by Love, serve one another. Finish the task: Translate the Scriptures into every language. Uncle Cam."

Visitors can read Cam's favorite Bible verses displayed on six pedestals. At a seventh pedestal, one can press a button and hear Cam's voice from his last public speech. The impression is powerful, as if the Founder is speaking from the grave: "There will be in glory among the redeemed, some from every tribe, nation and language." His millennial vision, though his eyes were closed, was undimmed, fixed in eternity upon the terrible Apocalypse and the judgment of the Second Coming.

It was, in a bizarre way, proof of Fundamentalism's final triumph over Nelson Rockefeller. Today, Nelson Rockefeller's voice is not heard or revered. Nor did the institution that carried his dream survive him. Nelson's IBEC is gone, swallowed up by larger European capital.[60] The historical significance of IBEC's disappearance was not lost on some observers. "The Rockefeller dream of using a private company to develop the economies of backward lands is apparently over," commented the *Wall Street Journal* in 1980.[61] IBEC, which never paid a dividend, had passed into history within two years of the death of its founder. Only Fazenda Bodoquena survived as a Rockefeller holding. David continued the family's partnership with Moreira Salles until the Brazilian was replaced by a new partner, Robert O. Anderson,[62] former director of Chase Manhattan Bank and chairman of ARCO, the Atlantic Refining Company spin-off of the old Standard Oil Trust.

ARCO now was stripping coal in the Powder River Basin (where the Sioux had fought Custer), plumbing the depths of Alaska's Prudhoe Bay for oil, and prospecting for oil in China (including China's claimed waters between Hainan Island and the coast of northern Vietnam). Closer to Bodoquena, the lands of Peru's Mayoruna Indians near the Brazilian border had been the site of ARCO drilling, and the Ganso Azul field near SIL's Yarinacocha base now belonged to ARCO, thanks to Anderson's purchase of Sinclair Oil in 1979. But the most germane development for the Rockefeller/Moreira Salles investment in Bodoquena was ARCO's purchase of Anaconda, the third-largest American copper company, in 1977, just two years after the *Engineering and Mining Journal* confirmed that Project RADAM's all-powerful aerial scanners had found significant deposits of copper in the Bodoquena hills. Anderson, a devotee of ranching (he owned a 100,000-acre spread in New Mexico) may have bought into more than beef. Fazenda Bodoquena, already by 1972 the eighth-largest agribusiness in Brazil (in comparison, King Ranch do Brazil ranked twenty-ninth, and IBEC's Sementes Agroceres S.A., sixtieth[63]), was turning out to be Nelson Rockefeller's biggest Brazilian success story.

But few would know it. In a twist of official fate, the life of Nelson Rockefeller was more open to public scrutiny before his death than after it. Nelson's papers, open to selective researchers during his lifetime, were closed on his death by the family and sealed in the archives that bore his name. In the interest of a vague security to the nation and clearer security to the family name, the records of Nelson's dreams and life were condemned to a basement vault, like the remains of their creator, under ground. They were not reopened for a decade, and then only in part. By 1994, many of these records were still unprocessed or censored, an ironic legacy of a life that had always sought recognition.

Cam's dream, in contrast, flourished in the apocalyptic fears of the Reagan years. Wycliffe's membership increased an astounding 72 percent in the three years that followed Chester Bitterman's martyrdom and Reagan's ascension to power, to over 5,600 members. In 1984, Wycliffe, under its SIL alias, entered its 1,000th tribe.[64] In 1988, SIL withdrew from Bolivia; in 1991, from Ecuador, proclaiming its task completed. New Testaments had been translated for every tribe. Evangelical Fundamentalist pastors had been left behind, too.

SIL computer centers in the United States, England, the Philippines, Peru, Colombia, and Australia hum into the night. Programs now help translators perform grammatical, statistical, and phonetic analyses, speeding the translation of languages joined by a common root.[65] But with only six years left to reach another 3,500 Bibleless tribes, the millennial goal seems unlikely to be fulfilled by the year 2000. New languages are always being discovered, and after them, new dialects.

Ten years after Townsend's death, his influence was still felt in Brazil. At the First Global Forum on the Environment, held in Rio de Janeiro, SIL's translators were participating in workshops, showing its video on bilingual education, and exhibiting its materials at its booth. SIL was larger than ever, wealthy with tangible assets like computers, new airplanes (including a jet), even a linguistics campus in Texas (assisted by a $100,000 gift from Sunoco's Pew family[66]). But SIL's heyday had clearly passed. Now it was only one voice among many, only one booth among hundreds.

Now Indian voices can be heard, many of them asserting their rights; challenging the ongoing efforts to flood or burn their homelands; confronting the continual incursions of promised reserves by cattle ranchers, settlers, and mining companies; and warning the conquerors that pharaonic visions will lead to their own destruction. The source of much of the world's oxygen lies within the 1 million square miles of the Amazon basin: almost two-thirds of the trees on the planet. Yet, despite this role as the lung of the earth, much of the Amazon rain forest is being burned down and turned into the source of dangerous increases of carbon dioxide in the atmosphere. In 1992 Canadian investigators reported that Brazil's rain forest alone was being burned at a rate of an acre every minute; every thirty seconds, an area the size of a football field was being destroyed by fire; every year, the equivalent of one-half the size of California was being devoured by flames.

Whatever the actual rate of destruction, most observers agree that the gases released into the upper atmosphere are creating a greenhouse effect, allowing the sun's rays to enter and preventing heat from escaping. Soil protected for centuries by the forest's 200-foot-high canopy is now exposed to the sun and increasing doses of pesticides, herbicides, and fertilizers. Its fertility has declined, often leaving a sun-baked wasteland and prompting still further slashing and burning of virgin forest. Fortunes are being made, but not by small farmers or would-be settlers.

In 1992, there were 30 million homeless people in Brazil, 7 million of them children. Rio was still a city besieged by the poor. Many of these poor people were swept off the streets by the army before delegates to the Global Forum arrived and were sent to unknown destinies, some, it was rumored, to graves, many to work in clearing the Amazon or on the ranches that are responsible for 80 percent of the deforestation.

Exports of beef and lumber continue to grow, keeping up profits for multinational corporate exporters and their Brazilian junior partners, and keeping up debt payments to banks like Chase Manhattan, which in 1982 led a $400-million loan syndicate to finance Brazil's offshore oil-drilling program—ample reasons for President George Bush to have been the only head of state at the Rio summit to refuse to sign the proposed treaty to protect the world's environment. So the Amazon's holocaust goes on in the names of national sovereignty and an elusive progress, with 50,000 fires in the Brazilian Amazon in September 1991 alone, to clear land that can support, on the average, only one head of cattle per acre.

This is one legacy of Nelson Rockefeller's "shining dream" of a conquered Amazon. Another, of course, is the survival of the Special Group, the supersecret small team from the National Security Council that Nelson was the first to chair and that Ronald Reagan and George Bush inherited to give "plausible deniability" its widest scope to date. This secret general staff, operating out of a White House basement office, waged covert warfare in the name of democracy against Soviet communism, against alleged enemy agents in other democracies, against Nicaragua's Sandinista government despite Congress's legislated prohibition, and ultimately against the United States' own Constitution. "To save the village we had to destroy it," was its rationale in Vietnam; to allegedly save democracy, both at home and abroad, they risked destroying it in both places.

This Rockefeller legacy, too, was global in scope, leaving behind few happy, prosperous people, many dictatorships, and much debt. In 1986, almost a decade after eight South American governments signed the Amazon Pact committing their countries to an integrated economic development of the Amazon basin (but not to protection of Indian land rights), and ten years after David Rockefeller led a bankers' delegation to Brazil to help the military regime secure additional loans, Latin Americans were again rioting against the visit of a Rockefeller. This time it was David. Argentines, upset over the sharp decline in real wages caused by government austerity measures imposed to repay Argentina's whopping $50 billion debt, blamed David. Chase Manhattan and other American banks had lent the military dictatorship billions of dollars during its twenty-year reign; when the generals finally handed over the government to elected civilians in 1984, it handed over the regime's debt as well, and David expected the new civilian government to pay, prompting a top adviser to the Argentine president to call him a "bloodsucker" and senators and at least one cabinet member to refuse to meet with him.

When he last visited Argentina in 1980, there had been protests then, too, over his perceived closeness with the military regime and the expense involved in renting the country's leading opera house to give him a posh reception. But he had faced nothing like this. Now, in 1986, water cannons and rubber bullets had to be used by police to stop protesters from marching too near the American club in downtown Buenos Aires, where David, now chairman of the Americas Society (an offspring of his old Business Group for Latin America), was conferring with American businessmen with interests in Argentina. More than eighty demonstrators were arrested, and five were hurt; windows were smashed and eggs and rocks were thrown against the heavily armed police. A United States flag was burned.[67]

Relegated to the back pages of U.S. newspapers, most reports, with the exception of a *New York Times* story, focused on the riot rather than its root cause. And even the *Times* led its account by describing the violence and noting that one of those gravely injured was a young member of the Communist party. Since Nelson's youth, Rockefellers were always fair game for communists, as communists were for Nelson. The *Times* pointed out that the Communist party had helped sponsor the march, although as only one of seven political parties in the Peronist-led coalition that had organized it. U.S. support for military dictatorships, whether Péron's or the supposedly more exotic "new military" species, was part of Nelson Rockefeller's legacy to Latin America; but it was not mentioned. The specter of an International Communist Conspiracy exploiting a nation's anger sufficed, as always.

But then Soviet Premier Mikhail Gorbachev gave a promise—and warning—to a startled President Reagan that "we are going to take your enemy away." With the collapse of a Soviet Union ruined by an arms race and a stifling police state and inefficient bureaucratic centralism also went the rationale for illegal arms sales like those of the Iran-Contra scandal, coups like Brazil's, and military interventions like Vietnam. *Nation-building*, the Rostowian term used to describe the soft side of the Cold War's counterinsurgency operations, has yet to find favor among Americans when applied just in Somalia, much less globally, to create a "New World Order" that appears only vaguely democratic—and more exclusively corporate in its multinational reach.

But there will always be enemies to demonize and indigenous peoples to conquer with love or bullets. That is because indigenous peoples, despite all they have been forced to face, survive. Their survival continues the cultural challenge to Euro-American delusions about a model of development that requires economic "austerity" deprivations and inhumane policies to pay off debts to foreign and domestic corporate entities, particularly banks, controlled by wealthy minorities, the origins of whose fortunes owe much to the plunder of tribal lands.

The conquest of the American West was marked by such policies toward tribal peoples as killing off their food base (the American buffalo), forced removal, religious persecution, and deculturation by missionaries and by the breakup of families by mandatory attendance at the BIA's boarding schools. These were subtler means of genocide, just as deadly as massacres and the deliberate distribution of disease-infected army blankets. This conquest, complete with its search-and-destroy cavalry sweeps, happened decades before the Soviet Union came into existence. The Rockefellers and the Townsends, in different ways, were part of that saga. Given the continued dynamics of unrestrained corporate expansion, their heirs could be part of the next conquest as well, starting out, like Nelson Rockefeller and William Cameron Townsend, on a road paved with good intentions.

Brazil's rubber tappers, once the hapless vanguard of the world market's penetration of the jungle, recently learned that lesson. Trying to save the rain forest with the very market forces that were destroying it, the rubber gatherers went into business with Cultural Survival Enterprises of Cambridge, Massachusetts, to produce "non-timber forest products," such as food products made with Brazil nuts, as an alternative to razing the rain forest. The Americans had been inspired to come to the aid of the rubber tappers by the martyrdom of Chico Mendes, who was assassinated in 1988 by landowners in Rondônia for organizing the *seringueiros* to defend their rights. It did not take long, however, before the anthropologists of Cultural Survival and the producers of Ben and Jerry's Rainforest Crunch candy and ice cream found their need to make profits conflicting with the economic survival of nut gatherers, who began complaining in 1991 of being squeezed by their American backers to repay a $100,000 loan the Americans gave to help the tappers set up a nut-shelling and processing factory.[68] Market forces alone could not meet human needs; left unguided, market forces ran amok, beyond the control of the nut gatherers. With huge companies setting prices, pressuring the nut gatherers' cooperative to be "more competitive," and lenders dictating terms and costs of loans, the prospects for the tappers maintaining their independence were questionable. Their plight was not unlike that facing Brazil as a whole or other countries struggling to retain national sovereignty in the new world order of the multinational corporations. Like Nelson's, the tappers' dream of everyone profiting was being shattered by the reality that an expanding marketplace does not make profits neutral, that someone profits and someone does not, and that expanding markets historically lead to ever-newer frontiers where the weak are conquered by the strong.

Yet, in the end, it is the voice of indigenous peoples and their regard for the sacredness of the earth, their traditional respect for the earth as a living force, that offers alternative values to wanton waste and destruction. The European invasion of the Americas, begun by Columbus and pursued by Rockefeller and Townsend, has left little that is sustainable as a mode of production when left unrestrained. The destruction of the environment and the waste of resources is not accidental, but endemic, overwhelming even the private enterprises that seek to profit by desperate government regulation through environmental services and products. But even in this new industry, some companies grow and many die, and private capital, with all its powers of persuasion in the halls of government, tends to concentrate to the detriment, not the benefit, of political democracy. Where profit is its own reward, its conversion from means to ends is inevitable.

So is the destruction of human beings. The burning of the rain forests is destroying not only the origin of 25 percent of all pharmaceuticals that benefit the world, not only much of the world's species of plants and animals, not only a vast treasure of knowledge of these riches, but whole groups of people.

Perhaps this is the real historical meaning of William Cameron Townsend's reaching every tribe with the Word and Nelson Rockefeller's reaching them with "development." Both methods were destructive to tribal ways of communal sharing and respect for the land. Both stories told of the same result: It was not God being brought to tribal cultures, but an alien culture of possessive individualism grown to such a giant corporate scale, with its own rapacious, competitive needs, that it could only devour them.

In 1976, with the publication of the book *Genocide in Paraguay*, Nazi holocaust chronicler Elie Wiesel, himself a survivor, analyzed the complicity of silence that linked the death camps of Germany with what was happening to the Aché Indians of Paraguay:

> . . . Our society prefers not to know anything of all that. Silence everywhere. Hardly a few words in the press. Nothing is discussed at the UN, nor among the politicized intellectuals or moralists. The great consciences kept quiet. Of course, we had an excuse! We didn't know. But now, after having read these testimonies, we know. Henceforth, we shall be responsible. And accomplices.

For some, this was an obnoxious burden of citizenship; for the governments involved, it was a cause for continuing denial; and for others who were seeking the warm bosom of corporate respectability and foundation grants, it was grounds for lofty refutation.

As the "Age of Genocide" described by anthropologists in the 1970s continued toward the twenty-first century, questions persisted, challenging the ongoing policy of plausible denial: Must crimes against humanity be the result of written policy deliberations to be recognized as crimes? Who shares responsibility when the destruction of cultures and peoples results from good intentions guided by alien goals and a blindness toward crimes by the powerful? What have these questions to do with international rights and international law in an increasingly interdependent world?

Adolf Berle, ironically, studied this issue even while chairing a sugar corporation that profited from low wages paid on Dominican plantations to descendants of Indian and African slaves. Among his papers are notes on the Universal Declaration of Human Rights, passed by the United Nations on December 10, 1948, when the ovens of Auschwitz were barely cool and memories were still fresh of just how far civilized people could descend:

> Everyone, as a member of society, has the right to social security and is entitled to realization, through national effort and international co-operation and in accordance with the organization and resources of each State, of the economic, social and cultural rights indispensable for the dignity and the free development of his personality.

Berle also studied the Genocide Convention signed by United Nations members three years later. In 1951, members of the United Nations, informed of the many ways that crimes against humanity had been carried out, gave genocide an explicit definition in Article II to the Convention on the Prevention and Punishment of the Crime of Genocide:

> In the present Convention, genocide means any of the following acts committed with intent to destroy, in whole or in part, a national, ethnic, racial or religious group, such as:
>
> •Killing members of the group;
>
> •Causing serious bodily or mental harm to members of the group;
>
> •Deliberately inflicting on the group conditions of life calculated to bring about its physical destruction in whole or in part;
>
> •Imposing measures intended to prevent births within the group;
>
> •Forcibly transferring children from one group to another group.

This was not an argument against *ethnocide*, the term applied in recent years to the destruction of an indigenous group as a people through policies like forced removal or forced assimilation, even though people are not being killed. But the Convention on Genocide was also not ambiguous in its definitions. Genocide is limited to deliberate acts that intend the physical destruction of all or part of a human group. Punishment is not limited, however, to those who commit a physical liquidation; it is also applicable to those who are in "complicity in genocide . . . whether they are constitutionally responsible rulers, public officials or private individuals."[69] In a democracy, it was assumed, citizens bear some responsibility for what is done in their name by their governments, even more so if they are aware of crimes and do not try to stop them.

There was nothing inevitable, therefore, about the unwillingness of successive administrations in Washington to press the United Nations to enforce the Convention on Genocide in Guatemala or Brazil or Indonesia. That failure was deliberate, a choice as clear as Nelson Rockefeller's choice of dictatorships over democracies that had policies he disliked, a choice as clear as William Cameron Townsend's Hail, Caesar doctrine of faith. In the Dollar Zone of the Western Hemisphere, that choice continues.

Only a few among the powerful have chosen a different route. One of them is Davison L. Budhoo, a former World Bank economist and Caribbean specialist who resigned in 1988 from his $100,000-a-year job as a senior official to the Washington, D.C.–based International Monetary Fund (IMF). In one section of his seven-part letter of resignation to the director of the IMF, Budhoo castigated the Fund for its "hypocrisy" in allowing millions of people to starve while turning a blind eye to the "Third World military expenditure binge, in deference to the arms exporters—its major shareholders." With the "concurrence of the Fund," Budhoo wrote,

> arms expenditures in developing countries rose from 7 billion [dollars] in 1975 to over 14 billion in 1980 and above 21 billion in 1986 . . . yet in 1985, over 1 billion Third World People lived in . . . absolute poverty, and over 500 million were in the throes of famine and incurable malnutrition. . . . We have no qualms in forcing governments to crush millions upon millions of their own people to death—look at the extremely serious allegations made recently by UNICEF against us in this respect—but when it comes to arms merchandising we are hypocritical enough to throw our hands up in the air and talk of "national sovereignty."

Claiming he had been haunted by his participation in "our own peculiar Holocaust," Budhoo wondered if "the heirs of those whom we have dismembered" would one day "clamor for another Nuremberg."[70]

It has not happened yet, even as huge arms expenditures continue in the Third World despite the end of the Cold War. But the clamor against the crime itself, genocide, has been spreading; the struggle for or against communism no longer can be offered as a rationale for such a terrible excess as genocide during wars between nation-states, civil wars, or campaigns of internal repression. Beyond the norms of international laws against aggression, human rights, it is now increasingly argued, stand above the benefits or exigencies of political alliances.

The recent unwillingness of the United States and other governments of the West to intervene promptly and forcefully against the Serbs in their "ethnic cleansing" of Muslims in Bosnia appalled many Americans; so did the failure to stop the Rwandan government from committing an even greater genocide, slaughtering as many as 500,000 Tutsi people, Rwanda's minority tribal group. But Americans did not need to look outside their own hemisphere for examples of genocide.

In 1991, protests erupted throughout the world against the West's

Quincentennial celebration of Christopher Columbus's expedition to the Americas. That year, while honoring Pope John Paul II during his visit to Mato Grosso with a Xavante chief's headdress of blue macaw feathers, representatives from thirty-two Indian nations (linguistic groups made up of many more tribes) in Brazil informed him they would protest celebrations marking the 500th anniversary of Colombus's landing. "Amerindia was invaded, not discovered," said the daughter of a Guarani chief whom the Pope had met eleven years earlier during his first visit, since murdered. Many of the Indians wore T-shirts with the names of murdered tribesmen and the dates of their deaths. Over 140 murders of Indians had been documented since the Pope's previous visit.[71]

Many more were not documented. The numbers sometimes staggered the imagination. In 1992, ten years after Guatemalan Indians seized the Brazilian Embassy to protest the massacres, the dead were still being counted by international investigators. But now the hemispherewide links between genocide and "development" were no longer in the shadows of a coincidental site for desperate protest; in October 1991, Indians from South America's Amazon basin had been greeted in broad daylight by Guatemalan Indians hosting the first international conference of indigenous peoples at Quetzaltenango. As official commemorations of Columbus's 1492 landing took place the following year, Amerindians mourned the holocaust that had destroyed millions of their people, celebrated their own indigenous consciousness, and watched—somewhat surprised—how fast many Euro-Americans throughout the hemisphere were moved by the power of that consciousness.

In August 1993, millions of Americans were startled by national television broadcasts reporting that Brazil's Yanomami Indians, having fought mining companies' efforts to delay the demarcation of their lands, had suffered a massacre at the hands of miners. The American public witnessed scenes of Indian women and children innocently naked and defenseless before a well-armed aggression from the "civilized" world. Then came word that Brazilian authorities had quarantined the area. The bodies of the slain Indians, it seemed, could not be found. They had disappeared.

A month later, after the charred remains were found and the murders exposed by chief Davi Kopenawa Yanomami as having an economic motive, came news of another Indian event, this one far north of the Amazon, in Central America. While Guatemala's human rights leader struggled to hold on to the presidency he had won, a long line of Indian women streamed down from the Guatemalan highlands and entered the capital. American military advisers and missionaries watched from the sidelines as hundreds of women passed silently by, carrying in their hands small crosses bearing the names of loved ones who had died at the hands of the military. Cakchiquel Indian leader Francisco Cali had conveyed the full horror of their suffering to the public the previous year:

100,000 killed in the previous fifteen years, more than 1 million displaced, 250,000 children losing one or both parents, 50,000 widowed, and 40,000 "disappeared."

As they had so often in the past, the women were taking their grievances to the capital city. But now they were hopeful that with the new civilian government and the recent awarding of the Nobel Peace Prize to Rigoberta Menchú, one of their own and daughter of one of the campesino leaders who died in the Spanish Embassy massacre over a decade before, the reporters could take their plight beyond editors and governments, to the people of the world.

Six months later, Nelson and David Rockefeller's dream of a hemispheric Dollar Zone seemed to be becoming reality. The North American Free Trade Agreement (NAFTA) between the United States, Mexico, and Canada finally had been pushed through Congress by the latest Trilateral Commission member to occupy the White House, Democratic president Bill Clinton. NAFTA went into legal effect on January 1, 1994. And as it did, the Indians of Chiapas, Mexico, revolted.

Armed with machetes, guns, and even wooden models of rifles, they seized towns, battled Mexican federal troops and issued a manifesto to the world, calling for economic justice and political reform in all Mexico. They especially wanted a new and fair national election; they, like many in Mexico, believed the fifty-year reign by the Institutional Revolutionary Party (PRI) had resorted to fraud in the last election to defeat the main opposition candidate, Senator Cuauhtémoc Cárdenas, the son of the late president Lázaro Cárdenas.

The name of Cárdenas was not the only one to haunt the Rockefellers. For their name, the Indian rebels chose the "Zapatista Liberation Army"; Zapata's spirit, they proclaimed, was still alive. For their mediators in negotiations with the embarrassed PRI regime in Mexico City, they chose Chiapas's Catholic Bishop Samuel Ruis, a former critic of SIL when it was still officially in Mexico, and Guatemala's Rigaberta Menchú. The choice was no accident of history, for this was a Mayan revolt against genocide and ethnocide that straddled the border of both countries. It had roots in the landing of Columbus and the subsequent European invasion that fostered an "American dream"—and a Rockefeller "shining dream"—that had become the Indians' nightmare. They called on the world to support them.

And if the citizens of the industrialized nations, though knowing, still did nothing, and the murders and ethnocide continued—in Mexico, in Guatemala, in the Amazon, in tribal areas throughout the world—they could be sure that history would one day ask: Was this, too, simply God's Will?

Or thy will?

APPENDIX A

The Rockefeller Mission to the Americas (1969)

Rockefeller's entourage was huge. It included "special advisers" from IBEC (such as Richard Aldrich and Berent Friele) and AIA (such as John Camp and Jerome Levinson); a staff of thirty, which included AIA's Flor Brennan, Nelson's confidential secretary Ann Whitman, and aides Hugh Morrow and Nancy Maginnes; and an "advance group" of seventeen, which included Joseph Persico and Joseph Canzeri. The official list of "advisory members" of the mission actually totaled thirty-four people, including IBM chairman Arthur K. Watson; bankers William F. Butler (Chase) and George Woods (First Boston Corporation); and top officials of Rockefeller institutions, such as Robert Goldwater (Museum of Primitive Art), Clifton Wharton (Agricultural Development Council), Emil M. Mrak (former chancellor of the University of California at Davis and director of IBEC Research Institute, and current director of Universal Foods, Nestlé Foundation and Lilly, McNeal Libby), and Detlev W. Bronk (trustee of the Rockefeller Brothers Fund and past president of Rockefeller University).

Many had substantial expertise in Brazilian affairs. Among them:

■ *Dr. Harold B. Gotaas*, Nelson's CIAA public health head and chief adviser on sanitation in the Amazon during the Rubber Development Corporation's World War heyday. Gotaas was now dean of Northwestern University's Technological Institute.

■ *Andrew McLellan*, labor adviser. As AFL-CIO Inter-American representative, he had traveled to Brazil shortly after the 1964 military coup to offer, through U.S. Military Attaché Colonel Vernon Walters, revised labor regulations for the Castelo Branco purge of labor leaders.

■ *George D. Woods*, former chairman of First Boston Corporation, International Finance Corporation, and the World Bank, which would soon underwrite bank loans to finance the Trans-Amazon Highway's penetration of Brazil's rain forest. A member of the Rockefeller Foundation's board of trustees, Woods was also a director of the *New York Times* and the Kaiser Industries holding company, whose Kaiser Aluminum owned nine subsidiaries in Brazil, including mines in the Brazilian Amazon.

■ *W. Kenneth Riland*, Nelson's personal physician and chief physician of the U.S. Steel Corporation, which had been mining in Brazil since the 1920s. U.S. Steel owned eight subsidiaries in Brazil and shares in three joint ventures. In 1967, it had discovered one of the world's largest lodes of high-grade iron ore in the Amazon jungle in the state of Pará at the Serra dos Carajás, ancestral home of the Xikrín Indians.

■ *Augustine R. Marusi*, formerly head of São Paulo's Alba corporation and the chairman of Borden, the chemical firm controlled by the family of SIL ally Sam Milbank.

■ *Clark Reynolds*, Stanford University food economist, who was then conducting a study of financial growth in Brazil, Colombia, Argentina, and Mexico.

Others were veterans of Nelson's CIAA days, including:

■ *Victor Borella*, the CIAA's labor expert, formerly of Rockefeller Center and a member of Rockefeller's staff.

■ *Monroe Wheeler*, CIAA's cultural publications chief and former director of exhibitions and publications. Wheeler was a trustee of the Museum of Modern Art (which Nelson had called "Mother's Museum" while chairing the board).

■ *George Beebe*, who had covered Latin America for the *Miami Herald* since the days when Nelson Rockefeller was head of CIAA and Roosevelt's assistant secretary of state for Latin America; Beebe was now the *Herald's* senior managing editor and a director of the Inter-American Press Association, a CIA conduit.

■ *Kenneth Holland*, former CIAA education director and now president of the Institute of International Relations, the CIA conduit that administered the Fulbright Scholarship and student exchanges from its offices at U.N. Plaza. Holland had served on the OAS Task Force on Education and was considered well informed on student affairs during the tumultuous 1960s.

And then there were the counterinsurgency experts from economic and military fields:

■ *General Robert Porter*, former chief of the Southern Command. Twice decorated by the Brazilian military junta, Porter had overseen U.S. military operations against Che Guevara in Bolivia.

■ *Leroy S. Wehrle*, former chief of AID operations in Laos and Vietnam; with the Harvard Development Center and a member of John 3rd's Asia Society.

■ *David Bronheim*, AID's former deputy U.S. coordinator of the Alliance for Progress and now director of the Rockefeller-backed Center for Inter-American Relations.

APPENDIX B

Members of the Rockefeller Commission on CIA Abuses (1975)

■ *C. Douglas Dillon*, Nelson Rockefeller's confidant and President Kennedy's treasury secretary. As an undersecretary of state in the Eisenhower administration, Dillon had participated in deliberations over the fate of Cuba's Fidel Castro and the Congo's Patrice Lumumba, both marked for assassination by the CIA. In 1971 he was named chairman of the Rockefeller Foundation board of trustees; he was already a director of the Institute of International Education, which had received CIA funds.

■ *General Lyman Lemnitzer*, former chairman of the Joint Chiefs of Staff, who was active in planning the Bay of Pigs invasion and supported the CIA's desire for direct U.S. military intervention, only to be overruled by Kennedy.

■ *Lane Kirkland*, the Georgetown University School of Foreign Service graduate who became AFL-CIO's top researcher and executive assistant to its president, George Meany, during the Kennedy-Johnson years. At that time, he was a director and strong supporter of the CIA-funded American Institute for Free Labor Development, which operated mostly in Latin America in cooperation with corporate leaders. When the CIA was exposed using labor and student unions and private foundations, Kirkland served on Johnson's commission to find some means of continuing the CIA's pet projects without their having to bear the CIA stigma. The commission simply recommended substituting overt government and private funding of the same projects that the CIA covertly had backed. AFL-CIO's secretary-treasurer at the time of the Rockefeller Commission on CIA Abuses, Kirkland was also a member of Nelson Rockefeller's Commission on Critical Choices.

■ *John T. Connor*, director of David Rockefeller's Chase Manhattan Bank, former commerce secretary in the Johnson administration, and president of Allied Chemical, in which the Rockefellers held $52 million in stock.

■ *Erwin Griswold*, former Harvard Law School dean and until recently the Johnson-appointed U.S. solicitor general. In March 1971, he argued on behalf of the Nixon administration that publication by the *New York Times* of the Pentagon Papers was a threat to Nixon's presidential powers over foreign affairs. In March 1972, he argued before the Supreme Court that the U.S. Army's surveillance of citizens opposing the Vietnam War violated neither federal law nor those citizens' First Amendment rights to freedom of assembly or speech. He lost both cases.

■ *Edgar F. Shannon, Jr.*, president of the University of Virginia. Shannon had no experience with the CIA. In 1975, he would join the board of the Rockefellers' prestigious Colonial Williamsburg Foundation.

■ *Ronald Reagan*, former actor and, until recently, governor of California. Reagan's appointment was seen by many as Ford's attempt to placate the right wing of his party. Reagan had no experience with the CIA, and attended few of the commission's sessions

NOTES

INTRODUCTION

1. Pereira's statements to Father Edgar Smith were first reported in Norman Lewis, "Genocide: From Fire and Sword to Arsenic and Bullets—Civilization Has Sent Six Million Indians to Extinction," *Sunday Times* (London), February 23, 1969.

2. For the estimate of 200,000 Indians, see Adrian Cowell, *London Observer*, June 20, 1971, p. 20, quoting Brazilian anthropologist Paulo Duarte; and Shelton H. Davis, *Victims of the Miracle* (Cambridge: Cambridge University Press, 1977), p. 5. For the lower estimate of below 100,000, see Darcy Ribeiro, "Culturas e Línguas Indígenas do Brasil," *Educação e Ciências Sociales,* Vol. 2, No. 6 (Rio de Janeiro: Brazilian Center of Educational Research, 1957); an English translation, "Indigenous Cultures and Languages in Brazil," can be found in *Indians of Brazil in the Twentieth Century*, ed. Janice H. Hopper (Washington, D.C.: Institute for Cross Cultural Research, 1967), pp. 79–160. In 1971 Duarte estimated there were fewer than 80,000 Indians surviving in Brazil; by his figures, some 120,000 had died. Others put the number of survivors at fewer than 50,000; using Ribeiro's 1957 figure, that would mean some 50,000 men, women, and children had died. In either case, for such a fate to have occurred so consistently in such a short period of time throughout an area as vast as the Brazilian Amazon, the result could have come only from a cause national in scope and power over the nation's development: the Brazilian military regime's development policy, officially titled "Operation Amazon" in 1965. Under international law, those who put into effect a policy that deliberately and systematically results in the destruction of a race, nation, or ethnic group are guilty of genocide.

3. Lewis, "Genocide."

4. Ibid.

5. *Atlas* magazine (London), January 1970.

6. Authors' interview with William Cameron Townsend, Waxhaw, N.C., September 1977.

7. Lewis, "Genocide."

8. Philip Agee, *Inside the Company* (Harmondsworth, Eng.: Penguin, 1975), p. 612; Victor Marchetti and John Marks, *The CIA and the Cult of Intelligence* (New York: Alfred A. Knopf, 1974), p. 123.

9. Major Olimpio Alver Machado, "Indian Guard Trained in Brazil," *International Policy Academy Review,* October 1970, pp. 9, 14.

10. *Jornal do Brasil,* August 27, 1972; see also Ben Munetar, "Agent Exposes Secret Concentration Camp in Crenaque, Brazil," *Wassaja,* November 1973.

11. *Veja* magazine, May 31, 1972, p. 21.

12. Max G. White (U.S. Geological Survey), "Probing the Unknown Amazon Basin—A Roundup of 21 Mineral Exploration Programs in Brazil," *Engineering and Mining Journal,* May 1973, pp. 72–76; and "Project Radam Maps the Unknown in Brazil," *Engineering and Mining Journal,* November 1975, pp. 165–68.

1: The Baptist Burden

1. B. J. Matteson to John D. Rockefeller, Jr., September 11, 1924, Western Trip—1924 file, Papers of John D. Rockefeller, Jr., Rockefeller Family Archives, Rockefeller Archive Center, Tarrytown, New York.

2. Quoted in Joe Alex Morris, *Nelson Rockefeller* (New York: Harper & Bros., 1960), p. 21.

3. See correspondence of August 23, 1893, of Frank Rockefeller to George D. Rogers, noting that all his lands "in Comanche and Kiowa Counties [Kansas]" had been deeded to John D. Rockefeller. Papers of John D. Rockefeller, Sr., Correspondence—1879–1894 Series, Rockefeller, Frank—Personal and Ranch No. 2 folder, Rockefeller Family Archives, Rockefeller Archive Center. See also Rockefeller, Frank—Personal and Ranch No. 1 folder and Box 82, Folders 609 and 610, Business Investments (1888–1891) series; *New York Times*, April 3, 1910, p. 8; and JDR Gifts (1913–1949) folder in the Rockefeller Foundation Archives for extensive documentation of the Rockefeller's investments in railroad stocks and bonds.

4. A. A. Bacone to J. D. Rockefeller, April 14, 1883, Papers of J. D. Rockefeller, Sr.—Office Correspondence, Bacone School file, Box 2, Folder 15, Rockefeller Archive Center. Rockefeller donations to Bacone totaled $10,500.

5. A millenarian who believed the spreading of Bible reading could hasten the Second Coming of the Lord and the prophesied Millennial Kingdom of a 1,000-year peace, Moody warned, "I say to the rich men of Chicago, their money will not be worth much if communism and infidelity sweep the land." See William G. McLaughlin, *Modern Revivalism* (New York: Ronald Press, 1959), p. 269.

6. References to Rockefeller's contributions to a Baptist mission railroad car working the Lake Superior region are located in the Duluth Mesabe & Northern Railway files, Papers of John D. Rockefeller, Sr., Box 1, Folder 1, Rockefeller Family Archives, Rockefeller Archive Center.

7. A. A. Bacone to J. D. Rockefeller, December 1890, Bacone file, Papers of John D. Rockefeller, Sr., in ibid.

8. James R. Thorpe to Robert W. Gumbel, May 8, 1926, Western Trip—1926 file, Papers of John D. Rockefeller, Jr., in ibid. Thorpe informed Gumbel that "it is claimed there are immensely valuable coal reserves on 200,000 acres."

9. Quoted in Raymond B. Fosdick, *John D. Rockefeller, Jr.: A Portrait* (New York: Harper & Bros., 1956), p. 167.

10. J. D. Rockefeller, Jr., Diary of Western Trip—Summer of 1924, Entry for July 16, 1924, Western Trip—1924 file, Rockefeller Family Archives, Rockefeller Archive Center.

11. Televised interview of Nelson Rockefeller by David Frost, New York, July 20, 1971.

2: The Fundamentalist Controversy

1. "Dr. Stratton Assails John D. Jr. for His Recent Praise of the Religion of Today," *New York Times,* December 2, 1924, p. 16.

2. Allan Nevins, ed., "The Memoirs of Frederick T. Gates," *American Heritage* (April 1955), p. 70.

3. J. D. Rockefeller—Cutler correspondence, 1917–1923, Appendix CC, Office of the Messrs. Rockefeller—OMR Series John D. Rockefeller, Sr., 1918–1937, Box 37, Folder 286, Rockefeller Family Archives, Rockefeller Archive Center, Tarrytown, New York.

4. William B. Riley, "Corporate Control: The Peril of Christian Education," in *Inspiration or Evolution?* (Cleveland: Union Gospel Press, 1926).

5. Gerald T. White, *Formative Years in the Far West* (New York: Appleton, 1962), p. 298.

6. Raymond B. Fosdick, *John D. Rockefeller, Jr.: A Portrait* (New York: Harper & Bros., 1956), p. 83.

7. John D. Rockefeller to Starr Murphy, December 9, 1920; JDR Gifts—December 15, 1920 (for Medical Education—1920–21), General Education Board, Rockefeller Boards, Office of the Messrs. Rockefeller, Rockefeller Archive Center.

8. John D. Rockefeller, Jr., to John D. Rockefeller, Sr., July 28, 1921, in ibid.

9. John D. Rockefeller, Sr., to John D. Rockefeller, Jr., August 1, 1921, in ibid.

10. Quoted in Peter Collier and David Horowitz, *The Rockefellers* (New York: Holt, Rinehart & Winston, 1976), p. 133.

11. Wolf Plume and Black Bull to John D. Rockefeller, Jr., April 16, 1926, Western Trip—1924 file, Papers of John D. Rockefeller, Jr., Rockefeller Family Archives, Rockefeller Archive Center.

12. Joe Alex Morris, *Nelson Rockefeller* (New York: Harper & Bros., 1960), p. 77.

13. John D. Rockefeller, Jr., to William G. Nelson, May 6, 1926, Western Trip—1924 file, Office of the Messrs. Rockefeller, Papers of John D. Rockefeller, Jr.—Personal Series, Rockefeller Family Archives, Rockefeller Archive Center.

14. William G. Nelson, Blackfeet Agency, U.S. Indian Field Service, to John D. Rockefeller, Jr., June 7, 1926, in ibid.

15. Harry M. Ralston to John D. Rockefeller, April 26, 1926, in ibid.

16. Memorandum dictated by Kenneth Chorley, January 4, 1924, in ibid.

17. Charles L. White to Raymond Fosdick, January 11, 1924, in ibid.

18. Herbert Welsh to Kenneth Chorley, November 19, 1924, in ibid.

19. John Collier to Raymond Fosdick, July 30, 1924, American Indian Defense Association—1923–1924 file, 169 TM, in ibid.

20. John Collier, *Indians of the Americas* (New York: New American Library, 1947), p. 134.

21. Quoted in Kenneth R. Philp, *John Collier's Crusade for Indian Reform: 1920–1954* (Tucson: University of Arizona Press, 1977), pp. 80, 81.

22. See Herbert Welsh to Kenneth Chorley, November 19, 1924, and John Collier to Raymond B. Fosdick, July 30, 1924, Indian Rights Association file, 169 IN, Office of the Messrs. Rockefeller, Papers of John D. Rockefeller, Jr.—Personal Series, Rockefeller Family Archives, Rockefeller Archive Center.

3: RETHINKING MISSIONS

1. Joe Alex Morris, *Nelson Rockefeller* (New York: Harper & Bros., 1960), p. 80.

2. Quoted in ibid., p. 59.

3. Quoted in ibid., p. 50.

4. Quoted in Peter Collier and David Horowitz, *The Rockefellers* (New York: Holt, Rinehart & Winston, 1976), pp. 104–5.

5. Gates's letter to John D. Rockefeller was printed in the *Boston Herald*, April 17, 1905.

6. Ibid.

7. Dorothy Berg, *American Policy and the Chinese Revolution, 1925–28* (New York: Macmillan, 1947), p. 68.

8. Ibid.

9. Statistics from William A. Brown, "The Protestant Rural Movement in China, 1920–37," in *American Missionaries in China* (Cambridge, Mass.: Harvard University Press, 1966).

10. E. I. Vaughn to Wickliffe Rose, December 3, 1920. Memorandum Part V—"General Impression of Present Conditions," Record Group (hereafter RG) II,1, 319, Guatemala, Folder 183, Records of International Health Board, Rockefeller Foundation Archives, Rockefeller Archive Center, Tarrytown, New York.

11. *Interchurch World Bulletin of North America*, April 1920.

12. Ibid.

13. Papers of John D. Rockefeller, Jr., Religious Interests, ICM—Institute on Social and Religious Surveys, Folder 329, Rockefeller Archive Center.

14. "Proceedings of the Meeting of the Layman's Foreign Mission Inquiry," Hotel Roosevelt, 1932.

15. Quoted in Raymond B. Fosdick, *John D. Rockefeller, Jr.: A Portrait* (New York: Harper & Bros., 1956), p. 219.

16. Ibid.

4: The Apostolic Vision

1. Quoted in Ethel E. Wallis and Mary A. Bennett, *Two Thousand Tongues to Go* (London: Hodder & Stoughton, 1966), p. 48.

2. Quoted in James C. Hefley and Marti Hefley, *Uncle Cam* (Waco, Tex.: Word Books, 1974), p. 66.

3. Quoted in ibid., p. 38.

4. Quoted in Wallis and Bennett, *Two Thousand Tongues,* p. 49.

5. *Central American Bulletin,* September 15, 1920, pp. 10–11.

6. Ibid., January 15, 1921, pp. 12–14.

7. See William H. McNeill, *Plagues and Peoples* (Garden City, N.Y.: Anchor Books, 1978).

8. Wallis and Bennett, *Two Thousand Tongues,* p. 48.

9. See *New York Times,* September 7, 1926, p. 20, and January 16, 1927, p. 8. The Dargue flight was also a direct response to competition by German companies in Latin America, particularly Scadta in Colombia, which wanted to extend its lines between South America and the United States.

10. Quoted in Hefley and Hefley, *Uncle Cam,* p. 69.

11. Quoted in ibid.

12. David Stoll, *Fishers of Men or Founders of Empires? The Wycliffe Bible Translators in Latin America* (London: Zed Press, 1982), p. 39. Stoll quotes a village elder who recalled the dispute.

13. Hefley and Hefley, *Uncle Cam,* p. 70.

14. Colonel J. White to Wickliffe Rose, August 11, 1918, Box 33, Yellow Fever Commission, Records of the International Health Board, Rockefeller Foundation Archives, Rockefeller Archive Center, Tarrytown, New York.

15. Quoted in Hefley and Hefley, *Uncle Cam,* pp. 71–72.

16. Quoted in ibid., p. 72.

17. Quoted in ibid., p. 74.

18. Quoted in Hugh Steven, ed., *A Thousand Trails* (White Rock, British Columbia: CREDO Publishing Corp., 1984), p. 216.

19. Quoted in Hefley and Hefley, *Uncle Cam,* p. 64.

20. Quoted in ibid., pp. 75–76.

21. Ibid.

5: The Rites of Political Passage

1. Quoted in Joe Alex Morris, *Nelson Rockefeller* (New York: Harper & Bros., 1960), p. 90.

2. Quoted in Robert Grant Irving, *Indian Summer: Lutyens, Baker, and Imperial Delhi* (New Haven, Conn.: Yale University Press, 1981), p. 351.

3. Quoted in Morris, *Nelson Rockefeller,* p. 91.

4. Quoted in ibid., p. 87.

5. Quoted in ibid.

6. Quoted in ibid.

7. Geoffrey Hellman, "Best Neighbor," *The New Yorker,* April 18, 1942.

8. Judith Brown, *Gandhi and Civil Disobedience* (Cambridge: Cambridge University Press, 1977), p. 386.

9. Quoted in Morris, *Nelson Rockefeller,* p. 89.

10. Quoted in ibid., p. 90.

11. Quoted in Hellman, "Best Neighbor."

12. Paraphrase of Paine's remarks by Josephus Daniels in *Shirt-Sleeve Diplomat* (Chapel Hill, N.C.: University of North Carolina Press, 1947), p. 444.

13. Quoted in Myer Kutz, *Rockefeller Power* (New York: Simon & Schuster, 1974), p. 127.

14. Ibid., pp. 126–27.

15. Diego Rivera, *My Art, My Life* (New York: Citadel Press, 1958), p. 43; see also Bertram Wolfe, *The Fabulous Life of Diego Rivera* (New York: Stein & Day, 1963), pp. 144, 146–47.

16. *New York World Telegram,* May 3, 1933.

17. Quoted in Morris, *Nelson Rockefeller,* p. 102.

18. *New York World Telegram,* May 12, 1933.

19. Josephus Daniels to Jonathan Daniels, November 28, 1933, Papers of Josephus Daniels (hereafter cited as Daniels Papers), Library of Congress, Washington, D.C.

20. Ibid.

21. Quoted in James C. Hefley and Marti Hefley, *Uncle Cam* (Waco, Tex.: Word Books, 1974), p. 78.

22. Aarón Sáenz's career is reviewed in James C. Hefley, *Aarón Sáenz: Mexico's Revolutionary Capitalist* (Waco, Tex.: Word Books, 1970).

23. Frank Tannenbaum, *Peace by Revolution: An Interpretation of Mexico* (New York: Columbia University Press, 1933), p. 179.

24. Ibid., p. 302.

25. Quoted in Hefley and Hefley, *Uncle Cam,* p. 80.

26. Quoted in ibid., p. 82.

27. William Cameron Townsend, *Tolo: The Volcano's Son* (Huntington Beach, Calif.: Wycliffe Bible Translators, 1981), p. 85.

28. See Carey McWilliams, *Factories in the Field* (Santa Barbara, Calif.: Peregrine, 1971).

29. Ramírez to Townsend, June 4, 1935, Papers of William Cameron Townsend, General Director of the Wycliffe Bible Translators, located at Jungle Aviation and Radio Service headquarters, Waxhaw, North Carolina (hereafter cited as Townsend Archives).

30. Hefley and Hefley, *Uncle Cam,* p. 89.

31. Legters to Townsend, November 14, 1935, Townsend Archives.

32. Kenneth R. Philp, *John Collier's Crusade for Indian Reform: 1920–1954* (Tucson: University of Arizona Press, 1977), p. 90.

33. Ibid., p. 172.

34. Hefley and Hefley, *Uncle Cam,* p. 90.

35. Information on Gamio's career was taken from Juan Comas, *The Life and Work of Manuel Gamio: A Posthumous Homage* (Mexico City: Anthropology Department, UNAM [National Autonomous University of Mexico], 1956).

36. Adolfo Gilly, *La Revolución Interrumpida* (Mexico City: Ediciones El Caballito, 1971), p. 291.

37. *New York Times,* October 7, 1935, p. 34.

38. W. C. Townsend to Ambassador Daniels, December 18, 1935, Townsend Archives.

39. Daniels, *Shirt-Sleeve Diplomat,* pp. 136, 255–62.

40. James C. Hefley and Hugh Steven, *Miracles in Mexico* (Chicago: Moody Press, 1972), p. 23.

41. Daniels Papers, Box 664, State Dept. Dispatch (1933–1935), Presidential Trip, December 2–12, 1935.

42. Ethel E. Wallis and Mary A. Bennett, *Two Thousand Tongues to Go* (London: Hodder & Stoughton, 1966), p. 88.

43. William Cameron Townsend and Richard S. Pittman, *Remember All the Way* (Huntington Beach, Calif.: Wycliffe Bible Translators, 1975), pp. 64–65.

44. Ibid., p. 36.

45. Hefley and Hefley, *Uncle Cam,* p. 102.

6: Good Neighbors Make Good Allies

1. *Dallas Morning News,* December 8, 1959.

2. Quoted in Russell Lynes, *Good Old Modern* (New York: Atheneum, 1973), p. 151.

3. Peter Collier and David Horowitz, *The Rockefellers* (New York: Holt, Rinehart & Winston, 1976), p. 202. See also Josephus Daniels's account of Nelson's visit and interpretation of the Rivera incident in his *Shirt-Sleeve Diplomat* (Chapel Hill, N.C.: University of North Carolina Press, 1947), pp. 444–46.

4. Quoted in ibid., pp. 202–3.

5. Max Winkler, "The Dollar Abroad," *Information Service* 5, Supplement 1 (March 1929), Foreign Policy Associates, New York.

6. Gómez's relations with Creole are described in Harvey O'Connor, *World Crisis in Oil* (New York: Monthly Review Press, 1962).

7. Quoted in Joe Alex Morris, *Nelson Rockefeller* (New York: Harper & Bros., 1960), pp. 111–12.

8. Quoted in ibid., p. 16.

9. Quoted in ibid., p. 114

10. Quoted in ibid., p. 112.

11. Senate Temporary National Economic Committee, 76th Cong. 3rd sess., *Investigation of Concentration of Economic Power* (Washington, D.C.: Government Printing Office, 1941).

12. Quoted in Frank Gervasi, *The Real Rockefeller* (New York: Atheneum, 1964), p. 69.

13. Quoted in Morris, *Nelson Rockefeller,* p. 115.

14. Quoted in James C. Hefley and Marti Hefley, *Uncle Cam* (Waco, Tex.: Word Books, 1974), p. 103.

15. Ibid.

16. Josephus Daniels to Franklin Delano Roosevelt, March 22, 1938, President's Secretary's File (hereafter PSF)—Mexico, Franklin D. Roosevelt Library.

17. Quoted in O'Connor, *World Crisis in Oil,* p. 112.

18. Daniels to Franklin Delano Roosevelt, March 29, 1938, Roosevelt Library.

19. Quoted in S. Shepard Jones and Denys P. Myers, eds., *Documents on American Foreign Relations, January 1938–June 1939* (Boston: World Peace Foundation, 1939), pp. 123–24.

20. Adolf Berle, *Navigating the Rapids* (New York: Harcourt, 1973), p. 177.

21. Quoted in Hefley and Hefley, *Uncle Cam,* p. 107.

22. Lázaro Cárdenas to W. C. Townsend, August 9, 1938, Townsend Archives.

23. W. C. Townsend to Cordell Hull, September 10, 1938, in ibid.

24. Press Conference, January 12, 1940, No. 614-A, President's Personal File (hereafter PPF) no. 1P, Roosevelt Library.

25. Committee on Cooperation, *Annual Report,* 1929, p. 8.

26. Ibid., p. 5.

27. See Gerard Colby, *Du Pont Dynasty: Behind the Nylon Curtain* (Secaucus, N.J.: Lyle Stuart, 1984), pp. 330–46.

28. Committee on Cooperation, *Annual Report,* 1934, p. 2.

7: The Mexican Tightrope

1. Quoted in Joe Alex Morris, *Nelson Rockefeller* (New York: Harper & Bros., 1960), pp. 118–19.

2. W. C. Townsend, *The Truth About Mexico's Oil* (Los Angeles: Inter-American Fellowship, 1940), pp. 4–5.

3. Robert Bottome to N. Rockefeller, March 16, 1940, Compañía de Fomento Venezuela file, Office of the Messrs. Rockefeller, Business Files, Rockefeller Family Archives, Rockefeller Archive Center, Tarrytown, New York.

4. Robert Bottome to Nelson Rockefeller, August 15, 1940, in ibid.

5. Carl Spaeth to Nelson Rockefeller, September 19, 1940, in ibid.

6. See Lloyd C. Gardner, *Economic Aspects of New Deal Diplomacy* (Madison: University of Wisconsin Press, 1954), pp. 153–68.

7. Ruml to H. Hopkins, December 28, 1938, Papers of Harry Hopkins, Box 97, Ruml file, Franklin D. Roosevelt Library.

8. Cable, Hopkins to Ruml, January 4, 1939, in ibid.

9. Anna Rosenberg to President Franklin D. Roosevelt, March 13, 1939, PPF, in ibid.

10. Quoted in Geoffrey Hellman, "Best Neighbor," *The New Yorker*, April 18, 1942.

11. Morris, *Nelson Rockefeller*, p. 124.

12. Ibid., pp. 129–30.

13. Will Clayton Memoir, Oral History Project, Columbia University, New York City.

14. Townsend, *The Truth About Mexico's Oil*, p. 26.

15. Ibid., p. 46.

16. Quoted in Ray Eldon Hiebert, *Courtier to the Crowd: The Story of Ivy Lee and the Development of Public Relations* (Ames, Iowa: Iowa State University Press, 1966), pp. 290–91.

17. Quoted in E. David Cronon, *Josephus Daniels in Mexico* (Madison: University of Wisconsin Press, 1960), p. 235.

18. Townsend, *The Truth About Mexico's Oil*, p. 64.

19. Collier's life is told by Kenneth R. Philp, *John Collier's Crusade for Indian Reform: 1920–1954* (Tucson: University of Arizona Press, 1977).

20. John Collier, Memorandum for Secretary Ickes, May 7, 1936, RG 75—Records of the Bureau of Indian Affairs, National Archives.

21. Quoted in James C. Hefley and Marti Hefley, *Uncle Cam* (Waco, Tex.: Word Books, 1974), pp. 114–15.

22. Josephus Daniels to Franklin D. Roosevelt, January 31, 1939, PSF—Mexico, PSF—Diplomatic (Box 61), Roosevelt Library.

23. Lázaro Cárdenas to Franklin D. Roosevelt, November 27, 1940, PPF 7214, in ibid.

24. W. C. Townsend to Franklin D. Roosevelt, Pan American Day [April 14], 1940, Townsend Archives.

8: The Coordinator

1. Franklin D. Roosevelt to Nelson Rockefeller, January 30, 1941, RG 229, Box 410, TR-47, U.S. Section of Inter-American Indian Institute folder, National Archives.

2. Joe Alex Morris, *Nelson Rockefeller* (New York: Harper & Bros., 1960), p. 137.

3. RG 229, Box 543, Records of the Immediate Office of the Coordinator, minutes of meetings and minutes of the Interdepartmental Committee on Inter-American Affairs, August 16, 1940. National Archives (located at National Records Center, Suitland, Maryland).

4. Quoted in Frank Gervasi, *The Real Rockefeller* (New York: Atheneum, 1964), p. 83.

5. Quoted in Morris, *Nelson Rockefeller*, p. 166.

6. Quoted in ibid., p. 146.

7. Laurance Duggan to Sumner Welles, December 29, 1942; see also David Green, *The Containment of Latin America: A History of the Myths and Realities of the Good Neighbor Policy* (Chicago: Triangle Books, 1971), p. 135.

8. Josephus Daniels to Franklin D. Roosevelt, September 4, 1939, PSF—Mexico, Franklin D. Roosevelt Library.

9. Laurance Rockefeller to William "Bud" H. McClave, June 28, 1941; McClave to L. Rockefeller, January 16, 1941; Office of the Messrs. Rockefeller, Business Files—Panama (118P), Rockefeller Family Archives, Rockefeller Archive Center, Tarrytown, New York. Laurance Rockefeller to Jesse Knight (American Colombian Corporation), December 2, 1941, in ibid.

10. Franklin Field to Nelson Rockefeller, March 27, 1942, and Field to A. Moore Montgomery, March 27, 1942, RG 229, Box 158, Inter-American Escadrille (Folders 3 and 4), National Archives.

11. Laurance Rockefeller to Edsel Ford, July 25, 1940, RG II, Office of the Messrs. Rockefeller, Business Files—Inter-American Escadrille folder, Rockefeller Family Archives, Rockefeller Archive Center.

12. James E. Farris to David L. Behneke, August 25, 1941, in ibid.

13. Carleton Beals, *Lands of the Dawning Morrow* (New York: Bobbs-Merrill, 1948), p. 179.

14. Message of President Oscar Benavides to the Peruvian Legislature, December 9, 1937. Copy located in CIAA files, RG 229, Box 411, U.S. Section of Inter-American Indian Institute—GG 1338 folder, National Archives.

15. *Moody's Manual of Investments* (New York: Frederic Hatch & Company, 1944), p. 1859.

16. Franklin D. Roosevelt to Nelson Rockefeller, January 21, 1942, and Nelson Rockefeller to Franklin D. Roosevelt, February 5, 1942, White House Official Files, Box 287, Peru folder, Roosevelt Library.

17. Nelson Rockefeller to Franklin D. Roosevelt, February 5, 1942, in ibid.

9: The Sword of the Spirit

1. CIAA contract No. OEM Cr-250, RG 229, Box 29, Schools and Institutions, National Archives.

2. Ethel E. Wallis and Mary A. Bennett, *Two Thousand Tongues to Go* (London: Hodder & Stoughton, 1966), p. 178.

3. James C. Hefley and Marti Hefley, *Uncle Cam* (Waco, Tex.: Word Books, 1974), p. 120.

4. *Translation* magazine (Wycliffe Bible Translators), 1944, p. 8.

5. W. C. Townsend, "Progress Report," April 1943, Townsend Archives.

6. "Nazi, Axis and Anti-Democratic Propaganda Addresses to or Against the Indians of the Americas," marked "Confidential" by CIAA, E-AC-5200; RG 229, Box 411, Race—Indians, National Archives.

7. Sol Tax, "Ethnic Relations in Guatemala," *América Indígena* 2 (October 1942), pp. 43–47.

8. *América Indígena* 2 (September 1942).

9. Harold E. Davis, Memorandum, November 8, 1943, "Inter-American Activities in the U.S. Education Programs, Schools and Institutions," RG 229, Central Files, Box 29, National Archives. On ACLS, Rockefeller Foundation grants, beginning with $25,000 in 1927, mushroomed in 1941. By 1964, the foundation had funneled over $6 million into ACLS and had made similar large grants to the Modern Language Association. See Arthur Bernon Tourtellot, ed., *Toward the Well-Being of Mankind: Fifty Years of the Rockefeller Foundation* (Garden City, N.Y.: Doubleday, 1964), pp. 174–75.

10. W. C. Townsend, draft memo, n. d. (c. 1942), Townsend Archives.

11. PSF Diplomatic files, Box 61, Mexico, 1940, Franklin D. Roosevelt Library.

12. George P. Murdoch et al., *Outline of Cultural Materials* (New Haven, Conn.: Human Relations Area Files, Yale University, 1967), pp. xiii–xiv. SIL linguists had assisted the data-collecting project of anthropologist Morris Swadesh in Mexico for Yale's Human Relations Area Files project; copies of the files were passed to Rockefeller's CIAA under a purchase agreement and were then renamed the Strategic Index of the Americas.

13. Files on Indians, grouped under "race," CIAA Central Files, R6229, National Archives.

14. EAC 5200 Central Files, RG 229, Box 410, National Indian Institute folder, CIAA files, in ibid.

15. Robert Redfield, *Boletín Indigenista* 3 (December 1943), pp. 213–15.

16. Clyde Kluckhohn, *Mirror for Man: A Survey of Human Behavior and Social Attitudes* (Greenwich, Conn.: Fawcett, 1967), p. 151.

17. W. C. Townsend, "Dear Fellow Workers," November 27, 1943, Townsend Archives.

18. *Boletín Indigenista* 3 (Summer 1943), pp. 111–13.

19. The Bulnes story is recounted in Cuauhtémoc González Pacheco, *Capital Extranjero en la Selva de Chiapas, 1863–1982* (Mexico City: Instituto de Investigaciones Económicas, UNAM [National Autonomous University of Mexico], 1983).

20. Wallis and Bennett, *Two Thousand Tongues*, pp. 163–64.

21. Hefley and Hefley, *Uncle Cam*, p. 125.

22. Ibid., p. 137.

10: The Shining Dream

1. Felisberto C. de Camargo to Berent Friele, November 29, 1941, RG 229, General Records, Central Files, Commercial and Financial, Country Files—Brazil—Box 172, Rubber file, National Archives.

2. "Vargas Suggests U.S. Might Join in Conference of Amazon Nation," October 13, 1940, typed reprint of article, RG 229, Box 76, Amazon Basin Project—9 folder, in ibid.

3. Stanley E. Hilton, *Hitler's Secret War in South America: German Military Espionage and Allied Counterespionage in Brazil, 1939–45* (Baton Rouge: Louisiana State University Press, 1981), p. 19.

4. William C. Burdett, American consul general, Rio de Janeiro, "The Ford Rubber Plantations in Brazil," June 5, 1938, RG 229, Box 172, Brazil—Rubber folder, National Archives.

5. Earl P. Hanson to Carl Spaeth, August 10, 1941, RG 229, Box 173, Investments folder, in ibid.

6. Nelson Rockefeller to Berent Friele, September 21, 1941, RG 229, Box 76, Amazon Basin Project file, in ibid.

7. Jefferson Caffery to Berent Friele, in ibid.

8. See P. C. Mangelsdorft to Henry M. Miller, Jr., June 23, 1941, 323—Agriculture, 1941, Rockefeller Foundation Archives, Rockefeller Archive Center, Tarrytown, New York.

9. Schultes's briefings on the political beliefs of his Colombian colleagues were included in the survey of Bogotá's agricultural education institutions by Henry M. Miller, Jr., of the Rockefeller Foundation. Miller's November 1941 trip was an outgrowth of the foundation's collaboration with Vice President Wallace and Nelson Rockefeller in stimulating Latin American agriculture to meet U.S. war needs. H. M. Miller, Jr., interviews, November 10–15, 1941, in ibid.

10. Earl Bressman (Department of Agriculture) to Nelson A. Rockefeller, December 12, 1941, RG 229, Box 270, Strategic Materiels folder, National Archives.

11. Earl Parker Hanson, *Journey to Manaos* (New York: Reynal & Hitchcock, 1938), p. 306.

12. Berent Friele to Morris Llewellyn Cooke, November 28, 1942, RG 229, Box 1261, folder 02.7, National Archives.

13. Project Authorization, "Amazon Basin Development Project," February 12, 1942, in ibid.

14. Quoted in Stewart Alsop, *Nixon and Rockefeller* (Garden City, N.Y.: Doubleday, 1960), p. 87.

15. Berent Friele to Nelson Rockefeller and Richard Kleberg, "Brazilian Political Situation," March 6, 1942, RG 229, Box 175, Spaeth Data file, National Archives.

16. Carl Spaeth to Milo Perkins, March 17, 1942, RG 229, Box 172, Rubber file, in ibid.

17. Nelson Rockefeller to Sumner Welles, March 7, 1942, in ibid.

18. Quoted in Joe Alex Morris, *Nelson Rockefeller* (New York: Harper & Bros., 1960), p. 158.

19. J. C. King to Berent Friele, April 28, 1942, RG 229, Box 76, "Amazon Basin Project I" file, National Archives.

20. Ibid.

21. J. C. King to Nelson Rockefeller, June 17, 1942, p. 9, in ibid.

22. Ibid.

23. Ibid.

24. John F. Simmons ["For the Ambassador"], Counselor of Embassy, Rio de Janeiro, to the Secretary of State [Cordell Hull], Report No. 7244, May 7, 1942, Subject: Rubber Procurement in Brazil, RG 66, Box 92, Brazil—Rubber 1942–1945 folder, National Archives.

25. J. C. King to Rockefeller, June 17, 1942, RG 229, Box 76, "Amazon Basin Project I" file, p. 14, National Archives.

26. Ernest Maes to Charles Collier, July 31, 1941, in ibid.

27. Ernest Maes to Charles Collier, June 25, 1941. Memo attached to letter from John Collier to Nelson Rockefeller, October 21, 1940, in ibid.

28. Harold Ickes to Nelson Rockefeller, January 5, 1942, in ibid. Ickes's figures were exaggerated, especially for Nicaragua.

29. Nelson Rockefeller to Harold Ickes, February 5, 1942, in ibid.

30. In 1900 the Standard Oil Trust had invested $75 million in the International Crude Rubber Company, headed by, among others, Standard Oil's William Rockefeller. Rockefeller later switched to the U.S. Rubber Company, a firm set up in 1892 by an official of W. R. Grace & Company. By 1903, U.S. Rubber's purchasing agent, General Rubber Company, was doing a thriving business in Indian-produced rubber in Pará and Manaus.

The other wing of the Rockefeller family, led by Nelson's father, John D. Rockefeller, Jr., and Nelson's maternal grandfather, Senator Nelson Aldrich, also jumped into the rubber boom. They invested in the Intercontinental Rubber Company, a venture of Thomas Fortune Ryan, Bernard Baruch, and the Guggenheims. Senator Aldrich also followed Ryan into the Amazon of Africa, the Congo. There they gained a forest monopoly in the Belgian Congo known as the American Congo Company. The group's major concern, Intercontinental Rubber, soon developed a soiled reputation for its association with Belgium's King Leopold, whose atrocities against Africans in the Congo rivaled the Peruvian Amazon Company's infamy in the Putumayo in the Peruvian Amazon. To force the rubber collectors to work, Leopold raised taxes as a pretext for unleashing troops on villages, holding women and children as hostages. If production fell, that was taken as proof of rebellion, and villages were burned and looted. In one district, 6,000 Africans were killed and mutilated every six months; by 1908 an incredible 8 million people had perished. The horrors perpetrated by King Leopold in the Belgian Congo made headlines throughout Europe and the United States, but the Rockefeller association with Intercontinental Rubber was ignored in the American press, despite the telling presence of Edward Aldrich on Intercontinental's board as late as 1918. See Howard and Ralph Wolf, *Rubber* (New York: Covici-Friede, 1936), and entry for Intercontinental Rubber in "Industrial Section," *Moody's Manual of Railroads and Corporation Securities* (New York: Frederic Hatch & Company, 1918).

31. For a study of the rubber industry, see Loren G. Polhamus, *Rubber: Botany Production and Utilization* (New York: Interscience Publishers, 1962).

32. Ernest Maes, "Brazilian Indian Labor and Indian Administration in Relation to the Rubber Collection Program," June 1942, RG 229, Box 411—Information; Science and Education file, U.S. Section of Inter-American Indian Institute, National Archives.

33. John Collier to Nelson Rockefeller, June 12, 1942, RG 229, Box 410, in ibid.

34. Nelson Rockefeller to John Collier, June 27, 1942, in ibid.

35. J. C. King to B. Friele, October 27, 1942, RG 229, Box 126; Rockefeller to Friele, November 16, 1942, RG 229, Box 1261, folder 02.7, Berent Friele—Coordinator (General), November 16, 1942–September 1943, National Archives.

11: THE DANCER

1. J. D. Le Cron, "Revised Project Authorization: A Project for the Improvement of Rural Diet in Mexico," draft, October 23, 1942, RG 229, General Records, Central Files 3, Information, Box 411, Inter-American Indian Institute folder, National Archives.

2. The CIAA, with help from Yale University's Institute of Human Relations, compiled a variety of glossaries on Amazonia. See the CIAA's "Battle of the Amazon" by John McClintock (Pr. 32.4602; Am), "Glossary of Brazilian-Amazonian Terms" (Pr. 32.4613; B73), and "Glossary of Useful Amazonian Flora" (Pr. 32.4613; Am 2/5), all dated 1943. A "Preliminary Bibliography on Amazonia" (Pr 32.4613: AmI/prelim.) was compiled in 1942, RG 229, in ibid.

3. Candido M. da Silva Rondon, "Problema Indígena," *América Indígena* 3 (January 1943), pp. 23–24.

4. This was done by deliberate design. See memorandum to Jean Pajus from Board of Economic Warfare, December 1, 1942, RG 229, Box 411, U.S. Section of Inter-American Indian Institute folder, National Archives.

5. *Boletín Indigenista* 3 (January 1943), p. 19.

6. Minutes of the Executive Committee of the Interdepartmental Committee on Inter-American Affairs,

August 30, 1940, RG 229, Box 543, Records of the Immediate Office of the Coordinator, Minutes of Meetings, National Archives.

7. Berent Friele to Nelson Rockefeller, August 23, 1943, RG 229, Box 175, Research—Miscellaneous folder, in ibid.

8. Senate Subcommittee on War Mobilization, *Cartels and National Security,* Report No. 4 (Washington, D.C.: Government Printing Office, 1944), p. 82.

9. Joseph Borkin, *The Crime and Punishment of I.G. Farben* (New York: Free Press, 1978), p. 143.

10. I. F. Stone, *P.M.,* April 5, 1943, p. 10.

11. I. F. Stone, "Officials Defied FDR's Orders," *P.M.* 8 (September 28, 1942). See also *The Nation,* September 2, 1942.

12. See Robert E. Sherwood, *Roosevelt and Hopkins* (New York: Harper & Bros., 1948), p. 756.

13. William O. Douglas, *Go East, Young Man* (New York: Random House, 1974), pp. 364–65.

14. Frank Gervasi, *The Real Rockefeller* (New York: Atheneum, 1964), p. 98.

15. Quoted in Joe Alex Morris, *Nelson Rockefeller* (New York: Harper & Bros., 1960), p. 181.

16. Quoted in ibid., pp. 181–82.

17. Interview with J. D. Le Cron, Columbia University Oral History Project, cited in Peter Collier and David Horowitz, *The Rockefellers* (New York: Holt, Rinehart & Winston, 1976), p. 683.

18. Ibid., p. 696.

19. James J. Matles and James Higgins, *Them and Us* (Boston: Beacon Press, 1974), p. 139.

20. See Bruce Catton, *The Warlords of Washington* (New York: Harcourt, 1948).

21. Quoted in Morris, *Nelson Rockefeller,* pp. 186–87.

22. Ibid., p. 835.

12: PREEMPTING THE COLD WAR

1. Carleton Beals, *Lands of the Dawning Morrow* (New York: Bobbs-Merrill, 1948), pp. 75–76.

2. Joe Alex Morris, *Nelson Rockefeller* (New York: Harper & Bros., 1960), p. 191.

3. Quoted in Frank Gervasi, *The Real Rockefeller* (New York: Atheneum, 1964), p. 106.

4. Quoted in Morris, *Nelson Rockefeller,* pp. 193–94.

5. Quoted in Gervasi, *The Real Rockefeller,* p. 102.

6. Ibid., p. 194.

7. Quoted in William Appleman Williams, *The Tragedy of American Diplomacy* (Cleveland: World, 1959), p. 238.

8. Editorial, *América Indígena,* April 1945.

9. Nelson Rockefeller to Adolf Berle, February 1, 1945, Berle Papers, Franklin D. Roosevelt Library.

10. Quoted in David Green, *The Containment of Latin America: A History of the Myths and Realities of the Good Neighbor Policy* (Chicago: Triangle, 1971), pp. 139–40.

11. Quoted in Morris, *Nelson Rockefeller,* p. 198.

12. Quoted in Green, *The Containment of Latin America,* pp. 180-81.

13. Quoted in ibid.

14. Quoted in Morris, *Nelson Rockefeller,* p. 201.

15. Quoted in Peter Collier and David Horowitz, *The Rockefellers* (New York: Holt, Rinehart & Winston, 1976), p. 236.

16. Quoted in Morris, *Nelson Rockefeller,* p. 202.

17. Green, *The Containment of Latin America,* p. 250.

18. Quoted in Gervasi, *The Real Rockefeller,* p. 113.

19. Quoted in Collier and Horowitz, *The Rockefellers,* p. 237.

20. W. Averell Harriman and Eli Abel, *Special Envoy to Churchill and Stalin, 1941–1946* (New York: Random House, 1975), p. 455.

21. Quoted in Collier and Horowitz, *The Rockefellers,* p. 239n.

22. Quoted in Green, *The Containment of Latin America,* p. 249.

23. Quoted in Morris, *Nelson Rockefeller,* p. 218.

24. Len Giovannitti and Fred Freed, *The Decision to Drop the Bomb* (New York: Coward-McCann, 1965), p. 73.

25. James Desmond, *Nelson Rockefeller: A Political Biography* (New York: Macmillan, 1964), p. 126.

26. Gervasi, *The Real Rockefeller,* pp. 121–22.

27. Desmond, *Nelson Rockefeller,* p. 132.

28. Ibid.

13: Latin America's First Cold War Coup

1. E. A. P. Palmer to A. Moore Montgomery, CIAA Commercial and Financial Division, October 11, 1941, RG 229, Box 172, National Archives.

2. Adolf Berle, Memorandum of April 26, 1945, Berle Papers, Franklin D. Roosevelt Library.

3. Frank Waring to Nelson Rockefeller, November 19, 1943, RG 229, Box 229, Industrial Development folder, National Archives.

4. Adolf Berle, "Management of Companhia Vale do Rio Doce," May 24, 1945, Memorandum to State Department, Berle Papers.

5. OSS Report No. 13886, May 20, 1942, Modern Military Records, National Archives.

6. Adolf Berle, Memorandum of Conversation, February 15, 1945, Berle Papers.

7. Harry S. Truman to Adolf Berle, September 13, 1945, Box 77, in ibid.

8. Paraphrase of telegram sent to the department, September 18, 1945, "Re: Political Situation in Brazil," Diary papers, in ibid.

9. Address of Ambassador Adolf Berle before the Journalists Syndicate, Hotel Quitandinha, September 29, 1945, in ibid.

10. Adolf Berle, diary entry for October 4, 1945, summary of confidential telegram sent by Ambassador Berle, October 1, 1945, in ibid.

11. Summary of cable, October 30, 1945, in ibid.

12. Berle, diary entry, October 30, 1945, in ibid.

13. William A. Wieland to Berle, November 13, 1945, in ibid.

14. Department of State, Division of Brazilian Affairs, Memorandum of Conversation, Philip C. Chalmers, "Subject: Political Situation in Brazil," November 1, 1945, in ibid.

15. *Washington Post,* November 28, 1945.

16. Philip Chalmers, Memorandum of Conversation, "Petroleum Refineries in Brazil," October 29, 1945, Berle Papers.

17. Adolf Berle, memorandum, November 16, 1945, in ibid.

18. Peter Seaborn Smith, *Oil and Politics in Modern Brazil* (Toronto: Macmillan, 1976), pp. 56, 71.

19. Memorandum of Conversation, subject: "Petroleum Refining in Brazil," November 23, 1945, participants: Adolf Berle and Messrs. Rayner, Lottus, and Chalmers, Berle Papers.

20. Philip Chalmers, memorandum of telephone conversation, December 5, 1945, in ibid.

21. Philip Chalmers to Spruille Braden, "Newspaper Reports of Ambassador Berle's Recall," December 3, 1945; Philip Chalmers to Ellis G. Briggs, November 28, 1945, in ibid.

22. Adolf Berle, memorandum, December 14, 1945, in ibid.

23. *New York Times,* December 6, 1946.

24. James Forrestal, *Diaries,* vol. 4, May 2, 1947, Papers of James Forrestal, Library of Congress.

25. Captain Bart W. Gillespie, Memorandum, "Suggested Plan for Assuring Navy of Sufficient Petroleum in the Event of Another War," p. 5, Appendix, SWNCC 289, and "Petroleum Reserves in South America," April 17, 1946, RG 218, Records of the U.S. Joint Chiefs of Staff, CCS 463.7 South America (4-17-46), National Archives.

26. Enclosure, p. 1, in ibid.

27. Gillespie, Appendix, p. 3, in ibid.

14: AMERICAN WINGS OVER THE AMAZON

1. Quoted in Ethel E. Wallis and Mary A. Bennett, *Two Thousand Tongues to Go* (London: Hodder & Stoughton, 1966), p. 181.

2. Agreement Between the Ministry of Public Education of Peru and Mr. William C. Townsend; copy on file in the Western History Collection of the University of Oklahoma at Norman.

3. Quoted in Wallis and Bennett, *Two Thousand Tongues,* p. 181.

4. Quoted in Jamie Buckingham, *Into the Glory* (Plainfield, N.J.: Logos, 1974), p. 25.

5. W. C. Townsend to Prentice Cooper, July 20, 1946, Townsend Archives.

6. W. C. Townsend to P. Cooper, October 24, 1946, in ibid.

7. Quoted in Buckingham, *Into the Glory,* p. 32.

8. James C. Hefley and Marti Hefley, *Uncle Cam* (Waco, Tex.: Word Books, 1974), p. 153.

9. Richard Ellsworth Day, *Breakfast Table Autocrat* (Chicago: Moody Press, 1946), p. 59.

10. *Translation* magazine (Wycliffe Bible Translators), Winter 1966.

11. Quoted in Vernon A. Walters, *Silent Missions* (Garden City, N.Y.: Doubleday, 1978), p. 165.

12. W. C. Townsend to Prentice Cooper, October 24, 1946, Townsend Archives.

13. Tad Szulc, *Twilight of the Tyrants* (New York: Holt, Rinehart & Winston, 1959), p. 184.

14. Hefley and Hefley, *Uncle Cam,* p. 162. The "Hail, Caesar" characterization of SIL's policy was originally coined by author David Stoll in *Fishers of Men or Founders of Empires? The Wycliffe Bible Translators in Latin America* (London: Zed Press, 1982).

15. "Second Inter-American Indian Conference and the Final Act," Papers of Philleo Nash, White House Central File (1946–1953), National Indian Institute, Department of Interior, Harry S. Truman Library, Independence, Missouri.

16. Ibid.

17. Ibid.

18. Ibid.

19. John Collier, "Has Roxas Betrayed America?" *Saturday Review of Literature,* January 11, 1947, p. 15; John Collier, *America's Colonial Record* (London: Fabian Publications, 1947), pp. 6–14.

20. Willard F. Barber, Memorandum on Conversation with Mr. W. C. Townsend, September 22, 1950, cited in Stoll, *Fishers of Men or Founders of Empires?,* pp. 81, 96.

21. See R. Immerman, *The CIA in Guatemala* (Austin: University of Texas Press, 1982), pp. 81–82.

22. William Cameron Townsend, *Lázaro Cárdenas: Mexican Democrat* (Ann Arbor, Mich.: George Wahr, 1952), p. 367.

15: THE PRETENDER AT BAY

1. During the war, when Laurance took his job with the navy, James McDonnell wrote him to ask for a little inside promotion for the company with Navy Secretary James Forrestal. McDonnell subsequently grew from a fifty-one-man staff at the time of Pearl Harbor to a vast operation with 5,000 workers, sending regular dividends to Laurance's accountants.

When Laurance moved to the Fighter Desk in early 1945, he sold his 20 percent holding in McDonnell. He wanted to avoid charges of impropriety, taking a large capital gain. How large can be judged from what his 20 percent holding cost him the following year when he reacquired it after mustering out of the navy. What had cost him $10,000 in 1939 now cost $405,000. He paid it, cheerfully; when he sold his 73,000 shares four years later, they were worth $8 million. See McDonnell file, Office of the Messrs. Rockefeller, Rockefeller Family Archives, Rockefeller Archive Center, Tarrytown, New York.

2. Chase Bank Files, Rockefeller Family Archives, in ibid.

3. Frank Gervasi, *The Real Rockefeller* (New York: Atheneum, 1964), pp. 125, 126.

4. Harrison, who had been the CIAA's assistant coordinator; Lockwood, CIAA former general counsel; Jamieson, former director of CIAA's Press Division; and Berent Friele, former CIAA director in Brazil. Martha Dalrymple, former Associated Press reporter who had been Jamieson's CIAA aide, came on board. Stacy May, an economist at Dartmouth College who had been wartime director of planning and statistics for Vice President Wallace's War Production Board, was recruited as an adviser, as was the sagelike Beardsley Ruml, now chairman of RCA.

5. Joe Alex Morris, *Nelson Rockefeller* (New York: Harper & Bros., 1960), p. 238.

6. Peter Collier and David Horowitz, *The Rockefellers* (New York: Holt, Rinehart & Winston, 1976), p. 260.

7. Cited in Morris, *Nelson Rockefeller*, p. 243.

8. Darcy Ribeiro, "Indigenous Cultures and Languages of Brazil," in *Indians of Brazil in the Twentieth Century*, ed. Janice H. Hopper (Washington, D.C.: Institute for Cross Cultural Research, 1967), p. 96, Table II. Of eighty-seven indigenous groups who were destroyed between 1900 and 1957, only six had succumbed in agricultural areas; fifty-nine groups were wiped out in extractive regions, constituting the overwhelming number of the 800,000 Indians who "disappeared" from the estimated population of 1 million Indians in 1900.

9. Joseph Jensen to Laurance Rockefeller, February 6, 1947, Memo, "Brazil-Phosphate Development Project," Rockefeller Archive Center.

10. Morris, *Nelson Rockefeller*, p. 248.

11. *New York Times*, August 14, 1946, p. 8.

12. Gervasi, *The Real Rockefeller*, p. 129.

13. *New York Times*, December 11, December 15, 1948.

14. Ibid., April 23, 1949, and May 7, 1949.

15. Morris, *Nelson Rockefeller*, p. 254.

16. Memorandum, "Future Work," August 23, 1946, Rockefeller Foundation Archives, Box 30, Folder 308, Rockefeller Archive Center.

17. *Who's Who in America*, 37th ed. (1972–1973) (Chicago: Marquis Who's Who, 1972).

16: The Latin Road to Power

1. Capus Waynich to Murphy, October 30, 1950, Cross Ref.—PPF, Folder 689, Harry S. Truman Library, Independence, Missouri.

2. *Partners in Progress, Report by the International Development Advisory Board* (New York: Simon & Schuster, 1951), p. 4.

3. Ibid., p. 60.

4. Ibid.

5. The charges were made in Frank Gervasi, *The Real Rockefeller* (New York: Atheneum, 1964), p. 138, and Joe Alex Morris, *Nelson Rockefeller* (New York: Harper & Bros., 1960), p. 278. Copies were, in fact, sent to the secretaries of state, treasury, defense, interior, agriculture, commerce, and labor. The vice president, the attorney general, the director of the Budget and Defense Mobilization, and the administrators of the ECA and Defense Production were sent copies. So were key members of Congress. The copies were sent out on March 9, 1951, the same day that Truman wrote Rockefeller. See PPF-689 (Nelson Rockefeller), Harry S. Truman Library.

6. House Committee on Foreign Affairs, *Hearings on the Mutual Security Program* (Washington, D.C.: Government Printing Office, 1951), pp. 354–56.

7. Peter Collier and David Horowitz, *The Rockefellers* (New York: Holt, Rinehart & Winston, 1976), p. 269.

8. G. William Domhoff, *Who Rules America?* (Englewood Cliffs, N.J.: Prentice-Hall, 1967), p. 87.

9. John Camp to Nelson Rockefeller, November 24, 1952, Camp Papers, Rockefeller Archive Center.

10. Rockefeller Foundation chairman John Foster Dulles, as chief partner of the Sullivan Cromwell law firm in 1936, had personally drafted United Fruit's 1936 contract with the Ubico dictatorship that gave the banana company its ninety-nine-year lease with exceptional tax benefits. Nelson's former assistant at the State Department, John Moors Cabot, owned stock in United Fruit and had been U.S. ambassador to Guatemala. His brother, Thomas C. Cabot, Jr., had briefly been president of United Fruit. John J. McCloy, as president of the World Bank, had denied Guatemala loans after reviewing its agrarian reform and liberal labor laws; within a year, as chairman of Chase, McCloy would sit on United Fruit's board. John McClintock, Nelson's former chief of the CIAA's Basic Economic Division, was now United Fruit's vice president and chief troubleshooter for Central America.

11. Adolf Berle, diary entry, October 12, 1952, Berle Papers. Franklin D. Roosevelt Library.

12. These records were described by one of King's superiors as "one of the most important and promising opportunities offered MIS [Military Intelligence Service] in financial intelligence." The files provided King with information on German espionage and sabotage systems in Latin America and on German penetration of Latin American armies, political groups, industry, and finance. RG 319, Army Intelligence, 1941–1945, Folder 210.68 M/a, National Archives, Suitland, Maryland.

13. Adolf Berle to Allen Dulles, May 11, 1951, Berle Papers.

17: IN THE WAKE OF WAR—AND THE CIA

1. Victor Marchetti and John Marks, *The CIA and the Cult of Intelligence* (New York: Alfred A. Knopf, 1974), p. 28.

2. CIA cables on SIL in 1952, released under the Freedom of Information Act, are in the authors' possession, courtesy of David Stoll.

3. Ethel E. Wallis and Mary A. Bennett, *Two Thousand Tongues to Go* (London: Hodder & Stoughton, 1966), p. 288.

4. Ibid., p. 281; and James C. Hefley and Marti Hefley, *Uncle Cam* (Waco, Tex.: Word Books, 1974), p. 173.

5. L. Fletcher Prouty, *The Secret Team* (Englewood Cliffs, N.J.: Prentice-Hall, 1973), p. 60.

6. Wallis and Bennett, *Two Thousand Tongues,* p. 310.

7. The Director's Column, *Translation* magazine (Wycliffe Bible Translators), January 1953.

8. *Central American Bulletin,* September 1955, p. 3.

9. Arbenz offered compensation of $1,185,000, exactly what United Fruit claimed the land was worth when the company paid its taxes.

10. Memorandum of Conversation, Department of State, May 25, 1953, 611-14/5-2553, National Archives.

11. John Hill to Henry Holland, June 7, 1954, State Department Archives, released under Freedom of Information Act Case 840606 to Blanche Wiesen Cook, *The Declassified Eisenhower* (Garden City, N.Y.: Doubleday, 1981), pp. 270–71.

12. Stephen Schlesinger and Stephen Kinzer, *Bitter Fruit: The Untold Story of the American Coup in Guatemala* (Garden City, N.Y.: Anchor Press/Doubleday, 1983), p. 112.

13. Ibid., p. 116.

14. Ibid., p. 126.

15. David Stoll, *Fishers of Men or Founders of Empires? The Wycliffe Bible Translators in Latin America* (London: Zed Press, 1982), p. 49.

16. Ibid., p. 48.

17. Harvey O'Connor, *World Crisis in Oil* (New York: Monthly Review Press, 1962), p. 251.

18. William Cameron Townsend and Richard Pittman, *Remember All the Way* (Huntington Beach, Calif.: Wycliffe Bible Translators, 1975), p. 27.

19. *New York Times,* October 1, 1953, p. 11.

20. Ibid.

21. W. Cameron Townsend, "President Odría's Visit to Eastern Peru: A New Day for the Jungle," *Peruvian Times,* August 7, 1953, p. 3.

22. *Time* (international edition), January 6, 1958, p. 25.

23. *Aviation Week,* May 5, 1958, p. 120.

24. *El Comercio* (Lima), February 28, 1953, pp. 5, 19.

25. *La Prensa* (Lima), August 8, 1953.

26. Ibid., pp. 1, 3.

27. *El Comercio,* August 19, 1953.

28. *La Prensa,* August 13, 1953, p. 2.

29. Robert G. Le Tourneau, *Mover of Men and Mountains* (Chicago: Moody Press, 1967).

30. Memo, Nelson Rockefeller to Louise A. Boyer, October 20, 1955, RG III B, Papers of Nelson Rockefeller—Personal, AIA-IBEC files, Box 7, Folder 72, Rockefeller Archive Center, Tarrytown, New York.

31. James C. Hefley and Marti Hefley, *Dawn over Amazonia* (Waco, Tex.: Word Books, 1972), p. 187.

32. Russell T. Hitt, *Jungle Pilot: The Life and Witness of Nate Saint* (Grand Rapids, Mich.: Zondervan, 1973), p. 152.

33. Dwight D. Eisenhower, Memorandum for the Files, October 1954, Lieutenant General James H. Doolittle file, Ann Whitman file, Administrative Series, Box 13, DDE—Papers of the President of the United States, Dwight D. Eisenhower Library.

34. Quoted in William R. Corson, *The Armies of Ignorance* (New York: Dial Press, 1977), p. 347.

18: IKE'S COLD WAR GENERAL

1. Frank Gervasi, *The Real Rockefeller* (New York: Atheneum, 1964), p. 145.

2. Walter Bowart, *Operation Mind Control* (New York: Dell, 1978), p. 108.

3. Robert Chin, CIA associate legislative counsel, to James Mitchie, investigator, Senate Subcommittee on Administrative Practice and Procedure, October 29, 1975, cited in Senate Subcommittee on Health of the Committee on Labor and Public Welfare and the Subcommittee on Administrative Practice and Procedure of the Committee on the Judiciary, 94th Cong., 1st sess., September 10, 12 and November 7, 1975, Joint Hearings. *Biomedical and Behavioral Research* (Washington, D.C.: Government Printing Office, 1978), p. 997.

4. John Collier, letter, Institute of Ethnic Affairs, May 8, 1954; "Statement of the Institute of Ethnic Affairs," July 8, 1954; "Terminating the American Indian," February 13, 1954; all in papers of John Collier, Yale University Library, New Haven.

5. Martha Dalrymple, *The AIA Story: Two Decades of International Cooperation* (New York: American International Association for Economic and Social Development, 1968), p. 96.

6. Peter Collier and David Horowitz, *The Rockefellers* (New York: Holt, Rinehart & Winston, 1976), p. 264.

7. "Rockefeller's IBEC," *Fortune,* February 1955.

8. Peter Seaborn Smith, *Oil and Politics in Modern Brazil* (Toronto: Macmillan, 1976), pp. 77, 91.

9. *New York Times,* January 16, 1952, p. 38; August 17, 1953, p. 29; January 27, 1953, p. 29; January 22, 1953, p. 3; January 24, 1953, p. 1; January 31, 1953, sec. 4, p. 2; February 10, 1953, p. 22; and May 13, 1953, p. 36.

10. See Arthur T. Moses, *Case Study of the Agricultural Program of ACAR in Brazil* (New York: National Planning Association, 1955). Nelson's coffee firm in El Salvador was called PROCAFE.

11. Robert Webb Coghill, "Memo: Personal Notes Relative to the Brazilian Petroleum Problem," April 15, 1953, O.C, C. D. Jackson, President's Official File, Box 854, File 164, Brazil (1), Dwight D. Eisenhower Library.

12. *New York Times,* June 19, 1953, p. 20; June 26, 1953, p. 5; and July 20, 1953, p. 11.

13. Cited in Marcos Arruda, Herbet de Souza, and Carlos Afonso, *Multinationals and Brazil* (Toronto: Brazilian Studies, 1975), pp. 79–80.

14. Shelton H. Davis, *Victims of the Miracle* (Cambridge: Cambridge University Press, 1977), p. 51. See also Roberto Cardoso de Oliveira, "Relationio de Uma Investigacão Sobre Terras em Mato Grosso," *SPI 1954* (Rio de Janeiro, 1955), pp. 173–84.

15. Tad Szulc, *Twilight of the Tyrants* (New York: Holt, Rinehart & Winston, 1959), pp. 95–96.

16. Harvey O'Connor, *World Crisis in Oil* (New York: Monthly Review Press, 1962), pp. 175, 96–98.

17. *Dallas Morning News,* December 17, 1954.

18. Adolf Berle, diary entry, January 3, 1955, Berle Papers, Franklin D. Roosevelt Library.

19. Corell Bell, *Negotiations from Strength: A Study in the Policies of Power* (London: Chatto & Windus, 1962), p. 91.

20. Adolf Berle, diary entry, January 3, 1955, Berle Papers.

21. Senate Select Committee to Study Governmental Operations with Respect to Intelligence Activities, *Supplementary Detailed Staff Reports on Foreign and Military Intelligence*, Book IV, Final Report (Washington, D.C.: Government Printing Office, 1976), pp. 50–51. Nelson was appointed chairman of the OCB's 5412 Committee. This Planning Coordination Group, or "Special Group" as it came to be called, was composed of Nelson (representing the president), Undersecretary of State Herbert Hoover, Jr. (representing Secretary Dulles), Defense Undersecretary Robert B. Anderson (representing Defense Secretary Wilson), and Allen Dulles (representing the CIA).

22. William R. Corson, *The Armies of Ignorance* (New York: Dial Press, 1977), p. 343.

23. Stuart H. Leroy, "The CIA's Use of the Press a 'Mighty Wurlitzer,'" *Columbia Journalism Review,* September/October 1974.

24. Congressional Reference Service catalog of CIA covert actions (CR5 75-50F), entered into the Congressional Record by Rep. Michael Harrington, September 30, 1975, pp. 31023–24.

25. Ibid.

26. Ibid.

27. See Christopher Simson, *Blowback: America's Recruitment of Nazis and Its Effects on the Cold War* (New York: Weidenfeld & Nicolson, 1988).

28. Robert Winters, "Allen Did Truth Serum Tests for U.S. Military," *Montreal Gazette,* February 25, 1984.

29. Adolf Berle, diary entry, March 27, 1957, Berle Papers.

30. John D. Marks, *The Search for the "Manchurian Candidate"* (New York: Times Books, 1979), p. 135. CIA ARTICHOKE program documents A/B, I,76/4 "Total Isolation" (March 21, 1955); A/B,I, 76/17: "Total Isolation-Supplementary Report No. 2" (April 27, 1955); and A/B,I, 76/12: "Total Isolation—Additional Comments" (May 19, 1955). Copies of these and thousands of other documents were released to researchers, including the authors, by the CIA in 1978 as a direct result of legal pressure by author John Marks and congressional investigators.

31. Gottlieb's role is described in the Church Committee Report (1976) and in Marks, *Search for the "Manchurian Candidate,"* p. 79.

32. MKULTRA subproject 35-10, May 16, 1955.

33. Marks, *Search for the "Manchurian Candidate,"* p. 203. The CIA's MKULTRA exploded with projects; over $655,000 went into Geshickter's experiments alone, and his hospital became a medical safehouse for other CIA-funded operations, including the African-American Institute (AAI). Arthur Felberbaum, a former contracts officer for the AAI, told of bringing stressed-out African exchange students to the hospital during the year after CIA funding of AAI was revealed by the *New York Times.* Interview with Arthur Felberbaum, March 1978.

34. "CIA Documents Tell of 1954 Project to Create Involuntary Assassins," *New York Times,* February 9, 1978, p. A17.

35. Ibid.

36. Arthur Bernon Tourtellot, ed., *Toward the Well-Being of Mankind: Fifty Years of the Rockefeller Foundation* (Garden City, N.Y.: Doubleday, 1964), p. 182.

37. Joseph B. Smith, *Portrait of a Cold Warrior* (New York: G. P. Putnam's Sons, 1976), pp. 268, 271–72.

38. Ibid., p. 274.

39. See Arthur M. Schlesinger, Jr., *A Thousand Days: John F. Kennedy in the White House* (Boston: Houghton Mifflin, 1965), p. 322.

40. Nelson Rockefeller, memorandum, "How the Planning Coordination Group Should Function," August 9, 1955, White House Central Files (Confidential File), Subject Series, Box 61, "Psychological Warfare" folder, Eisenhower Library.

41. Warren Hinckle, Robert Sheer, and Sol Stern, "The University on the Make," *Ramparts Special Collectors Edition* (San Francisco: Ramparts Magazine, 1968), pp. 56, 58.

42. Colonel Edward G. Lansdale, memorandum, "Some Thoughts on a Magsaysay Foundation," April 12, 1957, pp. 8–9, Office of the Messrs. Rockefeller, Rockefeller Boards, Rockefeller Brothers Fund, Box 22, Folder 220: Ramón Magsaysay Award Foundation, 1957–1958 folder, Rockefeller Archive Center Tarrytown, New York.

43. J. B. Smith, *Portrait of a Cold Warrior,* p. 179.

44. "Philippine Diplomat Explains Why Group Won Awards," *Charlotte News*, November 3, 1973.

45. Harper Woodward's fellow members of the CAT board included the CIA's George Doole and Hugh Grundy; Samuel S. Walker, director of Equitable Life Assurance and a board member of the Free Europe Committee, a CIA conduit; Arthur B. Richardson, chairman of Chesebrough-Pond's (formerly a subsidiary of Standard Oil of New Jersey); General Claire Chennault, cofounder (with William D. Pawley) of the Flying Tigers; and Brackley Shaw, an analyst on international aviation who had served under Air Force Secretary Stuart Symington during the Truman administration. See 1956 *Aviation Directory* listing for Civil Air Transport.

19: Disarming Disarmament

1. Joe Alex Morris, *Nelson Rockefeller* (New York: Harper & Bros., 1960), p. 300.

2. James Desmond, *Nelson Rockefeller: A Political Biography* (New York: Macmillan, 1964), p. 147.

3. Peter Collier and David Horowitz, *The Rockefellers* (New York: Holt, Rinehart & Winston, 1976), p. 275.

4. Frank Gervasi, *The Real Rockefeller* (New York: Atheneum, 1964), p. 176.

5. C. D. Jackson, "Log: From Quantico to Geneva—June, July, 1955," C. D. Jackson Papers, Box 72, Quantico Meetings (1) folder, Dwight D. Eisenhower Library.

6. Stewart Alsop, *Nixon and Rockefeller* (New York: Doubleday, 1960), p. 95.

7. Morris, *Nelson Rockefeller,* p. 300.

8. Jackson, "Log: From Quantico to Geneva," p. 2.

9. Vernon A. Walters, *Silent Mission* (Garden City, N.Y.: Doubleday, 1978), p. 289.

10. Desmond, *Nelson Rockefeller,* p. 150.

11. Dwight D. Eisenhower, interview, John Foster Dulles Oral History Collection, Princeton University, cited in Herbert S. Palmer, *Eisenhower and the American Crusades* (New York: Macmillan, 1972), p. 406.

12. Collier and Horowitz, *The Rockefellers,* p. 274.

13. "Psychological Aspects of United States Strategy," Quantico II Final Report to Nelson Rockefeller, November 1955, p. 22; White House Central Files (Confidential File), 1953–1961, Box 61, Nelson Rockefeller (4). Declassified through a Freedom of Information Act review requested by the authors.

14. Stacy May, "Thresholds of Armament Effort—U.S. and USSR" (Paper 14), C. D. Jackson Papers, Box 73, Quantico Meetings (5) folder, November 1955, Eisenhower Library.

15. "Psychological Aspects of United States Strategy."

16. Harry Rositzke, *The CIA's Secret Operations* (New York: Thomas Co., 1977), p. 189.

17. *New York Times,* February 27, 1967, p. 2.

18. The Pentagon's concerns go back to 1944 and can be found in the Records of the Joint Chiefs of Staff, Military Records Division, National Archives.

19. *New York Times,* April 1, 1955, p. 37.

20. Texas Instruments' Director Lloyd V. Berkner was the trustee (and, by 1957, chairman) of the

Rockefeller Public Service Awards committee of Nelson Rockefeller's Public Service Foundation; Berkner had been a member of the Rockefeller-sponsored Byrd expedition to the South Pole. Executive Vice President (and, by 1957, President) Patrick Haggerty would also emerge basking in the Rockefeller glow, as a member of the international advisory committee of David's Chase Manhattan Bank and executive committee member (with David) of the Rockefeller Medical University and of the Trilateral Commission. Texas Instruments' then-president, John E. Jonsson, also served with David Rockefeller on the board of the Equitable Life Assurance Society, New York's insurance giant.

21. Peter Seaborn Smith, *Oil and Politics in Modern Brazil* (Toronto: Macmillan, 1976), pp. 108–9.

22. *New York Times,* September 9, 1955, p. 15; September 10, 1955, p. 3; and September 21, 1955, p. 50.

23. The members of the Special Group were Ventures' new president, Robert B. Anderson, the recently resigned deputy secretary of defense; Herbert Hoover, Jr., whose United Geophysical Co. had taken seismographic readings in the Sechura for Union Oil; and, of course, Nelson Rockefeller.

24. Gervasi, *The Real Rockefeller,* pp. 182–83.

25. Dwight Eisenhower to Nelson Rockefeller, December 23, 1955, Administration Series (Whitman File), Box 33, Rockefeller—1952–1955 folder, Eisenhower Library.

26. Morris, *Nelson Rockefeller,* pp. 304–5.

20: MESSENGERS OF THE SUN

1. Accounts vary as to how SIL discovered the Helio Courier. In 1959, Cam told biographers Wallis and Bennett that he chanced upon a flying demonstration at a field near Tulsa and was impressed by the plane's ability to take off at a sharp angle. By 1974, he was telling biographers Hefley and Hefley that he was returning to Sulphur Springs from Tulsa when suddenly "he saw a single engine plane—not a helicopter—hovering overhead, almost at a standstill! Hurrying to the nearby airport, Cam found and questioned the manager, who told him about the new Helio Courier." Cam then took Larry Montgomery to the Helio manufacturing plant at Pittsburgh, Kansas. See Ethel E. Wallis and Mary A. Bennett, *Two Thousand Tongues to Go* (London: Hodder & Stoughton, 1966); and James C. Hefley and Marti Hefley, *Uncle Cam* (Waco, Tex.: Word Books, 1974).

According to Lynn Bollinger, creator of the Helio, Larry Montgomery was alone when he introduced himself as a former air force officer. After inspecting the plane and making just one test flight, Montgomery allegedly put in a call to Cam and then bought it on the spot. When Bollinger quoted Montgomery a price of $27,500, the pilot pulled out a roll of bills and began peeling off over $12,000. "Put this down," Bollinger remembered Montgomery's saying, "and the Lord will provide the rest." Interview with Lynn Bollinger, Dallas, Texas, October 17, 1977. Actually, Quaker Oats heir Henry Crowell provided the rest.

2. Quoted in Hefley and Hefley, *Uncle Cam,* p. 193.

3. Office of the Coordinator, September 1940–December 1941, Box 458, RG 229, National Archives.

4. W. C. Townsend to George Cross, December 20, 1955, Townsend Archives.

5. Jaime Galarza, "Ecuador: Oil Orgy," *Prensa Latina Features,* ES-1657.71, p. 4.

6. John Camp to Ted Watson, March 8, 1948, AIA files, Camp Papers, Rockefeller Archive Center, Tarrytown, New York.

7. Quoted in Rosemary Kingsland, *A Saint Among Savages* (London: William Collins, 1980), p. 97.

8. Quoted in *Life,* January 30, 1956, p. 15.

9. Summer Institute of Linguistics, *Language and Faith* (Santa Ana, Calif.: Wycliffe Bible Translators, 1972), p. 46.

10. Hefley and Hefley, *Uncle Cam,* p. 193.

11. Billy Graham New York Crusade, Inc., Report of Receipts and Expenditures from Inception, May 17, 1956, to December 16, 1957, p. 3, included in Roger Hull, chairman of Billy Graham New York Crusade, Inc., to John D. Rockefeller, Jr., and John D. Rockefeller 3rd, December 18, 1957, Protestant Council subseries, Billy Graham Crusade, New York, 1956–60 folder, Religious Interests Series, RG II, Office of the Messrs. Rockefeller, Rockefeller Family Archives, Rockefeller Archive Center, Tarrytown, New York.

12. Elizabeth Elliot, *The Savage My Kinsman* (New York: Harper & Bros., 1961), p. 63.

21: The Hidden Persuaders

1. *New York Times,* April 23, 1956.

2. "Fundamentalist Revival," *The Christian Century,* June 19, 1957, p. 749.

3. *Advance,* June 14, 1957, p. 6.

4. Letter, Lindsley F. Kimball to Dana Creel, August 27, 1956, folder entitled "Protestant Council, Billy Graham Crusade, New York, 1956–60," Religious Interests Series, RG II, Office of the Messrs. Rockefeller, Rockefeller Family Archives, Rockefeller Archive Center, Tarrytown, New York.

5. Thomas C. Campbell, Jr., "Capitalism and Christianity," *Harvard Business Review,* July/August 1957.

6. John O. Pollack, *Billy Graham* (New York: Harper & Row, 1979), p. 116.

7. *New York Times,* December 8, 1957.

8. Billy Graham New York Crusade, Inc., Report of Receipts and Expenditures from Inception, May 17, 1956, to December 16, 1957, included in Roger Hull, chairman of Billy Graham New York Crusade, Inc., to John D. Rockefeller, Jr., and John D. Rockefeller 3rd, December 18, 1957, and Protestant Council subseries, Billy Graham Crusade, New York, 1956–60 folder, Religious Interests Series, RG II, Office of the Messrs. Rockefeller, Rockefeller Family Archives, Rockefeller Archive Center.

9. Adolf Berle to W. Averell Harriman, January 4, 1956, Berle Papers, Franklin D. Roosevelt Library.

10. Robinson Rojas, *Estados Unidos en Brazil* (Santiago, Chile: Prensa Latinamerica, 1965), pp. 62–66, cited in Jan Knippers Black, *United States Penetration of Brazil* (Philadelphia: University of Pennsylvania Press, 1977), p. 38n.

11. Martha Dalrymple, *The AIA Story: Two Decades of International Cooperation* (New York: American International Association for Economic and Social Development, 1968), pp. 57–58.

12. Richard M. Greenbaum to W. B. Dixon Stroud, November 16, 1956, Fazenda Bodoquena folder, Box 4, Public Relations Series, RG II, Office of the Messrs. Rockefeller, Rockefeller Family Archives, Rockefeller Archive Center.

13. Berent Friele to Nelson Rockefeller, April 30, 1956, Papers of Nelson Rockefeller, Personal File, Country Series, General (1945–1971) folder, in ibid. (with clippings from the *New York Times,* April 30, 1956, entitled "Survey Disavows Brazil's Oil Policy").

14. See *Engineering and Mining Journal,* November 1975, p. 151.

15. Kenneth Kadow to Nelson Rockefeller and Berent Friele, March 14, 1947, Brazil IBEC folder, Box 7, IBEC Subseries, RG II, Office of the Messrs. Rockefeller, Rockefeller Family Archives, Rockefeller Archive Center.

16. Berent Friele to Nelson Rockefeller, April 7, 1953, RG III, 4B, Box 24, Folder 254, in ibid.

17. Robin Hanbury-Tenison, *Report of a Visit to the Indians of Brazil* (London: Survival International/ Primitive Peoples Fund, 1971), p. 13.

18. Roberto Cardoso de Oliveira, *O Processo da Assimilação dos Terêna* (Rio de Janeiro: Museo Nacional, 1960), pp. 130–32, 146–47.

19. Nelson Rockefeller to Walther Moreira Salles, March 7, 1956, Moreira Salles folder, Box 17, RG III, 4B, Rockefeller Family Archives, Rockefeller Archive Center.

20. Berent Friele to Nelson Rockefeller, June 25, 1956, Box 24, RG III, 4B, in ibid.

21. Berent Friele to Nelson Rockefeller, April 7, 1953, in ibid; and Nelson Rockefeller to Walther Moreira Salles, March 7, 1956, Moreira Salles folder, Box 17, in ibid.

22. Nelson Rockefeller to Berent Friele, 1956, Folder 254, Box 24, RG III, 4B, in ibid.

23. Nelson Rockefeller to Walther Moreira Salles, May 25, 1956, Moreira Salles folder, Box 17, RG III, 4, in ibid.

24. Walther Moreira Salles to Berent Friele, December 31, 1955; and Nelson Rockefeller to Moreira Salles, January 13, 1956, Box 17, RG III, Moreira Salles folder, in ibid.

25. Richard Greenbaum to W. Dixon Stroud, November 16, 1956, Fazenda Bodoquena folder, Box 4, Public Relations Series, in ibid.

26. Richard Aldrich, news report, November 19, 1950, RG IV, Public Relations Series, Box 4, Brazil-R. Aldrich, Reports folder, in ibid.

27. For more on União and Gulf, see Peter Seaborn Smith, *Oil and Politics in Modern Brazil* (Toronto: Macmillan, 1976), pp. 51, 110, 114, 119–21; on João Moreira Salles, see "Who Is Who in the Banco Moreira Salles," Papers of Nelson A. Rockefeller, Personal File, countries series, Folder 123, in Rockefeller Archive Center.

28. George Washburne, report, November 28, 1955, pp. 36–37, Funds—Brazil—IFI folder, Box 7, IBEC subseries, Wayne G. Broehl Papers, in Rockefeller Archive Center.

29. Frank Jamieson to Henry Bagley, February 21, 1957, Fazenda Bodoquena folder, Box 4, in ibid.

30. IBEC Press Release, in ibid.

31. Henry M. Bagley to Francis M. Jamieson, February 20, 1957, in ibid.

32. These companies, backed by Chase's CIT Finance Corporation, arranged one- to five-year loans for purchasing American equipment. Using Point IV credits for old-fashioned profit making, IBEC became involved in a wider range of Third World operations, including mining in apartheid Rhodesia, a cement factory in Thailand, and an auto plant in Brazil.

33. Willard Price, "The Amazing Amazon," *Reader's Digest,* September 1952, p. 6.

34. Richard Aldrich to John D. Rockefeller 3rd, February 27, 1959, Japan Society File, Rockefeller Family Archives, cited in Peter Collier and David Horowitz, *The Rockefellers* (New York: Holt, Rinehart & Winston, 1976), pp. 706–7.

22: The Brotherhood

1. Quoted in Stephen R. Graubard, *Kissinger* (New York: W. W. Norton, 1973), p. 108.

2. Frank Gervasi, *The Real Rockefeller* (New York: Atheneum, 1964), p. 195.

3. Nelson Rockefeller to Alberto Lleras Camargo, August 9, 1958, Papers of Nelson A. Rockefeller, Personal Files, Box 24, Folder 108, Rockefeller Archive Center, Tarrytown, New York.

4. *Dallas Morning News,* November 5, 1958.

5. Joe Alex Morris, *Nelson Rockefeller* (New York: Harper & Bros., 1960), p. 330.

6. Adolf Berle, diary entry, January 29, 1958, Berle Papers, Franklin D. Roosevelt Library.

7. See Stephen Schlesinger and Stephen Kinzer, *Bitter Fruit: The Untold Story of the American Coup in Guatemala* (Garden City, N.Y.: Anchor Press/Doubleday, 1983), pp. 236–38.

8. Adolf Berle, diary entry, December 4, 1958, Berle Papers.

9. Adolf Berle, diary entry, April 3, 1958, in ibid.

10. Adolf Berle, diary entry, October 16, 1958, in ibid.

11. John T. O'Rourke, "Our Man in Havana, William D. Pawley," *Washington Daily News,* February 20, 1961, p. 3.

12. Oren Root, *Persons and Persuasions* (New York: W. W. Norton, 1974), p. 143.

13. Berent Friele to Nelson Rockefeller, April 17, 1959, Berent Friele folder, RG IV, Papers of Nelson A. Rockefeller, Personal Files, Box 16, Series E, Rockefeller Archive Center.

14. Adolf Berle, diary entry, May 17, 1956, Berle Papers.

15. Confidential Memorandum, "João Belchior Marques Goulart," April 25, 1956, Department of State, Division of Biographic Information, Whitman File, Box 4, Brazil (10) folder, Dwight D. Eisenhower Library.

16. Ibid.

17. Shelton H. Davis, *Victims of the Miracle* (Cambridge: Cambridge University Press, 1977), p. 113.

18. Adolf Berle, diary entry, July 16–30, 1956, Berle Papers.

19. Adolf Berle, diary entry, August 1, 1945, in ibid.

20. Adolf Berle, diary entry, September 17, 1957, in ibid.

21. Lucien Bodard, *Green Hell* (New York: Outerbridge & Dientsfrey, 1971), p. 267.

22. Ibid., p. 262; Davis, *Victims of the Miracle*, p. 3; and Darcy Ribeiro, *A Política Indigenista Brasileira* (Rio de Janeiro: Ministerio da Agricultura Serviço de Informação o Agricola [Atvalidade Agrária, 1], 1962). (An abbreviated English-language version of this last work can be found in *International Labor Review* 85 [1962], entitled "The Social Integration of Indigenous Populations in Brazil." It is quoted in Walter Dostal, ed., *The Situation of the Indian in South America* [Geneva: World Council of Churches, 1972], pp. 449–50.) Brazilian constitutions after 1910 explicitly incorporated Indian land-tenure rights enacted in the legislation of that year, which created the Service for the Protection of the Indian.

23. Bodard, *Green Hell*, pp. 262–63.

24. Dale W. Kietzman, "Tendências de Ordem Lexical de Aculturação Lingüística em Terêna," *Revista de Antropologia* (São Paulo), no. 6, pp. 15–21. Abstract in *International Journal of American Linguistics*, no. 27 (1961), p. 160. Kietzman's technical study preceded by seven years the publication of booklets and a reader by the SIL team working full-time among the Terêna. See Alan C. Wares, ed., *Bibliography of the Summer Institute of Linguistics*, vol. 1, *1935–1975* (Dallas: Summer Institute of Linguistics, 1979), pp. 57, 138.

25. The SIL team, Muriel Perkins and Muriel Ekdahl, were sent to the SPI post at Cachoerinha, a Terêna village about fifty miles northwest of Aquidauana. Ethel E. Wallis and Mary A. Bennett, *Two Thousand Tongues to Go* (London: Hodder & Stoughton, 1966), p. 249.

26. Samuel Guy Inman, *New Day in Guatemala* (Milton, Conn.: Worldview Press, 1957), p. 13.

27. Edward A. Jameson, "The Indian Conference Hear from Some Guatemalan Indians," memorandum of May 21, 1959, enclosure in Elmer F. Bennett, "Classified Report of the United States Delegation to the Fourth Inter-American Indian Conference, Guatemala City, Guatemala, May 16 to May 25, 1959," June 9, 1959, Papers of Elmer F. Bennett, Box 6, folder entitled "Guatemala Trip, Aug. 12–29," Dwight D. Eisenhower Library.

28. Jameson, "The Indian Conference," p. 3.

29. Bennett, "Classified Report of the United States Delegation," p. 1.

30. Ibid., pp. 4–5.

31. Ibid., p. 5.

32. Ibid.

33. Doris Stone to Elmer Bennett, May 27, 1959, Papers of Elmer F. Bennett, Box 6, "Guatemala Trip, Aug. 12–29," Eisenhower Library.

34. W. C. Townsend, press release, June 8, 1959. Papers of Elmer F. Bennett, Box 7, in ibid.

35. C. D. Jackson to Dwight D. Eisenhower, August 13, 1954, White House Central Files (Confidential File), Subject Series, Box 61, in ibid.

36. William Cameron Townsend, "Friendship Flight of the 'Marshall Rondon,'" manuscript, October 1959, Papers of Elmer F. Bennett, Box 6, in ibid.

37. James C. Hefley and Marti Hefley, *Uncle Cam* (Waco, Tex.: Word Books, 1974), p. 209.

38. H.R. 776, "Townsend's bill," introduced by Representatives Jarman and Allott and backed in the Senate by South Dakota's William Langer, a former Rockefeller Foundation fellow and CIA officer, amended the Federal Property and Administrative Services Act of 1949.

39. Hefley and Hefley, *Uncle Cam*, p. 210.

23: Ascent of the Hawk

1. "Negro Protests Close Local Diners," and "Merchants, Police Confer on Lunch Counter Service," *Charlotte Observer*, February 10, 1960.

2. *Charlotte Observer*, November 13, 1956.

3. Quoted in James C. Hefley and Marti Hefley, *Uncle Cam* (Waco, Tex.: Word Books, 1974), pp. 200, 205.

4. "Billy Graham Speaks at Belk Devotional," *Charlotte News*, October 23, 1958.

5. *Dallas Morning News*, July 4, 1960.

6. Senate Select Committee to Study Governmental Operations with Respect to Intelligence Activities, *Alleged Assassination Plots Involving Foreign Leaders* (Washington, D.C.: Government Printing Office, 1975), p. 92.

7. Quoted in Peter Wyden, *Bay of Pigs* (New York: Simon & Schuster, 1979), pp. 39–40; and *Alleged Assassination Plots,* pp. 93–94.

8. Quoted in Thomas Kanza, *Conflict in the Congo* (Harmondsworth, Eng.: Penguin, 1972), p. 241.

9. Greg Lanning with Marti Mueller, *Africa Undermined: Mining Companies and the Underdevelopment of Africa* (New York: Penguin, 1979), pp. 239, 242.

10. *Alleged Assassination Plots,* p. 235.

11. Peter Collier and David Horowitz, *The Rockefellers* (New York: Holt, Rinehart & Winston, 1976), p. 298.

12. *Alleged Assassination Plots,* p. 235.

13. Ibid., p. 18.

14. Ibid., p. 55.

15. Ibid., p. 52.

16. Ibid., p. 21.

17. Quoted in Blanche Wiesen Cook, *The Declassified Eisenhower* (Garden City, N.Y.: Doubleday, 1981), pp. 211–12.

18. *Alleged Assassination Plots,* p. 21.

19. See Rayburn Library folder, in files of Rockefeller Brothers Fund, Rockefeller Archive Center, Tarrytown, New York.

20. *Dallas Morning News,* December 19, 1959.

21. James Desmond, *Nelson Rockefeller: A Political Biography* (New York: Macmillan, 1964), p. 241.

22. Nelson Rockefeller, speech before World Affairs Council of Philadelphia, April 22, 1960, Rockefeller 1959–1960 folder, Dwight D. Eisenhower Library.

23. Nelson Rockefeller, Law Day Speech at University of Chicago, May 1, 1960, in ibid.

24. Quoted in G. Bernard Noble, *Christian A. Herter* (New York: Cooper Square Publishers, 1962), pp. 80–81.

25. Quoted in L. Fletcher Prouty, *The Secret Team* (Englewood Cliffs, N.J.: Prentice-Hall, 1973), p. 378.

26. Quoted in Desmond, *Nelson Rockefeller,* p. 261.

27. Ibid., p. 264.

28. *Houston Chronicle,* July 13, 1960.

29. Quoted in Collier and Horowitz, *The Rockefellers,* p. 342.

30. Quoted in Desmond, *Nelson Rockefeller,* p. 282.

31. Adolf Berle, diary entry, July 25, 1960, Berle Papers, Franklin D. Roosevelt Library.

32. Collier and Horowitz, *The Rockefellers,* p. 329n.

33. Interview with Roswell Gilpatric, Oral History Project, p. 3, John F. Kennedy Library.

34. Henry Kissinger to Adolf Berle, October 17, 1960, Berle Papers.

35. N. Rockefeller to A. Berle, October 25, 1960, in ibid.

36. Rockefeller Foundation, "International Relations," December 1960, in ibid.

37. Frank Gervasi, *The Real Rockefeller* (New York: Atheneum, 1964), p. 241.

38. David Halberstam, *The Best and the Brightest* (New York: Random House, 1972; reprint, Greenwich, Conn.: Fawcett, 1973), p. 46 (page citations throughout these notes are to the reprint edition).

39. *Alleged Assassination Plots,* p. 48.

40. Memorandum, Lynn Bollinger to International Cooperation Administration, Office of Transportation: *Ready to Go: A Low Cost Proven Air and Radio Communications System for Underdeveloped Countries,* March 9, 1961. A copy is in the authors' possession.

41. Authors' interview with confidential source, New York City, November 12, 1977.

42. Letter, Ronald Holden to Herbert L. Fenster, "RE: GAC Claim Against CIA; My Client: Jungle Aviation and Radio Service," March 2, 1977, p. 3. A copy is in the authors' possession.

43. Memorandum, Nathan C. Fitts to Laurence R. Houston, June 5, 1962, "Subject: Contract with General Aircraft Corporation Inc. Involving Services of Laurence J. Montgomery." A copy is in the authors' possession.

44. Authors' interview with Laurence J. Montgomery, Cross Anchor, S.C., September 12, 1977.

45. Memorandum, Larry Montgomery to Lynn Bollinger, August 21, 1961. A copy is in the authors' possession.

46. L. Fletcher Prouty, "Precis: Project Eagle. A Plan for the Development of the Continent of Africa," March 1961. A copy is in the authors' possession.

47. G. William Domhoff, *Who Rules America Now?* (New York: Simon & Schuster, 1983), p. 138.

24: DEADLY INHERITANCE

1. Peter Wyden, *Bay of Pigs* (New York: Simon & Schuster, 1979), pp. 139, 100.

2. For a fuller account of Helms's role, see Thomas Powers, *The Man Who Kept the Secrets: Richard Helms and the CIA* (New York: Alfred A. Knopf, 1979).

3. Wyden, *Bay of Pigs,* pp. 109-10, 139.

4. Jordan A. Schwarz, *Liberal: Adolph Berle and the Vision of an American Era* (New York: Free Press, 1987), p. 326.

5. Adolf Berle, diary entry, January 9, 1961, Berle Papers, Franklin D. Roosevelt Library.

6. Adolf Berle, diary entry, February 27, 1961, in ibid.

7. "U.S. Assistance to Colombia in Combatting Guerrillas: Secret Position Paper Prepared for the State Visit by Colombian President Lleras; April 5–16, 1960." Department of State, declassified by a request of the authors under the Freedom of Information Act, Box 7, Whitman Papers, Dwight D. Eisenhower Library.

8. Ibid.

9. Adolf Berle, diary entry, February 27, 1961, Berle Papers.

10. Ibid.

11. Adolf Berle, diary entry, March 2, 1961, in ibid.

12. Jan Knippers Black, *United States Penetration of Brazil* (Philadelphia: University of Pennsylvania Press, 1977), p. 39.

13. Adolf Berle, diary entry, March 2, 1961, Berle Papers.

14. Wyden, *Bay of Pigs,* p. 147.

15. CIA Information Report No. C5-3/470, 587, cited in ibid., p. 169.

16. William R. Corson, *The Armies of Ignorance* (New York: Dial Press, 1977), pp. 383–85.

17. Quoted in Wyden, *Bay of Pigs,* p. 271.

18. Quoted in ibid.

19. Ibid., p. 168.

20. Senate Select Committee to Study Governmental Operations with Respect to Intelligence Activities, *Alleged Assassination Plots Involving Foreign Leaders* (Washington, D.C.: Government Printing Office, 1975), pp. 92–93, 97. Attorney General Robert Kennedy also was not informed; nor was Bissell's former student at Yale University, National Security Adviser McGeorge Bundy. See ibid., pp. 118–19, 121–23.

21. Ibid., pp. 96–98.

22. Ibid., pp. 81–82.

23. Ibid., p. 81. The committee reported that "the support chief recalled that Colonel J. C. King, head of the Western Hemisphere Division, gave him $50,000 in Bissell's office to pay the Cuban if he successfully assassinated Castro."

24. Wyden, *Bay of Pigs,* pp. 271–72.

25. Arthur M. Schlesinger, Jr., *A Thousand Days: John F. Kennedy in the White House* (Boston: Houghton Mifflin, 1965), p. 288.

26. Quoted in Wyden, *Bay of Pigs*, p. 209.

27. Quoted in Joseph B. Smith, *Portrait of a Cold Warrior* (New York: G. P. Putnam's Sons, 1976), p. 351.

28. Quoted in Paul B. Fay, Jr., *The Pleasure of His Company* (New York: Harper & Row, 1966), pp. 174–75.

29. Quoted in Wyden, *Bay of Pigs*, p. 306.

30. Interview with Roswell Gilpatric, p. 17, Oral History Project, John F. Kennedy Library; and Philip Yancey, "Wycliffe: A Mission in Search of a Future," *Christianity Today*, February 19, 1982, p. 21.

31. Interview with Gilpatric, p. 40.

32. Richard Alan White, *The Morass: United States Intervention in Central America* (New York: Harper & Row, 1984), p. 87.

33. William R. Kintner, *New Frontiers of War: Political Warfare Present and Future* (Chicago: Henry Regnery Co., 1962), p. 287.

34. See Philip Agee, *Inside the Company* (Harmondsworth, Eng.: Penguin, 1975), pp. 156–205.

35. Ibid., p. 172.

36. *Diario del Ecuador* (Quito), September 21, 1958. The Cubans were photographed by reporters investigating the disappearance of Dr. Robert Tremblay, a Canadian psychiatrist and fortune seeker who then committed suicide or was killed by the Huaorani during an expedition into their oil-rich territory.

37. The two companies, Norsul Oil and Mining of Albany, Georgia, and Phoenix Ecuador Oil of Toronto, actually fronts for Texaco and Gulf, respectively, got the concession in August.

38. Quoted in James C. Hefley and Marti Hefley, *Uncle Cam* (Waco, Tex.: Word Books, 1974), p. 223.

39. See Peter Seaborn Smith, *Oil and Politics in Modern Brazil* (Toronto: Macmillan, 1976), pp. 125–28, 136–37.

40. Adolf Berle, diary entry, May 23, 1961, Berle Papers.

41. Quoted in deLesseps S. Morrison, *Latin American Mission: An Adventure in Hemisphere Diplomacy* (New York: Simon & Schuster, 1965), p. 86.

42. Quoted in ibid.

43. Quoted in Jerome Levinson and Juan de Onis, *The Alliance That Lost Its Way* (Chicago: Quadrangle, 1970), pp. 71–72.

44. Freeport Sulphur was controlled by the Whitneys, the Standard Oil heirs whose scion, John Hay Whitney, was one of Nelson's closest friends. "Jock" Whitney had headed Freeport Sulphur. Rockefeller Foundation trustee Robert Lovett and later Jean Mauzé (third husband of Nelson's sister Babs) represented the Rockefeller holdings on Freeport's board. Nelson's second cousin, Godfrey Rockefeller, also sat on Freeport's board, representing the interests of the William Rockefeller branch of the family in New York's First National City Bank, then headed by Godfrey's brother, James Stillman Rockefeller.

45. Quoted in Milt Machlin, *The Search for Michael Rockefeller* (New York: G. P. Putnam's Sons, 1972), p. 242.

46. Quoted in ibid.

47. During World War II, De Bruyn had served as an Allied intelligence officer in Japanese-occupied New Guinea, living among the tribes while reporting on Japanese troop movements.

48. Adrian A. Gerbans, *The Asmat of New Guinea: The Journal of Michael Clark Rockefeller* (New York: Museum of Primitive Art, 1967), p. 43.

49. Machlin, *The Search for Michael Rockefeller*, p. 9.

50. *Time*, December 1, 1961, p. 17.

51. *Life*, December 1, 1961.

52. Machlin, *The Search for Michael Rockefeller*, p. 225.

53. Frank Gervasi, *The Real Rockefeller* (New York: Atheneum, 1964), p. 246.

25: BUILDING THE WARFARE STATE

1. *New York Times*, February 22, 1960.

2. *New York Times*, March 5, 1960.

3. Jack Newfield, "The Case Against Nelson Rockefeller," *New York,* March 9, 1970.

4. *New York Times,* November 21, 1974.

5. William R. Kintner, "The Scope of U.S. Actions, Abroad," p. 11, Joseph Dodge Papers, Dwight D. Eisenhower Library.

6. *Time,* November 3, 1961, p. 14.

7. IBEC *Annual Report,* 1959 (see reference to Fluid Power Division), 1961 (see Bellows-Valvair division description), and 1963.

8. Peter Collier and David Horowitz, *The Kennedys* (New York: Summit Books, 1984; reprint, New York: Warner Books, 1985), p. 265 (page citations throughout these notes are to the reprint edition).

9. Seymour Melman, *Pentagon Capitalism: The Political Economy of War* (New York: McGraw-Hill, 1970) p. 78.

10. Adolf Berle, Diary File, Box XXII, December 29, 1961, Berle Papers, Franklin D. Roosevelt Library.

11. Adolf Berle to Richard Goodwin, November 28, 1961, in ibid.

12. Adolf Berle, diary entry, July 7, 1961, in ibid.

13. A. A. Berle, "Psychological Offensive in Latin America" [Confidential], June 29, 1961, Box XXII, p. 3, in ibid.

14. Ibid., pp. 16, 5, 4.

15. Ibid., pp. 19–20.

16. Cable, A. Berle to N. Rockefeller, October 19, 1961, Box 220, Berle Papers.

17. Roger E. Boulton, *Defense Purchases and Regional Growth* (Washington, D.C.: Brookings Institution, 1966), pp. 9, 153, 169.

18. The official story of AIA's operations can be found in Martha Dalrymple, *The AIA Story: Two Decades of International Cooperation* (New York: American International Association for Economic and Social Development, 1986); the AIA's credit operations for agriculture in Minas Gerais, Brazil, are described in Arthur T. Mosher, *Case Study of Agricultural Program of ACAR in Brazil* (New York: National Planning Association, 1955).

19. Elizabeth A. Cobbs, "Entrepreneurship as Diplomacy: Nelson Rockefeller and the Development of the Brazilian Capital Market," *Business History Review* 63 (Spring 1989), p. 113.

20. "Latin American Information Committee, Programing Session, Arden House, May 15 and 16, 1961," attachment to letter from M. J. Rathbone (Standard Oil of New Jersey) to C. D. Jackson (Time, Inc.), LAIC file, C. D. Jackson Papers, Eisenhower Library.

26: Miracles Déjà Vu

1. James C. Hefley and Marti Hefley, *Uncle Cam* (Waco, Tex.: Word Books, 1974), p. 224.

2. *Charlotte Observer,* February 6, 1962.

3. Arthur M. Schlesinger, Jr., *A Thousand Days: John F. Kennedy in the White House* (Boston: Houghton Mifflin, 1965), pp. 582–83.

4. "State Visit by Colombia President Lleras, April 4–16, 1960. Position Paper: U.S. Assistance to Colombia in Combatting Guerrillas," *Secret,* Department of State, Colombia file, Dwight D. Eisenhower Library. Declassified in August 1982 and released to the authors pursuant to their request for mandatory review under the Freedom of Information Act.

5. Helio Courier Owners List, July 8, 1975, provided to the authors by Theodore Dinsmoor, attorney for Lynn Bollinger, president of General Aircraft.

6. *Charlotte Observer,* October 14, 1961.

7. Charlotte got the inside track because Joseph Robinson, Charlotte branch manager of the Wachovia Bank and head of the city's Belk-dominated Chamber of Commerce, raised $50,000 for the fair. Robinson looked to New York for Charlotte's future. He made six trips to New York that year to induce companies to move to Charlotte, more trips than he made to any other city. Robinson was closely allied with John Belk, who was elected vice president of the Chamber of Commerce that December. In 1964, when Wachovia

Bank assigned Robinson to its Winston-Salem office despite his protests, the Belks would come to his rescue with a job, so he could remain in Charlotte.

By 1962 Charlotte's Chamber of Commerce would be led by veterans from Rockefeller interests. Former Chase Manhattan Bank vice president Patrick Calhoun was chairman of the chamber's education committee and vice president of the North Carolina National Bank, where Tom Belk was director. B. L. Ray, director of Standard Oil of New Jersey, chaired the chamber's aviation committee. It was he who welcomed one of Laurance Rockefeller's new Eastern Airlines jetliners to Charlotte's airport in February 1962. The Eastern jet also sported a new name that was symbolic of the importance that the Rockefeller-owned airline placed on the home of the Belks: "The City of Charlotte: Spearhead of the New South." *Charlotte Observer,* February 6, 1962.

8. John Belk would become mayor of Charlotte. In 1961 Irwin was already a rising politician-businessman; a sitting member of North Carolina's House of Representatives, he had been a delegate to the 1960 Democratic Convention with then-Governor Luther Hodges. And like Sanz de Santamaría, Irwin Belk was committed to the Cold War, serving on the regional board of the CIA's [Radio] Free Europe Committee.

9. This point was originally made by David R. Goldfield in *Cotton Fields and Skyscrapers* (Baton Rouge: Louisiana State University Press, 1982).

10. "JFK Tells Division, 'I'm Proud of You,'" *Charlotte Observer,* October 13, 1961.

11. Ibid.

12. Victor Daniel Bonilla, *Servants of God or Masters of Men?* (Harmondsworth, Eng.: Penguin, 1972), pp. 224–36. On Texaco's board, and privy to many of its secrets, was Augustus Long, a member of the President's Foreign Intelligence Advisory Board. Long was also a director of Freeport Sulphur, the former owner of Cuban nickel that was currently hopeful of exploiting New Guinea copper. In the world of high finance and global mining, it seemed almost a small circle of friends.

13. Hefley and Hefley, *Uncle Cam,* p. 225.

14. Bonilla, *Servants of God,* pp. 207–11, 225.

15. Hefley and Hefley, *Uncle Cam,* p. 225.

16. Ibid., p. 226.

17. Robert G. Schneider to Robert Forbes Woodward, October 10, 1961, letter with attached proposal, "An Idea for Inter-American Friendship," John F. Kennedy Library (originally released under the Freedom of Information Act to David Stoll).

18. Interview with Roswell Gilpatric, Oral History Project, Kennedy Library, p. 46.

19. Philip Agee, *Inside the Company* (Harmondsworth, Eng.: Penguin, 1975), pp. 233–34, 279–81, 283, 292–94.

20. Schlesinger, *A Thousand Days,* p. 767.

21. Ibid.

22. Ibid., p. 768.

23. Agee, *Inside the Company,* pp. 279–80, 283–95.

24. Ibid., pp. 151, 229.

25. Senate Select Committee to Study Governmental Operations with Respect to Intelligence Activities, Final Report, Book II, *Intelligence Activities and the Rights of Americans* (Washington, D.C.: Government Printing Office, 1976), pp. 85, 77, citing Senate Subcommittee on Constitutional Rights, *Federal Data Banks, Computers and the Bill of Rights: Hearings Before the Senate Subcommittee on Constitutional Rights* (Washington, D.C.: Government Printing Office, 1971), p. 1137 (specifically, letter on army intelligence reports and daily summaries from Deputy Attorney General Warren Christopher to Major General William P. Yarborough, Assistant Chief of Staff for Intelligence, May 15, 1968), and pp. 1123–38.

26. Survey Report of General William P. Yarborough, February 26, 1962, National Security File, Box 319, Special Group Meetings—Fort Bragg (6) folder, Kennedy Library.

27. Senate Select Committee to Study Governmental Operations with Respect to Intelligence Activities, *Alleged Assassination Attempts Involving Foreign Leaders* (Washington, D.C.: Government Printing Office, 1975), p. 195.

28. Ibid., pp. 200–201, 206.

29. Survey report by General Yarborough.

30. Ibid.

31. Ibid., "Observations and Suggestions Bearing Upon Improvement of Counter Insurgency Capabilities," p. 2.

32. Ibid., p. 3.

33. Ibid., p. 4.

34. Chart, "Organization for Treatment of Counterinsurgency Matters in the Department of Defense," in ibid. Lansdale, as assistant to the undersecretary of defense, was the top "focal point" in this chart.

35. Ibid., Section 3: Survey Team Activities—Colombia, p. 8.

36. Ibid., "Secret Supplement—Colombian Survey Report."

37. Ibid., p. 5.

38. "El Instituto Linguistico de Verano," *Boletín de Antropología* (Medellín, Colombia: University of Antigua, 1976), pp. 9–13.

39. APCO map of Macarena Mountains, purchased in Colombia, in the authors' possession.

27: CAMELOT VERSUS POCANTICO: THE DECLINE AND FALL OF JOHN F. KENNEDY

1. White House statement, July 19, 1962.

2. Jerome Levinson and Juan de Onis, *The Alliance That Lost Its Way* (Chicago: Quadrangle, 1970), p. 82.

3. Victor Marchetti and John Marks, *The CIA and the Cult of Intelligence* (New York: Alfred A. Knopf, 1974), p. 123.

4. Arthur M. Schlesinger, Jr., *A Thousand Days: John F. Kennedy in the White House* (Boston: Houghton Mifflin, 1965), p. 803.

5. The CIA officer was William Harvey. The attorney general's intervention won the enmity of many in King's old-boy network, including Harvey. See Senate Select Committee to Study Governmental Operations with Respect to Intelligence Activities, *Alleged Assassination Plots Involving Foreign Leaders* (Washington, D.C.: Government Printing Office, 1975) p. 148n.

6. *New York Times,* July 16, 1961, p. 3.

7. David Wise and Thomas B. Ross, *The Invisible Government* (New York: Random House, 1964), p. 325.

8. Quoted in Nikita S. Khrushchev, *Khrushchev Remembers* (Boston: Little, Brown, 1970), pp. 497–98.

9. Robert Kennedy, *Thirteen Days: A Memoir of the Cuban Missile Crisis* (New York: W. W. Norton, 1969), pp. 36–37; and Gregg Herken, *Counsels of War* (New York: Alfred A. Knopf, 1985), p. 364.

10. Adolf Berle, diary entry, October 29, 1962, Berle Papers, Franklin D. Roosevelt Library.

11. Adolf Berle, diary entry, November 20, 1962, in ibid.

12. Ibid.

13. Schlesinger, *A Thousand Days,* p. 635.

14. Quoted in George F. McManus, *The Inside Story of Steel Wages and Prices, 1958–1967* (Philadelphia: Chilton, 1967), p. 48.

15. Ibid., p. 192.

16. *Life,* July 6, 1962, p. 33.

17. In 1960, Rockefeller Brothers, Inc.'s J. Richardson Dilworth presided over the union of American Overseas Finance Company, controlled by IBEC and CIT Financial Corporation, and the Transoceanic Development Corporation, Ltd., controlled by Kuhn, Loeb (Dilworth's former employer), First Boston Corp. and S. G. Warburg & Co. of London. The resulting company, Transoceanic AOFC, Ltd., held a portfolio of $26.6 million worth of holdings in twenty-nine countries and was majority controlled by A. O. Investing Company, which, in turn, was controlled by IBEC.

IBEC also directly had holdings in foreign investment banks and private development companies such as Lima's Inversiones Abancay, S.A.; Bogotá's Compañia Administradora Finibec, Ltda.; the Middle East

Development Corporation (with offices in Beirut, Cairo, and the Hague); the Industrial and Mining Bank of Iran (one of the Shah's favorites); and the Industrial Credit and Investment Corporation of Pakistan.

IBEC directors and Rockefeller confidants sat on the boards of similar foreign financial holding companies and mutual funds. In 1958, IBEC Chairman Robert Purcell was also a director of Canada's Mutual Fund, Ltd.; Investor International Mutual; and the Anelex Corporation. In addition, Nelson's IBEC, which went public in 1962 and began selling shares as a company with over $100 million in assets, had its Crescinco mutual funds investing in companies throughout Latin America, including in Brazil alone over 100 companies.

18. *Newsweek,* November 19, 1962, pp. 34–35; and *U.S. News and World Report,* November 19, 1962, pp. 50–52.

19. See Myer Kutz, *Rockefeller Power* (New York: Simon & Schuster, 1974), p. 222.

20. Peter Wyden, *Bay of Pigs* (New York: Simon & Schuster, 1979), p. 100.

21. Quoted in Peter Collier and David Horowitz, *The Kennedys* (New York: Warner Books, 1985), pp. 304–5.

22. Ibid.

23. Ibid., p. 303.

24. David Halberstam, *The Best and the Brightest* (Greenwich, Conn.: Fawcett, 1973), p. 360.

25. Adolf Berle, diary entry, September 25, 1962, Berle Papers.

26. Adolf Berle, diary entry, February 4, 1963, in ibid.

27. Adolf Berle, diary entry, March 12, 1963, in ibid.

28. *Houston Chronicle,* April 1, 1963.

29. Interview with Roswell Gilpatric, Oral History Project, pp. 93–94, John F. Kennedy Library.

30. *New York Times,* May 10, 1963.

31. Quoted in Frank Gervasi, *The Real Rockefeller* (New York: Atheneum, 1964), pp. 253–56.

32. Ibid., p. 255.

33. *Houston Observer,* September 3, 1963.

34. *Chicago Tribune,* April 26, 1963.

35. Associated Press report by Jack Bell, October 21, 1963.

36. Ibid.

37. Ibid.

38. Maxwell Taylor, *Swords and Plowshares* (New York: W. W. Norton, 1972), p. 301.

39. Halberstam, *The Best and the Brightest,* p. 360.

40. Thomas Powers, *The Man Who Kept the Secrets: Richard Helms and the CIA* (New York: Alfred A. Knopf, 1979), p. 132.

41. Wise and Ross, *Invisible Government,* p. 254.

42. Gilpatric, Oral History, p. 94.

43. *Houston Chronicle,* November 17, 1963.

44. On Argentina, see Joseph B. Smith, *Portrait of a Cold Warrior* (New York: G. P. Putnam's Sons, 1976), p. 373; on Ecuador, see Philip Agee, *Inside the Company* (Harmondsworth, Eng.: Penguin, 1975), pp. 283–96.

45. *Miami Herald,* December 24, 1966.

46. Stephen Schlesinger and Stephen Kinzer, *Bitter Fruit: The Untold Story of the American Coup in Guatemala* (Garden City, N.Y.: Anchor Press/Doubleday, 1983), pp. 243–44.

47. *New York Times,* April 28, 1963; Richard Gott, *Rural Guerrillas in Latin America* (Harmondsworth, Eng.: Penguin, 1973), p. 85.

48. According to author Peter Dale Scott, Standard Fruit director Seymour Weiss was a charter member of the Information Council of the Americas (INCA). An IRS investigation of Weiss for an alleged money-laundering scheme with mobster Meyer Lansky and payoffs to politicians was dropped after the murder of Weiss's alleged partner, Governor Huey Long, a presidential hopeful and probably the prime target of these federal investigations during the Roosevelt administration. Weiss was subsequently jailed for fraud in 1940. See T. Harry Williams, *Huey Long* (New York: Bantam, 1969), pp. 865–67; William Ivy Hair, *The Kingfish and His*

Realm (Baton Rouge: Louisiana State University Press, 1991), p. 286; New York Times, July 18, 1939, and November 20, 1940; Hank Messick, Lansky (New York: G. P. Putnam's Sons, 1971), p. 83; Peter Dale Scott, Deep Politics and the Death of JFK (Berkeley: University of California Press, 1993), pp. 97–99.

In 1940, Standard Fruit's vice president, Lucca Vaccaro, was indicted, along with Long's brother and the entire New Orleans dock board, for extortion and embezzlement. See Scott, Deep Politics, p. 100; New York Times, July 24, 1940; Charles Rappleye and Ed Becker, All-American Mafioso: The Johnny Roselli Story (Garden City, N.Y.: Doubleday, 1991), p. 151. Carlos Marcello's rise in New Orleans crime was based on his partnership in gambling, drugs, and protection rackets with Lansky, Frank Costello, and Lucky Luciano. He and John Roselli, who was involved in CIA assassination plots against Fidel Castro, reportedly ensured labor "peace" for Standard Fruit on the docks of New Orleans, New Jersey, and New York. They also ensured that casino gambling concessions in Guatemala, where Standard Fruit purchased bananas, would be continued despite the opposition of President Castillo Armas of 1954 coup fame; the president's opposition ended shortly after Roselli visited Guatemala City: Castillo Armas was assassinated by one of his own guards, in the classic mode of an inside job.

Other INCA members with ties to Standard Fruit were Eberhard Deutsch, Standard Fruit's general counsel, and William I. Monaghan and Manuel Gil, both of whom were Standard Fruit employees. Monaghan, a former FBI agent, resigned to join the Reily Coffee Company, where Lee Harvey Oswald also was employed at the time. The coffee company was owned by Eustis Reily, an INCA member, and William B. Reily, a supporter of the Free Cuba Committee, a conduit for donations to the Cuban Revolutionary Council (CRC), of which Gil was a leader in New Orleans. See Scott, Deep Politics, p. 95; and Harold Weisberg, Oswald in New Orleans (New York: Canyon Books, 1967), p. 362.

49. Schlesinger, A Thousand Days, p. 230.

50. Ibid., p. 227.

51. On Pier 13, see Stanley Penn, "On the Waterfront," in Nicolas Gage, ed., Mafia: USA (New York: Dell, 1972), p. 323. On Standard Fruit, Guatemala, organized crime (particularly John Roselli), and the CIA, see Scott, Deep Politics, pp. 108–11.

52. New York Herald Tribune, October 6, 1963.

53. Schlesinger, A Thousand Days, p. 428.

54. Quoted in ibid., p. 1023.

55. William Manchester, The Death of a President (New York: Harper & Row, 1967), p. 123.

56. Schlesinger, A Thousand Days, p. 934.

57. Alleged Assassinations Plots, p. 174.

58. Interview with Walter Sheridan, Oral History Project, Kennedy Library.

59. Seymour Freidin and George Bailey, The Experts (New York: Macmillan, 1968), p. 85.

60. Collier and Horowitz, The Kennedys, p. 317.

61. Schlesinger, A Thousand Days, p. 1029.

62. Collier and Horowitz, The Kennedys, p. 319.

28: To Turn a Continent

1. Interview with Lincoln Gordon, July 10, 1969, p. 16, Oral History Project, Lyndon B. Johnson Library.

2. Joseph B. Frantz, interview with Nelson Rockefeller, February 21, 1979, Oral History Project, in ibid.

3. Arthur M. Schlesinger, Jr., A Thousand Days: John F. Kennedy in the White House (Boston: Houghton Mifflin, 1965), p. 1019.

4. Memorandum, John A. McCone to Lyndon Johnson, December 3, 1963, Johnson Library.

5. Lyndon B. Johnson to Adolf Berle, December 19, 1963, Berle Papers, Franklin D. Roosevelt Library.

6. Interview with Lincoln Gordon, p. 14, Oral History Project, Johnson Library.

7. Adolf Berle, diary entry, October 19, 1961, Berle Papers.

8. Berent Friele to Walter Crawford, October 9, 1961, AIA Archives, Box 7, September/October 1961 folder, Rockefeller Archive Center, Tarrytown, New York.

9. See Philip Agee, diary entry for February 10, 1964, in *Inside the Company* (Harmondsworth, Eng.: Penguin, 1975), p. 321.

10. Memorandum, John F. Kennedy to Fowler Hamilton, February 2, 1962, John F. Kennedy Library.

11. Jerome Levinson and Juan de Onis, *The Alliance That Lost Its Way* (Chicago: Quadrangle, 1970), p. 145.

12. Jan Knippers Black, *United States Penetration of Brazil* (Philadelphia: University of Pennsylvania Press, 1977), p. 68.

13. Ibid.

14. Donald E. Syrud, *Foundations of Brazilian Economic Growth* (Stanford, Calif.: Hoover Institution Press, 1974), p. 17.

15. Ibid., p. 14.

16. AIA Report, March 11, 1961, AIA Archives, Box 15, Folder 134, Rockefeller Archive Center.

17. Philip M. Glick to Lawrence H. Levy and John R. Camp (AIA), March 15, 1962, in ibid.

18. Philip M. Glick to Walter Crawford (AIA-Rio), March 26, 1962, in ibid.

19. John R. Camp, "Suggestion for Rural Development in Brazil," November 1960. Proposal to the International Cooperative Administration, AIA Archives, Box 7, Folder 58, in ibid.

20. Flor P. Brennan to John Camp, November 9, 1962, AIA Archives, Box 7, Folder 63, Projects: Brazil, in ibid.

21. Walter Crawford to Berent Friele, "Subject: Ideas on Establishing a Foundation for the Development of the Planalto Central," February 6, 1963, AIA Archives, Box 7, Folder 63, in ibid.

22. *Engineering and Mining Journal,* November 1975, pp. 170–71.

23. Preliminary Report of the Planalto Pre-Survey Group, 1963, p. 27, AIA Archives, Box 8, Folder 65, Rockefeller Archive Center.

24. Ibid., pp. 20, 23.

25. Berent Friele to Adolf Berle, February 7, 1961, AIA Archives, Box 7, Folder 59, Brazil, in ibid.

26. John Camp to Walter L. Crawford, March 15, 1963, in ibid.

27. Philip Glick to John Camp, October 30, 1962, in ibid.

28. Crawford to Camp, March 2, 1963, in ibid.

29. Crawford to Camp, March 28, 1963, in ibid.

30. Preliminary Report of the Planalto Pre-Survey Group, pp. 83, 17, 32, AIA Archives, Box 8, Folder 65, in ibid.

31. Central Intelligence Agency, "Economic Deterioration and Leftist Gains in Brazil." Microfilm copies of these CIA research reports can be obtained through University Publications of America, 44 North Market Street, Frederick, Md. 21701.

32. Alfred Métraux, "Disparition des Indiens dans le Brésil Central," *Bulletin of the International Committee on Urgent Anthropological and Ethnological Research* (Vienna), no. 5 (1962), p. 131.

33. Darcy Ribeiro, *A Política Indigenista Brasileira* (Rio de Janeiro: Ministerio da Agricultura Serviço de Informação o Agricola [Atvalidade Agrária, 1], 1962), p. 99.

34. Carlos de Araújo Neto Moreira, "Relatório Sôbre a Situação Atual dos Indios Kayapó," *Revista de Antropologia,* São Paulo, nos. 1 and 2 (1959), pp. 49–64.

35. Roberto Cardoso de Oliveira, "The Role of Indian Posts in the Process of Assimilation," *América Indígena* (Mexico City), no. 2 (1960), pp. 89–95; Roberto Cardoso de Oliveira, *O Processo da Assimilação dos Terêna* (monograph), 1960, Rio de Janeiro; "A Situacão Atual dos Tapirape," *Boletim do Museu Paraense,* Emílio Goeldi; Nova Serie, Antropologia (Belém, Pará), 1959, no. 3, pp. 3–4.

36. "Germ Warfare Against Indians Is Charged in Brazil," *Medical Tribune and Medical News,* December 8, 1969.

37. Noel Nutels, "Medical Problems of Newly Contacted Indian Groups," in *Biomedical Challenges Presented by the American Indian* (Washington, D.C.: Pan American Health Organization, 1968), pp. 68–76.

38. When McChristian arrived in Greece, the CIA had just conducted its first counterinsurgency campaign with mostly conventional methods in conjunction with the Greek Army. The Joint United States Military Advisory Group (JUSMAG) was being used as a cover by CIA officers who were carrying out a mop-up campaign of arrests and terror directed by Station Chief Thomas Karamessines. Like McChristian,

Karamessines went on to fame in intelligence circles as CIA deputy director of plans. See Yiannis Roubatis and Karen Wynn, "CIA Operations in Greece," and Philip Agee, "The American Factor in Greece: Old and New," in Philip Agee and Louis Wolf, eds., *Dirty Work: The CIA in Western Europe* (Secaucus, N.J.: Lyle Stuart, 1978).

39. *New York Times,* November 1, 1961, pp. 1, 12; *New York Times,* November 2, 1961, p. 6.

40. Agee, *Inside the Company,* pp. 226–34.

41. Ibid., p. 243.

42. Donald Johnson to W. C. Townsend, April 2, 1962, Townsend Archives.

43. Donald Johnson to W. C. Townsend, June 14, 1962, in ibid.

44. Interview with Roswell Gilpatric, Oral History Project, Kennedy Library.

45. Jerry Elder to Cameron Townsend, December 4, 1962, Townsend Archives.

46. Lawrence W. Routh to Kenneth L. Waters, January 9, 1961, in ibid.

47. The Pew Memorial Fund's $1,000 covered the cost of rebuilding, modernizing, and installing radio equipment. See Fred Hufnegel to W. C. Townsend, July 16, 1961, in ibid.

48. Peter Seaborn Smith, *Oil and Politics in Modern Brazil* (Toronto: Macmillan, 1976), pp. 157–58, citing *Journal do Brasil* statistics.

49. Ethel E. Wallis and Mary A. Bennett, *Two Thousand Tongues to Go* (London: Hodder & Stoughton, 1966), p. 48.

50. James Wilson to Robert Schneider, December 31, 1961, Townsend Archives.

51. Memorandum, Jim Wilson to Robert Schneider, December 30, 1961, "Re: Spirit of Philadelphia," in ibid.

52. Jim Wilson to Dale Kietzman, October 24, 1961, in ibid.

53. Jim Wilson to W. C. Townsend, January 10, 1962, in ibid.

54. Ibid.

55. This latter estimate was made by the Ministry of Interior's Investigation Commission in 1967; see Norman Lewis, *The Missionaries* (New York: McGraw-Hill, 1988).

56. Jim Wilson to W. C. Townsend, August 20, 1962, Townsend Archives.

57. John Camp, Memorandum, May 3, 1963, AIA Archives, Rockefeller Archive Center.

58. Memorandum No. 14 for National Security Council Executive Meeting, December 11, 1963, Vice Presidential Security File, Box 4, National Security Council folder, Johnson Library.

59. Memorandum, Benjamin H. Read to McGeorge Bundy, December 27, 1963, White House Central File, Confidential File, Box 7, Folder CO 37-Brazil, in ibid.

60. William Cameron Townsend to President Johnson, December 16, 1963, Townsend Archives.

61. W. C. Townsend to Carlos Sanz de Santamaría, February 13, 1964, in ibid.

62. Ibid.

63. Jim Wilson to Robert Schneider, cc: Townsend and Kietzman, November 20, 1961, in ibid.

29: Operation Brother Sam

1. Jan Knippers Black, *United States Penetration of Brazil* (Philadelphia: University of Pennsylvania Press, 1977), p. 83.

2. Adolf Berle, diary entry, April 2, 1964, Berle Papers, Franklin D. Roosevelt Library.

3. Black, *United States Penetration of Brazil,* p. 41.

4. Rio Embassy Telegram A-927, February 3, 1964, p. 2, in National Security File, Country File—Brazil, folder: Brazil—Cables Vol. 1, Lyndon B. Johnson Library.

5. Black, *United States Penetration of Brazil,* p. 131.

6. Philip Agee, *Inside the Company* (Harmondsworth, Eng.: Penguin, 1975), p. 615.

7. See Ronald Radosh, *American Labor and U.S. Foreign Policy: The Cold War in the Unions from Gompers to Lovestone* (New York: Random House, 1970), chap. 13.

8. Agee, *Inside the Company,* pp. 609, 602, and 620, respectively. The banks were First National City Bank of New York (which then handled the banking of Bethlehem Steel, co-owner of the giant manganese lode in Amapá with the Antunes group), First National Bank of Boston (whose directors included Thomas Cabot, past president of United Fruit, and Paul C. Cabot, director also of M. A. Hanna [Mining] and Company and cousin of recent ambassador to Brazil John Moors Cabot), and Royal National Bank of Canada (the principal bank of J. Peter Grace's Brazilian Traction Light and Power [later called Brascan, Ltd.], Rio and São Paulo's largest electric and telephone company).

9. Black, *United States Penetration of Brazil,* p. 76.

10. Ibid., p. 70.

11. Agee, *Inside the Company,* p. 321.

12. Alfred Stepan, *The Military in Politics: Changing Patterns in Brazil* (Princeton, N.J.: Princeton University Press, 1971), pp. 31–42, 167–68.

13. Black, *United States Penetration of Brazil,* chap. 17.

14. Office of the Deputy Chief of Staff for Military Operations, U.S. Department of the Army, "Doctrinal Guidance for the Future," Army Information.

15. Joseph Novitski, "Latin Lands Turning to Europe," *New York Times,* May 4, 1971, pp. 1, 7.

16. Adolf Berle, diary entry, April 2, 1964, Berle Papers.

17. Black, *United States Penetration of Brazil,* p. 112. According to reports in *Fortune* magazine, Gordon left an identical impression with representatives of the Mesquita family, owners of the powerful daily newspaper *O Estado de São Paulo,* the major voice of coffee barons and of Lacerda's UDN party.

18. Adolf Berle, diary entry, April 2, 1964, Berle Papers.

19. Eugene H. Methvin, "Labor's New Weapon for Democracy," *Reader's Digest* (October 1966), pp. 21–28.

20. William Blum, *The CIA: A Forgotten History* (London: Zed Books, 1980), p. 197.

21. Black, *United States Penetration of Brazil,* p. 84.

22. Norman Blume, "Pressure Groups and Decision-Making in Brazil," *Studies in Comparative International Development* 3, no. 11 (1967–1968), p. 217.

23. Agee, *Inside the Company,* p. 362.

24. Jerome Levinson and Juan de Onis, *The Alliance That Lost Its Way* (Chicago: Quadrangle, 1970), p. 89.

25. Black, *United States Penetration of Brazil,* p. 83.

26. *Dicionario Histórico-Biográfico Brasileiro 1930–1983* (Rio de Janeiro: Forensa Universitaria, 1984), p. 3047.

27. Black, *United States Penetration of Brazil,* p. 83.

28. Adolf Berle, diary entry, April 2, 1964, Berle Papers.

29. Within a year, the Brazilian navy, in turn, would provide an oceanographic vessel to Hanna Mining to help Hanna develop plans to build deep-water loading facilities at Sepetiba Bay, sixty miles south of Rio de Janeiro. The concession was granted by Castelo Branco's presidential decree in accordance with a development plan previously proposed by Roberto Campos and rejected by Goulart.

30. Black, *United States Penetration of Brazil,* p. 45. Walters later would deny knowing about O'Meara's presence in Brazil except for a visit six months before the coup, but he did confirm reassuring O'Meara then that "things would fall into place pretty quickly."

31. Cable, Lincoln Gordon to Secretary of State Dean Rusk et al., March 27, 1964, National Security File, Country File—Brazil, Box 10, folder: Brazil—Cables Vol. 2, Lyndon B. Johnson Library.

32. Lincoln Gordon to Dean Rusk et al., March 29, 1964, in ibid.

33. Adolf Berle, diary entry, May 14, 1964, Berle Papers.

34. CIA Intelligence Information Cable, March 30, 1964, Document No. 13, National Security File, Country File—Brazil, Box 10, folder: Brazil—Cables Vol. 2, Johnson Library..

35. See João Goulart, "Address to the Sergeants, March 30, 1964," in Richard Fager and Wayne A. Cornellius, eds., *Political Power in Latin America: Seven Confrontations* (Englewood Cliffs, N.J.: Prentice-Hall, 1970), pp. 182–86.

36. *Dicionario Histórico-Biográfico Brasileiro 1930–1983,* pp. 3046–48.

37. John L. Chew, Rear Admiral and Vice Director for Operations, Joint Chiefs of Staff, to Carrier Task Group, March 31, 1964, Document No. 7, National Security File, Country File—Brazil, Box 10, folder: Brazil—Cables Vol. 2, Johnson Library.

38. Lewis H. Diuguid, "LBJ's Plan in Brazil Coup," *Washington Post,* December 29, 1976; copy in ibid.

39. Black, *United States Penetration of Brazil,* p. 70.

40. Ibid., p. 69.

41. Dean, American Embassy Brasília, to Secretary of State [Rusk], April 1, 1964, 10 P.M.. Document No. 001073, National Security File, Country File—Brazil, Box 10, folder: Brazil—Cables Vol. 3 (4/64), Johnson Library.

42. Andres Gunder Frank, *Latin America: Underdevelopment or Revolution?* (New York: Monthly Review Press, 1967), pp. 105–6. After the coup, the National Labor Federation would be declared illegal, and government intervenors would take over 409 unions, 43 labor federations, and 4 labor confederations.

43. Cable, Lincoln Gordon to Secretary of State Dean Rusk, April 2, 1964, National Security File, Country File—Brazil, Box 10, folder: Brazil—Cables Vol. 3 (4/64), Johnson Library.

44. Interview with Lincoln Gordon, p. 26, Oral History Project, in ibid.

45. Tad Szulc, "U.S. May Abandon Effort to Deter Latin Dictators," *New York Times,* March 19, 1964, p. 1.

46. Vernon A. Walters, *Silent Missions* (Garden City, N.Y.: Doubleday, 1978), pp. 388–89.

47. Senate Committee on Foreign Relations, *Hearings on the Nomination of Lincoln Gordon to Be the Assistant Secretary of State for Inter-American Affairs, February 7, 1966* (Washington, D.C.: Government Printing Office, 1966), pp. 44–45.

48. CIA Intelligence information cable, April 6, 1964, National Security File, Country File—Brazil, Box 10, Johnson Library.

49. Blum, *The CIA,* p. 187; Agee, *Inside the Company,* pp. 364–65.

50. Agee, *Inside the Company,* pp. 366, 379. The agents were former ambassador to Mexico Manuel Pio Correa, Lyle Fontoura, and Colonel Canara Sena.

51. *Ultima Hora,* April 8, 1964.

52. Peter Seaborn Smith, *Oil and Politics in Modern Brazil* (Toronto: Macmillan, 1976), p. 170.

53. By then, Brazilians and Americans had already put together a consortium that was interested in developing oil from Brazil's oil shale. Using Brazil's contacts with Soviet technicians to create a Cold War scare, the consortium gained a hearing from Assistant Secretary Mann and McGeorge Bundy, chairman of the National Security Council. Its lobbyist was Fowler Hamilton, former chief of AID and law partner of Undersecretary of State George Ball. Castelo Branco ended up breaking the agreement with the Soviets, acceding to the wishes of the syndicate led by Adolf Berle's friend, coup oil broker Alberto Byington. Byington's role in the oil-shale scheme is outlined in correspondence between Irvin Hoff (of the U.S. Cane Sugar Refiners Association) and presidential aide Bill Moyers, October 24, 1964, and December 9, 1964 (Moyer's draft), and Henry W. Clark (vice president of Atlanta Steamship Company) to McGeorge Bundy, October 14, 1964. The four letters are attached to an October 14, 1964, report entitled "Brazil: Unprecedented Opportunity for Free World," in White House General Files, CO-31, Box 16, folder CB37-Brazil, 11/22/63–10/21/65, Johnson Library.

54. *New York Times,* October 2, 1964.

55. Ibid., June 18, 1964.

56. Paulo R. Schilling, "Brazil: The Rebellion of the Downtrodden," *Marcha* (Montevideo), July 16, 1971, reprinted by Latin American Documentation Center, Mexico City (Document 9b), November 1971.

57. *New York Times,* November 7, 1964.

58. Ibid., November 23, 1964.

59. Ibid., December 15, 1964.

60. Levinson and de Onis, *The Alliance That Lost Its Way,* pp. 117–20.

61. Cable (No. 39), Central Intelligence Agency, October 15, 1965, National Security File, Country File—Brazil, folder: Brazil—Cables Vol. 5 (9/65–11/65), Johnson Library.

62. *Moody's Municipal and Government Manual* (New York: Frederic Hatch & Company, 1965), p. 2926.

63. Walters, *Silent Missions,* pp. 400–401.

64. Marek Lubomirski to Richard Aldrich, December 13, 1963, Broehl Papers, Box 7, Funds—Brazil folder, Rockefeller Archive Center, Tarrytown, New York.

65. Lubomirski to Aldrich, January 22, 1965, in ibid.

66. Berent Friele to Nelson Rockefeller, March 23, 1964, Papers of Nelson Rockefeller, Countries Series, Box 16, Folder 107, Rockefeller Family Archives, in ibid.

67. Friele to Rockefeller, April 9, 1964, in ibid.

68. Nelson Rockefeller to Pascoal Ramieri Mazzilli, April 3, 1964, in ibid.

69. International Basic Economy Corporation, *Annual Report,* 1964, p. 3.

70. Black, *United States Penetration of Brazil,* p. 78.

71. *New York Times,* April 3, 1964.

72. Michael C. Jensen, "The Pews of Philadelphia," *New York Times,* October 10, 1971; G. William Domhoff, *Who Rules America?* (Englewood Cliffs, N.J.: Prentice-Hall, 1967), p. 87.

73. Senate Committee on Rules and Administration, 93rd Cong., 2nd sess. *Hearings on the Nomination of Nelson A. Rockefeller of New York to Be Vice President of the United States* (Washington, D.C.: Government Printing Office, 1974), p. 657.

74. *New York Times,* July 19, 1964, pp. 1, 6.

75. Holmes Alexander, "LBJ and the Gordian Knot of Brazil," *New Haven Register,* April 18, 1964.

76. Norman Mailer, *Cannibals and Christians* (New York: Dial Press, 1966), p. 32.

77. *Houston Chronicle,* December 3, 1974. Based on testimony of J. Richardson Dilworth at vice presidential confirmation hearings that Nelson Rockefeller's 1964 dividend income amounted to about $5 million.

30: BENEATH THE EYEBROWS OF THE JUNGLE

1. Tad Szulc, *Latin America* (New York: Times Books, 1965), pp. 21, 89.

2. *Peruvian Times,* January 17, 1964, p. 3.

3. *Moody's Industrial Manual* (New York: Frederic Hatch & Company, 1965), p. 1642.

4. Jean-François G. Landeau, *Strategies of U.S. Independent Oil Companies Abroad* (Ann Arbor, Mich.: University Microfilms International Research Press, 1977), Exhibit 7, p. 101.

5. *New York Times,* January 15, 1964, p. 39.

6. W. C. Townsend to Sen. Michael Monroney, June 25, 1963, Townsend Archives.

7. W. C. Townsend to Lynn Bollinger, June 25, 1963, in ibid.

8. *Peruvian Times,* October 16, 1953, p. 5.

9. Ibid., January 31, 1964.

10. *La Crónica,* March 13, 14, 16, 1964; *El Comercio,* March 13, 16, 1964.

11. *La Crónica,* March 14, 15, 1964; *El Expreso,* March 27, 1964.

12. *El Expreso,* March 18, 20, 22, 1964; "Quienes Empujan a los Indios en sus Tropelias?" *El Comercio,* March 21, 1964.

13. *La Tribuna,* March 11, 1964.

14. *El Comercio,* March 13, 1964.

15. *El Expreso,* March 13, 1964.

16. Ibid., March 18, 1964.

17. Authors' interviews in Lima, September 1976; military historian Victor Villanueva also attributes International Petroleum (IPC) with being the supplier of the napalm used by the Peruvian air force against Campa Indian villages during the CIA's counterinsurgency campaign against MIR in 1965. According to Villanueva, IPC was eager to show its loyalty to the government in hopes of staving off pressure on Belaúnde to nationalize IPC's oil properties (Michael F. Brown and Eduardo Fernández, *War of Shadows: The Struggle for Utopia in the Peruvian Amazon* [Berkeley, Calif.: University of California Press, 1991], pp. 113–14).

18. *El Expresso*, March 20, 1964; *La Tribuna*, March 20, 21, 1964; *El Comercio*, March 21, 1964.

19. Photographs taken on March 22, 1964, in the authors' possession.

20. *El Expreso,* March 21, 1964.

21. *New York Times,* January 7, 1964, p. 5.

22. Cable, air force attaché, U.S. Embassy (Lima) to Chief of Staff, U.S. Air Force, March 31, 1964, National Security File, Country File—Peru, folder: Peru—Cables Vol. 6 (11/63–11/65), Lyndon B. Johnson Library.

23. State Department Memorandum, briefing "Possible Points for Discussion with the New Peruvian Ambassador," February 7, 1964, White House Central File, Confidential File, Box 11, folder CO234—Peru, in ibid.

24. Sherman Kent (Central Intelligence Agency, Office of National Estimates), Special Memorandum No. 19-65: "Prospects in Peru," July 29, 1965, in National Security File, Country File—Peru, folder: Peru—Cables Vol. 6 (11/63–11/65), in ibid.

25. Philip Agee, *Inside the Company* (Harmondsworth, Eng.: Penguin, 1975), pp. 268–69.

26. Ibid., p. 313.

27. Cable, American Embassy—Lima [Ambassador Jones] to Secretary of State [Dean Rusk], February 4, 1964, National Security File, Country File—Peru, folder: Peru—Cables Vol. 3 (11/63–11/65), Johnson Library.

28. Intelligence Information Cable ["sanitized" copy], Central Intelligence Agency, February 10, 1964, "Subject: Plans of the MIR for Revolutionary Action," in ibid.

29. Agee, *Inside the Company,* p. 321.

30. Brown and Fernández, *War of Shadows,* p. 93.

31. *La Prensa,* March 31, 1964.

32. Authors' interviews with L. Fletcher Prouty, former Defense Department liaison with the CIA, Washington, D.C., August 1977.

33. Authors' interviews with former U.S. government official and other confidential sources, Washington, D.C., 1977. Reports of the CIA support for the coup were also heard during interviews in Peru and in Bolivia in 1976, when the authors visited Iquitos, Pucallpa, Lima, Cuzco, the Lake Titicaca region, and La Paz.

34. Cole Blasier, "The United States and the Revolution," in *Beyond the Revolution: Bolivia Since 1952,* ed. James M. Mally and Richard Thorn (Pittsburgh: University of Pittsburgh Press, 1971), pp. 93–95.

35. Authors' interviews with L. Fletcher Prouty.

36. The Council for Latin America took over the Latin American Information Committee's extensive book program, partly financed by foundations serving as CIA conduits. This program became an important aspect of Johnson's International Education Program, which David also advised for propaganda efforts in Latin America and Vietnam. National Security File, Name File, David Rockefeller folder, Johnson Library.

37. David Rockefeller, "What Private Enterprise Means to Latin America," *Foreign Affairs,* April 1, 1966, p. 408.

38. John D. Rockefeller 3rd, "Opening Address to the Conference on Subsistence and Peasant Economies," February 28, 1965, in *Subsistence Agriculture and Economic Development,* ed. Clifton R. Wharton, Jr. (Chicago: Aldine, 1969), p. 3.

39. José L. Vasquez Calzada, *El Desbalance Entre Recursos de Poblacion en Puerto Rico* (San Juan: School of Medicine, University of Puerto Rico, November 1966), p. 8.

40. See J. M. Stycos, "Female Sterilization in Puerto Rico," *Eugenics Quarterly* 1, no. 1 (1954), pp. 3–9; and Harriet Presser, *Sterilization and Fertility Decline in Puerto Rico,* Population Monograph Series 13 (Berkeley, Calif.: California Institute of International Studies, 1973).

41. Mario C. Vasquez, "The Interplay Between Power and Wealth," and Henry F. Dobyns and Mario C. Vasquez, "The Transformation of Manors into Producers' Cooperatives," reports for Comparative Studies of Cultural Change, Department of Anthropology, Cornell University, Ithaca, New York, 1964. Comparative Studies of Cultural Change was the formal name of Cornell's social science research program in Peru, which was financed through the U.S. Agency for International Development under contract AID/csd-296 between AID and Cornell.

42. By 1966, Holmberg's Vicos project, begun in 1952 with grants from the Carnegie Corporation as part of the already established Cornell Peru Project, had received $621,772 through the Agency for International Development's research division under contract AID/csd-296. See State Department, Agency for International Development, Contract Service Division, *AID-Financed University Contracts* (Washington, D.C.: Government Printing Office, 1962–1967). The Vicos project's Pentagon ties were revealed by Holmberg's successor, William F. Whyte, in 1969 in "The Role of the U.S. Professor in Developing Countries," *American Sociologist* 4, no. 1 February 1969, p. 27n. Whyte reported that in February 1966, the year Holmberg died, "A barrage of attacks in one Lima newspaper, aimed particularly at the indirect link of our Peruvian associates with the Pentagon, led us to return the unexpended balance (more than $100,000), even though we felt we needed the money more than the Pentagon did." Writing two years earlier, in 1967, for the quarterly magazine of the Milbank Memorial Fund (headed by SIL-funder Sam Milbank), Whyte had listed the Advanced Research Projects Agency among the funding institutions, but did not reveal that ARPA was an arm of the Department of Defense. See Whyte, "Cultural Change and Stress in Rural Peru," *Milbank Memorial Fund Quarterly* 44, no. 4. If the Cornell program was still receiving Pentagon money in 1967, as Whyte reported then, its financial ties may have extended beyond the February 1966 termination date given by Whyte in 1969.

43. H. F. Waterhouse, *A Time to Build* (Columbia, S.C.: University of South Carolina Press, 1964), p. 11.

44. House Appropriations Committee, *Defense Appropriations Hearings for 1965*, Vol. 14 (Washington, D.C.: Government Printing Office, 1965), p. 138.

45. Waterhouse, *A Time to Build,* p. 11.

46. Office of the Assistant Secretary of Defense for International Security Affairs, *Military Assistance Facts* (Washington, D.C.: U.S. Department of Defense, 1969), p. 21.

47. U.S. Agency for International Development, Statistics and Reports Division, *Operations Report* as of June 30, 1964, and June 30, 1965.

48. "The IPA Faculty," *IPA Review*, January 1967, p. 16.

49. Irving Louis Horowitz, ed., *The Rise and Fall of Project Camelot* (Cambridge, Mass.: MIT Press, 1974), pp. 4, 184.

50. "Working Paper," December 5, 1964, Document No. 3, in ibid., pp. 56–59.

51. *Washington Star,* 1965, p. 1.

52. Horowitz, *The Rise and Fall of Project Camelot*, pp. 50–51.

53. House Committee on Foreign Affairs, Subcommittee on Internal Organization and Movements, 89th Cong., 1st sess., *Winning the Cold War: The U.S. Ideological Offensive,* Hearings (July 8, 13, and 14, and August 7, 1965), published in House Committee on Foreign Affairs, 89th Cong., 1st sess., *Behavioral Sciences and National Security*, Report 4, December 6, 1965 (Washington, D.C.: Government Printing Office, 1965).

54. E. W. Kenworthy, "Unit at Cornell Aided by Conduits," *New York Times*, February 27, 1967, p. 1.

31: MISTAKEN IDENTITIES

1. Quoted in James C. Hefley and Marti Hefley, *Dawn over Amazonia* (Waco, Tex.: Word Books, 1972), pp. 113–14.

2. Quoted in ibid., p. 115.

3. Quoted in ibid., p. 35.

4. Matthew Huxley and Cornell Capa, *Farewell to Eden* (New York: Harper & Row, 1964), pp. 142–44.

5. This story was repeated often in interviews about SIL's work throughout Latin America. SIL itself occasionally referred to this social tension. See Jerry Long, *Amazonia Reborn* (Portland, Ore.: Multnomah Press, 1970), p. 23.

6. W. C. Townsend, Memorandum, July 21, 1964, Townsend Archives.

7. W. C. Townsend to Ben Elson, January 15, 1964, in ibid.

8. David Stoll, *Fishers of Men or Founders of Empires? The Wycliffe Bible Translators in Latin America* (London: Zed Press, 1982), p. 132.

9. Eugene Loos to W. C. Townsend, April 24, 1964, Townsend Archives.

10. Chief Tariri to W. C. Townsend, July 7, 1964, in ibid.

11. W. C. Townsend to Ethel Wallis, August 7, 1964, in ibid.

12. Harold Key to W. C. Townsend, April 14, 1964, in ibid.

13. W. C. Townsend to Kenneth Watters, January 14, 1964; W. C. Townsend to Marion Slocum, March 16, 1964; W. C. Townsend to Harold Key, February 7, 1964, in ibid.

14. William Cameron Townsend to Ben Elson, September 3, 1964, in ibid.

15. Ibid.

16. Eugene Loos to W. C. Townsend, September 5, 1964, in ibid.

17. Quoted in Jamie Buckingham, *Into the Glory* (Plainfield, N.J.: Logos, 1974), pp. 115–17.

18. W. C. Townsend to Ben Elson, September 3, 1964, Townsend Archives.

19. *Translation* magazine (Wycliffe Bible Translators), Winter 1966, p. 9.

20. Victor Marchetti and John Marks, *The CIA and the Cult of Intelligence* (New York: Alfred A. Knopf, 1974), p. 124.

21. Armando Artola, *¡Subversión!* (Lima: Editorial Juridica, 1976), p. 22.

22. *New York Times,* October 11, 1964, p. 128.

23. Marchetti and Marks, *The CIA and the Cult,* p. 124.

24. Stoll, *Fishers of Men or Founders of Empires?,* pp. 150–51.

25. The CIA provided one of King Hurley's larger "Twin" Helio models for Montgomery and Prouty's use on a no-cost basis. The Twin was flown to New Orleans on May 15 from the CIA's Special Warfare Center at Eglin Air Force base in Florida, where Montgomery had worked in 1961 after his return from the Congo. Montgomery and Prouty flew it from there to Peru and back during the last two weeks of May, hoping to commence a joint manufacturing venture with the Peruvians. (See Memorandum, L. F. Prouty to L. L. Bollinger, May 5, 1964. Copy in the authors' possession.) SIL's Jerry Elder had a similar idea in a December 6, 1960, proposal to Bollinger, who replied with enthusiasm on January 8, 1961. Elder was acting as an agent for Helio with Peru's General Van Oordt.

26. Marchetti and Marks, *The CIA and the Cult,* pp. 124–25.

27. Norman Gall, "The Legacy of Che Guevara," *Commentary,* December 1967.

28. Michael F. Brown and Eduardo Fernández, *War of Shadows: The Struggle for Utopia in the Peruvian Amazon* (Berkeley, Calif.: University of California Press, 1991), p. 114.

29. Cited in Richard Gott, *Guerrilla Movements in Latin America* (Garden City, N.Y.: Doubleday, 1971), pp. 416–17, 420.

30. Stoll, *Fishers of Men or Founders of Empires?,* p. 150.

31. Gall, "Legacy of Che Guevara."

32. Ministerio de Guerra, *Las Guerrillas en el Perú* (Lima, 1966), pp. 60–64.

33. Brown and Fernández, *War of Shadows,* p. 84. Belaúnde claimed Guevara wore his black beret even in the tropical Amazonian heat.

34. *New York Times,* October 9, 1965 (supplement), p. 3.

32: Poisons of the Amazon

1. Nicole Maxwell, *Witch Doctor's Apprentice* (Boston: Houghton Mifflin, 1961), pp. 319–23.

2. Ibid.

3. Russell Warren Howe, "Asset Unwittingly: Covering the World for the CIA," *More,* May 1978, p. 25; John M. Crewdson and Joseph B. Treaster, "Worldwide Propaganda Network Built and Controlled by the C.I.A.," *New York Times,* December 26, 1977, p. 37.

4. David Atlee Phillips, *The Night Watch: Twenty-five Years of Peculiar Service* (New York: Atheneum, 1977), p. 133.

5. David Wise and Thomas B. Ross, *The Espionage Establishment* (New York: Random House, 1967), p. 137n.

6. Interview with confidential source, July 1977.

7. John D. Marks, *The Search for the "Manchurian Candidate"* (New York: Times Books, 1979), pp. 112–13.

8. Maxwell, *Witch Doctor's Apprentice,* p. 324.

9. Interviews with a former ANDCO employee and a former anthropologist in the area, 1977.

10. Gordon Thomas, *Journey into Madness: The True Story of Secret CIA Mind Control and Medical Abuse* (New York: Bantam Books, 1989), p. 251.

11. "Brazil," Report for the President, SR-17, November, 1948, Central Intelligence Agency, pp. 29–30, Harry S. Truman Library.

12. JAARS planned to purchase older Helios from the Peruvian army in 1964 with commissions from sales of newer Helios that SIL, acting as Lynn Bollinger's Helio agent, would sell to the Peruvians. "The three [Peruvian Army] planes could be readied for Brazil in short order," JAARS's Bernie May assured Cam. Memorandum, Bernie May to W. C. Townsend, February 12, 1964, Re: Helio Sale, Attached: Memorandum from May to Eugene Loos, February 11, 1964, Townsend Archives.

13. Dale Kietzman to James Wilson et al., October 28, 1964, in ibid.

14. Ibid.

15. "Brazil Builds First All Weather Cross Continent Road," *Brazil Bulletin,* January 1968, p. 3.

16. Memorandum re: Development in Amazona and Acre, Dale Kietzman to James Wilson et al., October 29, 1964, Townsend Archives.

17. "Emphasis on Brazil: The Awakening Giant of South America," *Translation* magazine (Wycliffe Bible Translators), Winter 1966.

18. Dale Kietzman, "Indians and Cultural Areas of Twentieth Century Brazil," in *Indians of Brazil in the Twentieth Century,* ed. Janice H. Hopper (Washington, D.C.: Institute for Cross Cultural Research, 1967), pp. 16, 43. The word *warlike* was attached to the Mayorunas and Cintas Largas; *wild groups* was used to describe Indians on the Paraguay side of the Paraná River.

19. See Darcy Ribeiro, *A Política Indigenista Brasileira* (Rio de Janeiro: Minesterio da Agricultura Serviço de Informação o Agricola [Atvaldade Agrâria, 1], 1962), pp. 38–39.

20. Kietzman, "Indians and Cultural Areas," pp. 7, 12, 50.

21. Ribeiro, *A Política Indigenista Brasileira,* pp. 38–39.

22. Kietzman, "Indians and Cultural Areas," pp. 4, 6.

23. *The Nation,* February 27, 1967.

24. Rex D. Hopper to Johan Galtung, April 5, 1965, National Security File, Agency File, Box 19, folder: Defense: Project Camelot, Lyndon B. Johnson Library.

25. Marks, *Search for the "Manchurian Candidate,"* p. 109.

26. Richard Helms, Deputy Director for Plans, to John McCone, Director of Central Intelligence, June 9, 1964, "eyes only—secret" memorandum (declassified November 13, 1975) on "Sensitive Research Programs" in Senate Subcommittee on Health of the Committee on Labor and Public Welfare and Subcommittee on Administrative Practice and Procedure of the Committee on the Judiciary, *Biomedical and Behavioral Research 1974, Joint Hearings on Human-Use Experimentation Programs of the Department of Defense and Central Intelligence Agency* (Washington, D.C.: Government Printing Office, 1976), pp. 970–72.

27. Maxwell, *Witch Doctor's Apprentice,* pp. 329–30.

28. Thomas, *Journey into Madness,* p. 251.

29. Marks, *Search for the "Manchurian Candidate,"* p. 203.

30. Ibid., p. 113.

31. Ibid., p. 62.

32. A CIA linguistics contract with Professor Anthony Oettinger was approved by the Harvard Corporation and confirmed by Vice President L. G. Wiggins and Dean Franklin Ford in 1968. (See Memorandum, L. G. Wiggins to Franklin L. Ford, September 16, 1968, reprinted in *How Harvard Rules* [Cambridge, Mass.: The Old Mole, 1969], p. 47.) Years later, when Harvard Medical School's Dr. Martin T. Orne's hypnosis experi-

ments were revealed to have been funded in 1962 by two CIA fronts—Adolf Berle's Human Ecology Fund and Boston's Scientific Engineering Institute—Harvard officials tried to protect Orne's identity as an alleged unwitting asset. (See *Harvard Crimson,* Editorial, February 11, 1978.)

33. Richard Evans Schultes to John C. Cady (Point IV Country Director for Colombia, headquartered at the U.S. Embassy in Bogotá), May 3, 1952, Rubber Investigations Files, Records of the Bureau of Plant Industry, Department of Agriculture, National Archives.

34. Authors' interview with Timothy Plowman, Cambridge, Mass., November 1977.

35. Quoted in Marks, *Search for the "Manchurian Candidate,"* p. 202.

36. Homer V. Pinkley, "Plant Admixtures to *Ayahuasca,* the South American Hallucinogenic Drink," *Lloydia* 32, no. 3 (September 1969). Pinkley presented this paper to the tenth annual meeting of Schultes's Society for Economic Botany, held at Kennett Square, Pennsylvania, home of the famed Longwood Gardens, the estate of Pierre S. du Pont II, the late munitions and chemical millionaire. Pinkley acknowledged the assistance of SIL's M. "Bub" Borman and Carolyn Orr, translators among, respectively, the Kofán and Quichua Indians (p. 313). Pinkley also drew upon previous linguistic work by SIL's Rachel Saint, Glen Turner, John Lindskoog, Bruce Moore, and Orville Johnson (translators for the Huaorani, Shuar, Cayapa, Colorado, and Secoya tribes, respectively), and the botanical work of former SIL anthropologist Ken Kensinger.

37. Army Research Task Summary, fiscal year 1961 (Washington, D.C.: Department of the Army, 1961), Vol. 1, p. 222. Taylor's contract was DA-108-405-735.

38. Margaret B. Kreig, *Green Medicine: The Search for Plants That Heal* (New York: Rand McNally, 1964), p. 130.

39. Ibid., p. 122.

40. "Expert Hunts Secrets of Old Witchdoctors," *Los Angeles Times,* September 20, 1959.

41. *Technical Abstract Bulletin,* 67-11, June 1, 1967, Defense Documentation Center, Department of Defense, Alexandria, Virginia. (The bulletin was published biweekly.)

42. Ibid.

43. *Technical Abstract Bulletin,* April 15, 1966.

44. Authors' interview with former ANDCO employee, 1977.

33: Death of a Continental Revolution

1. Shelton Davis and Robert O. Mathews, *The Geological Imperative: Anthropology and Development in the Amazon Basin of South America* (Cambridge, Mass.: Anthropological Resource Center, 1976), p. 72.

2. *La Crónica,* February 21, 1964.

3. Sherman Kent, Office of National Estimates, Central Intelligence Agency, Special Memorandum No. 19-65, Subject: Prospects in Peru, July 29, 1965, National Security File, Country File—Peru, folder: Peru—Cables Vol. 6 (11/63–11/65), Lyndon B. Johnson Library.

4. Armando Artola, *¡Subversión!* (Lima: Editorial Jurídica, 1976), pp. 22–23.

5. Che Guevara, *Guerrilla Warfare* (New York: Vintage Books, 1961), pp. 30–35, 80–81.

6. Authors' interview with Christopher Roper, London, February 25, 1978.

7. Authors' interview with confidential source, Lima, November 9, 1976.

8. "Gestapo Official Is Linked to U.S. Intelligence," *New York Times,* February 8, 1983.

9. *El Espectador* (Bogotá), December 8, 12, 1963.

10. Victor Daniel Bonilla, "The Destruction of the Colombian Indian Groups," in *The Situation of the Indian in South America,* ed. Walter Dostal (Geneva: World Council of Churches, 1972), p. 58.

11. *El Espectador,* December 8, 1963.

12. Ibid., December 17, 1963, p. 8-A.

13. *St. Petersburg Times,* May 5, 1988, p. 4a.

14. Testimony of Mike Tsalickis before the First Colombian-Brazilian Universities Scientific Conference on Investigations of the Amazon, 1974; addenda No. 2 and No. 3.

15. *St. Petersburg Times,* May 5, 8, 1988.

16. Roberto Fabrico, "To Die in Cuba," *Tropic* (Sunday magazine of the *Miami Herald*), November 6, 1977, p. 23. The headquarters for the raid, code-named JMWAVE, were located at the former Richmond Naval Station at the University of Miami South Campus near Perrine, Florida. Fabrico's main source for his article was paramilitary expert Bradley Ayers, who claimed to have met "Colonel Roselli," Mafia assassin John Roselli, during the mobster's visits to the base to recruit sharpshooters for an assassination team—allegedly to kill Castro.

17. For more on Barbie and Bolivia, see Charles Ashman and Robert J. Wagman, *The Nazi Hunters* (New York: Pharos Books, 1988), pp. 146–51; Albert Brun, "Barbie robe colecta nacional en Bolivia," *Diario La Republica* (La Paz), May 15, 1987, p. 20.

18. Michael F. Brown and Eduardo Fernández, *War of Shadows: The Struggle for Utopia in the Peruvian Amazon* (Berkeley, Calif.: University of California Press, 1991), p. 93.

19. Ladislas Farago, *Aftermath* (New York: Avon, 1975), pp. 89–92, 220, 274, 467.

20. "Pombo's Diary," September 28, 1966, in Daniel James, ed., *The Complete Bolivian Diaries of Che Guevara and Other Captured Documents* (New York: Stein & Day, 1968).

21. Robert Scheer, ed., *The Diary of Che Guevara* (New York: Bantam Books, 1968), entry for July 1, 1967.

22. Ibid., entry for January 19, 1967, pp. 50–51.

23. *Washington Post*, May 17, 1975.

24. *The Diary of Che Guevara*, p. 120.

25. Ibid., p. 121.

26. Ibid., entry for May 29, 1967, p. 118.

27. Ibid.

28. Ibid., entry for March 31, 1967, p. 86.

29. Quoted in Richard Gott, *Rural Guerrillas in Latin America* (Harmondsworth, Eng.: Penguin, 1973), p. 525.

30. Ibid., p. 527.

31. On JAARS's "transport," see David Stoll, *Fishers of Men or Founders of Empires? The Wycliffe Bible Translators in Latin America* (London: Zed Press, 1982), pp. 150–51. On the 1961 willingness to engage in "espionage," see Jerry Elder to Cameron Townsend, December 4, 1962, Townsend Archives. Stoll also quotes SIL's James Wroughton; SIL's Eugene Loos subsequently sent Stoll his own denial: "We know of no [SIL] flights made in that area at that time, and none of our linguistic personnel were working in that area at that time."

32. *Diary of Che Guevara*, entry for September 18, 1967, p. 178.

33. Andrew St. George, "How the U.S. Got Che," *True* magazine, April 1969.

34. *Diary of Che Guevara*, entry for September 26, 1967, p. 182.

35. Michele Ray, "In Cold Blood: How the CIA Executed Che," *Ramparts* magazine, 1969, pp. 147–48.

36. Felix Rodriguez and John Weisman, *Shadow Warrior* (New York: Simon & Schuster, 1989), p. 163.

37. Ibid., p. 164.

38. Ibid., p. 168.

39. Ibid., p. 171.

40. Ibid., p. 172.

41. Ibid., pp. 174–75.

42. Ibid., p. 178.

43. Victor Marchetti and John Marks, *The CIA and the Cult of Intelligence* (New York: Alfred A. Knopf, 1974), p. 125.

34: The Enemy Within

1. *Washington Post*, September 9, 1979.

2. Ralph de Toledano, *RFK: The Man Who Would Be President* (New York: New American Library/Signet, 1968), p. 339.

3. Jerome Levinson and Juan de Onis, *The Alliance That Lost Its Way* (Chicago: Quadrangle, 1970), p. 151. Levinson and de Onis interviewed Thorbine Reid, II, the former deputy director of the Peace Corps in Peru, who was in an auto with Kennedy and Ernesto Siracusa, the U.S. deputy chargé d'affaires, and witnessed the confrontation.

4. Ibid.

5. Cable, J. Wesley Jones to Robert F. Kennedy, November 15, 1965, National Security File, Country File—Peru, folder: Peru—Cables Vol. 6 (11/63-11/65), Lyndon B. Johnson Library.

6. Memorandum, "Subject: Peruvian Oil Problem," Grant G. Helleker (acting executive secretary, State Department) to McGeorge Bundy, July 6, 1965, National Security File, Country File—Peru, folder: Peru—Memos and Misc. Vol. 1 (11/63–11/65), in ibid.

7. Levinson and de Onis, *The Alliance That Lost Its Way*, p. 159.

8. *El Comercio* (domincal sup.), November 14, 1965. Quoted also in Jones cable to Kennedy. Also, Peter Collier and David Horowitz, *The Rockefellers* (New York: Holt, Rinehart & Winston, 1976), p. 417.

9. *El Comercio* (domincal sup.), November 14, 1965. Also, Jones cable to Kennedy.

10. Quoted in Collier and Horowitz, *The Rockefellers*, p. 417.

11. Memorandum, William Bowdler to McGeorge Bundy, October 16, 1965, with attached copies of Jones's cable. The USIA director passed along a copy of the cable to President Johnson's aide Marvin Watson. National Security File, Country File—Peru folder: Peru—Cables Vol. 6 (11/63–11/65), Johnson Library.

12. Quoted in de Toledano, *RFK*, p. 352.

13. Jack Newfield, *Robert Kennedy: A Memoir* (New York: E. P. Dutton, 1969), p. 95.

14. Quoted in de Toledano, *RFK*, p. 329.

15. Quoted in ibid.

16. Quoted in ibid., p. 330.

17. Quoted in Newfield, *Robert Kennedy*, p. 56.

18. Quoted in ibid., p. 122.

19. Quoted in ibid., p. 128.

20. Quoted in ibid., p. 137.

21. Billy Graham to Lyndon Johnson, December 29, 1963, Name File, Billy Graham folder, Johnson Library.

22. Billy Graham to Lyndon Johnson, April 10, 1964, in ibid.

23. R. W. Komer, Memorandum for the President, August 1, 1966, with attached note: "Note that the President wants Billy to visit Vietnam for Christmas, 1966," in ibid.

24. Memorandum on Graham's appearance on Bible Study Hour, no author, April 28, 1967, in ibid.

25. Memorandum, Rev. Calvin Thielman, May 8, 1967, in ibid.

35: Apocalypse Now: The Tribes of Indochina

1. IBEC, annual reports of various years. See also Wayne G. Broehl, Jr., *United States Business Performance Abroad: The Case Study of the International Basic Economy Corporation* (Washington, D.C.: National Planning Association, 1968).

2. Reeve Hankins, ROLIBEC International (Thailand) Ltd., to Leo Denlea, Jr., May 15, 1971, IBEC series, Box 74, ROLIBEC International folder, Rockefeller Archive Center, Tarrytown, New York.

3. Operational Chart for ROLIBEC Far East, in ibid.

4. ROLIBEC International (Thailand), Ltd., Monthly Operation Report, September 1972, in ibid.

5. Reeve Hankins to A. B. Palmer, September 13, 1971, in ibid.

6. Hankins to Denlea, November 30, 1971, IBEC series, Box 74, ROLIBEC International folder, in ibid.

7. President Dwight D. Eisenhower, speech before the National Governors Conference, Seattle, Washington, August 4, 1953.

8. Quoted in Robert Boyd, "N.C. Minister Renews Friendship with LBJ," *Charlotte Observer*, September 19, 1965.

9. Calvin Thielman to Lyndon B. Johnson, July 17, 1967, attached to Marvin Watson to the President [Lyndon B. Johnson], August 25, 1967, EXFG999, Container 430, folder 3/1/67–9/13/67, Lyndon B. Johnson Library.

10. Ibid.

11. Memorandum for the Record, May 8, 1967, White House Central Files, EXFG105-4, CD 291, Billy Graham folder, in ibid.

12. James C. Hefley, *By Life or by Death* (Grand Rapids, Mich.: Zondervan, 1969), p. 45; Richard Pittman to W. C. Townsend, June 9, 1962, Townsend Archives.

13. W. C. Townsend, "Wycliffe's First Martyr," article for *Translation* magazine (Wycliffe Bible Translators), written March 20, 1963, Townsend Archives.

14. W. C. Townsend to Richard Pittman, August 26, 1964, in ibid.

15. Memorandum, LJM [Lawrence J. Montgomery] (via NL) to CB [Chick Barquin], April 9, 1964. A copy is in the authors' possession. Montgomery, on Barquin's request, provided the address of the Missionary Aviation Fellowship in Fullerton, California, the names of the MAF's top officers (Grady Parrot, president, Jim Truxton, vice president, Charles Mellis, secretary-treasurer, and Betty Greene, director), as well as MAF's areas of operations: Mexico, Honduras, Ecuador, Congo (Leopoldville), Sudan, Britain, Ethiopia, Philippines, New Guinea, and Brazil. He also provided C&MA's Andrianoff's address in Vientiane. The memorandum indicates that Montgomery's relationship with the CIA, whether as a witting or unwitting contracted agent and asset, nevertheless continued after he was phased out of the Southeast Asia contract that sent his trainee, Sam Mustard, to Laos in 1962.

16. Kenneth Pike and Ruth M. Brend, eds., *The Summer Institute of Linguistics: Its Work and Contributions* (The Hague: Mouton, 1977), pp. 46–47, 50.

17. See Robert L. Mole, *The Montagnards of South Vietnam: A Study of Nine Tribes* (Rutland, Vt.: Tuttle, 1970).

18. See Howard Sochurek, "Slow Train Through Viet Nam's War," *National Geographic*, September 1964; and Howard Sochurek, "American Special Forces in Action in Viet Nam," *National Geographic,* January 1965.

19. Quoted in Howard Sochurek, "Viet Nam's Montagnards," *National Geographic*, April 1968, p. 448.

20. Ibid., p. 401.

21. Ibid., p. 487.

22. Quoted in ibid.

23. Clifton R. Wharton, Jr., to Nicolaas G. M. Luykx, II, July 5, 1967, Agricultural Development Council Archives, RG III, B1.23, Box 8, Folder 89: Michigan State University, Luykx, Nicolaas G. M., II, Rockefeller Archive Center.

24. "Research Proposal," attached to letter, Nicolaas G. M. Luykx, II, to Clifton R. Wharton, Jr., July 16, 1967, in ibid. See also Luykx to Wharton, November 4, 1968, in ibid.

25. John H. Bodley, *Victims of Progress* (Palo Alto, Calif.: Mayfield Publishing, 1982), pp. 73–74.

26. Alfred W. McCoy and Cathleen B. Read, *The Politics of Heroin in Southeast Asia* (New York: Harper & Row, 1972), pp. 135–36, 140–42.

27. The financial linkage began with the Thai border police, whose training and arming was carried out by the CIA through a front, Sea Supply, Inc. Based in Bangkok, Sea Supply was headed by Willis Bird. In 1962, Bird was indicted in the United States for allegedly seeking to defraud the government in Laos. Bird chose to take up permanent residence in Bangkok. See McCoy and Read, *The Politics of Heroin*, pp. 130, 138, 141, 144; Christopher Robbins, *Air America* (New York: G.P. Putnam's Sons, 1979), p. 253.

From Bangkok, the money thread led back to Miami. Sea Supply's counsel was Miami lawyer Paul L. E. Helliwell, former OSS chief of intelligence in China, who directed a network of CIA proprietaries in Latin America and the Far East (*Washington Post*, March 24, 1980, pp. A21–A22). Helliwell's Miami office doubled as Thai Counsel General. See also *First Principles* (published by Journal of the Center for National Security Studies, Washington, D.C.), June 1980, p. 9.

28. McCoy and Read, *The Politics of Heroin*, p. 352. The Youngs' story is told on pp. 265–66, 297–307, 310–15, and 339–42.

29. Ibid., pp. 304–8.

30. These mineral resources were identified for readers of *National Geographic* in a map. See Peter T. White,

"Hopes and Fears in Booming Thailand," *National Geographic* 132, no. 1 (July 1967), pp. 76–125. The map is on p. 82.

31. Testimony of Lieutenant General Austin W. Betts, House Appropriations Committee, Department of Defense Subcommittee, *Department of Defense Appropriations for 1970,* Part V (Washington, D.C.: Government Printing Office, 1969), p. 182.

32. *Technical Abstract Bulletin,* June 1, 1967, Defense Documentation Center, Department of Defense, Alexandria, Virginia.

33. Ibid., May 1, 1967, and June 1, 1967.

34. Cited in *Subliminal Warfare: The Role of Latin American Studies* (New York: North American Congress on Latin America, 1970). This report by NACLA, which alerted the authors to the *Technical Abstract Bulletins* cited above, remains the best and, to this day, only serious, well-researched critique of American social sciences studies funded by the Pentagon.

35. *Technical Abstract Bulletin,* June 15, 1967, Defense Documentation Center, Department of Defense, Alexandria, Virginia.

36. For a fictional European account of the practical worth of these sensory devices, see Pierre Boulle, *Ears of the Jungle* (New York: Vanguard Press, 1972). For a factual review, see the *Armed Forces Journal,* February 15, 1971.

37. Executive Secretary, American Advisory Council for Thailand, "Trip on Behalf of the American Advisory Council for Thailand to Thailand, November 22–December 17, 1968," p. 1. Cited in Eric R. Wolf and Joseph G. Jorgensen, "Anthropology on the Warpath in Thailand," *The New York Review,* November 19, 1970, p. 28.

38. Jason Study Minutes, July 3, 1967, p. 308, as cited by Drs. Eric R. Wolf and Joseph Jorgensen, members of the Ethics Committee of the American Anthropology Association and of the faculty of the University of Michigan, in "Antropología en Pos de Guerra," *América Indígena* 31, no. 2 (April 1971), p. 437.

39. One example is Stanford Research Institute's 1965 "Special Study of Mobility in the Mekong Delta Area of South Vietnam." SRI's chairman, Ernest Arbuckle, was a director of Castle and Cooke, 50 percent owner of the Thai-America Steel Company, and owner of Dole (pineapples) Philippines; Arbuckle was also a director of Utah Construction and Mining Company, which built B-52 bases in Thailand. He was dean of the Stanford University Business School.

40. Arthur Bernon Tourtellot, ed., *Toward the Well-Being of Mankind: Fifty Years of the Rockefeller Foundation* (Garden City, N.Y.: Doubleday, 1964), pp. 120–21.

41. Ibid., p. 195.

42. Figures from *100 Companies and Their Subsidiary Corporations, Listed According to Net Value of Military Prime Contract Awards, Fiscal Year 1968* (Washington, D.C.: Department of Defense, Comptroller, Directorate for Information Operations).

43. Jules Henry, "Capital's Last Frontier," *The Nation,* April 25, 1966.

44. Peter Collier and David Horowitz, *The Rockefellers* (New York: Holt, Rinehart & Winston, 1976), p. 418.

45. McCoy and Read, *The Politics of Heroin,* pp. 166–81.

46. Ibid., p. 163.

47. *New York Times,* July 19, 1966.

48. Harry Magdoff, *The Age of Imperialism* (New York: Monthly Review Press, 1969), p. 176.

49. Henry, "Capital's Last Frontier."

50. McCoy and Read, *The Politics of Heroin,* pp. 275–99.

51. Don A. Schanche, *Mister Pop* (New York: David McKay, 1970) p. 303.

52. "Conversing with the CIA," *Christianity Today,* October 19, 1975, pp. 62–63.

36: "Nation-Building" Through War

1. Victor Marchetti and John Marks, *The CIA and the Cult of Intelligence* (New York: Alfred A. Knopf, 1974), p. 245.

2. Quoted in Gordon Thomas, *Journey into Madness: The True Story of Secret CIA Mind Control and Medical Abuse* (New York: Bantam Books, 1989), p. 246.

3. Ibid., p. 259.

4. Pamphlet for conference, "Investment Conditions in Vietnam," New York City, February 28, 1958, p. 67, Papers of John D. Rockefeller 3rd, Asia Society, Rockefeller Archive Center, Tarrytown, New York.

5. Ibid., pp. 70–71, 73.

6. "Founder Denies Language Institute Is Tied to CIA," *Washington Post*, July 20, 1979.

7. See Gerald C. Hickey, *The Highland People of South Vietnam: Social and Economic Development* (Santa Monica, Calif.: RAND, 1967), pp. iv, 16–23. Hickey was a member of the U.S. Mission Council Subcommittee for Highland Affairs at the U.S. Embassy in Saigon. All of Hickey's linguistic classifications were based on SIL's research: "Long discussions with informants also were made possible by the linguistic assistance of a group of the Summer Institute of Linguistics" (p. 11). Members of the Christian and Missionary Alliance also assisted Hickey in his discussion with informants. Hickey's ARDA contract number was DAHC15 67 C0142.

8. W. C. Townsend to Rev. Calvin Thielman, February 28, 1967, Townsend Archives.

9. Senate Committee on Government Operations, 93rd Cong., 2nd sess., *Disclosure of Corporate Ownership* (Metcalf Committee Report) (Washington, D.C.: Government Printing Office, 1974), p. 121.

10. "Wycliffe Bible Translators May Leave County," *Santa Ana Register,* August 25, 1967.

11. *Dallas Morning News*, May 24, 1967.

12. Ibid., September 16, 1967.

13. Philip Knightly, *The First Casualty* (New York: Harcourt, 1975), pp. 381 and captions of photographs, pp. 390–95.

14. "Wycliffe World News," *Translation* magazine (Wycliffe Bible Translators), Spring 1966.

15. Les Troyer to W. C. Townsend, February 14, 1967, Townsend Archives.

16. Of the top twenty of AID's service contractors, a fifth were CIA conduits: Air America, the African-American Institute, the American Institute for Free Labor Development, the Asia Foundation, and the Pathfinder Fund. Two other organizations among the top twenty AID contractors, the Population Council and the International Executive Service Corps, were headed by Nelson's brothers John D. Rockefeller 3rd and David Rockefeller. *Top 20 Institutions in Value of Technical Services Contracts* (Washington, D.C.: Agency for International Development, 1971).

17. Peter Collier and David Horowitz, *The Rockefellers* (New York: Holt, Rinehart & Winston, 1976), p. 370.

18. Robert Purcell to Nelson Rockefeller, April 14, 1964, RG III, 4B, Papers of Nelson A. Rockefeller—Personal, AIA-IBEC files, Box 26, Robert Purcell folder, Rockefeller Family Archives, Rockefeller Archive Center.

19. Howard Kresge to W. C. Townsend, April 12, 1968, Townsend Archives. Kresge, who advised Cam on AID's standardized accounting procedures and other matters of concern to SIL, was given the Christian Service Award by the Church World Services in 1971 .

20. William Westmoreland, *A Soldier Reports* (Garden City, N.Y.: Doubleday, 1976), p. 108.

21. Ibid., p. 315.

22. Howard Sochurek, "Viet Nam's Montagnards," *National Geographic*, April 1968, p. 444.

23. Ibid., p. 463.

24. Memorandum, John P. Roche to Douglas Cater, February 23, 1967, White House Central Files, Box 193, Lyndon B. Johnson Library. Roche had been national chairman of the liberal Americans for Democratic Action and was an adviser to Vice President Hubert Humphrey.

37: TET: THE YEAR OF THE MONKEY

1. Vine Deloria, Jr., *Custer Died for Your Sins* (New York: Macmillan, 1969), p. 192.

2. Ibid.

3. Rex Weyler, *Blood of the Land* (New York: Vintage Books, 1984), pp. 149–50. See also, Beth Wood, "LDS Placement Program, To Whose Advantage," *Akwesasne Notes,* Winter 1978, p. 16.

4. *New York Times,* December 15, 1967, p. 11.

5. Jack Newfield, *Robert Kennedy: A Memoir* (New York: E. P. Dutton, 1969), p. 48.

6. Four Texans were named in Senate Rules Committee hearings in connection with payoffs and loans to Baker: Thomas E. Webb, Clint Murchison, Jr., Robert H. Thompson, and Bedford Wynne. Webb was involved in a Florida land-development loan from Hoffa's Teamsters Pension Fund, and Murchison's Tecon Corporation allegedly paid Webb to negotiate the loan (see John Masher, "Murchison Associate Reveals Baker Tieup in Joint Venture," *Dallas Morning News,* January 29, 1964). Webb and Murchison employee Thompson were also involved in questionable loans to Baker arranged by Dallas banker Robert H. Stewart. Finally, Wynne took a "salary" from Murchison's Sweetwater Development Company that was criticized in an army audit of Sweetwater's construction of a North Carolina desalination plant built with federal contracts. Baker, after recommending Wynne hire the law firm of New York Congressman Emmanuel Celler to help in the project, received $2,500 of the $10,000 Sweetwater paid the Celler firm in legal fees ("Didn't Know Firm, Murchison States," *Dallas Morning News,* February 5, 1965). Both Stewart and Wynne were directors of the Great Southwest Corporation, a venture in real estate holdings located between Dallas and Fort Worth, in which Nelson Rockefeller and his brothers had a large stake through Rockefeller Center, Inc. This was part of Nelson's growing business ties with conservative Texan oil and financial principals, including Robert B. Anderson, a major stockholder in Delada Oil, controlled by Bedford Wynne's uncle, T. L. Wynne (and after Anderson's sellout to return to the Eisenhower administration, 50-percent-controlled by Nelson's IBEC), and real estate developer Trammel Crow, a director of Great Southwest. Control of Southwest, according to congressional investigators, "was tightly centered in the Rockefeller and Wynne families" (House Committee on Banking and Currency, *Staff Report, The Penn Central Failure and the Role of Financial Institutions* [Washington, D.C.: Government Printing Office, 1970], part III, p. 30; see also *Congressional Record,* January 26, 1965, p. 1313, and Senate Committee on Rules, *Construction of the District of Columbia Stadium* [Washington, D.C.: Government Printing Office, 1964], pp. 859–87). On Stewart, see Senate Committee on Rules, *Financial or Business Interests of Officers or Employees of the Senate* (Washington, D.C.: Government Printing Office, 1964), p. 987ff. On Delada, see Bernard B. Nossiter, "Ex-Treasury Chief Received Oil Funds," *Washington Post,* June 16, 1970.

In 1966, Baker was convicted of fraud and taking bribes and was subsequently imprisoned. Wynne, Murchison, and Webb denied any wrongdoing and were not charged with any crime.

7. Mary Bishop, *Billy Graham: The Man and His Ministry* (New York: Grosset & Dunlap, 1978), p. 61.

8. James C. Hefley, *By Life or by Death* (Grand Rapids, Mich.: Zondervan, 1964), p. 160.

9. Ibid., p. 145.

10. Quoted in Townsend Hoopes, *The Limits of Intervention* (New York: David McKay, 1969), p. 145.

11. Quoted in ibid., pp. 129–30.

12. Richard Pittman to W. C. Townsend, February 18, 1968, Townsend Archives.

13. Newfield, *Robert Kennedy,* pp. 205–6.

14. Kennedy first thought he would announce his candidacy at a March 10 rally for Cesar Chavez in California. Chavez was failing to persuade farmworkers to adhere to nonviolence. But then Kennedy thought better of it. He did not want to exploit his friendship with Chavez or his support for the Mexican American field workers. Chavez had already lost thirty-five pounds, and his doctors had called Kennedy to ask him to persuade Chavez to give it up. So Kennedy delayed announcing his candidacy.

15. Ben Elson to W. C. Townsend, March 11, 1968, Townsend Archives.

16. Hoopes, *Limits of Intervention,* p. 195.

17. Johnson had already been shaken in December by the loss of $900 million in gold, the greatest loss for any month up to that date, but the loss of another $1 billion in the first ten days of March sent him into a panic.

18. *New York Times,* March 13, 1968.

19. Joseph Califano to Lyndon Johnson, March 1, 1968, Name File, Nelson Rockefeller folder, Lyndon B. Johnson Library.

20. Quoted in Doris Kearns, *Lyndon Johnson and the American Dream* (New York: Harper & Row, 1976), p. 343.

21. Quoted in Hoopes, *Limits of Intervention,* p. 185.

22. Ibid., p. 213.

23. Quoted in ibid., p. 219.

24. White House diary entry, March 31, 1968, Diary File, Box 14, Johnson Library.

25. Ibid.

26. See David Landau, *Kissinger: The Uses of Power* (New York: Houghton Mifflin, 1992), pp. 193–97.

27. White House diary entry, April 23, 1968, 7:30 P.M., Diary File, Johnson Library.

28. *Dallas Morning News,* January 28, 1979.

38: Nelson's Last Charge

1. Curt Gentry, *J. Edgar Hoover: The Man and the Secrets* (New York: W. W. Norton, 1991), p. 571.

2. Quoted in Mark Lane and Dick Gregory, *Code Named Zorro* (Englewood Cliffs, N.J.: Prentice-Hall, 1977), p. 52.

3. James C. Hefley and Marti Hefley, *Uncle Cam* (Waco, Tex.: Word Books, 1974), p. 253.

4. L. J. Davis, "An American Fortune: The Hunts of Dallas," *Harper's* (April 1981), p. 86.

5. Jack Newfield, *Robert Kennedy: A Memoir* (New York: E. P. Dutton, 1969), pp. 302–3.

6. Remarks of Governor Rockefeller and the President, June 10, 1968, Diary File, Lyndon B. Johnson Library.

7. Quoted in Joseph Persico, *The Imperial Rockefeller* (New York: Simon & Schuster, 1981), p. 76.

8. Quoted in Peter Collier and David Horowitz, *The Rockefellers* (New York: Holt, Rinehart & Winston, 1976), p. 359.

9. Quoted in Persico, *The Imperial Rockefeller*, p. 81.

10. *Dallas Morning News,* January 29, 1979.

11. Quoted in Seymour Hersh, *The Price of Power* (New York: Summit, 1983), p. 18.

12. Quoted in ibid.

13. Quoted in ibid. Nixon had first learned of Kissinger's willingness to spy on the Paris talks on September 10 through his own top foreign policy researcher, Richard Allen. Nixon's thirty-two-year-old aide had been a great admirer of Kissinger's hard line toward the Soviet Union and had worked out with Kissinger the compromise on the Vietnam plank that avoided a floor battle at the Miami convention. On September 12, Kissinger called Allen at Nixon's research headquarters at the former American Bible Society offices in Manhattan and explained that he had friends at the Paris negotiations and "had a way to contact them." Allen informed Mitchell, stressing the importance of "protecting the source." On September 22, Allen briefed Nixon directly in a confidential memorandum. Ibid., p. 13.

14. Quoted in ibid., p. 20.

15. Quoted in ibid.

16. Ibid., p. 21.

17. Quoted in ibid., p. 23.

18. William Safire, *Before the Fall: An Inside Look at the Pre-Watergate White House* (Garden City, N.Y.: Doubleday, 1975), p. 33.

39: Invasion of the Amazon

1. Speech, Lyndon B. Johnson, April 23, 1968, National Security File, Subject File, "OAS" folder, Lyndon B. Johnson Library.

2. In May 1967, Secretary General José A. Mora of Uruguay allowed the OAS's director of administrative affairs to move against U.S. control of the OAS's finances. Lawrence W. Acker, formerly deputy comptroller at the U.S. Defense Department, was informed of this fact as OAS treasurer, as were Acker's principal assistants, Oscar C. Lightner and Edwin Barrett, both Americans. Two other division chiefs in the treasurer's

office were rumored to be scheduled for reassignment as well. Reports by the OAS General Secretariat to the OAS Council about the organization's financial condition were described as "misrepresentations" in State Department memorandums that ended up in the National Security Council's files. "An unanswerable question at present is, 'Why remove the financial staff unless it is for shifting the control of financial matters from U.S. influence or returning it to its former undisciplined state with its questionable fiscal control of funds.'" Memorandum, Edward S. Little to Barbara Watson, "Serious Developments in the Organization of American States," June 22, 1967, National Security File, in ibid.

3. Memorandum, Sol Linowitz to Dean Rusk, June 21, 1967, National Security File, Subject File, "AID" folder, in ibid.

4. Sol Linowitz to Dean Rusk and Covey Oliver, June 27, 1967, in ibid.

5. Galo Plaza to W. C. Townsend, March 13, 1968, Townsend Archives.

6. Alexandro Moreano, "Capitalismo y Lucha de Clases en la Primera Mitad del Siglo XX," *Ecuador: Pasado y Presente* (Quito: Editorial Universitaria, 1975), p. 173.

7. David Stoll, *Fishers of Men or Founders of Empires? The Wycliffe Bible Translators in Latin America* (London: Zed Press, 1982), p. 296.

8. Rosemary Kingsland, *A Saint Among Savages* (London: William Collins, 1980), p. 127.

9. Quoted in Stoll, *Fishers of Men or Founders of Empires?*, p. 296.

10. OAS Press Release, Galo Plaza address, May 18, 1983; see also memorandum (with attachment), Walt Rostow to the President, June 24, 1968; both in National Security File, Subject File, "OAS" folder Vol. II, Johnson Library.

11. OAS press release, "Berle Warns of Hemisphere 'Empire' Unless OAS Gets Needed Backing," January 14, 1969.

12. Quoted in Joseph Persico, *The Imperial Rockefeller* (New York: Simon & Schuster, 1981), p. 100.

13. The IRI's experiments were also conducted at Fazenda Jangada and Capin Colonião in São Paulo, at Fazenda Aroeira Bonita near São Joaquim da Barra, Minas Gerais, at IBEC's SASA farm at Jacarezinho, Paraná, at fields near Anápolis, Minas Gerais, and at Fazenda Ubatriba at Apucarana, Paraná. See IRI— Brazil, Progress Reports to IRI trusts, RG III, 4B, Box 7, Folders 60–61 and Folder 65 (Coffee Research in Brazil), Rockefeller Archive Center, Tarrytown, New York.

14. Robert Russell (executive vice president of the IRI) to Nelson Rockefeller, March 29, 1957, RG III, 4B, Box 8, "AIA/IBEC," Robert Russell folder, in ibid.

15. Robert Russell to Nelson Rockefeller, August 12, 1957, in ibid.

16. Robert Russell to Nelson Rockefeller, March 15, 1958, in ibid.

17. Quoted in Martha Dalrymple, *The AIA Story: Two Decades of International Cooperation* (New York: American International Association of Economic and Social Development, 1968), p. 167.

18. IBEC Research Institute description, RG III, 4B, Box 7, Folder 47, Rockefeller Archive Center.

19. Robert Purcell to Nelson Rockefeller, August 15, 1963, RG III, 4B, Box 26, Robert Purcell folder, Rockefeller Family Archives, in ibid.

20. Elizabeth A. Cobbs, "Entrepreneurship as Diplomacy: Nelson Rockefeller and the Development of the Brazilian Capital Market," *Business History Review* 63 (Spring 1989), p. 113.

21. Richard Aldrich and Humberto Monteiro to Marshall Humberto de Castelo Branco, January 19, 1965, Broehl Papers, Box 7, Rockefeller Archive Center.

22. Quoted in Cobbs, "Entrepreneurship as Diplomacy," p. 111.

23. Quoted in ibid.

24. Deltec International, *Annual Report,* 1978. Deltec's investment in Anápolis real estate was through a subsidiary, Companhia City de Disenvolvimento.

25. *New York Times,* March 1, 2, 12, July 11, 1991; March 20, 1992.

26. Berent Friele to Adolf Berle, February 7, 1961, New York office, AIA Archives, Box 7, Folder 59, Brazil, Rockefeller Archive Center.

27. John R. Camp, "Suggestions for Rural Development in Brazil," November 1960 proposal to the

International Cooperative Administration, attached as "Exhibit 1, Preliminary Report of the Planalto Pre-Survey Group," AIA Archives, Box 7, Folder 58, in ibid.

28. Walter Crawford to Berent Friele, February 6, 1963, AIA Archives, Box 7, Folder 63, in ibid.

29. Berent Friele to Walter Crawford, December 16, 1964, AIA Archives, Box 7, Folder 50, in ibid.

30. Walter Crawford to Berent Friele, February 6, 1963, AIA Archives, Box 7, Folder 63, in ibid.

31. "Condensed Progress Report, April–June, 1962," p. 5, AIA Archives, Box 15, Folder 134, in ibid.

32. Dalrymple, AIA Story, p. 172.

33. By 1967, IBEC had 119 subsidiaries and principal affiliates in 33 countries. In Brazil alone, IBEC owned ranches, factories, retail subsidiaries, and the country's largest mutual fund.

34. "Brazilians Cry 'Plot over Amazon Plan,'" Washington Post, June 6, 1965, p. 8.

35. Ibid.

36. National Security File, Agency File, Boxes 3 and 4, Alliance for Progress, Vols. I and II, particularly Bowdler to McGeorge Bundy, July 28, 1965, in Alliance for Progress, Vol. II, Johnson Library.

37. Brazil Division to the Coordinator [Nelson Rockefeller], September 16, 1942, RG 229, Box 78, Country File, Brazil, National Archives.

38. New York Times, November 26, 1942.

39. Fato Novo, June 10, 1970.

40. Jornal do Brasil, December 1967; statement by Patrick Holt, general counsel, U.S. Senate Foreign Relations Committee, in Jan Knippers Black, United States Penetration of Brazil (Philadelphia: University of Pennsylvania Press, 1977), pp. 89–90.

41. Carlos Lacerda, Brasil Entre a Verdade e a Mentira (Rio de Janeiro: Block Editores, 1965). Cited in Black, United States Penetration of Brazil, p. 71.

42. Keith L. Storrs, "Brazil's Independent Foreign Policy, 1961–1964," unpublished Ph.D. dissertation, Cornell University, 1973. Cited in Black, United States Penetration of Brazil, p. 69.

43. Washington Star, April 17, 1967.

44. Time, December 16, 1966.

45. Adolf Berle, diary entry, October 2, 1968, Berle Papers, Franklin D. Roosevelt Library.

46. Adrian Cowell, The Decade of Destruction (New York: Henry Holt, 1990), p. 157.

47. "How the Big Find Was Made," in "Carajas: Staggering Iron Ore Reserves in Isolated Splendor," Engineering and Mining Journal, November 1975, p. 151.

48. Charles J. V. Murphy, "The King Ranch South of the Border," Fortune, July 1969, pp. 132–36.

49. Ernest McCrary, "The Amazon Basin—New Mineral Province for the 80s," Engineering and Mining Journal, February 1972, p. 82.

50. Shelton Davis, "The Indian Situation in Brazil Today," Indígena magazine (Berkeley, Calif.), 1973; Cenpes e Gremio Pilitecnico (Brazil), May 1973; and Memorandum, Report on "Tembé and Urubu-Kaapor Indians" (Geneva: World Council of Churches, 1972). See also "La Política de Genocidio Contra los Indios de Brasil," report by Brazilian anthropologists to the Forty-first International Congress of Americanists, Mexico City, 1974, p. 9.

51. Murphy, "The King Ranch South of the Border," p. 144.

52. Deltec International, Ltd., 10K report to the Securities and Exchange Commission, 1969. All of International Packers, Ltd.'s debentures were retired, IPL becoming in March 1969 a wholly owned subsidiary of Deltec International, Limited, the new parent company resulting from the merger of Deltec Panamerica S.A. and IPL. Deltec International, Ltd., also became the parent of Deltec Panamerica's Deltec Banking Corporation, Deltec's Bahamas-based investment bank, which held about 20 percent of Banco de Investimento do Brasil (BIB) in partnership with Nelson Rockefeller's IBEC, Walther Moreira Salles's Unão de Bancos Brasileiros (in which IBEC also had a holding), and smaller European and Canadian (Brascan, Ltd.) investors. BIB was folded into Deltec's organizational directory in Deltec's 1970 10K report, as was Deltec Banking and Companhia Swift do Brasil. Moreira Salles, IBEC and Unãio director, was given a seat on the board of the parent company, Deltec International, Ltd., overseeing Deltec's vast empire, including

Swift do Brasil's cattle ranch joint venture with King Ranch in Pará, Companhia Agro Pecuario do Pará. This meant that IBEC and Nelson in particular, through IBEC's representation on Deltec's board by Walther Moreira Salles, shared responsibility for decisions made by Deltec's board concerning Swift's cattle ranch in Pará and were indirectly involved in the vast Swift-Armour beef processing operations in Argentina and Brazil. Furthermore, beyond IBEC's board interlock with Deltec through Moreira Salles (who could hardly be described by Nelson as a disinterested party or remote associate in Brazil), BIB itself was very active in raising capital for some twenty-eight new projects in the north and northeastern regions, where most of the Amazon investments were taking place.

53. Richard Aldrich to Robert Purcell, December 19, 1957, RG III, 4B, Papers of Neslon A. Rockefeller—Personal, AIA-IBEC files, Box 1, "AIA-Brazil," Folder 7, Rockefeller Family Archives, Rockefeller Archive Center.

54. In 1971, Chicago's First National Bank and J. Henry Schroder Banking Corporation would join Bank of America in arranging a special $18 million revolving credit in Eurodollars for Deltec Banking Corporation, while Irving Trust and Chase served as registration and transfer agent, respectively, for Deltec's purchase of International Packers through a stock sale on the New York Stock Exchange. See *Moody's Industrial Manual* (New York: Frederic Hatch & Company, 1972), p. 1761.

55. Georg Grünberg, "Urgent Research in North-West Mato Grosso," *Bulletin of the International Committee on Urgent Anthropological and Ethnological Research* (Vienna), No. 8 (1966), pp. 143–52.

56. Norman Lewis, "Genocide: From Fire and Sword to Arsenic and Bullets—Civilization Has Sent Six Million Indians to Extinction," *Sunday Times* (London), February 23, 1969, p. 55.

57. Ibid., p. 41.

58. Darcy Ribeiro, "Indigenous Cultures and Languages of Brazil," in *Indians of Brazil in the Twentieth Century*, ed. Janice H. Hopper (Washington, D.C.: Institute for Cross Cultural Research, 1967), p. 134.

59. Lewis, "Genocide," p. 41.

60. Ibid., p. 51.

61. *New York Times,* August 2, 1974.

62. Lewis, "Genocide," p. 41.

63. Both Shelton Davis and Adrian Cowell estimated 200,000; however, one of Davis's key sources, Darcy Ribeiro, estimated close to 100,000 Indians at most. See Adrian Cowell, *London Observer,* June 20, 1971, p. 20; Shelton Davis, *Victims of the Miracle* (Cambridge: Cambridge University Press, 1977), p. 5; and Ribeiro, "Indigenous Cultures," pp. 107–8. In 1953, Ribeiro, using SPI's figures with collaboration by Eduardo Galvão, had counted 150,000, a figure he later dismissed as "overly optimistic." Cowell cites as his source Brazilian anthropologist Paulo Duarte, who claimed that of 200,000 Indians in Brazil in 1963, only about 80,000 survived by 1971.

64. Lewis, "Genocide," p. 55.

65. *Jornal do Brasil,* October 10, 1967.

66. Ibid., cited by Lewis, "Genocide," p. 44.

67. On tribes, see Walter Dostal, ed., *The Situation of the Indian in South America* (Geneva: World Council of Churches, 1972), Appendage 32, pp. 434–42, and Appendage 33, "A Selected Bibliography for the Study of Discrimination Against the Indians of Brazil," by Pedro Agostinho, Georg Grünberg, and Silvio Coelho dos Santos, pp. 443–53. On SIL, see Luiz Emygdio de Mello Filho, director of the National Museum, Federal University of Rio de Janeiro, to the President of FUNAI, Report on the Work of the Summer Institute of Linguistics, December 15, 1977. A copy is in the authors' possession. For FUNAI maps, see *SIL in Brazil: Annual Report, 1976* (Brasília: Summer Institute of Linguistics, 1976).

68. Dale Kietzman, "Indians and Cultural Areas of Twentieth Century Brazil," in *Indians of Brazil in the Twentieth Century,* ed. Janice H. Hopper (Washington D. C.: Institute for Cross Cultural Research, 1967), pp. 1–50, especially maps of culture areas I–VIII.

69. Kietzman, "Indians and Cultural Areas," p. 32.

70. Jim Wilson to "Uncle Cam," April 24, 1968, Townsend Archives.

71. W. C. Townsend to Ben Elson, September 5, 1968, in ibid.

72. "Brazil Military Moves into Other Social Areas," *Los Angeles Times,* March 13, 1967.

73. Cowell, *The Decade of Destruction,* pp. 52–56.

1. Letter, William W. Rogers, "Dear Friends," October 21, 1968, Rockefeller Brothers Fund Archives, Box 31, Brazil Project folder, Rockefeller Archive Center, Tarrytown, New York.

2. Ibid.

3. Ibid.

4. Henry W. Bagley to James Hyde, November 21, 1968, in ibid.

5. Letter, William W. Rogers, "Dear Friends," December 9, 1968, Box 31, Brazil Project folder, in ibid.

6. See Shelton Davis, "Custer Is Alive and Well in Brazil," *Indian Historian,* Winter 1973, p. 5; Darcy Ribeiro, "Indigenous Cultures and Languages in Brazil," in *Indians of Brazil in the Twentieth Century,* ed. Janice H. Hopper (Washington, D.C.: Institute for Cross Cultural Research, 1967), pp. 79–160.

7. Arthur Oakley Brooks was vice chairman and partner of Wood, Struthers & Winthrop, Inc., vice president of the Pine Street Fund, and president of the De Vegh Mutual Fund. Samuel R. Milbank controlled all three firms, serving as, respectively, chairman, president, and director.

8. Martha Dalrymple, *The AIA Story: Two Decades of International Cooperation* (New York: American International Association for Economic and Social Development, 1968), p. 267.

9. Tom Alexander, "A Wild Plan for South America's Wilds," *Fortune,* December 1967, p. 203.

10. International Mining's subsidiary was the South American Gold and Platinum Company, Harder's original firm, which strip-mined gold and platinum in the hills above the Chocó district's San Juan and Atrato rivers and also owned a gold mine in Segovia, Colombia.

11. Michael Kramer and Sam Roberts, *"I Never Wanted to Be Vice-President of Anything!"* (New York: Basic Books, 1976), p. 26.

12. Adolf Berle, diary entry, January 9, 1969, Berle Papers, Franklin D. Roosevelt Library.

13. Quoted in Joseph Persico, *The Imperial Rockefeller* (New York: Simon & Schuster, 1981), p. 103.

14. *Dallas Morning News,* May 31, 1969.

15. *New York Times,* June 1, 1969.

16. Adolf Berle, diary entry, March 21, 1968, Berle Papers.

17. Quoted in Persico, *The Imperial Rockefeller,* p. 103.

18. *Dallas Morning News,* June 2, 1969.

19. *New York Times,* June 3, 1969, p. 2.

20. Ibid.

21. The authors wish to acknowledge Lucien Bodard's poetic writing in *Green Hell* (New York: Outerbridge & Dientsfrey, 1971), p. 242, for this and other analogies used in this section.

22. Berent Friele to Nelson Rockefeller, September 24, 1969, RG III, 4B, Countries series, Box 16, Folder 107, Rockefeller Archive Center.

23. Berent Friele to Nelson Rockefeller, October 8, 1969, RG III, 4B, Countries series, Box 16, Folder 107, in ibid.

24. *New York Times,* June 20, 1969, p. 12.

25. Ibid.

26. John P. Wiley, director, USAID-Paraguay, to Walter Crawford, regional representative of the Inter-American Rural Development Program (AIA), April 21, 1963, AIA Archives, Paraguay, Box 8, Folder 67, Rockefeller Archive Center.

27. Walter L. Crawford, "Agricultural Production and Credit in Paraguay," report prepared for the AIA in September 1963, AIA Archives, Paraguay, Box 8, Folder 67, in ibid.

28. Philip Agee, *Inside the Company* (Harmondsworth, Eng.: Penguin, 1975), p. 592.

29. Associated Press report from Montevideo, *Dallas Morning News,* June 22, 1968.

30. Persico, *The Imperial Rockefeller,* p. 103.

31. Quoted in ibid., pp. 105–6.

41: Forging the Dollar-Zone

1. Nelson Rockefeller, *The Rockefeller Report on the Americas* (Chicago: Quadrangle Books, 1969), p. 45.

2. Seymour Hersh, *The Price of Power* (New York: Summit, 1983), p. 106.

3. *Rockefeller Report*, p. 61.

4. *New York Times*, August 16, 1969, p. 2.

5. Victor Marchetti and John Marks, *The CIA and the Cult of Intelligence* (New York: Alfred A. Knopf, 1974), p. 242.

6. *Rockefeller Report*, p. 64.

7. Nelson rested his case on price alone, comparing the lower wholesale prices for Argentine and Paraguayan canned beef to lean cuts of fresh domestic beef. Brazilian beef, in which he had a vested interest, was not mentioned. The nutritional value of lean meat versus canned meat, including the usually higher fat content and added preservative chemicals in canned meat, was ignored. See ibid., p. 79.

8. Since such Rockefeller financial holdings were hidden from researchers and the general public by holding companies' corporate shell games, no conflict of interest was ever acknowledged. Rather, it was Nelson's concerns about the diet of the American poor that were aired in the local press.

9. *New York Times*, October 28, 1969, p. 18.

10. Thomas Powers, *The Man Who Kept the Secrets: Richard Helms and the CIA* (New York: Alfred A. Knopf, 1979), p. 226.

11. *New York Times*, December 4, 1969, p. 25.

12. Ibid., December 8, 1969, p. 18.

13. *Newsweek*, January 15, 1970, p. 28.

14. *Rockefeller Report*, p. 58.

15. Ibid., p. ix.

16. Ibid.

17. *New York Times*, December 14, 1969, p. 19.

18. Ibid.

19. *Atlas* magazine (New York), February 1970, p. 8.

20. Ibid.

21. Ibid.

22. Susan Branford and Oriel Glock, *The Last Frontier: Fighting over Land in the Amazon* (London: Zed Books, 1985), p. 185.

23. Brazil, Congresso, "Parecer ao projeto de lei do Congresso" Nacional No. 16 de 1967, emenda no. 1 ao projeto lei. No. 16/67, Brasília, 1968, note 35, p. 219, cited in Cecelima Medina, "The Legal Status of Indians in Brazil," *Indian Law Journal*, September 1977, p. 23.

24. Companies that were staking claims included ALCOA, controlled by the Mellon (Gulf Oil) family of Pittsburgh, which took out a large bauxite-exploration concession northwest of Santarém. Nearby, ALCAN, ALCOA's Canadian spin-off, did likewise, with a 247,000-acre exploration concession that yielded a projected $90 million bauxite-mining project.

25. Marcos Arruda, Herbet de Souza, and Carlos Afonso, *Multinationals and Brazil* (Toronto: Brazilian Studies, 1974), p. 163.

26. Jerry Shields, *The Invisible Billionaire: Daniel Ludwig* (Boston: Houghton Mifflin, 1986), p. 296.

27. By 1957, David Rockefeller's Chase Manhattan, Chemical Bank, and New York Trust had done $150 million in shared business with Ludwig, allowing him to pyramid tanker collateral and the labor of cheap seamen from the Cayman Islands into an empire and $350 million in personal worth. Personal investments in companies like Union Oil of California, AVCO, and McLean Industries brought huge returns when Ludwig blocked mergers and had to be bought out. See Arruda, de Souza, and Afonso, *Multinationals and Brazil*, p. 163.

28. Shields, *The Invisible Billionaire*, p. 315.

29. Martha Dalrymple, *The AIA Story: Two Decades of International Cooperation* (New York: American International Association for Economic and Social Development, 1968), p. 172.

30. Peter Seaborn Smith, *Oil and Politics in Modern Brazil* (Toronto: Macmillan, 1976), p. 121.

31. Arruda, de Souza, and Afonso, *Multinationals and Brazil*, p. 101.

32. These board members included investment banker Paul Manheim, a partner of New York's Lehman Brothers with a specialty in sugar plantations (including former holdings in Cuba); John F. Gallagher of Sears, Roebuck (the same firm that produced Assistant Secretary of State Charles Appleton Meyer) and vice chairman of David Rockefeller's Council for Latin America; J. Peter Grace, chairman of W. R. Grace & Company and another leading figure in David's Council for Latin America; and Lewis B. Harder, chairman of both the International Mining Company and the Molybdenum Corporation.

33. *Moody's Industrial Manual* (New York: Frederic Hatch & Company, 1972), p. 2914.

34. "Rondônia, Capital do Estando," *Visão*, August 28, 1972; "La Política de Genocidio Contra los Indios de Brasil," report by Brazilian anthropologists to the Forty-first International Congress of Americanists, Mexico City, 1974, p. 19. On CBMM's owners, see *Dicionario Histórico-Biográfico Brasileiro 1930–1983* (Rio de Janeiro: Forensa Universitaria, 1984), p. 3047.

35. Kleberg, congratulating Johnson for expressing support for the junta right after the coup, sent Johnson a copy of a letter backing the coup from a Brazilian associate of Nelson's, Teodoro Barbosa.

36. *Governmental Operations with Respect to Intelligence Activities* (hereafter Church Committee Hearings), 94th Cong., 1st sess., vol. 7, *Covert Action, December 4 and 5, 1975* (Washington, D.C.: Government Printing Office, 1976).

37. Dalrymple, *AIA Story*, pp. 178–85.

38. Church Committee Hearings, Testimony of U.S. Ambassador to Chile Edward Korry, December 4, 1975, p. 42.

39. Dalrymple, *AIA Story*, p. 263.

40. Church Committee Hearings, p. 166.

41. J. C. Louis and Harvey Z. Yazijian, *The Cola Wars* (New York: Everest House, 1980), p. 224.

42. Senate Select Committee to Study Governmental Operations with Respect to Intelligence Activities, *Alleged Assassination Plots Involving Foreign Leaders* (Washington, D.C.: Government Printing Office, 1976), p. 228.

43. Church Committee Hearings, vol. 7, p. 170.

44. *Newsweek*, January 10, 1977, p. 25.

45. David Rockefeller, Emílio Collado, and Walter B. Wriston, "A Reappraisal of the Alliance for Progress," February 1963, papers of Merwin L. Bohan, Harry S. Truman Library, Independence, Missouri.

46. *The American College Dictionary* (New York: Random House, 1963), p. 616.

47. Cited in "The New Military," *Newsweek*, January 5, 1970, p. 27.

48. Council for Latin America, *Report* 6 (January 1990), pp. 6–7; see also American Chamber of Commerce in Peru, *Bulletin*, April 1970, p. 3.

49. Alfred Stepan, *The Military in Politics: Changing Patterns in Brazil* (Princeton, N.J.: Princeton University Press, 1971), pp. 31–42, 167–68.

50. See "The New Military," pp. 27–28; Stepan, *The Military in Politics*, p. 129.

51. General Aurelio de Lyra Tavares served as a liaison officer with U.S. forces invading Germany. Admiral of the Fleet Augusto Hamman Rademaker Grunewald served in South Atlantic escort duty.

52. See "The New Military," p. 102.

53. Branford and Glock, *The Last Frontier*, p. 45.

54. *Brazil: A New Economic Survey by First National City Bank*, pamphlet (New York: First National City Bank, 1974), p. 42.

55. Rockefeller Foundation Archives, RG 1.2, Projects, Box 122, Hudson Institute (1970–1976) folder, Rockefeller Archive Center, Tarrytown, New York. Nelson had given more than $50,000 to the Hudson Institute (*New York Times*, October 20, 1974, p. 66).

56. Darcy Ruato, "Brasil proyecto un Gigantesco Lago Artificial en la Amazonia," *El Espectador* (Bogotá), December 26, 1971.

57. Memorandum, Report on "Tembe and Urubús-Kaapor Indians" (Geneva: World Council of Churches, 1972).

58. Indígena and American Friends of Brazil, *Supysáua: A Documentary Report on the Conditions of Indian Peoples in Brazil* (Berkeley, Calif., 1974).

59. Shelton Davis, "Custer Is Alive and Well in Brazil," *Indian Historian,* Winter 1973, p. 58; see also Joseph Novitski, "Brazil Seen Moving Toward Forced Relocation of Tribes," *New York Times,* July 14, 1971.

60. IBEC, *Annual Report,* 1971.

61. Robert G. Hummerstone, "Cutting a Road Through Brazil's 'Green Hell,'" *New York Times Magazine,* March 5, 1972, p. 38.

62. Ibid.

63. *Folha da Tarde,* March 10, 1971.

64. Hummerstone, "Cutting a Road."

65. Ibid.

66. "The Amazon Basin—New Mineral Province for the '70s," *Engineering and Mining Journal,* February 1972, p. 82. W. R. Grace participated in a joint tin-mining venture in Rondônia with CESBRA (Companhia Estanifera do Brasil), a firm controlled by the Patino tin-mining group of Bolivia. "Rondônia, Capital do Estanho," *Visão,* August 28, 1972, pp. 96, 100. The CESBRA group controlled five of seven companies reportedly allowed by FUNAI to explore Cintas Largas lands in the Aripuanã Indian Park. *A Folha de São Paulo,* April 28, 1970; *Jornal do Brasil,* November 21, 1972; *Brazilian Information Bulletin,* no. 13 (Spring 1974), p. 16; Shelton H. Davis, *Victims of the Miracle* (Cambridge: Cambridge University Press, 1977), p. 86; "Brazil: More Tin," *Mining Journal,* February 25, 1972, p. 160; "Tin Road Sparks Boom," *Brazilian Bulletin,* August 1972, p. 8; and Secretaria de Planejamento da Presidência da República, *Atlas de Rondônia* (Rio de Janeiro: Fundação Instituto Brasíleiro de Geografia e Estatística and Governo do Territorio Federal de Rondônia, 1975), pp. 31–32. The atlas carried a foreword by Colonel Humberto da Silva Guedes, then military governor of Rondônia territory.

67. "La Política de Genocidio Contra los Indios de Brasil," a forty-six-page report smuggled out of Brazil and submitted to the Forty-first International Congress of Americanists convened in Mexico City in September 1974. It was signed "by a group of Brazilian anthropologist-patriots who cannot for the moment reveal their names, due to the fascist regime in Brazil." A copy is in the authors' possession

68. *Rockefeller Report,* pp. 63–64.

69. Senate Committee on Foreign Relations, Subcommittee on Western Hemisphere Affairs, United States Policies and Programs in Brazil, *Hearings,* 92nd Cong., 1st sess. (Washington, D.C.: Government Printing Office), p. 7.

70. Agency for International Development, *U.S. Overseas Loans and Grants of Assistance from International Organizations, Obligations and Loan Authorizations, July 1, 1945–June 30, 1972* (Washington, D.C.: Government Printing Office, 1974).

71. Olimpio Alves Machado, "Indian Guard Trained in Brazil," *IPA Review* 4 (October 1970), pp. 9, 14.

72. *Jornal do Brasil,* August 27, 1972, cited in Ben Muneta, "Agent Exposes Secret Concentration Camp in Crenaque, Brazil," *Wassaja,* November 1973.

73. Cited in Don Bonafede, "Guards Turned Slaughterers of Brazil's Indians," *Washington Post,* June 9, 1966.

74. *Correio Brasiliense,* October 15, 1970, also cited in Adrian Cowell, *The Tribe That Hides from Man* (New York: Stein & Day, 1974), p. 205.

75. Norman Lewis, "Genocide: From Fire and Sword to Arsenic and Bullets—Civilization Has Sent Six Million Indians to Extinction," *Sunday Times* (London), February 23, 1969, p. 41.

76. "Visita del Doctor Galo Plaza al Instituto Indigenista Interamericano," *América Indígena* 28, no. 4 (October 1968), p. 1153.

77. *Foundation Directory* (New York: Foundation Research Center, 1970). That year, the Woodward Foundation also gave $150,000 to the Moody Bible Institute and $25,000 to the Evangelical Alliance Mission. The Woodward Foundation was controlled by R. Beavens Woodward, Jr. See New York state corporate filing for Woodward Foundation and obituary of Harper Woodward, *New York Times,* April 17, 1981.

42: In the Age of Genocide

1. Richard Arens, ed., *Genocide in Paraguay* (Philadelphia: Temple University Press, 1976).

2. Ibid., pp. 184–87.

3. Philip Knightly and Callin Lambert, "The Killing of a Colombian Indian Tribe," *Atlas* magazine (New York), January 1971, pp. 47–48.

4. Victor Daniel Bonilla, "The Destruction of the Colombian Indian Groups," in *The Situation of the Indian in South America*, ed. Walter Dostal (Geneva: World Council of Churches, 1972), p. 68.

5. *El Espectador* (Bogotá), January 29, 1968.

6. The concessions granted by the Lleres Restrepo government were huge: Cities Service was given four exploratory blocks totaling 967,342 acres of land. Texaco, which already owned producing fields to the south on both sides of the Colombia-Ecuador border, was granted six blocks totaling another 1.4 million acres.

7. Bonilla, "The Destruction of the Colombian Indian Groups," pp. 67–68.

8. *El Espectador,* February 27, 1970.

9. This essay and those that follow are in Dostal, ed., *The Situation of the Indian in South America.*

10. Confidential report by Colombian government investigators, drawing on interviews of Forest Zander, director of SIL's Colombia branch, January 1971. A copy is in the authors' possession.

11. "The Declaration of Barbados: For the Liberation of the Indians," in Dostal, ed., *The Situation of the Indian,* pp. 376–81.

12. See Edward Dozier's classic study of the Hano-Tewa people's use of language to resist assimilation by the Hopi people, "Resistance to Acculturation and Assimilation in an Indian Pueblo," *American Anthropologist* 53 (1951), pp. 56–66; and *Hane: A Tewa Indian Community in Arizona* (New York: Holt, Rinehart & Winston, 1966).

13. Perhaps the strongest criticism of the ambiguities of SIL's bilingual education program in Latin America and its admitted goal of Hispanization was by Bolivian anthropologist Xavier Albó. See his "The Future of Oppressed Languages in the Andes," in David L. Browman and Ronald A. Schwarz, eds., *Peasants, Primitives, and Proletariats: The Struggle for Identity in South America* (New York: Houston Publishers, 1979), pp. 267–88.

14. Wade Coggins, "Study Attracts Mission Work Among Latin American Indians," *Evangelical Missions Quarterly* (Summer 1972), p. 203.

15. Editorial, *Christianity Today*, October 8, 1971.

16. A. R. Tippett, "Taking a Hard Look at the Barbados Declaration," *Evangelical Mission Quarterly* (Summer 1972).

17. Quoted in Edward B. Fiske's article on Graham in the *New York Times Magazine,* June 8, 1969.

18. Ibid.

19. "La Misión de Bardesio ena Preparar la Llegada de B. Graham, en 1977," *El Día* (Mexico City), July 17, 1976; "Esta en México Nelson Bardesio, Afirma un Periódico Canadiense," *El Día*, July 11, 1976.

20. A. J. Langguth, *Hidden Terrors: The Truth About U.S. Police Operations in Latin America* (New York: Pantheon, 1978), pp. 234–39, 245–46. See also North American Congress on Latin America, *Report,* January 1974.

21. Langguth, *Hidden Terrors,* p. 252. Kidnapped by Tupamaros guerrillas in 1972, Bardesio confessed on tape, giving details of assassinations and of the Brazilian junta's and the CIA's ties to death squads then murdering Uruguayan senators, even across the border in Argentina.

22. "Dallas Minister Attends Briefings on World Policy," *Dallas Morning News,* August 12, 1971.

23. Mary Bishop, *Billy Graham: The Man and His Ministry* (New York: Grosset & Dunlap, 1978), pp. 54–57.

24. Ibid., p. 57.

25. The tribes were the Guararo and the Piratapuyo. See David Stoll, *Fishers of Men or Founders of Empires? The Wycliffe Bible Translators in Latin America* (London: Zed Press, 1982), pp. 175–76.

26. Ibid., p. 152; authors' interviews in Lima, 1976.

27. "Se inicia explotacíon petrolera en los Llanos," *El Tiempo* (Bogotá), March 12, 1971, pp. 1, 9.

28. Dostal, ed., *The Situation of the Indian,* pp. 392–96.

29. Map, "Areas de Colonizacíon Frente (a Regiones de Frontera Socio Economicas)," in *La Colonización en Colombia: Una Evaluación del Proceso* (Bogotá: Subgerencia de Ingenieria, Division de Colonizaciones, 1973). The Division of Colonization was an agency of INCORA, the Colombian Institute of Agrarian Reform. A copy of this map is in the authors' possession.

30. "Importante Convenio con la Continental Petroleum y la Shell," Inter Press Service, January 29, 1972.

31. *Peruvian Times,* May 25, 1973, and December 7, 1973, p. 13.

32. Dostal, ed., *The Situation of the Indian,* pp. 392 (map), 395.

33. Jonathan Kendell, "Peru: River of Expense, Trickle of Oil," *New York Times,* October 12, 1975.

34. *New York Times,* January 6, 1971, p. 4; January 11, 1971, p. 10; January 12, 1971, p. 14; "Bolivia: Brazil's Geopolitical Prisoner," North American Congress on Latin America, *Latin America and Empire Report* 8, no. 2 (February 1974), p. 25.

35. June Nash, "Ethnology in a Revolutionary Setting," in Michael A. Rynkiewich and James P. Spradley, eds., *Ethics and Anthropology: Dilemmas in Fieldwork* (New York: Wiley, 1976), p. 161.

36. *Presencia,* August 8, 1971.

37. *Visão,* May 24, 1971.

38. *Jornal do Brasil,* July 6, 1971.

39. Memorandum, William N. Radford (foreign affairs analyst, Congressional Research Service), November 14, 1974, p. 3, Hutchinson Papers, Box 295, "Rockefeller, Nelson—Activities in Latin America," Gerald R. Ford Library. See also *Village Voice,* October 24, 1974.

40. *Washington Post,* August 28, 29, 1971. The U.S. military attaché was Major Robert J. Lundin, U.S. Air Force.

41. *New York Times,* August 25, 1971, p. 3.

42. June Nash, *We Eat the Mines and the Mines Eat Us* (New York: Columbia University Press, 1979), p. xl.

43. Richard Patch's study, *Attitudes Toward Sex: Reproduction Patterns of Aymara and Quechua Speaking People* (Hanover, N.H.: West Coast American Service, 17, March 1970), took a Malthusian approach toward poverty, charging it was linked to *machismo* in Latin American culture and bestial "sexual activity, either heterosexual or homosexual" that produces an ideal male who "is unworried, pugnacious and violent." Patch was a veteran of Cornell University's Vicos project in Peru.

44. *Forjando un Mañana Mejor,* pamphlet (La Paz: n.p., 1975), probably published by Ministerio de Educación y Cultura, Instituto Lingüístico de Verano (SIL).

45. Shelton Davis, "Custer Is Alive and Well in Brazil," *Indian Historian* (Winter 1973), p. 12.

46. W. Jesco Von Puttkamer, "Brazil Protects Her Cintas Largas," *National Geographic* (September 1971), p. 421.

47. Davis, "Custer Is Alive."

48. James C. Hefley and Marti Hefley, *Uncle Cam* (Waco, Tex.: Word Books, 1974), p. 244.

49. Townsend did not back down, despite criticisms. See William Cameron Townsend, "The USSR as We Saw It," *Christian Herald,* October 1975.

50. Hefley and Hefley, *Uncle Cam,* p. 259.

51. "Biennial Report" (Mexico City: Wycliffe Bible Translators/SIL, May 1971), pp. 1–3.

43: CRITICAL CHOICES

1. *New York Times,* December 8, 1971.

2. *Foreign Affairs,* January 1972.

3. Deltec International, *Annual Report,* 1971.

4. Wayne G. Broehl, Jr., *United States Business Performance Abroad: The Case Study of the International Basic Economy Corporation* (Washington, D.C.: National Planning Association, 1968), p. 123.

5. Quoted in Joseph Persico, *The Imperial Rockefeller* (New York: Simon & Schuster, 1981), p. 140.

6. *Official Report of the New York Special Commission on Attica* (New York, 1972), pp. 325, xi.

7. Richard Reeves, "The Nationwide Search for Nelson Rockefeller," *New York,* September 2, 1974, p. 8.

8. Persico, *Imperial Rockefeller,* p. 243; *New York Times,* October 15, 1974, p. 1.

9. See Armando Uribe, *The Black Book of American Intervention in Chile* (Boston: Beacon Press, 1975), pp. 30–33.

10. Seymour Hersh, *The Price of Power* (New York: Summit, 1983), p. 317.

11. Ibid., p. 112. The official was Roger Morris, who earlier had worked on African affairs under Walter Rostow.

12. *New York Times,* December 4, 1974, p. 29. The witness was A. Russell Ash, who was head of staff security in the NSC.

13. Hersh, *The Price of Power,* pp. 462–63n.

14. Joseph B. Frantz, interview with Nelson Rockefeller, February 21, 1974, pp. 15–16, Oral History Project, Lyndon B. Johnson Library.

15. Elizabeth A. Cobbs, "Entrepreneurship as Diplomacy: Nelson Rockefeller and the Development of the Brazilian Capital Market," *Business History Review,* no. 1 (Spring 1989), p. 116.

16. *Dicionário Histórico-Biográfico Brasíleiro, 1930–1983* (Rio de Janeiro: Forensa Universitaria, 1984), p. 3047 (entry for Walther Moreira Salles).

17. Shelton H. Davis, *Victims of the Miracle* (Cambridge: Cambridge University Press, 1977), p. 82.

18. Quoted in Martin Mayer, *The Bankers* (New York: Ballantine Books, 1974), pp. 482–83.

19. Arthur Bernon Tourtellot, ed., *Toward the Well-Being of Mankind* (Garden City, N.Y.: Doubleday, 1964), p. 147. Columbia's Russian Institute was founded in 1946 with a $250,000 Rockefeller Foundation grant.

20. Robert J. Donovan, *Confidential Secretary: Ann Whitman's Twenty Years with Eisenhower and Rockefeller* (New York: Dutton, 1988), p. 190.

21. Persico, *Imperial Rockefeller,* p. 236.

22. Edward Teller, *Energy: A Plan for Action* (New York: Commission on Critical Choices, 1975), p. 28.

23. Nelson Rockefeller, *Vital Resources* (Lexington, Mass.: D. C. Heath, 1972), p. 44.

24. Rex Weyler, *Blood of the Land* (New York: Vintage Books, 1984), pp. 144–49.

25. Suzanne Gordon, *Black Mesa—The Angel of Death* (New York: John Day, 1973).

26. Jonathan M. Samet, Daniel M. Kutvirt, Richard J. Waxweiler, and Charles R. Key, "Uranium Mining and Lung Cancer in Navajo Men," *New England Journal of Medicine* 310, no. 23 (June 7, 1984).

27. Mark and Judith Miller, "The Politics of Energy vs. the American Indian," *Akwesasne Notes,* Spring 1979, p. 20.

28. See Jeff Gillenkirk and Mark Dowie, "The Great Indian Power Grab," *Mother Jones,* January 1982.

29. "An Empty Black Pit," *Akwesasne Notes,* Early Autumn 1973, p. 4.

30. Weyler, *Blood of the Land,* p. 71.

31. Marguerite Merington, *The Custer Story: The Life and Intimate Letters of General George A. Custer and His Wife Elizabeth* (New York: Devin-Adair, 1950), p. 234.

32. Weyler, *Blood of the Land,* p. 74.

33. Sixty-one violent deaths were documented at the reservation between March 1973 and March 1976, a rate of 170 per 100,000. Denver's murder rate in 1974 was 20.2 per 100,000; the U.S. average was 9.7. Bruce Johansen and Roberto Maestras, *Wasi'chu: The Continuing Indian Wars* (New York: Monthly Review Press, 1979), p. 83, citing *FBI Uniform Crime Reports* (Washington, D.C.: Government Printing Office, 1975).

34. Quoted in James D. Theberge and Roger W. Fontane, *Latin America: Struggle for Progress* (Lexington, Mass.: D. C. Heath, 1977), p. 23.

35. Robert Hartmann, interview with Nelson Rockefeller, December 2, 1977, p. 7, Cannon Papers, Box 35, Gerald Ford Library.

36. Persico, *Imperial Rockefeller,* p. 245.

37. Ibid., p. 10.

1. *New York Times,* October 19, 1974, p. 1. Loan to Henry Kissinger is described in Senate Committee on Rules and Administration, *Hearings, The Nomination of Nelson A. Rockefeller of New York to Be Vice President of the United States* (Washington, D.C.: Government Printing Office, 1974), p. 883; on Rockefeller's cronies, see ibid., pp. 529 ff., 634–40.

2. AIA: $1,626,751; Center for Inter-American Relations: $50,878; Government Affairs Foundation: $1,026,180; IBEC Research Institute: $140,416; IRI Research Institute: $60,251; Lincoln Center: $7,565; Museum of Modern Art: $2,563,420; Museum of Primitive Art: $6,592,179; Rockefeller Brothers Fund: $830,510; Rockefeller University: $13,463. Total: $12,911,613.

3. AIA: $1,626,751; Center for Inter-American Relations: $50,878; IBEC Research Institute: $140,416; IRI Research Institute: $60,251; U.S. Government–Latin American Mission: $760,481. Total: $2,638,777.

4. University of the Andes Foundation: $56,218; Pan American Foundation: $6,240; Puerto Rico Flood Relief Fund: $10,000; Puerto Rican-Hispanic Sports Council: $5,175; Nicaraguan Relief Fund: $25,535. Total: $103,168.

5. Totals are from a list in the *New York Times;* October 20, 1974, p. 66.

6. *New York Times,* October 13, 1974, p. 1.

7. *New York Times,* December 4, 1974, p. 29.

8. See House Committee on Armed Services, Report of the Special Subcommittee on Intelligence, *Inquiry into the Alleged Involvement of the Central Intelligence Agency in the Watergate and Ellsberg Matters* (Washington, D.C.: Government Printing Office, 1973).

9. Quoted in Carl Oglesby, *The Yankee and Cowboy War* (Kansas City, Kans.: Sheed Andrews & McMeel, 1976), p. 48.

10. Peter Wyden, *Bay of Pigs* (New York: Simon & Schuster, 1979), p. 300.

11. Quoted in Oglesby, *The Yankee and Cowboy War,* p. 48.

12. See Senate Select Committee to Study Governmental Operations with Respect to Intelligence Activities, Final Report, *Intelligence Activities and the Rights of Americans,* Book 2 (Washington, D.C.: Government Printing Office, 1976), pp. 111–15.

13. Cited in Oglesby, *The Yankee and Cowboy War,* p. 273.

14. Senate Intelligence Committee, *Intelligence Activities and the Rights of Americans,* p. 288, n85a.

15. Memorandum, William V. Broe to William Colby, "Subject: Potential Flap Activities," May 21, 1973, p. 60; the Central Intelligence Agency declassified a highly sanitized version of that report on August 15, 1975. A copy is in the authors' possession.

16. See Seymour Hersh, "Hunt Tells of Early Work for a CIA Domestic Unit," *New York Times,* December 31, 1974, p. 1.

17. See Tad Szulc, "Why Rockefeller Tried to Cover up the CIA Probe," *New York,* September 5, 1977.

18. The CIA's Morse Allen, who headed project ARTICHOKE, conducted "Manchurian Candidate" (i.e., programmed assassin) experiments in 1954. In December, the same month Rockefeller was appointed to the Special Group, Director Allen Dulles shifted the project to Sidney Gottlieb's MKULTRA team. Rockefeller was briefed on all covert operations by Dulles in March 1955 and subsequently approved the MKULTRA's use of a floor of Georgetown University Hospital's new research wing as a source of "human patients and volunteers for experimental use." See John D. Marks, *The Search for the "Manchurian Candidate"* (New York: Times Books, 1979), pp. 182–92 and 202–3n.

19. Michael Turner, interview with Nelson Rockefeller, December 21, 1977, p. 34, Cannon Papers, Box 35, Gerald Ford Library.

20. Ibid., pp. 35–36.

21. Rockefeller University was one of the CIA's illegal storage sites for the poisons. Botulism toxia was secretly stored for the CIA by Dr. William Beers; shellfish poison was kept by Drs. Bertil Hille, Martin Rizack, and Edward Reich. The continued storage was in violation not only of federal law, but of the Geneva Convention of 1925 and the recent joint Washington-Moscow-London Convention of 1972, signed by

President Nixon. For the 1972 convention's text and a list of collaborators in the CIA's illegal stockpiling, see Senate Select Committee to Study Governmental Operations with Respect to Intelligence Activities, *Hearings, Volume 1: Unauthorized Storage of Toxic Agents* (Washington, D.C.: Government Printing Office, 1976), Exhibits 10 and 11 (pp. 212–29).

22. Nicole Maxwell, *Witch Doctor's Apprentice* (Secaucus, N.J.: Carol Publishers, 1990), p. 368.

23. Senate Select Committee to Study Governmental Operations with Respect to Intelligence Activities, *Alleged Assassination Plots Involving Foreign Leaders* (Washington, D.C.: Government Printing Office, 1975), p. 338.

24. Ibid., p. 193n. See other references to J. C. King on pp. 81, 94, 97, 115, and 338. King signed a sworn affidavit of his testimony on July 29, 1975.

25. *Los Angeles Times,* January 8, 1977.

26. "Colby Reads Ten Names That Colby Sought to Omit," *New York Times,* November 21, 1975, p. 54.

27. See Adolf Berle, diary entry, September 21, 1956, Berle Papers, Franklin D. Roosevelt Library.

45: SIL Under Siege

1. Quoted in Jim Catelli, "The Church and the CIA," National Catholic News Service, June 13, 1975. See also Gary MacEoin, "U.S. Mission Efforts Threatened by CIA 'Dirty Tricks,'" *The St. Anthony Messenger,* March 1975.

2. See Ed Plowman, "Some Missionaries Help CIA," *The National Courier,* October 7, 1975, p. 4; James Robison, "Spy Role of Missionaries Told," *Chicago Tribune,* August 2, 1975, sec. 2, p. 11; Richard F. Rashke, "CIA Funded, Manipulated Missionaries," *National Catholic Reporter* 2 (August 1, 1975), p. 1.

3. See David Mutchlin, *The Church as a Political Factor in Latin America* (New York: Praeger, 1971).

4. Quoted in Rashke, "CIA Funded Missionaries."

5. "Proposal for Socio-Linguistic and Education Research Project," Academy for Educational Development (La Paz, 1976), p. 2. A copy is in the authors' possession.

6. Ibid., p. 7.

7. Ibid., p. 21.

8. James C. Hefley and Edward E. Plowman, *Washington: Christians in the Corridors of Power* (Wheaton, Ill.: Tyndale House, 1975), pp. 155–56.

9. Ibid., p. 63.

10. Quoted in Laurie Nadel and Hesh Wiener, "Would You Sell a Computer to Hitler?" *Computer Decisions* (February 1977), p. 25.

11. Jeff Stein, "CIA's 'Secret Army' Moves from Thailand to Bolivia," *Latinamerica Press* (Lima), Pacific News Service, December 21, 1978, pp. 7–8.

12. Hefley and Plowman, *Washington,* p. 157.

13. Quoted in Stein, "CIA's 'Secret Army.'"

14. "Slave Camp Denounced in Bolivia," *El Excelsior* (La Paz), June 23, 1977.

15. Gerhard Pieters, "Bolivia Here We Come," *Sunday Times* (London), March 12, 1978.

16. "Union Oil Venture in Bolivian Jungle Is First Under New Hydrocarbon Law," *Business Latin America,* April 5, 1973, p. 112; "Getty Oil Unit Gets Stake in Texaco-Bolivian Contract," *Wall Street Journal,* August 12, 1976, p. 15.

17. See Jürgen Riester, "Indians of Eastern Bolivia: Aspects of Their Present Situation," IWIGIA Document No. 18 (Copenhagen: International Work Group in Indigenous Affairs, 1975), pp. 32–43; "Hoy es el Día de la Integración Nacional," *El Diario* (La Paz), October 18, 1976, p. 1.

18. Authors' interview with Ronald D. Olson, Tumi Chucua, Beni, Bolivia, October 19, 1976. Olson was quite expansive about his beliefs about the Cold War, Guevara, Allende, the lack of democracy in Bolivia, and that "man is inherently evil, not good." Unfortunately, as with almost all the interviews conducted with SIL over the years, the space requirements of this book prohibit an exposition of Olson's particular views.

19. *El Excelsior,* June 23, 1977.

20. Riester, "Indians of Eastern Bolivia," p. 55.

21. These denials were also heard by the authors during their visit to an SIL team working with Africans in a Bantustan near Johannesburg, South Africa, 1978.

22. Roger Michael, "Missionaries Get 'Miracle' Copters," *Charlotte Observer,* April 15, 1974.

23. Stein, "CIA's 'Secret Army.'"

24. *Washington Star,* January 8, 1976.

25. Ibid.

26. During their six months of travels in 1976 through five Amazon basin countries (Ecuador, Peru, Bolivia, Brazil, and Colombia), two Central American countries (Guatemala and Panama), and Mexico, the authors heard and read criticisms of SIL from a wide range of sources, including Indian leaders and peasants, university professors in various fields, ethnologists, botanists and anthropologists in the field, Red Cross officials, attorneys, businessmen, labor organizers, soldiers, journalists, government officials, and missionaries. There was also praise for SIL from many of the same types of sources, particularly military officers, businessmen, Fundamentalist Christian missionaries, and government officials. Most of the latter, however, expressed their opinions as defenses of SIL against a much wider base of opposition, and this was reflected to some degree in the press in 1975 in most of these countries (with the notable exceptions of Guatemala and Brazil, where ultrarightists, military dictatorships, and death squads made open criticism less prudent).

In Peru, the forty-four articles and editorials containing criticisms of SIL or calls for its expulsion were printed during the period November 19 to December 16 in *El Comercio, La Crónica, El Expreso, La Prensa,* and *El Correo,* Peru's leading sources of printed news and opinion. See particularly *El Correo,* December 7 (a number of articles in the newspaper's Sunday supplement, "Suceso") and three earlier denunciations on September 28 and October 9 and 17; editorials in *La Crónica,* November 29 ("SIL and Ideological Penetration"), December 2 ("The Ideology Which SIL Transmits"), December 7 ("Native Communities Face the SIL"), and December 24; *El Expreso,* December 15; *El Comercio,* November 26, as well as earlier denunciations on February 29 and March 1; "Professors and Students of Linguistics of the U.N.M.S.M. to Public Opinion," Lima, September 22 (mimeographed statement); "Critique of the Work of the Summer Institute of Linguistics," San Marcos University, Department of Linguistics, October 2 (mimeographed statement); and *Latinamerica Press* (Lima), December 18.

In Mexico, see *El Excelsior,* April 22, 1976 (most criticisms in Mexico came later in the decade). In Bolivia, see Jürgen Riester, "Indians of Eastern Bolivia: Aspects of Their Present Situation," IWIGIA Document No. 18 (Copenhagen: International Work Group for Indigenous Affairs, 1975). In Panama, see *Prensa Latina,* September 24, 1975, and "Acerca del Instituto Lingüístico de Verano," April 1976, position paper by the Frente de Trabajadores de la Cultura (Cultural Workers Front). The latter is an analysis that describes SIL as a "case of cultural penetration"; the position paper was approved by the Second Central American Sociology Congress held in Panama City that month; the full text was published in *El Día* (Mexico City), May 29, 1976. In Colombia, see *El Puebla* (Cali), October 26, 1975; *Alternativa* (Bogotá), June 30, 1975; and the debates in the Colombian Congress in *Anals de Congreso,* October 4 (p. 940), 15 (pp. 953, 957–58), 21 (pp. 9, 14, 15, 21, 991–95), and November 20 (pp. 927, 938–43, 950–58, 990–98, 1169–1182, and 1249–1250).

In Ecuador, see Gonzalo Oviedo, "La Educación Bilingüe," *El Mercurio,* February 1975; "Denuncian que Instituto Lingüístico Busca Dividir a Comunidades Indígenas," *Ultima Noticias* (Quito), February 17, 1975; "Misioneros en el Ecuador: Científicos o Colonialistas?" *Nueva* (Quito), no. 19, May 1975, pp. 56–64; *El Pionero* (Santo Domingo de los Colorados), April 12, 1975; and "Misiones Protestantes para el Impero: El Caso del Instituto Lingüístico de Verano," Asociación Escuela del Departamento de Antropología, Pontífica Universidad Católica del Ecuador, Quito, April 1975 (this last is essentially a translation of the report on SIL published earlier by the North American Congress on Latin America; ironically, the chairman of NACLA's board, Princeton theologian Richard Shaull, had once been considered by Cam as a possible contact for support for SIL).

Many, but not all, of the above sources are also cited, with some recounting of the stories, in David Stoll, *Fishers of Men or Founders of Empires? The Wycliffe Bible Translators in Latin America* (London: Zed Press, 1982), in chapters 6 and 7, pp. 165–236.

27. Philip Agee, *Inside the Company* (Harmondsworth, Eng.: Penguin, 1975), p. 192.

28. Seymour Hersh, *The Price of Power* (New York: Summit, 1983), p. 269.

29. Agee, *Inside the Company*, p. 614.

30. Cable, AMEMBASSY BOGOTA (Viron Vaky) to SECSTATE [Henry Kissinger], October 14, 1975. Declassified. A copy is in the authors' possession.

31. Ibid.

32. Cable, AMEMBASSY BOGOTA (Viron Vaky) to SECSTATE, November 20, 1975. Declassified. Cited in Stoll, *Fishers of Men or Founders of Empires?*, p. 184.

33. Cable, AMEMBASSY LIMA (Dean) to SECSTATE, November 20, 1975; cited in ibid., p. 204.

34. Dean had been the State Department's liaison to the Department of the Army's assistant chief of staff for intelligence in 1961, where the director of intelligence for the Joint Chiefs of Staff was General Robert Breitweiser, the same general who later paid a visit to Peru around the time the U.S. Marine Corps helicopters were sent into the Peruvian Amazon in 1964. That year, Dean was in neighboring Brazil working as a political officer in Brasília during the CIA/Pentagon-backed military coup. It was Dean who reported President Goulart's hurried flight in and out of the capital and Darcy Ribeiro's brave stand as brief head of Goulart's besieged and abandoned government.

35. Interview with Stefano Varese, Oaxaca, Mexico, July 1976.

36. The leading voices of the Peruvian critique were Marcel D'Ans, anthropologist at the Manu National Park (a reserve set up for the Machiguenga Indians), and linguist Alfredo Torero. See Marcel D'Ans, "Encounter in Peru," in Peter Aaby and Soren Hvalkof, eds., *Is God an American? An Anthropological Perspective on the Missionary Work of the Summer Institute of Linguistics* (Copenhagen: International Work Group for Indigenous Affairs/London: Survival International, 1981), pp. 148–62, and Torero's comments in *El Expreso* (Lima), January 31 and February 6, 1972.

37. "CIA: We'll Continue to Use Clergy," *Miami Herald*, December 13, 1975, p. 2-AW.

38. David Butler, *The Fall of Saigon* (New York: Simon & Schuster, 1985), p. 58.

39. Quoted in Carolyn Paine Miller, *Captured!* (Chappaqua, N.Y.: Christian Herald Books, 1977).

40. Butler, *The Fall of Saigon*, p. 53.

41. Quoted in Miller, *Captured!*, p. 34.

42. Philip Buchen, Counsel to President Ford, to Senator Mark Hatfield, November 5, 1975. A copy is in the authors' possession.

43. Nelson understood that, bitterly describing the appointment as having "given George Bush the deep six by putting him in the CIA." Robert Hartmann, interview with Nelson Rockefeller, December 2, 1988, p. 42, Cannon Papers, Box 35, Gerald Ford Library.

44. Quoted in Miller, *Captured!*, p. 266.

45. Quoted in ibid., p. 273.

46. See Kenneth A. Briggs, "Churches Angered by Disclosures, Seek to Ban Further CIA Use of Missionaries in Intelligence Work," *New York Times*, January 29, 1976.

47. *Washington Star,* January 8, 1976.

46: The Betrayal

1. *New York Times,* December 4, 1974, p. 29.

2. *New York Times*, August 29, 1975.

3. Quoted in Peter Lisagor, "The Rockefeller Nod," *New York Post*, June 17, 1975.

4. Quoted in Robert J. Donovan, *Confidential Secretary: Ann Whitman's Twenty Years with Eisenhower and Rockefeller* (New York: Dutton, 1988), pp. 187–88.

5. Robert Hartmann, interview with Nelson Rockefeller, December 2, 1977, p. 37, Cannon Papers, Box 35, Gerald Ford Library.

6. Bruce Johansen and Roberto Maestras, *Wasi'chu: The Continuing Indian Wars* (New York: Monthly Review Press, 1979), p. 128; *Rapid City Journal*, April 24, 1977.

7. Rex Weyler, *Blood of the Land* (New York: Vintage Books, 1984), p. 177; Ron Ridenhour with Arthur Lublow, "Bringing the War Home," *New Times* 5 (November 1975), no. 11, p. 18.

8. Hartmann, interview with Nelson Rockefeller, pp. 20–21.

9. Ibid., p. 21.

10. Quoted in Joseph Persico, *The Imperial Rockefeller* (New York: Simon & Schuster, 1981), p. 272.

11. Hartmann, interview with Nelson Rockefeller, p. 22.

12. Trevor Armbrister, interview with Nelson Rockefeller, October 21, 1977, pp. 20–21, Gerald Ford Library.

13. Ibid., p. 26.

14. John Stockwell, *In Search of Enemies* (London: Futura Publications, 1979), p. 19. Stockwell was chief of the CIA's Angola Task Force.

15. Quoted in Persico, *Imperial Rockefeller*, p. 271.

16. Armbrister, interview with Nelson Rockefeller, pp. 37–38.

17. Michael Turner, interview with Nelson Rockefeller, December 21, 1977, p. 45, and Hartmann, interview with Nelson Rockefeller, pp. 44–45, Gerald Ford Library.

18. Hartmann, interview with Nelson Rockefeller, pp. 44–45.

19. Ibid., p. 41.

20. Ibid., pp. 67–68.

47: The Great Tribulation

1. AMEMBASSY (Robert Dean) to SECSTATE (Kissinger), May 20, 1976. Declassified; a copy is in the authors' possession.

2. *Correo* (Lima), April 26, 1976; *La Prensa* (Lima), May 25, 1976.

3. Jerry Elder to W. C. Townsend, December 4, 1962, Townsend Archives.

4. Cables, Robert Dean to Henry Kissinger, June 2, April 28, 1976, released under the Freedom of Information Act to David Stoll and quoted in his *Fishers of Men or Founders of Empires? The Wycliffe Bible Translators in Latin America* (London: Zed Press, 1982), p. 206.

5. See ibid., p. 204, including letter from Lambert Anderson to Jimmy Carter, June 7, 1977.

6. Cable, Robert Dean to Henry Kissinger, March 10, 1976, June 21, 1976, in ibid.

7. *In Other Words*, March 1977, p. 2.

8. In the fall of 1976, the authors found SIL translators working feverishly at the Pôrto Velho base with New Tribes missionaries preparing for the glorious advance for the Lord. A year later, the military junta ordered SIL's expulsion from the tribes by December 1977.

9. Napoleon A. Chagnon, *Yanomamö: The Fierce People* (New York: Holt, Rinehart & Winston, 1968).

10. Napoleon Chagnon, Philip le Quesne, and James M. Cook, "Yanomamö Hallucinogens: Anthropological, Botanical, and Chemical Findings," *Current Anthropology* 12 (February 1971), no. 1, p. 72n.

11. *In Other Words*, February 1977, p. 5.

12. *O Estado de São Paulo*, March 1, 1975.

13. Quoted in *O Estado de São Paulo*, February 8, 1975.

14. *Manchete*, July 24, 1976, pp. 66–77.

15. Authors' interview with Yasushi Toyotomi, sheriff of FUNAI, Pôrto Velho, Brazil, October 22, 1976.

16. *Translation*, September–October 1973, p. 6.

17. Authors' interview with David Judd, business manager, SIL base, Pôrto Velho, Brazil, October 22, 1976.

18. Ibid.

19. Authors' interview with William Cameron Townsend, Waxhaw, N.C., September 1977.

20. Miguel Chase Sardi, "The Present Situation of the Indians in Paraguay," in *The Situation of the Indian in South America*, ed. Walter Dostal (Geneva: World Council of Churches, 1972), p. 184.

21. Quoted in Mark Münzel, "The Aché Indians, Genocide in Paraguay," in Richard Arens, ed., *Genocide in Paraguay* (Philadelphia: Temple University Press, 1976), p. 10.

22. *New York Times,* January 20, 1975, p. 41.

23. "Pamela Woolworth in Stock Deal for Cattle Venture in Paraguay," *New York Times*, Papers of Nelson A. Rockefeller, Personal File, Countries series, Box 55, Folder 499, Rockefeller Family Archives, Rockefeller Archive Center, Tarrytown, New York.

24. Sardi, "The Present Situation of the Indians in Paraguay," pp. 175, 203–5, 210–11.

25. *AIA Report*, April–June 1967, p. 8, American International Association for Economic and Social Development (AIA) Archives, Quarterly Series, Box 15, Rockefeller Archive Center. For more background on AIA's role in bringing Brazil into colonization schemes and expanded agribusiness in eastern Paraguay, see *AIA Quarterly Reports* for January–March and October–December 1964, January–March 1965, and July–September 1966; and Walter Crawford (AIA), "Observations and Suggestions on Rural Development in Paraguay," report to John P. Wiley (U.S. AID Director for Paraguay), April 21, 1963, and letter of May 13, 1963; Crawford to Flor Brennan (AIA, New York Office), July 25, 1963; Walter Crawford, "Agricultural Production and Credit in Paraguay," memorandum, September 1963; Crawford to John Camp (AIA, New York Office), September 23, 1963; all in AIA Archives, Box 8, Folder 67, Rockefeller Archive Center.

26. Mark Münzel, "Manhunt," in Arens, ed., *Genocide in Paraguay*, p. 33.

27. Norman Lewis, "The Camp at Cecilio Baez," in ibid., p. 62.

28. Quoted in *New York Times*, March 7, 1975, and cited in Chaim F. Shatan, "Genocide and Bereavement," in Arens, ed., *Genocide in Paraguay*, p. 102.

29. Ignatius Suharno and Kenneth L. Pike, eds., *From Baudi to Indonesian* (Irian Jaya: Cenderawasih University, Summer Institute of Linguistics, 1976).

30. *International Petroleum Encyclopedia, 1983* (Tulsa, Okla.: PennWell Publishing Company, 1983), p. 236.

31. *New York Times,* October 24, 1974, p. 20.

32. *New York Times,* December 31, 1976, p. 6.

33. *Wall Street Journal,* July 18, 1977, p. 8.

34. Quoted in William Shawcross, *The Shah's Last Ride* (New York: Simon & Schuster, 1988), p. 141.

35. *New York Times,* August 24, 1977, p. 17.

36. Ibid., March 9, 1978, sec. II, p. 9.

37. Shawcross, *The Shah's Last Ride,* p. 28.

38. Ibid., p. 285, citing documents produced by the Iran Central Bank in December 1979.

39. IBEC 10-K-1 filing, Securities and Exchange Commission. Rodman Rockefeller's salary was $106,667 in 1979.

40. Mary and Laurance Rockefeller, "How South America Guards Her Green Legacy: Parks, Plans, and People," *National Geographic*, January 1967, p. 104. Laurance conveyed to readers some sense of the global scope assumed so casually by corporate conservationists like the Rockefellers, when he recalled their first encounter with the Iguaçu Falls: "When Mary and I saw it, we exclaimed simultaneously, 'The Congo!' "

41. Quoted in Joseph Persico, *The Imperial Rockefeller* (New York: Simon & Schuster, 1981), p. 154.

42. *Dallas Morning News,* February 17, 1979.

48: Thy Will Be Done

1. "Philippine Diplomat Explains Why Group Won Award," *Charlotte News,* November 3, 1973.

2. Quoted in Walden Bello and Severina Rivera, eds., *The Logistics of Repression: The Role of U.S. Assistance in Consolidating the Martial Law Regime in the Philippines* (Washington, D.C.: Friends of the Filipino People, 1977), p. 55.

3. Jon Landaburu, "The Double-Edged Sword: The SIL in Colombia," *Survival International Review*, cited in David Stoll, *Fishers of Men or Founders of Empires? The Wycliffe Bible Translators in Latin America* (London: Zed Press, 1982), p. 252.

4. Elmer F. Bennett, "Classified Report of the United States Delegation to the Fourth Inter-American Indian

Conference, Guatemala City, Guatemala, May 16 to May 25, 1959," June 9, 1959, Papers of Elmer F. Bennett, Box 6, "Guatemala Trip, Aug. 12–29," Dwight D. Eisenhower Library. See also Edward A. Jameson, "The Indian Conference Hear from Some Guatemalan Indians," memorandum of May 21, 1959, enclosure in ibid.; and *Boletín Indigenista* 19, no. 2 (June 1959), p. 67.

5. Guillermo Bonfil Batalla, ed., *Indianidad y Descolonización in América Latina: Documentos de la Segunda Reunion de Barbados* (Mexico City: Nueva Imagen, 1979), pp. 397–400.

6. Inter-American Indian Institute, *Anuario Indigenista* (Mexico City: 1980), pp. 219–20.

7. *Newsweek,* October 25, 1976, p. 70.

8. "Evangelical Vote Is a Major Target," *New York Times,* June 29, 1980.

9. "Thunder on the Right: An Unholy War Breaks Out over Evangelical Politics," *People*, October 13, 1980, p. 34.

10. *Texas Business,* December 1979.

11. *IWIGIA Newsletter,* no. 19 (June 1978), pp. 2–6.

12. *Moody's Industrial Manual* (New York: Frederic Hatch & Company, 1977), p. 3898.

13. Philip Berryman, "The Color of Blood Will Never Be Forgotten," in *The Religious Roots of Rebellion: Christians in Central American Revolutions* (Maryknoll, N.Y.: Orbis Press, 1984), p. 178.

14. Walter Crawford to John Camp, September 21, 1961; see also "Latin American contact list," AIA Archives, general series, Box 7, Folder 61, Rockefeller Archive Center, Tarrytown, New York.

15. Supervivencia Infantil, Minestero de Salud (Ministry of Health), *Plan de Accion 1987* (Guatemala City: Minestero de Salud, 1986).

16. For a comprehensive overview of the plight of Guatemala's Indians during this period, see Luisa Frank and Philip Wheaton, *Indian Guatemala: Path to Liberation: The Role of Christians in the Indian Process* (Washington, D.C.: EPICA, 1984).

17. Stephen Schlesinger and Stephen Kinzer, "Guatemala's Election," *New York Times,* January 28, 1982, p. A23.

18. *Bible World* 77 (September–October 1985), p. 8.

19. José Castaneda, "Dos Justos Homenajes," *Guatemala Indígena* 17, nos. 1–2 (1982).

20. Christine Krueger, Ph.D., *Security and Development Conditions in the Guatemalan Highlands* (Washington, D.C.: Washington Office on Latin America, 1985), p. 1; Steven Drier, "Insurgency in Guatemala," *Focus,* July 1985, pp. 2–9.

21. "A Christian Soldier," *Newsweek*, December 13, 1982, p. 57; also, in the same issue of *Newsweek*, "Beans-and-Bullets Politics," pp. 56–58, and "Reagan's Friendly Persuasion," pp. 53–55; "Reagan Promises to Provide Brazil a $1.2 Billion Loan," *New York Times*, December 2, 1982; and "Reagan, the Discreet Suitor, Finds Brazil Willing," *New York Times*, December 3, 1982.

22. Stoll, *Fishers of Men or Founders of Empires?,* p. 3.

23. Authors' interviews with confidential sources, Bogotá, Colombia, December 1976.

24. Jorge G. Castañeda, *Utopia Unarmed: The Latin American Left After the Cold War* (New York: Alfred A. Knopf, 1993), p. 116.

25. *Chicago Tribune,* February 16, 1982, sec. 3, p. 1.

26. See Don Richardson, "Who Really Killed Chet Bitterman?" *Mission Frontier,* April 3, 1981, pp. 1, 4–7.

27. Billy Graham, speech at Wycliffe Bible Translators Golden Jubilee Rally, Anaheim Convention Center, Anaheim, California, May 9, 1981. Cited in Stoll, *Fishers of Men or Founders of Empires?,* p. 273.

28. Interview by Gerard Colby of Kenneth Pike and other SIL anthropologists and linguists, International Linguistics Center, Dallas, June 29, 1992.

29. Betty Blair, "Aftermath of a Martyrdom," *Charisma,* May 1982, p. 31.

30. *El Comercio* (Bogotá), June 27, 1981.

31. *In Other Words,* February 1981, p. 6.

32. Mary Helen Spooner, "Misery in Bolivia's Mines," *Financial Times,* December 30, 1984.

33. *National Reporter,* Winter 1986, p. 19; *Time,* December 4, 1989, p. 51; *Progressive,* May 1989, p. 8; Richard Alan White, *The Morass: United States Intervention in Central America* (New York: Harper & Row, 1984), p. 159.

34. *Maryknoll Magazine,* October 1980, pp. 12–15. Also cited in Stoll, *Fishers of Men or Founders of Empires?,* p. 209.

35. *Program for Agricultural and Craft Development for the Inhabitants of Chimaltenango Harmed by the Violence* (Chimaltenango, Guatemala: St. Anne's Parish, 1986), cited in *Who Pays the Price? The Cost of War in the Guatemalan Highlands* (Washington, D.C.: Washington Office on Latin America, 1988), p. 37.

36. "Eleven Beheaded in Guatemala," *Washington Post,* June 7, 1982 (of the eleven, ten were women); John Dinges, "Political Killings Are Continuing in North Guatemalan Countryside," *Washington Post,* July 17, 1982; Alan Riding, "Guatemalan Refugees Flood Mexico," *New York Times,* August 18, 1982; Gordon D. Mott, "Refugees Who Fled to Mexico Tell of Army's Atrocities," *San Jose Mercury News,* August 22, 1982; Okland Ross, "Tales of Horror Haunt Camps," *Toronto Globe,* August 22, 1982.

37. William Wallace, "Missionaries with a Mission?" *The Nation,* May 30, 1981.

38. Raymond Bonner, "Guatemala Junta's Chief Says God Guides Him," *New York Times,* June 10, 1982.

39. Raymond Bonner, "Guatemala Leader Reports Aid Plan," *New York Times,* May 20, 1982, p. A6.

40. Donna Eberwine, "To Ríos Montt, with Love Lift," *The Nation,* February 26, 1983, p. 239.

41. Marlisle Simons, "Guatemalans Are Adding a Few Twists to 'Pacification,'" *New York Times,* September 12, 1982, Section IV, p. 3.

42. Eberwine, "To Ríos Montt, with Love Lift," p. 238, quoting a State Department official whose statement had been reported in *The Forerunner,* monthly newsletter of Marantha Campus Ministries, which was represented at the State Department briefing.

43. Raymond Bonner, "Behind the Guatemala Coup: A General Takes Over and Changes Its Course," *New York Times,* March 29, 1982.

44. Bonner, "Guatemala Leader Reports Aid Plan.'"

45. Simons, "Guatemalans Are Adding a Few Twists to 'Pacification.'"

46. Eberwine, "To Ríos Montt, with Love Lift," p. 239.

47. Quoted in Raymond Bonner, "Guatemala Enlists Religion in Battle," *New York Times,* July 12, 1982.

48. Cited in Frank and Wheaton, *Indian Guatemala,* pp. 78–79.

49. *Who Pays the Price?,* p. 41.

50. Cultural Survival, Inc., and Anthropology Resource Center, *Voices of the Survivors: The Massacre at Finca San Francisco, Guatemala* (Cambridge, Mass.: Cultural Survival, Inc., 1983), p. 86; *Special Update, Guatemala: The Roots of Revolution* (Washington, D.C.: Washington Office on Latin America, February 1983), p. 15; "Special Report on Guatemala," *Survival International,* August 1982.

51. *Who Pays the Price?,* p. 71.

52. Simons, "Guatemalans Are Adding a Few Twists to 'Pacification.'" The *New York Times* reporter wrote, "The country's traditionally conservative Conference of Bishops noted May 27 that 'never in our history have such extremes been reached, with the assassinations now falling into the category of genocide.'"

53. "Guatemalan Vows to Aid Democracy," *New York Times,* December 6, 1982, p. A12.

54. Eberwine, "To Ríos Montt, with Love Lift," p. 239.

55. "Guatemalan Vows to Aid Democracy," p. A12.

56. *New York Times,* February 17, 1983, p. A8.

57. *New York Times,* March 15, 1983, p. A12.

58. Victor Perera, *Unfinished Conquest: The Guatemalan Tragedy* (Berkeley, Calif.: University of California Press, 1993), pp. 91–92.

59. Quoted in James C. Hefley, "Cam Townsend, 1896–1982," *Christianity Today,* May 21, 1982.

60. Nelson's battered company was finally given safe haven and his son was given a seat on the board of a major player in the corporate world when IBEC was bought by Booker McConnell, Ltd., the English firm that had built upon royalties from Agatha Christie mysteries to become a $1.5 billion conglomerate.

61. *Wall Street Journal,* July 1, 1980, p. 9.

62. *Dicionário Histórico-Biográfico Brasileiro, 1930–1983* (Rio de Janeiro: Forensa Universitaria, 1984), p. 3047.

63. *Visão,* August 28, 1972, pp. 258, 260.

64. *JAARS Prayerline*, Waxhaw, N.C., Jungle Aviation and Radio Services, Inc., December 1984.

65. Eliot King, "Serving the Spiritual," *Micro Discovery,* August 1983.

66. The $100,000 donation was made in 1980 by the Pew Memorial Trust. *Foundation Grant Index* (New York: The Foundation Center and Columbia University Press, 1982).

67. Lydia Chavez, "Argentines Riot Against Rockefeller," *New York Times,* January 15, 1986.

68. In 1991, one of Brazil's leading indigenous rights organizations, People of the Forest Alliance, issued a scathing attack on Cultural Survival's Rainforest Marketing program. "Cultural Survival reveals that 40% of its profits from sales of products would go back to grassroots organizations. We have not seen any returns." Cultural Survival's director of finance, Walter Gates, explained why. "We are applying the profits to the loan"—a $100,000 loan given to the rubber gatherers' cooperative in 1990 to set up its nut-shelling and processing factory. "From time to time, the producers have been a little unhappy with us," he said. "So we invited [one of them] up here to see for himself some of the problems we have in marketing the products." One of CSE's major problems, explains CSE founder Jason Clay, is that the cooperative is being forced to become competitive on the world market. A "short term subsidy" from CSE—the price it paid for the co-ops' nuts—"could easily wane in a few years" so "it is important to find new markets." Inevitably, CSE began looking to "Fortune 500 Companies" for marketing its nontimber forest products. See Charlotte Dennett Colby, "Has Rainforest Crunch Turned Sour?" *Toward Freedom,* October 1992.

69. Convention on the Prevention and Punishment of the Crime of Genocide, 1951, Articles III and IV.

70. Davison L. Bulhoo, *Enough Is Enough: Dear Mr. Camdessus . . . Open Letter of Resignation to the Managing Director of the International Monetary Fund* (New York: Apex Press, 1990), pp. 2, 11.

71. "Indians Tell Pope They Will Protest Columbus Parties," *St. Albans Messenger,* October 17, 1991.

SELECTED BIBLIOGRAPHY

BOOKS

Aaby, Peter, and Soren Hvalkof, eds. *Is God an American? An Anthropological Perspective on the Missionary Work of the Summer Institute of Linguistics.* Copenhagen: International Work Group for Indigenous Affairs; London: Survival International, 1981.

Abels, Jules. *The Rockefeller Billions.* New York: Macmillan, 1965.

Agee, Philip. *Inside the Company.* Harmondsworth, Eng.: Penguin Books, 1975.

Agee, Philip, and Louis Wolf, eds. *Dirty Work: The CIA in Western Europe.* Secaucus, N.J.: Lyle Stuart, 1978.

Alsop, Stuart. *Nixon and Rockefeller.* Garden City, N.Y.: Doubleday, 1960.

Anderson, Thomas P. *Matanza.* Lincoln, Neb.: University of Nebraska Press, 1971.

Arens, Richard, ed. *Genocide in Paraguay.* Philadelphia: Temple University Press, 1976.

Arruda, Marcos, Herbet de Souza, and Carlos Afonso. *Multinationals and Brazil.* Toronto: Brazilian Studies, 1975.

Artola, Armando. *¡Subversion!* Lima: Editorial Juridica, 1976.

Asad, Talal, ed. *Anthropology and the Colonial Encounter.* Atlantic Highlands, N.J.: Humanities Press, 1975.

Atlas de Rondônia. Rio de Janeiro: IBGE, 1975.

Baer, Werner. *Industrialization and Economic Development in Brazil.* Homewood, Ill.: Richard D. Irwin, Inc., 1965.

Beals, Carleton. *Banana Gold.* Philadelphia: J. P. Lippincott Company, 1932.

———. *Lands of the Dawning Morrow.* New York: Bobbs-Merrill, 1948.

Beekman, John, and James C. Hefley. *Peril by Choice.* Grand Rapids, Mich.: Zondervan, 1968.

Bell, Corell. *Negotiations from Strength: A Study in the Policies of Power.* London: Chatto & Windus, 1962.

Bello, Walden, and Severina Rivera, eds. *The Logistics of Repression: The Role of U.S. Assistance in Consolidating the Martial Law Regime in the Philippines.* Washington, D.C.: Friends of the Filipino People, 1977.

Berg, Dorothy. *American Policy and the Chinese Revolution, 1925–28.* New York: Macmillan, 1947.

Berle, Adolf. *Navigating the Rapids.* New York: Harcourt Brace Jovanovich, 1973.

Berryman, Philip. "The Color of Blood Will Never Be Forgotten," in *The Religious Roots of Rebellion: Christians in Central American Revolutions.* Maryknoll, N.Y.: Orbis Press, 1984.

Bishop, Mary. *Billy Graham: The Man and His Ministry.* New York: Grosset & Dunlap, 1978.

Black, Jan Knippers. *United States Penetration of Brazil.* Philadelphia: University of Pennsylvania Press, 1977.

Blair, John M. *The Control of Oil.* New York: Pantheon, 1976.

Blaufarb, Douglas A. *The Counterinsurgency Era: U.S. Doctrine and Performance, 1950 to the Present.* New York: Free Press, 1977.

Blomberg, Rolf. *The Naked Aucas.* London: Allen & Unwin, 1956.

Blum, William. *The CIA: A Forgotten History.* London: Zed Books, 1980.

Bodard, Lucien. *Green Hell.* New York: Outerbridge & Dientsfrey, 1971.

Bodley, John H. *Victims of Progress.* Palo Alto, Calif.: Mayfield Publishing, 1982.

Bonfil Batalla, Guillermo, ed. *Indianidad y Descolonización in América Latina: Documentos de la Segunda Reunion de Barbados.* Mexico City: Nueva Imagen, 1979.

Bonilla, Victor Daniel. *Servants of God or Masters of Men?* Harmondsworth, Eng.: Penguin, 1972.

Borkin, Joseph. *The Crime and Punishment of I.G. Farben.* New York: Free Press, 1978.

Borsage, Robert, and John Marks. *The CIA File.* New York: Grossman Publishers, 1976.

Boulton, Roger E. *Defense Purchases and Regional Growth.* Washington, D.C.: Brookings Institution, 1966.

Bowart, William. *Operation Mind Control.* New York: Dell, 1978.

Branford, Susan, and Oriel Glock. *The Last Frontier: Fighting over Land in the Amazon.* London: Zed Books, 1985.

Brazil: A New Economic Survey. New York: First National City Bank, 1974.

Broehl, Wayne G., Jr. *United States Business Performance Abroad: The Case Study of the International Basic Economy Corporation.* Washington, D.C.: National Planning Association, 1968.

Browman, David L., and Ronald A. Schwarz, eds. *Peasants, Primitives, and Proletariats: The Struggle for Identity in South America.* New York: Houston Publishers, 1979.

Brown, Judith. *Gandhi and Civil Disobedience.* Cambridge: Cambridge University Press, 1977.

Brown, Michael F., and Eduardo Fernández. *War of Shadows: The Struggle for Utopia in the Peruvian Amazon.* Berkeley, Calif.: University of California Press, 1991

Brown, William A. "The Protestant Rural Movement in China, 1920–37," in *American Missionaries in China.* Cambridge, Mass.: Harvard University Press, 1966.

Buckingham, Jamie. *Into the Glory.* Plainfield, N.J.: Logos, 1974.

Butler, David. *The Fall of Saigon.* New York: Simon & Schuster, 1985.

Calzada, José L. Vasquez. *El Desbalance Entre Recursos de Poblacion en Puerto Rico.* San Juan, Puerto Rico: School of Medicine, University of Puerto Rico, 1966.

Cardoso de Oliveira, Roberto. *O Processo de Assimilação dos Terêna.* Rio de Janeiro: Museo Nacional, 1960.

Castañeda, Jorge G. *Utopia Unarmed: The Latin American Left After the Cold War.* New York: Alfred A. Knopf, 1993.

Catton, Bruce. *The Warlords of Washington.* New York: Harcourt, 1948.

Chagnon, Napoleon A. *Yanomamö: The Fierce People.* New York: Holt, Rinehart, & Winston, 1968.

Chase, Allen. *Falange: The Axis Secret Army in the Americas.* New York: G. P. Putnam's Sons, 1943.

Chomsky, Noam, and Howard Zinn. *The Pentagon Papers.* Boston: Beacon Press, 1971.

Cockburn, Alexander, and Susanna B. Hecht. *The Fate of the Forest: Developers, Destroyers and Defenders of the Amazon.* London: Verso, 1989

Colby, Gerard. *Du Pont Dynasty: Behind the Nylon Curtain.* Secaucus, N.J.: Lyle Stuart, 1984.

Colby, William. *Honorable Men.* New York: Simon & Schuster, 1978.

Collier, John. *America's Colonial Record.* London: Fabian Publications, 1947.

————. *Indians of the Americas.* New York: New American Library, 1947.

Collier, Peter, and David Horowitz. *The Rockefellers: An American Dynasty.* New York: Holt, Rinehart & Winston, 1976.

————. *The Kennedys.* New York: Warner Books, 1984.

Colson, Charles W. *Born Again.* Lincoln, Va.: Elsen Books Publishing Company, 1976.

Comas, Juan. *The Life and Work of Manuel Gamio: A Posthumous Homage.* Mexico City: Anthropology Department, UNAM (National Autonomous University of Mexico), 1956.

"Convention on the Prevention and Punishment of the Crime of Genocide," in *Indian Rights—Human Rights: Handbook for Indians in International Human Rights Complaint Procedures.* Washington, D.C.: Indian Law Resource Center, 1984.

Cook, Blanche Wiesen. *The Declassified Eisenhower.* Garden City, N.Y.: Doubleday, 1981.

Corry, Steven. *Toward Indian Self Determination in Colombia.* London: Survival International, 1976.

Corson, William R. *The Armies of Ignorance.* New York: Dial Press, 1977.

Cotlaw, Lewis. *The Twilight of the Primitive.* New York: Macmillan, 1971.

Cowan, George. *The Word That Kindles.* Chappaqua, N.Y.: Christian Herald, 1979.

Cowell, Adrian. *The Decade of Destruction.* New York: Henry Holt, 1990.

————. *The Tribe That Hides from Man.* New York: Stein & Day, 1974.

Cronon, E. David. *Josephus Daniels in Mexico.* Madison: University of Wisconsin Press, 1960.

Dalrymple, Martha. *The AIA Story: Two Decades of International Cooperation.* New York: American International Association for Economic and Social Development, 1968.

Daniels, Josephus. *Shirt-Sleeve Diplomat.* Chapel Hill, N.C.: University of North Carolina Press, 1947.

Davis, Shelton H. *Victims of the Miracle.* Cambridge: Cambridge University Press, 1977.

Davis, Shelton, and Robert O. Mathews. *The Geological Imperative: Anthropology and Development in the Amazon Basin of South America.* Cambridge, Mass.: Anthropological Resource Center, 1976.

de Castro, Josué. *Death in the Northeast.* New York: Random House, 1966.

de Toledano, Ralph. *RFK: The Man Who Would Be President.* New York: New American Library, 1968.

Deloria, Vine, Jr. *Custer Died for Your Sins.* New York: Macmillan, 1969.

Desmond, James. *Nelson Rockefeller: A Political Biography.* New York: Macmillan, 1964.

Dicionário Histórico-Biográfico Brasileiro 1930–1983. Rio de Janeiro: Forensa Universitaria, 1984.

Dickson, Paul. *Think Tanks.* New York: Ballantine Books, 1971.

Diment, Eunice. *Kidnapped!* Exeter, Eng.: Paternoster, 1976.

Domhoff, G. William. *Who Rules America?* Englewood Cliffs, N.J.:Prentice-Hall, 1967.

———. *Who Rules America Now?* New York: Simon & Schuster, 1983.

Donovan, Robert J. *Confidential Secretary: Ann Whitman's Twenty Years with Eisenhower and Rockefeller.* New York: Dutton, 1988.

Douglas, William O. *Go East, Young Man.* New York: Random House, 1974.

Dostal, Walter, ed. *The Situation of the Indian in South America.* Geneva: World Council of Churches, 1972.

Dozier, Edward. *Hane: A Tewa Indian Community in Arizona.* New York: Holt, Rinehart & Winston, 1966.

Efron, Daniel H., Bo Holmstedt, and Nathan S. Kline. *Endopharmacologic Search for Psychoactive Drugs.* Washington, D.C.: Government Printing Office, 1967.

Elliot, Elizabeth. *No Graven Images.* New York: Harper & Row, 1966.

———. *The Savage My Kinsman.* New York: Harper & Bros., 1961.

———. *Through the Gates of Splendor.* New York: Harper & Bros., 1956.

Emery, Gennet Maxon. *Protestantism in Guatemala.* Cuernavaca: Centro Intercultural de Documentación (CIDOC), 1970.

Fager, Richard, and Wayne A. Cornellius, eds. *Political Power in Latin America: Seven Confrontations.* Englewood Cliffs, N.J.: Prentice-Hall, 1970.

Falla, Ricardo. *Massacres in the Jungle: Ixcán, Guatemala, 1975–1982.* Boulder, Colo.: Westview, 1994

Farago, Ladislas. *Aftermath.* New York: Avon Books, 1975.

Fay, Paul B., Jr. *The Pleasure of His Company.* New York: Harper & Row, 1966.

Fernández Artucio, Hugo. *The Nazi Underground in South America.* New York: Farrar & Rinehart, 1942.

Forjando un Mañana Mejor, 1955–1975. La Paz, Bolivia: Ministerio de Educación y Cultura, Instituto Lingüístico de Verano, 1975.

Forrestal, James V., Walter Millis, and E. S. Duffield, eds. *The Forrestal Diaries.* New York: Viking, 1951.

Fosdick, Harry. *The Living of These Days.* New York: Harper & Bros., 1956.

Fosdick, Raymond B. *Chronicle of a Generation.* New York: Harper & Bros., 1958.

———. *John D. Rockefeller, Jr.: A Portrait.* New York: Harper & Bros., 1956.

Frank, Luisa, and Philip Wheaton. *Indian Guatemala: Path to Liberation: The Role of Christians in the Indian Process.* Washington, D.C.: EPICA, 1984.

Friedin, Seymour, and George Bailey. *The Experts.* New York: Macmillan, 1968.

Fuller, Daniel P. *Give the Winds a Mighty Voice: The Story of Charles E. Fuller.* Waco, Tex.: Word Books, 1972.

Gage, Nicolas, ed. *Mafia: USA.* New York: Dell, 1972.

Gardner, Lloyd C. *Economic Aspects of New Deal Diplomacy.* Madison: University of Wisconsin Press, 1954.

Garrard, Martha. *More Glimpses of Bolivia.* Santa Ana, Calif.: Wycliffe Bible Translators, 1970.

Gentry, Curt. *J. Edgar Hoover: The Man and the Secrets.* New York: W. W. Norton, 1991.

Gervasi, Frank. *The Real Rockefeller.* New York: Atheneum, 1964.

Gilly, Adolfo. *La Revolución Interrumpida.* Mexico City: Ediciones El Caballito, 1971.

Giovannitti, Len, and Fred Freed. *The Decision to Drop the Bomb.* New York: Coward-McCann, 1965.

Goldfield, David R. *Cotton Fields and Skyscrapers.* Baton Rouge: Louisiana State University Press, 1982.

Gordon, Suzanne. *Black Mesa—The Angel of Death*. New York: John Day, 1973.

Gott, Richard. *Guerrilla Movements in Latin America*. Garden City, N.Y.: Doubleday, 1971.

———. *Rural Guerrillas in Latin America*. Harmondsworth, Eng.: Penguin Books, 1973.

Graham, Billy. *Peace with God*. New York: Spire Books, 1968.

Graubard, Stephen R. *Kissinger*. New York: W. W. Norton, 1973.

Green, David. *The Containment of Latin America: A History of the Myths and Realities of the Good Neighbor Policy*. Chicago: Triangle Books, 1971.

Guevara, Che. *Guerrilla Warfare*. New York: Vintage Books, 1961.

Hair, William Ivy. *The Kingfish and His Realm*. Baton Rouge: Louisiana State University Press, 1991.

Halberstam, David. *The Best and the Brightest*. Greenwich, Conn.: Fawcett, 1973.

Halstead, Bruce. *Dangerous Marine Animals*. Cambridge, Md.: Cornell Maritime Press, 1959.

Hanbury-Tenison, Robin. *Report of a Visit to the Indians of Brazil*. London: Survival International/Primitive Peoples Fund, 1971.

Hanson, Earl Parker. *Journey to Manaos*. New York: Reynal & Hitchcock, 1938.

Harriman, W. Averell, and Eli Abel. *Special Envoy to Churchill and Stalin, 1941–1946*. New York: Random House, 1975.

Hefley, James C. *Aarón Sáenz: Mexico's Revolutionary Capitalist*. Waco, Tex.: Word Books, 1970.

———. *By Life or by Death*. Grand Rapids, Mich.: Zondervan, 1969.

———. *God's Freelancers*. Orange, Calif.: Wycliffe Associates, 1978.

———. *No Time for Tombstones*. Wheaton, Ill.: Tyndale, 1976.

Hefley, James C., and Marti Hefley. *Dawn over Amazonia*. Waco, Tex.: Word Books, 1972.

———. *Uncle Cam*. Waco, Tex: Word Books, 1974.

Hefley, James C., and Edward E. Plowman. *Washington: Christians in the Corridors of Power*. Wheaton, Ill.: Tyndale House, 1975.

Hefley, James C., and Hugh Steven. *Miracles in Mexico*. Chicago: Moody Press, 1972.

Herken, Gregg. *Counsels of War*. New York: Alfred A. Knopf, 1985.

Hersh, Seymour. *The Price of Power*. New York: Summit, 1983.

Hickey, Gerald C. *Highland People of South Vietnam*. Santa Monica, Calif.: Rand Corp., 1967.

Hiebert, Ray Eldon. *Courtier to the Crowd: The Story of Ivy Lee and the Development of Public Relations*. Ames, Iowa: Iowa State University Press, 1966.

Hill, Samuel S., Jr. *Southern Churches in Crisis*. Boston: Beacon Press, 1966.

Hilton, Stanley E. *Hitler's Secret War in South America: German Military Espionage and Allied Counterespionage in Brazil, 1939–45*. Baton Rouge: Louisiana State University Press, 1981.

Hitt, Russell T. *Jungle Pilot: The Life and Witness of Nate Saint*. Grand Rapids, Mich.: Zondervan, 1973.

Holland, James R. *The Amazon*. New York: H. S. Barnes & Company, 1971.

Hoopes, Townsend. *The Limits of Intervention*. New York: David McKay, 1969.

Hopper, Janice H., ed. *Indians of Brazil in the Twentieth Century*. Washington, D.C.: Institute for Cross Cultural Research, 1967.

Horowitz, Irving Louis, ed. *The Rise and Fall of Project Camelot*. Cambridge, Mass.: MIT Press, 1974.

Howard, Philip. *Charles Gallandet Trumbull: Apostle of the Victorian Life*. Philadelphia: Sunday School Times Company, 1941.

Huxley, Matthew, and Cornell Capa. *Farewell to Eden*. New York: Harper & Row, 1964.

Hymes, Dell, ed. *Reinventing Anthropology*. New York: Vintage Books, 1972.

Immerman, Richard. *The CIA in Guatemala*. Austin: University of Texas Press, 1982.

Inman, Samuel Guy. *New Day in Guatemala*. Wilton, Conn.: Worldview Press, 1951.

International Petroleum Encyclopedia. Tulsa, Okla.: PennWell Publishing Company, 1983.

Irving, Robert Grant. *Indian Summer: Lutyens, Baker, and Imperial Delhi*. New Haven, Conn.: Yale University Press, 1981.

Jacques, Julian. *The Origin of Consciousness in the Breakdown of the Bicameral Mind*. Boston: Houghton Mifflin, 1976.

Johansen, Bruce, and Roberto Maestras. *Wasi'chu: The Continuing Indian Wars*. New York: Monthly Review Press, 1979.

Jones, S. Shepard, and Denys P. Myers, eds. *Documents on American Foreign Relations, January 1938–June 1939*. Boston: World Peace Foundation, 1939.

Jorstad, Erling. *The Politics of Doomsday: Fundamentalists of the Far Right*. New York: Abendon Press, 1970.

Kanza, Thomas. *Conflict in the Congo*. Harmondsworth, Eng.: Penguin, 1972.

Kearns, Doris. *Lyndon Johnson and the American Dream*. New York: Harper & Row, 1976.

Kennedy, Robert. *Thirteen Days: A Memoir of the Cuban Missile Crisis*. New York: W. W. Norton, 1969.

Khrushchev, Nikita S. *Khrushchev Remembers*. Boston: Little, Brown, 1970.

Kingsland, Rosemary. *A Saint Among Savages*. London: Collins, 1980.

Kintner, William R. *The Front Is Everywhere*. Norman, Okla.: University of Oklahoma Press, 1950.

————. *New Frontiers of War: Political Warfare Present and Future*. Chicago: Henry Regnery, 1962.

Kluckhohn, Clyde. *Mirror for Man: A Survey of Human Behavior and Social Attitudes*. Greenwich, Conn.: Fawcett, 1967.

Knightly, Philip. *The First Casualty*. New York: Harcourt, 1975.

Kramer, Michael, and Sam Roberts. *"I Never Wanted to Be Vice-President of Anything!"* New York: Basic Books, 1976.

Kreig, Margaret B. *Green Medicine: The Search for Plants That Heal*. New York: Rand McNally, 1964.

Kunstadter, Peter, ed. *Southeast Asian Tribes, Minorities and Nations*. Princeton, N.J.: Princeton University Press, 1967.

Kutz, Myer. *Rockefeller Power*. New York: Simon & Schuster, 1974.

Lacerda, Carlos. *Brasíl Entre a Verdade e a Mentira*. Rio de Janeiro: Block Editores, 1965.

Landau, David. *Kissinger: The Uses of Power*. Boston: Houghton Mifflin, 1992.

Landeau, Jean-François G. *Strategies of U.S. Independent Oil Companies Abroad*. Ann Arbor, Mich.: University Microfilms International Research Press, 1977.

Lane, Mark, and Dick Gregory. *Code Named Zorro*. Englewood Cliffs, N.J.: Prentice-Hall, 1977.

Langguth, A. J. *Hidden Terrors: The Truth About U.S. Police Operations in Latin America.* New York: Pantheon, 1978.

Lanning, Greg, with Marti Mueller. *Africa Undermined: Mining Companies and the Underdevelopment of Africa.* Harmondsworth, Eng.: Penguin, 1979.

Lansdale, Edward G. *In the Midst of Wars.* New York: Harper & Row, 1972.

Latham, Earl. *John D. Rockefeller: Robber Baron or Industrial Statesman?* Boston: D. C. Heath, 1949.

Le Tourneau, Robert G. *Mover of Men and Mountains.* Chicago: Moody Press, 1967.

Levinson, Jerome, and Juan de Onis. *The Alliance That Lost Its Way.* Chicago: Quadrangle, 1970.

Lewis, David Mayberry. *The Savage and the Innocent.* London: Evans Brothers, 1965.

Lewis, Norman. *The Missionaries.* New York: McGraw-Hill, 1988.

Long, Jerry. *Amazonia Reborn.* Portland, Ore.: Multnomah Press, 1970.

Louis, J. C., and Harvey Z. Yazijian. *The Cola Wars.* New York: Everest House, 1980.

McCann, Thomas. *An American Company: The Tragedy of United Fruit.* New York: Crown Publishers, 1976.

McCoy, Alfred W., and Cathleen B. Read. *The Politics of Heroin in Southeast Asia.* New York: Harper & Row, 1972.

MacDougall, Malcolm D. *We Almost Made It.* New York: Crown Publishers, 1977.

McGarvey, Patrick J. *CIA: The Myth and the Madness.* Harmondsworth, Eng.: Penguin, 1973.

Machlin, Milt. *The Search for Michael Rockefeller.* New York: G. P. Putnam's Sons, 1972.

McIntyre, Thomas J., with John C. Obert. *Fear Brokers: Peddling the Hate Politics of the New Right.* Boston: Beacon Press, 1981.

McLaughlin, William G. *Modern Revivalism.* New York: Ronald Press, 1959.

———. *Revivals, Awakenings and Reform.* Chicago: University of Chicago, 1978.

McManus, George F. *The Inside Story of Steel Wages and Prices, 1958–1967.* Philadelphia: Chilton, 1967.

McNeill, William H. *Plagues and Peoples.* Garden City, N.Y.: Anchor Books, 1978.

McWilliams, Carey. *Factories in the Field.* Santa Barbara, Calif.: Peregrine, 1971.

Magdoff, Harry. *The Age of Imperialism.* New York: Monthly Review Press, 1969.

Mailer, Norman. *Cannibals and Christians.* New York: Dial Press, 1966.

Mally, James M., and Richard Thorn, eds. *Beyond the Revolution: Bolivia Since 1952.* Pittsburgh: University of Pittsburgh Press, 1971.

Manchester, William. *The Death of a President.* New York: Harper & Row, 1967.

Manz, Beatriz. *Refugees of a Hidden War: The Aftermath of Counterinsurgency in Guatemala.* Albany, N.Y.: State University of New York Press, 1988.

Marchetti, Victor, and John Marks. *The CIA and the Cult of Intelligence.* New York: Alfred E. Knopf, 1974.

Marks, John. *The Search for the "Manchurian Candidate."* New York: Times Books, 1979.

Marsden, George M. *Fundamentalism and American Culture: The Shaping of Twentieth Century Evangelicalism, 1870–1925.* New York: Oxford University Press, 1980.

Matles, James J., and James Higgins. *Them and Us.* Boston: Beacon Press, 1974.

Matthiessen, Peter. *At Play in the Fields of the Lord.* New York: Random House, 1965.

———. *The Cloud Forest.* New York: Viking Press, 1961.

Maxwell, Nicole. *Witch Doctor's Apprentice*. Boston: Houghton Mifflin, 1961. (Reissue. Secaucus, N.J.: Carol Publishers, 1990.)

Mayer, Martin. *The Bankers*. New York: Ballantine Books, 1974.

Meggers, Betty. *Amazonia: Man and Culture in a Counterfeit Paradise*. Chicago: Aldine Atherton, 1971.

Melman, Seymour. *Pentagon Capitalism: The Political Economy of War*. New York: McGraw-Hill, 1970.

Merington, Marguerite. *The Custer Story: The Life and Intimate Letters of General George A. Custer and His Wife Elizabeth*. New York: Devin-Adair, 1950.

Mole, Robert L. *The Montagnards of South Vietnam: A Study of Nine Tribes*. Rutland, Vt.: Tuttle, 1970.

Morales, Edmundo. *Cocaine: White Gold Rush in Peru*. Tucson: University of Arizona Press, 1989.

Morris, Joe Alex. *Nelson Rockefeller*. New York: Harper & Row, 1960.

———. *Those Rockefeller Brothers*. New York: Harper & Bros., 1953.

Morrison, deLesseps S. *Latin American Mission: An Adventure in Hemisphere Diplomacy*. New York: Simon & Schuster, 1965.

Mosher, Arthur T. *Case Study of the Agricultural Program of ACAR in Brazil*. New York: National Planning Association, 1955.

Murdoch, George P., et al. *Outline of Cultural Materials*. New Haven, Conn.: Human Relations Area Files, Yale University, 1967.

Mutchlin, David. *The Church as a Political Factor in Latin America*. New York: Praeger, 1971.

Nash, June. *We Eat the Mines and the Mines Eat Us*. New York: Columbia University Press, 1979.

Newfield, Jack. *Robert Kennedy: A Memoir*. New York: E. P. Dutton, 1969.

The New York Times, ed. *The Pentagon Papers*. New York: New York Times, 1971.

Niebuhr, Reinhold. *Moral Man and Immoral Society*. New York: Charles Scribner's Sons, 1932.

Nimuendaju, Curt. *The Tukuna*. Berkeley, Calif.: University of California Press, 1952.

Noble, G. Bernard. *Christian A. Herter*. New York: Cooper Square Publishers, 1962.

Nutels, Noel. "Medical Problems of Newly Contacted Indian Groups," in *Biomedical Challenges Presented by the American Indian*. Washington, D.C.: Pan American Health Organization, 1968.

O'Connor, Harvey. *World Crisis in Oil*. New York: Monthly Review Press, 1962.

Oglesby, Carl. *The Yankee and Cowboy War*. Kansas City, Kans.: Sheed Andrews & McMeel, 1976.

Ogelsby, Carl, and Richard Shaull. *Containment and Change*. New York: Macmillan, 1967.

O'Neil, John Cochrane. *Paul's Letter to the Romans*. Harmondsworth, Eng.: Penguin, 1975.

Orr, J. Edwin. *Evangelical Awakenings in Latin America*. Minneapolis, Minn.: Bethany Fellowship, Inc., 1978.

Pacheco, Cuauhtémoc González. *Capital Extranjero en la Selva de Chiapas, 1863–1982*. Mexico City: Instituto de Investigaciones Económicas, UNAM (National Autonomous University of Mexico), 1983.

Parmet, Herbert S. *Eisenhower and the American Crusades*. New York: Macmillan, 1972.

Patch, Richard. *Attitudes Toward Sex: Reproduction Patterns of Aymara and Quechua Speaking People*. Hanover, N.H.: West Coast American Service, 1970.

Perera, Victor. *Unfinished Conquest: The Guatemalan Tragedy*. Berkeley, Calif.: University of California Press, 1993.

Perez Ramirez, Gustavo. *Planas: Las Contradicciones del Capitalismo*. Bogotá: Ediciones Tercer Mundo, 1971.

————. *Planas: Uno Año Despues.* Bogotá: Editorial America Latina, 1971.

Phillips, David Atlee. *The Night Watch: Twenty-five Years of Peculiar Service.* New York: Atheneum, 1977.

Philp, Kenneth R. *John Collier's Crusade for Indian Reform: 1920–1954.* Tucson: University of Arizona Press, 1977.

Pike, Kenneth, and Ruth M. Brend, eds. *The Summer Institute of Linguistics: Its Work and Contributions.* The Hague: Mouton, 1977.

Polhamus, Loren G. *Rubber: Botany Production and Utilization.* New York: Interscience Publishers, 1962.

Pollack, John O. *Billy Graham.* New York: Harper & Row, 1979.

————. *A Foreign Devil in China.* Minneapolis, Minn.: World Wide Publications, 1971.

————. *Moody Without Sankey.* London: Hodder & Stoughton, 1966.

Powers, Thomas. *The Man Who Kept the Secrets: Richard Helms and the CIA.* New York: Alfred A. Knopf, 1979.

Prouty, L. Fletcher. *The Secret Team.* Englewood Cliffs, N.J.: Prentice-Hall, 1973.

Radosh, Ronald. *American Labor and U.S. Foreign Policy: The Cold War in the Unions from Gompers to Lovestone.* New York: Random House, 1970.

Rappleye, Charles, and Ed Becker. *All-American Mafioso: The Johnny Roselli Story.* Garden City, N.Y.: Doubleday, 1991.

Riley, William B. "Corporate Control: The Peril of Christian Education," in *Inspiration or Evolution?* Cleveland: Union Gospel Press, 1926.

Rivera, Diego. *My Art, My Life.* New York: The Citadel Press, 1958.

Robbins, Christopher. *Air America: The Story of the CIA's Secret Airlines.* New York: G. P. Putnam's Sons, 1979.

Rockefeller, John D. *Random Reminiscences of Men and Events.* Tarrytown, N.Y.: Sleepy Hollow Press and the Rockefeller Archive Center, 1984.

Rockefeller, Michael. *The Asmat of New Guinea: The Journal of Michael Clark Rockefeller.* New York: Museum of Primitive Art, 1967.

Rockefeller, Nelson. *Partners in Progress, Report by the International Development Advisory Board.* New York: Simon & Schuster, 1951.

————. *The Rockefeller Report on the Americas: The Official Report of a United States Presidential Mission for the Western Hemisphere.* Chicago: Quadrangle Books, 1969.

————. *Unity, Freedom, and Peace: A Blueprint for Tomorrow.* New York: Random House, 1968.

————. *Vital Resources.* Lexington, Mass.: D. C. Heath, 1972.

Rodriguez, Felix, and John Weisman. *Shadow Warrior.* New York: Simon & Schuster, 1989.

Rojas, Robinson. *Estados Unidos en Brazil.* Santiago, Chile: Prensa Latinamerica, 1965.

Rondon, Cândido Mariano do Silva. *Lectures.* New York: Greenwood Press, 1916.

Root, Oren. *Persons and Persuasions.* New York: W. W. Norton, 1974.

Rositzke, Harry. *The CIA's Secret Operations.* New York: Thomas Company, 1977.

Rossi, Sanna Barlow. *God's City in the Jungle.* Huntington Beach, Calif.: Wycliffe Bible Translators, 1975.

Rusher, William A. *The Rise of the Right.* New York: Morrow, 1984.

Rynkiewich, Michael A., and James P. Spradley, eds. *Ethics and Anthropology: Dilemmas in Fieldwork.* New York: Wiley, 1976.

Safire, William. *Before the Fall: An Inside Look at the Pre-Watergate White House*. Garden City, N.Y.: Doubleday, 1975.

Sampson, Anthony. *The Seven Sisters: The Great Oil Companies and the World They Shaped*. New York: Viking, 1975.

Sandeen, Ernest. *The Roots of Fundamentalism: British and American Millenarianism, 1800–1930*. Chicago: University of Chicago Press, 1970.

Schanche, Don A. *Mister Pop*. New York: David McKay, 1970.

Scheer, Robert, ed. *Diary of Che Guevera*. New York: Bantam Books, 1968.

Scheflin, Alan W., and Edward M. Otpon, Jr. *The Mind Manipulators*. New York: Paddington Press, 1978.

Schlesinger, Arthur M., Jr. *A Thousand Days: John F. Kennedy in the White House*. Boston: Houghton Mifflin, 1965.

Schlesinger, Stephen, and Stephen Kinzer. *Bitter Fruit: The Untold Story of the American Coup in Guatemala*. Garden City, N.Y.: Anchor Press/Doubleday, 1983.

Schorr, Daniel. *Clearing the Air*. New York: Berkley Medallion Books, 1978.

Schultes, Richard Evans. *Hallucinogenic Plants*. New York: Golden Press, 1976.

Schwarz, Jordan A. *Liberal: Adolph Berle and the Vision of an American Era*. New York: Free Press, 1987.

Scott, Peter Dale. *Deep Politics and the Death of JFK*. Berkeley, Calif.: University of California Press, 1993.

Shawcross, William. *The Shah's Last Ride*. New York: Simon & Schuster, 1988.

Sherwood, Robert E. *Roosevelt and Hopkins*. New York: Harper & Bros., 1948.

Shields, Jerry. *The Invisible Billionaire: Daniel Ludwig*. Boston: Houghton Mifflin, 1986.

Simpson, Eyler N. *The Ejido: Mexico's Way Out*. Chapel Hill: University of North Carolina Press, 1937.

Simson, Christopher. *Blowback: America's Recruitment of Nazis and Its Effects on the Cold War*. New York: Weidenfeld & Nicolson, 1988.

Skidmore, Thomas E. *Politics in Brazil, 1930–1964: An Experiment in Democracy*. New York: Oxford University Press, 1967.

Smith, Joseph B. *Portrait of a Cold Warrior*. New York: G. P. Putnam's Sons, 1976.

Smith, Peter Seaborn. *Oil and Politics in Modern Brazil*. Toronto: Macmillan, 1976.

Stepan, Alfred. *The Military in Politics: Changing Patterns in Brazil*. Princeton, N.J.: Princeton University Press, 1971.

Steven, Hugh, ed. *A Thousand Trails*. White Rock, British Columbia: CREDO Publishing Corp., 1984.

Stockwell, John. *In Search of Enemies: A CIA Story*. London: Future Publications, 1979.

Stoll, David. *Fishers of Men or Founders of Empires? The Wycliffe Bible Translators in Latin America*. London: Zed Press, 1982.

Suharno, Ignatius, and Kenneth L. Pike, eds. *From Baudi to Indonesian*. Irian Jaya: Cenderawasih University/Summer Institute of Linguistics, 1976.

Summer Institute of Linguistics. *Language and Faith*. Santa Ana, Calif.: Wycliffe Bible Translators, 1972.

———. *SIL in Brazil: Annual Report*. Brasília: Summer Institute of Linguistics, 1976.

Swain, Tony. *Plants in the Development of Modern Medicine*. Cambridge, Mass.: Harvard University Press, 1972.

Syrud, Donald E. *Foundations of Brazilian Economic Growth*. Stanford, Calif.: Hoover Institution Press, 1974.

Szulc, Tad. *Twilight of the Tyrants*. New York: Holt, 1959.

Tanzer, Michael. *The Political Economy of International Oil and the Underdeveloped Countries*. Boston: Beacon Press, 1969.

Taylor, Maxwell. *Swords and Plowshares*. New York: W. W. Norton, 1972.

Teller, Edward. *Energy: A Plan for Action*. New York: Commission on Critical Choices, 1975.

Theberge, James D., and Roger W. Fontane. *Latin America: Struggle for Progress*. Lexington, Mass.: D. C. Heath, 1977.

Thomas, Gordon. *Journey into Madness: The True Story of Secret CIA Mind Control and Medical Abuse*. New York: Bantam Books, 1989.

Tourtellot, Arthur Bernon, ed. *Toward the Well-Being of Mankind: Fifty Years of the Rockefeller Foundation*. Garden City, N.Y.: Doubleday, 1964.

Townsend, William Cameron. *Lázaro Cárdenas: Mexican Democrat*. Ann Arbor, Mich.: George Wahr, 1952.

———. *They Found a Common Language*. New York: Harper & Row, 1972.

———. *Tolo: The Volcano's Son*. Huntington Beach, Calif.: Wycliffe Bible Translators, 1981.

Townsend, William Cameron, and Richard S. Pittman. *Remember All the Way*. Huntington Beach, Calif.: Wycliffe Bible Translators, 1975.

———. *The Truth About Mexico's Oil*. Los Angeles: Inter-American Fellowship, 1940.

Tyler, William G. *The Brazilian Industrial Economy*. Lexington, Mass.: Lexington Books/D.C. Heath, 1981.

Uribe, Armando. *The Black Book of American Intervention in Chile*. Boston: Beacon Press, 1975.

Wallis, Ethel. E. *Aucas Downriver: Dayuma's Story Today*. New York: Harper & Row, 1973.

———. *The Dayuma Story*. Old Tappan, N.J.: Spire, 1979.

———. *Lengthened Cords*. Glendale, Calif.: Wycliffe Bible Translators, 1958.

———. *Tariri: My Story*. New York: Harper & Row, 1965.

Wallis, Ethel E., and Mary A. Bennett. *Two Thousand Tongues to Go*. London: Hodder & Stoughton, 1966.

Walters, Vernon A. *Silent Missions*. Garden City, N.Y.: Doubleday, 1978.

Wares, Alan C. *Bibliography of the Summer Institute of Linguistics*. Dallas: Summer Institute of Linguistics, 1979.

Waterhouse, H. F. *A Time to Build*. Columbia, S.C.: University of South Carolina Press, 1964.

Weil, Andrew. *The Natural Mind*. Boston: Houghton Mifflin, 1972.

Weisberg, Harold. *Oswald in New Orleans*. New York: Canyon Books, 1967.

Westmoreland, William. *A Soldier Reports*. Garden City, N.Y.: Doubleday, 1976.

Weyler, Rex. *Blood of the Land*. New York: Vintage, 1984.

Wharton, Clifton R., Jr., ed. *Subsistence Agriculture and Economic Development*. Chicago: Aldine, 1969.

White, Gerald T. *Formative Years in the Far West*. New York: Appleton, 1962.

White, John Wesley. *What Does It Mean to Be Born Again?* Minneapolis, Minn.: Bethany Fellowship, 1977.

White, Richard Alan. *The Morass: United States' Intervention in Central America*. New York: Harper & Row, 1984.

Who Pays the Price? The Cost of War in the Guatemalan Highlands. Washington, D.C.: Washington Office on Latin America, 1988.

Williams, Douglas, ed. *Mission Supplement*. Huntington Beach, Calif.: Wycliffe Bible Translators, 1976.

Williams, T. Harry. *Huey Long*. New York: Bantam Books, 1969.

Williams, William Appleman. *The Tragedy of American Diplomacy*. Cleveland: World, 1959.

————, ed. *The Shaping of American Diplomacy, Volume 2: 1914:1968*. Chicago: Rand-McNally, 1970.

Wilson, Forbes. *The Conquest of Copper Mountain*. New York: Atheneum, 1981.

Wise, David, and Thomas B. Ross. *The Espionage Establishment*. New York: Random House, 1967.

————. *The Invisible Government*. New York: Random House, 1964.

Wolf, Eric. *Sons of the Shaking Earth*. Chicago: University of Chicago Press, 1959.

Wolfe, Bertram. *The Fabulous Life of Diego Rivera*. New York: Stein & Day, 1963.

Woodward, Bob, and Carl Bernstein. *The Final Days*. New York: Simon & Schuster, 1976.

Wyden, Peter. *Bay of Pigs*. New York: Simon & Schuster, 1979.

Young, Perry Deane. *God's Bullies: Power Politics and Religious Tyranny*. New York: Holt, Rinehart & Winston, 1982.

United States Government Publications

Agency for International Development. *Top 20 Institutions in Value of Technical Services Contracts*. Washington, D.C.: Government Printing Office, 1971.

Agency for International Development. *U.S. Overseas Loans and Grants of Assistance from International Organizations: July 1, 1945–June 30, 1972*. Washington, D.C.: Government Printing Office, 1973.

Agency for International Development. *AID-Financed University Contracts*. Washington, D.C.: Government Printing Office, 1962–1967.

Commission on CIA Activities Within the United States (Nelson Rockefeller, Chairman). *Report to the President*. Washington, D.C.: Government Printing Office, 1975.

Committee on Appropriations, U.S. House of Representatives. *Defense Appropriations Hearings for 1965*. Washington, D.C.: Government Printing Office, 1965.

Committee on Appropriations, U.S. House of Representatives, Department of Defense Subcommittee, Hearings. *Department of Defense Appropriations for 1970* (particularly Part V, Testimony of Lt. Gen. Austin W. Betts). Washington, D.C.: Government Printing Office, 1969.

Committee on Armed Services, U.S. House of Representatives, Report of the Special Subcommittee on Intelligence. *Inquiry into the Alleged Involvement of the Central Intelligence Agency in the Watergate and Ellsberg Matters*. Washington, D.C.: Government Printing Office, 1973.

Committee on Banking and Currency, U.S. House of Representatives. *Staff Report, The Penn Central Failure and the Role of Financial Institutions,* part III. Washington, D.C.: Government Printing Office, 1970.

Committee on Foreign Affairs, U.S. House of Representatives. *Hearings on the Mutual Security Program*. Washington, D.C.: Government Printing Office, 1951.

Committee on Foreign Affairs, U.S. House of Representatives, 89th Congress, 2nd Session. Subcommittee on Internal Organization and Movements, Part 8. *Winning the Cold War: The U.S. Ideological Offensive*. Hearings (July 8, 13, and 14 and August 7, 1965) in House Committee on Foreign Affairs, 89th Congress, 1st Session. *Behavioral Sciences and National Security,* Report 4, December 6, 1965. Washington, D.C.: Government Printing Office, 1965.

Committee on Foreign Relations, U.S. Senate. *Hearings on the Nomination of Lincoln Gordon to Be the Assistant Secretary of State for Inter-American Affairs.* Washington, D.C.: Government Printing Office, 1966.

Committee on Government Operations, Subcommittees on Intergovernmental Relations, and on Budgeting, Management and Expenditures, U.S. Senate. *Disclosure of Corporate Ownership* (Metcalf Committee Report). Washington, D.C.: Government Printing Office, 1974.

Committee on Interior and Insular Affairs, U.S. Senate, 94th Congress, 2nd Session, Special Subcommittee on Integrated Oil Operations. *The Structure of the U.S. Petroleum Industry: A Summary of Survey Data.* Washington, D.C.: Government Printing Office, 1976.

Committee on Rules, U.S. Senate, 88th Congress, 2nd Session. *Construction of the District of Columbia Stadium.* Washington, D.C.: Government Printing Office, 1964.

Committee on Rules, U.S. Senate, 88th Congress, 2nd Session, Hearings. *Financial or Business Interests of Officers or Employees of the Senate.* Washington, D.C.: Government Printing Office, 1964.

Committee on Rules and Administration, U.S. Senate, 93rd Congress, 2nd Session, Hearings. *The Nomination of Nelson A. Rockefeller of New York to Be Vice President of the United States.* Washington, D.C.: Government Printing Office, 1974.

Congressional Reference Service Catalog of CIA Covert Actions (CR5 75-50F) entered into the *Congressional Record* by Rep. Michael Harrington, September 30, 1975.

Department of the Army, *Army Research Task Summary,* 1961.

Department of Defense, Defense Documentation Center, *Technical Abstract Bulletin,* 1967.

Department of Defense, Comptroller, Directorate for Information Operations, *100 Companies and Their Subsidiary Corporations, Listed According to Net Value of Military Prime Contract Awards,* Fiscal Year 1968.

Department of Defense, Office of the Assistant Secretary of Defense for International Security Affairs, *Military Assistance Facts,* 1969.

Select Committee on Intelligence and Subcommittee on Health and Scientific Research of the Committee on Human Resources, U.S. Senate, Joint Hearings. *Project MKULTRA: The CIA's Program of Research in Behavioral Modification.* Washington, D.C.: Government Printing Office, 1977.

Select Committee to Study Governmental Operations with Respect to Intelligence Activities, U.S. Senate, Interim Report. *Alleged Assassination Plots Involving Foreign Leaders.* Washington, D.C.: Government Printing Office, 1975.

Select Committee to Study Governmental Operations with Respect to Intelligence Activities, U.S. Senate, Final Report. Book II. *Intelligence Activities and the Rights of Americans.* Washington, D.C.: Government Printing Office, 1976.

Select Committee to Study Governmental Operations with Respect to Intelligence Activities, U.S. Senate, Final Report. Book III. *Supplementary Detailed Staff Reports on Intelligence Activities and the Rights of Americans.* Washington, D.C.: Government Printing Office, 1976.

Select Committee to Study Governmental Operations with Respect to Intelligence Activities, U.S. Senate, Final Report. Book IV. *Supplementary Detailed Staff Reports on Foreign and Military Intelligence.* Washington, D.C.: Government Printing Office, 1976.

Select Committee to Study Governmental Operations with Respect to Intelligence Activities, U.S. Senate, Hearings, Volume 1. *Unauthorized Storage of Toxic Agents.* Washington, D.C.: Government Printing Office, 1976.

Select Committee to Study Governmental Operations with Respect to Intelligence Activities, U.S. Senate, Hearings (December 4 and 5, 1975), Volume 7. *Covert Action.* Washington, D.C.: Government Printing Office, 1976.

Subcommittee on Constitutional Rights, U.S. Senate. *Federal Data Banks, Computers, and the Bill of Rights.* Washington, D.C.: Government Printing Office, 1976.

Subcommittee on Health of the Committee on Labor and Public Welfare and the Subcommittee on Administrative Practice and Procedure of the Committee on the Judiciary, U.S. Senate, 94th Congress, 1st Session, Joint Hearings (September 10, 12 and November 7, 1975). *Biomedical and Behavioral Research.* Washington, D.C.: Government Printing Office, 1978.

Subcommittee on War Mobilization, Committee on Military Affairs, U.S. Senate, 78th Congress, 2nd Session, Report No. 4. *Cartels and National Security, Part 1. Findings and Recommendations.* Washington, D.C.: Government Printing Office, 1944.

Temporary National Economic Committee, U.S. Senate, 76th Congress, 3rd Session. Report. *Investigation of Concentration of Economic Power.* Washington, D.C.: Government Printing Office, 1941.

Articles and Annuals

Alexander, Holmes. "LBJ and the Gordian Knot of Brazil." *New Haven Register,* April 18, 1964.

Alexander, Tom. "A Wild Plan for South America's Wilds." *Fortune,* December 1967.

American Chamber of Commerce in Peru. *Bulletin,* April 1970.

Arcand, Bernard. "The Urgent Situation of the Cuiva Indian of Colombia." Copenhagen: International Work Group for Indigenous Affairs, 1972. IWGIA Document 7.

Berdickensky, Bernardo. "The Araucanian Indian in Chile." Copenhagen: International Work Group for Indigenous Affairs, 1972. IWGIA Document 20.

Bernstein, Jacob. "America's Lost Identity: Reflections on the U.S. Quincentenary Commission." *Toward Freedom,* October 1992.

"Billy Graham Speaks at Belk Devotional." *Charlotte News,* October 23, 1958.

Blair, Betty. "Aftermath of a Martyrdom." *Charisma,* May 1982.

Blume, Norman. "Pressure Groups and Decision-Making in Brazil." *Studies in Comparative International Development,* Vol. 3, No. 11 (1967–68).

Bodley, John H. "Tribal Survival in the Amazon: The Campa Case." Copenhagen: International Work Group for Indigenous Affairs, 1975. IWGIA Document No. 5.

"Bolivia: Brazil's Geopolitical Prisoner." *Latin America and Empire Report,* North American Congress on Latin America, Vol. 7, No. 2, February 1974.

Bonafede, Don. "Guards Turned Slaughterers of Brazil's Indians." *Washington Post,* June 9, 1966.

Boyd, Robert. "N.C. Minister Renews Friendship with LBJ." *Charlotte Observer,* September 19, 1965.

"Brasil Proyecta un Gigantesco Lago Artificial en la Amazonia." *Inter-Press Service,* December 26, 1971.

"Brazil Builds First All Weather Cross Continent Road." *Brazil Bulletin,* January 1968.

"Brazil Military Moves into Other Social Areas." *Los Angeles Times,* March 13, 1967.

"Brazilians Cry 'Plot over Amazon Plan.'" *Washington Post,* June 6, 1965.

Campbell, Thomas, Jr. "Capitalism and Christianity." *Harvard Business Review,* July/August 1957.

"Carajas: Staggering Iron Ore Reserves in Isolated Splendor." *Engineering and Mining Journal,* November 1975.

Cardoso de Oliveira, Roberto. "The Role of Indian Posts in the Process of Assimilation." *América Indígena,* Vol. 20, No. 2 (1960).

Castaneda, José. "Dos Justos Homenajes." *Guatemala Indígena,* Vol. 17, Nos. 1–2, 1982.

Catelli, Jim. "The Church and the CIA." National Catholic News Service, June 13, 1975.

Chagnon, Napoleon, Philip le Quesne, and James M. Cook. "Yanomamö Hallucinogens: Anthropological, Botanical, and Chemical Findings." *Current Anthropology,* Vol. 12, No. 1, February 1971.

Chapianno, Jean. "The Brazilian Indigenous Problem and Policy: The Aripuanã Park." Copenhagen and Geneva: International Work Group for Indigenous Affairs and Documentation and Information Center for Indigenous Affairs in the Amazon Region, 1975. IWGIA Document 19.

Chavez, Lydia. "Argentines Riot Against Rockefeller." *New York Times,* January 15, 1986.

"CIA Documents Tell of 1954 Project to Create Involuntary Assassins." *New York Times,* February 9, 1978.

Cobbs, Elizabeth A. "Entrepreneurship as Diplomacy: Nelson Rockefeller and the Development of the Brazilian Capital Market." *Business History Review,* Vol. 63, No. 1 (Spring 1989).

Coggins, Wade. "Study Attracts Mission Work Among Latin American Indians." *Evangelical Missions Quarterly,* Summer 1972.

Colby, Charlotte Dennett. "Has Rainforest Crunch Turned Sour?" *Toward Freedom,* October 1992.

"Colby Reads Ten Names That Colby Sought to Omit." *New York Times,* November 21, 1975.

Collier, John. "Has Roxas Betrayed America?" *Saturday Review of Literature,* January 11, 1947.

———. "Terminating the American Indian." *Bulletin of the Institute of Ethnic Affairs,* February 13, 1954.

"Conversing with the CIA." *Christianity Today,* October 19, 1975.

Council for Latin America. *Report,* Volume 6, No. 2, January 1990.

Crewdson, John M., and Joseph B. Treaster. "Worldwide Propaganda Network Built and Controlled by the C.I.A." *New York Times,* December 26, 1977.

"Critique of the Work of the Summer Institute of Linguistics." Department of Linguistics, San Marcos University, October 2, 1975.

"Dallas Minister Attends Briefings on World Policy." *Dallas Morning News,* August 12, 1971.

Davis, L. J. "An American Fortune: The Hunts of Dallas." *Harper's,* April 1981.

Davis, Shelton. "Custer Is Alive and Well in Brazil." *Indian Historian,* Winter 1973.

Deltec International, Ltd. *Annual Reports,* 1970–1977.

"Denuncian que Instituto Lingüístico Busca Dividir a Comunidades Indígenas." *Ultima Noticias,* February 17, 1975.

Dinges, John. "Political Killings Are Continuing in North Guatemalan Countryside." *Washington Post,* July 17, 1982.

Diuguid, Lewis H. "LBJ's Plan in Brazil Coup." *Washington Post,* December 29, 1976.

Dozier, Edward. "Resistance to Acculturation and Assimilation in an Indian Pueblo." *American Anthropologist,* Vol. 53, 1951.

Drier, Steven. "Insurgency in Guatemala." *Focus,* July 1985.

Dun & Bradstreet's Directory (annual).

"Economic Deterioration and Leftist Gains in Brazil." *Central Intelligence Agency [Research Report, 1963].* Available in microfilm from University Publications of America, Inc., Frederick, Maryland.

"Eleven Beheaded in Guatemala." *Washington Post,* June 7, 1982.

"Emphasis on Brazil: The Awakening Giant of South America." *Translation,* Winter 1966.

"An Empty Black Pit," *Akwesasne Notes,* Early Autumn 1973.

"Está en México Nelson Bardesio, Afirma un Periódico Canadiense." *El Día,* July 11, 1976.

"Evangelical Vote Is a Major Target." *New York Times,* June 29, 1980.

Fabiro, Roberto. "To Die in Cuba." *Tropic* (Sunday magazine of the *Miami Herald*), November 6, 1977.

Foundation Directory. New York: Foundation Center, 1972 (other volumes of this annual also used).

Foundation Grants Index. New York: Foundation Center, 1982 (other volumes of this annual also used).

Fuerst, René. "Bibliography of the Indigenous Problem and Policy of the Brazilian Amazon Region (1957–1972)." Copenhagen: International Work Group for Indigenous Affairs, 1975. IWGIA Document 6.

"Fundamentalist Revival." *Christian Century,* June 19, 1957.

Galarza, Jaime. "Ecuador: Oil Orgy." *Prensa Latina Features,* ES-1657.71. Cited in "Ecuador Oil Up for Grabs," *NACLA's Latin America and Empire Report,* Vol. 4, No. 8, November 1975.

Gall, Norman. "The Legacy of Che Guevara." *Commentary,* December 1967.

"Germ Warfare Against Indians Is Charged in Brazil." *Medical Tribune and Medical News,* December 8, 1969.

"Gestapo Official Is Linked to U.S. Intelligence." *New York Times,* February 8, 1983.

"Getty Oil Unit Gets Stake in Texaco-Bolivian Contract." *Wall Street Journal,* August 12, 1976.

Gossain, Juan. "Violencia en los Llanos." *El Espectador,* February 27, 1970.

Grünberg, Georg. "Urgent Research in North-West Mato Grosso." *Bulletin of the International Committee on Urgent Anthropological and Ethnological Research* (Vienna), No. 8, 1966.

"Guatemala: The Roots of Revolution." Washington, D.C.: Washington Office on Latin America, February 1983.

Las Guerrillas en el Perú. Lima: Ministerio de Guerra, 1966.

Hart, Laurie. "Story of the Wycliffe Bible Translators: Pacifying the Last Frontiers." *NACLA's Latin America and Empire Report,* Vol 7., No. 10, December 1973.

Hefley, James C. "Cam Townsend, 1896–1982." *Christianity Today,* May 21, 1982.

Hellman, Geoffrey. "Best Neighbor." *The New Yorker,* April 18, 1942.

Henry, Jules. "Capital's Last Frontier." *The Nation,* April 25, 1966.

Hersh, Seymour. "Hunt Tells of Early Work for a CIA Domestic Unit." *New York Times,* December 31, 1974.

Hinckle, Warren, Robert Sheer, and Sol Stern. "The University on the Make." *Ramparts Special Collectors Edition.* Ramparts Magazine Inc., 1968.

Howe, Russell Warren. "Asset Unwittingly: Covering the World for the CIA." *More,* May 1978.

"Hoy es el Día de la Integración Nacional." *El Diario* (La Paz), October 18, 1976.

Hummerstone, Robert G. "Cutting a Road Through Brazil's 'Green Hell.'" *New York Times Magazine,* March 5, 1972.

"Ideology Which SIL Transmits." *La Crónica,* December 2, 1975.

"Importante Convenio con la Continental Petroleum y la Shell." Inter-Press Service, January 29, 1972.

"Indian Situation in Brazil Today." *Indígena,* 1973.

"Indians Tell Pope They Will Protest Columbus Parties." *St. Albans Messenger,* October 17, 1991.

"El Instituto Lingüístico de Verano." *Boletín de Antropología,* University of Antigua, 1976.

Inter-American Indian Institute. *Anuario Indigenista,* 1980.

International Basic Economy. *Annual Reports,* 1959–1979.

International Petroleum Encyclopedia (annual).

Investment Companies (annual, published by Arthur Weisberger & Company).

"IPA Faculty." *IPA Review,* January 1967.

Jensen, Michael C. "The Pews of Philadelphia." *New York Times,* October 10, 1971.

Jungle Gems, 1971–72. Riberalta, Bolivia: Tumi Chucua School, Instituto Lingüístico de Verano (Summer Institute of Lingustics), 1972.

Junqueira, Carmen. "The Brazilian Indigenous Problem and Policy: The Example of the Xingu National Park." Copenhagen: International Work Group for Indigenous Affairs, 1975. IWGIA Document 13.

Kenworthy, E. W. "Unit at Cornell Aided by Conduits." *New York Times,* February 27, 1967.

Kietzman, Dale W. "Tendências de ordem lexical de aculturação lingüística em Terêna." *Revista de Antropologia,* No. 6. (Abstract in *International Journal of American Linguistics,* University of Chicago Press, No. 27, 1961.)

King, Elliot. "Serving the Spiritual." *Micro Discovery,* August 1983.

Knightly, Phillip, and Callin Lambert. "The Killing of a Colombian Indian Tribe." *Atlas,* January 1971.

Leroy, Stuart H. "The CIA's Use of the Press a 'Mighty Wurlitzer.'" *Columbia Journalism Review,* September/October 1974.

Lewis, Norman. "Eastern Bolivia: The White Promised Land." Copenhagen: International Work Group for Indigenous Affairs, 1978. IWGIA Document No. 31

———. "Genocide: From Fire and Sword to Arsenic and Bullets—Civilization Has Sent Six Million Indians to Extinction." *Sunday Times Magazine* (London), February 23, 1969.

Lisagor, Peter. "The Rockefeller Nod." *New York Post,* June 17, 1975.

Lizot, Jacques. "The Yanomami in the Face of Ethnocide." Copenhagen: International Work Group for Indigenous Affairs, 1978. IWGIA Document No. 22.

MacEoin, Gary. "U.S. Mission Efforts Threatened by CIA 'Dirty Tricks.'" *St. Anthony Messenger,* March 1975.

Machado, Maj. Olimpio Alver. "Indian Guard Trained in Brazil." *International Police Academy Review,* October 1970.

Medina, Cecilima. "The Legal Status of Indians in Brazil." *Indian Law Journal,* September 1977.

Methvin, Eugene H. "Labor's New Weapon for Democracy." *Reader's Digest,* October 1966.

Métraux, Alfred. "Disparition des Indiens dans le Brésil Central." *Bulletin of the International Committee on Urgent Anthropological and Ethnological Research* (Vienna), 1962.

Michael, Roger. "Missionaries Get 'Miracle' Copters." *Charlotte Observer,* April 15, 1974.

Miller, Mark, and Judith Miller. "The Politics of Energy vs. the American Indian." *Akwesasne Notes,* Spring 1979.

"La Misíon de Bardesio era Preparar la Llegada de B. Graham, en 1977." *El Día,* July 17, 1976.

"Misiones Protestantes Para El Impero: El Caso del Instituto Lingüístico de Verano." Associación Escuela del Departamento de Antropología, Pontífica Universidad Católica del Ecuador, April 1975.

Moody's Industrial Manual, annual, various years used.

Moody's Manual of Banks and Finance, annual, various years used.

Moody's Manual of Investments, 1944.

Moody's Municipal and Government Manual, 1965.

Moreira, Carlos de Araújo Neto. "Relatório Sôbre a Situação Atual dos Indios Kayapó." *Revista de Antropologia,* 1959.

Mott, Gordon D. "Refugees Who Fled to Mexico Tell of Army's Atrocities." *San Jose Mercury News,* August 22, 1982.

Munetar, Ben. "Agent Exposes Secret Concentration Camp in Crenaque, Brazil." *Wassaja,* November 1973.

Münzel, Mark. "The Aché: Genocide Continues in Paraguay." Copenhagen: International Work Group for Indigenous Affairs, 1978. IWGIA Document No. 17.

———. "The Aché Indians: Genocide in Paraguay." Copenhagen: International Work Group for Indigenous Affairs, 1978. IWGIA Document No. 11.

Murphy, Charles J. V. "The King Ranch South of the Border." *Fortune,* June 1969.

"Native Communities Face the SIL." *La Crónica,* December 7, 1975.

"Negro Protests Close Local Diners." "Merchants, Police Confer on Lunch Counter Service." *Charlotte Observer,* February 10, 1960.

Nevins, Allan, ed. "The Memoirs of Frederick T. Gates." *American Heritage,* April 1955.

"The New Military." *Newsweek,* January 5, 1970.

Newbold, Stokes. "Receptivity to Communist Fomented Agitation in Rural Guatemala." *Economic Development and Cultural Change,* Vol. 5, No. 4, 1957.

Novitski, Joseph. "Latin Lands Turning to Europe." *New York Times,* May 4, 1971.

O'Rourke, John T. "Our Man in Havana, William D. Pawley." *Washington Daily News,* February 20, 1961.

Oviedo, Gonzalo. "La Educacion Bilingüe." *El Mercurio,* February 1975.

"Pamela Woolworth in Stock Deal for Cattle Venture in Paraguay." *New York Times,* February 7, 1956.

"Philippine Diplomat Explains Why Group Won Award." *Charlotte News,* November 3, 1973.

Pieters, Gerhard. "Bolivia Here We Come." *Sunday Times* (London), March 12, 1978.

Plowman, Ed. "Some Missionaries Help CIA." *National Courier,* October 7, 1975.

"La Politica de Genocidio Contra los Indios de Brasil." Report by Brazilian anthropologists to the Forty-first International Congress of Americanists, Mexico City, 1974.

Presser, Harriet. "Sterilization and Fertility Decline in Puerto Rico." *Population Monograph Series,* Series 13, Berkeley, Calif., 1973.

Price, Willard. "The Amazing Amazon." *Reader's Digest,* September 1952.

"Project RADAM Maps the Unknown in Brazil." *Engineering and Mining Journal,* November 1975.

Rashke, Richard. "CIA Funded, Manipulated Missionaries." *National Catholic Reporter,* August 1, 1975.

Ray, Michele. "In Cold Blood: How the CIA Executed Che." *Ramparts,* 1969.

Redfield, Robert, and Ernest Maes, letters, quoted in editorial. *Boletín Indigenista,* Vol. 3, No. 4, December 1943.

Reed, Charles H. "Linguaje y Educación Bilingüe en Vietnam." *Shucniqui Tandanacuy Ishcay Shimipi Yachachingapac, Documento Final,* Palacio Legislativo, Ecuador, 1974.

Reeves, Richard. "The Nationwide Search for Nelson Rockefeller." *New York,* September 2, 1974.

Ribeiro, Darcy. "Culturas e Línguas Indígenas do Brasil." *Educação e Ciências Sociales,* Vol. 2, No. 6, Brazilian Center of Educational Research, 1957. Translation in Janice H. Hopper, ed., *Indians of Brazil in the Twentieth Century* (Washington, D.C.: Institute for Cross Cultural Research, 1967).

———. *A Política Indigenista Brasileira.* Rio de Janeiro: Minesterio da Agricultura Serviço de Informação o Agricola, 1962. English translation of excerpts in Pedro Agostinho, Georg Grünberg, and Sílvio Coelhos dos Santos, "A Selected Bibliography for the Study of Discrimination Against the Indians in Brazil," in Walter Dostal, ed., *The Situation of the Indian in South America* (Geneva: World Council of Churches, 1972). Abbreviated English version, "The Social Integration of Indigenous Populations in Brazil," in *International Labor Review,* 1962.

Richardson, Don. "Who Really Killed Chet Bitterman?" *Mission Frontier,* April 3, 1981.

Riding, Alan. "Guatemalan Refugees Flood Mexico." *New York Times,* August 18, 1982.

Riester, Jürgen. "Indians of Eastern Bolivia: Aspects of Their Present Situation." Copenhagen: International Work Group for Indigenous Affairs,1975, IWGIA Document No. 18.

Robison, James. "Spy Role of Missionaries Told." *Chicago Tribune,* August 2, 1975.

Rockefeller, David. "What Private Enterprise Means to Latin America." *Foreign Affairs,* April 1, 1966.

Rockefeller, Mary, and Laurance Rockefeller. "How South America Guards Her Green Legacy: Parks, Plans and People." *National Geographic,* January 1967.

"Rockefeller's IBEC." *Fortune,* February 1955.

Rondon, Candido M. da Silva. "Problema Indígena." *América Indígena,* January 1943.

"Rondônia, Capital do Estanho." *Visão,* August 28, 1972.

Ross, Okland. "Tales of Horror Haunt Camps." *Toronto Globe,* August 22, 1982.

Ruato, Darcy. "Brasil proyecto un Gigantesco Lago Artificial en la Amazonia." *El Espectador* (Bogotá), December 26, 1971.

St. George, Andrew. "How the U.S. Got Che." *True,* April 1969.

Samet, Jonathan M., Daniel M. Kutvirt, Richard J. Waxweiler, and Charles R. Key. "Uranium Mining and Lung Cancer in Navajo Men." *New England Journal of Medicine,* Vol. 310, No. 23, June 7, 1984.

Schilling, Paulo R. "Brazil: The Rebellion of the Downtrodden." *Marcha* (Montevideo), July 16, 1971. Reprinted by Latin American Documentation Center (Mexico City), Document 9b, November 1971.

Schlesinger, Stephen, and Stephen Kinzer. "Guatemala's Election." *New York Times,* January 28, 1982.

"Se Inicia Explotacíon Petrolera en los Llanos." *El Tiempo,* March 12, 1971.

"SIL and Ideological Penetration." *La Crónica,* November 29, 1975.

Siverts, Henning. "Tribal Survival in the Alto Marañon: The Aguaruna Case." Copenhagen: International Work Group for Indigenous Affairs, 1975, IWGIA Document No. 10.

"Slave Camp Denounced in Bolivia." *El Excelsior* (La Paz), June 23, 1977.

Sochurek, Howard. "American Special Forces in Action in Viet Nam." *National Geographic,* January 1965.

———. "Slow Train Through Viet Nam's War." *National Geographic,* September 1964.

———. "Viet Nam's Montagnards." *National Geographic,* April 1968.

"Special Report on Guatemala." *Survival International,* August 1982.

Spooner, Mary Helen. "Misery in Bolivia's Mines." *Financial Times,* December 30, 1984.

Standard & Poor's Directory of Corporations (annual).

Stone, I. F. *P.M.,* April 5, 1943.

———. "Officials Defied FDR's Orders." *P.M.,* September 28, 1942.

Stycos, J. M. "Female Sterilization in Puerto Rico." *Eugenics Quarterly,* Vol. 1, No. 1, 1954.

Subliminal Warfare: The Role of Latin American Studies. New York: North American Congress on Latin America, 1970.

Szulc, Tad. "U.S. May Abandon Effort to Deter Latin Dictators." *New York Times,* March 19, 1964.

———. "Why Rockefeller Tried to Cover Up the CIA Probe." *New York,* September 5, 1977.

Tax, Sol. "Ethnic Relations in Guatemala." *América Indígena,* October 1942.

"Thunder on the Right: An Unholy War Breaks Out over Evangelical Politics." *People,* October 13, 1980.

Tippett, A. R. "Taking a Hard Look at the Barbados Declaration." *Evangelical Mission Quarterly,* Summer 1972.

Townsend, W. C. "The Guatemalan Indian and the San Antonio Mission Station." *Central American Bulletin,* September 15, 1920.

———. "Romish Priesthood in Guatemala." *Central American Bulletin,* January 15, 1928.

———. "Tolo: The Volcano's Son." *Revelation,* April–October 1936.

———. "The USSR as We Saw It." *Christian Herald,* October 1975.

———. "Were They Missionaries or 'Just' Linguists?" *Christian Herald,* April 1976.

———. "Wycliffe's First Martyr." Article for *Translation* magazine, written March 20, 1963.

"Union Oil Venture in Bolivian Jungle Is First Under New Hydrocarbon Law." *Business Latin America,* April 5, 1973.

Varese, Stefano. "The Forest Indians in the Present Political Situation in Peru." Copenhagen: International Work Group for Indigenous Affairs, 1975, IWGIA Document No. 8.

Vasquez, Mario. "The Interplay Between Power and Wealth." And with Henry F. Dobyns, "The Transformation of Manors into Producers' Cooperatives." Unpublished manuscripts. Department of Anthropology, Cornell University. Ithaca, New York.

"Visita del doctor Galo Plaza al Instituto Indigenista Interamericano." *América Indígena,* Vol. 8, No. 4, October 1968.

"Voices of the Survivors." Cultural Survival and Anthropology Resource Center, September 1983.

Von Puttkamer, W. Jesco. "Brazil Protects Her Cintas Largas." *National Geographic,* September 1971.

Wasserstrom, Robert. "Revolution in Guatemala: Peasants and Politics Under the Arbenz Government." *Comparative Studies in Society and History,* Vol. 17, No. 4, October 1975.

White, Max G. "Probing the Unknown Amazon Basin—A Roundup of 21 Mineral Exploration Programs in Brazil." *Engineering and Mining Journal,* May 1973.

White, Peter T. "Hopes and Fears in Booming Thailand." *National Geographic,* July 1967.

Who's Who in America, 1972–73. Chicago: Marquis Who's Who, 1972 (other volumes of this annual also used).

Whyte, William F. "Cultural Change and Stress in Rural Peru." *Milbank Memorial Fund Quarterly,* Vol. 55, No. 4, 1967.

———. "The Role of the U.S. Professor in Developing Countries." *American Sociologist,* Vol 4. No. 1, February 1969.

Winters, Robert. "Allen Did Truth Serum Tests for U.S. Military." *Montreal Gazette,* February 25, 1984.

Wolf, Eric R., and Joseph G. Jorgensen. "Anthropology on the Warpath in Thailand." *The New York Review,* November 19, 1970.

———. "Antropología en Pos de Guerra." *América Indígena,* Vol. 31, No. 2, April 1971.

Wood, Beth. "LDS Placement Program, to Whose Advantage." *Akwesasne Notes,* Winter 1978.

Wycliffe Bible Translators. *Translation,* 1944.

———. *Translation,* Winter 1966.

Yancey, Philip. "Wycliffe: A Mission in Search of a Future." *Christianity Today,* February 19, 1982.

Periodicals and Newspapers

AIFLD Report
Akwesasne Notes
Alternativa (Bogotá)
The Andean Report
Andean Times
Anthropology Resource Center newsletter
Atlas magazine
Aviation Directory
Aviation Week
Beyond (JAARS newsletter)
Boletín Indigenista (Mexico City)
Brazil Herald (Rio de Janeiro)
Brazilian Information Bulletin
Bulletin of the American Anthropological Association
Business Latin America
Business Week
Central American Bulletin
Charlotte News and Observer
Chicago Tribune
Christian Century
Christian Science Monitor
Christianity Today
El Comercio (Quito)
El Comercio (Lima)
Conservative Digest
Correo (Lima)
La Crónica (Lima)
Cultural Survival newsletter
Current Anthropology
Dallas Morning News
El Día (Mexico City)
El Diario (La Paz)
Engineering and Mining Journal
El Espectador (Bogotá)
Evangelical Mission Quarterly
El Excelsior (La Paz)
El Expreso (Lima)
Facts on File
Financial Times
Focus
Foreign Affairs
Fortune
Harvard Crimson
Houston Chronicle
In Other Words
Indígena (Berkeley, California)

International Police Academy Review
IWGIA Newsletter
Jornal do Brasil (Rio de Janeiro)
Latin America Economic Report (London)
Latinamerica Press (Lima)
Life
The Lima Times
Miami Herald
Mother Jones
NACLA Report on the Americas
Nation
National Catholic Reporter
National Geographic
New England Journal of Medicine
New York magazine
New York Times
New York Times Magazine
News from Survival International
Newsweek
O Estado de São Paulo (São Paulo)
O Globo (Rio de Janeiro)
Oil and Gas Journal
The Oklahoma Daily (Norman)
Peruvian Times (Lima)
La Prensa (Lima)
Prensa Latina (Panama City)
Progressive
St. Albans Messenger (Vermont)
St. Petersburg Times (Florida)
San Jose Mercury News (California)
Technical Abstract Bulletin
Texas Business
El Tiempo (Bogotá)
El Tiempo (Quito)
Time
Toronto Globe
Translation
La Tribuna (Pôrto Velho)
Ultima Noticias (Quito)
U.S. News and World Report
Village Voice
Visão
Wall Street Journal
Washington Post
Washington Star-News
Wycliffe Associates Newsletter

MANUSCRIPT COLLECTIONS

Dwight D. Eisenhower Library (Abilene, Kansas)
Ann Whitman file
White House Central Files
    Confidential File
    Official File
White House Office File
    Office of the Special Assistant for National Security Affairs
Papers of:
    Elmer Bennett
    Mark Bortman
    Joseph Dodge
    General James Doolittle
    Gordon Gray
    C. D. Jackson
Department of State, Colombia file
U.S. Council on Foreign Economic Policy
U.S. President's Advisory Committee on Government Organization

Franklin D. Roosevelt Library (Hyde Park, New York)
President's Official Files
President's Personal File
President's Secretary's file
President's Special Committee to Study the Rubber Situation
Papers of:
    Adolf Berle, Jr.
    Morris L. Cooke
    Harry L. Hopkins

Gerald Ford Library (Ann Arbor, Michigan)
Papers of:
    James M. Cannon
        Robert Hartmann, interview with Nelson Rockefeller, December 2, 1977
        Trevor Armbrister, interview with Nelson Rockefeller, October 21, 1977
        Mike Turner, interview with Nelson Rockefeller, December 21, 1977
    Leo Cherne
    Edward Hutchinson
        Congressional Research Service investigation of Nelson A. Rockefeller

Harry S. Truman Library (Independence, Missouri)
White House Central Files
    Confidential File
    Official File
President's Official Files
    Secretary's File
    Permanent File
Post-Presidential Papers
Papers of:
    Henry Bennett
    Merwin Bohan
    William A. Brophy
    Clark Clifford
    Oscar Chapman
    Kenneth Iverson
    Herschel V. Johnson
    Edward G. Miller, Jr.

Dillon S. Myer
Philleo Nash
Sidney Souers
James Webb

John F. Kennedy Library (Boston, Massachusetts)
National Security Files (including Special Group Meetings)
White House Central Files
Oral history interview with Roswell Gilpatric
Oral history interview with Walter Sheridan
Papers of Luther H. Hodges
Papers of Arthur Schlesinger, Jr.

Library of Congress (Washington, D.C.)
Papers of Josephus Daniels

Lyndon B. Johnson Library (Austin, Texas)
Confidential File
    Countries Series
National Security File
    Country Series (particularly Brazil and Peru)
Name File (particularly David Rockefeller and Billy Graham)
Oral history interview with Lincoln Gordon
Oral history interview with Thomas C. Mann
Oral history interview with Nelson Rockefeller
Oral history interview with Laurance Rockefeller
White House Central Files
    Country Series
White House Diary Files

National Security Archives (Washington, D.C.)
Research records of John Marks, author of *The Search for the "Manchurian Candidate"*

Rockefeller Archive Center (Tarrytown, New York)
Papers of:
    Wayne G. Broehl
    John R. Camp
    Raymond Fosdick
    Frederick T. Gates
    Benjamin Washburn
Archives of:
    The Agricultural Development Council
    The American International Association for Economic and Social Development (AIA)
    The Asia Society
    The General Education Board
    The International Basic Economy Corporation (IBEC)
    The International Education Board
    Laura Spellman Rockefeller Memorial
    The Rockefeller Family
        John D. Rockefeller
    The Office of the Messrs. Rockefeller General Files
        John D. Rockefeller, Senior, 1918–1937
        John D. Rockefeller, Jr., Personal Papers
        John D. Rockefeller 3rd Papers
        Nelson Aldrich Rockefeller Papers
        Business Interests, 1886–1961
        Civic Interests, 1899–1961

Economic Reform Interests, 1894–1961
Educational Interests, 1896–1961
Religious Interests, 1894–1962
Rockefeller Boards, 1899–1961
World Affairs, 1896–1961
The Population Council
The Rockefeller Brothers Fund
The Rockefeller Foundation
Rockefeller Sanitary Commission
Sealantic Fund

Townsend Archives (Waxhaw, North Carolina)
Papers of William Cameron Townsend

University of Oklahoma (Norman, Oklahoma)
Western History Collections
Papers of Elmer Thomas

United States National Archives (Washington, D.C.)
Diplomatic Branch—Records and Analysis Reports
Modern Military Records
Records of the Office of Strategic Services (OSS)
Records of the Joint Chiefs of Staff
Department of Agriculture Records
Office of Foreign Agricultural Relations
Department of State Records

Washington National Archives Record Center (Suitland, Maryland)
Record Group 218, Records of the U.S. Joint Chiefs of Staff, South America
Record Group 319, Army Intelligence
Record Group 229, Records of the Office of Inter-American Affairs and the Coordinator of Inter-American
Affairs, particularly:
Amazon Basin Project
Berent Friele
Brazil-Rubber
Commercial and Financial Division
Industrial Development
Inland Waterways
Inter-American Indian Institute
Investments
Minutes of Meetings
National Indian Institute
Rubber, 1942
Rubber Investigations
Spaeth Data
Strategic Materials

Yale University Library (New Haven, Connecticut)
The Private Papers of John Collier

Selected Interviews

Philip Agee, Amsterdam.
Javier Albó, La Paz, Bolivia.
Consuelo Alfaro, Lima, Peru.
John Alsop, Mexico City, Mexico.

Rolando Andrade, Lima, Peru.
Jomingo Antuni Ch, Cuenca, Ecuador.
Nestor Arboleda, Quito, Ecuador.
Nell Arvelo-Jiménez, Madison, Wisconsin.
Consuelo Ayacucho, Lima, Peru.
Felípe Ayala, Iquitos, Peru.
Monsignor Correa Yepes Belarmino, Bishop of Vaupés, Bogotá, Colombia.
Oskar Beltran Figuerido, Villavicencio, Colombia.
Cesar Benalcazar, Quito, Ecuador.
Barbara Bentley, London, England.
Marie Berg, SIL base, Lomalinda, Colombia.
Jacob Bernstein, New York City, New York (phone interview).
John Bishop, SIL base at Limoncocha, Ecuador.
José Blandon, Bayano, Panama.
Gertrude Blom, San Cristóbal de las Casas, Chiapas, Mexico.
Edward Boer, Chapel Hill, North Carolina.
Lynn Bollinger, Dallas, Texas.
Victor Daniel Bonilla, Bogotá, Colombia.
Roger Booth and Anne-Marie Seiler-Baldiger, Leticia, Colombia, and Basel, Switzerland.
Randy Borman, SIL base at Limoncocha, Ecuador.
Rev. Roy Bourgeois, La Paz, Bolivia.
Robert K. Brown, Boulder, Colorado.
Herbert Brussow, SIL base at Lomalinda, and Villavicencio, Colombia.
José Maria Bulnes, Mexico City, Mexico.
Donald Burns, La Paz, Bolivia.
Luis Campos, Quito, Ecuador.
Franklin Canelos, Quito, Ecuador.
Monsignor Marceliano Canyes, Bishop of Amazonas, Leticia, Colombia.
Carlos Carrasco, Lima, Peru.
Stephen Corry, London, England.
Montezuma Cruz, Pôrto Velho, Brazil.
Jaime Curtain, Panama City, Panama.
Col. Geoffrey de Meiss, Zurich, Switzerland (phone interview).
Isabel and Ricardo de Pozas, Mexico City, Mexico.
Fabio Dickson, Leticia, Colombia.
Martin Diskin, Managua, Nicaragua.
Julio Dixon, Panama City, Panama.
Norma Duffy, SIL base at Limoncocha, Ecuador.
Eduardo Escobar, Lima, Peru.
Carlos Esparza, Mexico City, Mexico.
Eduardo Espinel, SENA, Vallavicencio, Colombia.
Antonio Escobar Grizales, Villavicencio, Colombia.
Roger Fenton, Leticia, Colombia.
Robert Fink, Washington, D.C.
Jay Fippinger, Des Moines, Iowa.
Orville and Helen Floden, St. Petersburg, Florida.
René Fuerst, Geneva, Switzerland.
Jim Garrison, New Orleans, Louisiana.
Walter Gates, Boston, Massachusetts (phone interview).
Roger Ginger and Orville Johnson, SIL base at Limoncocha, Ecuador.
Margaret and James Goff, Lima, Peru.
Richard Gott, London, England.
Joe Grimes, SIL base, Tumi Chucua, Bolivia.
Allen Gus Grouget, Roslyn, Virginia.
Paco Guerrera, Cuernevaca, Mexico.
Jacinto Gutiérrez, Puira, Peru.
Jerry Hemming, Miami, Florida.

Jim Higgins, Underhill, Vermont (phone interview).
Barbara Hoch, SIL base at Tumi Chucua, Bolivia.
Ray Howell, Waxhaw, North Carolina.
Darryl Hunt, Lima, Peru.
Javier Hurtado, La Paz, Bolivia.
Rev. Gregorio Iriarte, La Paz, Bolivia.
Elan Jaworki, Lima, Peru.
Herman Jesson, Los Angeles, California.
David Judd, business manager, SIL base, Pôrto Velho, Brazil.
Darryl Keener, Long Beach, California.
John Kelly, Washington, D.C.
Ken Kensinger, Bennington, Vermont.
Tom Kirby, Villavicencio, Colombia.
Jim Kostman, Washington, D.C.
Michael Lambert, Boston, Massachusetts.
James Larrick, Winston-Salem, North Carolina.
Rocque Lima, Lima, Peru.
Rev. Raul Macín, Mexico City, Mexico.
Scott Malone, Washington, D.C.
Victor·Marchetti, Vienna, Virginia.
John Marks, Washington, D.C.
La Plaz Martinéz, Leticia, Colombia.
Bonnie Mass, Boston, Massachusetts.
Frank Maurovitch, Lima, Peru.
Nicole Maxwell, Bogotá, Colombia.
Bernie May, Waxhaw, North Carolina.
Daniel McCurry, Quito, Ecuador.
Jim Miller, SIL base at Lomalinda, Colombia.
Nancy Modierno, San Cristóbal de las Casas, Chiapas, Mexico.
Lawrence J. Montgomery, Cross Anchor, South Carolina.
Thomas Moore, New York City, New York.
Filiberto Morales, Panama City, Panama.
Chip Morris, San Cristóbal de las Casas, Chiapas, Mexico.
Solomon Nahmad, Mexico City, Mexico.
Jim Nathans, San Cristóbal de las Casas, Chiapas, Mexico.
Marguerita Nolasco, Mexico City, Mexico.
William Nyman, Bogotá, Colombia.
Max Oldenberg, Leticia, Colombia.
Ronald D. Olson, Tumi Chucua, Beni, Bolivia.
Gonzales Olvido, Quito, Ecuador.
Manuel Palacios, Machala, Ecuador.
Jorge Pantaleis, La Paz, Bolivia.
Napoleon Peralta, Bogotá, Colombia.
José Pereira, Quito, Ecuador.
Kenneth Pike, International Linguistics Center, Dallas, Texas.
Daoina Pinheira, Pôrto Velho, Brazil.
Timothy Plowman, Cambridge, Massachusetts.
Dennis Popp, La Jolla, California.
Paul Powlson, Yarinacocha, Peru.
Inez Pozzi-Escot, Lima, Peru.
Harry Priest, SIL base at Tumi Chucua, Bolivia.
Monsignor Léonides E. Proaño, Bishop of Riobamba, Ecuador.
L. Fletcher Prouty, Washington, D.C.
Thomas Quigley, Washington D.C.
Chris Rack, Boston, Massachusetts.
Robert Raffauf, Boston, Massachusetts.
Rev. Luis Rainoso, Lima, Peru.

Richard Rashke, Washington, D.C.
Scott Robinson, Tlayacapan, Mexico.
Armando Rojas, Puerto Cabezas, Nicaragua.
Steve Romanoff, Worcester, Massachusetts.
Nemesio Rodriguez, Mexico City, Mexico.
Jesus San Roman, Iquitos, Peru.
José Roman, Iquitos, Peru.
Christopher Roper, London, England.
Timothy Ross, Bogotá, Colombia.
Bishop Samuel Ruiz Garcia, San Cristóbal de las Casas, Chiapas, Mexico.
Rachel Saint, SIL base at Limoncocha, Ecuador.
Caio Julio Salles Lanhoso Martins, Pôrto Velho, Brazil.
Padre Juan Santos Ortiz, Ecuador.
Rev. Paul Schlener, Marco, Brazil.
Ned Seelye, SIL base at Limoncocha, Ecuador.
Allan Shannon, Lima, Peru.
Richard Smith, Lima, Peru.
Gustavo Solis, Lima, Peru.
Rudolfo Stavenhagen, Mexico City, Mexico.
John Stockwell, Austin, Texas.
David Stoll, Boston, Massachusetts.
Paul Strike, Quito, Ecuador.
Sandy Tolan and Nancy Pistero, Prescott, Arizona (phone interview).
William Cameron Townsend, Waxhaw, North Carolina.
Yasushi Toyotomi, sheriff of FUNAI, Pôrto Velho, Brazil.
Mike Tsalickis, Tarpon Springs, Florida.
Fernando Umano, Puerto Lleras, Colombia.
Cam Uynh, Des Moines, Iowa.
Franz Vanderhoff, Mexico City, Mexico.
Erik Van Lennep, Strafford, Vermont (phone interview).
Stefano Varese, Oaxaca, Mexico, and Lima, Peru.
Dan Velie, SIL base at Yarinacocha, Peru.
Jay Vick, SIL base at Tumi Chucua, Bolivia.
Nelson Villagomez, Quito, Ecuador.
Claudio Mena Villamares, Quito, Ecuador.
Robert Wasserstrom, San Cristóbal de las Casas, Chiapas, Mexico.
Steve Weisman, London, England.
Thomas Weisman, Zurich, Switzerland.
Rev. Philip Wheaton, Washington, D.C.
Rev. William Wipfler, New York.
Consuelo Yanez, Quito, Ecuador.
Jim Yost, SIL base at Limoncocha, Ecuador.
W. Vaughn Young, Los Angeles, California.
Pilar Zarillas, Lima, Peru.

Former Peace Corps members, Washington, D.C.
Former employees of the Amazon Natural Drug Company.
Former CIA employee, Dar es Salaam, Tanzania.
Journalists, Bogotá, Colombia.
Confidential sources, Guatemala City, Guatemala.
Confidential sources, Leticia, Colombia.
Confidential sources, Lima, Peru.
Brazilian nut merchants, Pôrto Velho, Brazil.
News reporters, Pôrto Velho, Brazil.
Cuna Indians [names withheld], Bayano, Panama.
Cuna Indians [names withheld], Panama City, Panama.
Lacondón Indians [names withheld], San Cristóbal de las Casas, Chiapas, Mexico.

INDEX

Amazon basin (*cont.*)
development of, 152, 315, 316, 450, 475, 482, 517, 669; resources of, 133, 140–42, 633, 652, 655, 669–70. *See also* Bolivia; Brazil; Colombia; Ecuador; Peru; *names of specific commodities*
Amazon Development Corporation, 139, 147, 616n
Amazon Natural Drug Company (ANDCO), 497–98, 505, 509, 511, 514–15, 521–22, 738
Amazon/Orinoco link, 138, 154–55, 615–16, 633–34. *See also* "Great Lakes" proposal
Amazon Pact, 823
Amazon rain forest, 133, 134–35, 140, 152, 247, 822, 825–26
Amazon Rosewood and Commerce Company, 519
Amazon Valley Corporation, 138, 139, 140, 149
America Indígena magazine, 101, 153
American Advisory Council for Thailand, 559
American Agricultural Chemical Company, 21
American and Foreign Power Company, 425
American Anthropological Association, 557, 743
American Baptist Education Society, 20
American Baptist Foreign Mission Society, 24
American Baptist Home Mission Society, 15, 24
American Bible Society, 49, 121, 124, 881n13
American Coffee Corporation, 135, 181, 258
American Council of Learned Societies, 126, 842n9
American Farm Bureau Federation, 166
American Friends of Vietnam, 568
American Independent Party, 590
American Indian Defense Association, 12, 99
American Indian Movement (AIM): in U.S., 719, 740, 763; in Brazil, 803
American Institute for Free Labor Development (AIFLD), 441, 442, 444, 879n16
American International Association for Economic and Social Development (AIA): AIA/AID conflict, 429, 613; as antirevolutionary, 313, 729; in Brazil, 216, 251–58, 295, 297–98, 301, 424, 613; CIAA and, 848n4; in Colombia, 380; and colonization of Amazon, 232, 613–14; founded, 212; in Paraguay, 777; in Venezuela, 218–19
American Light and Power, 444, 447, 452
American Linguistic Society, 73
American Linseed Company, 21
American Molasses Company, 191, 538n
American Moravian Church, 783

American Oil Company. *See* AMOCO
American Overseas Investing Company, 306, 862n17
American Smelting and Refining Company (ASARCO), 703, 783
American Universities Research Program, 555
American University, 479, 558
Americas Society, 824
AM/LASH. *See* Cubela, Rolando
AMOCO, 514, 522. *See also* Standard Oil of Indiana
Amnesty International, 818
Anaconda Copper, 703, 719, 821. *See also* Atlantic Richfield Company
Anderson, Lambert, 771
Anderson, Robert B., 328, 422, 538–39, 851n21, 880n6
Anderson, Robert O., 789, 821
Anderson Clayton Company, 608
Andrada e Silva, José Bonifácio de, 698
Andrade, Victor, 174, 302, 694, 729
Andrianoff, Rev. T. J., 552
Anelex Corporation, 863n17
Angleton, James, 734, 758
Anglo Frigorífico, 608
Anglo Meat Processing, 298
Anglo-Mexican Oil Company, 188
Angola, CIA's covert war in, 738, 766
Anthropology, American: and Rockefeller-funded network, 126, 476–77; and U.S. counterinsurgency, 128–30, 320–21, 477–80. *See also* Barbados Conferences; Project Camelot; Strategic Index of the Americas
Antunes, Augusto T. A.: in Amapá, 316, 428, 613–14, 659; on BIB board, 660; on Chase Advisory Board, 790; and ICOMI, 316, 428, 613–14, 659, 774
Antunes Foundation, 429, 614, 659
A.O. Investing Company, 862n17
Applied anthropology, 128–30
APRA party, Peru, 396–97, 457, 469, 516
Arab oil: embargo, 716; fields, 192
Araguaia River massacre, 144
Aranha, Oswaldo, 138
Arbenz Guzmán, Jacobo, 232, 238–41, 243, 262, 319
Arbor Acres: in southern Africa, 782; in Thailand, 547
Arbuckle, Ernest, 878n39
ARCO. *See* Atlantic Richfield Company
Arévalo, Juan, 412
Argentina: anti-American protests in, 641,

610–11; and mining, 183, 188, 190, 360, 432, 440, 616–17; and oil, 181–82, 192, 257–58; and ranching, 618–20; Rockefeller holdings, 648, 784–86, 855n32
—and Bolivia, 276, 298, 302, 529
—financial affairs of, 182, 403, 421, 426, 618, 648
—government: army, 442–43, 515, 638–39; foreign relations of, 134, 166, 181, 350–51; Ministry of Agriculture, 427; Ministry of Labor, 147; Ministry of Planning and Economic Coordination, 451; National Department of Mineral Production, 662; supreme court of, 450, 451, 638
—human rights in, 650–61
—Indians of: Indian labor and CIAA, 145–47; tribal peoples, 620–29. *See also* Indian tribes
—military coups in, 186–87, 261–62, 440, 443, 632
—and nationalism, 299, 772–75
—politics in, 183–87, 450, 452, 650
—*See also* Alliance for Progress; Amazon basin; American International Association for Economic and Social Development; Bodoquena; Brazilian junta; CIA; Goulart, João; International Basic Economy Corporation; King, John Caldwell; Moreira Salles, Walther; Operation Amazon; Quadros, Jânio; Rockefeller, Nelson; Summer Institute of Linguistics; Vargas, Getúlio
Brazil Herald, 631
Brazilian-American Association of New York, 135
Brazilian-American Chamber of Commerce, 611, 671
Brazilian Election Factbook, 503
Brazilian ethnology, bibliography of, 501
Brazilian Expeditionary Force, 260, 442
Brazilian Foundation, 427
Brazilian Institute of Agrarian Reform, 624
Brazilian Institute for Democratic Action (IBAD), 442
Brazilian Investexport, 695
Brazilian junta, strategy in: Bolivia, 665, 694; Chile, 664; Uruguay, 665
Brazilian Labor Party (PTB), 184, 190
Brazilian Petroleum Company. *See* Petrobrás
Breitweiser, Gen. Robert W., 471, 895n34
Bressler, Dr. Harvey, 183
Brett, Gen. George, 199n
Brewster, Owen, 192
Brezhnev, Leonid, 798

Brito, Francisco de, 1–2
Brizola, Lionel, 425, 525
Brookings Institution, 29–30, 62, 708
Brooks, Arthur Oakley, 632–33, 885n7
Brú tribe, Vietnam, 573, 757
Bryan, William Jennings, 20, 26
Brzezinski, Zbigniew, 644, 715, 768
Buchen, Philip, 757
Buckley, William, 504–5, 509, 514–15, 567
Budhoo, Davison L., 828
Buell, Edgar "Pop," 565, 748
Bulganin, Nikolai, 272
Bulnes, Jaime, 130
Buna artificial rubber, 155, 156
Bunche, Ralph, 327, 340
Bundy, McGeorge: as Ford Foundation president, 720; in Johnson administration, 437, 490, 541, 543, 868n53; in Kennedy administration, 339, 375, 399; reliance on CIA, 339
Bundy, William, 339
Bunker, Ellsworth, 576, 581
Bureau of Indian Affairs, U.S. Department of the Interior (BIA): in American West, 4, 9, 11, 27, 29; under Collier, 94, 99, 126, 147; cuts in, 256; Indians confront, 717, 719; model for FUNAI, 652, 803; philosophy of, 477; revisions in, 576–77; and tribal police, 4, 676
Bureau of Native Affairs, New Guinea, 366
Burke, Adm. Arleigh, 355
Burke, Charles H., 15, 28, 30
Burns, Donald: in Bolivia, 746, 746n; at Chicago dedication, 283; education, 480; in Peru, 483, 484, 489, 691
Burns, Nadine, 484, 691
Bush, George: as head of CIA, 696, 734, 758, 765; as president, 823; as vice-president, 796–97
Business Advisory Council (BAC), 160, 383
Business Group for Latin America, 474, 824
Business Roundtable, 803–4
Butcher, Willard C., 783, 789
Buzomi, Fr. Francesco, 553
Byington, Alberto, 440, 443, 445, 868n53
Byrnes, James, 178

Cabell, Gen. Charles, 352, 415
Cabell, Earl, 415
Cabot, John Moors, 351, 424, 849n10
Cabot, Paul C., 426n
Cabot, Thomas C., Jr., 849n10
Café Filho (Brazilian v.p.), 261

Caffery, Jefferson, 135, 143, 148–49
Cali, Francisco, 829
California Institute of Technology, 478
California Orange Growers Association, 63, 65
Calles, Gen. Plutarco Elias, 72
Caltex, 779
"Cam." *See* Townsend, William Cameron
Camacho, Gen. Manuel Ávila, 102, 118, 125
Cambodia, 238, 547, 758–59
Cambuhy Coffee & Cotton Estates, Ltd., 301
Cameron, D. Ewen, 284
Camirí oil, 276, 496, 525
Camp, John, 232, 429, 831
Camp Wycliffe, 65, 73, 85, 249
Campos, Milton, 216
Campos, Roberto, 436, 437, 450, 610, 615
Cannon, James, 637, 762
Cantrell, William, 690
Canyes, Fr. Eduardo. *See* Canyes, Bishop
   Marceliano
Canyes, Bishop Marceliano, 387–89, 473, 519,
   521, 590
Canzeri, Joseph, 591, 786, 788, 831
Capa, Cornell, 287–88, 484
Capuchins, 387, 519
Carbon and carbon gas, in Amazon, 669
Cárdenas, Amalia, 198, 799, 802
Cárdenas, Gen. Lázaro: as benefactor of Cam,
   74, 83, 131, 166, 198, 209, 287; and foreign
   relations, 98, 169, 322; meets Nelson
   Rockefeller, 93; as Mexican president, 61, 66,
   67, 71–72, 84, 102; as supporter of Indians,
   97, 206
Cárdenas Solarzano, Cuauhtémoc, 799, 802, 830
Cárdenas Museum (Waxhaw, N.C.), 799, 820
Cardin, Christian, 573
Cargill Agricola e Comercial, S.A. (CASCA), 217,
   307
Caribbean Free Trade Association, 645
Carlsen, William, 565
Carranza, Venustiano, 70
Carrion, Alejandro, 813
Carter, Jimmy, 760–63, 768, 774, 788, 795
Cassiterite, 620, 652–54, 773, 774
Castelo Branco, Humberto de, 425, 444, 449,
   450, 654
Castillo Armas, Carlos, 243, 244, 312
Castillo-Cárdenas, Gonzalo, 686
Castle and Cooke, 878n39
Castro, Fidel: assassination plots against, 266,
   348, 354, 739; and Cuban revolution, 311,
   313; and Guevara, 515, 525; and ICBMs,

374; as law student, 203; relationship with
   U.S. of, 325, 416, 517
Castro, Raúl, 325
Catavi, Bolivia, massacre, 153, 157
Cater, Douglas, 575
Caterpillar Tractor, 695
Catholic Action, 807
Catholic Bishops Conference, 818
Catholic church. *See* Roman Catholic church
Catholic Relief Services, 745
Celler, Emmanuel, 880n6
Center for Research in the Social Sciences, 558,
   558n
Central American Bulletin, 44
Central American Common Market, 645
Central American Mission (C.A.M.), 43, 47, 48,
   238
Central Brazil Foundation, 152
Central Highlands, Vietnam, 546–47, 568
Central Intelligence Agency. *See* CIA
Central University, Quito, 636
Cerro de Pasco Corporation, 486, 703
Chagnon, Napoleon, 773
Champion, George, 293, 689, 783, 791
Chang, Juan Pablo ("El Chino"), 525, 532–33
Chapin, Dwight, 596
Charismatic Renewal, 770
Charlotte, North Carolina, 323, 324, 384–85,
   860n7
Chase International Investment Corporation,
   568
Chase Manhattan Bank: board of directors of,
   789–91; and Iran, 787; in Latin America,
   451, 458, 459, 654–55, 659; and Vietnam
   lobby, 568. *See also* Rockefeller, David
Chase National Bank: and Batista regime, 313;
   Latin American Department of, 211, 258,
   285n, 412; links with Nelson Rockefeller, 75,
   154, 190, 257. *See also* Chase Manhattan
   Bank; Rockefeller, David
Chase Sardi, Miguel, 680, 685, 775
Chavez, Cesar, 542, 880n14
Cheney, Dick, 765, 768
Chennault, Anna, 595, 595n, 596
Chennault, Gen. Claire, 595n, 852n45
Chesebrough-Pond's, 852n45
Chevron Resources, 692, 719
Chiang Kai-shek, 35, 170, 238, 595n
Chiang Mai, Thailand, 556–57, 565, 743, 757
Chiapas, Mexico, 130–31, 201–2, 802, 830
Chicol, Joe, 63
Chile, 158, 164, 166, 243, 663–64, 703, 744

Chilean Development Corporation, 663
China: China lobby, 595n; at Dumbarton Oaks, 161; missions in, 32–35, 123; nationalism in, 34; Nixon in, 709
Chinlund, Edwin, 293n
"Chino, El." *See* Chang, Juan Pablo
Chiriboga Villagomez, José, 277–78, 281–82, 287, 321
Chou En-lai, 740
Christian and Missionary Alliance (C&MA), 246, 366, 549, 552–53, 565, 571, 757
Christian Century magazine, 292
Christian Church of the Word, 816
Christian Democratic Party, Chile, 662, 663
Christian Herald, 46
Christian Television Network, 386
Christopher, Warren, 392
Chrysler Corporation, 404, 634. *See also* Hanna–National Steel–Chrysler complex
Church, Frank, 745, 804
Church of the Word by Gospel Outreach, 809
Churchill, Winston, 157, 158, 164, 171
CIA (Central Intelligence Agency): administration of, 144, 264, 357, 690, 733, 734; in Africa, 327–28, 738, 766; and Amazon hallucinogens and poisons, 504–5, 508–9; and Bay of Pigs, 333, 343, 347–56; and drug traffic, 524; in Far East, 222, 343, 556, 565, 566, 877n27; in Guatemala, 233, 239, 241, 242, 262, 413; organizations used as fronts by, 180, 341, 375, 662, 879n16; in Philippines, 208, 209, 221, 234, 235–38; in South America, 275, 349, 431, 471–72, 490–91, 503, 515, 745; tactics of, 256, 264–65, 398, 448, 467, 497, 690, 737; and U-2 flights, 271, 331; use of missionaries, 564–65, 743–45, 751–52, 756–59; use of social scientists, 557–58; use of tribal people in war, 503–4, 565, 574. *See also* Colby, William; Dulles, Allen; "Family Jewels"; Helio Courier airplane; Helms, Richard; King, John Caldwell; Lansdale, Edward; Mind control experiments; Rockefeller, Nelson
CIAA: administration of, 107, 108, 112, 115, 154, 159, 180, 212; and development schemes, 113–15, 135, 139, 152, 181–82, 201, 224; and Indians, 121, 124, 126–27, 144; as intelligence unit, 137, 169; and *Partners in Progress*, 226–28, 256; personnel on Rockefeller campaign staff, 311; programs of, 145, 146, 150–51, 167; in wartime, 113, 154–55, 156, 180

CIMI. *See* Missionary Indigenist Council
CIT Financial Corporation of New York, 306, 855n32
Cities Service Oil, 801
Civil Aeronautics Board, 721
Civil Affairs Office (CAO), Philippines, 235
Civil Air Transport (CAT), 269, 595n, 852n45
Civil Irregular Defense Groups (CIDG) 553, 575
Civil Operations and Rural Development Support (CORDS), 566–67
Clandestine Services for the Western Hemisphere, 144, 733. *See also* King, John Caldwell
Clark, Leonard, 285
Clayton, Will, 115, 139
Clifford, Clark, 583, 585, 587, 594
Cline, Ray, 734
Clinton, Bill, 830
CNPI. *See* National Council for the Protection of the Indian
Coal: in Amazon basin, 133; in Vietnamese Central Highlands, 568
Cobb, Jerry, 522
Coca, Gen. Ariel, 813
Coerr, Wymberly, 602
Coffee, 239, 240, 258–59, 379
Coffin, William Sloane, 761, 795
Coggins, Wade, 689
Cohen, Patrick, 552–53
Coherent Radiation company, 725
COINTELPRO program, FBI, 392, 731
Colby, William, 566–67, 735, 737, 756, 758, 765
Cold War: ideology, 583, 665, 694; strategy, 191, 220–21, 226–28, 645, 745
Colgate-Palmolive, 804
Collazo, Oscar, 223–24
Collier, Charles, 144, 145
Collier, John: as Commissioner of Indian Affairs, 67, 89, 99, 145, 145n, 147, 207, 257; founds American Indian Defense Association, 13; heads Institute of Ethnic Affairs, 256–257; and National Indian Institute, 107; as supporter of Indians, 29, 127, 460n, 677
Collier, Peter, 540
Colombia: American interests in, 116, 143; military in, 312, 393, 684; protest in, 349, 636; resources of, 136, 152, 379–81. *See also* Amazon basin
Colombian Finance Corporation, 380
Colombian National Oil Company, 692
Colonization in Paraguay, 777n

First Global Forum on the Environment, 822, 823

First Inter-American Conference on Indian Life, Mexico, 96–97, 99, 100–101, 124, 207, 677

First National Bank of Boston, 190, 867n8

First National Bank of Chicago, 620

First National Bank of Dallas, 569

First National City Bank, New York, 312, 459, 562, 570, 660, 669, 867n8

First Union National Bank, 385

Fish, Hamilton, 97

Fitzgerald, Desmond, 662

Flanagan, Mannie, 130

Fleming, Peter, 284

Flipse, Joseph, 565

Fluorspar, 557

Fontainha Geyer, Paulo, 660

Forbes, Alexander E., 46

Ford, Gerald: and foreign affairs, 744–45, 757; and Nelson Rockefeller, 729, 764–65, 780, 796; as president, 729, 764–65, 767; as vice-president, 716, 721–22

Ford Foundation, 569, 720

Ford Motor Company, 134–35, 337

Fordlândia rubber plantation, 134

Foreign Intelligence Advisory Board, 6, 411, 664, 690, 707

Foreign Ministers Conference (1942), 156

Foreign Operations Administration, 256

Foreign Policy Association, 118

Foreign Policy Research Institute, 371, 503, 510

Foreign Service Institute, 398

Food for the Hungry, 748, 752

Forrestal, James V., 96, 847n1

Fort Bragg, North Carolina, 291, 358, 359, 392, 479

Fort Sill, Oklahoma, 60n, 122

Forty-first International Congress of Americanists, 888n67

Fosdick, Dr. Harry Emerson, 12, 26, 82, 176

Fosdick, Raymond: as head of Rockefeller Foundation, 36, 191, 220–21; as a liberal, 12, 28, 37, 89; as trustee of Brookings Institution, 30

Fourth Russell Tribunal on Human Rights, 803

Fox, Edward, 472

Franco, Gen. Francisco, 312, 388

Frear, James A., 29

Free Asia Committee, 234

Free Cuba Committee, 864n48

Free Europe Committee, 852n45

Free Trade Zone, 319, 607, 645, 668

Freeport Sulphur Company, 325, 363, 364, 542, 778, 859n44

Frei, Eduardo, 663, 707

Friele, Berent: and Bodoquena purchase, 30; Brazilian-American business associations of, 135; and CIAA in Brazil, 133, 137–38; and IBEC in Brazil, 258, 298, 452; advice to Nelson Rockefeller, 154, 181; on South American tour, 831

Fries, Charles, 122, 124

French Indochina, 133, 208. See also Vietnam

Fubini, Eugene G., 339, 372

Fuentes Roldan, Alfredo, 320

Fulbright, William, 415

Fuller, Charles, 63, 65, 123, 200, 201

Fuller Theological Seminary, 689

FUNAI (National Foundation for the Indian): and Amazon development, 670; created, 4, 624; and Indian tribes, 673, 698, 803; mission and philosophy of, 652, 774; and missionaries, 627, 651, 772

Fundamentalism, Christian: backers of, 123, 202, 248, 284, 292–95; and election of Reagan, 803–6; and Fundamentalist Controversy, 24–27, 176, 407–8; and Indian ethnicity, 483, 687, 689, 750–51; and modernism, 21, 26–27, 32–39, 795; nexus with politics, 408, 454, 796–97, 804–5; and Religious Roundtable, 803; and *Rethinking Missions*, 39–40; and Rockefellers, 22, 293; and settling American frontier, 20; in South, 34, 122, 323, 324, 385–86, 804; in Vietnam, 510, 549, 553, 747. *See also* Fosdick, Dr. Harry Emerson; Gates, Frederick; Mott, John; Summer Institute of Linguistics; Wycliffe Bible Translators

Fundamentalism, Islamic, 783, 796, 798

Fundamentalists: in American politics, 454, 544, 590; as missionaries, 26, 525, 819. *See also* Summer Institute of Linguistics; Wycliffe Bible Translators

F.W. Woolworth, 776

Gaitán, Jorge, 204, 392

Gallagher, John F., 887n32

Gallegos, Rómulo, 218–19

Gallotti, Antonio, 660, 790

Galo Plaza: at Chapultepec, 168; and OAS, 601–3, 645, 663, 677; as president of Ecuador, 209, 222, 277, 285, 496; and Nelson Rockefeller, 285–86, 602, 637; and SIL, 287; at U.N. founding, 174

Galvão, Eduardo Encas, 501
Gamio, Manuel, 68, 100, 198, 207, 319
Gandhi, Mohandas K., 52, 54–57
Ganso Azul Oil Company, 245
Ganso Azul oil field, Peru, 120, 151, 193, 245, 260, 459, 514
Garcia, Frank, 306
Gardner, John, 787
Gates, Frederick, 20–21, 33, 37
Gates, Walter, 900n68
Geisel, Gen. Ernesto, 774
Geneen, Harold, 425, 753
General Accounting Office, 426
General Advisory Committee on Foreign Assistance Programs, 474, 572–73. *See also* Rockefeller, David
General Aircraft, 340, 341
General Education Board, 21, 82, 215, 377
General Electric, 160
General Motors, 383, 442, 641
General Rubber Company, 844n30
Geneva Accord (1962), 547
Geneva Agreement (1954), 588
Geneva Convention (1925), 575, 892n21
Geneva Summit Conference (1955), 270, 332
Genocide: in Amazon, 1–3, 623–24, 676–77, 835n2, 884n63; and Barbados Conference, 680; and counterinsurgency warfare, 359; link with development, 827, 828, 829, 848n8; in Paraguay, 775–78. *See also* Indians: massacres of
Genocide Convention, U.N., 827–28
Genocide in Paraguay, 775, 778, 826
Geophysical Service, Inc. (GSI), 276, 570
Georgetown University: Hospital, 266, 505; School of Foreign Service, 602
Gerardi, Bishop Juan, 818
Germany: in Latin America during World War II, 118, 125, 134, 138, 849n12; postwar plans for at Yalta, 170–71; prewar competition in Latin America, 91, 92, 96, 97, 116–18
Geschickter, Dr. Charles, 265–66, 505
Getty Oil, 750
Geyer, Georgie Ann, 412
Giancana, Sam, 739
Giap. *See* Vo Nguyen Giap
Gil, Manuel, 413, 864n48
Gilpatric, Roswell: and counterinsurgency, 358, 375, 398; and Institute of Defense Analysis, 478; promotes K. T. Young, 560; in Special Group, 343; as undersecretary of defense, 335, 337, 434

Gilpatrick, Chadbourne, 221, 267, 562
Glick, Philip, 429
Golbery do Couto e Silva, Gen., 444, 450, 713
Gold, in Amazon, 133, 670
Gold crisis (1968), 585, 714, 880n17
Goldberg, Arthur, 724, 725
Goldwater, Barry: backs Nixon in 1968, 579–80; Kennedy consults, 355; Nelson Rockefeller courts in 1976, 761; on Nixon sellout to Rockefeller, 335; presidential campaign of, 404, 406, 407, 408, 410, 453, 454
Gómez, Juan Vicente, 77, 217
González Videla, Gabriel, 663
Good Neighbor Policy, 84, 97, 153, 155, 166, 283, 349, 356
Goodell, Charles, 592
Goodwin, Richard, 356, 356n, 377, 584
Goodyear, Charles, 146
Goodyear Rubber Company, 136
Gorbachev, Mikhail, 824
Gordon, Lincoln: as ambassador to Brazil, 421, 424, 444, 445–46, 617; appointed assistant secretary of state for Latin American affairs, 449; courts Galo Plaza for OAS, 602
Gospel Missionary Union, 284
Gospel Outreach, 816
Gottlieb, Dr. Sidney, 265, 325, 354, 505, 508, 567, 732
Goulart, João: as labor minister, 261; leftist leanings of, 296, 314, 443, 445; meets Nelson Rockefeller and Berle, 316; overthrow of, 439, 440–41, 448, 449; presidency of, 404, 423, 425, 426, 431
Governors' conferences, 329, 370, 422
Grace, J. Peter, 312, 397, 660, 662, 673, 703, 712, 717, 887n32
Graham, Billy: in American politics, 399, 544, 580, 690; Fundamentalist backing of, 40, 202, 290, 324, 761; Rockefellers' funding of crusades, 290, 294, 689; and SIL, 290, 486, 812, 820; support of Vietnam missions, 552. *See also* Billy Graham Crusade
Grau San Martín, Ramón, 89
Gray, Gordon, 332
Gray, L. Patrick, 731
"Great Lakes" proposal, 138, 154–55, 615–16, 633–34, 669
Great Southwest Corporation, 579, 880n6
Green, James, 799
Green Berets: in Amazon, 358, 359, 433–34, 491, 503, 530; and counterinsurgency, 375;

and Fort Bragg display, 387; in Vietnam, 291, 358, 549
Greene, Betty, 200, 201, 552
Greene, Jerome, 30
Gregory, Don, 363, 367
Grenfell, Sir Wilfred, 31
Grew, Joseph, 175, 177
Griset, Eugene and Lula, 50
Griset, Loren, 744
Grünberg, Georg, 620, 622, 686
Guatemala: banana industry in, 849n10; coups in, 209, 264, 412, 730; massacre in, 815–16; Ministry of Education, 319; plan for invasion of, 241, 243; revolution in, 232
Guelier, Lidea, 813
Guerrilla Army of the Poor, 806, 809, 817
Guevara, Ernesto Lynch (Che): in Bolivia, 517, 523, 525–34, 639, 693; in CIA custody, 244; in Congo, 490, 493; and Cuban revolution, 325, 392, 515; death of, 533–34; at Punta del Este, 361–62
Guevara, Hector Cordero, 493
Guggenheim family, 326, 844n30
Gulf Oil: benefactor of IBAD, 412; in Bolivia, 276, 525, 528, 692; in Brazil, 189, 258, 304; in Colombia, 143, 387, 395; in Venezuela, 77
Guzmán, Loyola, 696

Hagerty, James, 263
Haggerty, Patrick, 761, 791, 853n20
Haig, Alexander, 720, 721, 762, 790, 812
Haldeman, H. R., 595, 730
Halstead, Dr. Bruce, 509
Hamilton, Fowler, 429, 868n53
Hammer, Armand, 756
Hanbury-Tenison, Robin, 677
Haney, Albert, 241
Haney, Ted, 747
Hanks, Nancy, 787
Hanna Mining, 188, 360, 404, 426, 435, 442, 652, 867n29
Hanna–National Steel–Chrysler complex, 404, 426, 426n, 435
Hannah, John, 743
Hanson, Earl Parker, 135, 137
Harder, Lewis B., 633, 662, 712, 887n32
Harding, Warren G., 25
Harding, William Barkley, 152
Harnoncourt, René d', 147
Harper, William R., 22
Harrar, J. George, 572
Harriman, William Averell: as governor of New

York, 295, 310; as heir, 83; and Marshall Plan, 424; and Paris peace talks, 587, 595; at State Department, 204, 228, 230; and test ban, 405; at U.N. founding, 174
Harrison, Wallace, 211, 295n, 315, 638
Hartmann, Robert, 764
Harvard University: anthropology at, 100, 129, 366, 698; Bundy as dean of arts and sciences, 339; K. T. Young teaches at, 559; Kissinger at, 309, 335, 355–56; Michael Rockefeller at, 364; and research funding, 873n32. *See also* Peabody Museum
Hatfield, Mark, 756–57, 759
Hawkins, Jack, 351
Haya de la Torre, Victor, 396, 457, 469, 516
Heckathorne, Malcolm "Mac," 341
Helio Aircraft Corporation, 340, 384
Helio Courier airplane, 269, 282, 327, 340–42, 352, 384, 565, 853n1, 872n25
Helliwell, Paul L. E., 877n27
Helms, Jesse, 805
Helms, Richard: and Bay of Pigs, 347, 730; and Bolivia, 530; and Chile, 664; as CIA chief, 399, 567, 732
Hemisphere Economic Policy, 95, 96
Henry, Jules, 564
Heraud, Javier, 470
Hernandez, Aurelio, 529
Hernández de Alba, Gregorio, 387, 395
Hersh, Seymour, 735
Herter, Christian, 320, 326
HEW, 126, 256, 265, 266
Hickenlooper Amendment, 458, 635
Hickey, Gerald C., 568
Higher War College, Brazil, 260, 442, 667
Highlander Education Project, 552
Hispanoil, 809
Hitler, Adolf, 97–98, 155
Hizballah, 504
Hmong (Meo) tribe: in Laos, 548, 555, 565, 574; resettlement to Bolivia, 748, 749, 752
Ho Chi Minh: accepts offer of peace talks, 587; and Diem, 267, 359; fights the French, 208; and Vietnam War, 265, 543, 547, 573
Ho Chi Minh Trail, 548, 573–74, 757
Hobbing, Enno, 381, 708n
Hodges, Luther, 378, 379, 381, 382–83, 861n8
Hoffa, Jimmy, 579, 739
Hoffman, Albert, 508
Holland, Henry, 312
Holland, Kenneth, 339, 832
Holland, Spessard, 321

Holmberg, Allen, 476
Holtzman, Elizabeth, 725
Honduras, 242, 243, 635
Hoopes, Townsend, 583, 585, 587
Hoover, Herbert, 30
Hoover, Herbert, Jr., 251
Hoover, J. Edgar, 113, 165, 184, 578, 708, 851n21. *See also* FBI
Hopkins, Harry, 88, 92, 95, 162
Hopper, Janice, 501, 503, 625
Hopper, Rex, 479, 503, 625
Horowitz, David, 540
House, Roy Temple, 122
Howard, Lisa, 416
Hruska, Roman, 592
Hudson Institute, 615, 633, 887n55
Hughes, Charles Evans, 25
Hughes, Howard, 731
Hukbalahap (Huks), 205, 234, 235, 236
Hull, Cordell: appointed secretary of state, 72; competition with Welles, 156; convenes Dumbarton Oaks, 160–61; diplomacy of in Latin America, 84, 86, 101, 157; and Nelson Rockefeller, 96, 143, 175; resigns, 162
Human Ecology Fund, 874n32
Hummerstone, Robert, 671
Humphrey, Hubert, 543, 588, 591, 594, 596
Hunt, E. Howard, 244, 708, 710, 730, 734
Hunt, H. L., 324, 408, 486
Hunt, Nelson Bunker, 408, 415, 486, 570, 590, 805
Huntington, Samuel P., 561, 564, 768
Hussein, Saddam, 783
Huxley, Matthew, 484

IBAD. *See* Brazilian Institute for Democratic Action
IBEC. *See* International Basic Economy Corporation
ICBM. *See* Minuteman; Titan II
Ickes, Harold, 88, 99, 145
ICOMI (Industria e Comercio de Minerios), 613, 659, 774. *See also* Antunes, Augusto T. A.; Bethlehem Steel
IDAB. *See* International Development Advisory Board
IFI. *See* Inter-American Finance and Investment Corporation
I.G. Farben, 97, 155, 156
Igorot tribes, Philippines, 800
III. *See* Inter-American Indian Institute
Indian Claims Commission, 719

Indian Defense Association, 28
Indian languages. *See* Tribal languages
Indian New Deal, 99
Indian Reorganization Act of 1934, 99
Indian reservations: in Brazil, 317, 610, 681; in U.S., 577, 719–20, 763, 891n33
Indian Rights Association, 28–30
Indian tribes (of North and South America):
—discussed: Aché, 504, 681, 775, 803, 826; Auca, 250, 493, 603–6; Aymará, 472, 746; Ayoreo (Moro), 680, 750; Beiço-de-Pau, 622, 623–24, 625, 628; Blackfoot, 16–17, 26; Cakchiquel, 41, 46, 240, 244, 806, 929; Campa, 489, 491–93, 510, 512, 514–15, 534, 684, 801, 869n17; Canelas, 623, 625, 626–27; Cintas Largas, 1–3, 620, 624–27, 673, 698, 712, 773–74, 888n66; Colorado, 285, 286, 287, 874n36; Creek, 13, 719; Guajibo, 681, 691–92, 753; Guaraní, 525, 528–29, 623, 829; Ixil Maya, 243, 806, 807–9, 815, 816; Kadiwéu, 300–301, 319, 625; Karajá, 319, 436, 625, 670; Kayapó, 215, 618, 670; Kekchí, 239, 806, 818; Kofán, 603, 685, 874n36; Kréen-Akaróre, 618, 626, 628; Lacondón, 125–26, 130–31; Mapuche, 664, 698; Matses, 461, 465–66, 481–82, 493, 514, 522, 821; Maxacalí, 215, 623, 625, 676; Miskito, 783, 810; Nambikuára, 87n, 623; Navajo, 15, 577, 717–18, 780, 803; Otomi, 108, 150; Parukotó-Charúma, 25–26; Pipil, 50, 143, 813; Quechua (Peru), 456–57, 486, 493, 515, 746; Quichua (Ecuador), 284, 285, 874n36; Secoya, 603, 874n36; Shapra, 250, 484, 486; Shoshone, 576–77, 719; Sibundoy, 386–87, 519, 681; Sioux, 577, 719, 763, 803; Suruí, 504, 652, 712; Tembé, 619, 670; Terêna, 300–301, 318–19, 360, 432, 856n25; Urubús-Kaapor, 619, 670; Xavante, 152, 315, 319, 624–25, 803, 828; Xikrín, 67, 618, 625, 626; Yanomami, 773–74, 829; Yaqui, 15, 123
—other tribes mentioned: Aguatatec, 240; Amahuaca, 514; Amarajaeiri, 801; Angaité, 777; Apache, 718; Apalaí, 670; Apinayé, 319; Arauca, 681; Arikiéna, 670; Black Carib, 240; Borôros, 623; Botocudos, 215; Carib, 144; Carijona, 811; Catio, 633; Chimayo, 15; Chippewa, 15; Chulupí, 681; Comanche, 711; Cree, 719; Cuiva, 681; Eastern Ojibway, 719; Embera, 633; Gorotíre, 670; Guajajara, 319; Havasupai-Walappa, 719; Hixkaryána,

Joint Brazil-U.S. Development Commission, 259

Joint Post-War Development Group for Vietnam, 668

Joint U.S. Military Advisory Group, Greece, 433, 865n38

Jones, James A., 805

Jones, James Wesley, 471, 538

Jonsson, John Erik, 570, 761, 853n20

Journey to Manaos, 137

J.P. Morgan Company, 76

Jungle Aviation and Radio Service. *See* JAARS

Jungle warfare bases: in Bolivia, 512; in Brazil, 489, 503, 511, 534, 628; in Colombia, 395, 511

Junqueira, Antonio, 624

"Junta, the," 92, 95, 108

Juruna, Mário, 803

Kahn, Herman, 615–16, 633, 686

Kaolin, in Brazilian Amazon, 655

Karamessines, Thomas, 865–66n38

Kasavubu, Joseph, 326

Keating, Kenneth, 399, 537

Kendall, Donald, 579, 701

Kennan, George, 214

Kennecott Copper, 703, 717

Kennedy, Edward, 584, 736

Kennedy, Jacqueline, 391–92, 415, 416

Kennedy, John Fitzgerald: appointments from Rockefeller Studies panels, 335–39; assassination of, 415–16, 738; and Berle, 375; and business, 357, 389, 401–3; in Colombia, 391–92; and Cuba, 343, 351–57, 405, 414; and David Rockefeller, 402–4, 411, 665–66; and foreign affairs, 410, 414; forms administration, 335, 337; liberalism of, 405, 414; and Nelson Rockefeller, 335, 371, 406–7, 411; and Peru, 397, 398, 458; popularity of, 405, 421; presidential campaign, 324, 329, 415; as senator, 267. *See also* Counterinsurgency doctrine; Ngo Dinh Diem; Project Eagle; Rockefeller, Nelson: and Kennedys

Kennedy, Robert Francis: assassination of, 591; and CIA, 416, 536, 538; elected senator, 536–44; and ITT, 404, 425; in JFK administration, 355, 357, 371, 398–400, 405; as JFK campaign manager, 336; policy conflicts with Nelson Rockefeller and Johnson, 537, 538–40, 541–42, 576–77; presidential campaign (1968), 586, 589, 590, 880n14; and Vietnam, 542–44

Kensinger, Ken, 874n36

Kerr-McGee company, 718

Khomeini, Ayatollah Ruhollah, 783, 796

Khrushchev, Nikita, 273, 274, 328, 333, 374, 400

Khuzestan Water and Power Authority, 788

Kibwe, Jean-Baptiste, 341n

Kidd, Baron, 593

Kietzman, Dale, 202, 318, 437, 488–89, 500, 558, 570, 651

Kietzman, Harriet, 318

Kim Il-Sung, 208

Kimball, Linsley, 293

Kindberg, Will, 489

King, Coretta, 336

King, John Caldwell (J. C.): in Amazon, 140, 143–44, 424, 446, 509, 511, 522; in Argentina, 233; and assassination plots, 325, 348, 354, 393, 410–11, 735, 738–39; in CIA, 149, 265, 325, 393, 497; and Cuba, 353, 356, 410–11; dies, 739–40; in Guatemala, 241; at Johnson & Johnson, 116, 138–39, 299; and Mafia, 348; and 1964 Brazil coup, 441, 446; in Peru, 494, 496–99. *See also* Amazon Natural Drug Company

King, Rev. Martin Luther King, Jr., 336, 578, 589, 731, 760

King, Rev. Martin Luther King, Sr., 795

King Hurley Company, 384, 490

King Ranch: do Brasil, 618–19, 821; in Texas, 75, 298, 761

Kintner, William, 327n, 359, 371, 390, 510, 748

Kirby, Alan, 579

Kirby, Fred, 579

Kirkpatrick, Gen. Lyman, 504

Kissinger, Henry: advises Nelson Rockefeller, 355, 452, 709; on Chase Advisory Board, 791; and foreign affairs, 601, 696, 707, 709, 765, 766; at Harvard, 309, 335, 355–56; and Nelson's death, 795, 796; at Paris peace talks, 587, 595–96, 881n13

Kissinger, Nancy Maginnes, 709, 831

Kleberg, Richard J., Jr., 75, 139, 298, 618, 662

Kluckhohn, Clyde, 129–30

Knightly, Philip, 571

Knowland, William F., 238

Komer, Robert, 566

Korean War, 208, 222, 225, 245, 258, 260, 302

Korry, Edward, 663

Kosygin, Aleksei, 543

Kreig, Margaret, 497, 509

Kresge, Howard, 573
Kruel, Gen. Armoury, 447
Kubisch, Jack B., 775
Kubitschek, Juscelino: and Bolivian controversy, 303; and R. Campos, 437; as governor, 278; on Inter-American Committee, 663; as president of Brazil, 295–308, 314, 315
Kuhn, Loeb, 715n
Kuparuk oil fields, 718
Kurulu tribe, New Guinea, 366
Ky. *See* Nguyen Cao Ky
Kyes, Roger, 251

Labor movement: in Bolivia, 153–54; in Brazil, 190, 431, 443–44, 450; in Mexico, 84; in Uruguay, 641
Lacerda, Carlos, 261, 424, 441, 614, 617, 629
Land reform: in Brazil, 430; in Cuba, 314; in Guatemala, 238, 240, 244
Landabaru, Jon, 801
Langer, William, 856n38
Lansdale, Edward: and Cuba, 266, 312; and counterinsurgency, 343, 358, 375; in Philippines, 208, 235, 268; and Vietnam, 238, 265, 560, 565, 571
Lansing, Robert, 39
Lansky, Meyer, 517, 863n48
Laos, 238, 547, 556, 743
LaRotta, Ramón, 392
Latin American Business Highlights, 212
Latin American Free Trade Association, 645
Latin American Information Committee (LAIC), 381, 474, 708, 870n36
Latin American Institute, 496
Laymen's Foreign Missions Inquiry, 39
Lead, in Amazon, 652, 669
League of Nations, 37, 156, 272
Lechín, Juan, 472
Le Cron, J. D., 159
Le Duc Tho, 709
Lee, Ivy, 19, 26, 97, 744
Legters, L. L., 47, 51, 60, 67, 87n, 124, 436, 697
LeMay, Gen. Curtis, 400, 569, 590
Lemnitzer, Gen. Lyman, 356, 359, 833
Le Tourneau, Robert, 245, 246, 247, 248–49, 514
Lewis, Drew, 767
Lewis, Norman, 4, 651, 778
Liberal party, Colombia, 164, 204, 387, 392
Liberal party, New York, 310, 538
Liddy, G. Gordon, 732
Light Companies of Brazil, 660

Lightner, Oscar C., 881n2
Lilienthal, David, 108, 668, 669, 788
Lilly Foundation, 569n
Limited war concept, 371, 375, 472
Limoncocha SIL base, Ecuador, 290, 360, 433, 487, 509, 603, 605
Lincoln Center for the Performing Arts, 295n, 355
Lindholm, Donald, 771
Lindsay, Frank, 372n
Lindsay, John V., 592
Lindskoog, John, 874n36
Linguistic Society of America, 66
Linhares, José, 187, 188, 189
Link, Walter, 360
Linowitz, Sol, 603
Lisu tribe, Thailand, 557
Litton Industries, 670–71
Lleras Camargo, Alberto: at Chapultepec, 168; as Colombian president, 176, 310, 312; and Cuba, 349–50; and "Great Lakes" proposal, 633; and Nelson Rockefeller, 168, 174, 310; as OAS chief, 209, 387; relations with U.S., 380, 391, 416; at U.N. founding, 174
Lloyd Aereo Boliviano, 118, 152
Lobatón, Guillermo, 491, 493
Lockett, Thomas, 128
Lockwood, John, 180, 210
Lodge, Henry Cabot, 342, 410
Loma Linda University, 509–10
Lomalinda SIL base, Colombia, 395, 487
Lon Nol, 758
London School of Economics, 312
Long, Huey, 863n48
Loos, Eugene, 485, 490, 499
López Contreras, Gen. Eleázar, 217
López Michelsen, Alfonso, 752
López Portillo, José, 802
Los Angeles Bible House, 42
Lott, Henrique, 654
Love, George, 426n
Lovett, Robert, 221, 337, 859n44
Lucas, Gen. Benedicto, 814
Luce, Don, 565
Luce, Henry, 287–88, 293n, 295n
Luciano, Lucky, 864n48
Ludwig, Daniel K., 406, 613, 633, 654–55, 670, 886n27. *See also* Antunes, Augusto T. A.; Chase Manhattan Bank
Lumumba, Patrice, 325, 339, 340, 493
Luykx, Nicolaas G. M. II, 555
Lyon, Floyd, 487

National Association of Evangelicals, 123
National Association of Manufacturers, 383
National Aviation, 793
National Bank for Economic Development, 437
National Bilingual Education Program, 483, 746n
National Commission on Critical Choices, 710
National Committee for the Alliance for
　Progress, 474
National Congress of American Indians, 577
National Council for the Protection of the Indian
　(CNPI), 500
National Council of Churches, 745, 748, 819
National Defense Council, 160
National Foundation for the Indian. *See* FUNAI
National Geographic magazine, 522, 552, 575,
　698, 794
National Indian Institute, 103, 107, 126, 144,
　206, 239, 677, 809
National Information Service, 450, 639
National Institutes of Health, 256, 265, 740
National Integration Plan, Brazil, 652
National Intelligence Service, Peru, 515
National Iranian Oil Company, 787
National liberation movements: Colombia, 392,
　684; Guatemala, 811–12; Peru, 489, 493,
　525, 533–34; Philippines, 800; Vietnam,
　547, 552, 567, 581, 583, 709
National Petroleum Council, Brazil, 190
National Research Council, 615
National Security Agency, 339, 372
National Security Council: in Eisenhower
　administration, 251, 263, 274–75; formerly
　SNWCC, 192; in Johnson administration,
　530; in Kennedy administration, 327, 331,
　338, 357, 398, 437; wiretaps on, 708. *See
　also* Special Group
Nationalist party, Puerto Rico, 224–25
Native American Rights Fund, 720
NATO. *See* North Atlantic Treaty Organization
Natural gas deposits: in Peru, 462; in Southeast
　Asia, 561n
Natural Resources Planning Board, 559
Navigators, 123, 202, 290
Negociación Azucarera Nepeña, S.A., 456
Nehru, Jawaharlal, 53, 238, 370
Nelson Rockefeller Collection, Inc., The, 779
Neves, Luis, 623
New Deal, 160, 249, 357, 400
New Federalism, 711
New Peoples Army, Philippines, 800
New Tribes Mission, 500, 773, 775, 777–78
Newfield, Jack, 542, 577, 591–92

Ngo Dinh Diem, 238, 267, 410, 560
Ngo Dinh Nhu, 410
Nguyen Cao Ky, 562, 570, 571, 587
Nguyen Ngoc Loan, 582
Nguyen Van Thieu, 564, 587, 709
Nicaragua, 218, 635
Nickel: in Amazon, 669; in Cuba, 363
Niebuhr, Reinhold, 292, 408
Niemeyer, Oscar, 315, 638
Nitze, Paul, 115
Nixon, Richard M.: and CIA, 730, 731; duplicity
　of on Vietnam, 709–10; and Fundamentalist
　support, 288, 689; and Latin America, 6,
　635, 664, 702; 1960 campaign, 329, 330,
　334–35, 336; 1968 campaign, 536, 578–79;
　paranoia of, 280, 645, 708–9; resignation of,
　691, 700–710, 721–22; trip to China, 709;
　as vice-president, 274, 315
Nobel Peace Prize, 268, 580, 677, 830
Noriega, Manuel, 813
North American Free Trade Agreement
　(NAFTA), 830. *See also* Free Trade Zone
North Atlantic Treaty Organization (NATO), 5,
　273
North Vietnam. *See* Democratic Republic of
　Vietnam
Northern Baptist Convention, 11, 24, 26
Nova Ruiz, Gen. 394
Noval, Joaquin, 320
Nuclear arms policies, 405–6, 409
Nyman, Will, 64

O, For a Thousand Tongues, 208
OAS. *See* Organization of American States
Obregón, Alvaro, 70
O'Brien, Conor Cruise, 341n
O'Brien, Lawrence, 731
Occidental Petroleum, 692, 756
O'Donnell, Kenneth, 415
Odría, Manuel: and Cam, 199, 244, 249; coups
　involving, 206, 247, 311, 397; and
　Ecuador/Peru border dispute, 277; and U.S.
　companies, 278, 458, 496
O'Dwyer, Paul, 211
Oettinger, Anthony, 873n32
Office of the Coordinator of Inter-American
　Affairs. *See* CIAA
Office of Population, 475
Office of the Presidential Assistant for
　Community Development, Philippines, 267
Office of Strategic Services (OSS), 113, 130,
　182, 184, 221, 358

299, 614, 639–40; and wartime rubber, 119, 135–37, 147–49

—and CIA, 267–68, 278, 736, 740

—and destruction of Rivera mural, 57–60

—in Eisenhower administration: chairs Committee on Government Organization, 255–56; chairs Special Group, 251, 268, 278, 851n21; as special assistant for Cold War affairs, 262, 263, 270–75

—and Far East, 53, 55–57, 268, 308, 368, 547, 592, 709

—in Ford administration: chairs commission on CIA abuses, 735–40; and Domestic Council, 761–62; and National Security Council, 765; leaves office, 766–69; as vice-president, 696, 722, 723–29, 734;

—and Fundamentalism, 293, 330, 408

—as governor of New York, 310–11, 312, 385, 537, 706, 716

—and IBEC, 212, 573, 782

—and Indians, 10–11, 15–16, 31, 78–81, 103, 107–8, 128, 143–47, 150–54, 157, 168, 198, 300–301, 318, 430, 638, 650–51, 673–75, 740, 780

—and Johnson, 473, 537, 538, 587, 711

—and Kennedys: criticizes JFK administration, 403, 406, 409, 453; and Cuban missile crisis, 355, 399; influences early JFK administration, 335–39, 371–72, 375–77, 380–81, 398; on Johnson as vice-president, 422; opposes Robert Kennedy, 577, 591

—and J. C. King, 138–39, 140, 141, 142–43, 144, 149, 265

—and Latin America: Argentina, 157, 162, 169; Bolivia, 157; changing view toward national self-determination, 54, 82–83, 94, 214, 216, 278–79, 299, 306, 313–14, 316, 362–63, 410, 428–29, 453, 455, 607, 647, 666, 694, 697, 714, 729; consolidates holdings in, 712; contacts in, 164, 285, 377; Ecuador, 285; and expanded CIA operations in, 274–75; free trade in, 330, 334, 474–75, 667–68; interlocking of business and philanthropic interests in, 118, 168, 213–14, 586, 780; theory of development in, 667, 887n55; tour of (1969), 607, 634–42, 831–32

—and Middle East, 275, 279, 783, 787

—and military-industrial complex, 328–31

—and Nixon, 334–35, 594, 596, 707–8, 715

—and nuclear war, 328, 370–71, 372, 374

—personal characteristics and family relations of: aging and death, 787, 795, 821–22; ambi-

tion, 158, 331; appearance of, 210, 455; as art collector, 57, 80, 364, 723, 779, 793; early life and education, 9–11, 15–17, 27, 31–32, 54; family assets of, 150, 779–80; family influence on, 18, 54, 331, 724; marriages of, 53–57, 367, 407; and Michael, 311, 363, 455, 792, 796; personal style of, 80, 108, 165, 166, 219, 230

—as presidential candidate: presidential ambitions, 309–22; 1960 campaign, 329–31, 333–35, 336; 1964 candidacy, 403, 404, 453, 454; 1968 candidacy, 536, 588, 589, 591–94; 1976 race, 760–61, 764–65

—reaction to Cuban revolution, 313–14

—and Roosevelt administration, 92, 103, 107, 156, 377, 400, 677; as assistant secretary of state for Latin America, 163–82

—and State Department, 5, 157, 162, 643

—and Truman administration: and Congress, 228–29; Dulles opposes, 176; fired by Truman, 178, 179; and IDAB, 221–22, 225, 230, 286; Marshall supports, 203; postwar planning, 166; and U.N. headquarters, 211

—and Venezuela, 116, 217, 219–20, 406–7, 588, 610, 636

—See also Bodoquena; CIAA; IBEC; Moreira Salles, Walther; Rockefeller Brothers Fund; Rockefeller Center; Special Group

Rockefeller, Rodman: at IBEC, 634, 781–83; and Michael, 364, 369; and Nelson, 285n, 407, 792, 796

Rockefeller, Steven, 368, 407, 593, 787, 792

Rockefeller, Steven, Jr., 795

Rockefeller, William, 82, 844n30

Rockefeller, Winthrop, 18, 211, 298, 306, 407, 712, 761

Rockefeller Brothers Fund, 212, 220, 293, 297, 329, 663, 725, 787; Special Studies Project, 309, 335, 339, 375, 424

Rockefeller Brothers, Inc., 212

Rockefeller Center, 57, 75–76, 210, 211, 220, 226, 725

Rockefeller Commission on CIA Abuses, 735–37, 833–34

Rockefeller family: back Saigon regime, 560; business associations of, 562, 570, 726–28, 784–86; and Fundamentalism, 292, 293; in Latin America, 714–15, 663. *See also individual family members*

Rockefeller Family Fund, 725

Rockefeller Foundation: in India, 562; management of, 168, 191, 211, 220, 266–67, 293,

Standard Oil of New Jersey (*cont.*)
258, 296, 303–4, 442, 450, 608; in
Caribbean, 276, 313, 362, 364–65; in China,
54, 88; in Colombia, 35–36, 395, 692; in
Dutch East Indies/Indonesia, 54, 364, 368; in
Ecuador, 285, 496; and Germany, 98; in
Guatemala, 36; and I.G. Farben, 97, 155; and
Japan, 98; in Mexico, 35, 83, 97–98, 101; in
Middle East, 35, 231; and Navajo Indian
lands, 15; in Paraguay, 775; in Peru, 35, 245,
278, 458, 514, 517, 666; refinery threat,
706; and Rockefeller Foundation, 36; in
Thailand, 561; in U.S. Southwest, 717n, 718;
in Venezuela, 77; in World War II, 155. *See
also* Creole Petroleum; International
Petroleum Company; King Ranch
Standard Oil of New York (Mobil Oil; Socony),
211, 246, 461, 560, 717n, 718
Standard Oil of Ohio, 276
Standard Oil Trust, 6, 15, 19, 77, 82
Stanford University, 478, 878n39
Stassen, Harold, 176, 177, 271, 272
State Department. *See* U.S. government: State
Department
State-War-Navy Coordinating Committee
(SWNCC), 192, 221, 276. *See also*
Rockefeller, John D. 3rd
Stauffer Chemical, 608
Stennis, John, 405–6
Stettinius, Edward, 160, 162, 163, 170, 173,
174, 178
Stevenson, Adlai E., 352, 415
Stewart, Lyman, 24, 34, 64
Stewart, Milton, 24
Stewart, Robert H., 880n6
Stewart, W. L., 24
Stimson, Henry, 149, 169, 170
Stoll, David, 490
Stone, Doris, 320, 801
Strategic Bombing Survey, 130
Strategic Index of the Americas, 129, 147n, 152,
842n12. *See also* Anthropology, American
Stratton, Dr. John Roach, 20
Strauss, Louis, 226
Stroessner, Alfredo, 640, 775
Strong, Gen. Robert V., 199n
Struharik, Paul, 757, 758
Student protests, 166, 631, 635–37, 640–41
Sucrest sugar refiners, 313, 456
Sugar, 69, 70, 313
Suharno, Ignatius, 779
Suharto, 778

Sukarno, 238, 364, 410
Sullivan, William, 708, 739
Summer Institute of Linguistics (SIL): in
Amazon basin, 201, 206, 434, 436, 500;
anti-Catholicism of, 323, 590; and Asia
Foundation, 571; and aviation, 282–83, 288;
bases: *see* Limoncocha, Lomalinda, Tumi
Chucua, Yarinacocha; in Bolivia, 530, 571; in
Brazil, 4, 318, 432, 500–501, 625, 692; collaborators with, 126–28, 205, 318–19, 363,
509, 625, 692; in Colombia, 387, 395, 473,
684, 691, 752; and counterinsurgency, 128,
130, 433, 482, 575, 743; criticisms of, 686,
751, 801, 894n26; in Ecuador, 285, 287,
360, 499; in Far East, 208, 758, 759; financial supporters of, 290, 487, 569, 678,
743–44, 813; and First Indian Conference,
100, 168; founding of, 40, 67, 73, 86,
122–24; in Guatemala, 239, 240, 244, 811;
and Islam, 798; in Mexico, 131, 201, 802; in
Peru, 124, 206, 247, 459, 479, 482–83, 540,
771, 799; in Philippines, 208, 236, 571, 799,
800; and Rockefeller Foundation, 44, 433,
439; in Vietnam, 289, 387, 546, 552–53,
571, 757. *See also* Campos, Roberto; JAARS;
Ribeiro, Darcy; Townsend, William Cameron;
Wycliffe Bible Translators
Sun Oil Company (Sunoco), 40, 435, 443, 486,
718
Superintendency for the Development of the
Amazon (SUDAM), 618, 670
Superior Oil, 692
Survival International, 677
Swadesh, Morris, 842n12
Sweetwater Development Company, 880n6
Swift, Geraldine, 620, 633
Swift, Harold, 619
Swift-Armour, S.A., 618–19. *See also* Deltec
International, Ltd.; Swift do Brasíl
Swift company, 298. *See also* Swift do Brasíl
Swift do Brasíl, 633
SWNCC. *See* State-War-Navy Coordinating
Committee
Szulc, Tad, 449, 459, 650

Taft, Robert, 231
Tammany Hall, 310, 541
Tanganyika Concessions, Ltd., 326
Tannenbaum, Frank, 62, 67, 130
Taos Pueblo, N.M., 9, 28, 254
Tariri, 484–85, 487
Távora, Juárez, 260

Tax, Sol, 126, 130
Taylor, Dr. Dermot B., 509
Taylor, Gen. Maxwell, 355, 371, 398, 478
Taylor, Thomas A., 620, 633, 712
Teamsters' Pension Fund, 579, 880n6
Teller, Edward, 370, 717, 762–63
Tello, Dr. Julio César, 80
Tenneco, 717n
Tennessee Valley Authority, 669, 763
Texas Gulf Producing Company, 246, 459
Texas Instruments, 276, 569, 852–53n20
Texas International, 761
Texas Oil Company (Texaco): in Bolivia, 276, 756; in Brazil, 189, 258, 436, 442, 443, 450; in Colombia, 387, 395; in Ecuador, 277, 603, 685; in Guatemala, 276, 806; in Paraguay, 775; in Peru, 459, 514
Texas Pacific, 561n
Thai-America Steel Company, 878n39
Thai National Police, 556, 559
Thaibec Investment Service, 547
Thailand, 238, 547–48, 557, 743, 855n32
Thela Comercial, S.A., 307
"Theology of Liberation," 690, 691
Thermo Electron, 725
Thielman, Rev. Calvin, 545, 546, 549, 552, 569
Thieu. *See* Nguyen Van Thieu
Third Century Corporation, 716
Third World development, 191, 226–28, 229–30, 263, 273, 283, 425
Thompson, Kenneth, 399
Thompson, Robert H., 880n6
Thompson, Gen. Robert T., 582–83
Thompson, Warren, 475
Tidmarsh, Dr. Wilfrid, 284–85
Time-Life, Inc., 287, 293n, 381
Tin, 153, 548, 673–74, 888n66
Tippett, A. R., 689
Titan II (ICBM), 372, 374
Titicaca, Lake, 472, 517, 692
Tito, Josip, 351
Toledano, Lombardo, 84, 170
Tolentino, Enrique, 757, 758
Tolo: The Volcano's Son, 64, 806
Torres, Gen. Juan José, 692, 693–94, 695, 750
Torres Restrepo, Fr. Camilo, 684
Torresola, Griselio, 225
Torrijos, Omar, 813
Townsend, Elaine, 198, 200, 201, 699
Townsend, Elvira, 44, 50, 61, 131–32
Townsend, Grace, 201, 202
Townsend, Paul (Cam's brother), 63, 249

Townsend, Paul (Guatemalan missionary), 820
Townsend, William Cameron ("Cam"): in Brazil, 360, 460, 499; and Cárdenas, 85, 100–101, 132, 209, 799; career at SIL, 4, 486, 699, 752, 835n1; in Colombia, 385, 387–89, 473, 754; and Daniels, 60, 70, 74, 85, 86, 100; in Ecuador, 283, 359–60; in Guatemala, 36–52, 238, 322, 810; and Inter-American Indian conferences, 100, 321, 697, 699, 802–3; and Korean War, 208–9; and linguistics, 44, 68, 699; in Mexico, 60, 98, 130–31, 382; as novelist, 64, 806; personal life of, 42, 198, 201, 282, 814, 815, 820; and Peru, 197, 246, 460, 756, 799, 814; plans for Pacific area, 121–25, 208, 236; praises Nelson Rockefeller, 209; and public relations, 484–87, 489, 570; relations with Latin American leaders, 168, 244, 245, 435, 438–39, 469, 603, 627, 697; and Religious Roundtable, 803, 805; supporters of, 200, 247, 248, 324, 342, 570; and U.S. government and politics, 102–3, 205, 324, 390, 569, 590, 743, 856n37; in USSR, 699, 798; and Venezuela, 91; and Vietnam, 545, 549. *See also* JAARS; Summer Institute of Linguistics; Wycliffe Bible Translators
Trade Expansion Act of 1962, 402, 425
Trafficante, Santos, 348, 354, 405, 413, 517, 739–40
Trans-Amazonian highway system, 232, 500, 620, 652, 669–70, 673, 676, 688
Trans-Andean Highway, 120, 246
Trans-Andean pipeline, 692, 754, 756
Trans-Chaco Highway, 680
Translation magazine, 123, 574, 748
Transoceanic AOFC, Ltd., 862n17
Transoceanic Development Corporation, Ltd., 862n17
Treaty of Rio de Janeiro, 233
Tremblay, Dr. Robert, 859n36
Tribal languages: Cakchiquel, 44–46; Huao, 604; Montagnard, 387; Quechua, 80, 153, 203, 250, 483; Tagalog, 208, 236; in Yucatán, 126
Tribal studies, Vietnam, 558
Tricontinental Conference, 529
Trilateral Commission, 645, 715, 768, 853n20
Trotman, Dawson, 123, 132, 202, 290
Troyer, Les, 571
True, Clara, 29
Truett, Rev. George W., 324
Trujillo, Rafael, 218, 312, 393, 739

Truman, Harry S.: assassination attempt, 223–25; becomes president, 173, 175, 177; and Berle, 185, 190; and Cam, 288; criticizes Standard Oil, 155; and Latin American policy, 177, 189, 209; and Nelson Rockefeller, 178–79, 220, 230; as vice-presidential candidate, 163

Truth About Mexico's Oil, The, 98, 101

Tsalickis, Mike, 519, 520–23

Tshombe, Moise, 326, 327, 341, 341n

Tucci, Nicolo, 159, 172

Tulane University, 320, 478

Tumi Chucua SIL base, Bolivia, 697, 747

Tungsten, in Far East, 548, 557

Tunney Amendment, 766

Túpac Amaru Front, Peru, 491, 492

Turbay Ayala, Julio, 811

Turner, Glenn, 874n36

Tweedy, Bronson, 327

Ubico, Gen. Jorge, 48–49, 50, 118, 807

Udall, Stewart, 577, 717

Unevangelized Field Mission, 500, 773

União de Bancos Brasileiros, 611, 622

União Democrática Nacional party (UDN), Brazil, 184, 189, 190, 192, 441, 443, 867n17

União refinery. *See* Refinaria Exploração de Petrólio União, S.A.

Union Carbide, 451, 618

Union of Indian Nations, Brazil, 803

Union of Soviet Socialist Republics (USSR): bilingual programs in, 699; collapses, 824; at Geneva, 272–73; in Latin America, 329, 374, 694; at Paris Summit, 328, 331; propaganda of, 425; at U.N., 161, 165, 169; at Yalta, 164, 165, 170–72

Union Oil of California, 24, 245, 514, 561n, 750, 886n27

Union Theological Seminary, 20, 292, 293, 295n, 408, 761

United Fidelity Union Life Insurance Company, 569

United Fruit: agriculture school in Honduras, 285n; CIAA assistance to, 115; in Ecuador, 285, 602; and First National Bank of Boston, 190; in Guatemala, 36, 232, 412, 849n10; and Guatemalan land reform, 238, 240, 244

United Kingdom, 161, 171, 177, 585–86

United Nations: in Africa, 327, 340, 341, 341n; charter of, 176, 177, 399–400; Food and Agriculture Organization, 814; founding of, 5, 156, 165, 169, 170, 173–77; General Assembly, 176; headquarters of, 211, 315, 638; and human rights, 219, 243, 575, 803, 826; Security Council, 175, 243

United Nuclear, 718

U.S. Business Advisory Council for the Alliance for Progress, 539

U.S. Chamber of Commerce, 383

U.S. government:

—administrative departments and agencies: Atomic Energy Commission, 773; cabinet, 263, 337–39; Central Intelligence Agency, *see* CIA; Civil Rights Commission, 763; Department of Agriculture, 136, 139, 505, 508; Department of Commerce, 108, 383–84; Department of Defense, 199, 255, 333, 378, 477; Department of Health, Education and Welfare, 126, 256, 265, 266; Department of the Interior, 13 (*see also* Bureau of Indian Affairs); Department of Justice, 155, 188 (*see also* FBI); Department of the Treasury, 279; Geological Survey, 5, 450; Information Agency (USIA), 256, 275, 381, 435, 556; National Academy of Science, 615; Works Progress Administration, 88, 92

—Congress: House of Representatives, 175, 228, 729; Senate, 155, 192, 310, 327, 332, 543, 579, 745

—embassies abroad: Lima, 200; Rio de Janeiro, 431; Saigon, 581; Teheran, 787

—military: Air Force, 130, 199, 450, 616–17; Army, 122, 287, 445, 447, 557; Joint Chiefs, 327; Marine Corps, 467; missions, 170, 218, 219, 555, 556, 675; National War College, 260; Navy, 122, 130, 192, 215, 447, 522, 561

—State Department: and African nationalism, 326; Bureau of Intelligence Research, 113, 348, 359; Bureau of Latin American Affairs, 159, 172, 375, 601; Foreign Service, 398, 664; International Division, 165, 169, 173; International Information Agency, 256; in Latin America, 98, 157, 189, 241, 313, 314, 381, 648; Nelson Rockefeller's proposals to, 96, 221, 225, 228; Office of Facts and Figures, 180; Office of Philippines and Southeast Asian Affairs, 560; Office of Policy Coordination (CIA), 207, 208; and Overseas Private Investment Corporation, 548; policies of, 130, 332, 348, 451, 828

U.S. Industrial Mission to Brazil, 138

U.S. Marshal's Services Special Operations Group, 720